CLYMER®
YAMAHA
OUTBOARD SHOP MANUAL
2-90 HP TWO-STROKE • 1999-2002 (Includes Jet Drives)

The World's Finest Publisher of Mechanical How-to Manuals

PRIMEDIA
Business Magazines & Media

P.O. Box 12901, Overland Park, KS 66282-2901

Copyright ©2003 PRIMEDIA Business Magazines & Media Inc.

FIRST EDITION
First Printing March, 2003

Printed in U.S.A.

CLYMER and colophon are registered trademarks of PRIMEDIA Business Magazines & Media Inc.

This book was printed at Von Hoffmann an ISO certified company.

ISBN: 0-89287-827-4

Library of Congress: 2003102478

AUTHOR: Mark Rolling.

TECHNICAL PHOTOGRAPHY: Mark Rolling.

TECHNICAL ILLUSTRATIONS: Mike Rose.

WIRING DIAGRAMS: Bob Caldwell.

EDITOR: Jason Beaver.

PRODUCTION: Shara Pierceall.

COVER: Mark Clifford Photography, Los Angeles, California.

All rights reserved. Reproduction or use, without express permission, of editorial or pictorial content, in any manner, is prohibited. No patent liability is assumed with respect to the use of the information contained herein. While every precaution has been taken in the preparation of this book, the publisher assumes no responsibility for errors or omissions. Neither is any liability assumed for damages resulting from use of the information contained herein. Publication of the servicing information in this manual does not imply approval of the manufacturers of the products covered.

All instructions and diagrams have been checked for accuracy and ease of application; however, success and safety in working with tools depend to a great extent upon individual accuracy, skill and caution. For this reason, the publishers are not able to guarantee the result of any procedure contained herein. Nor can they assume responsibility for any damage to property or injury to persons occasioned from the procedures. Persons engaging in the procedure do so entirely at their own risk.

General Information	1
Troubleshooting	2
Lubrication, Maintenance and Tune-Up	3
Timing, Synchronization and Adjustment	4
Fuel System	5
Ignition and Electrical Systems	6
Power Head	7
Gearcase	8
Jet Drive	9
Manual Starter	10
Tilt/Trim and Midsection	11
Oil Injection System	12
Remote Control	13
Index	14
Wiring Diagrams	15

CLYMER PUBLICATIONS
PRIMEDIA Business Magazines & Media

Chief Executive Officer Timothy M. Andrews
President Ron Wall

EDITORIAL

Editor
James Grooms

Associate Editor
Jason Beaver

Technical Writers
Ron Wright
Ed Scott
George Parise
Mark Rolling
Michael Morlan
Jay Bogart

Production Supervisor
Dylan Goodwin

Lead Production Editor
Shirley Renicker

Production Editors
Greg Araujo
Shara Pierceall

Associate Production Editors
Susan Hartington
Holly Messinger
Darin Watson

Technical Illustrators
Steve Amos
Mitzi McCarthy
Bob Meyer
Mike Rose

MARKETING/SALES AND ADMINISTRATION

Vice President, PRIMEDIA Business Directories & Books
Rich Hathaway

Marketing Manager
Elda Starke

Advertising & Promotions Coordinator
Melissa Abbott

Associate Art Directors
Chris Paxton
Tony Barmann

Sales Manager/Marine
Dutch Sadler

Sales Manager/Manuals
Ted Metzger

Sales Manager/Motorcycles
Matt Tusken

Sales Coordinator
Marcia Jungles

Operations Manager
Patricia Kowalczewski

Customer Service Manager
Terri Cannon

Customer Service Supervisor
Ed McCarty

Customer Service Representatives
Susan Kohlmeyer
April LeBlond
Courtney Hollars
Jennifer Lassiter
Ernesto Suarez
Shawna Davis

Warehouse & Inventory Manager
Leah Hicks

The following product lines are published by PRIMEDIA Business Directories & Books.

More information available at *primediabooks.com*

Contents

QUICK REFERENCE DATA IX

CHAPTER ONE
GENERAL INFORMATION 1

Manual organization 1	Special tools 20
Warnings, cautions and notes 2	Precision measuring tools 20
Safety 2	Electrical system fundamentals 28
Serial number and model identification 3	Basic mechanical skills 30
Engine operation 5	Engine identification codes 36
Fasteners 5	Technical abbreviations 37
Shop supplies 8	Metric tap and drill sizes 38
Galvanic corrosion 10	Conversion formulas 38
Propellers 12	Specifications 39
Basic tools 17	

CHAPTER TWO
TROUBLESHOOTING 40

Preliminary inspection 41	Ignition system 72
Operating requirements 41	Tilt and trim system 88
Starting difficulty 41	Power head 95
Fuel system 43	Cooling system 97
Starting system 51	Gearcase 99
Charging system 57	Starting system troubleshooting 101
Fuse and wire harness 63	Fuel system troubleshooting 102
Warning system 64	Ignition system troubleshooting 103
Oil injection system 70	Specifications 104

CHAPTER THREE
LUBRICATION, MAINTENANCE AND TUNE-UP 109
Lubrication 109
Maintenance 118
Tune-up 127
Engine break-in 130
Specifications 131
Maintenance schedule 132
Fluid capacities 133
Oil and fuel mixing rates 133
Spark plug specifications 134

CHAPTER FOUR
TIMING, SYNCHRONIZATION AND ADJUSTMENT 135
Timing, synchronization and adjustments 135
Test propellers 182
Wide open throttle speed 183
Specifications 183

CHAPTER FIVE
FUEL SYSTEM 185
Fuel system safety 185
Fuel system components service 185
Carburetor 208
Reed housing/intake manifold 228
Recirculation system 233
Specifications 234

CHAPTER SIX
IGNITION AND ELECTRICAL SYSTEMS 236
Battery 236
Starting system components 243
Starter motor 248
Charging system components 257
Ignition system components 261
Warning system components 271
Specifications 273

CHAPTER SEVEN
POWER HEAD 275
Service considerations 275
Power head break-in 276
Service recommendations 276
Lubricants, sealants and adhesives 277
Fasteners and torque 278
Power head removal/installation 278
Flywheel removal/installation 285
Power head disassembly 286
Power head components cleaning and inspection ... 306
Power head assembly 319
Specifications 335

CHAPTER EIGHT
GEARCASE 340
Gearcase operation 340
Propeller 342
Gearcase removal/installation 346
Water pump 354
Gearcase disassembly/assembly 362
Sacrificial anodes 422
Component inspection 423
Gearcase pressure test 426
Specifications 427

CHAPTER NINE
JET DRIVE 429
Jet drive operation 429
Jet drive repair 431
Specifications 441

CHAPTER TEN
MANUAL STARTER 442
Repair 444
Specifications 462
Starter rope length 462

CHAPTER ELEVEN
TILT/TRIM AND MIDSECTION 463
Manual tilt system removal and installation 463
Power tilt/trim system removal/installation 465
Tilt/trim relay replacement 470
Tilt/trim sender replacement 470
Electric trim motor removal/installation 471
Tilt/trim system electric motor repair 475
Manual release valve removal and installation..... 481
Hydraulic system filling and bleeding 482
Midsection 483
Specifications 494

CHAPTER TWELVE
OIL INJECTION SYSTEM 496
System operation 496
Oil level sensor removal/installation 497
Oil reservoir removal/installation 498
Oil hoses and check valves 499
Oil pump 502
Driven gear 506
Bleeding air from the system 506
Specifications 507
Oil reservoir capacity 507
Oil pump identification 507

CHAPTER THIRTEEN
REMOTE CONTROL 508
Neutral throttle operation 508
Throttle/shift cable removal/installation 509
Remote control 512
Specifications 520

INDEX 521

WIRING DIAGRAMS 525

Quick Reference Data

STANDARD TORQUE SPECIFICATIONS

Screw or nut size	N•m	in.-lb.	ft.-lb.
Metric			
M5 bolt	5	44	–
M6 bolt	8	70	–
M8 bolt	18	156	13
M10 bolt	36	–	27
M12 bolt	43	–	32
M14 bolt	81.3	–	60
8 mm nut	5	44	–
10 mm nut	8	70	–
12 mm nut	18	156	13
14 mm nut	36	–	27
17 mm nut	43	–	32

MAINTENANCE SCHEDULE

After each use	Check for loose nuts, bolts, spark plugs
	Check the propeller
	Check the oil reservoir level*
	Flush the cooling system
	Lubricate the jet drive bearings*
	Check for and correct leaking fluids
	Wash the exterior of gearcase and drive shaft housing
	Touch up paint damage on external surfaces
Before each use	Check for and correct fuel leakage
	Check the steering and controls for proper operation
	Check the oil reservoir level*
	Check for a proper cooling system operation (water stream)
	Check for proper operation of the lockout assembly
	(continued)

MAINTENANCE SCHEDULE (continued)

Initial 10 hours or one month	Lubricate the swivel tube, tilt tube and steering system
	Check throttle operation
	Check shift linkages for proper operation
	Check tightness of all accessible nuts and bolts
	Check power tilt and trim operation*
	Check choke lever operation*
	Inspect fuel filter for contamination
	Inspect fuel hoses and connections
	Adjust the idle speed (see Chapter Four)
	Inspect mid-section components (see Chapter Eleven)
	Inspect the spark plug(s)
	Adjust the oil pump linkage (see Chapter Four)*
	Inspect oil reservoir for water or contamination*
	Check electrical wiring and connections
	Check power head for water and exhaust leakage
	Check gearcase lubricant level and condition
	Check condition and charge level of battery
	Check carburetor synchronization and adjustments
	Check cylinder compression (see Chapter Two)
	Adjust the lockout assembly (see Chapter Four)
Initial 50 hours or 90 days	Lubricate the swivel tube, tilt tube and steering system
	Adjust the carburetor(s)
	Inspect fuel filter for contamination
	Check spark plug condition and gap
	Check and adjust the ignition timing (see Chapter Four)
	Check the oil injection system*
	Check electrical wiring and connections
	Check power head for water and exhaust leakage
	Check gearcase lubricant level and condition
	Inspect the water pump impeller (see Chapter Eight)
	Check the propeller
	Check propeller nut for tightness
	Clean and inspect sacrificial anodes
	Check all accessible nuts and bolts for tightness
	Check cylinder compression (see Chapter Two)
	Adjust the lockout assembly (see Chapter Four)
Each 100 hours of usage or 180 days	Lubricate the swivel tube, tilt tube and steering system
	Check carburetor synchronization and adjustments
	Inspect fuel filter for contamination
	Check fuel hoses and clamps for leakage
	Check the spark plug condition and gap
	Check the power tilt/trim fluid level (see Chapter Eleven)
	Inspect the mid-section components
	Check the oil injection system*
	Check electrical wiring and connections
	Check power head for water and exhaust leakage
	Check gearcase lubricant level and condition
	Check the condition and charge level of the battery (see Chapter Six)*
	Clean and inspect sacrificial anodes
	Check all accessible nuts and bolts for tightness
	Check the propeller nut for tightness
	Check cylinder compression
	Adjust the lockout assembly (see Chapter Four)
Each 200 hours of usage or one year	Inspect fuel tank, hoses and clamps
	Clean or replace the fuel filter
	Replace the water pump impeller
	Check fuel valve for proper operation*

*This maintenance item may not apply to all models.

FLUID CAPACITIES

Model	Capacity (approximate)
Fuel tank	
2 hp	1.2 L (0.32 gal.)
3 hp	1.4 L (0.37 gal.)
4 and 5 hp	2.8 L (0.74 gal.)
Gearcase	
2 hp	45 ml (1.5 oz.)
3 hp	74 ml (2.5 oz.)
4 and 5 hp	100 ml (3.4 oz.)
6 and 8 hp	160 ml (5.4 oz.)
9.9 and 15 hp	251 ml (8.5 oz.)
20 and 25 hp (two-cylinder)	370 ml (12.5 oz.)
25 hp (three-cylinder) and 30 hp	200 ml (6.8 oz.)
40 and 50 hp	430 ml (14.5 oz.)
60-90 hp	500 ml (16.9 oz.)
Oil Reservoir	
20 and 25 hp (two-cylinder)	0.7 L (0.74 qt.)
28 jet, 35 jet, 40 hp and 50 hp	1.5 L (1.59 qt.)
60 and 70 hp	2.8 L (2.96 qt.)
65 jet and 75-90 hp	3.3 L (3.49 qt.)

OIL AND FUEL MIXING RATES

Quantity of fuel	Oil for 50:1 ratio	Oil for 100:1 ratio
3.8 L (1 gal.)	76 cc (2.6 oz.)	38 cc (1.25 oz.)
7.6 L (2 gal.)	152 cc (5.2 oz)	76 cc (2.6 oz.)
11.4 L (3 gal.)	228 cc (7.8 oz.)	114 cc (3.9 oz.)
15.4 L (4 gal.)	304 cc (10.4 oz.)	152 cc (5.2 oz.)
18.9 L (5 gal.)	380 cc (12.8 oz.)	190 cc (6.4 oz.)
22.8 L (6 gal.)	456 cc (15.6 oz.)	228 cc (7.8 oz.)
26.6 L (7 gal.)	530 cc (18.2 oz.)	265 cc (9.1 oz.)
30.8 L (8 gal.)	608 cc (20.8 oz.)	304 cc (10.4 oz.)
34.2 L (9 gal.)	684 cc (23.4 oz.)	342 cc (11.7 oz.)
37.8 L (10 gal.)	760 cc (25.6 oz.)	380 cc (12.8 oz.)
41.6 L (11 gal.)	832 cc (28.2 oz.)	416 cc (14.1 oz.)
45.6 L (12 gal.)	912 cc (31.2 oz.)	456 cc (15.6 oz.)

SPARK PLUG SPECIFICATIONS

Model	NGK plug	Champion plug	Gap
2 hp	B5HS	L90 C	0.6 mm (0.024 in.)
3 hp	B6HS-10	L86C	1.0 mm (0.040 in.)
4 and 5 hp	B7HS	L82C	0.6 mm (0.024 in.)
6-40 hp	B7HS-10	L82C	1.0 mm (0.040 in.)
28 jet	B7HS-10	L82C	1.0 mm (0.040 in.)
35 jet and 50-90 hp	B8HS-10	L78C	1.0 mm (0.040 in.)

BATTERY REQUIREMENTS

Model	Minimum CCA rating	Amp hour rating
6-30 hp (except 28 jet)	210	40-70
35 jet and 50-90 hp	380	70-100

CHARGING SYSTEM CAPACITY

Model	Maximum output
6-25 hp (two-cylinder)	
Lighting coil output	80 watt
Battery charging output	6 amp
25 hp (three-cylinder) and 30 hp	8 amp
28 jet, 35 jet, 40 hp and 50 hp	
Lighting coil output	80 watt
Battery charging output	6 amp
60 and 70 hp	6 amp
65 jet and 75-90 hp	10 amp

BATTERY CHARGE PERCENTAGE

Specific gravity reading	Percentage of charge remaining
1.120-1.140	0
1.135-1.155	10
1.150-1.170	20
1.160-1.180	30
1.175-1.195	40
1.190-1.210	50
1.205-1.225	60
1.215-1.235	70
1.230-1.250	80
1.245-1.265	90
1.260-1.280	100

BATTERY CAPACITY

Accessory draw	Provides continuous power for:	Approximate recharge time
80 amp-hour battery		
5 amps	13.5 hours	16 hours
15 amps	3.5 hours	13 hours
25 amps	1.6 hours	12 hours
105 amp-hour battery		
5 amps	15.8 hours	16 hours
15 amps	4.2 hours	13 hours
25 amps	2.4 hours	12 hours

Chapter One

General Information

This detailed and comprehensive manual covers Yamaha two-stroke outboard engines (2-90 hp models).

This manual can be used by anyone from a first time do-it-yourselfer to a professional mechanic. The text provides step-by-step information on maintenance, tune-up, repair and overhaul. Hundreds of illustrations guide the reader through every job.

A shop manual is a reference that should be used to find information quickly. Clymer manuals are designed with that in mind. All chapters are thumb tabbed and important items are indexed at the end of the manual. All procedures, tables, photos and instructions in this manual are designed for the reader who may be working on the machine or using the manual for the first time.

Keep the manual in a handy place such as a toolbox or boat. It will help to better understand how the boat runs, lower repair and maintenance costs and generally increase enjoyment of the boat.

Frequently used specifications and capacities from individual chapters are summarized in the *Quick Reference Data* at the front of the book. Specifications concerning specific systems are at the end of each chapter.

Tables 1-4 are at the end of this chapter.

Table 1 lists engine identification codes.
Table 2 lists technical abbreviations.
Table 3 lists metric tap and drill sizes.
Table 4 lists conversion formulas.
Table 5 lists standard torque specifications.

MANUAL ORGANIZATION

All dimensions and capacities are expressed in U.S. standard and metric units of measurement.

This chapter provides general information on shop safety, tool use, service fundamentals and shop supplies. The tables at the end of the chapter include general engine information.

Chapter Two provides methods and suggestions for quick and accurate diagnosis and repair of problems. Troubleshooting procedures discuss typical symptoms and logical methods to pinpoint the trouble.

Chapter Three explains all periodic lubrication and routine maintenance necessary to keep the outboard operating well. Chapter Three also includes recommended tune-up procedures, eliminating the need to constantly consult other chapters on the various assemblies.

Subsequent chapters describe specific systems, providing disassembly, repair, assembly and adjustment procedures in simple step-by-step form.

Some of the procedures in this manual specify special tools. When possible, the tool is illustrated in use. Well-equipped mechanics may be able to substitute similar tools or fabricate a suitable replacement. However, in some cases, the specialized equipment or expertise may make it impractical for the home mechanic to attempt the procedure. When necessary, such operations are identified in the text with the recommendation to have a dealership or specialist perform the task. It may be less expensive to have them perform these jobs, especially when considering the cost of the equipment. This is true with machine work for power head rebuilds, as machinists spend years perfecting their trade and even professional mechanics will often rely upon their services.

WARNINGS, CAUTIONS AND NOTES

The terms WARNING, CAUTION and NOTE have specific meanings in this manual.

A WARNING emphasizes areas where injury or even death could result from negligence. Mechanical damage may also occur. WARNINGS *are to be taken seriously*.

A CAUTION emphasizes areas where equipment damage could result. Disregarding a CAUTION could cause permanent mechanical damage, though injury is unlikely.

A NOTE provides additional information to clarify or make a procedure easier. Disregarding a NOTE could cause inconvenience, but would not cause equipment damage or injury.

SAFETY

Professional mechanics can work for years and never sustain a serious injury or mishap. Follow these guidelines and practice common sense to safely service the engine.

1. Do not operate the engine in an enclosed area. The exhaust gasses contain carbon monoxide, an odorless, colorless, and tasteless poisonous gas. Carbon monoxide levels build quickly in small, enclosed areas and can cause unconsciousness and death in a short time. Make sure the work area is properly ventilated or operate the engine outside.
2. *Never* use gasoline or any extremely flammable liquid to clean parts. Refer to *Handling Gasoline Safely* and *Cleaning Parts* in this chapter.
3. Never smoke or use a torch in the vicinity of flammable liquids, such as gasoline or cleaning solvent.
4. After removing the engine cover, allow the engine to air out before performing any service work. Review *Fuel System Service Precautions* at the beginning of Chapter Five or Chapter Six.
5. Use the correct tool type and size to avoid damaging fasteners.
6. Keep tools clean and in good condition. Replace or repair worn or damaged equipment.
7. When loosening a tight or stuck fastener, always consider what would happen if the wrench should slip. In most cases, it is safer to pull on a wrench or a ratchet than it would be to push on it. Be careful; protect yourself accordingly.
8. When replacing a fastener, make sure to use one with the same measurements and strength as the old one. Refer to *Fasteners* in this chapter for additional information.
9. Keep your work area clean and uncluttered. Keep all hand and power tools in good condition. Wipe greasy and oily tools after using them. They are difficult to hold and can cause injury. Replace or repair worn or damaged tools. Do not leave tools, shop rags or anything that does not belong in the hull.
10. Wear safety goggles during all operations involving drilling, grinding, or the use of a cold chisel, or *anytime* the safety of your eyes is in question (when debris may spray or scatter). *Always* wear safety goggles when using solvent and compressed air.
11. Do not carry sharp tools in clothing pockets.
12. Always have an approved fire extinguisher available. Make sure it is rated for gasoline (Class B) and electrical (Class C) fires.
13. Do not use compressed air to clean clothes, the boat/engine or the work area. Debris may be blown into eyes or skin. *Never* direct compressed air at yourself or someone else. Do not allow children to use or play with any compressed air equipment.
14. When using compressed air to dry rotating parts, hold the part so it cannot rotate. Do not allow the force of the air to spin the part. The air jet is capable of rotating parts at extreme speed. The part may become damaged or disintegrate, causing serious injury.

Handling Gasoline Safely

Gasoline is a volatile flammable liquid and is one of the most dangerous items in the shop.

Because gasoline is used so often, many people forget that it is hazardous. Only use gasoline as fuel for gasoline internal combustion engines. Do not use it as a cleaner or degreaser. Keep in mind, gasoline is always present in the fuel tank, fuel lines and carburetor or fuel rail. To avoid a

GENERAL INFORMATION

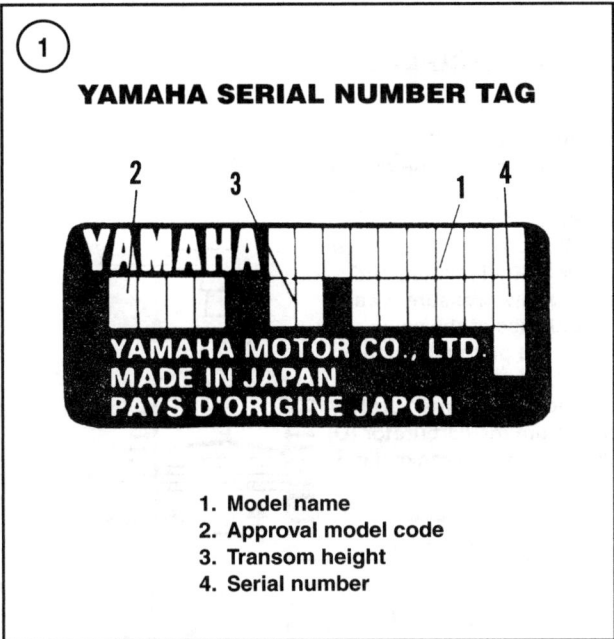

1. Model name
2. Approval model code
3. Transom height
4. Serial number

disastrous accident when working around the fuel system, carefully observe the following precautions:
1. *Never* use gasoline to clean parts. See *Cleaning Parts* in this section.
2. When working on the fuel system, work outside or in a well-ventilated area.
3. Do not add fuel to the fuel tank or service the fuel system while the boat is near an open flame, sparks or where someone is smoking. Gasoline vapor is heavier than air. It collects in low areas and is much more easily ignited than liquid gasoline.
4. Allow the engine to cool completely before working on any fuel system component.
5. When draining a carburetor or fuel fitting, catch the fuel in a plastic container and then pour it into an approved gasoline storage device.
6. Do not store gasoline in glass containers. If the glass breaks, a serious explosion or fire may occur.
7. Immediately wipe up spilled gasoline with rags. Store the rags in a metal container with a lid until they can be properly disposed of, or place them outside in a safe place for the fuel to evaporate.
8. Do not pour water onto a gasoline fire. Water spreads the fire and makes it more difficult to extinguish. Use a class B, BC or ABC fire extinguisher to extinguish the fire.
9. Always turn OFF the engine before refueling. Do not spill fuel onto the engine components. Do not overfill the fuel tank. Leave an air space at the top of the tank to allow room for the fuel to expand because of temperature fluctuations.

Cleaning Parts

Cleaning parts is one of the more tedious and difficult service jobs performed in the home garage. Many types of chemical cleaners and solvents are available for shop use. Most are poisonous and extremely flammable. To prevent chemical exposure, vapor buildup, fire and serious injury, observe each product warning label and note the following:
1. Read the entire product label before using any chemical. Always know what type of chemical is being used and whether it is poisonous and/or flammable.
2. Do not use more than one type of cleaning solvent at a time. If mixing chemicals is called for, measure the proper amounts according to the manufacturer.
3. Work in a well-ventilated area.
4. Wear chemical-resistant gloves.
5. Wear safety glasses.
6. Wear a vapor respirator if the instructions call for it.
7. Wash hands and arms thoroughly after cleaning parts.
8. Keep chemical products away from children and pets.
9. Thoroughly clean all oil, grease and cleaner residue from any part that must be heated.
10. Use a nylon brush when cleaning parts. Metal brushes may cause a spark.
11. When using a parts washer, only use the solvent recommended by the equipment manufacturer. Make sure the parts washer is equipped with a metal lid that will lower in case of fire.

SERIAL NUMBER AND MODEL IDENTIFICATION

Before troubleshooting the engine, verify the model name, model number, horsepower and serial number of the engine. The model must be correctly identified before any service is performed on the engine. In many cases, the tables list specifications by horsepower, type of lubrication system, type of starting system and/or model name. Identification tags for most models are located on the port side clamp bracket or on the swivel bracket near the tiller control handle. Refer to **Figure 1** to review the various forms of information on the tag.

The first numerals in the model name (1, **Figure 1**) indicate the horsepower rating. The letters following the numbers indicate the engine characteristics. Some models have an additional letter preceding the numbers. This letter also identifies the engine characteristics. The final let-

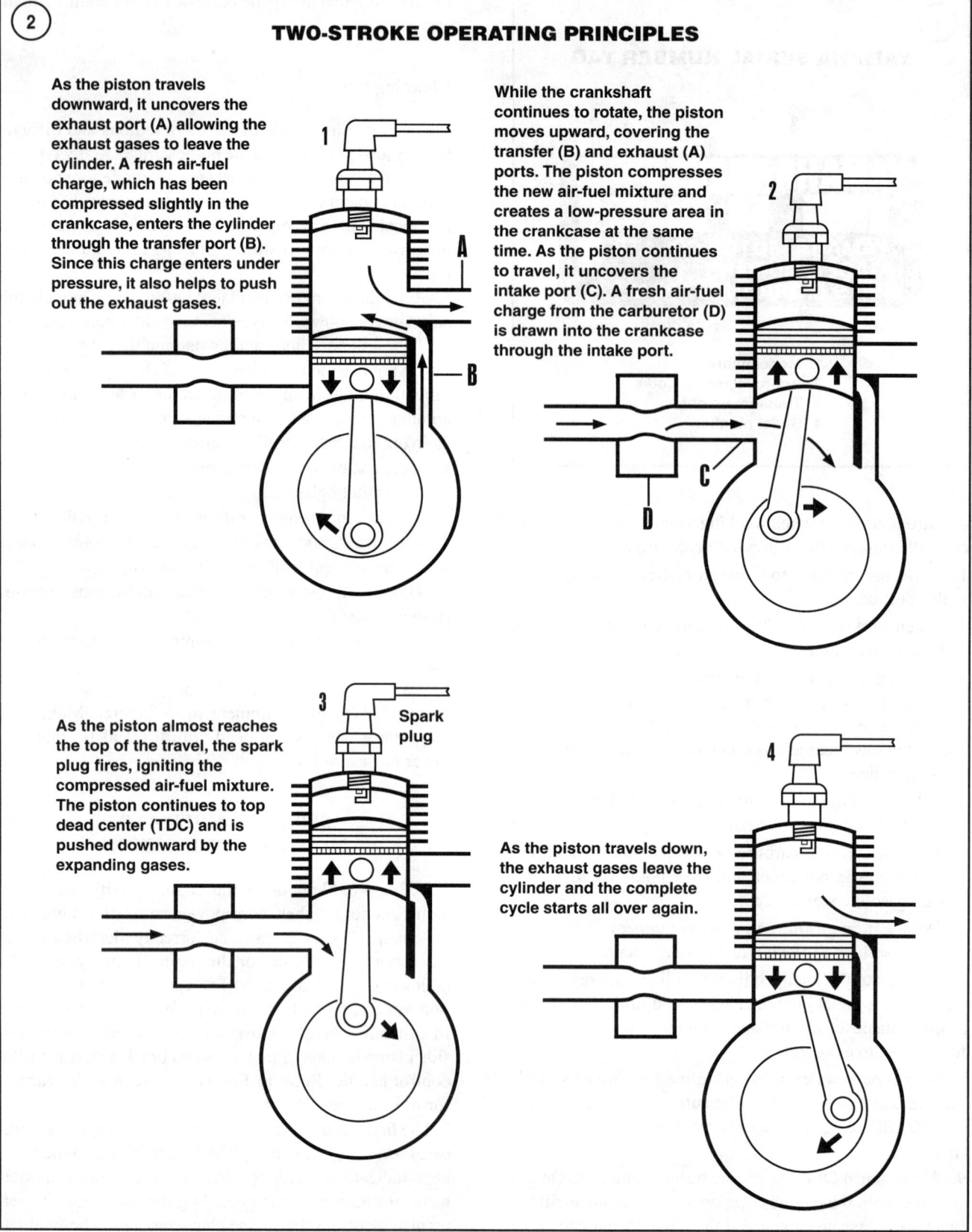

GENERAL INFORMATION

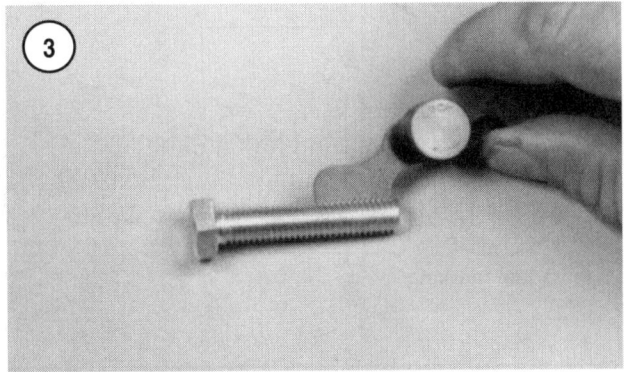

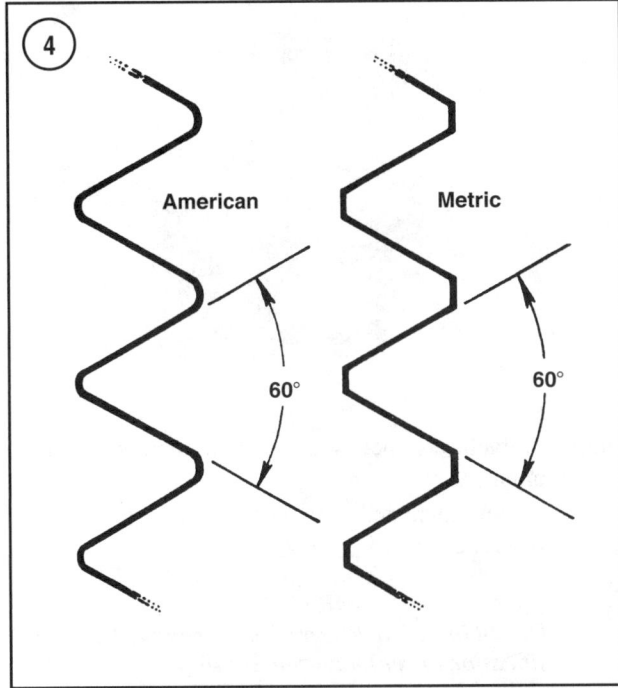

ter in the model name is the year model code. A number 2 or 3 follows the year model code on 25 hp models. This numeral indicates the number of cylinders. Refer to **Table 1** and the information on the tag to identify the horsepower, year model and engine characteristics. In addition, the information on the tag is required when purchasing replacement parts for Yamaha outboards.

ENGINE OPERATION

All marine engines, whether two- or four-stroke, gasoline or diesel, operate on the Otto cycle intake, compression, power and exhaust phases. All Yamaha engines covered in this manual are of two-stroke design. **Figure 2** shows typical gasoline two-stroke engine operation.

FASTENERS

Proper fastener selection and installation is important to ensure that the engine operates as designed and can be serviced efficiently. The choice of original equipment fasteners is not arrived at by chance. Make sure replacement fasteners meet all the same requirements as the originals.

Threaded Fasteners

Threaded fasteners secure most of the components on the boat and engine. Most are tightened by turning them clockwise (right-hand threads). If the normal rotation of the fastener being tightened loosens, the fastener may have left-hand threads. If a left-hand threaded fastener is expected, it is noted in the text.

Nuts, bolts and screws are manufactured in a wide range of thread patterns. To join a nut and bolt, the diameter of the bolt and the diameter of the hole in the nut must be the same and the threads must be properly matched.

The best way to tell if the threads on two fasteners match is to turn the nut on the bolt (or the bolt into the threaded hole in a piece of equipment) with fingers only. Make sure both pieces are clean; remove Loctite or other sealer residue from threads if present. If force is required, check the thread condition on each fastener. If the thread condition is good but the fasteners jam, the threads are not compatible. A thread pitch gauge (**Figure 3**) can also be used to determine pitch.

NOTE
To ensure the fastener threads are not mismatched or cross-threaded, start all fasteners by hand. If a fastener is hard to start or turn, determine the cause before tightening it with a wrench.

Two dimensions are required to match the thread size of the fastener: the number of threads in a given distance and the outside diameter of the threads.

Two systems are currently used to specify threaded fastener dimensions: the U.S. Standard system and the metric system. Although fasteners may appear similar, close inspection shows that the thread designs are not the same (**Figure 4**). Pay particular attention when working with unidentified fasteners; mismatching thread types can damage threads.

NOTE
Most Yamaha engines (especially the 40 hp models) are manufactured with predominantly International Organization for Standardization (ISO) metric fasten-

ers, though some models may be equipped with components using U.S. Standard fasteners depending on the model and application.

U.S. Standard fasteners are sorted by grades (hardness/strength). Bolt heads are marked to represent different grades; no marks means the bolt is grade zero, two marks equal grade two, three marks equal grade five, four marks equal grade six, five marks equal grade seven and six marks equal grade eight. It is important when replacing fasteners to make sure the replacements are of equal or greater strength than the original.

U.S. Standard fasteners generally come in two pitches: coarse and fine. The coarse bolts/screws have fewer threads per inch than the fine. They are normally referred to by size such as 1/2-16 or 3/8-24. In these names the first number, 1/2 or 3/8 in the example, represent the measurement of the bolt diameter from the top of the threads to the top of the other side. The second number represents the number of threads per inch (16 or 24 in the case of the examples).

International Organization for Standardization (ISO) metric threads come in three standard thread sizes: coarse, fine and constant pitch. The ISO coarse pitch is used for most common fastener applications. The fine pitch thread is used on certain precision tools and instruments. The constant pitch thread is used mainly on machine parts and not for fasteners. The constant pitch thread, however, is used on all metric thread spark plugs.

The length (L, **Figure 5**), diameter (D) and distance between thread crests (pitch) (T) classify metric screws and bolts. The numbers 8—1.25 × 130 identify a typical bolt. This indicates the bolt has diameter of 8 mm. The distance between thread crests is 1.25 mm and the length is 130 mm.

NOTE
*When purchasing a bolt from a dealership or parts store, it is important to know how to specify bolt length. The correct way to measure bolt length is to measure the length, starting from underneath the bolt head to the end of the bolt (**Figure 6**). Always measure bolt length in this manner to avoid purchasing or installing bolts that are too long.*

The grade marking located on the top of the fastener (**Figure 5**) indicates the strength of metric screws and bolts. The higher the number, the stronger the fastener. Unnumbered fasteners are the weakest.

Many screws, bolts and studs are combined with nuts to secure particular components. To indicate the size of a

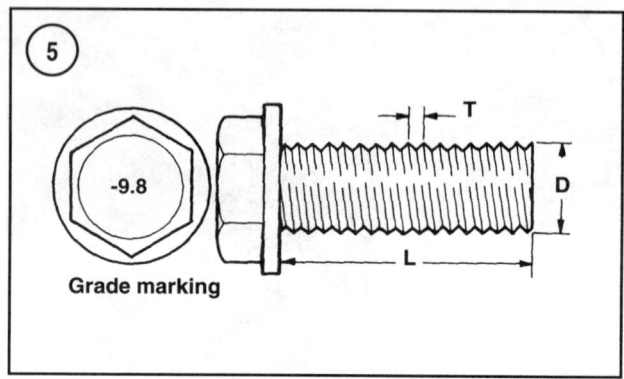

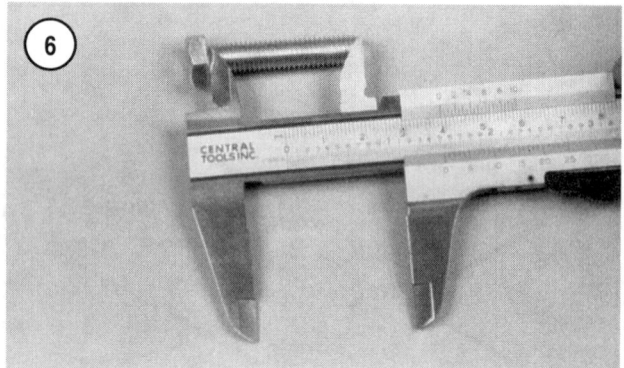

nut, manufacturers specify the internal diameter and the thread pitch.

The measurement across two flats on a nut or bolt indicates the wrench size.

WARNING
Do not install fasteners with a strength classification lower than what was originally installed by the manufacturer. Doing so may cause equipment failure and/or damage.

Torque Specifications

The materials used during the manufacturing of the engine may be subjected to uneven stresses if the fasteners of the various subassemblies are not installed and tightened correctly. Fasteners that are improperly installed or work loose can cause extensive damage. It is essential to use an accurate torque wrench, described in this chapter, with the torque specifications in this manual. Torque specifications are listed at the end of each chapter. If a torque is not listed, use the general torque specifications in **Table 5** of this chapter.

Specifications for torque are provided in Newton-meters (N•m), foot-pounds (ft.-lb.) and inch-pounds

GENERAL INFORMATION

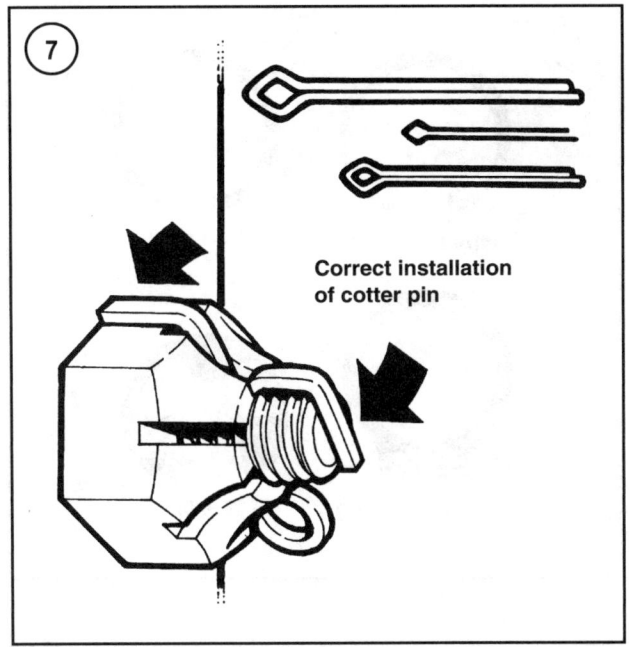

Correct installation of cotter pin

(in.-lb.). Torque specifications for specific components (including all critical torque figures) are at the end of the appropriate chapters. Torque wrenches are covered in the *Basic Tools* section of this chapter.

Self-Locking Fasteners

Several types of bolts, screws and nuts incorporate a system that creates interference between the two fasteners. Interference is achieved in various ways. The most common type is the nylon insert nut and a dry adhesive coating on the threads of a bolt.

Self-locking fasteners offer greater holding strength than standard fasteners, which improves their resistance to vibration. Most self-locking fasteners cannot be reused. The materials used to form the lock become distorted after the initial installation and removal. It is a good practice to discard and replace self-locking fasteners after their removal. Do not replace self-locking fasteners with standard fasteners.

Washers

There are two basic types of washers: flat washers and lockwashers. Flat washers are simple discs with a hole to fit a screw or bolt. Lockwashers prevent a fastener from working loose. Washers can be used as spacers and seals, or to help distribute fastener load and to prevent the fastener from damaging the component.

As with fasteners, when replacing washers make sure the replacement washers are the same design and quality.

NOTE
Give as much care to the selection and purchase of washers as given to bolts, nuts and other fasteners. Avoid washers that are made of thin and weak materials. These will deform and crush the first time they are used in a high torque application, allowing the nut or bolt to loosen.

Cotter Pins

A cotter pin is a split metal pin inserted into a hole or slot to prevent a fastener from loosening. In certain applications, the fastener must be secured in this way. For these applications, a cotter pin and castellated (slotted) nut are used.

To use a cotter pin, first make sure the diameter is correct for the hole in the fastener. After correctly tightening the fastener and aligning the holes, insert the cotter pin through the hole and bend the ends over the fastener (**Figure 7**). Cut the arms to a suitable length to prevent them from snagging on clothing, or worse, skin; remember that exposed ends of the pin cut flesh easily. When the cotter pin is bent and its arms cut to length, it must be tight. If it can be wiggled, it is improperly installed.

Unless instructed to do so, never loosen a torqued fastener to align the holes. If the holes do not align, tighten the fastener just enough to achieve alignment.

Cotter pins are available in various diameters and lengths. Measure length from the bottom of the head to the tip of the shortest pin.

Do not reuse cotter pins as their ends may break, causing the pin to fall out and allowing the fastener to loosen.

Snap Rings

Snap rings (**Figure 8**) are circular-shaped metal retaining clips. They help secure parts and gears in place such as shafts, pins or rods. External type snap rings retain items on shafts. Internal type snap rings secure parts within housing bores. In some applications, in addition to securing the component(s), snap rings of varying thickness also determine endplay. These are usually called selective snap rings.

There are two basic types of snap rings: machined and stamped snap rings. Machined snap rings (**Figure 9**) can be installed in either direction, since both faces have sharp edges. Stamped snap rings (**Figure 10**) have a sharp edge and a round edge. When installing a stamped snap ring in a thrust application, install the sharp edge facing away from the part producing the thrust.

Observe the following when installing snap rings:
1. Wear eye protection when removing and installing snap rings.
2. In some applications, it may be necessary to replace snap rings after removing them.
3. Compress or expand snap rings only enough to install them. If overly expanded, they lose their retaining ability.
4. After installing a snap ring, make sure it seats completely.
5. Remove and install snap rings with snap ring pliers. See *Snap Ring Pliers* in this chapter.

E-rings and circlips are used when it is not practical to use a snap ring. Remove E-rings with a flat blade screwdriver by prying between the shaft and E-ring. To install an E-ring, center it over the shaft groove and push or tap it into place.

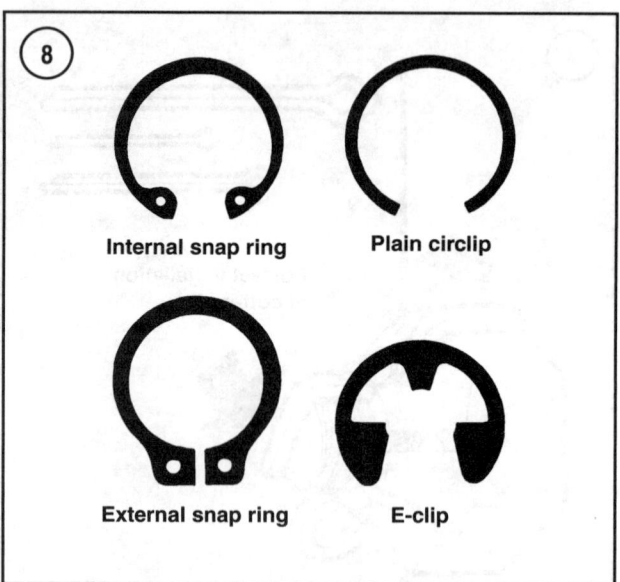

SHOP SUPPLIES

Lubricants

Periodic lubrication helps ensure long life for any type of equipment. The *type* of lubricant used is just as important as the lubrication service itself, although in an emergency the wrong type of lubricant is usually better than no lubricant at all. The following information describes the types of lubricants most often used on marine equipment. Be sure to follow the manufacturer's recommendations for lubricant types.

NOTE
*For more information on Yamaha recommended lubricants, please refer to **Quick Reference Data** at the beginning of this manual or the information and tables in Chapter Three.*

Generally, all liquid lubricants are called *oil*. They may be mineral-based (including petroleum bases), natural-based (vegetable and animal bases), synthetic-based or emulsions (mixtures). *Grease* is oil to which a thickening base was added so that the end product is semi-solid. Grease is often classified by the type of thickener added; lithium soap is commonly used.

Two-stroke engine oil

Lubrication for a two-stroke engine is provided by oil mixed into the incoming air-fuel mixture. Some of the oil mist settles out in the crankcase, lubricating the crankshaft, bearings and lower end of the connecting rod. The

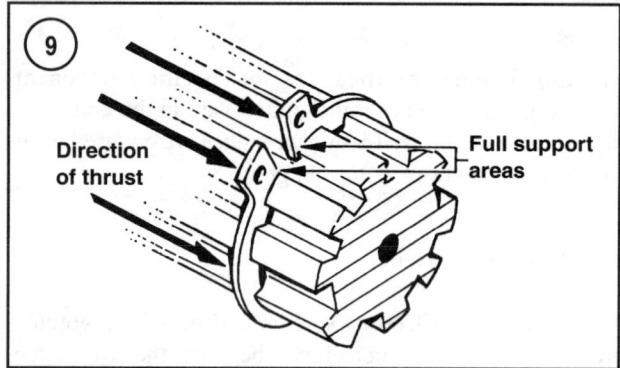

rest of the oil enters the combustion chamber to lubricate the piston, rings and the cylinder wall. This oil is burned with the air-fuel mixture during the combustion process.

Engine oil must have several special qualities to work well in a two-stroke engine. It must mix easily and stay in suspension with gasoline. When burned, it can not leave behind excessive deposits. It must also withstand the high operating temperature associated with two-stroke engines.

The National Marine Manufacturer's Association (NMMA) has set standards for oil used in two-stroke, water-cooled engines. This is the NMMA TC-W (two-cycle, water-cooled) grade. It indicates the oil's performance in the following areas:
1. Lubrication (prevention of wear and scuffing).
2. Spark plug fouling.
3. Piston ring sticking.
4. Preignition.

GENERAL INFORMATION

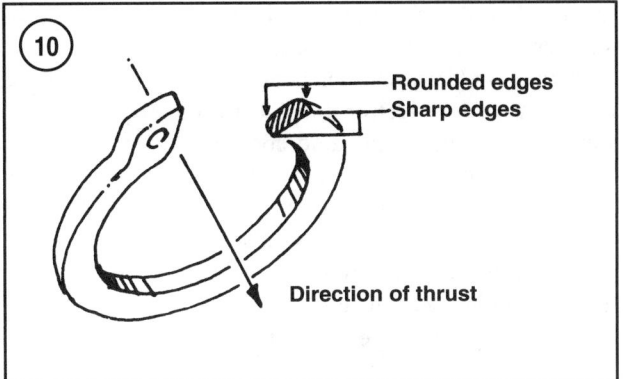

5. Piston varnish.
6. General engine condition (including deposits).
7. Exhaust port blockage.
8. Rust prevention.
9. Mixing ability with gasoline.

In addition to oil grade, manufacturers specify the ratio of gasoline to oil required during break-in and normal engine operation.

Gearcase oil

Gearcase lubricants are assigned SAE viscosity numbers under the same system as four-stroke engine oil. Gearcase lubricant falls into the SAE 72-250 range. Some gearcase lubricants, such as SAE 85-90, are multigrade.

Three types of marine gearcase lubricant are generally available: SAE 90 hypoid gearcase lubricant is designed for older manual-shift units; Type C gearcase lubricant contains additives designed for the electric shift mechanisms; High viscosity gearcase lubricant is a heavier oil designed to withstand the shock loading of high performance engines or engines subjected to severe duty use. Always use a gearcase lubricant of the type specified by the gearcase manufacturer.

Greases

Grease is lubricating oil with thickening agents added to it. The National Lubricating Grease Institute (NLGI) grades grease. Grades range from No. 000 to No. 6, with No. 6 being the thickest. Typical multipurpose grease is NLGI No. 2. For specific applications, manufacturers may recommend water-resistant type grease or one with an additive such as molybdenum disulfide (MoS2).

Cleaners, Degreasers and Solvents

Many chemicals are available to remove oil, grease and other residue.

Before using cleaning solvents, consider how they will be used and disposed of, particularly if they are not water-soluble. Local ordinances may require special procedures for the disposal of many types of cleaning chemicals. Refer to *Safety and Cleaning Parts* in this chapter for more information on their use.

Use electrical contact cleaner to clean wiring connections and components without leaving any residue. Carburetor cleaner is a powerful solvent used to remove fuel deposits and varnish from fuel system components. Use this cleaner carefully, as it may damage finishes.

Generally, degreasers are strong cleaners used to remove heavy accumulations of grease from engine and frame components.

Most solvents are used in a parts washing cabinet for individual component cleaning. For safety, use only non-flammable or high flash point solvents.

Gasket Sealant

Sealants are used in combination with a gasket or seal and are occasionally used alone. Follow the manufacturer's recommendation when using sealants. Use extreme care when choosing a sealant different from the type originally recommended. Choose sealants based on their resistance to heat, various fluids and their sealing capabilities.

One of the most common sealants is RTV, or room temperature vulcanizing sealant. This sealant cures at room temperature over a specific time period. This allows the repositioning of components without damaging gaskets.

Moisture in the air causes the RTV sealant to cure. Always install the tube cap as soon as possible after applying RTV sealant. RTV sealant has a limited shelf life and does not cure properly if the shelf life has expired. Keep partial tubes sealed and discard them if they have surpassed the expiration date.

Applying RTV sealant

Clean all old gasket residue from the mating surfaces. Remove all gasket material from blind threaded holes; it can cause inaccurate bolt torque. Spray the mating surfaces with aerosol parts cleaner and then wipe with a lint-free cloth. The area must be clean for the sealant to adhere.

Apply RTV sealant in a continuous bead 2-3 mm (0.08-0.12 in.) thick. Circle all the fastener holes unless otherwise specified. Do not allow any sealant to enter these holes. Assemble and tighten the fasteners to the specified torque within the time frame recommended by the RTV sealant manufacturer (usually within 10-15 minutes).

Gasket Remover

Aerosol gasket remover can help remove stubborn gaskets. This product can speed up the removal process and prevent damage to the mating surface that may be caused by using a scraping tool. Most of these types of products are very caustic. Follow the gasket remover manufacturer's instructions.

Threadlocking Compound

A threadlocking compound is a fluid applied to the threads of fasteners. After tightening the fastener, the fluid dries and becomes a solid filler between the threads. This makes it difficult for the fastener to work loose from vibration, or heat expansion and contraction. Some threadlocking compounds also provide a seal against fluid leaks.

Before applying threadlocking compound remove any old compound from both thread areas and clean them with aerosol parts cleaner. Use the compound sparingly. Excess fluid can run into adjoining parts.

Threadlocking compounds come in different strengths. Follow the particular manufacturer's recommendations regarding compound selection. Two manufacturers of threadlocking compound are ThreeBond and Loctite, which offer a wide range of compounds for various strength, temperature and repair applications.

Applying threadlock

Make sure surfaces are clean. If a threadlock was previously applied to the component, remove this residue.

Shake the container thoroughly and apply to both parts, then assemble the parts and/or tighten the fasteners.

GALVANIC CORROSION

A chemical reaction occurs whenever two different types of metal are joined by an electrical conductor and immersed in an electrolytic solution such as water. Electrons transfer from one metal to the other through the electrolyte and return through the conductor.

The hardware on a boat is made of many different types of metal. The boat hull acts as a conductor between the metals. Even if the hull is wooden or fiberglass, the slightest film of water on the hull provides conductivity by acting as electrolyte. This combination creates a good environment for electron flow. Unfortunately, this electron flow results in galvanic corrosion of the metal involved, causing one of the metals to be corroded or eroded away. The amount of electron flow, and therefore the amount of corrosion, depends on several factors:
1. The types of metal involved.
2. The efficiency of the conductor.
3. The strength of the electrolyte.

Metals

The chemical composition of the metal used in marine equipment has a significant effect on the amount and speed of galvanic corrosion. Certain metals are more resistant to corrosion than others. These electrically negative metals are commonly called *noble*; they act as the cathode in any reaction. Metals that are more subject to corrosion are electrically positive; they act as the anode in a reaction. The more noble metals include titanium, 18-8 stainless steel and nickel. Less noble metals include zinc, aluminum and magnesium. Galvanic corrosion becomes more excessive as the difference in electrical potential between the two metals increases.

In some cases, galvanic corrosion can occur within a single piece of metal. For example, brass is a mixture of zinc and copper, and, when immersed in an electrolyte, the zinc portion of the mixture will corrode away as a galvanic reaction occurs between the zinc and copper particles.

Conductors

The hull of the boat often acts as the conductor between different types of metal. Marine equipment, such as the engine/gearcase of the outboard can act as the conductor. Large masses of metal, firmly connected together, are more efficient conductors than water. Rubber mountings and vinyl-based paint can act as insulators between pieces of metal.

Electrolyte

The water in which a boat operates acts as the electrolyte for the corrosion process. The more efficient a conductor is, the more excessive and rapid the corrosion will be.

Cold, clean freshwater is the poorest electrolyte. Pollutants increase conductivity; therefore, brackish or saltwa-

GENERAL INFORMATION

ter is an efficient electrolyte. This is one of the reasons that most manufacturers recommend a freshwater flush after operating in polluted, brackish or saltwater.

Protection from Galvanic Corrosion

Because of the environment in which marine equipment must operate, it is practically impossible to totally prevent galvanic corrosion. However, there are several ways in which the process is slowed. After taking these precautions, the next step is to *fool* the process into occurring only in certain places. This is the role of sacrificial anodes and impressed current systems.

Slowing corrosion

Some simple precautions can help reduce the amount of corrosion taking place outside the hull. These precautions are not substitutes for the corrosion protection methods discussed under *Sacrificial Anodes* and *Impressed Current Systems* in this chapter, but they can help these methods reduce corrosion.

Use fasteners made of metal more noble than the parts they secure. If corrosion occurs, the parts they secure may suffer but the fasteners are protected. The larger secured parts are more able to withstand the loss of material. Also major problems could arise if the fasteners corrode to the point of failure.

Keep all painted surfaces in good condition. If paint is scraped off and bare metal exposed, corrosion rapidly increases. Use a vinyl- or plastic-based paint, which acts as an electrical insulator.

Be careful when applying metal-based antifouling paint to the boat. Do not apply antifouling paint to metal parts of the boat or the outboard engine/gearcase. If applied to metal surfaces, this type of paint reacts with the metal and results in corrosion between the metal and the layer of paint. Maintain a minimum 25 mm (1 in.) border between the painted surface and any metal parts. Organic-based paints are available for use on metal surfaces.

Where a corrosion protection device is used, remember that it must be immersed in the electrolyte along with the boat to provide any protection. If the outboard is raised out of the water when the boat is docked, any anodes on the engine will be removed from the corrosion process rendering them ineffective. (Of course, the engine requires less protection when raised out of the water/electrolyte.) Never paint or apply any coating to anodes or other protection devices. Paint or other coatings insulate them from the corrosion process.

Any change in boat equipment, such as the installation of a new stainless steel propeller, changes the electrical potential and may cause increased corrosion. Always consider this fact when adding equipment or changing exposed materials. Install additional anodes or other protection equipment as required to ensure the corrosion protection system is up to the task. The expense to repair corrosion damage usually far exceeds that of additional corrosion protection.

Sacrificial anodes

Sacrificial anodes are specially designed to do nothing but corrode. Properly fastening such pieces to the boat causes them to act as the anode in any galvanic reaction that occurs; any other metal in the reaction acts as the cathode and is not damaged.

Anodes are usually made of zinc, a less noble material. Some anodes are manufactured of an aluminum and indium alloy. This alloy is less noble than the aluminum alloy in drive system components, providing the desired sacrificial properties. The aluminum and indium alloy is more resistant to oxide coating than zinc anodes. Oxide coating occurs as the anode material reacts with oxygen in the water. An oxide coating insulates the anode, dramatically reducing corrosion protection.

Anodes must be used properly to be effective. Simply fastening anodes to the boat in random locations does not do the job.

First determine how much anode surface is required to adequately protect the equipment surface area. A good starting point is provided by the Military Specification MIL-A-818001, which states that one square inch of new anode protects either:

1. 800 sq. in. of freshly painted steel.
2. 250 sq. in. of bare steel or bare aluminum alloy.
3. 100 sq. in. of copper or copper alloy.

This rule is valid for a boat at rest. If underway, additional anode areas are required to protect the same surface area.

The anode must be in good electrical contact with the metal that it protects. If possible, attach an anode to all metal surfaces requiring protection.

Quality anodes have inserts around the fastener holes that are made of a more noble material. Otherwise, the anode could erode away around the fastener hole, allowing the anode to loosen or possibly fall off, thereby losing needed protection.

Impressed Current System

An impressed current system can be added to any boat. The system generally consists of the anode, controller and reference electrode. The anode in this system is coated with a very noble metal, such as platinum, so that it is almost corrosion-free and can last almost indefinitely. The reference electrode, under the hull waterline, allows the control module to monitor the potential for corrosion. If the module senses that corrosion is occurring, it applies positive battery voltage to the anode. Current then flows from the anode to all other metal components, regardless of how noble or non-noble these components may be. Essentially, the electrical current from the battery counteracts the galvanic reaction to dramatically reduce corrosion damage.

Only a small amount of current is needed to counteract corrosion. Using input from the sensor, the control module provides only the amount of current needed to suppress galvanic corrosion. Most systems consume a maximum of 0.2 Ah at full demand. Under normal conditions, these systems can provide protection for 8-12 weeks without recharging the battery. Remember that this system must have constant connection to the battery. Often the battery supply to the system is connected to a battery switching device causing the operator to inadvertently shut off the system while docked.

An impressed current system is more expensive to install than sacrificial anodes, but considering the low maintenance requirements and the superior protection it provides, the long-term cost may be lower.

PROPELLERS

The propeller is the final link between the engine drive system and the water. A perfectly maintained engine and hull are useless if the propeller is the wrong type, damaged or deteriorated. Although propeller selection for a specific application is beyond the scope of this manual, the following provides the basic information needed to make an informed decision. A professional at a reputable marine dealership is the best source for a propeller recommendation.

How a Propeller Works

As the curved blades of a propeller rotate through the water, a high-pressure area forms on one side of the blade and a low-pressure area forms on the other side of the blade (**Figure 11**). The propeller moves toward the low-pressure area, carrying the boat with it.

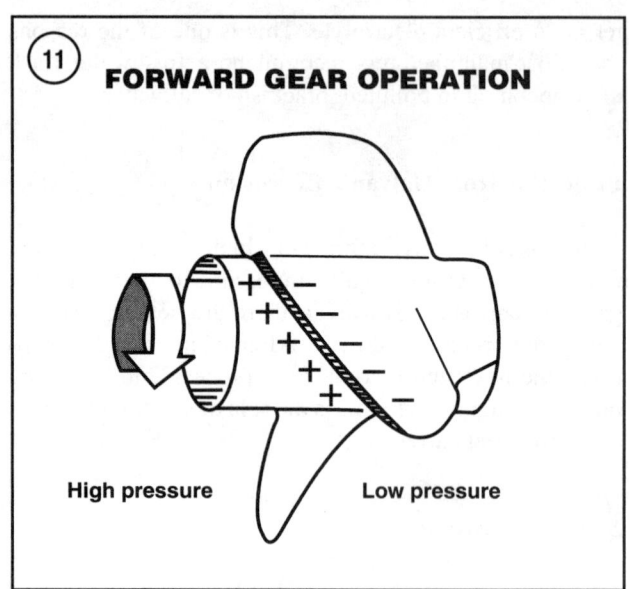

Propeller Parts

Although a propeller is usually a one-piece unit, it is made of several different parts (**Figure 12**). Variations in the design of these parts make different propellers suitable for different applications.

The blade tip is the point of the blade furthest from the center of the propeller hub or propeller shaft bore. The blade tip separates the leading edge from the trailing edge.

The leading edge is the edge of the blade nearest the boat. During forward operation, this is the area of the blade that first cuts through the water.

The trailing edge is the surface of the blade furthest from the boat. During reverse operation, this is the area of the blade that first cuts through the water.

The blade face is the surface of the blade that faces away from the boat. During forward operation, high-pressure forms on this side of the blade.

The blade back is the surface of the blade that faces toward the boat. During forward gear operation, low-pressure forms on this side of the blade.

The cup is a small curve or lip on the trailing edge of the blade. Cupped propeller blades generally perform better than non-cupped propeller blades.

The hub is the center portion of the propeller. It connects the blades to the propeller shaft. On most drive systems, engine exhaust is routed through the hub; in this case, the hub is made up of an outer and inner portion, connected by ribs.

A diffuser ring is used on through-hub exhaust models to prevent exhaust gasses from entering the blade area.

GENERAL INFORMATION

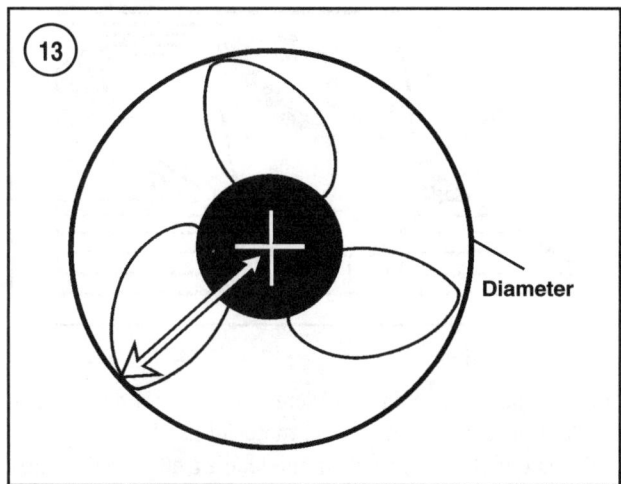

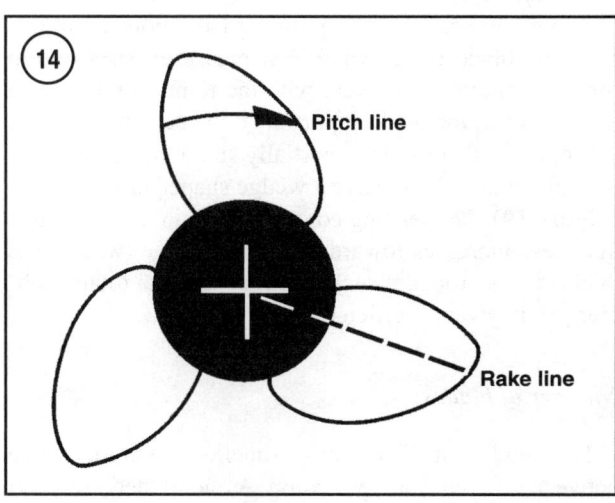

Propeller Design

Changes in length, angle, thickness and material of propeller parts make different propellers suitable for different applications.

Diameter

Propeller diameter is the distance from the center of the hub to the blade tip, multiplied by two. Essentially it is the diameter of the circle formed by the blade tips during propeller rotation (**Figure 13**).

Pitch and rake

Propeller pitch and rake describe the placement of the blades in relation to the hub (**Figure 14**).

Pitch describes the theoretical distance the propeller would travel in one revolution. In A, **Figure 15**, the propeller would travel 10 in. in one revolution. In B, **Figure 15**, the propeller would travel 20 in. in one revolution. This distance is only theoretical; during typical operation, the propeller achieves only 75-85% of its pitch. Slip rate describes the difference in actual travel relative to the pitch. Lighter, faster boats typically achieve a lower slip rate than heavier, slower boats.

Propeller blades can be constructed with constant pitch (**Figure 16**) or progressive pitch (**Figure 17**). On a progressive propeller, the pitch starts low at the leading edge and increases toward the trailing edge. The propeller pitch specification is the average of the pitch across the entire

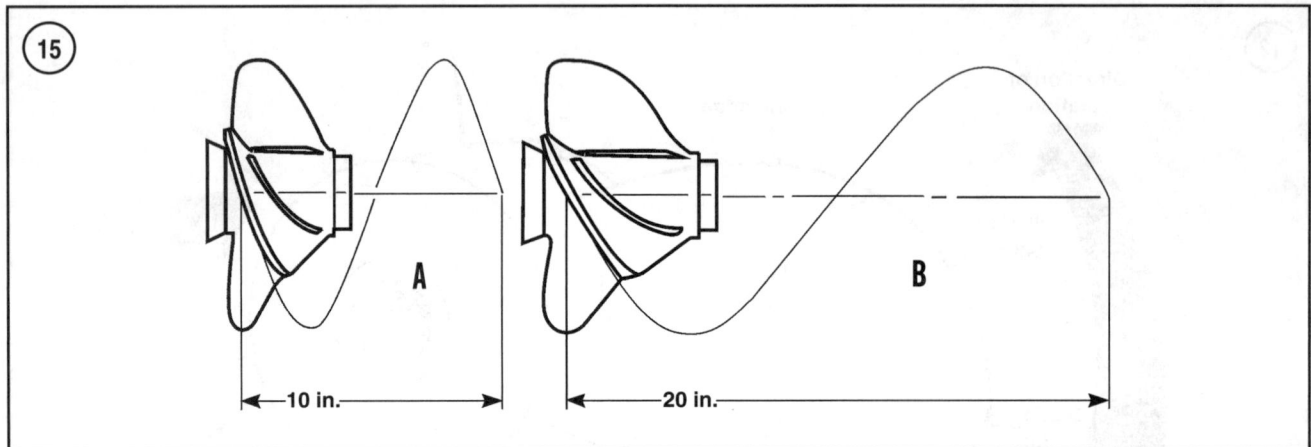

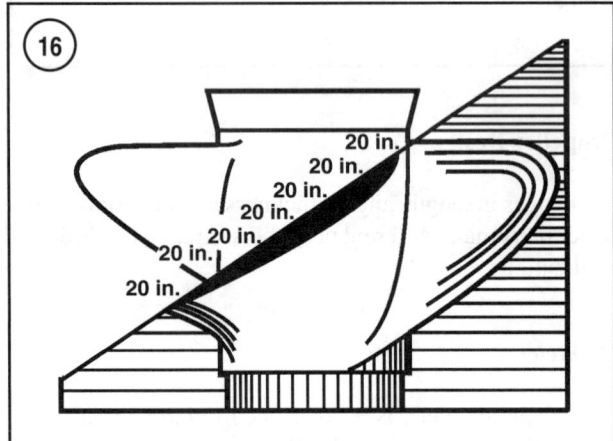
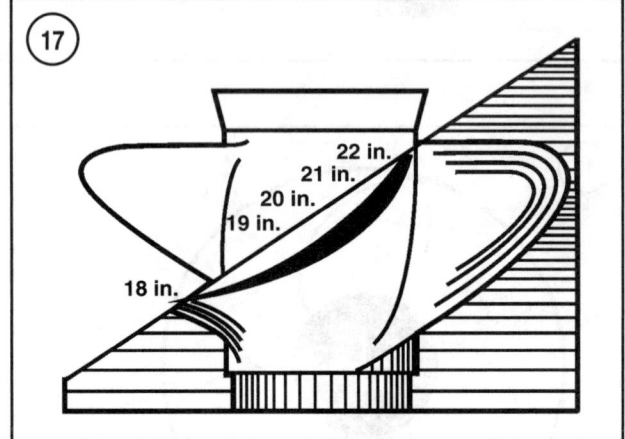

blade. Propellers with progressive pitch usually provide better overall performance than constant pitch propellers.

Blade rake is specified in degrees and is measured along a line from the center of the hub to the blade tip. A blade that is perpendicular to the hub (A, **Figure 18**) has 0° rake. A blade that is angled from perpendicular (B, **Figure 18**) has a rake expressed by its difference from perpendicular. Most propellers have rakes ranging from 0-20°. Lighter, faster boats generally perform better using a propeller with a greater amount of rake. Heavier, slower boats generally perform better using a propeller with less rake.

Blade thickness

Blade thickness is not uniform at all points along the blade. For efficiency, blades are as thin as possible at all points while retaining enough strength to move the boat. Blades are thicker where they meet the hub and thinner at the blade tips. This construction is necessary to support the heavier loads at the hub section of the blade. Overall blade thickness is dependent on the strength of the material used.

When cut along a line from the leading edge to the trailing edge in the central portion of the blade, the propeller blade resembles an airplane wing. The blade face, where high-pressure exists during forward rotation, is almost flat. The blade back, where low-pressure exists during forward rotation, is curved, with the thinnest portions at the edges and the thickest portion at the center.

Propellers that run only partially submerged, as in racing applications, may have a wedge shaped cross-section (**Figure 19**). The leading edge is very thin and the blade thickness increases toward the trailing edge, where it is thickest. If a propeller such as this type is run totally submerged, it is very inefficient.

Number of blades

The number of blades on a propeller is a compromise between efficiency and vibration. A one-bladed propeller

GENERAL INFORMATION

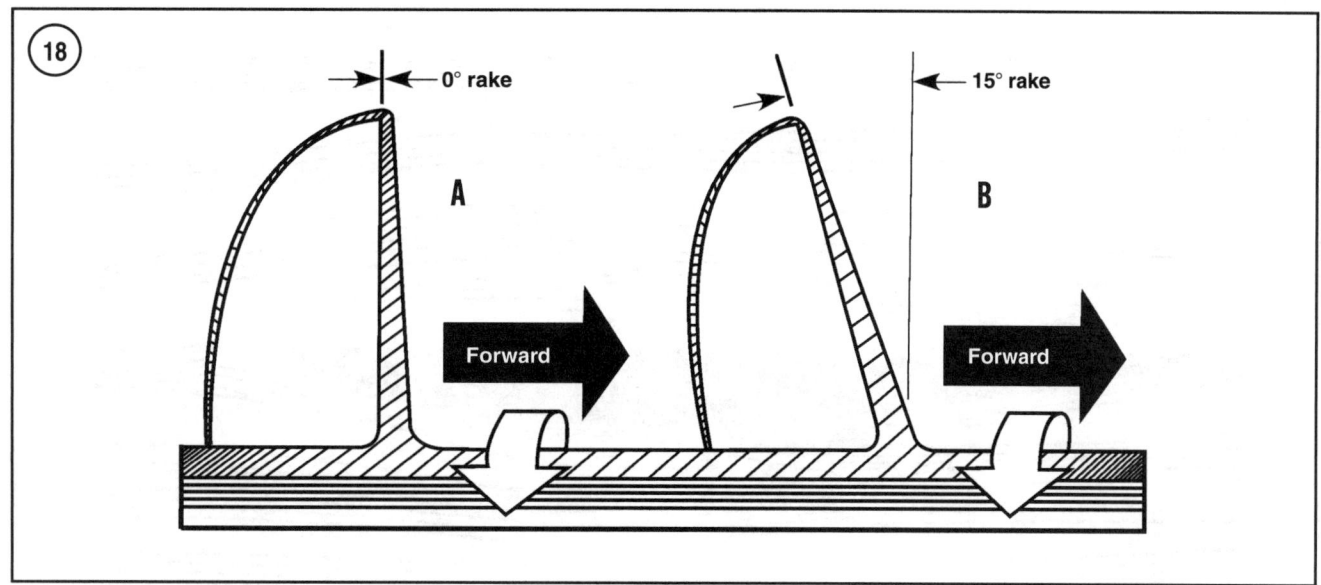

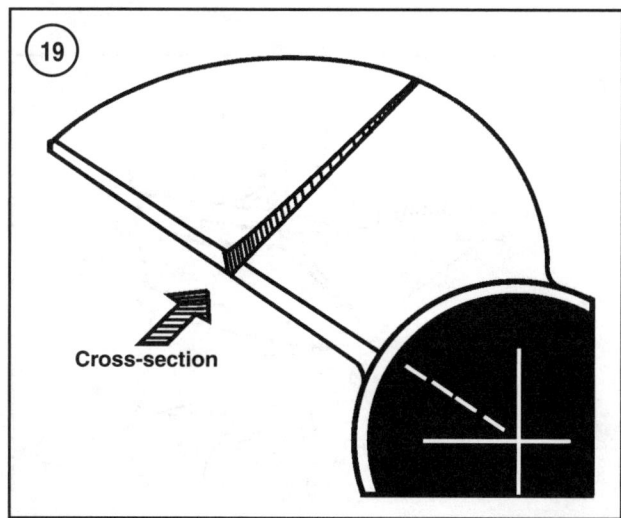

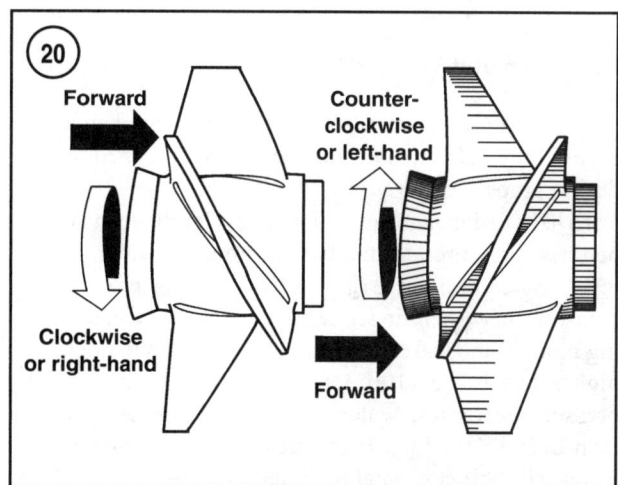

would be the most efficient, but it would create an unacceptable amount of vibration. As blades are added, efficiency decreases, but so does vibration. Most propellers have three or four blades, representing the most practical trade-off between efficiency and vibration.

Material

Propeller materials are chosen for strength, corrosion resistance and economy. Stainless steel, aluminum, plastic and bronze are the most commonly used materials. Bronze is quite strong but rather expensive. Stainless steel is more common than bronze because of its combination of strength and lower cost. Aluminum alloy and plastic materials are the least expensive but usually lack the strength of stainless steel. Plastic propellers are more suited for lower horsepower applications.

Direction of rotation

Propellers are made for both right-hand and left-hand rotations although right-hand is the most commonly used. As viewed from the rear of the boat while in forward gear, a right-hand propeller turns clockwise and a left-hand propeller turns counterclockwise. Off the boat, the direction of rotation is determined by observing the angle of the blades (**Figure 20**). A right-hand propeller's blade slant from the upper left to the lower right; a left-hand propeller's blades are opposite.

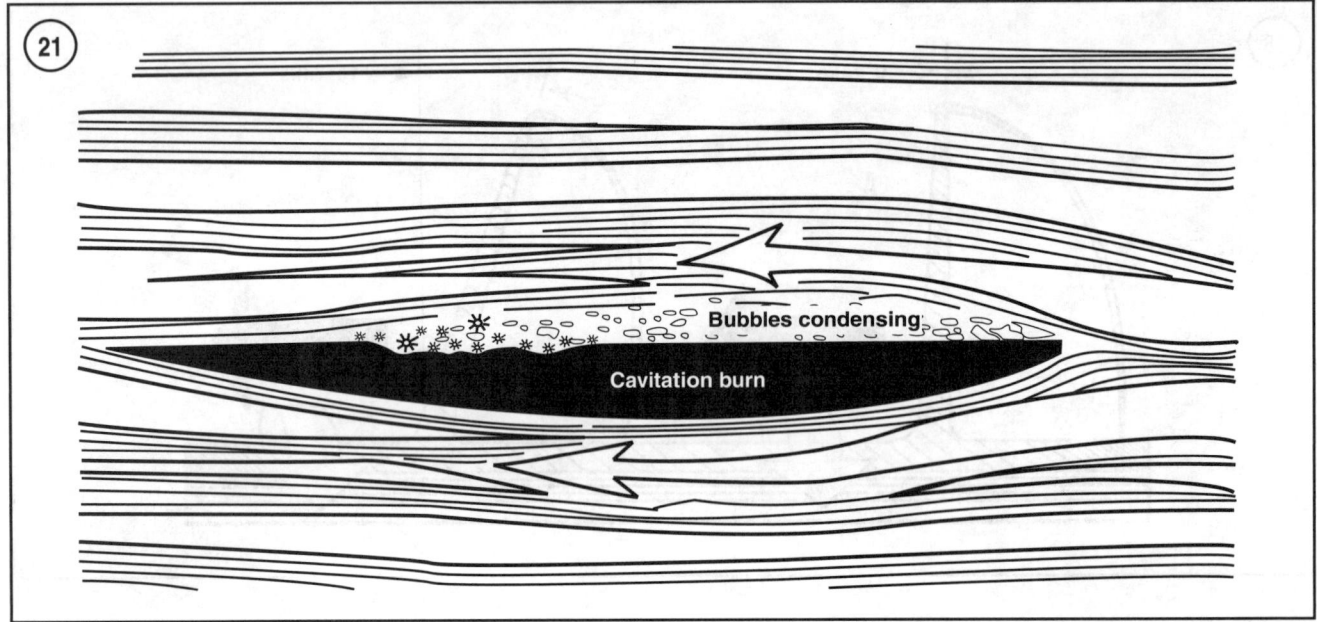

Cavitation and Ventilation

Cavitation and ventilation are *not* interchangeable terms; they refer to two distinct problems encountered during propeller operation.

To help understand cavitation, consider the relationship between pressure and the boiling point of water. At sea level, water boils at 212° F (100° C). As pressure increases, such as within an engine cooling system, the boiling point of the water increases—it boils at a temperature higher than 212° F (100° C). The opposite is also true. As pressure decreases, water boils at a temperature lower than 212° F (100° C). If the pressure drops low enough, water will boil at normal room temperature.

During normal propeller operation, low pressure forms on the blade back. Normally the pressure does not drop low enough for boiling to occur. However, poor propeller design, damaged blades or using the wrong propeller can cause unusually low pressure on the blade surface (**Figure 21**). If the pressure drops low enough, boiling occurs and bubbles form on the blade surfaces. As the boiling water moves to a higher pressure area of the blade, the boiling ceases and the bubbles collapse. The collapsing bubbles release energy that erodes the surface of the propeller blade.

Corroded surfaces, physical damage or even marine growth combined with high-speed operation can cause low pressure and cavitation on outboard gearcase surfaces. In such cases, low pressure forms as water flows over a protrusion or rough surface. The boiling water forms bubbles that collapse as they move to a higher pressure area toward the rear of the surface imperfection.

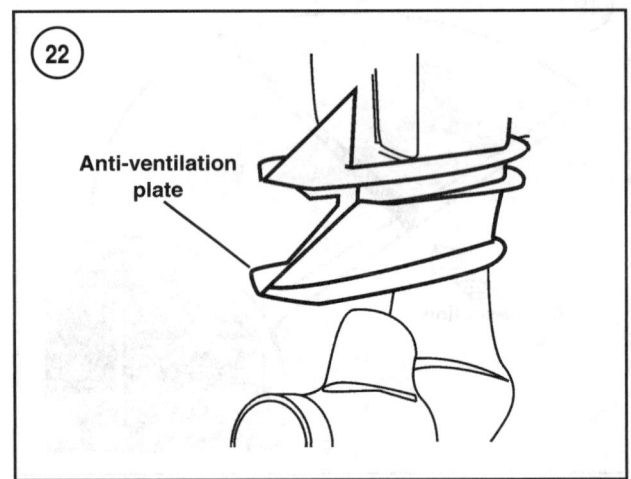

This entire process of pressure drop, boiling and bubble collapse is called *cavitation*. The ensuing damage is called *cavitation burn*. Cavitation is caused by a decrease in pressure, not an increase in temperature.

Ventilation is not as complex a process as cavitation. Ventilation refers to air entering the blade area, either from above the water surface or from a through-hub exhaust system. As the blades meet the air, the propeller momentarily loses its bite with the water and subsequently loses most of its thrust. An added complication is that the propeller and engine over-rev, causing very low pressure on the blade back and massive cavitation.

Most marine drive systems have a plate (**Figure 22**) above the propeller designed to prevent surface air from

GENERAL INFORMATION

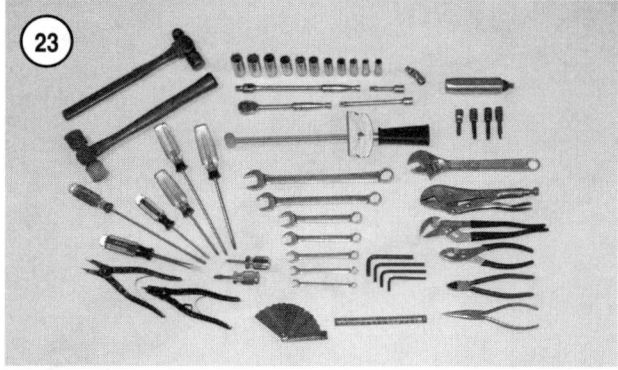

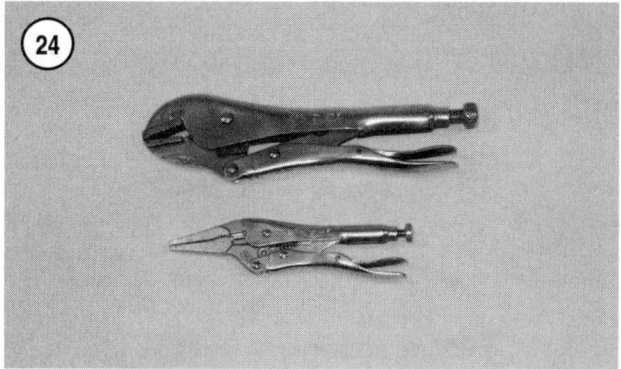

entering the blade area. This plate is an *anti-ventilation plate*, although it is often incorrectly called an *anticavitation plate*.

Most propellers have a flared section at the rear of the propeller called a diffuser ring. This feature forms a barrier, and extends the exhaust passage far enough aft to prevent the exhaust gases from ventilating the propeller.

A close fit of the propeller to the gearcase is necessary to keep exhaust gasses from exiting and ventilating the propeller. Using the wrong propeller attaching hardware can position the propeller too far aft, preventing a close fit. The wrong hardware can also allow the propeller to rub heavily against the gearcase, causing rapid wear to both components. Wear or damage to these surfaces allows the propeller to ventilate.

BASIC TOOLS

Most of the procedures in this manual can be carried out with simple hand tools and test equipment familiar to the home mechanic. Always use the correct tools for the job at hand. Keep tools organized and clean. Store them in a tool chest with related tools organized together.

After using a tool, wipe off dirt and grease with a clean cloth and return the tool to its correct place. Wiping tools off is especially important when servicing the craft in areas where they can come in contact with sand. Sand is very abrasive and causes premature wear to engine parts.

Quality tools are essential. The best are constructed of high-strength alloy steel. These tools are light, easy to use and resistant to wear. Their working surface is devoid of sharp edges and the tool is carefully polished. They have an easy-to-clean finish and are comfortable to use. Quality tools are a good investment.

When purchasing tools to perform the procedures covered in this manual, consider the potential frequency of use. If starting a tool kit, consider purchasing a basic tool set (**Figure 23**) from a large tool supplier. These sets are available in many tool combinations and offer substantial savings when compared to individually purchased tools. As work experience grows and tasks become more complicated, specialized tools can be added.

Screwdrivers

Screwdrivers of various lengths and types are mandatory for the simplest tool kit. The two basic types are the slotted tip (flat blade) and the Phillips tip. These are available in sets that often include an assortment of tip sizes and shaft lengths.

As with all tools, use a screwdriver designed for the job. Make sure the size of the tip conforms to the size and shape of the fastener. Use them only for driving screws. Never use a screwdriver for prying or chiseling metal. Repair or replace worn or damaged screwdrivers. A worn tip may damage the fastener, making it difficult to remove.

Phillips screwdrivers are sized according to their point size. They are numbered one, two, three and four. The degree of taper determines the point size; the No. 1 Phillips screwdriver is the most pointed. The points are more blunt as the number increases.

Pliers

Pliers come in a wide range of types and sizes. Though pliers are useful for holding, cutting, bending and crimping, they should never be used to turn bolts or nuts.

Each design has a specialized function. Slip-joint pliers are general-purpose pliers used for gripping and bending. Diagonal cutting pliers are needed to cut wire and can be used to remove cotter pins. Needlenose pliers are used to hold or bend small objects. Locking pliers (**Figure 24**), sometimes called vise-grips, are used to hold objects very tightly. They have many uses ranging from holding two parts together to gripping the end of a broken stud. Use caution when using locking pliers, as the sharp jaws damage the objects they hold.

Snap Ring Pliers

Snap ring pliers (**Figure 25**) are specialized pliers with tips that fit into the ends of snap rings to remove and install them.

Snap ring pliers are available with fixed action (either internal or external) or convertible (one tool works on both internal and external snap rings). They may have fixed tips or interchangeable ones of various sizes and angles. For general use, select convertible type pliers with interchangeable tips.

WARNING
Snap rings can slip and fly off when removing and installing them. Also, the snap ring plier tips may break. Always wear eye protection when using snap ring pliers.

Hammers

Various types of hammers are available to fit a number of applications. A ball-peen hammer is used to strike another tool, such as a punch or chisel. Soft-faced hammers are required when a metal object must be struck without damaging it. *Never* use a metal-faced hammer on engine components, as damage does occur in most cases.

Always wear eye protection when using hammers. Make sure the hammer face is in good condition and the handle is not cracked. Select the correct hammer for the job and make sure to strike the object squarely. Do not use the handle or the side of the hammer to strike an object.

When striking a hammer against a punch, cold chisel or similar tool, the face of the hammer should be at least 1/2 in. larger than the head of the tool. When it is necessary to strike hard against a steel part without damaging it, use a brass hammer. Brass will give when used on a harder object.

Wrenches

Box-end, open-end and combination wrenches (**Figure 26**) come in a variety of types and sizes.

The number stamped on the wrench refers to the distance between the work areas. This size must match the size of the fastener head.

The box-end wrench is an excellent tool because it grips the fastener on all sides. This factor reduces the chance of the tool slipping. The box-end wrench is designed with ei-

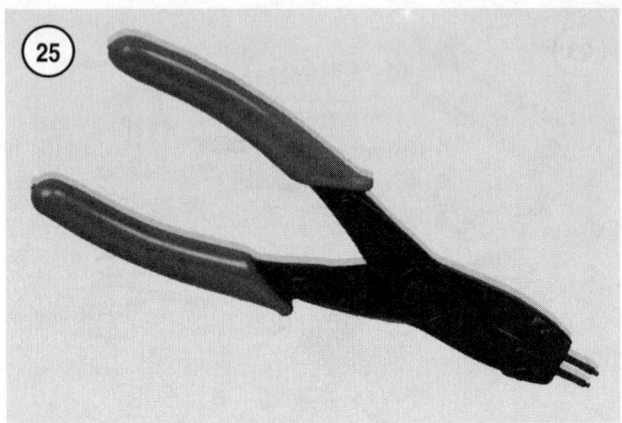

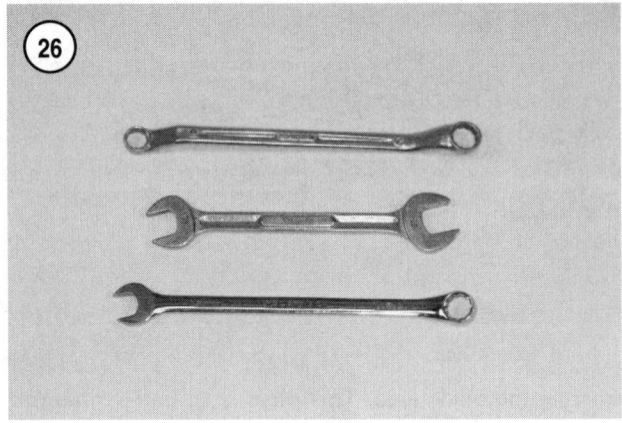

ther a six or 12-point opening. For stubborn or damaged fasteners, the six-point provides superior holding ability by contacting the fastener across a wider area at all six edges. For general use, the 12-point works well. It allows the wrench to be removed and reinstalled without moving the handle over such a wide arc.

An open-end wrench is fast and works best in areas with limited overhead access. It contacts the fastener at only two points, and can slip under heavy force, or if the tool or fastener is worn. A box-end wrench is preferred in most instances, especially when breaking loose and applying the final tightness to a fastener.

The combination wrench has a box-end on one end, and an open-end on the other. This combination makes it a very convenient tool.

Adjustable Wrenches

An adjustable wrench or Crescent wrench can fit nearly any nut or bolt head that has clear access around its entire perimeter. Adjustable wrenches are best used as a backup wrench to keep a large nut or bolt from turning while the

GENERAL INFORMATION

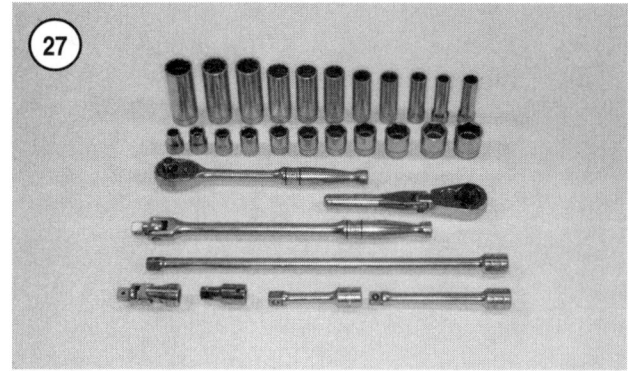

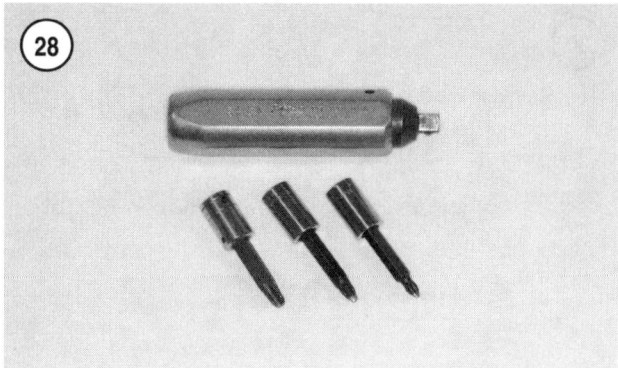

other end is being loosened or tightened with a box-end or socket wrench.

Adjustable wrenches contact the fastener at only two points, which makes them more subject to slipping off the fastener. The fact that one jaw is adjustable and may loosen only aggravates this shortcoming. Make certain the solid jaw is the one transmitting the force.

Socket Wrenches, Ratchets and Handles

Sockets that attach to a ratchet handle (**Figure 27**) are available with six-point or 12-point openings and different drive sizes. The drive size (1/4, 3/8, 1/2 and 3/4 in.) indicates the size of the square hole that accepts the ratchet handle. The number stamped on the socket is the size of the work area and must match the fastener head.

As with wrenches, a six-point socket provides superior-holding ability, while a 12-point socket needs to be moved only half as far to reposition it on the fastener.

Sockets are designated for either hand or impact use. Impact sockets are made of thicker material for more durability. Compare the size and wall thickness of two sockets, say a 19-mm hand socket and a 19-mm impact socket. Use impact sockets when using an impact driver or air tools. Use hand sockets with hand-driven attachments.

WARNING
Do not use hand sockets with air or impact tools, as they may shatter and cause injury. Always wear eye protection when using impact or air tools.

Various handles are available for sockets. The speed handle is used for fast operation. Flexible ratchet heads in varying lengths allow the socket to be turned with varying force, and at odd angles. Extension bars allow the socket setup to reach difficult areas. The ratchet is the most versatile. It allows the user to install or remove the nut without removing the socket.

Sockets combined with any number of drivers make them undoubtedly the fastest, safest and most convenient tool for fastener removal and installation.

Impact Driver

An impact driver provides extra force for removing fasteners, by converting the impact of a hammer into a turning motion. This makes it possible to remove stubborn fasteners without damaging them. Impact drivers and interchangeable bits (**Figure 28**) are available from most tool suppliers. When using a socket with an impact driver make sure the socket is designed for impact use. Refer to *Socket Wrenches, Ratchets and Handles* in this chapter.

WARNING
Do not use hand sockets with air or impact tools as they may shatter and cause injury. Always wear eye protection when using impact or air tools.

Impact drivers are great for the home mechanic as they offer many of the advantages of air tools without the need for a costly air compressor to run them.

Allen Wrenches

Allen or setscrew wrenches (**Figure 29**) are used on fasteners with hexagonal recesses in the fastener head. These wrenches come in L-shaped bar, socket and T-handle types. Allen bolts are sometimes called socket bolts.

Torque Wrenches

A torque wrench is used with a socket, torque adapter or similar extension to measure torque while tightening a fastener. Torque wrenches come in several drive sizes (1/4, 3/8, 1/2 and 3/4) and have various methods of reading the torque value. The drive size is the size of the square drive that accepts the socket, adapter or extension.

Common types of torque wrenches include the deflecting beam (A, **Figure 30**) the dial indicator (B) and the audible click (C).

When choosing a torque wrench, consider the torque range, drive size and accuracy. The torque specifications in this manual provide an indication of the range required.

A torque wrench is a precision tool that must be properly cared for to remain accurate. Store torque wrenches in cases or separate padded drawers within a toolbox. Follow the manufacturer's instructions for care and calibration.

Torque Adapters

Torque adapters or extensions extend or reduce the reach of a torque wrench. The torque adapter shown on the top of **Figure 31** is used to tighten a fastener that cannot be reached because of the size of the torque wrench head, drive, and socket. If a torque adapter changes the effective lever length the torque reading on the wrench will not equal the actual torque applied to the fastener. It is necessary to recalibrate the torque setting on the wrench to compensate for the change of lever length. When using a torque adapter at a right angle to the drive head, calibration is not required, since the effective length has not changed.

To recalculate a torque reading when using a torque adapter, use the following formula, and refer to **Figure 31**.

$$TW = \frac{TA \times L}{L + A}$$

TW is the torque setting or dial reading on the wrench.

TA is the torque specification (the actual amount of torque that should be applied to the fastener).

A is the amount that the adapter increases (or in some cases reduces) the effective lever length as measured along the centerline of the torque wrench (**Figure 31**).

L is the lever length of the wrench as measured from the center of the drive to the center of the grip.

The effective length of the torque wrench measured along the centerline of the torque wrench is the sum of **L** and **A** (**Figure 31**).

Example:
TA = 20 ft.-lb.
A = 3 in.
L = 14 in.
$$TW = \frac{20 \times 14}{14 + 3} = \frac{280}{17} = 16.5 \text{ ft. lb.}$$

In this example, the torque wrench would be set to the recalculated torque value (TW = 16.5 ft.-lb.). When using a beam-type wrench, tighten the fastener until the pointer aligns with 16.5 ft.-lb. In this example, although the torque wrench is pre-set to 16.5 ft.-lb., the actual torque is 20 ft.-lb.

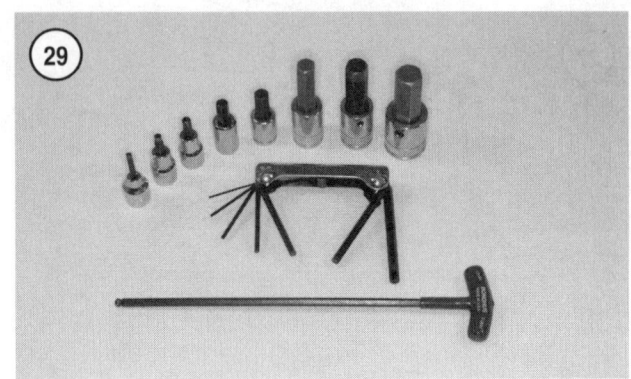

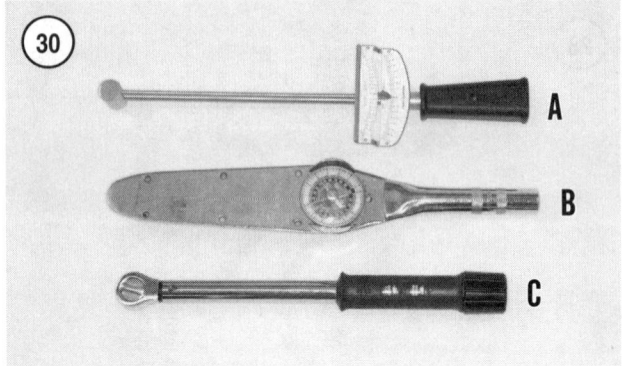

SPECIAL TOOLS

Some of the procedures in this manual require special tools. These are described in the appropriate chapter and are available from either the outboard manufacturer or a tool supplier.

In many cases, an acceptable substitute may be found in an existing tool kit. Another alternative is to make the tool. Many schools with a machine shop curriculum welcome outside work that can be used as practical shop applications for students.

PRECISION MEASURING TOOLS

The ability to accurately measure components is essential to successfully rebuilding an engine. Equipment is manufactured to close tolerances, and obtaining consistently accurate measurements is essential to determining which components require replacement or further service.

Each type of measuring instrument is designed to measure a dimension with a certain degree of accuracy and within a certain range. When selecting the measuring tool, make sure it is applicable to the task.

As with all tools, measuring tools provide the best results if cared for properly. Improper use can damage the

GENERAL INFORMATION

HOW TO MEASURE TORQUE WRENCH EFFECTIVE LENGTH

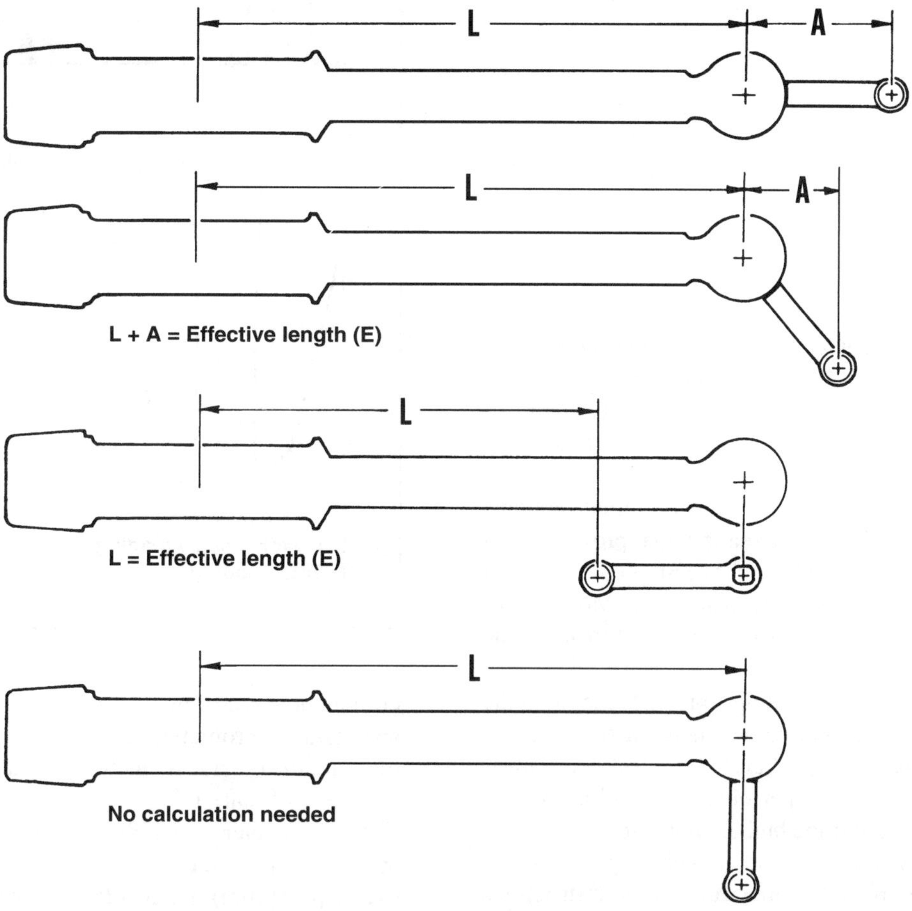

L + A = Effective length (E)

L = Effective length (E)

No calculation needed

tool and result in inaccurate results. If any measurement is questionable, verify the measurement using another tool. A standard gauge is usually provided with measuring tools to check accuracy and calibrate the tool if necessary.

Precision measurements can vary according to the experience of the person performing the procedure. Accurate results are only possible if the mechanic possesses a feel for using the tool. Heavy-handed use of measuring tools produces less accurate results than if the tool is grasped gently by the fingertips so the point at which the tool contacts the object is easily felt. This feel for the equipment produces more accurate measurements and reduces the risk of damaging the tool or component. Refer to the following sections for specific measuring tools.

Feeler Gauge

The feeler or thickness gauge (**Figure 32**) is used for measuring the distance between two surfaces.

A feeler gauge set consists of an assortment of steel strips of graduated thickness. Each blade is marked with its thickness. Blades can be of various lengths and angles for different procedures.

A common use for a feeler gauge is to measure valve clearance. Wire (round) type gauges are used to measure spark plug gap.

To obtain a proper measurement using a feeler gauge, make sure the proper-sized blade passes through the gap with some slight drag. The blade should not need to be forced through, and should not have any play up-and-down between the surfaces being measured.

Calipers

Calipers are excellent tools for obtaining inside, outside and depth measurements. Although not as precise as a micrometer, they allow reasonable precision, typically to within 0.05 mm (0.002 in.). Most calipers have a range up to 150 mm (6 in.).

Calipers are available in dial, vernier or digital versions. Dial calipers have a dial gauge readout that provides convenient reading. Vernier calipers have marked scales that are compared to determine the measurement. Most convenient of all, the digital caliper uses an LCD to show the measurement.

To help ensure accurate readings, properly maintain the measuring surfaces of the caliper. There must not be any dirt or burrs between the tool and the object being measured. Never force the caliper closed around an object; close the caliper around the highest point so it can be removed with a slight drag. Some calipers require calibration. Always refer to the manufacturer's instructions when using a new or unfamiliar caliper.

To read a vernier caliper refer to **Figure 33**. The fixed scale is marked in 1 mm increments. Ten individual lines on the fixed scale equal 1 cm. The movable scale is marked in 0.05 mm (hundredth) increments. To obtain a reading, establish the first number by the location of the 0 line on the movable scale in relation to the first line to the left on the fixed scale. In this example, the number is 10 mm. To determine the next number, note which of the lines on the movable scale align with a mark on the fixed scale. A number of lines will seem close, but only one aligns exactly. In this case, 0.50 mm is the reading to add to the first number. The result of adding 10 mm and 0.50 mm is a measurement of 10.50 mm.

Micrometers

A micrometer is an instrument designed for linear measurement using the decimal divisions of the inch or meter (**Figure 34**). While there are many types and styles of mi-

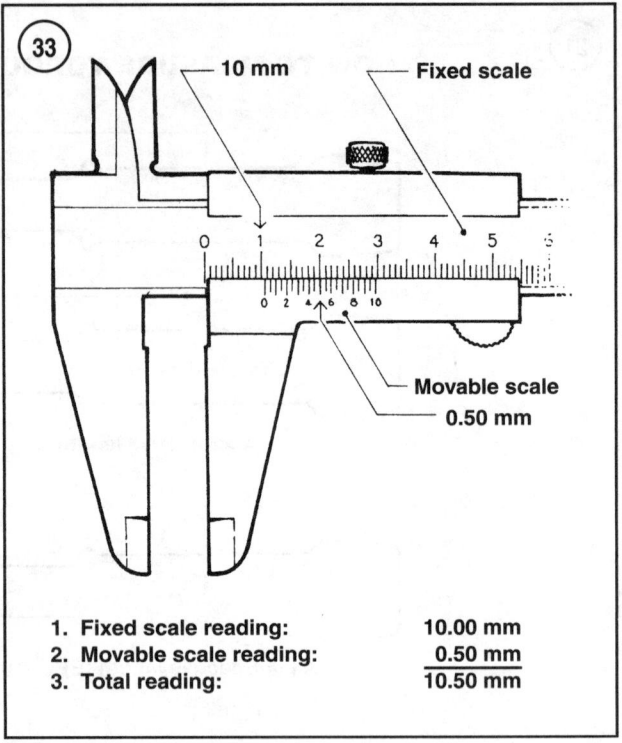

crometers, most of the procedures in this manual call for an outside micrometer. The outside micrometer is used to measure the outside diameter of cylindrical forms and the thickness of materials.

A micrometer size indicates the minimum and maximum size of a part that it can measure. The usual sizes are 0-1 in. (0-25 mm), 1-2 in. (25-50 mm), 2-3 in. (50-75 mm) and 3-4 in. (75-100 mm).

Micrometers covering a wider range of measurement are available, using a large frame with interchangeable anvils of various lengths. This type of micrometer offers a cost savings; however, its overall size may make it less convenient.

Reading a Micrometer

When reading a micrometer, numbers are taken from different scales and added together. The following sections describe how to take measurements with various types of outside micrometers.

For accurate results, properly maintain the measuring surfaces of the micrometer. There cannot be any dirt or burrs between the tool and the measured object. Never force the micrometer closed around an object. Close the micrometer around the highest point so it can be removed with a slight drag. **Figure 35** shows the markings and parts of a standard inch micrometer. Be familiar with

GENERAL INFORMATION

DECIMAL PLACE VALUES*

0.1	Indicates 1/10 (one tenth of an inch or millimeter)
0.010	Indicates 1/100 (one one-hundreth of an inch or millimeter)
0.001	Indicates 1/1000 (one one-thousandth of an inch or millimeter)

*This chart represents the values of figures placed to the right of the decimal point. Use it when reading decimals from one-tenth to one one-thousandth of an inch or millimeter. It is not a conversion chart (for example: 0.001 in. is not equal to 0.001 mm).

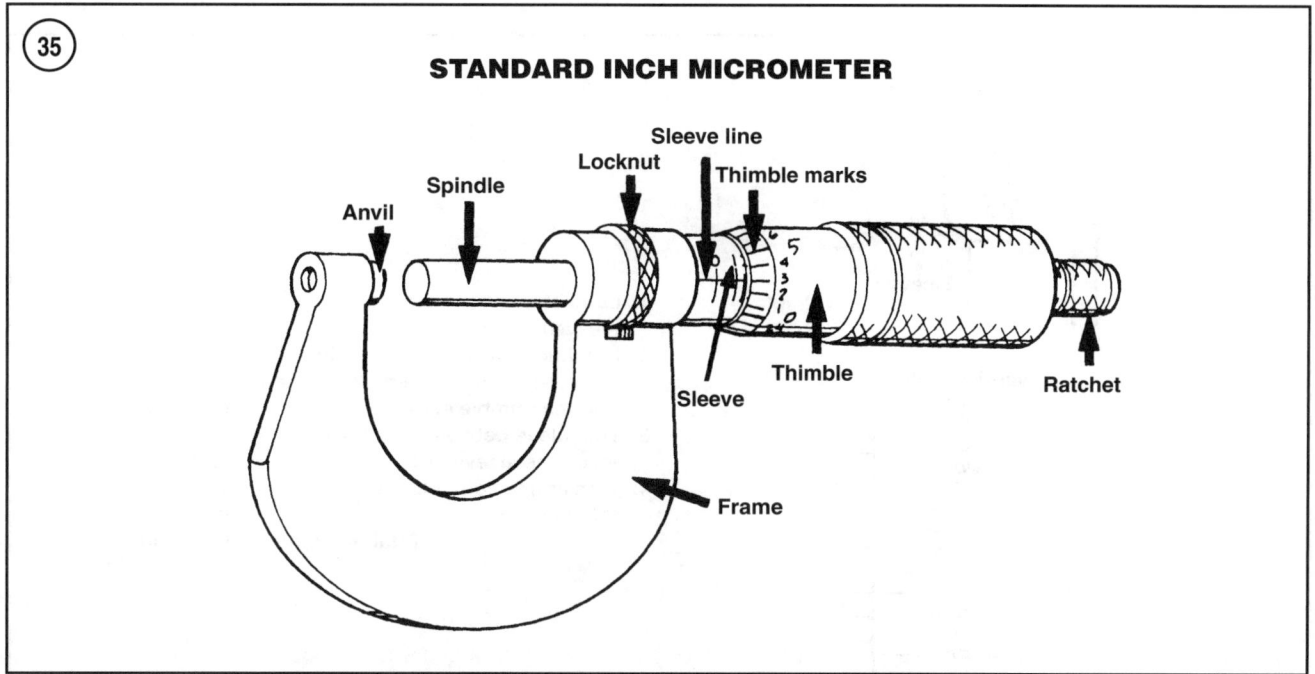

STANDARD INCH MICROMETER

these terms before using a micrometer in the following sections.

Standard inch micrometer

The standard inch micrometer is accurate to one-thousandth of an inch or 0.001. The sleeve is marked in 0.025 in. increments. Every fourth sleeve mark is numbered 1, 2, 3, 4, 5, 6, 7, 8, 9. These numbers indicate 0.100 in., 0.200 in., 0.300 in., and so on.

The tapered end of the thimble has twenty-five lines marked around it. Each mark equals 0.001 in. One complete turn of the thimble will align its zero mark with the first mark on the sleeve or 0.025 in.

When reading a standard inch micrometer, perform the following steps while referring to **Figure 36**.

1. Read the sleeve and find the largest number visible. Each sleeve number equals 0.100 in.
2. Count the number of lines between the numbered sleeve mark and the edge of the thimble. Each sleeve mark equals 0.025 in.
3. Read the thimble mark that aligns with the sleeve line. Each thimble mark equals 0.001 in.

NOTE
If a thimble mark does not align exactly with the sleeve line, estimate the amount between the lines. For accurate readings in ten-thousandths of an inch (0.0001 in.), use a vernier inch micrometer.

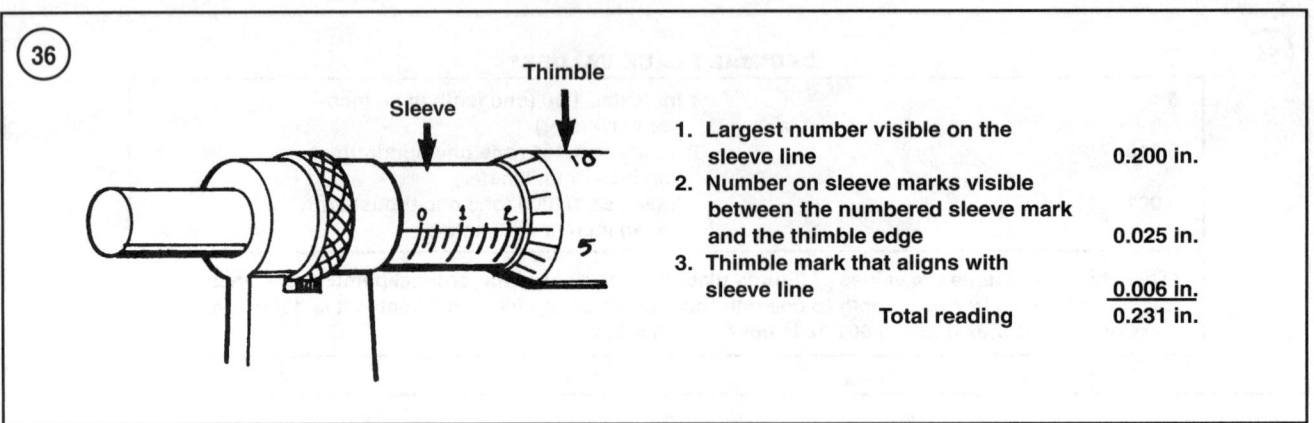

1. Largest number visible on the sleeve line	0.200 in.
2. Number on sleeve marks visible between the numbered sleeve mark and the thimble edge	0.025 in.
3. Thimble mark that aligns with sleeve line	0.006 in.
Total reading	0.231 in.

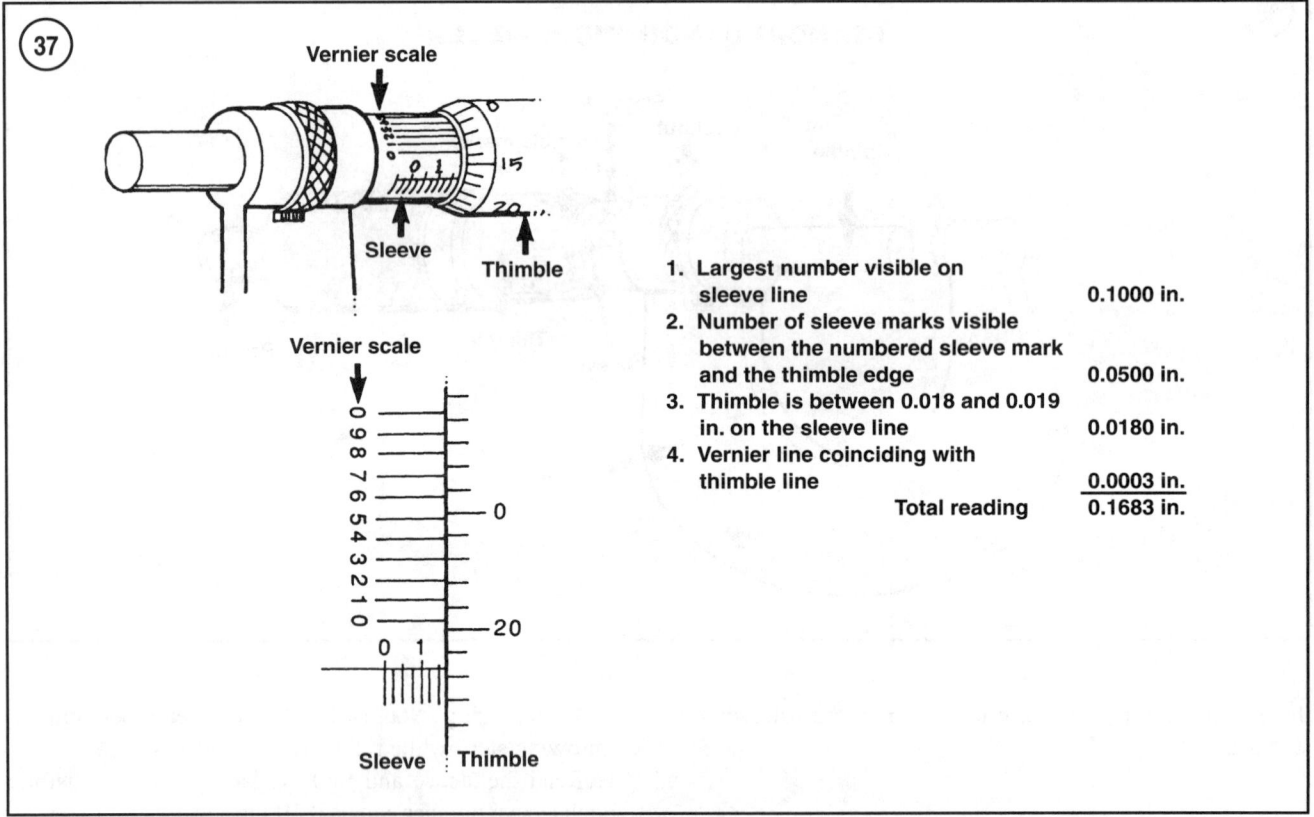

1. Largest number visible on sleeve line	0.1000 in.
2. Number of sleeve marks visible between the numbered sleeve mark and the thimble edge	0.0500 in.
3. Thimble is between 0.018 and 0.019 in. on the sleeve line	0.0180 in.
4. Vernier line coinciding with thimble line	0.0003 in.
Total reading	0.1683 in.

4. Add the readings from Steps 1-3.

Vernier inch micrometer

A vernier inch micrometer is accurate to one ten-thousandth of an inch or 0.0001 in. It has the same marking as a standard inch micrometer with an additional vernier scale on the sleeve (**Figure 37**).

The vernier scale consists of 11 lines marked 1-9 with a 0 on each end. These lines run parallel to the thimble lines and represent 0.0001 in. increments.

When reading a vernier inch micrometer, perform the following steps while referring to **Figure 37**.

1. Read the micrometer in the same way as a standard micrometer. This is the initial reading.

2. If a thimble mark aligns exactly with the sleeve line, reading the vernier scale is not necessary. If they do not align, read the vernier scale in Step 3.

GENERAL INFORMATION

STANDARD METRIC MICROMETER

Figure 38

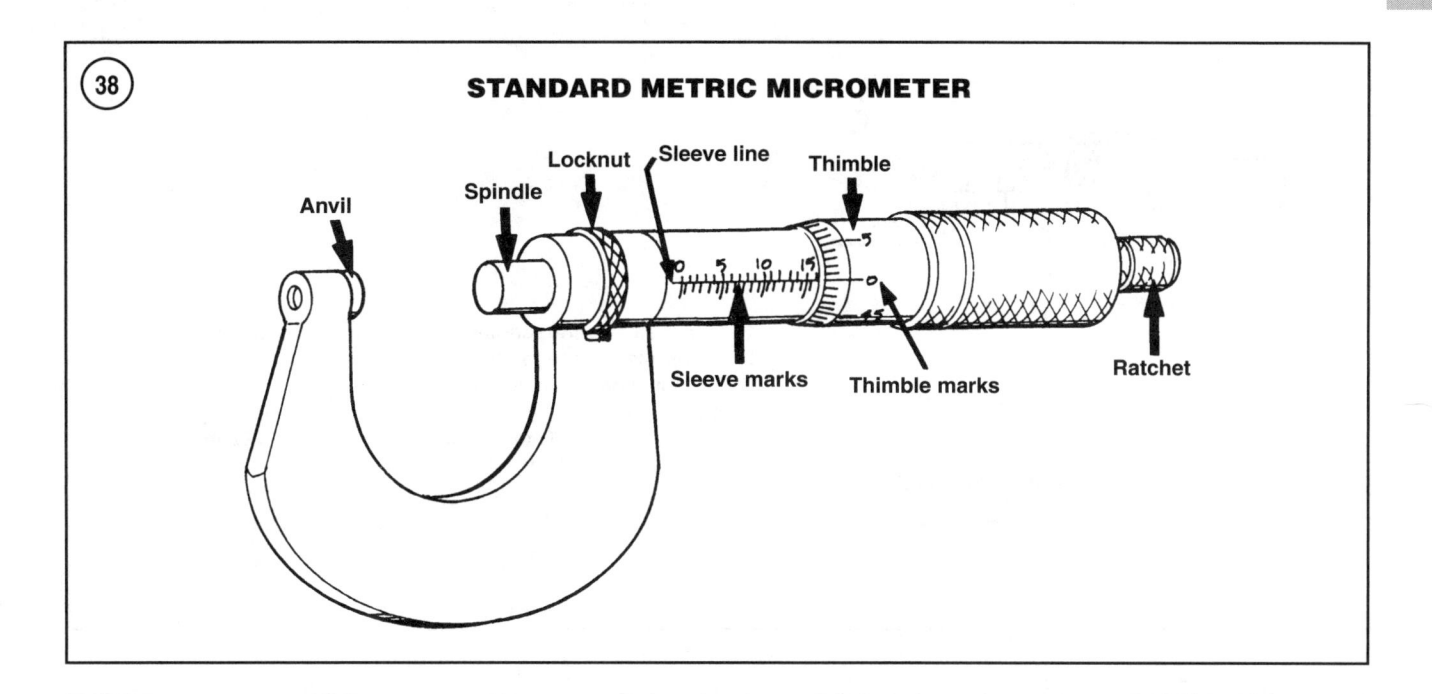

3. Determine which vernier scale mark aligns with one thimble mark. The vernier scale number is the amount in ten-thousandths of an inch to add to the initial reading from Step 1.

Metric micrometer

The standard metric micrometer (**Figure 38**) is accurate to one one-hundredth of a millimeter (0.01 mm). The sleeve line is graduated in millimeter and half millimeter increments. The marks on the upper half of the sleeve line equal 1.00 mm. Every fifth mark above the sleeve line is identified with a number. The number sequence depends on the size of the micrometer. A 0-25 mm micrometer, for example, has sleeve marks numbered 0 through 25 in 5 mm increments. This numbering sequence continues with larger micrometers. On all metric micrometers, each mark on the lower half of the sleeve equals 0.50 mm.

The tapered end of the thimble has fifty lines marked around it. Each mark equals 0.01 mm.

One complete turn of the thimble aligns the 0 mark with the first line on the lower half of the sleeve line or 0.50 mm.

When reading a metric micrometer, add the number of millimeters and half-millimeters on the sleeve line to the number of one one-hundredth millimeters on the thimble. Perform the following steps while referring to **Figure 39**.

1. Read the upper half of the sleeve line and count the number of lines visible. Each upper line equals 1 mm.

2. See if the half-millimeter line is visible on the lower sleeve line. If so, add 0.50 mm to the reading in Step 1.

3. Read the thimble mark that aligns with the sleeve line. Each thimble mark equals 0.01 mm.

NOTE
If a thimble mark does not align exactly with the sleeve line, estimate the amount between the lines. For accurate readings in two-thousandths of a millimeter (0.002 mm), use a metric vernier micrometer.

4. Add the readings from Steps 1-3.

Metric vernier micrometer

A metric vernier micrometer (**Figure 40**) is accurate to two-thousandths of a millimeter (0.002 mm). It has the same markings as a standard metric micrometer with the addition of a vernier scale on the sleeve. The vernier scale consists of five lines marked 0, 2, 4, 6, and 8. These lines run parallel to the thimble lines and represent 0.002-mm increments.

When reading a metric vernier micrometer, refer to **Figure 40** and perform the following steps.

1. Read the micrometer in the same way as a standard metric micrometer. This is the initial reading.

2. If a thimble mark aligns exactly with the sleeve line, reading the vernier scale is not necessary. If they do not align, read the vernier scale in Step 3.

39

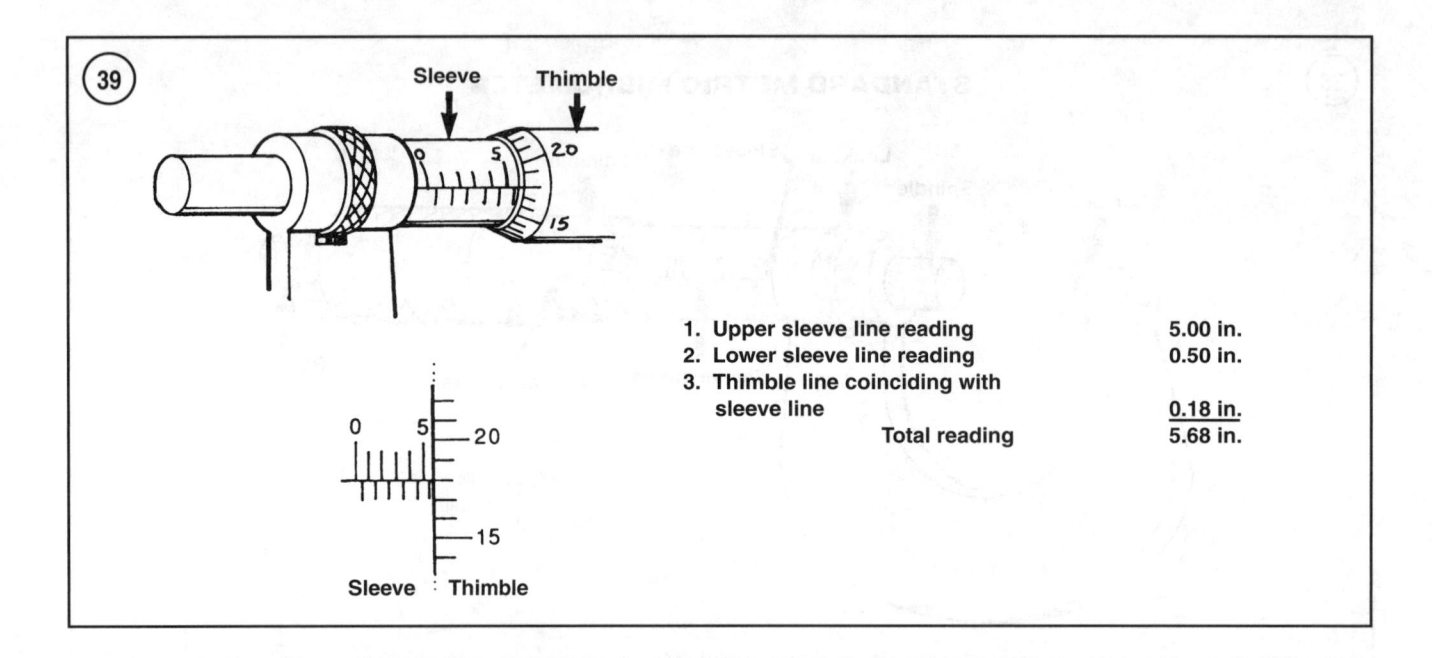

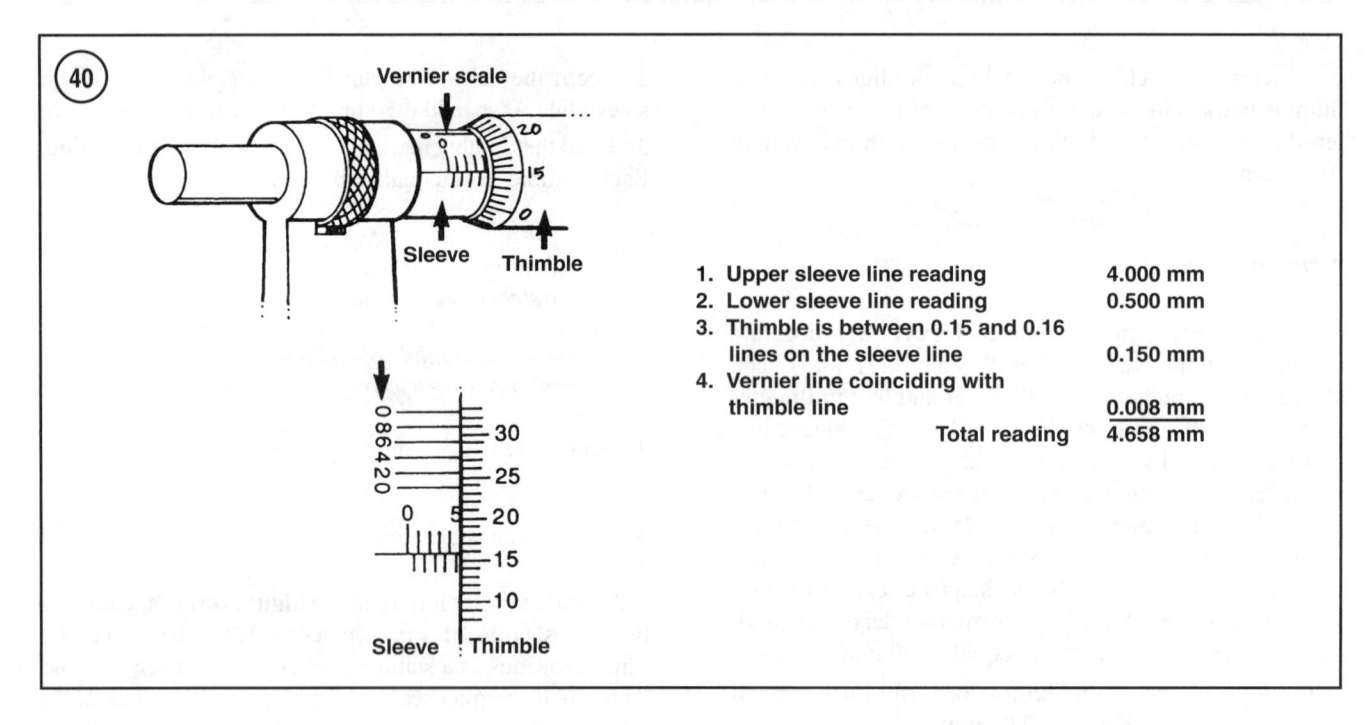

1. Upper sleeve line reading	5.00 in.
2. Lower sleeve line reading	0.50 in.
3. Thimble line coinciding with sleeve line	0.18 in.
Total reading	5.68 in.

40

1. Upper sleeve line reading	4.000 mm
2. Lower sleeve line reading	0.500 mm
3. Thimble is between 0.15 and 0.16 lines on the sleeve line	0.150 mm
4. Vernier line coinciding with thimble line	0.008 mm
Total reading	4.658 mm

3. Determine which vernier scale mark aligns exactly with one thimble mark. The vernier scale number is the amount in two-thousandths of a millimeter to add to the initial reading from Step 1.

Micrometer Adjustment

Before using a micrometer, check its adjustment as follows:

1. Clean the anvil and spindle faces.
2A. Check a 0-1 in. or 0-25 mm micrometer as follows:
   a. Turn the thimble until the spindle contacts the anvil. If the micrometer has a ratchet stop, use it to ensure the proper amount of pressure is applied.
   b. If the adjustment is correct, the 0 mark on the thimble will align exactly with the 0 mark on the sleeve line. If the marks do not align, the micrometer is out of adjustment.

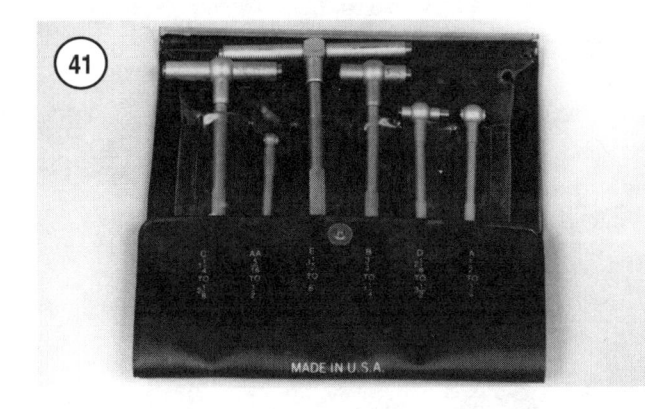

GENERAL INFORMATION

27

    c. Follow the manufacturer's instructions to adjust the micrometer.

2B. To check a micrometer larger than 1 in. or 25 mm use the standard gauge supplied by the manufacturer. A standard gauge is a steel block, disc or rod that is machined to an exact size.

    a. Place the standard gauge between the spindle and anvil, and measure the outside diameter or length. If the micrometer has a ratchet stop, use it to ensure the proper amount of pressure is applied.

    b. If the adjustment is correct, the 0 mark on the thimble will align exactly with the 0 mark on the sleeve line. If the marks do not align, the micrometer is out of adjustment.

    c. Follow the manufacturer's instructions to adjust the micrometer.

Micrometer Care

Micrometers are precision instruments. Use and maintain them with great care.

Note the following:

1. Store micrometers in protective cases or separate padded drawers in a toolbox.

2. When in storage, make sure the spindle and anvil faces do not contact each other or another object. If they do, temperature changes and corrosion may damage the contact faces.

3. Do not clean a micrometer with compressed air. Dirt forced into the tool causes wear.

4. Lubricate micrometers with WD-40 to prevent corrosion.

Telescoping and Small Bore Gauges

Use telescoping gauges (**Figure 41**) and small hole gauges to measure bores. Neither gauge has a scale for direct readings. Use an outside micrometer to determine the reading.

To use a telescoping gauge, select the correct size gauge for the bore. Compress the movable post and carefully insert the gauge into the bore. Carefully move the gauge in the bore to make sure it is centered. Tighten the knurled end of the gauge to hold the movable post in position. Remove the gauge and measure the length of the posts. Telescoping gauges are typically used to measure cylinder bores.

To use a small-bore gauge, select the correct size gauge for the bore. Carefully insert the gauge into the bore. Tighten the knurled end of the gauge to carefully expand the gauge fingers to the limit within the bore. Do not overtighten the gauge, as there is no built-in release. Excessive tightening can damage the bore surface and the tool. Remove the gauge and measure the outside dimension. Small hole gauges are typically used to measure valve guides.

Dial Indicator

A dial indicator (**Figure 42**) is a gauge with a dial face and needle used to measure variations in dimensions and movements, such as crankshaft and gear shaft runout limits.

Dial indicators are available in various ranges and graduations and with three basic types of mounting bases: magnetic, clamp, or screw-in stud. When purchasing a dial indicator, select the magnetic stand type (B, **Figure 42**) with a continuous dial (A).

Cylinder Bore Gauge

The cylinder bore gauge is a very specialized precision tool that is only needed for major engine repairs or rebuilds. The gauge set shown in **Figure 43** is comprised of a dial indicator, handle and a number of different length adapters (anvils) used to fit the gauge to various bore sizes. The bore gauge can be used to measure bore size, taper and out-of-round. When using a bore gauge, follow the manufacturer's instructions.

Compression Gauge

A compression gauge (**Figure 44**) measures the combustion chamber (cylinder) pressure (usually in psi or kg/cm^2). An engine is capable of mechanically generating on the compression stroke. The gauge adapter is either inserted or screwed into the spark plug hole to obtain the reading. Disable the engine so it does not start and hold the throttle in the wide-open position when performing a compression test. An engine that does not have adequate compression cannot be properly tuned.

Multimeter

A multimeter (**Figure 45**) is an essential tool for electrical system diagnosis. The voltage function indicates the voltage applied or available to various electrical components. The ohmmeter function tests circuits for continuity, or lack of continuity, and measures the resistance of a circuit.

Some less expensive models contain a needle gauge and are known as analog meters. Most high-quality (but not necessarily expensive) meters available today contain digital readout screens. Digital multimeters are often known as DVOMs. When using an analog ohmmeter, the needle must be zeroed or calibrated according to the meter manufacturer's instructions. Some analog and almost all digital meters are self-zeroing and no manual adjustment is necessary.

Some manufacturers' specifications for electrical components are based on results using a specific test meter. Results may vary if using a meter not recommended by the manufacturer is used.

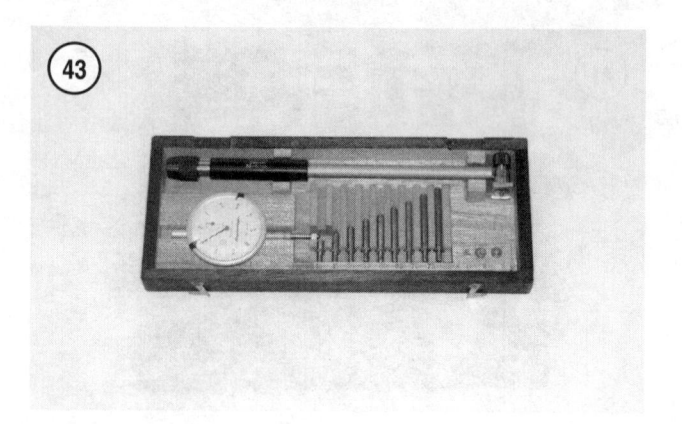

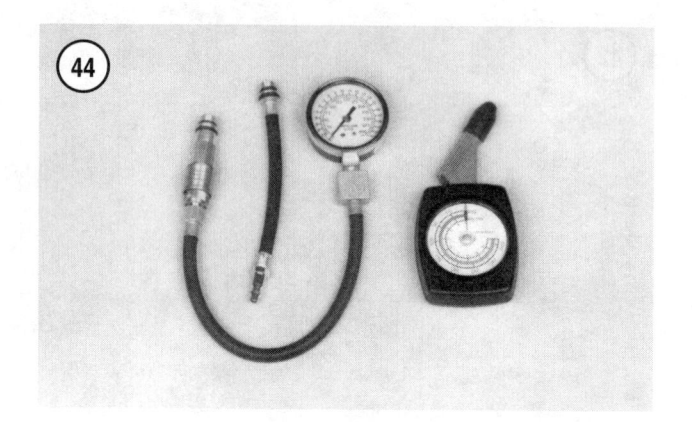

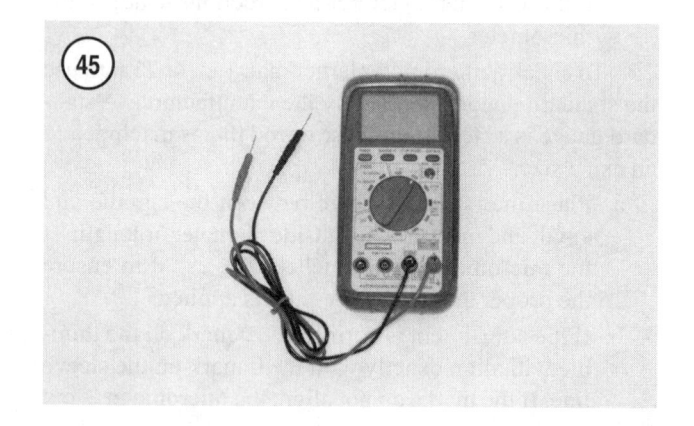

ELECTRICAL SYSTEM FUNDAMENTALS

A thorough study of the many types of electrical systems used in engines today is beyond the scope of this manual. However, a basic understanding of electrical basics is necessary to perform simple diagnostic tests.

Voltage

Voltage is the electrical potential or pressure in an electrical circuit and is expressed in volts. The more pressure (voltage) in a circuit, the more work that can be performed.

Direct current (DC) voltage means the electricity flows in one direction. All circuits powered by a battery are DC circuits.

Alternating current (AC) means the electricity flows in one direction momentarily then switches to the opposite direction. Alternator output is an example of AC voltage. This voltage must be changed or rectified to direct current to operate in a 12-volt battery powered system.

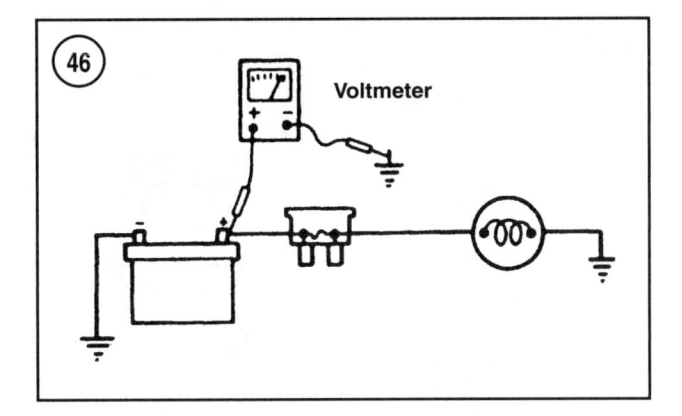

GENERAL INFORMATION

46 Voltmeter

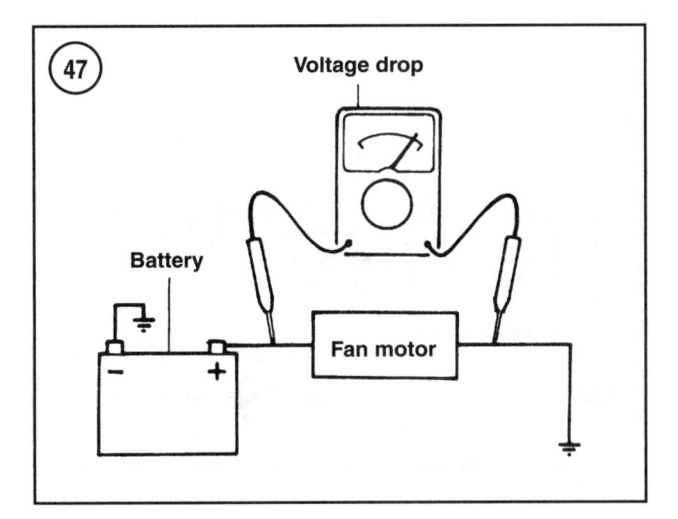

47 Voltage drop / Battery / Fan motor

is turned ON, but the example in **Figure 46** shows a measurement at the positive battery terminal, which should always have voltage if the battery is charged. The test light should light or the meter should display a reading. The reading should be within one volt of battery voltage. If the voltage is less, there is a problem in the circuit.

Voltage drop test

Resistance causes voltage to drop. This resistance can be measured in an active circuit by using a voltmeter to perform a voltage drop test. A voltage drop test compares the difference between the voltage available at the start of a circuit to the voltage at the end of the circuit. But it does so while the circuit is operational. If the circuit has no resistance, there will be no voltage drop. The greater the resistance, the greater the voltage drop will be. A voltage drop of one volt or more usually indicates excessive resistance in the circuit.

1. Connect the positive meter test lead to the electrical source (where electricity is coming from).
2. Connect the negative meter test lead to the electrical load (where electricity is going). See **Figure 47**.
3. If necessary, activate the component(s) in the circuit.
4. A voltage reading of 1 volt or more indicates excessive resistance in the circuit. A reading equal to battery voltage indicates an open circuit.

Resistance

Resistance is the opposition to the flow of electricity within a circuit or component and is measured in ohms. Resistance causes a reduction in available current and voltage.

Resistance is measured in an inactive circuit with an ohmmeter. The ohmmeter sends a small amount of current into the circuit and measures how difficult it is to push the current through the circuit.

An ohmmeter, although useful, is not always a good indicator the actual ability of a circuit under operating conditions. This fact is due to the low voltage (6-9 volts) that the meter uses to test the circuit. The voltage in an ignition coil secondary winding can be several thousand volts. Such high voltage can cause the coil to malfunction, even though it tests acceptable during a resistance test.

Resistance generally increases with temperature. Perform all testing with the component or circuit at room temperature. Resistance tests performed at high temperatures may indicate high resistance readings and result in the unnecessary replacement of a component.

Measuring voltage

Unless otherwise specified, perform all voltage tests with the electrical connectors attached.

When measuring voltage, select a meter range one scale higher than the expected voltage of the circuit to prevent damage to the meter. To determine the actual voltage in a circuit, use a voltmeter. To simply check if voltage is present, use a test light.

NOTE
When using a test light, either lead can be attached to ground.

1. Attach the negative meter test lead to a good ground (bare metal). Make sure the ground is not insulated with a rubber gasket or grommet.
2. Attach the positive meter test lead to the point being checked for voltage (**Figure 46**).
3. If necessary for the circuit being checked, turn ON the ignition switch. This will be necessary if the point being checked only has power applied when the ignition switch

Resistance and continuity test

> *CAUTION*
> *Only use an ohmmeter on a circuit that has no voltage present. The meter will be damaged if it is connected to a live circuit. Remember, if using an analog meter, it must normally be calibrated each time it is used or the scale is changed.*

A continuity test can determine if the circuit is complete. This type of test is performed with an ohmmeter or a self-powered test lamp.

1. Disconnect the negative battery cable.
2. Attach one test lead (ohmmeter or test light) to one end of the component or circuit.
3. Attach the other test lead to the opposite end of the component or circuit (**Figure 48**).
4. A self-powered test light will come on if the circuit has continuity or is complete. An ohmmeter will indicate either low or no resistance if the circuit has continuity. An open circuit is indicated if the meter displays infinite resistance.

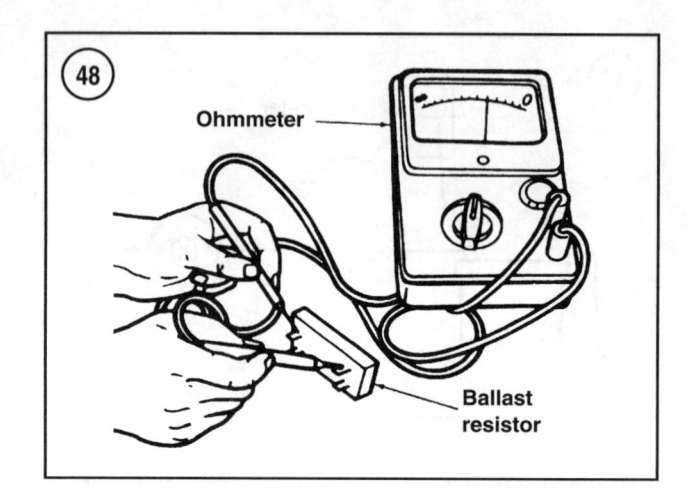

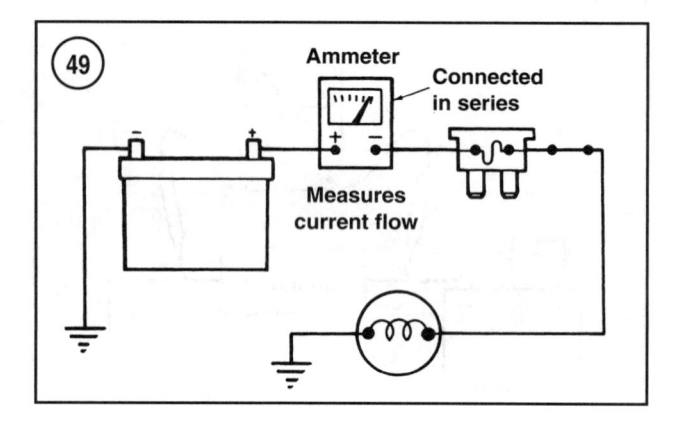

Amperage

Amperage is the unit of measure for the amount of current within a circuit. Current is the actual flow of electricity. The higher the current, the more work that can be performed up to a given point. If the current flow exceeds the circuit or component capacity, the system will be damaged.

Measuring amps

An ammeter measures the current flow or amps of a circuit (**Figure 49**). Amperage measurement requires that the circuit be disconnected and the ammeter be connected in series to the circuit. Always use an ammeter that can read higher than the anticipated current flow to prevent damage to the meter. Connect the positive test lead to the electrical source and the negative test lead to the electrical load.

BASIC MECHANICAL SKILLS

Most of the service procedures covered are straightforward and can be performed by anyone reasonably handy with tools. It is suggested, however, to consider your own capabilities carefully before attempting any operation involving major disassembly.

1. *Front*, as used in this manual, refers to the front of the engine or the side of the engine facing the boat; the front of any component is the end closest to the front of the engine or boat. The *left* and *right* sides refer to the position of the parts as viewed by the boat operator sitting and facing forward. These rules are simple, but confusion can cause a major inconvenience during service.

2. When disassembling engine or drive components, mark the parts for location and mark all parts that mate together. Small parts, such as bolts, can be identified by placing them in plastic sandwich bags. Because many types of ink fade when applied to tape, use a permanent ink pen. Seal the bags and label them with masking tape and a marking pen. If reassembly will take place immediately, place nuts and bolts in a cupcake tin or egg carton in the order of disassembly.

3. Protect finished surfaces from physical damage or corrosion. Keep gasoline off painted surfaces.

4. Use penetrating oil to free frozen or tight bolts, then strike the bolt head a few times with a hammer and punch. (Use a screwdriver on screws.) Avoid the use of heat where possible, as it can warp, melt or affect the temper of parts. Heat also ruins finishes, especially paint and plastics.

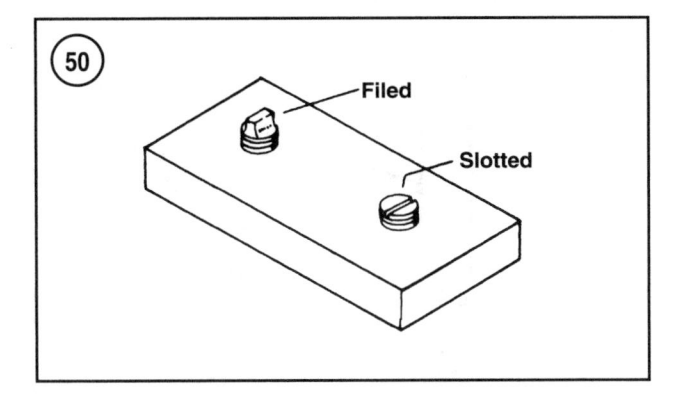

5. Unless otherwise noted, no parts removed or installed (other than bushings and bearings) in the procedures given in this manual should require unusual force during disassembly or assembly. If a part is difficult to remove or install, find out why before proceeding.
6. Cover all openings after removing parts or components to prevent things like dirt or small tools from falling in.
7. Read each procedure *completely* while looking at the actual parts before starting a job. Make sure you *thoroughly* understand what is to be done and then carefully follow the procedure, step by step.
8. For the Do-it-Yourselfer, recommendations are occasionally made to refer service or maintenance to a dealership or a specialist in a particular field. In these cases, the work will be done more quickly and economically than performing the job yourself.
9. In procedural steps, the term *replace* means to discard a defective part and replace it with a new or exchange unit. *Overhaul* means to remove, disassemble, inspect, measure, repair or replace defective parts, reassemble and install major systems or parts.
10. Some operations require the use of a hydraulic press. If a suitable press is not available, it would be wiser to have these operations performed by a shop equipped for such work, rather than to try to do the job yourself with makeshift equipment that may damage the engine.
11. Repairs go much faster and easier if the machine is clean before beginning work.
12. If special tools are required, make arrangements to get them before starting. It is frustrating and time-consuming to start a job and then be unable to complete it.
13. Make diagrams or take a picture wherever similar-appearing parts are found. For instance, crankcase bolts often are not the same length. You may think you can remember where everything came from, but mistakes are costly. You may also get sidetracked and not return to work for days or even weeks—in which time, carefully laid out parts may have become disturbed.
14. When assembling parts, be sure all shims and washers are put exactly where they came out.
15. Whenever a rotating part butts against a stationary part, look for a shim or washer. Use new gaskets if there is any doubt about the condition of the old ones. A thin coating of silicone sealant on non-pressure type gaskets may help them seal more effectively.
16. If it becomes necessary to purchase gasket material to make a gasket for the engine, measure the thickness of the old gasket (at an uncompressed point) and purchase gasket material with the same approximate thickness.
17. Heavy grease can be used to hold small parts in place if they tend to fall out during assembly. However, keep grease and oil away from electrical components, unless otherwise directed.
18. Never use wire to clean out jets and air passages. They are easily damaged. Use compressed air to blow out the carburetor only if the diaphragm is removed first.
19. Take your time and do the job right. Do not forget that a newly rebuilt engine must be broken in just like a new one.

Removing Frozen Fasteners

If a fastener cannot be removed, several methods may be used to loosen it. First, apply penetrating oil such as Liquid Wrench, WD-40 or PB Blaster. Apply it liberally and let it penetrate for 10-15 minutes. Rap the fastener several times with a small hammer. Do not hit it hard enough to cause damage. Reapply the penetrating oil if necessary.

For frozen screws, apply penetrating oil as described, then insert a screwdriver in the slot and rap the top of the screwdriver with a hammer. This loosens the corrosion so the screw can be removed in the normal way. If the screw head is too damaged to use this method, grip the head with locking pliers and twist the screw out.

Avoid applying heat unless specifically instructed, as it may melt, warp or remove the temper from parts.

Removing Broken Fasteners

If the head breaks off a screw or bolt, several methods are available for removing the remaining portion. If a large portion of the remainder projects out, try gripping it with locking pliers. If the projecting portion is too small or a sufficient grip cannot be obtained on the protruding piece, file it to fit a wrench or cut a slot in it to fit a screwdriver (**Figure 50**).

If the head breaks off flush (which too often happens in this situation), use a screw extractor. To do this, center-punch the exact center of the remaining portion of the screw or bolt. Drill a small hole in the screw and tap the extractor into the hole. Back the screw out with a wrench on the extractor (**Figure 51**).

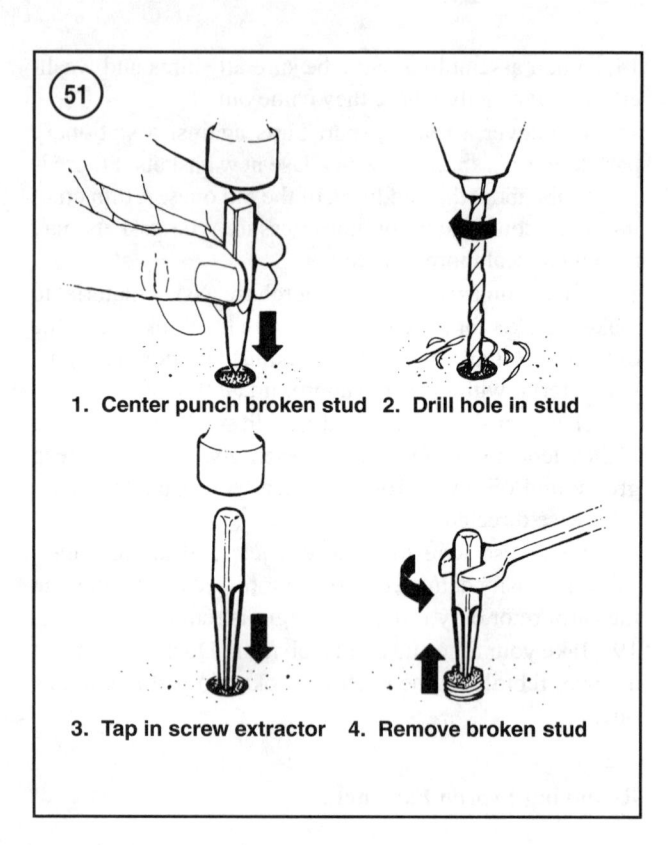

NOTE
Broken screw extraction sometimes fails to remove the fastener from the bore. If this occurs, or if the screw is drilled off-center and the threads are damaged, a threaded-insert will be necessary to repair the bore. Check for one at a local dealership or supply store and follow the manufacturer's instructions for installation.

Repairing Damaged Threads

Occasionally, threads are stripped through carelessness or impact damage. Often the threads can be repaired by running a tap (for internal threads on nuts) or die (for external threads on bolts) through the threads (**Figure 52**). Use only a specially designed spark plug tap to clean or repair spark plug threads.

If an internal thread is damaged, it may be necessary to install a Helicoil or some other type of thread insert. Follow the manufacturer's instructions when installing the insert.

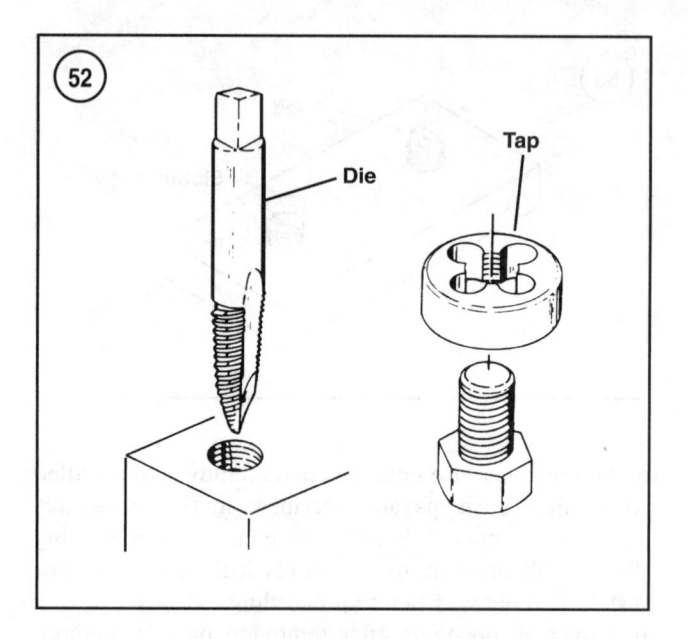

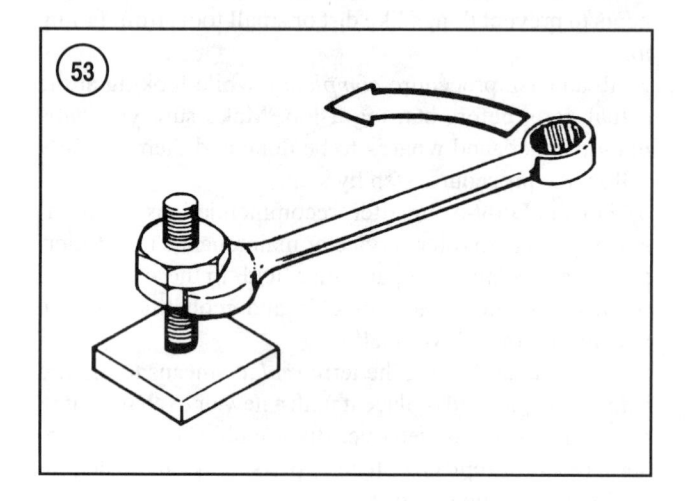

If it is necessary to drill and tap a hole, refer to **Table 3** for metric tap drill sizes.

Stud Removal/Installation

A stud removal tool that makes the removal and installation of studs easier is available from most tool suppliers. If one is not available, thread two nuts onto the stud and tighten them against each other to lock them in place, then remove the stud by turning the lower nut (**Figure 53**).

NOTE
If the threads on the damaged stud do not allow installation of the two nuts, it is necessary to remove the stud with a pair of locking pliers or a stud remover.

GENERAL INFORMATION

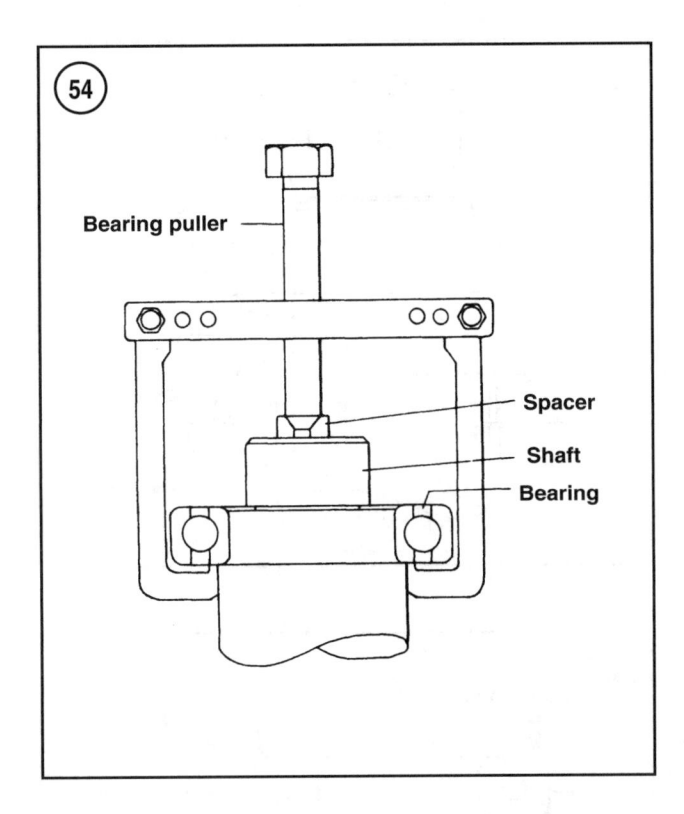

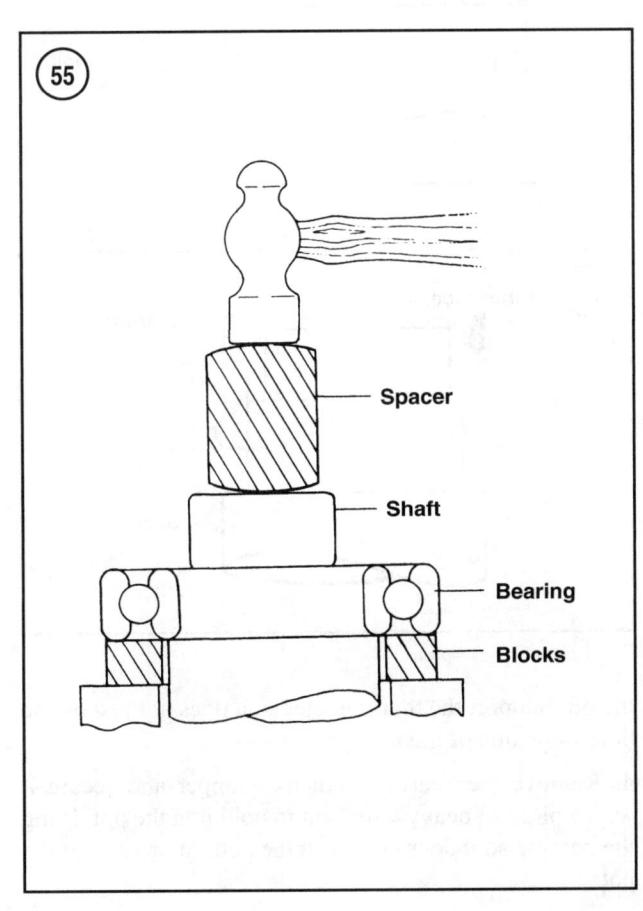

Removing Hoses

When removing stubborn hoses, do not exert excessive force on the hose or fitting. Remove the hose clamp and carefully insert a small screwdriver or pick tool between the fitting and hose. Apply a spray lubricant under the hose and carefully twist the hose off the fitting. Clean the fitting of any corrosion or rubber hose material with a wire brush. Clean the inside of the hose thoroughly. Do not use any lubricant when installing the hose (new or old). The lubricant may allow the hose to come off the fitting, even with the clamp secure.

Bearings

Bearings are used in the engine and gearcase assembly to reduce power loss, heat and noise resulting from friction. Because bearings are precision parts, it is necessary to maintain them with proper lubrication and maintenance. If a bearing is damaged, replace it immediately. When installing a new bearing, try not to damage it. Bearing replacement procedures are included in the individual chapters where applicable; however, use the following sections as a guideline.

NOTE
Unless otherwise specified, install bearings with the manufacturer's mark or number facing outward.

Removal

While bearings are normally removed only when damaged, there may be times when it is necessary to remove a bearing that is in good condition. However, improper bearing removal will damage the bearing, shaft, and/or case half. Note the following when removing bearings.

1. When using a puller (**Figure 54**) to remove a bearing from a shaft, take care not to damage the shaft. Always place a piece of metal between the end of the shaft and the puller screw. In addition, place the puller arms next to the inner *(not outer)* bearing race.
2. When using a hammer to remove a bearing from a shaft, do not strike the hammer directly against the shaft. Instead, use a brass or aluminum spacer between the hammer and shaft (**Figure 55**) and make sure to support both bearing races with wooden blocks as shown.
3. The ideal method of bearing removal is with a hydraulic press. In order to prevent damage to the bearing and shaft or case, note the following when using a press:

a. Always support the inner and outer bearing races with a suitable size wooden or aluminum spacer ring (**Figure 56**). If only the outer race is supported, pressure applied against the balls and/or the inner race will damage them.
b. Always make sure the press ram (**Figure 56**) aligns with the center of the shaft. If the ram is not centered, it may damage the bearing and/or shaft.
c. The moment the shaft is free of the bearing, it will drop to the floor. Secure or hold the shaft to prevent it from falling.

Installation

1. When installing a bearing in a housing, apply pressure to the *outer* bearing race (**Figure 57**). When installing a bearing on a shaft, apply pressure to the *inner* bearing race (**Figure 58**).
2. When installing a bearing as described in Step 1, use some type of driver. Never strike the bearing directly with a hammer or the bearing will be damaged. When installing a bearing, use a driver, a piece of pipe or a socket with a diameter that matches the bearing race. **Figure 59** shows the correct way to use a socket and hammer to install a bearing on a shaft.
3. Step 1 describes how to install a bearing in a case half or over a shaft. However, when installing a bearing over a shaft *and* into a housing at the same time, a tight fit is required for both outer and inner bearing races. In this situation, install a spacer underneath the driver tool so that pressure is applied evenly across both races. See **Figure 60**. If the outer race is not supported as shown, the balls or rollers will push against the outer bearing race and damage it.

Installing an interference fit bearing over a shaft

When a tight fit is required, the bearing inside diameter will be smaller than the shaft. In this case, driving the bearing on the shaft using normal methods may cause bearing damage. Instead, heat the bearing before installation. Note the following:

1. Secure the shaft so that it is ready for bearing installation. Also, take this opportunity (while the parts are cold) to size and gather the appropriate spacers and drivers for installation.
2. Clean the bearing surface on the shaft of all residue. Remove burrs with a file or sandpaper.
3. Fill a suitable pot or beaker with clean mineral oil. Place a thermometer rated higher than 120° C (248° F) in the oil. Support the thermometer so it does not rest on the bottom or side of the pot.

4. Remove the bearing from its wrapper and secure it with a piece of heavy wire bent to hold it in the pot. Hang the bearing so it does not touch the bottom or sides of the pot.

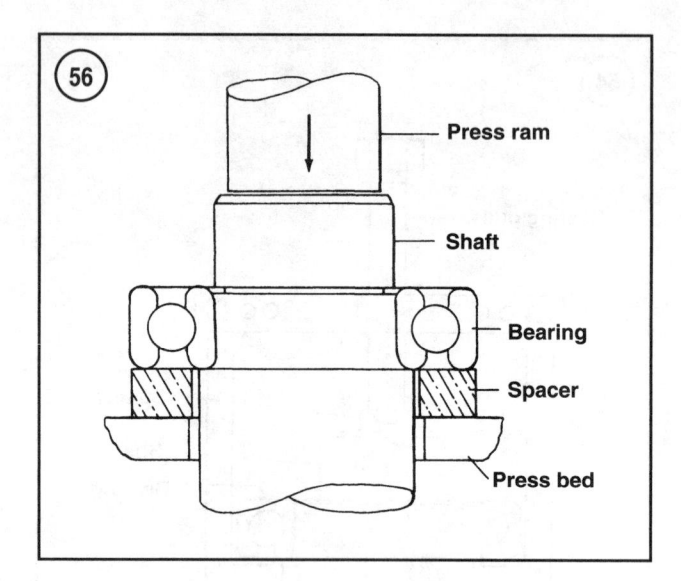

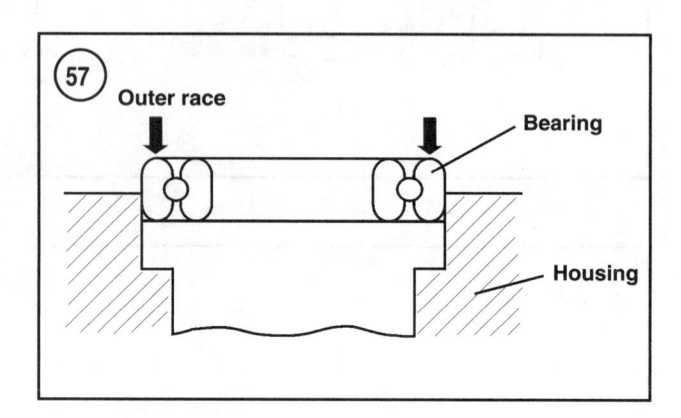

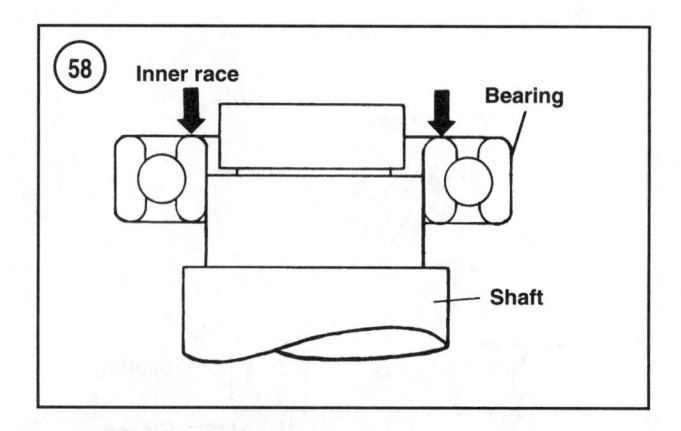

GENERAL INFORMATION

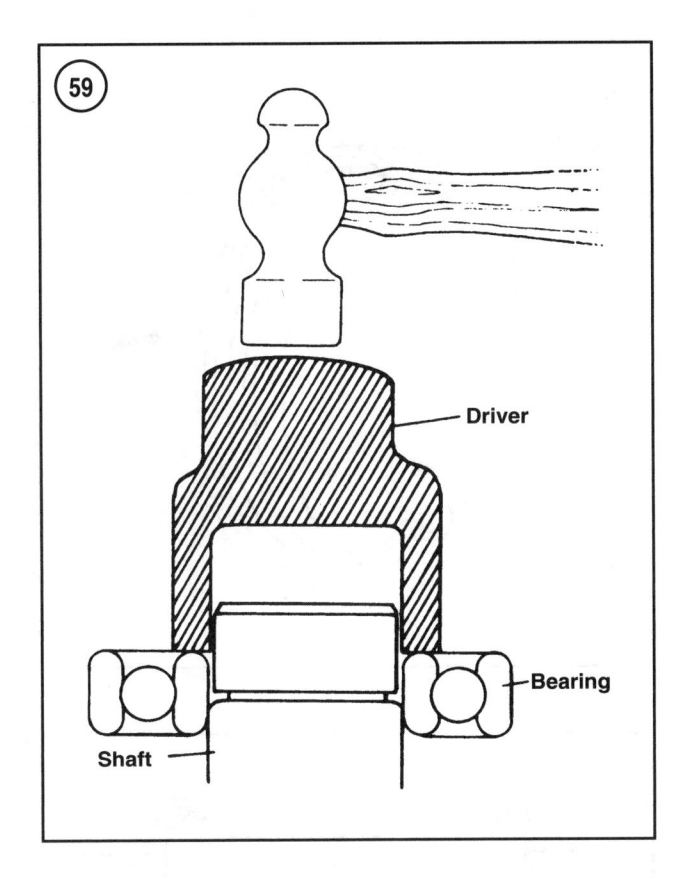

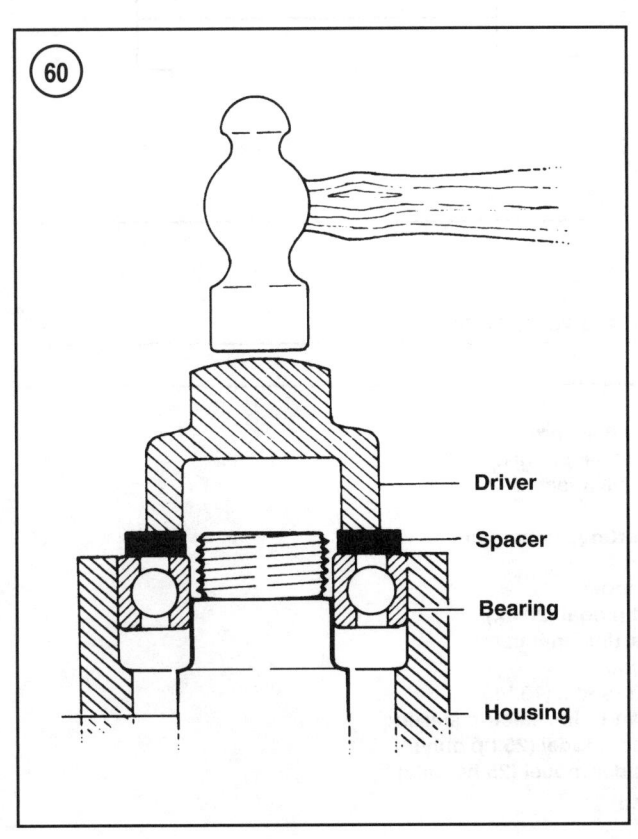

5. Turn the heat on and monitor the thermometer. When the oil temperature rises to approximately 120° C (248° F), remove the bearing from the pot and quickly install it. If necessary, place a socket on the inner bearing race and tap the bearing into place. As the bearing chills, it will tighten on the shaft so work quickly when installing it. Make sure the bearing is installed completely.

Replacing an interference fit bearing in a housing

Bearings are generally installed in a housing with a slight interference fit. Driving the bearing into the housing using normal methods may damage the housing or bearing. Instead, heat the housing (to make the inner diameter of the bore larger) and chill the bearing (to make the outer diameter slightly smaller) before installation. This makes bearing installation much easier.

CAUTION
Before heating the crankcases in this procedure to remove the bearings, wash the cases thoroughly with detergent and water. In order to prevent a possible fire hazard, rinse and rewash the cases as required to remove all traces of oil and other chemical deposits.

1. While the parts are still cold, determine the proper size and gather all necessary spacers and drivers for installation.
2. Place the new bearing in a freezer to chill it and slightly reduce the outside diameter.
3. While the bearing is chilling, heat the housing to a temperature of about 100° C (212° F) in an oven or on a hot plate. An easy way to check if the housing is hot enough is to drop tiny drops of water on the case; if they sizzle and evaporate immediately, the temperature is correct. Heat only one housing at a time.

CAUTION
Do not heat the housing with a propane or acetylene torch. Never bring a flame into contact with the bearing or housing. The direct heat will destroy the case hardening of the bearing and will likely warp the housing.

4. Remove the housing from the oven or hot plate using a thick kitchen potholder, heavy protective gloves or heavy shop cloths.

NOTE
A suitable size socket and extension works well for removing and installing bearings.

5. Hold the housing with the bearing side down and tap the bearing out. Repeat for all bearings in the housing.

NOTE
Always install bearings with the manufacturer's mark or number facing outward.

6. While the housing is still hot, install the chilled new bearing(s) into the housing. Install the bearings by hand, if possible. If necessary, lightly tap the bearing(s) into the housing with a socket placed on the outer bearing race. *Do not* install new bearings by driving on the inner bearing race. Drive each bearing into the bore until it seats completely.

Seal Replacement

Seals (**Figure 61**) are used to contain oil, water, grease or combustion gasses in a housing or shaft. Improper removal of a seal can damage the components. Improper installation of the seal can damage the seal. Note the following:
1. Prying is generally the easiest and most effective method of removing a seal from a housing. However, always place a rag underneath the pry tool to prevent damage to the housing.
2. Pack waterproof grease in the seal lips before installing the seal.
3. In most cases, install seals with the manufacturer's numbers or marks facing out.
4. Install seals with a socket placed on the outside of the seal as shown in **Figure 62**. Drive the seal squarely into the housing. Never install a seal by hitting directly against the top of the seal with a hammer.

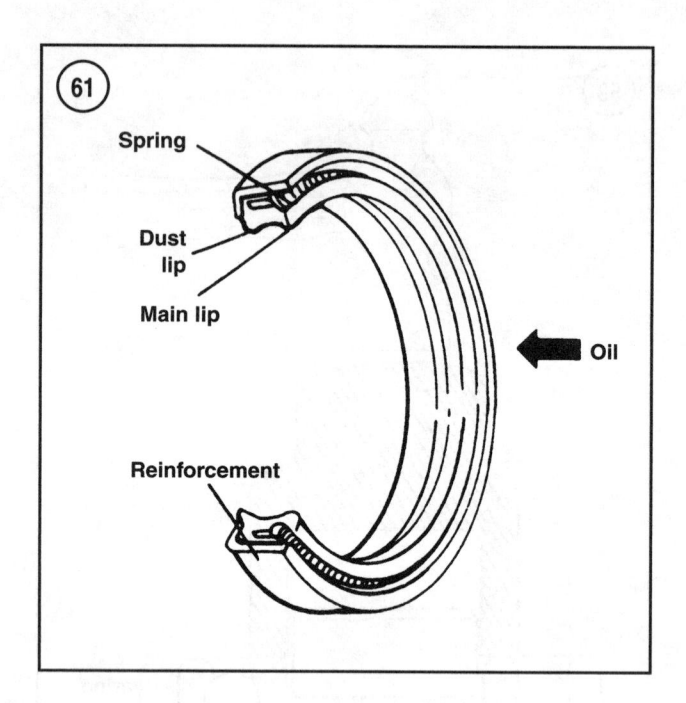

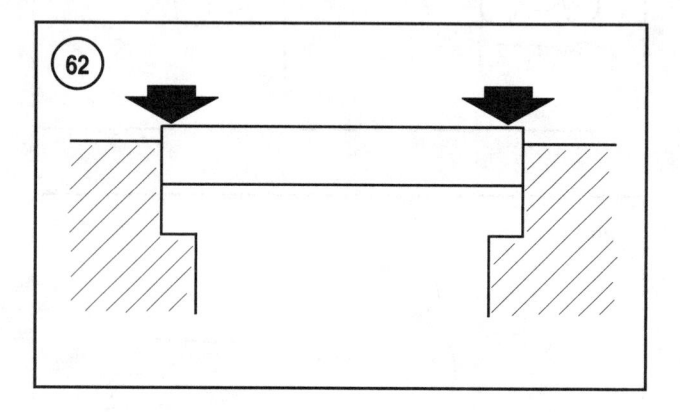

Table 1 ENGINE IDENTIFICATION CODES

Model characteristic codes	
Letter before the horsepower rating	
C	C series models, premix
E	Enduro models, premix,
P	Pro series, oil injected
Letters following the horsepower rating	
E	Electric starting, manual tilt
H	Tiller control
J	Jet drive model
L	Long shaft model (20 in.)
M	Manual starting, manual tilt
R	Tiller control
S	Short shaft model (15 in.)
T	Power tilt and trim, electric starting
2	Two-cylinder model (25 hp only)
3	Three-cylinder model (25 hp only)
	(continued)

GENERAL INFORMATION

Table 1 ENGINE IDENTIFICATION CODES (continued)

Model characteristic codes	
Year model codes	
W	1998 year model
X	1999 year model
Y	2000 year model
Z	2001 year model
A	2002 year model

Table 2 TECHNICAL ABBREVIATIONS

ABDC	After bottom dead center
Ah	Amperage hour
ATDC	After top dead center
BBDC	Before bottom dead center
BDC	Bottom dead center
BTDC	Before top dead center
C	Celsius (Centigrade)
cc	Cubic centimeters
CDI	Capacitor discharge ignition
CKP	Crankshaft position
CMP	Camshaft positioin
CT	Cylinder temperature
CTP	Closed throttle position
cu. in.	Cubic inches
DOHC	Dual-overhead camshafts
ECU	Electronic control unit
EFI	Electronic fuel injection
EM	Exhaust manifold
F	Fahrenheit
ft.-lb.	Foot-pounds
g	Gram
gal.	Gallons
hp	Horsepower
IAC	Idle air control
IAT	Intake air temperature
in.	Inches
kg	Kilogram
kg/cm^2	Kilograms per square centimeter
kgm	Kilogram meters
km	Kilometer
L	Liter
m	Meter
MAG	Magneto
MAP	Manifold absolute pressure
mm	Millimeter
MPEFI	Multi-Port Sequential Electronic Fuel Injection
N.A.	Not available
N•m	Newton-meters
oz.	Ounce
OHC	Overhead camshaft
psi	Pounds per square inch
pto	Power take off
pts.	Pints
qt.	Quarts
rpm	Revolutions per minute
WOT	Wide open throttle

Table 3 METRIC TAP AND DRILL SIZES

Metric tap (mm)	Drill size	Decimal equivalent	Nearest fraction
3 × 0.50	No. 39	0.0995	3/32
3 × 0.60	3/32	0.0937	3/32
4 × 0.70	No. 30	0.1285	1/8
4 × 0.75	1/8	0.125	1/8
5 × 0.80	No. 19	0.166	11/64
5 × 0.90	No. 20	0.161	5/32
6 × 1.00	No. 9	0.196	13/64
7 × 1.00	16/64	0.234	15/64
8 × 1.00	J	0.277	9/32
8 × 1.25	17/64	0.265	17/64
9 × 1.00	5/16	0.3125	5/16
9 × 1.25	5/16	0.3125	5/16
10 × 1.25	11/32	0.3437	11/32
10 × 1.50	R	0.339	11/32
11 × 1.50	3/8	0.375	3/8
12 × 1.50	13/32	0.406	13/32
12 × 1.75	13/32	0.406	13/32

Table 4 CONVERSION FORMULAS

Multiply	By	To get equivalent of
Length		
Inches	25.4	Millimeter
Inches	2.54	Centimeter
Miles	1.609	Kilometer
Feet	0.3048	Meter
Millimeter	0.03937	Inches
Centimeter	0.3937	Inches
Kilometer	0.6214	Mile
Meter	3.281	Mile
Fluid volume		
U.S. quarts	0.9463	Liters
U.S. gallons	3.785	Liters
U.S. ounces	29.573529	Milliliters
Imperial gallons	4.54609	Liters
Imperial quarts	1.1365	Liters
Liters	0.2641721	U.S. gallons
Liters	1.0566882	U.S. quarts
Liters	33.814023	U.S. ounces
Liters	0.22	Imperial gallons
Liters	0.8799	Imperial quarts
Fluid volume (continued)		
Milliliters	0.033814	U.S. ounces
Milliliters	1.0	Cubic centimeters
Milliliters	0.001	Liters
Torque		
Foot-pounds	1.3558	Newton-meters
Foot-pounds	0.138255	Meter-kilograms
Inch-pounds	0.11299	Newton-meters
Newton-meters	0.7375622	Foot-pounds
Newton-meters	8.8507	Inch-pounds
Meters-kilograms	7.2330139	Foot-pounds
Volume		
Cubic inches	16.387064	Cubic centimeters
Cubic centimeters	0.0610237	Cubic inches

(continued)

GENERAL INFORMATION

Table 4 CONVERSION TABLES (continued)

Multiply	By	To get equivalent of
Temperature		
Fahrenheit	(F − 32) × 0.556	Centigrade
Centigrade	(C × 1.8) + 32	Fahrenheit
Weight		
Ounces	28.3495	Grams
Pounds	0.4535924	Kilograms
Grams	0.035274	Ounces
Kilograms	2.2046224	Pounds
Pressure		
Pounds per square inch	0.070307	Kilograms per square centimeter
Kilograms per square centimeter	14.223343	Pounds per square inch
Kilopascals	0.1450	Pounds per square inch
Pounds per square inch	6.895	Kilopascals
Speed		
Miles per hour	1.609344	Kilometers per hour
Kilometers per hour	0.6213712	Miles per hour

Table 5 GENERAL TORQUE SPECIFICATIONS

Screw or nut size	in.-lb.	ft.-lb.	N•m
U.S. Standard			
6-32	9	–	1.0
8-32	20	–	2.3
10-24	30	–	3.4
10-32	35	–	4.0
12-24	45	–	5.1
1/4-20	70	–	7.9
1/4-28	84	–	9.5
5/16-18	160	13	18
5/16-24	168	14	19
3/8-16	–	23	31
3/8-24	–	25	34
7/16-14	–	36	49
7/16-20	–	40	54
1/2-13	–	50	68
1/2-20	–	60	81
Metric			
5 mm	36	–	4
6 mm	70	–	8
8 mm	156	13	18
10 mm	–	26	35
12 mm	–	35	48
14 mm	–	60	81

Chapter Two

Troubleshooting

An orderly and logical approach is the best way to troubleshoot an outboard. A haphazard approach may eventually find the problem, but it can waste time and cause unnecessary parts replacement. Follow the step-by-step instructions provided in this chapter to troubleshoot in an efficient and timely manner.

The first step in any troubleshooting procedure is to define the symptoms as closely as possible, then localize the problem. Subsequent steps involve testing the areas that could cause the symptoms.

Never assume anything. Do not overlook the obvious. If the engine will not start, is the safety lanyard attached? Is the fuel system primed? Is the engine cranking slowly because the battery is discharged? Check for disconnected wiring or hoses. Is the proper starting procedures being followed? If the engine suddenly quits, check the easiest, most accessible problem first. Is there fuel in the tank? Is the fuel tank vent open, allowing air to enter the tank as it should? If nothing obvious is found in a quick check, delve deeper.

Learning to recognize and describe the symptoms will make diagnosis easier for you or the mechanic at a dealership or shop. Gather as many symptoms as possible to aid in diagnosis. Note whether the engine lost power gradually or all at once, and what color of smoke came from the exhaust. Remember that a more complicated machine is easier to troubleshoot because symptoms point to specific problems.

After the symptoms are defined, test and analyze areas that could cause problems. Guessing at the cause of a problem may provide a solution, but it can easily lead to frustration, wasted time and a series of expensive, unnecessary parts replacement.

Expensive equipment or complicated test gear is not necessary to determine whether repairs may be attempted at home. A few simple checks could save a large repair bill

TROUBLESHOOTING

This chapter provides sections covering model identification, preliminary inspection, operating requirements, starting difficulty, and system or component testing.

Tables 1-3 list common problems related to the starting, fuel and ignition systems. The probable cause(s) and corrective action(s) are also listed. **Tables 1-3** may refer to component test in this chapter for further testing. **Tables 4-15** list specifications for various components and systems on the engine.

PRELIMINARY INSPECTION

Most engine malfunctions can be corrected by checking and correcting a few simple items. If the following checks do not fix the problem, refer to **Tables 1-3** for starting, fuel and ignition system troubleshooting. Additional troubleshooting tips are provided in this chapter for the specific system or component.

1. Inspect the engine for loose, disconnected, dirty or corroded wiring.
2. Provide the engine with fresh fuel and the proper mix of Yamaha outboard engine oil as described in Chapter Three.
3. Check the battery for proper and clean connections as described in Chapter Three.
4. Fully charge the battery if necessary as described in Chapter Seven.
5. Use the proper equipment to test for spark at each cylinder as described in this chapter.
6. Check spark plug condition and gap settings as described in Chapter Three.
7. Place the lanyard safety switch in the RUN position.
8. Make sure the boat hull is clean and in good condition.

OPERATING REQUIREMENTS

An internal combustion engine requires three basic things to run properly: a fresh supply of fuel and air in the proper proportion, adequate compression in the combustion chamber and a source of ignition at the proper time (**Figure 1**). If any of these requirements are missing, the engine will not run. If any of these requirements are lacking, the engine will not run properly.

STARTING DIFFICULTY

Starting Procedures

If the engine is difficult to start, the problem may be with the engine or related to the starting procedure. Refer to the owner's manual for the proper starting procedure.

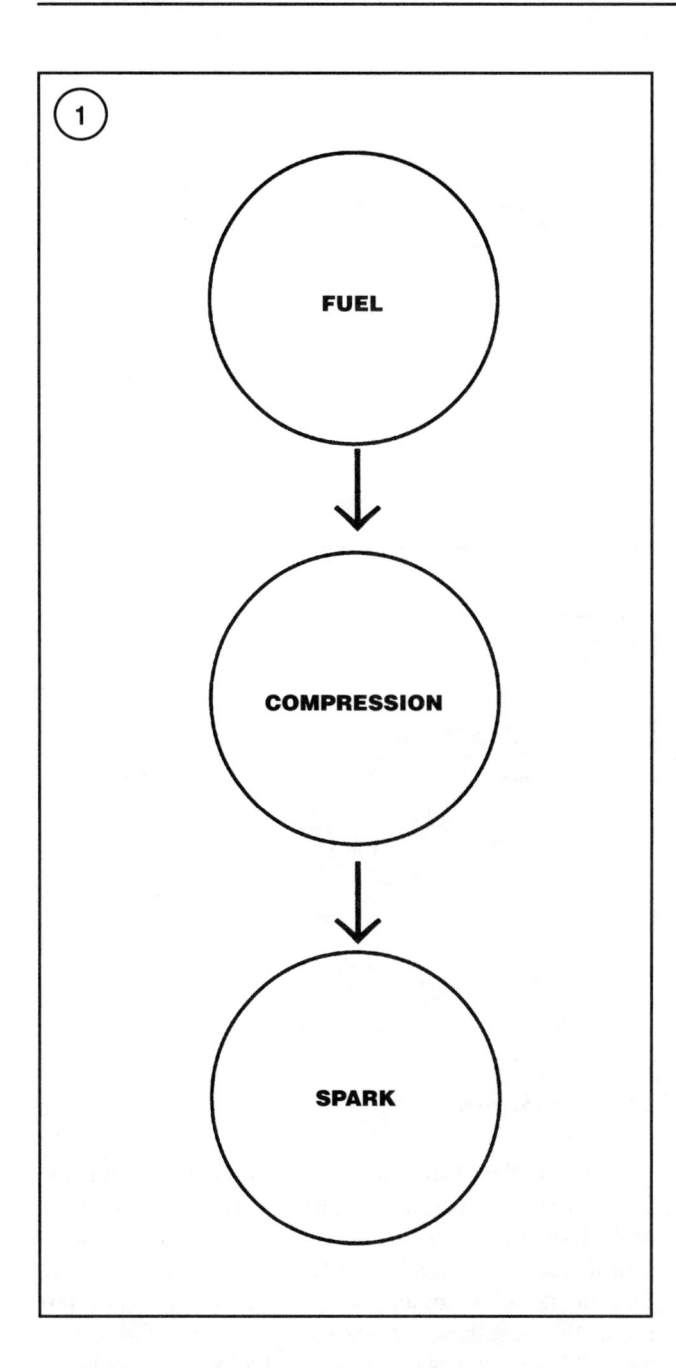

and lost time while the boat sits in a dealership service department. On the other hand, be realistic. Do not attempt repairs beyond your abilities. Service departments charge heavily for putting together a disassembled engine and some will not even take on such a job.

During continuity tests, if a component has failed open, the component has a broken circuit and is not functioning. If a component has a short circuit, a ground exists in the component, which results in an excessive flow of current. In either case, the component must be repaired or replaced.

CHAPTER TWO

Refer to **Table 1** to troubleshoot problems with the electric starting system. Manual starter repair is described in Chapter Ten.

NOTE
Some 28 jet, 45 jet and 50-90 hp models are equipped with the Prime-Start system to improve starting and cold engine operation. This system will not be able to start the engine with the throttle open. The throttle must be closed to create the intake manifold vacuum needed for the system to operate properly.

Determining a Fuel or Ignition Fault

It can be difficult to determine if a starting problem is related to fuel, ignition or other causes. If the engine will not start, first make sure the ignition system is operating. If the ignition system is operating properly, check the fuel system. Use a spark gap tester to check output from the ignition system at cranking speeds as described in this chapter. Spark gap testers are available from a variety of sources including Yamaha (part No. YM34487/90890-06754).

Spark test

WARNING
High voltage is present in the ignition system. Never touch wires or connections. Never perform ignition system testing in wet conditions. Never perform electrical testing when fuel or fuel vapor is present as arcing can cause a fire or explosion.

1. Remove the spark plug(s) (B, **Figure 2**) to prevent accidental starting.
2. Connect the alligator clip lead (A, **Figure 2**) of the spark tester to a suitable engine ground.
3. Attach the selected spark plug lead to the spark gap tester (C, **Figure 2**).
4. On 6-90 hp models, connect the remaining spark plug lead to the engine ground to prevent arcing.
5. Crank the engine while observing the spark gap tester (**Figure 3**). A strong, blue spark that jumps a 9 mm (0.35 in.) gap indicates adequate spark.
6. Repeat Steps 3-5 for the remaining cylinders.
7. Install the spark plug(s) and connect the lead(s) when testing is complete. Refer to **Table 1** for ignition system testing if the spark is lacking or weak on any of the cylinders. Refer to **Table 2** for fuel system troubleshooting if the ignition system is working but the engine will not start.

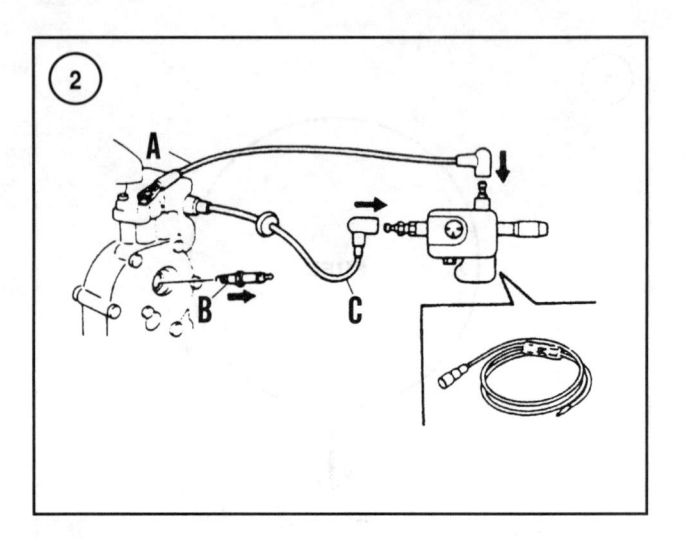

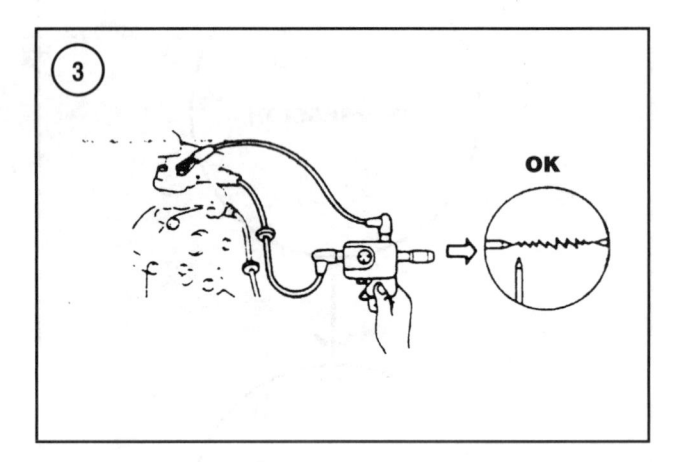

Checking the fuel system

Fuel related problems are common to outboard engines. Fuel has a relatively short shelf life. Fuel starts to lose some of its desirable qualities in as little as 14 days and becomes sour if it is stored for a long period. Gummy deposits may form in the carburetor and fuel passages as the fuel evaporates. Over time these deposits harden into varnish-like material. These deposits can also clog fuel filters, fuel hoses and the fuel pump. Also, fuel can become contaminated with water from condensation or other sources. Water causes the engine to run poorly or not at all.

Check the condition of the fuel if the engine has been stored and will not start. Carefully drain the fuel into a suitable container. Illustrations that show the specific location of the bowl drain screw (**Figure 4**) are in Chapter Five. Unusual odor, debris, cloudy appearance or the presence of water indicates a fuel related problem. If any of these condition are present, dispose of the old or contaminated fuel in an environmentally responsible manner.

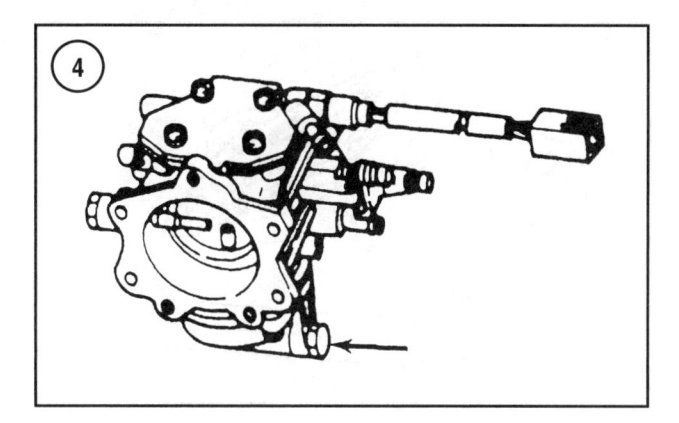

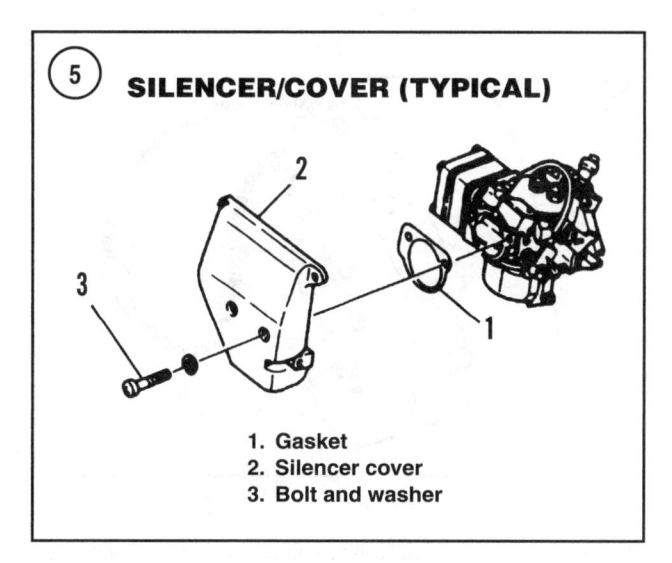

TROUBLESHOOTING

built-in fuel tanks are equipped with an antisiphon device to prevent fuel from siphoning from the fuel tank if a leak occurs in the fuel hose. These devices are necessary for safety but can cause problems if they malfunction. Temporarily run the engine using a portable fuel tank with a fresh fuel/oil mixture. Inspect the fuel tank pickup, antisiphon device and fuel tank vent if the engine performs properly on the temporary fuel tank. Always replace corroded or plugged antisiphon devices.

To check for a problem with the fuel pump, try gently squeezing the primer bulb when the symptom occurs. Perform a complete inspection of the fuel pump and fuel hoses if the symptom improves while the primer bulb is being squeezed. Fuel system repair is described in Chapter Five. Always check for and correct fuel leaks after working with fuel system components.

CAUTION
Never run an outboard without providing the engine with cooling water. Use either a test tank or flush test adapter if the engine cannot be operated under actual conditions. Remove the propeller before running the engine on a flush test adapter. Install a test propeller when operating the engine in a test tank. Refer to Chapter Four for information on test propellers.

Carburetor Tests

A rough running engine that smokes excessively is usually caused by a rich fuel/air mixture. The typical causes of a rich fuel/air mixture are a flooding carburetor, faulty recirculation system, stuck choke valve or faulty electrothermal valve. The most common cause is a flooding carburetor or improper float level adjustment. Weak spark or faulty spark plugs can also cause rough running and excessive smoking.

Other problems with the carburetor(s) can cause a lean fuel/air mixture that leads to poor performance or bogging on acceleration.

Rich fuel/air mixture

1. Disconnect and ground the spark plug lead(s) to prevent accidental starting.
2. On electric start models, disconnect the battery cables.
3. Remove the silencer cover (2, **Figure 5**, typical) as described in Chapter Five. Do not remove the carburetor(s) from the engine.
4. On 2-5 hp models, look into the front of the carburetor while opening the fuel valve on the integral fuel tank.

Contact a local marine dealership or automotive repair facility for information on the proper disposal of fuel. Clean and inspect the entire fuel system if contaminants are found in the float bowl. If the entire system is not thoroughly cleaned, the problems will continue. Replace all fuel filters.

If fuel cannot be drained from the float bowl, disassemble the carburetor(s) along with the fuel pump and hoses. Typically, the fuel inlet needle is stuck closed or blocked with debris. Repairs to the carburetor and other fuel system components are described in Chapter Five.

A faulty choke valve or Prime Start system can also cause starting difficulty. Test these components if other fuel system components test correctly and starting is still difficult.

FUEL SYSTEM

The fuel tank or fuel pump is usually the problem if the engine surges at higher speeds. Boats equipped with

5. On 6-90 hp models, look into the front of the carburetor while gently squeezing the primer bulb.
6. If fuel is flowing in the opening of the carburetor, remove the carburetor and repair it as described in Chapter Five.
7. Install the silencer cover as described in Chapter Five.
8. On electric start models, connect the battery cables.
9. Connect the spark plug lead(s).

Lean fuel/air mixture

CAUTION
Never operate an outboard that is not running properly. A fault in the fuel system may be causing the engine to operate with a lean fuel/air mixture. Operating the engine with a lean fuel mixture can lead to serious power head damage.

Blocked jets, passages, orifices or vent openings can cause either a rich or lean mixture. Symptoms of inadequate or excess fuel include bogging down during rapid acceleration, rough idle, poor performance at high speed or surging at any engine speed.

If the engine is bogging on acceleration, push in on the key switch or turn the choke lever on when the bogging occurs. The mixture is lean if the symptoms improve with the enriched fuel. The mixture is rich if the symptoms become worse. In either case, clean and inspect the carburetor(s) as described in Chapter Five.

Altitude adjustments

Changes to carburetor jets or carburetor adjustments may be required to correct engine malfunctions while operating at high elevation or extreme hot or cold climates. When operating in these conditions, contact a Yamaha dealership in the area for carburetor adjustment recommendations.

Reed Valve Test

WARNING
Be extremely careful when working with the fuel system. Never smoke around fuel or fuel vapor. Make sure no flame or source of ignition is present

A chipped or broken reed valve (**Figure 6**) can cause poor idle quality and rough running, primarily at lower engine speeds. An engine with damaged reed valves may run satisfactorily at higher engine speeds.

Test the engine for damaged reed valves while running at low speed in the water, in a test tank or on a flush/test adapter. Although variations exist in the number of carburetors and mounting arrangements for the silencer cover and carburetors, the testing procedures are the same.

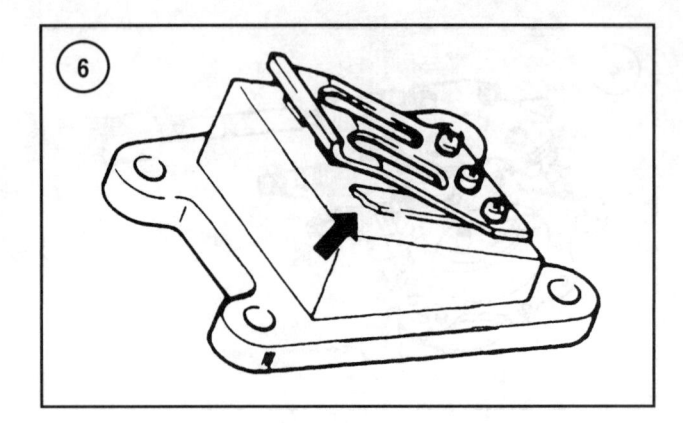

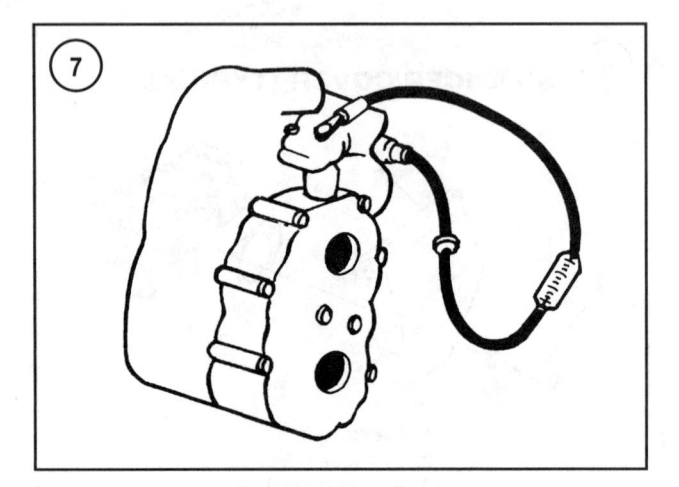

1. Remove the silencer cover (**Figure 5**) as described in Chapter Six.
2. If silencer cover bolts also secure the carburetor, install washers or spacers on the mounting bolts to compensate for the excess bolt length with the cover removed. Make sure the carburetor is securely mounted on the intake manifold before proceeding.
3. Observe the carburetor opening while running the engine at idle speed. If fuel spits out of the carburetor opening, there is a problem with the reed valve. Remove and inspect the reed valve and related components as described in Chapter Six.
4. Install the silencer cover as described in Chapter Six.

Compression Test

Older engines or engines with high operating hours often are hard to start, or have poor idle quality or poor performance. Perform a compression test if the fuel and

TROUBLESHOOTING

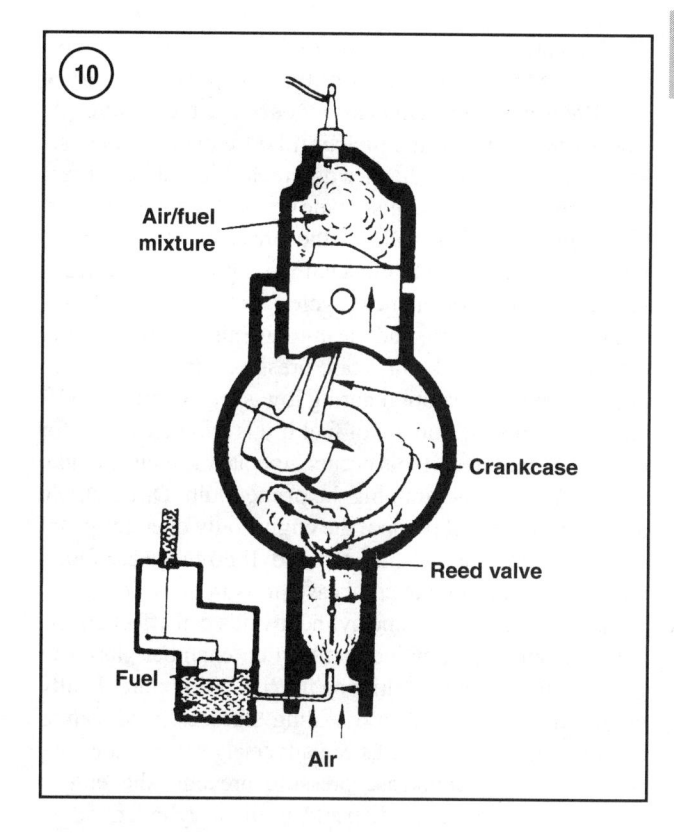

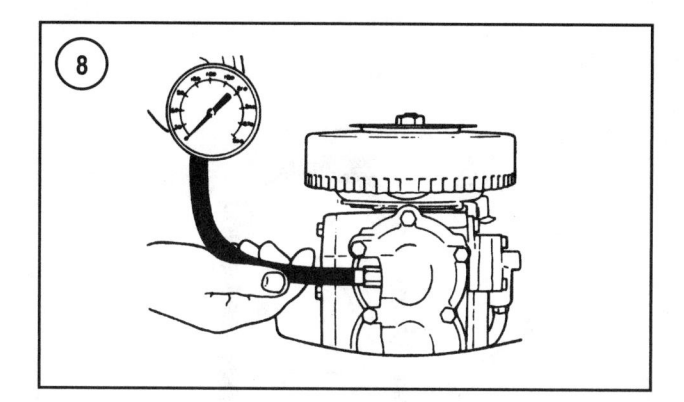

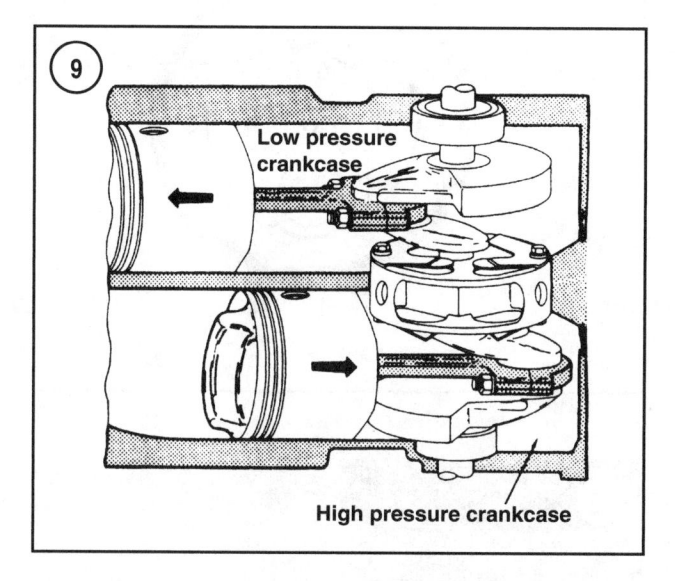

ignition system are not causing these symptoms. Avoid relying solely on the compression test as an indication of the condition of the engine. Sometimes a compression test will have satisfactory readings when there is something wrong in the outboard. Closer inspection of the piston, rings and cylinder walls may reveal scoring or scuffing not detected by the compression test. A leak-down test is a more reliable indicator of the piston, ring and cylinder wall condition. This equipment is far more costly and more difficult to use than a typical compression gauge. Have a reputable marine dealership perform a leak-down test if necessary.

1. Remove the spark plugs. To prevent arcing, ground the spark plug lead(s) using suitable jumper leads (**Figure 7**).
2. Remove the propeller as described in Chapter Eight.
3. Install the compression gauge in the No. 1 cylinder spark plug opening (**Figure 8**). Securely tighten the adapter to prevent leaks at the spark plug opening.
4. Manually hold the throttle valve(s) in the wide-open position.
5. Operate the electric or manual starter until the flywheel rotates at least six revolutions.
6. Record the compression reading.
7. Repeat Steps 3-6 for the remaining cylinders.
8. Install the propeller as described in Chapter Nine.
9. Compare the compression readings and note the highest and lowest readings. The lowest reading should be within 10% of the highest reading. One or more cylinders with significantly lower readings or a cylinder that reads 517 kPa (75 psi) or less indicates a problem. Remove the cylinder head or exhaust cover and inspect the piston and cylinder wall before attempting to troubleshoot or tune the engine. An engine with inadequate or unbalanced compression cannot be tuned properly and will not perform correctly. Power head repair is described in Chapter Seven.
10. Install the spark plug(s) and connect the lead(s).

Crankcase Seal Test

A two-stroke engine operates with alternating pressure and vacuum in the crankcase (**Figure 9**). As the piston moves up on the compression stroke, the volume in the crankcase increases and creates a vacuum. Atmospheric pressure forces fuel and air to flow through the carburetor, through the reed valve and into the crankcase (**Figure 10**).

As the piston moves down on the power stroke, the volume in the crankcase decreases forming pressure (**Figure 11**). Pressure in the crankcase closes the reed valve (A, **Figure 11**), trapping the fuel/air mixture in the crankcase. As the piston moves further downward, crankcase pressure increases until the piston moves past the transfer port (B, **Figure 11**). This allows the pressurized mixture to flow into the combustion chamber, providing a fresh fuel/air mixture for the next cycle.

Crankcase pressure and vacuum are also used to power the fuel pump. Weak crankcase pressure can contribute to poor fuel pump operation during low-speed operation. Often the engine will run out of fuel if it is allowed to idle for over a few minutes. If this occurs, operate the engine at idle speed while gently pumping the primer bulb. Disassemble and inspect the fuel pump if the engine only operates properly while the bulb is being pumped. If no faults are found with the fuel pump, the crankcase pressure may be weak.

Faulty pistons, rings and cylinder walls can affect crankcase pressure by allowing combustion chamber gasses to leak into the crankcase, diluting the fuel/air mixture. Faulty crankshaft seals, crankcase sealing surfaces, reed valves and cylinder block castings can adversely affect crankcase pressures. Low crankcase pressure prevents the engine from receiving adequate fuel and air in the cylinder, reducing engine efficiency. The engine will produce less power, causing bogging on acceleration and poor idle quality. In extreme cases, the engine can be tuned to idle at the correct out of gear speed, but will still stall when shifted into gear. The reduced efficiency prevents the engine from producing enough power to offset the load of the propeller. Typically, inadequate crankcase sealing only affects engine operation at lower speeds. At higher engine speeds the leak is a smaller percentage of the volume of air entering the engine and the symptoms are reduced.

If a crankcase or crankcase gasket leak is suspected, spray a soap and water solution onto the mating surfaces and casting while cranking the engine. Bubbles indicate the point of the leak. On multiple cylinder engines, internal leaks can occur. The symptoms are consistent with external leaks. Disassemble and inspect the engine components to find the leak. Before disassembling the power head, check for leaks at the intake manifold and reed housing. Faulty reeds or leaking gaskets will cause low crankcase pressure. Power head disassembly, inspection and repair procedures are described in Chapter Seven.

Fuel Enrichment System

Yamaha outboards are equipped with a fuel enrichment system to improve starting and cold engine operation. The

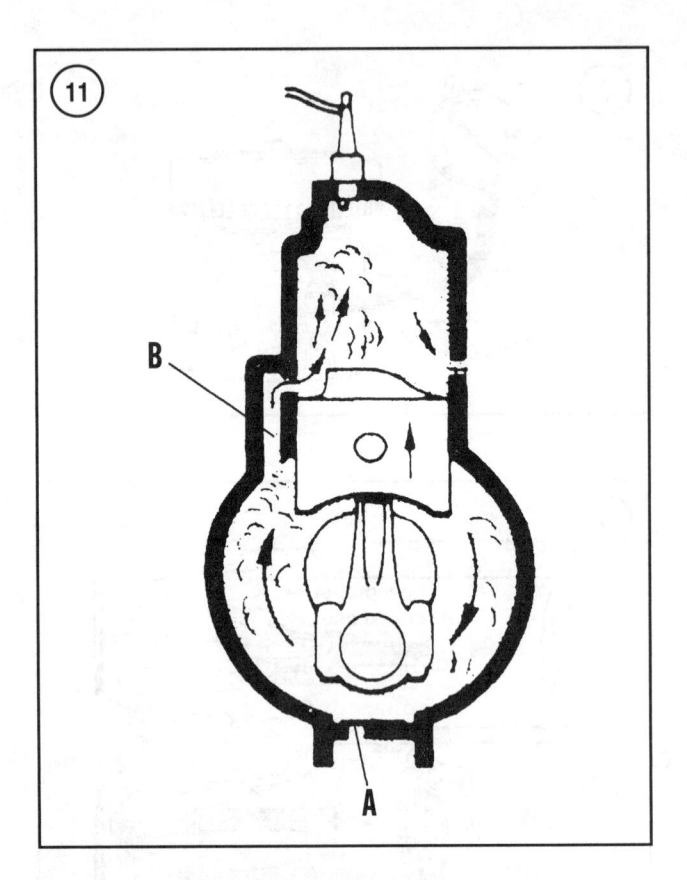

TROUBLESHOOTING

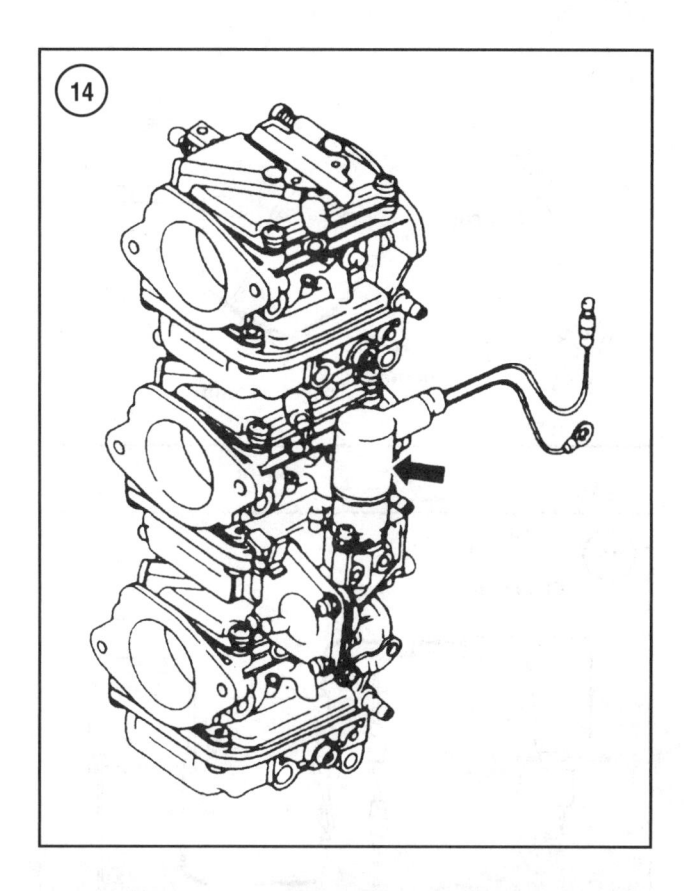

systems used include a manually operated choke valve, electrically operated choke valve and the Prime Start system.

Manual start models are equipped with a manually operated choke valve. Simply pull the choke knob (**Figure 12**) to close the choke valve. Closing the choke valve restricts air flow into the carburetor causing more fuel to enter the engine.

Most electric start models are equipped with a solenoid actuated choke valve (**Figure 13**). The solenoid moves a plunger that closes the choke valve(s). To activate the choke, push the control mounted choke switch while starting the engine. On some remote controls, the choke switch is integrated into the key switch. To activate the choke, push in on the key switch while starting the engine.

Oil injected 28 jet, 35 jet and 40-90 hp models are equipped with the Prime Start system. The battery charging coil, located under the flywheel, powers the carburetor mounted electrothermal valve (**Figure 14**). It allows fuel from the carburetor to flow directly into the engine during cold engine starting/running conditions. An internal valve functions as the pump that moves the fuel. The valve gradually decreases fuel delivery as the engine warms to normal operating temperature. The plunger retracts after the engine is switched off to provide automatic control of the enrichment system.

Test these systems if the engine is difficult to start and other systems are not faulty. Repair procedures for Prime Start system components are in Chapter Five.

NOTE
The Prime Start system will not operate properly unless the throttle is closed while the engine is started.

Choke solenoid test

The battery must be fully charged for this procedure.
1. Remove the silencer cover as described in Chapter Five.
2. Turn the key switch to the ON position. Do not activate the electric starter.
3. Observe the choke valves while repeatedly pushing in on the key switch or tripping the choke switch. The choke valve should close (**Figure 15**) with a smooth brisk motion each time the switch is activated and open (**Figure 16**) each time the switch is released.
   a. If the valve opens as specified, refer to **Table 2** and **Table 3** for other possible starting problem causes.
   b. If the choke valve opens and closes slowly, check for binding linkages and clean corrosion or other

contaminants from the choke plunger. Proceed to Step 4 if slow operation persists.
   c. If the choke valve does not move when the switch is activated, proceed to Step 4.
4. Calibrate a multimeter to the 20 VDC scale.
5. Disconnect the blue wire bullet connector from the choke solenoid.
6. Connect the positive test lead to the blue wire harness connector for the choke solenoid. Do not connect the test lead to the blue wire connected to the solenoid. Connect the negative test lead to the negative terminal on the solenoid.
7. Observe the meter while repeatedly pushing in on the key switch or tripping the choke switch. If the meter does not indicate battery voltage each time the switch activates and 0 volt each time the switch is released, repeat the test with the negative test lead connected to an engine ground.
   a. If there is only battery voltage with the negative lead connected to an engine ground, there is a fault in the solenoid ground wire or terminal. Repair the wire or terminal and retest.
   b. If there is low voltage with either negative wire connection point, test the key switch and related wiring as described in this chapter.
   c. If there is battery voltage at the meter, check for binding choke valve linkages. Replace the choke solenoid as described in Chapter Five if the battery voltage is correct and the choke does not operate.
8. Test the solenoid winding resistance as follows:
   a. Remove the choke solenoid as described in Chapter Five.
   b. Calibrate a volt/ohmmeter to the R × 1 scale.
   c. Connect the positive meter test lead to the blue solenoid wire (**Figure 17**). Connect the negative meter test lead to the black solenoid wire.
   d. If the meter does not indicate 3.7-4.0 ohms, replace the solenoid.
   e. Install the choke solenoid as described in Chapter Five.
9. Reconnect all wiring, then install the silencer cover as described in Chapter Five.

Electrothermal valve running test

The engine must be operated in the water, in a test tank or on a flush/test device for this procedure.

CAUTION
Never run an outboard without providing the engine with cooling water. Use either a test tank or flush test adapter if the engine cannot be operated under actual conditions. Remove the propeller before running the engine on a flush test adapter. Install a test propeller when operating the engine in a test tank. Refer to Chapter Four for information on test propellers.

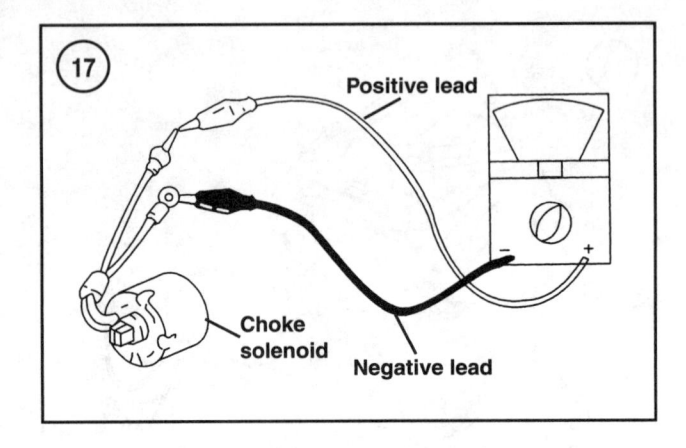

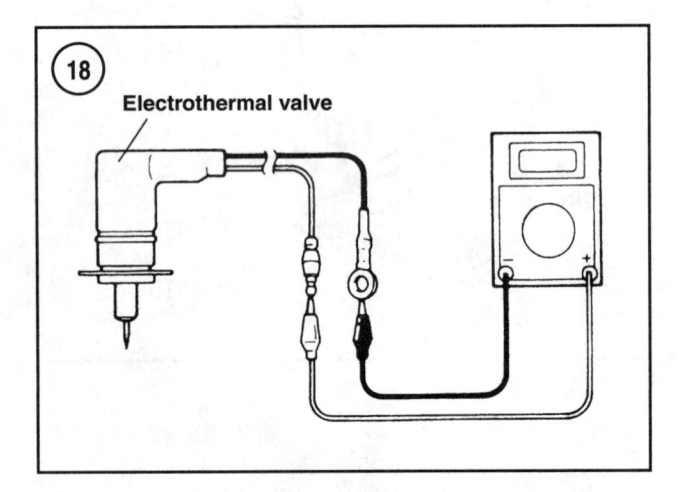

1. Make sure engine and electrothermal valve have cooled to room temperature.
2. Start the engine and immediately touch a finger to the top of the electrothermal valve (**Figure 14**). Keep the engine at idle speed for this test.
3. If the electrothermal valve does not begin to warm within a few minutes of engine operation, test the charging system output as described in this chapter. If the charging system test correctly, measure the electrothermal valve resistance and perform an operational test as described in this chapter.

Electrothermal valve resistance test

NOTE
Perform this test at a room temperature of 20° C (68° F). Allow the component to warm

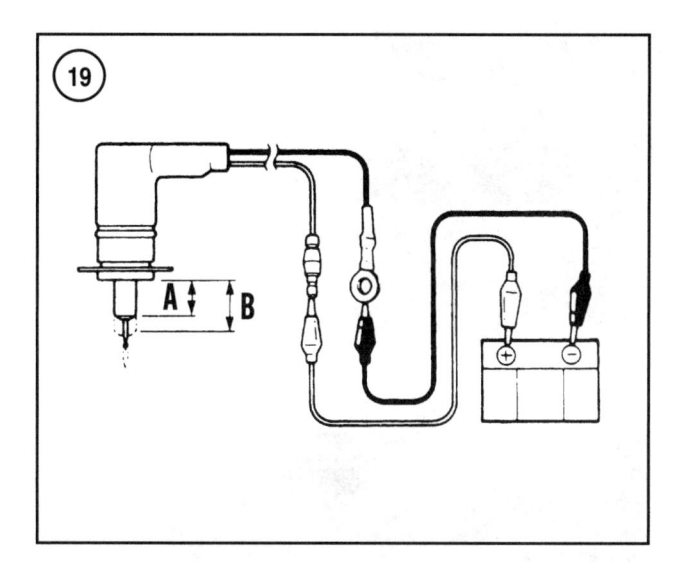

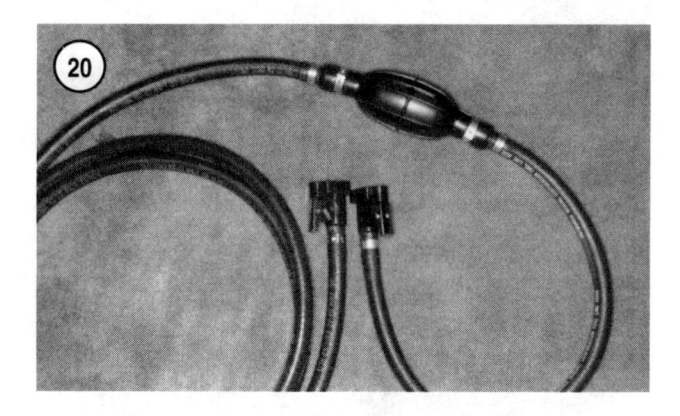

TROUBLESHOOTING

Electrothermal valve operational test

A fully charged battery, jumper wires and a measuring ruler are required for this test. Allow the engine to cool to room temperature before performing this test.

1. Remove the electrothermal valve as described in Chapter Five.
2. Use a permanent marker to mark the plunger at the point where it exits the electrothermal valve. Measure the distance from the mark to the valve body at the points indicated in A, **Figure 19**.
3. Using jumper leads, connect the blue wire of the valve to the positive terminal of a fully charged battery (**Figure 19**).
4. Using jumper wires, connect the black wires of the valve to the negative terminal of the battery (**Figure 19**).
5. Maintain this connection for 5-7 minutes. The valve should heat up after a few minutes.
6. With the wires still connected to the battery, measure the distance from the marking to the body of the valve at the points indicated in B, **Figure 19**.
7. If the measurement in Step 6 is not greater than the measurement in Step 2, replace the electrothermal valve.
8. Install the electrothermal valve as described in Chapter Five.

Fuel Supply Hose and Primer Bulb

NOTE
Run the engine at full throttle for several minutes to check for a faulty fuel supply hose or primer bulb.

A faulty fuel supply hose or primer bulb (**Figure 20**) can cause fuel starvation and lean operating conditions at higher engine speeds or can cause the engine to run out of fuel at idle speed.

A faulty check valve can prevent the primer bulb from pumping fuel or restrict fuel flow to the engine. Leaking at the check valve and hose connections can allow fuel and air leaks.

Faulty hoses and connections allow fuel to leak from the supply hose when the engine is at rest, and allow air to be drawn into the fuel when the engine is running.

The most effective method for troubleshooting a suspect fuel supply hose is to operate the engine using a suitable hose from an engine that is operating correctly. Test the primer bulb as described in Chapter Five if the symptoms disappear with the replacement hose. Inspect the hose connectors (**Figure 21**) for defects. Replace the hoses if the primer bulb tests correctly.

---

or cool to normal room temperature before testing. The resistance measurement will be higher if the component is tested at higher temperatures. The measurement will be lower at lower temperatures.

Use a digital volt/ohmmeter to measure the resistance of the winding in the electrothermal valve. Valve removal is not required for this test.

1. Disconnect and ground the spark plug leads to prevent accidental starting.
2. On electric start models, disconnect the battery cables.
3. Disconnect the bullet for the blue electrothermal valve wire. Disconnect the negative ground wire on the valve.
4. Calibrate the volt/ohmmeter to the R × 1 scale.
5. Connect the meter test leads to the electrothermal valve wires (**Figure 18**) and observe the meter reading. If the meter does not indicate 2.32-3.48 ohms, replace the electrothermal valve as described in Chapter Five.
6. Reconnect all wiring and the spark plug leads.

Recirculation System Test

During low speed operation, fuel and oil collect in certain areas in the power head. The recirculation system uses crankcase pressure and vacuum pulses to move the mixture to other locations in the power head, where it lubricates bearings and other components before entering the combustion chamber to be burned.

The recirculation system on some models only uses internal passages. Other models use external hoses and fittings. Some models use a combination of internal passages and external hoses. Refer to Chapter Five for hose routing on models so equipped.

Leaking external hoses allow an oily film to form on the external surfaces of the power head. Replace leaking hoses or faulty fittings to prevent oil leak and inadequate lubrication of the power head components.

A plugged recirculation system prevents movement of the fuel, causing it to eventually be drawn into the combustion chamber with the fuel/air mixture. This causes a rich fuel mixture, which causes the engine to run very rough, slow down and eventually stall. The symptoms occur only at lower engine speeds, since fuel generally does not collect at higher engine speeds. An engine with a faulty recirculation system will usually bog down when accelerated after idling for an extended time. This is due to a rich fuel mixture as the collected fuel is quickly drawn into the combustion chamber.

To check for a plugged recirculation system, operate the engine at a fast idle until the engine reaches full operating temperature. Return the engine to idle speed and quickly note the engine idle speed and running characteristics. If the symptoms surface fairly quickly after returning to idle speed, check for other problems.

If the recirculation system is suspect, check the condition of external hoses and the hose routing as described in Chapter Five. Test the check valve inside some hose fittings as described in this section.

A faulty recirculation system is not always caused by plugged passages or faulty check valves. A flooding or improperly adjusted carburetor can cause more of the mixture to collect than the system can move. Weak crankcase pressure or faulty reed valves reduce the systems capability for moving fuel and increases the volume of fuel that collects in the power head. Check these components if the symptoms persist and no faults are found with hoses or check valves.

Check valve fittings test

A hand-operated pressure/vacuum pump or syringe is required for this test.

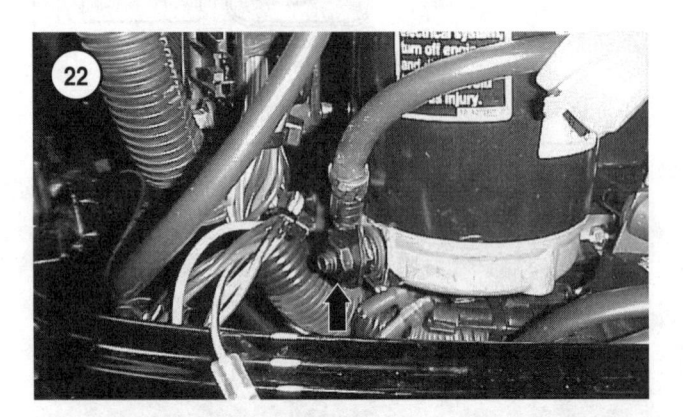

1. Disconnect and ground the spark plug lead(s) to prevent accidental starting.

2. On electric start models, disconnect the battery cables.

3. Remove the hose from the fitting. Connect a hand-operated pressure/vacuum pump or syringe and hose to the fitting. The hose must fit tightly on the check valve fitting. Clamp the hose on the fitting if necessary.

4. Alternately apply pressure and vacuum to the check valve fitting. The check valve should allow air to flow in one direction and not the other. Replace the check valve fitting if it allows air to flow in both directions or does not allow flow in one direction.

TROUBLESHOOTING

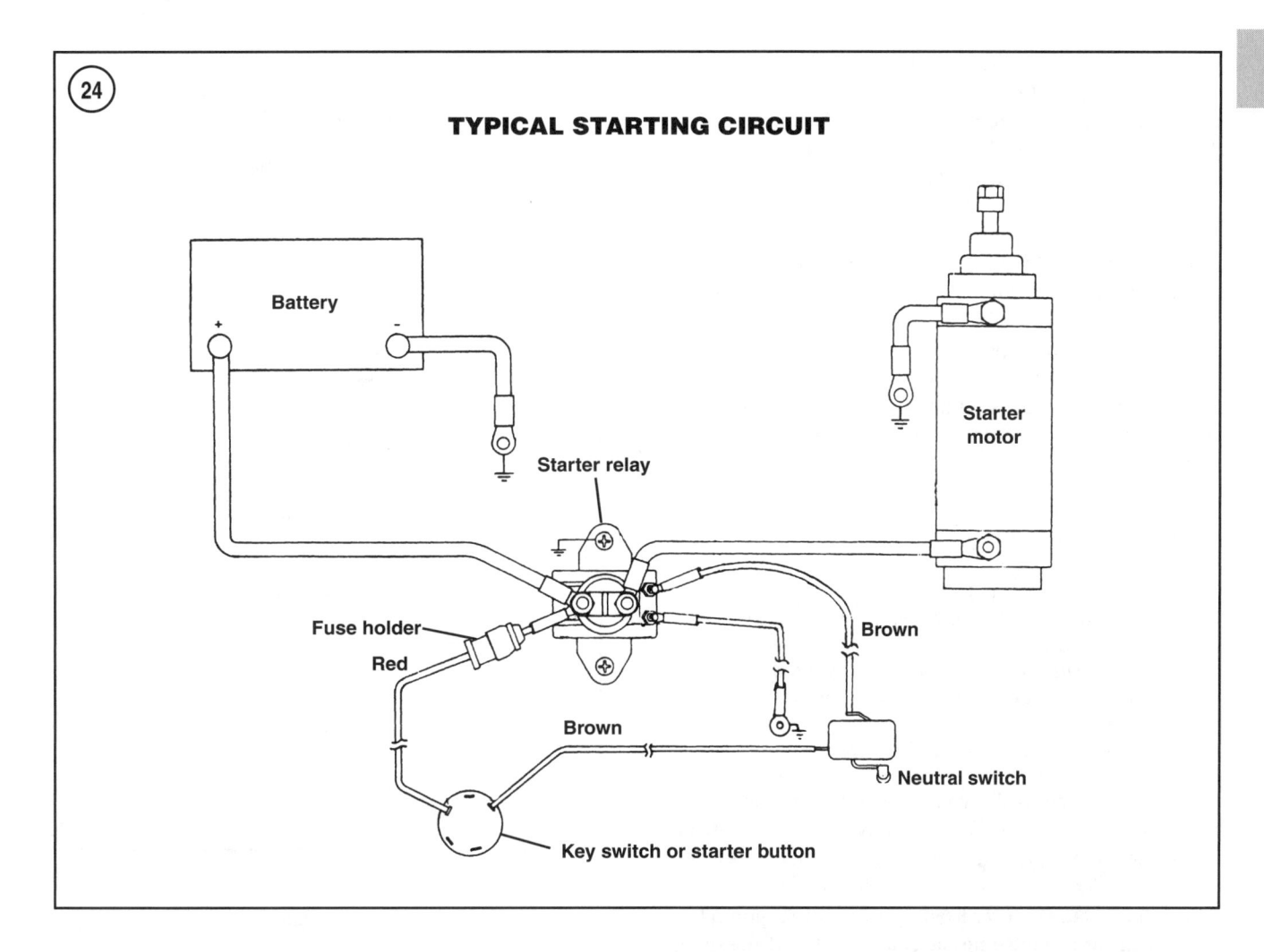

Figure 24 — TYPICAL STARTING CIRCUIT

5. Repeat the test for the remaining check valves on the engine.
6. Connect the spark plug lead(s).
7. On electric start models, connect the battery cables.

STARTING SYSTEM

The starting systems on 2-5 hp models have a manual starter. A manual starter or electric starter is used on 6-50 hp, E60 and E75 models. Electric starting is used on 60-90 hp models (except E60 and E75).

The common components of the electric starting system are the battery, starter button or key switch, starter relay, neutral safety switch, starter motor and wiring.

The electric starter motor (**Figure 22**) is similar in design to what is commonly used in automobiles. The mounting position of the electric starter on the power head allows the starter drive gear (**Figure 23**) to engage a flywheel mounted ring gear. The neutral safety switch (**Figure 24**) prevents the starter from operating when the engine is in gear. When the starter is disengaged, the flywheel kicks the drive gear down to the starter with assistance from the return spring (**Figure 25**).

The electric motor portion of the starter can produce a tremendous amount of torque, but only for a short period of time. Never operate the starter motor for over 20 seconds at a time and allow a two-minute cooling period between each attempt to start the engine. A large amount of electrical current is necessary to provide the torque to crank the engine. Battery requirements are in the *Quick Reference Data* section at the beginning of the manual. Weak or undercharged batteries are the leading cause of starting system problems. Battery maintenance and testing procedures are in Chapter Three.

Electric Starting System Operation

The key switch or starter button connects to the positive terminal of the battery through a series of harness and wire connections. When the start button is activated, current is directed first to the neutral switch (**Figure 24**), then to the starter relay. One terminal of the relay is connected to the battery positive terminal by a large diameter cable. The other large terminal is connected to a terminal on the starter motor (**Figure 22**). When the neutral switch supplies current to the relay, the relay makes an internal connection that allows current to flow from the battery positive terminal to the starter terminal. The relay arrangement allows the starter current to be controlled using the shortest wires possible. The starter motor attaches to and is grounded to the power head. Starter motor removal, repair and installation procedures are in Chapter Six. Refer to **Table 1** for starting system troubleshooting. Starting system component testing is described in this section.

Starter Cranking Voltage Test

CAUTION
Never operate the starter motor for over 20 seconds without allowing at least 2 minutes for the starter to cool down. Attempting to start the engine with a weak or undercharged battery can cause starter motor overheating and subsequent failure.

This test measures the voltage delivered to the starter motor during cranking. Test and fully charge the battery before performing this test. Refer to Chapter Seven for battery testing, maintenance and charging procedures. Check for a seized power head, gearcase or jet pump before repairing or replacing the starter motor. If possible, use an analog meter for this test. The readings may fluctuate on a digital meter and prevent accurate voltage measurement.

1. Disconnect and ground the spark plug leads to prevent accidental starting.
2. Calibrate a voltmeter to the 20 or 40 VDC scale. Connect the positive test lead to the large terminal on the starter motor (**Figure 22**). Carefully scrape the neoprene coating from the terminal nut to ensure a good connection.
3. Connect the negative test lead to an engine ground.
4. Crank the engine while observing the voltmeter.
   a. If there is no voltage, test the starter relay as described in this section.
   b. If the voltage is 9.5 VDC or greater, the starter relay is supplying adequate current for the starter. Replace or repair the starter if it does not rotate or rotates slowly.
   c. If the voltage is 9.4 volts or lower, check the battery terminals and cables, then replace or fully charge the battery. Repeat the test.

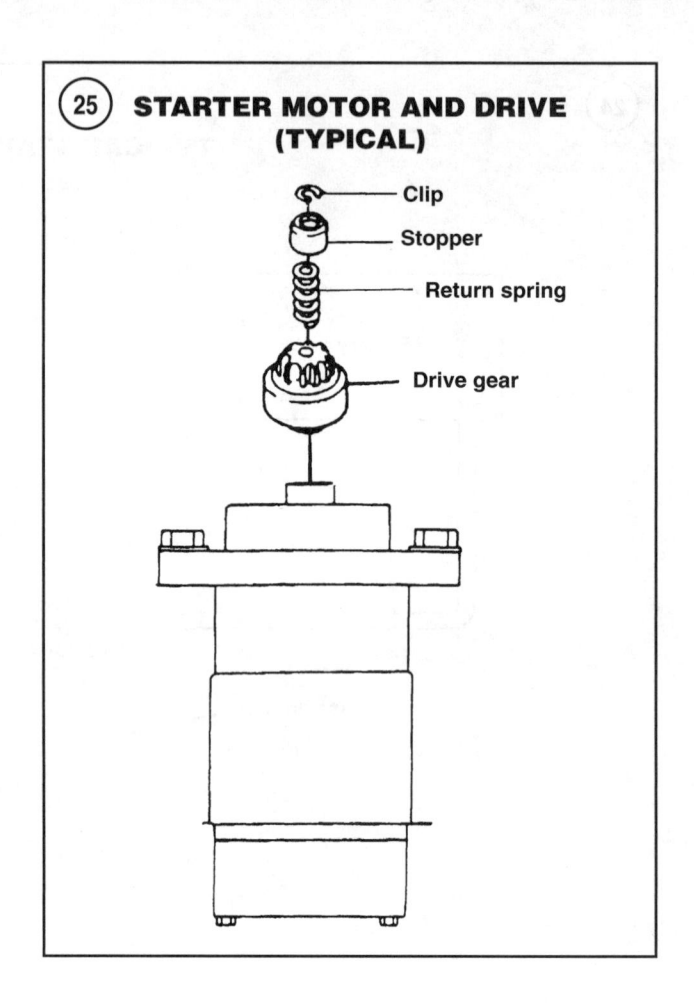

5. Reconnect the spark plug leads.

Starter Relay Tests

The starter relay allows a large current to pass from the battery to the starter motor. When the key switch or starter button is activated, current flows through the brown wire to the neutral switch, then to the relay. This current passes through a winding in the relay and returns to ground through the black relay ground wire. This creates a strong magnetic force that moves the relay plunger, connecting contacts that allow current flow to the starter. The first test checks the voltage supply and the ground wire for the relay. The relay function test checks for proper operation of the relay.

Starter relay voltage test

Refer to Chapter Six for starter relay and leads locations.

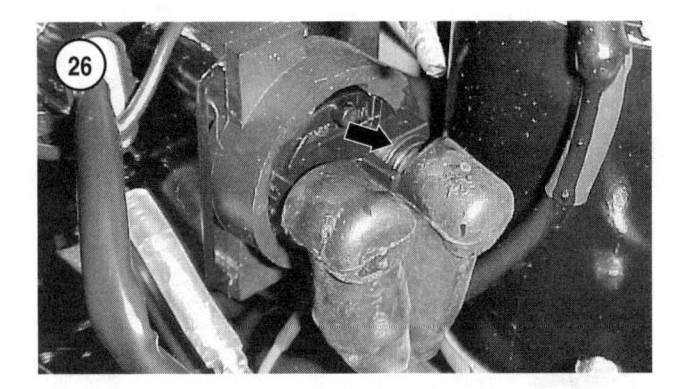

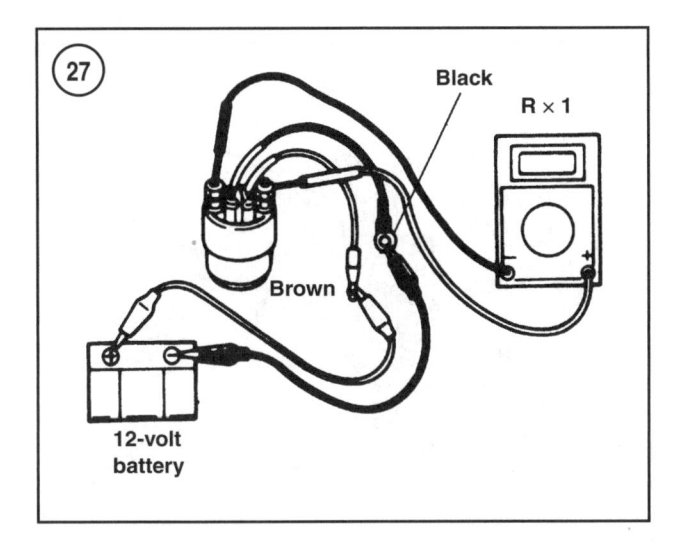

TROUBLESHOOTING

brown wire harness terminal. Do not connect the meter lead to the relay wire. Observe the meter while repeatedly depressing and releasing the starter button or turning the key switch to all three positions.

    a. *Starter button*—If the meter does not indicate battery voltage each time the button is depressed and 0 volt each time the button is released, test the fuses, neutral safety switch, starter button and related wiring.

    b. *Key switch*—If the meter does not indicate battery voltage each time the switch reaches the start position and 0 volt with the key in the off or run positions, test the fuses, neutral safety switch, key switch and related wiring.

8. Reconnect the brown engine harness wire to the brown starter relay wire. Route the wiring so it does not interfere with other components.

9. Connect the positive meter test lead to the positive battery cable terminal at the starter. Observe the meter while depressing the starter button or rotating the key switch to the START position. Repeat the test with the positive meter test lead connected to the starter cable terminal at the relay (**Figure 26**). The meter should indicate battery voltage at both test points.

    a. If there is only voltage at the starter relay terminal, the cable or cable terminals are faulty. Replace or repair the starter cable and retest.

    b. If there is no voltage at either test point, perform the relay function test described in this chapter.

10. Reconnect the positive battery starter cable to the starter terminal (**Figure 22**). Securely tighten the terminal and apply a coat of liquid neoprene to the terminal to help prevent unnecessary arcing and corrosion.

11. Connect the spark plug leads.

Starter relay function test

This test requires a fully charged battery, an analog multimeter and suitable jumper wires.

1. Remove the starter relay from the engine as described in Chapter Six.

2. Calibrate the multimeter to the R × 1 scale. Connect the negative meter test lead to one of the large terminals on the relay (**Figure 27**). Connect the positive test lead to the other large terminal.

3. Use a jumper wire to connect the black starter relay wire to the negative battery terminal (**Figure 27**).

4. Connect a jumper wire to the positive battery terminal. Observe the ohmmeter while repeatedly touching the jumper wire to the brown wire terminal of the relay. The meter should indicate continuity each time the connection in made and no continuity each time the connection is bro-

1. Disconnect and ground the spark plug leads to prevent accidental starting.

2. Disconnect the large diameter positive battery cable from the starter terminal (**Figure 22**). Cover the cable terminal to prevent it from contacting any components during testing. Route the cable so the terminal is positioned away from all components.

3. Calibrate a volt/ohmmeter to the 20 or 40 VDC scale.

4. Connect the negative meter test lead to a good engine ground.

5. Touch the positive meter test lead to the battery terminal of the relay. Check the wiring and terminals of the large diameter cable connecting the battery to the positive terminal if no voltage is recorded. If the wiring and terminals are not faulty, check for a faulty battery ground terminal or cable.

6. Touch the negative meter test lead to the black ground starter relay terminal. If battery voltage is present, repair or replace the starter relay ground wire.

7. Disconnect the brown wire connector from the relay connector. Connect the positive meter test lead to the

ken. Also, the relay should make a clicking noise each time the connection in made.

5. Replace the starter relay if it fails to perform as described.

6. Install the starter relay as described in Chapter Six.

Neutral Switch Test

The neutral switch prevents the electric starter from operating when the engine is in forward or reverse gear. A cable operated lockout mechanism is used on 4-50 hp (including E60 and E75) models with a manual starter. Lockout assembly repair procedures are in Chapter Ten and adjustment procedures are in Chapter Four.

On electric start models with tiller control, the neutral switch is mounted on the engine (**Figure 28**). The plunger portion of the switch contacts the shift linkages during shifting.

On electric start models with remote control, the switch is mounted in the remote control. Some engines are provided with both an engine- and control-mounted switch. Test both switches if so equipped.

Remote control models

A multimeter is required for this test.

1. Remove the remote control and rear cover as described in Chapter Thirteen. Do not remove the control handle.
2. Locate the neutral switch (4, **Figure 29**), then trace the switch wires to their connections on the remote control harness (7). Disconnect both switch wires.
3. Calibrate the multimeter to the R × 1 scale. Connect the meter test leads to each of the neutral safety switch leads.
4. With the control in the neutral gear position, the meter should indicate continuity. Shift the control handle into the FORWARD and REVERSE gear positions. The meter should indicate no continuity. Test the key switch and related wiring as described in this chapter if the meter readings test as specified. If they do not, proceed to Step 5.
5. Disassemble the remote control and remove the neutral switch as described in Chapter Thirteen. Test the switch as follows:
   a. Connect the ohmmeter to each of the switch wires (**Figure 30**).
   b. Observe the ohmmeter while depressing the switch lever (**Figure 30**). The meter should indicate continuity with the switch depressed and no continuity with the switch released. If it does not, replace the neutral safety switch.

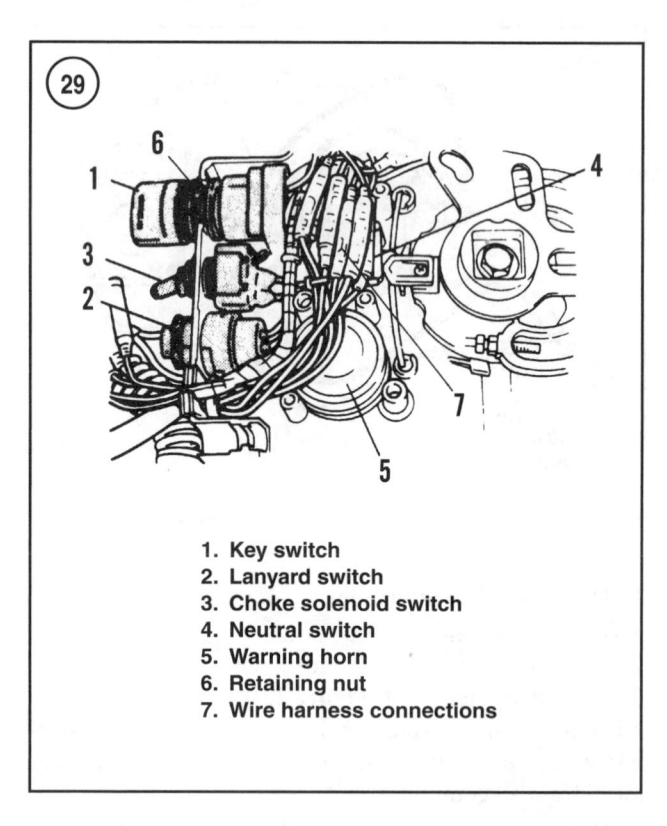

1. Key switch
2. Lanyard switch
3. Choke solenoid switch
4. Neutral switch
5. Warning horn
6. Retaining nut
7. Wire harness connections

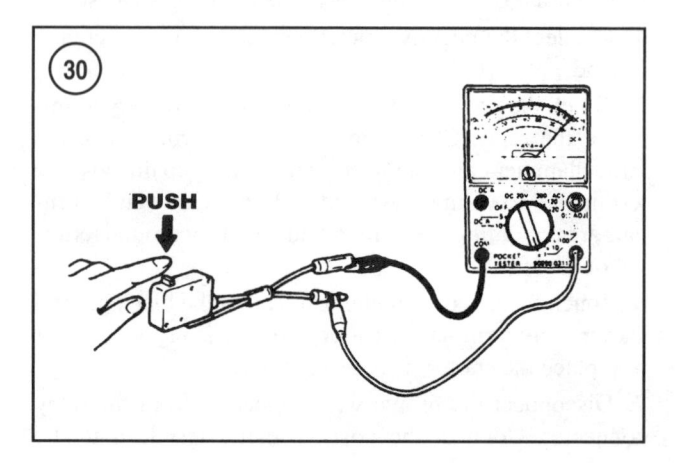

TROUBLESHOOTING

31

Br
Br

32

A B

Brown

1. Disconnect and ground the spark plug lead(s) to prevent accidental starting.
2. Disconnect the brown neutral switch wires from the starter relay and engine harness or starter button.
3. Calibrate the multimeter to the R × 1 scale. Connect the meter test leads to each of the neutral safety switch wires (**Figure 31**). Do not accidentally connect the test leads to the starter relay wire and wire harness or starter button wires.
4. Shift the control arm into NEUTRAL, FORWARD and REVERSE gear. The meter should read continuity each time the engine is shifted into neutral gear and no continuity each time the engine is shifted into forward or reverse gear.
   a. If the switch is operating correctly, proceed to Step 6, then test the starter button or key switch as described in this chapter.
   b. If the switch is not operating correctly, adjust the shift cables and linkages as described in Chapter Four and repeat the test. If the switch is still not operating correctly, proceed to Step 5.
5. Remove the neutral switch as described in Chapter Six.
   a. Measure the distance from the switch body to the tip of the plunger at the points indicated in A, **Figure 32**. If the measurement is not 19.5-20.5 mm (0.768-0.807 in.), the switch is worn or binding and must be replaced.
   b. Connect the meter test leads to each of the brown neutral switch wires. With the plunger in the relaxed position, the meter should indicate no continuity. If it does not, the switch has shorted and must be replaced.
   c. Observe the meter while slowly pushing the plunger into the body. Measure the distance from the switch body to the plunger tip (B, **Figure 32**) when the meter reading changes to continuity. If the change does not occur at a measured distance of 18.5-19.5 mm (0.728-0.768 in.), replace the switch.
   d. Install the neutral switch as described in Chapter Six.
6. Connect the neutral switch to the starter relay and engine wire harness or starter button. Route the wiring so it will not contact moving components.
7. Connect the spark plug leads.

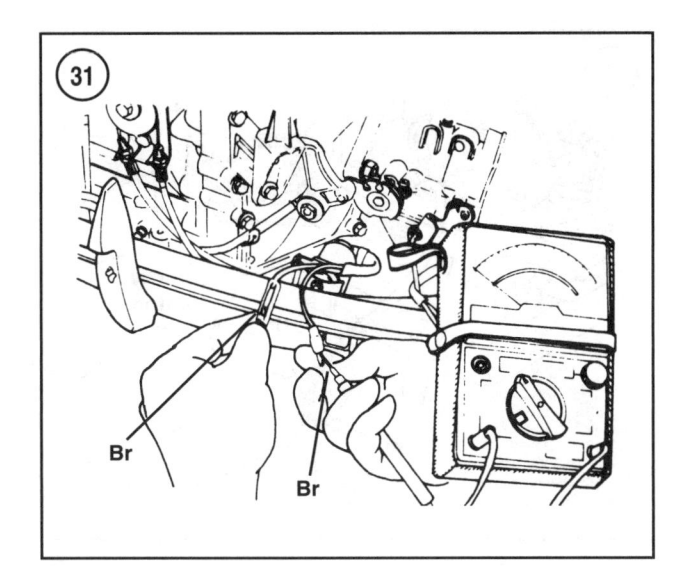

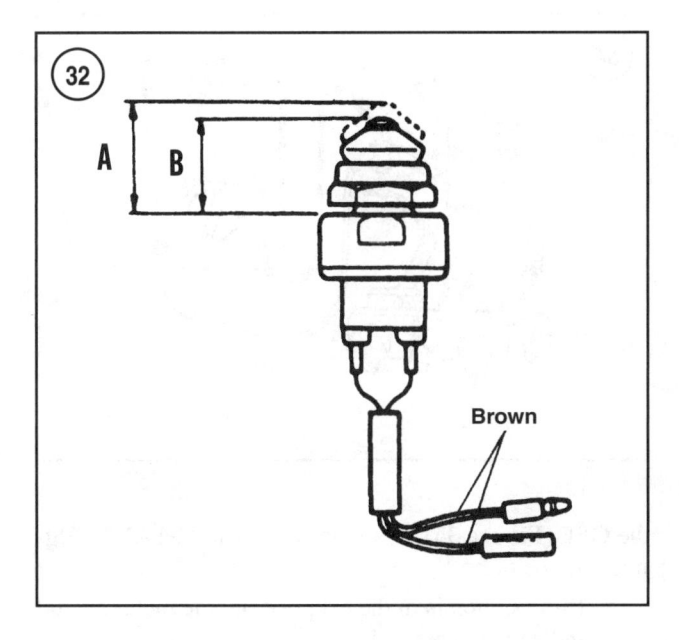

c. Install the switch in the remote control as described in Chapter Thirteen.

6. Reconnect the neutral switch wires to the remote control harness wires. Route the wiring to prevent contact with moving components.
7. Reassemble and install the remote control as described in Chapter Thirteen

Tiller control models

A multimeter and an accurate depth micrometer or vernier caliper are required for this test.

Starter Button Test

The starter button is used on 6-35 hp (except 28 jet) tiller control models with electric starting. One wire from the starter button connects to the battery positive terminal through a connection to the starter relay. The other wire connects to the neutral switch wire. When the button is de-

pressed, current flows through the neutral safety switch to the starter relay. A multimeter is required to test the starter button. Refer to Chapter Six for the starter button location.
1. Shift the engine into FORWARD gear. Disconnect and ground the spark plug leads to prevent accidental starting.
2. Disconnect the starter button wires from the starter relay and neutral switch.
3. Calibrate the multimeter to the 20 or 40 VDC scale. Connect the negative test lead to an engine ground. Observe the meter while connecting the positive test lead to the red wire that goes to the starter relay. If the meter does not indicate battery voltage, check for a blown fuse or a faulty wire connecting the battery positive terminal to the starter relay.
4. Calibrate the multimeter to the R × 1 scale. Connect the meter test leads to each of the starter button wires (**Figure 33**).
5. Observe the meter while repeatedly depressing and releasing the button. If the meter does not indicate continuity each time the button is depressed and no continuity each time the button is released, the button is shorted or has failed open. Replace the starter button as described in Chapter Six.
6. Connect the starter button wires to the starter relay and neutral switch wires.
7. Shift the engine into NEUTRAL gear. Connect the spark plug leads.

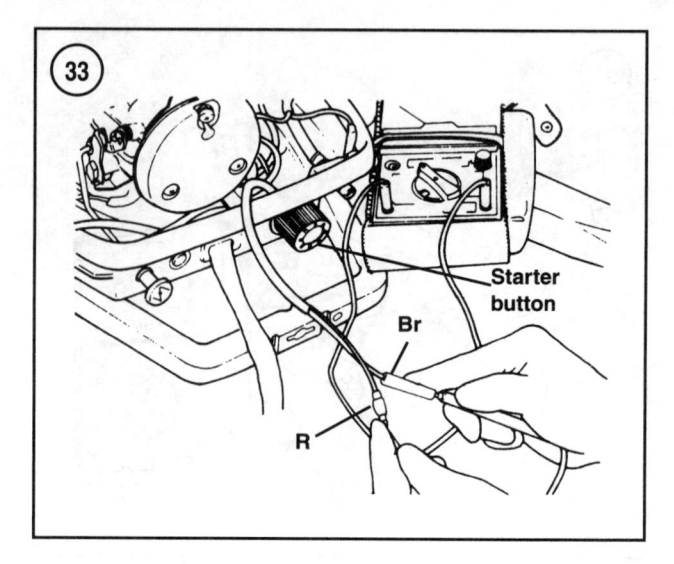

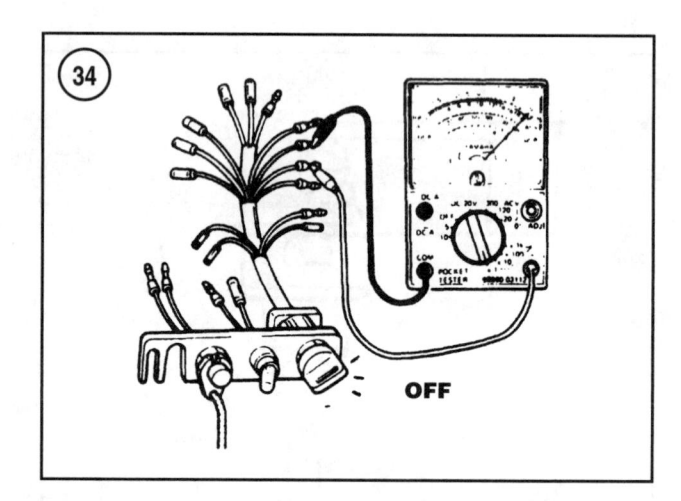

Key Switch Test

The key switch is mounted in the remote control or on the dash on remote control models. The switch is mounted in the tiller control housing on 28 jet, 35 jet and 40-85 hp models with tiller control and electric starting.
1. Disconnect the battery cables. Disconnect and ground the spark plug leads to prevent accidental starting.
2. Remove the key switch as described in Chapter Six.
3. Calibrate a multimeter to the R × 1 scale.
4. Connect the positive meter test lead to the white switch wire and the negative meter test lead to the black switch wire. Observe the meter while repeatedly turning the key switch to the OFF (**Figure 34**), ON (**Figure 35**) and START (**Figure 36**) positions.
   a. If the switch is in the off position, the meter should indicate continuity.
   b. If the switch is in the on position, the meter should indicate no continuity.
   c. If the switch is in the start position, the meter should indicate no continuity.
5. Connect the positive test lead to the red switch wire and the negative test lead to the yellow switch wire. Observe the meter while repeatedly turning the key switch to the OFF (**Figure 34**), ON (**Figure 35**) and START (**Figure 36**) positions.
   a. If the switch is in the off position, the meter should indicate no continuity.
   b. If the switch is in the on position, the meter should indicate continuity.
   c. If the switch is in the start position, the meter should indicate continuity.
6. Connect the positive test lead to the red switch wire and the negative test lead to the brown switch wire. Observe the meter while repeatedly turning the key switch to the OFF (**Figure 34**), ON (**Figure 35**) and START (**Figure 36**) positions.
   a. If the switch is in the off position, the meter should indicate no continuity.
   b. If the switch is in the on position, the meter should indicate no continuity.

TROUBLESHOOTING

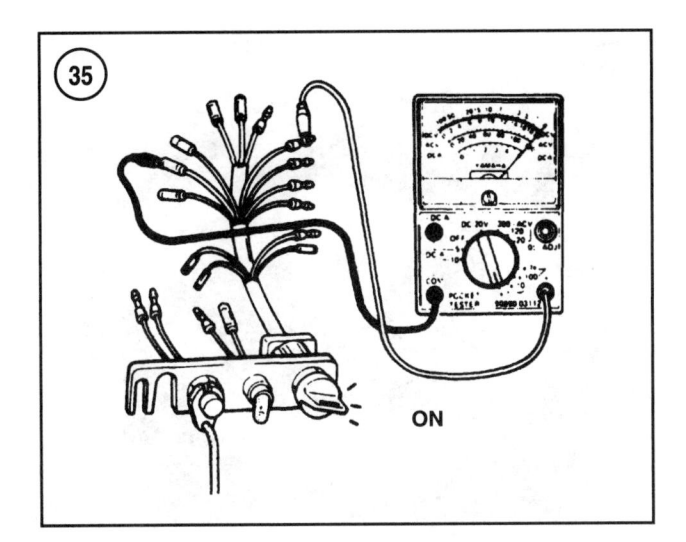

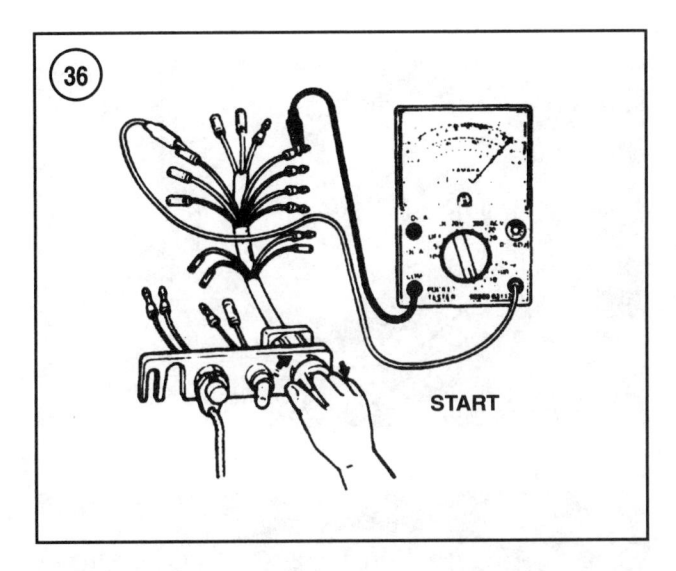

35

ON

36

START

c. If the switch is in the start position, the meter should indicate continuity.
7. Replace the switch if any test results are incorrect.
8. Install the key switch as described in Chapter Six.
9. Connect the battery cables and spark plug leads.

Choke switch test

The choke switch is used on models that have a key switch and a choke solenoid. The switch is either integrated into the key switch or mounted in the remote control (3, **Figure 29**).
1. Remove the remote control and rear cover as described in Chapter Thirteen. Do not remove the control handle.
2A. If the choke switch is mounted in the control, locate the choke switch (3, **Figure 29**), then trace the switch wires to their connections on the remote control harness (7). Disconnect both switch wires.
2B. If the choke switch is integrated into the key switch, disconnect the blue and black key switch wires from the remote control harness connections (7, **Figure 29**).
3. Calibrate the multimeter to the R × 1 scale. Connect the positive meter test lead to the blue switch wire. Connect the negative meter test lead to the black switch wire.
4A. If the choke switch is mounted in the control, activate the switch by placing the key switch in the RUN position, then turn the choke switch toward the key switch.
4B. If the choke switch is integrated into the key switch, activate the switch by turning the choke switch to the ON or START position while pushing straight in on the key switch.
5. Observe the meter while repeatedly activating then releasing the choke switch. The meter should indicate continuity each time the switch is activated and no continuity each time the switch is released. If the choke switch is integrated into the key switch, the test results should be the same with the key switch in both the run and start positions.
6. Replace the choke switch or key switch if any test results are incorrect.
7. Assemble and install the remote control as described in Chapter Thirteen.

CHARGING SYSTEM

The charging system maintains the battery charge level for starting the engine and onboard accessories. Accessories, such as depth sounders and trolling motors, can draw a considerable current from the battery. The charging system may not be able to keep up with the demand for current. Increased use of electrical accessories places a greater demand on the typical outboard charging system. Test all components of the charging system if the battery fails to maintain a charge. Determine the total amperage consumed by the accessories and compare the total with the charging system output specification in **Table 4**. The charging system will deliver considerably less output when the engine is operated at lower speeds. Install additional batteries or a battery with greater capacity as needed. Charge the battery at more frequent intervals if the amperage load is near or exceeding the charging system output. When two batteries are being used, install a battery switch (**Figure 37**) and connect the accessories to one of the batteries. The other battery provides a backup to start the engine if the accessory load discharges its battery. Battery maintenance and charging procedures are in Chapter Six.

The components of the charging system include the flywheel (**Figure 38**), battery charging coil (**Figure 39**), rectifier (**Figure 40**) or rectifier/regulator (**Figure 41**), the wiring and the battery.

Engines with a manual starter generally do not use a battery charging system. Some models have an optional lighting coil. The lighting coil is positioned under the flywheel like the battery charging coil and produces alternating current as the flywheel magnets rotate past it. The current produced by the lighting coil is only suitable for navigational lighting. The optional rectifier or rectifier/regulator can convert the current produced by the lighting coil to direct current, giving the system battery charging capability.

Models with electric starting have a battery charging coil under the flywheel (**Figure 42**) that produces alternating current. The battery charging coil is similar to the lighting coil used on manual start models. The current is directed to either a rectifier (**Figure 40**) or rectifier/regulator (**Figure 41**) where it is converted to direct current. The regulator portion of the rectifier/regulator limits the charging system output when necessary to prevent overcharging.

The battery charging coil and ignition charging coil are integrated into a single assembly (**Figure 43**) on 65 jet and 75-90 hp models. Replace the complete assembly if either coil fails.

NOTE
In addition to charging the battery, the charge coil produces the electrical pulses that operate the dash-mounted tachometer. If the tachometer is operating, the charge coil is producing alternating current.

Troubleshooting the charging system requires a multimeter. Use an analog meter when checking for continuity in a circuit. Use a digital volt/ohmmeter when measuring the voltage produced by the charging system.

NOTE
If the meter is set for diode tests, test results may be the reverse of what is described in the test procedure due to differences in make and model. Tests results are correct when meter reads continuity with the leads connected one way and no continuity with the test leads polarity are reversed.

System Output Test

This test checks for charging system output at the battery. The battery must be fully charged for this test.

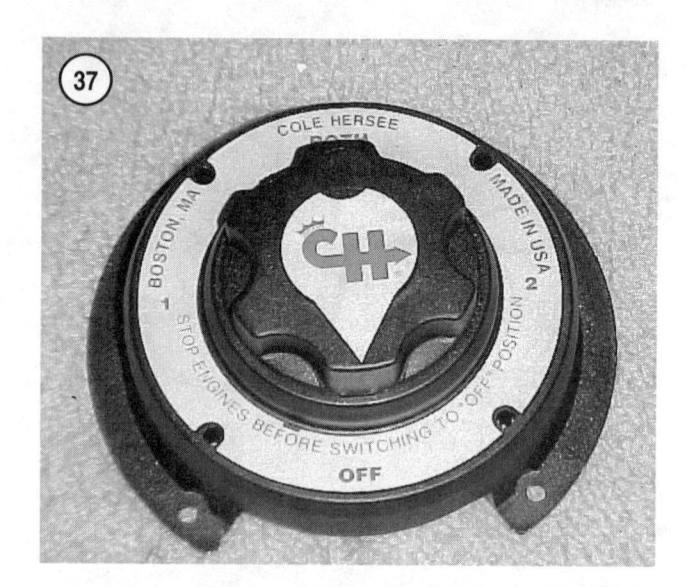

WARNING
Remove the propeller before running the engine. Stay clear of the propeller shaft while running an engine on a flush/test adapter. Disconnect the battery and all spark plug leads before removing or installing a propeller.

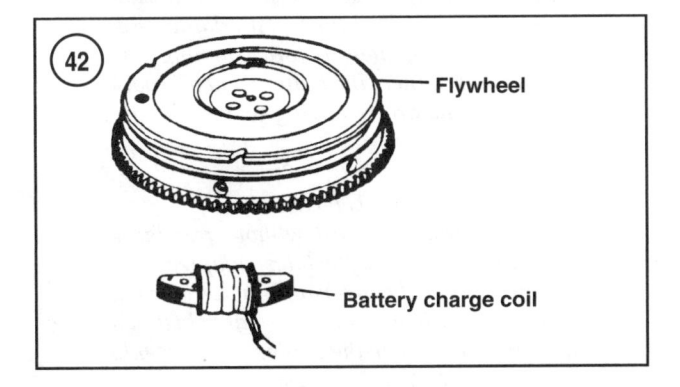

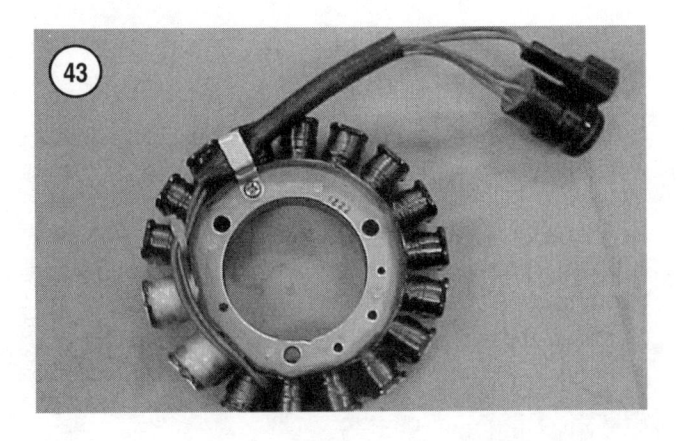

TROUBLESHOOTING

59

CAUTION
Never run an outboard without providing cooling water. Use a flush/test adapter if the engine cannot be operated under normal conditions or in a suitable test tank. Install a test propeller to run the engine in a test tank.

1. Calibrate an ohmmeter to measure 10-15 VDC.
2. Connect the positive meter test lead to the battery positive terminal. Connect the negative meter test lead to a suitable engine ground. Observe the meter and record the battery voltage.
3. Start the engine and run it at fast idle until the engine reaches normal operating temperature. Turn off all accessories.
4. Advance the throttle to approximately 2500 rpm. Record the voltage reading. If so equipped, note if the tachometer is functioning. Compare the engine running voltage reading with the engine off voltage reading.
    a. If the engine running reading is equal to or below the engine off reading, the charging system is not operating. Test all charging system components as described in this section.
    b. If the engine running voltage exceeds 14.0 volts, the charging system is overcharging. Check for faulty wiring or a low electrolyte level in the battery. Replace the rectifier/regulator to correct overcharging.
    c. If the engine running reading is 0.3 volt or higher than the engine off reading, the charging system is charging the battery. If the battery fails to maintain a charge, check for excessive accessory load or a faulty battery.
    d. If the tachometer is working, and the engine running reading is equal to or below the engine off reading, test the rectifier or rectifier/regulator as described in this chapter.
    e. If the tachometer is not working, and the engine running reading is equal to or below the engine off reading, test the battery charge coil and rectifier or rectifier/regulator as described in this chapter.
    f. If the tachometer is not working, and the engine running reading is 0.3 volt or higher than the engine off reading, substitute a known good tachometer and retest. If the tachometer still does not operate, test the rectifier or rectifier/regulator as described in this chapter.

NOTE
If the system is discharging, test all components of the charging system. Often, both the charge coil and the rectifier or rectifier/regulator are faulty. A fault with the flywheel magnets can cause decreased charging sys-

tem output; however, the same magnets are used to power the ignition system. Problems with the magnets will also cause ignition system problems as well.

Lighting/Battery Charge Coil Test

Determine which test to perform by the model, available test specifications, and whether or not the engine has battery charging capability. A rectifier (**Figure 40**) or rectifier/regulator (**Figure 41**) must be installed for the engine to have battery charging capability.
1. If the engine only has lighting capability, measure the lighting coil resistance. Test the lighting coil output on 9.9 hp, 15 hp, 28 jet, 35 jet 40 hp, 50 hp and E75 models.
2. If the engine has battery charging capability, measure the coil resistance on 6 hp, 8 hp, 28 jet, 35 jet and 40-90 hp models. Test the battery charging coil output on 9.9-90 hp (except E60) models.

NOTE
Replace the rectifier or rectifier/regulator if the charging system is not operating and the lighting/battery charge coil tests correctly.

NOTE
Use a meter with peak output voltage measuring capability to measure peak output voltage from the lighting or battery charging coil. If the coil is tested with the AC voltage scale, the test results will probably be low.

Lighting/battery charge coil resistance test

A digital volt/ohmmeter is required for this test. The lighting/battery charge coil can be tested without being removed from the engine. Ambient temperature will affect the measured resistance. Perform this test with the engine cooled or warmed to normal room temperature, approximately 20° C (68° F).
1. Disconnect the battery cables.
2. Disconnect and ground the spark plug leads to prevent accidental starting.
3. Calibrate a digital volt/ohmmeter to the R × 1 scale.
4. Locate the two green or green and green/white lighting/battery charge coil wires. The wires lead to the coil mounting location under the flywheel.
5. Disconnect the two green wires or one green and one green/white wires from the lighting harness or connections to the rectifier or rectifier/regulator.
6. Connect the positive meter test lead to the green lighting/battery charge coil wire (**Figure 44**). Connect the neg-

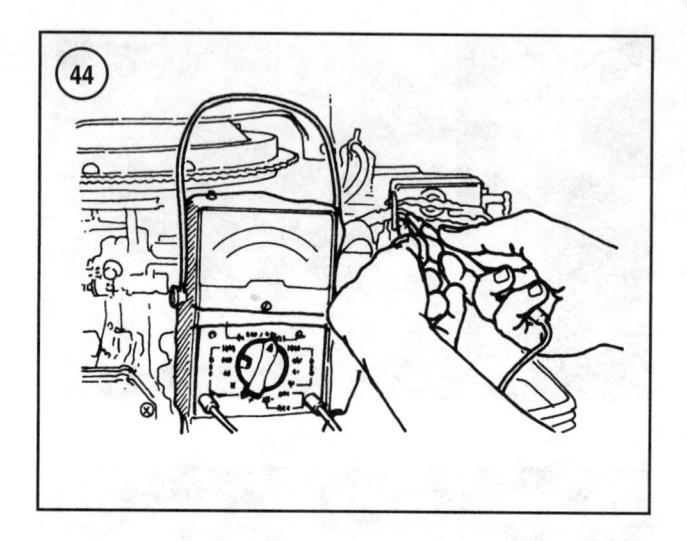

ative meter test lead to the remaining green or green/white coil lead. Do not connect the test leads to the lighting harness or rectifier/regulator wire. Record the resistance reading.
7. If the resistance reading is not within the specification in **Table 5**, replace the lighting/battery charge coil as described in Chapter Six.

WARNING
Stay clear of the propeller shaft while running an engine on a flush/test adapter. Remove the propeller before running the engine. Disconnect the battery and all spark plug leads before removing or installing a propeller.

CAUTION
Never run an outboard without providing cooling water. Use a flush/test adapter if the engine cannot be operated under normal conditions or in a suitable test tank. Install a test propeller to run the engine in a test tank.

Lighting coil output test (models with lighting coil only)

A common meter with peak output voltage capability, or Yamaha part No. J-39299/90890-06752 and YU-39991/90890-03169, and an accurate shop tachometer are required for this test.
1. Connect a shop tachometer to the engine. Follow the tachometer manufacturer's instructions.
2. Locate the two green or green and green/white lighting coil wires. The wires lead to the coil mounting location under the flywheel.

TROUBLESHOOTING

Figure 45

Figure 46

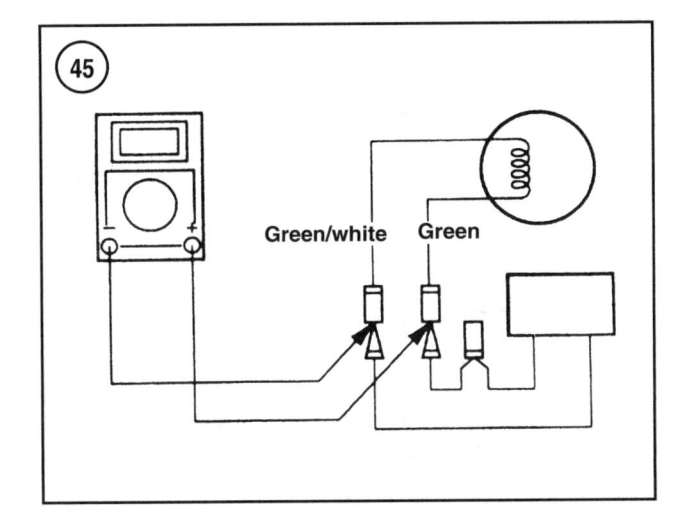

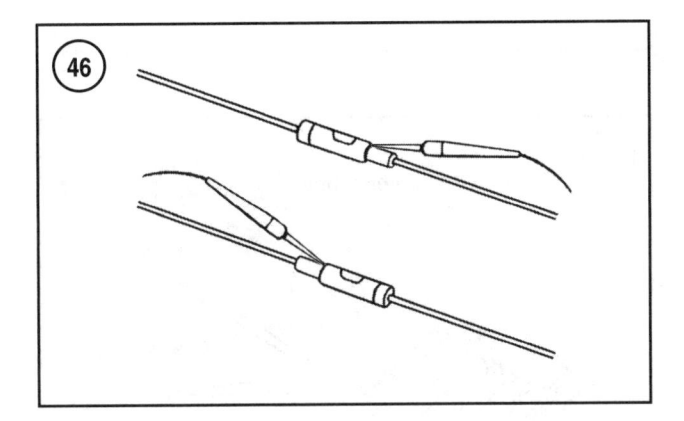

3. Refer to **Table 5** for the test specifications, then calibrate the multimeter to the correct peak AC voltage scale. Scale changes may be required when testing at different engine speeds.

4. Connect the positive meter test lead to the green lighting/battery charge coil wire (**Figure 45**). Connect the negative meter test lead to the remaining green or green/white coil wire. Do not connect the test leads to the lighting harness wires.

5. Start the engine and run it at fast idle until it reaches normal operating temperature. Record the output voltage while running the engine at the speed(s) listed in **Table 5**. Change the meter scale as required for the test specification. To check the voltage at cranking speed, disconnect and ground the spark plug leads. Note the meter readings while operating the manual starter.

6. If the coil output does not meet or exceed the minimum specification in **Table 5** at each listed engine speed, replace the lighting coil as described in Chapter Six.

7. Disconnect the shop tachometer. Reconnect the lighting coil wires to the lighting harness

Lighting/battery charge coil output test (models with battery charging capability)

A common meter with peak output voltage capability, or Yamaha part No. J-39299/90890-06752 and YU-39991/90890-03169, and an accurate shop tachometer are required for this test.

1. Connect a shop tachometer to the engine. Follow the tachometer manufacturer's instructions.

2. Locate the two green or green and green/white lighting/battery charge coil wires. The wires lead to the coil mounting location under the flywheel. Trace the wires to their bullet connection to the rectifier or rectifier/regulator wires. Do not disconnect the wires for this test.

3. Refer to **Table 5** for the test specifications, then calibrate the multimeter to the correct peak AC voltage scale. Scale changes may be required when testing at different engine speeds.

4. Connect the positive meter test lead to the green lighting/battery charge coil wire (**Figure 45**). Connect the negative meter test lead to the remaining green or green/white coil wire. Do not disconnect the wires. Slip the test lead probes between the bullet connector sleeves so they contact the terminals as shown in **Figure 46**.

5. Start the engine and run it at fast idle until it reaches normal operating temperature. Record the output voltage while running the engine at the speed(s) listed in **Table 5**. Change the meter scale as required for the test specification. To check the voltage at cranking speed, disconnect and ground the spark plug leads. Note the meter readings while operating the electric or manual starter.

6. If the coil output does not meet or exceed the minimum specification in **Table 5** at each designated engine speed, replace the battery charge/lighting coil as described in Chapter Six.

7. Disconnect the shop tachometer. Reconnect the lighting coil wires to the lighting harness.

Rectifier Test

A common multimeter is required for this test. Use an analog meter if possible. Refer to **Figure 47** for this procedure.

1. Remove the rectifier from the power head as described in Chapter Six.

2. Calibrate an ohmmeter to the R × 1 scale.

3. Connect the positive meter test lead to one of the green rectifier wires (**Figure 47**). Connect the negative meter test lead to the black rectifier wire. Note the meter reading, then repeat the test with the red test lead connected to the other green rectifier wire. If the meter indicates no

continuity for either test point, the rectifier has failed open and must be replaced.

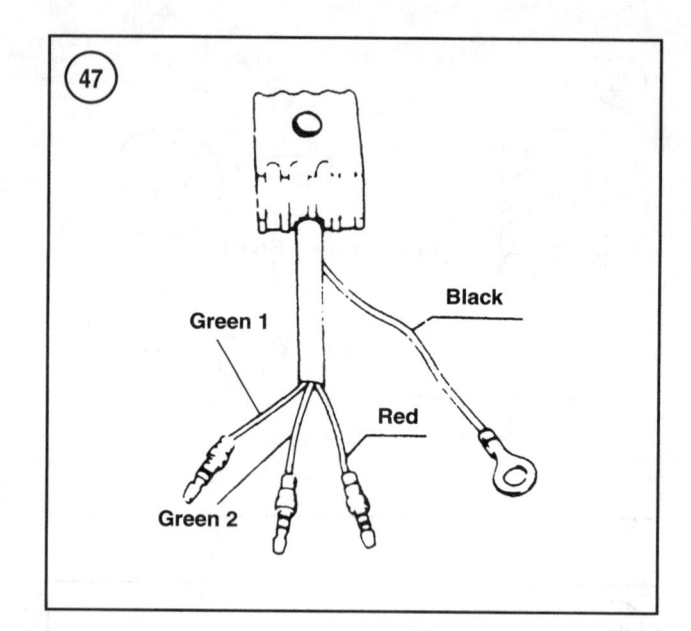

4. Connect the positive test lead to the red rectifier wire (**Figure 47**). Connect the negative test lead to the black rectifier wire and note the meter reading. If the meter indicates no continuity, the rectifier has failed open and must be replaced.

5. Connect the positive test lead to the red rectifier wire (**Figure 47**). Connect the negative test lead to one of the green rectifier wires. Note the meter reading, then repeat the test with the negative test lead connected to the other green rectifier wire. If the meter indicates no continuity on either test point, the rectifier has failed open and must be replaced.

6. Connect the positive test lead to one of the green rectifier wires (**Figure 47**). Connect the negative test lead to the other green rectifier wires. Note the meter reading and reverse the test lead connection points. If the meter indicates continuity for each connection point, the rectifier is shorted internally and must be replaced.

7. Connect the positive test lead to one of the green rectifier wires (**Figure 47**). Connect the negative test lead to the red rectifier wire. Note the meter reading, then repeat the test with the positive test lead connected to the other green rectifier wire. If the meter indicates continuity for either connection point, the rectifier is shorted internally and must be replaced.

8. Connect the positive test lead to the black rectifier wire (**Figure 47**). Connect the negative test lead to one of the green rectifier wires. Note the meter reading, then repeat the test with the negative test lead connected to the other green rectifier wire. If the meter indicates continuity for either connection point, the rectifier has shorted internally and must be replaced.

9. Install the rectifier on the power head as described in Chapter Six.

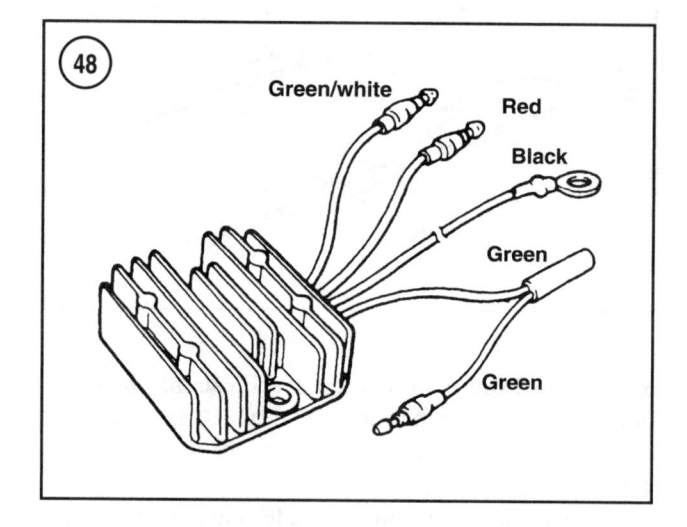

Rectifier/Regulator Test

A common multimeter is required for this test. Use an analog meter if possible. Refer to **Figure 48** for this procedure.

1. Remove the rectifier/regulator from the power head as described in Chapter Six.
2. Calibrate an ohmmeter to the R × 1 scale.
3. Connect the positive meter test lead to the red rectifier/regulator wire (**Figure 48**). Connect the negative meter test lead to the green/white wire to the rectifier/regulator. Note the meter reading, then repeat the test with the negative test lead connected to the green rectifier/regulator wire. If the meter indicates no continuity for either test point, the rectifier/regulator has failed open and must be replaced.

4. Connect the positive test lead to the red rectifier/regulator wire (**Figure 48**). Connect the negative test lead to the black rectifier/regulator wire. If the meter indicates no continuity, the rectifier/regulator has failed open and must be replaced.

5. Connect the positive test lead to the black rectifier/regulator wire (**Figure 48**). Connect the negative test lead to the green rectifier/regulator wire. If the meter indicates continuity, the rectifier/regulator has shorted and must be replaced.

6. Connect the positive test lead to the black rectifier/regulator wire (**Figure 48**). Connect the negative test lead to the red rectifier/regulator wire. If the meter indicates con-

TROUBLESHOOTING

indicates continuity for either test point, the rectifier/regulator has shorted internally and must be replaced.

10. Connect the positive test lead to the green rectifier/regulator wire (**Figure 48**). Connect the negative test lead to the green/white wire to the rectifier/regulator. If the meter indicates no continuity, the rectifier/regulator has failed open and must be replaced.

11. Connect the positive test lead to the green/white wire to the rectifier/regulator (**Figure 48**). Connect the negative test lead to the green rectifier/regulator wire. If the meter indicates continuity, the rectifier/regulator has shorted and must be replaced.

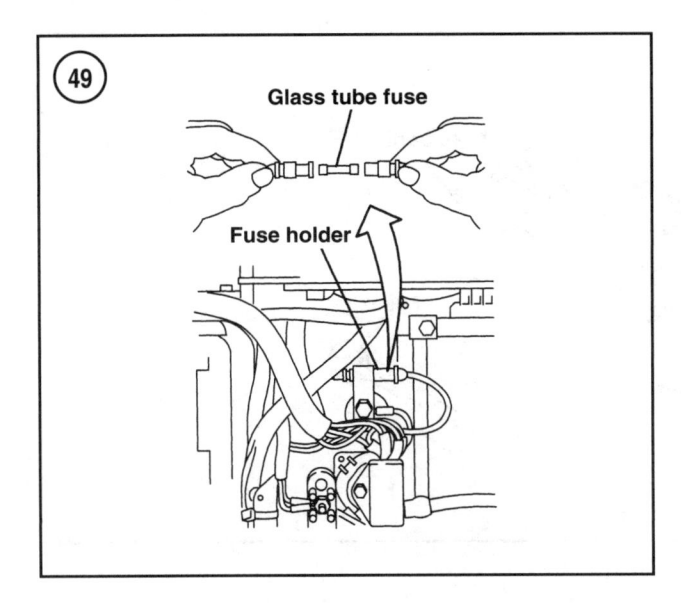

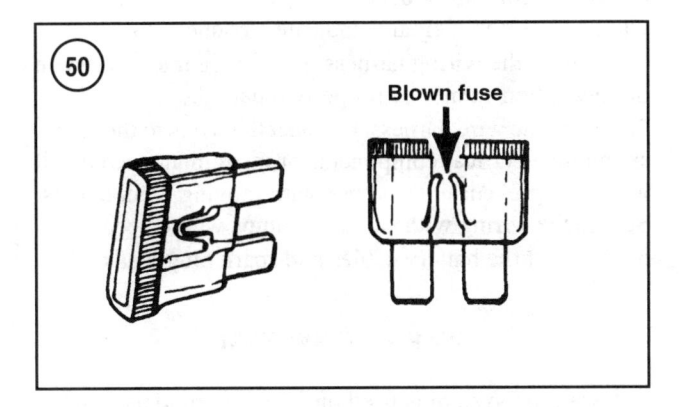

12. Install the rectifier/regulator as described in Chapter Six.

FUSE AND WIRE HARNESS

Fuse Test

Fuses are used on all electric start models to protect the electrical system against a short circuit or overload. Never replace a fuse without thoroughly inspecting the electrical system. Fuses are designed to open the circuit if an overload occurs. Never bypass a fuse or install a fuse with greater capacity than specified, or you may risk your safety or the safety of others. The most common symptom of a blown fuse is the electric starter will not operate and the dash-mounted gauges will not work. In some instances, the first symptom is that the tilt/trim system is not working. Use a common multimeter to test fuses. Never rely solely on a visual inspection to test fuses. Different types of fuses and mounting arrangements are used on the various models covered in this manual. **Figures 49-51** show the most commonly used fuse types and mounting arrangements.

1. Refer to the wiring diagrams at the end of the manual to identify the wire colors and capacity of the fuse(s).
2. Disconnect the battery cables.
3. Disconnect and ground the spark plug leads to prevent accidental starting.
4. Trace the indicated wire color to the fuse location. The fuse is located under the electrical component cover or in another easily accessible location on the power head.
5. Remove the fuse from the retainer. Visually check for a blown fuse (**Figure 50**). There is no need to test a blown fuse with a meter. Proceed to Step 7.
6. Calibrate the multimeter to the R × 1 scale. Touch the meter test leads to each fuse terminal. If the meter indicates no continuity, the fuse has failed open and must be replaced. If the fuse tests correctly, proceed to Step 9.
7. Thoroughly inspect the electrical system and correct the overload or short before replacing the fuse.

tinuity, the rectifier/regulator has shorted and must be replaced.

7. Connect the positive test lead to the black rectifier/regulator wire (**Figure 48**). Connect the negative test lead to the green/white wire to the rectifier/regulator. If the meter indicates no continuity, the rectifier/regulator has failed open and must be replaced.

8. Connect the positive test lead to the green rectifier/regulator wire (**Figure 48**). Connect the negative test lead to the black rectifier/regulator wire. Note the meter reading, then repeat the test with the positive test lead connected to the green/white wire to the rectifier/regulator. If the meter indicates no continuity for either test point, the rectifier/regulator has failed open and must be replaced.

9. Connect the positive test lead to the green rectifier/regulator wire (**Figure 48**). Connect the negative test lead to the red rectifier/regulator wire. Note the meter reading, then repeat the test with the positive test lead connected to the green/white wire to the rectifier/regulator. If the meter

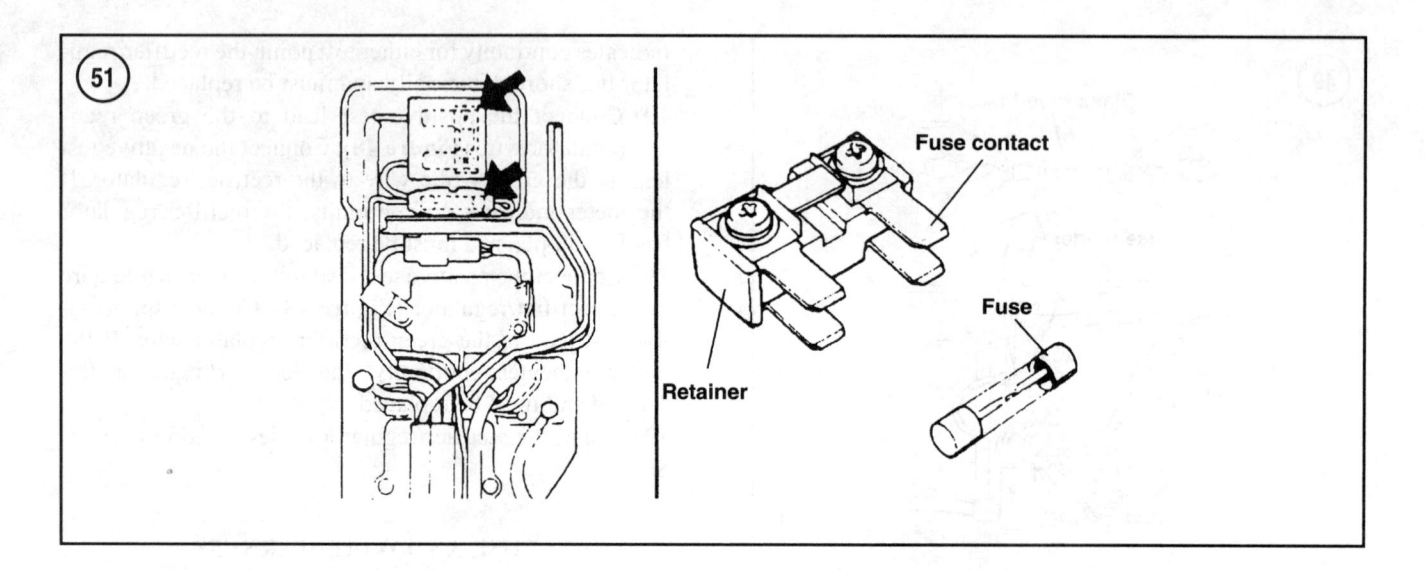

8. Clean the fuse terminals and contacts in the fuse holder, then install the fuse into the holder.
9. Route all wiring to prevent contact with moving components.
10. Connect the battery cables and spark plug leads.

Wire Harness Test

Due to the harsh operating environment, problems with the wiring harness are common. A problem may occur continuously or only intermittently. When there is an electrical problem and all components test correctly, the wire harness may be faulty. Check both the engine and instrument harnesses on remote control models. Gently twist, bend and pull on wire harness connectors when checking the leads for continuity to locate an intermittent fault.

Use a multimeter or self-powered test light to test the wire harness.

1. Disconnect the battery cables. Disconnect and ground the spark plug leads to prevent accidental starting.
2. Disconnect the engine harness from the instrument wire harness, if used. Disconnect the wire harness leads from the engine components or instruments.
3. Calibrate the meter to the R × 1 scale.
4. Connect the meter or test light lead to one of the harness wires (A, **Figure 52**). Touch the other test lead or test light probe to the corresponding harness pin connector (B, **Figure 52**) for the wire being checked. If the meter indicates no continuity or the test light does not illuminate, check the wiring or check for a faulty terminal. Repair as necessary.
5. Refer to the wiring diagrams at the end of the manual to determine connection points for each of the wires.

Check for continuity between the chosen wire and other wires only if the diagrams indicate a connection.
6. Replace the wiring harness if the open or shorted wire or connection cannot be properly repaired.
7. Install the wire harness. Connect the wires to the corresponding electrical components or instruments. Route all wiring to prevent interference with moving components. Secure the wiring with suitable clamps where necessary.
8. Connect the battery cables and spark plug leads.

WARNING SYSTEM

A warning system is used on 20-90 hp models to warn the operator of a problem with the engine. Continued operation with the warning system activated can lead to serious and expensive engine damage.

Warning System Operation

Warning system operation and component use will vary by model, type of control system and type of lubrication system. Overheat warning is present on all 20-90 hp models. Low oil level warning is used on all oil-injected models. Major components of the warning system include:
1. Thermoswitch.
2. Oil level sensor.
3. CDI unit
4. Warning horn.
5. Warning light.

Read the following descriptions to determine if the warning system is operating correctly. Test all applicable warning system components if there is a false warning or lack of warning.

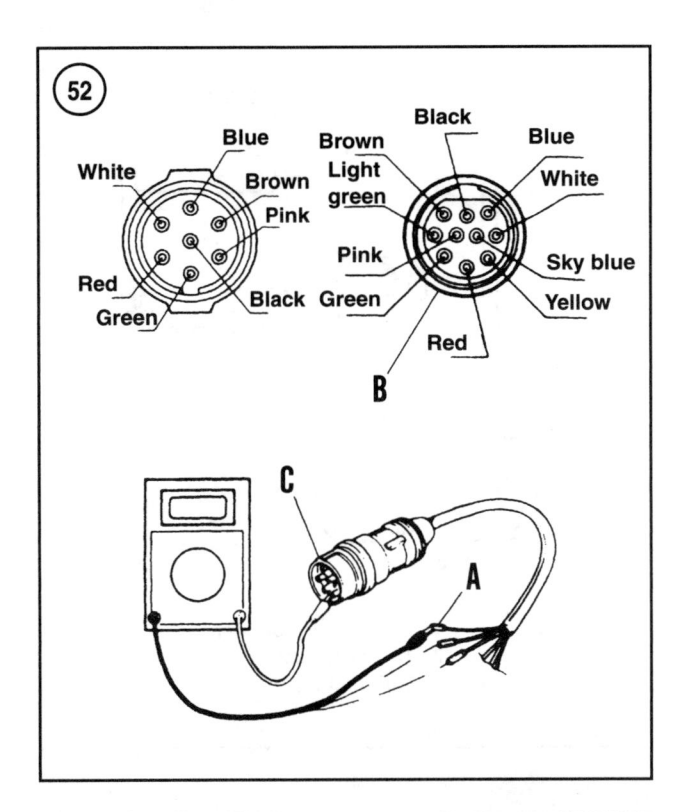

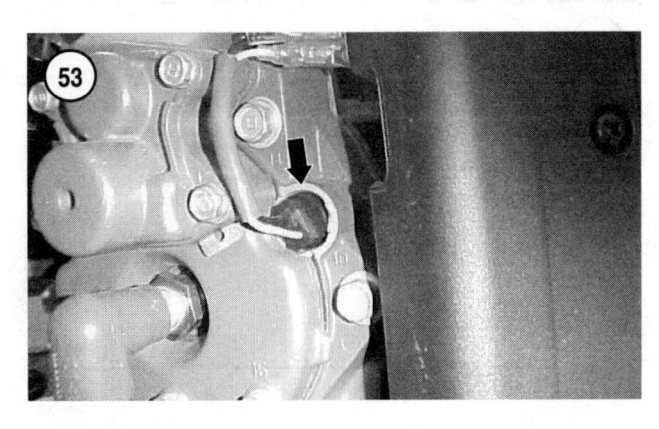

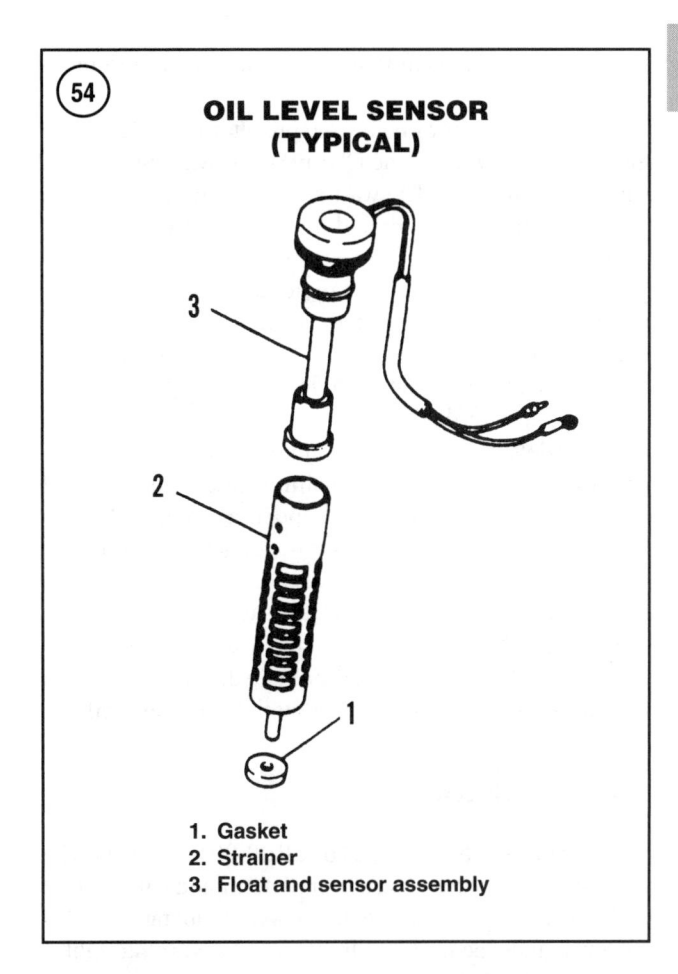

TROUBLESHOOTING

52

Connector pinouts:
- White, Blue, Brown, Black, Blue, White
- Red, Pink, Light green, Pink, Sky blue
- Green, Black, Green, Yellow, Red

A, B, C

53

54 OIL LEVEL SENSOR (TYPICAL)

1. Gasket
2. Strainer
3. Float and sensor assembly

or warning horn wires. The warning light illuminates or the warning horn sounds. On most models, grounding the wire also signals the CDI unit to initiate power reduction to help prevent engine damage. The CDI unit initiates an ignition misfire or retards ignition timing to reduce the engine speed to a maximum of approximately 2000 rpm. Full power is only restored after the engine is reduced to idle speed and the overheating is corrected.

Overheating

The thermoswitch (**Figure 53**) detects overheating. The switch mounts in the cylinder head or exhaust cover. One wire of the thermoswitch connects to an engine ground. The other wire connects to the CDI unit and the warning light or warning horn. The warning light is used on 20-30 hp tiller models. The warning horn is used on 40-90 hp tiller control models and all 20-90 hp models with remote control. The light or horn is powered by the battery on electric start models and the ignition system on manual start models.

If the engine reaches the predetermined temperature, the thermoswitch grounds the CDI unit and warning light

Low oil level

All oil injected models use an oil reservoir to supply oil to the gear driven pump. The oil level sensor (**Figure 54**) on oil-injected models detects low oil level in the reservoir and operates the oil level indicator panel used on some remote control models. One wire of the oil level sensor connects to an engine ground. The pink wire connects to the CDI unit and the warning light or warning horn. An engine-mounted warning light is used on 20-30 hp tiller models. A warning horn is used on 40-90 hp tiller control models and all 20-90 hp models with remote control. The light or horn is powered by the battery on most electric start models and the ignition system on manual start models.

If the oil level drops below the predetermined level, the thermoswitch grounds the CDI unit and warning light or warning horn wires. The warning light illuminates or the warning horn sounds. Grounding the wire also signals the CDI unit to initiate power reduction to help prevent engine damage. The CDI unit initiates an ignition misfire or retards ignition timing to reduce the engine speed to a maximum of approximately 2000 rpm. Full power is only restored after the engine is reduced to idle speed and the oil reservoir is refilled.

On models with the dash mounted oil level panel. The green oil level indicator light illuminates when the oil level is at or above the normal operating range. The yellow indicator light illuminates if the oil level drops below the normal operating range. The red indicator light illuminates if the oil level drops below the safe operating range.

Never operate the engine with the warning horn sounding or the low oil level light illuminated. The power head will fail if the engine is operated with insufficient oil.

Thermoswitch Test

A thermoswitch is installed on all 20-90 hp models. The thermoswitch switches on at a predetermined temperature and switches off at a slightly lower temperature. This switch sounds the horn or illuminates the warning light if the power head is overheating. One thermoswitch wire connects to the engine ground. The other wire connects to the CDI unit and warning horn or light.

A common multimeter, a liquid thermometer and a container of water that can be heated are required to test the thermoswitch.

1. Remove the thermoswitch as described in Chapter Six. Allow the switch to cool to room temperature before testing.
2. Calibrate the multimeter to the R × 1 scale.
3. Connect the positive meter test lead to one of the thermoswitch wires. Connect the negative meter test lead to the other thermoswitch wire.
4. If the meter indicates continuity with the switch at room temperature, the switch is shorted and must be replaced. No further testing is necessary.
5. Fill the container with cool tap water. Suspend the thermoswitch in the water so the tip is below the surface. Place the thermometer in the container with the thermoswitch (**Figure 55**).
6. Begin heating and gently stir the water while observing the meter and thermometer. Note the temperature when the meter switches to a continuity reading.

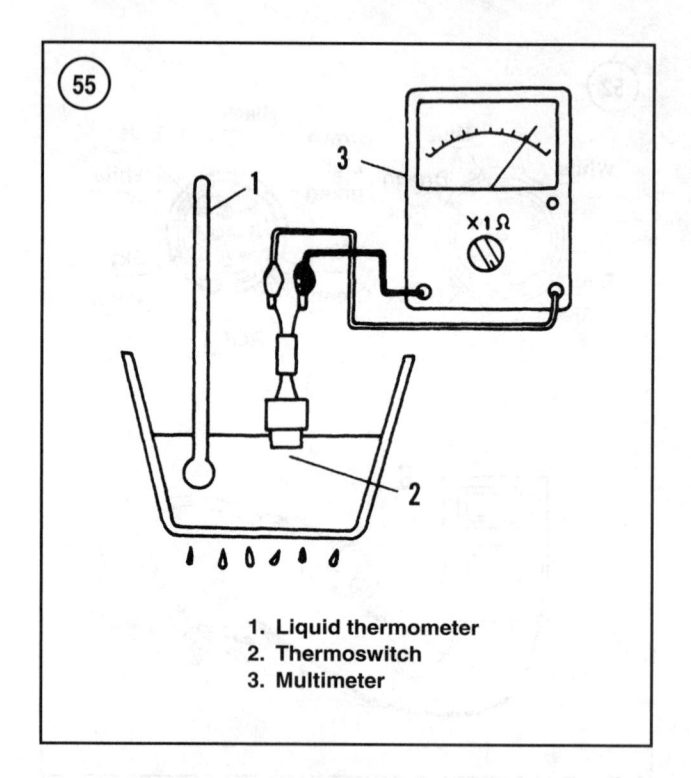

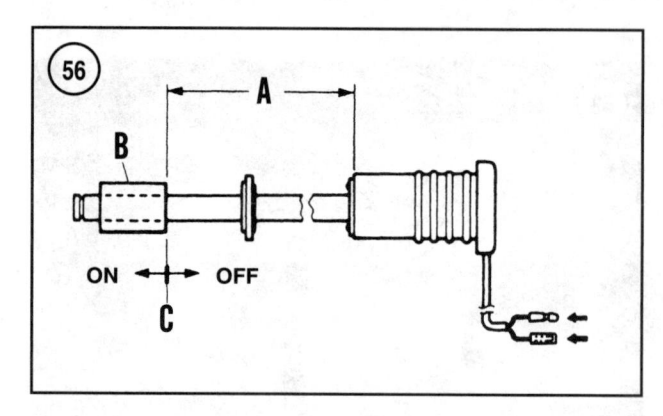

1. Liquid thermometer
2. Thermoswitch
3. Multimeter

7. Discontinue the test if the water begins to boil before the meter reading changes. Replace the thermoswitch.
8. Allow the water in the container to slowly cool while observing the meter and thermometer. Note the temperature when the meter changes to a no continuity reading.
9. Compare the switching temperatures with the specifications in **Table 6**. Replace the thermoswitch if the switching does not occur within the specified ranges.
10. Install the thermoswitch as described in Chapter Six.

Oil Level Sensor Test

The sensor contains a float/magnet assembly and one or two magnetically activated switches. The switches close

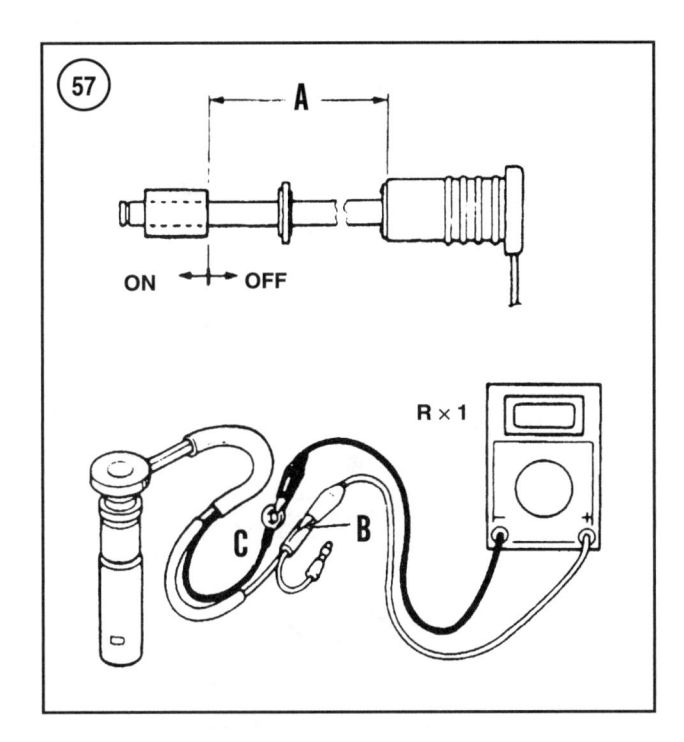

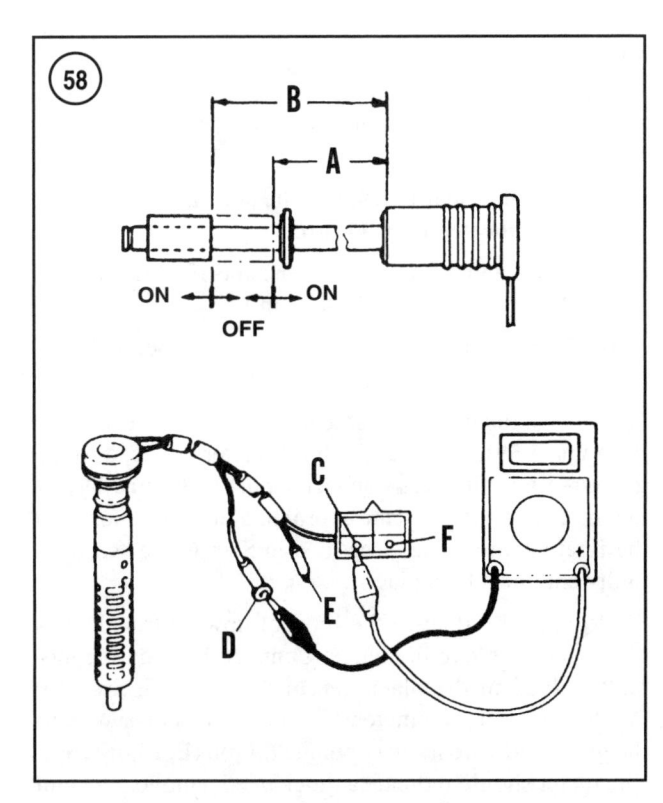

TROUBLESHOOTING

20 hp, 25 hp and 30 hp models

1. Remove the oil level sensor as described in Chapter Twelve. Carefully dry the sensor.
2. Calibrate the meter to the R × 1 scale.
3. Connect the positive meter test lead to the pink sensor wire. Connect the negative meter test lead to the black sensor wire.
4. Position the float (B, **Figure 56**) to the limit of upward travel or as close as possible to the wires. If the meter indicates continuity with the float in the full up position, the switch in the sensor is stuck or shorted and the sensor must be replaced.
5. Observe the meter while slowly moving the float downward or away from the wires. Stop moving the float at the exact point where the meter reading switches to continuity (C, **Figure 56**). Hold the float at the switching point and measure the distance from the top of the float to the body of the sensor (A, **Figure 56**). The measurement should be 56.3-59.3 mm (2.22-2.33 in.). Replace the sensor if it switches at a different level or if the float reaches the bottom of travel without activating the switch.
6. Install the oil level sensor as described in Chapter Twelve.

28 jet, 35 jet, 40 hp and 50 hp models

1. Remove the oil level sensor as described in Chapter Twelve. Carefully dry the sensor.
2. Calibrate the meter to the R × 1 scale.
3. Position the float to the limit of upward travel or as close as possible to the wires.
4A. On manual start models, connect the positive meter test lead to the pink sensor wire (B, **Figure 57**). Connect the negative meter test lead to the black sensor wire (C, **Figure 57**).
4B. On electric start models, connect the positive meter test lead to the pink sensor lead (E, **Figure 58**). Connect the negative meter test lead to the black sensor wire (D, **Figure 58**).
5. If the meter indicates continuity with the float in the full up position for both manual and electric start models, the sensor switch is struck or shorted and the sensor must be replaced.
6. Observe the meter while slowly moving the float downward or away from the wires. Stop moving the float at the exact point where the meter reads continuity. Hold the float at the switching point and measure the distance from the top of the float to the body of the sensor (A, **Figure 57** or B, **Figure 58**). The measurement should be 56.8-59.8 mm (2.24-2.35 in.). Replace the sensor if it

the circuit as the float magnet aligns with the switch. Switch testing procedures will vary by the model and type of control used. A multimeter and measuring ruler is required to test the sensor.

switches at a different level or if the float reaches the bottom of travel without activating the switch.

7. On electric start models, connect the positive meter test lead to the green wire harness connector pin (C, **Figure 58**). Connect the negative meter test lead to the black sensor wire (D, **Figure 58**). Position the float to the limit of upward travel or as close as possible to the sensor wires. If the meter indicates no continuity with the float in the full up position, the switch has failed open and the sensor must be replaced.

8. On electric start models, connect the positive meter test lead to the green/red wire harness connector pin (F, **Figure 58**). Connect the negative meter test lead to the black sensor wire (D, **Figure 58**). Position the float to the limit of upward travel. If the meter indicates continuity with the float in the full up position, the switch has shorted and the sensor must be replaced. Observe the meter while slowly moving the float downward. Stop moving the float at the exact point where the meter reading switches to continuity. Hold the float at the switching point and measure the distance from the top of the float to the body of the sensor (A, **Figure 58**). The measurement should be 32.8-35.8 mm (1.29-1.41 in.). Replace the sensor if it switches occurs at a different level or if the float reaches the limit of travel without activating the switch.

9. Install the oil level sensor as described in Chapter Twelve.

60-90 hp models

1. Remove the oil level sensor as described in Chapter Twelve. Carefully dry the sensor.
2. Calibrate the meter to the R × 100 scale.
3. Position the float to the limit of upward travel or as close as possible to the wires.
4. Connect the positive meter test lead to the green wire harness connector pin (D, **Figure 59**). Connect the negative meter test lead to the green/red wire harness connector pin (E, **Figure 59**). If the meter indicates continuity, the switches are shorted and the sensor must be replaced.
5. Connect the positive meter test lead to the green wire harness pin connector (D, **Figure 59**). Connect the negative test lead to the black sensor wire (C, **Figure 59**). If the meter indicates continuity with the float in the full up position, the switch is shorted and the sensor must be replaced. Observe the meter while slowly moving the float downward or away from the wires. Stop moving the float at the exact point where the meter reading switches to continuity. Hold the float at the switching point and measure the distance from the top of the float to the body of the sensor (A, **Figure 59**). The measurement should be 79.5-82.5 mm (3.13-3.25 in.) for 60 and 70 hp models and 5.8-8.8 mm (0.23-0.35 in.) for 65 jet and 75-90 hp models. Replace the sensor if it switches at a different level or if the float reaches the bottom of travel without activating the switch.

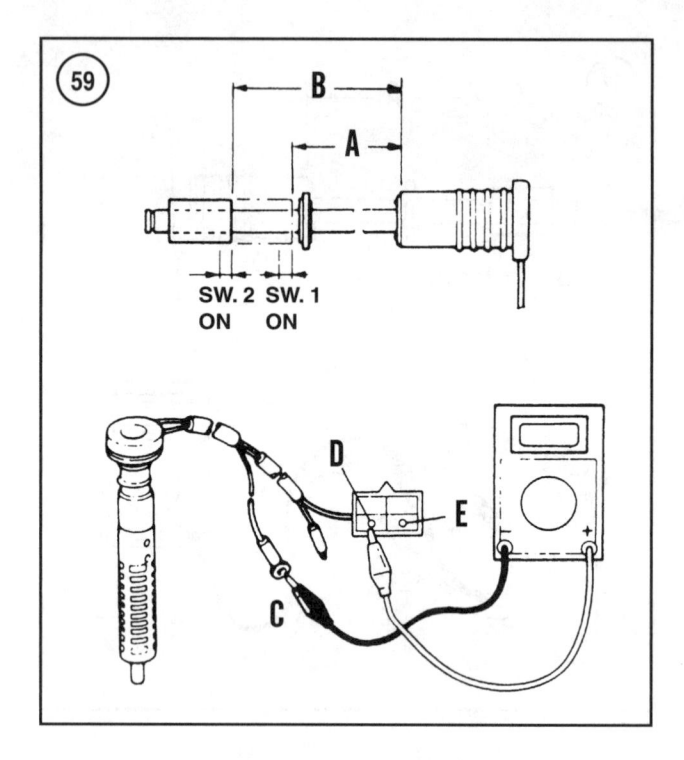

6. Position the float to achieve the specified distance at the points indicated in B, **Figure 59**.
   a. On 60 and 70 hp models, the specified distance is 114.5-117.3 mm (4.51-4.62 in.).
   b. On 65 jet and 75-90 hp models, the specified distance is 42.3-45.3 mm (1.67-1.78 in.).

7. Connect the positive test lead to the black sensor wire (C, **Figure 59**). Connect the black meter test lead to the green/red wire harness connector pin (E, **Figure 59**). If the meter does not indicate approximately 640 ohms with the float positioned as described in Step 6, the sensor is faulty and must be replaced.

8. Position the float to the limit of upward travel or as close as possible to the wires. Connect the negative meter test lead to the black sensor wire (C, **Figure 59**). While observing the meter, touch the red sensor wire to the green/red wire harness connector pin (E, **Figure 59**). The meter should indicate a quick needle movement and return to a no continuity reading. Repeat the test several times. Replace the sensor if it fails to perform as specified.

9. Install the oil level sensor as described in Chapter Twelve.

TROUBLESHOOTING

69

cannot be operated under normal conditions. Install a test propeller to run the engine in a test tank.

This test checks the power supply and wiring for the overheat warning system. The engine must be run under actual conditions or in a test tank for this procedure.

1. Start the engine and run it at a fast idle until it reaches normal operating temperature.
2. Advance the throttle to approximately 2000 rpm.
3. Locate the thermoswitch on the cylinder head or exhaust cover. Disconnect the pink or orange switch wire. Use a jumper wire to connect the pink or orange wire to an engine ground. Do not connect the thermoswitch lead to ground.
4. If the warning horn does not sound or the warning lamp does not illuminate with the pink or orange wire grounded, test the warning horn or light as described in this section. There is a faulty wire or connection if the horn or light tests correctly, but fails to operate with the pink or orange lead grounded. Repair the wire or connection before operating the engine.
5. Stop the engine and reconnect the thermoswitch wire. Repair any faulty wiring or connections before operating the engine.

Warning Light Test

A warning light on 20-50 hp manual start models illuminates when the oil level is low or the power head is overheated. A 1.5-volt AAA battery and suitable jumper wires are required to test the light.

1. Remove the warning light as described in Chapter Six.
2. Use two jumper wires to connect the positive contact of the AAA battery to the male terminal (A, **Figure 61**) of the warning light. Connect the negative contact of the AAA battery to the female terminal (B, **Figure 61**). The light should illuminate.
3. Reverse the lead connections. The light should not illuminate.
4. Replace the light if it fails to perform as specified.
5. Install the warning light as described in Chapter Six.

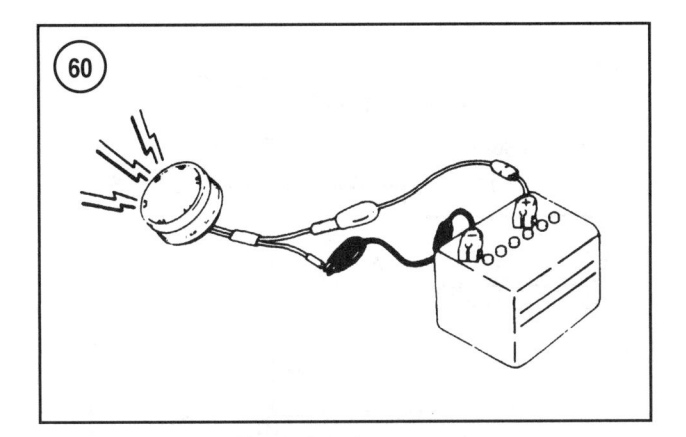

Oil Level Warning Panel Test

28 jet, 35 jet, 40 hp and 50 hp models with remote control and electric starting have an oil level warning panel. The green lamp illuminates when the oil level in the reservoir is within the normal range. The yellow lamp illuminates if the oil level drops below the normal range, indicating oil needs to be added to the reservoir. The red light illuminates if the level drops below the safe opera-

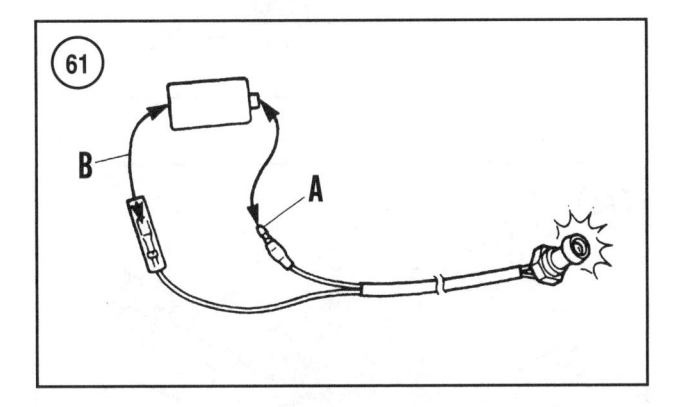

Warning Horn Test

WARNING
When performing tests using a battery, never make the final connection of a circuit at the battery terminal. Arcing may occur and ignite the explosive gasses near the battery.

A warning horn is used on all remote control 20-90 hp models and 28 jet, 35 jet, 40 hp and 50 hp models with tiller control and electric starting. Testing the warning horn requires a fully charged battery and suitable jumper wires.

1. Remove the warning horn as described in Chapter Six.
2. Use jumper wires to connect the warning horn wire to the battery terminals as indicated in **Figure 60**. Replace the warning horn if it fails to emit a load tone.
3. Install the warning horn as described in Chapter Six.

Overheat Warning Circuit Test

CAUTION
Never run an outboard without providing cooling water. Use a test tank if the engine

tion range. Never operate the engine without enough oil in the reservoir or the power head will be seriously damaged.

A 1.5-volt AAA battery and jumper wires are required to test the warning panel.

1. Disconnect the harness connections and wires, then remove the warning panel.
2. Connect the positive AAA battery contact to the yellow/red warning panel wire (**Figure 62**). Use a jumper wire to connect the negative AAA battery contact to the green wire harness connector pin. The green light should illuminate.
3. Connect the positive AAA battery contact to the yellow/red warning panel wire (**Figure 62**). Use a jumper wire to connect the negative battery contact to the black warning panel wire. The yellow light should illuminate.
4. Connect the positive AAA battery contact to the yellow/red warning panel wire (**Figure 62**). Use a jumper wire to connect the negative AAA battery contact to the green/red wire harness connector pin. The red light should illuminate.
5. Replace the warning panel if it fails to perform as specified in Steps 2-4.

OIL INJECTION SYSTEM

The primary components of the oil injection system include the oil reservoir, oil level sensor, oil pump, drive and driven gears, hoses, check valves, and fittings. Failure of any of these components can cause serious power head damage. Test these components if an oil related failure has occurred or if the oil injection system may not be operating properly. Refer to *Warning System* in this chapter to test the oil level sensor.

Drive/Driven Gear

Oil pump drive or driven gear failure will cause insufficient oil delivery to the power head. The oil pump output test in this section tests for gear failure. The pump can also be removed for visual inspection of the gears. Broken or missing gear teeth, discoloration or the presence of debris are sure signs for gear failure. To inspect the gears, remove the oil pump and driven gear as described in Chapter Twelve. Broken gear teeth can be caused by debris that has entered the crankcase or failure of the oil pump. Replace the oil pump and the gears to prevent a possible repeat failure.

Oil Pump Output Test

An accurate measuring container, shop tachometer and watch or clock are required for this test.

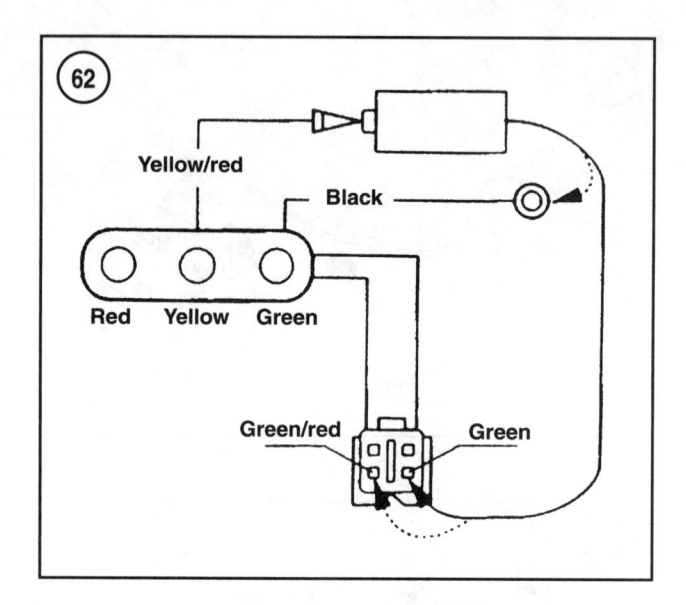

CAUTION
Supply the engine with a 50:1 fuel/oil mixture for the oil pump output test.

CAUTION
Never run an outboard without providing cooling water. Use either a test tank or flush/test adapter if the engine cannot be operated under actual conditions. Remove the propeller before running the engine on a flush/test adapter. Install a test propeller to run the engine in a test tank.

WARNING
Stay clear of the propeller shaft while running the engine on a flush/test adapter. Always disconnect the battery and spark plug

TROUBLESHOOTING

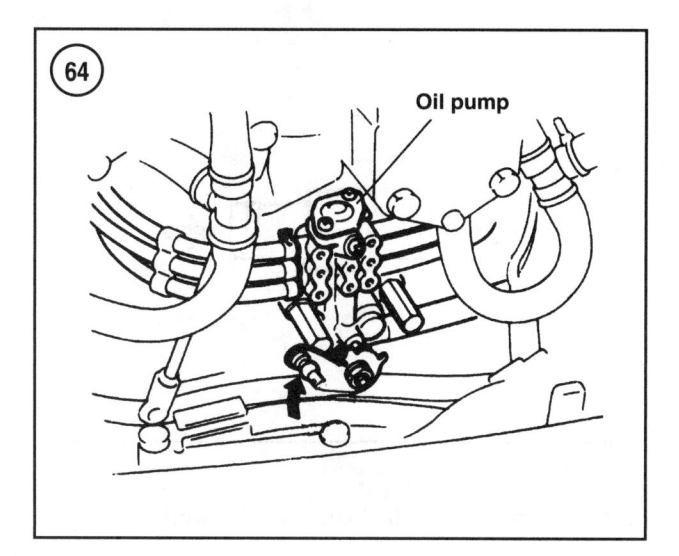

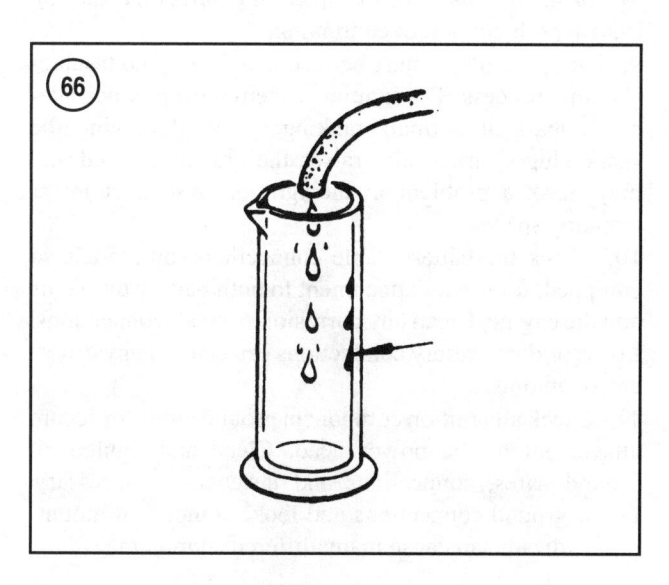

leads before removing or installing the propeller.

NOTE
The measuring container must have 0.1 cc graduations for accurate measurement of the pump output.

1. Run the engine at a fast idle for 10 minutes on a fresh 50:1 fuel/oil mixture. Shut off the engine, then install a shop tachometer following the manufacturer's instructions.

2. Disconnect the oil pump linkage (**Figure 63**) from the pump lever. Rotate the pump lever to the wide-open position (**Figure 64**). Refer to *Oil Pump Linkage Adjustment* in Chapter Four to determine the wide-open position. Typically, the pump lever is rotated in the clockwise direction until it contacts the stop.

3. Disconnect one of the oil pump discharge hoses from the intake manifold connection (**Figure 65**). Refer to the diagrams in Chapter Twelve to assist with oil hose routing and connection points. Direct the hose into the graduated container (**Figure 66**). Make sure the oil discharged from the hose does not contact the side of the container.

4. Start the engine and adjust the throttle to 1500 rpm. Record the oil level in the graduated container. Run the engine for three minutes, then reconnect the oil hose. Shut off the engine.

5. Record the oil level in the container. Subtract the earlier measurement from the last measurement to determine the oil pump output during the three minute run time. Repeat Steps 3-5 for each of the oil pump discharge hoses. Record the output from each hose.

6. The output from each hose should be within the specification in **Table 7**.

   a. If the output from each hose is below the specification, remove the oil pump and inspect the drive and driven gears as described in this chapter. Test the check valves as described in this chapter. Replace the oil pump if the gears and check valves test satisfactorily.

   b. If the output from each hose is above the specification, replace the oil pump. Installing an incorrect oil pump is usually the cause of excessive output. Verify the model name and serial number as described in Chapter One before ordering the replacement pump.

   c. If the output from the hoses is uneven, test the check valves as described in this section. Replace the oil pump if the valves test correctly and the output is above or below the specification from one or more of the hoses. Check for a faulty drive/driven gear if the output is below the specification.

Oil Hose Check Valves Test

CAUTION
Do not use compressed air to test oil hose check valves. The valves are not designed to withstand the pressure and volume produced by a mechanical compressor. Excessive air pressure or volume can damage or weaken the valve and lead to subsequent failure. Operating the engine with a damaged or failed check valve can result in insufficient lubrication and serious power head damaged.

An oil hose check valve ensures the oil flows through the hose in only one direction.
1. Remove the oil hose check valves as described in Chapter Twelve.
2. Connect the pressure tester to one of the fittings on the valve (**Figure 67**). Apply light pressure and note if air exits the opposite fitting. Connect the tester to the opposite fitting and repeat the test. Air should flow easily in the direction of the arrow on the valve and not flow in the other directory.
3. Repeat the test for each check valve on the engine.
4. Replace any check valve that fails to perform as specified.
5. Install the check valves as described in Chapter Twelve.

IGNITION SYSTEM

The ignition system on Yamaha outboards has reliable solid-state components. Commonly used components include the flywheel, ignition charge coil, pulser coil, CDI unit, ignition coil, spark plugs and the wiring. Except for the spark plugs, little maintenance or adjustment is required. All components, except the CDI unit, can be tested using a resistance or peak voltage output test. The best way to test the CDI unit is to use a process of elimination. If all other components of the ignition system test correctly, the source of an ignition system malfunction is probably the CDI unit.

Troubleshooting Notes and Precautions

Observe the following troubleshooting precautions to avoid damaging the ignition system or injuring yourself.
1. Do not reverse the battery connections. Reverse battery polarity will damage electronic components.
2. Do not spark the battery terminals with the battery cable connections to determine polarity.
3. Do not disconnect the battery cables while the engine is running.
4. Do not crank or run the outboard if any electrical components are not grounded to the power head.
5. Do not touch or disconnect any ignition components while the outboard is running.
6. Do not rotate the flywheel when performing ohmmeter tests. The meter will be damaged.
7. If there is a sudden unexplained timing change:
    a. Check the flywheel magnets for damage or a possible shift in magnet position. If the magnets are cracked, damaged or have shifted position, replace the flywheel. See Chapter Seven.
    b. Check the flywheel key for a sheared condition. See Chapter Seven.
8. The ignition system on electric start models requires that the electric starter crank the engine at normal speed in order for the ignition system to produce adequate spark. If the starter motor cranks the engine slowly or not at all, go to *Starting System* in this chapter and correct the starting system problem before continuing.
9. The spark plugs must be installed during the troubleshooting process. The ignition system must produce adequate spark at normal cranking speed. Removing the spark plug(s) artificially raises the cranking speed and may mask a problem in the ignition system at lower cranking speeds.
10. Check the battery cable connections, on models so equipped, for secure attachment to both battery terminals and the engine. Clean any corrosion from all connections. Loose or dirty battery connections can cause many different symptoms.
11. Check all ignition component ground wires for secure attachment to the power head. Clean and tighten all ground wires, connections and fasteners as necessary. Loose ground connections and loose component mounting hardware can cause many different symptom.

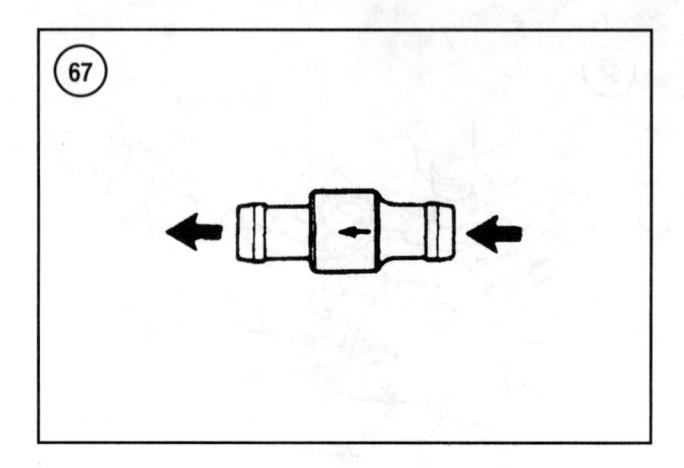

TROUBLESHOOTING

Resistance (Ohmmeter) Tests

The resistance values in the following test procedures are based on tests performed at a normal room temperature or 20° C (68° F). Actual resistance readings obtained during testing will generally be slightly higher if the components are hot and lower if the components are cold. Also, resistance readings may vary depending on the manufacturer of the ohmmeter. Use discretion before failing a component that is only slightly out of specification. Many ohmmeters have difficulty reading less than 1 ohm accurately. If this is the case, specifications of less than 1 ohm generally appear as a very low (continuity) reading. If possible, use an accurate digital ohmmeter to measure values of less than 1 ohm.

Peak Output Voltage Tests

Peak output voltage tests check the voltage output of the ignition charge coil, pulser coil or CDI unit. The test procedures may check voltage output only at normal cranking speed. If an ignition misfire or failure occurs only when the engine is running and cranking speed tests do not show any defects, perform the output tests at the engine speed at which the ignition symptom or failure occurs.

When checking peak voltage output of a component, observe the meter needle for fluctuations, which indicate erratic voltage output. The voltage output of the ignition charge coil and CDI unit may change with engine speed, but should not be erratic.

CAUTION
Do not run the engine without an adequate water supply and do not exceed 3000 rpm without an adequate load.

The term *peak volts* is used interchangeably with Direct Volts Adapter (DVA). Use the recommended meter and adapter (Yamaha part No. J-39299/90890-06752 and YU-39991/90890-03169) or another accurate meter with peak voltage capability whenever the specification is in DVA or peak volts.

WARNING
High voltage is present during ignition system operation. Do not touch ignition components, wires or test leads while cranking or running the engine.

CAUTION
Unless otherwise noted, perform all peak volt testing with the wires connected, but with the terminals exposed to accommodate test lead connections. All electrical components must be securely grounded to the power head when the engine is cranked or started or the components will be damaged.

System Description and Troubleshooting Sequence

Ignition system operation, components used and testing procedures vary by model. Refer to the appropriate system description to gain an understanding of the system before performing tests. The troubleshooting sequence follows the description.

2 hp model

Refer to **Figure 68**.

The ignition system has a flywheel, ignition charge coil, CDI unit and ignition coil.

Alternating current is generated as the flywheel magnets pass by the ignition charge coil. This current is directed to the CDI unit to be converted to direct current and stored in a capacitor. An electrical pulse from the charging current closes a switch in the CDI unit as the piston nears TDC. This releases the stored charge to the ignition coil. The coil increases the charge voltage to the level needed to jump the spark plug gap. The ignition system has a fixed ignition timing. Adjustment is not required. The stop switch prevents operation by shorting the ignition charge current to ground.

Perform the following tests to troubleshoot the ignition system.

1. Spark test.
2. Stop circuit test.
3. Ignition charge coil resistance test.
4. Ignition coil resistance test.

3-5 hp models

Refer to **Figure 69** or **Figure 70**.

The ignition system has a flywheel, ignition charge coil, two pulser coils, CDI unit and ignition coil.

Alternating current is generated as the flywheel magnets pass by the ignition charge coil. This current is directed to the CDI unit to be converted to direct current and stored in a capacitor. Electrical pulses are generated as the flywheel magnets pass by the pulser coils. These pulses close a switch in the CDI unit that releases the stored charge to the ignition coil. The coil increases the charge voltage to the level needed to jump the spark plug gap. The No. 1 pulser coil produces a stronger pulse at lower

68 IGNITION SYSTEM (2 HP MODEL)

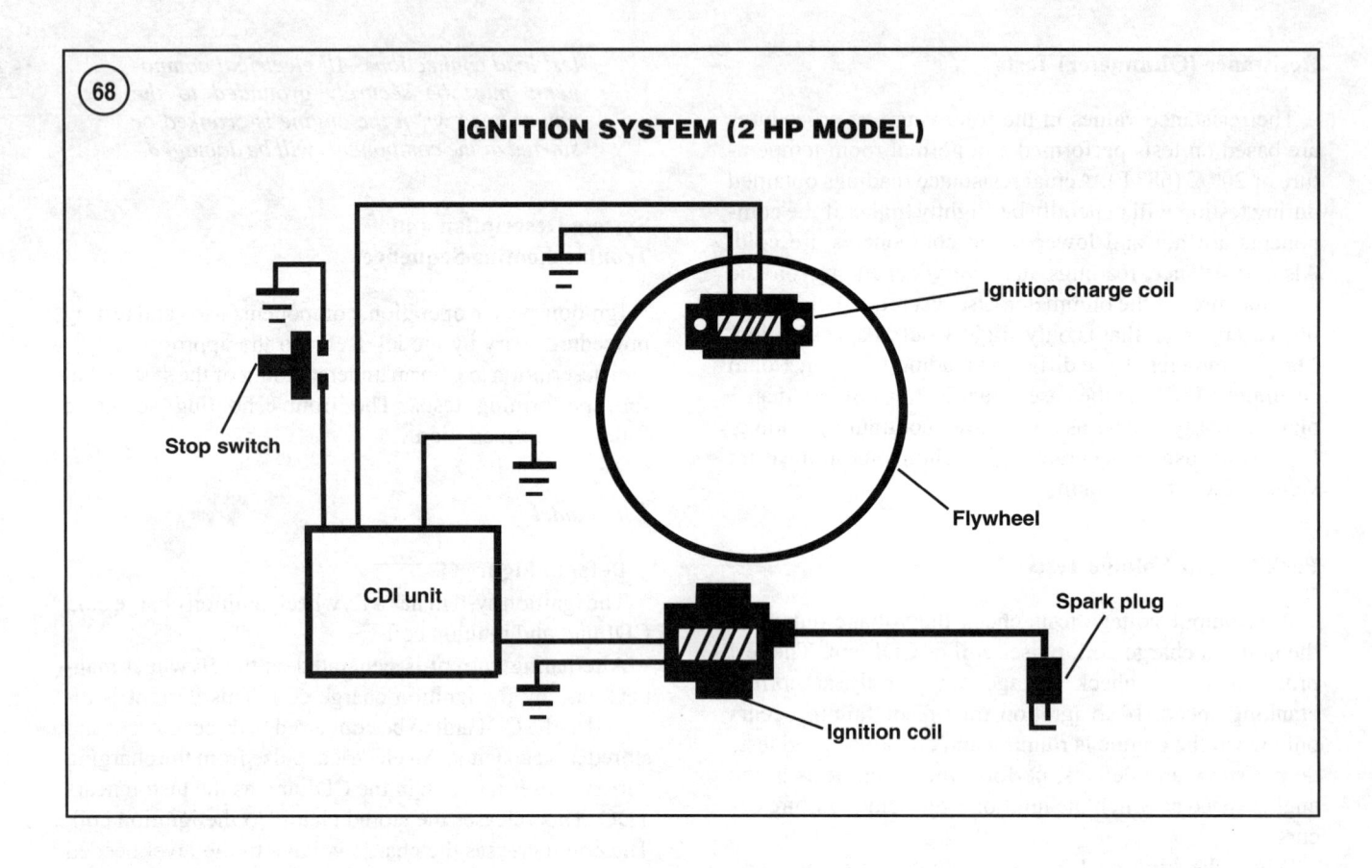

- Ignition charge coil
- Stop switch
- Flywheel
- CDI unit
- Spark plug
- Ignition coil

69 IGNITION SYSTEM (3 HP MODEL)

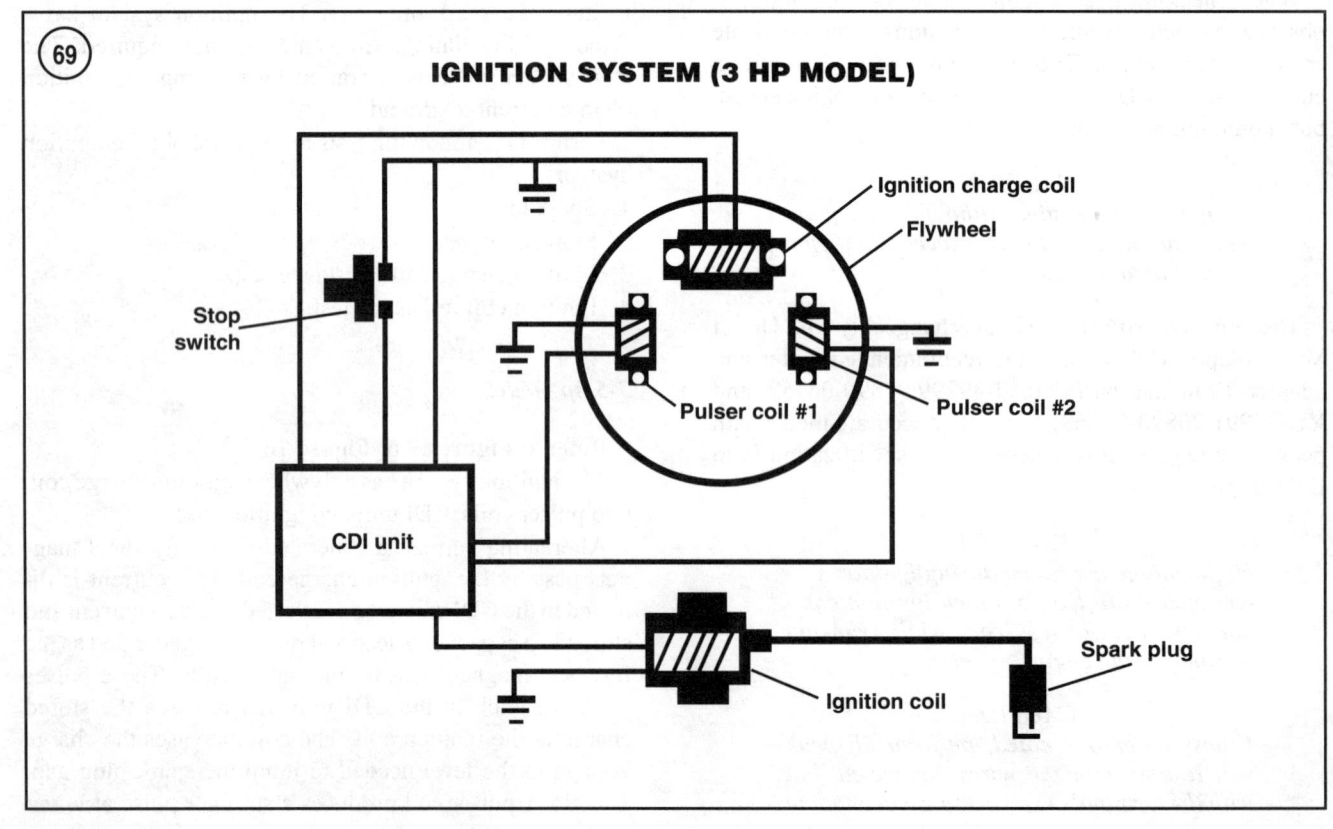

- Ignition charge coil
- Flywheel
- Stop switch
- Pulser coil #1
- Pulser coil #2
- CDI unit
- Spark plug
- Ignition coil

TROUBLESHOOTING

70

IGNITION SYSTEM (4 AND 5 HP MODELS)

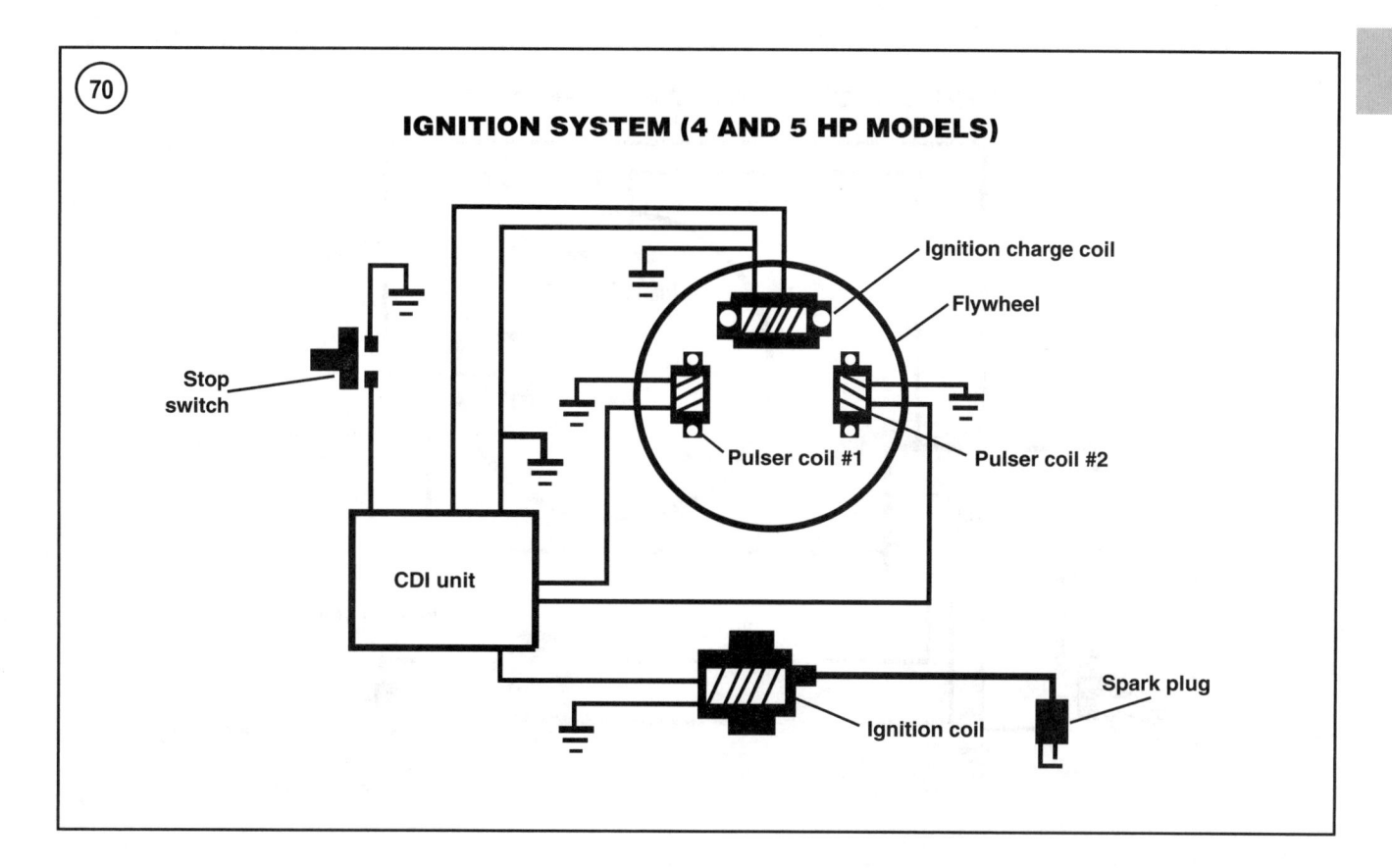

engine speeds and the No. 2 pulser coil produces a stronger pulse at higher engine speeds. The combined pulses provide automatic ignition timing advancement with increasing engine speeds. Test the pulser coil(s) if the ignition timing does not properly advance. The stop switch prevents operation by shorting the ignition charge current to ground.

Perform the following tests to troubleshoot the ignition system.
1. Spark test.
2. Stop circuit test.
3. Ignition charge coil resistance test.
4. Pulser coil resistance test.
5. Ignition coil resistance test.

6 and 8 hp models

Refer to **Figure 71**.

The ignition system has a flywheel, ignition charge coil, pulser coil, CDI unit and ignition coil.

Alternating current is generated as the flywheel magnets pass by the ignition charge coil. This current is directed to the CDI unit to be converted to direct current and stored in a capacitor. An electric pulse is generated as the flywheel triggering magnet passes by the pulser coil. The pulse closes a switch in the CDI unit that releases the stored charge to the ignition coil. The coil increases the charge voltage to the level needed to jump the spark plug gap. The pulser coil produces a pulse every 180° of flywheel rotation and the ignition coil produces spark at both plugs simultaneously. When one piston is near the bottom of its stroke, the other piston is nearing the top of its stroke. The pulser coil mounting base rotates with throttle movement to provide mechanical timing advancement. The stop switch or remote control stop circuit prevents operation by shorting the ignition charge current to ground.

Perform the following tests to troubleshoot the ignition system.
1. Spark test.
2. Stop circuit test.
3. Ignition charge coil resistance test.
4. Pulser coil resistance test.
5. Ignition coil resistance test.

9.9 and 15 hp models

Refer to **Figure 72**.

The ignition system has a flywheel, ignition charge coil, pulser coil, CDI unit and two ignition coils.

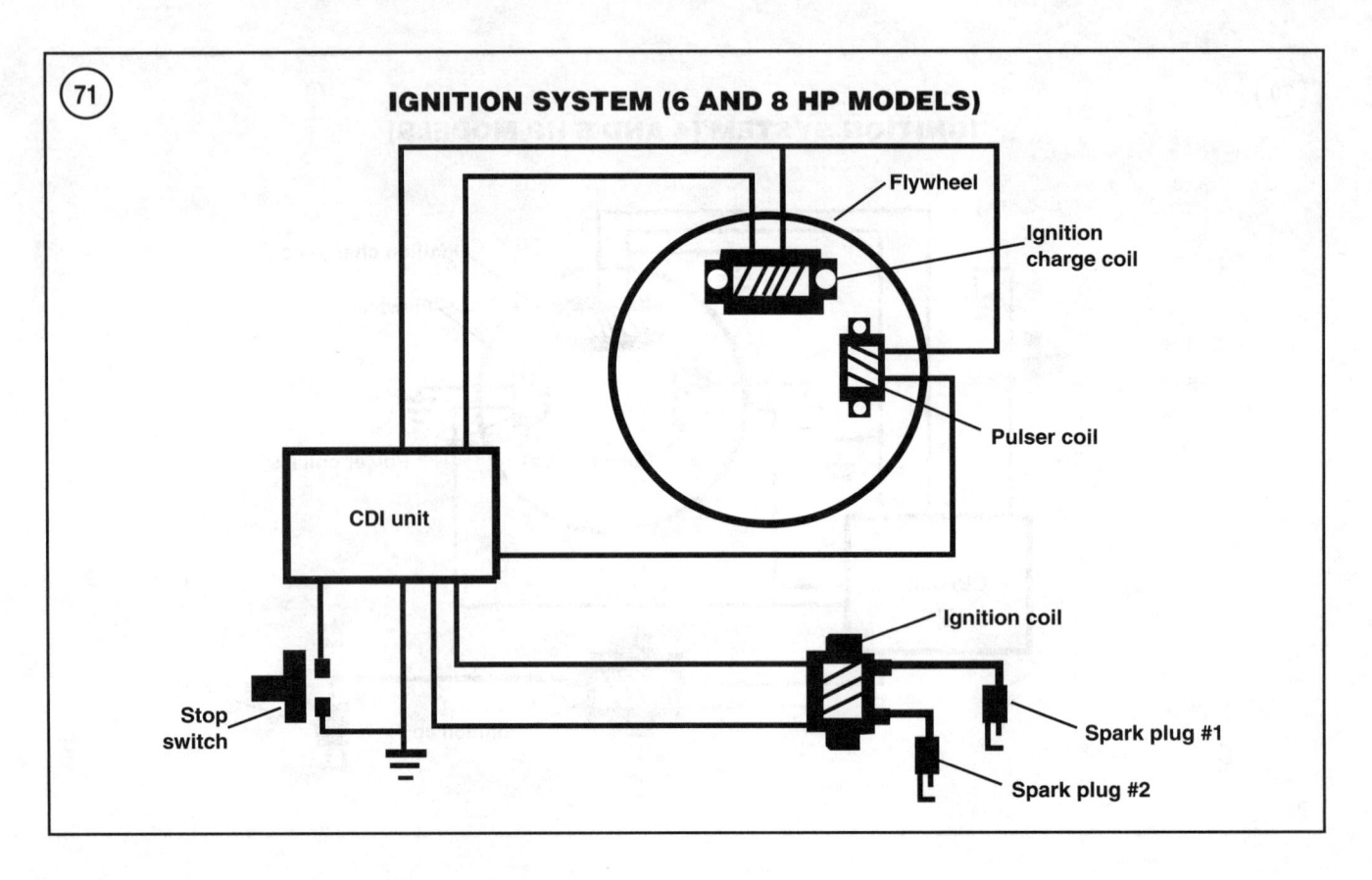

CHAPTER TWO

(71) IGNITION SYSTEM (6 AND 8 HP MODELS)

- Flywheel
- Ignition charge coil
- Pulser coil
- CDI unit
- Stop switch
- Ignition coil
- Spark plug #1
- Spark plug #2

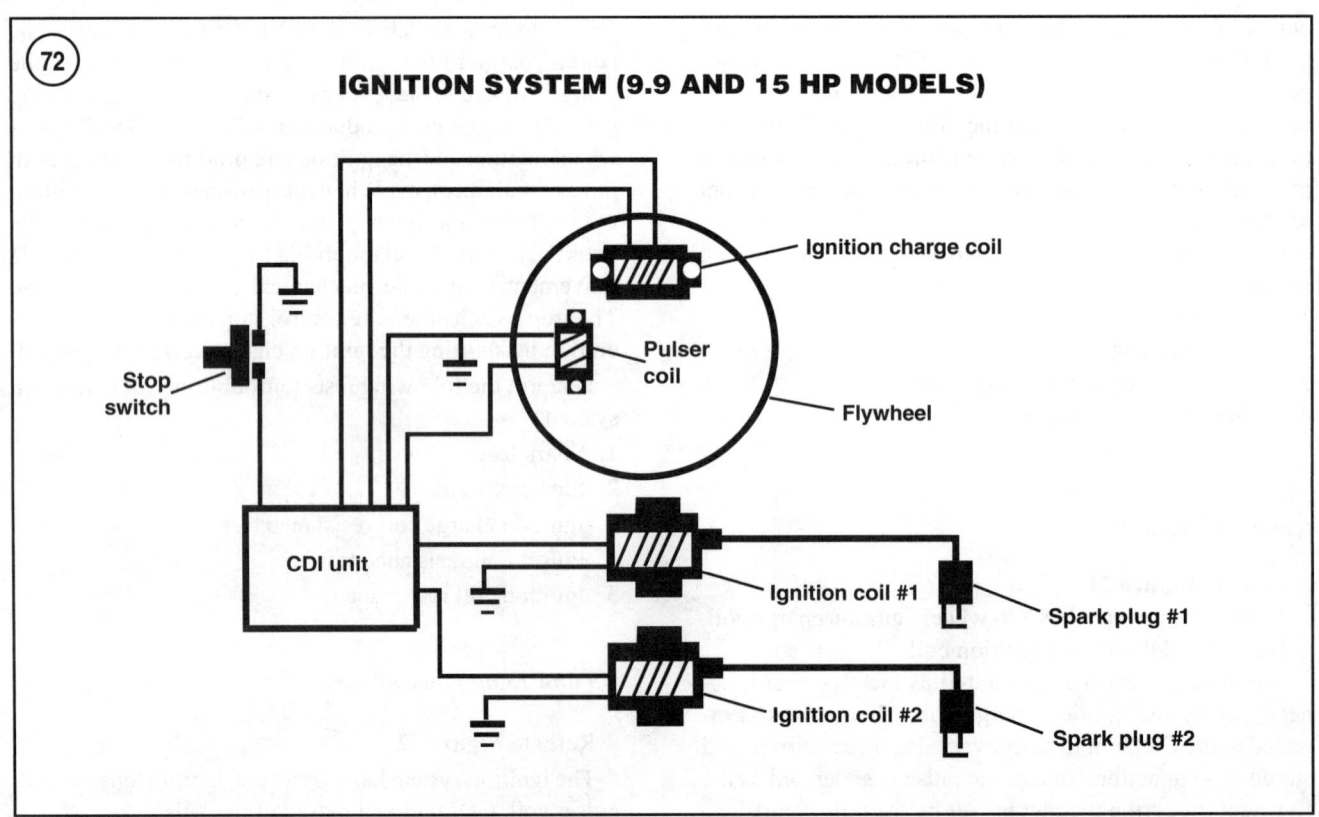

(72) IGNITION SYSTEM (9.9 AND 15 HP MODELS)

- Ignition charge coil
- Pulser coil
- Flywheel
- Stop switch
- CDI unit
- Ignition coil #1
- Spark plug #1
- Ignition coil #2
- Spark plug #2

TROUBLESHOOTING

73 IGNITION SYSTEM (20 AND 25 HP TWO-CYLINDER MODELS)

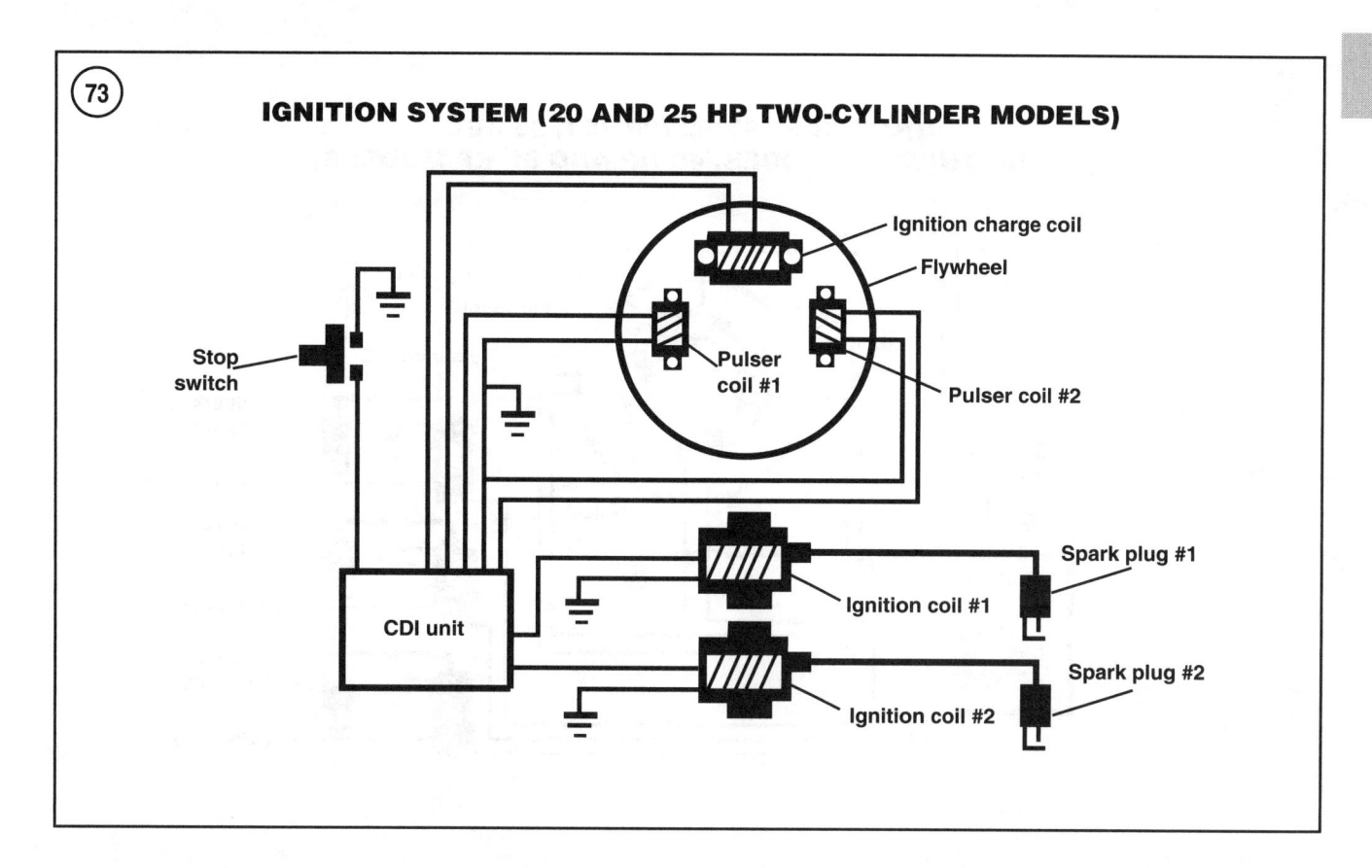

- Ignition charge coil
- Flywheel
- Stop switch
- Pulser coil #1
- Pulser coil #2
- CDI unit
- Ignition coil #1
- Spark plug #1
- Ignition coil #2
- Spark plug #2

Alternating current is generated as the flywheel magnets pass by the ignition charge coil. This current is directed to the CDI unit to be converted to direct current and stored in a capacitor. An electric pulse is generated as the flywheel magnets pass by the pulser coil. This pulse is directed to one of two switches in the CDI unit that release the stored charge to its corresponding ignition coil. The ignition coil increases the charge voltage to the level needed to jump the spark plug gap. The switch receiving the pulse is determined by the polarity of the triggering magnets in the flywheel. This ensures the spark is directed to the coil for the piston that is near its firing position. The pulser coil mounting base rotates with throttle movement to provide mechanical timing advancement. The stop switch or remote control stop circuit prevents operation by shorting the ignition charge current to ground.

1. Spark test.
2. Stop circuit test.
3. Ignition charge coil resistance test.
4. Pulser coil resistance test.
5. Ignition coil resistance test.
6. Ignition charge coil output test.
7. Pulser coil output test.
8. CDI unit output test.

20 and 25 hp two-cylinder models

Refer to **Figure 73**.

The ignition system has a flywheel, ignition charge coil, two pulser coils, CDI unit and two ignition coils.

Alternating current is generated as the flywheel magnets pass by the ignition charge coil. This current is directed to the CDI unit to be converted to direct current and stored in a capacitor. The triggering magnets in the flywheel pass by the pulser coil as its corresponding piston approaches its firing position. This creates an electrical pulse that is directed to a corresponding switch in the CDI unit. The switch then releases the stored charge to the corresponding ignition coil. The ignition coil increases the charge voltage to the level needed to jump the spark plug gap. The pulser coil mounting base rotates with throttle movement to provide mechanical timing advancement. The stop switch or remote control stop circuit prevents operation by shorting the ignition charge current to ground.

1. Spark test.
2. Stop circuit test.
3. Ignition charge coil output test.
4. Pulser coil output test.
5. CDI unit output test.

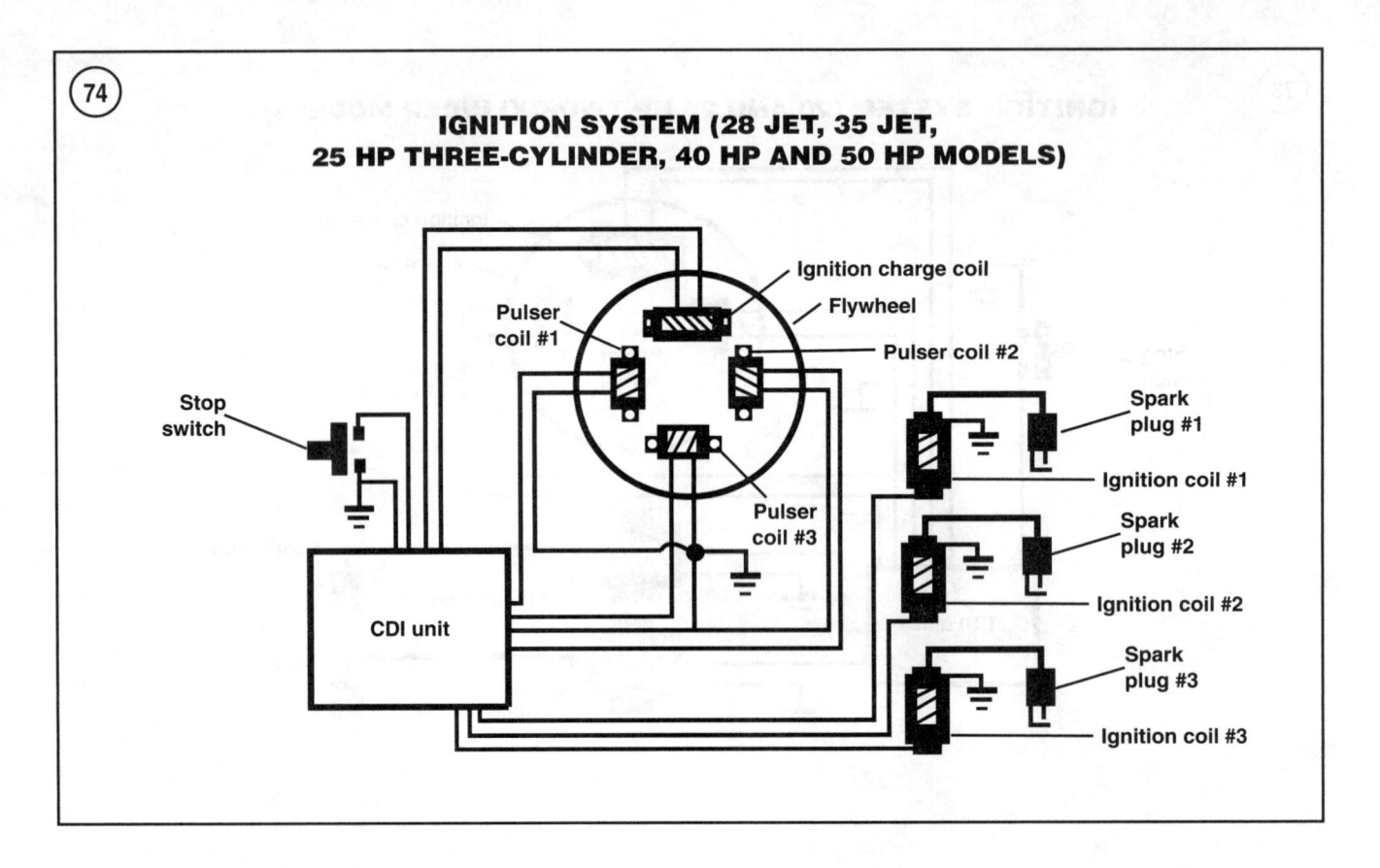

Figure 74 IGNITION SYSTEM (28 JET, 35 JET, 25 HP THREE-CYLINDER, 40 HP AND 50 HP MODELS)

25 hp three-cylinder and 30 hp models

Refer to **Figure 74**.

The ignition system has a flywheel, ignition charge coil, three pulser coils, CDI unit and three ignition coils.

Alternating current is generated as the flywheel magnets pass by the ignition charge coil. This current is directed to the CDI unit to be converted to direct current and stored in a capacitor. The triggering magnets in the flywheel pass by the pulser coil as its corresponding piston approaches its firing position. This creates an electrical pulse that is directed to a corresponding switch in the CDI unit. The switch then releases the stored charge to the corresponding ignition coil. The ignition coil increases the charge voltage to the level needed to jump the spark plug gap. The pulser coils mounting base rotates with throttle movement to provide mechanical timing advancement. The stop switch or remote control stop circuit prevents operation by shorting the ignition charge current to ground.

1. Spark test.
2. Stop circuit test.
3. Ignition charge coil output test.
4. Pulser coil output test.
5. CDI unit output test.

28 jet, 35 jet, 40 hp and 50 hp models

Refer to **Figure 74**.

The ignition system has a flywheel, ignition charge coil, three pulser coils, CDI unit and three ignition coils.

Alternating current is generated as the flywheel magnets pass by the ignition charge coil. This current is directed to the CDI unit to be converted to direct current and stored in a capacitor. The triggering magnets in the flywheel pass by the pulser coil as its corresponding piston approaches its firing position. This creates an electrical pulse that is directed to a corresponding switch in the CDI unit. The switch then releases the stored charge to the corresponding ignition coil. The ignition coil increases the charge voltage to the level needed to jump the spark plug gap. A linkage connects the throttle linkage to the timing indicator on the CDI unit. Moving the indicator electronically advances or retards the ignition timing. The stop switch or remote control stop circuit prevents operation by shorting the ignition charge current to ground.

1. Spark test.
2. Stop circuit test.
3. Ignition charge coil resistance test.
4. Pulser coil resistance test.
5. Ignition coil resistance test.

TROUBLESHOOTING

Figure 75 IGNITION SYSTEM (60-90 HP [EXCEPT E60 AND E75] MODELS)

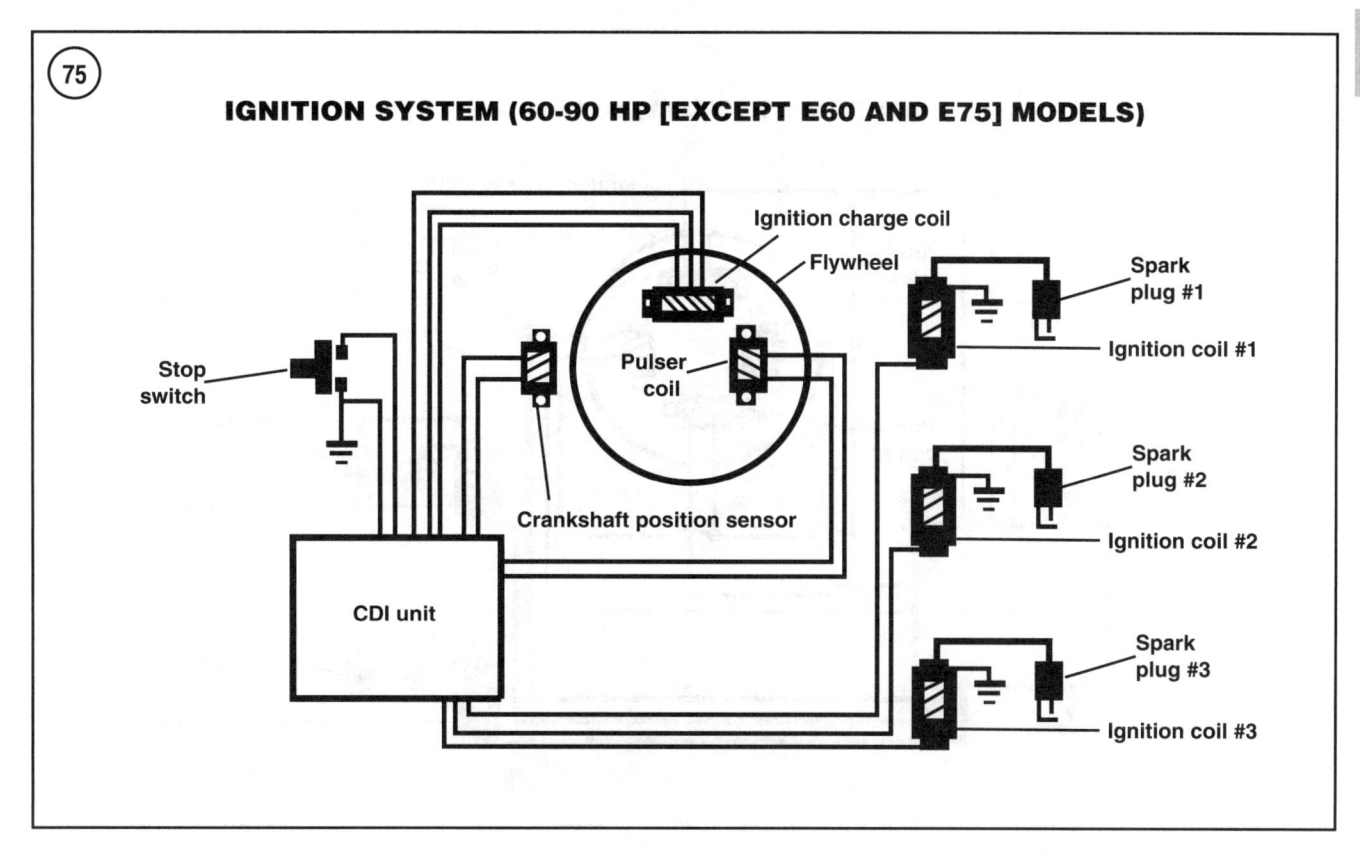

6. Ignition charge coil output test.
7. Pulser coil output test.
8. CDI unit output test.

60-90 hp (except E60 and E75) models

Refer to **Figure 75**.

The ignition system has a flywheel, ignition charge coil, crankshaft position sensor, pulser coil, CDI unit and three ignition coils.

Alternating current is generated as the flywheel magnets pass by the ignition charge coil. This current is directed to the CDI unit to be converted to direct current and stored in a capacitor. The triggering magnets in the flywheel pass by the pulser coil creating an electrical pulse that is directed to the ignition timing circuits in the CDI unit. An electrical pulse is also generated as the flywheel gear teeth pass by the crankshaft position sensor. These pulses are also directed to the timing circuits where they are used to determine the piston position for all three cylinders.

As each piston reaches its firing position, the timing circuits activate a switch that releases the stored charge to the corresponding ignition coil. The ignition coil increases the charge voltage to the level needed to jump the spark plug gap. A linkage connects the throttle linkage to the timing indicator on the CDI unit. Moving the indicator electronically advances or retards the ignition timing. The stop switch or remote control stop circuit prevents operation by shorting the ignition charge current to ground.

1. Spark test.
2. Stop circuit test.
3. Ignition charge coil resistance test.
4. Pulser coil resistance test.
5. Crankshaft position sensor resistance test.
6. Ignition coil resistance test.
7. Ignition charge coil output test.
8. Pulser coil output test.
9. Crankshaft position sensor output test.
10. CDI unit output test.

E60 model

Refer to **Figure 76**.

The ignition system has a flywheel, ignition charge coil, three pulser coils, CDI unit and three ignition coils.

Alternating current is generated as the flywheel magnets pass by the ignition charge coil. This current is directed to the CDI unit to be converted to direct current and stored in a capacitor. The triggering magnets in the fly-

76 IGNITION SYSTEM (E60 MODEL)

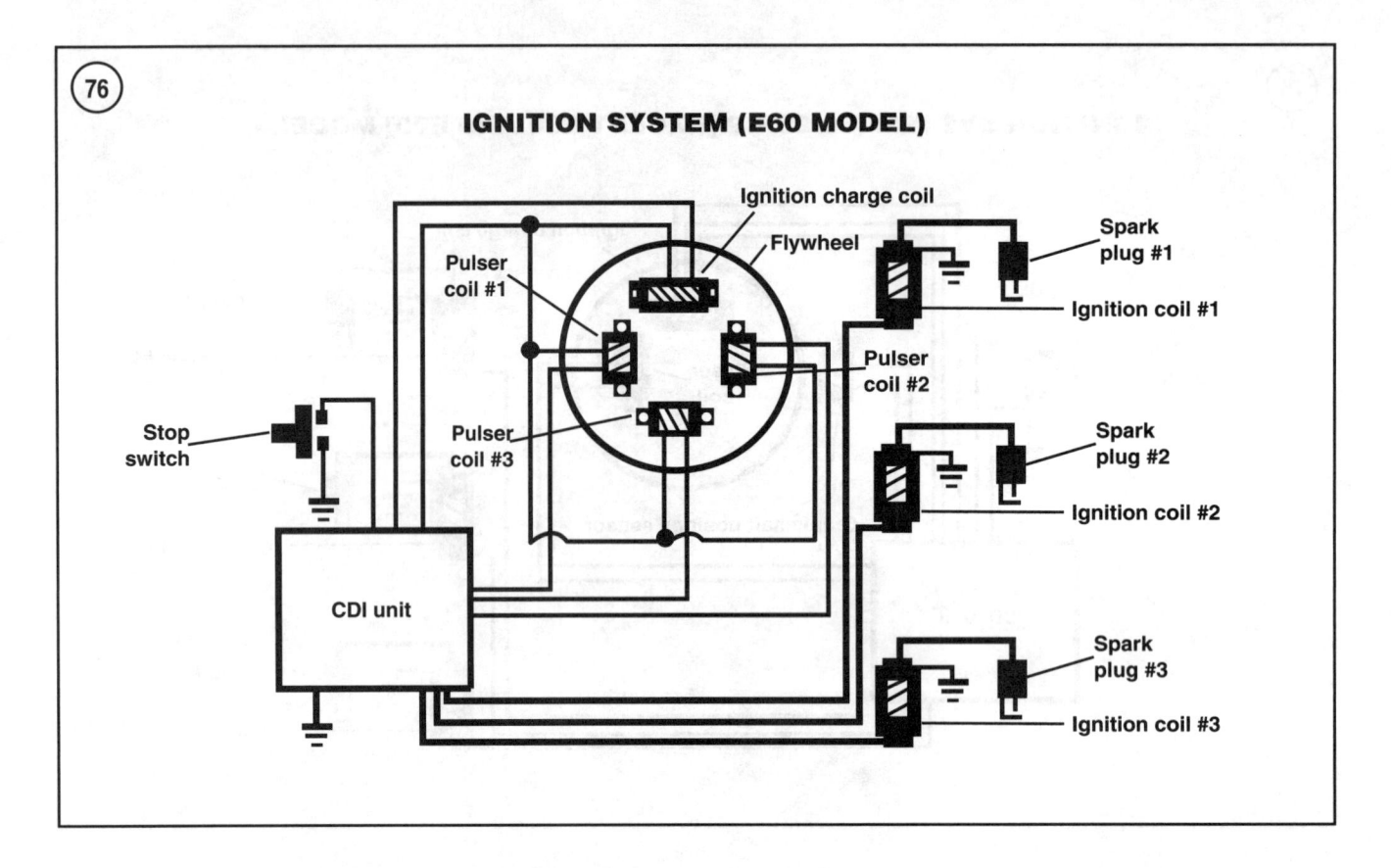

wheel pass by the pulser coil as its corresponding piston approaches its firing position. This creates an electrical pulse that is directed to a corresponding switch in the CDI unit. The switch then releases the stored charge to the corresponding ignition coil. The ignition coil increases the charge voltage to the level needed to jump the spark plug gap. The pulser coil mounting base rotates with throttle movement to provide mechanical timing advancement. The stop switch or remote control stop circuit prevents operation by shorting the ignition charge current to ground.

1. Spark test.
2. Stop circuit test.
3. Ignition charge coil resistance test.
4. Pulser coil resistance test.
5. Ignition coil resistance test.

E75 model

Refer to **Figure 77**.

The ignition system has a flywheel, ignition charge coil, two pulser coils, a CDI unit and three ignition coils.

Alternating current is generated as the flywheel magnets pass by the ignition charge coil. This current is directed to the CDI unit to be converted to direct current and stored in a capacitor. The triggering magnets in the fly-

wheel pass by the pulser coils creating electrical pulses that are directed to the ignition timing circuits in the CDI unit where they are used to determine the piston position for all three cylinders.

As each piston reaches its firing position, the timing circuits activate a switch that releases the stored charge to the corresponding ignition coil. The ignition coil increases the charge voltage to the level needed to jump the spark plug gap. The pulser coil mounting base rotates with throttle movement to provide mechanical timing advancement.

The stop switch or remote control stop circuit prevents operation by shorting the ignition charge current to ground.

1. Spark test.
2. Stop circuit test.
3. Ignition charge coil resistance test.
4. Pulser coil resistance test.
5. Ignition coil resistance test.
6. Ignition charge coil output test.
7. Pulser coil output test.
8. CDI unit output test.

Spark Test

Check for spark as described in this chapter under *Spark test* under *Starting Difficulty*. If any cylinders have

TROUBLESHOOTING

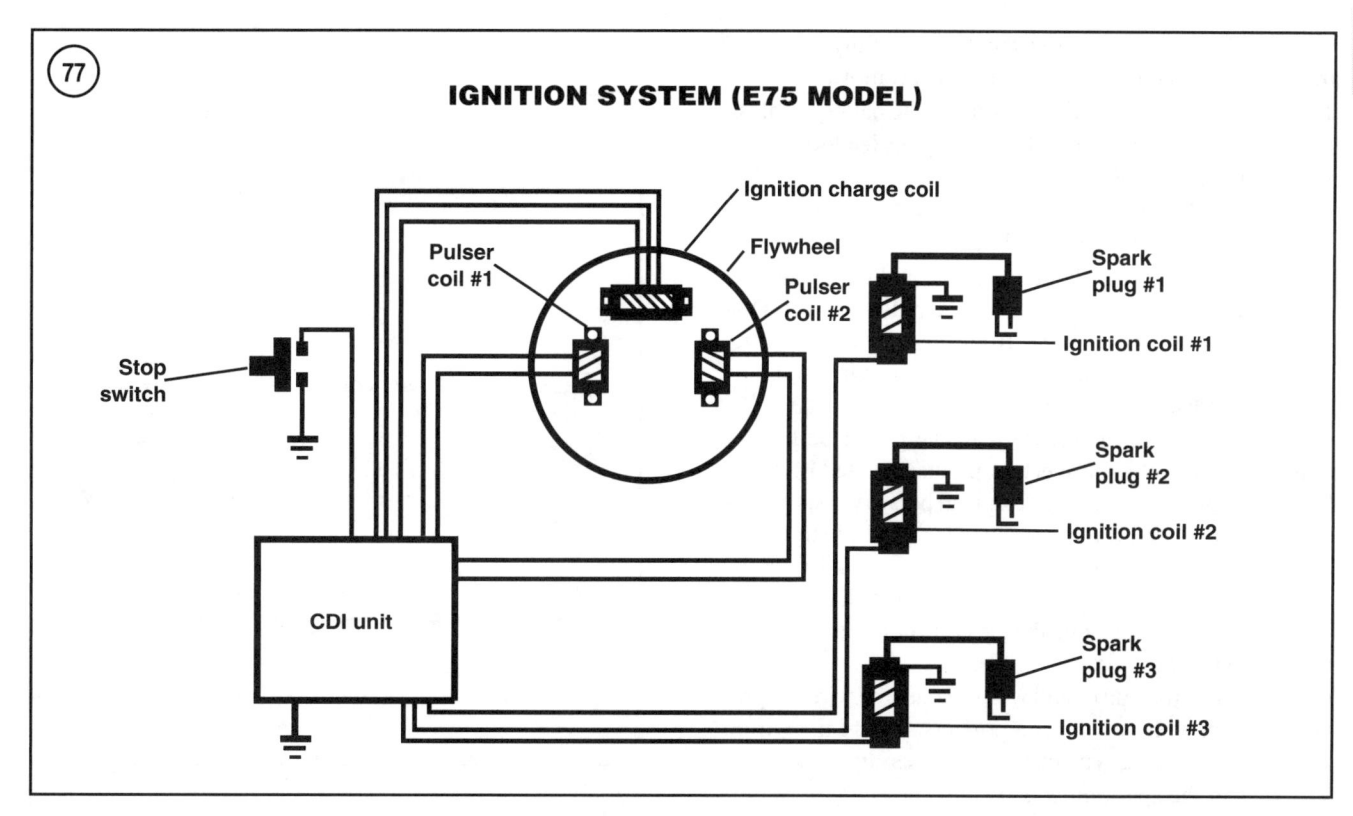

(77) IGNITION SYSTEM (E75 MODEL)

Diagram shows: Stop switch, Pulser coil #1, Ignition charge coil, Flywheel, Pulser coil #2, CDI unit, Ignition coils #1, #2, #3 and Spark plugs #1, #2, #3.

no spark or weak spark, perform the specified test procedures to determine the cause(s).

Stop Circuit Test

Pushing the stop button, tripping the lanyard safety switch or switching the ignition key off activates the stop circuit. Any of these actions cause the engine to stop running because the current required to operate the ignition system is diverted to engine ground. A failure in the stop circuit can cause the engine to have no spark or not be able to stop. A multimeter is required to test this circuit.

1. On electric start models, disconnect the battery cables.
2. Disconnect and ground the spark plug lead(s) to prevent accidental starting.
3. Locate and disconnect the white wire leading to the CDI unit. Refer to the wiring diagrams at the end of the manual and Chapter Six to assist with locating the CDI unit.
4. Calibrate the multimeter to the $R \times 1$ scale.
5. Connect the positive meter test lead to the white wire that was disconnected from the CDI unit. Do not connect the test lead to the CDI unit wiring. Connect the negative meter test lead to a good engine ground.
6. The meter should indicate continuity when:

   a. The key switch is in the OFF position.
   b. The engine mounted stop switch is depressed.
   c. The lanyard cord is removed from the lanyard safety switch or stop switch.

7. The meter should indicate no continuity when:

   a. The key switch is in the ON or START position.
   b. The engine-mounted stop switch is in the released or normal ON position.
   c. The lanyard cord is properly attached onto the lanyard safety switch or stop button.

8. If the circuit does not test correctly, disconnect the wiring for one of the switches and repeat the test. Replace the disconnected switch if the circuit now tests correctly. See Chapter Six. If the fault cannot be identified by isolating the switches, repair or replace the shorted or open white wire in the engine or instrument wiring harness.
9. Reconnect the spark plug lead(s).
10. On electric start models, connect the battery cables.

Pulser Coil Resistance Test

The pulser coil creates a pulsating current that is used to initiate spark at the plug. A faulty pulser coil can cause an intermittent spark or no spark on one coil or, on some models, all coils. Pulser coils are located under the flywheel (**Figure 78**). Follow the test carefully to avoid misdiagnosis and unnecessary flywheel removal.

1. On electric start models, disconnect the battery cables.
2. Disconnect and ground the spark plug lead(s) to prevent accidental starting.
3. Refer to the test specifications in **Table 9**, then calibrate the meter to the proper ohm scale.
4. Refer to the wiring diagrams at the end of the manual to identify the wire color used for the pulser coil(s). Disconnect the pulser coil wires from the CDI unit or other wire harness connections. The pulser coil wires must be isolated for accurate testing.
5. Connect the meter test leads to the pulser coil wires (**Figure 78**) or other connection points as listed in **Table 9**. Record the meter reading. Test lead polarity does not affect the test results. If the resistance is not within the specification, the pulser coil is shorted or open and must be replaced. If applicable, perform the pulser coil output test before replacing the coil. Pulser coil replacement is described in Chapter Six.
6. Reconnect the pulser coil wires. Route the wires to prevent contact with moving components. Secure the wiring with plastic locking type clamps as necessary.
7. Connect the spark plug leads.
8. On electric start models, connect the battery cables.

Crankshaft Position Sensor Resistance Test

The crankshaft position sensor is used on 60-90 hp (except E60 and E75) models. This sensor creates a pulsating current as a raised protrusion on the flywheel teeth pass next to the sensor coil. The pulsating current is directed to the CDI unit to provide an rpm reference and crankshaft positioning for each cylinder relative to TDC. A fault with this sensor can cause no spark or intermittent spark at the coil. Use a digital volt/ohmmeter for this test. To prevent misdiagnosis and unnecessary sensor replacement, perform the crankshaft position sensor output test before deciding to replace the crankshaft position sensor.

1. Disconnect the battery cables.
2. Disconnect and ground the spark plug lead(s) to prevent accidental starting.
3. Calibrate the ohmmeter to the automatic scaling or 100-500 ohms.
4. Locate the crankshaft position sensor next to the flywheel (**Figure 79**). Trace the sensor blue/white and blue/red wires to the connection on the CDI unit harness. Disconnect the wire connector.
5. Connect the meter test leads to the blue/white and blue/red sensor wire terminals. Do not inadvertently connect to the CDI unit wiring.
6. If the meter does not read 158-236 ohms, the sensor is shorted or open and must be replaced. To prevent misdiagnosis and unnecessary sensor replacement, perform the crankshaft position sensor output test, before deciding to replace the sensor. Sensor replacement is described in Chapter Six.
7. Reconnect the sensor harness to the CDI unit harness. Route the wires to prevent contact with moving components. Secure the wiring with plastic locking type clamps as necessary.
8. Connect the spark plug leads.

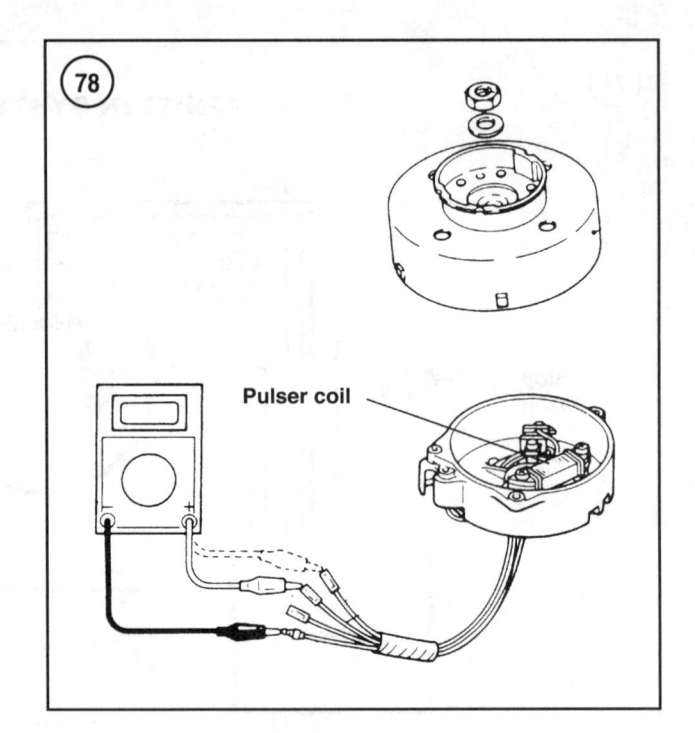

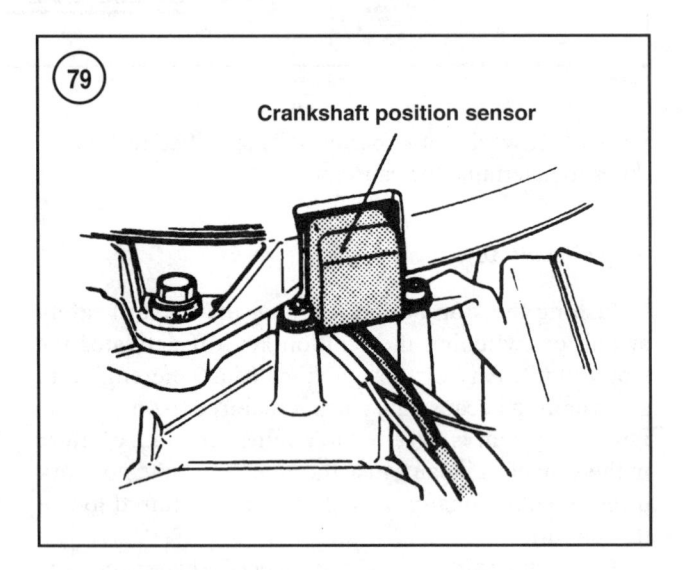

TROUBLESHOOTING

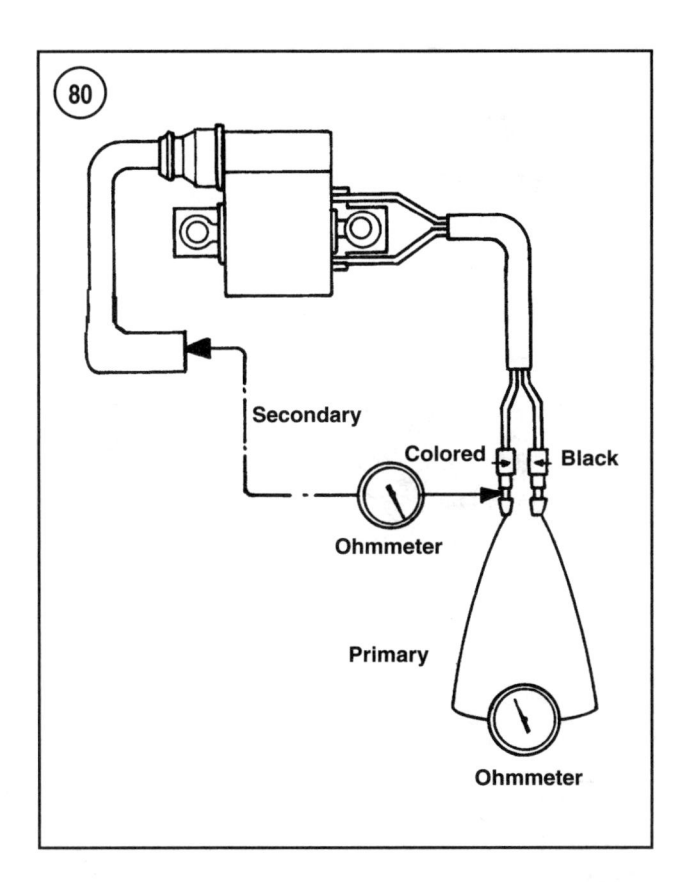

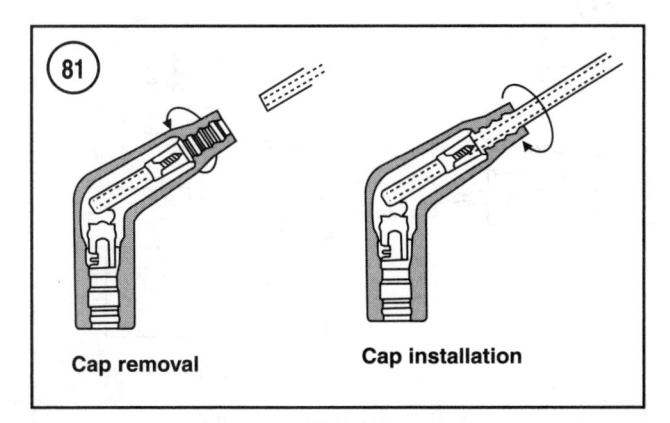

80

Secondary
Colored — Black
Ohmmeter
Primary
Ohmmeter

81

Cap removal   Cap installation

9. Connect the battery cables.

Ignition Coil Resistance Test

A problem with the ignition coil can cause or contribute to an intermittent misfire or no spark at the coil. This procedure can be performed without removing the coil from the engine. The spark plug cap contains a resistor to reduce radio interference from the ignition system. Remove the cap to measure the secondary resistance. Use an accurate digital ohmmeter for this procedure.

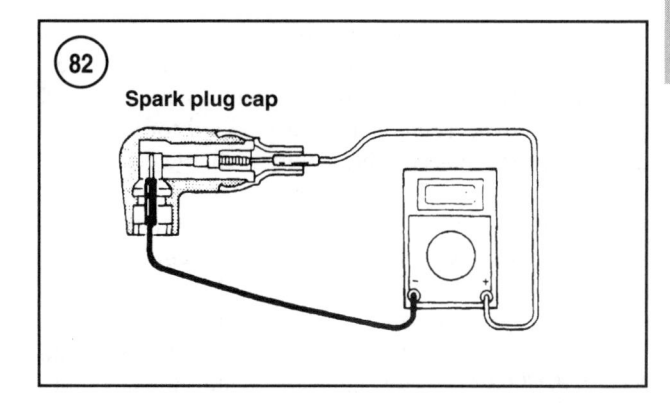

82

Spark plug cap

1. On electric start models, disconnect the battery cables.
2. Refer to *Ignition Charge Coil* in Chapter Six to locate the ignition coils and connecting leads. Disconnect the wire connections to the CDI unit, engine ground and spark plug.
3. Calibrate the digital ohmmeter to the R × 1 scale. Connect the negative meter test lead to the black coil wire (**Figure 80**). Connect the positive meter test lead to the orange or black/white coil wire.
4. The meter reading should be within the primary resistance specification in **Table 10**.
5. Carefully unthread the spark plug cap from the ignition coil (**Figure 81**). Remove both caps on 6 and 8 hp models.
6. Calibrate the meter to read 6000-7000 ohms. Connect the meter test leads to the contacts in the cap as shown in **Figure 82**. If the meter does not read 4000-6000 ohms of resistance, replace the spark plug cap.
7. Refer to **Table 10**, then calibrate the meter to the appropriate scale to measure the secondary resistance specification.
8. Connect the positive meter test lead to the orange or black/white coil wire. Connect the negative test lead to the core wire in the spark plug lead (**Figure 80**). Remove the cap for this test. If the meter reading is not within the secondary resistance specification in **Table 10**, replace the ignition coil. On 6 and 8 hp, repeat the test using the remaining spark plug lead.
9. Carefully thread the spark plug cap onto the lead (**Figure 82**). The screw portion of the cap should thread into the core of the cable and contact the core wire.
10. Reconnect the battery cables on electric start models.

Ignition Charge Coil Output Test

The ignition charge coil powers the ignition system. A fault with this component can cause an intermittent spark, weak spark or no spark. On certain models, a faulty charge coil can cause the engine to run properly at one speed range and misfire at another. The ignition charge coil is located under the flywheel (**Figure 83**). Perform the test carefully to avoid misdiagnosis and unnecessary flywheel removal. Flywheel removal is not required for testing as the coil wires are accessible. Ignition charge coil output specifications are in **Table 11**. Perform this test under actual operating conditions or with the engine running in a suitable test tank. Use a test propeller if the engine will be run in a test tank.

A common meter with peak output voltage capability, or Yamaha part No. J-39299/90890-06752 and YU-39991/90890-03169, and an accurate shop tachometer are required for this test.

Perform the output test with all wires connected. A test harness is required for the following models: On 60 and 70 hp (except E60) models, use Yamaha part No. YB-38831/90890-06767. On 65 jet and 75-90 hp models, use Yamaha part No. YB-6443/90890-06757.

WARNING
The ignition system produces very high voltage current. Never touch any part of your body to the test lead of any engine wiring while the flywheel is rotating. Never stand in water while testing or work around wiring or connections.

CAUTION
Never run an outboard without providing cooling water. Use either a test tank or run the engine under actual conditions. Install a test propeller to run the engine in a test tank.

1. Connect a shop tachometer to the engine. Follow the tachometer manufacturer's instructions.
2A. On 9.9-50 hp models, locate the brown and blue charge coil wires. The wires lead to the coil mounting location under the flywheel. Connect the meter test lead to the charge coil wires as shown in **Figure 84**. Test lead polarity does not affect the test results on these models. Do not disconnect the wires. Insert the test leads between the bullet connectors as shown in **Figure 85**.
2B. On 60-90 hp models, disconnect the ignition charge coil wire harness from the engine wire harness or CDI unit. Connect the test harness to the charge coil harness and engine or CDI harness as shown in **Figure 86**. Connect the meter test leads to the test harness wire colors specified in **Table 11**.
3. Refer to **Table 11** for the test specifications, then calibrate the multimeter to the correct peak AC voltage scale. Scale changes may be required to test at different engine speeds.
4. Start the engine and run it at fast idle until it reaches normal operating temperature. Record the output voltage while running the engine at the speeds listed in **Table 11**. Change the meter scale as required for the test specification. To check the voltage at cranking speed, disconnect and ground the spark plug leads. Note the meter readings while operating the electric or manual starter. Repeat the test for models requiring a second wire connection.

83

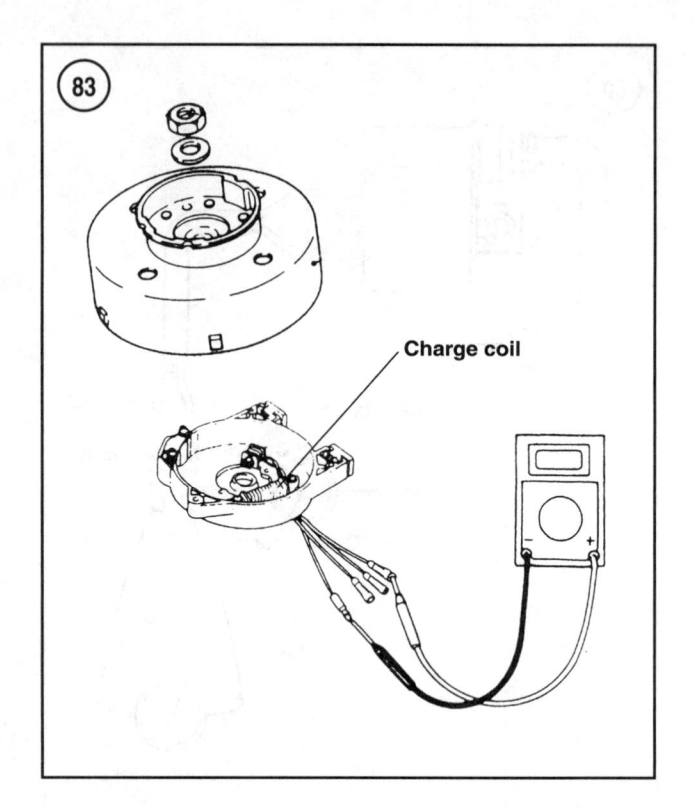

Charge coil

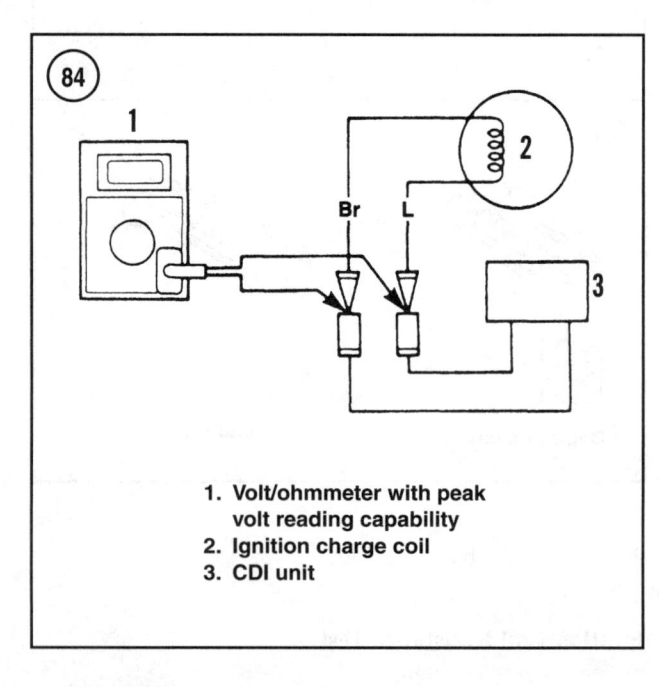

84
1. Volt/ohmmeter with peak volt reading capability
2. Ignition charge coil
3. CDI unit

TROUBLESHOOTING

85

⑧⑤

⑧⑥

3

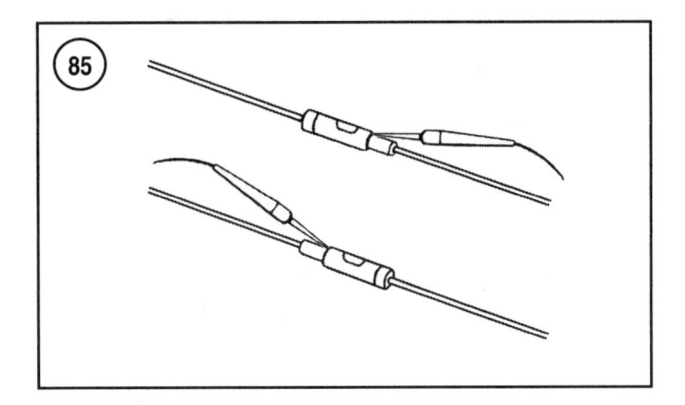

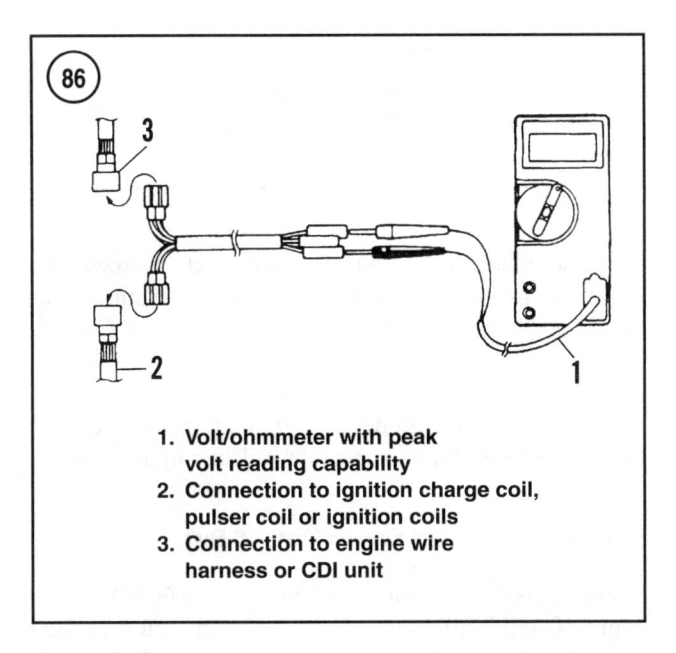

2   1

1. Volt/ohmmeter with peak volt reading capability
2. Connection to ignition charge coil, pulser coil or ignition coils
3. Connection to engine wire harness or CDI unit

5. If the coil output does not meet or exceed the minimum specification in **Table 11** at each designated engine speed, replace the ignition charge coil as described in Chapter Six.
6. Disconnect the shop tachometer.
7. On 60-90 hp models, remove the test harness and reconnect the charge coil harness.

Ignition Charge Coil Resistance Test

The ignition system is powered by the ignition charge coil. A fault with this component can cause an intermittent spark, weak spark or no spark. On certain models, a faulty charge coil can cause the engine to run properly and one speed range and misfire at another. The ignition charge coil is located under the flywheel (**Figure 83**). Perform the test carefully to avoid misdiagnosis and unnecessary flywheel removal. Flywheel removal is not required for testing as the coil wires are accessible. Ignition charge coil resistance specifications are in **Table 8**. All readings were obtained with the component warmed to 20° C (68° F). The coil resistance reading may be higher when tested at a higher temperature and lower when tested at a lower temperature.

1. On electric start models, disconnect the battery cables.
2. Disconnect and ground the spark plug lead(s) to prevent accidental starting.
3. Refer to the test specifications in **Table 8**, then calibrate the meter to the proper ohm scale.
4. Refer to the wiring diagrams at the end of the manual to identify the wire color used for the ignition charge coil. Disconnect the charge coil wires from the CDI unit, or other wire harness connections. The charge coil wires must be isolated for accurate testing.
5. Connect the meter test leads to the charge coil wires (**Figure 84**) or other connection points as listed in **Table 8** and note the meter reading. Test lead polarity does not affect the test results. If the resistance is not within the specification, the coil is shorted or open and must be replaced. If applicable, perform the ignition charge coil output test before replacing the coil. Ignition charge coil replacement is described in Chapter Six.
6. Reconnect the ignition charge coil wires. Route the wires to prevent contact with moving components. Secure the wires with plastic locking type clamps as necessary.
7. Connect the spark plug leads.
8. On electric start models, connect the battery cables.

Pulser Coil Output Test

The pulser coil creates a pulsating current that is used to initiate spark at the plug. A faulty pulser coil can cause an intermittent spark or no spark on one coil or, on some models, all coils. Pulser coils are located under the flywheel (**Figure 78**). Follow the test carefully to avoid misdiagnosis and unnecessary flywheel removal. Pulser coil output specifications are in **Table 12**. Perform this test under actual operating conditions or with the engine running in a suitable test tank. Use a test propeller if the engine will be run in a test tank.

A common meter with peak output voltage capability, or Yamaha part No. J-39299/90890-06752 and YU-39991/90890-03169, and an accurate shop tachometer are required for this test.

Perform the output test with all wires connected. A test harness is required for the following models: On 25 hp three-cylinder and 30 hp models, use Yamaha part No. YB-38832/90890-06772. On 28 jet, 35 jet, 40 hp and 50 hp models, use Yamaha part No. YB-06443/90890-06757. On 60-90 hp (except E60 and E75) models, use Yamaha part

No. YB-38831/90890-06767. On E75 models, use Yamaha part No. YB-38831/90890-06771.

> *WARNING*
> *The ignition system produces very high voltage current. Never touch any part of your body to any test lead of the engine wiring while the flywheel is rotating. Never stand in water while testing or work around wiring or connections.*

> *CAUTION*
> *Never run an outboard without providing cooling water. Use either a test tank or run the engine under actual conditions. Install a test propeller to run the engine in a test tank.*

1. Connect a shop tachometer to the engine. Follow the tachometer manufacturer's instructions.

2A. On 9.9 and 15 hp models, locate the white/red and black pulser coil wires. The wires lead to the coil mounting location under the flywheel. Connect the meter test leads to the pulser coil wires as shown in **Figure 87**. Do not disconnect the wires. Insert the test leads between the bullet connectors as shown in **Figure 85**.

2B. On 20 and 25 hp two-cylinder models, locate the white/red, white/black and black pulser coil wires. The wires lead to the coil mounting location under the flywheel. Connect the meter test leads to the pulser coil wires as shown in **Figure 87**. Do not disconnect the wires. Insert the test leads between the bullet connectors as shown in **Figure 85**. These models use two pulser coils. Refer to **Table 12** for test lead connection points. Test lead polarity does not affect the test results.

2C. On 25 hp three-cylinder and 30-90 hp models, disconnect the pulser coil wire harness from the engine wire harness or CDI unit. Connect the test harness to the pulser coil harness and engine or CDI harness as shown in **Figure 86**. Connect the meter test leads to the test harness wire colors specified in **Table 12**. Test lead polarity does not affect the test results.

3. Refer to **Table 12** for the test specifications, then calibrate the multimeter to the correct peak AC voltage scale. Scale changes may be required to test at different engine speeds.

4. Start the engine and run it at fast idle until it reaches normal operating temperature. Record the output voltage while running the engine at the speeds listed in **Table 12**. To check the voltage at cranking speed, disconnect and ground the spark plug leads. Note the meter readings while operating the electric or manual starter. Repeat the test for models using a multiple pulser coils connection. Use the wire colors specified in **Table 12**.

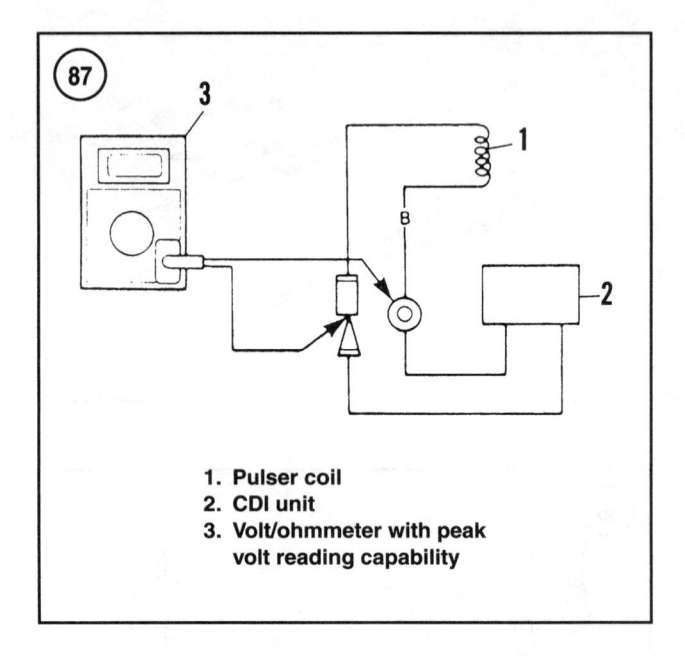

87
1. Pulser coil
2. CDI unit
3. Volt/ohmmeter with peak volt reading capability

5. If the pulser coil output does not meet or exceed the minimum specification in **Table 12** at each designated engine speed, replace the pulser coil as described in Chapter Six.

6. Disconnect the shop tachometer.

7. On 25 hp three-cylinder and 30-90 hp models, remove the test harness and reconnect the pulser coil harness.

Crankshaft Position Sensor Output Test

The crankshaft position sensor is used on 60-90 hp (except E60 and E75) models. A pulsating current is created as the flywheel teeth pass next to the sensor coil. The pulsating current is directed to the CDI unit to provide an rpm reference and crankshaft positioning for each cylinder relative to TDC. A fault with this sensor can cause no spark or intermittent spark at the coil.

Follow the test carefully to avoid misdiagnosis and unnecessary flywheel removal. Crankshaft position sensor output specifications are in **Table 13**. Perform this test under actual operating conditions or with the engine running in a suitable test tank. Use a test propeller if the engine will be run in a test tank.

A common meter with peak output voltage capability, or Yamaha part No. J-39299/90890-06752 and YU-39991/90890-03169, and an accurate shop tachometer are required for this test.

> *WARNING*
> *The ignition system produces very high voltage current. Never touch any part of your body to any test lead of the engine wiring*

TROUBLESHOOTING

while the flywheel is rotating. Never stand in water while testing or work around wiring or connections.

CAUTION
Never run an outboard without providing cooling water. Use either a test tank or run the engine under actual conditions. Install a test propeller to run the engine in a test tank.

1. Connect a shop tachometer to the engine. Follow the tachometer manufacturer's instructions.
2. Locate the crankshaft position sensor next to the flywheel (**Figure 80**). Trace the sensor blue/white and blue/red wires to the connection on the CDI unit harness.
3. Connect the meter test leads to the blue/white and blue/red sensor wire terminals. The CDI unit and crankshaft position sensor wire harnesses must remain connected for this test. Insert the test leads between the bullet connectors to contact the terminals (**Figure 85**). Test lead polarity does not affect the test results.
4. Refer to **Table 13** for the test specifications, then calibrate the multimeter to the correct peak AC voltage scale. Scale changes may be required to test at different engine speeds.
5. Start the engine and run it at fast idle until it reaches normal operating temperature. Record the output voltage while running the engine at the speeds listed in **Table 13**. Change the meter scale as required for the test specification. To check the voltage at cranking speed, disconnect and ground the spark plug leads. Note the meter readings while operating the electric or manual starter.
6. If the crankshaft position sensor output does not meet or exceed the minimum specification in **Table 13** at each designated engine speed, replace the sensor as described in Chapter Six.
7. Disconnect the shop tachometer.

CDI Unit

Failure of the CDI unit is relatively rare and replacement seldom corrects an ignition system malfunction. Replace the CDI unit if a constant or intermittent misfire has been verified with a spark tester and all other ignition system components and wiring test satisfactorily. Occasionally, the engine will experience a misfire only at higher engine speeds and all ignition components test correctly. Often, the misfire is caused by the overspeed prevention circuits in the CDI unit. The circuits initiate a misfire at a designated speed and higher. Normal operation resumes when the throttle is reduced enough to bring the engine rpm into the normal maximum range. An overspeed prevention system is used on Refer to **Table 15** to determine the maximum recommended operating speed. Refer to the following to determine the overspeed prevention activation speeds. On 20 and 25 hp two-cylinder models, the system activates at approximately 6300-6700 rpm. On 25 hp three cylinder and 30-90 hp models, the system activates at approximately 5800-6200 rpm.

If the overspeed prevention circuit may be causing a misfire, perform the following procedure.

1. Connect a shop tachometer to the engine following the manufacturer's instructions.
2. Observe the tachometer while an assistant operates the engine at the speed in which the misfire occurs.
3. Compare the engine speed with the specification in **Table 15**. Refer to the following for recommendations:
   a. If the engine is exceeding the maximum rated rpm, install a larger or higher pitch propeller to reduce engine speed (Chapter Eight).
   b. If the engine is well within the maximum rated rpm and is misfiring, test all components of the ignition and fuel systems. Replace the CDI unit only if all fuel and ignition system components test satisfactorily.
   c. If the engine is near the top of the maximum operating speed range and misfires intermittently, the engine is intermittently exceeding the maximum rated speed. Install the next larger or higher pitch propeller to prevent intermittent overspeed prevention.
   d. If the engine is near the bottom or below the maximum operating range and is misfiring, test all components of the ignition and fuel systems. Replace the CDI unit only if all fuel and ignition system components test satisfactorily.

CDI unit output test

The CDI unit converts alternating current from the flywheel and the ignition charge coil into direct current and stores it in a capacitor, then releases the charge to the correct ignition coil using input from the pulser coil and/or crankshaft position sensor. A faulty CDI unit can cause no spark on one or more of the cylinders. This test measures the peak voltage delivered to the ignition coil(s). Low output to one or more of the coils indicates a faulty pulser coil, crankshaft position sender or stop circuit. Test all of these components before performing this procedure.

Follow the test carefully to avoid misdiagnosis and part replacement. CDI unit output specifications are in **Table 14**. Perform this test under actual operating conditions or with the engine running in a suitable test tank. Use a test propeller if the engine will be run in a test tank.

A common meter with peak output voltage capability, or Yamaha part No. J-39299/90890-06752 and

YU-39991/90890-03169, and an accurate shop tachometer are required for this test.

Perform the output test with all wires connected.

WARNING
The ignition system produces very high voltage current. Never touch any part of your body to any test lead of the engine wiring while the flywheel is rotating. Never stand in water while testing or work around wet wiring or connections.

1. Connect a shop tachometer to the engine. Follow the tachometer manufacturer's instructions.
2. Connect the negative meter test lead to the black ground terminal for the ignition coil. Connect the positive meter test lead to the coil wire colors listed in **Table 14**. Insert the test leads between the bullet connectors as shown in **Figure 85**.
3. Refer to **Table 14** for the test specifications, then calibrate the multimeter to the correct peak AC voltage scale. Scale changes may be required to test at different engine speeds.
4. Start the engine and run it at fast idle until it reaches normal operating temperature. Record the output voltage while running the engine at the speeds listed in **Table 14**. Change the meter scale as required for the test specification. To check the voltage at cranking speed, disconnect and ground the spark plug leads. Note the meter readings while operating the electric or manual starter. Repeat the test using each pair of coil wires. Record the meter readings.
5. The CDI unit output should meet or exceed the minimum specification in **Table 14** at each designated engine speed. Refer to the following for repair recommendations.
   a. If the voltage is correct and there is no spark at the coil, check for faulty coil connections. Replace the coil if the connections are satisfactory.
   b. If there is no voltage, test all ignition system components and circuits as described in this chapter. Replace the CDI unit only if there is no spark, and all other components and circuits test correctly.
   c. If the voltage is low, test the ignition charge coil resistance and output, the stop circuit, the ignition coil resistance and the wiring. Replace the CDI unit only if all other ignition system components and circuits test satisfactorily.
6. Disconnect the shop tachometer.

TILT AND TRIM SYSTEM

Tilt and trim systems used on Yamaha outboards vary by model and horsepower.

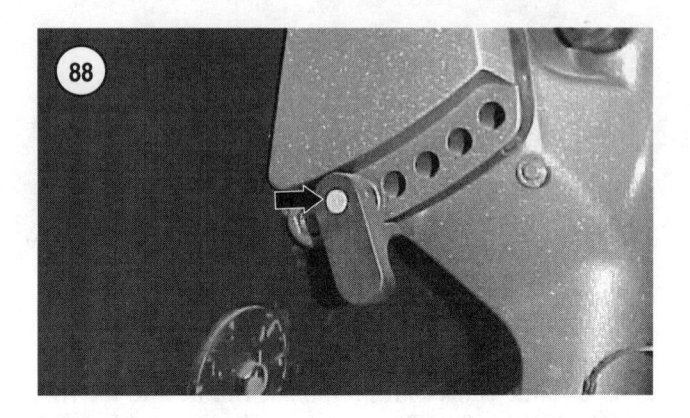

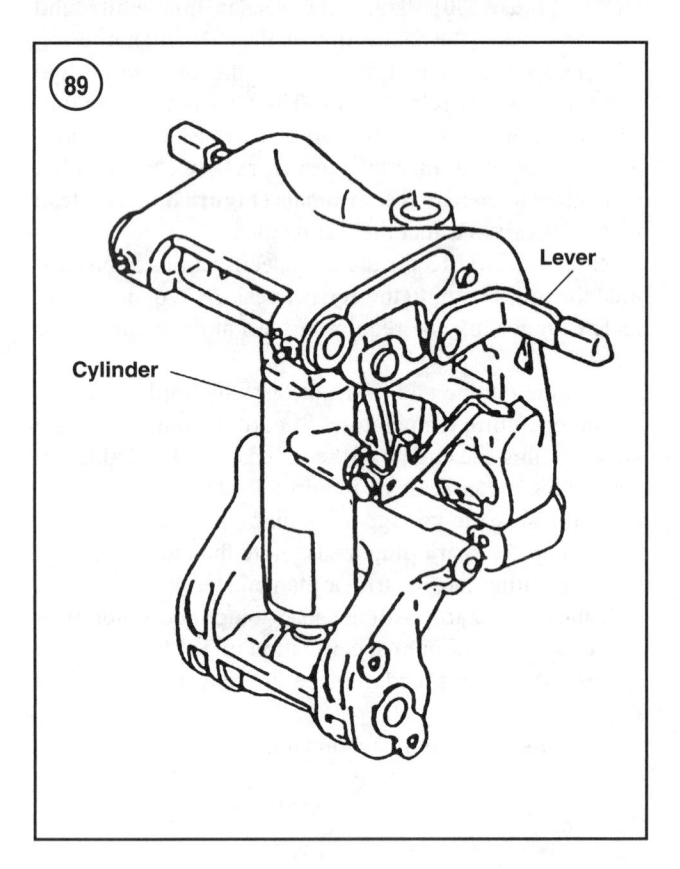

Tilt Pin and Reverse Lock Hook

A tilt pin (**Figure 88**) and reverse lock hook is used on 2-30 hp (except 28 jet) models. The tilt pin allows the engine to run slightly tilted in or out to change the running attitude of the boat or to enhance shallow water operation. The reverse lock hook prevents propeller thrust from moving the engine up or out in reverse gear. If the engine will not lock in reverse or cannot be tilted in forward or neutral gear, check for worn or damaged components. Refer to Chapter Eleven for information on repairing the reverse lock mechanism.

TROUBLESHOOTING

**SINGLE HYDRAULIC CYLINDER SYSTEM
(25 HP THREE-CYLINDER, 28 JET AND 30-50 HP MODELS)**

1. Electric motor
2. Hydraulic pump
3. Hydraulic cylinder

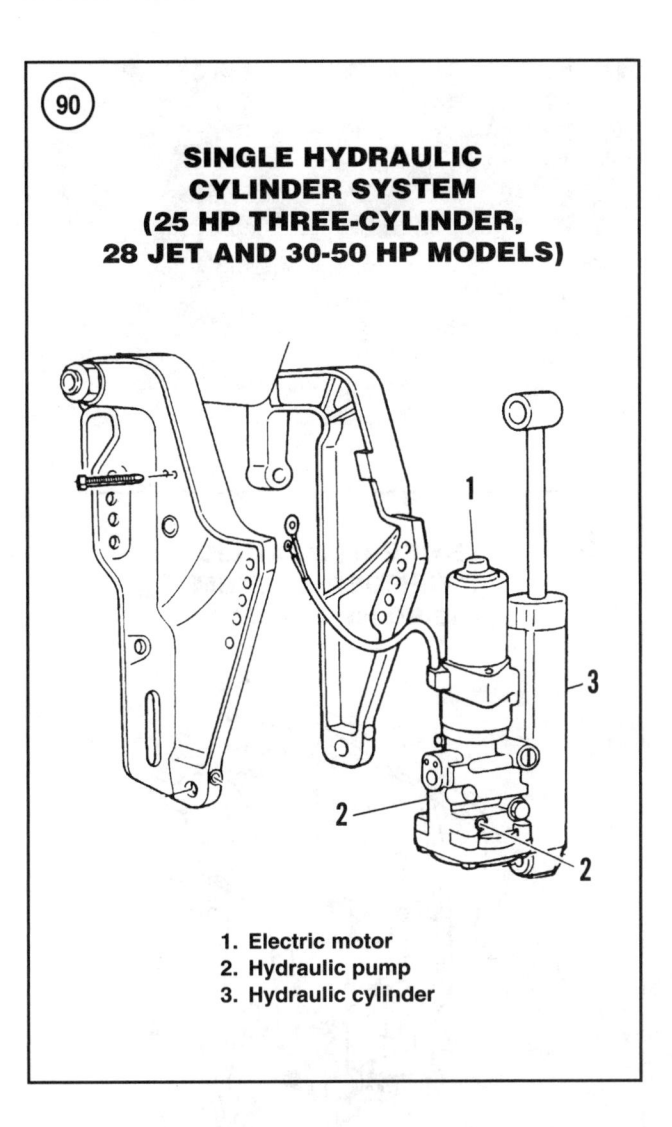

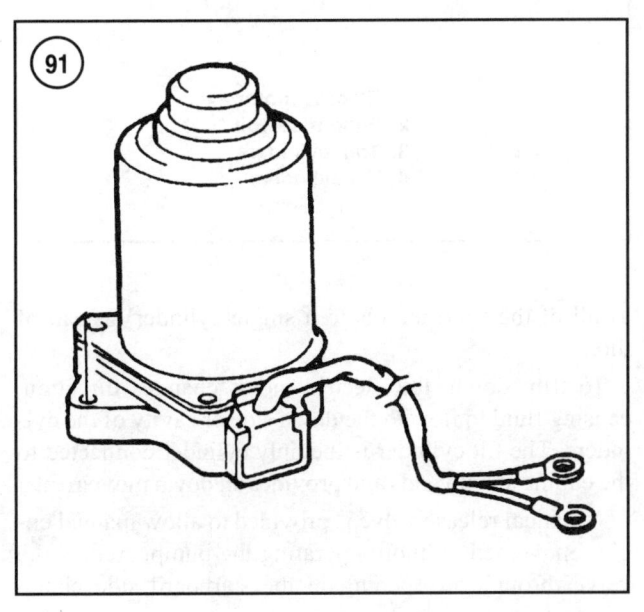

Manual Hydraulic Tilt

A manually operated hydraulic tilt system (**Figure 89**) is used on 28 jet, 35 jet and 40-90 hp models that are not equipped with power tilt and trim. This unit mounts between the clamp brackets in the same manner as power tilt and trim units. It provides hydraulic assistance for trailering or beaching the boat. It does not have enough force to trim out against the thrust of the propeller.

This system holds fluid under pressure in the hydraulic cylinder with internal valves. This allows the system to hold the engine in the tilt or trim position while underway or trailering. To change the trim or tilt system, move the lever to the released position, move the engine to the desired position then return the lever to the lock position.

Shock absorbing valves provide controlled fluid movement that allows the cylinder ram to extend at a controlled rate during impact with underwater objects. This system can help minimize impact damage.

The typical symptoms of a fault with this system include:
1. The engine tucks under while underway.
2. The engine trails out in reverse or when slowing down.
3. Leaking fluid.

This system is not serviceable. To troubleshoot the system, check the lever position. Replace the assembly if the lever is in the normal position and the fault still exists.

Single Cylinder Tilt/Trim System

A single cylinder electrically powered tilt and trim system is used on 25 hp three-cylinder, 28 jet and 30-50 hp models that are not equipped with a tilt pin and reverse lock hook or the manual hydraulic tilt system. The assembly mounts between the clamp brackets (**Figure 90**). It can move the engine up or out against propeller thrust, allowing the operator to change the running attitude while underway.

The major components include the electric motor, hydraulic pump and hydraulic cylinder. A bi-directional electric motor (**Figure 91**) drives the pump. Engine-mounted relays control the electric motor/pump rotation, reversing the motor direction controls fluid movement to and from the hydraulic cylinder. Fluid moves from the pump to the up side of the cylinder to trim the engine up. Fluid returns to the pump from the down side of the cylinder. Fluid is directed to the down side of the cylinder to trim the engine down. Fluid returns to the pump from the up side of the cylinder. The manual release valve (**Figure 92**) allows the engine to be moved up or down without operating the electric motor. If the system malfunctions, check the position of this valve first. Counterclockwise rotation releases the valve to move the engine. Clockwise rotation closes the valve to hold the engine in position.

Typical symptoms of a malfunction include:
1. The engine will not move up.
2. The engine will not move down.
3. The engine leaks down while trailering or tucks under while underway.
4. The engine trails out when in reverse or when slowing down.
5. Hydraulic fluid is leaking from the system.

If the electric motor is not operating, refer to troubleshooting procedures as described in this chapter. Replacement and repair of the electric motor is described in Chapter Eleven. If the motor is operating correctly and the above symptoms are present, check the fluid level and the manual release valve position as described in Chapter Eleven.

If both check satisfactorily, have the system repaired by a professional. Remove the system as described in Chapter Eleven and contact a Yamaha dealership for information. Removing the assembly from the engine can reduce expense and eliminate the inconvenience of transporting and storing the boat at the dealership.

Three Hydraulic Cylinder Tilt/Trim System

A three cylinder electrically powered tilt and trim system is used on 60-90 hp models that are not equipped with the manually operated hydraulic tilt system. The assembly mounts between the clamp brackets (**Figure 93**). It can move the engine up or out against propeller thrust, allowing the operator to change running attitude while underway.

The major components of the system include the bi-rotational electric motor and pump, fluid reservoir, trim cylinders and tilt cylinder. Engine-mounted relays control the electric motor/pump rotation. Reversing the motor direction controls fluid movement within the system. Fluid moves into the up side or up cavity of both trim rams and the tilt cylinder to trim up from a fully down position. The ends of the trim cylinder rams contact striker plates on the swivel housing. Fluid pressure causes all three hydraulic cylinders to extend and raise the engine. Frequently apply a coat of water resistant grease to the ends of the trim cylinder rams to prevent noisy operation while trimming up. When the trim cylinders reach the limit of extension, the tilt cylinder remains the only means for raising the engine further. Less power is then developed in the up direction as only one cylinder drives the system. This has an effect of limiting the trim range while underway at higher engine speeds. The engine will, however, have a greater tilt speed as all of the fluid travels to a single cylinder instead of three.

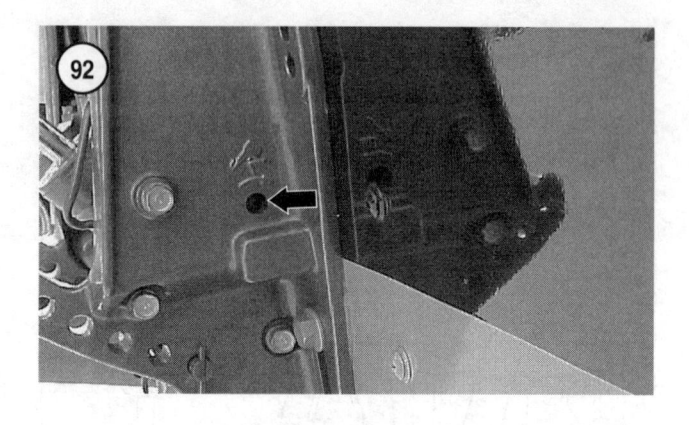

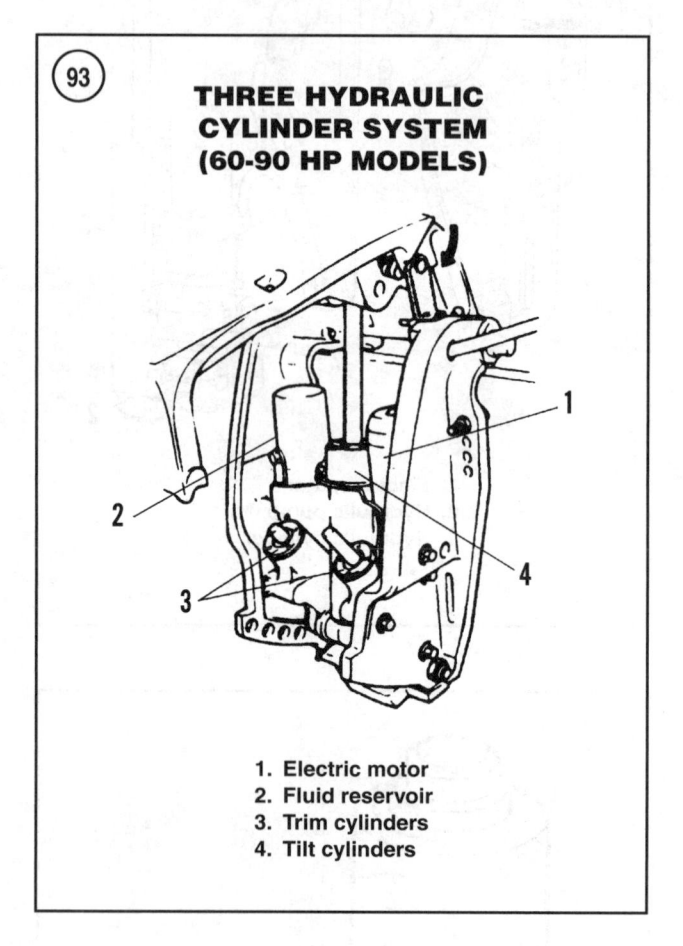

To trim down, the electric motor changes direction, causing fluid to flow to the down side or cavity of the cylinders. The tilt cylinder is the only cylinder connected to the engine at both ends and provides all down movement.

A manual release valve is provided to allow manual engine movement without operating the pump. Access the valve through an opening in the starboard side clamp

TROUBLESHOOTING

Figure 94: TILT/TRIM RELAY UNIT
- Terminal No. 1
- Positive
- Negative
- Terminal No. 2
- Sky blue
- Light green
- Black

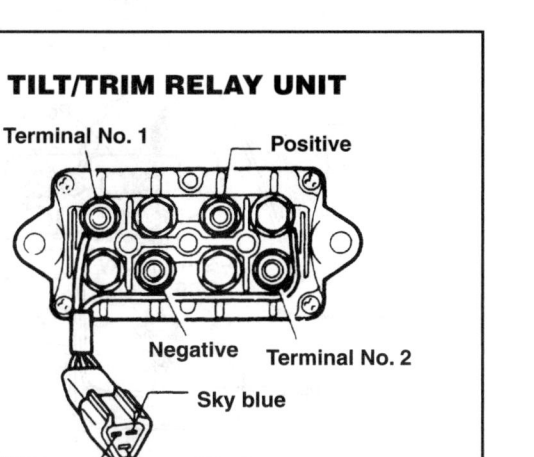

bracket. If the system malfunctions, check the position of this valve first. Counterclockwise rotation releases the valve to move the engine. Clockwise rotation closes the valve to hold the engine in position.

Typical symptoms of a malfunction include:
1. The engine will not move up.
2. The engine will not move down.
3. The engine leaks down from the tilt position only.
4. The engine tucks under while underway.
5. The engine trails out when in reverse or when slowing down.
6. Hydraulic fluid is leaking from the system.

If the electric motor is not operating, troubleshoot the electric part of the system as described in this section. Replacement and repair of the electric motor is described in Chapter Eleven. If the motor is operating correctly and the above symptoms are present, check the fluid level and the manual release valve position as described in Chapter Eleven.

If both check satisfactorily, have the system repaired by a professional. Removing the assembly from the engine can reduce expenses and eliminate the inconvenience of transporting and storing the boat at the dealership.

Electrical Tests

The major electrical components of the tilt/trim system include the electric motor, relay unit, trim position sender and switches. The bi-directional motor has a blue and a green wire. When the up trim or tilt is selected, the blue wire is connected to the positive battery terminal via wires and the relays. The green wire is connected to ground and the negative terminal by the same means. The electric motor and pump rotate in the direction that moves fluid to the up side of the cylinders. When the down direction is selected, the relays reverse the wire connection and motor rotation. A remote control, dash-mounted, tiller control or engine-mounted switch controls the relays. The red switch wire supplies battery voltage to the switch. When the switch is in the up position, the red wire connects to the blue wire contact in the switch. The blue wire directs the battery current to the up relay. When the switch is in the down position, the red wire connects to the green wire contact in the switch. The green wire directs the battery current to the down relay.

When battery current is supplied to either relay, the relay directs the current to the electric motor. The other relay provides the connection to ground for the electric motor. When energized, the relay opens the ground connection. Both relays must make the proper connection for the electric motor to operate.

The models covered in this manual use a single assembly that houses both relays (**Figure 94**). If either relay fails, replace the assembly.

If the trim motor fails to run in either direction, check for a blown fuse and disconnected or faulty wiring. Then test the trim switch and relay unit as described in this section to verify that the trim switch is supplying current to the relays and the relays are supplying current to the electric motor. Repair or replace the electric motor if all other components test correctly and the electric motor will not operate.

If the trim motor only fails to run in one direction, test the trim switches and relay unit as described in this section. A fault with the motor is unlikely. If the motor is able to operate in one direction, it can usually operate in the other.

Relay continuity test

A common multimeter is required for this procedure.
1. Remove the relay unit from the engine as described in Chapter Eleven. Refer to **Figure 94** for this procedure.
2. Calibrate the ohmmeter to the R × 1 scale.
3. Connect the positive meter test lead to the sky blue terminal connection. Connect the negative meter test lead to the black terminal connection. If the meter indicates no continuity, the relay unit has failed open and must be replaced.
4. Connect the positive test lead to the light green terminal connection. Connect the negative test lead to the black terminal connection. If the meter indicates no continuity, the relay unit has failed open and must be replaced.
5. Connect the positive test lead to terminal No. 1 on the relay unit. Connect the negative test lead to the negative terminal on the relay. If the meter indicates no continuity, the relay unit has failed open and must be replaced.
6. Connect the positive test lead to terminal No. 2 on the relay. Connect the negative test lead to the negative termi-

nal on the relay. If the meter indicates no continuity, the relay unit has failed open and must be replaced.

7. Connect the positive test lead to terminal No. 1 on the relay unit. Connect the negative test lead to the positive terminal on the relay. If the meter indicates continuity, the relay is shorted internally and must be replaced.

8. Connect the positive test lead to terminal No. 2 on the relay unit. Connect the negative test lead to the positive terminal on the relay. If the meter indicates continuity, the relay is shorted internally and must be replaced.

9. Perform an operational test on the relay unit as described in this chapter.

Relay operational test

A multimeter, jumper wires and a fully charged battery are required for this procedure. Refer to **Figure 95** for this procedure.

1. Remove the relay unit as described in Chapter Eleven.
2. Calibrate the meter to the R × 1 scale.
3. Use jumper wires to connect the positive battery terminal to the light green terminal and the negative battery terminal to the black terminal. Connect the positive test lead to the positive terminal on the relay. Connect the negative meter test lead to the negative terminal on the relay. If the meter indicates continuity, the relay is not switching internally and must be replaced. Disconnect the jumper wires then the meter test leads.
4. Use the jumper wires to connect the positive battery terminal to the sky blue terminal and the negative battery terminal to the black terminal. Connect the positive test lead to the negative terminal on the relay. Connect the negative test lead to terminal No. 1 on the relay unit. If the meter indicates no continuity, the relay is not switching internally and must be replaced.
5. Disconnect the jumper wires then the meter test leads.
6. Install the relay unit as described in Chapter Eleven.

Tilt/trim switch test

The tilt and trim system is controlled by a three-position switch mounted on the remote control handle, dash, tiller handle, engine cover or other locations in the boat. Most boats have two or more switches. Testing procedures are similar for all switches. This rocker type switch is spring loaded to center in the off position. Activate the up or down direction by moving the switch to the desired direction. A fused wire supplies battery current to the switch. Check the fuse before testing the switch. Refer to *Fuses and Wire Harness* in this chapter for the procedure.

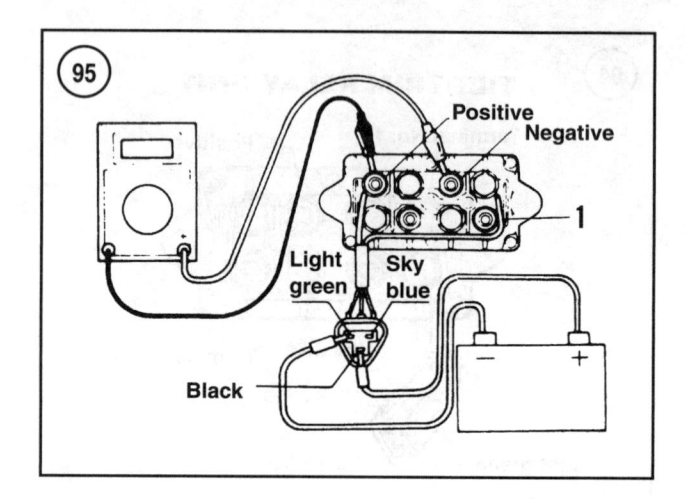

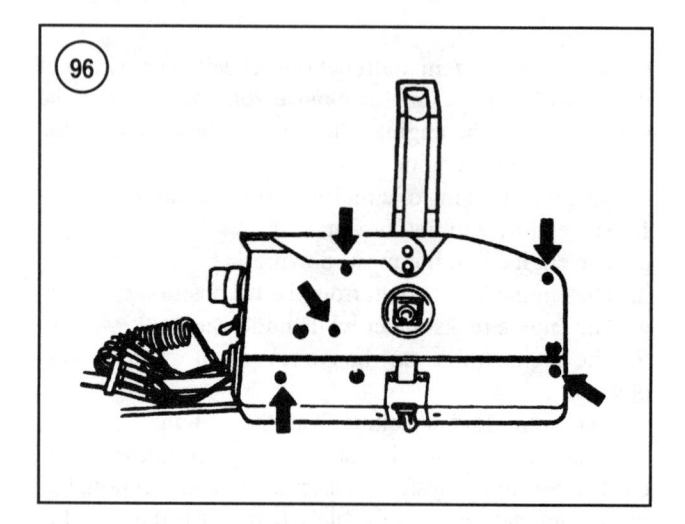

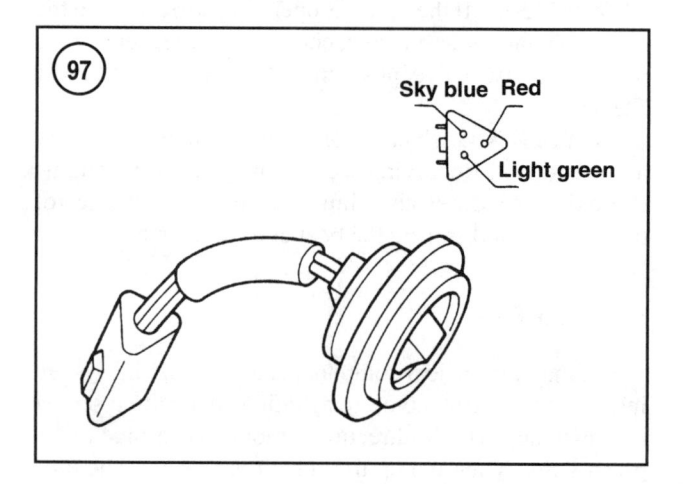

If the system fails to operate properly only when operating a single switch, test only that switch. If the system is not functioning when operating multiple switches, check for a blown fuse, faulty wiring, faulty relay or trim

TROUBLESHOOTING

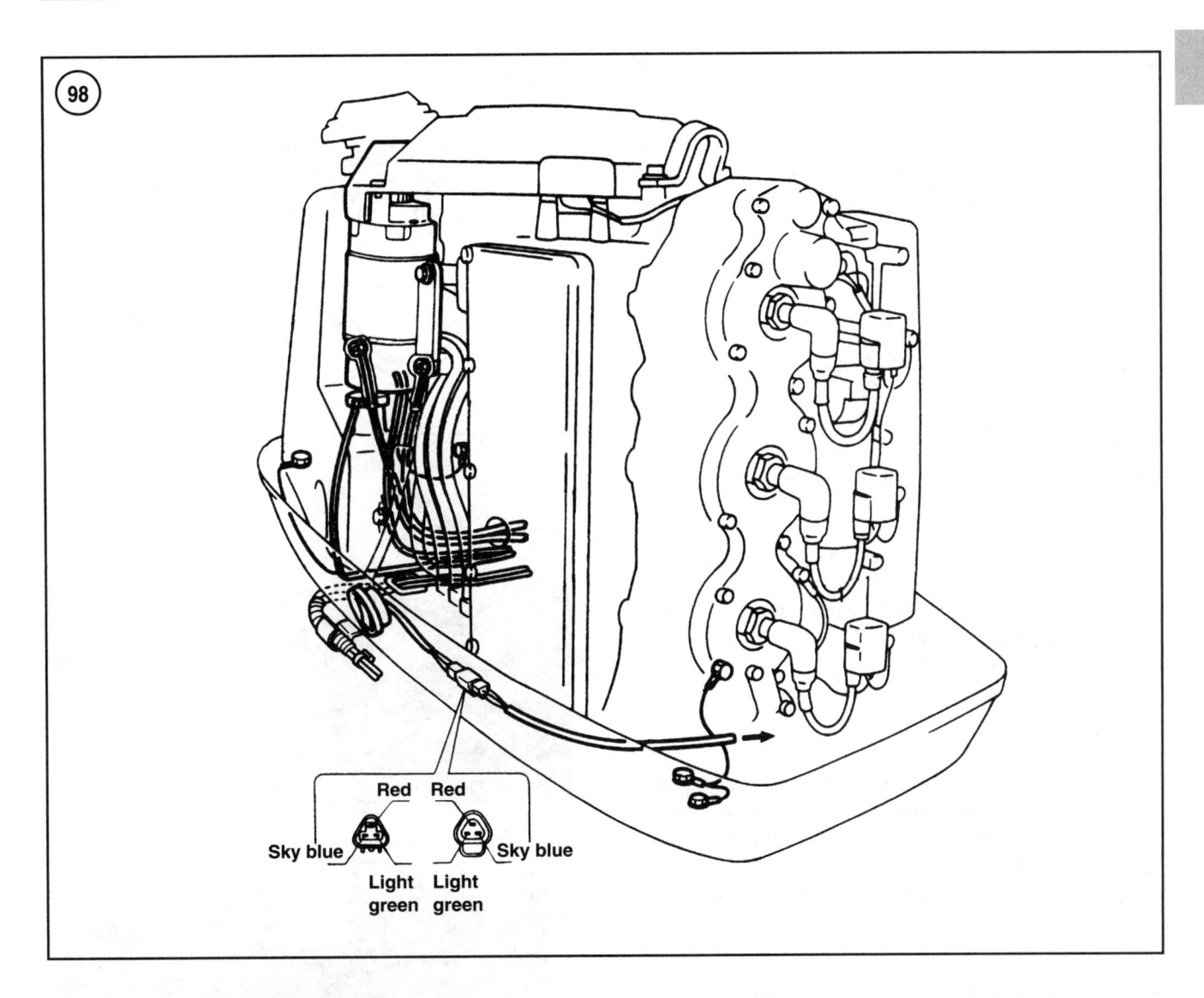

98

Red Red
Sky blue Sky blue
Light Light
green green

motor. Multiple switch failure can prevent the trim system from operating properly by activating both relays simultaneously. Disconnect the trim switches one at a time and check for proper operation. Test the switch if the system operates properly when that switch is disconnected.

A multimeter is required for this procedure.

1. Disconnect the battery cables.

2A. For a remote control mounted switch, remove the remote control and back cover (**Figure 96**) as described in Chapter Thirteen. Locate and disconnect the trim switch wires from the remote control harness.

2B. For a dash mounted switch, disconnect the trim switch wires from the instrument harness. Remove the switch from the dash if necessary for better access to the wire terminals (**Figure 97**).

2C. For a engine cover or tiller control mounted switch, locate and disconnect the trim switch wires (**Figure 98**) from the engine wire harness.

3. Calibrate the meter to the R × 1 scale. Do not connect test leads to the remote control, trim relay or engine wire harness.

4. Connect the positive test lead to the red wire pin on the switch. Connect the negative test lead to the sky blue wire pin on the switch. The meter should indicate no continuity with the switch in the OFF and DOWN positions. The meter should indicate continuity with the switch in the UP position. Replace the switch if it fails to perform as specified.

5. Connect the positive test lead to the red wire pin on the switch. Connect the negative test lead to the light green wire pin on the switch. The meter should indicate no continuity with the switch in the OFF and UP positions. The

meter should indicate continuity with the switch in the DOWN positions. Replace the switch if it fails to perform as specified.

6. Connect the positive test lead to the sky blue wire pin on the switch. Connect the negative test lead to the light green wire pin to the switch. If the meter indicates continuity when the switch is toggled to any of the three positions, the switch is shorted internally and must be replaced.

7A. For a remote control mounted switch, reconnect the trim switch wires, then route the wires to prevent interference with moving components. Install the back cover and remote control as described in Chapter Thirteen.

7B. For a dash mounted switch, install the switch if it was removed to access the wires. Reconnect the trim switch wires. Secure the wires with plastic locking clamps to prevent entanglement with other components.

7C. For an engine cover or tiller control mounted switch, connect the trim switch (**Figure 98**) to the engine wire harness. Route the wires to prevent interference with moving components. Secure the wires with plastic locking type clamps as necessary.

8. Connect the battery cables.

Trim position sender test

The trim position sender (**Figure 99**) is mounted on the inside of the port clamp bracket. The arm of the sender contacts the swivel bracket and moves as the engine tilts up and down. Movement of the arm changes the sender resistance and results in a varying voltage to the dash mounted gage. The voltage and gauge reading correspond to the engine tilt/trim angle. A multimeter is required to test the sender.

1. Remove the trim position sender as described in Chapter Eleven.
2. Calibrate an ohmmeter to measure 360-540 ohms of resistance.
3. Connect the positive test lead to the pink sender wire pin (**Figure 99**). Connect the negative test lead to the black sender wire pin. Note the meter reading while *slowly* moving the sender arm to the full range of travel. The resistance reading should change smoothly. The highest meter reading should not exceed 540 ohms and the lowest meter reading should not fall below 360 ohms. Replace the sender if the meter reading is erratic or the reading exceeds the specification.
4. Calibrate an ohmmeter to measure 800-1200 ohms of resistance.
5. Connect the positive test lead to the orange sender wire pin (**Figure 99**). Connect the negative test lead to the black sender wire pin. Note the meter reading while *slowly* moving the sender arm to the full range of travel. The resistance reading should change smoothly. The highest meter reading should not exceed 1200 ohms and the lowest meter reading should not fall below 800 ohms. Replace the sender if the meter reading is erratic or the reading exceeds the specification.

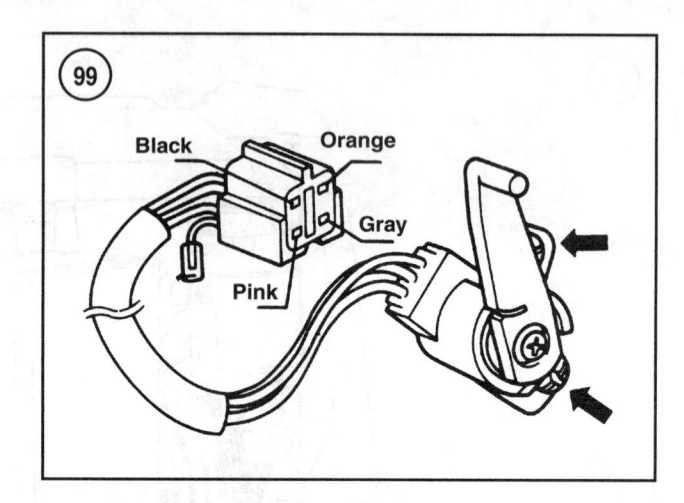

6. Install the trim position sender as described in Chapter Eleven. Adjust the sender as described in Chapter Four.

TROUBLESHOOTING

(**Figure 100**) or aluminum deposits (**Figure 101**) and perform a compression test as described in this chapter. Disassemble and inspect the power head if there is a problem with the compression or if there are aluminum deposits or physical damage on the spark plug(s).

A whirring noise that is most pronounced as the throttle is decreased is usually related to a problem with crankshaft and rod bearings. The bearing between the connecting rod and crankshaft may have failed. Improper storage preparation can lead to corrosion at the contact surfaces of the needle bearings (**Figure 102**). The contact surfaces may later develop ridges. Only major repair to the power head will correct this problem.

Sometimes a mechanics stethoscope (**Figure 103**) can help identify the probelm cylinder. Compare the noise from one area of the power head with noise from the same area but different cylinder. If the problem is related to a piston or rings, the noise will be more pronounced when the stethoscope probe contacts that cylinder head area. The noise will be more pronounced when the probe contacts the crankcase if the problem is related to that crankshaft or connecting rod.

Lubrication Failure

Insufficient lubrication will result in damage to internal components and possible power head failure. Insufficient lubrication is caused by not properly adding oil to the fuel on a premix model or failure of the automatic oil injection system. In either case, the engine will probably operate fine for a few minutes, then begin to slow down. The engine may eventually stall and not crank over with the starter. The engine may start after cooling down but will probably slow down and stop again. Continued operation will result in power head failure.

If the engine may have run without sufficient lubrication, perform a compression test as described in this chapter. The top cylinders generally suffer the most damage when oil is lacking or overheating has occurred. Disassemble and inspect the power head components. Insufficient lubrication normally causes the crankshaft and connecting rod components to have a bluish tinge. The pistons and cylinder wall may develop scuffing (**Figure 104**) and scoring, particularly near the exhaust port areas. Crankshaft seals may also look burned and the crankshaft components may not have a normal oil film. Take a sample of the fuel from the carburetor bowl on premix models. Apply a small amount of fuel to a white piece of cardboard and allow it to dry in a safe area. Residual oil in the fuel sample should leave a blue stain on the cardboard. This does not mean the oil was mixed in the proper ratio or that oil was present in the fuel in the carburetor at the ex-

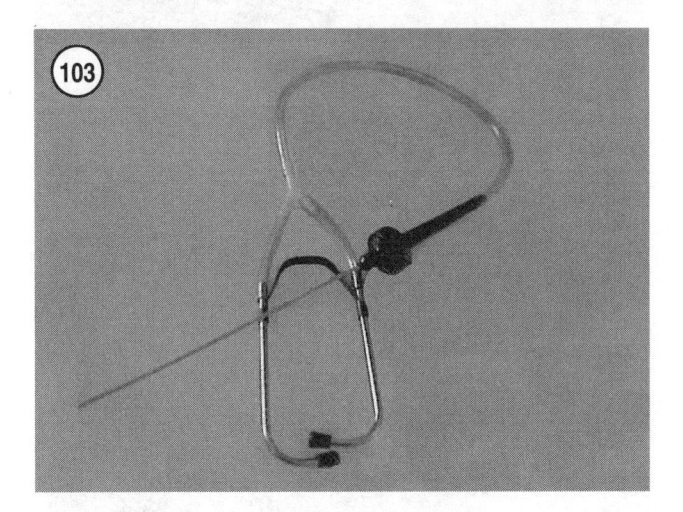

POWER HEAD

CAUTION
Operating an engine with an unusual noise may result in increased damage that renders a power head repair impossible.

This section covers power head testing and troubleshooting including engine noises, lubrication failure, detonation, preignition, engine seizure and water entering the cylinder(s).

Engine Noises

Some noise will occur in the power head during normal operation, but a ticking noise or a heavy knocking noise that intensifies when under heavy load (accelerating) may indicate a problem. A ticking noise commonly occurs when one or more of the cylinders has failed. The noise is generally caused by a piece of piston ring that has been embedded in the piston dome and is striking the cylinder head. Inspect the spark plug for damage

act time of failure. An improper fuel/oil mixture can result in excessive oil one minute and insufficient oil the next. On oil injected models, test and inspect the *entire* oil injection system if power head failure has occurred and insufficient lubrication may have been the cause.

Detonation

Detonation damage (**Figure 105**) is cause by heat and pressure in the combustion chamber becoming too great for the fuel. Fuel normally burns at a controlled rate that produces the expanding gasses to drive the piston down on the power stroke. If conditions in the engine allow heat and pressure to get too high, the fuel may explode violently. These violent explosions will cause serious damage to the piston and other power head components. Carbon deposits, overheating, lean fuel conditions, over advanced timing and lugging are some problems that lead to detonation. The octane rating of the fuel used must meet or exceed the octane requirement for the engine. Never use a fuel with lower than the recommended octane rating. It may cause detonation under normal operating conditions.

During detonation, the combustion chamber temperature and pressure rise dramatically, creating a strong shock wave that is often called a spark knock. Due to the normal noise generated by a two-stroke outboard engine, the noise may not be detectable while under way. If detonation occurs, the engine looses power and will idle roughly or stall. The engine may seize if the damage is great enough. A compression test will probably reveal that one or move cylinders has low compression. Inspect the spark plug(s) when they have been removed for the compression test. Aluminum deposits (**Figure 101**) are a sign of serious piston damage. Complete power head repair is required if detonation has occurred. Refer to Chapter Seven.

Preignition

Preignition is the premature ignition of the air/fuel charge in the combustion chamber. Preignition is caused by hot spots in the combustion chamber. Wrong heat range spark plugs, carbon deposits and inadequate cooling are some causes of preignition. Preignition will result in loss of power and eventually lead to serious damage to the piston and other power head components. Preignition may lead to detonation as the early ignition causes the heat and pressure in the combustion chamber to rise dramatically. Typically the piston suffers the most damage. Often the preignition causes localized heating in the piston dome that eventually heats the material to the melting point, causing a hole to form in the piston dome (**Figure 106**). A compression test and spark plug inspection will probably reveal low compression and aluminum deposits consistent with detonation failure.

TROUBLESHOOTING

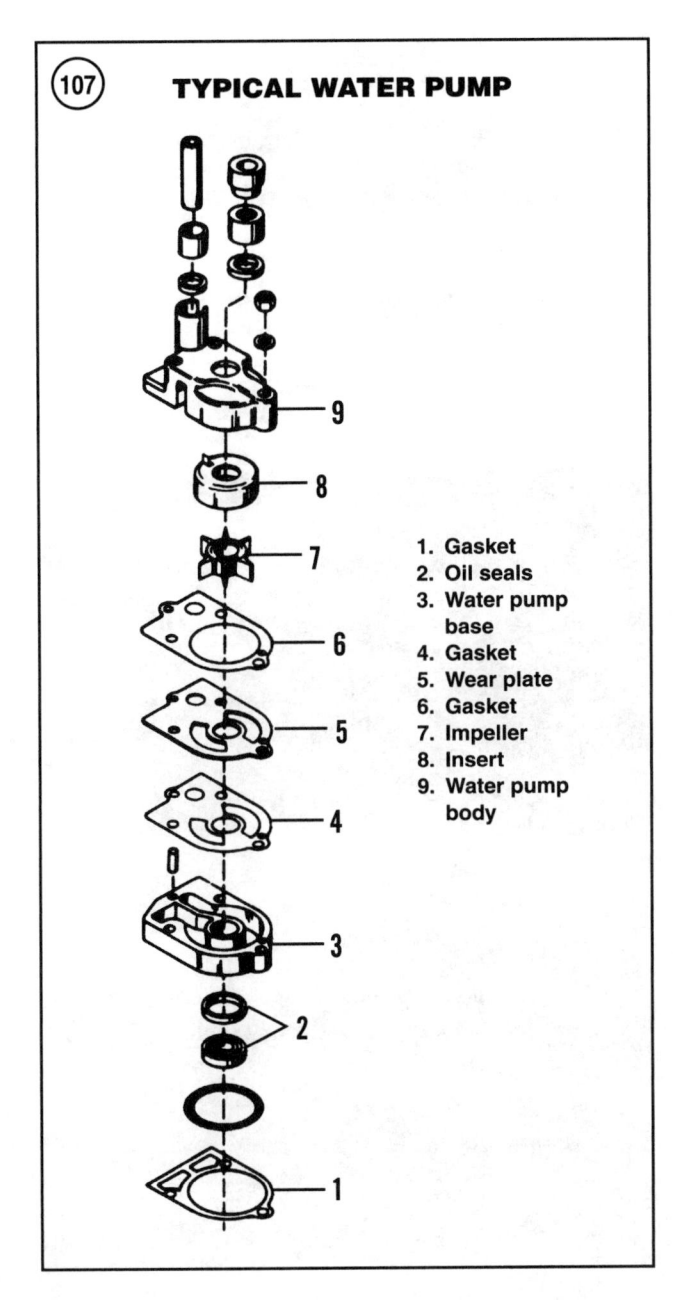

TYPICAL WATER PUMP

1. Gasket
2. Oil seals
3. Water pump base
4. Gasket
5. Wear plate
6. Gasket
7. Impeller
8. Insert
9. Water pump body

nation (Chapter Three) or check the jet pump for debris lodged in the impeller. If necessary, remove the gearcase (Chapter Eight) or jet pump (Chapter Nine) and check for flywheel rotation. Disassemble and inspect the power head if the flywheel cannot be rotated with the gearcase or jet pump removed. Always remove the manual starter if applicable (Chapter Ten) to check for flywheel rotation. The manual starter or lockout assembly can fail and prevent flywheel rotation.

Water Entering the Cylinder

Water can enter the cylinder from a number of areas. Water in the fuel, water entering through the carburetor, a leaking exhaust plate/cover and gaskets, a leaking cylinder head gasket and internal cylinder block flaws are some of the common causes. The typical symptom is rough running particularly at idle. The engine may run satisfactorily at higher engine speed. Water intrusion is normally discovered when the spark plug(s) are removed for inspection. Remove the cylinder head and exhaust cover if water or a white deposit is found on any of the plugs. The wet cylinder will usually have significantly less carbon deposits on the cylinder head and piston dome. The steam formed during combustion removes carbon deposits. Continued operation with water entering the cylinder will result in power head failure. Inspect the cylinder head gasket, cylinder head, exhaust plate and exhaust cover gaskets. A black or white deposit over a sealing surface or physical damage to the gasket indicates the point of the leak. Internal leakage due to a cylinder flaw can be difficult if not impossible to locate. Small cracks, pin holes and voids in the material may not be visually apparent and may not leak until the engine reaches normal operating temperature. Replace the cylinder block if water is entering the cylinder and no other causes are found. Refer to Chapter Seven for power head repair procedures.

Engine Seizure

Although the power head can seize at any operating speed, seizure at high speed is unlikely. The condition causing the seizure will result in a gradual loss of power and engine speed. The most common cause of engine seizure is power head failure, usually caused by detonation or preignition. Always inspect the gearcase or jet pump before removing and disassembling the power head. Gearcase or jet pump failure can prevent the crankshaft from rotating leading one to believe the power head has seized. Inspect the gearcase lubricant for metal contami-

COOLING SYSTEM

Water is drawn in by a water pump (**Figure 107**, typical) that is mounted on the gearcase or jet pump. The pump supplies water to the exhaust area of the power head first, then to the cylinder head and cylinder block. The water exits the power head near the power head mounting surface and travels out through the drive shaft housing. As the water travels through the power head, it absorbs heat and carries it away. If the engine is overheating, the water is not flowing through the power head with sufficient volume or is not absorbing the heat adequately.

Most models are equipped with a thermostat (**Figure 108**) to help maintain a minimum power head temperature. The thermostat by restricts exiting water until a minimum temperature is reached.

A stream of water (**Figure 109**) is visible at the rear of the lower engine cover when the water is exiting the power head. The fitting for the stream will commonly become blocked with debris and cease flowing. Clean the opening with a small stiff wire brush. Inspect the cooling system as described in this chapter if the water stream does not appear after the fitting has been cleaned.

Cooling System Inspection

Inspect the water pump if overheating is noticed on the temperature gauge, the water stream is weak or missing, or the overheat alarm sounds. Water pump disassembly, inspection and assembly procedures are in Chapter Eight.

Inspect and test the thermostat if overheating is occurring and the water pump checks satisfactorily. Refer to *Thermostat Testing* in this section.

Remove the water jacket covers and inspect the cooling system passages for debris or deposits if the engine is overheating and no problem can be found with the water pump or thermostat. Rocks, pieces of a failed water pump impeller, sand, shells and other debris may restrict water flow.

Salt, calcium or other deposits can form in the cooling passages, restricting water flow and preventing efficient heat transfer. Use a cleaner specifically designed to remove cooling system deposits. Make sure the cleaner is suitable for use on aluminum material. Always follow the manufacturer's instructions when using one of these products. These cleaners are usually available at marine specialty stores. Water jacket, thermostat and exhaust cover removal and installation procedures are in Chapter Seven.

Verifying Engine Temperature

If overheating is suspected, verify the engine temperature using Thermomelt sticks (**Figure 110**). They are made of material formulated to melt at a specified temperature. Mark the cylinder head near the thermoswitch (Chapter Six) with the sticks. On engines not equipped with an alarm system, hold the stick in contact with the cylinder head near the spark plug opening. The mark or stick melts if the surface reaches the temperature listed on the stick. Check the temperature during or immediately after the suspected overheating occurs. Use different temperature sticks to determine the approximate engine temperature. Stop the engine if the temperature exceeds 90° C (194° F) to avoid damaging the power head.

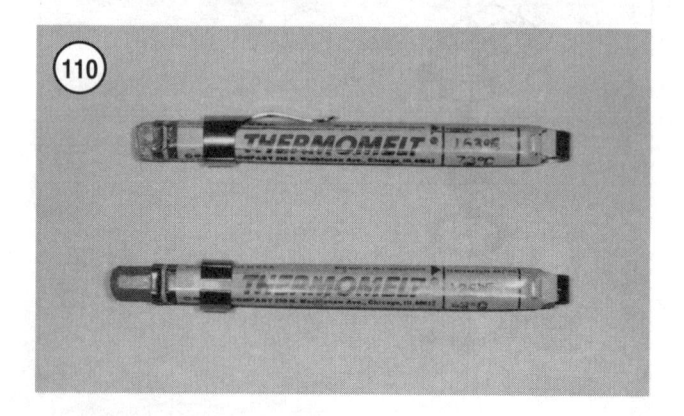

Perform this test with the boat in the water and running under actual conditions. Operating the engine unloaded in neutral gear may not generate enough heat to test the cooling system. Do not troubleshoot the cooling system while running the engine using a flush/test adapter. The volume of water flowing through the hose may not be the same as the water supplied by the water pump under normal conditions. Troubleshooting with a flush/test adapter may mask

TROUBLESHOOTING

mometer, piece of string and a container of water that can be heated is required for this procedure.

1. Remove the thermostat as described in Chapter Seven.
2. Tie the string to the thermostat and suspend the thermostat in the container of water (**Figure 111**).
3. Place the thermometer in the water and begin heating the water. Observe the thermostat and thermometer.
4. Note the temperature at which the thermostat begins to open (**Figure 112**). This should occur at 48-52° C (118-126° F).
5. Observe the thermostat and thermometer while continuing to heat the water. The thermostat should be fully open at approximately 60° C (140° F).
6. Allow the container of water to completely cool, then remove the thermostat. The thermostat should completely close when cooled to room temperature.
7. Replace the thermostat if it fails to close at room temperature or opens above or below the specified temperature.
8. Install the thermostat as described in Chapter Seven.

GEARCASE

Problems with the gearcase are generally related to leaks and failed internal components. Symptoms include unusual noise, shifting difficulty or slipping under load.

At the first sign of a problem, check the gearcase lubricant level and condition as described in Chapter Three. If the lubricant level is low or water is in the lubricant, pressure test the gearcase as described in Chapter Eight. If there are an excessive amount of larger metal particles in the lubricant (**Figure 113**), disassemble and inspect the gearcase as described in Chapter Eight.

Water in the Gearcase

Under certain conditions, a small amount of water may be present in the gearcase lubricant. The possible conditions included a gearcase that has not received normal maintenance for several years and has been stored with the gearcase in the water. Only a pressure test will determine if a faulty seal, gasket, O-ring or other components are allowing water into the gearcase. Gearcase pressure testing is described in Chapter Eight. Failure to correct the leak will eventually lead to extensive damage to internal gearcase components.

Lubricant Leaks

The presence of lubricant on the exterior of or on the surface below the gearcase indicates a leak. Pressure test

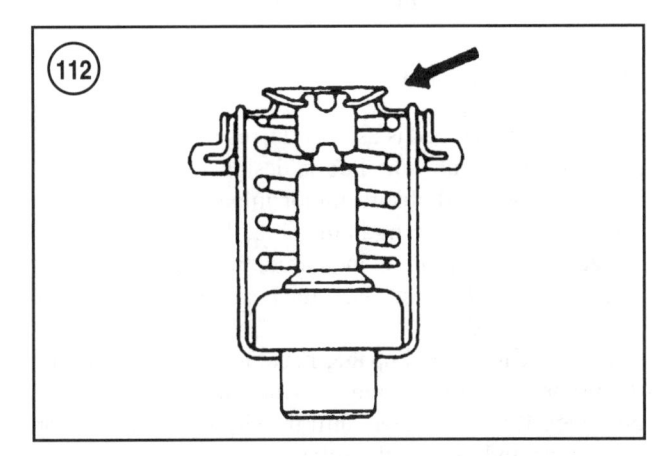

a real problem on smaller engines or cause overheating at high engine speeds with larger engines.

Thermostat Test

Test the thermostat if the engine is overheating or is unable to reach normal operating temperature. A liquid ther-the gearcase if there is a leak. Gearcase pressure testing is described in Chapter Eight. Failure to correct the leak will result in failure of the gears and bearings or the gearcase due to insufficient lubrication. Under certain conditions, the gearcase may vent lubricant through the shift shaft seal. This occurs if the gearcase is over-filled with lubricant and exposed to intense sunlight for an extended period of time. Over-filling prevents the formation of an air pocket at the top of the drive shaft bore. Lack of an air pocket will force fluid past the seal due to heat expansion. If there is a leak, pressure test the gearcase as described in Chapter Eight and refill the gearcase to the proper level as described in Chapter Three.

Knocking or Grinding Noise

Gearcase noise does occur during normal operation. Normal gearcase noise is barely noticeable. If a knocking or grinding noise is coming from the gearcase, gears or other components in the gearcase may be damaged. An inspection of the gearcase lubricant will reveal large metal particles. The gears may have been damaged by the propeller hitting an underwater object or from shifting into gear at high engine speed.

High-Pitched Whine

A high-pitched whine normally indicates a bearing problem or the gears are running out of alignment. The only way to verify a problem is to disassemble the gearcase and inspect the components (Chapter Eight). Occasionally, a high-pitched whine is created by the propeller during normal operation. Try a different, but suitable, propeller to check for this condition. On high-speed applications, a damaged propeller, gearcase housing or boat bottom can generate a hydro-dynamic vibration that causes a whine. Repair damaged components or surfaces.

Gearcase Vibration

Never run an engine with severe gearcase vibration as it places added stress on the gears, bearings and other gearcase components. Excessive vibration can compromise the durability of the entire engine. A damaged propeller or a bent propeller shaft often causes vibration.

A propeller can appear perfect but still be out of balance. Have the propeller trued and balanced at a reputable propeller repair shop or try a different, but suitable, propeller.

Always check for a bent propeller shaft if a vibration occurs. A bent propeller shaft is usually the result of an impact with an underwater object or other damage to the gearcase. Inspection of the propeller shaft and other components is described in Chapter Eight.

Slipping Under Load

Slipping under load is usually the result of failure of the propeller drive hub. The hub is designed to cushion the shifting action and absorb minor impact damage. If the propeller hub is spinning in the bore, the engine rpm will increase as the throttle is increased, but the boat will not increase speed. In most cases, the boat will not accelerate to planing speed.

To check for hub slippage, make a reference mark on the propeller shaft that aligns with a mark made on the propeller. Run the engine until the slippage occurs. Stop the engine and inspect the reference marking alignment. Have a new hub installed by a reputable propeller repair shop if the markings are not aligned after the engine has been run.

Shifting Difficulty

Hard shifting or difficulty engaging a gear is usually the result of improperly adjusted shift linkages or cables. Adjust the linkages and cables as described in Chapter Four. Disassemble and inspect the shifting components in the gearcase if shifting problems cannot be corrected with proper adjustment. Gearcase disassembly and inspection are described in Chapter Eight.

TROUBLESHOOTING

Table 1 STARTING SYSTEM TROUBLESHOOTING

Symptom	Possible causes	Corrective action
Electric starter does not energize	Engine not in neutral gear	Shift into NEUTRAL gear
	Weak or discharged battery	Test or charge the battery (Chapter Six)
	Dirty or corroded battery terminals	Thoroughly clean battery terminals
	Faulty neutral switch	Test neutral switch
	Faulty electric starter button	Test starter button
	Faulty ignition key switch	Test ignition key switch
	Faulty starter relay	Test starter relay
	Loose or dirty starter wire connection	Clean and tighten starter wire connections
	Faulty electric starter	Repair the electric starter
Electric starter engages flywheel (flywheel rotates slowly)	Weak or discharged battery	Test or charge the battery (Chapter Six)
	Dirty or corroded battery terminals	Thoroughly clean battery terminals
	Loose or dirty wire starter connections	Clean and tighten starter wire connections
	Engine is in gear	Correct for improper shift adjustment
	Faulty electric starter	Repair the electric starter
	Internal power head damage	Inspect power head for damage
	Internal gearcase damage	Inspect gearcase lubricant for debris
Electric starter engages (flywheel does not rotate)	Weak or discharged battery	Test or charge the battery (Chapter Six)
	Dirty or corroded battery terminals	Thoroughly clean battery terminals
	Loose or dirty wire starter connections	Clean and tighten starter wire connections
	Engine is in gear	Correct improper shift adjustment
	Water in the cylinder(s)	Inspect spark plug(s) for water contamination
	Damaged starter drive gear	Inspect starter drive gear
	Damaged flywheel gear teeth	Inspect flywheel gear teeth
	Faulty electric starter	Repair the electric starter
	Seized power head	Inspect power head for damage
	Seized gearcase	Inspect gearcase lubricant for debris
Electric starter (noisy operation)	Dirty or dry starter drive gear	Clean and lubricate starter drive gear
	Damaged starter drive gear teeth	Inspect starter drive gear
	Damaged or corroded flywheel gear	Inspect flywheel drive gear teeth
	Loose starter mounting bolt(s)	Tighten starter mounting bolt(s)
	Worn or dry starter bushing(s)	Repair electric starter (Chapter Six)
Manual starter does not engage flywheel	Worn or damaged drive pawl	Replace the drive pawl (Chapter Ten)
	Broken or damaged friction spring	Repair the friction spring
	Dry or binding rewind mechanism	Repair the manual starter
Manual starter engages the flywheel but does not rotate	Engine is in gear	Shift engine into NEUTRAL
	Misadjusted lockout assembly	Adjust the lockout assembly (Chapter Four)
	Damaged lockout assembly	Repair the manual starter (Chapter Ten)
	Worn or damaged rewind mechanism	Repair the manual starter
(continued)		

Table 1 STARTING SYSTEM TROUBLESHOOTING (continued)

Symptom	Possible causes	Corrective action
Manual starter engages the flywheel but does not rotate (cont.)	Frayed starter rope	Replace the starter rope (Chapter Ten)
	Corroded or binding starter sheave	Repair the manual starter
	Water in the cylinders	Inspect the spark plug(s) for water contamination
	Seized or damaged power head	Inspect power head for damage
	Seized or damaged gearcase	Inspect gearcase lubricant for debris
Manual starter rope does not rewind	Worn or frayed starter rope	Replace starter rope (Chapter Ten)
	Broken or damaged rewind spring	Replace rewind spring
	Dry, corroded or damaged rewind mechanism	Repair manual starter

Table 2 FUEL SYSTEM TROUBLESHOOTING

Symptom	Possible causes	Corrective action
Engine does not start	Closed fuel tank vent	Open the fuel tank vent
	Old or contaminated fuel	Provide the engine with fresh fuel
	Disconnected fuel hose	Connect fuel hose
	Faulty primer bulb	Check the primer bulb
	Choke valve not operating	Check choke valve operation
	Faulty Prime-Start system	Test Prime-Start system
	Air or fuel leaks in hose fittings	Inspect hose fittings for leakage
	Blocked fuel filter	Inspect the filter for contaminants
	Stuck carburetor inlet needle	Repair the carburetor(s) (Chapter Five)
	Improper float level adjustment	Repair the carburetor(s)
	Blocked carburetor passages	Repair the carburetor(s)
	Faulty fuel pump	Inspect fuel pump (Chapter Five)
Stalls or runs rough at idle	Old or contaminated fuel	Provide the engine with fresh fuel
	Improper idle speed adjustment	Adjust idle speed
	Closed or blocked fuel tank vent	Open or clear vent
	Blocked carburetor passages	Repair carburetor(s) (Chapter Five)
	Flooding carburetor	Check for carburetor flooding
	Faulty primer bulb	Check the primer bulb
	Air or fuel leaks at hose fittings	Inspect hose fittings for leakage
	Blocked fuel filter	Inspect the filter for contaminants
	Faulty fuel pump	Inspect fuel pump (Chapter Five)
	Worn or damaged reed valve	Check reed valves
	Low crankcase pressure	Check for crankcase leak
	Sticking choke valve	Check choke valve operation
	Faulty Prime-Start system	Test Prime-Start system
	Low crankcase pressure	Check for leaking crankcase
	Worn or damaged reed valves	Check for damaged reed valves
Idle speed too high	Improper idle speed adjustment	Adjust idle speed (Chapter Four)
	Improper throttle linkage adjustment	Adjust throttle linkages (Chapter Four)
	Binding throttle linkage(s)	Check linkage(s)
	Faulty Prime-Start system	Test Prime-Start system

(continued)

TROUBLESHOOTING

Table 2 FUEL SYSTEM TROUBLESHOOTING (continued)

Symptom	Possible causes	Corrective action
Hesitation during acceleration	Old or contaminated fuel	Supply the engine with fresh fuel
	Faulty fuel pump	Inspect the fuel pump
	Sticking choke valve	Check choke valve operation
	Faulty Prime-Start system	Test Prime-Start system
	Blocked carburetor passages	Repair carburetor(s)
	Blocked fuel filter	Inspect the filter(s) for contaminants
	Air or fuel leaks at hose fittings	Inspect hose fittings for leakage
	Closed or blocked fuel tank vent	Open or clear tank vent
	Flooding carburetor	Check for carburetor flooding
Misfire or poor high-speed performance	Old or contaminated fuel	Supply the engine with fresh fuel
	Faulty fuel pump	Inspect the fuel pump
	Sticking choke valve	Check choke valve operation
	Faulty primer bulb	Test the primer bulb (Chapter Five)
	Misadjusted throttle linkages	Adjust throttle linkages (Chapter Four)
	Blocked carburetor passages	Repair carburetor(s)
	Blocked fuel filter(s)	Inspect the filter(s) for contaminants
	Air or fuel leaks at hose fittings	Inspect hose fittings for leakage
	Closed or blocked fuel tank vent	Open or clear vent
Excessive exhaust smoke	Flooding carburetor	Check for carburetor flooding
	Blocked carburetor passages	Repair carburetor(s)
	Improper float level	Repair carburetor(s)
	Leaking accelerator pump	Repair carburetor(s)
	Sticking choke valve	Check choke valve operation
	Faulty Prime-Start system	Test Prime-Start system

Table 3 IGNITION SYSTEM TROUBLESHOOTING

Symptom	Possible causes	Corrective action
Engine does not start	Lanyard switch activated	Check lanyard switch
	Fouled spark plug(s)	Check or replace spark plug(s)
	Improper ignition timing adjustment	Adjust the ignition timing (Chapter Four)
	Faulty spark plug lead	Check for arcing spark plug lead
	Faulty spark plug cap	Test ignition coil and cap
	Shorted stop circuit	Test for shorted stop circuit
	Faulty ignition charge coil	Test ignition charge coil
	Faulty pulser coil	Test pulser coil
	Faulty crankshaft position sensor	Test crankshaft position sensor
	Faulty ignition coil	Test ignition coil
	Faulty CDI unit	Check CDI unit
Stalls or runs rough at idle	Fouled spark plug(s)	Check or replace spark plug(s)
	Improper ignition timing adjustment	Adjust the ignition timing (Chapter Four)
	Faulty spark plug cap	Test ignition coil and cap
	Faulty spark plug lead	Check for arcing spark plug lead
	Partially shorted stop circuit	Test stop circuit
	Faulty ignition charge coil	Test ignition charge coil
	Faulty pulser coil	Test pulser coil
	Faulty crankshaft position sensor	Test crankshaft position sensor
	Faulty ignition coil	Test ignition coil
	Faulty CDI unit	Check CDI unit

(continued)

Table 3 IGNITION SYSTEM TROUBLESHOOTING (continued)

Symptom	Possible causes	Corrective action
Idle speed too high	Improper ignition timing adjustment	Adjust the ignition timing (Chapter Four)
	Faulty pulser coil	Test pulser coil
	Faulty crankshaft position sensor	Test crankshaft position sensor
	Faulty CDI unit	Check low speed timing (Chapter Four)
Misfire or poor high-speed performance	Engine reaching rev limit	Check full speed engine rpm
	Fouled spark plug(s)	Check or replace spark plug(s)
	Improper ignition timing adjustment	Adjust the ignition timing (Chapter Four)
	Faulty spark plug lead	Check for arcing spark plug lead
	Faulty spark plug cap	Test ignition coil and cap
	Partially shorted stop circuit	Test for shorted stop circuit
	Faulty ignition charge coil	Test ignition charge coil
	Faulty pulser coil	Test pulser coil
	Faulty crankshaft position sensor	Test crankshaft position sensor
	Faulty ignition coil	Test ignition coil
	Faulty CDI unit	Check CDI unit
Engine will not stop	Faulty stop circuit	Test stop circuit

Table 4 CHARGING SYSTEM CAPACITY

Model	Maximum output
6-25 hp (two-cylinder)	
Lighting coil output	80 watt
Battery charging output	6 amp
25 hp (three-cylinder) and 30 hp	8 amp
28 jet, 35 jet, 40 hp and 50 hp	
Lighting coil output	80 watt
Battery charging output	6 amp
60 and 70 hp	6 amp
65 jet and 75-90 hp	10 amp

Table 5 BATTERY CHARGE COIL TEST SPECIFICATIONS

Model	Specification
6 and 8 hp	
Lighting/charge coil resistance	0.36-0.44 ohm
9.9 and 15 hp	
Lighting only models	
Coil output	
At 1500 rpm	12 VAC*
Battery charge models	
Coil output	
At cranking speed	11 VAC*
At 1500 rpm	13 VAC*
20 and 25 hp (two-cylinder)	
Battery charge coil output	
At cranking speed	4 VAC*
At 1500 rpm	13 VAC*
25 (three-cylinder) and 30 hp	
Battery charge coil output	
At cranking speed	4 VAC*
At 1500 rpm	25 VAC*
At 3500 rpm	25 VAC*
	(continued)

TROUBLESHOOTING

Table 5 BATTERY CHARGE COIL TEST SPECIFICATIONS (continued)

Model	Specification
28 jet, 35 jet, 40 hp and 50 hp	
Lighting only models	
Coil resistance	0.56-0.84 ohm
Coil output	
At 3000 rpm	12 VAC*
At 5500 rpm	13.5-16.5 VAC
Battery charging models	
Coil output	
At cranking speed	9 VAC*
At 1500 rpm	25 VAC*
At 3500 rpm	25 VAC*
60 and 70 hp (except E60)	
Battery charge/lighting coil resistance	0.57-0.85 ohm
Battery charge coil output	
At cranking speed	8 VAC*
At 1500 rpm	25 VAC*
At 3500 rpm	25 VAC*
E60	
Battery charge/lighting coil resistance	0.41-0.50 ohm
65 jet and 75-90 hp (except E75)	
Battery charge/lighting coil resistance	0.4-0.6 ohm
Battery charge coil output	
At cranking speed	10 VAC*
At 1500 rpm	25 VAC*
At 3500 rpm	25 VAC*
E75	
Battery charge/lighting coil resistance	0.36-0.54 ohm
Lighting only models	
Coil output	
At cranking speed	8 VAC*
At 1500 rpm	30 VAC*
At 3500 rpm	75 VAC*
Battery charging models	
Coil output	
At cranking speed	8 VAC*
At 1500 rpm	25 VAC*
At 3500 rpm	25 VAC*

*Minimum voltage output at designated engine speed.

Table 6 THERMOSWITCH TEST SPECIFICATIONS

Model	Temperature
20 hp, 25 hp and 30 hp	
Switching on	90-96° C (194-205° F)
Switching off	76-90° C (169-194° F)
28 jet, 35 jet, 40 hp and 50 hp	
With pink lead	
Switching on	90-96° C (194-205° F)
Switching off	76-90° C (169-194° F)
With orange lead	
Switching on	38-52° C (100-126° F)
Switching off	26-34° C (79-93° F)
60-90 hp (except E60)	
Switching on	84-90° C (183-194° F)
Switching off	60-74° C (140-165° F)
E60	
Switching on	87° C (189° F)
Switching off	67° C (153° F)

Table 7 OIL PUMP OUTPUT SPECIFICATIONS

Model	Output @ 1500 rpm
20 hp	0.7-0.9 cc
25 hp (two-cylinder)	0.7-0.9 cc
25 hp (three-cylinder)	0.8-0.9 cc
30 hp	0.8-0.9 cc
28 jet, 35 jet, 40 hp and 50 hp	1.1-2.1 cc
60 and 70 hp	1.7-2.7 cc
65 jet and 75-90 hp	2.4-3.8 cc

Table 8 IGNITION CHARGE COIL RESISTANCE SPECIFICATIONS

Model	Test points	Ohms
2 hp	Brown wire and ground	317-387
3-5 hp	Brown wire and black wire	248-302
6 and 8 hp	Brown wire and black wire	81-99
9.9 and 15 hp	Brown wire and blue wire	248-372
28 jet, 35 jet, 40 hp and 50 hp	Brown wire and blue wire	368-552
60 and 70 hp (except E60)	Brown wire and blue wire	136-204
E60	Brown wire and black wire	148-182
65 jet and 75-90 hp (except E75)	Brown wire and red wire	64-96
	Blue wire and red wire	191-288
E75	Brown wire and red wire	48-72
	Blue wire and red wire	428-642

Table 9 PULSER COIL RESISTANCE SPECIFICATIONS

Model	Test points	Ohms
3 hp		
High speed coil	Black wire and red/white wire	30-36
Low speed coil	Black wire and green/white wire	279-341
4 and 5 hp		
High speed coil	Black wire and white/red wire	30-36
Low speed coil	Black wire and white/green wire	248-303
6 and 8 hp	Black wire and white/red wire	92-112
9.9 and 15 hp	Black wire and white/red wire	352-528
28 jet, 35 jet, 40 hp and 50 hp		
Pulser coil No. 1	Black wire and white/red wire	168-252
Pulser coil No. 2	Black wire and white/black wire	168-252
Pulser coil No. 3	Black wire and white/green wire	168-252
60 and 70 hp (except E60)	White/red wire and white/black wire	240-360
E60		
Pulser coil No. 1	Black wire and white/red wire	117-143
Pulser coil No. 2	Black wire and white/black wire	117-143
Pulser coil No. 3	Black wire and white/green wire	117-143
65 jet and 75-90 hp (except E75)	White/red wire and white/black wire	241-362
E75		
Pulser coil No. 1	White/red wire and white/green wire	256-384
Pulser coil No. 2	White/black wire and white/green wire	256-384

Table 10 IGNITION COIL RESISTANCE SPECIFICATIONS

Model	Primary resistance (ohm)	Secondary resistance (ohms)
2 hp	0.18-0.24	2700-3700
3 hp	0.08-0.12	2080-3120
4 and 5 hp	0.14-0.22	3200-4800
6 and 8 hp	0.25-0.35	6800-10,200

(continued)

TROUBLESHOOTING

Table 10 IGNITION COIL RESISTANCE SPECIFICATIONS (continued)

Model	Primary resistance (ohm)	Secondary resistance (ohms)
9.9 and 15 hp	0.05-0.07	1680-2520
28 jet, 35 jet, 40 hp and 50 hp	0.18-0.24	2720-3680
60-90 hp (except E60)	0.18-0.24	3260-4880
E60	0.18-0.26	3840-5760

Table 11 IGNITION CHARGE COIL OUTPUT SPECIFICATIONS

Model	Cranking speed (volts)	1500 rpm volts	3500 rpm volts
9.9 and 15 hp			
Brown and blue wires	200	250	*
20 and 25 hp (two-cylinder)			
Brown and blue wires	125	125	*
25 hp (three cylinder) and 30 hp			
Brown and blue wires	210	205	115
28 jet, 35 jet, 40 hp and 50 hp			
Brown and blue wires	145	160	130
60 and 70 hp (except E60)			
Brown and blue wires	150	160	120
65 jet and 75-90 hp (except E75)			
Red and brown wires	60	170	150
Red and blue wires	100	135	135
E75			
Red and brown wires	40	145	160
Red and blue wires	105	135	160

*It is not necessary to test output voltage at this engine speed.

Table 12 PULSER COIL OUTPUT SPECIFICATIONS

Model	Cranking speed (volts)	1500 rpm volts	3500 rpm volts
9.9 and 15 hp			
Black wire and white/red wire	5	5	*
20 and 25 hp (two-cylinder)			
Black wire and white/black wire	5.5	15	*
Black wire and white/red wire	5.5	15	*
25 hp (three-cylinder) and 30 hp			
Black wire and white/red wire (No. 1)	4	11	2
Black wire and white/black wire (No. 2)	4	11	2
Black wire and white/green wire (No. 3)	4	11	1
28 jet, 35 jet, 40 hp and 50 hp			
Black wire and white/red wire (No. 1)	3	9	15
Black wire and white/black wire (No. 2)	3	9	15
Black wire and white/green wire (No. 3)	3	9	15
60 and 70 hp (except E60)			
White/red wire and white/black wire	2.5	6.5	10
65 jet and 75-90 hp (except E75)			
White/red wire and white/black wire	5	14	20
E75			
White/red wire and white/green wire	3.5	8	12
White/black wire and white/green wire	3.5	8	12

*It is not necessary to test output voltage at this engine speed.

Table 13 CRANKSHAFT POSITION SENSOR OUTPUT SPECIFICATIONS

Model	Cranking speed (volts)	1500 rpm volts	3500 rpm volts
60 and 70 hp (except E60)			
Blue/red wire and blue/white wire	5.0	20.0	16.0
75-90 hp (except E75)			
Blue/red wire and blue/white wire	5.5	25.0	20.0

Table 14 CDI UNIT OUTPUT SPECIFICATIONS

Model	Cranking speed (volts)	1500 rpm volts	3500 rpm volts
9.9 and 15 hp			
Coil black wire and black/white wire	170	215	*
Coil black wire and black/orange wire	170	215	*
20 and 25 hp (two-cylinder)			
Coil black wire and black/white wire	105	110	*
Coil black wire and black/orange wire	105	110	*
25 hp (three-cylinder) and 30 hp			
Coil black wire and black/orange wire	190	185	105
Coil black wire and black/white wire	190	185	105
Coil black wire and black/yellow wire	190	185	105
28 jet, 35 jet, 40 hp and 50 hp			
Coil black wire and black/orange wire	125	140	110
Coil black wire and black/white wire	125	140	110
Coil black wire and black/yellow wire	125	140	110
60 and 70 hp (except E60)			
Coil black wire and black/white wire	105	145	105
75-90 hp (except E75)			
Coil black wire and black/white wire	130	155	130
E75			
Coil black wire and black/white wire	105	140	145

*It is not necessary to test output voltage at this engine speed.

Table 15 MAXIMUM ENGINE OPERATING SPEED

Model	Engine speed (rpm)
2 hp	4000-5000
3-5 hp	4500-5500
6 hp	4000-5000
8 hp	4500-5500
9.9 and 15 hp	4500-5500
20 and 25 hp (two-cylinder)	5000-6000
25 hp (three-cylinder)	4500-5500
28 jet	4500-5500
30 hp	4500-5500
35 jet	4500-5500
40-60 hp	4500-5500
65 jet	4500-5500
70 hp	5000-6000
75-90 hp	4500-5500

Chapter Three

Lubrication, Maintenance and Tune-Up

Performing regular maintenance and tune-ups is the most effective way to ensure smooth running and trouble free performance. This chapter includes lubrication, maintenance and tune-up procedures for the Yamaha outboards covered in this manual. Engine break-in procedures are at the end of this chapter.

Table 2 lists the maintenance schedules for Yamaha outboards. Maintenance schedules are also listed in the *Quick Reference Data* at the front of the manual. **Table 3** lists fluid capacities. **Table 4** lists fuel-to-oil mixing ratios. **Table 5** lists spark plug specifications. **Tables 1-5** are at the end of this chapter.

LUBRICATION

Lubrication is the most important maintenance item for an outboard. An outboard will not operate for long without lubrication. Lubricant for the power head, gearcase and other components prevents excessive wear, guards against corrosion and provides smooth operation of turning and sliding surfaces such as tilt tubes, swivel brackets and control linkages. Power head, gearcase and jet pump lubrication procedures are in this chapter.

Power Head Lubrication

Two methods are used to lubricate the internal components of a two-stroke Yamaha outboard: premix and oil injection. Both methods introduce the lubricant into the internal power head components. The lubricant provides protection as it passes through the engine, and is eventually burned with the fuel during combustion. Become familiar with proper fuel and oil mixing on premix models. On oil injection models, become familiar with proper use of Precision Blend oil injection and its warning system. Chapter Two describes the warning system operation.

During new engine break-in or after power head repair, the engine must be provided with double the normal fuel/oil mixture. Use a 50:1 fuel/oil mixture in the fuel tank for oil injected models in addition to the oil provided by the oil injection system. For premix models, add twice the normal amount of oil to the fuel.

All 2-15 hp models use the premix method. Some 20-90 hp models also use this method. Precision Blend oil injection is available for 20-90 hp models.

CHAPTER THREE

Engine Oil Recommendation

The manufacturer recommends Yamalube Two-Cycle Outboard Oil. This oil meets or exceeds the TCW-3 standards set by the National Marine Manufacturers Association (NMMA). If Yamalube is not available, use a major engine manufacturer's oil that meets or exceeds the NMMA TC-W3 specification. Look for the NMMA logo on the container (**Figure 1**). If possible, avoid mixing different brands as a gel-like deposit may form in the oil reservoir on oil injected models.

CAUTION
Never use oil that is not specified for two-stroke water cooled engines. Do not substitute automotive motor oil. It will not provide adequate lubrication for the internal engine components. Operating the engine without adequate lubrication will result in serious power head damage or engine seizure.

Premix Models

The oil mixed with the fuel is an essential part of the lubrication system. The fuel/oil passes through the entire fuel system and into the engine. Some of the oil collects on internal components to provide protection. The recirculation system moves residual oil that collects in certain areas of the power head to other areas of the power head. The oil lubricates bearings and other components as it moves through the various passages and passes into the combustion chamber for lubrication and burning.

Premix oil must be mixed correctly for proper oil delivery. Too little oil can result in insufficient lubrication and possible power head damage. Too much oil will not decrease wear in the engine and may cause spark plug fouling, excessive smoke, lean fuel conditions and increased combustion chamber deposits. Lean fuel conditions and increased combustion chamber deposits can lead to preignition or detonation damaged pistons (**Figure 2**).

Fuel to oil ratios vary by model and usage. 2-30 hp premix (except 28 jet) models require a 100:1 fuel/oil ratio for normal recreational use and a 50:1 fuel/oil ratio for heavy commercial use after break-in. 28 jet and 40-90 hp premix models require a 50:1 fuel/oil ratio for all applications after break-in.

The oil and fuel must be thoroughly mixed for correct engine operation. If the oil is poured into the fuel, it will settle on the bottom of the tank. The engine may operate with a very rich oil mixture one minute and a lean oil mixture the next. The engine will run erratically until the oil is mixed with the fuel by wave action or movement of the vessel.

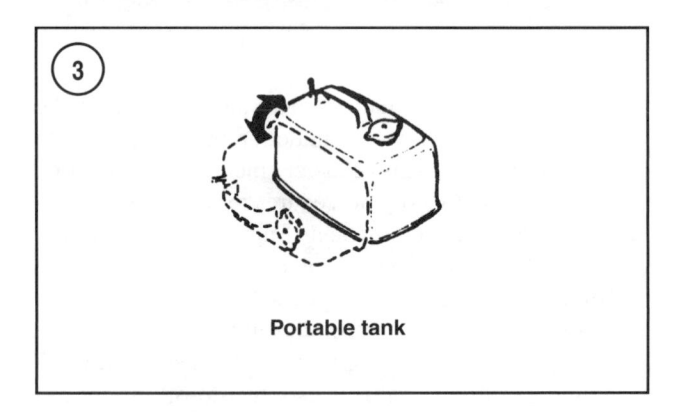

CAUTION
Only mix fuel and oil when it will be used within a few weeks. Fuel begins to deteriorate in as little as 14 days. Also, the oil may settle on the bottom of the tank and cause an inconsistent fuel/oil delivery to the engine.

When using a portable fuel tank, pour in all of the oil and half of the fuel. Install the fill cap and shut the vent or

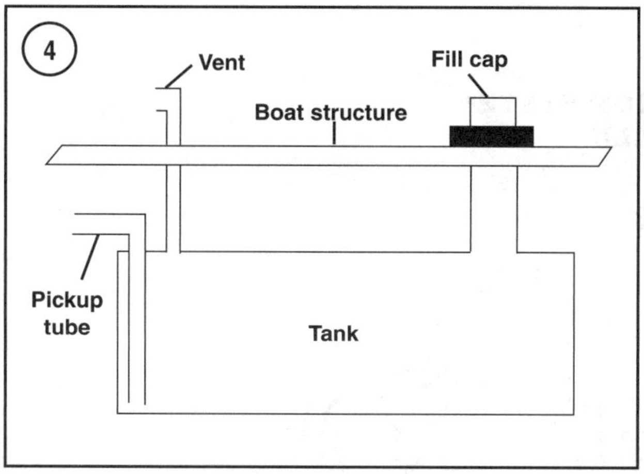

LUBRICATION, MAINTENANCE AND TUNE-UP

4 Vent — Fill cap — Boat structure — Pickup tube — Tank

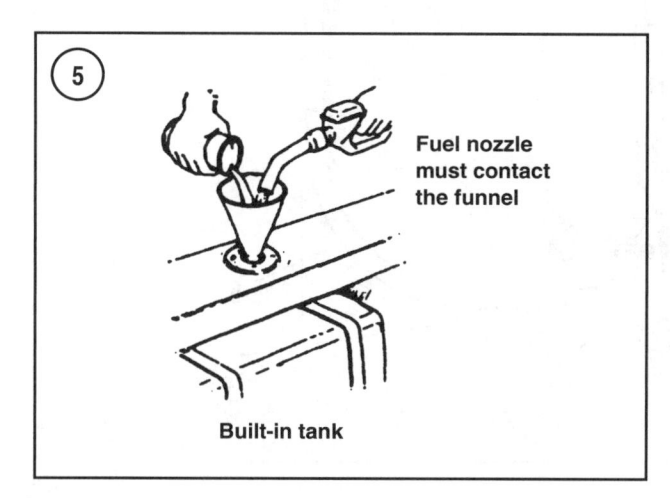

5 Fuel nozzle must contact the funnel — Built-in tank

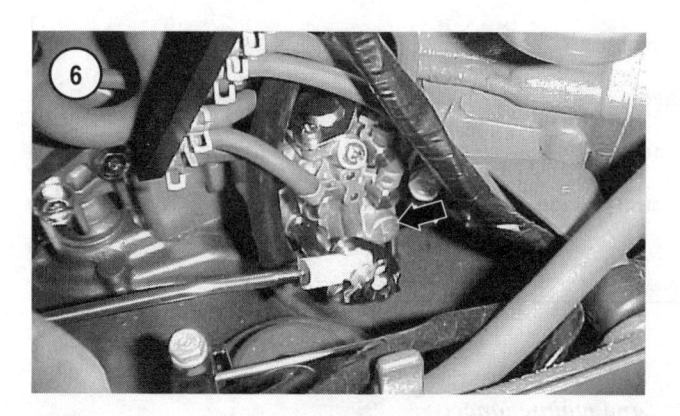

6

7 OIL INJECTION SYSTEM (20-60 HP MODELS) — Engine cover — Warning lamp — Oil tank cap — Oil reservoir — Oil level sensor — Oil injection pump — Remote control box — Battery — Fuel tank — Warning horn (remote control models)

valve. Disconnect the fuel line if the tank is equipped with an automatic fuel tank vent. Disconnecting the fuel line closes the vent on most tanks with this feature. Carefully tip the tank onto its side, then back to the upright position (**Figure 3**) several times to mix the fuel. Remove the fill cap and add the other half of the fuel. Install the fill cap and repeat the mixing procedure. If the temperature is be-low 0° C (32° F), add the specified amount of oil to 3.8 L (1 gal.) of fuel and mix as described. Add the remaining fuel and repeat the mixing process.

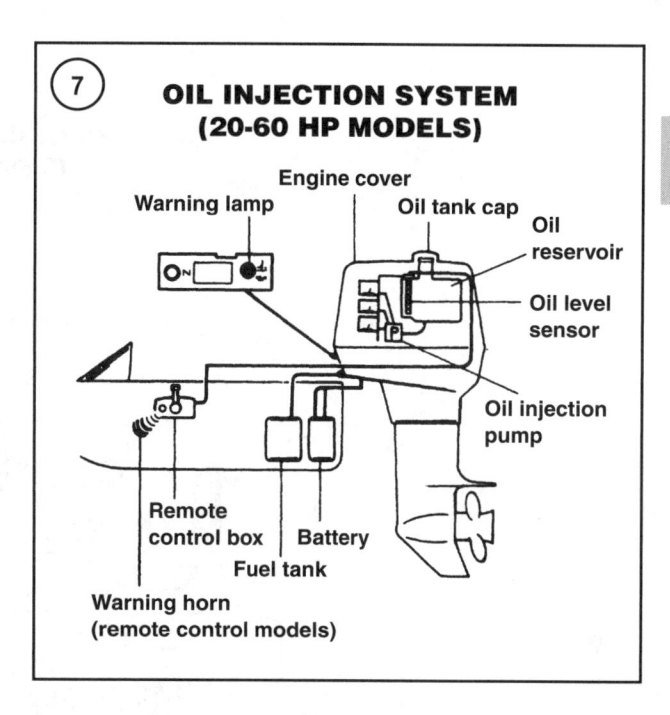

If the boat is equipped with a built-in fuel tank (**Figure 4**), mix the required amount of oil and 3.8 L (1 gal.) of fuel into a suitable container. Carefully mix the oil into the fuel. Insert a large metal funnel and filler neck and pour the mixture in when the fuel is added to the tank (**Figure 5**).

Table 4 lists the amount of oil needed for an amount of fuel in both the 50:1 and 100:1 ratios.

Oil Injected Models

Oil injection eliminates the need to mix fuel and oil after break-in. A gear-driven variable rate oil pump (**Figure 6**) delivers the correct amount of oil to the engine at all speeds. **Figure 7** is a typical oil injection system. The oil is injected directly into the engine at the intake manifold. Air and fuel flowing into the engine disperse the oil throughout the power head. Oil never enters the carburetor. This reduces the formation of deposits in the carburetor during extended storage. A warning system monitors the oil level in the oil reservoir and a horn and/or lamp warns the operator when the reservoir needs to be filled. If the oil level drops below a critical level, the warning system will reduce power to help prevent power head damage.

CAUTION
Never operate the engine without adequate oil in the reservoir. The power head will be

FUEL/OIL INJECTION SYSTEM (TYPICAL)

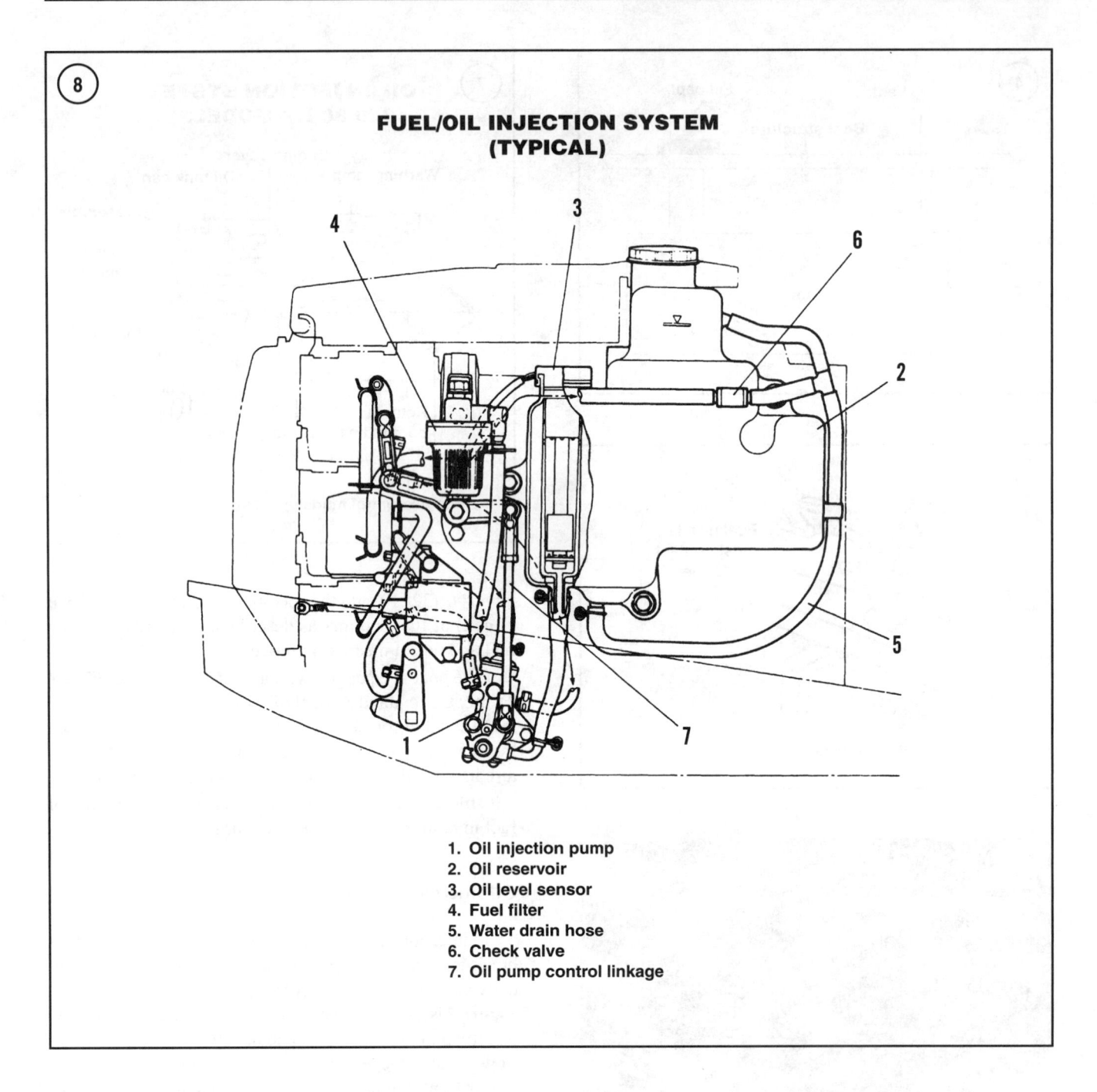

⑧

1. Oil injection pump
2. Oil reservoir
3. Oil level sensor
4. Fuel filter
5. Water drain hose
6. Check valve
7. Oil pump control linkage

serious damaged or seize if the engine is operated without adequate lubrication.

Routinely check the oil level before operating the engine. Inspect the areas around the oil hoses, oil pump and the reservoir for oily residue. Oily residue could indicate an oil leak. Correct any oil leak in the oil injection system before operating the engine. Check for leaks when performing routine maintenance and when the engine cover is removed.

Oil injection system inspection and maintenance

Check the oil pump control linkage (7, **Figure 8**) for free movement and proper adjustment. Oil pump adjustment is described in Chapter Four.

Inspect the water drain tube (1, **Figure 9**) for the presence of water by removing the hose over a suitable container. Drain a few ounces from the reservoir and quickly reconnect the hose. Completely drain the reservoir and all

LUBRICATION, MAINTENANCE AND TUNE-UP

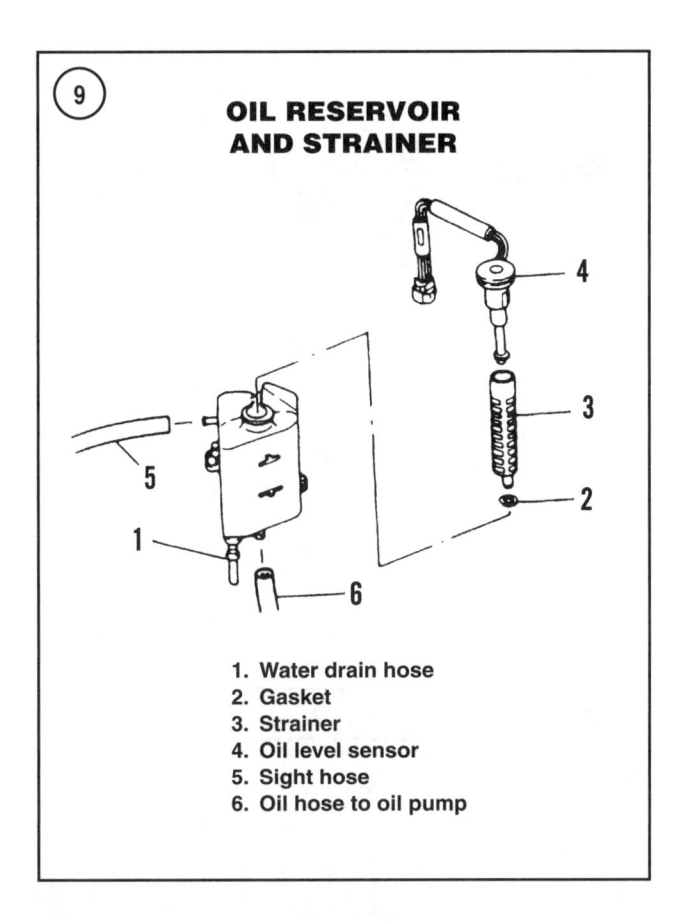

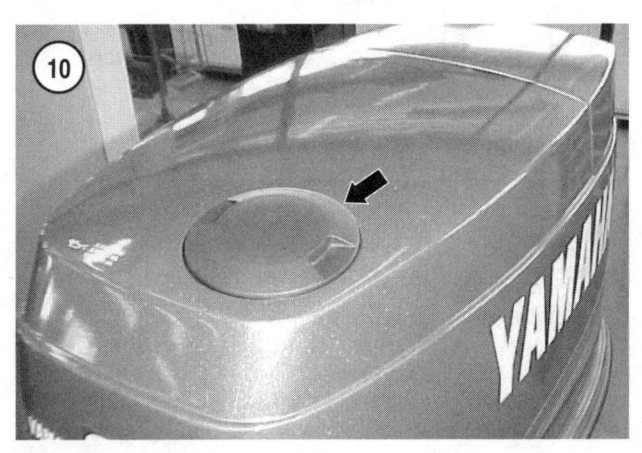

9. OIL RESERVOIR AND STRAINER

1. Water drain hose
2. Gasket
3. Strainer
4. Oil level sensor
5. Sight hose
6. Oil hose to oil pump

oil hoses if there is water or other contaminants in the oil. Removal, inspection and installation of the oil injection components are described in Chapter Twelve.

Remove the oil level sensor (4, **Figure 9**) to access the oil strainer (3). Remove the strainer and clean it with a soft brush and mild solvent. Dry the components with compressed air before installing them into the reservoir. Removal and installation procedures for these and other oil injection components are in Chapter Twelve.

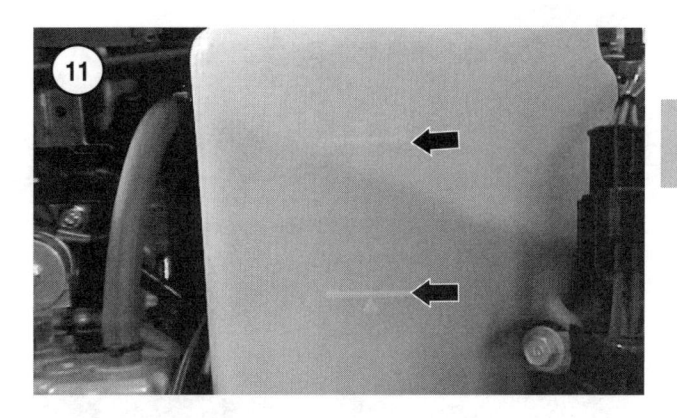

CAUTION
*The oil strainer and gasket (2 and 3, **Figure 9**) must be installed correctly for the oil injection system to operate properly. An improperly installed gasket or strainer can block oil flow to the oil pump, causing inadequate lubrication for the power head. Follow the procedures in Chapter Twelve to remove or install oil injection system components.*

Oil level check and filling procedure

CAUTION
Never overfill the oil reservoir. The oil may seep past the fill cap and leak from the oil fill opening. Leaking occurs when the oil expands from heat or when the engine is placed in the full tilt position. When properly filled, an air space allows for heat expansion and tilting of the engine.

Check the oil level before operating the engine and after running the engine for two or more hours at higher throttle settings. Only use the recommended oil as described in this chapter.

Most models are equipped with an opening in the engine cover for access to the oil fill cap (**Figure 10**). On some models, the engine cover must be removed to access the oil fill cap.

On 20-70 hp models, use the marks on the translucent oil reservoir (**Figure 11**) to check the oil level.

On 75-90 hp models, read the dash-mounted gauge to determine the oil level. These models have a reservoir (**Figure 12**) that does not have fill and add marks.

To add oil, wipe debris or contaminants from the oil fill cap and surrounding surfaces. Remove the cap and use a clean funnel to pour oil into the reservoir. Check the fill cap seal for deteriorated or damaged surfaces. Replace the seal if necessary. Install and securely tighten the fill cap.

Drain oil using the water drain tube if the oil reservoir is overfilled.

Gearcase Lubrication

Change the gearcase lubricant after the first 10 hours of use for a new engine or a new gearcase, or after major gearcase repair. After the first 10 hours, change the gearcase lubricant at 50 hour intervals or once a season (whichever occurs first). Use Yamaha gearcase lubricant or a suitable gearcase lubricant that meets or exceeds marine GL5 specifications.

Refer to the recommendations on the container for the proper application. Check the gearcase lubricant level and condition at regular intervals (**Table 2**). Correct problems before they lead to gearcase component failure.

CAUTION
Never use automotive gear lubricant in an outboard gearcase. These lubricants are not suitable for marine applications. Using them can lead to increased wear and corrosion of internal components.

Lubricant level and condition check

Level/vent and drain/fill plug locations may be different from the illustration. Refer to Chapter Eight for model specific information.

1. Place the engine in the upright position (**Figure 13**) for at least one hour before checking the lubricant level.
2. On electric start models, disconnect the battery cables.
3. Disconnect and ground the spark plug lead(s) to prevent accidental starting.

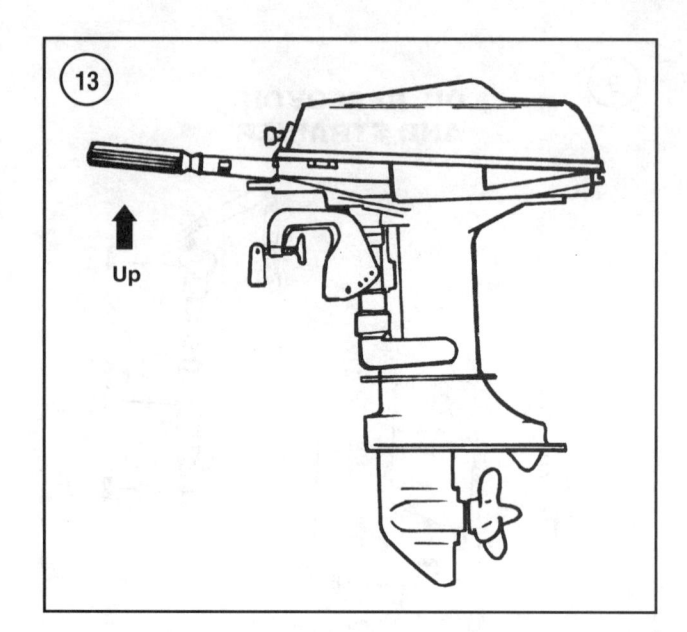

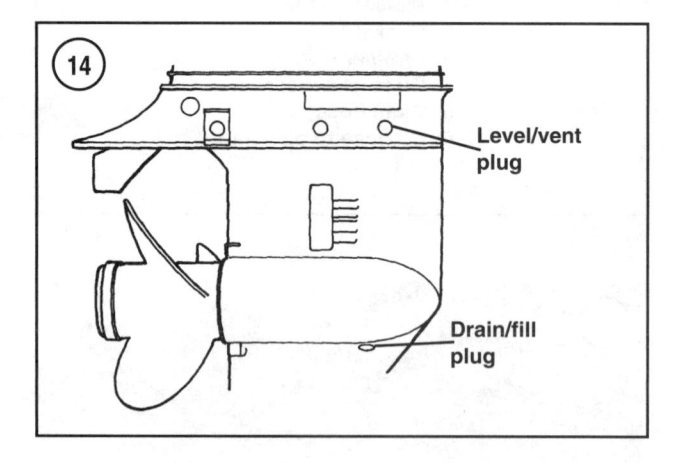

CAUTION
Operating the engine with a low lubricant level or water contaminated lubricant will result in serious damage to internal gearcase components. Inspect the sealing washer on the drain/fill and level/vent plugs when they are removed. Replace missing or damaged plugs.

4. Slowly loosen and remove the drain/fill plug (**Figure 14**). Drain a small sample of lubricant from the gearcase. Quickly replace the drain plug and securely tighten.

5. Inspect the lubricant for water or a milky appearance. Pressure test the gearcase to determine the source of the leak if either condition is present. Gearcase pressure testing is described in Chapter Eight.

LUBRICATION, MAINTENANCE AND TUNE-UP

7. Remove the level/vent plug (**Figure 14**). The lubricant level should be even with the bottom of the threaded level/vent plug opening. Add lubricant to the drain plug opening (**Figure 15**) until it is full. If more than an ounce is required to fill the gearcase, pressure test the gearcase as described in Chapter Eight.
8. After adding lubricant, allow the gearcase to sit in a shaded area for at least one hour and check the lubricant level again. Top it off if necessary.
9. On electric start models, connect the battery cables.
10. Connect the spark plug lead(s).

Gearcase lubricant change

Level/vent and drain/fill plug locations may be different from the illustration. Refer to Chapter Eight for model specific information.

1. Place the engine in the upright position (**Figure 13**).
2. On electric start models, disconnect the battery cables.
3. Disconnect and ground the spark plug lead(s) to prevent accidental starting.

CAUTION
Operating the engine with a low lubricant level or water contaminated lubricant will result in serious damage to internal gearcase components. Inspect the sealing washer on the drain/fill and level/vent plugs when they are removed. Replace missing or damaged plugs.

NOTE
Some gearcases use two level/vent plugs. Refer to the illustrations in Chapter Eight to determine the quantity and location(s) of the plug(s). If so equipped, remove both level/vent plugs to check the lubricant level or fill the gearcase.

4. Place a suitable container under the gearcase (**Figure 16**). Remove the drain/fill plug and level/vent plug(s) (**Figure 14**).
5. Allow the gearcase to drain completely, then tilt the engine to ensure the drain/fill plug is at the lowest point.
6. Inspect the lubricant for water or a milky appearance. Pressure test the gearcase to determine the source of the leak if either condition is present. Gearcase pressure testing is described in Chapter Eight.

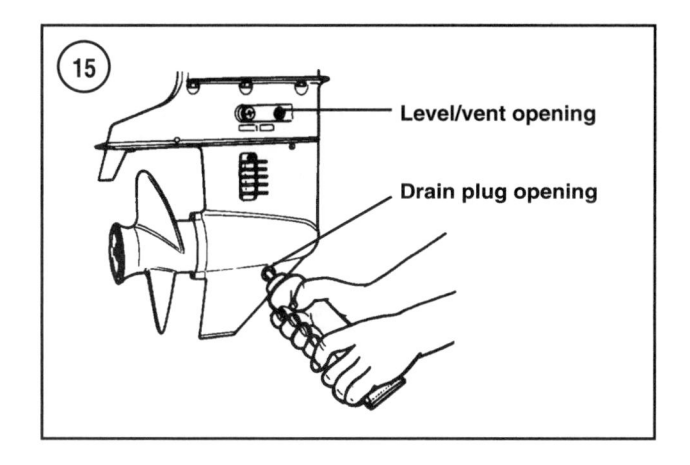

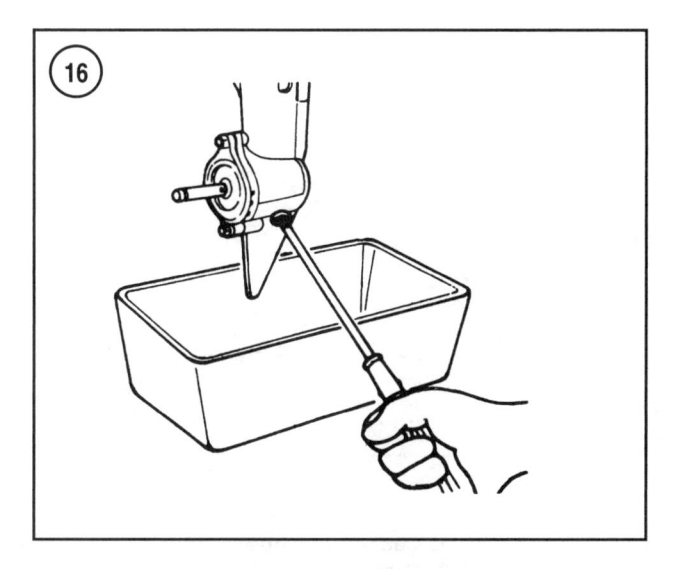

NOTE
A small amount of very fine metal particles is usually present in the gearcase lubricant. These fine particles form during normal operation and their presence does not indicate

NOTE
A small amount of very fine metal particles is usually present in the gearcase lubricant. These fine particles form during normal operation and their presence does not indicate a problem. Large particles, however, indicate a potential problem in the gearcase.

6. Rub a small amount of the lubricant sample between your finger and thumb. Disassemble and inspect the gearcase for damaged components if the lubricant feels contaminated or gritty. Refer to Chapter Eight for disassembly and inspection procedures.

NOTE
Some gearcases use two level/vent plugs. Refer to the illustrations in Chapter Eight to determine the quantity and location(s) of the plug(s). If so equipped, remove both level/vent plugs to check the lubricant level or fill the gearcase.

a problem. Large particles, however, indicate a potential problem in the gearcase.

7. Rub a small amount of the lubricant sample between your finger and thumb. Disassemble and inspect the gearcase for damaged components if the lubricant feels contaminated or gritty. Refer to Chapter Eight for disassembly and inspection procedures.
8. Return the engine to the upright position (**Figure 13**).
9. Use a pump type dispenser or squeeze tube to *slowly* pump gearcase lubricant into the fill/drain opening (**Figure 15**) until it flows out of the level/vent opening(s). On models with two level/vent openings, continue until lubricant flows from each opening.
10. Without removing the pump from the drain/fill opening, install and securely tighten the level/vent plug(s). Remove the pump and *quickly* install the drain/fill plug. Tighten the drain fill plug securely.
11. Allow the gearcase to sit in a shaded area for at least one hour and check the lubricant level again. Top it off if necessary.
12. On electric start models, connect the battery cables.
13. Connect the spark plug lead(s).
14. Dispose of the drained gearcase lubricant in a responsible manner. Many marine or automotive parts retailers accept used oil and gearcase lubricant for recycling.

Jet Drive Lubrication

A jet drive unit is attached to the drive shaft housing in place of a propeller drive gearcase. Jet drive units require maintenance at frequent intervals. Lubricate the drive shaft bearings after each operating period and when preparing the engine for extended storage. Use Yamaha All-Purpose Grease or a grease that meets or exceeds NLGI No. 1 rating.

NOTE
Slight discoloration of the expelled jet drive grease is normal during the break-in period. Inspect the drive shaft seals and bearings if the expelled grease is dark gray, contains metal particles or has a significant amount of water.

1. Locate the capped vent hose (1, **Figure 17**) on the port side of the jet drive.
2. Disconnect the vent hose from the fitting.
3. Connect a grease gun to the fitting on the jet drive. Pump grease into the fitting until grease exits the vent hose (3, **Figure 17**).
4. Inspect the exiting grease. Disassemble the jet drive and inspect the internal components if metal particles, dark gray coloration or a significant amount of water is present. Refer to Chapter Nine for disassembly, inspection and assembly procedures.
5. Wipe the expelled grease from the hose and connect the hose to the jet drive grease fitting.

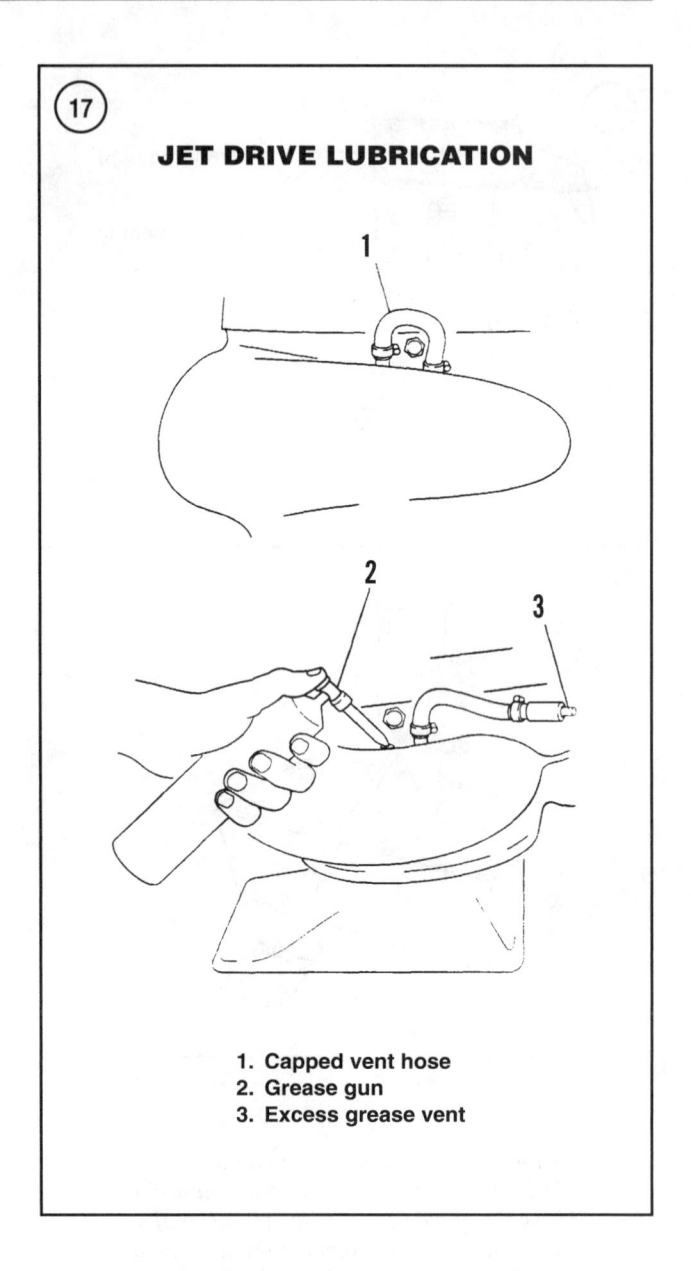

JET DRIVE LUBRICATION

1. Capped vent hose
2. Grease gun
3. Excess grease vent

Other Lubrication Points

Other lubrication points include the throttle and shift linkages, steering cable, swivel shafts, tilt tube, tilt lock mechanism and reverse lock mechanism. In certain application, lubrication is required for the gearcase bearing carrier. Refer to **Table 2** for maintenance intervals and a description of the lubricating points.

LUBRICATION, MAINTENANCE AND TUNE-UP

Throttle and shift linkages

Apply a light film of Yamaha All-Purpose Grease to pivot points and sliding surfaces of the throttle and shift linkages (**Figure 18**, typical). To identify the lubrication points, have an assistant move the throttle and shift controls while observing the linkages. Only a small amount of grease is required. Use just enough grease to leave a film on the surfaces.

Steering cable

CAUTION
The steering cable must be in the retracted position when grease is injected into the fitting. The cable can become hydraulically locked if grease is injected with the cable extended. Refer to the cable manufacturer's recommendation for the type and frequency of lubrication.

Apply Yamaha All-Purpose Grease to the pivot point and sliding surfaces of the steering cable (**Figure 19**, typical). Some steering cables are equipped with a grease fitting (**Figure 20**). Regular lubrication of the steering cable will dramatically increase its life.

Swivel shaft and tilt tube

Locate the fittings on the swivel housing (**Figure 21** and **Figure 22**), and lubricate the swivel shaft and tilt tube. Inject Yamaha All-Purpose Grease into the fittings until grease comes out of the joints.

Tilt lock and reverse lock mechanism

Raise the engine to the full tilt position to access the reverse lock mechanism pivot points (**Figure 23**, typical). Engage the tilt lock or secure the engine with an overhead support during this procedure. Apply a light coat of Yamaha All-Purpose Grease to the pivot points and sliding surfaces of the tilt lock and reverse lock mechanism. Only a small amount of grease is required. Use only enough grease to leave a film on the surfaces. Refer to the illustrations in Chapter Eleven to identify the tilt lock and reverse lock components and pivot points.

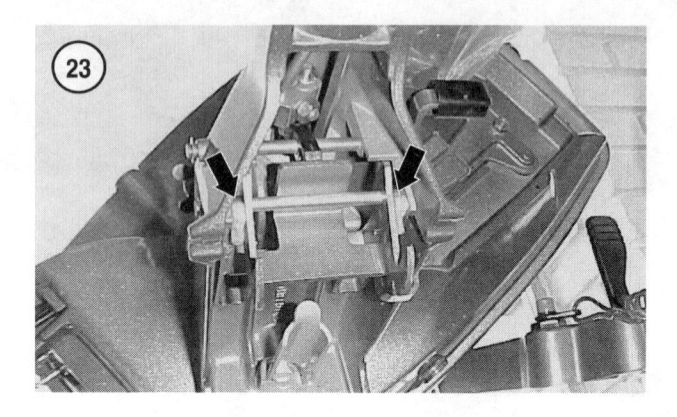

Bearing carrier

If the engine is operated frequently in saltwater, remove the bearing carrier (**Figure 24**) and clean all salt deposits from the carrier and gearcase housing. Salt deposits can build up at the carrier-to-housing contact area and eventually damage the housing. Install a new O-ring (**Figure 24**) during assembly. Refer to Chapter Eight for bearing carrier removal and installation procedures.

MAINTENANCE

This section includes maintenance procedures for the propeller shaft and propeller, cooling system, electrical system, fuel system and corrosion prevention. Preparation for storage, fitting out and instructions for engines that have been submerged are also included.

Propeller Shaft and Propeller Maintenance

Remove the propeller nut, attaching hardware and the propeller as described in Chapter Eight. Clean deposits and old grease from the propeller shaft and propeller splined sections.

Inspect the propeller for bent blades (**Figure 25**), cracked surfaces, nicks or missing blade sections. Dress small nicks in the propeller blade with a file. Replace the propeller or have it repaired if there are cracks, blade sections are missing or it is significantly bent.

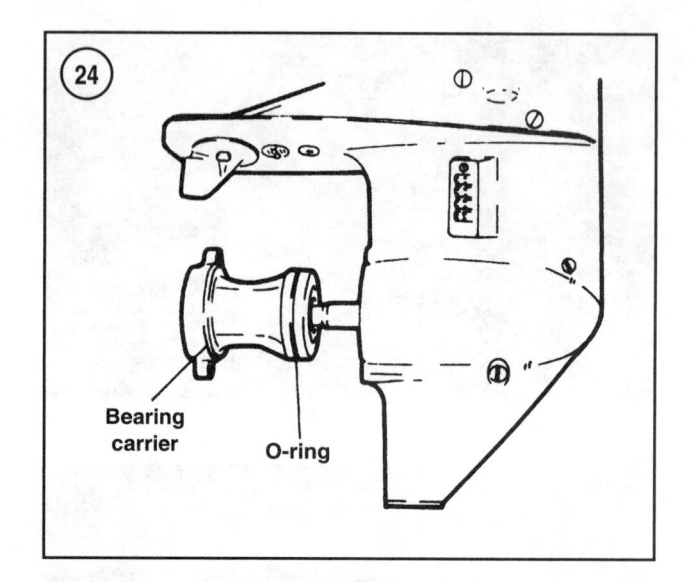

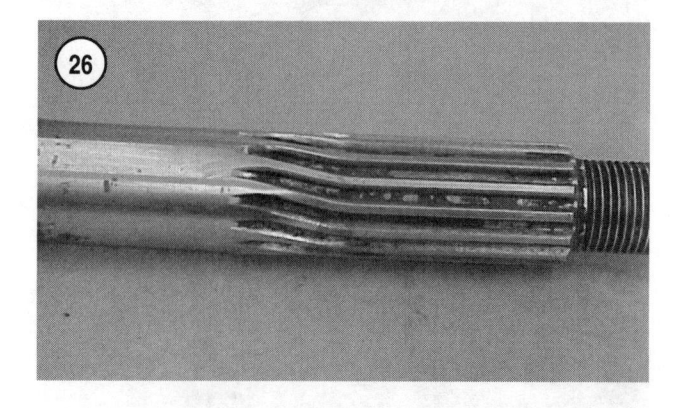

Inspect the propeller shaft for twisted splines (**Figure 26**) or a bent shaft. Replace the propeller shaft (Chapter Eight) if it is bent or splines are twisted.

Apply Yamaha All-Purpose Grease or equivalent to the propeller shaft and install the propeller as described in Chapter Eight.

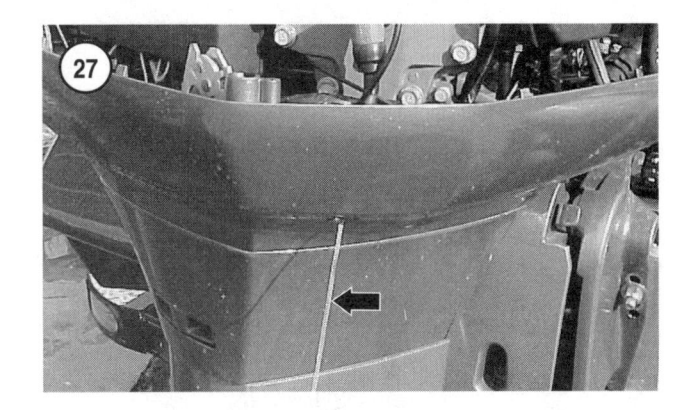

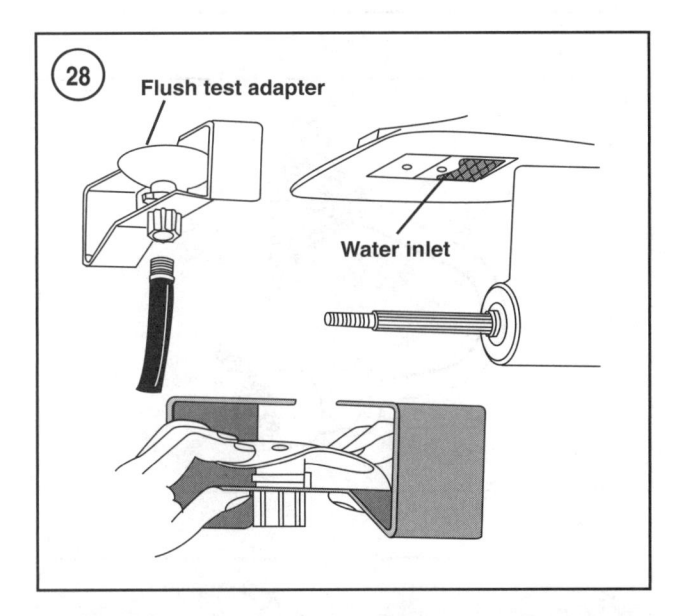

LUBRICATION, MAINTENANCE AND TUNE-UP

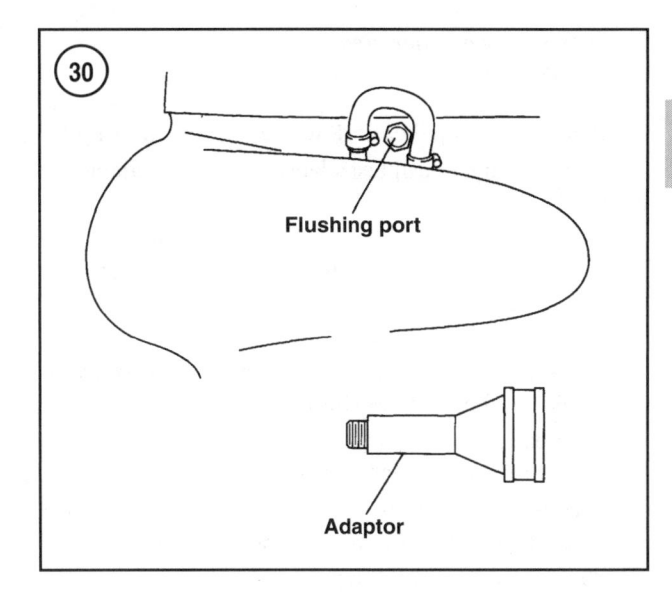

the water pump may not be operating at good efficiency. Inspect the water pump after every 50 hour period of operation, once a year or whenever the engine is running warmer than normal. Water pump inspection and repair is described in Chapter Eight.

Flush the cooling system at regular intervals to help prevent corrosion and deposit buildup in the cooling system. Flush the system after each operation in salt or brackish water, polluted water or water that is laden with silt or sand. Inspect the water pump more frequently if the engine is operated in these conditions. The type of drive system and water inlet placement determines the type of flush/test adapter required.

For the water screen located under the antiventilation plate, use the type of adapter shown in **Figure 28**.

For the water screen located on the sides of the gearcase, use the type of adapter shown in **Figure 29**.

For jet drive models, use the thread-in type adapter (Yamaha part No. 6EO-28193-00-94). See **Figure 30**.

Flushing the cooling system

WARNING
Stay clear of the propeller shaft while running an engine on a flush/test adapter. Remove the propeller before running the engine on a flush/test adapter. Disconnect the battery cables and spark plug lead(s) before removing or installing the propeller.

CAUTION
Never run the engine without providing cooling water. Use either a test tank or

Cooling System Maintenance

Inspect the cooling system for proper operation every time the engine is run. A stream of water exiting the lower back of the engine (**Figure 27**) indicates the water pump is operating. Never run the engine if it is overheating or if

flush/test adapter. Remove the propeller before running the engine.

1. Remove the propeller as described in Chapter Eight.
2A. When using a flush/test adapter, install the adapter as follows:
   a. On jet drive models, remove the plug from the flushing port (**Figure 30**). Thread the adapter fully into the port.
   b. For a propeller drive gearcase, slip the flush test adapter over the antiventilation plate (**Figure 28**) or sides of the gearcase (**Figure 29**).
   c. Thread a garden hose onto the adapter. Connect the hose to a freshwater supply.
   d. Turn the water on. Make sure the cup(s) on the adapter completely cover the water screen(s).
2B. Use a test tank as follows:
   a. Fill the test tank with freshwater.
   b. On a portable engine, install the engine in the test tank and securely tighten the clamp screws (**Figure 31**).
   c. On a permanently attached engine, place the engine in the full tilt position. Move the boat or tank to position the engine over the tank. Tilt the engine downward until it is in the upright position. Make sure the water screen is well below the water line. Add water as needed.
3. Run the engine at a fast idle in neutral gear until the engine reaches full operating temperature.
4. Run the engine at fast idle for a minimum of 10 minutes and the water exiting the lower cover (**Figure 27**) is clear. Monitor the engine temperature. Stop the engine if it begins to overheat.
5. Bring the engine back to idle speed for a few minutes and stop the engine.
6. Remove the flush/test adapter or remove the engine from the test tank. Place the engine in the upright position for several minutes to drain the cooling system passages.
7. Install the propeller as described in Chapter Eight.

Electrical System Maintenance

Many problems with an outboard engine are caused by insufficient maintenance to the electrical system. Components requiring maintenance include:
1. Cranking battery.
2. Wiring and electrical connections.
3. Starter motor.

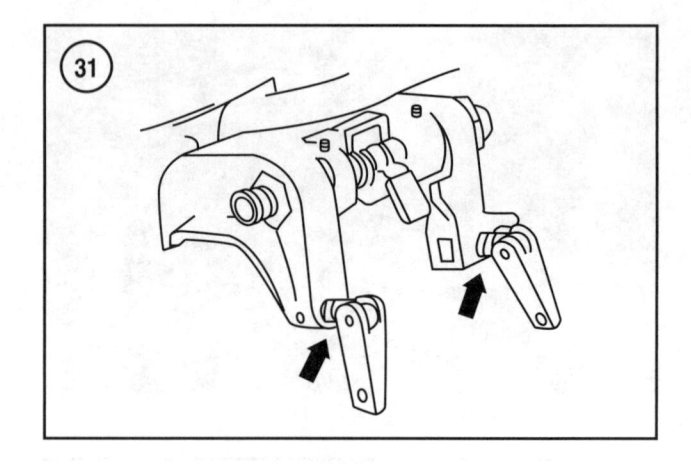

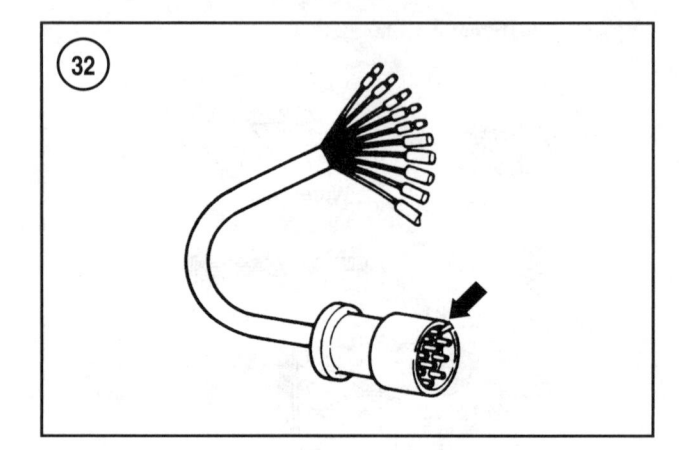

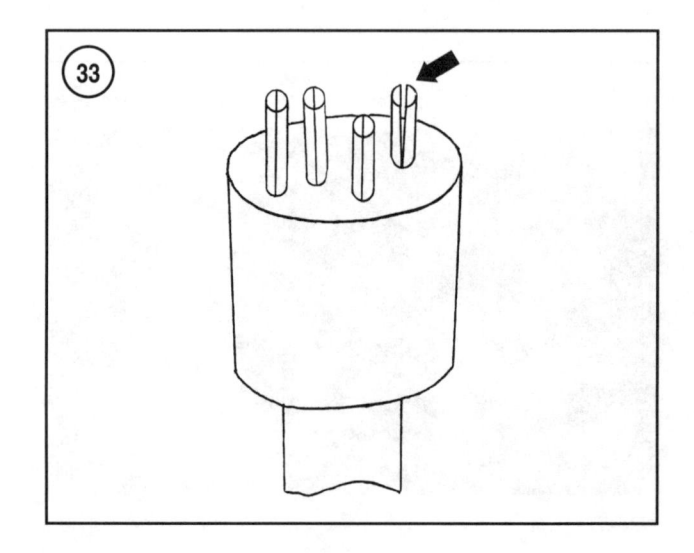

Cranking battery

The cranking battery requires more maintenance than any other component related to the engine. Unlike automobiles, boats may not be run for several weeks or longer.

LUBRICATION, MAINTENANCE AND TUNE-UP

34 Loose connector

35 Bent pin

36

scrape corrosion from the contacts. Apply a light coat of Yamaha All-Purpose Grease or equivalent to the main harness plug to seal out moisture and prevent corrosion.

CAUTION
Apply only enough grease to leave a light film on electrical contacts. Excessive grease can seep into electrical components, such as relays, and cause a malfunction.

The male pins of the main harness connector tend to squeeze together and may not make good contact with the female end. Use a very small blade screwdriver and slightly spread the pins (**Figure 33**) to maintain a reliable connection. Disconnect and inspect the wire connectors for corrosion and loose connectors (**Figure 34**) or bent terminal pins (**Figure 35**).

Starter motor

Only use a light coat of grease where required. Excess grease may attract dirt or debris and lead to starter malfunctions. Refer to Chapter Six if removal or disassembly is required to access the pinion drive and armature shaft.

1. Disconnect the battery cables. Disconnect and ground the spark plug leads to prevent accidental starting.
2. Disconnect the starter cable terminal (**Figure 36**) and clean corrosion from the cable terminal and terminal post. Reconnect the cable and securely tighten the nut. To prevent corrosion, apply a coat of Liquid Neoprene to the terminal. Liquid Neoprene is available from marine or automotive parts retailers.
3. Rotate the pinion drive gear clockwise to expose the helical splines on the armature shaft (**Figure 37**). Apply a light coat of Yamaha All-Purpose Grease or equivalent to the splines. Release the pinion drive gear and apply the same grease to the armature shaft and the teeth on the pinion drive gear. Reconnect the battery cables and check for proper electric starter operation.

Fuel System

Fuel requirements

Always use a major brand of fuel from a facility that sells a large amount of fuel. Fuel has a relatively short shelf life.

Use fuel with a minimum average octane rating of 86. This fuel should meet the requirement for an engine operated under normal conditions. Use a higher octane rating

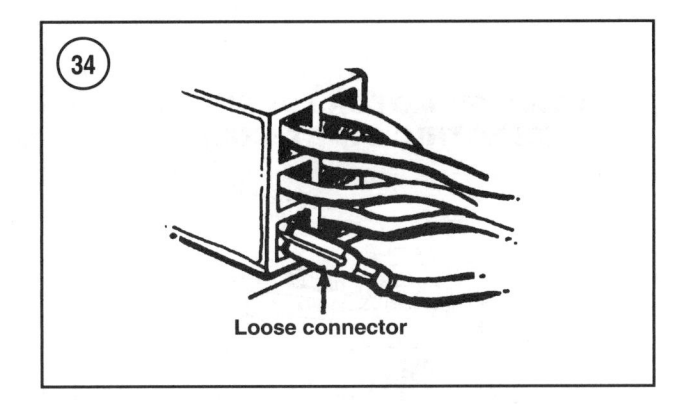

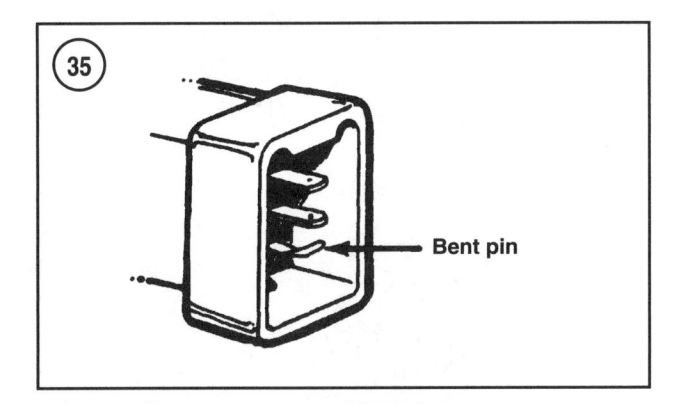

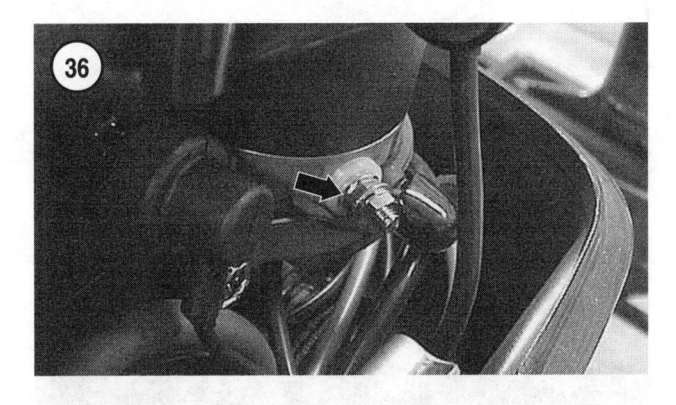

Without proper maintenance, the battery will lose its charge and begin to deteriorate. Marine engines are exposed to more moisture than automobiles resulting in more corrosion on the battery terminals. Clean the terminals and charge the battery at 30-day intervals when the engine is in long-term storage. Battery testing, changing and maintenance are described in Chapter Six.

Wiring and electrical connections

Periodically inspect the main harness connector (**Figure 32**) for corrosion or faulty pin connections. Carefully

if the engine is used for commercial or heavy-duty service.

Using premium grade fuel from a major supplier has advantages. The higher octane rating provides added protection against detonation. Major brands generally have a high turnover of fuel, helping to ensure fresh fuel for the engine. Premium grade fuel normally contains a high quality detergent that helps keep the internal components of the power head and fuel system clean.

CAUTION
Never run an outboard on old or stale fuel. Serious power head damage could occur from using fuel that has deteriorated. Varnish-like deposits that form as fuel deteriorates can block fuel flow, resulting in lean fuel mixture. A lean fuel mixture leads to preignition and detonation damage. Dispose of fuel that has been stored for a long time without proper treatment. Fuel should not be stored over 60 days even with proper treatment. Contact a local marine dealership or an automotive repair facility for information on disposal of old or stale fuel.

Fuel additives

Use fuel stabilizer such as Sta-Bil to help prevent the formation of gum or varnish-like deposits in the fuel system during extended storage. Add Yamaha Ring Free or a similar additive into the fuel on a continual basis. This type of additive with a good quality oil can reduce deposits on the piston rings and in the combustion chamber. Mix the additives into the fuel in the concentrations listed on the container.

Fuel filter

Clean, inspect or replace the fuel filter at the intervals in **Table 3**. Most of the lower horsepower engines use an inline-type fuel filter (**Figure 38**). This type of fuel filter is not serviceable. Visually inspect the filter through the translucent body. Replace the filter if contaminants can be seen or if it has become dark. Replacement procedures for this type of filter are in Chapter Six.

Most higher horsepower engines use the serviceable canister-type fuel filter (**Figure 39**). Inspect, clean or replace this filter at the intervals in **Table 2**. Water from the fuel system tends to collect in the bottom of the canister or this filter. Inspect the fuel system components, including the fuel tank, for contamination if water is in the canister.

Some outboards are equipped with a large spin-on type fuel filter (**Figure 40**). This type of filter is mounted on the boat structure and connects to the fuel line between the primer bulb and the fuel tank. This filter separates most of the water from the fuel before it reaches the engine. Service this fuel filter when servicing other fuel filters on the engine.

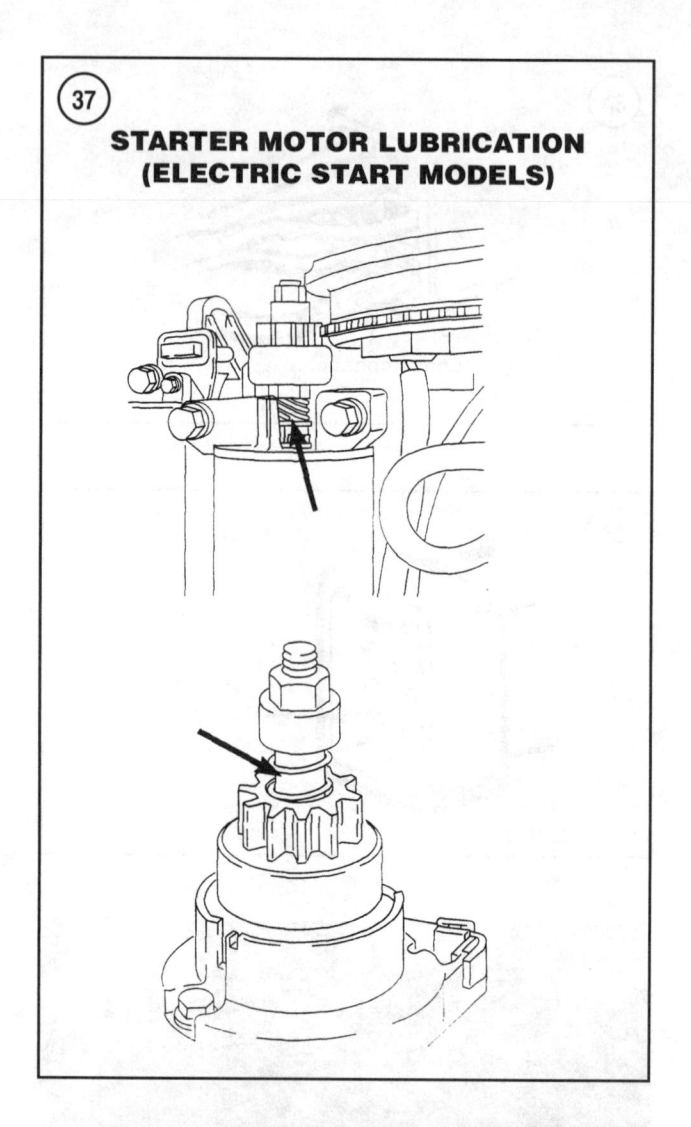

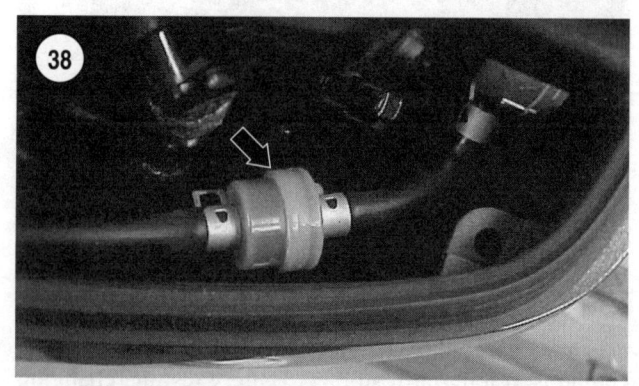

LUBRICATION, MAINTENANCE AND TUNE-UP

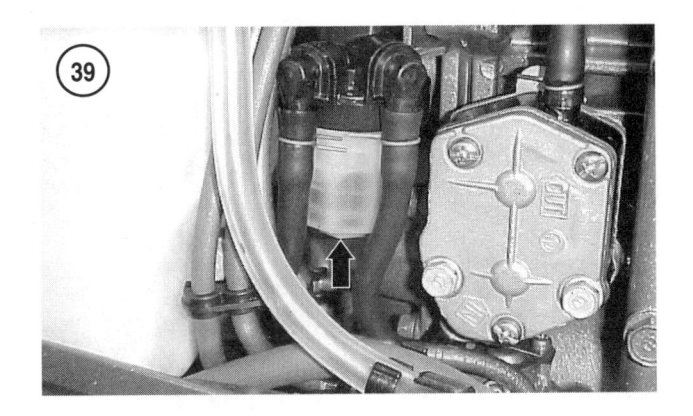

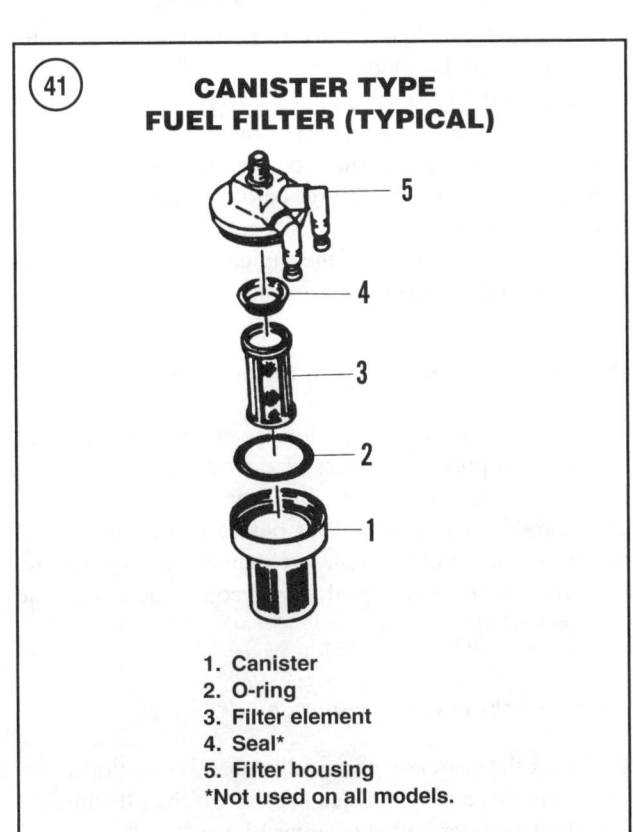

Servicing the canister-type fuel filter

1. On electric start models, disconnect the battery cables.
2. Disconnect and ground the spark plug lead to prevent accidental starting.
3. Place a suitable container or shop towels under the filter to capture spilled fuel.
4. While supporting the filter housing (5, **Figure 41**), carefully twist the canister (1), counterclockwise as viewed from the bottom, to remove the canister. Clean up any spilled fuel.
5. Empty the canister into a see-through container and check for contaminants. Inspect the fuel tank if there is water or a significant amount of debris in the fuel.
6. Remove and inspect the O-ring (2, **Figure 41**) and replace it if it is pinched or damaged.
7. Carefully pull the filter element (3, **Figure 41**) and upper seal (4) from the filter housing. Some models do not use a seal in this location.
8. Clean the canister and filter element using a mild solvent (**Figure 42**). Do not scrub the screen. Use a toothpick to remove the gummy material that collects in the bottom of the canister.
9. Inspect the filter element for deposits, debris or damage to the screen. Replace the screen if the screen is damaged or the element cannot be adequately cleaned.
10. Inspect the canister for cracks or damaged threads. Replace the canister if it is not in excellent condition.
11. Install the filter element into the canister with the open end facing upward. Position the seal (4, **Figure 41**) between the element and the filter housing. Some models do not use a seal in this location.

WARNING
Be careful when installing the canister on the filter housing. Make sure the canister threaded section is not cross-threaded during installation. A fuel leak could occur and

---

Figure 41: CANISTER TYPE FUEL FILTER (TYPICAL)

1. Canister
2. O-ring
3. Filter element
4. Seal*
5. Filter housing

*Not used on all models.

cause a fire or an explosion. Always check the entire fuel system for leaks after servicing the fuel system. Correct fuel leaks before putting the engine into service.

12. Install the O-ring into the recess in the canister. Carefully thread the canister onto the filter housing and hand-tighten it. Other means of tightening can crack or damage the canister.
13. Squeeze the primer bulb to fill the fuel system while checking for leaks. Correct any fuel leak before putting the engine into service.
14. Connect the spark plug leads.
15. On electric start models, connect the battery cables.

Fuel Hoses, Hose Clamps and Valves

At the recommended intervals (**Table 2**), check the entire fuel system for leaking hoses or connections. Check the condition of all fuel hose clamps. Remove and replace plastic locking type clamps (**Figure 43**) that appear old or have become brittle. They are relatively inexpensive and replacing them can prevent future problems. Carefully tug on the fuel hoses to check for a tight fit at the connections. Inspect spring type hose clamps (**Figure 44**). Replace clamps that are corroded, appear distorted, are damaged or have weak spring tension. Always replace damaged or questionable hose clamps.

Replace fuel hoses that have become hard or brittle, have a cracked or weathered appearance, have a spongy feel or are leaking. Only use the recommended hose available from a Yamaha or marine dealership. Fuel hoses available from automotive parts stores may not meet the demands placed upon the hose or may not meet Coast Guard requirements.

Check the fuel valve (**Figure 45**) used on 2-5 hp models for proper operation and indication of leaks. Replace the fuel valve if it is hard to move or appears to be leaking.

Corrosion Prevention

Corrosion prevention increases the life and reliability of the engine.

Decrease corrosion in the power head cooling passages by flushing the cooling system as described in this chapter as soon as possible after running the engine in salt, brackish or polluted water.

Clean and inspect external mounted anodes (**Figure 46**) at the recommended intervals (**Table 2**). Frequently test the electrical continuity of the anodes as described in Chapter Eight. Clean, inspect and test the anodes more frequently if the engine is run or stored in salt, brackish or polluted wa-

ter. Use a stiff brush to remove vegetation or powdery deposits. Replace the anode if it has lost 40% or more of its original material. Never paint or cover the anode with a protective coating. Doing so will dramatically decrease its ability to protect underwater components from corrosion. Always clean the mounting area before installing the anode to ensure a proper connection. Inspect the anode mounting area if corrosion is noted on the engine components and the anode is not experiencing corrosion.

Preparation for Storage and Fitting Out

The objective when preparing the engine for long term storage is to prevent unnecessary corrosion or deterioration during the storage period. If stored properly, the engine should operate as well as before it was stored. All major systems require some preparation during storage. Perform any maintenance that will come due during the storage period.

Preparing the engine for storage

1. Check the gearcase lubricant level and condition as described in this chapter. Check and top off the tilt/trim system fluid as described in Chapter Eleven.

LUBRICATION, MAINTENANCE AND TUNE-UP

nect the fuel supply hose at the engine and fuel tank. Direct the outlet end of the hose into the fuel tank and pump the primer bulb to remove residual fuel from the hose. Reconnect the fuel hose to prevent contamination during the storage period.

13. Check all water drain openings to make sure they are clear.
14. On oil injected models, fill the oil reservoir to reduce the air space in the reservoir. This can dramatically reduce condensation and the formation of water in the reservoir.
15. Store the engine in a protected area. If possible, store the engine in the upright position. Place a piece of cardboard or another suitable material under the engine to capture fluids that may leak from the engine.

Applying the storage sealing agent

1. Remove the silencer cover from the carburetor(s) as described in Chapter Five.
2. Run the engine at idle speed in a test tank or on a flush/test adapter for 10 minutes or until the engine reaches normal operating temperature.
3. Raise the engine speed to 1500 rpm. Spray a sealing agent for outboard engines into the carburetor(s) until the engine stalls. Try to spray evenly into all carburetors on multicarburetor engines.
4. Remove the engine from the test tank or remove the flush/test adapter. Place the engine in the upright position for several minutes to drain water from the cooling passages.
5. Remove each spark plug and pour approximately 1 oz. of Yamalube Two-Stroke Outboard Oil or equivalent into each cylinder. Crank the engine over a few times to distribute the oil.
6. Install the spark plugs.

Fitting out

When taking the engine out of storage, perform all required maintenance, service the water pump, and replace the impeller as described in Chapter Eight. The impeller will deteriorate during extended storage. Prepare and run the engine as follows:

1. Change or correct all lubricant levels.
2. Supply the engine with fresh fuel. If the engine has been in storage for one year or longer, operate the engine on a 50:1 fuel/oil mixture for the first few hours. This applies to oil injected engines as well.
3. Open the fuel valve (2-5 hp models) or pump the primer bulb and check for carburetor flooding as de-

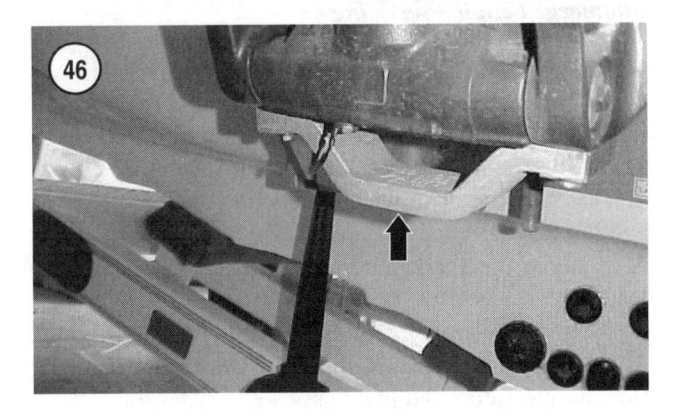

2. Lubricate the propeller shaft as described in this chapter. Remove the battery from the boat and maintain it as described in Chapter Six.
3. Check all electrical harnesses for corrosion or faulty connections and repair as necessary. Apply grease to the terminals as described in this chapter.
4. Lubricate all steering, throttle and shift linkages.
5. Lubricate all pivot and swivel shafts.
6. Lubricate the jet drive if so equipped.
7. Drain fuel from the engine-mounted fuel tank. Treat the fuel in portable or built-in tanks with an additive such as Sta-Bil.
8. Clean the exterior of the gearcase and midsection to remove vegetation, dirt or deposit buildup.
9. Wipe down the components under the engine cover and apply a good corrosion preventative spray such as CR66 or an equivalent.
10. Inspect, clean or change the fuel filter(s). Clean the screen for the oil injection system.
11. Flush the cooling system and treat the internal components of the power head with a storage sealing agent to prevent corrosion during the storage period. Refer to the procedures in this section.
12. Drain each carburetor float bowl. Refer to the diagrams in Chapter Five to locate the drain fitting. Discon-

scribed in Chapter Two. Flooding is common after long term storage.

4. Install the battery as described in Chapter Six.
5. Supply the engine with cooling water and start it.
6. Run the engine at idle speed until it reaches operating temperature. Check for proper operation of the cooling, fuel, electrical and oil injection systems. Stop the engine immediately if a fuel or oil leak is noted, overheating is detected or the warning system activates. Correct any problems before continuing.
7. Avoid running at wide-open throttle for an extended period of time during the first hour of operation.
8. Avoid continued operation if the engine is not operating properly. Continued operation may damage the power head or other components. Refer to Chapter Two for troubleshooting and testing procedures.

Submersion

If the engine has been completely submerged, three factors need to be considered. Was the engine running when the submersion occurred? Was the engine submerged in salt, brackish or heavily polluted water? How long has the engine been out of the water?

Submerged while running

Completely disassemble and inspect the power head if the engine was submerged while running. Internal damage to the power head, such as a bent connecting rod, is likely when this occurs. Refer to Chapter Seven for power head repair procedures.

Submerged in salt, brackish or heavily polluted water

Many components of the engine will corrode after submersion in salt, brackish or heavily polluted water. The symptoms may not occur for some time after the event. Salt crystals will form in areas of the engine and promote intense corrosion in those areas. The wire harness and connectors are the most commonly affected components. It is difficult to remove all of the salt crystals from the connectors. Replace the wire harness and all connectors to ensure a reliable repair. The starter motor, relays and any switch or sensor on the engine will probably fail if they are not thoroughly cleaned or replaced.

Retrieve and service the engine as soon as possible. Wash all debris from the engine with freshwater upon retrieval. If sand, silt or any other gritty material is in the engine cover, disassemble and inspect the power head as described in Chapter Seven.

Perform the submerged engine service procedures as soon as possible. Have a qualified assistant help perform the required service if necessary.

Thoroughly clean the engine and submerge it in a barrel or tank of clean freshwater if it cannot be serviced within a few hours of retrieval. This protective submersion will prevent exposure to air and decrease the potential for corrosion. This will not preserve the engine indefinitely. Service the engine within a few days of protective submersion.

Submerged engine servicing

1. Remove the engine cover and wash all material from the engine with freshwater. Completely disassemble and inspect the internal power head components if there is sand, silt or other gritty material inside the engine cover.
2. Dry the exterior of the engine with compressed air or another means.
3. Remove the spark plugs and ground the spark plug leads.
4. Remove the propeller as described in Chapter Eight.
5. Drain all water and residual fuel from the carburetor float bowls, filters and fuel hoses.
6. Position the engine with the spark plug openings facing downward. Slowly rotate the flywheel clockwise to force water from the cylinders. Use the manual starter or manually turn the flywheel on electric start models.
7. Rotate the flywheel several times to make sure the crankshaft is turning over freely. Disassemble and inspect the internal power head components if there is interference or binding.

WARNING
Rubbing alcohol is extremely flammable. Never smoke when using rubbing alcohol. Never use rubbing alcohol around a flame, sparks or another source of ignition.

8. Position the engine with the spark plug openings facing downward and pour rubbing alcohol into the carburetor opening(s). Allow the engine to set for a few minutes and slowly rotate the flywheel one complete revolution.
9. Position the engine with the spark plug opening facing upward and pour rubbing alcohol into the spark plug opening(s).
10. Slowly rotate the flywheel one complete revolution. Position the engine with the spark plug opening(s) facing downward and drain the alcohol from the cylinders. Rotate the flywheel to remove residual alcohol from the power head.

LUBRICATION, MAINTENANCE AND TUNE-UP

pression cannot be tuned properly. Refer to Chapter Two for compression testing procedures and recommendations.

Spark Plug(s)

Service the spark plug(s) during a tune-up. Although spark plugs can be cleaned and gapped to restore performance, they will not last as long as new plugs. Replace spark plugs that are not like new. Both standard type and surface gap plugs are used on Yamaha outboards. Remove the plugs and compare them to the plugs shown in **Figure 48** for standard type plugs and **Figure 49** for surface gap plugs. Spark plugs can give an indication of problems with the engine, sometimes before symptoms occur.

Correct spark plug

The correct spark plug is vital to the performance and durability of the outboard. Refer to **Table 5** for the correct spark plug. Refer to the spark plug manufacture's application guide if using a different brand spark plug.

Spark plug removal

CAUTION
Dirt or other foreign material surrounding the spark plug can fall into the spark plug opening when the spark plug is removed. Foreign material in the cylinder can cause serious power head damage.

1. Clean the area around the spark plug(s) using compressed air or a suitable brush.
2. Disconnect the spark plug lead(s) by carefully twisting the cap back and forth on the plug while pulling outward. Pulling on the lead instead of the cap can damage the lead.
3. If there is corrosion at the spark plug threaded opening, apply a penetrating oil on the threaded opening and allow it to soak for several hours.
4. Remove the spark plugs using the correct size spark plug wrench. A metric wrench is required on many of the plugs. Arrange the plugs in the order of the cylinder from which they were removed.
5. Closely examine each spark plug for the conditions shown in **Figure 48** for standard type plugs or **Figure 49** for surface gap plugs. Spark plug condition indicates engine condition and can warn of developing problems.
6. Check each plug brand and part number. All plugs must be identical.
7. Discard the spark plugs. Although they can be cleaned and reused if they are in good condition, they will not last

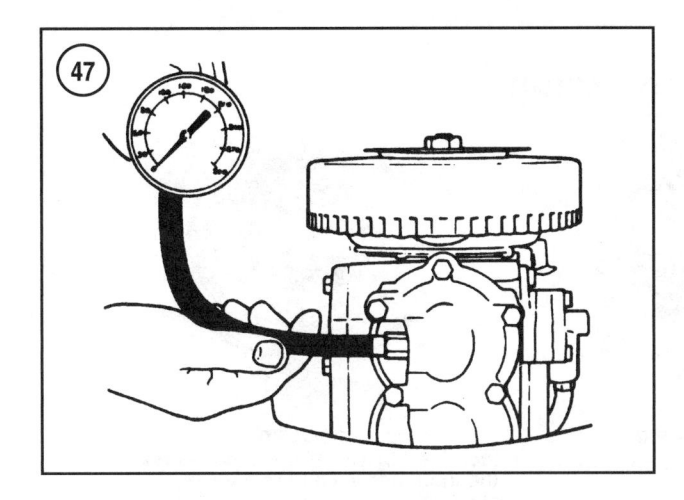

11. Place the engine in the normal upright position. Pour one teaspoon of Yamalube Two-Stroke Outboard Oil into the cylinder(s) and carburetor opening(s).
12. Rotate the flywheel several revolutions to distribute the oil.
13. On oil injected models, remove, clean and reinstall the oil reservoir, screen and oil hoses as described in Chapter Twelve.
14. Disconnect and air dry all electrical connections.
15. Remove, disassemble and inspect the starter motor as described in Chapter Six.
16. Provide the engine with a fresh supply of fuel and oil mixed at a 50:1 ratio.
17. Provide the engine with cooling water, then start the engine and run it at idle speed for at least one hour to remove any residual water. If the engine cannot be started, refer to Chapter Two for troubleshooting procedures.
18. Perform all routine maintenance before putting the engine into service. Install the propeller as described in Chapter Eight.

TUNE-UP

A tune-up is a series of test, adjustment and inspection procedures to return the engine to factory specification. A properly tuned and maintained engine will perform better and last longer. A tune-up can also improve fuel economy and reduce exhaust emissions.

This section includes the necessary adjustments, inspections and spark plug replacement procedures.

Compression Test

Perform a compression test (**Figure 47**) before beginning a tune-up. An engine with weak or unbalanced com-

SPARK PLUG CONDITION

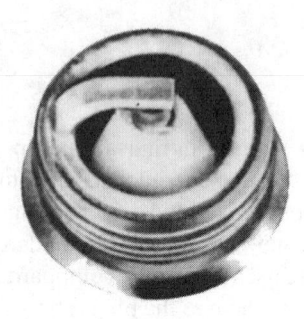

NORMAL
- Identified by light tan or gray deposits on the firing tip.
- Can be cleaned.

GAP BRIDGED
- Identified by deposit buildup closing gap between electrodes.

OIL FOULED
- Identified by wet black deposits on the insulator shell bore and electrodes.
- Caused by excessive oil entering combustion chamber through worn rings and pistons, excessive clearance between valve guides and stems or worn or loose bearings. Can be cleaned. If engine is not repaired, use a hotter plug.

CARBON FOULED
- Identified by black, dry fluffy carbon deposits on insulator tips, exposed shell surfaces and electrodes.
- Caused by too cold a plug, weak ignition, dirty air cleaner, too rich fuel mixture or excessive idling. Can be cleaned.

ADDITIVE FOULED
- Identified by dark gray, black, yellow or tan deposits or a fused glazed coating on the insulator tip.
- Caused by using gasoline additives. Can be cleaned.

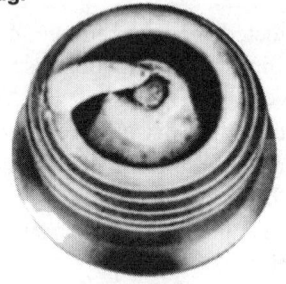

WORN
- Identified by severely eroded or worn electrodes.
- Caused by normal wear. Should be replaced.

FUSED SPOT DEPOSIT
- Identified by melted or spotty deposits resembling bubbles or blisters.
- Caused by sudden acceleration. Can be cleaned.

OVERHEATING
- Identified by a white or light gray insulator with small black or gray brown spots with bluish-burnt appearance of electrodes.
- Caused by engine overheating, wrong type of fuel, loose spark plugs, too hot a plug or incorrect ignition timing. Replace the plug.

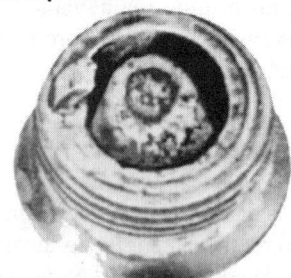

PREIGNITION
- Identified by melted electrodes and possibly blistered insulator. Metallic deposits on insulator indicate engine damage.
- Caused by wrong type of fuel, incorrect ignition timing or advance, too hot a plug, burned valves or engine overheating. Replace the plug.

LUBRICATION, MAINTENANCE AND TUNE-UP

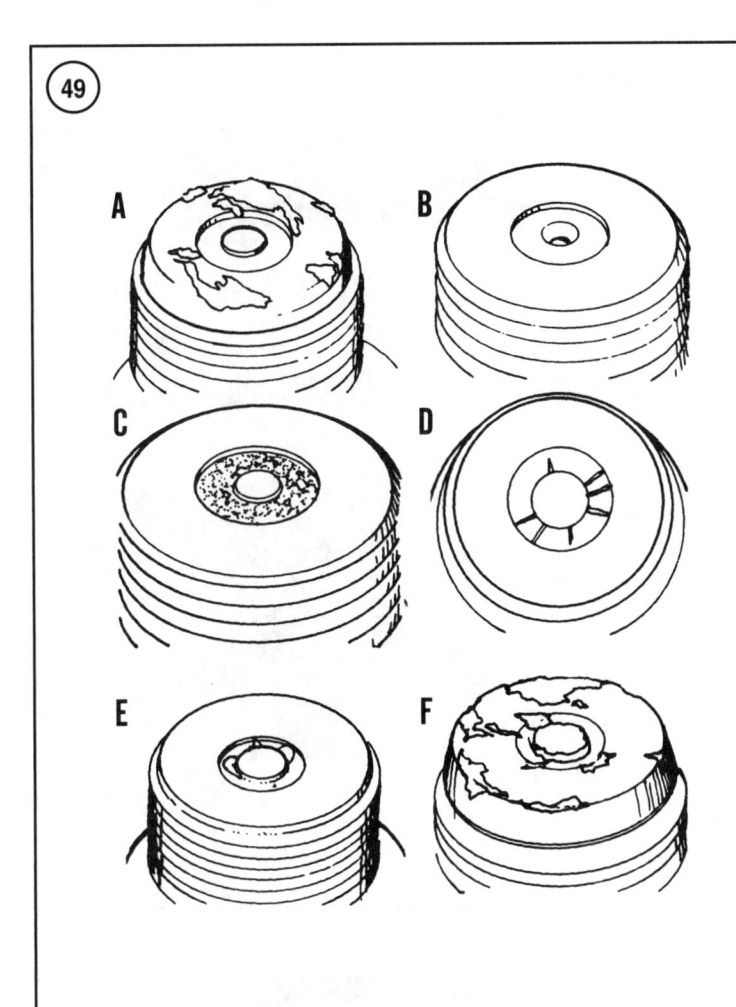

**SPARK PLUG ANALYSIS
(SURFACE GAP SPARK PLUGS)**

A. Normal—Light tan or gray colored deposits indicate that the engine/ignition system condition is good. Electrode wear indicates normal spark rotation.
B. Worn out—Excessive electrode wear can cause hard starting or a misfire during acceleration.
C. Cold fouled—Wet oil or fuel deposits are caused by "drowning" the plug with raw fuel mix during cranking, overich carburetion or an improper fuel:oil ratio. Weak ignition will also contribute to this condition.
D. Carbon tracking—Electrically conductive deposits on the firing end provide a low-resistance path for the voltage. Carbon tracks form and can cause misfires.
E. Concentrated arc—Multi-colored appearance is normal. It is caused by electricity consistently following the same firing path. Arc path changes with deposit conductivity and gap erosion.
F. Aluminum throw off—Caused by preignition. This is not a plug problem but the result of engine damage. Check engine to determine cause and extent of damage.

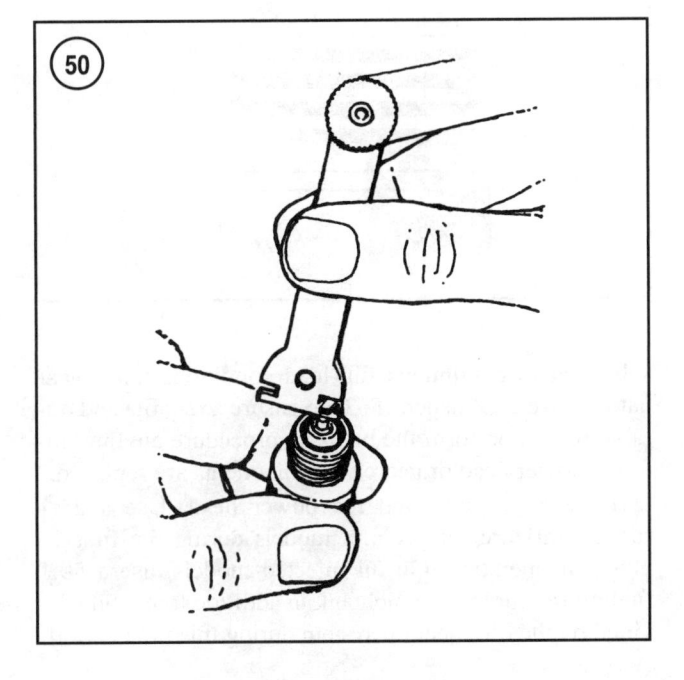

as long as new plugs. New plugs are relatively inexpensive and are far more reliable.

Gapping standard type spark plugs

New spark plugs must be carefully gapped to ensure a consistent spark. Use a special spark plug gapping tool (**Figure 50**) and feeler gauges (**Figure 51**) or a combination tool (**Figure 52**) to adjust the gap.

1. Insert the appropriate size gauge (**Table 5**) between the electrodes (**Figure 53**). If the gap is correct, there will be a slight drag as the gauge passes between the electrodes.

CAUTION
Never attempt to narrow the spark plug gap by tapping the spark plug on a hard object. This can damage the spark plug and possibly fracture the insulator. Always use a gapping tool to increase or narrow the spark plug gap.

2. Carefully bend the side electrode with a gapping tool (**Figure 50**) to adjust the gap. Always measure the gap after the adjustment.

3. Inspect the spark plug threads in the power head and clean them with a thread chaser (**Figure 54**) as necessary. Occasionally, the aluminum material from the spark plug opening will come out with the spark plug. A threaded insert can be installed into the cylinder head to repair this condition. Have a reputable marine dealership or machine shop perform this procedure.

4. Make sure the gasket is installed on the spark plug.

5. Wipe the opening clean before installing the new plug. Screw the plug into the power head by hand until it seats. Very little force is required. If force is necessary, the threads may be dirty or the plug may be cross-threaded. Unscrew the plug and clean the threads before attempting to install the plug.

6. Tighten the spark plug to the specification in **Table 1**. If a torque wrench is not available, seat the plug finger-tight, then tighten the plug an additional 1/4 turn of the wrench.

7. Inspect the spark plug lead and cap before connecting it to the spark plug. Replace the lead if the insulation is damaged or deteriorated. Replace the cap if the contacts are corroded or the cap is cracked.

8. Install the cap on the plug. Push until the spark plug terminal fully seats into the cap.

Timing and Carburetor Adjustment

Timing adjustments can easily be made at lower engine speeds. To check the ignition timing at higher speeds, the engine should be tested under actual operating conditions with a timing light installed (**Figure 55**). Timing adjustments will require an assistant. One to operate the boat and one to check the timing.

Carburetor adjustments involve carburetor synchronization, idle mixture and idle speed adjustments (**Figure 56**). Perform the carburetor synchronization and linkage adjustments before adjusting the carburetor(s). Make final adjustments under actual running conditions. This generally provides the smoothest and most efficient operation.

Ignition timing, carburetor synchronization, idle mixture and idle speed adjustment are described in Chapter Four.

ENGINE BREAK-IN

During the first few hours of running, many of the internal power head and gearcase components should not be subjected to continuous full-load conditions until wear patterns are established. To help ensure a reliable and durable repair, perform the break-in procedure anytime internal power head or gearcase components are replaced.

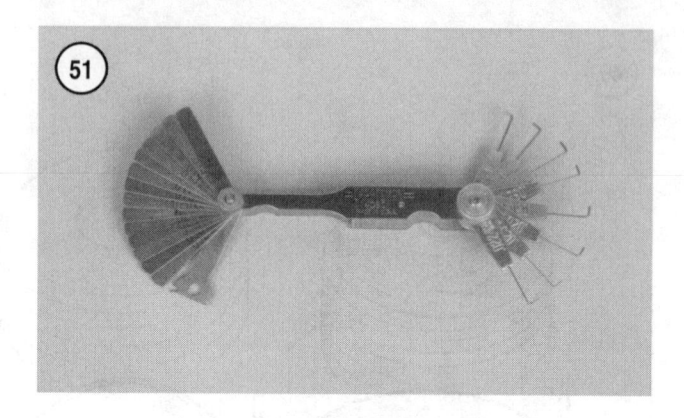

If the repair involved the power head, Use a 25:1 fuel/oil mixture for pre-mix models during the first 10 hours of operation. On oil injected models, use a 50:1 fuel/oil mixture in the fuel tank in addition to the oil provided by the oil injection system during this time period.

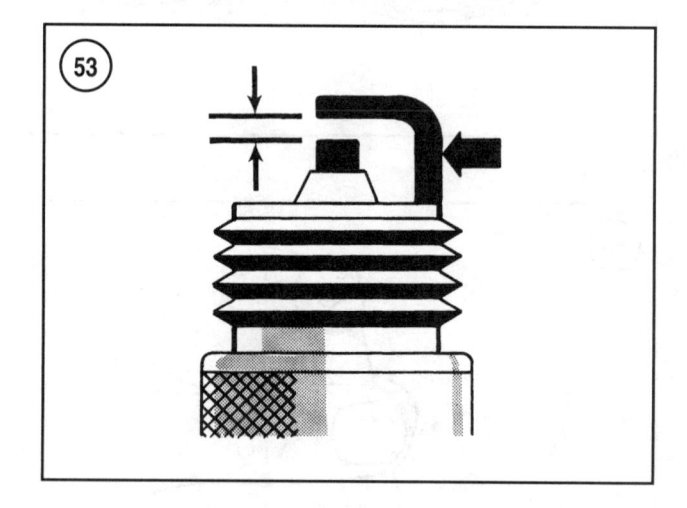

LUBRICATION, MAINTENANCE AND TUNE-UP

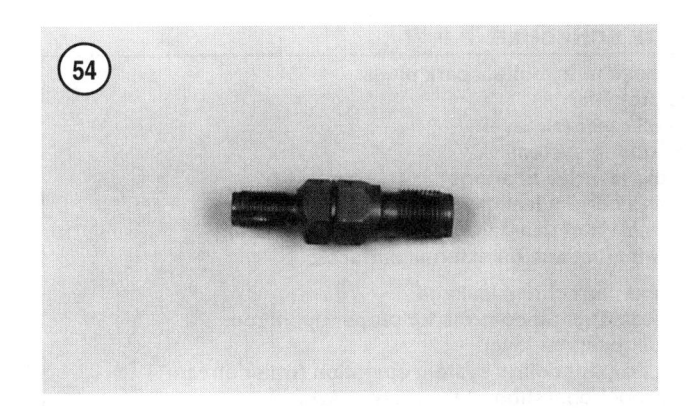

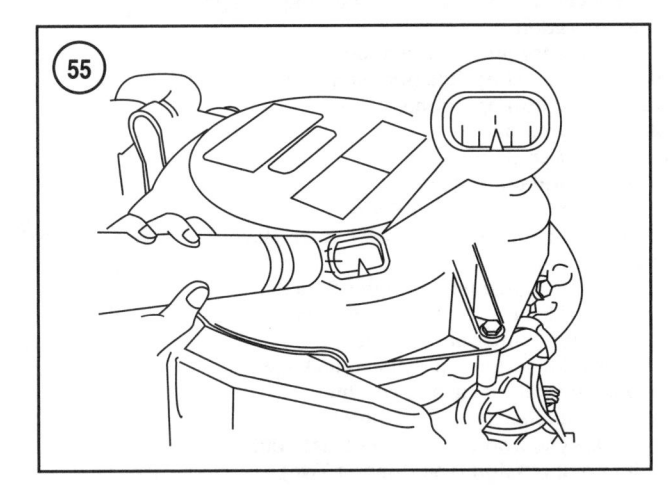

Operate the engine at fast idle, approximately 1500 rpm, in neutral for the first 10 minutes. During the next 50 minutes, change the throttle setting frequently and avoid full throttle operation, except to quickly plane the boat. Do not exceed 3000 rpm during the 50 minute time period.

During the second hour of operation, use full throttle only as needed to plane the boat, then reduce the throttle setting to a maximum of 3/4 open. Vary the throttle setting frequently during the second hour of operation.

During the third hour of operation, run the engine at varying throttle openings. Occasionally advance the throttle to full open for a short period, up to five minutes, then reduce the throttle setting to 3/4 open or lower to allow the engine to cool.

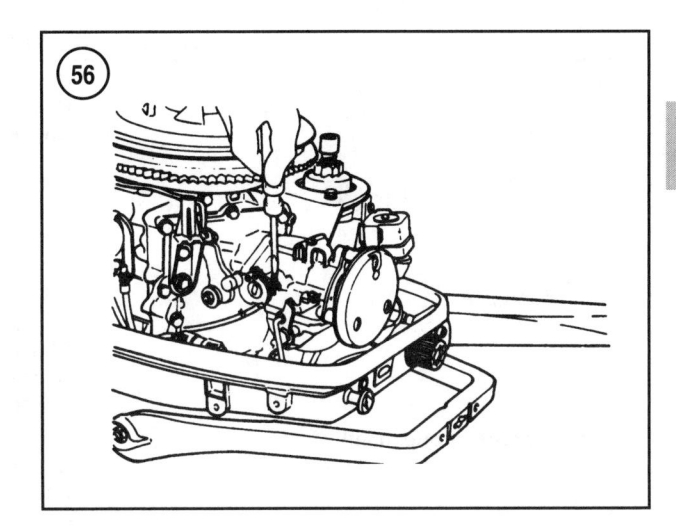

During the remaining seven hours of the ten hour break-in period, avoid continuous full-throttle operation and do not operate the engine at any one throttle setting for more than 15 minutes.

After the ten hour break-in period, the engine can be operated at any speed at or below the maximum recommended by the manufacturer. Refer to Chapter Two for engine operating speed recommendations.

If the repair involved the gearcase, change the gearcase lubricant as described in this chapter. Fine metal particles commonly form on the drain/fill plug during new gear break-in. Fine particles do not indicate a problem within the gearcase. Larger or gritty particles indicate a potential problem. Disassemble and inspect and the gearcase before continuing operation.

If the repair involved the power head, use the standard fuel/oil mixture as recommended in this chapter. If the engine is equipped with oil injection, monitor the amount of fuel burned and the oil used from the reservoir. If the oil use is not consistent with the fuel burned, test the oil pump output as described in Chapter Two.

Table 1 TORQUE SPECIFICATIONS

Fastener	N•m	in.-lb.	ft.-lb.
Gearcase plugs	7	62	–
Spark plug			
2-15 hp	25	–	18
20 and 25 hp (two-cylinder)	25	–	18
25 hp (three-cylinder) and 30 hp	20	–	15
28 jet, 35 jet, 40 hp and 50 hp	25	–	18
60-90 hp	25	–	18

Table 2 MAINTENANCE SCHEDULE

After each use	Check for loose nuts, bolts, spark plugs
	Check the propeller
	Check the oil reservoir level*
	Flush the cooling system
	Lubricate the jet drive bearings*
	Check for and correct leaking fluids
	Wash the exterior of gearcase and drive shaft housing
	Touch up paint damage on external surfaces
Before each use	Check for and correct fuel leakage
	Check the steering and controls for proper operation
	Check the oil reservoir level*
	Check for a proper cooling system operation (water stream)
	Check for proper operation of the lockout system
Initial 10 hours or one month	Lubricate the swivel tube, tilt tube and steering system
	Check throttle operation
	Check shift linkages for proper operation
	Check tightness of all accessible nuts and bolts
	Check power tilt and trim operation*
	Check choke lever operation*
	Inspect fuel filter for contamination
	Inspect fuel hoses and connections
	Adjust the idle speed (see Chapter Four)
	Inspect mid-section components (see Chapter Eleven)
	Inspect the spark plug(s)
	Adjust the oil pump linkage (see Chapter Four)*
	Inspect oil reservoir for water or contamination*
	Check electrical wiring and connections
	Check power head for water and exhaust leakage
	Check gearcase lubricant level and condition
	Check condition and charge level of battery
	Check carburetor synchronization and adjustments
	Check cylinder compression (see Chapter Two)
	Adjust the lockout assembly (see Chapter Four)
Initial 50 hours or 90 days	Lubricate the swivel tube, tilt tube and steering system
	Adjust the carburetor(s)
	Inspect fuel filter for contamination
	Check spark plug condition and gap
	Check and adjust the ignition timing (see Chapter Four)
	Check the oil injection system*
	Check electrical wiring and connections
	Check power head for water and exhaust leakage
	Check gearcase lubricant level and condition
	Inspect the water pump impeller (see Chapter Eight)
	Check the propeller
	Check propeller nut for tightness
	Clean and inspect sacrificial anodes
	Check all accessible nuts and bolts for tightness
	Check cylinder compression (see Chapter Two)
	Adjust the lockout assembly (see Chapter Four)
Each 100 hours of usage or 180 days	Lubricate the swivel tube, tilt tube and steering system
	Check carburetor synchronization and adjustments
	Inspect fuel filter for contamination
	Check fuel hoses and clamps for leakage
	Check the spark plug condition and gap
	Check the power tilt/trim fluid level (see Chapter Eleven)
	Inspect the mid-section components.
	Check the oil injection system*
	Check electrical wiring and connections
	Check power head for water and exhaust leakage
	(continued)

LUBRICATION, MAINTENANCE AND TUNE-UP

Table 2 MAINTENANCE SCHEDULE (continued)

Each 100 hours of usage or 180 days (cont.)	Lubricate the swivel tube, tilt tube and steering system Check gearcase lubricant level and condition Check the condition and charge level of the battery (see Chapter Six)* Clean and inspect sacrificial anodes Check all accessible nuts and bolts for tightness Check the propeller nut for tightness Check cylinder compression Adjust the lockout assembly (see Chapter Four)
Each 200 hours of usage or one year	Inspect fuel tank, hoses and clamps Clean or replace the fuel filter Replace the water pump impeller Check fuel valve for proper operation*

*This maintenance item may not apply to all models.

Table 3 FLUID CAPACITIES

Model	Capacity (approximate)
Fuel tank	
2 hp	1.2 L (0.32 gal.)
3 hp	1.4 L (0.37 gal.)
4 and 5 hp	2.8 L (0.74 gal.)
Gearcase	
2 hp	45 ml (1.5 oz.)
3 hp	74 ml (2.5 oz.)
4 and 5 hp	100 ml (3.4 oz.)
6 and 8 hp	160 ml (5.4 oz.)
9.9 and 15 hp	251 ml (8.5 oz.)
20 and 25 hp (two-cylinder)	370 ml (12.5 oz.)
25 hp (three-cylinder) and 30 hp	200 ml (6.8 oz.)
40 and 50 hp	430 ml (14.5 oz.)
60-90 hp	500 ml (16.9 oz.)
Oil reservoir	
20 and 25 hp (two-cylinder)	0.7 L (0.74 qt.)
28 jet, 35 jet, 40 hp and 50 hp	1.5 L (1.59 qt.)
60 and 70 hp	2.8 L (2.96 qt.)
65 jet and 75-90 hp	3.3 L (3.49 qt.)

Table 4 OIL AND FUEL MIXING RATES

Quantity of fuel	Oil for 50:1 ratio	Oil for 100:1 ratio
3.8 L (1 gal.)	76 cc (2.6 oz.)	38 cc (1.25 oz.)
7.6 L (2 gal.)	152 cc (5.2 oz)	76 cc (2.6 oz.)
11.4 L (3 gal.)	228 cc (7.8 oz.)	114 cc (3.9 oz.)
15.4 L (4 gal.)	304 cc (10.4 oz.)	152 cc (5.2 oz.)
18.9 L (5 gal.)	380 cc (12.8 oz.)	190 cc (6.4 oz.)
22.8 L (6 gal.)	456 cc (15.6 oz.)	228 cc (7.8 oz.)
26.6 L (7 gal.)	530 cc (18.2 oz.)	265 cc (9.1 oz.)
30.8 L (8 gal.)	608 cc (20.8 oz.)	304 cc (10.4 oz.)
34.2 L (9 gal.)	684 cc (23.4 oz.)	342 cc (11.7 oz.)
37.8 L (10 gal.)	760 cc (25.6 oz.)	380 cc (12.8 oz.)
41.6 L (11 gal.)	832 cc (28.2 oz.)	416 cc (14.1 oz.)
45.6 L (12 gal.)	912 cc (31.2 oz.)	456 cc (15.6 oz.)

Table 5 SPARK PLUG SPECIFICATIONS

Model	NGK plug	Champion plug	Gap
2 hp	B5HS	L90 C	0.6 mm (0.024 in.)
3 hp	B6HS-10	L86C	1.0 mm (0.040 in.)
4 and 5 hp	B7HS	L82C	0.6 mm (0.024 in.)
6-40 hp	B7HS-10	L82C	1.0 mm (0.040 in.)
28 jet	B7HS-10	L82C	1.0 mm (0.040 in.)
35 jet and 50-90 hp	B8HS-10	L78C	1.0 mm (0.040 in.)

Chapter Four

Timing, Synchronization and Adjustment

For an outboard engine to deliver maximum efficiency, performance and reliability, the ignition and fuel systems must be correctly adjusted. This adjustment procedure is referred to as *synch and link*.

Failure to properly synch and link an engine will not only result in a loss of engine performance and efficiency, but also can lead to power head damage. Perform all synch and link adjustments during a tune-up or whenever any ignition or fuel system components are replaced, serviced or adjusted.

Adjustments to the shift linkages, jet, drive, lockout assembly (neutral only start) and trim position sender are required after removal or repairs of related components, and at the intervals specified in Chapter Three.

Tighten all fasteners to the specification for the size of fastener listed in Chapter Three unless the instructions list a torque specification. **Tables 1-8** list synch and link specifications. All tables are at the end of this chapter.

TIMING, SYNCHRONIZATION AND ADJUSTMENTS

On a typical engine, a synch and link procedure will generally involve the following:

1. Synchronizing and adjusting the ignition and fuel systems linkages.
2. Making sure the fuel system throttle plate(s) fully open and close, and all throttle plates are synchronized to open and close at exactly the same time.
3. Synchronizing the ignition system spark advance with throttle plate(s) operation to provide optimum off-idle acceleration and smooth part-throttle operation.
4. Adjusting the oil injection pump linkage.
5. Adjusting the ignition timing at idle and wide-open throttle engine speeds.
6. Setting the idle speed.

Synch and link procedures for Yamaha outboard engines differ according to engine model, type of starting system, type of lubrication system and optional equipment. This chapter is divided by model for fast and easy reference. Each section specifies the appropriate procedure and sequence to follow.

Read *Safety Precaution* and *General Information* in this chapter before performing the synch and link procedures.

Safety Precautions

Wear approved eye protection at all times, especially when machinery is in operation. Wear approved ear protection during all running tests and in the presence of noisy machinery. Keep loose clothing tucked in and long hair secured.

When making or breaking any electrical connection, always disconnect the negative battery cable. When performing tests that require cranking the engine without starting, disconnect and ground the spark plug leads to prevent accidental starts and sparks.

Securely cap or plug all disconnected fuel lines to prevent fuel discharge when the engine is cranked or the primer bulb is squeezed.

Thoroughly read all manufacturer's instructions and safety sheets for test equipment and special tools being used.

Do not substitute parts unless they meet or exceed the original manufacturer's specifications.

Never run an outboard engine without an adequate water supply. Never run an outboard engine at wide-open throttle without an adequate load. Never exceed 3000 rpm in neutral with no load.

Safely performing on-water tests requires two people; one person to operate the boat, and one person to monitor the gauges or test instruments. All personnel must remain seated inside the boat at all times. Do not lean over the transom while the boat is under way. Use extensions to allow gauges and meters to be located in the normal seating area.

A test propeller is an economical alternative to the dynometer. A test propeller is also a convenient alternative to on-water testing. **Table 1** lists the part numbers for test propellers available from a Yamaha or marine dealership. A test propeller can also be made by modifying the diameter of a standard low pitch aluminum propeller until the recommended wide-open throttle speed can be obtained with the engine in a test tank or on the trailer backed into the water. Propeller repair stations can provide the modification service. Normally, approximately 1/3 to 1/2 of the outer blade surface is removed. However, it is better to remove too little, than too much. It may take several tries to achieve the correct full throttle speed, but once achieved, no further modifications will be required. Many propeller repair stations have experience with this type of modification and may be able to recommend a starting point.

Be careful when tying the boat to a dock as considerable thrust is developed by the test propeller. Some docks may not be able to withstand the load.

Test propellers also allow simple tracking of engine performance. The full-throttle test speed of an engine fitted with a correctly modified test propeller can be tracked from season to season. It is not unusual for a new or rebuilt engine to show a slight increase in test propeller speed as complete break-in is achieved and then to hold that speed over the normal service life of the engine. As the engine begins to wear out, the test propeller speed will show a gradual decrease.

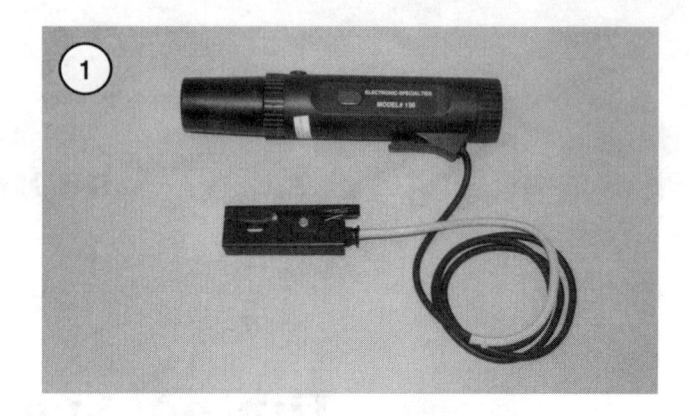

General Information

Perform synch and link adjustments with the engine running under actual operating conditions to be as accurate as possible. Carburetor idle speed adjustments are very sensitive to engine load and exhaust system back pressure. If the adjustments are made with the engine running on a flushing device, the adjustments will not be correct when the engine is operated in the water under load.

CAUTION
*Do not run the engine without an adequate water supply and do not exceed 3000 rpm without an adequate load. Refer to **Safety Precautions** in this chapter.*

Ignition Timing

All models use some form of timing marks that allow the ignition timing to be checked using a suitable strobo-

TIMING, SYNCHRONIZATION AND ADJUSTMENT

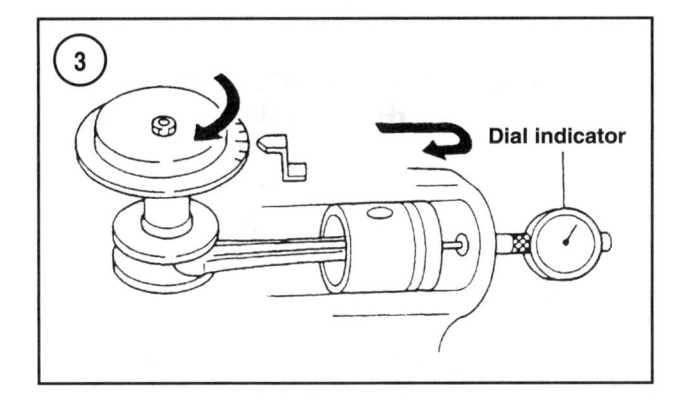

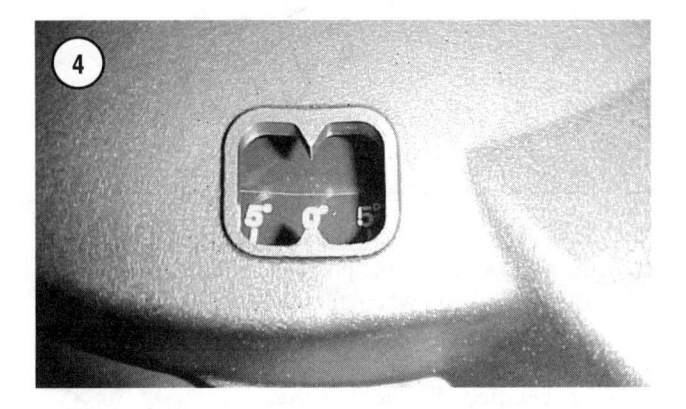

scopic timing light (**Figure 1**). On models with adjustable timing, a linkage adjustment is made to bring the timing into specification. If the timing is not within specification on models with nonadjustable timing, there is either a mechanical or electrical defect in the system. Chapter Two covers ignition troubleshooting for all models.

The maximum timing check will be most accurate at wide-open throttle. This method is not always practical, however, as the outboard must be operated at full throttle in forward gear under load to verify maximum timing advance. If possible, use a test tank and test propeller, as timing an engine while speeding across open water can be hazardous. Refer to *Safety Precautions* in the previous section.

The maximum timing advance on some models can be set by holding the ignition linkage in the full-throttle position while the engine is being cranked. While acceptable where noted, this procedure is not as accurate as the wide-open throttle check. Whenever possible, check the maximum timing specification at wide-open throttle with a test propeller.

Wide-Open Throttle Speed Verification

All outboard engines have a specified wide-open throttle (WOT) speed range. When the engine is mounted on a boat and run at wide-open throttle, the engine speed should be within the specified range. If the engine speed is above or below the specified range, the engine is damaged. **Table 2** lists the maximum wide-open throttle speed range for all models.

NOTE
Use an accurate shop tachometer for checking WOT speed. Do not use the boat tachometer for WOT verification.

Operating an engine with a propeller that will not allow the engine to reach its specified range is called over-propping. This causes the combustion chamber temperature to rise dramatically, leading to preignition and detonation (Chapter Two).

Operating an engine with a propeller that allows an engine to exceed its specified range is called over-speeding. Over-speeding an engine will lead to mechanical failure of the reciprocating engine components. Some engines are equipped with an rpm limit module that shorts out the ignition system to limit engine speed. Over-speeding these engines can cause ignition misfire symptoms that can cause troubleshooting difficulty.

Changing the pitch, diameter or style of the propeller changes the load on the engine and the resulting WOT engine speed. If the WOT engine speed exceeds the specified range, install a propeller with more pitch or a larger diameter and recheck engine speed. If the WOT engine speed is below the specified range, install a propeller with less pitch or smaller diameter and recheck engine speed.

Required Equipment

Static adjustment of the ignition timing and/or verification of the timing pointer requires a dial indicator (**Figure 2**) to position the No. 1 piston at top dead center (TDC) accurately before timing adjustments are made. The No. 1 spark plug must be removed for this procedure. The dial indicator is threaded into the spark plug opening. Adjustments to the timing pointer synchronize the pointer to the actual piston position relative to TDC. See **Figure 3**.

All ignition timing checks and adjustments require a stroboscopic timing light connected to the No. 1 spark plug lead. As the engine is cranked or operated, the light flashes each time the spark plug fires. When the light is pointed at the moving flywheel, the mark on the flywheel (**Figure 4**) appears to stand still. The appropriate timing marks will be aligned if the timing is correctly adjusted.

CAUTION
*Factory timing specifications are in **Table 4** and **Table 5**. Occasionally the manufacturer*

will modify their specifications during production. If the engine has a decal attached to the power head silencer cover, always follow the specification on the decal, instead of the specification in **Table 4** and **Table 5**.

NOTE
Timing lights with built-in features, such as a timing advance function, are not recommended for outboard engines. A basic high-speed timing light with an inductive pickup, such as Yamaha part No. YM-33277 is recommended.

Use an accurate shop tachometer to determine engine speed during timing adjustment. Do not rely on the tachometer installed in a boat to provide accurate engine speed readings. Use Yamaha part No. YU-8036-A or another suitable tachometer.

Timing, Synchronization and Carburetor Adjustment (2 hp Model)

The ignition timing is non-adjustable and timing pointer adjustment is not required. This model does not use a timing pointer. Only the idle speed adjustment is required on this model.

Idle speed adjustment

1. Disconnect and ground the spark plug lead to prevent accidental starting.
2. Carefully turn the adjusting screw (**Figure 5**) clockwise until it is lightly seated. Turn the screw out counterclockwise 1 1/2 turns.
3. Remove the propeller as described in Chapter Eight and install a test propeller. The test propeller part number is in **Table 1**.
4. Connect the spark plug lead. Connect a suitable shop tachometer to the spark plug lead.
5. Place the engine in a suitable test tank. Securely tighten the clamp screws. Start the engine and advance the throttle to approximately 1500 rpm in NEUTRAL gear for ten minutes or until the engine reaches full operating temperature.
6. Place the throttle control in the idle position. Turn the screw (**Figure 5**) clockwise until the engine speed begins to drop, then note the screw position.
7. Slowly turn the screw (**Figure 5**) counterclockwise until the engine speed increases then begins to drop. Note the screw position.

8. Adjust the screw to the position midway between the two noted points and where the engine attains the highest and most consistent speed. If the speed is not within the range specified in **Table 7**, turn the screw clockwise to attain the specified idle speed range.

9. Slowly advance the throttle, then bring it down to the idle position. Check for binding linkages or readjust the idle speed if the engine does not return to the specified range within 30-40 seconds.

10. Rapidly advance the throttle while checking for hesitation. Readjust the screw to minimize hesitation. Counterclockwise rotation reduces hesitation in most cases. Readjust the screw only a slight amount. Do not adjust the screw enough to exceed the idle speed limits.

11. Stop the engine and remove it from the test tank.

12. Remove the test propeller and install the running propeller as described in Chapter Eight.

Timing, Synchronization and Carburetor Adjustments (3 hp Model)

The ignition timing is not adjustable on this model and timing pointer adjustment is not required. Perform the following adjustments and checks:

1. Pilot screw adjustment.
2. Idle speed adjustment.
3. Ignition timing check.
4. Throttle cable adjustment.

TIMING, SYNCHRONIZATION AND ADJUSTMENT

6 PILOT SCREW ADJUSTMENT (3 HP MODEL)

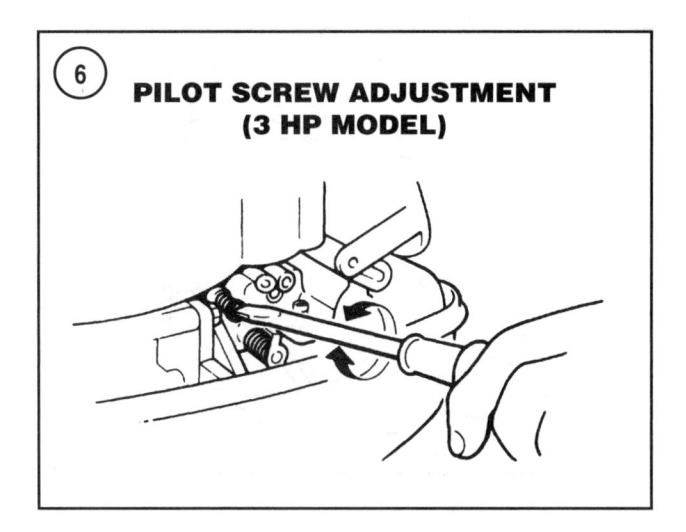

7 IDLE SPEED ADJUSTMENT (3 HP MODEL)

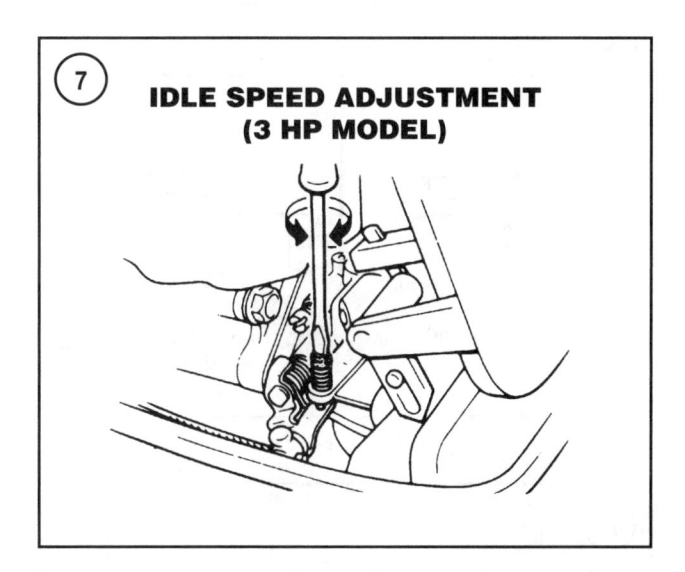

Pilot screw adjustment

1. Disconnect and ground the spark plug lead to prevent accidental starting.
2. Carefully turn the pilot screw clockwise until it is lightly seated (**Figure 6**).
3. Turn the pilot screw counterclockwise to the middle of the adjustment range in **Table 6**.

Idle speed adjustment

1. Turn the idle speed screw (**Figure 7**) counterclockwise until there is a gap between the screw tip and the carburetor throttle lever. Slowly rotate the screw clockwise until the tip just contacts the lever. Turn the screw one complete turn clockwise to slightly open the throttle.

2. Remove the propeller as described in Chapter Eight and install a test propeller. The test propeller part number is in **Table 1**.
3. Connect the spark plug lead. Connect a suitable shop tachometer to the spark plug lead.
4. Place the engine in a suitable test tank. Securely tighten the clamp screws. Start the engine and advance the throttle to approximately 1500 rpm in NEUTRAL gear for ten minutes or until the engine reaches full operating temperature.
5. Place the throttle control in the idle position and note the idle speed. Turn the screw (**Figure 7**) until the idle speed is in the middle of the specification in **Table 7**. Clockwise screw rotation increases idle speed. Counterclockwise rotation decreases idle speed.
6. Shift the engine into FORWARD gear. Allow the idle to stabilize for a few minutes, then note the in-gear idle speed. If the in-gear idle speed is not within the specification in **Table 7**, readjust the idle speed screw.
7. Shift the engine into NEUTRAL gear. Allow the idle to stabilize for a few minutes, then note the idle speed. The neutral gear idle speed must remain within the specification in **Table 7**. If necessary, readjust the idle speed screw until both the in-gear and in-neutral idle speeds are within the specification. Several adjustments may be required.
8. Shift the engine into FORWARD gear and allow the idle to stabilize for a few minutes. Slowly advance the throttle, then bring it down to the idle position. Check for binding linkages or readjust the idle speed if the engine does not return to the specified range within 30-40 seconds.
9. Rapidly advance the throttle while checking for hesitation. If necessary, readjust the pilot screw (**Figure 6**) to minimize hesitation. Counterclockwise rotation reduces hesitation in most cases. Readjust the screw only a slight amount. Do not exceed the adjustment limits in **Table 6**.
10. Check the ignition timing as described in this section.

Ignition timing check

1. Remove the propeller as described in Chapter Eight and install a test propeller. The test propeller part number is in **Table 1**.
2. Connect a timing light to the spark plug lead (**Figure 8**).
3. Connect a shop tachometer to the spark plug lead. Do not allow the timing light and tachometer pickups to touch during this procedure.
4. Place the engine in a suitable test tank. Securely tighten the clamp screws. Start the engine and advance the throttle to approximately 1500 rpm in NEUTRAL gear for

ten minutes or until the engine reaches full operating temperature.

5. Place the throttle in the idle position and allow the idle speed to stabilize for a few minutes. Direct the flashing light at the timing windows (**Figure 8**) on the port side of the power head. The timing mark should appear in the left window (**Figure 9**) at idle speed.

6. Shift the engine into FORWARD gear. Observe the tachometer and timing window while advancing the throttle to the maximum timing speed specified in **Table 6**. The timing mark should appear in the right window (**Figure 9**) at the maximum timing speed.

7. If the timing mark does not appear as specified in Step 5 and Step 6, check for a sheared flywheel drive key as described in Chapter Seven, faulty pulser coil or faulty CDI unit as described in Chapter Two.

8. Return the throttle to idle. Shift the engine into NEUTRAL. Stop the engine and remove it from the test tank.

9. Remove the test propeller and install the running propeller as described in Chapter Eight.

Throttle cable adjustment

1. Disconnect and ground the spark plug lead to prevent accidental starting.

2. Locate and loosen the throttle cable anchor screw (**Figure 10**). The cable should slide freely in the anchor.

3. Place the throttle grip in the idle position (**Figure 11**). Rotate the carburetor throttle lever to the idle position (**Figure 12**). The lever must be in contact with the idle speed screw tip.

4. Lightly pull on the cable wire to remove slack. Hold the throttle lever in NEUTRAL and securely tighten the cable anchor screw (**Figure 10**).

5. Rotate the throttle grip to the full throttle position (**Figure 13**) and check the position of the carburetor throttle lever. If the lever does not move to the full open position as shown in **Figure 13**, check for a faulty cable. If the cable is not faulty, loosen the anchor screw and readjust the cable to achieve full movement to the idle and full throttle positions. Securely tighten the cable anchor screw when it is properly adjusted.

6. Connect the spark plug lead. Run the engine and check for proper throttle operation. Readjust as necessary. Do not operate the engine if there is binding or improper operation.

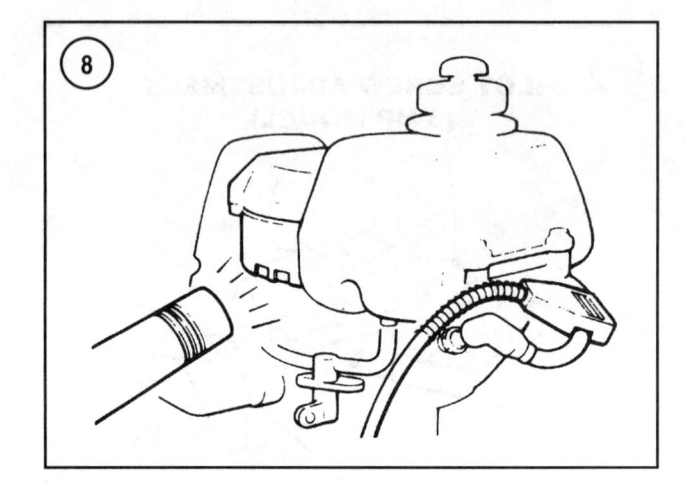

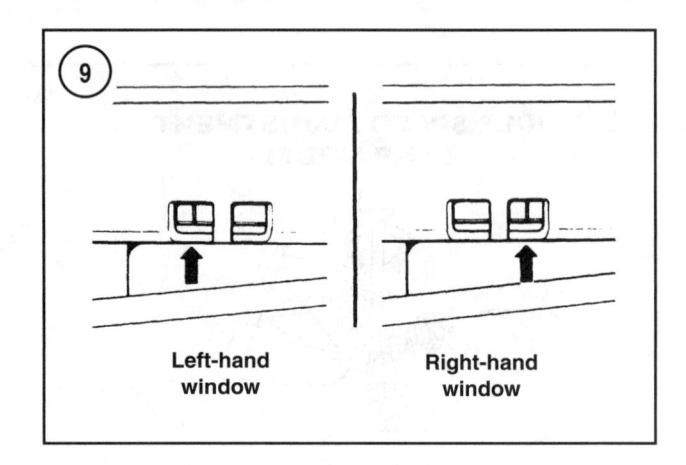

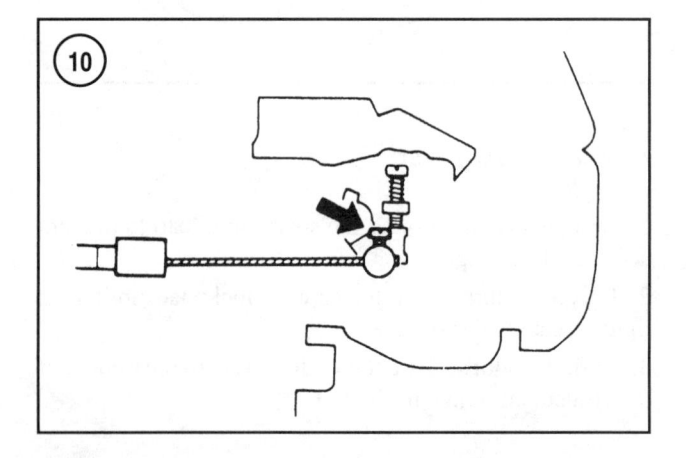

Timing, Synchronization and Carburetor Adjustments (4 and 5 hp Models)

The ignition timing is not adjustable on this model and timing pointer adjustment is not required. Perform the following adjustments and checks:

TIMING, SYNCHRONIZATION AND ADJUSTMENT

PILOT SCREW ADJUSTMENT (4 AND 5 HP MODELS)

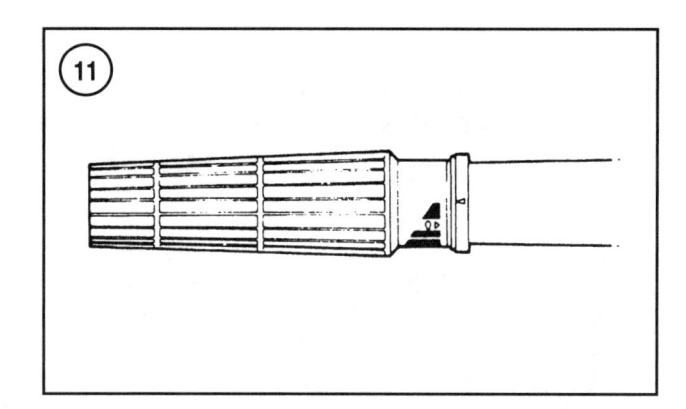

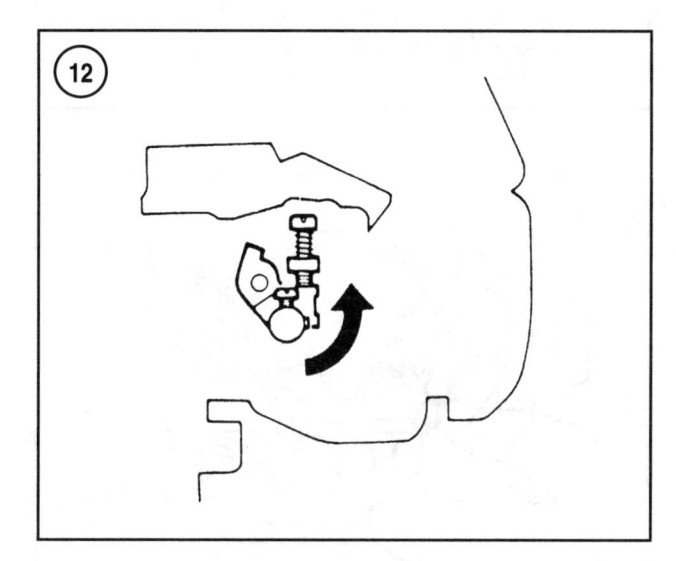

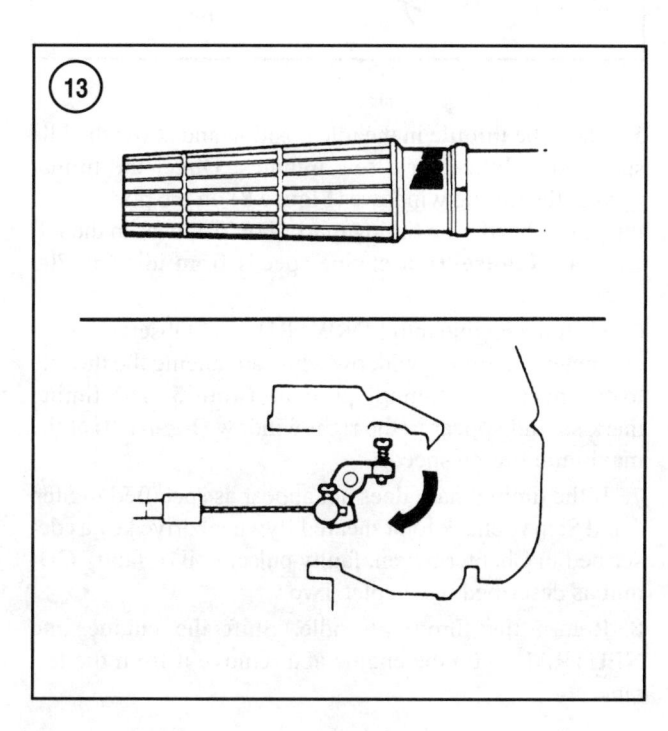

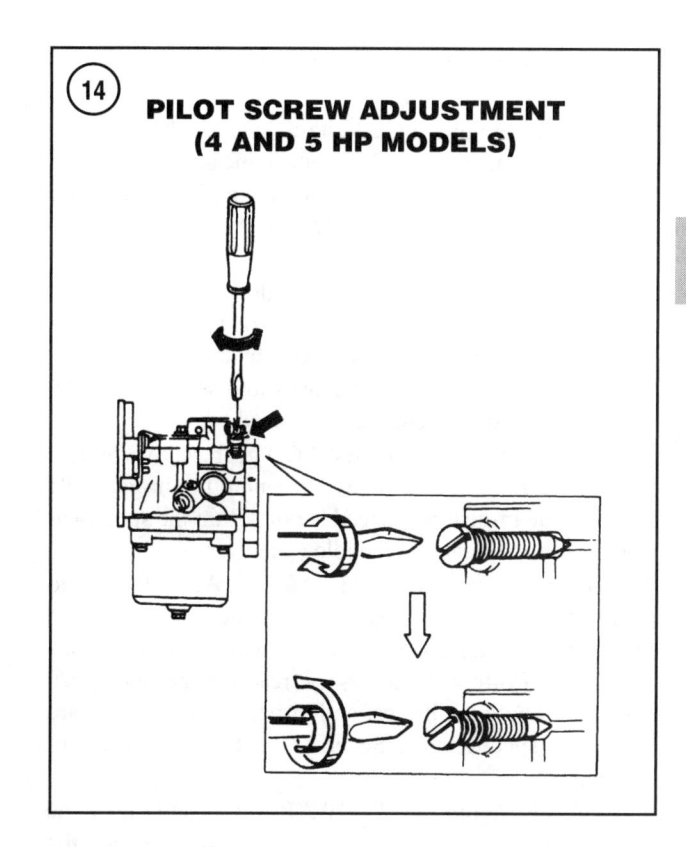

1. Pilot screw adjustment.
2. Idle speed adjustment.
3. Ignition timing check.
4. Throttle cable adjustment.

Pilot screw adjustment

1. Disconnect and ground the spark plug lead to prevent accidental starting.
2. Carefully turn the pilot screw clockwise until it is lightly seated (**Figure 14**).
3. Turn the pilot screw counterclockwise to the middle of the adjustment range in **Table 6**.

Idle speed adjustment

1. Turn the idle speed screw (**Figure 15**) counterclockwise until there is a gap between the screw tip and the carburetor throttle lever. Slowly rotate the screw clockwise until the tip just contacts the lever. Turn the screw one complete turn clockwise to slightly open the throttle.
2. Remove the running propeller as described in Chapter Nine and install a test propeller. The test propeller part number is in **Table 1**.

3. Connect the spark plug lead. Connect a shop tachometer to the spark plug lead.

4. Place the engine in a suitable test tank. Securely tighten the clamp screws. Start the engine and advance the throttle to approximately 1500 rpm in NEUTRAL gear for ten minutes or until the engine reaches full operating temperature.

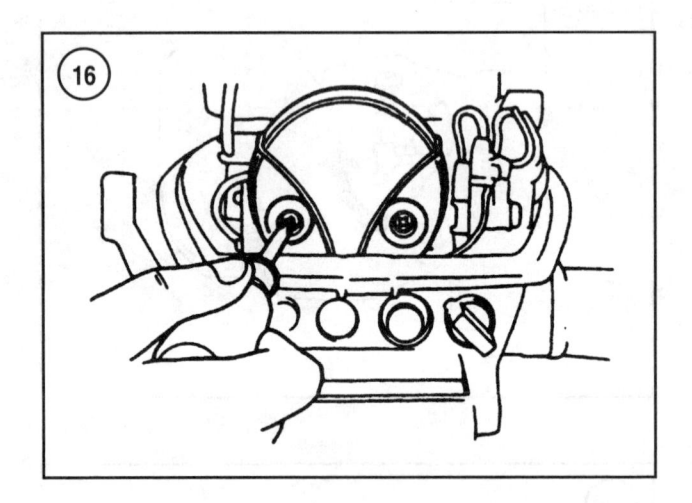

5. Place the throttle control in the idle position and note the idle speed. Turn the screw (**Figure 15**) until the idle speed is in the middle of the specification in **Table 7**. Clockwise screw rotation increases idle speed. Counterclockwise rotation decreases idle speed.

6. Shift the engine into FORWARD gear. Allow the idle to stabilize for a few minutes, then note the in-gear idle speed. If the in-gear idle speed is not within the specification in **Table 7**, readjust the idle speed screw.

7. Shift the engine into NEUTRAL gear. Allow the idle to stabilize for a few minutes, then note the idle speed. The in-neutral gear idle speed should remain within the specification in **Table 7**. If necessary, readjust the idle speed screw until both the in-gear and in-neutral idle speeds are within the specification. Several adjustments may be required.

8. Shift the engine into FORWARD gear and allow the idle to stabilize for a few minutes. Slowly advance the throttle, then bring it down to the idle position. Check for binding linkages or readjust the idle speed if the engine does not return to the specified range within 30-40 seconds.

9. Rapidly advance the throttle while checking for hesitation. If necessary, readjust the pilot screw (**Figure 14**) to minimize hesitation. Counterclockwise rotation reduces hesitation in most cases. Readjust the screw only a slight amount. Do not exceed the adjustment limits in **Table 6**.

10. Check the ignition timing as described in this chapter.

Ignition timing check

1. Remove the running propeller as described in Chapter Eight and install a test propeller. The test propeller part number is in **Table 1**.

2. Connect a timing light to the spark plug lead (**Figure 8**).

3. Connect a shop tachometer to the spark plug lead. Do not allow the timing light and tachometer pickups to touch during this procedure.

4. Place the engine in a suitable test tank. Securely tighten the clamp screws. Start the engine and advance the throttle to approximately 1500 rpm in NEUTRAL gear for ten minutes or until the engine reaches full operating temperature.

5. Place the throttle in the idle position and allow the idle speed to stabilize for a few minutes. Direct the timing light at the timing windows (**Figure 8**) on the port side of the power head. The timing mark should appear in the left window (**Figure 9**) at engine speeds from idle to 1700 rpm.

6. Shift the engine into FORWARD gear. Observe the tachometer and timing window while advancing the throttle to the maximum timing speed in **Table 5**. The timing mark should appear in the right window (**Figure 9**) at the maximum timing speed.

7. If the timing mark does not appear as specified in Step 5 and Step 6, check for a sheared flywheel drive key as described in Chapter Seven, faulty pulser coil or faulty CDI unit as described in Chapter Two.

8. Return the throttle to idle. Shift the engine into NEUTRAL. Stop the engine and remove it from the test tank.

TIMING, SYNCHRONIZATION AND ADJUSTMENT

4. Rotate the carburetor throttle lever (C, **Figure 17**) to the idle position. The lever should contact the tip of the idle speed screw.
5. Without disturbing the throttle lever or throttle grip setting, lightly pull on the cable wire to remove slack. Securely tighten the cable anchor screw (D, **Figure 17**).
6. Rotate the throttle grip several times to the full throttle and idle positions. Make sure the carburetor throttle lever is slightly away from the stop (E, **Figure 17**) at the full throttle position and just contacts the idle speed screw at idle. Readjust as necessary.
7. Install the silencer cover and secure it with the two screws (**Figure 16**).

Timing, Synchronization and Carburetor Adjustments (6 and 8 hp Models)

These models use mechanical timing advancement. Timing pointer and ignition timing adjustments are required. Perform the following adjustments and checks:
1. Timing pointer adjustment.
2. Static timing adjustment.
3. Throttle linkage adjustment.
4. Pilot screw adjustment.
5. Idle speed adjustment.
6. Ignition timing check.

Timing pointer adjustment

Use Yamaha part No. YU-3097/90890-01252 and YU-1256 or another suitable dial indicator and universal mount for this procedure.

NOTE
All reference to the flywheel is as viewed from the top of the flywheel.

1. Remove both spark plugs and ground the spark plug leads.
2. On electric start models, disconnect the battery cables.
3. Shift the engine into NEUTRAL gear.
4. Carefully pry the mounting base linkage from the throttle arm connector (**Figure 18**).
5. Attach the dial indictor mount to one of the head bolts. Install the dial indictor into the mount with the indicator stem in the No. 1 spark plug opening. Adjust the mount to position the stem in direct contact with the piston as it nears the top of its compression stroke.
6. Slowly rotate the flywheel clockwise while observing the dial indicator. Stop when the flywheel reaches the top of its stroke. This is the point of rotation when the needle on the dial indicator just reverses its direction as the fly-

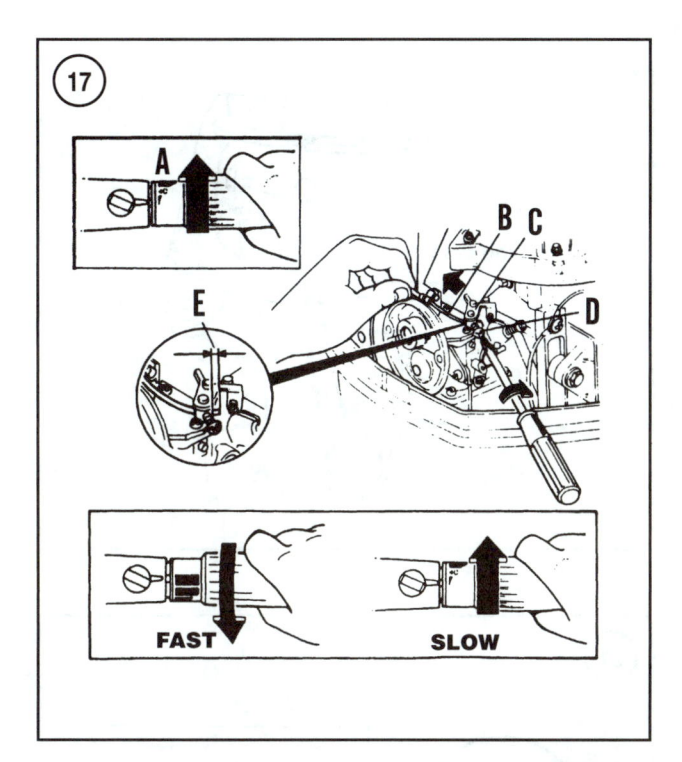

9. Remove the test propeller and install the running propeller as described in Chapter Eight.

Throttle cable adjustment

1. Remove the two screws and silencer cover from the front of the carburetor (**Figure 16**) as described in Chapter Five.
2. Place the throttle grip (A, **Figure 17**) in the lowest speed setting.
3. Loosen the cable anchor screw (D, **Figure 17**). The cable wire should slide freely through the anchor for the adjustment procedure.

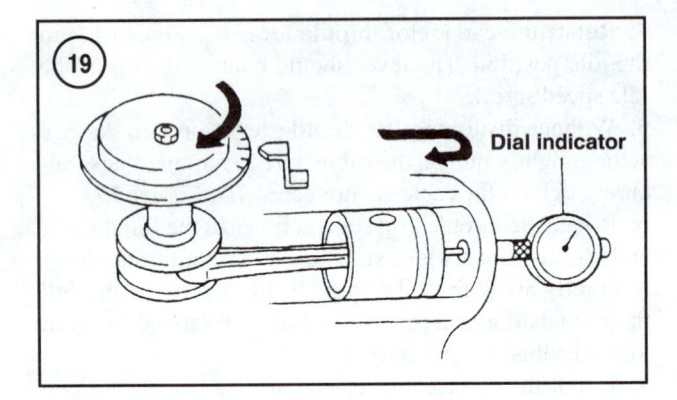

wheel is rotated (**Figure 19**). Keep the flywheel in this position while adjusting the pointer.

7. Loosen the mounting bolt and move the pointer (**Figure 20**) until it aligns with the *0* or *TDC* mark on the flywheel. Securely tighten the mounting bolt after adjustment.

8. Remove the dial indicator and mount. Perform the static timing adjustments as described in this chapter.

Static timing adjustment

1. Observe the timing pointer while slowly rotating the flywheel in the clockwise direction. Stop when the timing pointer perfectly aligns with the 35° BTDC mark on the flywheel (**Figure 21**).
2. Move the mounting base (A, **Figure 22**) until the mark on the base aligns with the mark on the flywheel. If the mounting base does not just contact the stopper plate (B, **Figure 22**) as the marks align, loosen the stopper retaining bolt and reposition the stopper plate. Securely tighten the bolt after adjustment.
3. Carefully snap the mounting base linkage onto the throttle arm connector (**Figure 18**).
4. Adjust the throttle linkage as described in this chapter.

Throttle linkage adjustment (tiller control)

1. Shift the engine into FORWARD gear.
2. Rotate the throttle grip to the full throttle position (**Figure 23**) while observing the carburetor lever (**Figure 24**). If the lever does not contact the stop just as the throttle grip reaches the full throttle position and the mounting base (A, **Figure 22**) contacts the stop, adjust the linkages as follows:
   a. Carefully pry the mounting base linkage from the throttle arm connector (**Figure 18**).
   b. Move the mounting plate until it contacts the stopper plate (**Figure 22**).
   c. Loosen all four adjusting nuts (**Figure 24**).

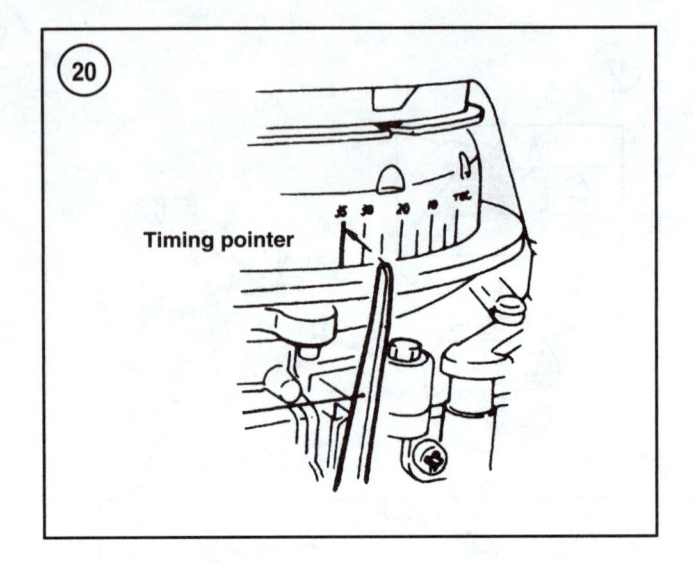

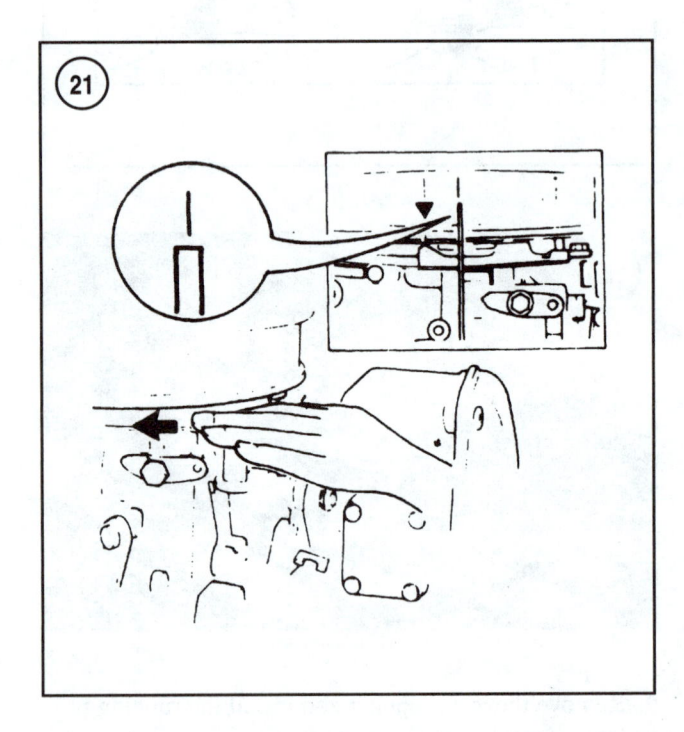

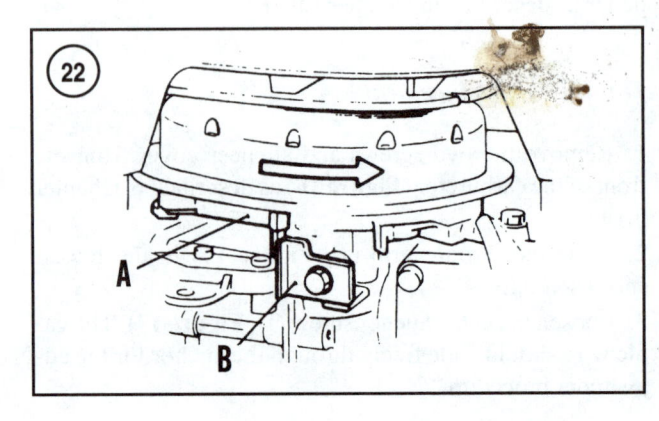

TIMING, SYNCHRONIZATION AND ADJUSTMENT

23

24
Carburetor lever
Adjusting nuts (outer)
Adjusting nuts (inner)

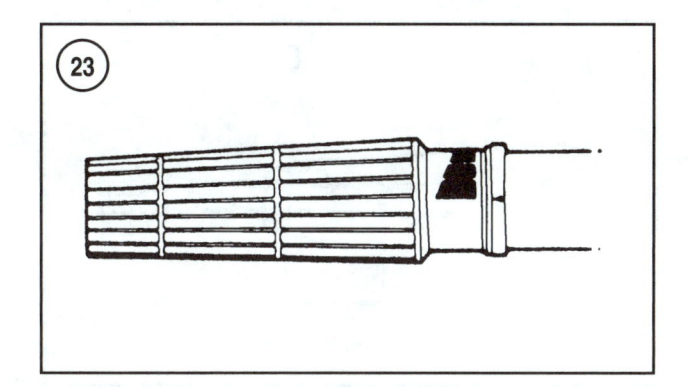

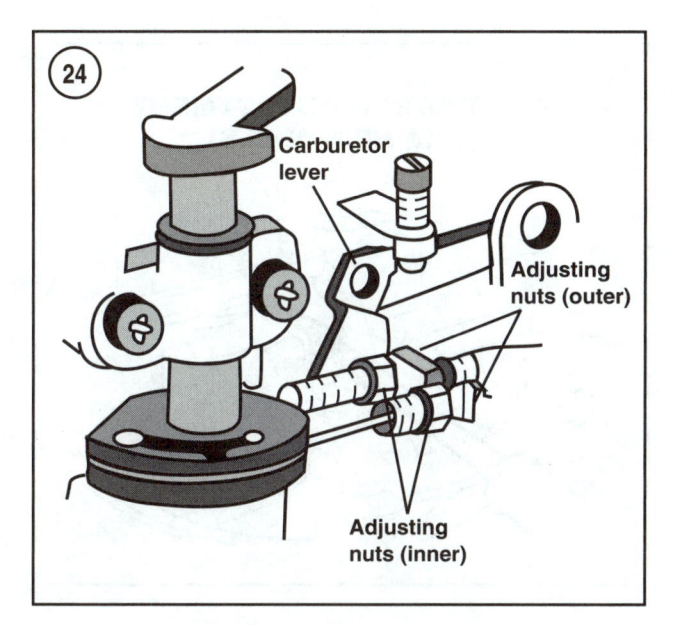

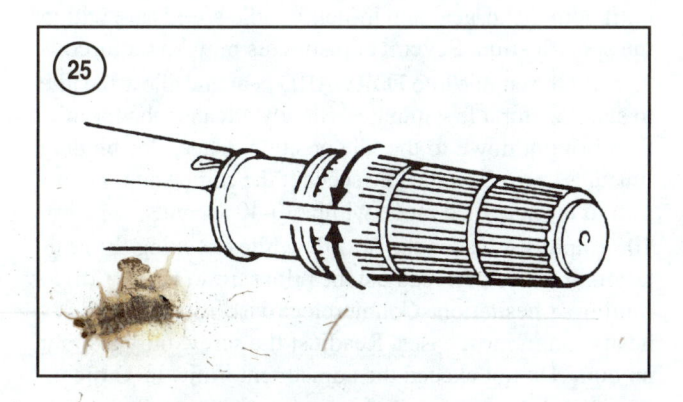

25

d. Turn the adjusting nuts until the carburetor throttle lever just touches the stop. The grip should remain in the full throttle position.

e. Without disturbing the throttle lever, turn the four adjusting nuts (**Figure 24**) until they just contact the cable mounting bracket.

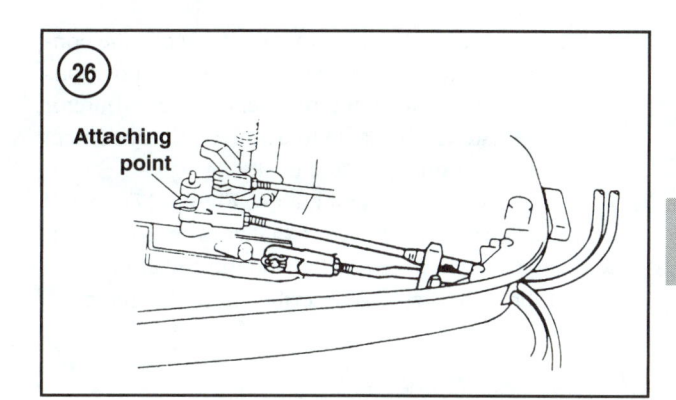

26
Attaching point

f. Check for free play in the throttle grip. If the grip does not rotate approximately 3 mm (0.125 in.) at the points shown in **Figure 25**, loosen the outer adjusting nut (**Figure 24**) to achieve the desired free play.

g. Securely tighten the four adjusting nuts and check the free play and throttle lever stop. Readjust as necessary.

h. Adjust the length of the mounting base linkage until the connectors align on both ends. Then carefully snap the mounting base linkage on the throttle arm connector (**Figure 18**).

3. Install the spark plugs. Do not connect the spark plug leads at this time.

4. Adjust the pilot screw as described in this chapter.

Throttle cable adjustment (remote control)

1. Shift the engine into FORWARD gear.
2. Observe the carburetor lever while an assistant slowly moves the remote control handle to full throttle. If the lever does not contact the stop just as the control handle reaches full throttle, adjust the cable as follows:

a. Place the remote control handle in the NEUTRAL gear idle speed position.

b. Disconnect the throttle cable from the attaching point (**Figure 26**, typical).

c. Open the latch and pull the cable from the lower cover or power head mounted retainer.

d. Loosen the jam nut (A, **Figure 27**) and rotate the cable end (B) until the cable fits over the connection point and into the retainer without moving the linkages.

e. Check the cable end for adequate thread engagement (C, **Figure 27**). A minimum of 8 mm (0.31 in.) of engagement is required. Position the cable anchor into a different groove on the cable as required.

f. Fit the cable on the attaching points. Move the control handle to the full throttle and idle positions while checking for full movement of the carburetor lever. Readjust the cable to achieve full movement to the full throttle and idle positions.

g. Securely tighten the jam nut (A, **Figure 27**). Install the fasteners and engage the latch to secure the cable to the mounting bracket and throttle arm.

3. Adjust the pilot screw as described in this chapter.

Pilot screw adjustment

1. Disconnect and ground the spark plug lead to prevent accidental starting.
2. On electric start models, disconnect the battery cables.
3. Carefully turn the pilot screw clockwise until it is lightly seated (**Figure 28**).
4. Turn the pilot screw counterclockwise to the middle of the adjustment range in **Table 6**.
5. Adjust the idle speed as described in this chapter.

Idle speed adjustment

1. Turn the idle speed screw (**Figure 29**) counterclockwise until there is a gap between the screw tip and the carburetor throttle lever. Slowly rotate the screw clockwise until the tip just contacts the lever. Turn the screw one complete turn clockwise to slightly open the throttle.
2. Remove the running propeller as described in Chapter Eight and install a test propeller. The test propeller part number is in **Table 1**.
3. Connect the spark plug leads. Connect a shop tachometer to the spark plug lead.
4. On electric start models, connect the battery cables.
5. Place the engine in a test tank. Securely tighten the clamp screws. Start the engine and advance the throttle to approximately 1500 rpm in NEUTRAL gear for ten minutes or until the engine reaches full operating temperature.
6. Place the throttle control in the idle position and note the idle speed. Turn the screw (**Figure 29**) until the idle speed is in the middle of the specification in **Table 7**. Clockwise screw rotation increases idle speed. Counterclockwise rotation decreases idle speed.
7. Shift the engine into FORWARD gear. Allow the idle to stabilize for a few minutes, then note the in-gear idle speed. If the in-gear idle speed is not within the specification in **Table 7**, readjust the idle speed screw.
8. Shift the engine into NEUTRAL gear. Allow the idle to stabilize for a few minutes, then note the idle speed. The in-neutral gear idle speed should remain within the specification in **Table 7**. If necessary, readjust the idle speed screw

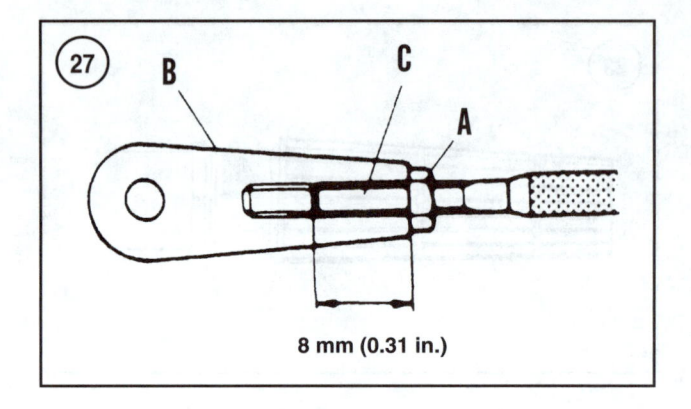

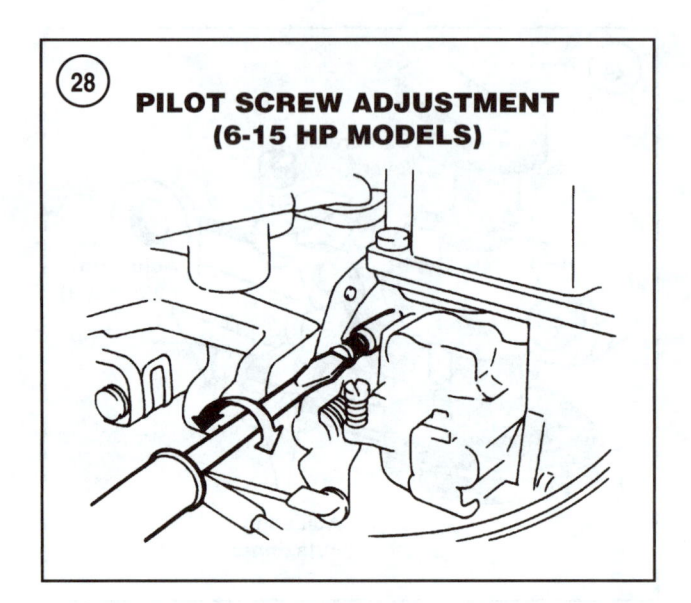

until both the in-gear and in-neutral idle speeds are within the specification. Several adjustments may be required.

9. Shift the engine into FORWARD gear and allow the idle to stabilize for a few minutes. Slowly advance the throttle, then bring it down to the idle position. Check for binding linkages or readjust the idle speed if the engine does not return to the specified range within 30-40 seconds.
10. Rapidly advance the throttle while checking for hesitation. If necessary, readjust the pilot screw (**Figure 28**) to minimize hesitation. Counterclockwise rotation reduces hesitation in most cases. Readjust the screw only a slight amount. Do not exceed the adjustment limits in **Table 6**.
11. Check the ignition timing as described in this chapter.

Ignition timing check

1. Remove the running propeller as described in Chapter Eight and install a test propeller. The test propeller part number is in **Table 1**.

TIMING, SYNCHRONIZATION AND ADJUSTMENT

Figure 29 IDLE SPEED ADJUSTMENT (6 AND 8 HP MODELS)

Figure 30 (showing labels A, B, C, D, E, F)

ten minutes or until the engine reaches full operating temperature.

5. Place the throttle in the idle position and allow the idle speed to stabilize for a few minutes. Direct the flashing light at the timing pointer and flywheel mark. When the light flashes, the timing pointer should align with the flywheel mark specified in **Table 4**.

6. Shift the engine into FORWARD gear. Observe the tachometer and timing window while advancing the throttle to the maximum timing speed in **Table 5**. The timing pointer should align with the maximum timing mark specified in **Table 5**.

7. Return the throttle to idle. Shift the engine into NEUTRAL. Stop the engine and remove it from the test tank.

8. If the timing pointer does not align with the specified marks, readjust the static timing.

9. Remove the test propeller and install the running propeller as described in Chapter Eight.

Timing, Synchronization and Carburetor Adjustments (9.9 and 15 hp Models)

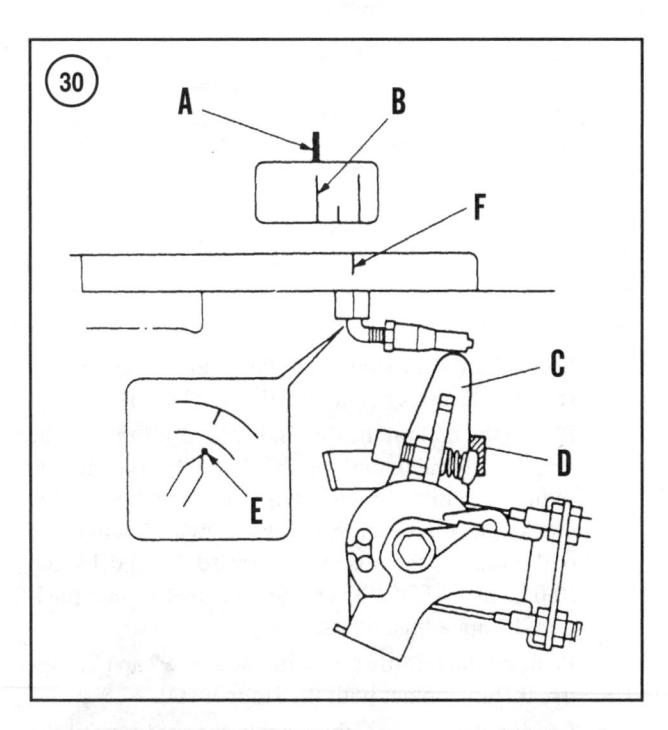

These models use mechanical timing advancement. Static ignition timing adjustments and an ignition timing check are required. Perform the following adjustments and checks:

1. Static timing adjustment.
2. Throttle linkage adjustment.
3. Pilot screw adjustment.
4. Idle speed adjustment.
5. Ignition timing check.

Static timing adjustment

1. Remove both spark plugs and ground the spark plug leads.
2. On electric start models, disconnect the battery cables.
3. Shift the engine into NEUTRAL gear.
4. Observe the mark on the manual starter housing (A, **Figure 30**) and timing marks on the flywheel (B) while rotating the flywheel clockwise. Stop when the 30° BTDC mark on the flywheel aligns with the mark on the manual starter housing (A, **Figure 30**).
5. Move the throttle arm (C, **Figure 30**) until it contacts the stopper (D).
6. With the flywheel marks aligned to 30° BTDC, the mark on the mounting base (E, **Figure 30**) should align with the lower marking on the flywheel (F). If necessary, adjust as follows:

2. Connect a timing light to the No. 1 (top) spark plug lead.

3. Connect a shop tachometer to the spark plug lead. Do not allow the timing light and tachometer pickups to touch during this procedure.

4. Place the engine in a suitable test tank. Securely tighten the clamp screws. Start the engine and advance the throttle to approximately 1500 rpm in NEUTRAL gear for

a. Loosen the jam nut (**Figure 31**) and carefully unthread the linkage from the mounting base connector.
b. Thread the dial indicator mount into the No. 1 spark plug opening. Install the dial indictor into the mount with the indicator stem in the No. 1 spark plug opening. Adjust the mount to position the stem in direct contact with the piston as it nears the top of its compression stroke (**Figure 32**).
c. Slowly rotate the flywheel clockwise while observing the dial indicator. Stop when the flywheel reaches the top of its stroke. This is the point of rotation when the needle on the dial indicator just reverses its direction as the flywheel is rotated.
d. Rotate the dial on the dial indicator until the needle aligns with the *0* mark on the dial. Observe the dial indicator while slowly rotating the flywheel counterclockwise. Stop the flywheel when the dial indicates the piston has moved down 4.22 mm (0.166 in.) BTDC. Keep the flywheel in this position during adjustment.
e. Position the throttle arm (C, **Figure 30**) in contact with the stopper (D). Move the mounting base until the mark (E, **Figure 30**) aligns with the mark on the flywheel (F).
f. Adjust the length of the linkage connecting the throttle arm (C, **Figure 30**) to the mounting base (E) until it can be installed without disturbing the marking alignment.
g. Connect the linkage to the mounting base and securely tighten the jam nut (**Figure 31**).
h. Remove the dial indicator and mount. Do not install the spark plugs at this time.

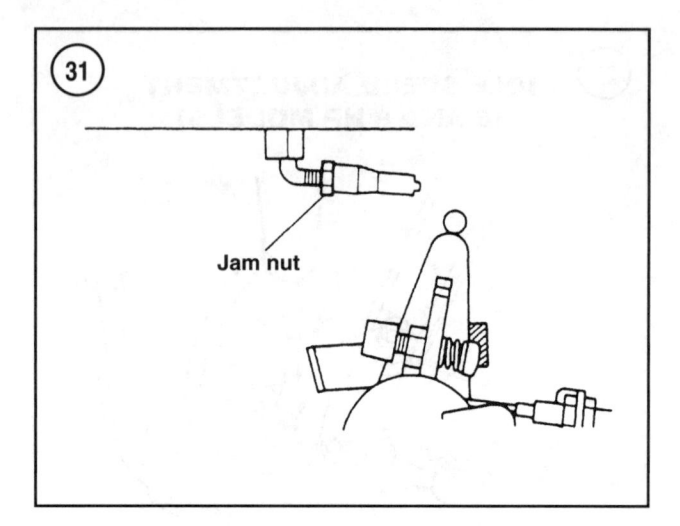

7. Rotate the flywheel until the mark on the manual starter housing (A, **Figure 33**) aligns with the 5° ATDC mark on the flywheel (B).

8. Move the throttle arm until the screw cap (C, **Figure 33**) contacts the stopper (D).

9. With the flywheel mark aligned to 5° ATDC, the mark on the mounting base (E, **Figure 33**) should align with the lower mark on the flywheel (F). If necessary, adjust as follows:

a. Thread the dial indicator mount into the No. 1 spark plug opening. Install the dial indictor into the mount with the indicator stem in the No. 1 spark plug opening. Adjust the mount to position the stem in direct contact with the piston as it nears the top of its compression stroke (**Figure 32**).
b. Slowly rotate the flywheel clockwise while observing the dial indicator. Stop when the flywheel reaches the top of its stroke. This is the point of rotation when the needle on the dial indicator just reverses its direction as the flywheel is rotated.
c. Rotate the dial on the dial indicator until the needle aligns with the *0* mark on the dial. Observe the dial indicator while slowly rotating the flywheel in the clockwise direction. Stop the flywheel when the dial indicates the piston has moved down 0.13 mm (0.005 in.) ATDC. Keep the flywheel in this position during adjustments.
d. Position the throttle arm with the screw cap (C, **Figure 33**) in contact with the stopper (D).
e. Loosen the jam nut, then rotate the screw until the mark on the mounting base (E, **Figure 33**) aligns with the flywheel mark (F). Securely tighten the jam nut.
f. Remove the dial indicator and mount.

10. Install the spark plugs. Do not connect the leads at this time.

11. Adjust the throttle linkage as described in this chapter.

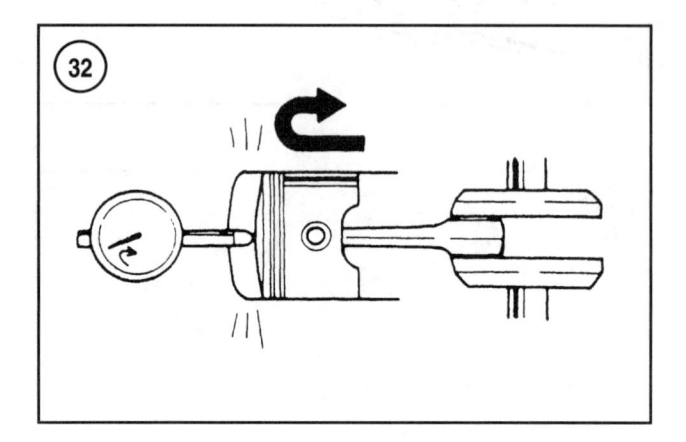

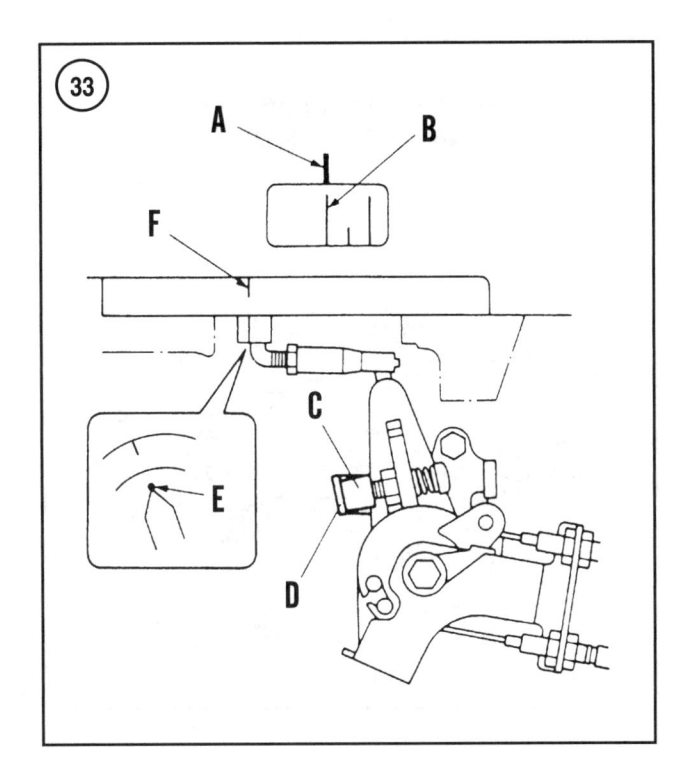

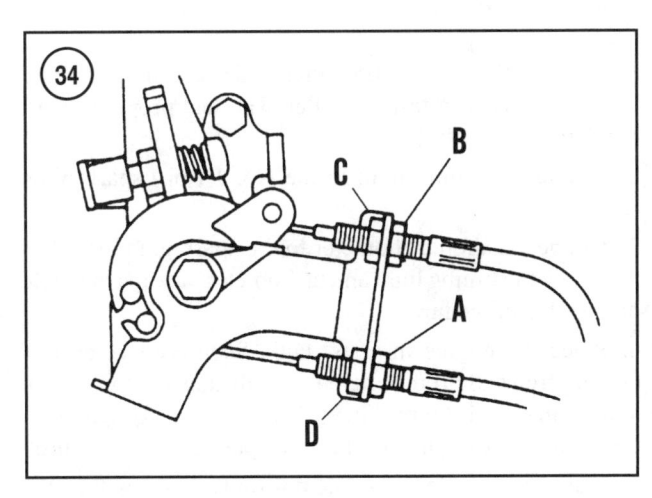

TIMING, SYNCHRONIZATION AND ADJUSTMENT

5. Check the amount of free play in the throttle grip (**Figure 25**). Adjust the nuts (C and D, **Figure 34**) until there is a slight amount of free play.

6. Securely tighten the jam nuts (A and B, **Figure 34**).

*Throttle cable adjustment
(remote control models)*

1. Shift the engine into FORWARD gear.

2. Observe the carburetor lever while an assistant slowly moves the remote control handle to full throttle. If the lever does not contact the stop just as the control handle reaches full throttle, adjust the cable as follows:

   a. Place the remote control handle in the NEUTRAL gear idle speed position.
   b. Disconnect the throttle cable from the attaching point (**Figure 26**, typical).
   c. Open the latch and pull the cable from the lower cover or power head mounted retainer.
   d. Loosen the jam nut (A, **Figure 27**) and rotate the cable end (B) until the cable will fit over the connection point and into the retainer without moving the linkages.
   e. Check the cable end for adequate thread engagement (C, **Figure 27**). A minimum of 8 mm (0.31 in.) of engagement is required. Position the cable anchor into a different groove on the cable as required.
   f. Fit the cable on the attaching points. Move the control handle to the full throttle and idle positions while checking for full movement of the carburetor lever. Readjust the cable to achieve full movement to the full throttle and idle positions.
   g. Securely tighten the jam nut (A, **Figure 27**). Install the fasteners and engage the latch to secure the cable to the mounting bracket and throttle arm.

3. Adjust the pilot screw as described in this chapter.

*Throttle linkage adjustment
(tiller control models)*

1. Rotate the throttle grip to the idle position (**Figure 11**).

2. Loosen the jam nuts (A and B, **Figure 34**).

3. Adjust the nuts (C and D, **Figure 34**) until the stop screw cap (C, **Figure 33**) just contacts the stop (D, **Figure 33**) with the throttle grip in the idle throttle position.

4. Place the throttle grip in the full throttle position. If the throttle arm (C, **Figure 31**) does not contact the stop (D), readjust the nuts (C and D, **Figure 34**).

Pilot screw adjustment

1. Disconnect and ground the spark plug lead to prevent accidental starting.

2. On electric start models, disconnect the battery cables.

3. Carefully turn the pilot screw clockwise until it is lightly seated (**Figure 28**).

4. Turn the pilot screw counterclockwise to the middle of the adjustment range in **Table 6**.

5. Adjust the idle speed as described in this chapter.

Idle speed adjustment

1. Loosen the anchor screw (**Figure 35**). Turn the idle speed screw (**Figure 35**) counterclockwise until there is a gap between the screw tip and the carburetor throttle lever. Slowly rotate the screw clockwise until the tip just contacts the lever. Turn the screw one complete turn clockwise to slightly open the throttle. Securely tighten the anchor screw.
2. Remove the running propeller as described in Chapter Eight and install a test propeller. The test propeller part number is in **Table 1**.
3. Connect the spark plug leads. Connect a shop tachometer to the spark plug lead.
4. On electric start models, connect the battery cables.
5. Place the engine in a test tank. Securely tighten the clamp screws. Start the engine and advance the throttle to approximately 1500 rpm in NEUTRAL gear for ten minutes or until the engine reaches full operating temperature.
6. Place the throttle control in the idle position and note the idle speed. If the in-neutral idle speed is not within the specification in **Table 7**, adjust the idle speed as follows:
   a. Fully loosen the anchor screw (**Figure 35**).
   b. Turn the idle speed screw (**Figure 35**) until the idle speed is in the middle of the idle speed range (**Table 7**). Clockwise screw rotation increases idle speed. Counterclockwise rotation decreases idle speed.
   c. Without disturbing the linkages, securely tighten the anchor screw.
7. Shift the engine into FORWARD gear. Allow the idle to stabilize for a few minutes, then note the in-gear idle speed. If the in-gear idle speed is not within the specification in **Table 7**, readjust the idle speed screw.
8. Shift the engine into NEUTRAL gear. Allow the idle to stabilize for a few minutes, then note the idle speed. The in-neutral gear idle speed should remain within the specification in **Table 7**. If necessary, readjust the idle speed screw until both the in-gear and in-neutral idle speeds are within the specification. Several adjustments may be required.
9. Shift the engine into FORWARD gear and allow the idle to stabilize for a few minutes. Slowly advance the throttle, then bring it down to the idle position. Check for binding linkages or readjust the idle speed if the engine does not return to the specified range within 30-40 seconds.
10. Rapidly advance the throttle while checking for hesitation. If necessary, readjust the pilot screw (**Figure 28**) to minimize hesitation. Counterclockwise rotation reduces hesitation in most cases. Readjust the screw only a slight amount. Do not exceed the adjustment limits in **Table 6**.
11. Check the ignition timing as described in this chapter.

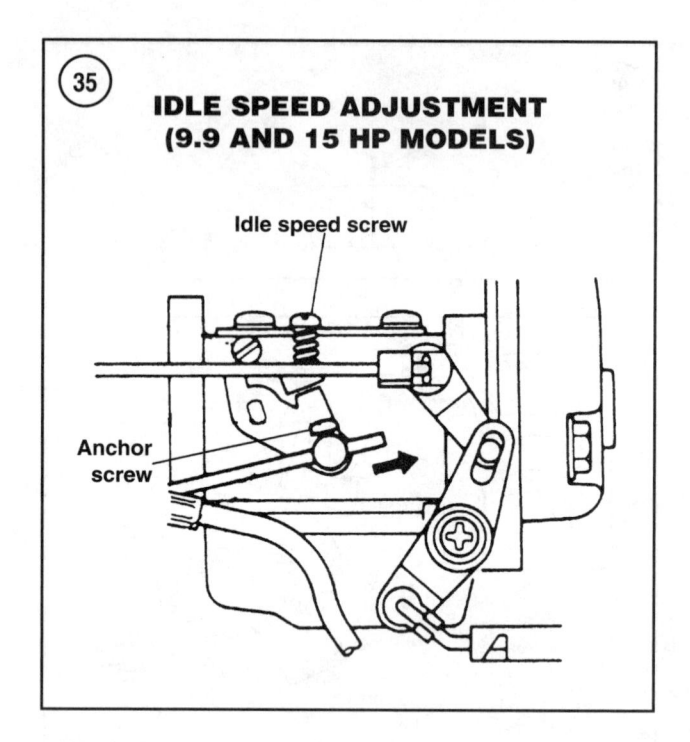

Ignition timing check

1. Remove the running propeller as described in Chapter Eight and install a test propeller. The test propeller part number is in **Table 1**.
2. Connect a timing light to the No. 1 (top) spark plug lead.
3. Connect a shop tachometer to the spark plug lead. Do not allow the timing light and tachometer pickups to touch during this procedure.
4. Place the engine in a test tank. Securely tighten the clamp screws. Start the engine and advance the throttle to approximately 1500 rpm in NEUTRAL gear for ten minutes or until the engine reaches full operating temperature.
5. Place the throttle in the idle position and allow the idle speed to stabilize for a few minutes. Direct the timing light at the mark on the manual starter housing (A, **Figure 33**) and flywheel marks (B). When the light flashes, the mark on the manual starter housing should align with the idle speed timing mark specified in **Table 4**.
6. Shift the engine into FORWARD gear. Observe the tachometer and timing marks while advancing the throttle to the maximum timing speed in **Table 5**. The manual starter housing mark should align with the maximum timing marking specified in **Table 5**.
7. Return the throttle to idle. Shift the engine into NEUTRAL. Stop the engine and remove it from the test tank.

TIMING, SYNCHRONIZATION AND ADJUSTMENT

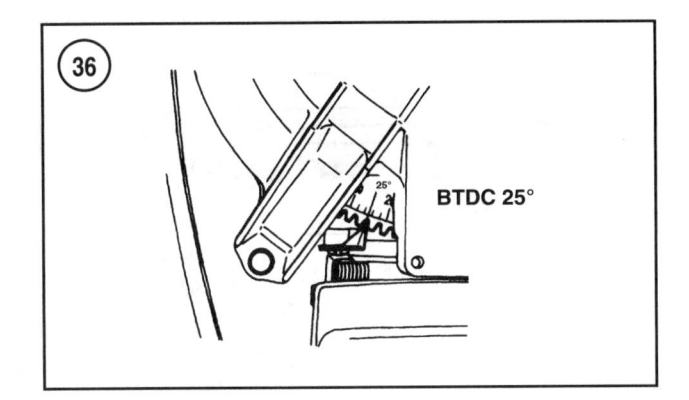

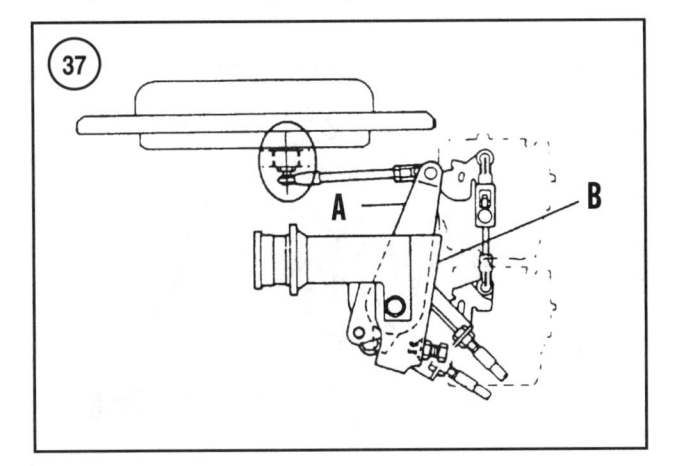

36

BTDC 25°

37

A   B

8. If the marks do not align as specified, readjust the static timing.

9. Remove the test propeller and install the running propeller as described in Chapter Eight.

Timing, Synchronization and Carburetor Adjustments (20 and 25 hp Two-Cylinder Models)

These models use mechanical timing advancement. Static ignition timing, carburetor pickup timing and ignition timing checks are required. Perform the following adjustments and checks:

1. Static timing adjustment.
2. Carburetor synchronization.
3. Pickup timing adjustment.
4. Throttle linkage/cable adjustment.
5. Dashpot adjustment.
6. Pilot screw adjustment.
7. Idle speed adjustment.
8. Neutral speed limiter adjustment.
9. Ignition timing check.

Static timing adjustment

1. Remove both spark plugs and ground the spark plug leads.
2. On electric start models, disconnect the battery cables.
3. Shift the engine into NEUTRAL gear.
4. Observe the timing pointer and timing marks on the flywheel (**Figure 36**) while rotating the flywheel clockwise. Stop when the 25° BTDC mark on the flywheel aligns with the timing pointer.
5. Move the throttle arm (A, **Figure 37**) until it contacts the full advance stopper (B). With the arm in contact with the stopper, the mark on the mounting base should align with the mark on the flywheel as shown in **Figure 37**. If necessary, adjust as follows:
   a. Loosen the jam nut, then carefully pry the linkage ball joint from the mounting base connector.
   b. Thread the dial indicator mount into the No. 1 spark plug opening. Install the dial indictor into the mount with the indicator stem in the No. 1 spark plug opening. Adjust the mount to position the stem in direct contact with the piston as it nears the top of its compression stroke (**Figure 32**).
   c. Slowly rotate the flywheel clockwise while observing the dial indicator. Stop when the flywheel reaches the top of its stroke. This is the point of rotation when the needle on the dial indicator just reverses its direction as the flywheel is rotated.
   d. Rotate the dial on the dial indicator until the needle aligns with the *0* mark on the dial. Observe the dial indicator while slowly rotating the flywheel in the counterclockwise. Stop the flywheel when the dial indicates the piston has moved down 3.34 mm (0.131 in.) BTDC. Keep the flywheel in this position during linkage adjustments.
   e. Position the throttle arm (A, **Figure 37**) in contact with the full advance stopper (B). Move the mounting base until its mark aligns with the mark on the flywheel as shown in **Figure 37**.
   f. Adjust the length of the linkage connecting the throttle arm to the mounting base until it can be installed without disturbing the marking alignment.
   g. Connect the linkage to the mounting base and securely tighten the jam nut.
   h. Remove the dial indicator and mount. Do not install the spark plugs at this time.
6. Observe the timing pointer and timing marks on the flywheel (**Figure 38**) while rotating the flywheel clockwise. Stop when the 7° ATDC mark on the flywheel aligns with the timing pointer.
7. Move the throttle arm (A, **Figure 39**) until it contacts the cap on the full retard stop screw (B). Hold the arm

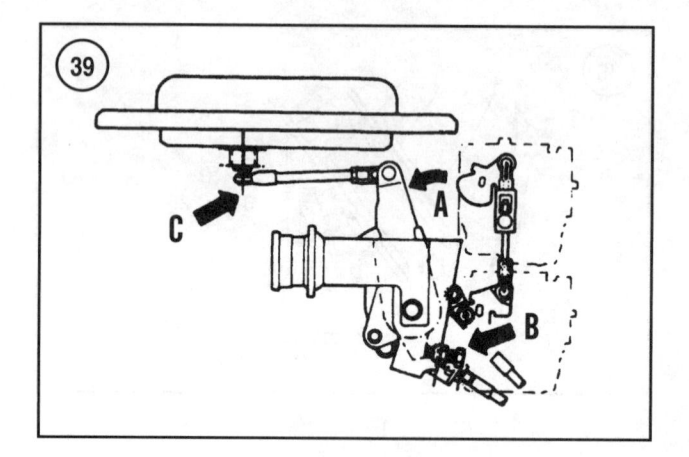

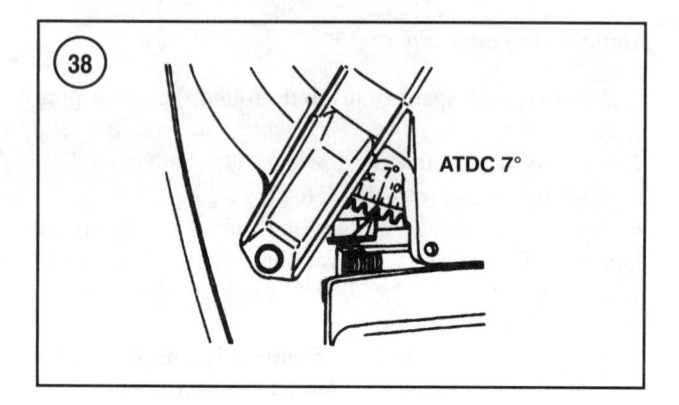

against the cap and check the alignment of the mounting base and flywheel marks (C, **Figure 39**). If the marks do not align, loosen the jam nut on the stop screw and rotate the screw until the marks align. Securely tighten the jam nut after adjustment. The throttle arm should be in contact with the stop screw during adjustments.
8. Synchronize the carburetors as described in this chapter.

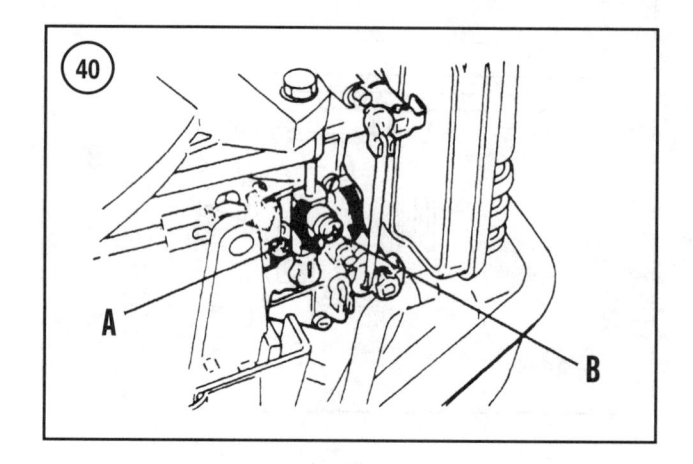

Carburetor synchronization

1. Remove the silencer cover from the carburetors as described in Chapter Five.
2. Fully loosen the throttle linkage screw (B, **Figure 40**).
3. Look into the lower carburetor opening (**Figure 41**) and rotate the idle speed screw (A, **Figure 40**) until the throttle plate just reaches its closed position.
4. Loosen the throttle lever screws (1, **Figure 42**) to allow both carburetor plates to fully close. Securely tighten the lever screws.
5. Gently hold the throttle linkage in position to ensure the throttle plates are closed, then securely tighten the linkage screw (2, **Figure 42**).
6. Observe the throttle plates (**Figure 41**) while turning the idle speed screw (A, **Figure 40**) clockwise. Stop when the throttle plates just start to move.
7. Install the silencer cover on the carburetors as described in Chapter Five.
8. Adjust the pickup timing as described in this chapter.

Pickup timing adjustment

1. Observe the timing pointer and timing marks on the flywheel (**Figure 43**) while rotating the flywheel clockwise. Stop when the 3° ATDC mark on the flywheel aligns with the timing pointer.
2. Move the throttle arm (A, **Figure 39**) toward the rear of the engine until it just contacts the throttle roller.
3. Inspect the marks on the mounting base and flywheel (**Figure 37**). If the mark on the mounting base does not align with the mark on the flywheel as the roller contacts the throttle arm and the center of the roller aligns with the mark on the arm (**Figure 43**), loosen the throttle roller screw and adjust the roller. Securely tighten the roller screw after adjustment.

TIMING, SYNCHRONIZATION AND ADJUSTMENT

42

1. Throttle lever screws
2. Throttle linkage screw
3. Throttle roller

43 PICKUP TIMING ADJUSTMENT (20 AND 25 HP TWO-CYLINDER MODELS)

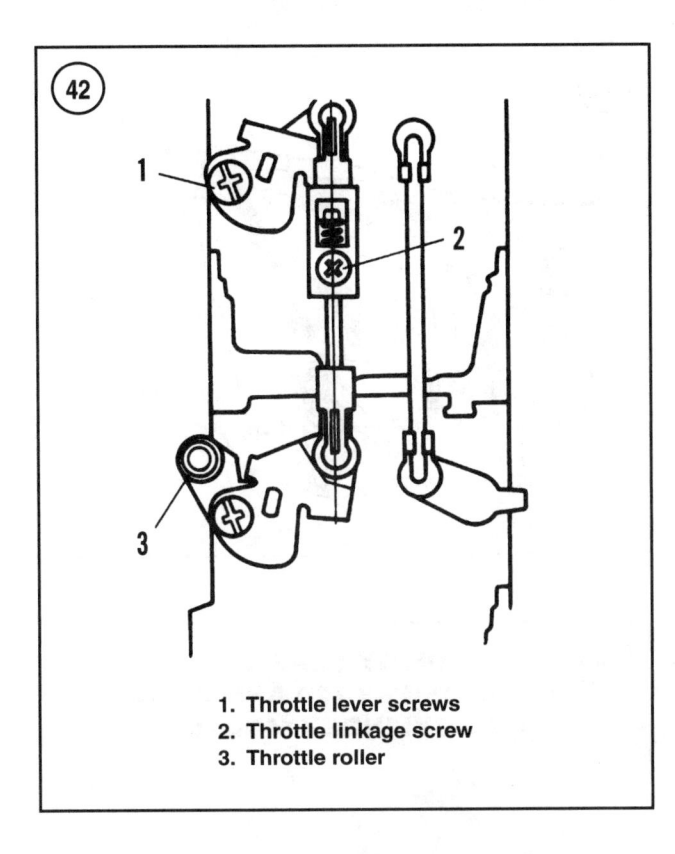

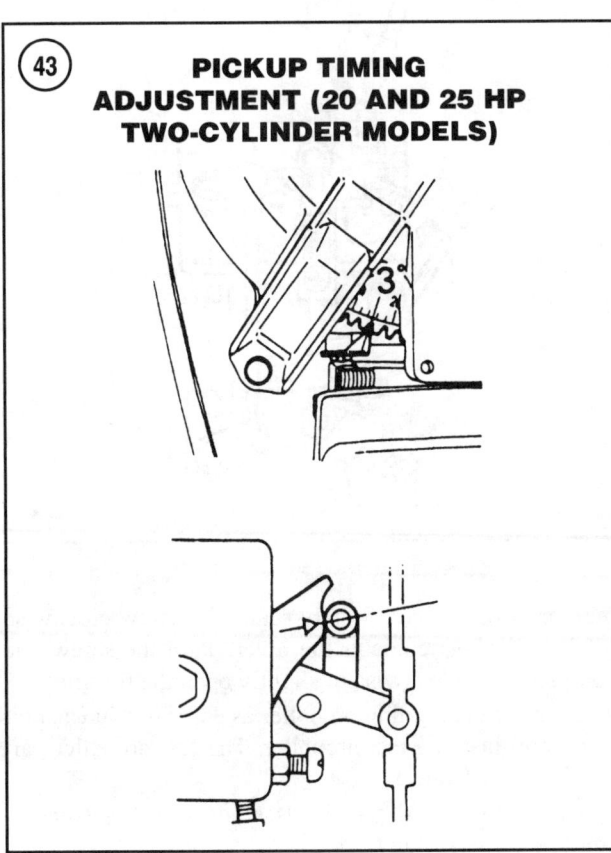

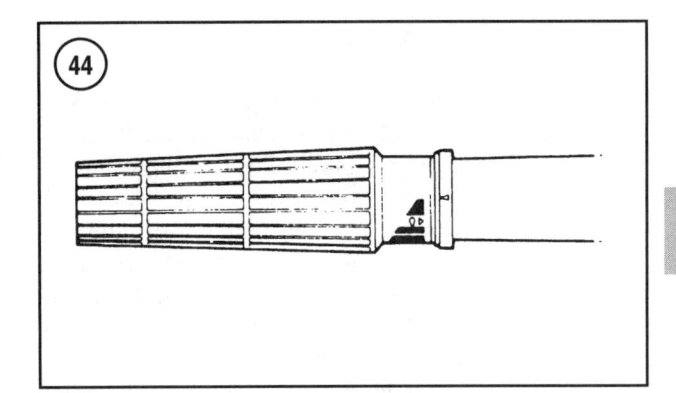

44

4. Install the spark plugs. Do not connect the spark plug leads at this time.

Throttle linkage adjustment (tiller control models)

1. Shift the engine into FORWARD gear. Rotate the throttle grip to the idle position (**Figure 44**).
2. Loosen the jam nuts (A and B, **Figure 34**).
3. Adjust the nuts (C and D, **Figure 34**) until the throttle arm (A, **Figure 39**) contacts the full retard stop screw (B) with the grip in the idle position.
4. Place the throttle grip in the full throttle position. If the throttle arm (A, **Figure 37**) does not just contact the stop (B) as the grip reaches the full throttle position, readjust the nuts (C and D, **Figure 34**).
5. Check the amount of free play in the throttle grip (**Figure 25**). Adjust the nuts (C and D, **Figure 34**) until there is approximately 3 mm (0.12 in.) of free play.
6. Securely tighten the jam nuts (A and B, **Figure 34**).

Throttle cable adjustment (remote control models)

1. Shift the engine into FORWARD gear.
2. Observe the carburetor lever while an assistant slowly moves the remote control handle to full throttle. If the lever does not contact the stop just as the control handle reaches full throttle, adjust the cable as follows:
   a. Place the remote control handle in the NEUTRAL gear idle speed position.
   b. Disconnect the throttle cable from the attaching point (**Figure 26**, typical).
   c. Open the latch and pull the cable from the lower cover or power head mounted retainer.
   d. Loosen the jam nut (A, **Figure 27**) and rotate the cable end (B) until the cable will fit over the connec-

tion point and into the retainer without moving the linkages.

e. Check the cable end for adequate thread engagement (C, **Figure 27**). A minimum of 8 mm (0.31 in.) of engagement is required. Position the cable anchor into a different groove on the cable as required.

f. Fit the cable on the attaching points. Move the control handle to the full throttle and idle positions while checking for full movement of the carburetor lever. Readjust the cable to achieve full movement to the full throttle and idle positions.

g. Securely tighten the jam nut (A, **Figure 27**). Install the fasteners and engage the latch to secure the cable to the mounting bracket and throttle arm.

3. Adjust the dashpot as described in this chapter.

Dashpot adjustment

1. Place the throttle in the idle position.
2. Inspect the dashpot plunger. If the plunger does not allow the throttle arm (**Figure 45**) to contact the full retard stop and maintain light contact with the arm, adjust the dashpot as follows:
    a. Loosen the screws (**Figure 45**).
    b. Move the throttle arm (**Figure 45**) against the full ignition retard stop.
    c. Push the dashpot toward the throttle arm until the plunger is just fully retracted.
    d. Hold the dashpot in position and securely tighten the mounting screws.
3. Place the throttle in the full throttle position. The plunger should fully extend from the dashpot. Replace the dashpot if the plunger fails to fully extend.

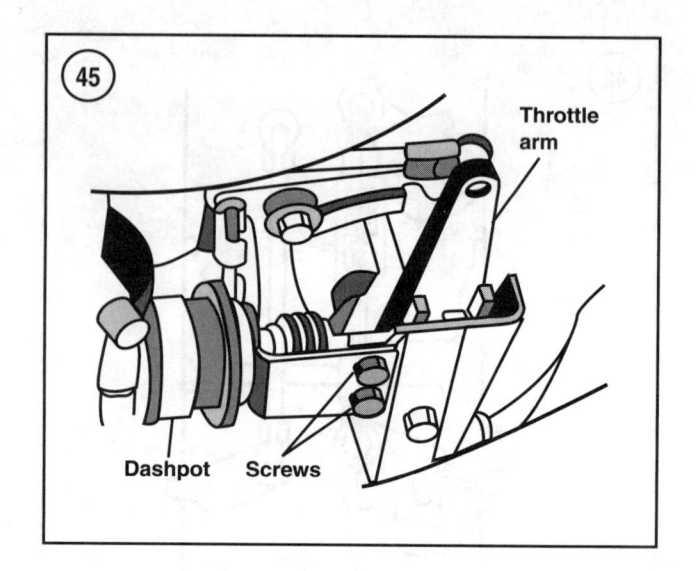

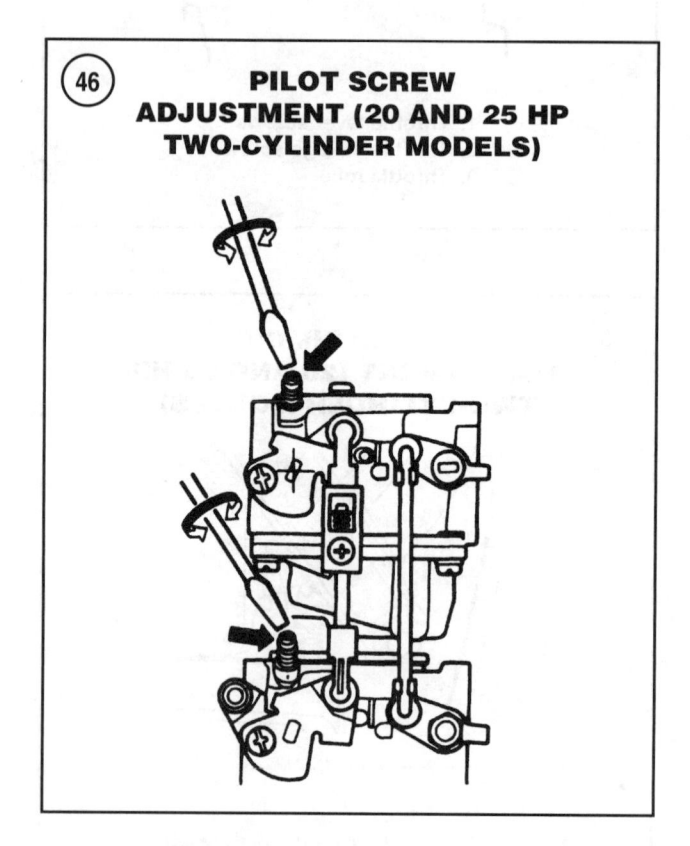

Pilot screw adjustments

1. Disconnect and ground the spark plug lead to prevent accidental starting.
2. On electric start models, disconnect the battery cables.
3. Carefully turn the pilot screw for the upper carburetor clockwise until it is lightly seated (**Figure 46**).
4. Turn the pilot screw counterclockwise to the middle of the turns out range in **Table 6**.
5. Repeat Steps 3 and 4 for the bottom carburetor pilot screw.
6. Adjust the idle speed as described in this chapter.

Idle speed adjustment

1. Turn the idle speed screw (**Figure 47**) counterclockwise until there is a gap between the screw tip and the carburetor throttle lever. Slowly rotate the screw clockwise until the tip just contacts the lever. Turn the screw one complete turn clockwise to slightly open the throttle.
2. Remove the running propeller as described in Chapter Eight and install a test propeller. The test propeller part number is in **Table 1**.
3. Connect the spark plug leads. Connect a shop tachometer to the spark plug lead.

TIMING, SYNCHRONIZATION AND ADJUSTMENT

Figure 47 IDLE SPEED ADJUSTMENT (20 AND 25 HP TWO-CYLINDER MODELS)

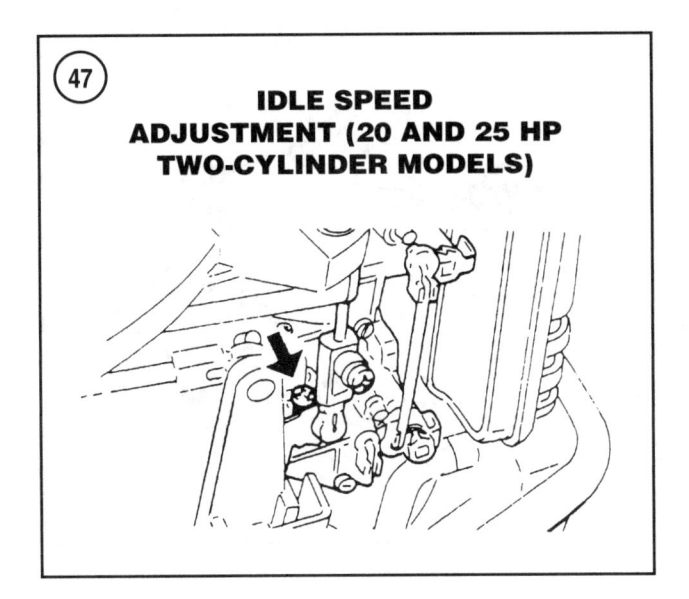

Figure 48 NEUTRAL SPEED LIMITER ADJUSTMENT (20 AND 25 HP TWO-CYLINDER MODELS)
Adjusting screw

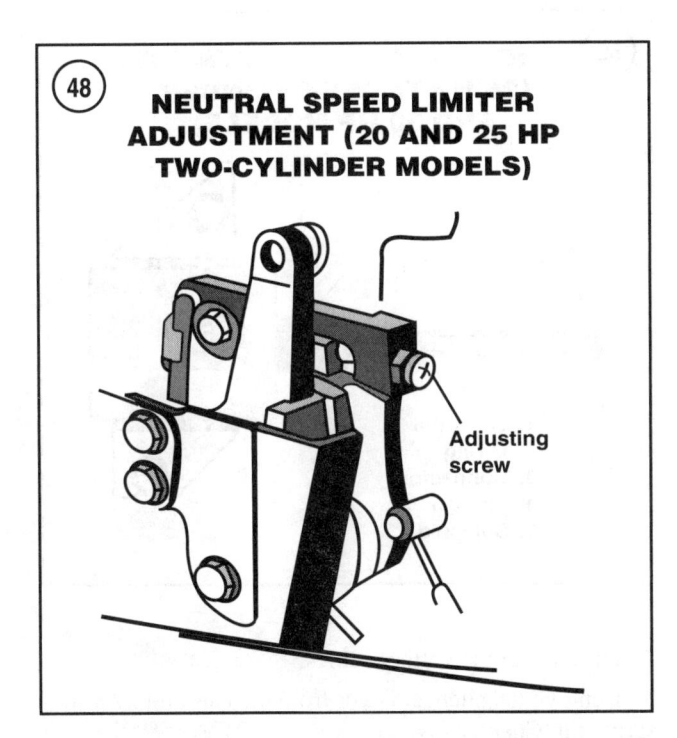

4. On electric start models, connect the battery cables.
5. Place the engine in a test tank. Securely tighten the clamp screws. Start the engine and advance the throttle to approximately 1500 rpm in NEUTRAL gear for ten minutes or until the engine reaches full operating temperature.
6. Place the throttle control in the idle position and note the idle speed. If the in-neutral idle speed is not within the specification in **Table 7**, adjust the idle speed as follows:
   a. Turn the idle speed screw (**Figure 47**) until the idle speed is in the middle of the idle speed range in Table 7. Clockwise screw rotation increases idle speed. Counterclockwise rotation decreases idle speed.
   b. Check the throttle arm to throttle roller alignment as described in this chapter under *Pickup timing adjustment*. Readjust the roller as necessary.
7. Shift the engine into FORWARD gear. Allow the idle to stabilize for a few minutes, then note the in-gear idle speed. If the in-gear idle speed is not within the specification in **Table 7**, readjust the idle speed screw.
8. Shift the engine into NEUTRAL gear. Allow the idle to stabilize for a few minutes, then note the idle speed. The in-neutral gear idle speed should remain within the specification in **Table 7**. If necessary, readjust the idle speed screw until both the in-gear and in-neutral idle speeds are within the specification. Several adjustments may be required.
9. Shift the engine into FORWARD gear and allow the idle to stabilize for a few minutes. Slowly advance the throttle, then bring it down to the idle position. Check for binding linkages or readjust the idle speed if the engine does not return to the specified range within 30-40 seconds.
10. Rapidly advance the throttle while checking for hesitation. If necessary, readjust the pilot screws (**Figure 46**) as described in this chapter to minimize hesitation. Counterclockwise rotation reduces hesitation in most cases. Readjust the screws only a slight amount. Do not exceed the adjustment limits in **Table 6**.
11. Adjust the neutral speed limiter as described in this chapter.

Neutral speed limiter adjustment

1. Adjust the idle speed as described in this section.
2. Shift the engine into NEUTRAL gear.
3. Observe the tachometer while slowly advancing the throttle. Proper adjustment limits the in-neutral speed to 3500-4100 rpm. If the in-neutral speed is above or below the specification, turn the adjustment screw (**Figure 48**) to achieve the specified limit. Clockwise rotation decreases the limiter speed. Counterclockwise rotation increases the limiter speed.
4. Return the engine to idle speed and turn the engine OFF.
5. Check the ignition timing as described in this chapter.

Ignition timing check

1. Remove the running propeller as described in Chapter Eight and install a test propeller. The test propeller part number is in **Table 1**.

2. Connect a timing light to the No. 1 (top) spark plug lead.

3. Connect a shop tachometer to the spark plug lead. Do not allow the timing light and tachometer pickups to touch during this procedure.

4. Place the engine in a test tank. Securely tighten the clamp screws. Start the engine and advance the throttle to approximately 1500 rpm in NEUTRAL gear for ten minutes or until the engine reaches full operating temperature.

5. Place the throttle in the idle position and allow the idle speed to stabilize for a few minutes. Direct the timing light at the timing pointer and flywheel marks (**Figure 38**). When the light flashes, the timing pointer should align with the idle speed timing mark specified in **Table 4**.

6. Shift the engine into FORWARD gear. Observe the tachometer and timing pointer while advancing the throttle to the maximum timing speed in **Table 5**. The timing pointer (**Figure 36**) should align with the maximum timing mark specified in **Table 5**.

7. Return the throttle to idle. Shift the engine into NEUTRAL. Stop the engine and remove it from the test tank.

8. If the marks do not align as specified, readjust the static timing.

9. Remove the test propeller and install the running propeller as described in Chapter Eight.

Timing, Synchronization and Carburetor Adjustments (25 hp Three-Cylinder and 30 hp Models)

These models use mechanical timing advancement. Static ignition timing, carburetor pickup timing and ignition timing checks are required. Perform the following adjustments and checks:

1. Choke valve adjustment.
2. Carburetor synchronization.
3. Timing pointer adjustment.
4. Static timing adjustment.
5. Pilot screw adjustment.
6. Idle speed adjustment.
7. Neutral speed limiter adjustment.
8. Pickup timing adjustment.
9. Throttle linkage/cable adjustment.
10. Ignition timing check.

Choke valve adjustment

This procedure is only required on electric start models.
1. Disconnect the spark plug leads to prevent accidental starting.

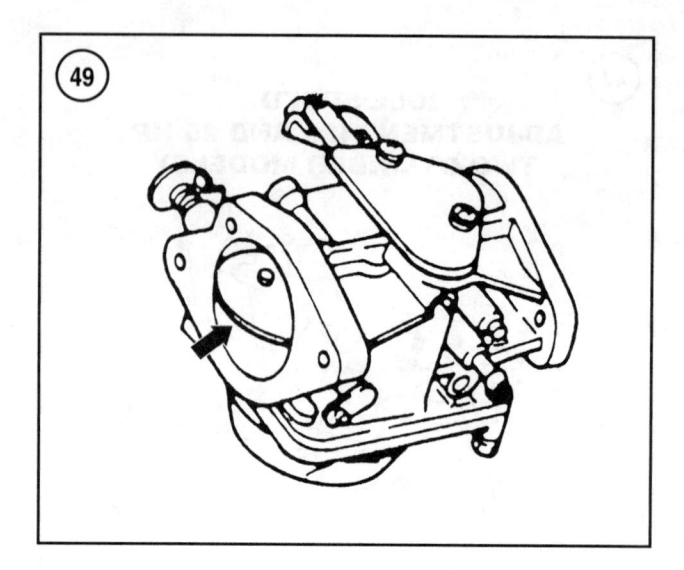

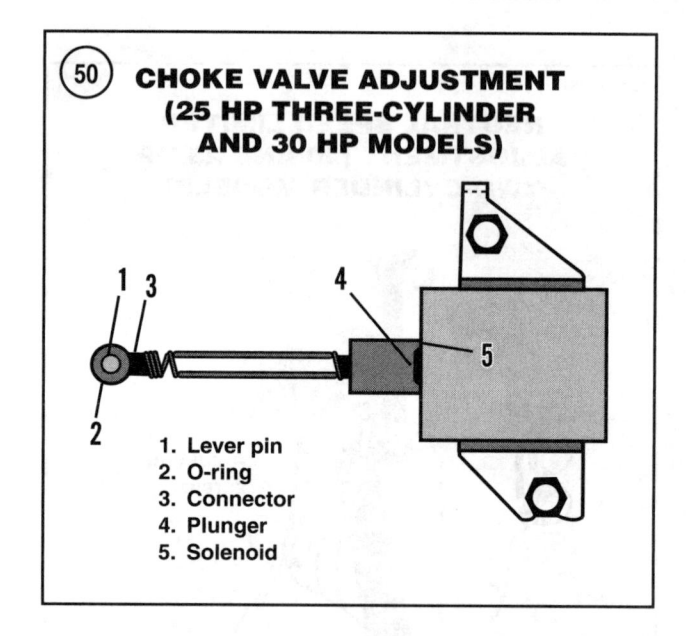

2. Disconnect the battery cables.

3. Remove the silencer cover from the carburetors as described in Chapter Five.

4. Move the choke lever on the bottom carburetor to fully close the choke valve (**Figure 49**).

5. Adjustment is correct when the mark on the choke plunger (4, **Figure 50**) is flush with the choke solenoid body (5).

6. If necessary, adjust the choke valve as follows:
  a. Remove the O-ring (2, **Figure 50**) to free the linkage from the choke lever pin (1).
  b. Rotate the connector (3, **Figure 50**) to achieve the length necessary for proper adjustment.

TIMING, SYNCHRONIZATION AND ADJUSTMENT

⑤¹ CARBURETOR SYNCHRONIZATION (25 HP THREE-CYLINDER AND 30 HP MODELS)

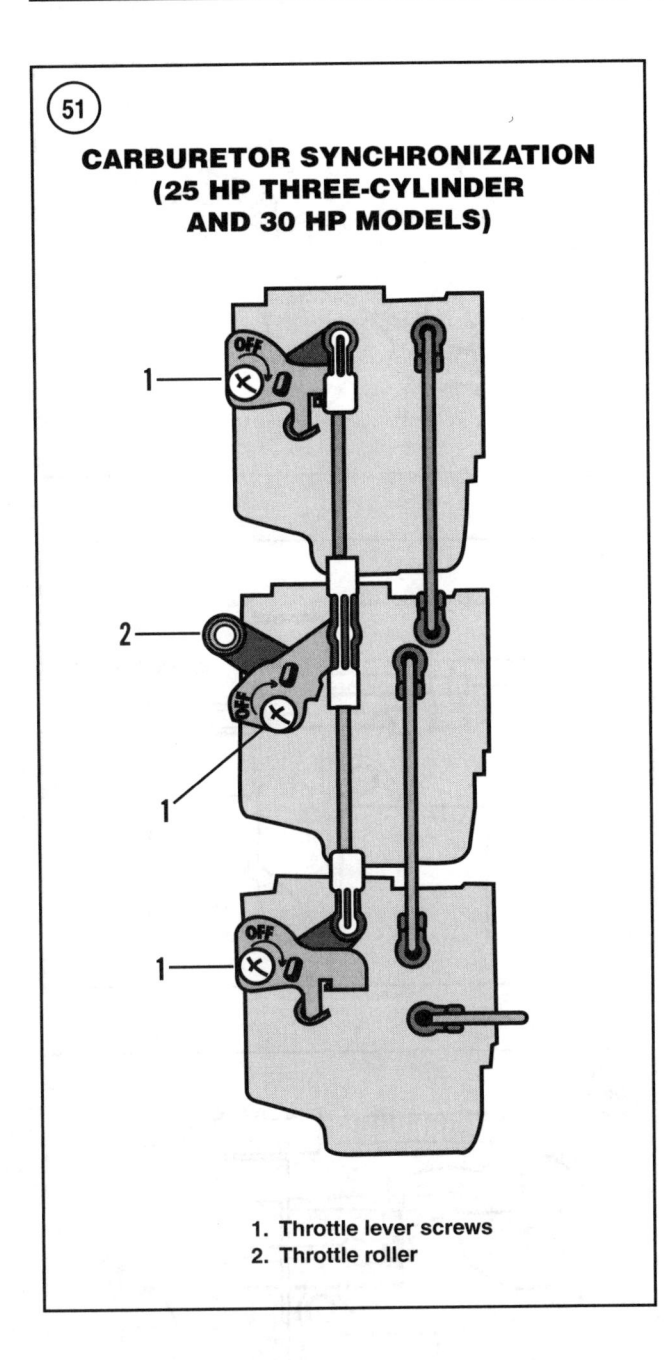

1. Throttle lever screws
2. Throttle roller

⑤² IDLE SPEED ADJUSTING SCREW (25 HP THREE-CYLINDER AND 30 HP MODELS)

c. After adjustment, hook the connector onto the choke valve pin. Install the O-ring onto the pin to hold the connector.
d. Check for proper adjustment. Readjust as necessary.

Carburetor synchronization

NOTE
The carburetor lever screws on 25 hp three-cylinder and 30 hp models use left-hand threads. Turn the screws clockwise to loosen them and counterclockwise to tighten them.

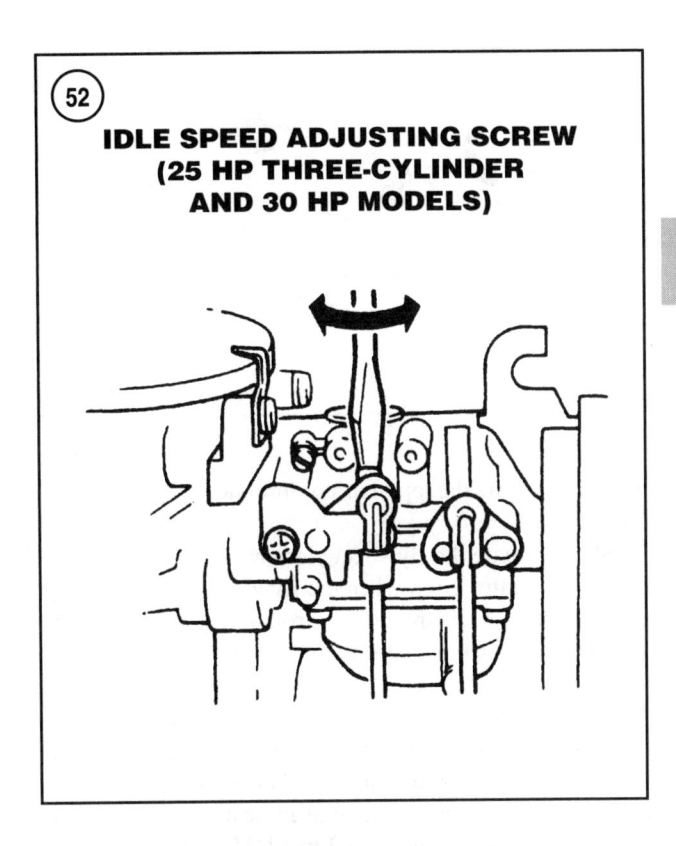

1. Fully loosen the upper and lower throttle lever screws (1, **Figure 51**).
2. Look into the top carburetor opening (**Figure 41**) and rotate the idle speed screw (**Figure 52**) until the throttle plate is fully closed.
3. Push down lightly on the throttle roller to remove slack from the linkage, then securely tighten the upper and lower screws.
4. Observe the throttle plates (**Figure 41**) while turning the idle speed screw (**Figure 52**) clockwise. Stop when the throttle plates just start to move.
5. Install the silencer cover onto the carburetors as described in Chapter Five.
6. Adjust the timing pointer as described in this chapter.

Timing pointer adjustment

1. Remove the three spark plugs.
2. Thread the dial indicator mount into the No. 1 spark plug opening. Install the dial indictor into the mount with the indicator stem in the No. 1 spark plug opening. Adjust the mount to position the stem in direct contact with the

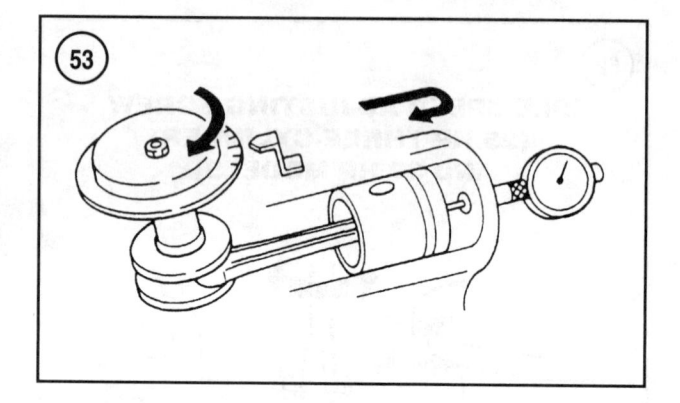

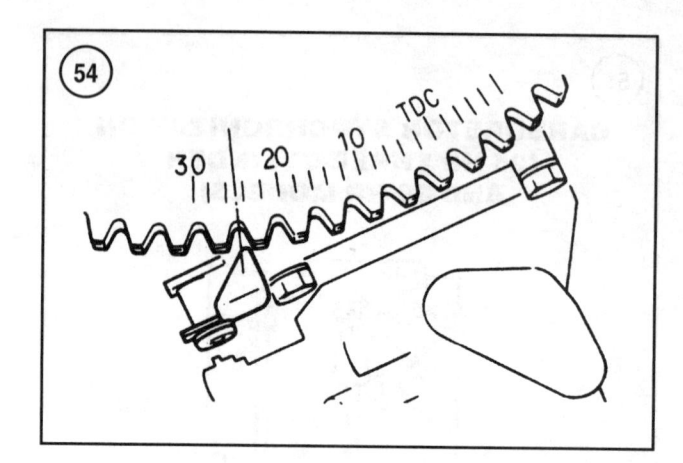

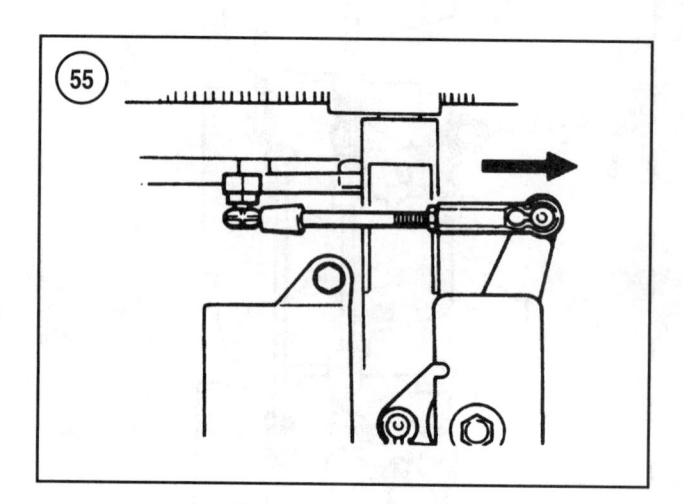

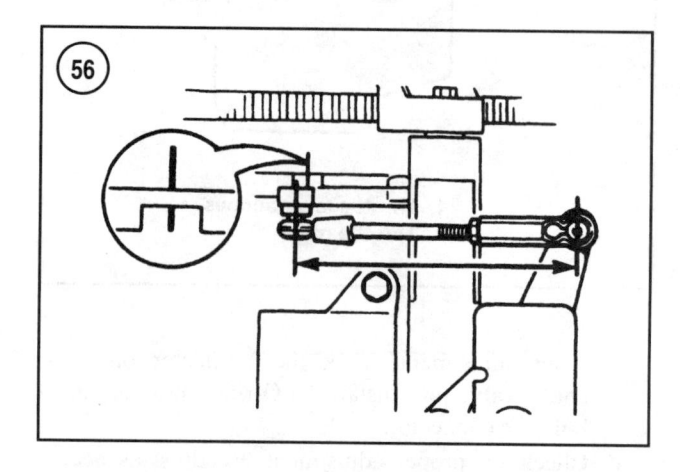

piston as it nears the top of its compression stroke (**Figure 53**).

3. Slowly rotate the flywheel clockwise while observing the dial indicator. Stop when the flywheel reaches the top of its stroke. This is the point of rotation when the needle on the dial indicator just reverses its direction as the flywheel is rotated.

4. Rotate the dial on the dial indicator until the needle aligns with the *0* mark on the dial. Observe the dial indicator while slowly rotating the flywheel counterclockwise. Stop the flywheel when the dial indicates the piston has moved down 3.55 mm (0.140 in.) BTDC. Keep the flywheel in this position during the pointer adjustment.

5. Loosen the pointer screw and move the pointer until it aligns with the 25° BTDC mark on the flywheel (**Figure 54**). Securely tighten the pointer screw.

6. Remove the dial indicator. Do not install the spark plugs at this time.

Static timing adjustment

1. Observe the timing pointer and timing marks on the flywheel (**Figure 54**) while rotating the flywheel clockwise. Stop when the 25° BTDC mark on the flywheel aligns with the timing pointer.

2. Move the throttle arm until it contacts the full advance stop (**Figure 55**). With the arm in contact with the stopper, the mark on the mounting base should align with the marking on the flywheel as shown in **Figure 56**. If necessary, adjust as follows:
   a. Carefully pry the linkage from the connector on the mounting base.
   b. Move the mounting base until the flywheel mark and mounting base align as shown in **Figure 56**.
   c. Loosen the jam nut and rotate the mounting base end of the linkage until the linkage connectors align with the throttle arm and mounting base connectors (**Figure 56**).
   d. Connect the linkage to the mounting base and securely tighten the jam nut.

3. Observe the timing pointer and timing marks on the flywheel (**Figure 57**) while rotating the flywheel clockwise. Stop when the 5° ATDC mark on the flywheel aligns with the timing pointer.

TIMING, SYNCHRONIZATION AND ADJUSTMENT

57

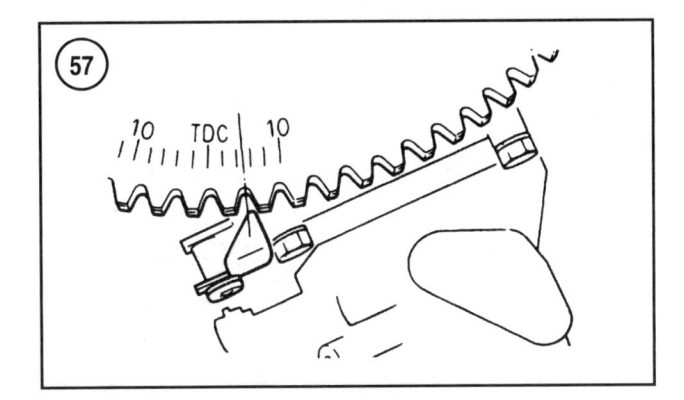

58

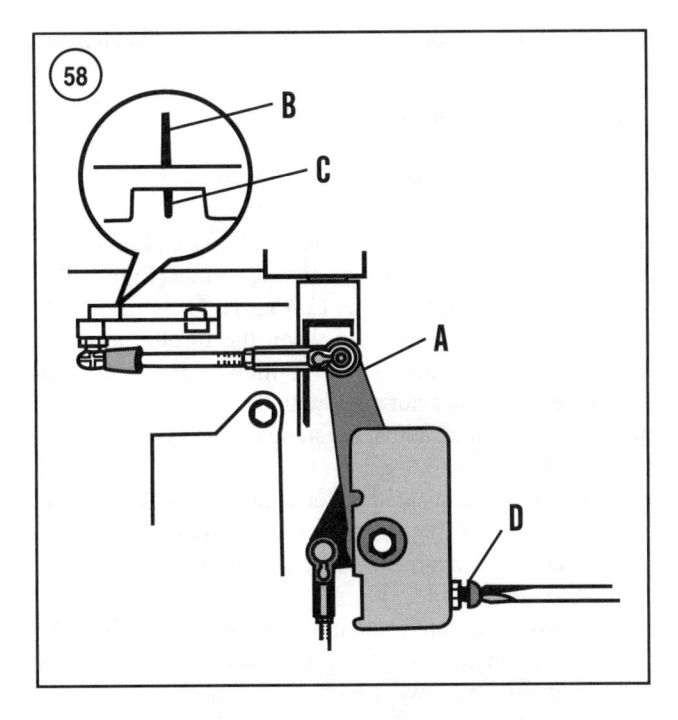

4. Move the throttle arm (A, **Figure 58**) until it contacts the cap on the full retard stop screw (D). Hold the arm against the cap and check the alignment of the mounting base mark (C, **Figure 58**) and flywheel mark (B). If the marks do not align, loosen the jam nut on the stop screw and rotate the screw until the marks align. Securely tighten the jam nut after adjustment. The throttle arm must be in contact with the stop screw during adjustments.

5. Install the spark plugs. Do not connect the spark plug leads at this time.

6. Adjust the pilot screws as described in this chapter.

Pilot screw adjustments

1. Disconnect and ground the spark plug leads to prevent accidental starting.

59 IDLE SPEED ADJUSTING SCREW (25 HP THREE-CYLINDER AND 30 HP MODELS)

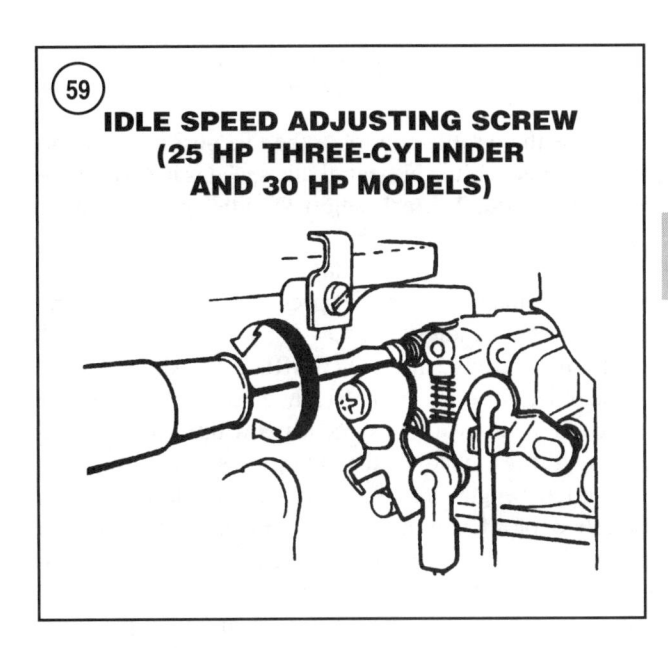

2. On electric start models, disconnect the battery cables.

3. Carefully turn the pilot screw for the upper carburetor clockwise until it is lightly seated (**Figure 59**).

4. Turn the pilot screw counterclockwise to the middle of the turns out range in **Table 6**.

5. Repeat Steps 3 and 4 for the middle, then bottom, carburetor pilot screws. The adjustment specification may vary by the carburetor position on the engine.

6. Adjust the idle speed as described in this section.

Idle speed adjustment

1. Turn the idle speed screw (**Figure 52**) counterclockwise until there is a gap between the screw tip and the carburetor throttle lever. Slowly rotate the screw clockwise until the tip just contacts the lever. Turn the screw one complete turn clockwise to slightly open the throttle.

2. Remove the running propeller as described in Chapter Eight and install a test propeller. The test propeller part number is in **Table 1**.

3. Connect the spark plug leads. Connect a shop tachometer to the spark plug lead.

4. On electric start models, connect the battery cables.

5. Place the engine in a test tank. Securely tighten the clamp screws. Start the engine and advance the throttle to approximately 1500 rpm in NEUTRAL gear for ten minutes or until the engine reaches full operating temperature.

NOTE
On 25 hp three-cylinder and 30 hp models, the idle speed is different for models

equipped with power tilt and trim versus models without this option.

6. Place the throttle control in the idle position and note the idle speed. If the in-neutral idle speed is not within the specification in **Table 7**, adjust the idle speed. Turn the idle speed screw (**Figure 52**) until the idle speed is in the middle of the idle speed range in **Table 7**. Clockwise screw rotation increases idle speed. Counterclockwise rotation decreases idle speed.

7. Shift the engine into FORWARD gear. Allow the idle to stabilize for a few minutes, then note the in-gear idle speed. If the in-gear idle speed is not within the specification in **Table 7**, readjust the idle speed screw.

8. Shift the engine into NEUTRAL gear. Allow the idle to stabilize for a few minutes, then note the idle speed. The in-neutral gear idle speed should remain within the specification in **Table 7**. If necessary, readjust the idle speed screw until both the in-gear and in-neutral idle speeds are within the specification. Several adjustments may be required.

9. Shift the engine into FORWARD gear and allow the idle to stabilize for a few minutes. Slowly advance the throttle, then bring it down to the idle position. Check for binding linkages or readjust the idle speed if the engine does not return to the specified range within 30-40 seconds.

10. Rapidly advance the throttle while checking for hesitation. If necessary, readjust the pilot screws (**Figure 59**) to minimize hesitation. Counterclockwise rotation reduces hesitation in most cases. Readjust the screws only a slight amount. Do not exceed the adjustment limits in **Table 6**. Adjust each screw the same amount and in the same rotational direction.

11. Adjust the neutral speed limiter as described in this chapter.

Neutral speed limiter adjustment

The neutral speed limiter adjusting screw threads into a link arm located directly below the throttle arm. The link arm contacts the shift linkages.

1. Adjust the idle speed as described in this chapter.
2. Shift the engine into NEUTRAL gear.
3. Observe the tachometer while slowly advancing the throttle. Proper adjustment limits the in-neutral speed to 3700-3800 rpm. If the in-neutral speed is above or below the specification, turn the adjustment screw to achieve the specified limit. Clockwise rotation decreases the limited speed. Counterclockwise rotation increases the limited speed.
4. Return the engine to idle speed and turn the engine OFF.

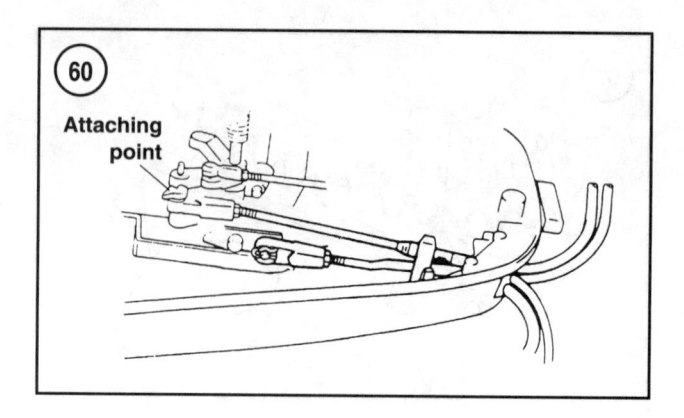

5. Adjust the pickup timing as described in this chapter.

Pickup timing adjustment

1. Adjust the idle speed as described in this section.
2. Shift the engine into FORWARD gear.
3. Connect a timing light to the No. 1 spark plug lead.
4. Direct the timing light at the timing pointer (**Figure 57**).
5. Observe the throttle roller (2, **Figure 51**) while slowly advancing the throttle. Stop when the throttle arm just contacts the roller and note the ignition timing. If the center of the roller does not align with the mark on the arm at the point of contact, adjust the static timing as described in this chapter.
6. If the timing indicated is not within the pickup timing specification in **Table 3**, adjust it as follows:
   a. Return the engine to idle and shift into NEUTRAL. Stop the engine.
   b. Loosen the screw and move the roller slightly in the direction necessary for proper adjustment. Securely tighten the screw.
   c. Start the engine and recheck the pickup timing. Repeat the process until the roller just contacts the throttle arm at the specified ignition timing.
   d. Synchronize the carburetors and adjust the idle speed as described in this chapter.
7. Adjust the throttle linkages or cables as described in this chapter.

Throttle linkage adjustment
(tiller control models)

1. Shift the engine into FORWARD gear. Rotate the throttle grip to the idle position (**Figure 44**).
2. Loosen the jam nuts (A and B, **Figure 34**).
3. Adjust the nuts (C and D, **Figure 34**) until the throttle arm (A, **Figure 39**) contacts the full retard stop screw (B) with the grip in the idle position.

TIMING, SYNCHRONIZATION AND ADJUSTMENT

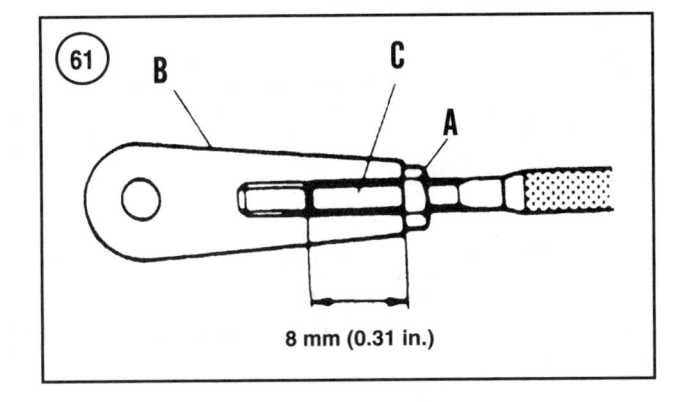

61
B, C, A
8 mm (0.31 in.)

4. Move the throttle grip to the full throttle position. If the throttle arm (A, **Figure 37**) does not just contact the stop (B) as the grip reaches the full throttle position, readjust the nuts (C and D, **Figure 34**).

5. Check the amount of free play in the throttle grip (**Figure 25**). Adjust the nuts (C and D, **Figure 34**) until approximately 3 mm (0.12 in.) of free play is present.

6. Securely tighten the jam nuts (A and B, **Figure 34**).

7. Check the ignition timing as described in this chapter.

*Throttle cable adjustment
(remote control models)*

1. Shift the engine into FORWARD gear.
2. Observe the carburetor lever while an assistant slowly moves the remote control handle to full throttle. If the lever does not contact the stop just as the control handle reaches full throttle, adjust the cable as follows:
   a. Place the remote control handle in the NEUTRAL gear idle speed position.
   b. Disconnect the throttle cable from the attaching point (**Figure 60**, typical).
   c. Open the latch and pull the cable from the lower cover or power head mounted retainer.
   d. Loosen the jam nut (A, **Figure 61**) and rotate the cable end (B) until the cable will fit over the connection point and into the retainer without moving the linkages.
   e. Check the cable end for adequate thread engagement (C, **Figure 61**). A minimum of 8 mm (0.31 in.) of engagement is required. Position the cable anchor into a different groove on the cable as required.
   f. Fit the cable on the attaching points. Move the control handle to the full throttle and idle positions while checking for full movement of the carburetor lever. Readjust the cable to achieve full movement to the full throttle and idle positions.

   g. Securely tighten the jam nut (A, **Figure 61**). Install the fasteners and engage the latch to secure the cable to the mounting bracket and throttle arm.

3. Check the ignition timing as described in this chapter.

Ignition timing check

1. Remove the running propeller as described in Chapter Eight and install a test propeller. The test propeller part number is in **Table 1**.
2. Connect a timing light to the No. 1 (top) spark plug lead.
3. Connect a shop tachometer to the spark plug lead. Do not allow the timing light and tachometer pickups to touch during this procedure.
4. Place the engine in a test tank. Securely tighten the clamp screws. Start the engine and advance the throttle to approximately 1500 rpm in NEUTRAL gear for ten minutes or until the engine reaches full operating temperature.
5. Place the throttle in the idle position and allow the idle speed to stabilize for a few minutes. Direct the timing light at the timing pointer and flywheel marks (**Figure 57**). When the light flashes, the timing pointer should align with the idle speed timing mark specified in **Table 4**.
6. Shift the engine into FORWARD gear. Observe the tachometer and timing pointer while advancing the throttle to the maximum timing speed in **Table 5**. The timing pointer (**Figure 54**) should align with the maximum timing mark specified in **Table 5**.
7. Return the throttle to idle. Shift the engine into NEUTRAL. Stop the engine and remove it from the test tank.
8. If the marks do not align as specified, readjust the static timing.
9. Remove the test propeller and install the running propeller as described in Chapter Eight.

Timing, Synchronization and Carburetor Adjustments (28 Jet, 35 Jet, 40 hp and 50 hp Models)

These models use an electronic timing advancement with a CDI unit mounted timing indicator. A static ignition timing adjustment and timing check are required. Perform the following adjustments and checks.

1. Static timing adjustment.
2. Carburetor synchronization.
3. Throttle cable adjustment.
4. Pilot screw adjustment.
5. Idle speed adjustment.

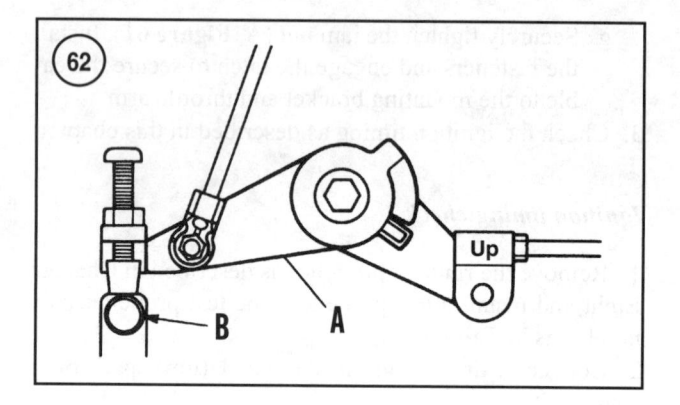

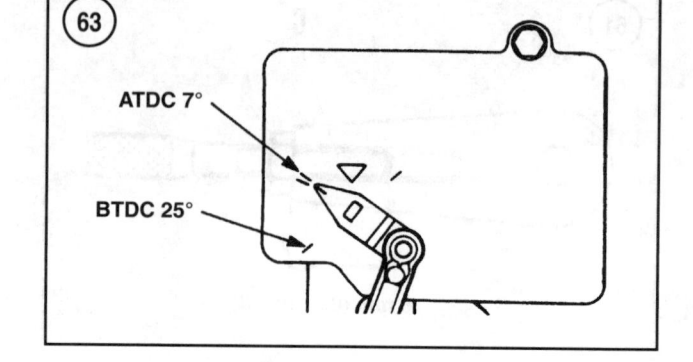

6. Ignition timing check.
7. Pickup timing adjustment.

Static timing adjustment

1. On electric start models, disconnect the battery cables.
2. Disconnect and ground the spark plug leads to prevent accidental starting.
3. Move the throttle arm (A, **Figure 62**) until the adjusting screw cap contacts the full retard stop (B).
4. Locate the timing indicator on the CDI unit (**Figure 63**). If the indicator does not align with the 7° ATDC mark on the CDI unit as indicated, adjust it as follows:
   a. Loosen the jam nut on the full retard adjusting screw.
   b. Hold the throttle arm to keep the adjusting screw cap (B, **Figure 64**) in contact with the stop.
   c. Rotate the adjusting screw until the measurement is 20.0 mm (0.79 in.) at the points indicated (A, **Figure 64**). Securely tighten the jam nut.
   d. Loosen the jam nut (A, **Figure 65**) on the indicator linkage. Carefully pry the linkage from the indicator.
   e. Keep the adjusting screw in contact with the stopper (C, **Figure 65**) and adjust the length of the indicator linkage until the 7° ATDC mark would align with the pointer if the linkage were installed.
   f. Carefully snap the linkage onto the indicator and securely tighten the jam nut.
5. Move the throttle arm until it contacts the cap on the full advance adjusting screw (D, **Figure 65**). Loosen the jam nut on the adjusting screw.
6. Keep the throttle arm in contact with the adjusting screw cap, then rotate the screw (D, **Figure 65**) until the indicator aligns with the 25° BTDC mark on the CDI unit. Securely tighten the adjusting screw.
7. Adjust the throttle cable as described in this chapter.

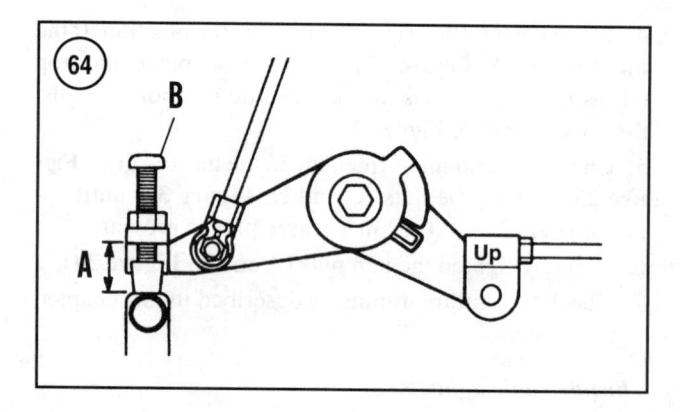

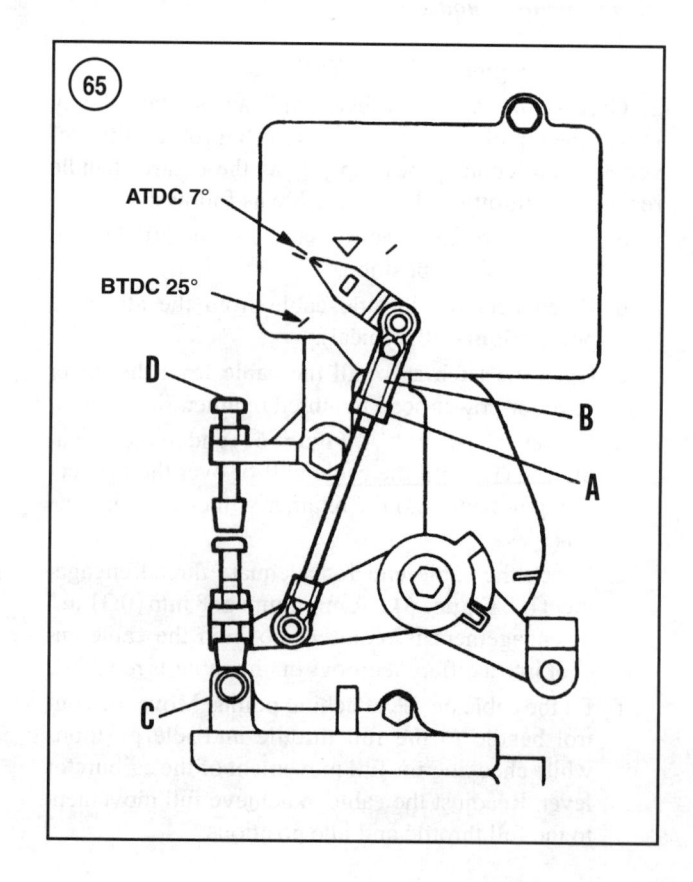

TIMING, SYNCHRONIZATION AND ADJUSTMENT

Figure 66 IDLE SPEED ADJUSTMENT (28 JET, 35 JET, 40 HP AND 50 HP MODELS)

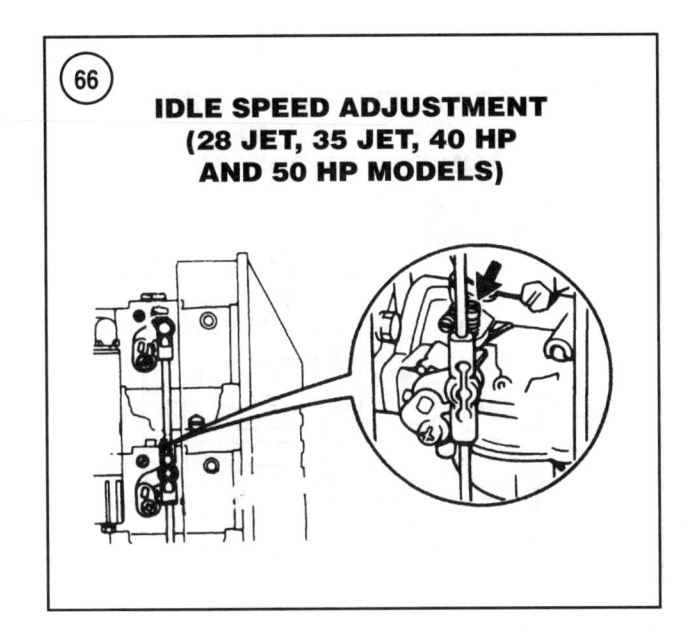

Figure 67

Figure 68

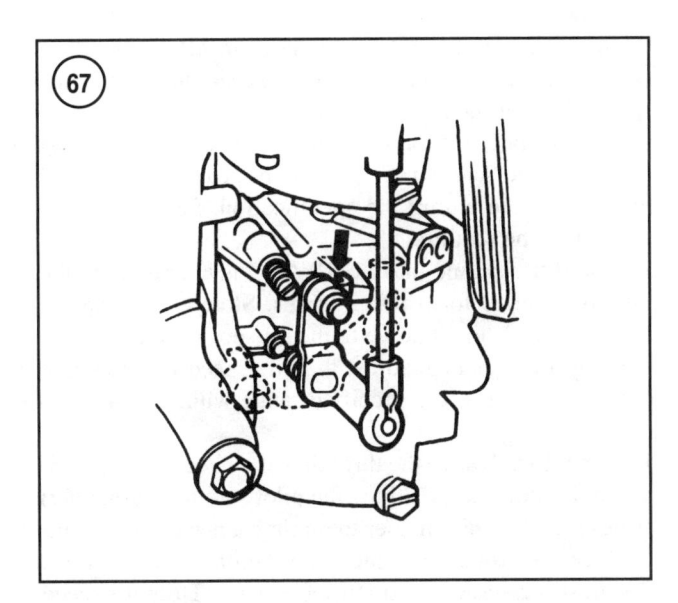

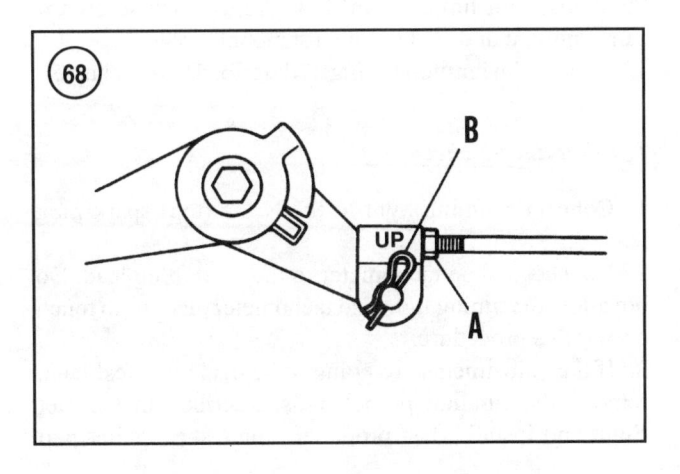

Carburetor synchronization

NOTE
The carburetor lever screws on 28 jet, 35 jet, 40 hp and 50 hp models use left-hand threads. Turn the screws clockwise to loosen them and counterclockwise to tighten them.

1. Move the throttle arm until its adjusting screw contacts the full retard stop (**Figure 62**).
2. Remove the silencer cover from the carburetors as described in Chapter Five.
3. Look into the top carburetor opening (**Figure 41**) and rotate the idle speed screw (**Figure 66**) until the throttle plate is fully closed.
4. Fully loosen the upper and middle throttle lever screws (1, **Figure 51**).
5. Push down lightly on the throttle roller to remove slack from the linkage, then securely tighten the upper and middle screws.
6. Observe the throttle plates (**Figure 41**) while turning the idle speed screw (**Figure 66**) clockwise. Stop when the throttle plates just start to move.
7. Install the silencer cover on the carburetors as described in Chapter Five.
8. Adjust the throttle cable as described in this chapter.

Throttle cable adjustment

1. Shift the engine into FORWARD gear.
2. Observe the carburetor lever (**Figure 67**) while slowly advancing the throttle to the wide-open limit. If the throttle lever does not contact the stop just as the throttle setting reaches the wide-open limit, adjust it as follows:
    a. Place the throttle control in the NEUTRAL position.
    b. Loosen the jam nut (A, **Figure 68**), then remove the pin (B) from the throttle linkage connector.
    c. Pull the connector from the throttle arm. Move the throttle arm (A, **Figure 62**) until the full retard adjusting screw contacts the stopper (B).
    d. Rotate the connector on the end of the cable until the cable can be installed over the throttle arm pin without moving the arm. Be sure the *UP* mark on the connector faces upward.
3. Check for proper full-throttle lever positioning as described in Step 2. If the adjustment is not correct, adjust the static timing as described in this chapter.
4. Adjust the pilot screws as described in this chapter.

Pilot screw adjustment

NOTE
On 35 jet and 50 hp models, the pilot screw adjustment is different for models with electric starting versus manual start models.

1. Disconnect and ground the spark plug leads to prevent accidental starting.
2. On electric start models, disconnect the battery cables.
3. Carefully turn the pilot screw (**Figure 69**) for the upper carburetor clockwise until it is lightly seated.
4. Turn the pilot screw counterclockwise to the middle of the adjustment range in **Table 6**.
5. Repeat Steps 3 and 4 for the middle, then bottom, carburetor pilot screws.
6. Adjust the idle speed as described in this section.

Idle speed adjustment

1. Turn the idle speed screw (**Figure 66**) counterclockwise until there is a gap between the screw tip and the carburetor throttle lever. Slowly rotate the screw clockwise until the tip just contacts the lever. Turn the screw one complete turn clockwise to slightly open the throttle.
2. Remove the running propeller as described in Chapter Eight and install a test propeller. The test propeller part number is in **Table 1**. Do not install the test propeller if the adjustment will be made under actual running conditions.
3. Connect the spark plug leads. Connect a shop tachometer to the spark plug lead.
4. On electric start models, connect the battery cables.
5. Place the engine in a test tank or operate the vessel under normal conditions in an area away from other boat traffic. Adjust the idle speed while a qualified assistant operates the boat. When using a test tank, securely tighten the clamping screws.
6. Start the engine and advance the throttle to approximately 1500 rpm in NEUTRAL gear for ten minutes or until the engine reaches full operating temperature.
7. Move the throttle control to the idle position and note the idle speed. If the in-neutral idle speed is not within the specification in **Table 7**, adjust the idle speed. Turn the idle speed screw (**Figure 66**) until the idle speed is in the middle of the idle speed range in **Table 7**. Clockwise screw rotation increases idle speed. Counterclockwise rotation decreases idle speed.
8. Shift the engine into FORWARD gear. Allow the idle to stabilize for a few minutes, then note the in-gear idle speed. If the in-gear idle speed is not within the specification in **Table 7**, readjust the idle speed screw.
9. Shift the engine into NEUTRAL gear. Allow the idle to stabilize for a few minutes, then note the in-neutral idle speed. The in-neutral gear idle speed should remain within the specification in **Table 7**. If necessary, readjust the idle speed screw until both the in-gear and in-neutral idle speeds are within the specification. Several adjustments may be required.
10. Shift the engine into FORWARD gear and allow the idle to stabilize for a few minutes. Slowly advance the throttle, then bring it down to the idle position. Check for binding linkages or readjust the idle speed if the engine does not return to the specified range within 30-40 seconds.
11. Rapidly advance the throttle while checking for hesitation. If necessary, readjust the pilot screws (**Figure 69**) as described in this chapter to minimize hesitation. Counterclockwise rotation reduces hesitation in most cases. Readjust the screws in small increments. Do not exceed the adjustment limits in **Table 6**. Adjust each screw the same amount and in the same rotational direction.
12. Check the ignition timing as described in this chapter.

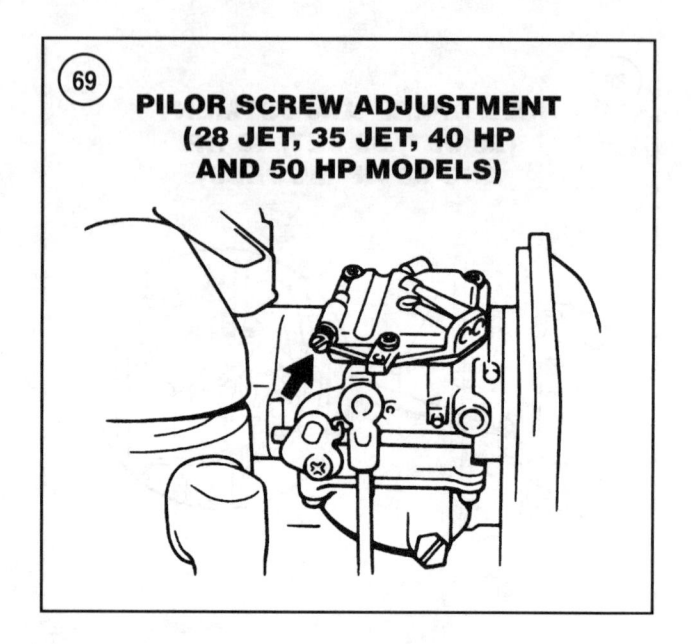

Ignition timing check

1. Connect a timing light to the No. 1 (top) spark plug lead.
2. Connect a shop tachometer to the spark plug lead. Do not allow the timing light and tachometer pickups to touch during this procedure.
3. If the adjustments are going to be made in a test tank, remove the running propeller as described in Chapter Eight and install a test propeller. The test propeller part

TIMING, SYNCHRONIZATION AND ADJUSTMENT

Figure 70

Figure 71 — PICKUP TIMING ADJUSTMENT

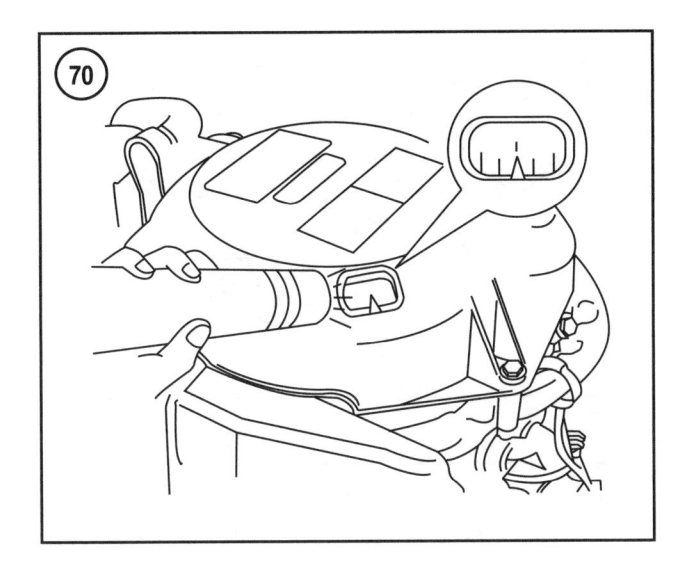

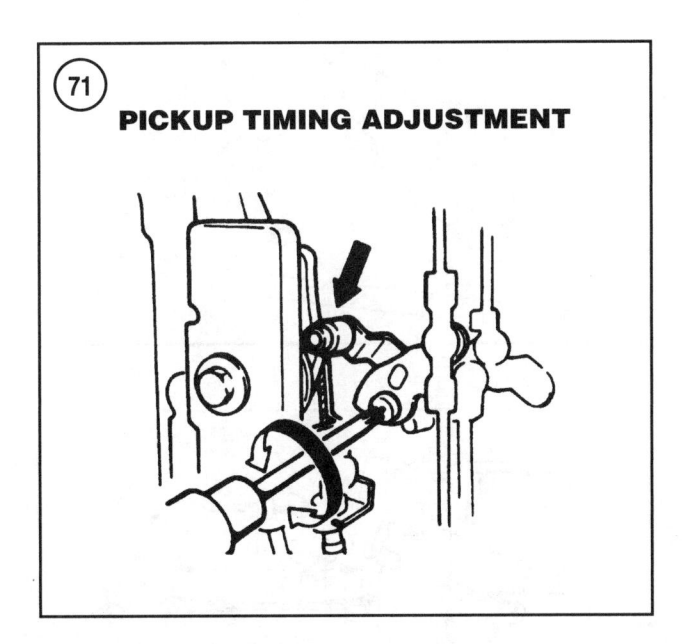

number is in **Table 1**. Do not install a test propeller if the adjustment will be made under actual operating conditions; have a qualified assistant operate the boat while you perform the check.

4. Start the engine and advance the throttle to approximately 1500 rpm in NEUTRAL gear for ten minutes or until the engine reaches full operating temperature.
5. Move the throttle to the idle position and allow the idle speed to stabilize for a few minutes. Direct the timing light at the timing pointer and flywheel marks (**Figure 70**). When the light flashes, the timing pointer should align with the idle speed timing mark specified in **Table 4**.
6. Shift the engine into FORWARD gear. Observe the tachometer and timing pointer while advancing the throttle to the maximum timing speed in **Table 5**. The timing pointer (**Figure 70**) should align with the maximum timing mark specified in **Table 5**.
7. Return the throttle to idle. Shift the engine into NEUTRAL. Stop the engine.
8. If the markings do not align as specified, readjust the static timing as described in this section and recheck the timing. Check for a sheared flywheel key as described in Chapter Seven or faulty ignition system component as described in Chapter Two if the timing remains incorrect.
9. Remove the test propeller if one was installed.
10. Adjust the pickup timing as described in this chapter.

Pickup timing adjustment

1. Adjust the pickup timing while an assistant operates the vessel in a clear area. Shift the engine into FORWARD gear.
2. Connect a timing light to the No. 1 spark plug lead.
3. Direct the timing light at the timing pointer (**Figure 70**).
4. Observe the throttle roller (**Figure 71**) while slowly advancing the throttle. Stop when the throttle arm just contacts the roller and note the ignition timing. If the center of the roller does not align with the mark on the roller, adjust the static timing as described in this chapter
5. If the timing is not within the pickup timing specification in **Table 3**, adjust it as follows:
   a. Return the engine to idle and shift into NEUTRAL. Stop the engine.
   b. Loosen the screw (**Figure 71**) and move the roller slightly in the direction necessary for proper adjustment. Securely tighten the screw.
   c. Start the engine and recheck the pickup timing. Repeat the process until the roller just contacts the throttle arm at the specified ignition timing.
   d. Synchronize the carburetors and adjust the idle speed as described in this chapter after adjusting the pickup timing.
6. Adjust the throttle linkages or cables as described in this chapter.

Timing, Synchronization and Carburetor Adjustments (60-90 hp [Except E60 and E75] Models)

These models use an electronic timing advancement with a CDI unit mounted timing indicator. Perform the following adjustments.

1. Timing pointer adjustment.
2. Link rod adjustment.
3. Static timing adjustment.

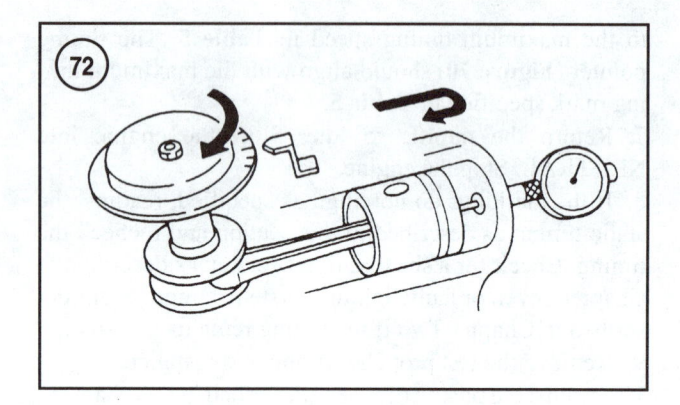

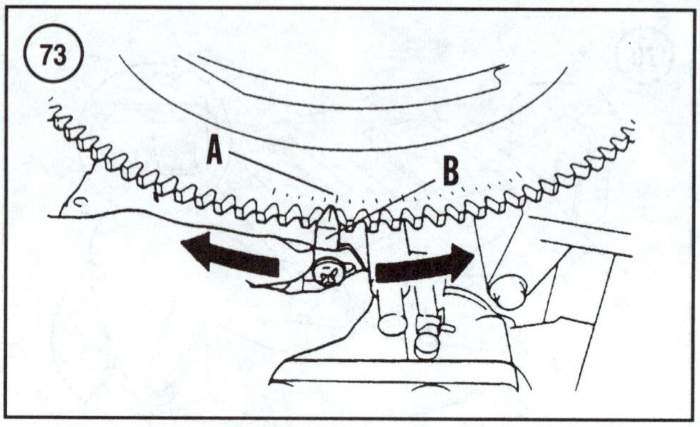

CHAPTER FOUR

4. Carburetor synchronization.
5. Pilot screw adjustment.
6. Throttle cable adjustment.
7. Ignition timing adjustment.
8. Idle speed adjustment.
9. Pickup timing adjustment.

Timing pointer adjustment

1. On electric start models, disconnect the battery cables.
2. Remove the three spark plugs. Ground the spark plug leads.
3. Thread the dial indicator mount into the No. 1 spark plug opening. Install the dial indictor into the mount with the indicator stem in the No. 1 spark plug opening. Adjust the mount to position the stem in direct contact with the piston as it nears the top of its compression stroke (**Figure 72**).
4. Slowly rotate the flywheel clockwise while observing the dial indicator. Stop when the flywheel reaches the top of its stroke. This is the point of rotation when the needle on the dial indicator just reverses its direction as the flywheel is rotated.
5. Loosen the screw and move the pointer (B, **Figure 73**) until it aligns with the 0° TDC mark on the flywheel (A). Securely tighten the pointer screw.
6. Remove the dial indicator and install the spark plugs. Do not connect the spark plug leads at this time.
7. Adjust the link rods as described in this chapter.

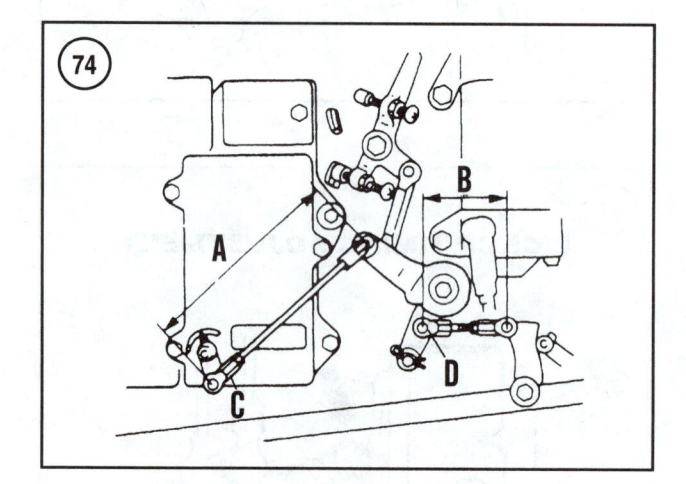

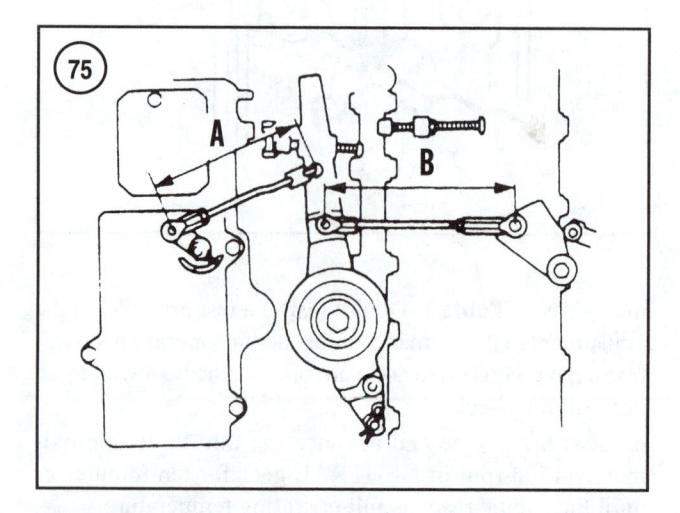

Link rod adjustment

1. Carefully pry the throttle sensor linkages (C and D, **Figure 74**) from the timing indicator lever, throttle arm and throttle cam ball joints.
2A. On 60 and 70 hp models, rotate the connector to adjust the timing indicator-to-throttle arm linkage distance to a length of 129.0 mm (5.08 in.) at the points indicated (A, **Figure 74**). Adjust the throttle arm-to-throttle cam linkage distance to a length of 58.0 mm (2.28 in.) at the points indicated (B, **Figure 74**).

2B. On 65 jet and 75-90 hp models, rotate the connector to adjust the timing indicator-to-throttle arm linkage distance to a length of 93.5 mm (3.68 in.) at the points indicated (A, **Figure 75**). Adjust the throttle arm-to-throttle

TIMING, SYNCHRONIZATION AND ADJUSTMENT

76 FULL RETARD TIMING ADJUSTMENT (60 AND 70 HP MODELS)

77 FULL RETARD TIMING ADJUSTMENT (65 JET AND 75-90 HP MODELS)

78 FULL ADVANCE TIMING ADJUSTMENT (60 AND 70 HP MODELS)

79 FULL ADVANCE TIMING ADJUSTMENT (65 JET AND 75-90 HP MODELS)

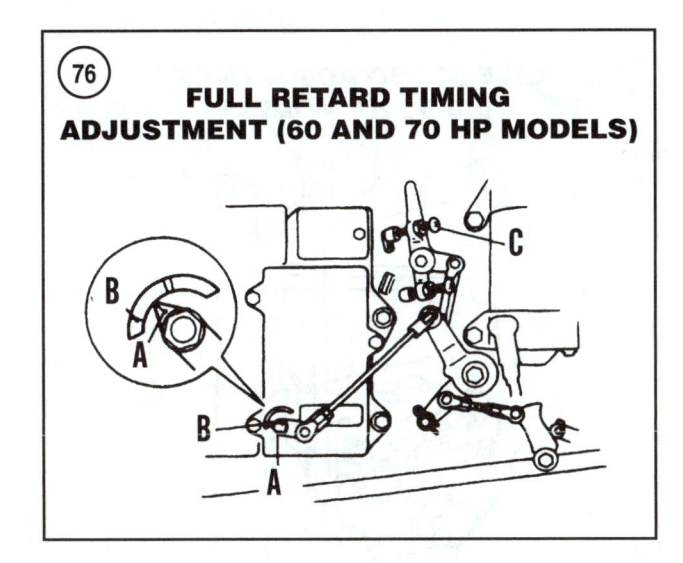

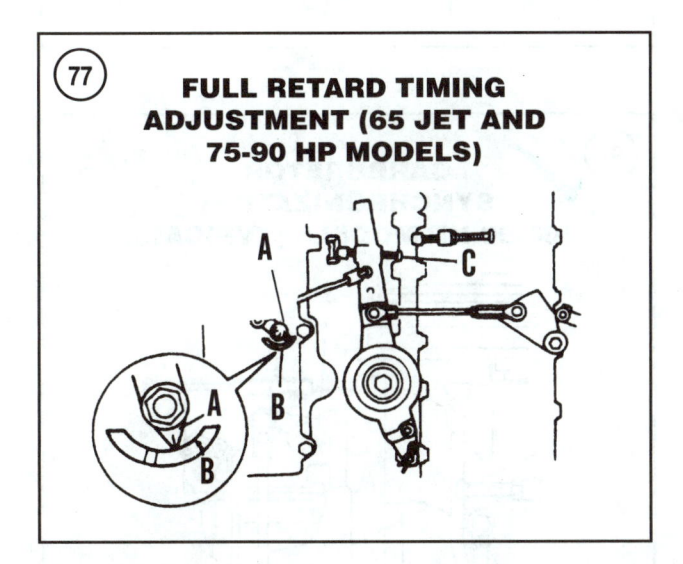

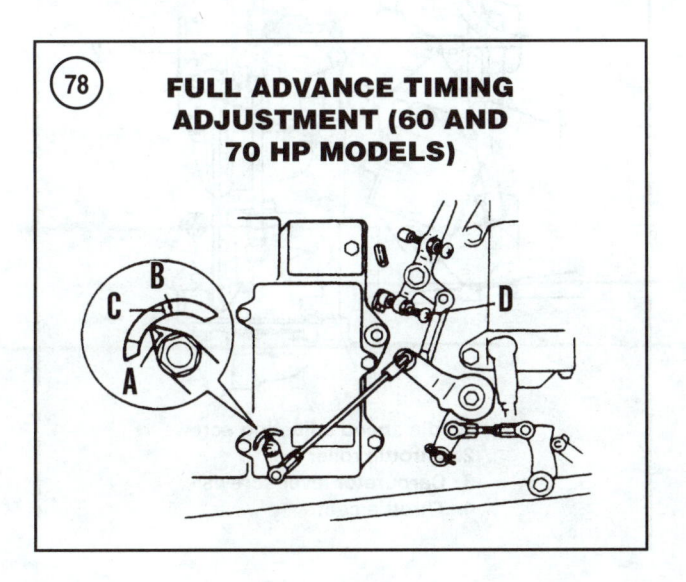

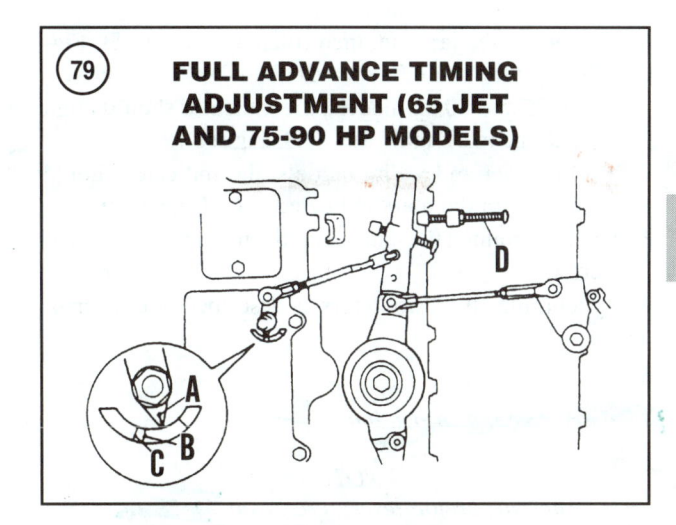

cam linkage distance to a length of 120.5 mm (4.74 in.) at the points indicated (B, **Figure 75**).

3. Connect the linkages to the timing indicator, throttle arm and throttle cam. Snap the connectors onto the ball joints.

4. Adjust the static timing as described in this chapter.

Static timing adjustment

1A. On 60 and 70 hp models, move the throttle lever until the full retard adjusting screw (C, **Figure 76**) on the timing stop lever contacts the stop. Keep the screw cap in contact with the stop during the adjustment. Loosen the jam nut, then rotate the screw (C, **Figure 76**) until the timing indicator (A) aligns with the mark (B) on the CDI unit. Securely tighten the jam nut.

1B. On 65 jet and 75-90 hp models, move the throttle lever until the full retard adjusting screw (C, **Figure 77**) contacts the stop. Keep the screw cap in contact with the stop during the adjustment. Loosen the jam nut, then rotate the screw (C, **Figure 77**) until the timing indicator (A) aligns with the mark (B) on the CDI unit. Securely tighten the jam nut.

2A. On 60 and 70 hp models, move the throttle lever until the full advance adjusting screw (D, **Figure 78**) on the timing stop lever contacts the stop. Keep the screw cap in contact with the stop during the adjustment. Loosen the jam nut, then rotate the screw (D, **Figure 78**) until the timing indicator (A) aligns with the mark for the engine model.

  a. On 60 hp models, the indicator should align with the mark indicated in B, **Figure 78**.
  b. On 70 hp models, the indicator should align with the mark indicated in C, **Figure 78**.

2B. On 65 jet and 75-90 hp models, move the throttle lever until it contacts the cap on the full advance adjusting screw (D, **Figure 79**). Keep this position during adjust-

ment. Loosen the jam nut, then rotate the screw (D, **Figure 79**) until the timing indicator aligns with the mark.
   a. On 75 and 80 hp models, the indicator should align with the mark indicated in B, **Figure 79**.
   b. On 65 jet and 90 hp models, the indicator should align with the mark indicated in C, **Figure 79**.
3. Securely tighten the jam nut on the full advance adjusting screw.
4. Synchronize the carburetors as described in this chapter.

Carburetor synchronization

NOTE
The carburetor lever screws on 60-90 hp models use left-hand threads. Turn the screws clockwise to loosen them and counterclockwise to tighten them.

1. Move the throttle arm until the full retard adjusting screw contacts the retard stop (see *Static timing adjustment*).
2. Remove the silencer cover from the carburetors as described in Chapter Five.
3. Look into the middle carburetor opening and rotate the idle speed screw (**Figure 80**) until the throttle plate is fully closed.
4. Fully loosen the upper and middle carburetor lever screws (3, **Figure 81**).
5. Push down lightly on the throttle roller to remove slack from the linkage, then securely tighten the upper and middle screws.
6. Observe the throttle plates while turning the idle speed screw (**Figure 80**) clockwise. Stop when the throttle plates just start to move.
7. Install the silencer cover onto the carburetors as described in Chapter Five.
8. Adjust the pilot screws as described in this chapter.

Pilot screw adjustment

1. Disconnect and ground the spark plug lead to prevent accidental starting.
2. On electric start models, disconnect the battery cables.
3. Carefully turn the pilot screw (**Figure 82**) for the upper carburetor clockwise until it is lightly seated.
4. Turn the pilot screw counterclockwise to the middle of the adjustment range in **Table 6**.
5. Repeat Steps 3 and 4 for the middle, then bottom, carburetor pilot screws.
6. Adjust the throttle cable as described in this chapter.

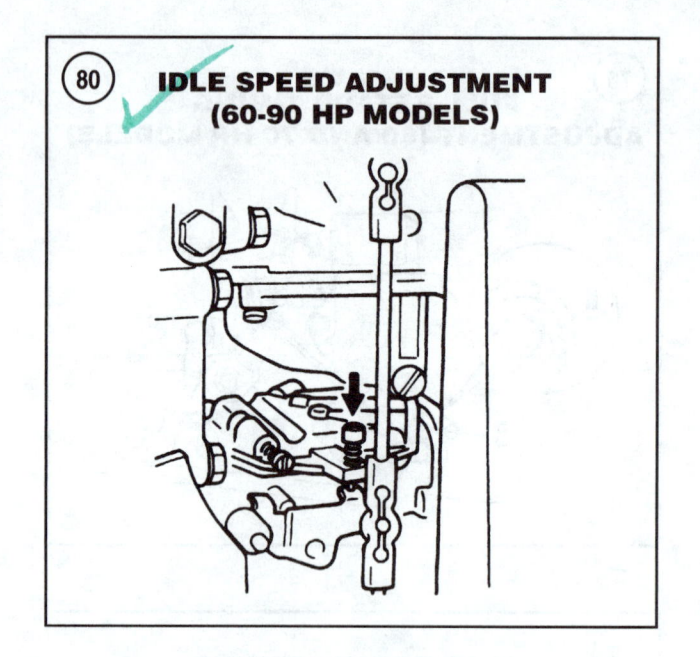

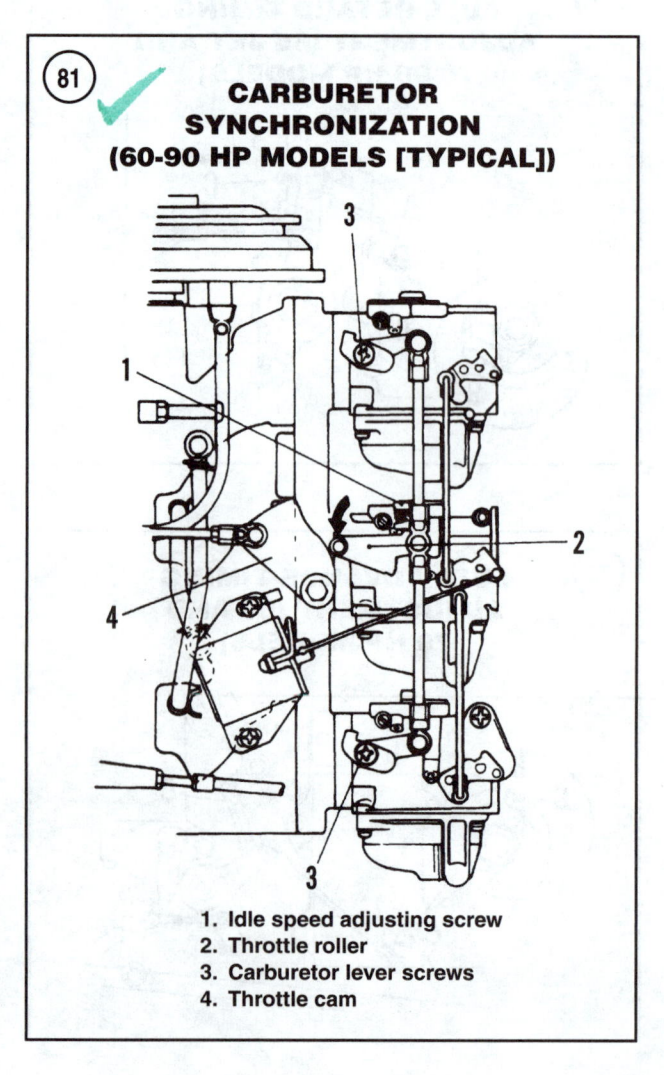

80   IDLE SPEED ADJUSTMENT (60-90 HP MODELS)

81   CARBURETOR SYNCHRONIZATION (60-90 HP MODELS [TYPICAL])

1. Idle speed adjusting screw
2. Throttle roller
3. Carburetor lever screws
4. Throttle cam

TIMING, SYNCHRONIZATION AND ADJUSTMENT

82 PILOT SCREW ADJUSTMENT (60-90 HP MODELS)

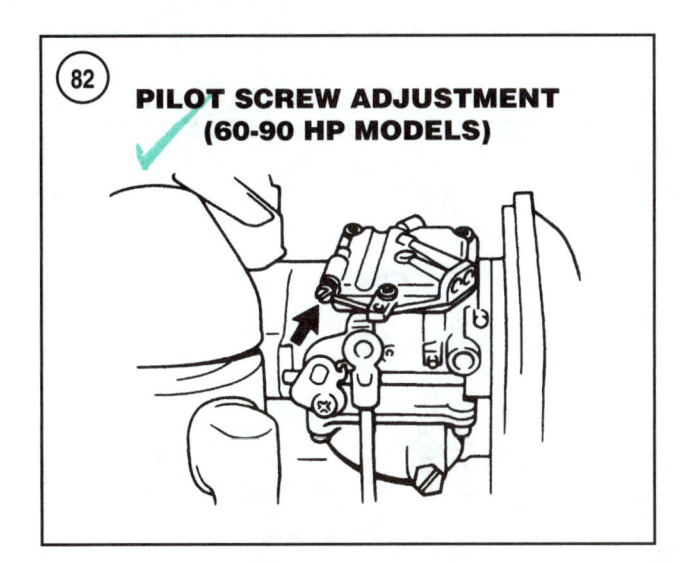

83

Throttle cable adjustment

1. Shift the engine into FORWARD gear.
2. Observe the carburetor levers while an assistant slowly moves the remote control handle to full throttle. If the levers do not contact the stop just as the throttle control reaches full throttle, adjust the cable as follows:
   a. Move the shift selector to the NEUTRAL gear idle speed position.
   b. Disconnect the throttle cable from the attaching point (**Figure 60**, typical).
   c. Open the latch and pull the cable from the lower cover or power head mounted retainer.
   d. Loosen the jam nut (A, **Figure 61**) and rotate the cable end (B) until the cable will fit over the connection point and into the retainer without moving the linkages.
   e. Check the cable end for adequate thread engagement (C, **Figure 61**). A minimum of 8 mm (0.31 in.) of engagement is required. Position the cable anchor into a different groove on the cable as required.
   f. Fit the cable onto the attaching points. Move the control handle to the full throttle and idle positions while checking for full movement of the carburetor lever. Readjust the cable to achieve full movement to the full throttle and idle positions.
   g. Securely tighten the jam nut (A, **Figure 61**). Install the fasteners and engage the latch to secure the cable to the mounting bracket and throttle arm.
3. Adjust the ignition timing as described in this chapter.

Ignition timing adjustment

Perform this adjustment under actual running conditions. Adjust the ignition timing while a qualified assistant operates the controls. Operate the boat in a safe area away from boat traffic.

1. On electric start models, connect the battery cables.
2. Connect the spark plug leads.
3. Connect a timing light to the No. 1 (top) spark plug lead.
4. Connect a shop tachometer to the spark plug lead. Do not allow the timing light and tachometer pickups to touch during this procedure.
5. Start the engine and advance the throttle to approximately 1500 rpm in NEUTRAL gear for ten minutes or until the engine reaches full operating temperature. Check and adjust the ignition timing while a qualified assistant operates the boat.
6. Move the throttle to the idle position and allow the idle speed to stabilize for a few minutes. Direct the timing light at the timing pointer and flywheel marks (**Figure 83**). When the light flashes, the timing pointer should align with the full retard timing mark specified in **Table 4**. If necessary, adjust as follows:
   a. On 60 and 70 hp models, loosen the jam nut on the full retard adjusting screw (C, **Figure 76**).
   b. On 65 jet and 75-90 hp models, loosen the jam nut on the full retard adjusting screw (C, **Figure 77**).
   c. Keep the cap on the adjusting screw in contact with the stop during the adjustment.
   d. Direct the timing light at the timing pointer (**Figure 83**). Rotate the full retard adjusting screw until the timing pointer aligns with the full retard timing specification in **Table 4**.
   e. Securely tighten the jam nut.
7. Shift the engine into FORWARD gear. Observe the tachometer and timing pointer while an assistant advances the throttle to wide open. The engine should reach the speed range in **Table 5**.
8. Direct the timing light at the timing pointer (**Figure 83**). If the timing pointer does not align with the maxi-

mum timing mark specified in **Table 5**, adjust it as follows:
  a. On 60 and 70 hp models, loosen the nut on the full advance adjusting screw (D, **Figure 78**).
  b. On 65 jet and 75-90 hp models, loosen the nut on the full advance adjusting screw (D, **Figure 79**).
  c. Keep the cap on the adjusting screw in contact with the stop during the adjustment.
  d. Direct the timing light at the timing pointer (**Figure 83**). Rotate the full advance adjusting screw until the timing pointer aligns with the full advance timing specification in **Table 5**.
  e. Securely tighten the jam nut.
9. Return the throttle to idle. Shift the engine into NEUTRAL.
10. If timing adjustment was required, readjust the throttle cable as described in this chapter.
11. Adjust the idle speed as described in this chapter.

Idle speed adjustment

Perform this adjustment under actual running conditions. Adjust the idle speed while a qualified assistant operates the controls. Operate the boat in a safe area away from boat traffic.
1. Adjust the ignition timing as described in this chapter.
2. Turn the idle speed screw (**Figure 80**) counterclockwise until there is a gap between the screw tip and the carburetor throttle lever. Slowly rotate the screw clockwise until the tip just contacts the lever. Turn the screw one complete turn clockwise to slightly open the throttle.
3. Connect a suitable shop tachometer to the spark plug lead.
4. Start the engine and advance the throttle to approximately 1500 rpm in NEUTRAL gear for ten minutes or until the engine reaches full operating temperature.
5. Move the throttle control to the idle position and note the idle speed. If the in-neutral idle speed is not within the specification in **Table 7**, adjust the idle speed. Turn the idle speed screw (**Figure 80**) until the idle speed is in the middle of the idle speed range in **Table 7**. Clockwise screw rotation increases idle speed. Counterclockwise rotation decreases idle speed.
6. Have an assistant shift the engine into FORWARD gear. Allow the idle to stabilize for a few minutes, then note the in-gear idle speed. If the in-gear idle speed is not within the specification in **Table 7**, readjust the idle speed screw.
7. Have an assistant shift the engine into NEUTRAL gear. Allow the idle to stabilize for a few minutes, then note the idle speed. The in-neutral gear idle speed should remain within the specification in **Table 7**. If necessary,

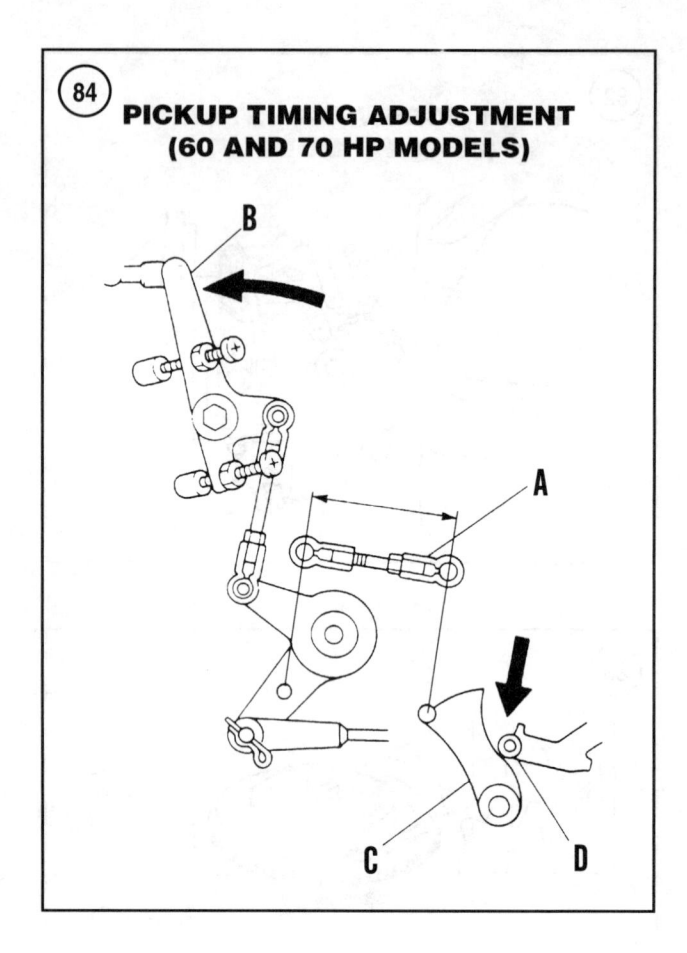

84 PICKUP TIMING ADJUSTMENT (60 AND 70 HP MODELS)

readjust the idle speed screw until both the in-gear and in-neutral idle speeds are within the specification. Several adjustments may be required.
8. Shift the engine into FORWARD gear and allow the idle to stabilize for a few minutes. Slowly advance the throttle, then bring it down to the idle position. Check for binding linkages or readjust the idle speed if the engine does not return to the specified range within 30-40 seconds.
9. Rapidly advance the throttle while checking for hesitation. If necessary, readjust the pilot screws (**Figure 82**) to minimize hesitation. Counterclockwise rotation reduces hesitation in most cases. Readjust the screws only a slight amount. Do not exceed the adjustment limits in **Table 6**. Adjust each screw the same amount and in the same rotational direction.
10. Adjust the pickup timing as described in this chapter.

Pickup timing adjustment

1. Move the throttle to the idle position. Stop the engine.
2A. On 60 and 70 hp models, move the throttle arm until the full retard adjusting screw on the timing stop lever

TIMING, SYNCHRONIZATION AND ADJUSTMENT

85 PICKUP TIMING ADJUSTMENT (65 JET AND 75-90 HP MODELS)

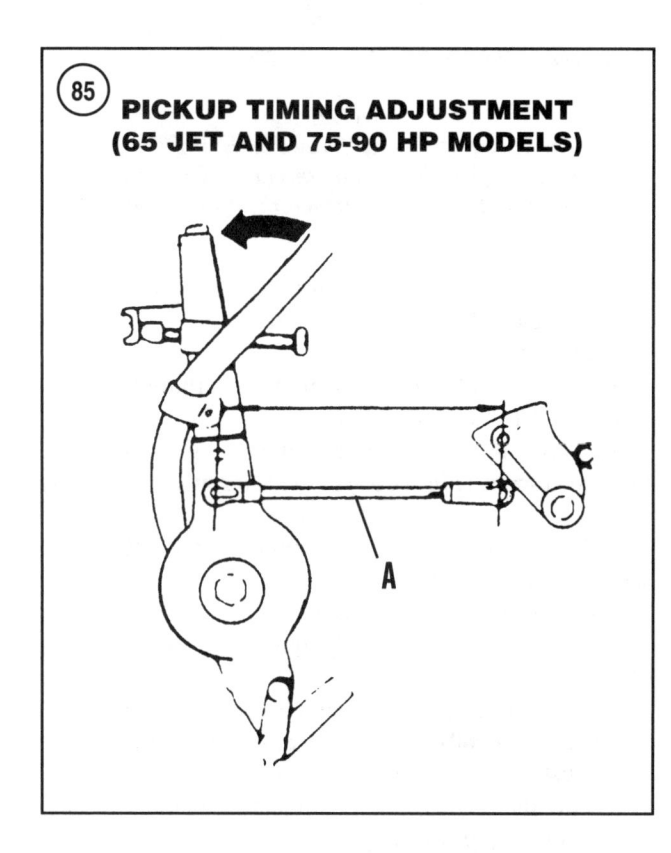

(B, **Figure 84**) contacts the stop. Keep the adjusting screw cap in contact with the stop during adjustments.

2B. On 65 jet and 75-90 hp models, move the throttle arm until the cap on the full retard screw contacts the stop as described in **Figure 85**.

3. Carefully pry the throttle cam linkage (A, **Figure 84** or A, **Figure 85**) from the ball sockets on the throttle arm and throttle cam.

4. Move the throttle cam (C, **Figure 84**) until it makes very light contact with the throttle roller (D).

5. Loosen the jam nut, then adjust the length of the throttle cam linkage until the linkage can be installed with the throttle cam making light contact with the roller. A slight gap of up to 0.4 mm (0.016 in.) between the throttle cam and roller is acceptable. Do not adjust the length to the point that the roller is opening the throttle. The roller must spin freely.

6. If the linkage length was changed, adjust the throttle cable as described in this chapter.

7. Connect a timing light to the No. 1 spark plug lead.

8. Have an assistant operate the boat in a clear area away from boat traffic.

9. Direct the timing light at the pointer (**Figure 83**). Shift the engine into FORWARD gear.

10. Observe the throttle cam and roller while an assistant slowly advances the throttle. Stop when the throttle cam just contacts the throttle arm and note the ignition timing. Do not advance the throttle to the point that the throttle plates actually open.

11. If the ignition timing is not within the pickup timing specification in **Table 3**, stop the engine and readjust the length of the throttle arm-to-throttle cam linkage. Several adjustments may be required.

Timing, Synchronization and Carburetor Adjustments (E60 and E75 Models)

These models use an electronic timing advancement with a CDI unit mounted timing indicator. Perform the following adjustments.

1. Timing pointer adjustment.
2. Static timing adjustment.
3. Carburetor synchronization.
4. Pilot screw adjustment.
5. Throttle cable adjustment.
6. Ignition timing adjustment.
7. Idle speed adjustment.
8. Pickup timing adjustment.

Timing pointer adjustment

1. On electric start models, disconnect the battery cables.

2. Remove the three spark plugs. Ground the spark plug leads.

3. Thread the dial indicator mount into the No. 1 spark plug opening. Install the dial indictor into the mount with the indicator stem in the No. 1 spark plug opening. Adjust the mount to position the stem in direct contact with the piston as it nears the top of its compression stroke (**Figure 72**).

4. Slowly rotate the flywheel clockwise while observing the dial indicator. Stop when the flywheel reaches the top of its stroke. This is the point of rotation when the needle on the dial indicator just reverses its direction as the flywheel is rotated.

5. Rotate the dial on the dial indicator until the needle aligns with the *0* mark on the dial. Observe the dial indicator while slowly rotating the flywheel counterclockwise. Stop the flywheel when the dial indicates the piston has moved the specified distance down from TDC. Keep the flywheel in this position during the pointer adjustment.

   a. On E60 models, stop when the piston moves down exactly 2.42 mm (0.095 in.).
   b. On E75 models, stop when the piston moves down exactly 3.41 mm (0.134 in.).

6. Loosen the screw and move the pointer until it aligns with the specified mark on the flywheel (**Figure 54**). Securely tighten the pointer screw.
   a. On E60 models, adjust the pointer to align with the 19° BTDC mark.
   b. On E75 models, adjust the pointer to align with the 22° BTDC mark.
7. Inspect the mark on the flywheel (B, **Figure 58**) and the mounting base (C). If the marks do not align, check for a sheared flywheel key as described in Chapter Seven or improper timing pointer adjustment.
8. Remove the dial indicator. Do not install the spark plugs at this time.
9. Adjust the static timing as described in this chapter.

Static timing adjustment

1. Position the flywheel at the full advance position as described in the timing pointer adjustment procedures.
2A. On E60 models, move the throttle lever until the full advance adjusting screw (D, **Figure 78**) on the timing stop lever contacts the stop. Keep the screw cap in contact with the stop during the adjustment. Loosen the jam nut, then rotate the adjusting screw until the marks on the flywheel (B, **Figure 58**) and mounting base (C) align just as the cap contacts the stop. Securely tighten the jam nut.
2B. On E75 models, move the throttle lever until the full advance adjusting screw (D, **Figure 79**) contacts the stop. Keep the screw cap in contact with the stop during the adjustment. Loosen the jam nut, then rotate the adjusting screw until the marks on the flywheel (B, **Figure 58**) and mounting base (C) align just as the cap contacts the stop. Securely tighten the jam nut.
3. Rotate the flywheel clockwise until the timing pointer aligns with the 2° ATDC mark on the flywheel.
4A. On E60 models, move the throttle lever until the full retard adjusting screw (C, **Figure 76**) on the timing stop lever contacts the stop. Keep the screw cap in contact with the stop during the adjustment. Loosen the jam nut, then rotate the adjusting screw until the marks on the flywheel (B, **Figure 58**) and mounting base (C) align just as the cap contacts the stop. Securely tighten the jam nut.
4B. On E75 models, move the throttle lever until the full retard adjusting screw (C, **Figure 77**) contacts the stop. Keep the screw cap in contact with the stop during the adjustment. Loosen the jam nut, then rotate the adjusting screw until the marks on the flywheel (B, **Figure 58**) and mounting base (C) align just as the cap contacts the stop. Securely tighten the jam nut.
5. Synchronize the carburetors as described in this chapter.

Carburetor synchronization

NOTE
The carburetor lever screws on E60-E75 hp models use left-hand threads. Turn the screws clockwise to loosen them and counterclockwise to tighten them.

1. Move the throttle arm until the full retard adjusting screw contacts the retard stop. Refer to *Static timing adjustment* in this chapter.
2. Remove the silencer cover from the carburetors as described in Chapter Five.
3. Look into the middle carburetor opening and rotate the idle speed screw (**Figure 80**) until the throttle plate is fully closed.
4. Fully loosen the upper and middle carburetor lever screws (3, **Figure 81**).
5. Push down lightly on the throttle roller to remove slack from the linkage, then securely tighten the upper and middle screws.
6. Observe the throttle plates while turning the idle speed screw (**Figure 80**) clockwise. Stop when the throttle plates just start to move.
7. Install the silencer cover on the carburetors as described in Chapter Five.
8. Adjust the pilot screws as described in this chapter.

Pilot screw adjustment

1. Disconnect and ground the spark plug lead to prevent accidental starting.
2. On electric start models, disconnect the battery cables.
3. Carefully turn the pilot screw (**Figure 82**) for the upper carburetor clockwise until it is lightly seated.
4. Turn the pilot screw counterclockwise to the middle of the adjustment range in **Table 6**.
5. Repeat Steps 3 and 4 for the middle, then bottom carburetor pilot screws.
6. Adjust the throttle cable as described in this chapter.

Throttle cable adjustment

1. Shift the engine into FORWARD gear.
2. Observe the carburetor levers while an assistant slowly moves the remote control handle to full throttle. If the levers do not contact the stop just as the throttle control reaches full throttle, adjust the cable as follows:
   a. Move the shift selector to the NEUTRAL gear idle speed position.
   b. Disconnect the throttle cable from the attaching point (**Figure 60**, typical).

TIMING, SYNCHRONIZATION AND ADJUSTMENT

c. Open the latch and pull the cable from the lower cover or power head mounted retainer.
d. Loosen the jam nut (A, **Figure 61**) and rotate the cable end (B) until the cable will fit over the connection point and into the retainer without moving the linkages.
e. Check the cable end for adequate thread engagement (C, **Figure 61**). A minimum of 8 mm (0.31 in.) of engagement is required. Position the cable anchor into a different groove on the cable as required.
f. Fit the cable on the attaching points. Move the control handle to the full throttle and idle positions while checking for full movement of the carburetor lever. Readjust the cable to achieve full movement to the full throttle and idle positions.
g. Securely tighten the jam nut (A, **Figure 61**). Install the fasteners and engage the latch to secure the cable to the mounting bracket and throttle arm.
3. Adjust the ignition timing as described in this chapter.

Ignition timing adjustment

Perform this adjustment under actual running conditions. Adjust the ignition timing while a qualified assistant operate the controls. Operate the boat in a safe area away from boat traffic.
1. On electric start models, connect the battery cables.
2. Connect the spark plug leads.
3. Connect a timing light to the No. 1 (top) spark plug lead.
4. Connect a shop tachometer to the spark plug lead. Do not allow the timing light and tachometer pickups to touch during this procedure.
5. Start the engine and advance the throttle to approximately 1500 rpm in neutral gear for ten minutes or until the engine reaches full operating temperature. Check and adjust the ignition timing while a qualified assistant operates the boat.
6. Move the throttle to the idle position and allow the idle speed to stabilize for a few minutes. Direct the timing light at the timing pointer and flywheel marks (**Figure 83**). When the light flashes, the timing pointer should align with the full retard timing mark specified in **Table 4**. If necessary, adjust it as follows:
   a. On E60 models, loosen the jam nut on the full retard adjusting screw (C, **Figure 76**).
   b. On E75 models, loosen the jam nut on the full retard adjusting screw (C, **Figure 77**).
   c. Keep the cap on the adjusting screw in contact with the stop during the adjustment.
   d. Direct the timing light at the timing pointer (**Figure 83**). Rotate the full retard adjusting screw until the timing pointer aligns with the full retard timing specification in **Table 4**.
   e. Securely tighten the jam nut.
7. Shift the engine into FORWARD gear. Observe the tachometer and timing pointer while the assistant advances the throttle to wide open. The engine should reach the speed range in **Table 5**.
8. Direct the timing light at the timing pointer (**Figure 83**). If the timing pointer does not align with the maximum timing mark specified in **Table 5**, adjust it as follows:
   a. On E60 models, loosen the nut on the full advance adjusting screw (D, **Figure 78**).
   b. On E75 models, loosen the nut on the full advance adjusting screw (D, **Figure 79**).
   c. Keep the cap on the adjusting screw in contact with the stop during the adjustment.
   d. Direct the timing light at the timing pointer (**Figure 83**). Rotate the full advance adjusting screw until the timing pointer aligns with the full advance timing specification in **Table 4**.
   e. Securely tighten the jam nut.
9. Return the throttle to idle. Shift the engine into NEUTRAL.
10. If timing adjustment was required, readjust the throttle cable as described in this chapter.
11. Adjust the idle speed as described in this chapter.

Idle speed adjustment

Perform this adjustment under actual running conditions. Adjust the idle speed while a qualified assistant operates the controls. Operate the boat in a safe area away from boat traffic.
1. Adjust the ignition timing as described in this chapter.
2. Turn the idle speed screw (**Figure 80**) counterclockwise until there is a gap between the screw tip and the carburetor throttle lever. Slowly rotate the screw clockwise until the tip just contacts the lever. Turn the screw one complete turn clockwise to slightly open the throttle.
3. Connect a shop tachometer to the spark plug lead.
4. Start the engine and advance the throttle to approximately 1500 rpm in NEUTRAL gear for ten minutes or until the engine reaches full operating temperature.
5. Place the throttle control in the idle position and note the idle speed. If the in-neutral idle speed is not within the specification in **Table 7**, adjust the idle speed. Turn the idle speed screw (**Figure 80**) until the idle speed is in the middle of the idle speed range in **Table 7**. Clockwise screw rotation increases idle speed. Counterclockwise rotation decreases idle speed.

6. Have an assistant shift the engine into FORWARD gear. Allow the idle to stabilize for a few minutes, then note the in-gear idle speed. If the in-gear idle speed is not within the specification in **Table 7**, readjust the idle speed screw.

7. Have an assistant shift the engine into NEUTRAL gear. Allow the idle to stabilize for a few minutes, then note the idle speed. The in-neutral gear idle speed should remain within the specification in **Table 7**. If necessary, readjust the idle speed screw until both the in-gear and in-neutral idle speeds are within the specification. Several adjustments may be required.

8. Shift the engine into FORWARD gear and allow the idle to stabilize for a few minutes. Slowly advance the throttle, then bring it down to the idle position. Check for binding linkages or readjust the idle speed if the engine does not return to the specified range within 30-40 seconds.

9. Rapidly advance the throttle while checking for hesitation. If necessary, readjust the pilot screws (**Figure 82**) to minimize hesitation. Counterclockwise rotation reduces hesitation in most cases. Readjust the screws only a slight amount. Do not exceed the adjustment limits in **Table 6**. Adjust each screw the same amount and in the same rotational direction.

10. Adjust the pickup timing as described in this chapter.

Pickup timing adjustment

1. Place the throttle in the idle position. Stop the engine.
2A. On E60 models, move the throttle arm until the full retard adjusting screw on the timing stop lever (B, **Figure 84**) contacts the stop. Keep the adjusting screw cap in contact with the stop during adjustments.
2B. On E75 models, move the throttle arm until the cap on the full retard screw contacts the stop as described in **Figure 85**.
3. Carefully pry the throttle cam linkage (A, **Figure 84** or A, **Figure 85**) from the ball sockets on the throttle arm and throttle cam.
4. Move the throttle cam (C, **Figure 84**) until it lightly contacts the throttle roller (D).
5. Loosen the jam nut, then adjust the length of the throttle cam linkage until the linkage can be installed with the throttle cam making light contact with the roller. A slight gap of up to 0.4 mm (0.016 in.) between the throttle cam and roller is acceptable. Do not adjust the length to the point that the roller is opening the throttle. The roller must spin freely.
6. If the linkage length was changed, adjust the throttle cable as described in this section.
7. Connect a timing light to the No. 1 spark plug lead.

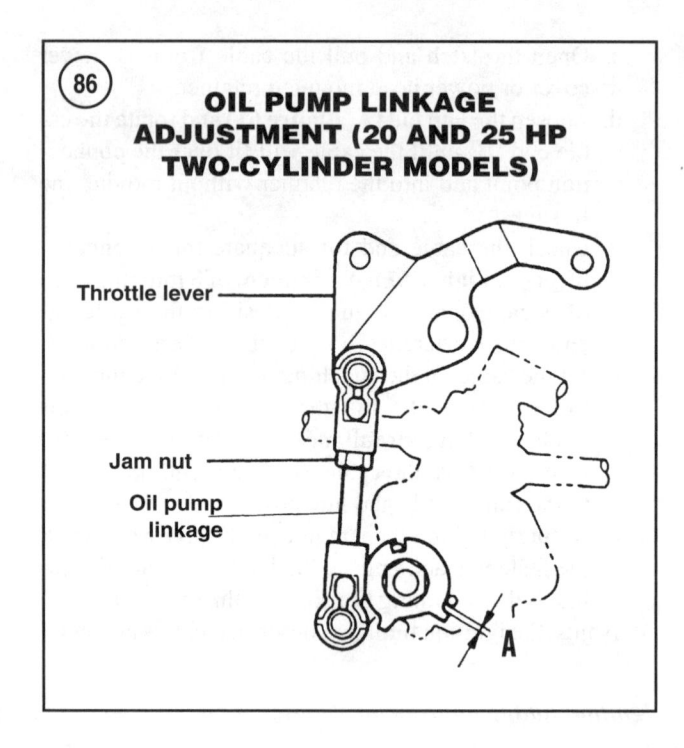

8. Have an assistant operate the boat in a clear area away from boat traffic.
9. Direct the timing light at the pointer (**Figure 83**). Shift the engine into FORWARD gear.
10. Observe the throttle cam and roller while an assistant slowly advance the throttle. Stop when the throttle cam just contacts the throttle arm and note the ignition timing. Do not advance the throttle to the point that the throttle plates actually open.
11. If the ignition timing is not within the pickup timing specification in **Table 3**, stop the engine and readjust the length of the throttle arm-to-throttle cam linkage. Several adjustments may be required.

**Oil Pump Linkage Adjustment
(20 and 25 hp Two-Cylinder Models)**

1. Disconnect and ground the spark plug leads to prevent accidental starting.
2. On electric start models, disconnect the battery cables.
3. Shift the engine into FORWARD gear. Advance the throttle to wide open.
4. Use feeler gauges to measure the clearance between the tab on the oil pump lever and the stop on the pump body (A, **Figure 86**).
5. If the clearance is not 0.5 mm (0.02 in.), adjust as follows:
   a. Carefully pry the oil pump linkage (**Figure 86**) from the ball socket on the throttle lever.

TIMING, SYNCHRONIZATION AND ADJUSTMENT

87

**OIL PUMP LINKAGE ADJUSTMENT
(25 HP THREE-CYLINDER,
28 JET AND 30-50 HP MODELS)**

Oil pump linkage

Jam nut

A

Stop

Pump lever

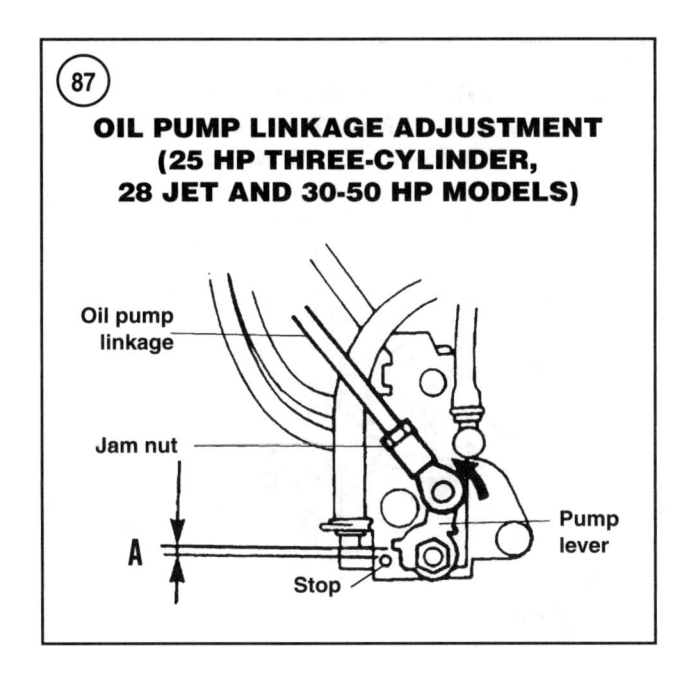

b. Loosen the jam nut, then rotate the connector until the linkage can be installed with the specified stop clearance.
c. Carefully snap the connector on the throttle lever ball socket. Securely tighten the jam nut.
d. Measure the clearance and readjust it as necessary. Several adjustments may be required.

6. Move the throttle to idle speed. Shift the engine into NEUTRAL gear. Connect the spark plug leads.
7. Move the throttle control from idle to full throttle and back to idle several times. If there is binding, inspect the linkage for improper installation or contact with other components. Correct the source of binding before operating the engine.
8. On electric start models, connect the battery cables.

Oil Pump Linkage Adjustment (25 hp Three-Cylinder, 28 Jet and 30-50 hp Models)

1. Disconnect and ground the spark plug leads to prevent accidental starting.
2. On electric start models, disconnect the battery cables.
3. Shift the engine into FORWARD gear.
4. Observe the oil pump lever and stop on the pump body while slowly advancing the throttle to wide open.
5A. On 25 hp three-cylinder and 30 hp models, if the tab on the lever does not contact the stop (**Figure 87**) just as the throttle reaches wide-open, adjust it as follows:
   a. Carefully pry the oil pump linkage (**Figure 87**) from the ball socket on the pump lever.
   b. Loosen the jam nut, then rotate the connector until the linkage can be installed with the lever just contacting the stop.
   c. Carefully snap the connector on the throttle lever ball socket. Securely tighten the jam nut.
   d. Check the lever-to-stop clearance for light contact. Readjust the linkage length as necessary.

5B. On 28 jet, 35 jet, 40 hp and 50 hp models, use feeler gauges to measure the clearance between the tab on the oil pump lever and the stop on the pump body (A, **Figure 87**).
6. If the clearance is not 1.0 mm (0.039 in.), adjust it as follows:
   a. Carefully pry the oil pump linkage (**Figure 87**) from the ball socket on the throttle lever.
   b. Loosen the jam nut, then rotate the connector until the linkage can be installed with the specified stop clearance.
   c. Carefully snap the connector onto the throttle lever ball socket. Securely tighten the jam nut.
   d. Measure the clearance and readjust as necessary. Several adjustments may be required.

7. Move the throttle to idle speed. Shift the engine into NEUTRAL gear. Connect the spark plug leads.
8. Move the throttle control from idle to full throttle and back to idle several times. If there is binding, inspect the linkage for improper installation or contact with other components. Correct the source of binding before operating the engine.
9. On electric start models, connect the battery cables.

Oil Pump Linkage Adjustment (60-90 hp Models)

1. Disconnect and ground the spark plug leads to prevent accidental starting.
2. On electric start models, disconnect the battery cables.
3. Shift the engine into FORWARD gear.
4. Move the throttle roller until the carburetor lever contacts the wide open stop on the carburetor body (**Figure 88** or **Figure 89**). Keep the lever in firm contact with the stop during adjustments.
5. Use feeler gauges to measure the clearance between the tab on the oil pump lever and the stop on the pump body (**Figure 90**).
6. If the clearance is not 1.0 mm (0.039 in.), adjust it as follows:
   a. Remove the retaining pin, then pull the oil pump linkage (**Figure 90**) from the post on the pump lever.
   b. Loosen the jam nut, then rotate the connector until the linkage can be installed on the post with the specified stop clearance.

88 OIL PUMP LINKAGE ADJUSTMENT (60 AND 70 HP MODELS)

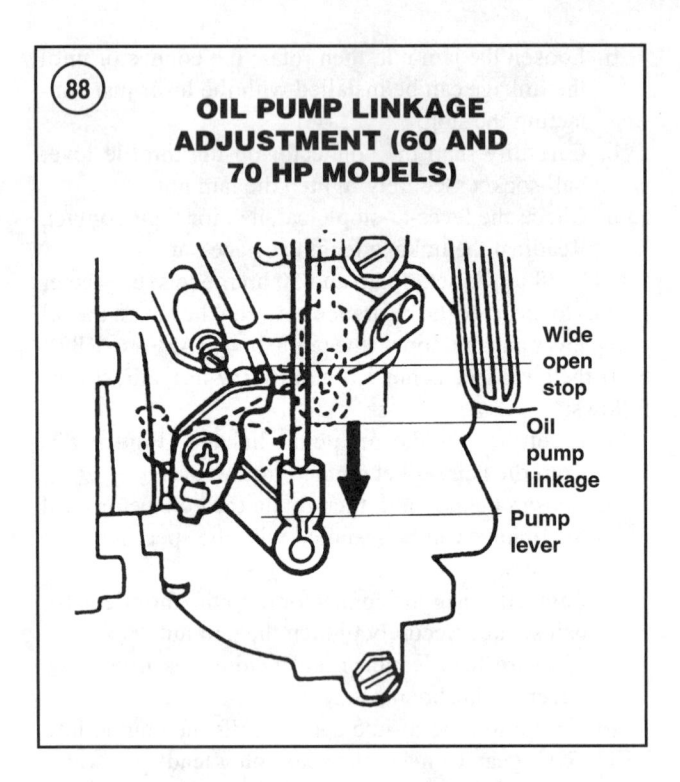

- Wide open stop
- Oil pump linkage
- Pump lever

89 OIL PUMP LINKAGE ADJUSTMENT (65 JET AND 75-90 HP MODELS)

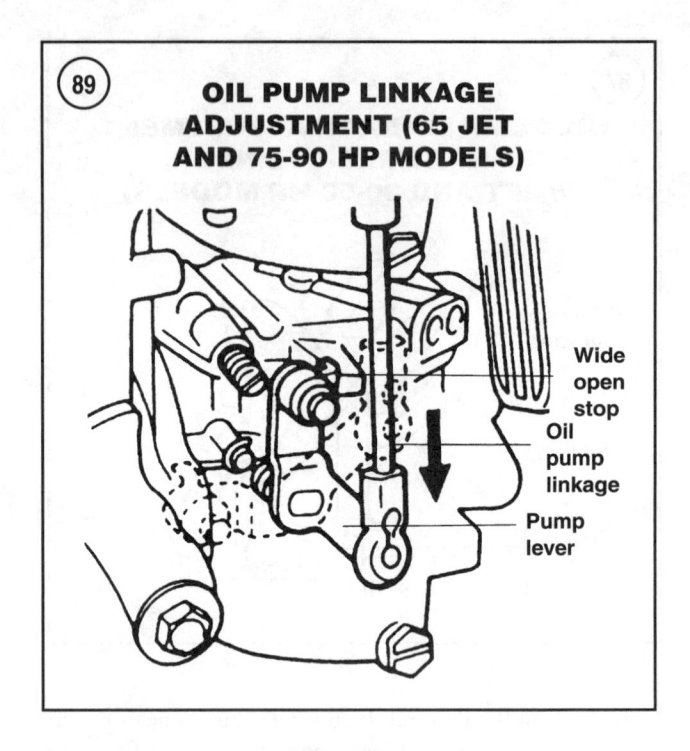

- Wide open stop
- Oil pump linkage
- Pump lever

90 OIL PUMP LINKAGE ADJUSTMENT (60-90 HP MODELS)

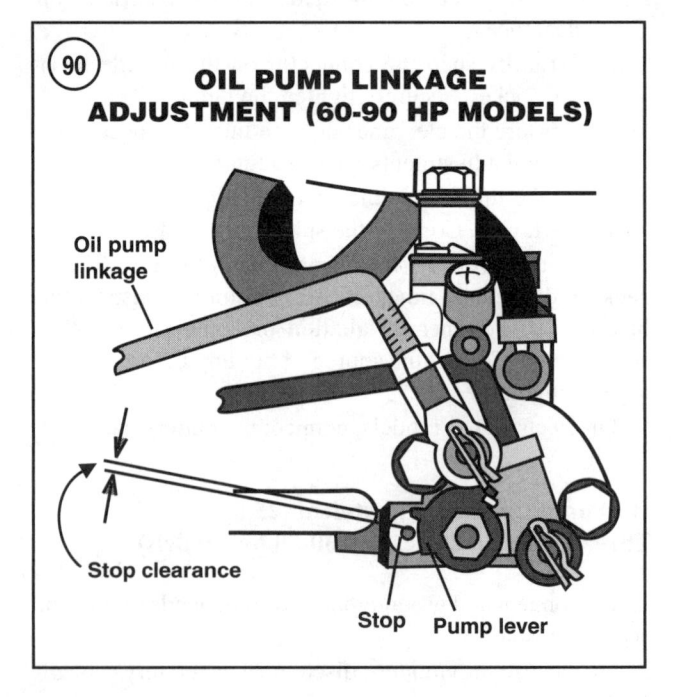

- Oil pump linkage
- Stop clearance
- Stop
- Pump lever

c. Fit the connector on the post on the pump lever. Install the retaining pin. Securely tighten the jam nut.
d. Measure the clearance and readjust as necessary. Several adjustment may be required.

7. Move the throttle to idle speed. Shift the engine into NEUTRAL gear. Connect the spark plug leads.

8. Move the throttle control from idle to full throttle and back to idle several times. If there is binding, inspect the linkage for improper installation or contact with other components. Correct the source of binding before operating the engine.

9. On electric start models, connect the battery cables.

Lockout Assembly Adjustment

1. Disconnect the spark plug lead(s) to prevent accidental starting.
2. Shift the engine into neutral gear.
3. On 4-50 hp models, loosen the lock nut and adjusting nut (**Figure 91**) to allow cable movement within the bracket.
4A. On 4-8 hp and 20-50 hp models, rotate the adjusting nut (B, **Figure 92**) until the edge of the plunger aligns with the center of the opening in the manual starter housing.
4B. On 9.9 and 15 hp models, rotate the adjusting nut (A, **Figure 93**) until the mark on the manual starter housing aligns with the edge of the stopper lever (B).
4C. On E60 and E75 models, loosen the locknut (**Figure 94**) to allow cable movement. Pull the cable until the mark on the slide aligns with the mark on the stopper (**Figure 94**). Hold the cable in position and securely tighten the locknut.
5. On 4-50 hp models, securely tighten the lock nut (**Figure 91**) against the cable bracket.

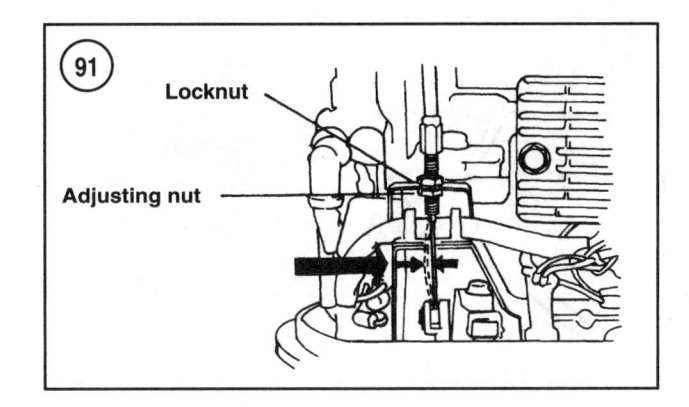

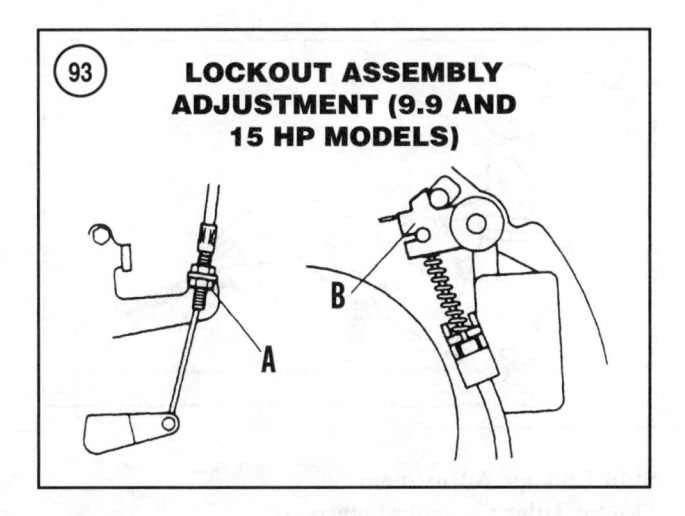

TIMING, SYNCHRONIZATION AND ADJUSTMENT

91 Locknut, Adjusting nut

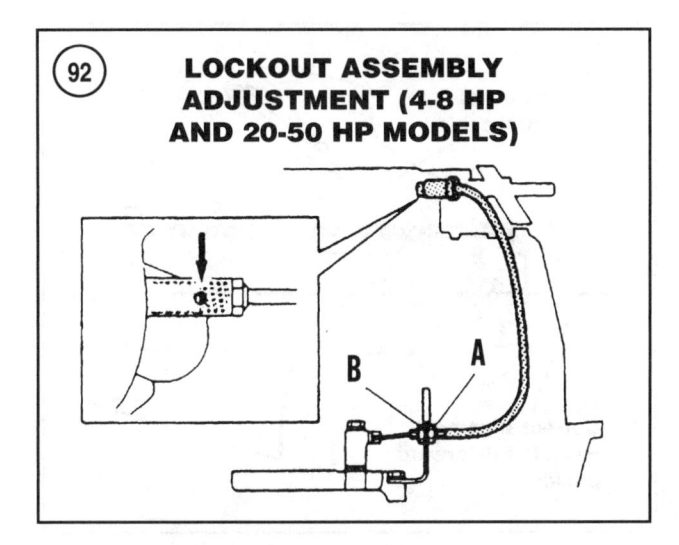

92 LOCKOUT ASSEMBLY ADJUSTMENT (4-8 HP AND 20-50 HP MODELS)

93 LOCKOUT ASSEMBLY ADJUSTMENT (9.9 AND 15 HP MODELS)

94 LOCKOUT ASSEMBLY ADJUSTMENT (E60 AND E75 MODELS) — Stopper marking, Slide marking, Lock nut

95 Slotted for adjustment purposes, Embossed lines

6. Shift the engine into FORWARD gear then pull the manual starter. Shift the engine into REVERSE gear then pull the manual starter.

7. Repeat the adjustments and check for worn or damaged components if the manual starter activates in either forward or reverse gears. Manual starter repair is described in Chapter Ten.

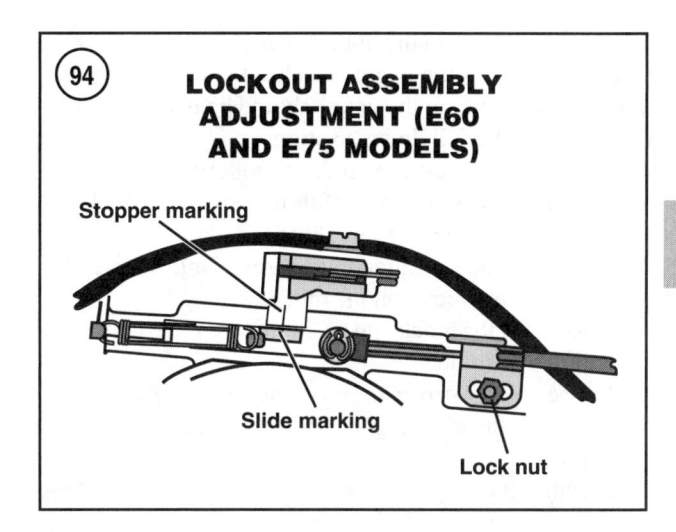

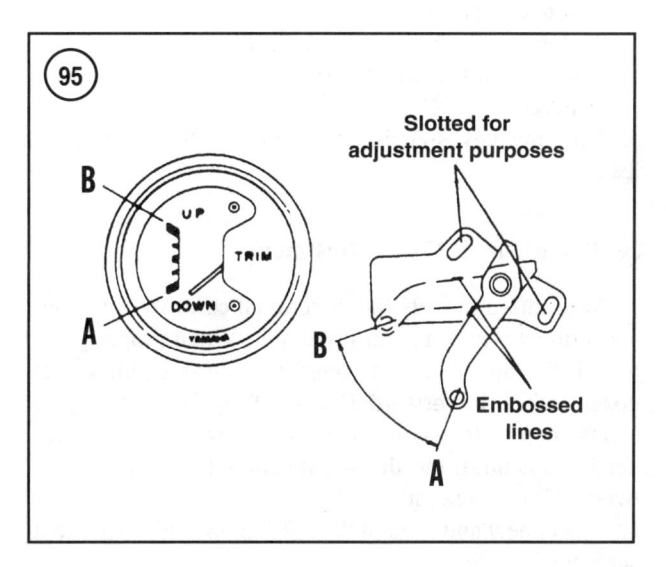

8. Connect the spark plug lead(s).

Tilt/Trim Sender Adjustment

To adjust the sender, it must be moved within the limits of the adjusting slot until the gauge reads correctly.

1. Disconnect and ground the spark plug leads to prevent accidental starting.

2. Turn the key switch to the RUN position. Do not engage the starter.

3A. On models using the analog gauge, check the reading on the gauge when the engine reaches the full down position. The gauge should reach the down mark (A, **Figure 95**) at the same time the engine reaches its down limit.

3B. On models using the digital gauge, check the reading (**Figure 96**) when the engine reaches the full down position. One segment on the gauge should be displayed with the engine in the full down position.
4. If necessary, adjust the sender as follows:
   a. Raise the engine to the full tilt position. Block the engine to keep it from falling.
   b. Loosen the two mounting screws until the sender will barely move on the mount.
   c. Remove the block and position the engine in the full down position.
   d. Use a screwdriver to move the sender (**Figure 96**) within the adjusting slot until the gauge reads correctly.
   e. Raise the engine to access the sender mounting screws and block the engine. Securely tighten the sender screws.
   f. Remove the block and operate the trim to the up and down limits while observing the gauge. Readjust as necessary.
5. Turn the key switch OFF. Connect the spark plug leads.

Jet Drive Thrust Gate Adjustment

On jet drive models the directional control cable connects directly onto the jet drive unit. When properly adjusted, the thrust gate is completely clear of the outlet nozzle when in forward (**Figure 97**). The thrust gate should completely cover the outlet nozzle when in reverse. In neutral, the thrust gate should be midway between these two points.
1. Disconnect and ground the spark plug leads to prevent accidental starting.
2. Place the control in FORWARD.
3. Loosen the cable retainer or jam nut and adjust the directional control cable until the pivot bracket aligns with the linkage that connects the cable bracket to the thrust gate (**Figure 97**). The thrust gate should be completely clear of the outlet nozzle. Securely tighten the cable retainer or jam nut.
4. Place the control in NEUTRAL.
5. Loosen the nut (**Figure 98**) and move the stop bracket until it just contacts the thrust gate lever.
6. Connect the spark plug leads.
7. Tie the vessel securely to a sturdy dock or another appropriate structure. Start the engine and only run it at idle speed.
8. Move the control to the FORWARD, REVERSE and NEUTRAL positions while checking for proper directional control. Perform additional cable and stop bracket adjustments as necessary.

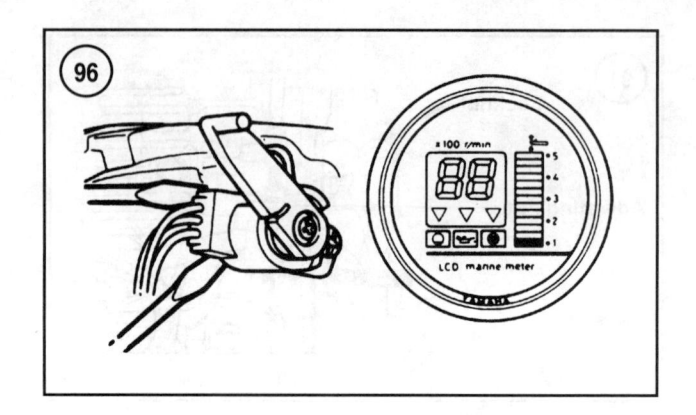

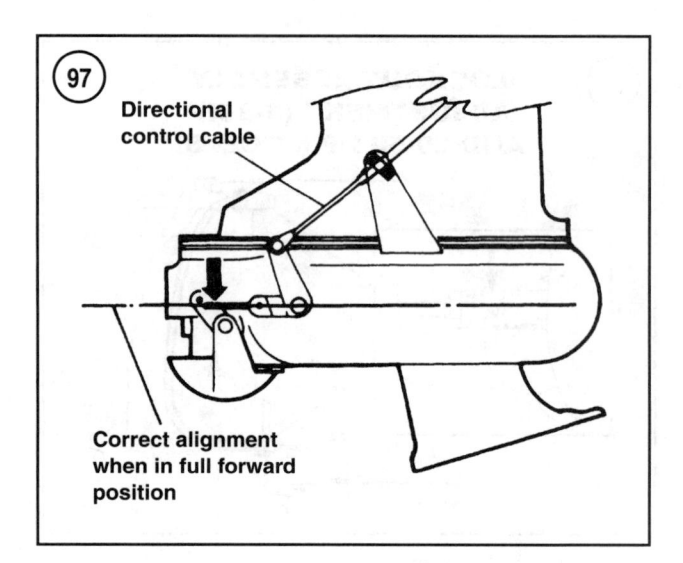

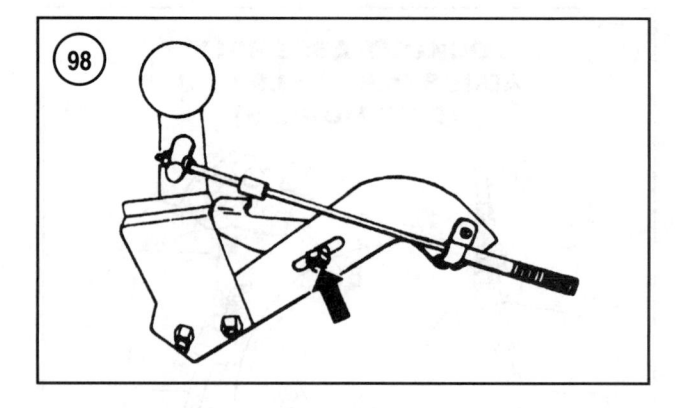

Shift Linkage Adjustment
(3-8 hp Tiller Control Models)

Make shift linkage adjustments at the upper-to-lower shift shaft clamp type connector (**Figure 99**).

1. Disconnect and ground the spark plug lead(s) to prevent accidental starting.

TIMING, SYNCHRONIZATION AND ADJUSTMENT

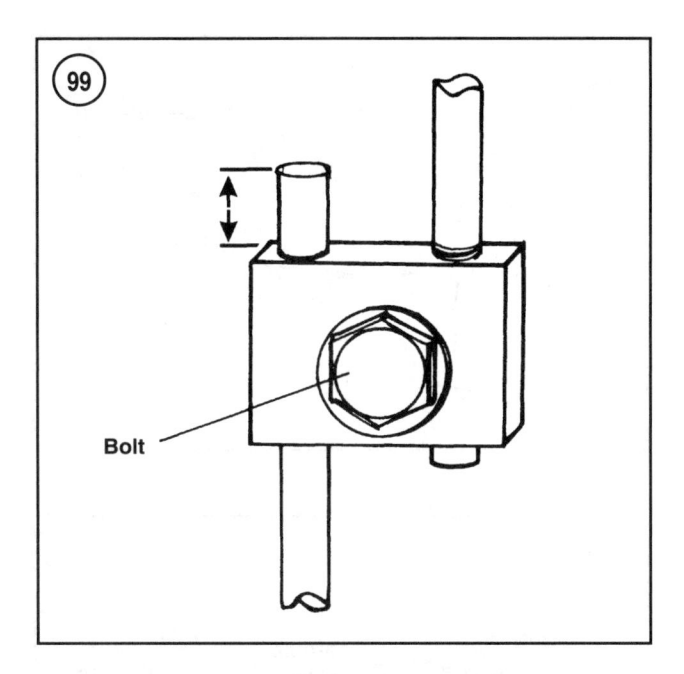

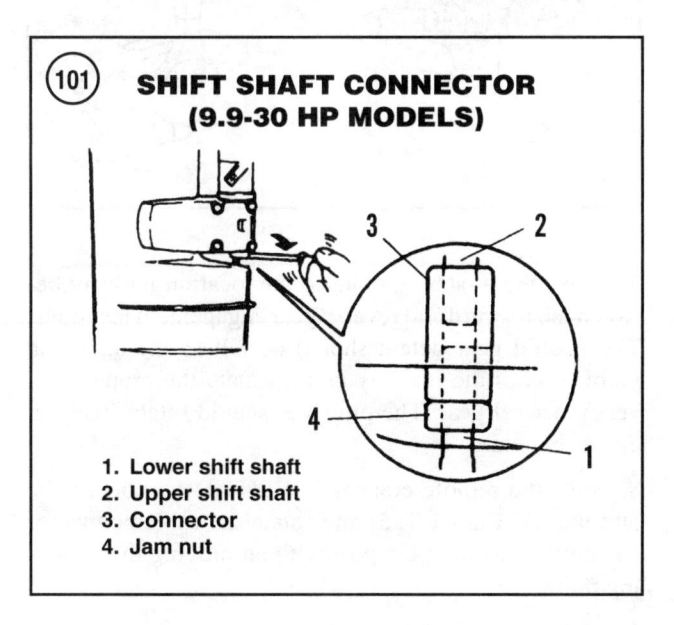

2. On electric start models, disconnect the battery cables.
3. Refer to *Gearcase Removal/Installation* in Chapter Eight to locate the shift shaft connector.
4. Loosen the connector bolt (**Figure 99**) until both shift shafts are just free to move. Move the shift selector (**Figure 100**) to the NEUTRAL position.
5. Move the lower shift shaft downward until the gearcase shifts into the neutral gear detent. The propeller can be rotated either direction in neutral gear.
6. Fit both shafts into their respective bores in the connector. The lower shaft must pass through the connector and protrude on the upper side (**Figure 99**). Securely tighten the connector bolt as described in *Gearcase Removal/Installation* in Chapter Eight.
7. Alternately shift the engine into the FORWARD and NEUTRAL gear positions, and rotate the propeller to check for proper clutch engagement. The propeller should spin in both directions in neutral gear. The propeller should lock when it is rotated counterclockwise in forward gear.
8. On 4-8 hp models, shift the engine into REVERSE gear and rotate the propeller clockwise. The propeller should lock.
9. Repeat the adjustment if the clutch engagement is incorrect. If adjustment fails to correct the clutch engagement, check for worn or damaged components in the gearcase (Chapter Eight).
10. Connect the spark plug lead(s).
11. On electric start models, connect the battery cables.
12. Run the engine in a test tank and check for proper shifting. Correct any faults before putting the engine into service.

Shift Linkage Adjustment (9.9-30 hp Tiller Control Models)

Make the shift adjustment at the upper-to-lower shift shaft threaded connector (**Figure 101**).

1. Disconnect and ground the spark plug lead(s) to prevent accidental starting.
2. On electric start models, disconnect the battery cables.
3. Check the shift adjustment as follows:
   a. Shift the engine into NEUTRAL gear and rotate the propeller. The propeller should spin freely in both directions.
   b. Shift the engine into FORWARD gear and rotate the propeller counterclockwise. The propeller should lock.
   c. Shift the engine into REVERSE gear and rotate the propeller clockwise. The propeller should lock.
   d. Shift the engine into NEUTRAL.

4. Shift adjustment is required if there is a clicking sound when the propeller is rotated in neutral gear or if the propeller fails to lock in forward or reverse gear. Adjust it as follows:
   a. Hold the connector with a wrench and use another wrench to loosen the jam nut (**Figure 102**).
   b. Remove the connector (3, **Figure 101**) from the lower shift shaft.
   c. Push down on the lower shift shaft until you feel the neutral detent. The propeller spins freely with the gearcase shifted into neutral.
   d. Place the shift selector (**Figure 100**) into NEUTRAL gear.
   e. Align the upper and lower shift shafts. Thread the connector (3, **Figure 101**) onto the lower shift shaft until all slack is removed from the upper shaft. Do not rotate the connector enough to move the lower shift shaft or shift selector.
   f. Hold the connector with a wrench and use another wrench to securely tighten the jam nut (**Figure 102**).

5. Check for proper adjustment as described in Step 3. Readjust as needed. If adjustment fails to correct the clutch engagement, check for worn or damaged components in the gearcase (Chapter Eight).
6. Connect the spark plug leads.
7. On electric start models, connect the battery cables.
8. Run the engine in a test tank and check for proper shifting. Correct any faults before putting the engine into service.

**Shift Cable Adjustment
(6-30 hp Remote Control Models)**

Make the shift cable adjustment at the cable end (**Figure 103**).

1. Disconnect and ground the spark plug lead(s) to prevent accidental starting.
2. On electric start models, disconnect the battery cables.
3. Shift the remote control lever into NEUTRAL gear (**Figure 104**).
4. Remove the retainer, then lift the cable end from the shift linkage attaching point (**Figure 103**).
5. Move the attaching point toward the front of the engine while an assistant rotates the propeller counterclockwise. Stop when the clutch engages forward gear and locks the propeller. Note the location of the attaching point.
6. Move the attaching point toward the rear of the engine while an assistant rotates the propeller clockwise. Stop when the clutch engages reverse gear and locks the propeller. Note the location of the attaching point.
7. Move the attaching point to the location midway between the forward and reverse gear engagement locations. The neutral gear detent should be felt as the attaching point reaches the midway point. Rotate the propeller to verify neutral gear. The propeller should rotate freely in either direction.
8. Shift the remote control to NEUTRAL. Loosen the jam nut (A, **Figure 105**) and rotate the cable connector (B) until it fits over the post without moving the attaching point.

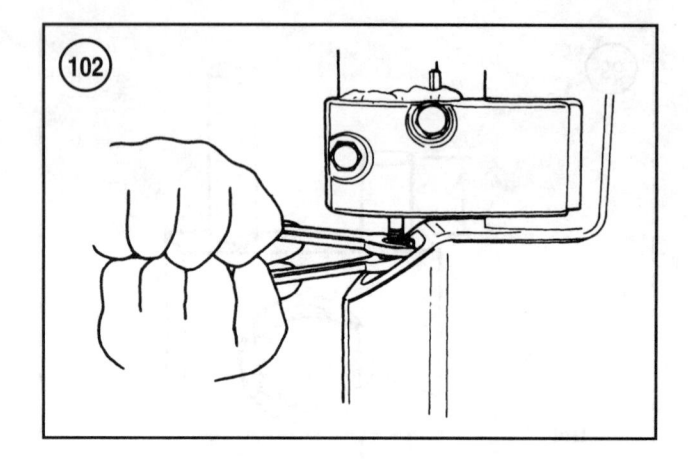

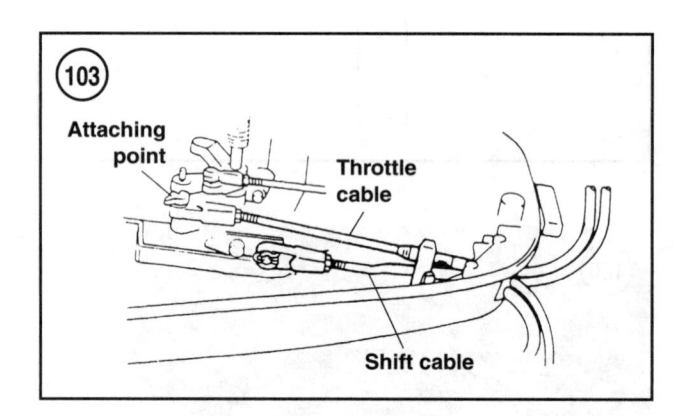

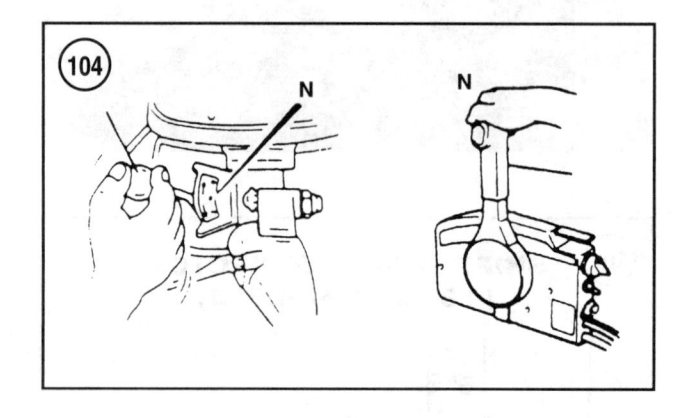

TIMING, SYNCHRONIZATION AND ADJUSTMENT

105
B C A
8 mm (0.31 in.)

106
A B
C D
8 mm (0.31 in.)

connector (3, **Figure 101**) maintains a minimum of 9.5 mm (0.374) thread engagement to the lower shift shaft.

e. Hold the shift shaft connector with a wrench and use another wrench to securely tighten the jam nut (**Figure 102**).

10. Fit the cable connector over the post on the attaching point and secure it with the locking pin or nut and washer. Securely tighten the jam nut (A, **Figure 105**) against the connector.

11. Check for proper clutch engagement as follows:
   a. Shift the remote control into FORWARD gear. Do not advance the throttle. Rotate the propeller counterclockwise to check for proper clutch engagement. If the propeller does not lock, repeat the adjustments.
   b. Shift the remote control into REVERSE gear. Do not advance the throttle. Rotate the propeller clockwise. If the propeller does not lock, repeat the adjustments.
   c. Shift the remote control into NEUTRAL and rotate the propeller in both directions. If the propeller does not rotate freely in either direction, repeat the adjustments.
   d. Check for worn or damaged components in the gearcase (Chapter Eight) if the clutch engagement cannot be corrected with the adjustments.

12. Connect the spark plug leads.
13. On electric start models, connect the battery cables.
14. Run the engine on a flush test adapter and check for proper shifting. Correct any faults before putting the engine into service.

Shift Cable Adjustment (40-90 hp Remote and Tiller Control Models)

1. Disconnect and ground the spark plug lead(s) to prevent accidental starting.
2. On electric start models, disconnect the battery cables.
3. Shift the remote control (**Figure 104**) or tiller control shift lever (A, **Figure 106**) into NEUTRAL gear.
   a. On tiller control models, move the shift lever to the midpoint between its forward and reverse limits of travel.
   b. On remote control models, shift the control to NEUTRAL. Move the lever toward the forward and reverse gear positions until there is a slight resistance. Do not move the shift cable. Note the limits in each position. Place the control handle at the midpoint between the limits of travel.
4. Remove the locking pin or nut and washers to free the shift cable end from the shift linkage.

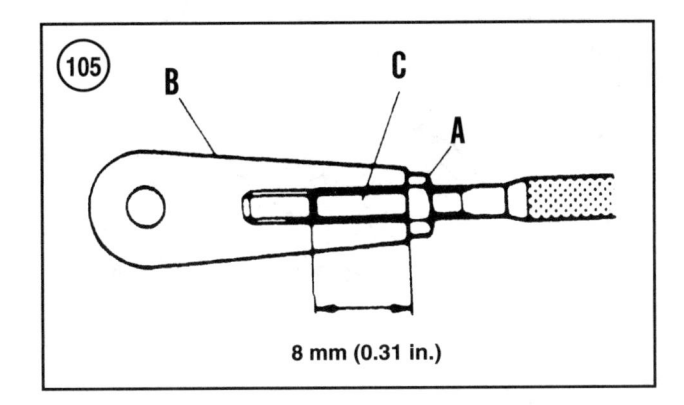

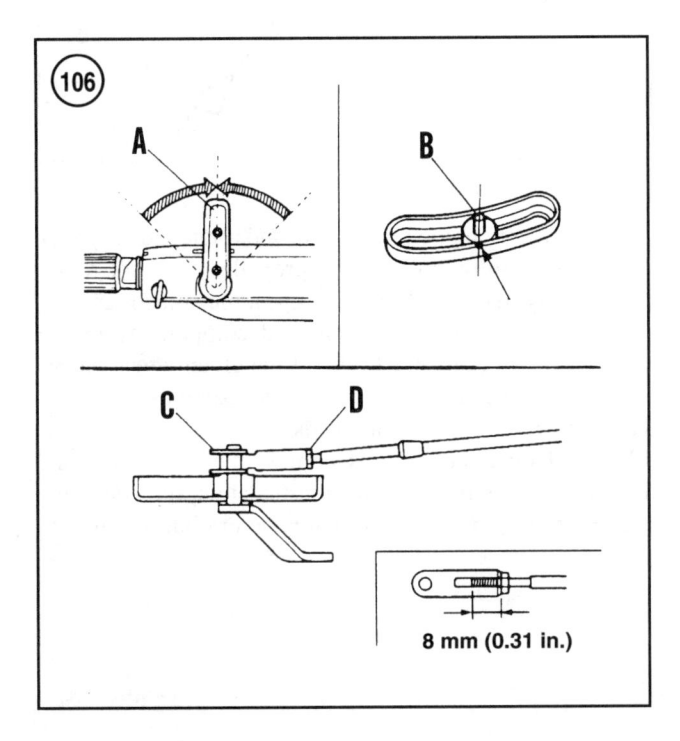

9. Check the cable end for adequate thread engagement (C, **Figure 105**). A minimum of 8 mm (0.315 in.) of engagement is required. If the engagement is less than the minimum correct it as follows:
   a. Hold the shift shaft connector with a wrench and use another wrench to loosen the jam nut (**Figure 102**).
   b. Rotate the shift shaft connector (3, **Figure 101**) until the attaching point moves forward a slight amount.
   c. Readjust the shift cable connector as described in Step 8.
   d. Check the cable connector for adequate thread engagement. Repeat this step until the thread engagement meets or exceeds the minimum. Make sure the

5. On 40 hp, 50 hp, E60 and E75 models, move the cable adjusting point (B, **Figure 106**) to the middle of the slot in the bracket. The center of the adjusting point should align with the mark on the bracket.

6. On 60-90 hp (except E60 and E75) models, move the cable adjusting point until the shift lever (A, **Figure 107**) aligns with the arrow (B) on the lower engine cover.

7. Spin the propeller to verify neutral gear. If the propeller does not spin freely in either direction, the shift shafts are not aligned correctly. Remove and reinstall the gearcase as described in Chapter Eight.

8. Loosen the jam nut (A, **Figure 105**) and rotate the cable connector (B) until it fits over the post without moving the attaching point.

9. Check the cable end for adequate thread engagement (C, **Figure 105**). A minimum of 8 mm (0.315 in.) of engagement is required.

10. Fit the cable connector over the post on the attaching point and secure it with the locking pin or nut and washer. Securely tighten the jam nut (A, **Figure 105**) against the connector.

11. Check for proper clutch engagement as follows:
  a. Shift the engine into FORWARD gear. Do not advance the throttle. Rotate the propeller counterclockwise to check for proper clutch engagement. If the propeller does not lock, repeat the adjustments.
  b. Shift the engine into REVERSE gear. Do not advance the throttle. Rotate the propeller clockwise. If the propeller does not lock, repeat the adjustments.
  c. Shift the engine into neutral and rotate the propeller in both directions. If the propeller does not rotate freely in either direction, repeat the adjustments.
  d. Check for worn or damaged components in the gearcase (Chapter Eight) if the clutch engagement cannot be corrected with the adjustments.

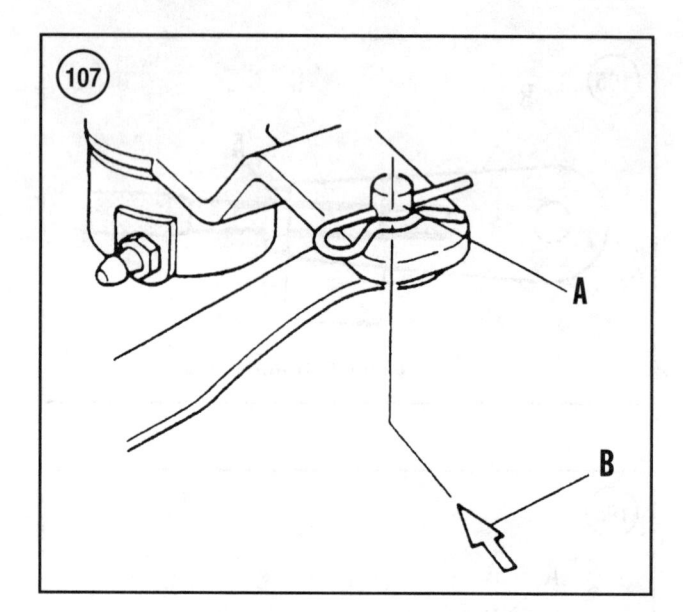

12. Connect the spark plug leads.

13. On electric start models, connect the battery cables.

14. Run the engine on a flush test adapter and check for proper shifting. Correct any faults before putting the engine into service.

Table 1 TEST PROPELLERS

Model	Part No.
2 hp	YB-1601
3-5 hp	YB-1630
6 and 8 hp	YB-1625
9.9 and 15 hp	YB-1619
20-30 hp	YB-1621
40 and 50 hp	YB-1611
60-90 hp	YB-1620

TIMING, SYNCHRONIZATION AND ADJUSTMENT

Table 2 WIDE OPEN THROTTLE SPEED

Model	Engine speed (rpm)
2 hp	4000-5000
3-5 hp	4500-5500
6 hp	4000-5000
8 hp	4500-5500
9.9 and 15 hp	4500-5500
20 and 25 hp (two-cylinder)	5000-6000
25 hp (three-cylinder)	4500-5500
28 jet	4500-5500
30 hp	4500-5500
35 jet	4500-5500
40-60 hp	4500-5500
65 jet	4500-5500
70 hp	5000-6000
75-90 hp	4500-5500

Table 3 PICKUP TIMING SPECIFICATIONS

Model	Timing
20 and 25 hp (two-cylinder)	3° ATDC
25 hp (three-cylinder)	2-4° ATDC
30 hp	1-3° ATDC
28 jet, 35 jet, 40 hp and 50 hp	7° ATDC
60 and 70 hp (except E60)	6-8° ATDC
E60	2° ATDC
65 jet and 75-90 hp (except E75)	7-9° ATDC
E75	2° ATDC

Table 4 IDLE/FULL RETARD TIMING SPECIFICATIONS

Model	Timing
3 hp	4-8° BTDC
4 and 5 hp	3-9° BTDC
6 and 8 hp	3-5° BTDC
9.9 and 15 hp	4-6° ATDC
20 and 25 hp (two-cylinder)	6-8° ATDC
25 hp (three-cylinder) and 30 hp	
With power tilt and trim	3-7° ATDC
Without power tilt and trim	4-6° ATDC
28 jet, 35 jet, 40 hp and 50 hp	6-8° ATDC
60 and 70 hp (except E60)	6-8° ATDC
E60	1-3° ATDC
65 jet and 75-90 hp (except E75)	7-9° ATDC
E75	1-3° ATDC

Table 5 MAXIMUM (FULL ADVANCE) IGNITION TIMING

Model	Maximum timing	Maximum timing speed (rpm)
2 hp	16-20° BTDC	5000
3 hp	18-24° BTDC	5000
4 and 5 hp	25-31° BTDC	5000
6 and 8 hp	34-36° BTDC	5000
9.9 and 15 hp	29-31° BTDC	4500-5500
20 and 25 hp (two-cylinder)	24-26° BTDC	4500-5000
25 hp (three-cylinder) and 30 hp	24-26° BTDC	4500-5000

(continued)

Table 5 MAXIMUM (FULL ADVANCE) IGNITION TIMING (continued)

Model	Maximum timing	Maximum timing speed (rpm)
28 jet, 35 jet, 40 hp and 50 hp	24-28° BTDC	4500-5500
60 hp, 65 jet and 90 hp (except E60)	21-23° BTDC	4500-5500
E60	18-20° BTDC	4500-5500
70-80 hp (except E75)	19-21° BTDC	4500-5500
E75	21-23° BTDC	4500-5500

Table 6 PILOT SCREW ADJUSTMENT SPECIFICATIONS

Model	Adjustment range (turns out)
3 hp	1–1 1/2
4 hp	1 1/2–2
5 hp	1 1/4–1 3/4
6 and 8 hp	7/8–1 3/8
9.9 and 15 hp	1 1/4–1 3/4
20 hp	1 3/4–3 1/4
25 hp (two-cylinder)	1 1/4–2 3/4
25 hp (three-cylinder) and 30 hp	
Top carburetor	1/2–1
Middle carburetor	1 1/2–2
Bottom carburetor	3/4–1 1/4
28 jet and 40 hp	1 1/4–1 3/4
35 jet and 50 hp	
Manual start	1 3/8–1 7/8
Electric start	1 1/8–1 3/8
60 hp	
Premix models	1 1/4–1 3/4
Oil injected models	1 1/8–1 5/8
70 hp	1–1 1/2
75 and 80 hp (except E75)	1 1/8–1 5/8
E75	1–1 1/2
65 jet and 90 hp	1–1 1/2

Table 7 IDLE SPEED SPECIFICATIONS

Model	Idle speed in gear (rpm)	Idle speed in neutral (rpm)
2 hp	1100-1200	*
3 hp	1000-1000	1150-1250
4 and 5 hp	950-1050	1100-1200
6 and 8 hp	750-850	850-950
9.9 and 15 hp	600-700	700-800
20 and 25 hp (two-cylinder)	600-700	700-800
25 hp (two-cylinder) and 30 hp		
With power tilt and trim	750-850	1000-1000
Without power tilt and trim	600-700	700-800
28 jet, 35 jet, 40 hp and 50 hp	650-750	750-850
60-90 hp (except E60 and E75)	650-750	750-850
E60	750-950	950-1050
E75	750-850	850-950

*This model is not equipped with neutral gear.

Chapter Five

Fuel System

This chapter describes removal, repair and installation of fuel system components including the:
1. Fuel tank.
2. Fuel hoses, fuel valves and connectors.
3. Fuel pump.
4. Carburetor.
5. Choke solenoid.
6. Electrothermal valve.
7. Reed housing/intake manifold.
8. Recirculation system.

Refer to the diagrams for help with fuel hose routing and component identification when removing and installing components. Refer to the expanded illustrations of carburetor and fuel pump components to disassemble or assemble the assemblies. Mark all hoses and corresponding fittings and connectors to ease reassembly.

Table 1 lists torque specifications for most fuel system fasteners. Use the standard tightening torque specifications for fasteners not listed in Chapter One. **Table 2** lists reed valve service specifications. **Table 3** lists float height specifications. **Tables 1-3** are located at the end of this chapter.

FUEL SYSTEM SAFETY

Be careful when working with the fuel system. Never smoke around fuel or fuel vapors. Make sure no flame or source of ignition is present in the work area. Flame or sparks can ignite fuel or fuel vapor resulting in a fire or explosion.

Wear protective eyewear when using compressed air (**Figure 1**) to clean carburetor parts. Work in a well ventilated area when repairing the fuel system. Take all necessary precautions against fires or explosions. Always disconnect the battery *before* servicing the outboard.

FUEL SYSTEM COMPONENTS SERVICE

Portable Remote Fuel Tank

Portable remote fuel tanks (**Figure 2**, typical) are used on 6-90 hp models. Several companies manufacture portable fuel tanks. Purchase replacement parts at a marine dealership or repair shop.

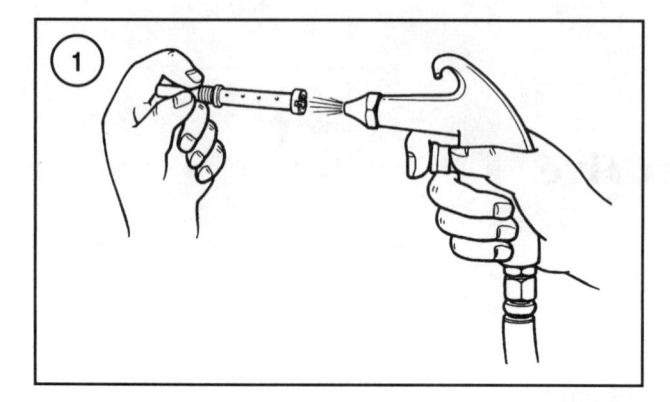

Portable remote fuel tanks require periodic cleaning and inspection. If there is water in the tank, inspect the remainder of the fuel system for potential contamination.

1. Remove the fuel hose connector (1, **Figure 2**) and fill cap (4). Pour the fuel into a suitable container.
2. Remove the screws that hold the fuel gauge assembly (3, **Figure 2**). Carefully remove the assembly from the tank. Never force the assembly or the float arm may be damaged. Remove and discard the gasket between the gauge assembly and the tank.
3. Check for free movement of the float arm on the gauge assembly (**Figure 3**). Replace the assembly if binding cannot be corrected by bending the float arm into the correct position. Inspect the float for deteriorated or physically damaged surfaces. Replace the float if it is damaged or if it appears to be saturated with fuel.
4. Add a small amount of solvent into the fuel tank. Block the fuel gauge opening with a shop towel and install the fill cap. Shake the tank for a few minutes. Drain the solvent and blow dry with compressed air.
5. Replace the tank if there is internal or external rusting, or physical damage. Replace the tank if there is a fuel leak or the tank is suspected of leaking. Repeat Step 4 if there are residual debris or deposits in the tank.
6. Install the fuel gauge assembly into the tank with a new gasket. Install and securely tighten the screws.
7. Check and correct fuel leaks.

Vessel Mounted Fuel Tank

Vessel mounted fuel tanks (**Figure 4**) are used on some 6-90 hp models. They can be difficult to access. Removable panels are used in some boats for access to the fitting and sender assembly. The major components that require service include the fuel pickup tube, fuel level sender, fuel fitting and the antisiphon device. These components are available from many different suppliers. Removal, inspection and installation procedures vary with the brand

PORTABLE REMOTE FUEL TANK (TYPICAL)

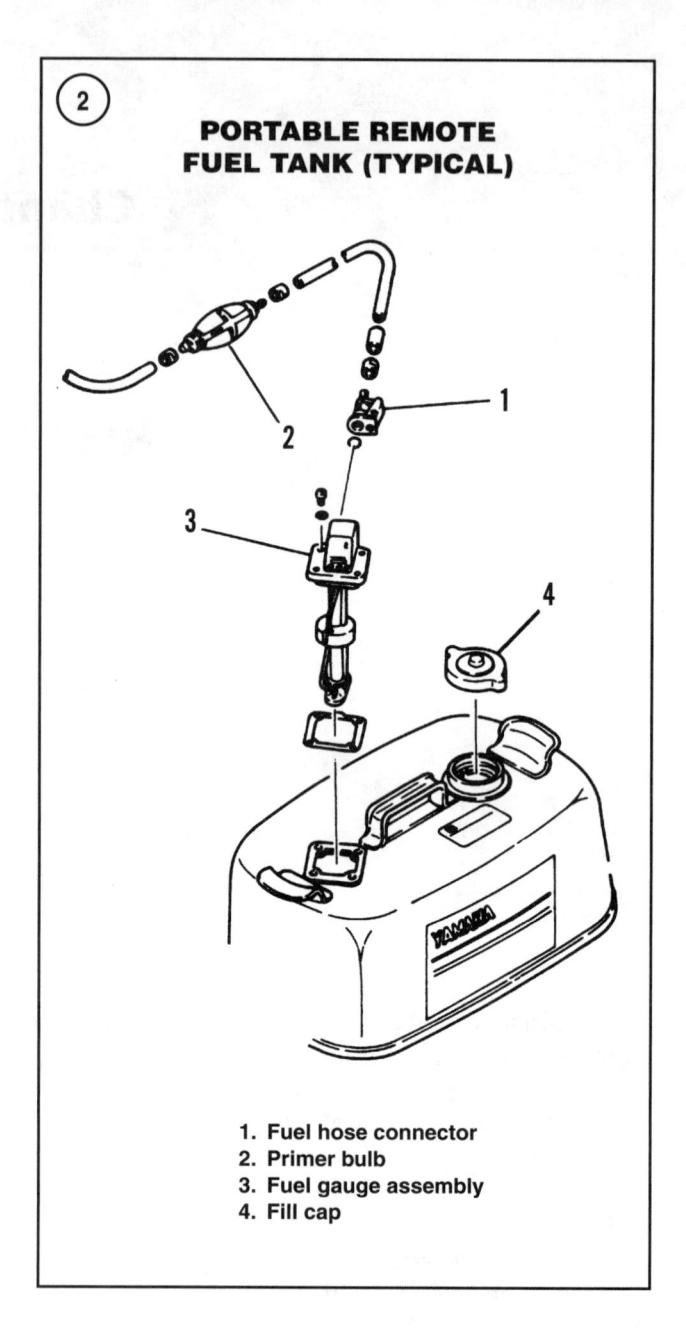

1. Fuel hose connector
2. Primer bulb
3. Fuel gauge assembly
4. Fill cap

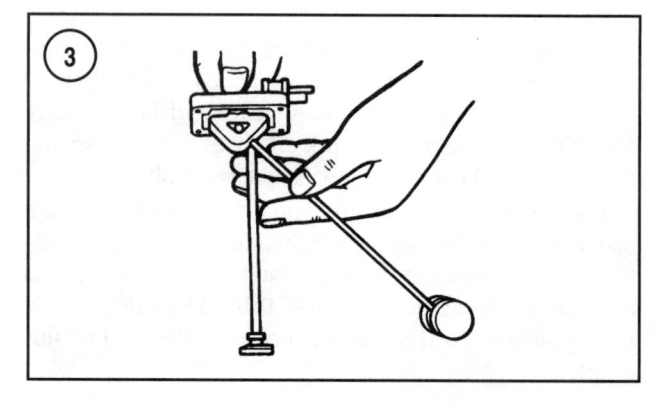

FUEL SYSTEM

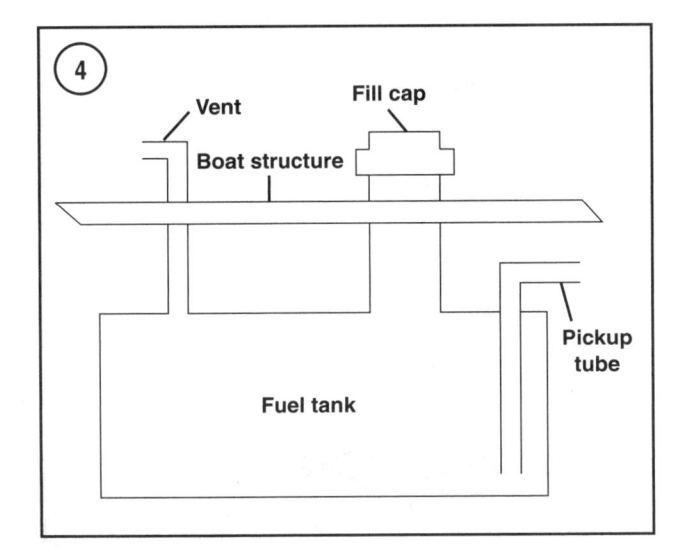

4
Vent — Fill cap
Boat structure
Pickup tube
Fuel tank

5

6

and model of the tank. Contact the tank manufacturer or boat manufacturer for specific instructions.

Integral Fuel Tank

Integral tanks (**Figure 5**) are mounted on 2-5 hp models. An optional valve (**Figure 6**) that allows the use of a

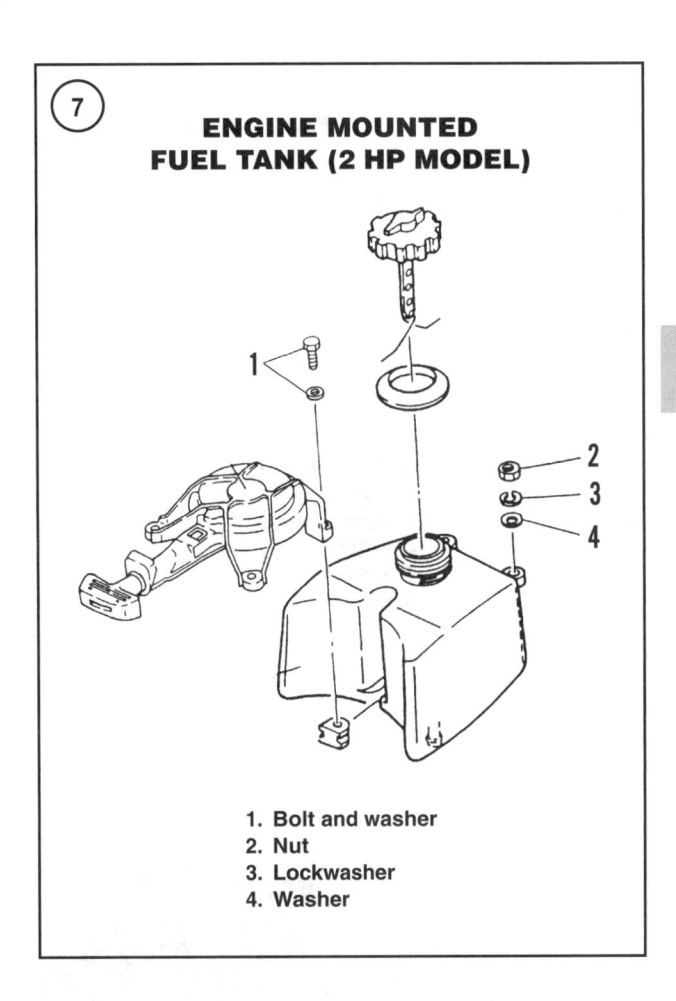

7 ENGINE MOUNTED FUEL TANK (2 HP MODEL)

1. Bolt and washer
2. Nut
3. Lockwasher
4. Washer

remote or integral valve is available for 4 and 5 hp models. Refer to **Figures 7-9**.

1. Turn the fuel valve to the OFF position.

2. Disconnect and ground the spark plug lead to prevent accidental starting.

3. Disconnect the fuel hose and clamp from the fuel tank fitting or valve (**Figure 10**). Use a shop towel for residual fuel that may spill from the valve, fitting or disconnected hose.

4A. On 2 hp models, remove the bolt and washer (1, **Figure 7**) from the manual starter mounting leg. Remove the two nuts (2, **Figure 7**) and washers (3 and 4), then lift the tank from the power head mount. Remove the grommet from the front mounting bolt opening in the tank.

4B. On 3 hp models, remove the bolt from the rear mounting leg of the manual starter. Remove the bolt and washer (3, **Figure 8**), then lift the tank from the power head mount. Pull the grommets (7, **Figure 8**) form the front and rear bolt openings.

4C. On 4 and 5 hp models, remove the two bolts (7, **Figure 9**), then lift the tank from the lower engine cover. Re-

⑧ ENGINE MOUNTED FUEL TANK (3 HP MODEL)

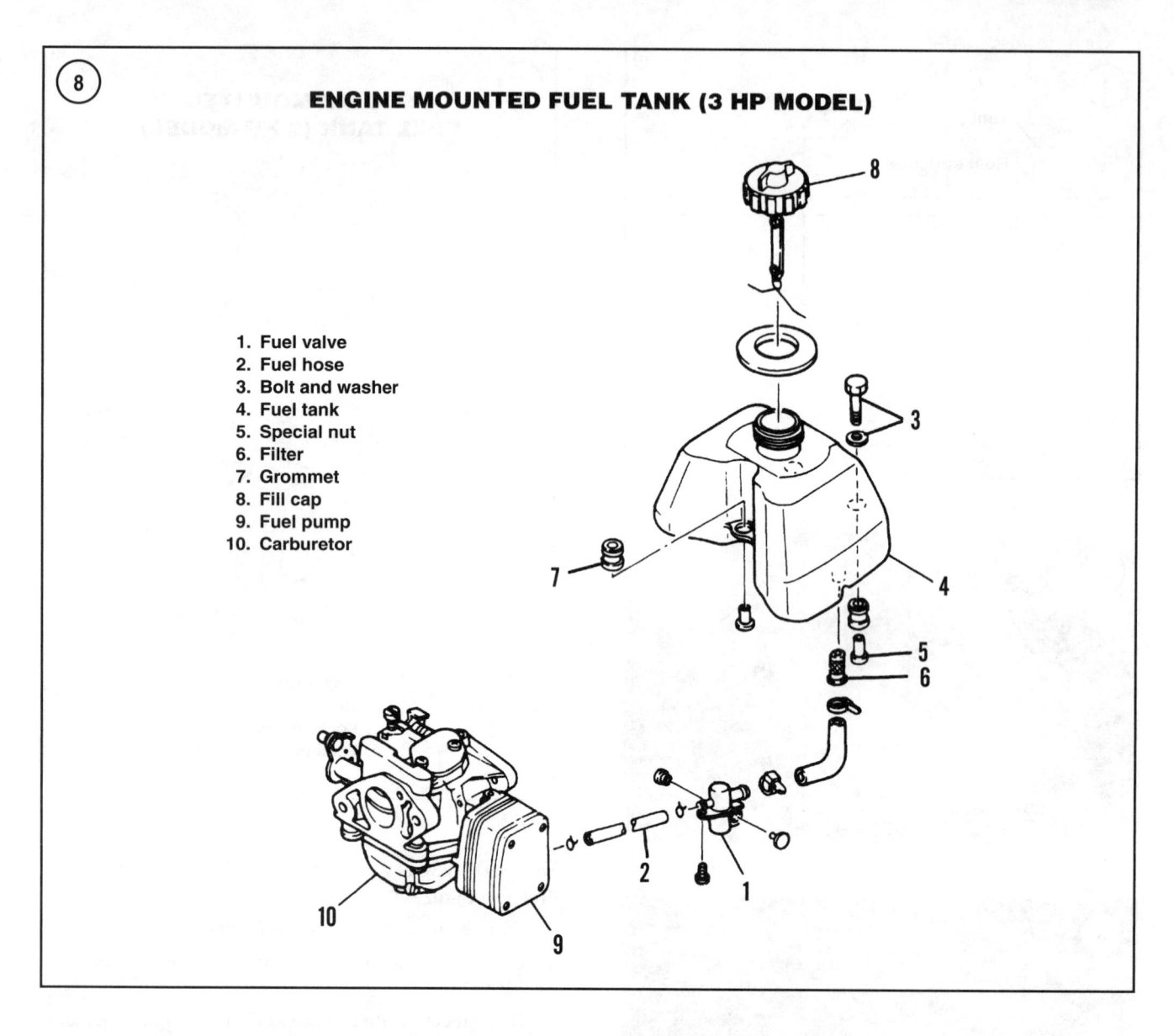

1. Fuel valve
2. Fuel hose
3. Bolt and washer
4. Fuel tank
5. Special nut
6. Filter
7. Grommet
8. Fill cap
9. Fuel pump
10. Carburetor

move the two cushions (4, **Figure 9**), grommets (5) and sleeves (6) from the tank or lower engine cover.

5. Remove the fill cap and empty the fuel into a suitable container.

6. Put a small amount of solvent into the fuel tank and install the fill cap. Shake the tank for a few minutes, then empty the tank. Thoroughly drain the fuel tank and dry it with compressed air. Inspect the tank for residual debris or contamination. Repeat the cleaning process until the tank is completely clean.

7. Remove the fuel valve or fitting from the fuel tank. Inspect the screen for debris or damage. Clean debris from the screen with a suitable solvent. Replace the screen if it is damaged. Open and close the valve to check for proper operation. Direct solvent into the opening, then open and close the valve. Replace the valve if it fails to block solvent flow when in the off position or allows flow in the on position. Replace the valve if solvent or fuel is leaking from the valve lever.

8. Inspect the tank for cracking or other physical damage. Replace the tank if damaged or suspected of leaking.

9. Tank installation is the reverse of removal. Inspect all fuel hoses and clamps. Replace fuel hoses that have cracks, holes or possible leaks. Replace any hose clamp that is corroded, distorted or has lost spring tension. Install all grommets, cushions, sleeves and washers onto the tank mounting surface during installation. Securely tighten the tank mounting bolts and nuts.

10. Fill the tank with a fresh fuel and oil mixture. Check for and correct any fuel leak. Connect the spark plug lead.

FUEL SYSTEM

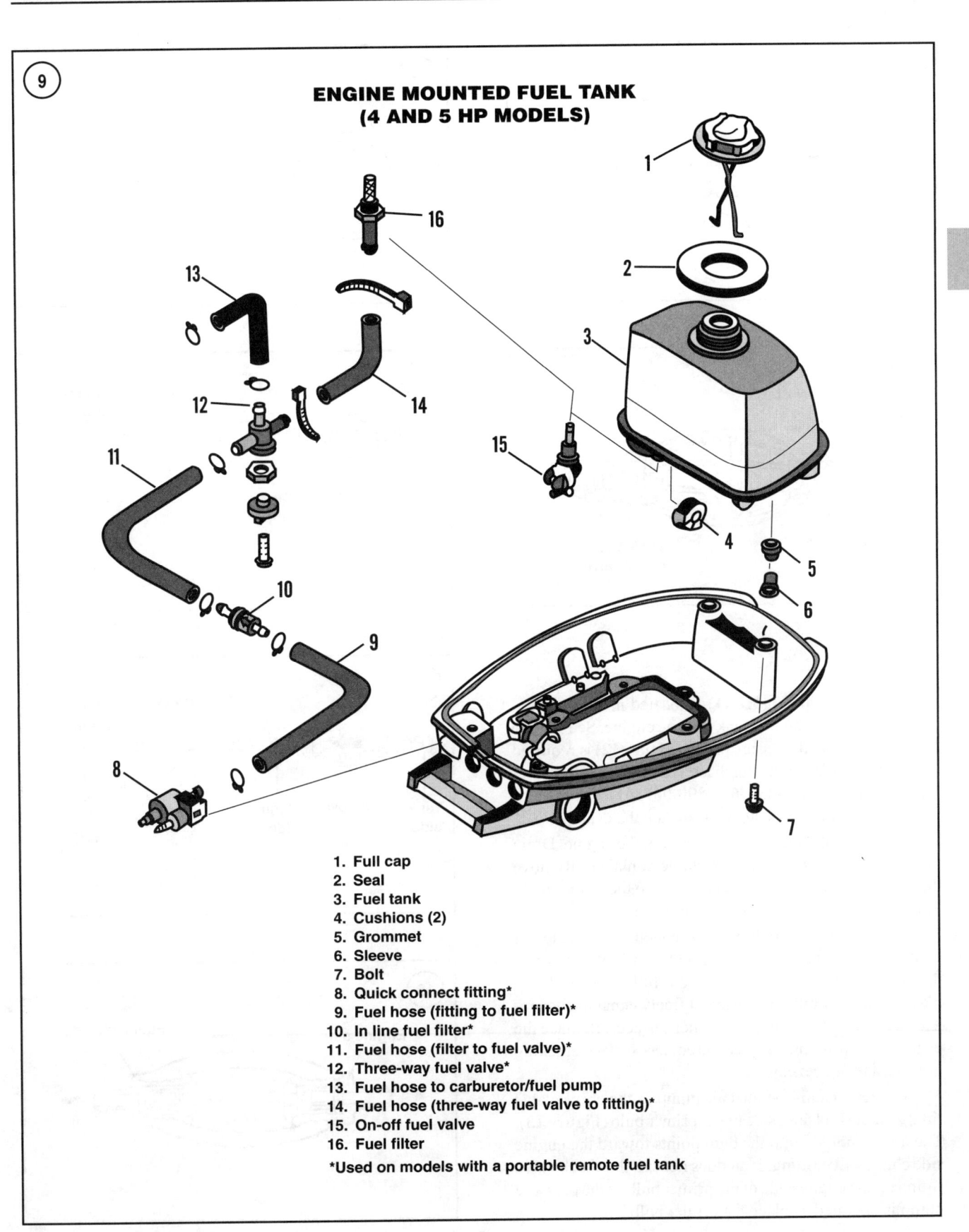

189

⑨

**ENGINE MOUNTED FUEL TANK
(4 AND 5 HP MODELS)**

1. Full cap
2. Seal
3. Fuel tank
4. Cushions (2)
5. Grommet
6. Sleeve
7. Bolt
8. Quick connect fitting*
9. Fuel hose (fitting to fuel filter)*
10. In line fuel filter*
11. Fuel hose (filter to fuel valve)*
12. Three-way fuel valve*
13. Fuel hose to carburetor/fuel pump
14. Fuel hose (three-way fuel valve to fitting)*
15. On-off fuel valve
16. Fuel filter

*Used on models with a portable remote fuel tank

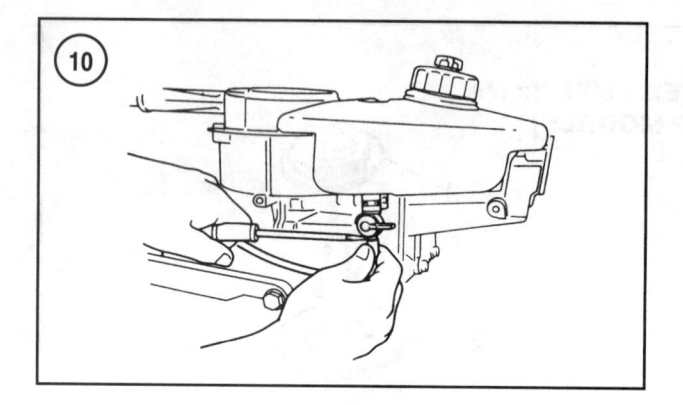

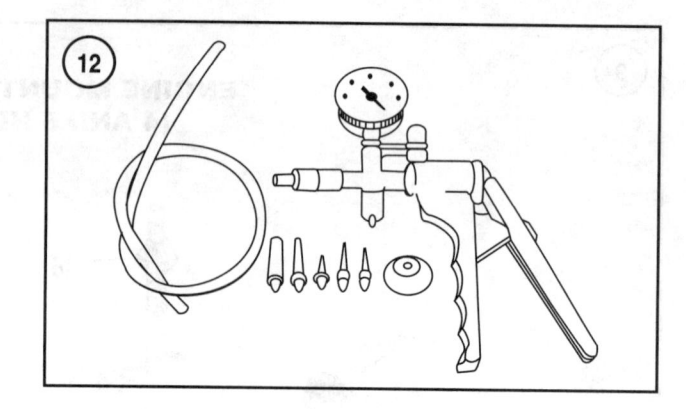

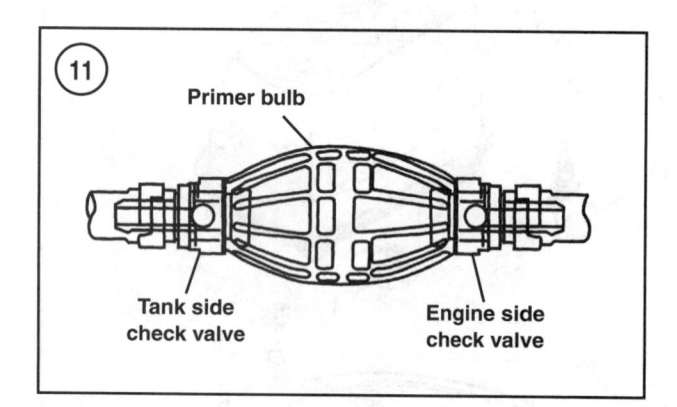

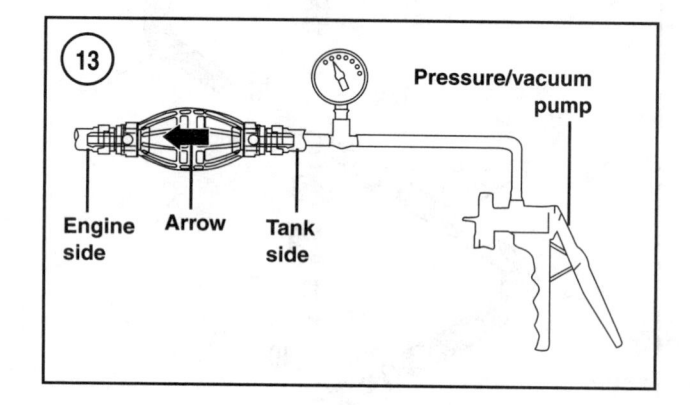

Primer Bulb

The primer bulb (**Figure 11**) is located in the fuel supply hose between the fuel tank and the engine. See **Figure 2**. A hand-operated pressure pump (**Figure 12**) is required to test the primer bulb. Purchase the pump (Miti-Vac or Yamaha part No. YB-35956/90890-06756) from an automotive parts store, tool supplier or Yamaha dealership.

1. Disconnect the fuel supply hose from the engine. Drain the fuel from the hose into a suitable container. Remove the hose clamps from both connections to the primer bulb. Pull the hoses from the primer bulb fittings.

2. Place the primer bulb over a container suitable for holding fuel. Direct the outlet side toward the container, then squeeze the primer bulb until it is fully collapsed. Replace the primer bulb if it does not freely expand when released or sticks together on the inner surfaces. Replace the primer bulb if it appears weathered, has surface cracking or is hard to squeeze.

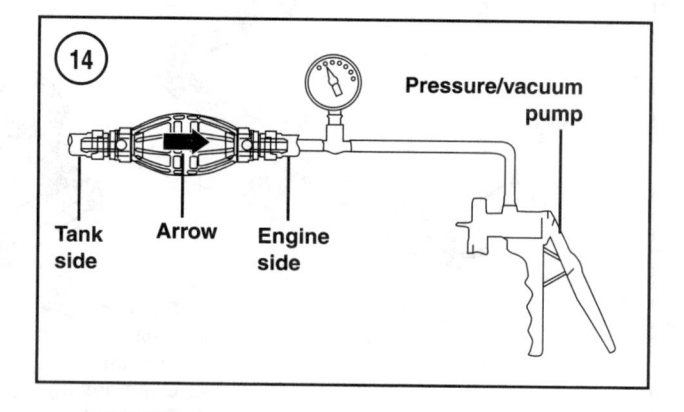

3. Connect a hand-operated air pump to the check valve fitting on the fuel tank side of the primer bulb (**Figure 13**). The arrow molded into the bulb points toward the engine side check valve fitting. If air does not exit the check valve fitting on the engine side of the primer bulb as the pressure pump is operated, replace the primer bulb.

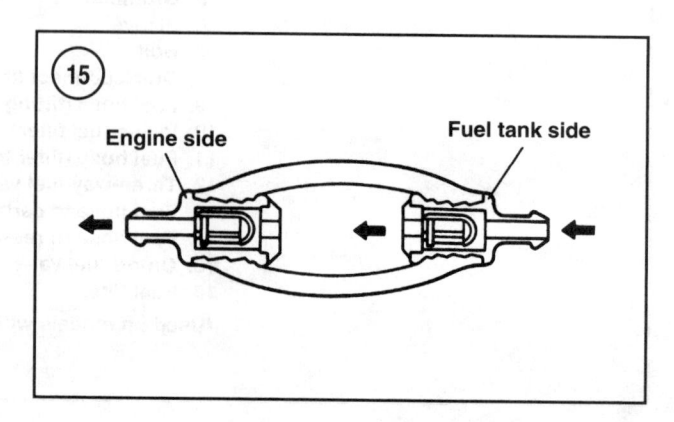

FUEL SYSTEM

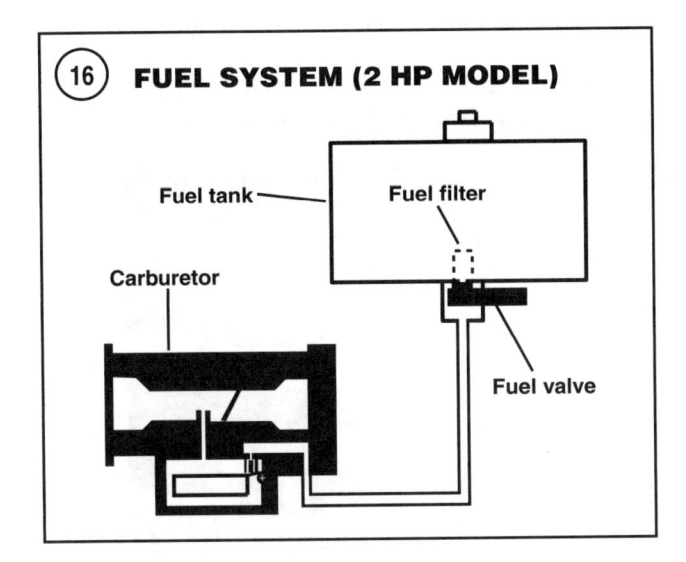

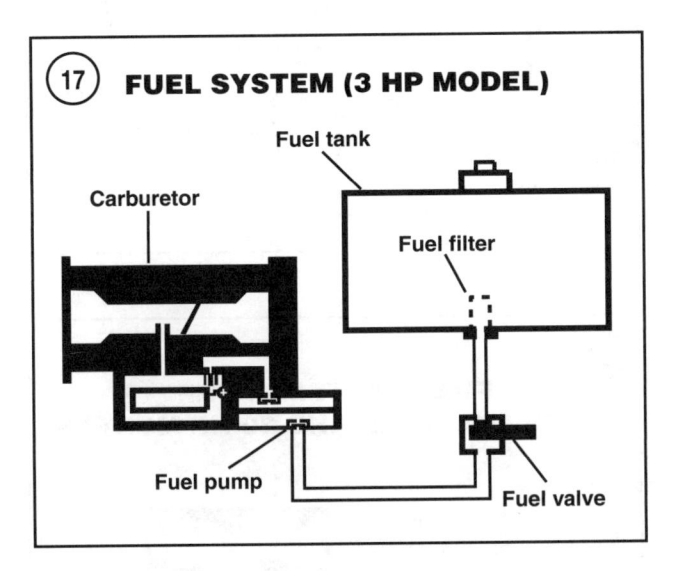

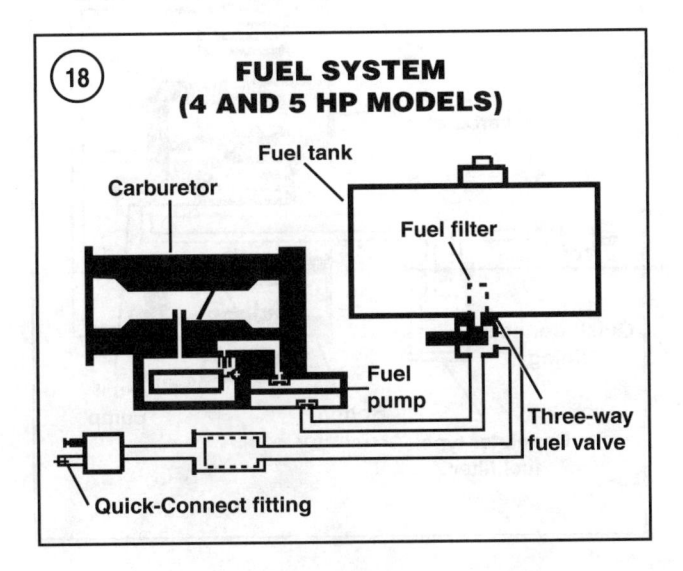

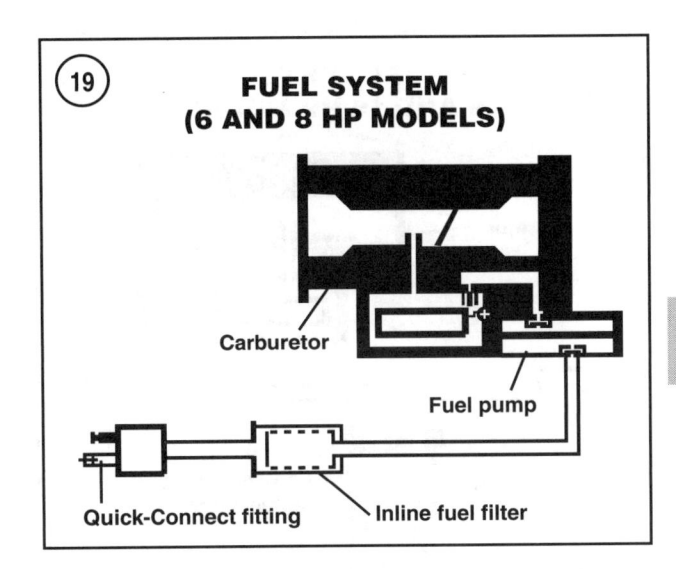

16 FUEL SYSTEM (2 HP MODEL)

- Fuel tank
- Fuel filter
- Carburetor
- Fuel valve

17 FUEL SYSTEM (3 HP MODEL)

- Fuel tank
- Carburetor
- Fuel filter
- Fuel pump
- Fuel valve

18 FUEL SYSTEM (4 AND 5 HP MODELS)

- Fuel tank
- Carburetor
- Fuel filter
- Fuel pump
- Three-way fuel valve
- Quick-Connect fitting

19 FUEL SYSTEM (6 AND 8 HP MODELS)

- Carburetor
- Fuel pump
- Quick-Connect fitting
- Inline fuel filter

4. Connect the pressure pump to the check valve fitting on the engine side of the primer bulb (**Figure 14**). The arrow molded into the bulb points toward the engine side check valve fitting. Air should not exit the fuel tank side check valve fitting as the pump is operated. Replace the primer bulb if air exits the fitting.

5. Submerge the primer bulb, with the air pump hose attached to the engine side, into clear water. Block the fuel tank fitting with a finger. Operate the pump and check for bubble formation on the primer bulb surface and fittings. Replace the primer bulb if leaking is indicated from the surfaces or leaking from the fittings cannot be corrected by installing new clamps. Thoroughly dry the primer bulb before installation.

6. Connect the fuel hoses to the primer bulb fittings. Note the direction of fuel flow before connecting the hoses (**Figure 15**). Use the arrow molded into the primer bulb for correct orientation.

Fuel Hoses

Fuel hose sizes and routing vary by model. Refer to **Figures 16-23** for correct routing and connection of hoses.

Only use the Yamaha replacement fuel hoses or other hoses that meet U.S. Coast Guard requirements for marine applications. Never install a fuel hose that is smaller in diameter than the original hose. Replace all fuel hoses at the same time unless unusual circumstances create the need to replace only one fuel hose. If one hose fails, other hoses are suspect.

Replace hoses that feel sticky to the touch, feel spongy, are hard and brittle, or have surface cracking. Always replace hoses that split on the end instead of cutting off the end and reattaching the hose. The hose will probably split again. To avoid hoses kinking or interfering with other components, never cut replacement hoses shorter or longer than the original.

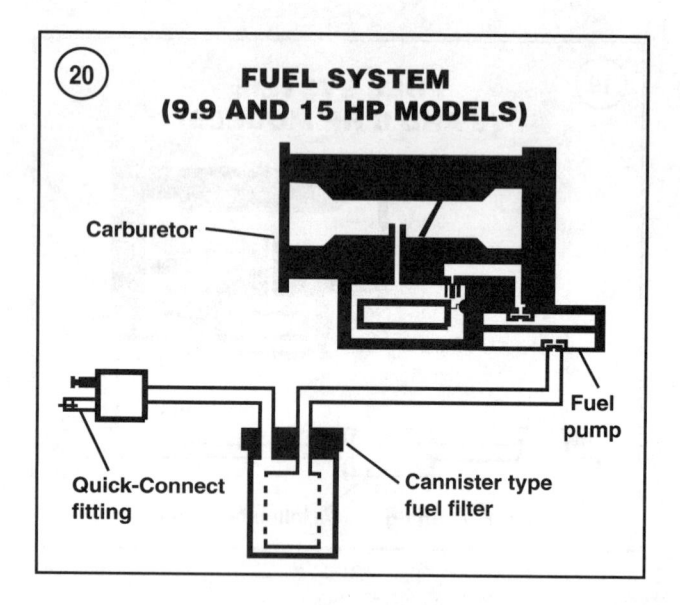

Fuel Hose Connectors

Connectors used on the fuel hoses include the plastic locking type hose clamps, spring type hose clamp and quick-connector.

Plastic locking type clamp

The plastic locking type clamps (**Figure 24**) must be cut for removal. Replace them with the correct Yamaha clamps. Some plastic locking type clamps are not suitable for the application and will fail. Always use the same width as the removed plastic locking clamp. A larger clamp may not clamp tightly to a smaller hose. A smaller clamp may not withstand the load and allow the hose to come off the fitting.

Pull the end through the clamp (**Figure 25**) until the hose is securely fastened and will not rotate on the fitting. Avoid pulling too tightly as the clamp may fail or be weakened and eventually loosen.

Spring type hose clamp

Remove spring type hose clamps by squeezing the ends together with pliers (**Figure 26**) while carefully moving the clamp away from the fitting. Replace spring type hose clamps that are corroded, bent, deformed or have lost spring tension.

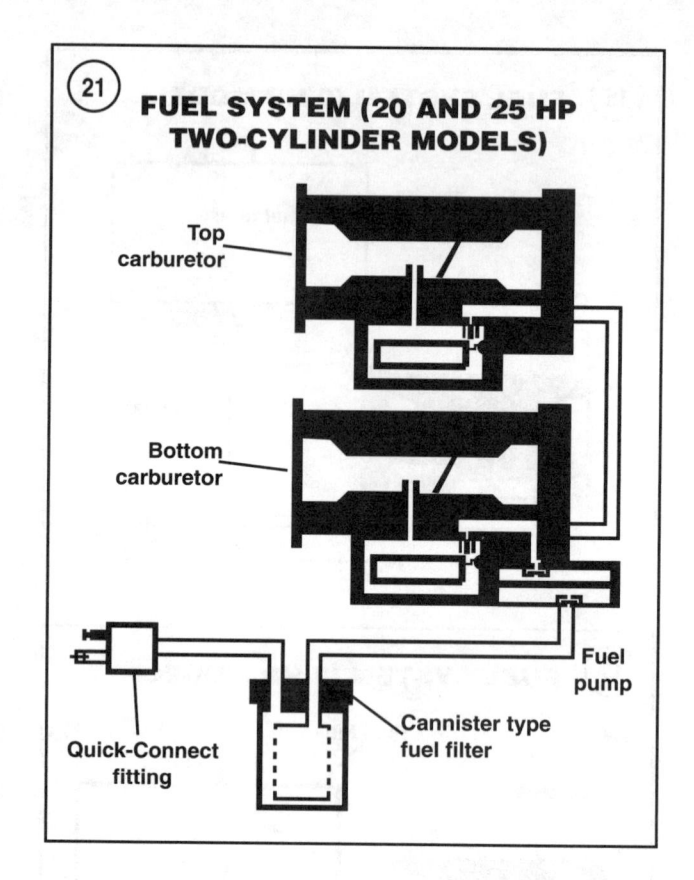

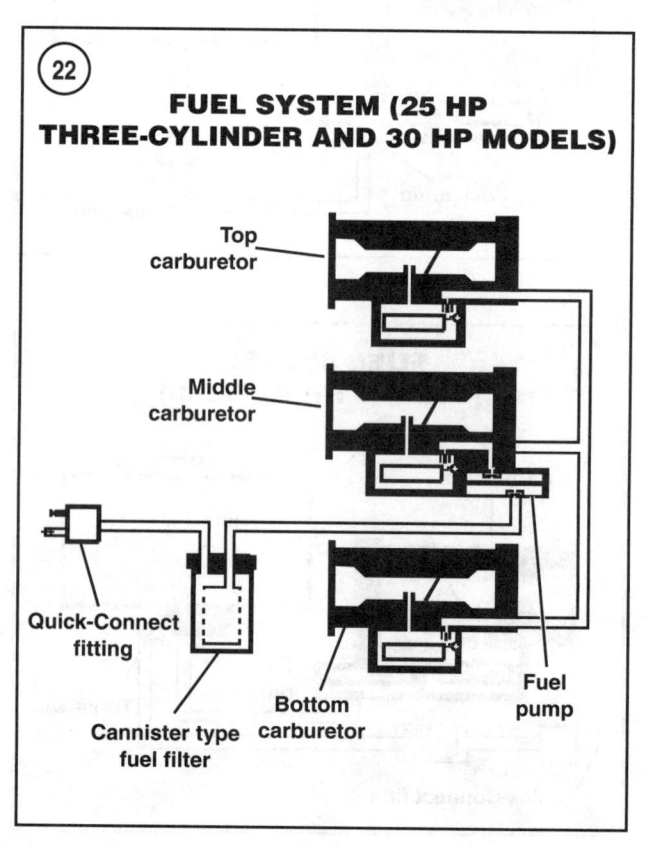

FUEL SYSTEM

23 FUEL SYSTEM (28 JET, 35 JET AND 40-90 HP MODELS)
- Top carburetor
- Middle carburetor
- Fuel pump
- Quick-Connect fitting
- Cannister type fuel filter
- Bottom carburetor

24

25

26

27 QUICK-CONNECTOR (TYPICAL)

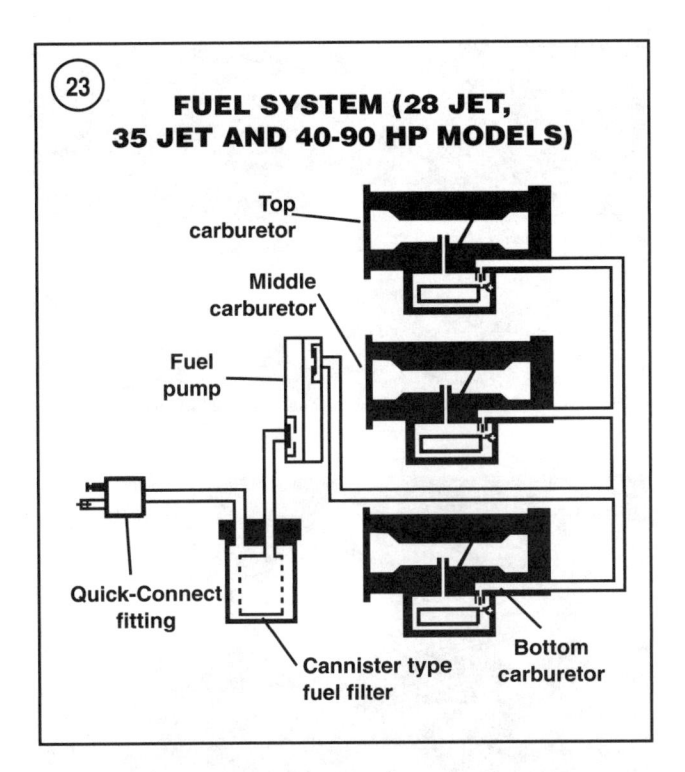

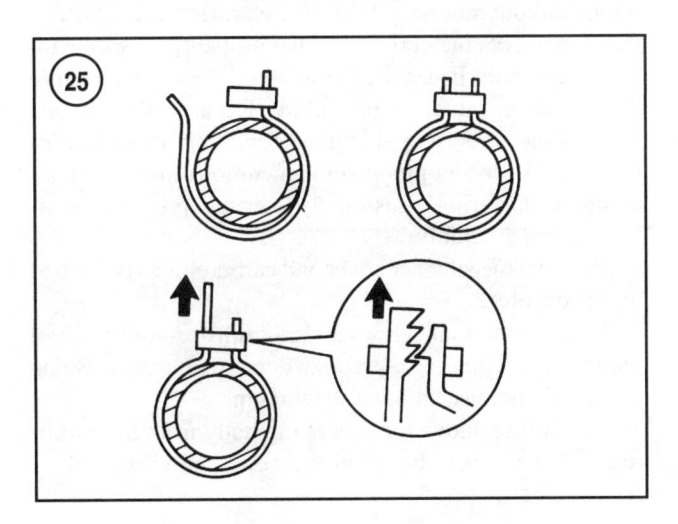

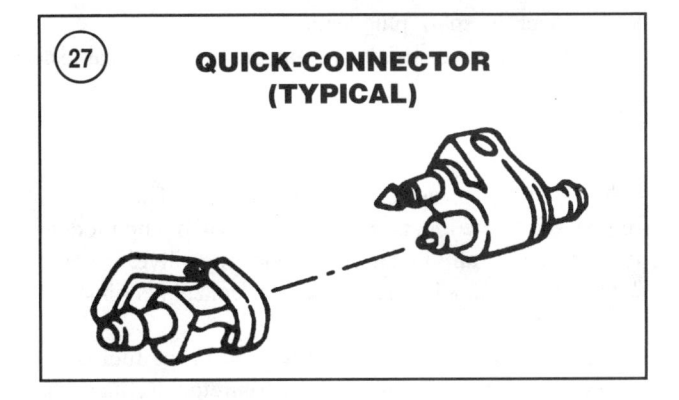

Quick-connector

A quick-connector type clamp (**Figure 27**) is used on 5-90 hp models to connect the fuel supply hose to the engine.

To disconnect this type of clamp, push on the locking lever, then pull the fuel supply hose from the engine fitting.

To connect the clamp, depress the locking lever, then carefully push the fuel supply hose onto the engine fitting. Make sure to align the lever side with the solid pin on the engine fitting. The pin with the check valve must fit into the opening in the connector that aligns with the fuel hose. Push firmly on the fitting, then release the locking lever. Pull on the hose to make sure the locking lever engages the groove in the solid pin.

Check for leaking at the quick-connector fittings on a frequent basis. Observe the connection while squeezing the primer bulb. Replace both fittings if there is leaking at the connection. Replace quick-connectors as follows:

1. On electric start models, disconnect the battery cables.
2. Disconnect and ground the spark plug lead(s) to prevent accidental starting.
3. Remove the hose clamps then pull the hose from the connector fittings.

4. Remove the mounting bolt. Pull the engine fitting from the lower engine cover.
5. Fit the replacement quick-connector on the lower engine cover. Align the fitting with the opening and install the mounting bolt. Securely tighten the bolt.
6. Connect the fuel supply quick-connector to the engine quick-connector.
7. Push the engine and fuel supply hoses onto their respective quick-connector fittings. Secure the hoses with the appropriate clamps. Route the hoses to avoid interference with moving components.
8. Squeeze the primer bulb while checking for leaks. Correct leaking as necessary.
9. Connect the spark plug lead(s).
10. On electric start models, connect the battery cables.

Fuel Valves

Fuel valves are used on 2-5 hp models. The valve is mounted into the fuel tank on 2 hp, 4 hp and 5 hp models. Remove and drain the tank to replace the valve. Refer to *Integral Fuel Tank* in this chapter for replacement instructions on these models.

On 3 hp models, the valve is located in the fuel hoses connecting the fuel tank to the carburetor. Replace the valve as follows:
1. Disconnect and ground the spark plug lead to prevent accidental starting.
2. Place the valve lever in the OFF position.
3. Disconnect the fuel hose from the carburetor fitting. Direct the hose into a container suitable for holding fuel.
4. Move the valve lever to the ON position and drain the fuel tank. If the tank will not drain, remove the integral fuel tank as described in this chapter.
5. Connect the fuel hose to the carburetor fitting and secure it with a suitable clamp. Remove the clamps and pull both hoses from the fuel valve fittings. Remove the screw to free the valve from the power head.
6. Open and close the valve to check for proper operation.
7. Install the replacement valve onto the power head and secure it with the screw. Tighten the screw to the specification in **Table 1**.

Fuel Pumps

Two types of fuel pumps are used on Yamaha outboards. A gravity fuel delivery system is used on the 2 hp model. A carburetor mounted fuel pump (**Figure 28**) is used on 3-30 hp (except 28 jet) models. A power head mounted fuel pump (**Figure 29**) is used on 28 jet and 40-60 hp models. Refer to the appropriate diagram (**Figures 16-23**) to assist with fuel hose routing and connections. Replace all gaskets, diaphragms, check valves and seals when servicing the fuel pump. Check for proper engine operation and correct any fuel leaks before putting the engine into service.

Carburetor mounted fuel pump

It is possible to repair the carburetor mounted fuel pump without removing the carburetor. However, it is difficult to access the carburetor that probably needs cleaning and repairs if debris, varnish-like deposits or brittle gaskets caused fuel pump failure. Repair only the fuel pump if the carburetor is in good condition. Refer to **Figures 30-34** for fuel pump component locations. Mark all components during disassembly to ensure proper orientation during assembly.
1. Remove the silencer cover and carburetor as described in this chapter.
2. Remove the four screws and carefully remove the fuel pump cover, outer gasket and outer diaphragm. Some models do not use an outer diaphragm.
3. Carefully remove the fuel pump body from the carburetor. Remove the check valve screws and check valves from the body.

FUEL SYSTEM

30

**CARBURETOR MOUNTED FUEL PUMP
(3, 6 AND 8 HP MODELS)**

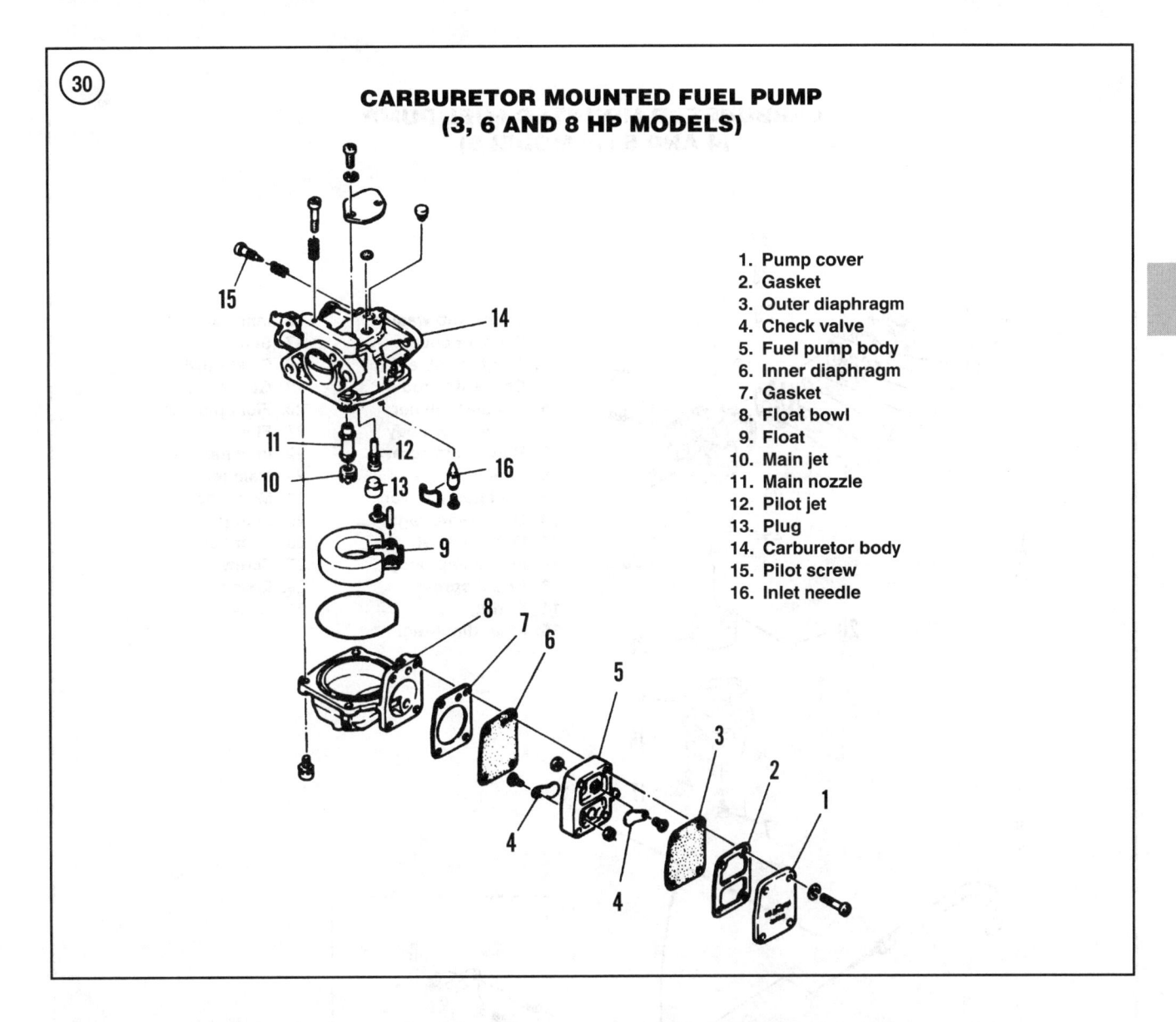

1. Pump cover
2. Gasket
3. Outer diaphragm
4. Check valve
5. Fuel pump body
6. Inner diaphragm
7. Gasket
8. Float bowl
9. Float
10. Main jet
11. Main nozzle
12. Pilot jet
13. Plug
14. Carburetor body
15. Pilot screw
16. Inlet needle

4. On 4 and 5 hp models, remove the boost spring (13, **Figure 31**) and cap (14) from the body.

5. Remove the inner diaphragm and gasket from the body or carburetor surfaces.

6. Clean all components with a suitable solvent. Carefully scrape gasket material from the fuel pump body, cover and carburetor surfaces. Never scratch or damage the gasket mating surfaces. Inspect the check valves and valve contact surfaces on the fuel pump body. Replace the body and valves if either surface is damaged or deteriorated.

7. Assembly is the reverse of disassembly. Note the following:
   a. Replace all gaskets, diaphragms and seals when assembling the fuel pump.
   b. Refer to the appropriate illustration during assembly to help ensure proper component orientation.
   d. Handle the diaphragm with care to avoid tearing the openings where the screws pass through the diaphragm and gaskets.
   e. Securely tighten the mounting screws.

8. Install the carburetor and silencer cover as described in this chapter.

9. Check for and correct any fuel leaks before putting the engine into service.

Power head mounted fuel pump

Deformed or damaged diaphragms, brittle gaskets and faulty check valves are some common causes of fuel

CHAPTER FIVE

③1

**CARBURETOR MOUNTED FUEL PUMP
(4 AND 5 HP MODELS)**

1. Screw and washer
2. Silencer cover
3. Throttle cable
4. Choke link rod
5. Nut and washer
6. Carburetor body
7. Bowl drain screw
8. Screw
9. Fuel pump cover
10. Outer diaphragm
11. Outer gasket
12. Fuel pump body
13. Boost spring
14. Spring cap
15. Inner diaphragm
16. Inner gasket
17. Screw
18. Float bowl
19. Gasket
20. Float pin
21. Float
22. Inlet needle
23. Main jet
24. Main nozzle
25. Pilot jet
26. Pilot screw
27. Screw
28. Cover
29. Gasket

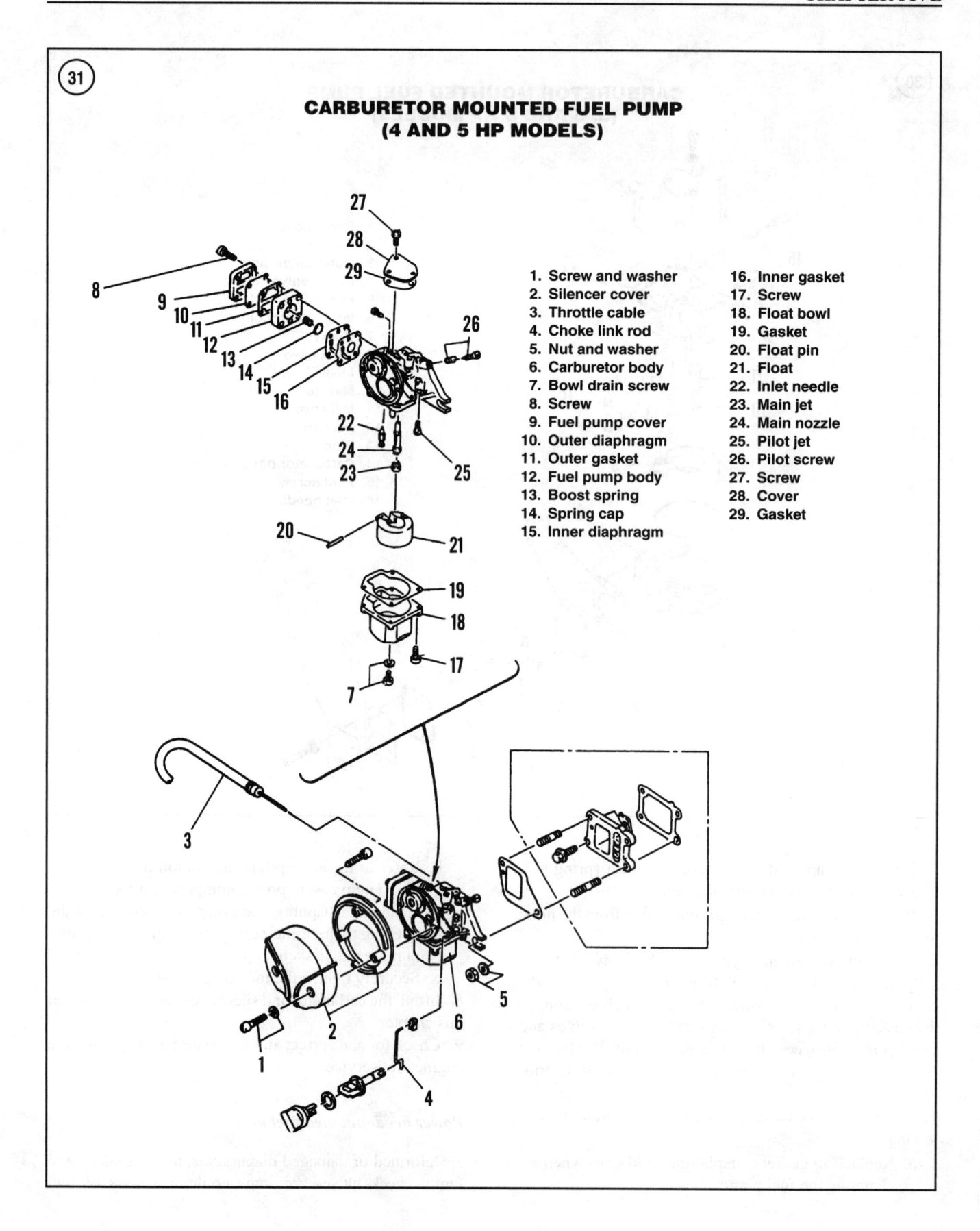

FUEL SYSTEM

32

CARBURETOR MOUNTED FUEL PUMP
(9.9 AND 15 HP MODELS)

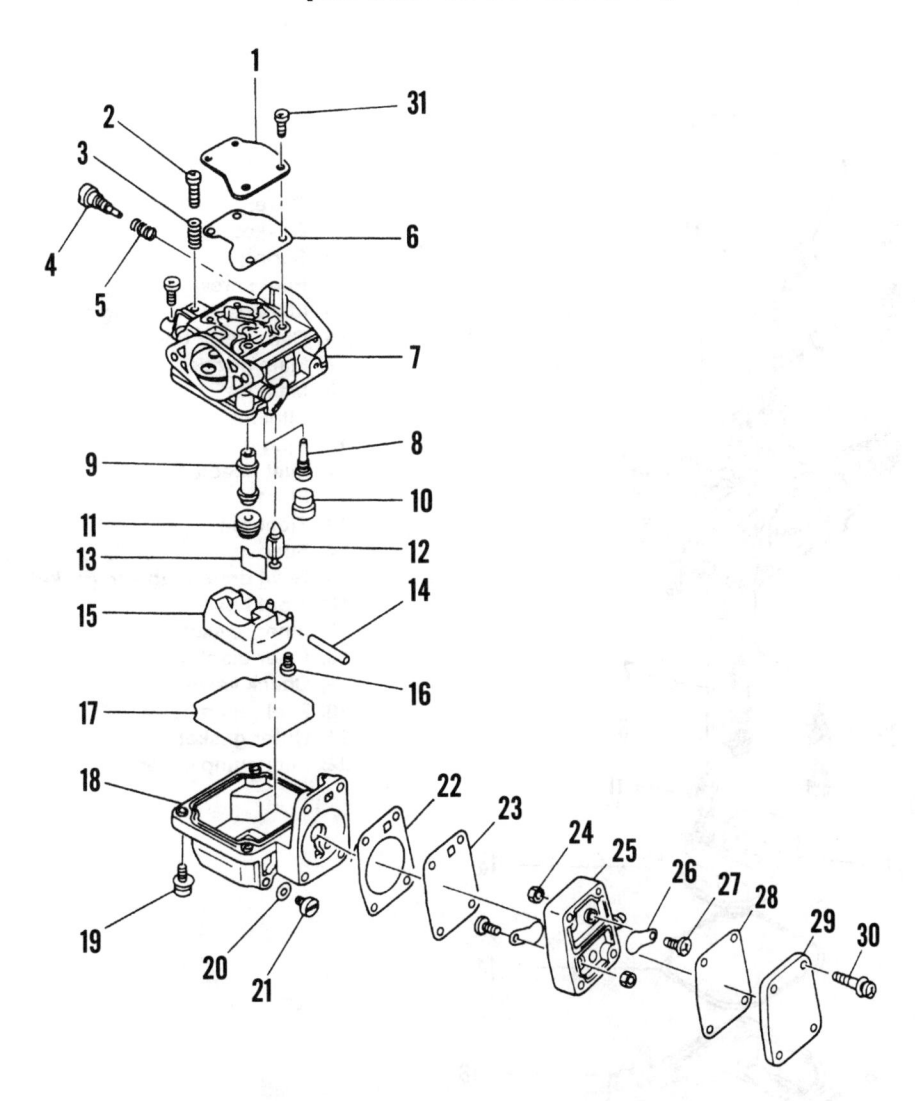

1. Cover
2. Idle speed adjusting screw
3. Spring
4. Pilot screw
5. Spring
6. Gasket
7. Carburetor body
8. Pilot jet
9. Main nozzle
10. Plug
11. Main jet
12. Inlet needle
13. Clip
14. Float pin
15. Float
16. Float pin screw
17. Seal
18. Float bowl
19. Screw
20. Gasket
21. Bowl drain screw
22. Inner gasket
23. Inner diaphragm
24. Nut
25. Fuel pump body
26. Check valve
27. Screw
28. Outer diaphragm
29. Fuel pump cover
30. Screw

CHAPTER FIVE

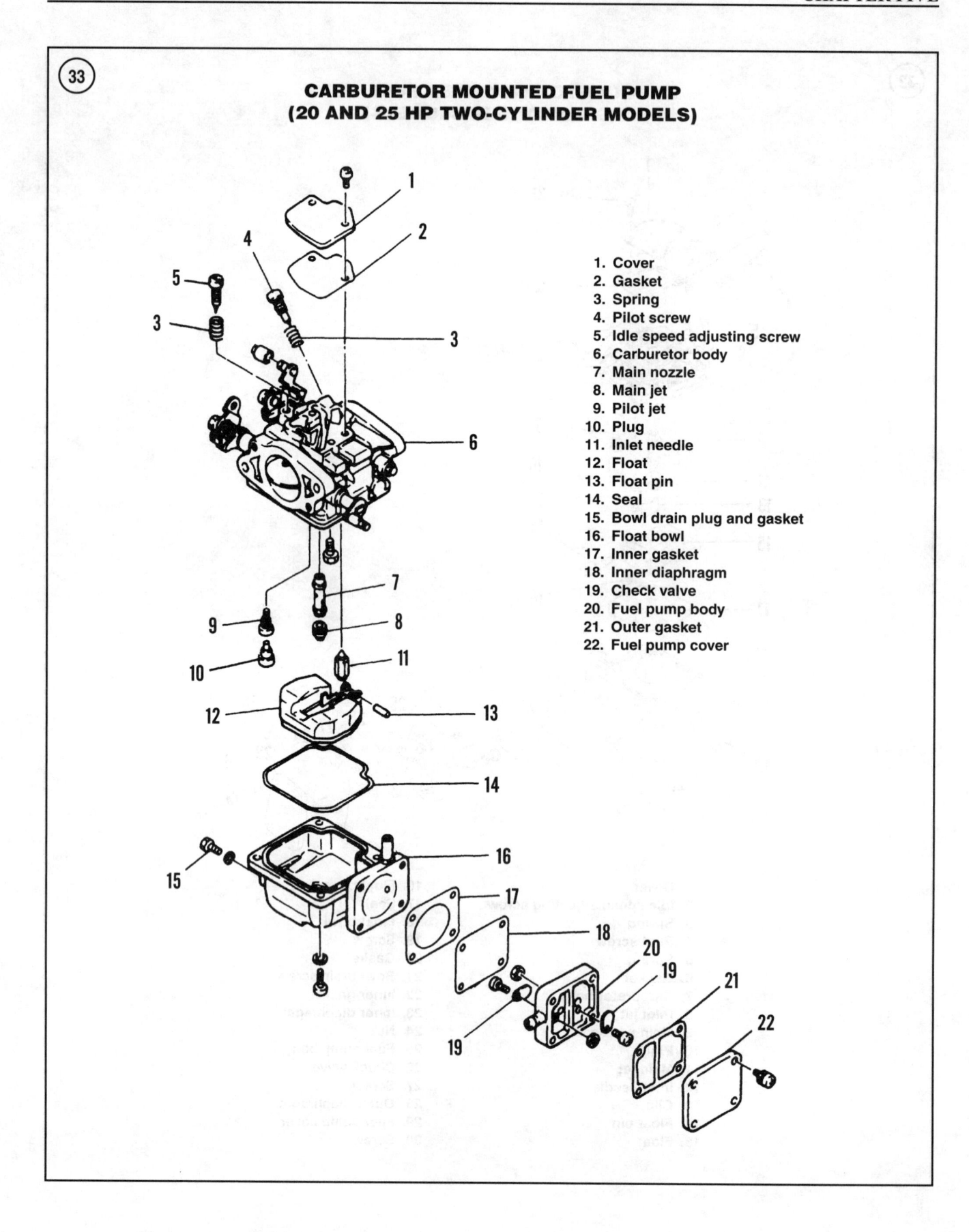

CARBURETOR MOUNTED FUEL PUMP
(20 AND 25 HP TWO-CYLINDER MODELS)

1. Cover
2. Gasket
3. Spring
4. Pilot screw
5. Idle speed adjusting screw
6. Carburetor body
7. Main nozzle
8. Main jet
9. Pilot jet
10. Plug
11. Inlet needle
12. Float
13. Float pin
14. Seal
15. Bowl drain plug and gasket
16. Float bowl
17. Inner gasket
18. Inner diaphragm
19. Check valve
20. Fuel pump body
21. Outer gasket
22. Fuel pump cover

FUEL SYSTEM

③④

**CARBURETOR MOUNTED FUEL PUMP
(25 HP THREE-CYLINDER AND 30 HP MODELS)**

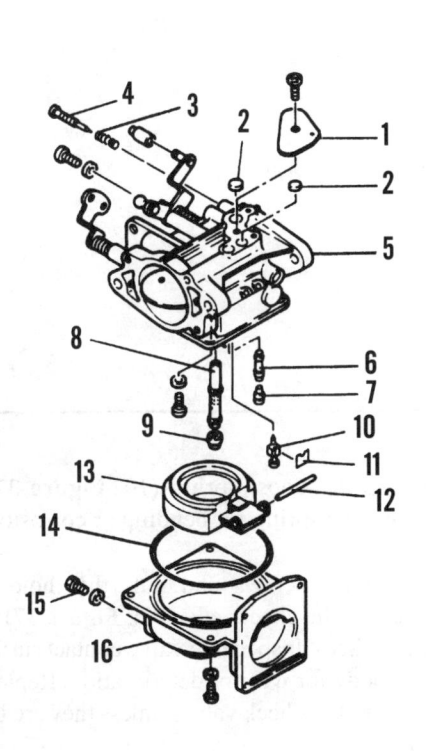

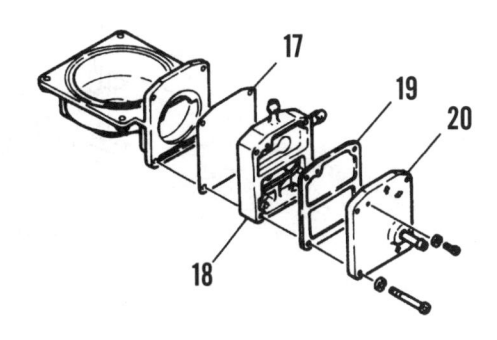

1. Cover
2. Seal
3. Spring
4. Pilot screw
5. Carburetor body
6. Pilot jet
7. Plug
8. Main nozzle
9. Main jet
10. Inlet needle
11. Clip
12. Float pin
13. Float
14. Seal
15. Bowl drain screw and gasket
16. Float bowl
17. Inner diaphragm
18. Fuel pump body
19. Outer gasket
20. Fuel pump cover

pump failure. Mark all components during disassembly to ensure proper orientation during assembly.

A pressure/vacuum tester (Miti-Vac or Yamaha part No. YB-35956/90890-06756) is required to pressure test the fuel pump upon assembly. Use a shop towel or suitable container to capture residual fuel that spills from disconnected hoses.

Refer to **Figure 35** or **Figure 36** for fuel pump mounting and hose routing.

1. On electric start models, disconnect the battery cables.
2. Disconnect and ground the spark plug lead(s) to prevent accidental starting.
3. Locate the inlet and outlet fittings on the fuel pump body. Cut and dispose of the plastic locking type clamps

CHAPTER FIVE

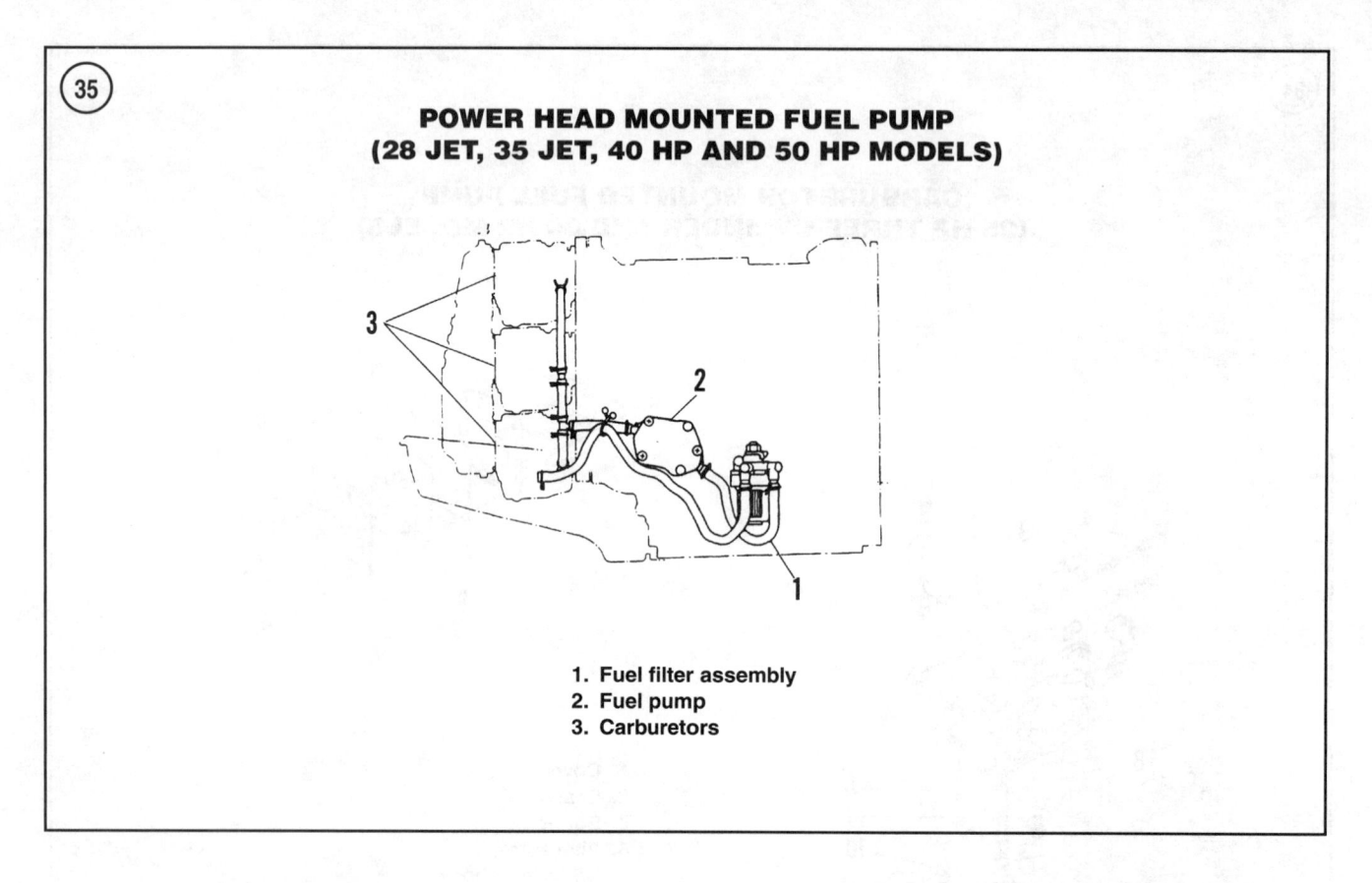

**POWER HEAD MOUNTED FUEL PUMP
(28 JET, 35 JET, 40 HP AND 50 HP MODELS)**

1. Fuel filter assembly
2. Fuel pump
3. Carburetors

used on some models. Remove spring type hose clamps by squeezing the ends together.

4. Position a container or shop towel under the fuel pump hoses, then carefully push the hoses from the fittings. Work carefully and do not tug on the hoses or use side force against the fittings. The fittings will break if excessive force is used. Gently twist difficult hoses to free them from the fittings.

5. Drain residual fuel from the hoses. Remove the two fuel pump mounting screws (5, **Figure 36**) and carefully pull the pump from the power head.

6. Remove the gasket (4, **Figure 36**) from the power head or fuel pump surfaces. Discard the gasket.

7. Remove the three screws (1, **Figure 37**) that hold the assembly together. Being careful to avoid damaging gasket surfaces, pry the fuel pump cover (2, **Figure 37**) from the fuel pump body (7).

8. Remove the outer gasket (4, **Figure 37**) and diaphragm (3) from the body. Be careful to avoid damaging the gasket mating surfaces if the gaskets must be scraped for removal. Discard all gaskets and diaphragms.

9. Use the same procedures to remove the back cover, diaphragm and gasket from the pump body.

10. Remove the boost spring (10, **Figure 37**) and cap (11). Inspect the spring for bending or corrosion. Replace as needed.

11. Remove the screws and nuts that hold the check valves. Inspect the check valves (6, **Figure 37**) for bent or corroded surfaces. Inspect the valve contact surfaces on the fuel pump body for wear or deterioration. Replace the fuel pump body and/or check valves unless they are in excellent condition.

12. Use a straightedge to check the fuel pump body, outer cover and inner cover for warped surfaces. Replace warped components.

13. Inspect gasket and diaphragm contact surfaces on the body and covers for scratches, nicks or deteriorated surfaces. Replace components that have damaged surfaces.

14. Assembly is the reverse of disassembly. Note the following:
   a. Install new gaskets and diaphragms during assembly.
   b. Use the screw openings in the diaphragms and gaskets to assist with proper orientation.
   c. Carefully position the diaphragm over the boost spring and cap. The spring and cap are easily dislodged.
   d. Align the screw openings while holding the components together.

FUEL SYSTEM

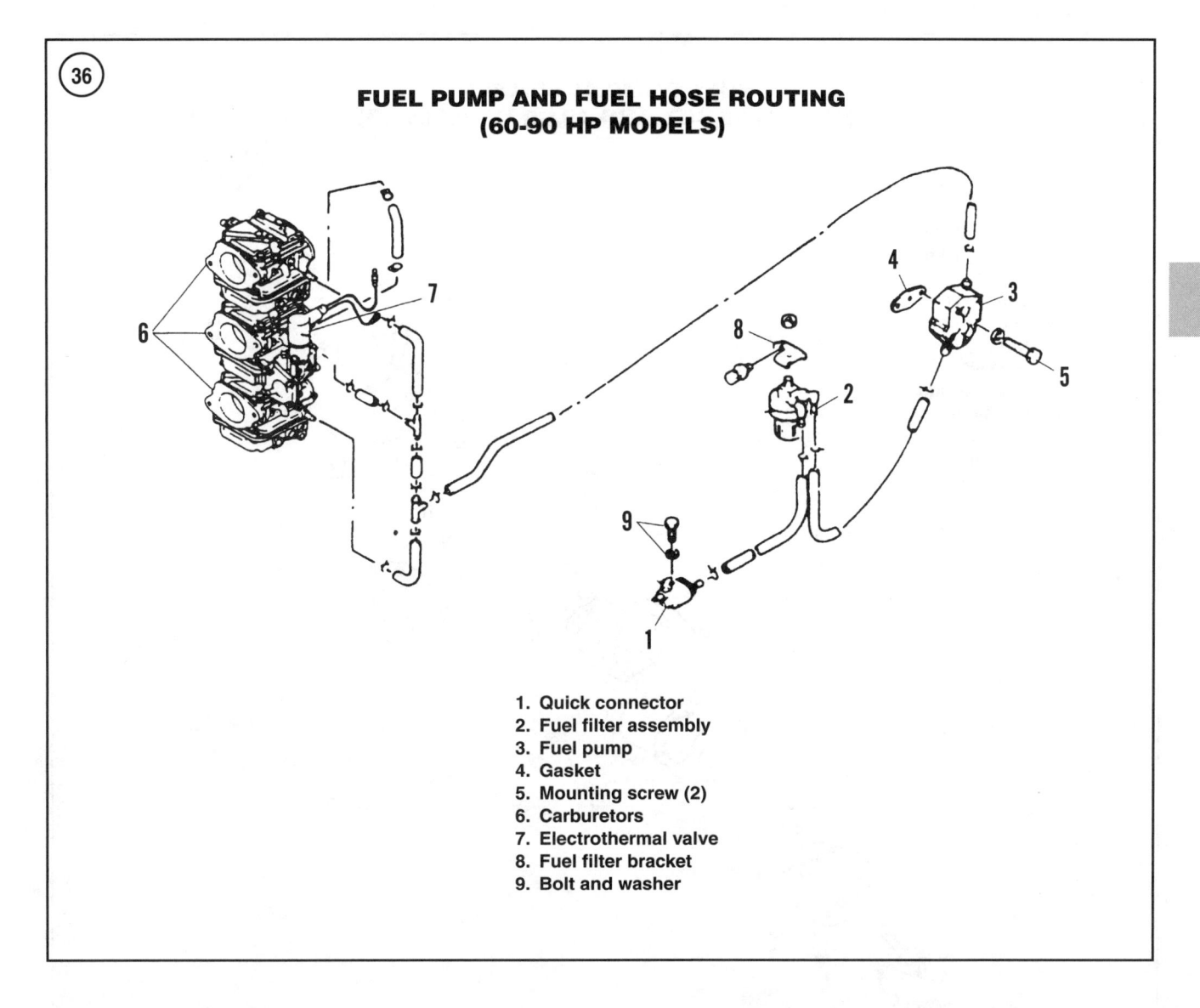

**FUEL PUMP AND FUEL HOSE ROUTING
(60-90 HP MODELS)**

1. Quick connector
2. Fuel filter assembly
3. Fuel pump
4. Gasket
5. Mounting screw (2)
6. Carburetors
7. Electrothermal valve
8. Fuel filter bracket
9. Bolt and washer

e. Evenly and securely tighten the three screws to hold the assembly together.

15. Pressure test the fuel pump as described in this section.

16. Install a new gasket (4, **Figure 36**) onto the back cover of the fuel pump. Slip the two mounting screws through the pump and gasket to hold the gasket.

17. Install the fuel pump onto the power head. Make sure the mounting gasket is not dislodged during installation. Thread the mounting screws (5, **Figure 36**) into the power head openings. Evenly and securely tighten the mounting screws.

18. Connect the fuel hoses to the fuel pump fittings. The hose connected to the outlet side must be connected to the carburetors. The hose connected to the inlet side must be connected to the fuel filter.

19. Observe the fuel pump for indication of leaking while squeezing the primer bulb. Correct leaks before putting the engine into service.

20. Connect the spark plug leads.

21. On electric start models, connect the battery cables.

Fuel pump pressure test

A pressure/vacuum tester (Miti-Vac or Yamaha part No. YB-35956/90890-06756) is required for this procedure. Purchase the tester from an automotive or marine parts store or Yamaha dealership.

NOTE
Put a small amount of fuel in the fuel pump fittings before pressure testing the fuel

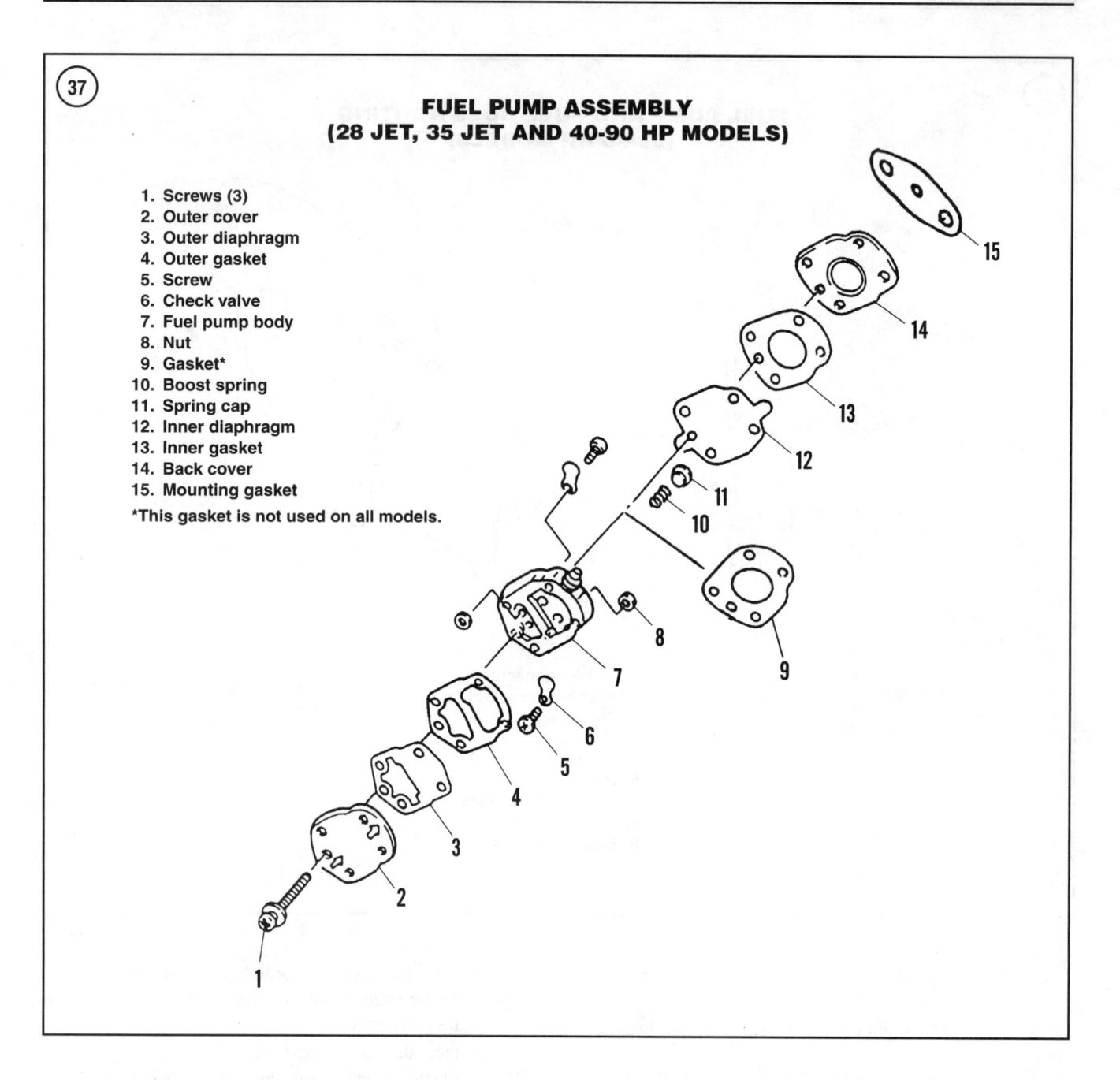

Figure 37. FUEL PUMP ASSEMBLY (28 JET, 35 JET AND 40-90 HP MODELS)

1. Screws (3)
2. Outer cover
3. Outer diaphragm
4. Outer gasket
5. Screw
6. Check valve
7. Fuel pump body
8. Nut
9. Gasket*
10. Boost spring
11. Spring cap
12. Inner diaphragm
13. Inner gasket
14. Back cover
15. Mounting gasket

*This gasket is not used on all models.

pump. The fuel is necessary to simulate the fuel present on the sealing surfaces during operation. Use only enough fuel to wet the inner components and check valve surfaces.

1. Connect a hand-operated vacuum/pressure pump to the *inlet fitting* of the fuel pump. Block the *outlet fitting* with a finger (A, **Figure 38**). Slowly apply pressure until it reaches 50 kPa (7.2 psi.). If the test pressure cannot be attained, the gaskets are faulty or the fuel pump is assembled incorrectly.

2. Connect the vacuum/pressure pump to the *inlet fitting* of the fuel pump. Do not block the *outlet fitting* (B, **Figure 38**). Apply a vacuum until it reaches 30 kPa (4.4 psi). The check valve is faulty if the test vacuum cannot be attained.

3. Connect the vacuum/pressure pump to the *outlet fitting* (C, **Figure 38**) of the fuel pump. Do not block the *inlet fitting*. Slowly apply pressure until it reaches 50 kPa (7.2 psi.). The check valve is faulty if the test pressure cannot be attained.

4. Disassemble, inspect and assemble the fuel pump if it fails the pressure test in Step 1. Disassemble and inspect the check valves and pump body if it fails the tests in Step 2 or

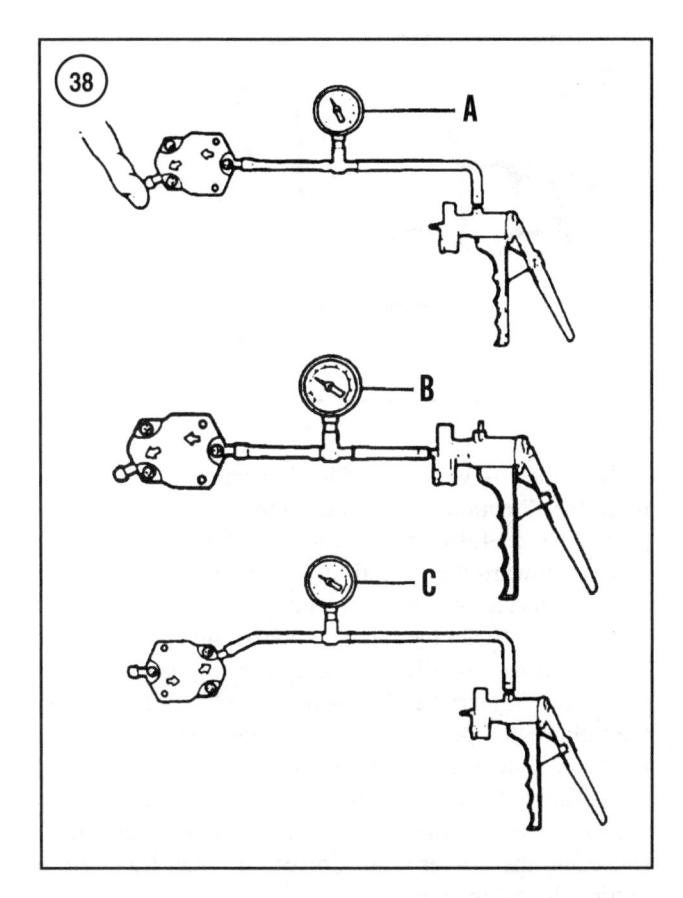

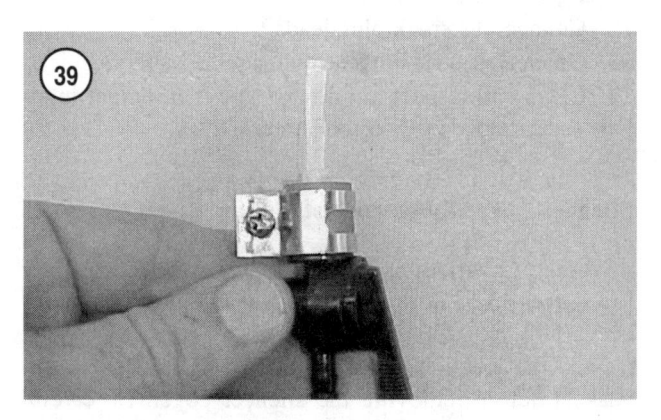

FUEL SYSTEM

203

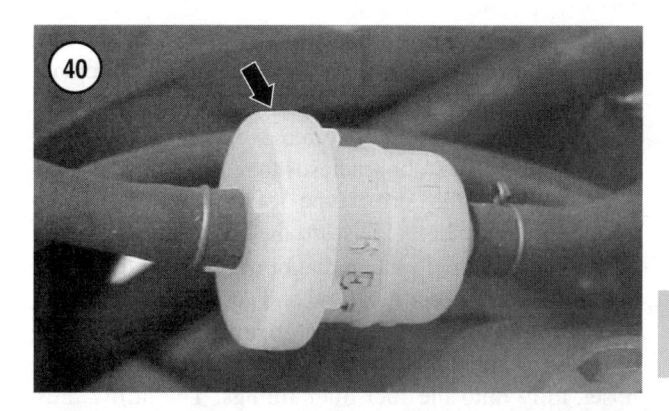

must be removed from the power head and drained so the filter can be cleaned and inspected. Refer to *Integral Fuel Tank* in this chapter for fuel filter removal, inspection and installation procedures.

Some 4 and 5 hp models and all 6 and 8 hp models are equipped with an inline type fuel filter (**Figure 40**). This filter is not serviceable and must be replaced if it is damaged or contaminated. Refer to *Fuel Filter* in Chapter Three to determine the need for replacement. Replace the fuel filter as described in this chapter.

All 20-90 hp models use a canister type fuel filter (**Figure 41**). This filter is fully serviceable. Cleaning and inspection procedures for this type of filter are Chapter Three. If necessary, replace the complete fuel filter assembly as described in this section.

Step 3. Replace the check valves if no faults are found with the pump body. Assemble the pump and retest. Replace the pump body if the pump fails the pressure test again.

Fuel Filter

Three different types of fuel filter are used on the Yamaha outboards in this manual.

All 2-5 hp models are equipped with a fuel filter mounted in the fuel tank fitting (**Figure 39**). The fuel tank

Inline type fuel filter replacement

1. On electric start models, disconnect the battery cables.
2. Disconnect and ground the spark plug lead(s) to prevent accidental starting.
3. Trace the fuel hose from the quick-connector fitting on the lower engine cover to the inline fuel filter (**Figure 40**).
4. Place a shop towel under the fuel filter to capture spilled fuel. Cut and remove plastic locking type clamps

at the fuel filter fittings. Squeeze the ends of spring type clamps and move them away from the fittings. Replace weak or corroded clamps.

5. Carefully twist and pull to remove the hoses from the filter fittings. Cut stubborn hoses to remove them and replace them with the correct type of fuel hose. Drain residual fuel from the hoses. Discard the fuel filter.

6. Refer to the fuel system diagrams (**Figures 16-19**) to determine the correct fuel flow and connection points.

7. Use the arrow on the filter (**Figure 42**) to determine the direction of fuel flow through the filter, then push the hoses fully onto the fuel filter fittings. The arrow must point toward the hose leading to the fuel pump or carburetor.

8. Install new plastic locking type hose clamps onto the fuel hose. Tighten the clamps until the hoses fit snug on the fittings. To open the spring type clamps, squeeze the ends together, slide them over the fittings, then release the ends. Tug on the hoses to verify a secure connection.

9. Route the fuel hoses and position the filter to prevent contact with any moving components.

10. Observe the fuel filter, fittings and hoses while squeezing the primer bulb. Correct any fuel leak before putting the engine into service.

11. Connect the spark plug leads.

12. On electric start models, connect the battery cables.

Canister type fuel filter replacement

1. On electric start models, disconnect the battery cables.

2. Disconnect and ground the spark plug lead(s) to prevent accidental starting.

3. Trace the fuel hose from the quick-connector fitting on the lower engine cover to the fuel filter assembly (**Figure 41**).

4. Place a shop towel under the fuel filter to capture spilled fuel. Cut and remove plastic locking type clamps at the fuel filter fittings. Squeeze the ends of spring type clamps and move them away from the fittings. Replace weak or corroded clamps.

5. Carefully twist and pull to remove the hoses from the filter fittings. Cut stubborn hoses to remove them and replace them with the correct type of fuel hose. Drain residual fuel from the hoses.

6. Remove the fasteners and pull the filter assembly from the power head or filter mounting bracket.

7. Fit the replacement filter assembly to the mount on the bracket or power head. Install the filter assembly mounting bolts and nuts, and tighten them securely.

8. Refer to **Figures 20-23** to determine the correct fuel flow and connection points for the specified model.

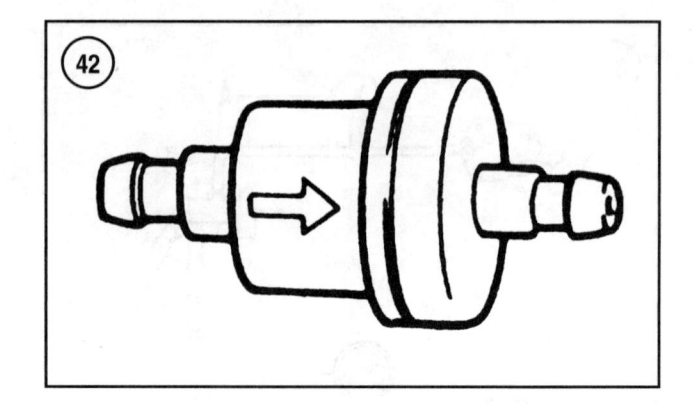

9. Note the arrows near the filter housing fittings to determine the direction of fuel flow through the filter, then push the hoses fully onto the fuel filter fittings. The arrow pointing toward the hose fitting is the outlet fitting. The hose connected to this fitting must be connected to the hose leading to the fuel pump or carburetor.

10. Install new plastic locking type hose clamps on the fuel hose. Tighten the clamps until the hoses fit snug on the fittings. To open spring type clamps, squeeze the ends together, slide them over the fittings, then release the ends. Tug on the hose to verify a secure connection.

11. Observe the fuel filter, fittings and hoses while squeezing the primer bulb. Correct any fuel leak before putting the engine into service.

12. Connect the spark plug leads.

13. On electric start models, connect the battery cables.

14. Clean and inspect the filter element at regular intervals as described in Chapter Three.

Silencer Cover Removal/Installation

Numerous variations exist for the silencer cover. Refer to **Figures 43-53** during the removal and installation procedures.

Note the location and orientation of all fasteners and gaskets before removing the silencer cover. Be careful when pulling the cover from the engine to avoid damaging the cover gasket or seal. Always replace torn or damaged gaskets during assembly.

1. Disconnect and ground the spark plug lead(s) to prevent accidental starting.

2. On electric start models, disconnect the battery cables.

3A. On 2 hp models, remove the screw (1, **Figure 43**) and throttle lever knob (2). Disconnect the black and white stop switch wires (4, **Figure 43**). Pull the choke knob (6, **Figure 43**) and O-ring (7) from the cover.

3B. On 6 and 8 hp models, remove the four screw (5, **Figure 46**) and upper cover from the silencer.

FUEL SYSTEM

SILENCER COVER AND CARBURETOR (2 HP MODEL)

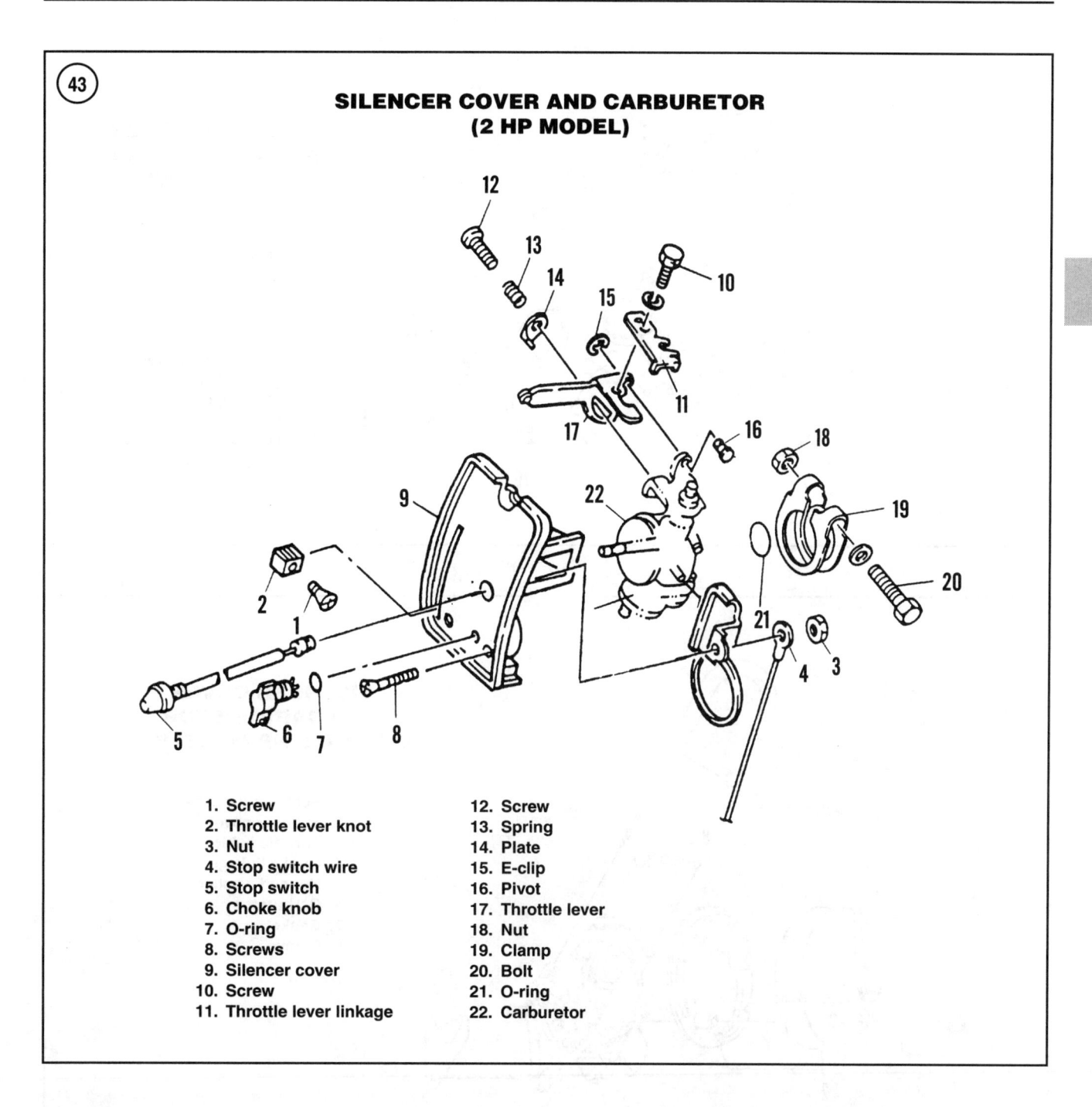

1. Screw
2. Throttle lever knot
3. Nut
4. Stop switch wire
5. Stop switch
6. Choke knob
7. O-ring
8. Screws
9. Silencer cover
10. Screw
11. Throttle lever linkage
12. Screw
13. Spring
14. Plate
15. E-clip
16. Pivot
17. Throttle lever
18. Nut
19. Clamp
20. Bolt
21. O-ring
22. Carburetor

3C. On 9.9 and 15 hp models, remove the screw (1, **Figure 47**) and washer (2), then pull the choke lever (3) from the silencer cover (5).

NOTE
The bolts that hold the silencer cover on 3 and 6-15 hp models also secure the carburetors to the intake manifold. To avoid unnecessary damage to the carburetor mounting gasket or seal, have an assistant support the carburetor until the bolts can be temporarily reinstalled.

4A. On 2 hp models, remove the two screws (8, **Figure 43**) and the silencer cover (9).

4B. On 4 and 5 hp models, remove the two screws and washer (1, **Figure 45**) and the silencer cover (2).

4C. On 3 and 6-15 hp models, have an assistant support the carburetor, then remove the two bolts (1, **Figure 44**, 1,

CHAPTER FIVE

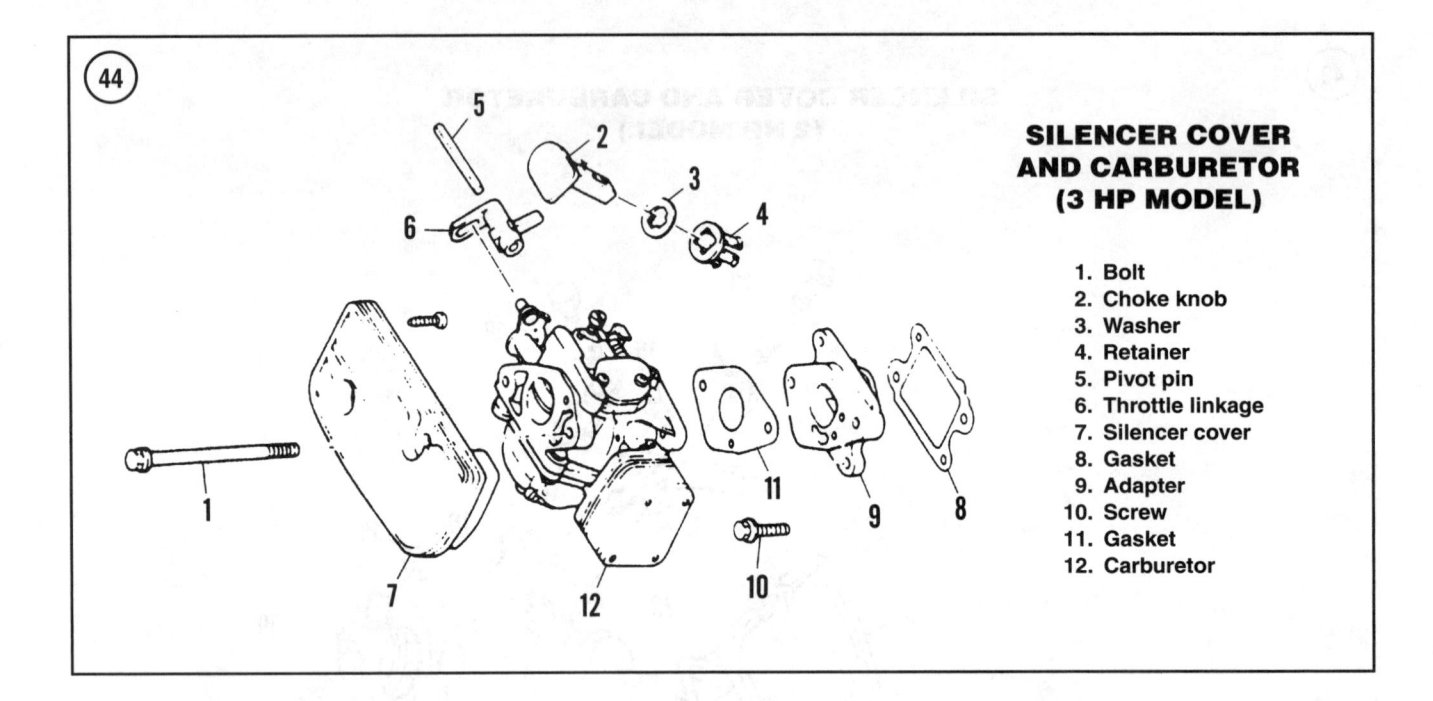

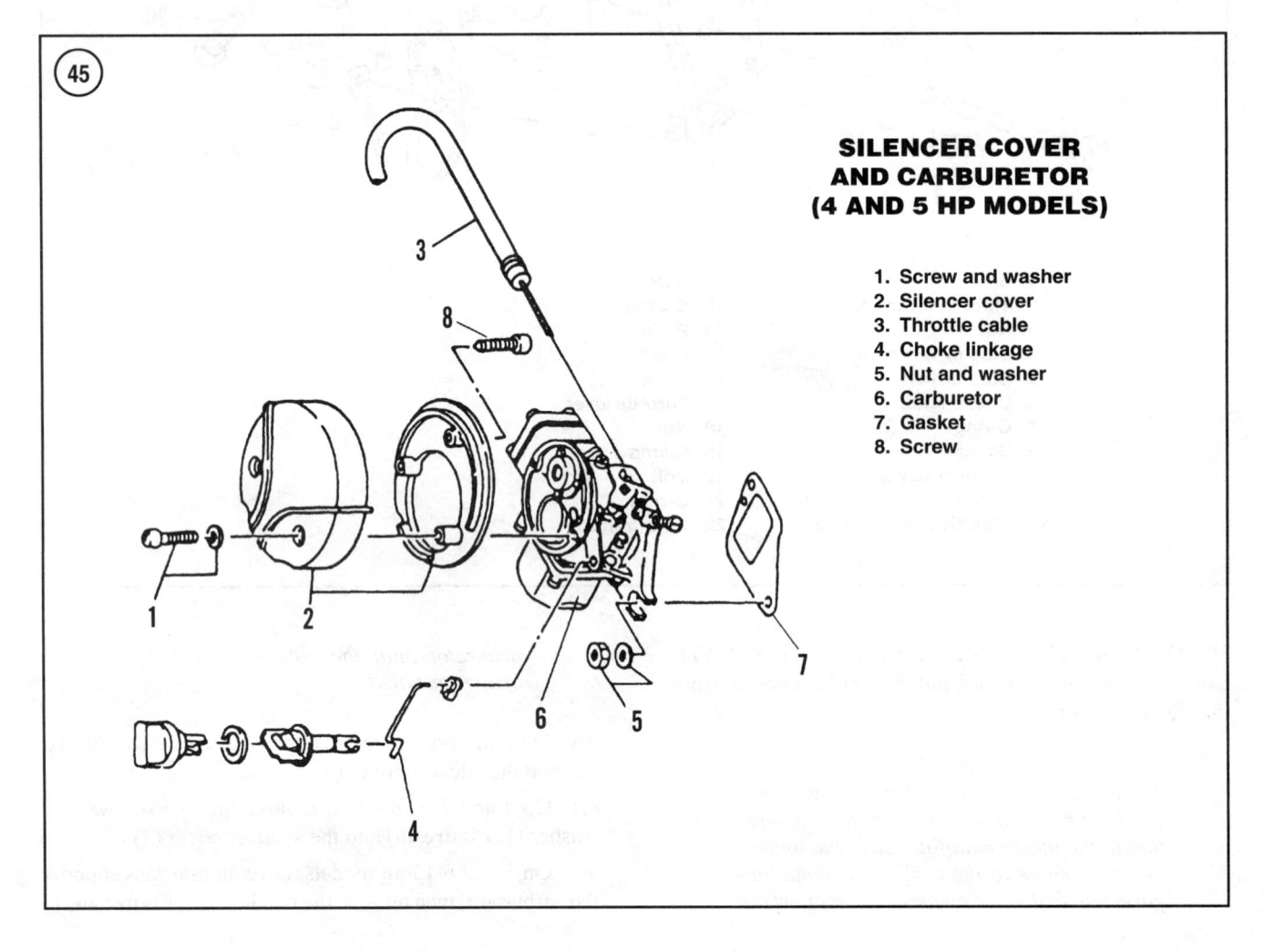

⑭ SILENCER COVER AND CARBURETOR (3 HP MODEL)

1. Bolt
2. Choke knob
3. Washer
4. Retainer
5. Pivot pin
6. Throttle linkage
7. Silencer cover
8. Gasket
9. Adapter
10. Screw
11. Gasket
12. Carburetor

⑮ SILENCER COVER AND CARBURETOR (4 AND 5 HP MODELS)

1. Screw and washer
2. Silencer cover
3. Throttle cable
4. Choke linkage
5. Nut and washer
6. Carburetor
7. Gasket
8. Screw

FUEL SYSTEM

⑦ 46

**SILENCER COVER AND CARBURETOR
(6 AND 8 HP MODELS)**

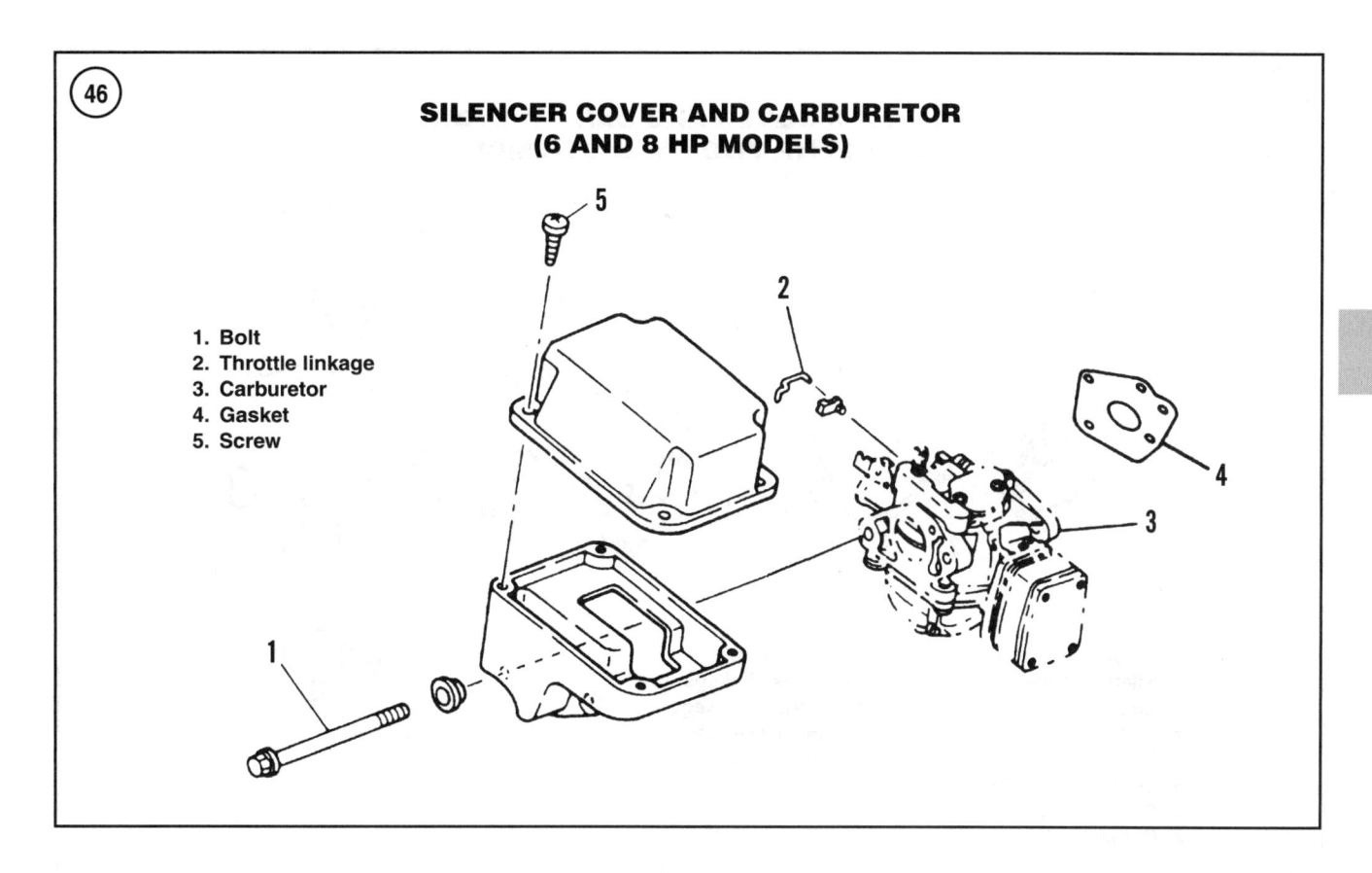

1. Bolt
2. Throttle linkage
3. Carburetor
4. Gasket
5. Screw

⑦ 47

**SILENCER COVER AND CARBURETORS
(9.9 AND 15 HP MODELS)**

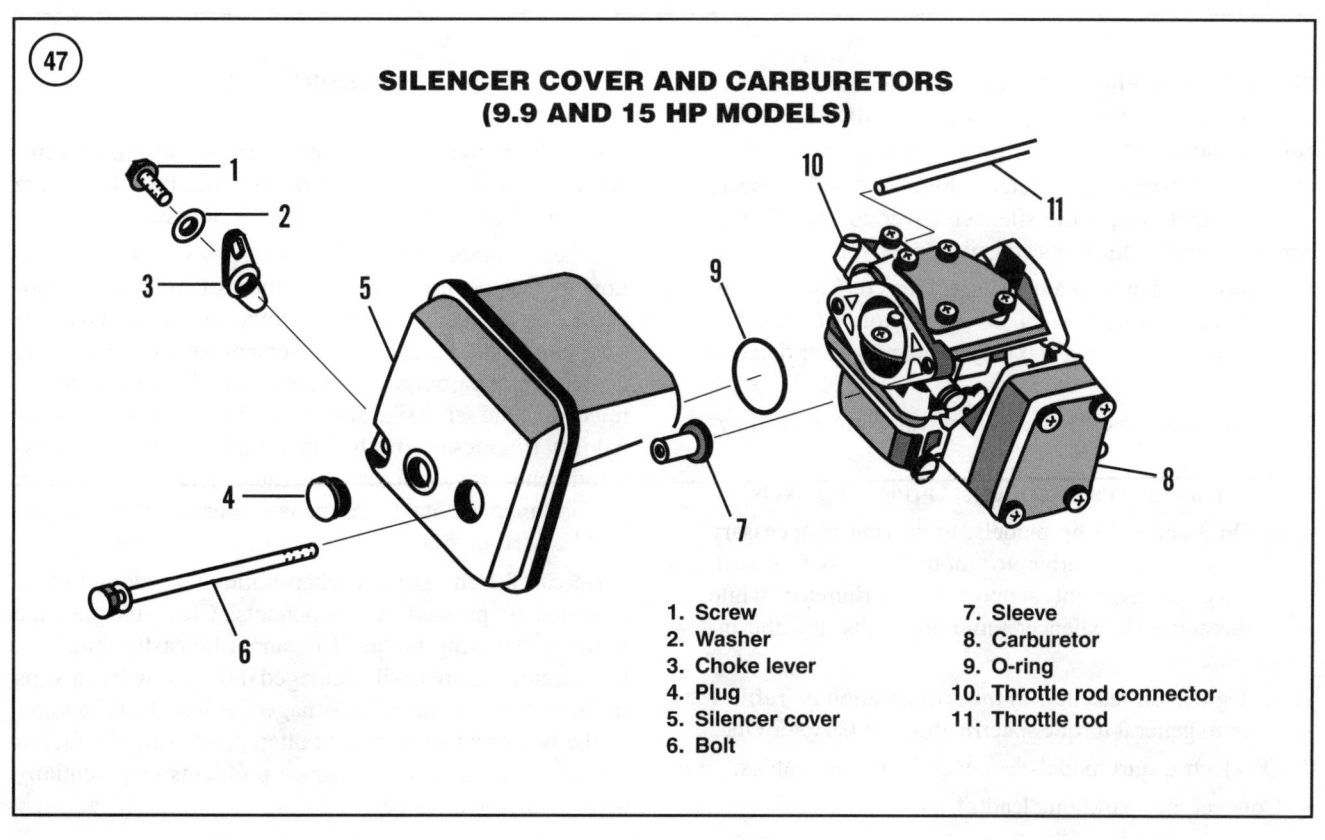

1. Screw
2. Washer
3. Choke lever
4. Plug
5. Silencer cover
6. Bolt
7. Sleeve
8. Carburetor
9. O-ring
10. Throttle rod connector
11. Throttle rod

208 CHAPTER FIVE

**48 SILENCER COVER AND CARBURETORS
(20 AND 25 HP TWO-CYLINDER MODELS)**

1. Screw and washer
2. Silencer cover
3. Seal
4. Gasket
5. Bolt and washer
6. Screw and washer
7. Silencer cover bracket
8. Choke knob
9. Choke linkage
10. Choke linkage
11. Throttle linkage
12. Hose clamps
13. Fuel hose
14. Seals
15. Gaskets

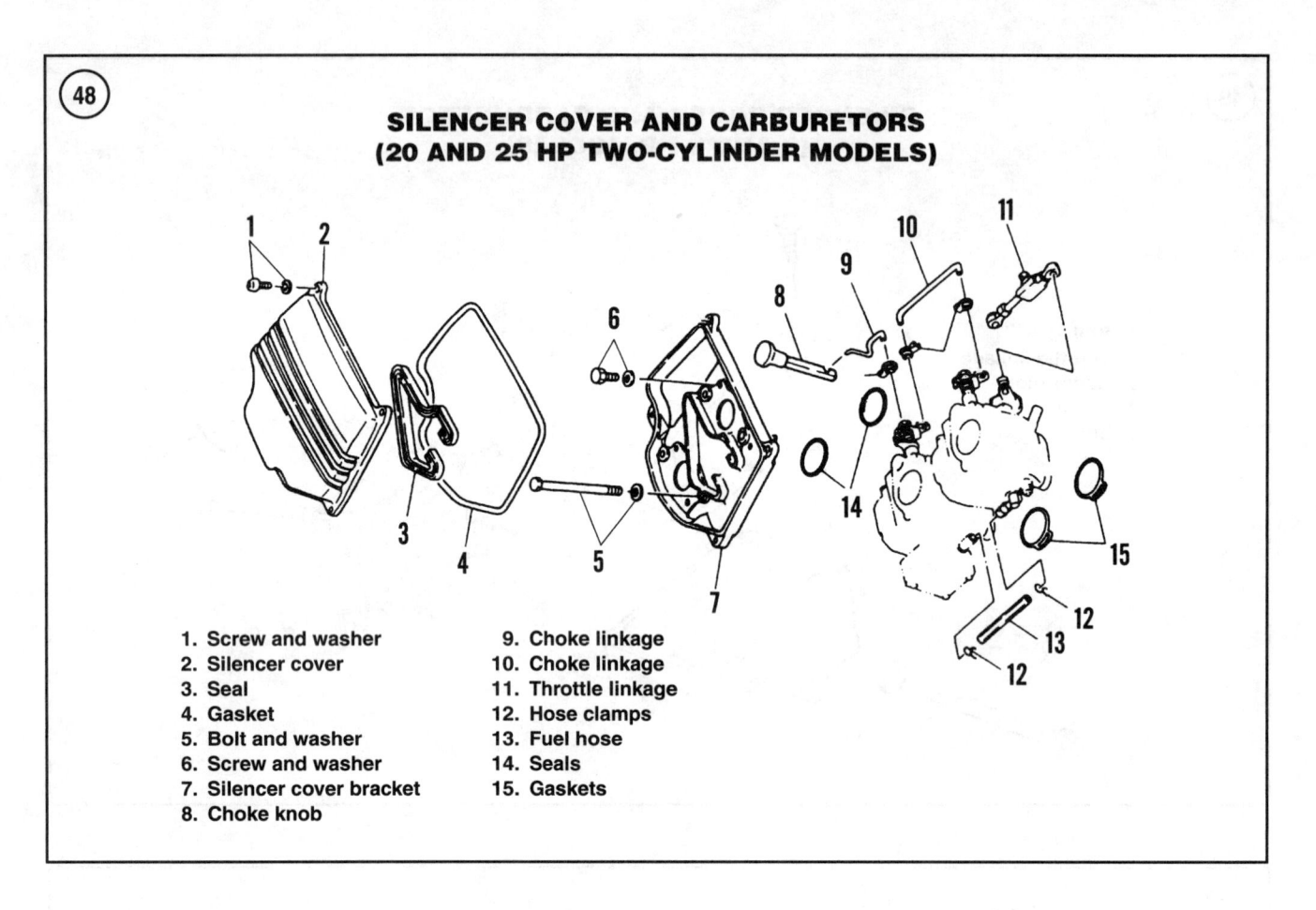

Figure 46 or 6, **Figure 47**) from the silencer cover. Remove the cover, then temporarily reinstall the bolts to hold the carburetor.

4D. On 20-90 hp models, refer to **Figures 48-53** to locate the bolts that secure the silencer cover to the silencer bracket. Remove the bolts and silencer cover.

5. Remove and inspect any seals, O-rings or gaskets from the silencer cover, bracket or carburetor. Replace the seals, gaskets or O-ring(s) if they are damaged or deteriorated.

6. Installation is the reverse of removal. Note the following:

  a. Replace any damaged seals, O-rings or gaskets.
  b. On 3 and 6-15 hp models, to prevent unnecessary damage to the carburetor mounting gasket or seal, have an assistant support the carburetor while threading the silencer mounting bolts into the intake.
  c. Tighten all fasteners to the specification in **Table 1** or to general torque specifications in Chapter One.

7. On electric start models, connect the battery cables.
8. Connect the spark plug lead(s).

CARBURETOR

Pay close attention when removing and installing components, especially carburetors, to avoid installing them in the wrong locations. Mark them if necessary.

When disassembling carburetors, pay very close attention to the location and orientation of internal components. Jets normally have a jet number stamped on the side or opening end. Purchase replacement jets from a Yamaha dealership or carburetor specialty shop. Replacement jets must have the same size and shape of opening as the original jets. Engines used at higher altitudes or in extreme environments may require alternate jets for optimum performance. Contact a Yamaha dealership if the engine will be used in these environments.

Be careful and patient when removing jets and other threaded or pressed-in components. Clean the passage without removing the jet if it cannot be easily removed. Carburetor jets are easily damaged if the screwdriver slips in the slot. Never install a damaged jet into the carburetor as the fuel or air flow may be altered. Altering the fuel or air flow can cause performance problems or potentially serious engine damage.

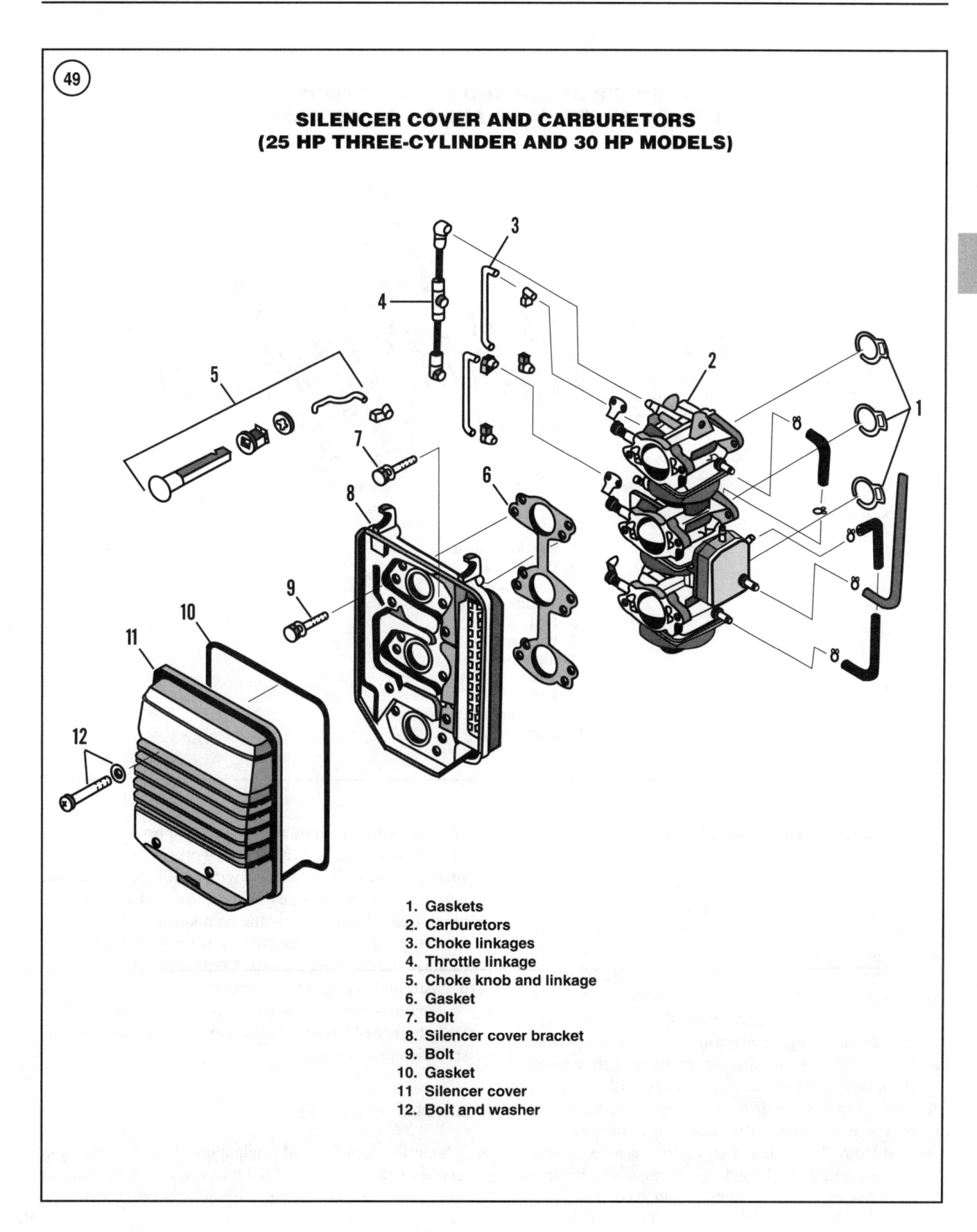

FUEL SYSTEM

**SILENCER COVER AND CARBURETORS
(25 HP THREE-CYLINDER AND 30 HP MODELS)**

1. Gaskets
2. Carburetors
3. Choke linkages
4. Throttle linkage
5. Choke knob and linkage
6. Gasket
7. Bolt
8. Silencer cover bracket
9. Bolt
10. Gasket
11 Silencer cover
12. Bolt and washer

CHAPTER FIVE

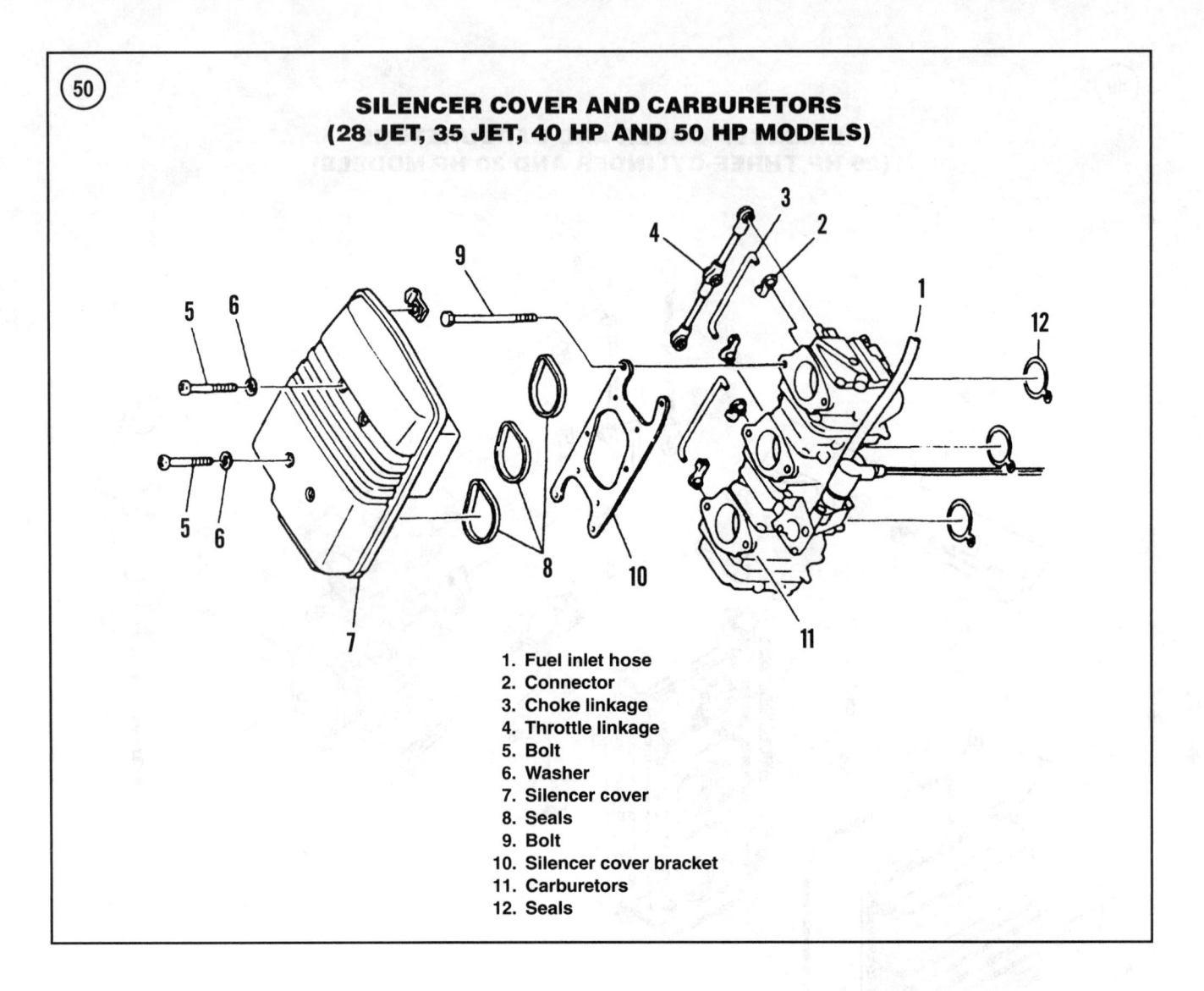

SILENCER COVER AND CARBURETORS (28 JET, 35 JET, 40 HP AND 50 HP MODELS)

1. Fuel inlet hose
2. Connector
3. Choke linkage
4. Throttle linkage
5. Bolt
6. Washer
7. Silencer cover
8. Seals
9. Bolt
10. Silencer cover bracket
11. Carburetors
12. Seals

To avoid fuel or air leaks, replace all gaskets, seals or O-rings when a fuel system component is disassembled.

The most important step in carburetor repair is the cleaning process. Use a good quality solvent to remove varnish-like deposits that commonly form in fuel systems. Spray-type carburetor cleaners available at automotive parts stores are effective in removing most stubborn deposits. Never use solvent that is not suitable for aluminum material. Some solvents may irreparably damage the carburetor casting. Remove all plastic or rubber components from the fuel pump, fuel filter or carburetor before cleaning them with solvent. Carefully scrape gasket material from the components with a razor scraper. Work carefully to avoid removing material or scratching sealing surfaces. Use a stiff bristle brush and solvent to remove deposits from the carburetor fuel bowl. Never use a wire brush as delicate sealing surfaces can be damaged. Use compressed air to blow out all passages and orifices (**Figure 1**). A piece of straw from a broom works well to clean out small passages. Never use stiff wire for this purpose as the wire may enlarge the size of the passage and alter the carburetor calibration. Allow the component to soak in the solvent if the deposits are difficult to remove. Never compromise the cleaning process. Continue to clean until all deposits and debris are removed.

Numerous variations exist for carburetor mounting. Refer to **Figures 43-53** during the carburetor removal and installation procedures.

Installation/Removal

Note the location and orientation of all fasteners and gaskets before removing the silencer cover. Be careful when pulling the cover from the engine to avoid damaging

FUEL SYSTEM

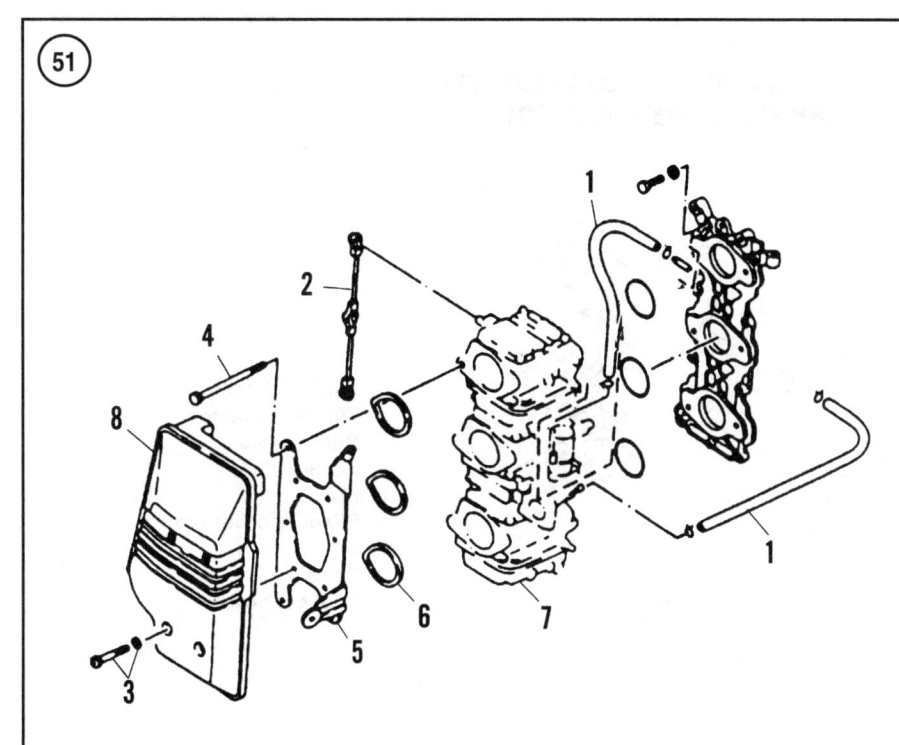

51

SILENCER COVER AND CARBURETORS (60 AND 70 HP MODELS)

1. Fuel inlet hose
2. Throttle linkage
3. Bolt and washer
4. Bolt
5. Silencer cover bracket
6. Seals
7. Carburetors
8. Silencer cover

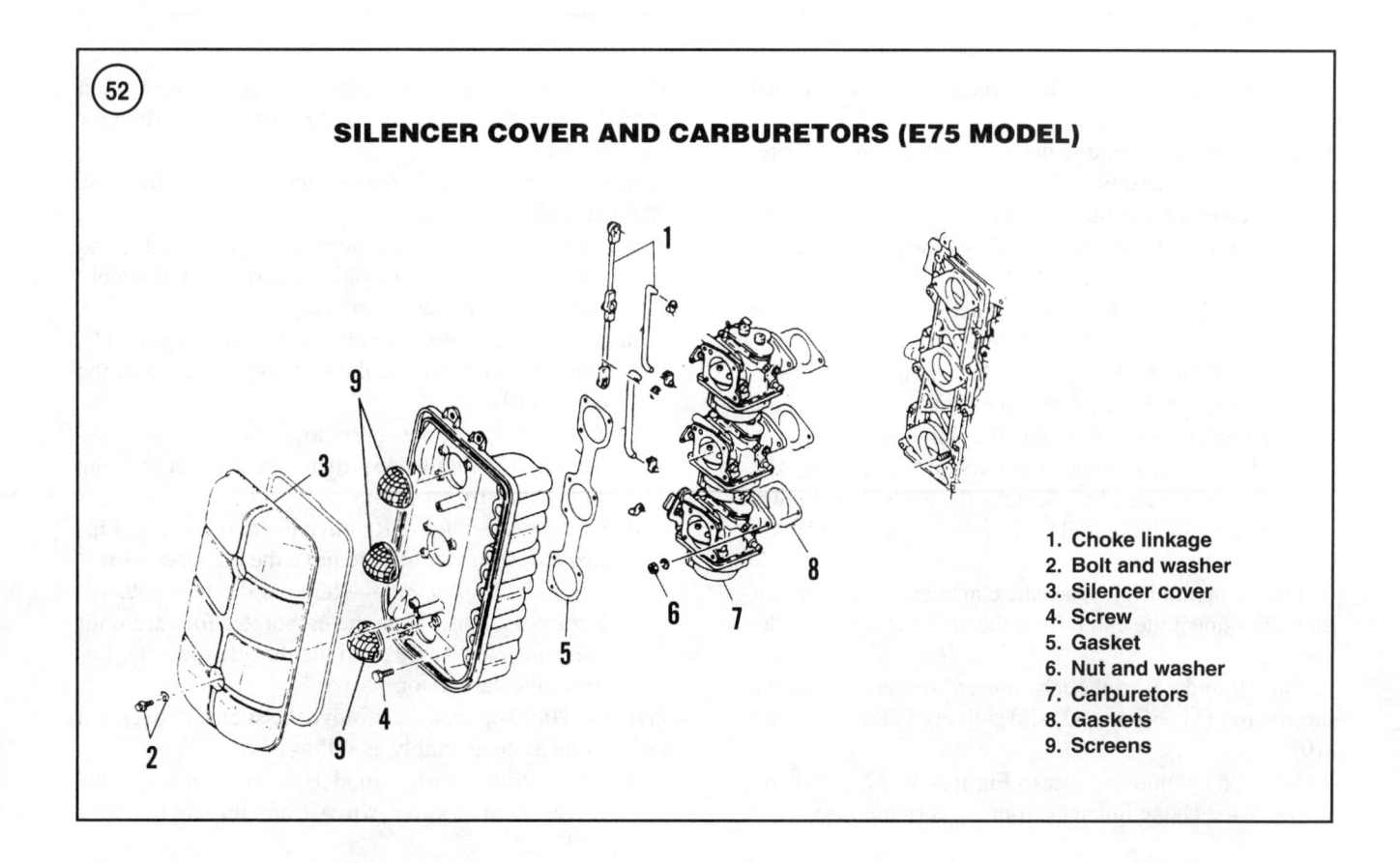

52

SILENCER COVER AND CARBURETORS (E75 MODEL)

1. Choke linkage
2. Bolt and washer
3. Silencer cover
4. Screw
5. Gasket
6. Nut and washer
7. Carburetors
8. Gaskets
9. Screens

SILENCER COVER AND CARBURETORS (75-90 HP [EXCEPT E75] MODELS)

1. Fuel inlet hose
2. Throttle linkage
3. Bolt and washer
4. Seals
5. Bolt
6. Silencer cover bracket
7. Carburetors
8. Seals
9. Silencer cover

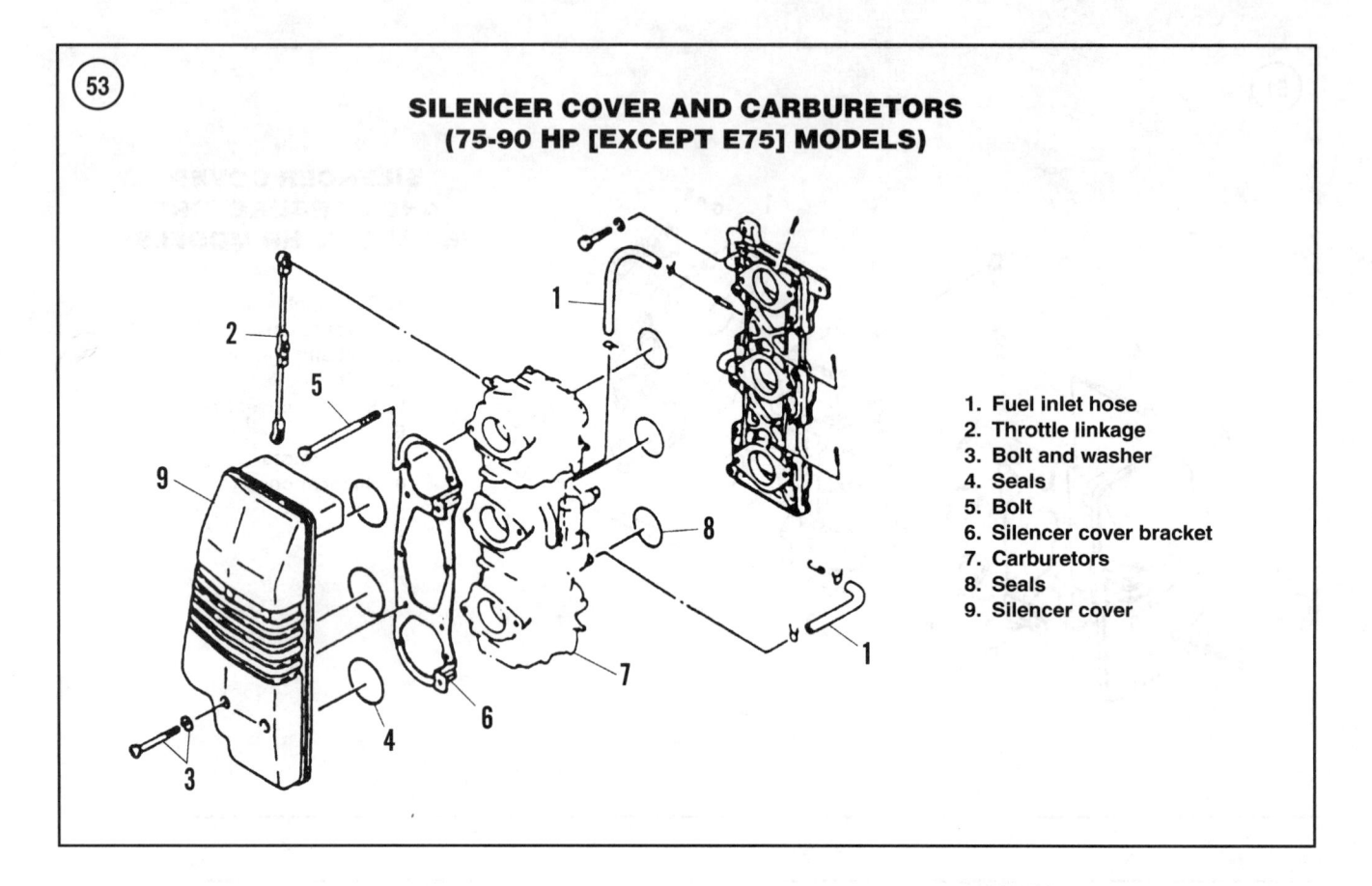

the cover gasket or seal. Always replace torn or damaged gaskets during assembly.

1. Disconnect and ground the spark plug lead(s) to prevent accidental starting.
2. On electric start models, disconnect the battery cables.
3. Place a suitable container or shop towel under the carburetor(s) to capture spilled fuel.
4A. On 2-5 hp models, close the fuel valve, then pull the fuel hose from the carburetor fitting.
4B. On 6-90 hp models, remove the clamp(s), then carefully pull the fuel hose(s) from the carburetor fittings.
5. Drain residual fuel from the disconnected hose(s).
6. On 2 hp models, remove the screw (12, **Figure 43**), spring (13) and plate (14). Remove the E-clip (15, **Figure 43**), then pull the linkage (11), throttle lever (17) and pivot (16).
7. On 3-5 hp models, loosen the clamp and anchor screw, then disconnect the cable from the carburetor throttle lever.
8. On 9.9 and 15 hp models, loosen the screw until the throttle rod (11, **Figure 47**) slides freely in the connector (10).
9. On 3-75 hp models, refer to **Figures 44-52**, then carefully pry the choke linkages from the carburetor(s).

10. On 20-90 hp models, refer to **Figure 48-53**, then carefully pry the throttle linkage from the carburetor throttle levers.
11A. On 2-15 hp models, remove the carburetor from the intake manifold as follows:
   a. *2 hp models*—Loosen the bolt (20, **Figure 43**) and nut (18), then carefully pull the carburetor assembly from the reed housing/intake.
   b. *3 hp models*—Remove the two bolts (1, **Figure 44**), then carefully remove the carburetor (12) from the adapter (9).
   c. *4 and 5 hp models*—Remove the two nuts and washers (5, **Figure 45**), then carefully remove the carburetor (6).
   d. *6 and 8 hp models*—Remove the two bolts (1, **Figure 46**), then carefully remove the carburetor (3).
   e. *9.9 and 15 hp models*—Remove the two bolts (6, **Figure 47**), then slide the carburetor forward until the connector is free from the throttle rod (11). Remove the carburetor.
11B. On 20-90 hp models, remove the silencer cover and carburetors as an assembly as follows:
   a. On Prime-Start models, disconnect the electrothermal valve wires from the engine wire

FUEL SYSTEM

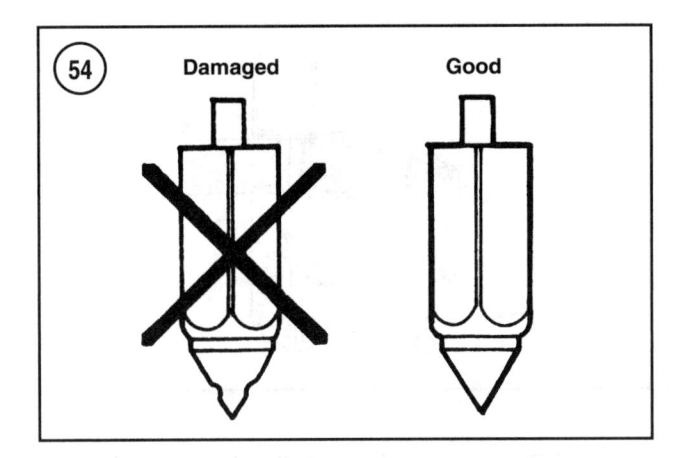

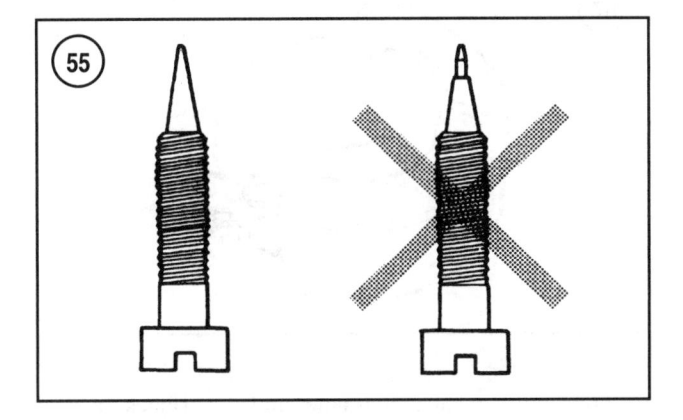

54 Damaged   Good

55

harness connections. Locate the hose fitting next to the electrothermal valve. Trace the hose to its connection onto the top of the No. 1 carburetor or intake manifold. Disconnect the hose from both fittings.

   b. Refer to **Figures 48-53** to locate the silencer bracket and carburetor mounting bolts.

   c. Support the silencer bracket while loosening the four or six mounting bolts.

   d. Remove the two or three carburetors and silencer bracket as an assembly. Mark the carburetor mounting location on each carburetor. Remove the bolts and separate the carburetors.

12. Remove the gasket, seal or O-ring from the carburetor mount. Do not reuse the carburetor mounting gaskets, seals or O-rings. Carefully scrape residual gasket material from the carburetor or intake manifold mating surfaces. Do not scratch the mating surfaces.

13. Installation is the reverse of removal. Note the following:

   a. Install new gaskets, seals and O-rings on the carburetor-to-intake mating surfaces. Make sure the openings in the gaskets match openings in the intake and carburetor.

   b. On 20-90 hp models, fit the mounting bolts through the silencer bracket and carburetors, then install the carburetors and bracket as an assembly.

   c. Tighten the mounting bolts to the specification in **Table 1** or Chapter One.

   d. Connect the fuel hoses to the carburetor fittings and clamps as described in this chapter under *Fuel Hose Connectors*.

   e. On 25-90 hp Prime-Start models, connect the electrothermal valve leads onto the engine wire harness connections.

14. Install the silencer cover as described in this chapter.

15. Observe all fuel hoses and connections while opening the fuel valve or squeezing the primer bulb. Repair fuel leaks before proceeding.

16. Perform applicable carburetor synchronization and adjustments as described in Chapter Four.

17. On electric start models, connect the battery cables.

18. Connect the spark plug lead(s).

Inspection

A clean working environment is essential for carburetor repairs. Mark all hose connections before removing them from the carburetor(s). On multi-carburetor engines, match each carburetor to its respective cylinder and repair *one* carburetor at a time.

Place all components on a clean work surface as they are removed from the carburetor and cleaned. Arrange these components in a manner consistent with the illustrations. This will save time and help ensure a proper repair.

Use a solvent designed for carburetor cleaning to clean all deposits from the carburetor passages, jets, orifices and float bowl. Use compressed air to blow through passages to help remove contaminants.

Carefully remove jets from the carburetor. Use the proper size screwdriver and maintain downward force while removing jets. If jets cannot be easily removed, soak the carburetor in solvent for several hours before attempting to remove them. Clean the carburetor without removing the jets if they are especially difficult to remove and the carburetor has a significant amount of deposits or corrosion. Replace the jets if they are damaged during removal.

Inspect the fuel inlet valve upon removal for damaged sealing surfaces (**Figure 54**). Inspect the valve seat for pitting, worn or irregular surfaces. Replace worn or damaged components. On some carburetors the seat is not available separately and the carburetor must be replaced if the seat is faulty.

Inspect the pilot screw for worn or damaged surfaces (**Figure 55**). Damage in this area is usually caused by excessive force when seating the screw. If the screw is damaged, inspect the seat in the screw opening for damage. Replace the screw if it is damaged. Replace the carburetor if the seat is damaged. The engine will not operate properly at lower speeds with a damaged screw or seat.

Use an accurate ruler to check the float height or drop settings (**Figure 56**). Set the float exactly as specified to help ensure maximum performance and durability. Float settings have a profound affect on fuel calibration.

Inspect the float (**Figure 57**) for fuel saturation and worn or damaged surfaces. Some floats are constructed with a translucent material that allows it to be visually inspected for saturation. On models using nontranslucent floats, gently press a thumbnail against the float surface. Remove the thumbnail and inspect the thumbnail indentation in the float. Replace the float if fuel appears in the indentation.

The float height can be adjusted without the carburetor being completely disassembled. The electrothermal valve can be serviced without the carburetor being removed or disassembled. Refer to the instructions in the disassembly/assembly procedures.

Disassembly/Assembly

2 hp models

Refer to **Figure 58** for this procedure.
1. Remove the silencer cover and carburetor as described in this chapter.
2. Position the carburetor over a container suitable for holding fuel, then remove the bowl drain screw (8, **Figure 58**) and gasket (9). Discard the drain screw gasket. Drain all fuel from the float bowl.
3. Remove the nut, lockwasher and plain washer from the choke valve shaft (6, **Figure 58**). Remove the shaft and choke valve.
4. Remove the throttle screw (10, **Figure 58**), throttle link bracket (19), cap (20), spacer (22) and throttle plunger (12).
5. Note the E-clip groove position on the throttle plunger (**Figure 59**). The E-clip must be installed in the original groove during assembly. Remove the E-clip (**Figure 60**), then separate the throttle plunger from the mixing chamber screw. Carefully pull the throttle valve from the throttle bore.
6. Remove the two screws (23, **Figure 58**) and float bowl (24). Remove and discard the gasket (25, **Figure 58**).
7. Remove the screw (26, **Figure 58**), then lift the float (27) and float pin (28) from the carburetor.
8. Remove the main nozzle (31, **Figure 58**), then carefully remove the main jet (**Figure 61**) from the nozzle.

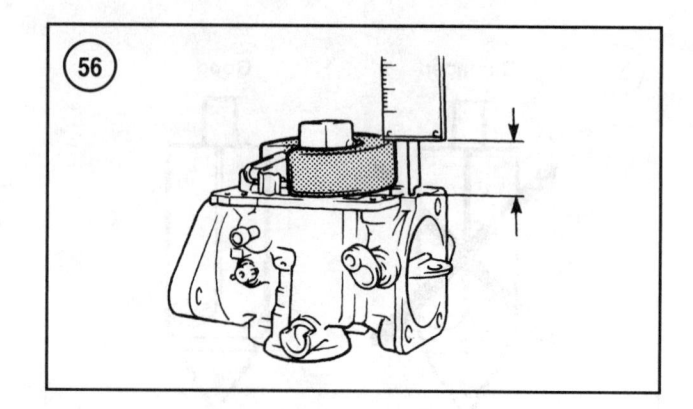

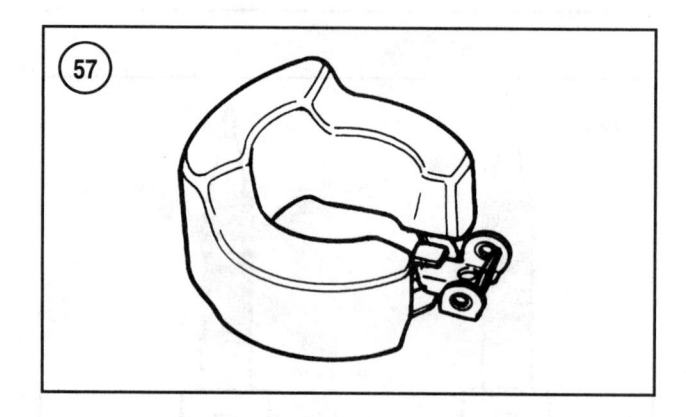

9. Thoroughly clean all passages and all surfaces. Inspect all components as described earlier in this section. Replace worn or damaged components.
10. Assembly is the reverse of disassembly. Note the following:
   a. Install new gaskets and seals in all locations.
   b. Apply Loctite 242 to the threads of the throttle screw (10, **Figure 58**).
   c. Install the E-clip in the same groove from which it was removed. If the E-clip was missing or dislodged before the position was checked, install the E-clip in the second groove.
   d. Apply a light coat of water-resistant grease to the throttle shaft and idle adjusting screw spring.
   e. Before installing the float bowl, adjust the float height as described in Step 11.
11. Adjust the float height as follows:
   a. Place the carburetor on a work surface with the bowl side facing up.
   b. Gently lift and drop the float several times to verify proper seating of the inlet needle.
   c. Measure the float height at the points indicated in A, **Figure 62**. If the float height is not in the range in **Table 3**, remove the float and gently bend the float tab (B, **Figure 62**) until the measurement is correct.

FUEL SYSTEM

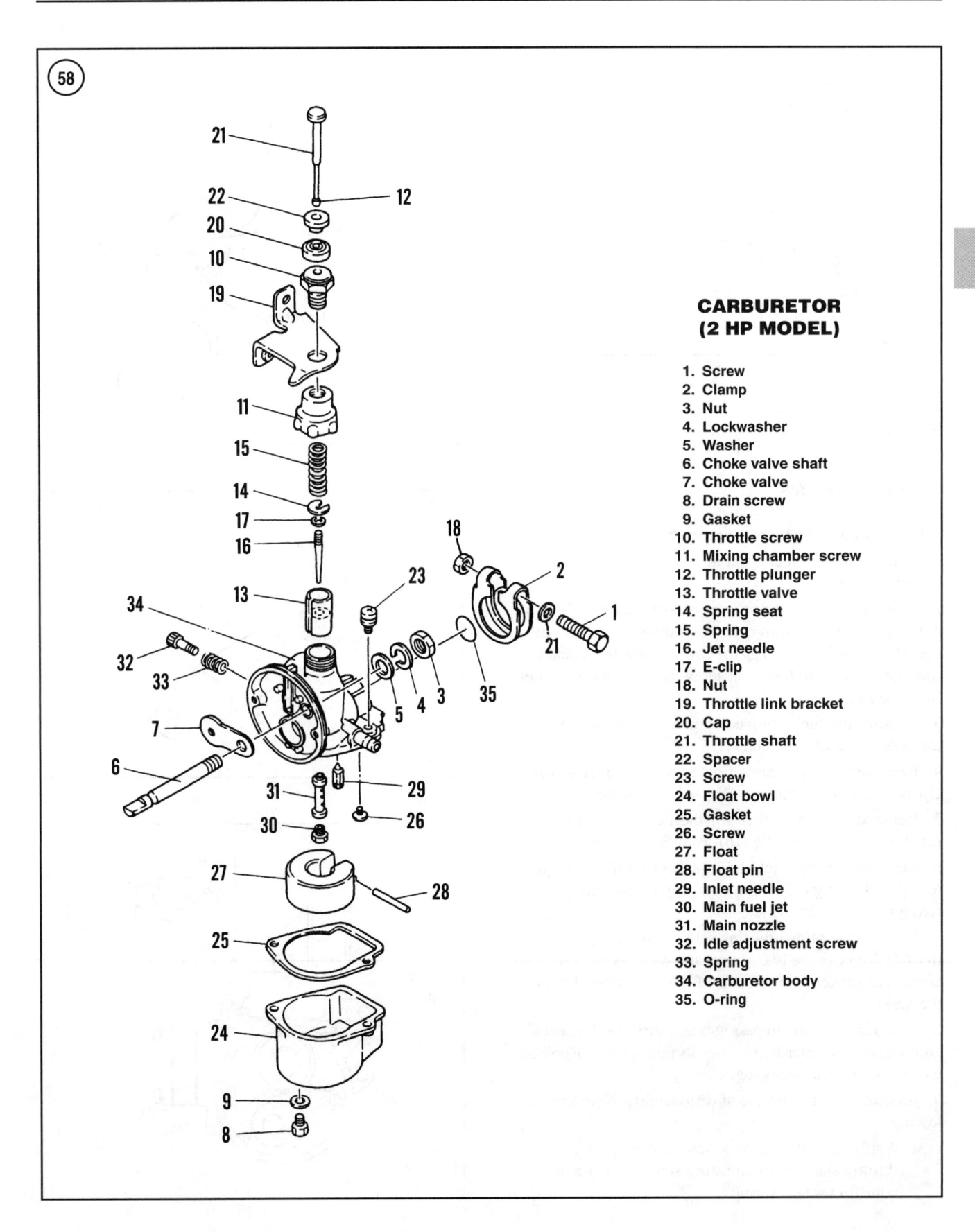

58

CARBURETOR (2 HP MODEL)

1. Screw
2. Clamp
3. Nut
4. Lockwasher
5. Washer
6. Choke valve shaft
7. Choke valve
8. Drain screw
9. Gasket
10. Throttle screw
11. Mixing chamber screw
12. Throttle plunger
13. Throttle valve
14. Spring seat
15. Spring
16. Jet needle
17. E-clip
18. Nut
19. Throttle link bracket
20. Cap
21. Throttle shaft
22. Spacer
23. Screw
24. Float bowl
25. Gasket
26. Screw
27. Float
28. Float pin
29. Inlet needle
30. Main fuel jet
31. Main nozzle
32. Idle adjustment screw
33. Spring
34. Carburetor body
35. O-ring

216

CHAPTER FIVE

---

⑤⁹ Clip position

Lean ↑
← 1st groove
← 2nd
← 3rd
← 4th
← 5th
Rich ↓

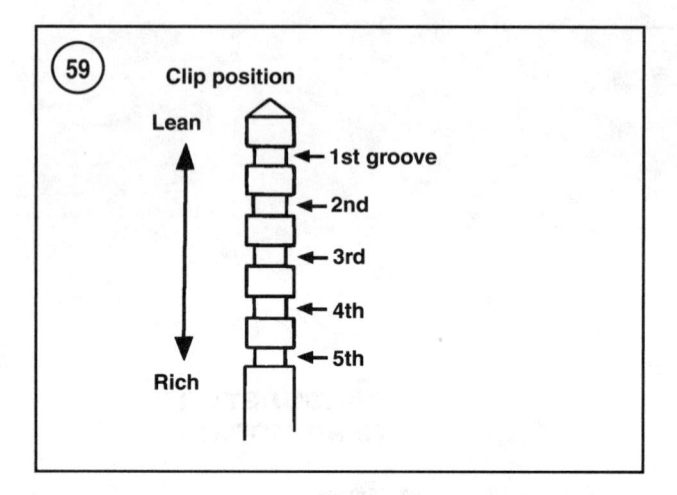

12. Install the carburetor and silencer cover as described in this chapter.

3, 6 and 8 hp models

Refer to **Figure 63** for this procedure.

1. Remove the silencer cover and carburetor as described in this chapter.

2. Position the carburetor over a container suitable for holding fuel, then remove the bowl drain screw and gasket. The screw is located on the corner of the bowl near the fuel pump. Discard the drain screw gasket. Drain all fuel from the float bowl.

3. Remove the fuel pump components from the carburetor as described in this chapter.

4. Remove the four screws, float bowl (8, **Figure 63**) and O-ring from the carburetor. Discard the O-ring.

5. Remove the screw, then lift the float (9, **Figure 63**), pivot pin and inlet needle (16) from the carburetor.

6. Remove the main jet and nozzle (10 and 11, **Figure 63**). Pull the plug (13, **Figure 63**) from the opening, then remove the pilot jet (12).

7. Remove the pilot adjusting screw and spring (15, **Figure 63**). Remove the two screws and washers, then lift the cover and gasket from the top of the carburetor. Discard the gasket.

8. Thoroughly clean all passages and surfaces. Inspect all components as described earlier in this section. Replace worn or damaged components.

9. Assembly is the reverse of disassembly. Note the following:

a. Apply a light coat of water-resistant grease to the throttle shaft, pilot adjusting screw spring and idle adjusting screw spring.

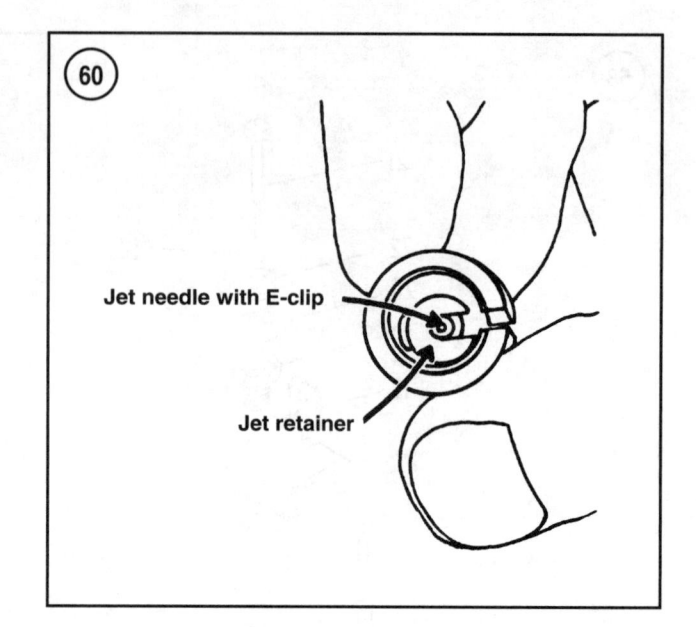

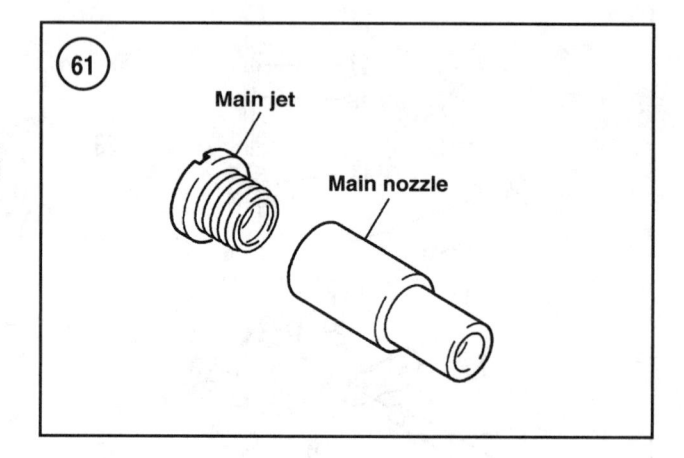

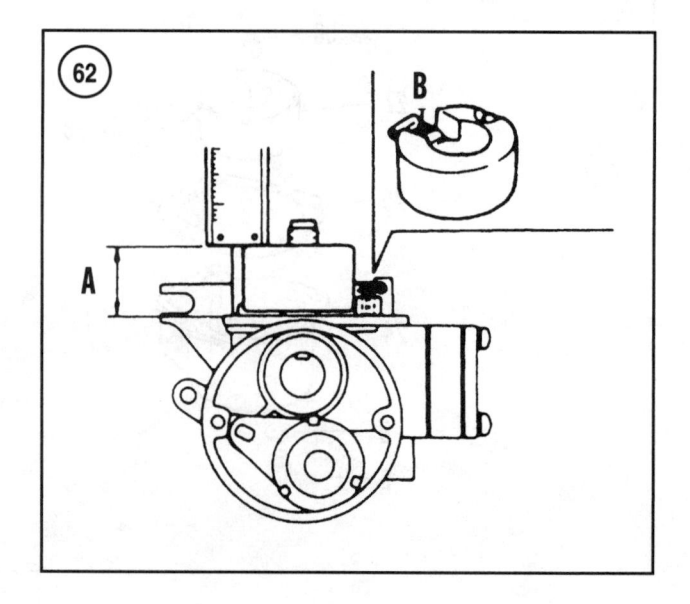

---

⑥⁰ Jet needle with E-clip
Jet retainer

⑥¹ Main jet
Main nozzle

⑥² A B

FUEL SYSTEM

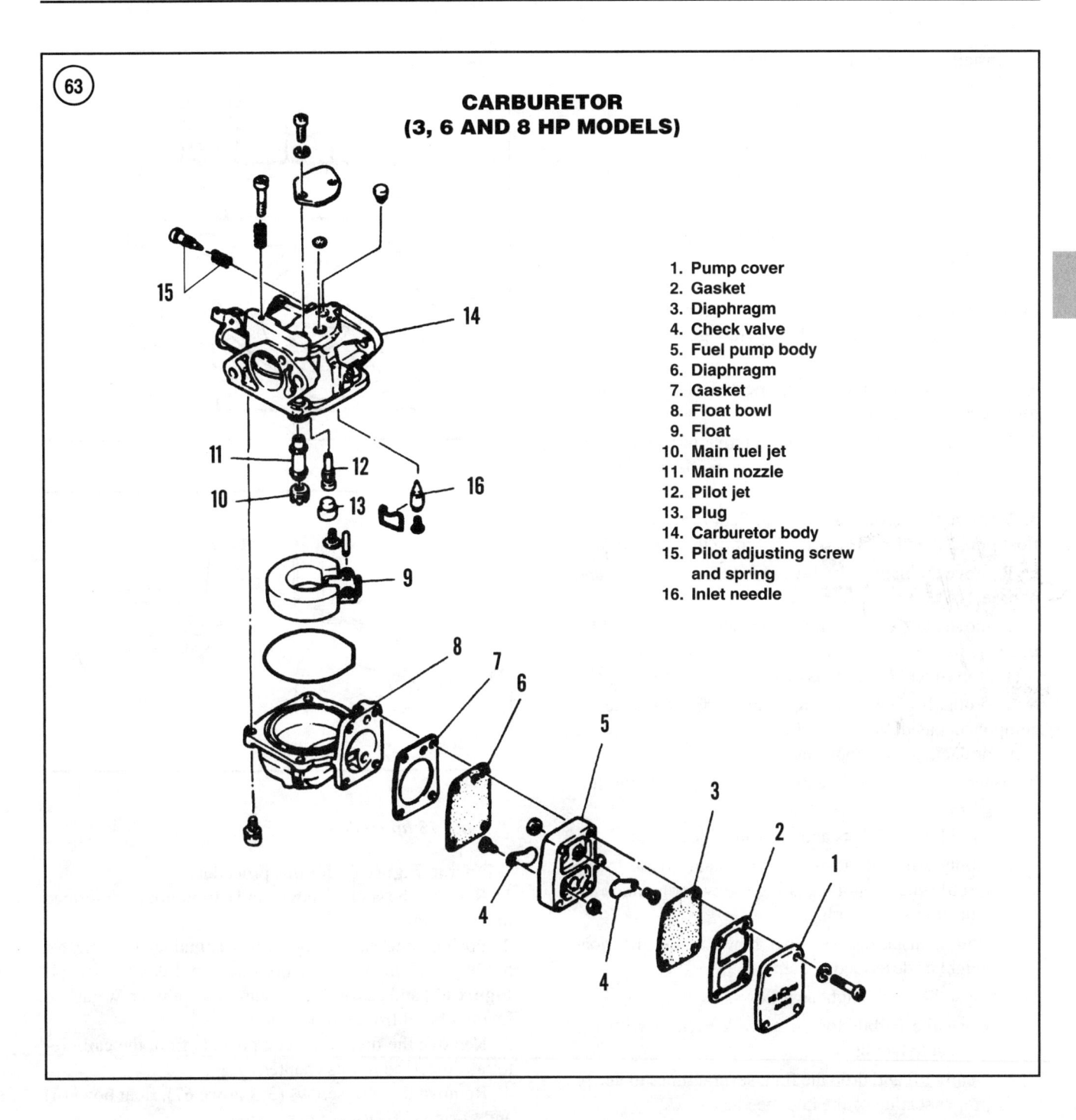

63 **CARBURETOR (3, 6 AND 8 HP MODELS)**

1. Pump cover
2. Gasket
3. Diaphragm
4. Check valve
5. Fuel pump body
6. Diaphragm
7. Gasket
8. Float bowl
9. Float
10. Main fuel jet
11. Main nozzle
12. Pilot jet
13. Plug
14. Carburetor body
15. Pilot adjusting screw and spring
16. Inlet needle

b. Fit the pull-off clip onto the groove in the inlet needle. Slip the clip over the tab of the float during installation.

10. Adjust the float height as follows:
   a. Place the carburetor on a work surface with the bowl side facing upward.
   b. Gently lift and drop the float several times to verify proper seating of the inlet needle.
   c. Measure the float height at the points indicated in **Figure 64**. If the float height is not in the range in **Table 3**, remove the float and gently bend the float tab (**Figure 65**) until the measurement is correct.
   d. Install the float bowl.

11. Install the fuel pump components as described in this chapter.

12. Install the carburetor and silencer cover as described in this chapter.

4 and 5 hp models

Refer to **Figure 66** for this procedure.

1. Remove the silencer cover and carburetor as described in this chapter.
2. Position the carburetor over a container suitable for holding fuel, then remove the bowl drain screw and gasket (7, **Figure 66**). Discard the drain screw gasket. Drain all fuel from the float bowl.
3. Remove the fuel pump components from the carburetor as described in this chapter.
4. Remove the four screws (17, **Figure 66**), float bowl (18) and gasket (19) from the carburetor. Discard the gasket.
5. Remove the screw, then lift the float (21, **Figure 66**), float pin (20) and inlet needle (22) from the carburetor.
6. Remove the main jet (23, **Figure 66**), nozzle (24) and pilot jet (25).
7. Remove the pilot adjusting screw and spring (26, **Figure 66**). Remove the three screws (27, **Figure 66**), then lift the top cover (28) and gasket (29). Discard the gasket.
8. Thoroughly clean all passages and surfaces. Inspect all components as described earlier in this section. Replace worn or damaged components.
9. Assembly is the reverse of disassembly. Note the following:
   a. Install new gaskets and seals in all locations.
   b. Apply a light coat of water-resistant grease to the throttle shaft, pilot adjusting screw spring and idle adjusting screw spring.
   c. Before installing the float bowl, adjust the float height as described in Step 10.
10. Adjust the float height as follows:
   a. Place the carburetor on a work surface with the bowl side facing up.
   b. Gently lift and drop the float several times to verify proper seating of the inlet needle.
   c. Measure the float height at the points indicated in A, **Figure 62**. If the float height is not in the range in **Table 3**, remove the float and gently bend the float tab (B, **Figure 62**) until the measurement is correct.
11. Install the fuel pump components as described in this chapter.
12. Install the carburetor and silencer cover as described in this chapter.

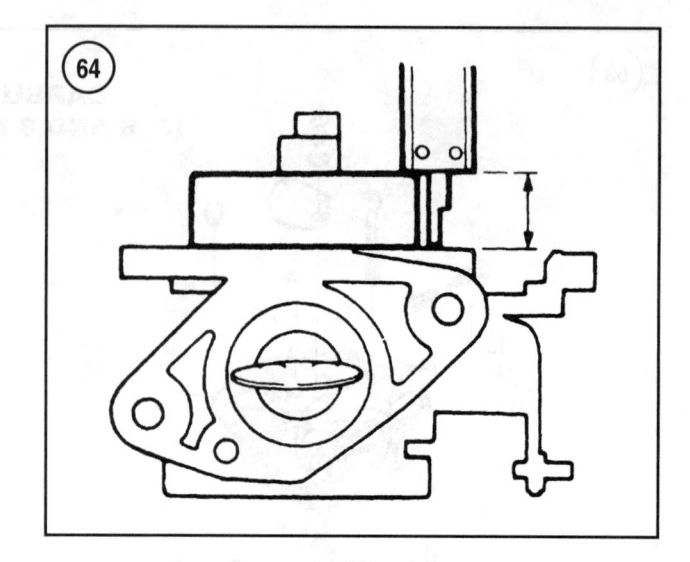

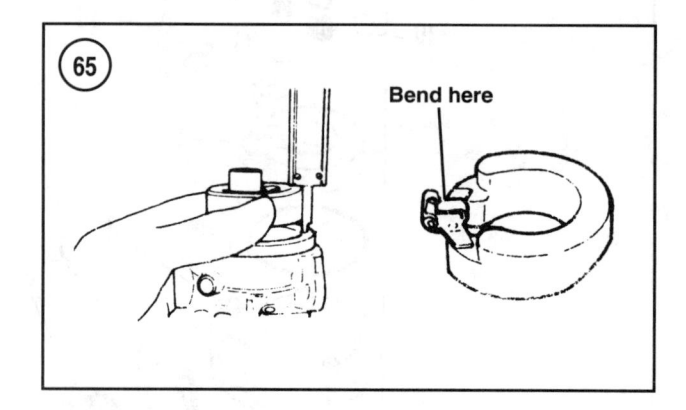

9.9 and 15 hp models

Refer to **Figure 67** for this procedure.

1. Remove the silencer cover and carburetor as described in this chapter.
2. Position the carburetor over a container suitable for holding fuel, then remove the float bowl drain screw (1, **Figure 67**) and gasket (2). Discard the drain screw gasket. Drain all fuel from the float bowl.
3. Remove the fuel pump components from the carburetor as described in this chapter.
4. Remove the four screws (3, **Figure 67**), float bowl (4) and O-ring (5). Discard the O-ring.
5. Remove the screw (6, **Figure 67**), then lift the float (8), float pin (7) and inlet needle (9) from the carburetor.
6. Remove the main fuel jet (12, **Figure 67**) and nozzle (11). Remove the plug (13, **Figure 67**), then unthread the pilot jet (14) from the carburetor.
7. Remove the four screws (15, **Figure 67**), then lift the top cover (16) and gasket (17) from the carburetor. Discard the gasket.

FUEL SYSTEM

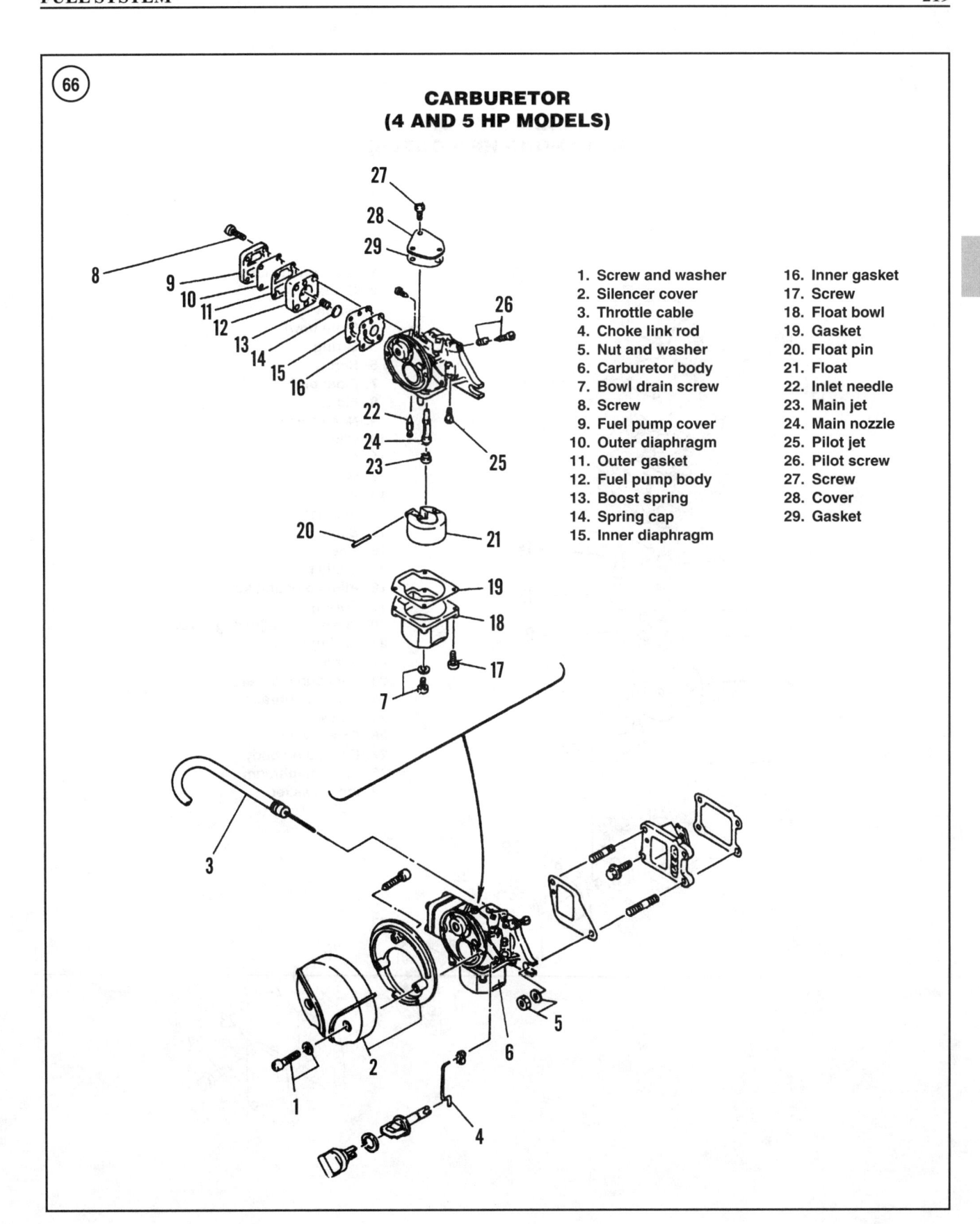

⑥⑥ CARBURETOR (4 AND 5 HP MODELS)

1. Screw and washer
2. Silencer cover
3. Throttle cable
4. Choke link rod
5. Nut and washer
6. Carburetor body
7. Bowl drain screw
8. Screw
9. Fuel pump cover
10. Outer diaphragm
11. Outer gasket
12. Fuel pump body
13. Boost spring
14. Spring cap
15. Inner diaphragm
16. Inner gasket
17. Screw
18. Float bowl
19. Gasket
20. Float pin
21. Float
22. Inlet needle
23. Main jet
24. Main nozzle
25. Pilot jet
26. Pilot screw
27. Screw
28. Cover
29. Gasket

CARBURETOR
(9.9 AND 15 HP MODELS)

1. Bowl drain screw
2. Gasket
3. Screw
4. Float bowl
5. O-ring
6. Screw
7. Float pin
8. Float
9. Needle valve
10. Clip
11. Main nozzle
12. Main jet
13. Plug
14. Pilot jet
15. Screw
16. Cover
17. Gasket
18. Pilot adjusting screw
19. Spring
20. Idle speed adjusting screw
21. Spring
22. Screw
23. Fuel pump cover
24. Outer diaphragm
25. Screw
26. Check valve
27. Fuel pump body
28. Inner diaphragm
29. Inner gasket

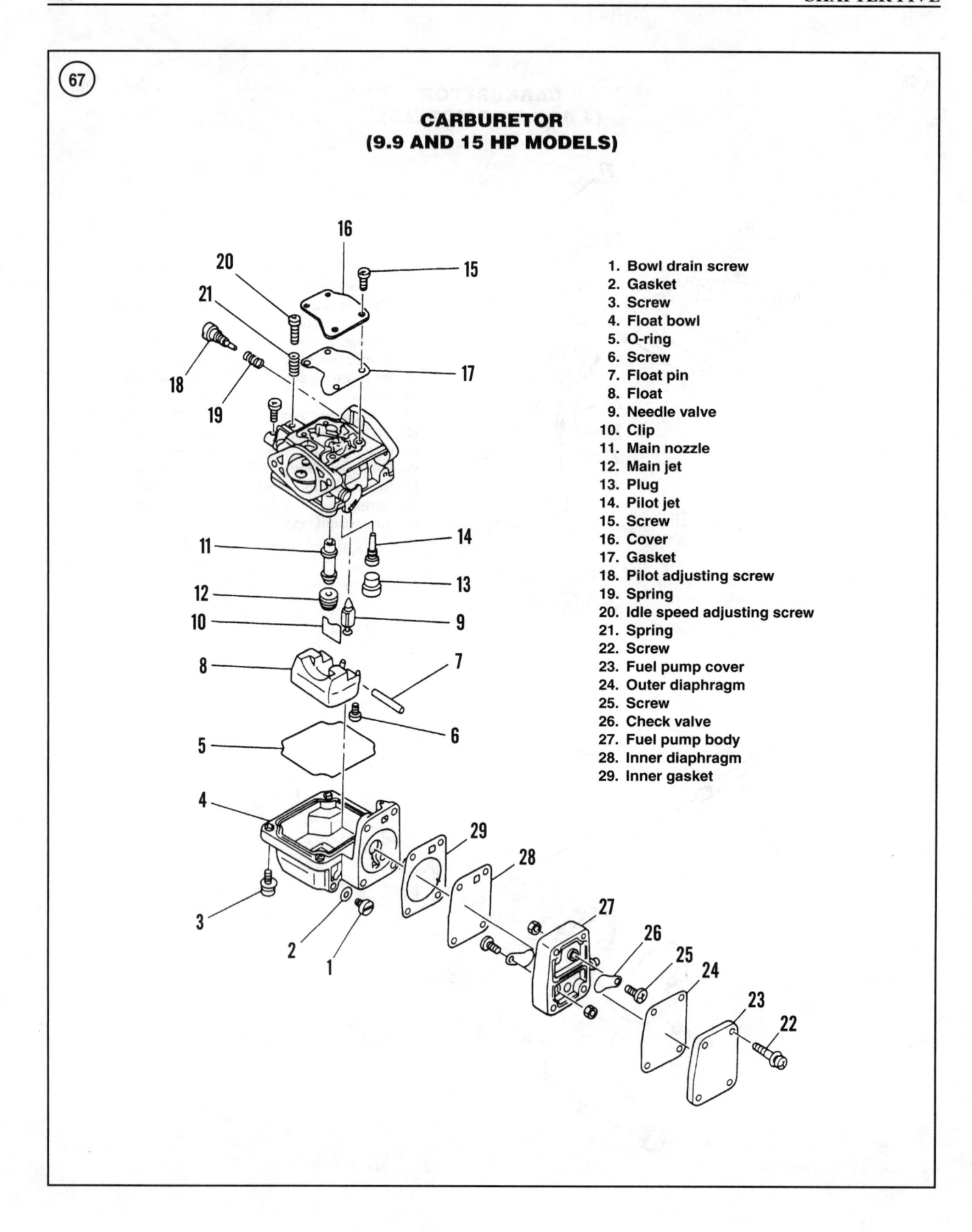

FUEL SYSTEM 221

4. Remove the four screws, float bowl (16, **Figure 69**) and O-ring (14). Discard the O-ring.
5. Remove the screw, then lift the float (12, **Figure 69**), float pin (13) and inlet needle (11) from the carburetor.
6. Remove the main fuel jet (8, **Figure 69**) and nozzle (7). Remove the plug (10, **Figure 69**), then unthread the pilot jet (9) from the carburetor.
7. Remove the two screws, then lift the top cover (1, **Figure 69**) and gasket (2) from the carburetor. Discard the gasket.
8. Remove the pilot adjusting screw (4, **Figure 69**) and spring (3), and the idle speed adjusting screw (5) and spring (3).
9. Assembly is the reverse of disassembly. Note the following:
   a. Install new gaskets and seals in all locations.
   b. Apply a light coat of water-resistant grease to the throttle shaft, pilot adjusting screw spring and idle adjusting screw spring.
10. Adjust the float height as follows:
    a. Place the carburetor on a work surface with the bowl side facing up.
    b. Gently lift and drop the float several times to verify proper seating of the inlet needle.
    c. Measure the float height at the points indicated in **Figure 68**. If the float height is not in the range in **Table 3**, remove the float and gently bend the float tab (**Figure 65**) until the measurement is correct.
    d. Install the float bowl.
11. For the lower carburetor, install the fuel pump components as described in this chapter.
12. Install the carburetor and silencer cover as described in this chapter.

25 hp three-cylinder and 30 hp models

Refer to **Figure 70** for this procedure.
1. Remove the silencer cover and carburetors as described in this chapter.
2. Position the carburetor over a container suitable for holding fuel, then remove the float bowl drain screw and gasket (15, **Figure 70**). Discard the drain screw gasket. Drain all fuel from the float bowl.
3. For the middle carburetor, remove the fuel pump components from the carburetor as described in this chapter.
4. Remove the four screws, float bowl (16, **Figure 70**) and O-ring (14). Discard the O-ring.
5. Remove the screw, then lift the float (13, **Figure 70**), float pin (12) and inlet needle (10) from the carburetor. Remove the pull-off clip from the needle.

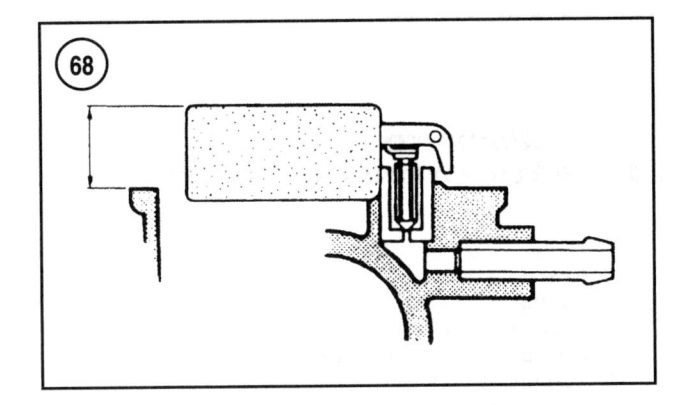

8. Remove the pilot adjusting screw (18, **Figure 67**) and spring (19), and the idle speed adjusting screw (20) and spring (21).
9. Assembly is the reverse of disassembly. Note the following:
   a. Install new gaskets and seals in all locations.
   b. Apply a light coat of water-resistant grease to the throttle shaft, pilot adjusting screw spring and idle adjusting screw spring.
   c. Fit the pull-off clip onto the groove in the inlet needle. Slip the clip over the tab of the float during installation.
10. Adjust the float height as follows:
    a. Place the carburetor on a work surface with the bowl side facing up.
    b. Gently lift and drop the float several times to verify proper seating of the inlet needle.
    c. Measure the float height at the points indicated in **Figure 68**. If the float height is not in the range in **Table 3**, replace the float.
    d. Install the float bowl.
11. Install the fuel pump components as described in this chapter.
12. Install the carburetor and silencer cover as described in this chapter.

20 and 25 hp two-cylinder models

Refer to **Figure 69** for this procedure.
1. Remove the silencer cover and carburetors as described in this chapter.
2. Position the carburetor over a container suitable for holding fuel, then remove the float bowl drain screw and gasket (15, **Figure 69**). Discard the drain screw gasket. Drain all fuel from the float bowl.
3. For the lower carburetor, remove the fuel pump components from the carburetor as described in this chapter.

**CARBURETOR
(20 AND 25 HP TWO-CYLINDER MODELS)**

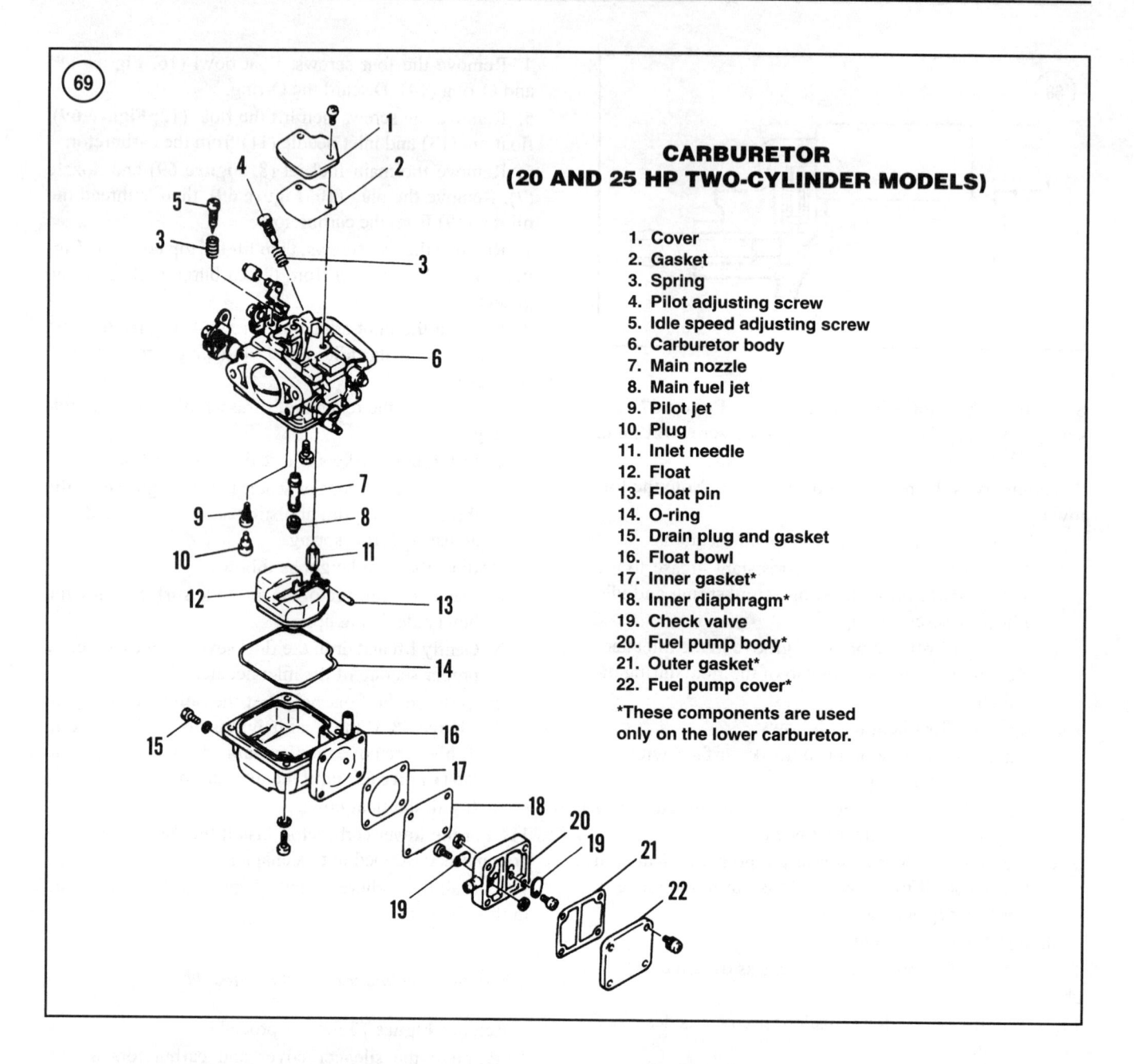

1. Cover
2. Gasket
3. Spring
4. Pilot adjusting screw
5. Idle speed adjusting screw
6. Carburetor body
7. Main nozzle
8. Main fuel jet
9. Pilot jet
10. Plug
11. Inlet needle
12. Float
13. Float pin
14. O-ring
15. Drain plug and gasket
16. Float bowl
17. Inner gasket*
18. Inner diaphragm*
19. Check valve
20. Fuel pump body*
21. Outer gasket*
22. Fuel pump cover*

*These components are used only on the lower carburetor.

6. Remove the main fuel jet (9, **Figure 70**) and nozzle (8). Remove the plug (7, **Figure 70**), then unthread the pilot jet (6) from the carburetor.
7. Remove the screw, then lift the top cover (1, **Figure 70**) and seals (2) from the carburetor. Discard the seals.
8. Remove the pilot adjusting screw (4, **Figure 70**) and spring (3).
9. Assembly is the reverse of disassembly. Note the following:
   a. Install new gaskets and seals in all locations.
   b. Apply a light coat of water-resistant grease to the throttle shaft and pilot adjusting screw spring.
10. Adjust the float height as follows:
   a. Place the carburetor on a work surface with the bowl side facing up.
   b. Gently lift and drop the float several times to verify proper seating of the inlet needle.
   c. Measure the float height at the points indicated in **Figure 64**. If the float height is not in the range in **Table 3**, replace the float and re-measure the height. Replace the inlet needle, then the valve seat if the measurement remains incorrect. The float is not adjustable on these models.
   d. Install the float bowl.

FUEL SYSTEM

70

**CARBURETOR
(25 HP THREE-CYLINDER AND 30 HP MODELS)**

1. Cover
2. Seal
3. Spring
4. Pilot adjusting screw
5. Carburetor body
6. Pilot jet
7. Plug
8. Main nozzle
9. Main jet
10. Inlet needle
11. Clip
12. Float pin
13. Float
14. O-ring
15. Bowl drain screw and gasket
16. Float bowl
17. Inner diaphragm*
18. Fuel pump body*
19. Outer gasket*
20. Fuel pump cover*

*These components used only on the middle carburetor.

---

11. For the middle carburetor, install the fuel pump components as described in this chapter.

12. Install the carburetor and silencer cover as described in this chapter.

28 jet, 35 jet and 40-90 hp choke valve models

Refer to **Figure 71** for this procedure.

1. Remove the silencer cover and carburetors as described in this chapter.

2. Position the carburetor over a container suitable for holding fuel, then remove the float bowl drain screw (7, **Figure 71**) and gasket (8). Discard the drain screw gasket. Drain all fuel from the float bowl.

3. Remove the four screws, float bowl and O-ring (9, **Figure 71**). Discard the O-ring.

4. Remove the screw, then lift the float (4, **Figure 71**), float pin and inlet needle (6) from the carburetor. Remove the pull-off clip from the needle.

5. Remove the main fuel jet (3, **Figure 71**) and nozzle (2). Remove the plug, then unthread the pilot jet (5, **Figure 71**) from the carburetor.

6. Remove the two screws, then lift the top cover and seals from the carburetor. Discard the seals.

7. Remove the pilot adjusting screw (1, **Figure 71**) and spring.

8. Assembly is the reverse of disassembly. Note the following:

   a. Install new gaskets and seals in all locations.

b. Apply a light coat of water-resistant grease to the throttle shaft and pilot adjusting screw spring.
c. Fit the pull-off clip onto the groove in the inlet needle. Slip the clip over the tab of the float during installation.

9. Adjust the float height as follows:
   a. Place the carburetor on a work surface with the bowl side facing up.
   b. Gently lift and drop the float several times to verify proper seating of the inlet needle.
   c. Measure the float height at the points indicated in **Figure 68**. If the float height is not in the range in **Table 3**, remove the float and gently bend the float tab (**Figure 65**) until the measurement is correct. If the tab is not used on the float, replace the float to correct the float height.
   d. Install the float bowl.

10. Install the carburetor and silencer cover as described in this chapter.

28 jet, 35 jet and 40-90 hp Prime-Start models

Refer to **Figure 72** for this procedure.

1. Remove the silencer cover and carburetors as described in this chapter.
2. Position the carburetor over a container suitable for holding fuel, then remove the float bowl drain screw (1, **Figure 72**) and O-ring (2). Discard the O-ring. Drain all fuel from the float bowl.
3. For the middle carburetor, remove the electrothermal valve and Prime-Start pump from the carburetor as described in this chapter.
4. Remove the four screws (10, **Figure 72**), float bowl (4) and O-ring (12). Discard the O-ring.
5. Remove the screw (13, **Figure 72**), then lift the float (15), float pin (14) and inlet needle (16) from the carburetor. Remove the pull-off clip (17, **Figure 72**) from the needle.
6. Remove the main fuel jet (20, **Figure 72**) and nozzle (21). Remove the plug (22, **Figure 72**), then unthread the pilot jet (23) from the carburetor.
7. Remove the screws and washers (3, **Figure 72**), then lift the top cover (4) and O-ring (5) from the carburetor. Discard the O-ring.
8. Remove the pilot adjusting screw (6, **Figure 72**) and spring (7), and the idle speed adjusting screw (8) and spring (9).
9. Assembly is the reverse of disassembly. Note the following:
   a. Install new gaskets and seals in all locations.
   b. Apply a light coat of water-resistant grease to the throttle shaft and pilot adjusting screw spring.

71 CARBURETOR (28 JET, 35 JET AND 40-90 HP MODELS WITH A CHOKE VALVE)

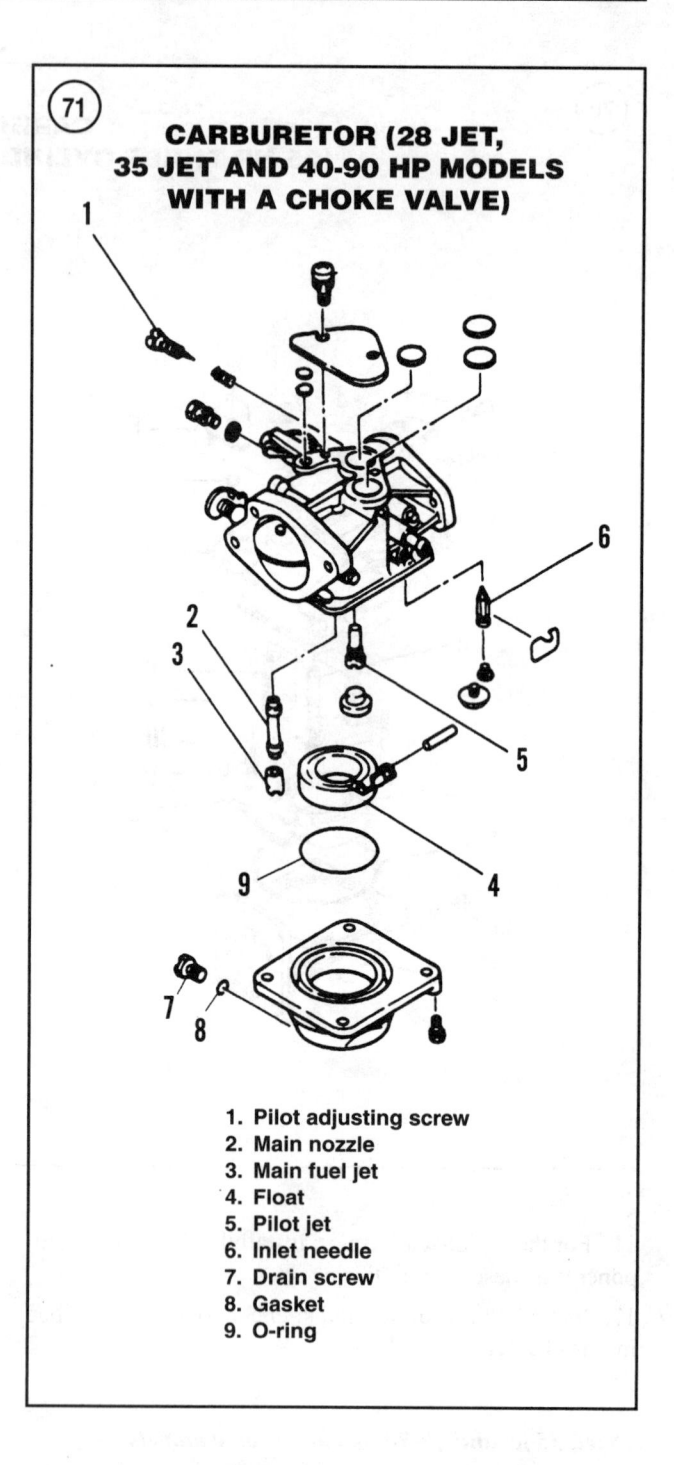

1. Pilot adjusting screw
2. Main nozzle
3. Main fuel jet
4. Float
5. Pilot jet
6. Inlet needle
7. Drain screw
8. Gasket
9. O-ring

10. Adjust the float height as follows:
    a. Place the carburetor on a work surface with the bowl side facing up.
    b. Gently lift and drop the float several times to verify proper seating of the inlet needle.
    c. Measure the float height at the points indicated in **Figure 64**. If the float height is not in the range in **Table 3**, remove the float and gently bend the float

FUEL SYSTEM

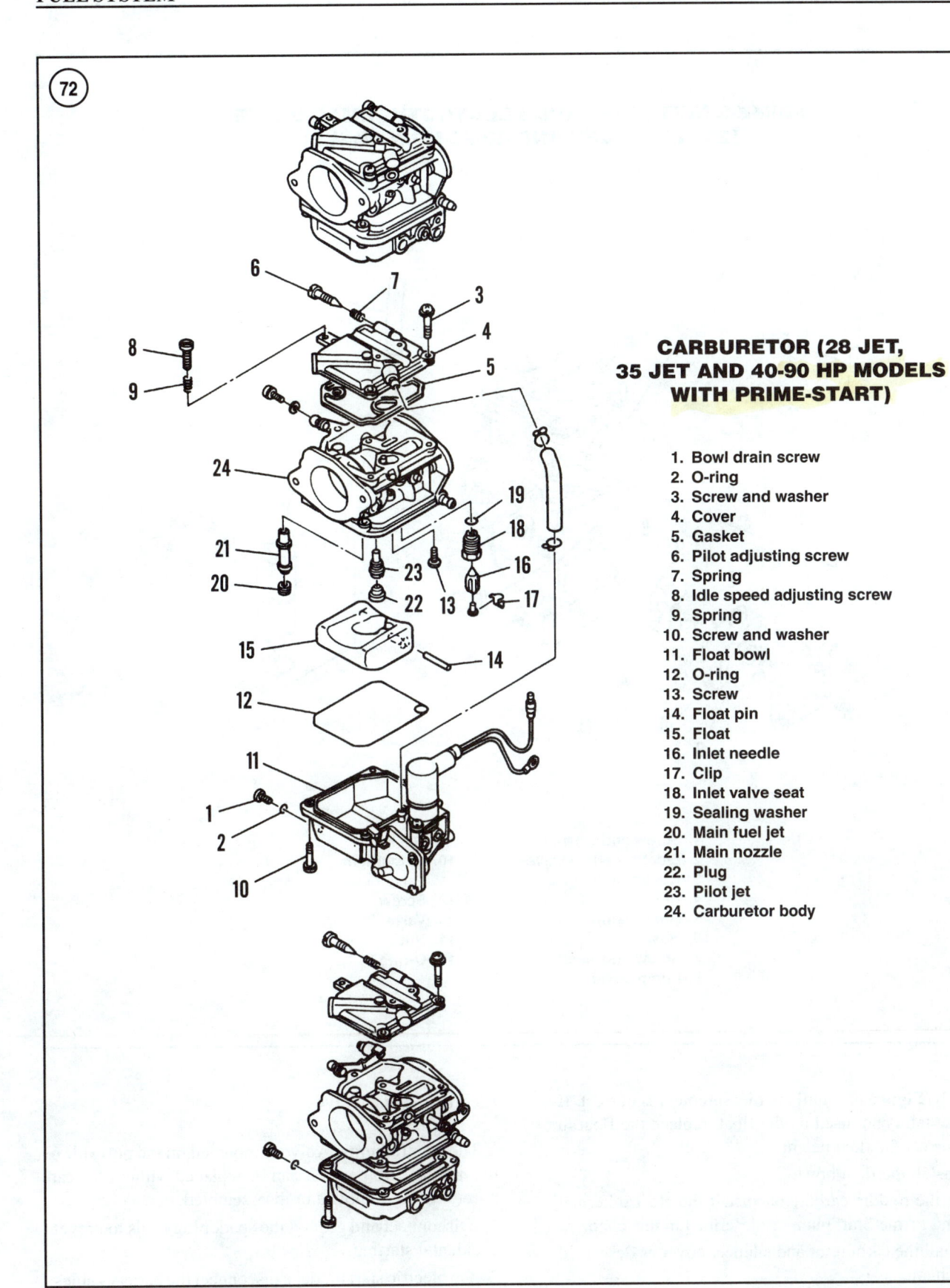

72

CARBURETOR (28 JET, 35 JET AND 40-90 HP MODELS WITH PRIME-START)

1. Bowl drain screw
2. O-ring
3. Screw and washer
4. Cover
5. Gasket
6. Pilot adjusting screw
7. Spring
8. Idle speed adjusting screw
9. Spring
10. Screw and washer
11. Float bowl
12. O-ring
13. Screw
14. Float pin
15. Float
16. Inlet needle
17. Clip
18. Inlet valve seat
19. Sealing washer
20. Main fuel jet
21. Main nozzle
22. Plug
23. Pilot jet
24. Carburetor body

CHAPTER FIVE

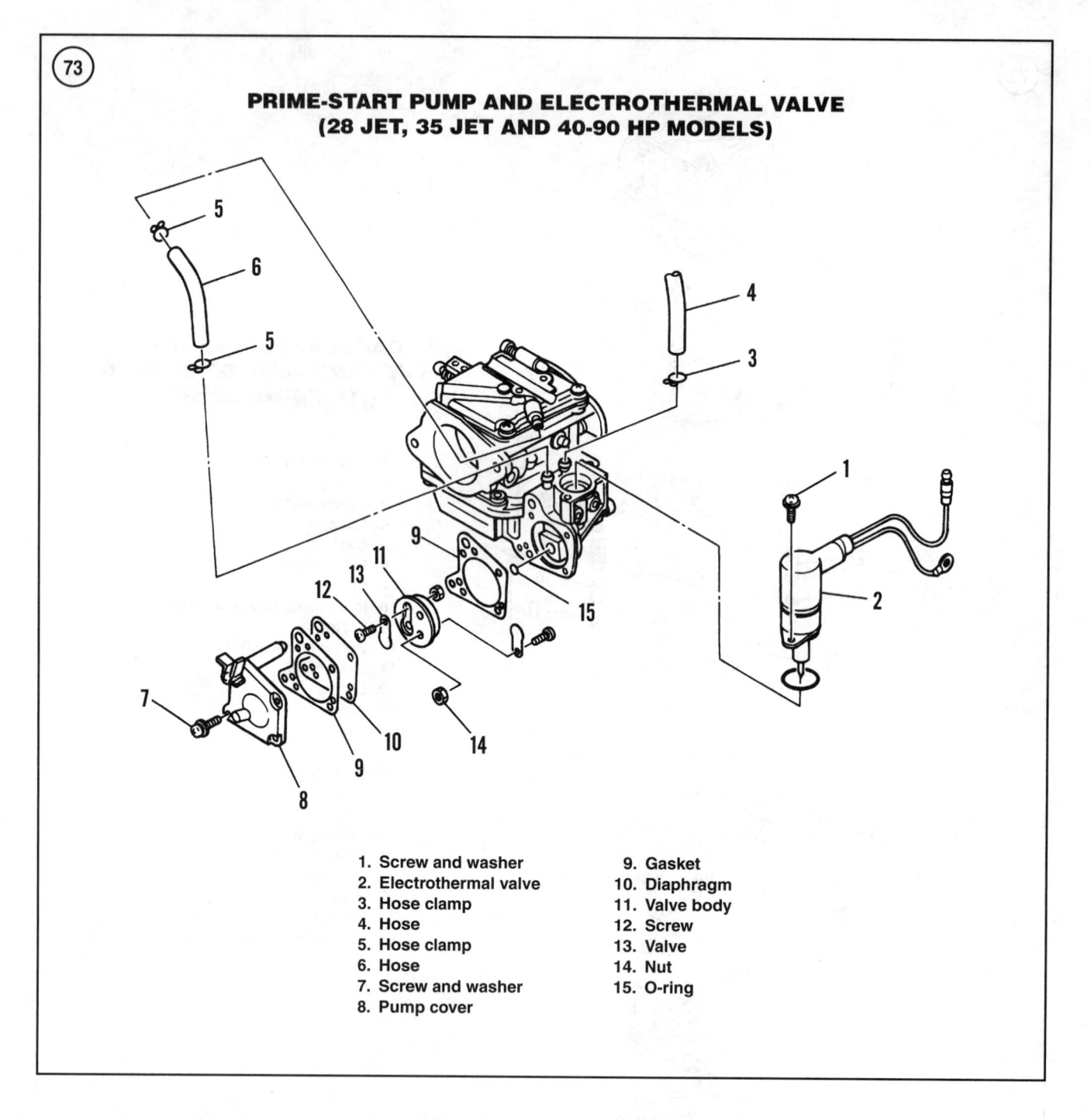

73) PRIME-START PUMP AND ELECTROTHERMAL VALVE (28 JET, 35 JET AND 40-90 HP MODELS)

1. Screw and washer
2. Electrothermal valve
3. Hose clamp
4. Hose
5. Hose clamp
6. Hose
7. Screw and washer
8. Pump cover
9. Gasket
10. Diaphragm
11. Valve body
12. Screw
13. Valve
14. Nut
15. O-ring

tab (**Figure 65**) until the measurement is correct. If the tab is not used on the float, replace the float to correct the float height.

   d. Install the float bowl.

11. For the middle carburetor, install the electrothermal valve and Prime-Start pump as described in this chapter.

12. Install the carburetor and silencer cover as described in this chapter.

Electrothermal Valve

The electrothermal valve is mounted on the port side of the middle carburetor. It can be replaced without the carburetor being removed or disassembled.

1. Disconnect and ground the spark plug leads to prevent accidental starting.

2. On electric start models, disconnect the battery cables.

FUEL SYSTEM

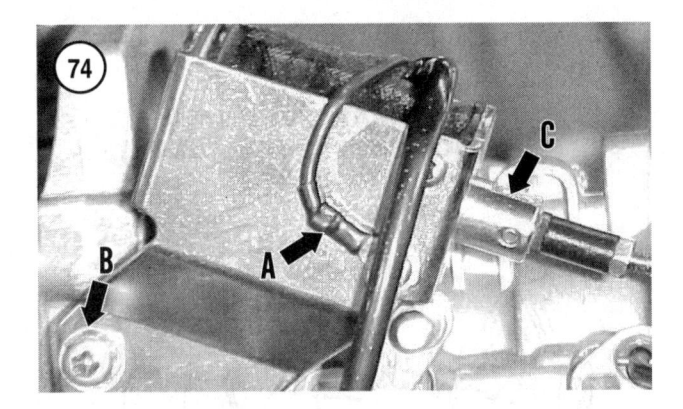

74

3. Use compressed air to blow all debris or contaminants from the electrothermal valve mounting surfaces. This will help prevent contaminants from entering the Prime-Start pump.
4. Disconnect the electrothermal valve wires from the engine ground terminal and the connector on the engine wire harness.
5. Remove the screws and washer (1, **Figure 73**), then carefully lift the electrothermal valve (2) from the carburetor. Remove the O-ring from the valve or valve bore in the carburetor. Discard the O-ring.
6. Use a lint-free shop towel to wipe debris or contaminants from the electrothermal valve bore in the carburetor. Contamination in the bore will eventually block passages in the Prime-Start pump.
7. Install a new O-ring onto the electrothermal valve. Apply a light coat of Yamaha All-Purpose Grease to the O-ring.
8. Insert the valve tip into its bore in the carburetor and seat the valve onto the carburetor. Rotate the valve to align the mounting screw openings. Install and securely tighten the screws.
9. Connect the electrothermal valve ground and engine harness connections. Route the wire to prevent interference with moving components. Secure the wires with plastic locking type clamps as needed.
10. Connect the spark plug leads.
11. Connect the battery cables.

Prime-Start Pump

The Prime-Start pump is installed on the side of the middle carburetor. The valve can be serviced without the carburetor being removed or disassembled. If there is debris or contamination in the pump, completely disassemble and clean all three carburetors.

Refer to **Figure 73** for this procedure.

1. Disconnect and ground the spark plug leads to prevent accidental starting.
2. On electric start models, disconnect the battery cables.
3. Remove the silencer cover as described in this chapter.
4. Remove the electrothermal valve as described in this chapter.
5. Remove the three screws and washers (7, **Figure 73**), then carefully remove the pump cover (8), gasket (9) and diaphragm (10). Discard the gasket and diaphragm.
6. Pull the valve body (11, **Figure 73**) from the carburetor. Remove and discard the O-ring (15, **Figure 73**).
7. Remove the screws (12, **Figure 73**) and nuts (14), then lift the valves (13) from the valve body.
8. Clean all removed components, except the electrothermal valve, in a suitable solvent and dry them with compressed air.
9. Inspect the valves for bent, chipped or damaged surfaces. Inspect the valve body for wear at the valve contact surfaces. Replace the valve body and valves if there are worn or damaged surfaces.
10. Assembly is the reverse of disassembly. Install new seals, gaskets, diaphragms and O-rings in all locations during assembly.
11. Install the electrothermal valve as described in this chapter.
12. Install the silencer cover as described in this chapter.
13. Connect the spark plug leads.
14. Connect the battery cables.

Choke Solenoid

The choke solenoid is located on the starboard side of the carburetors.
1. Disconnect the battery cables.
2. Disconnect and ground the spark plug leads to prevent accidental starting.
3. Disconnect the blue choke solenoid wire from the engine wire harness connection.
4. Disconnect the black choke solenoid terminal (A, **Figure 74**, typical) from the engine ground connection.
5. Remove the mounting screws (B, **Figure 74**, typical) and lift the solenoid from the mount.
6. Apply a light coat of Yamaha All-Purpose Grease or equivalent to the choke plunger (C, **Figure 74**, typical), then insert the plunger into the solenoid. Install the mounting screws and securely tighten them.
7. Connect the black choke solenoid terminal to the engine ground. Connect the blue solenoid wire to the engine wire harness connection.
8. Connect the spark plug leads.
9. Connect the battery cables.

228

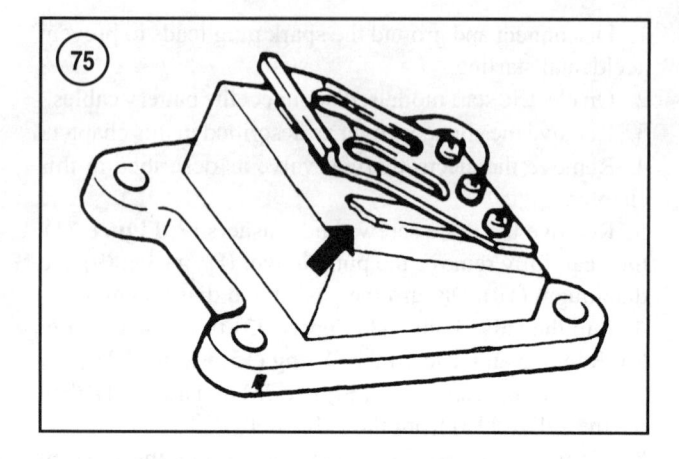

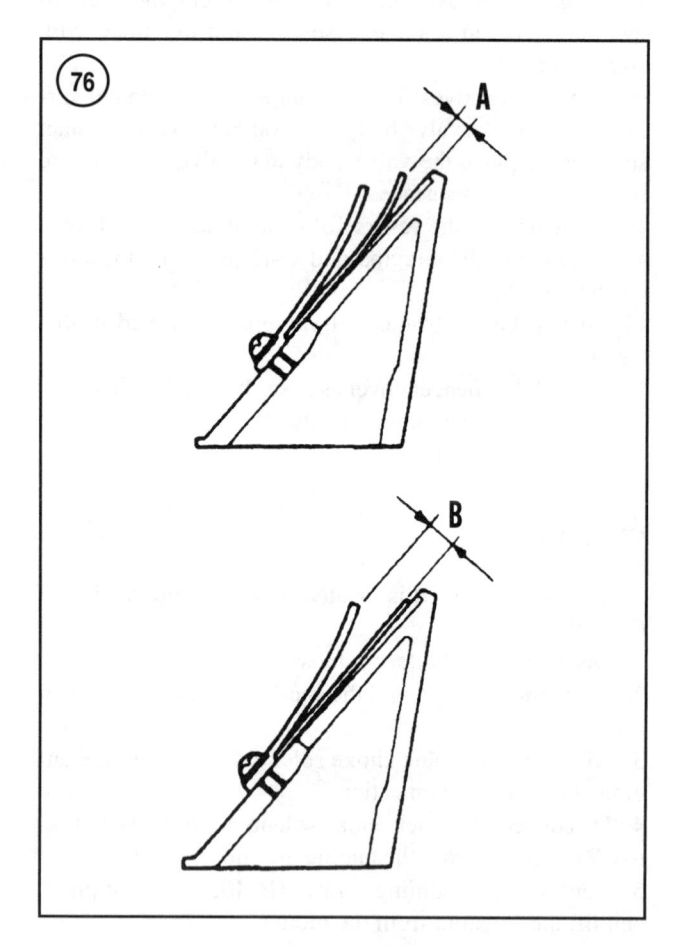

75

76

REED HOUSING/INTAKE MANIFOLD

Inspect the reed valves upon removal for bent, cracked or missing sections (**Figure 75**, typical). Measure the reed tip opening (A, **Figure 76**) and reed stop opening (B) during inspection and after installing new components. If the measurement(s) are incorrect, replace the reed valve and/or reed stop. Reed valve specifications are in **Table 2**.

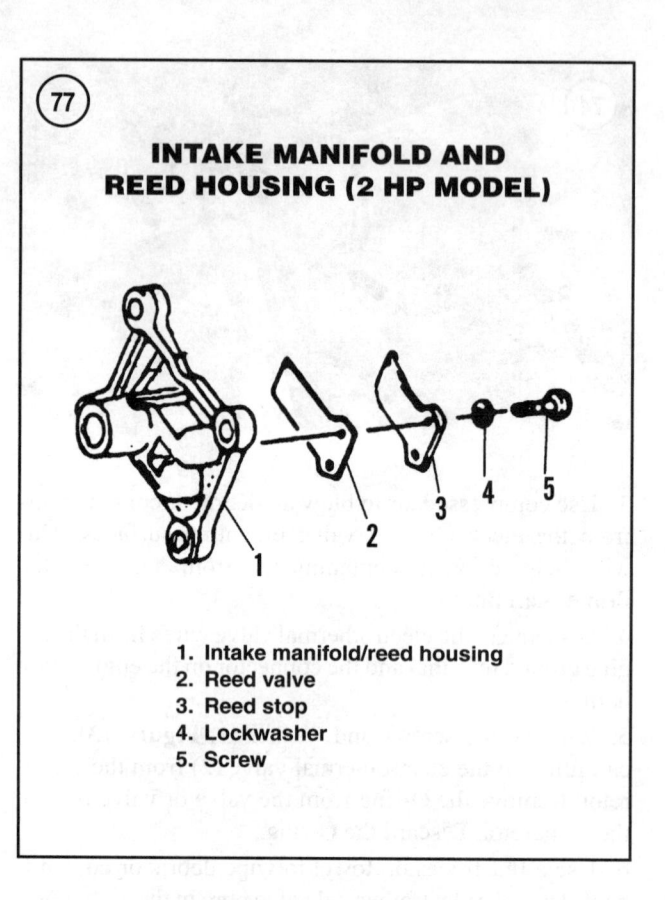

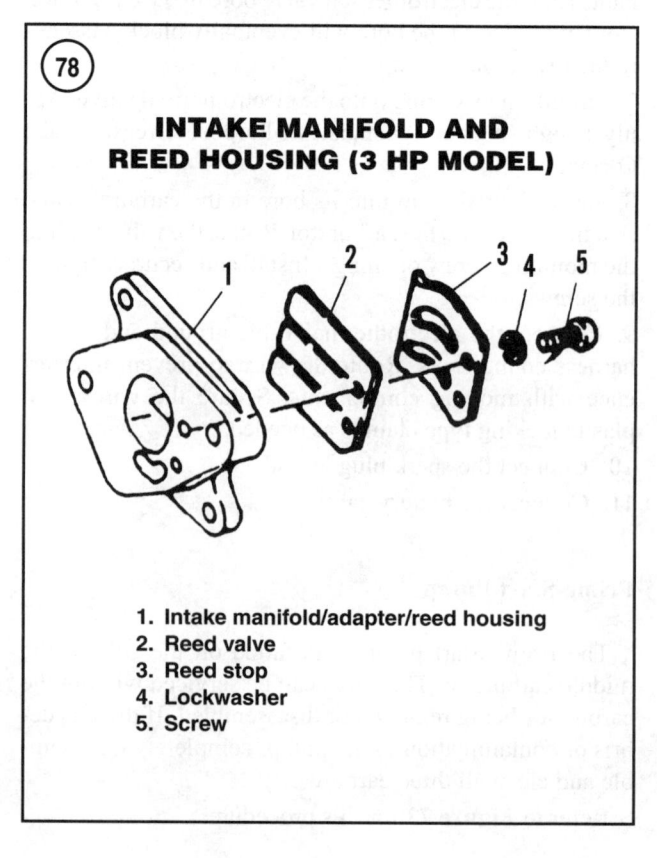

CHAPTER FIVE

77

INTAKE MANIFOLD AND REED HOUSING (2 HP MODEL)

1. Intake manifold/reed housing
2. Reed valve
3. Reed stop
4. Lockwasher
5. Screw

78

INTAKE MANIFOLD AND REED HOUSING (3 HP MODEL)

1. Intake manifold/adapter/reed housing
2. Reed valve
3. Reed stop
4. Lockwasher
5. Screw

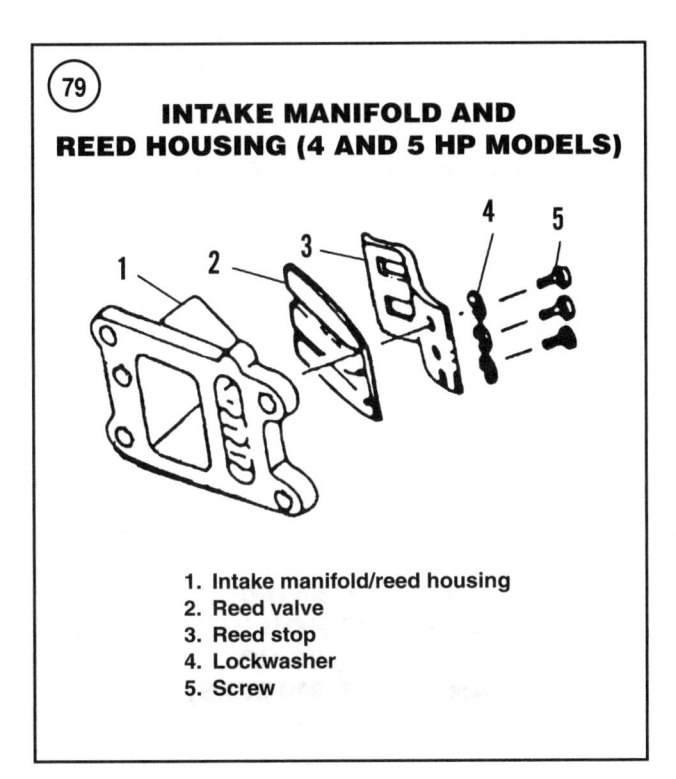

FUEL SYSTEM

79 INTAKE MANIFOLD AND REED HOUSING (4 AND 5 HP MODELS)

1. Intake manifold/reed housing
2. Reed valve
3. Reed stop
4. Lockwasher
5. Screw

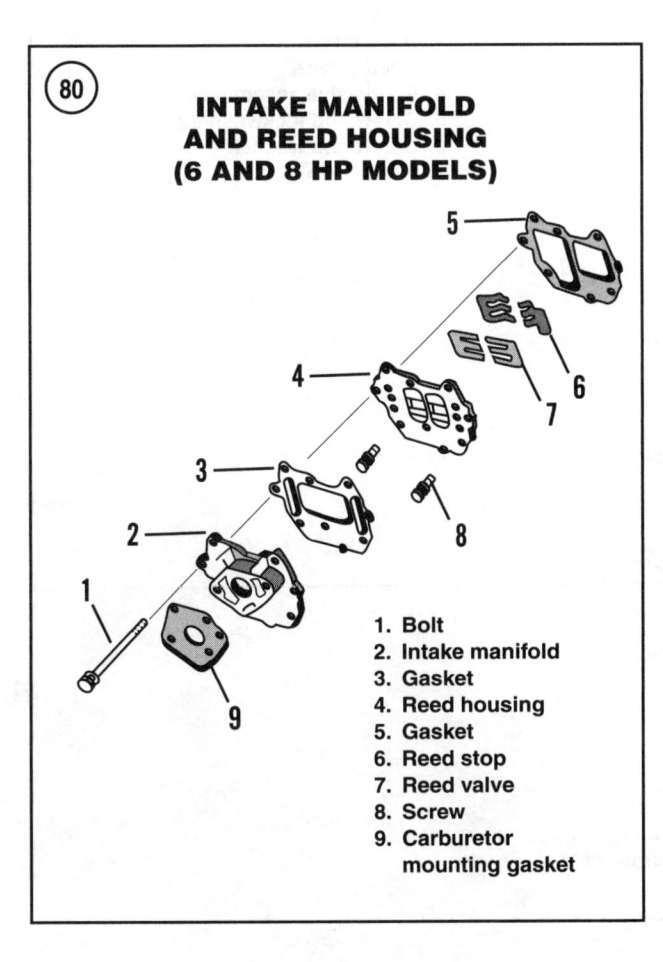

80 INTAKE MANIFOLD AND REED HOUSING (6 AND 8 HP MODELS)

1. Bolt
2. Intake manifold
3. Gasket
4. Reed housing
5. Gasket
6. Reed stop
7. Reed valve
8. Screw
9. Carburetor mounting gasket

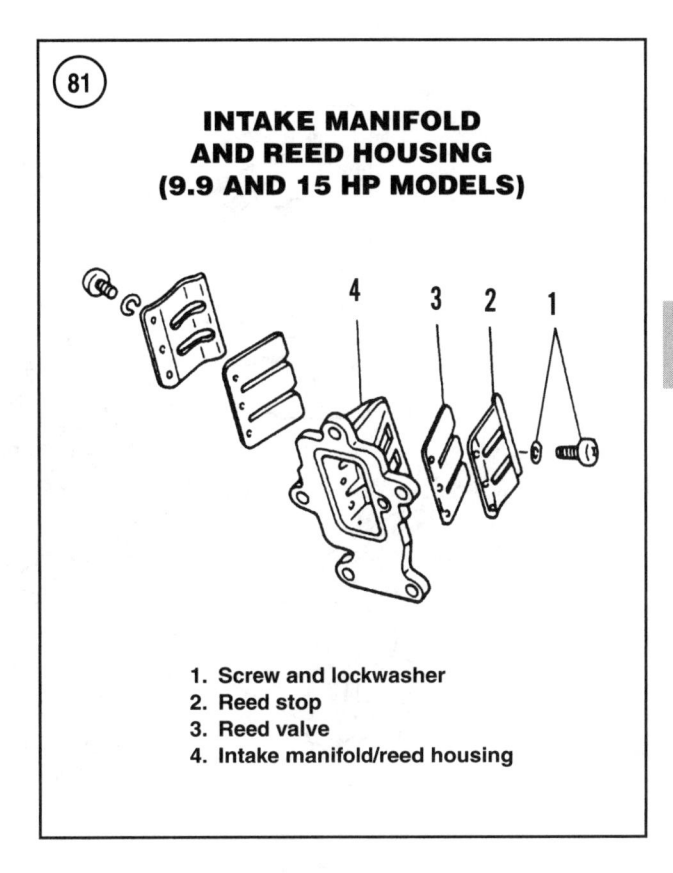

81 INTAKE MANIFOLD AND REED HOUSING (9.9 AND 15 HP MODELS)

1. Screw and lockwasher
2. Reed stop
3. Reed valve
4. Intake manifold/reed housing

Reed housing and intake manifold designs vary by model. Refer to **Figures 77-84** during the removal, disassembly and installation procedures.

Removal

1. Remove the carburetor as described in this chapter.
2. On oil injected models, disconnect the oil lines from the intake manifold fittings.
3. Remove the fasteners, then carefully pry the intake manifold, reed housing and plates from the crankcase cover. Remove and discard any gaskets.
4. Inspect the reeds for defects, then measure the reed tip and reed stop openings as described in this section. Remove the reed valves and stops only if they must be replaced. Remove them as follows:
   a. On 20-90 hp models, remove the screws, then carefully pull the reed assemblies from the intake manifold.
   b. Remove the screws, reed stops and reed valves from the engine.
5. Use a suitable solvent to thoroughly clean all components. Dry the components with compressed air. Clean all residual Loctite from the reed screw and screw openings.

230

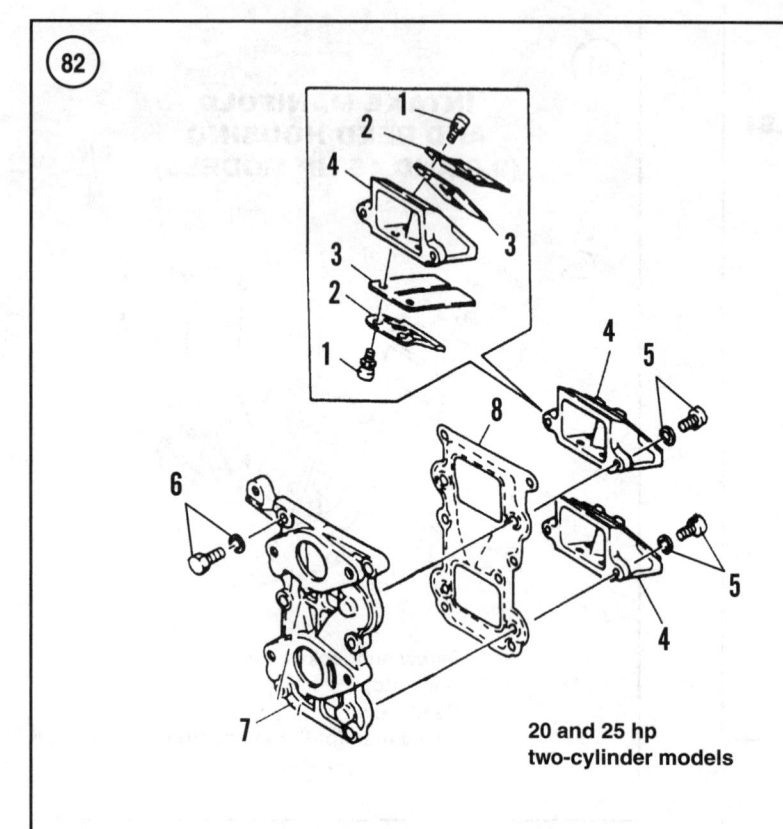

CHAPTER FIVE

⑧²

20 and 25 hp
two-cylinder models

25 and 30 hp
three-cylinder models

**INTAKE MANIFOLD
AND REED HOUSING
(20 HP, 25 HP
AND 30 HP MODELS)**

1. Screws
2. Reed stops
3. Reed valves
4. Reed valve assemblies
5. Screw and lockwashers
6. Screw and washer
7. Intake manifold
8. Gasket

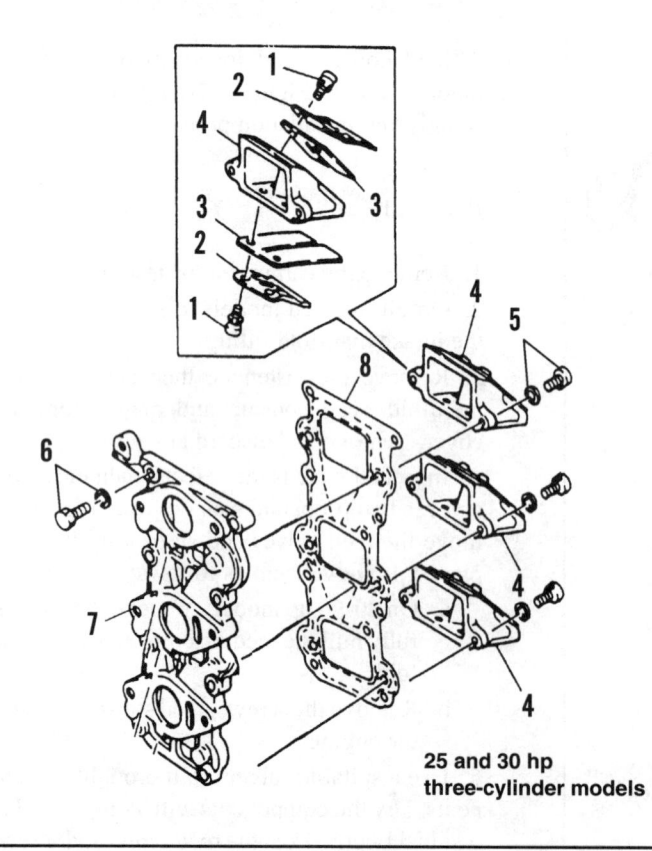

FUEL SYSTEM

**INTAKE MANIFOLD AND REED HOUSING
(28 JET, 35 JET, 40 HP AND 50 HP)**

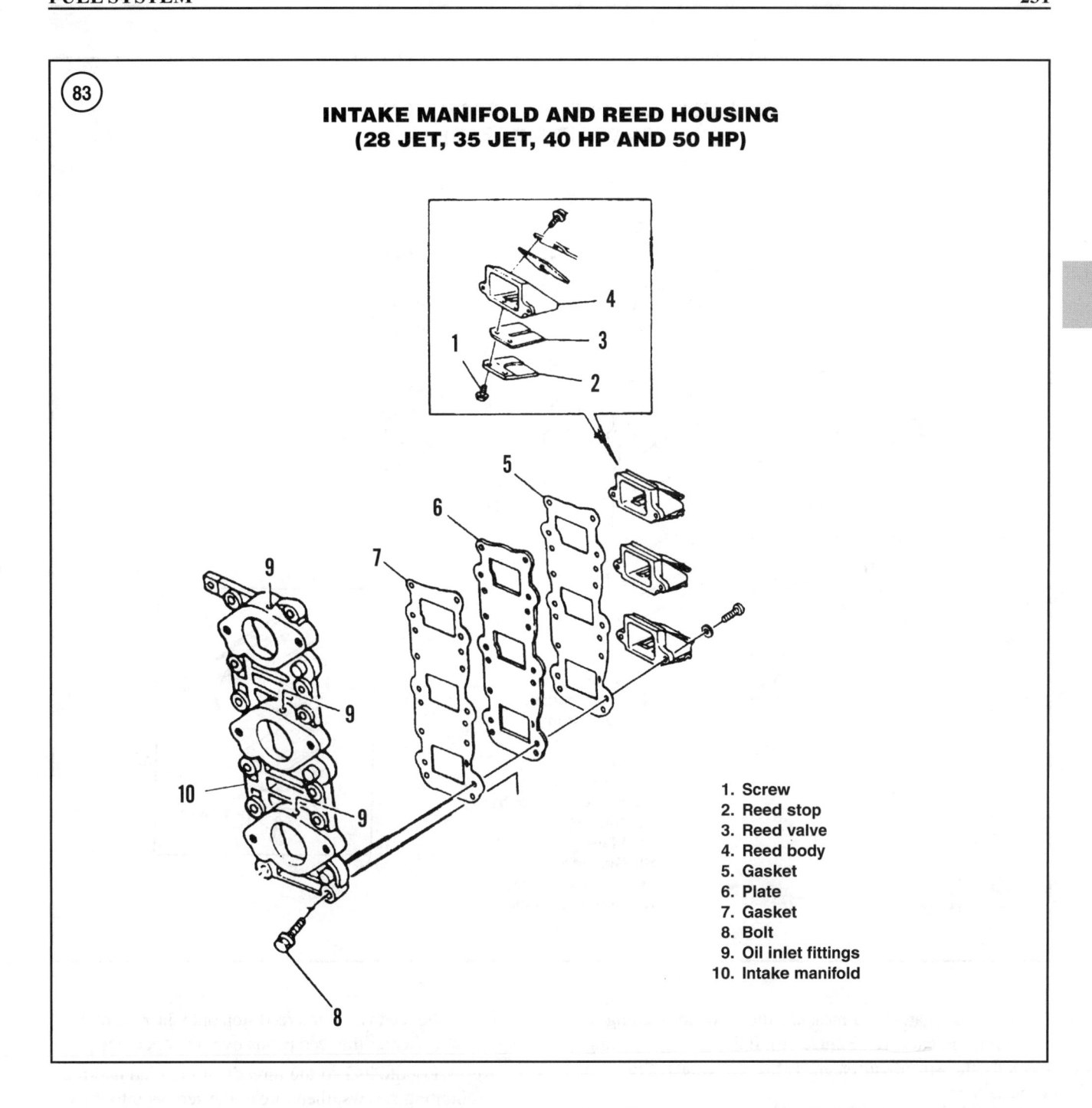

1. Screw
2. Reed stop
3. Reed valve
4. Reed body
5. Gasket
6. Plate
7. Gasket
8. Bolt
9. Oil inlet fittings
10. Intake manifold

Inspection

1. Inspect the reed valves for cracked, chipped or missing petals. Replace all reeds in the engine if any are faulty. The conditions contributing to reed failure may have affected other reed valves. Remove the cylinder head and inspect the piston and cylinder head if any petals are missing. Refer to Chapter Eight for cylinder head removal and installation procedures.

2. Inspect the reed contact surface for worn or irregular surfaces. Replace the reed body, intake manifold or reed mounting plate if these are any defects.

3. Inspect the screw opening for damaged or missing threads. The threads may be damaged during screw removal. Replace the component if the threads are damaged.

4. Inspect the reed stop for cracked or damaged surfaces and replace as needed.

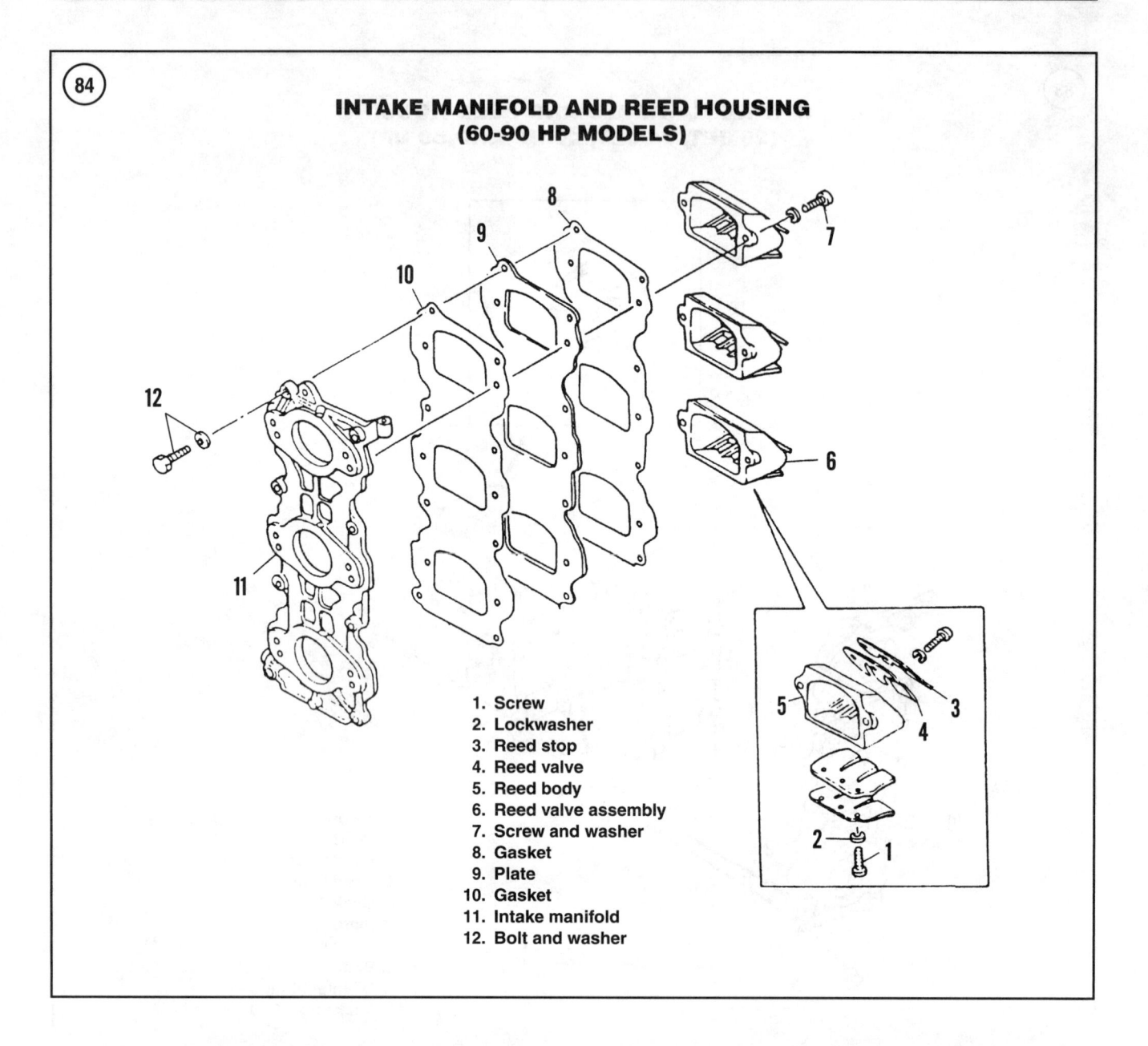

INTAKE MANIFOLD AND REED HOUSING (60-90 HP MODELS)

1. Screw
2. Lockwasher
3. Reed stop
4. Reed valve
5. Reed body
6. Reed valve assembly
7. Screw and washer
8. Gasket
9. Plate
10. Gasket
11. Intake manifold
12. Bolt and washer

5. Use feeler gauges to measure the reed tip opening at the points indicated (A, **Figure 76**). If the reed tip opening exceeds the specification in **Table 2**, replace the reed valves.
6. Use a depth micrometer to measure the distance from the tip of the reed valve to the reed stop surface (B, **Figure 76**). If the measurement is not within the reed stop opening specification in **Table 2**, replace the reed stop.

Installation

Refer to **Figures 77-84** during the assembly and installation procedures.

1. Install the reed valve and reed stop onto the reed mounting surface. Center the reed petals over the openings.
2. Apply Loctite 242 to the threads of the reed and reed stop mounting screws, then thread the screws into the intake manifold, reed plate or reed body. Check for properly centered reed petals, then tighten the screws to the specification in **Table 1**.
3. On 20-90 hp models, install new gaskets, then fit the reed valve assemblies onto the plate and intake manifold. Apply Loctite 242 to the threads, then hand-thread the reed assembly screws into the reed assemblies, plate and intake manifold. Tighten the screws evenly to the specification in **Table 1**.

FUEL SYSTEM

85 RECIRCULATION SYSTEM (4 AND 5 HP MODELS)

1. Hose: 120 mm (4.72 in.)
2. Hose: 100 mm (3.94 in.)
3. Hose: 70 mm (2.76 in.)

86 RECIRCULATION SYSTEM (28 JET, 45 JET, 40 HP AND 50 HP MODELS)

87 RECIRCULATION SYSTEM (60 AND 70 HP MODELS)

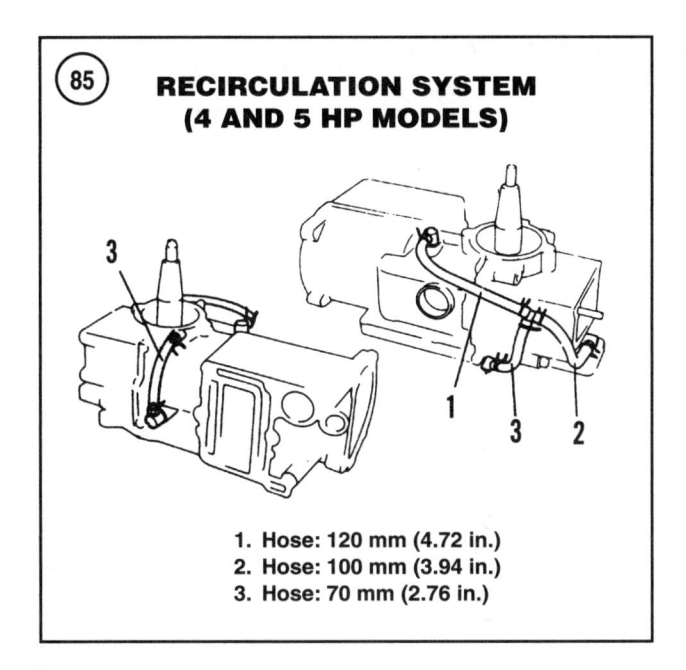

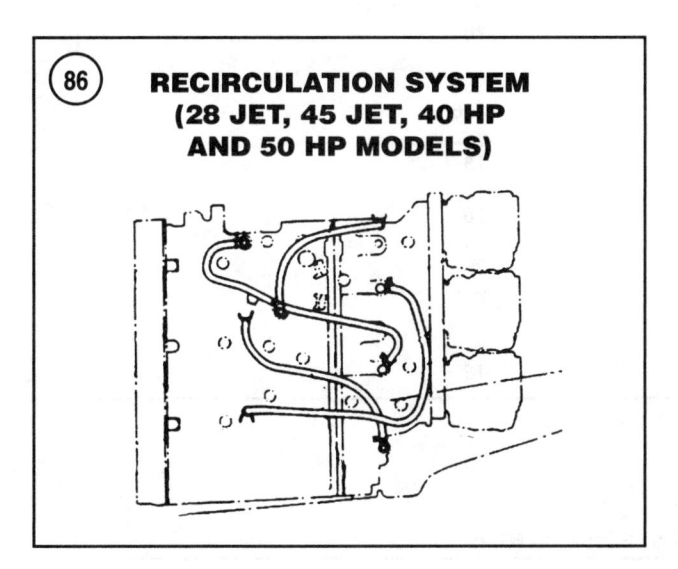

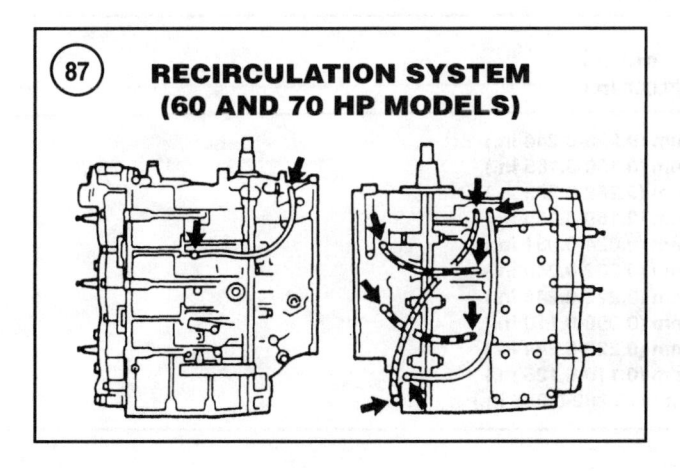

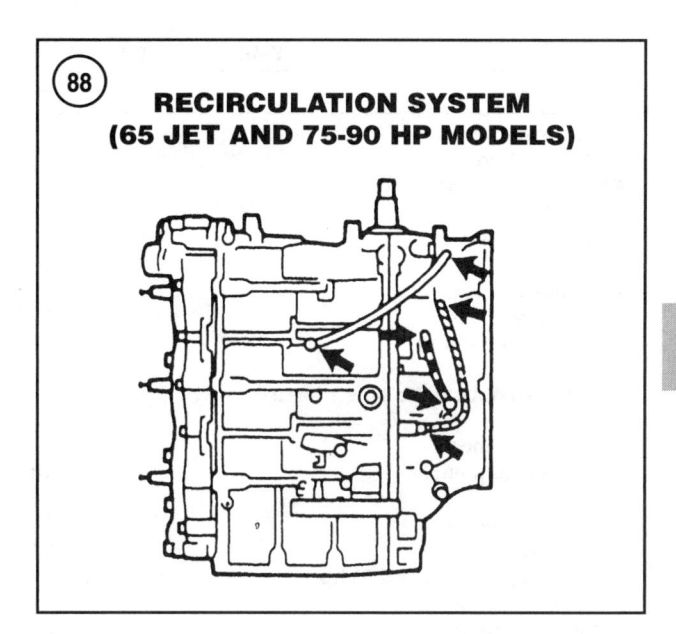

88 RECIRCULATION SYSTEM (65 JET AND 75-90 HP MODELS)

4. Install a new gasket, then install the intake manifold/reed housing assembly onto the intake manifold.
5. Apply Loctite 242 to the threads, then hand-thread the intake manifold bolts into the power head. Tighten the bolts in two steps to the specification in **Table 1**. Use a crossing pattern or the cast in torque sequence numbering on the intake manifold.
6. On oil injected models, connect the oil lines to the intake manifold fittings.
7. Install the carburetor(s) and silencer cover as described in this chapter.
8. On oil injected models, bleed air from the oil injection system as described in Chapter Twelve.

RECIRCULATION SYSTEM

Faulty hoses in the recirculation system result in oil and fuel leaks, hard starting, and rough idling. Inspect the recirculation hoses for tears, leaks or deterioration. Replace all of the recirculation hoses if any are faulty. The condition that contributed to failure of one hose is probably affecting the others. Only use the hose available from a Yamaha outboard dealership. An automotive vacuum hose is not suitable for the application.

To prevent hose kinking and blocked passages, never cut hoses longer or shorter than the original.

Note the hoses routing and connection points before removing them. Most models use a single hose or short sections of hose that are easy to route. Always route the hose to the fitting from which it was removed.

For models with multiple hose connection points, refer to **Figures 85-88**.

Table 1 FUEL SYSTEM TORQUE SPECIFICATIONS

Fastener	N•m	in.-lb.	ft.-lb.
Choke lever screw			
9.9 and 15 hp	3	26	–
Float bowl			
4 and 5 hp	2	18	–
Float bowl drain			
4 and 5 hp	3	26	–
Fuel pump cover			
4 and 5 hp	2	18	–
Fuel valve mounting			
3 hp	3	26	–
Intake/reed housing to power head			
2 hp			
First sequence	5	44	–
Second sequence	10	88	–
6 and 8 hp			
First sequence	6	53	–
Second sequence	11	97	–
28 jet, 35 jet, 40 hp and 50 hp			
First sequence	4	36	–
Second sequence	8	70	–
60 and 70 hp			
First sequence	4	36	–
Second sequence	8	70	–
65 jet and 75-90 hp			
First sequence	4	36	–
Second sequence	12	106	–
Main fuel jet			
4 and 5 hp	2	18	–
Silencer cover			
60-90 hp	2	18	–
Reed assembly to intake manifold			
20 hp, 25 hp and 30 hp	4	36	–
Reed valve/reed stop	1	9	–
Throttle rod connector			
9.9 and 15 hp	1	9	–
Top cover (carburetor)	2	18	–

Table 2 REED VALVE SPECIFICATIONS

Measurement	Specification
Maximum reed tip opening	
2 hp	0.3 mm (0.012 in.)
3-90 hp	0.2 mm (0.008 in.)
Reed stop opening	
2 hp	5.8-6.2 mm (0.228-0.244 in.)
3 hp	3.8-4.2 mm (0.150-0.165 in.)
4 and 5 hp	6.8-7.2 mm (0.268-0.283 in.)
6 and 8 hp	4.3-4.7 mm (0.169-0.185 in.)
9.9 hp	0.6-0.8 mm (0.024-0.031 in.)
15 hp	5.9-6.1 mm (0.232-0.240 in.)
20 and 25 hp (two-cylinder)	5.8-6.2 mm (0.228-0.244 in.)
25 hp (three-cylinder) and 30 hp	2.5-2.8 mm (0.098-0.110 in.)
28 jet, 35 jet, 40 hp and 50 hp	5.8-6.2 mm (0.228-0.244 in.)
60 hp	2.8-3.2 mm (0.110-0.126 in.)
65 jet and 70-90 hp	9.7-10.1 mm (0.382-0.398 in.)

FUEL SYSTEM

Table 3 FLOAT HEIGHT SPECIFICATIONS

Model	Float height
2 hp	16.8-17.8 mm (0.661-0.700 in.)
3 hp	12.0-16.0 mm (0.472-0.630 in.)
4 and 5 hp	21.5-22.5 mm (0.846-0.886 in.)
6 and 8 hp	12.0-16.0 mm (0.472-0.630 in.)
9.9 and 15 hp	12.5-15.5 mm (0.492-0.610 in.)
20 and 25 hp (two-cylinder)	14.0-15.0 mm (0.551-0.591 in.)
25 hp (three-cylinder)	14.5-17.5 mm (0.571-0.689 in.)
30 hp	13.5-16.5 mm (0.531-0.650 in.)
28 jet, 35 jet, 40 hp and 50 hp	14.0-16.0 mm (0.551-0.630 in.)
60 hp	
Premix models	12.0-16.0 mm (0.472-0.630 in.)
Oil injected models	13.0-15.0 mm (0.512-0.591 in.)
70 hp	13.0-15.0 mm (0.512-0.591 in.)
75 hp	
Premix models	16.5-21.5 mm (0.650-0.846 in.)
Oil injected models	13.0-15.0 mm (0.512-0.591 in.)
65 jet, 80 hp and 90 hp	13.0-15.0 mm (0.512-0.591 in.)

Chapter Six

Ignition and Electrical Systems

This chapter includes service procedures for the battery, starter motor, charging system and ignition system on outboard engines covered in this manual. Wiring diagrams are located at the end of the manual.

Table 1 lists tightening torque specifications. Use the standard torque specifications located in Chapter One for fasteners not listed in **Table 1**. **Tables 2-4** list battery charge percentage, battery capacity and battery requirements. **Table 5** lists electric starter motor specifications. All tables are located at the end of the chapter.

BATTERY

Batteries used in marine applications endure far more rigorous treatment than those used in automotive applications. Marine batteries (**Figure 1**) generally have a thicker exterior case to cushion the plates during tight turns and rough water operation. Thicker plates are also individually fastened within the case to help prevent premature failure. Spill-resistant caps on the battery cells help prevent electrolyte from spilling into the bilge. Automotive batteries should be used in a boat *only* during an emergency situation when a suitable marine battery is not available.

CAUTION
Sealed or maintenance-free batteries are not recommended for use with unregulated charging systems. Excessive charging during continued high-speed operation will cause the electrolyte to boil, resulting in a loss of electrolyte. Since water cannot be added to sealed batteries.

Rating Methods

The battery industry has developed specifications and performance standards to evaluate batteries and their energy potential. Several rating methods are available to provide meaningful information on battery selection.

Cold cranking amps (CCA)

CCA represents in amps the current flow the battery can deliver for 30 seconds at -17.8° C (0° F) without dropping below 1.2 volts per cell (7.2 volts on a standard 12 volt battery). The higher the number, the more amps it can deliver to crank the engine. CCA times 1.3 equals MCA.

IGNITION AND ELECTRICAL SYSTEMS

amps, without dropping below 1.75 volts per cell (10.5 volts on a standard 12 volt battery). The reserve capacity rating defines the length of time that a typical vehicle can be driven after the charging system fails. The 25 amp figure takes into account the power required by the ignition, lighting and other accessories. The higher the reserve capacity rating, the longer the vehicle could be operated after a charging system failure.

Amp-hour rating

The ampere hour rating method is also called the 20 hour rating method. This rating represents the steady current flow that the battery will deliver for 20 hours while at 26.7° C (80° F) without dropping below 1.75 volts per cell (10.5 volts on a standard 12 volt battery). The rating is actually the steady current flow times the 20 hours. For example, a 60 amp-hour battery will deliver 3 amps continuously for 20 hours. This rating method has been largely discontinued by the battery industry. CCA or MCA and reserve capacity ratings are now the most common battery rating methods.

Recommendations

Using a battery with inadequate capacity can cause hard starting or an inability to start the engine. Battery requirements are in **Table 4**. A battery with a capacity exceeding the minimum requirement is acceptable, and is highly recommended for a boat equipped with numerous electrical accessories (radios, depth finders, pumps). Consider adding an additional battery and installing a battery switch (**Figure 2**) on such applications. The switch allows starting and charging using one or both batteries. The switch can be turned off with the boat at rest or during storage to prevent discharge that occurs from some on-board accessories.

To determine the required capacity of a batteries, calculate the accessory current (amperage) draw rate of the accessory and refer to **Table 3**.

Two batteries may be connected in parallel to double the ampere-hour capacity while maintaining the required 12 volts. See **Figure 3**. For accessories that require 24 volts, batteries may be connected in series (**Figure 4**), but only accessories specifically requiring 24 volts should be connected to the system. If charging becomes necessary, batteries connected in a parallel or series circuit should be disconnected and charged individually.

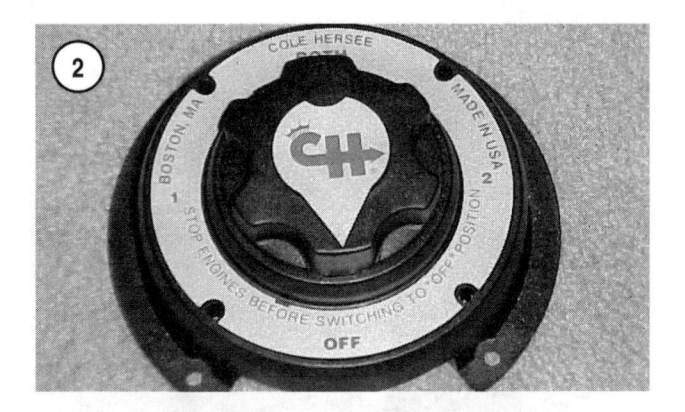

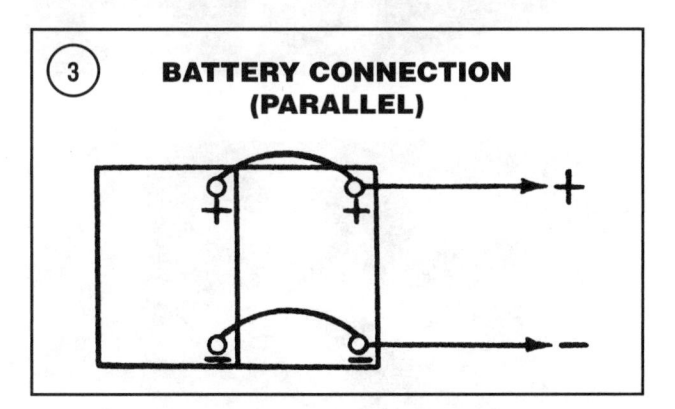

Marine cranking amps (MCA)

MCA is similar to the CCA test figure except that the test is run at 0° C (32° F) instead of 0° F (-17.8° C). This is more aligned with actual boat operating environments. MCA times 0.77 equals CCA.

Reserve capacity

Reserve capacity represents the time in minutes that a fully charged battery at 26.7° C (80° F) can deliver 25

Safety

The battery must be securely fastened in the boat to keep it from shifting or moving in the bilge area. The positive battery terminal (or the entire top of the battery) must also be covered with a nonconductive shield or boot.

If the battery is not properly secured it may contact the hull or metal fuel tank in rough water or while being transported. If the battery shorts against the metal hull or fuel tank, the short circuit will cause sparks and possibly an electrical fire. An explosion could occur if the fuel tank or battery case is compromised.

If the battery is not properly grounded and the battery contacts the metal hull, the battery will try to ground through the control cables or the wiring harness. Again, the short circuit will cause sparks and possibly an electrical fire. The control cables and boat wiring harness will be irreparably damaged.

Observe the following precautions to install a battery in a boat, especially a metal boat or a boat with a metal fuel tank.

1. Choose a location as far as practical from the fuel tank while still providing access for maintenance.
2. Secure the battery to the hull with a plastic battery box and tie-down strap (**Figure 5**) or a battery tray (**Figure 6**) with a nonconductive shield or boot covering the positive battery terminal.
3. Make sure all battery cable connections (two at the battery, two at the engine) are clean and tight. Do *not* use wing nuts to secure battery cables. If wing nuts are present, discard them and replace them with corrosion resistant hex nuts and lock washers to ensure positive electrical connections. Loose battery connections can cause an engine malfunction and failure of expensive components.
4. Periodically inspect the installation to make sure the battery is secured to the hull and the battery cable connections are clean and tight.

Removal, Care, Inspection and Installation

1. Remove the battery tray top or battery box cover. See **Figure 5** or **Figure 6**.
2. Disconnect the negative battery cable, then the positive battery cable.

NOTE
Some batteries have a built-in carry strap (Figure 1).

3. Attach a battery carry strap to the terminal posts. Remove the battery from the boat.
4. Inspect the entire battery case for cracks, holes or other damage.

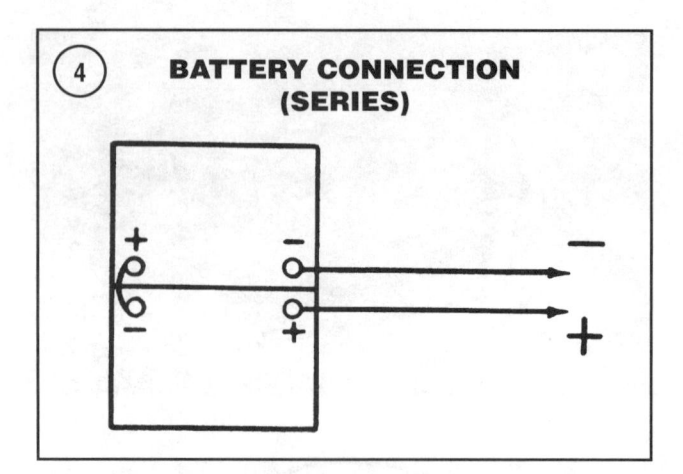

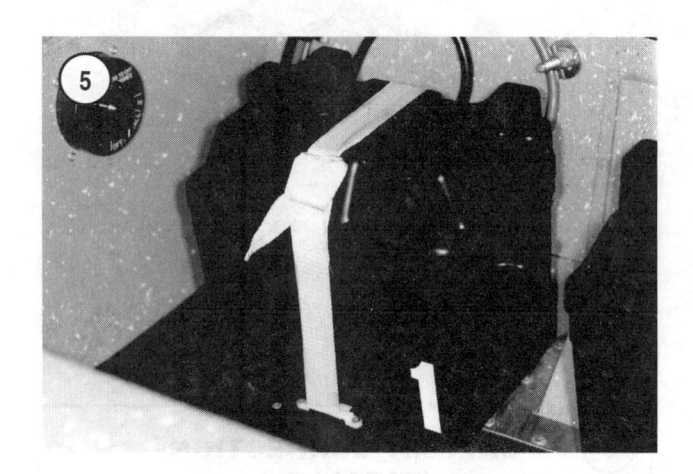

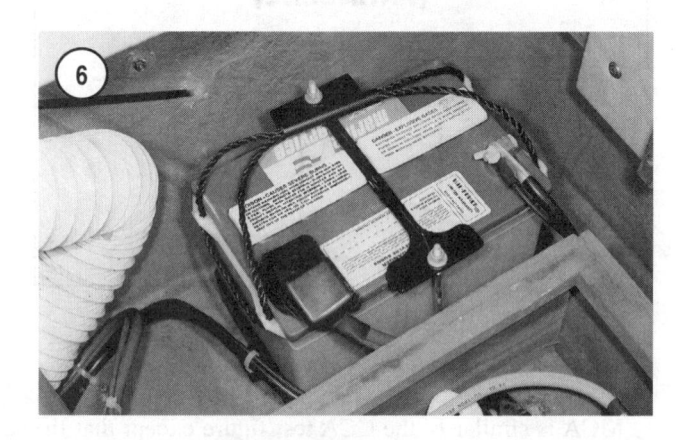

5. Inspect the battery tray or battery box for corrosion or deterioration. Clean as necessary with a solution of baking soda and water.

NOTE
Do not allow the baking soda cleaning solution to enter the battery cells in Step 5 or the electrolyte will be severely weakened.

IGNITION AND ELECTRICAL SYSTEMS

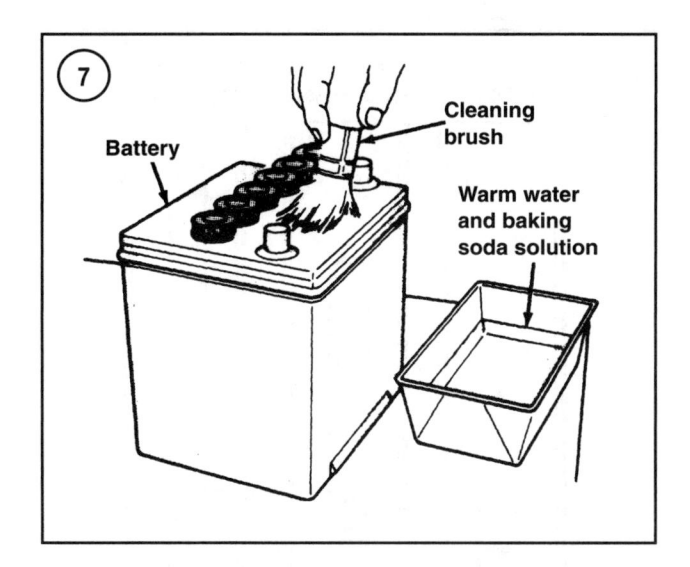

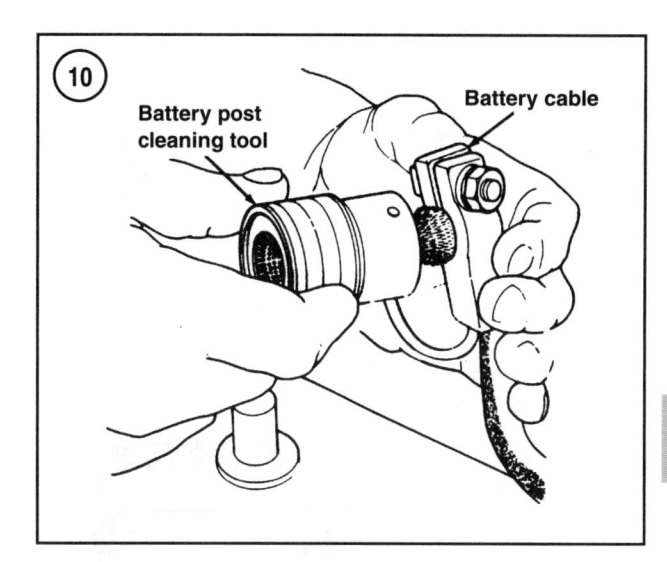

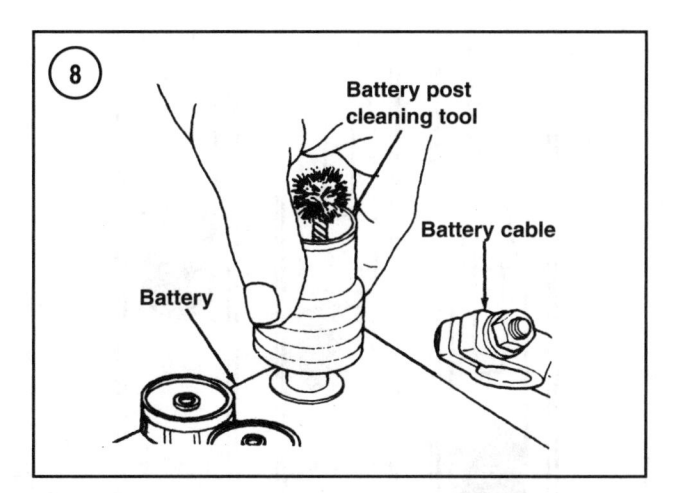

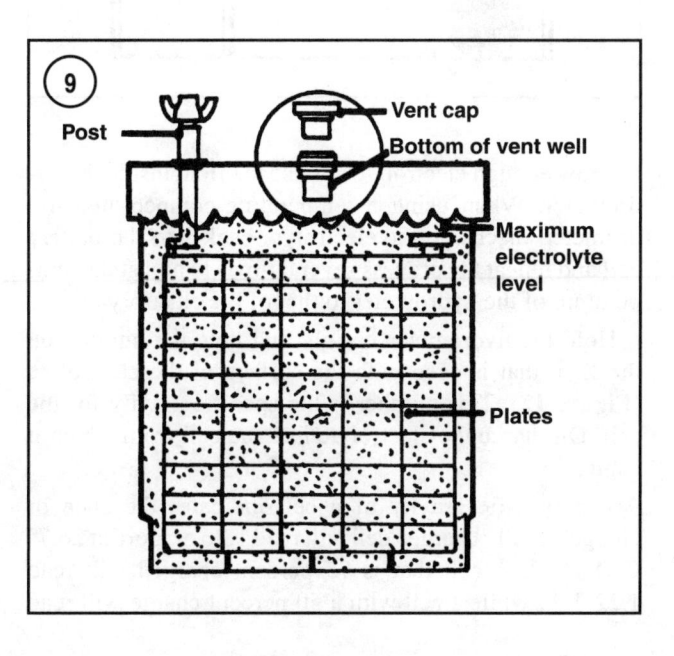

Figure 7 — Battery, Cleaning brush, Warm water and baking soda solution

Figure 8 — Battery post cleaning tool, Battery cable, Battery

Figure 9 — Post, Vent cap, Bottom of vent well, Maximum electrolyte level, Plates

Figure 10 — Battery post cleaning tool, Battery cable

6. Clean the top of the battery with a stiff bristle brush using the baking soda and water solution (**Figure 7**). Rinse the battery case with clear water and wipe it dry with a clean cloth or paper towel.

7. Clean the battery terminal posts with a stiff wire brush or battery terminal cleaning tool (**Figure 8**).

NOTE
Do not overfill the battery cells in Step 8. The electrolyte expands due to heat from the charging system and will overflow if the level is more than 4.8 mm (3/16 in.) above the battery plates.

8. Remove the filler caps and check the electrolyte level. Add distilled water, if necessary, to bring the level up to 4.8 mm (3/16 in.) above the plates in the battery case. See **Figure 9**.

9. Clean the battery cable clamps with a stiff wire brush (**Figure 10**).

10. Place the battery back into the boat and into the battery tray or battery box. If a battery tray is used, install and secure the retaining bracket.

11. Reconnect the positive battery cable first, then the negative cable.

CAUTION
Make sure the battery cables are connected to their proper terminals. Reversing the battery polarity will cause electrical and ignition system damage.

12. Securely tighten the battery connections. Coat the connections with petroleum jelly or a light grease to minimize corrosion. If a battery box is used, install the cover and secure the assembly with a tie-down strap.

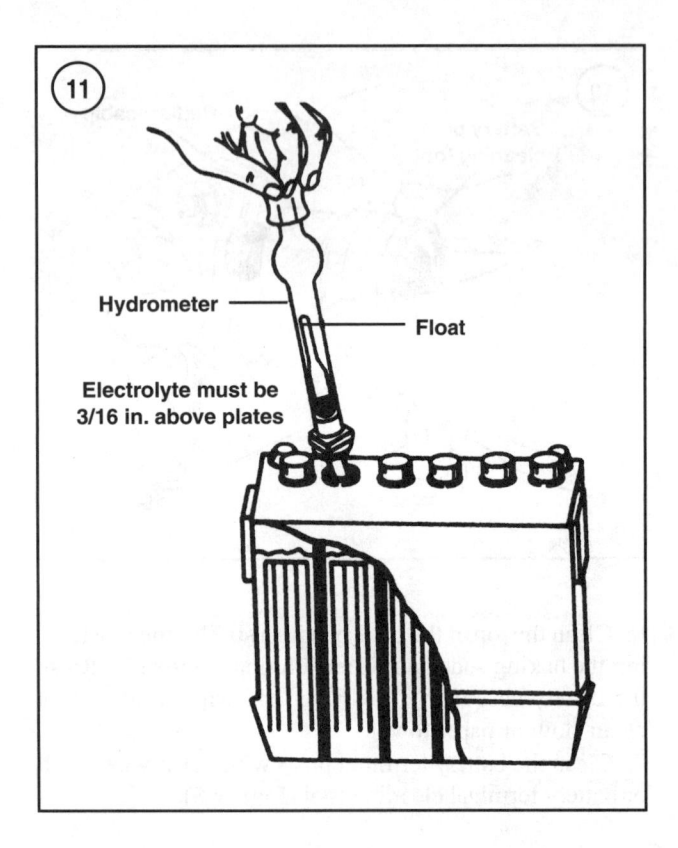

Battery Tests

Hydrometer test

On batteries with removable vent caps, the best method of checking the battery state of charge is to check the specific gravity of the electrolyte with a hydrometer. Use a hydrometer with numbered graduations from 1.100-1.300 points rather than one with color-coded bands. To use the hydrometer, squeeze the rubber bulb, insert the tip into a cell, then release the bulb to fill the hydrometer. See **Figure 11**.

NOTE
Do not test the specific gravity immediately after adding water to the battery cells, as the water will dilute the electrolyte and lower the specific gravity. To obtain an accurate hydrometer reading, charge the battery after adding water and before testing it with a hydrometer.

NOTE
*If a temperature-compensated hydrometer is **not** used, add 4 points specific gravity to the actual reading for every 10° above 26.7° C (80° F). Subtract 4 points specific gravity for every 10° below 26.7° C (80° F).*

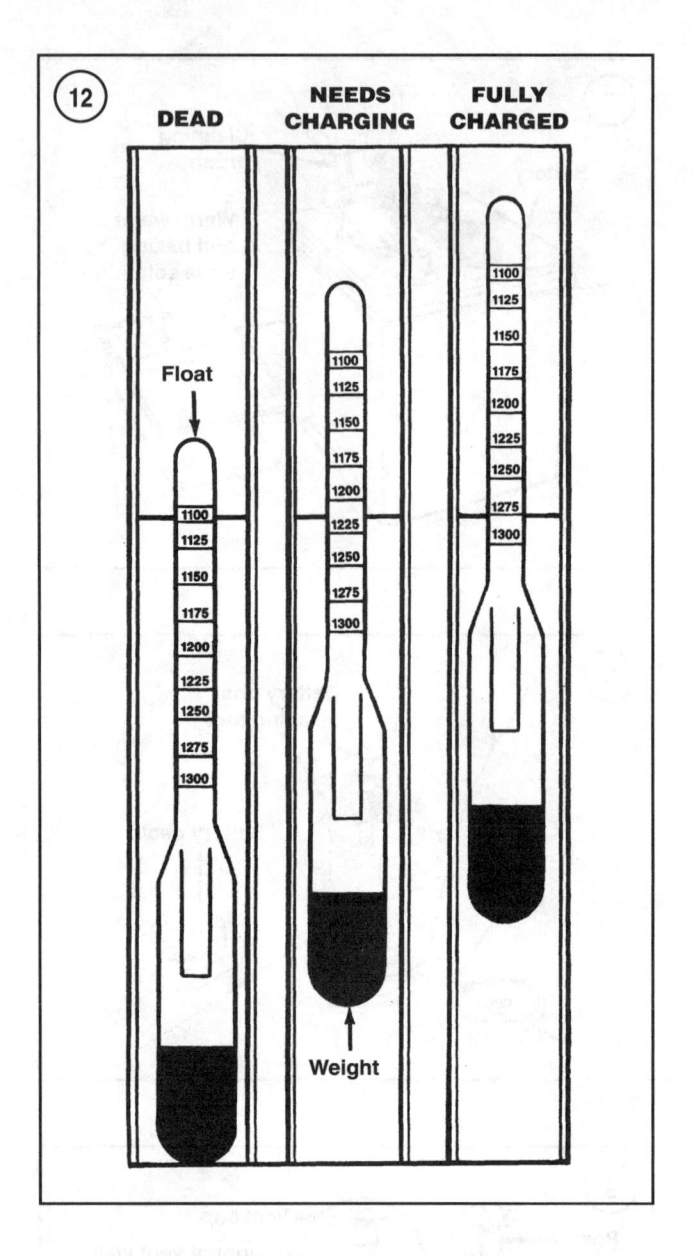

Draw enough electrolyte to raise the float inside the hydrometer. When using a temperature-compensated hydrometer, discharge the electrolyte back into the battery cell and repeat the process several times to adjust the temperature of the hydrometer to that of the electrolyte.

Hold the hydrometer upright and note the number on the float that is even with the surface of the electrolyte (**Figure 12**). This number is the specific gravity for the cell. Discharge the electrolyte into the cell from which it came.

The specific gravity of a cell indicates the state of charge. A fully charged cell will read 1.26 or more at 26.7° C (80° F). A cell that is 75 percent charged will read 1.22-1.23 while a cell with a 50 percent charge will read

IGNITION AND ELECTRICAL SYSTEMS

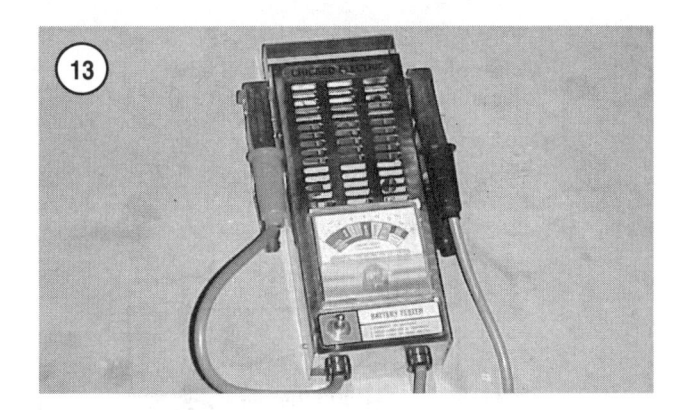

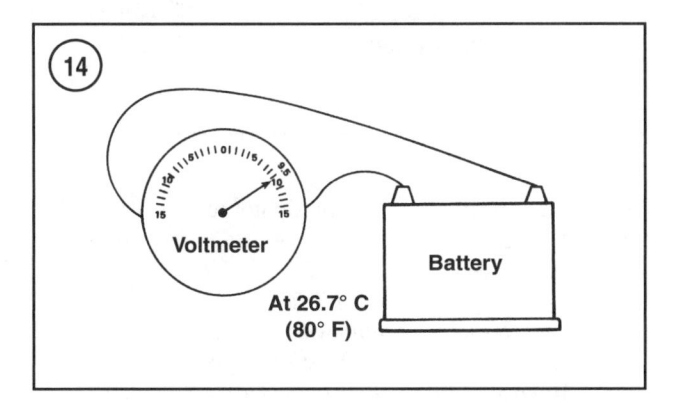

Figure 13

Figure 14 Voltmeter / Battery At 26.7° C (80° F)

1.17-1.18. Any cell reading 1.12 or less is discharged. All cells should be within 30 points specific gravity of each other. If there is over 30 points variation, the battery condition is questionable. Charge the battery and recheck the specific gravity. If 30 points or more variation remains between cells after charging, the battery has failed and should be replaced. Refer to **Table 2** for battery charge level based on specific gravity readings.

Open-circuit voltage test

On sealed or maintenance-free batteries, check the state of charge by measuring the open-circuit (no load) voltage of the battery. Use a digital voltmeter for best results. For the most accurate results, allow the battery to set at rest for at least 30 minutes to allow the battery to stabilize. Then, observing the correct polarity, connect the voltmeter to the battery and note the meter reading. If the open-circuit voltage is 12.7 volts or higher, the battery is fully charged. A reading of 12.4 volts means the battery is approximately 75 percent charged, a reading of 12.2 volts means the battery is approximately 50 percent charged and a reading of 12.1 volts means that the battery is approximately 25 percent charged.

Load test

Two common methods are used to load test batteries. A commercially available load tester (**Figure 13**) measures the battery voltage as it applies a load across the terminal. If a load tester is not available, measure the cranking voltage as follows:
1. Attach a voltmeter across the battery as shown in **Figure 14**.
2. Remove and ground the spark plug leads to the power head to prevent accidental starting.
3. Crank the engine for approximately 15 seconds while noting the voltmeter reading. Note the voltage at the end of the 15 second period.
4A. If the voltage is 9.5 volts or higher, the battery is sufficiently charged and of sufficient capacity for the outboard engine.
4B. If the voltage is below 9.5 volts, one of the following conditions is present:
   a. The battery is discharged or defective. Charge the battery and retest.
   b. The battery is of too small capacity for the outboard engine. Refer to *Recommendations* in this chapter.
   c. The starting system is drawing excessive current causing the battery voltage to drop. Refer to Chapter Two for starting system troubleshooting procedures.
   d. There is a mechanical defect in the power head or gearcase creating excessive load and current draw on the starting system. Inspect the power head and gearcase for mechanical defects.

Storage

Wet cell batteries slowly discharge when stored. They discharge faster when warm than when cold. Before storing a battery, clean the case with a solution of baking soda and water. Rinse the case with clean water and wipe it dry. Fully charge the battery, then store it in a cool, dry location. Check the electrolyte level and state of charge frequently during storage. If the specific gravity falls to 40 points or more below full charge (1.260), or the open circuit voltage falls below 12.4 volts, recharge the battery.

Charging

Maintain a good state of charge in batteries used for starting. Check the state of charge with a hydrometer or digital voltmeter as described in this chapter.

Remove the battery from the boat for charging, since a charging battery releases highly explosive hydrogen gas. In many boats, the area around the battery is not well ventilated and the gas may remain in the area for hours after the charging process has been completed. Sparks or flames occurring near the battery can cause it to explode spraying battery acid over a wide area.

If the battery cannot be removed for charging, make sure the bilge access hatches, doors or vents are fully open to allow adequate ventilation. Observe the following precautions when charging batteries:

1. Never smoke in close proximity to any battery.
2. Make sure all accessories are turned off before disconnecting the battery cables. Disconnecting a circuit that is electrically active will create a spark that can ignite explosive gas that may be present.
3. Always disconnect the negative battery cable first, then the positive cable.
4. On batteries with removable vent caps, always check the electrolyte level before charging the battery. Maintain the correct electrolyte level throughout the charging process.
5. Never attempt to charge a battery that is frozen.

WARNING
Be extremely careful not to create any sparks around the battery when connecting the battery charger.

6. Connect the charger to the battery. Connect the negative charger lead to the negative battery terminal and the positive charger lead to the positive battery terminal. If the charger output is variable, select a setting of approximately 4 amps. It is preferable to charge a battery slowly at low amp settings, rather than quickly at high amp settings.
7. If the charger has a dual voltage setting, set the voltage switch to 12 volts, then switch the charger on.
8. If the battery is severely discharged, allow it to charge for at least 8 hours. Check the charging process with a hydrometer. Consider the battery fully charged when the specific gravity of all cells does not increase when checked three times at one hour intervals, and all cells are gassing freely.

Jump Starting

If the battery becomes severely discharged, it is possible to jump start the engine from another battery in or out of a boat. Jump starting can be dangerous if the proper procedure is not followed. Always use caution when jump starting.

Check the electrolyte level of the discharged battery before attempting the jump start. If the electrolyte is not visible or if it appears to be frozen, do not jump start the discharged battery.

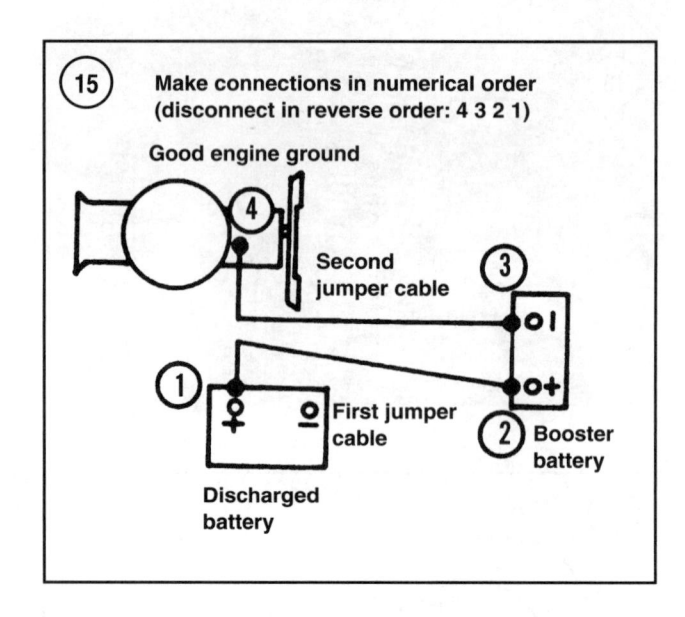

WARNING
Be extremely careful when connecting the booster battery to the discharged battery. Make sure the jumper cables are connected in the correct polarity.

1. Connect the jumper cables in the order and sequence shown in **Figure 15**.

WARNING
An electrical arc may occur when the final connection is made. This could cause an explosion if it occurs near the battery. For this reason, make the final connection to a good engine ground away from the battery and not to the battery itself.

2. Make sure all jumper cables are out of the way of moving engine parts.

CAUTION
Do not run the engine without an adequate water supply and do not exceed 3000 rpm without an adequate load.

3. Start the engine. Once it starts, run it at a moderate speed (fast idle).

CAUTION
Running the engine at high speed with a discharged battery can damage the charging system.

IGNITION AND ELECTRICAL SYSTEMS

4. Remove the jumper cables in the exact reverse of the order shown in **Figure 15**. Remove the cable at point 4, then 3, then 2 and finally 1.

STARTING SYSTEM COMPONENTS

This section describes removal, inspection and installation for electric starting system components. If the torque specification is not listed in **Table 1**, refer to Chapter One for general torque specifications.

Starter Relay
Removal/Installation

Starter relay mounting locations vary by model. Use the wiring diagrams located at the back of the manual to identify the starter relay wire colors. Refer to the following information and trace the wires to the relay (**Figure 16**).

On 6-15 hp models, the relay is located just aft of the starter motor on the starboard side of the power head.

On 20 and 25 hp two-cylinder models, the relay is located just below the flywheel on the port side of the power head.

On 25 hp three-cylinder and 30 hp models, the relay is located just below the starter motor. The starter motor is mounted on the starboard side of the power head.

On 28 jet, 35 jet, 40 hp and 50 hp models, the relay is located below and slightly aft of the starter motor. The starter motor is mounted on the starboard side of the power head.

On 60 and 70 hp models, the relay is located near the lower starboard side of the power head. A mounting bracket secures the relay to the lower engine cover. The main engine wire harness passes directly over the relay.

On 65 jet and 75-90 hp models, the relay is located on the electrical component mount at the rear and starboard side of the power head. The plastic electrical component cover (**Figure 17**) must be removed to access the starter relay, trim relays and rectifier/regulator.

1. Disconnect the cables from the battery. Disconnect and ground the spark plug leads to prevent accidental starting.
2. On 65 jet and 75-80 hp models, remove the plastic electrical component cover (**Figure 17**).
3. Mark all relay terminals with the wire color and note the wire routing before disconnecting the relay wires.
4. Carefully pull the rubber boots (**Figure 16**) away from the relay terminals. Remove the hex nuts and washers, then pull the two wires from the relay terminals.
5. Locate the brown and black wires leading to the relay. Unplug the brown and black wire bullet connectors from the relay. If the black wire does not have a bullet connector, trace the wire from the relay to its connection to the power head ground. Remove the screw and lock washer (5 and 6, **Figure 18**) to disconnect the wire.
6. Carefully pry the relay (4, **Figure 18**) from the rubber mount (3). Work carefully to avoid damaging the relay. If poor access prevents easy removal of the relay, remove the bolt and washer (2, **Figure 18**), then lift the relay and mounting bracket from the engine.
7. Inspect the rubber mount for tears or deterioration. If there are defects, carefully pull the mount from the arms of the mounting bracket (1, **Figure 18**).
8. If the mounting bracket was removed, fit the arms of the mounting bracket through the slots on each side of the rubber mount. Push the mount onto the bracket until the tabs on each arm protrude from the slots.
9. Align the large terminals with the arms of the relay mount, then insert the replacement relay into the mount. Push the relay in until the tabs in the mount opening capture the relay. Apply a light coat of window cleaning solution to the rubber mount for easier installation.
10. If the mounting bracket (1, **Figure 18**) was removed, install the bracket onto the power head, electrical component plate or lower engine cover. Secure the bracket with

18 STARTER RELAY REMOVAL/INSTALLATION

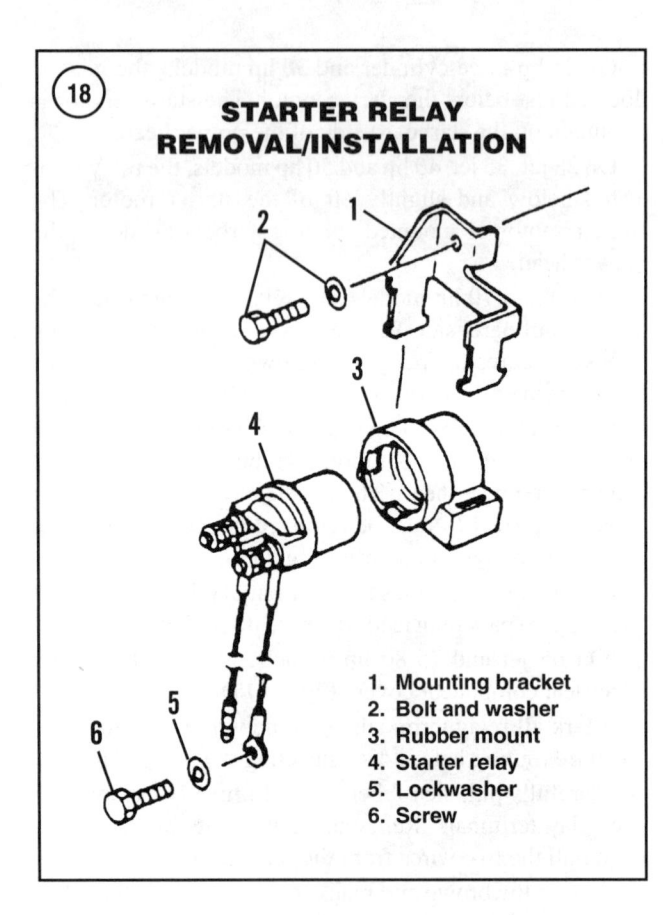

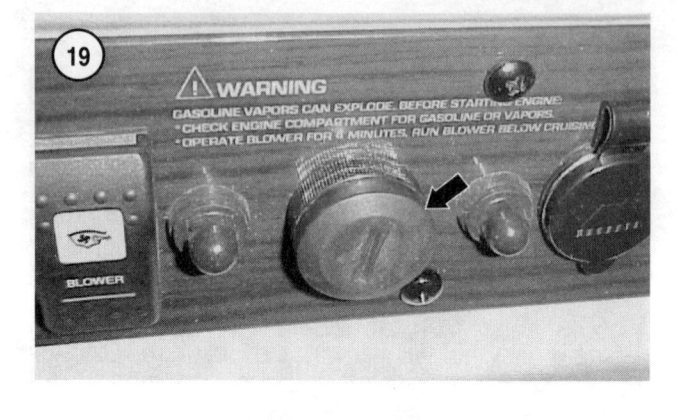

1. Mounting bracket
2. Bolt and washer
3. Rubber mount
4. Starter relay
5. Lockwasher
6. Screw

the bolt and washer (2, **Figure 18**). Tighten the mounting bolt to the general specification in Chapter One.

11. Reconnect the brown and black wires bullet connectors. If the black wire does not use a bullet connector, connect the black wire to the engine ground using the screw and lock washer (5 and 6, **Figure 18**).

12. Connect the large diameter wire terminals to the large terminals of the relay. Secure the terminals with the hex nuts and tighten the nuts securely.

13. Install the rubber boots (**Figure 16**) onto the terminals. The rubber boots must completely cover the terminals. Route the relay wiring as noted prior to removal.

14. On 65 jet and 75-90 hp models, install the plastic electrical component cover (**Figure 17**).

15. Connect the battery cables and spark plug leads.

Key Switch Removal/Installation

Key switch mounting locations vary by the type of control.

On remote control models, the switch mounts in the control box or on the dash (**Figure 19**).

On tiller control (28 jet, 35 jet and 40-90 hp) models, the key switch mounts into the tiller handle bracket on the front of the engine.

Remote control models

1. Disconnect the battery cables. Disconnect and ground the spark plug leads to prevent accidental starting.
2. If the switch is mounted in the remote control, disassemble the remote control and replace the key switch as described in Chapter Thirteen.
3. Remove a dash mounted key switch as follows:
   a. Record the color of the wire connected to the key switch terminals, then disconnect the wires.
   b. Pull the rubber seal from the outer nut. Remove the outer nut and pull the switch from the dash.
4. Install a dash mounted key switch as follows:
   a. Thread the inner nut fully on the shaft of the switch. Install the lock washer over the shaft.
   b. Insert the key switch into the dash. The drain holes in the switch body (**Figure 20**) must face downward.
   c. Thread the outer nut on the key switch. If the switch fits loosely in the opening, thread the inner

IGNITION AND ELECTRICAL SYSTEMS

**KEY SWITCH AND STOP/LANYARD SWITCH
(28 JET, 35 JET AND 40-90 HP [TYPICAL] MODELS)**

1. Bolt
2. Switch housing screws
3. Clamp screw
4. Terminals
5. Key switch
6. Switch housing
7. Lanyard switch

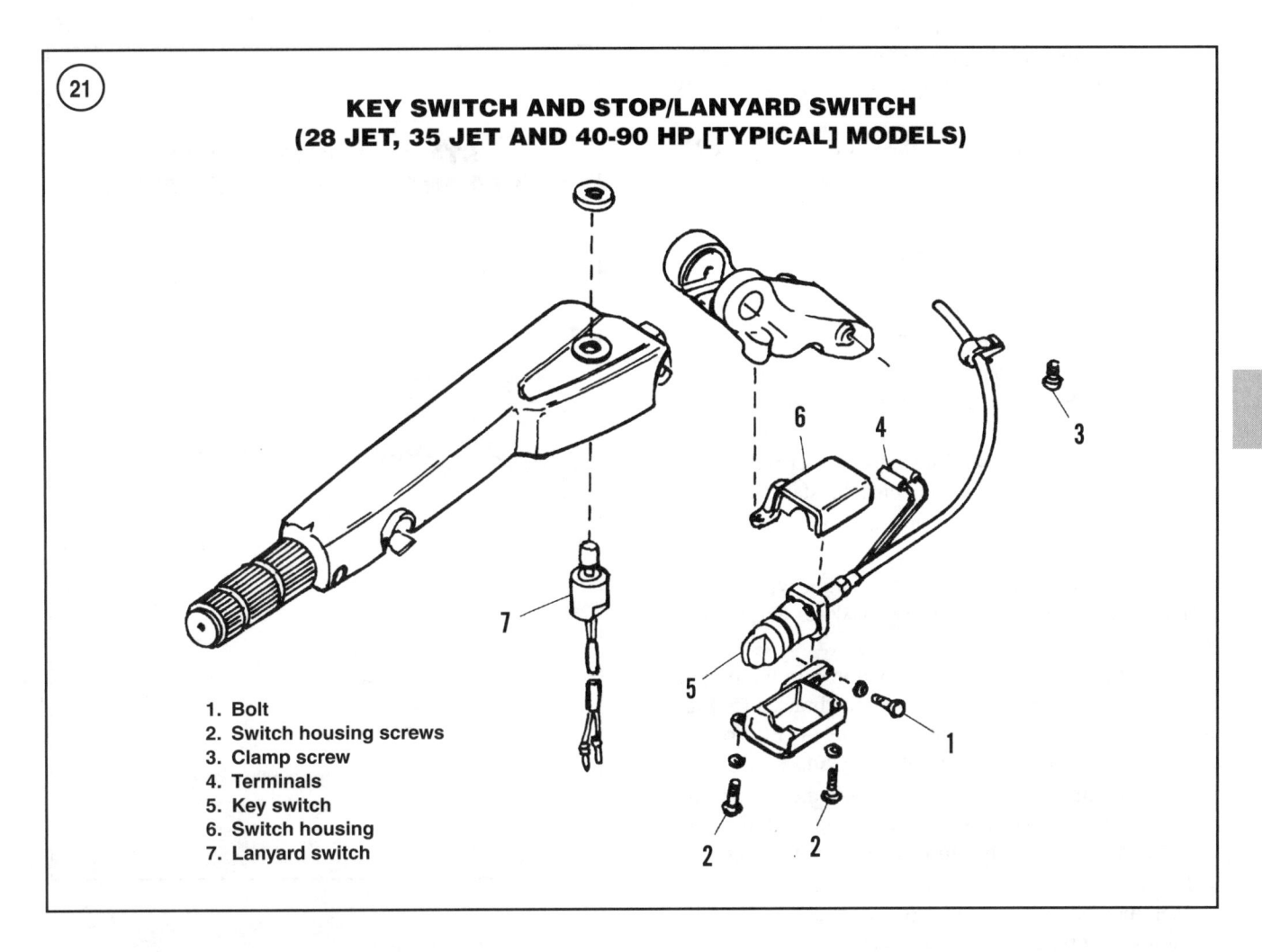

nut toward the dash until the switch is securely mounted.

d. Install the rubber seal into the outer nut. Use the ignition key to align the slot in the seal with the key slot in the switch.

e. Connect all wires to the corresponding terminals of the switch. When replacing the switch, refer to the switch manufacturer's instructions for wire connecting points.

5. Connect the battery cables and spark plug leads.

Tiller control models

Refer to **Figure 21**, typical for this procedure.

1. Disconnect the battery cables. Disconnect and ground the spark plug leads to prevent accidental starting.
2. Remove the screws (2, **Figure 21**) and upper cover (6) to free the key switch (5) from the housing.
3. Unplug the bullet terminals (4, **Figure 21**) from the lanyard switch (7) wires.
4. Trace the key switch wire harness to its connections to the engine wire harness, neutral safety switch and starter relay wires. Note the wire routing and connection points, then disconnect the key switch wires.
5. Remove the clamp screw (3, **Figure 21**, typical) to free the wire harness clamp. Guide the harness through the opening in the lower engine cover while removing the switch.
6. Guide the key switch wire harness through the opening in the lower engine cover. Connect all wires to their appropriate engine wire harness connections. Connect the bullet terminals (4, **Figure 21**) to the lanyard switch (7) wires.
7. Route all wiring to avoid pinching and potential interference with moving components. Secure the switch wire harness with the clamp screw (3, **Figure 21**).
8. Install the key switch (5, **Figure 21**) into its recess in the switch housing. The groove in the key switch body must fit over the ridge in the housing. Fit the switch wire harness into the slot in the rear of the switch housing.

9. Install the cover (6, **Figure 21**) onto the housing. The ridge in the housing must fit over the groove in the key switch body.

10. Install and securely tighten the screws (2, **Figure 21**) and washers.

11. Connect the battery cables and spark plug leads.

**Starter Button Removal/Installation
(6-30 hp [Except 28 Jet] Models)**

The starter button mounts on the front side of the lower engine cover. Refer to **Figure 22**, typical for this procedure.

1. Disconnect the battery cables. Disconnect and ground the spark plug leads to prevent accidental starting.
2. Remove the starter button nut and bracket used on some models.
3. Trace the brown and red starter button wires to the starter relay and neutral safety switch wires. Disconnect both wires.
4. Install the replacement starter button into the engine cover opening. If so equipped, install the bracket (5, **Figure 22**) onto the button. Thread the nut (4, **Figure 22**) onto the button and securely tighten the nut.
5. Route the starter button wire harness to the appropriate bullet connections on the starter relay and neutral safety switch wires. Connect the brown and red button wires.
6. Position the starter button wire harness so it will not contact moving components. Secure the harness with plastic locking type clamps as needed.
7. Connect the battery cables and spark plug leads.

Neutral Safety Switch Replacement

Mounting locations for the neutral safety switch vary by the type of control system used.

On remote control models, the switch is mounted with the control box. See **Figure 23**.

On tiller control models, the switch is located on the engine (**Figure 24**). The switch bracket is mounted on the lower engine cover or power head to position the switch plunger in direct contact with the shift linkages (**Figure 25**, typical).

NOTE
Some remote control models may be equipped with both a control box and engine mounted neutral safety switch. This is not a problem for starting system operation if both switches operate correctly.

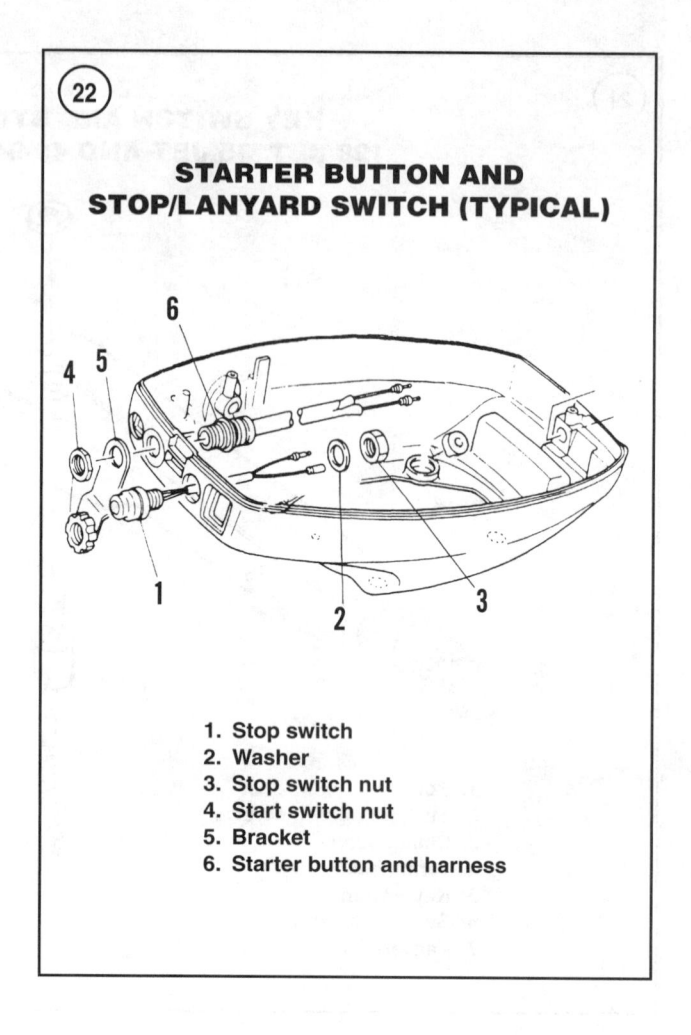

22

STARTER BUTTON AND STOP/LANYARD SWITCH (TYPICAL)

1. Stop switch
2. Washer
3. Stop switch nut
4. Start switch nut
5. Bracket
6. Starter button and harness

Remote control models

NOTE
Some Yamaha outboards are not equipped with a Yamaha control. Contact the manufacturer of the control or a reputable marine dealership for repair information.

Refer to **Figure 23**, typical for this procedure.

1. Disconnect the battery cables. Disconnect and ground the spark plug leads to prevent accidental starting.
2. Refer to Chapter Thirteen to disassemble the remote control to the point where the neutral safety switch is easy accessible.
3. Locate the two neutral switch wires then disconnect them from the remote control harness.
4. Remove the screw and retainer (2, **Figure 23**), then lift the switch (3) from the control.
5. Inspect the switch operating arm (1, **Figure 23**) and leaf spring (4) for cracks and worn surfaces. Replace if necessary.

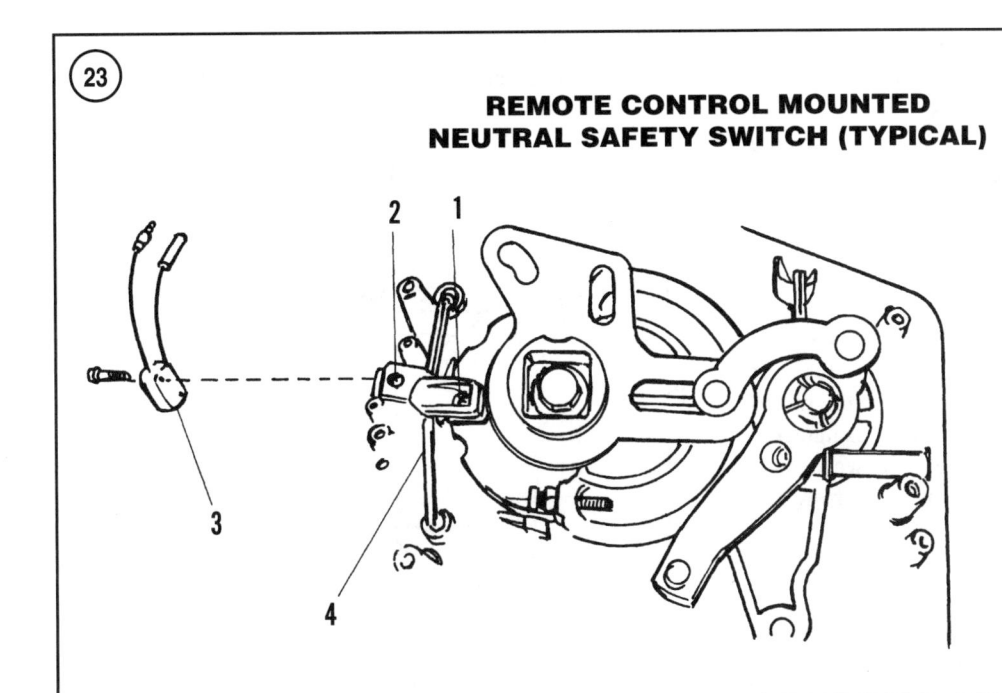

IGNITION AND ELECTRICAL SYSTEMS

23

REMOTE CONTROL MOUNTED NEUTRAL SAFETY SWITCH (TYPICAL)

1. Switch operating arm
2. Switch retainer
3. Neutral safety switch
4. Leaf spring

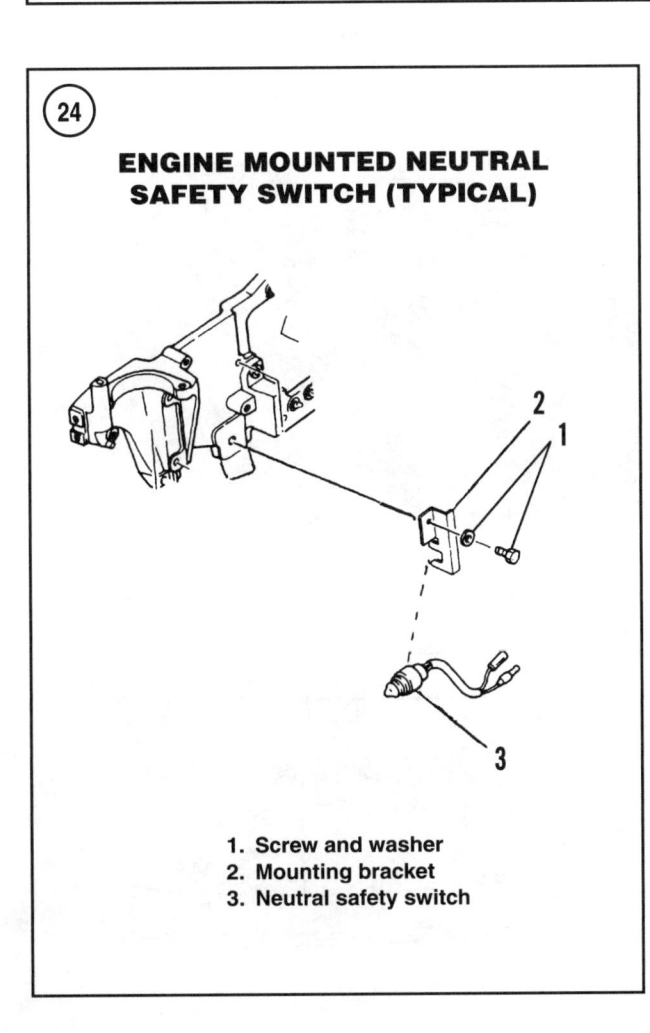

24

ENGINE MOUNTED NEUTRAL SAFETY SWITCH (TYPICAL)

1. Screw and washer
2. Mounting bracket
3. Neutral safety switch

25

6. Position the replacement switch on its mounts and secure it with the retainer and screw.

7. Connect the neutral safety switch wires to the remote control harness wires. Route the switch wires so they will not interfere with moving components. Secure the wires with plastic locking type clamps as needed.

8. Reassemble and install the remote control as described in Chapter Thirteen.

9. Connect the battery cables and spark plug leads.

Tiller control models

Mounting locations for the neutral safety switch vary by model. Refer to the wiring diagrams at the back of the manual to identify the switch wire colors and connection points. Trace the indicated wire to the neutral safety switch mounting bracket. See **Figure 24**.

1. Disconnect the battery cables. Disconnect and ground the spark plug leads to prevent accidental starting.
2. Disconnect the brown neutral safety switch wires from the starter relay and starter button or engine wire harness bullet connectors.
3. Shift the engine into FORWARD gear.
4. Loosen the large nut on the switch (3, **Figure 24**). Carefully slide the switch from the slot in the bracket. If the bracket is not equipped with a slot, remove the nut to free the switch from the bracket. If the large nut is inaccessible, remove the bracket mounting screw and washer (1, **Figure 24**), then remove the bracket and switch from the engine.
5. Install the switch into the bracket and secure it with the large nut.
6. Shift the engine into NEUTRAL gear. Check for proper alignment of the switch with the cam portion of the linkage. The tip of the plunger must contact the center of the cam. Loosen the nut and reposition the switch within the slot as necessary. Securely tighten the large nut after verifying proper alignment.
7. Connect the brown neutral safety switch wires to the starter relay and starter button or engine wire harness bullet connectors.
8. Route the switch wire harness to prevent contact with moving components. Secure the harness with plastic locking type clamps as needed.
9. Connect the battery cables and spark plug leads.

STARTER MOTOR

This section describes the starter motor removal, installation, disassembly, and assembly for a typical starter motor. The motor appearance, mounting methods, internal component appearances, and repair procedures vary by model. Procedures indicate when a model specific procedure is required. Refer to **Table 1** for torque specifications and general torque specifications in Chapter One if a specific torque is not listed.

Removal/Installation

1. Disconnect the battery cables. Disconnect and ground the spark plug leads to prevent accidental starting.
2. Locate the starter motor (**Figure 26**, typical) on the side of the power head.
3. Pull the insulating boot from the large starter wire terminal, then remove the terminal nut (**Figure 27**). If the

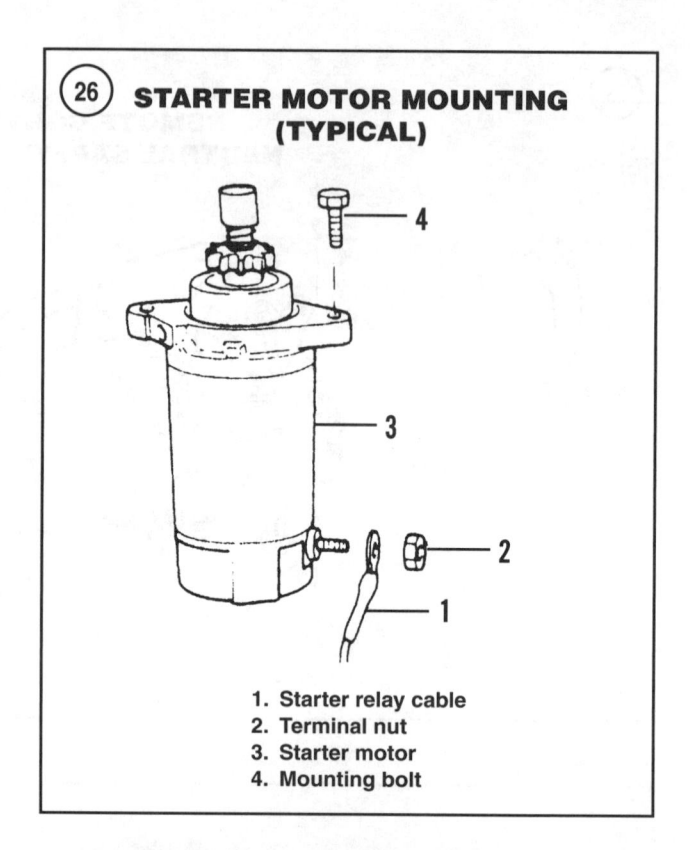

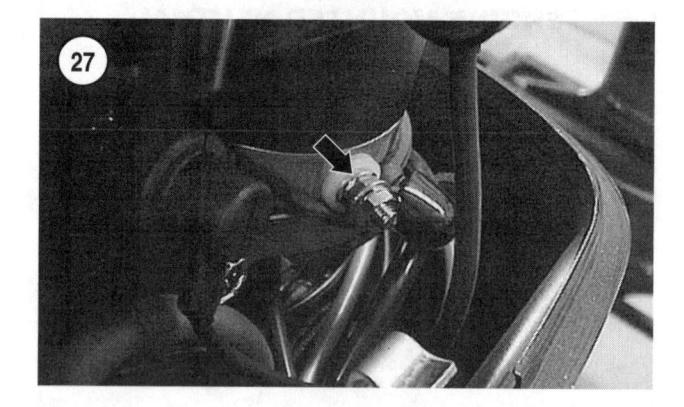

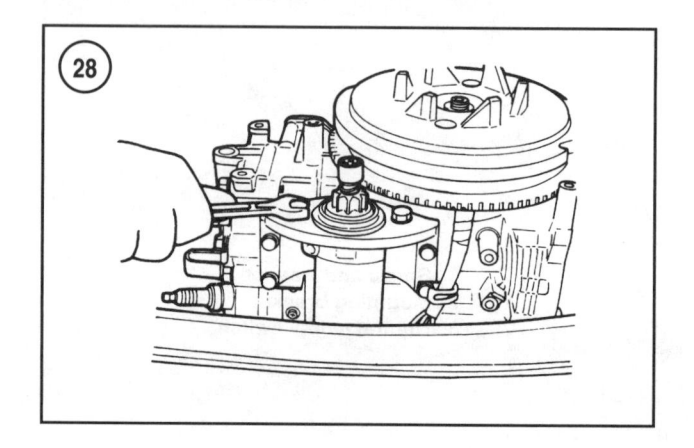

IGNITION AND ELECTRICAL SYSTEMS

**STARTER MOTOR COMPONENTS
(6-25 HP TWO-CYLINDER MODELS)**

1. Locking clip
2. Pinion stopper
3. Spring
4. Pinion drive
5. Throughbolts
6. Top cover
7. Frame
8. Armature
9. Composite washers
10. Metal washers
11. Ring
12. Bottom cover
13. Thrust washer
14. Brush plate
15. Brushes and springs

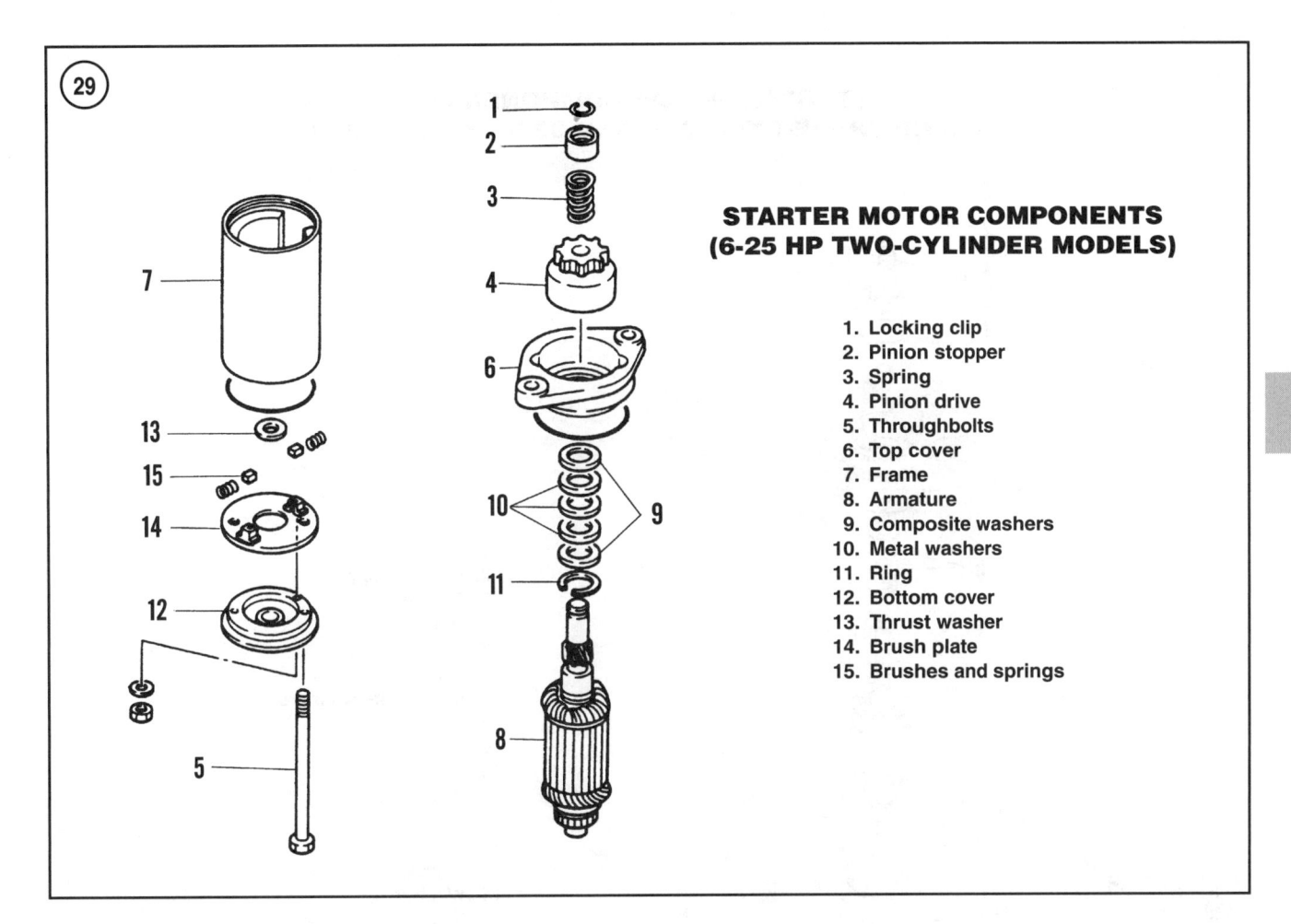

terminal is difficult to access, remove the starter mounting bolts and pull the starter away from the power head, then remove the terminal nut.

4. Support the starter, then locate and remove the starter mounting bolts (**Figure 28**). Note any grounding wires connected to the mounting bolts during removal.

   a. Two top mounted bolts are used on 6-50 hp models.

   b. Four side mounted bolts are used on 60-90 hp models.

5. If the starter terminal is difficult to access after starter installation, connect the cable and tighten the nut before installing the starter on the bracket.

6. Install the replacement starter motor onto the mounting bracket. Make sure no wires or hoses are pinched by the starter, then thread the mounting bolts into the starter and mounting bracket. Make sure the mounting bolts pass through any grounding wire terminal, if so equipped, before passing through the starter. Route the ground wire so it does not interfere with other components before tightening the mounting bolts.

7. Tighten the starter mounting bolts to the specification in **Table 1**.

8. Connect the large gauge wire terminal to the starter terminal (**Figure 27**). Securely tighten the terminal nut.

9. Slide the insulating boot onto the starter terminal. The boot must completely cover the terminal.

10. Connect the battery cables and spark plug leads.

CAUTION
Never strike the frame of the starter motor. The permanent magnets in the frame may crack or break and cause starter motor failure.

Disassembly

Refer to **Figures 29-32**.

1. Remove the starter as described in this chapter.

2. Clamp the starter lightly in a vise with protective jaws. Grasp the pinion drive and stopper (**Figure 33**), then pull them toward the starter to expose the locking clip. Care-

**STARTER MOTOR COMPONENTS
(25 HP THREE-CYLINDER AND 30-50 HP MODELS)**

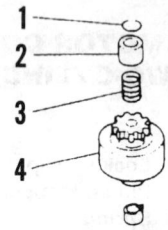

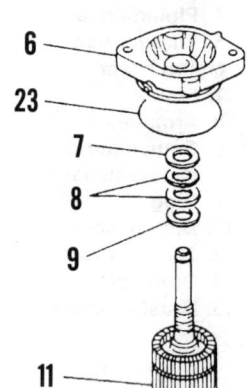

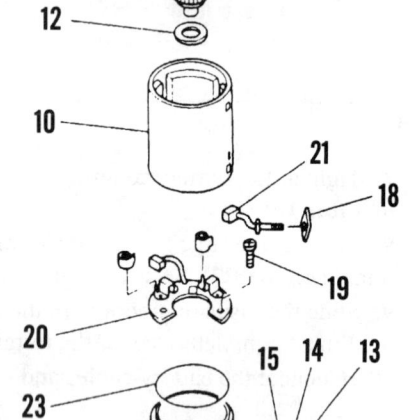

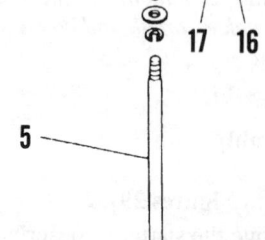

1. Locking clip
2. Pinion stopper
3. Spring
4. Pinion drive
5. Throughbolts
6. Top cover
7. Composite washers
8. Metal washers
9. Ring
10. Frame
11. Armature
12. Thrust washer
13. Terminal nut
14. Lock washer
15. Washer
16. Insulating bushing
17. O-ring
18. Insulating bushing
19. Screw
20. Brush plate
21. Positive brush
22. Bottom cover
23. O-ring

IGNITION AND ELECTRICAL SYSTEMS

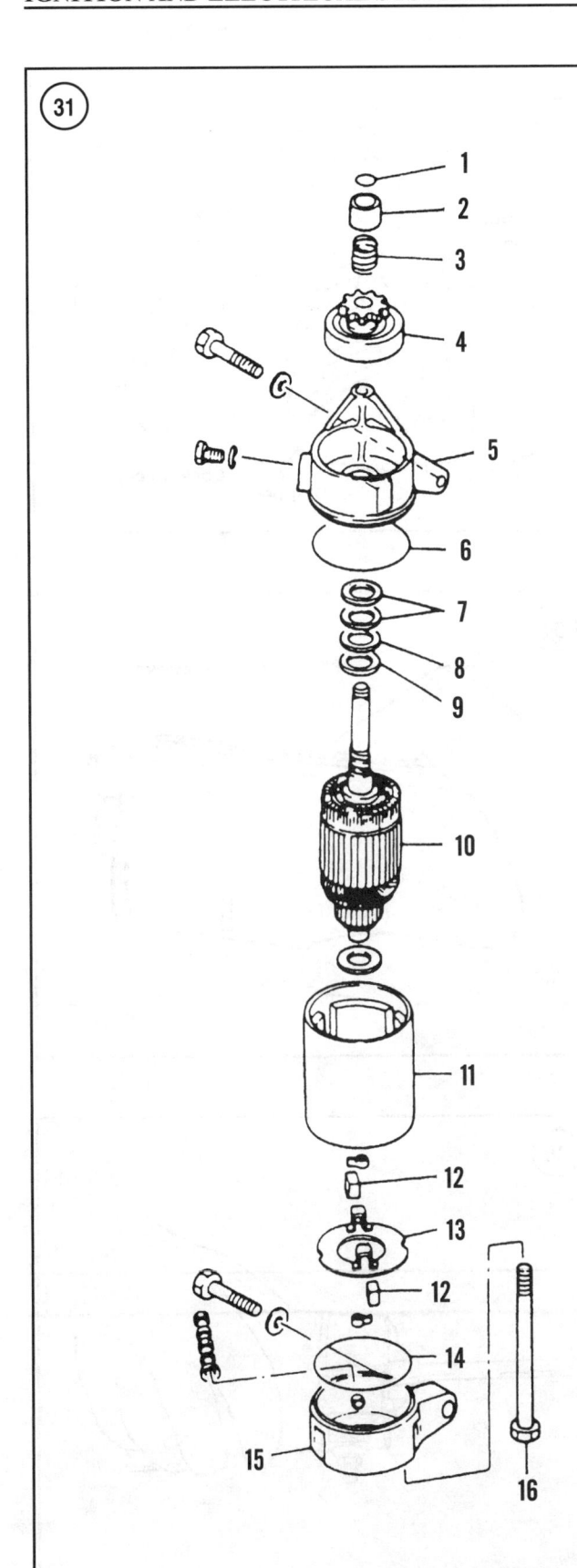

③¹

**STARTER MOTOR COMPONENTS
(60 AND 70 HP MODELS)**

1. Locking clip
2. Pinion stopper
3. Spring
4. Pinion drive
5. Top cover
6. O-ring
7. Composite washers
8. Metal washers
9. Ring
10. Armature
11. Frame
12. Brushes
13. Brush plate
14. O-ring
15. Bottom cover
16. Throughbolts

252

CHAPTER SIX

32 STARTER MOTOR COMONENTS (65 JET AND 75-90 HP MODELS)

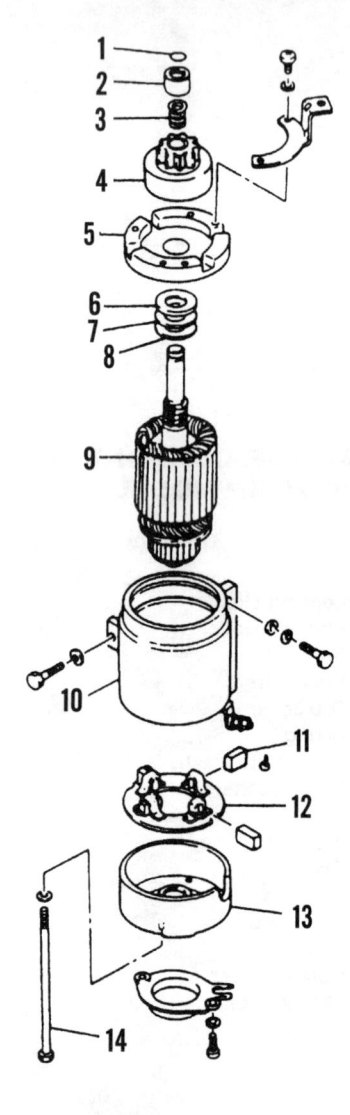

1. Locking clip
2. Pinion stopper
3. Spring
4. Pinion drive
5. Top cover
6. Composite washer
7. Metal washer
8. Ring
9. Armature
10. Frame
11. Brushes
12. Brush plate
13. Bottom cover
14. Throughbolts

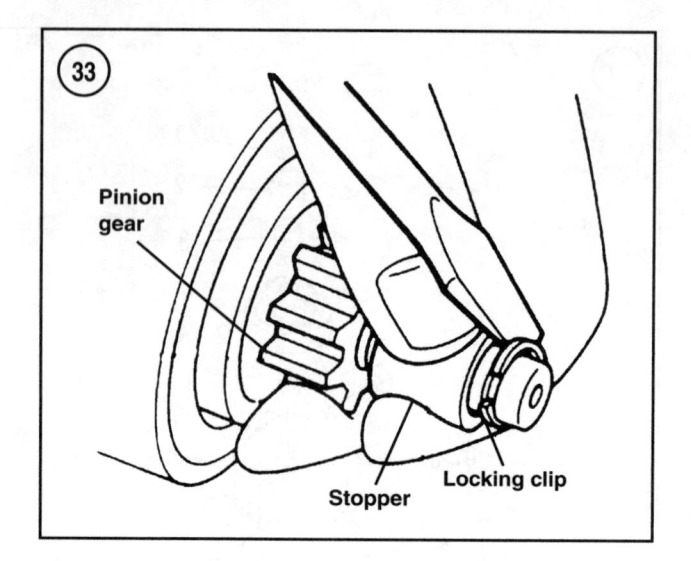

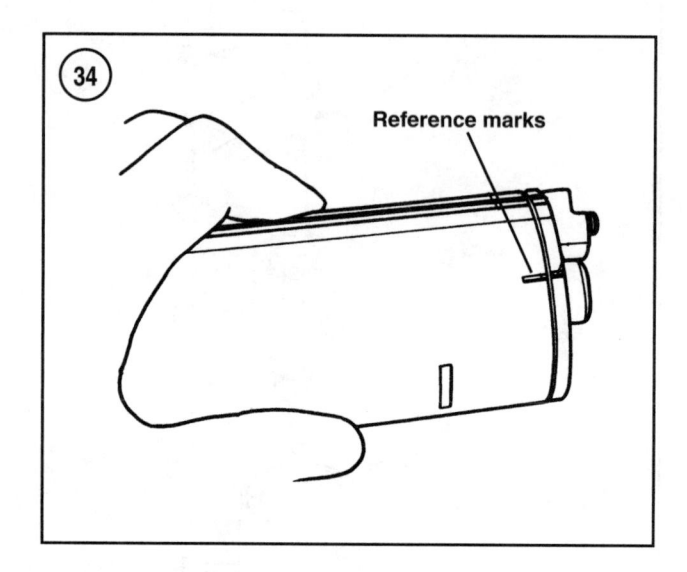

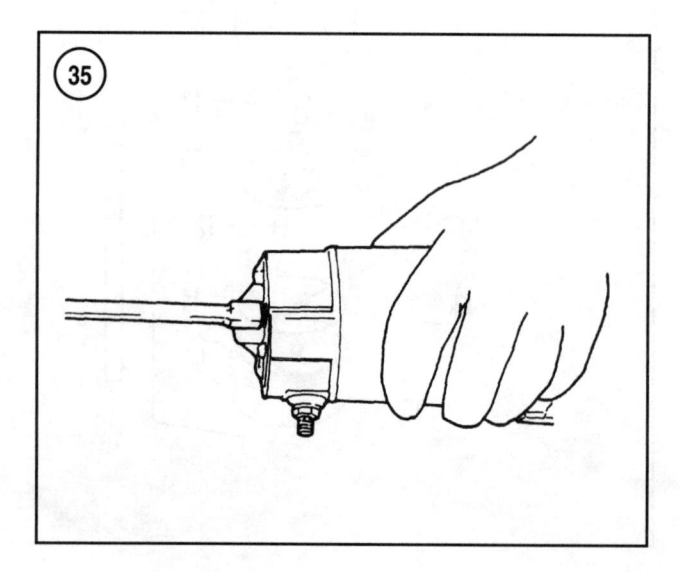

33

Pinion gear

Stopper

Locking clip

34

Reference marks

35

IGNITION AND ELECTRICAL SYSTEMS

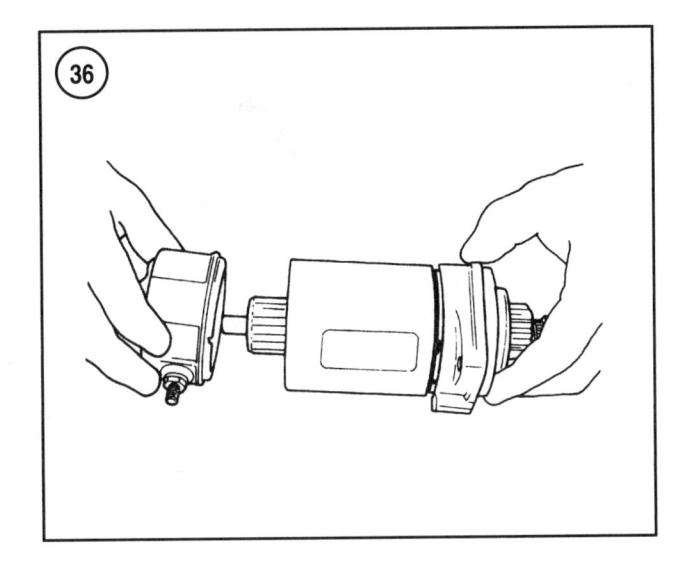

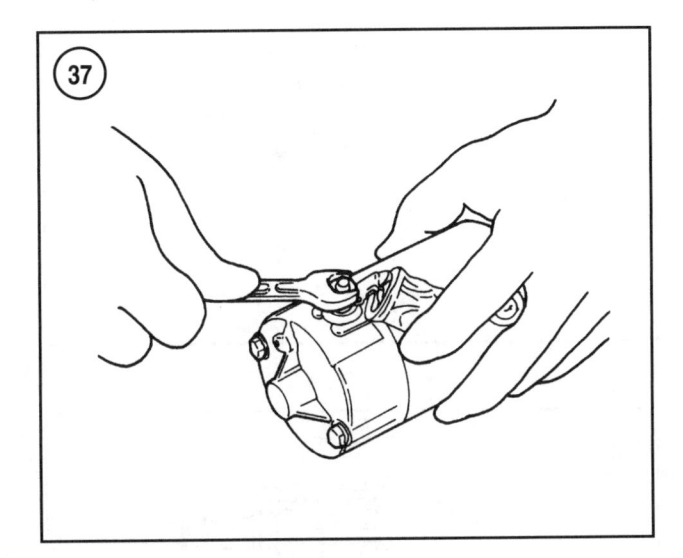

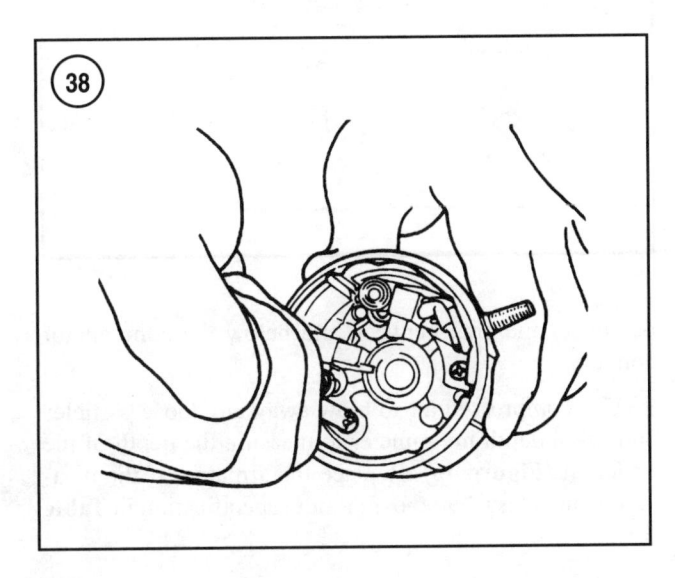

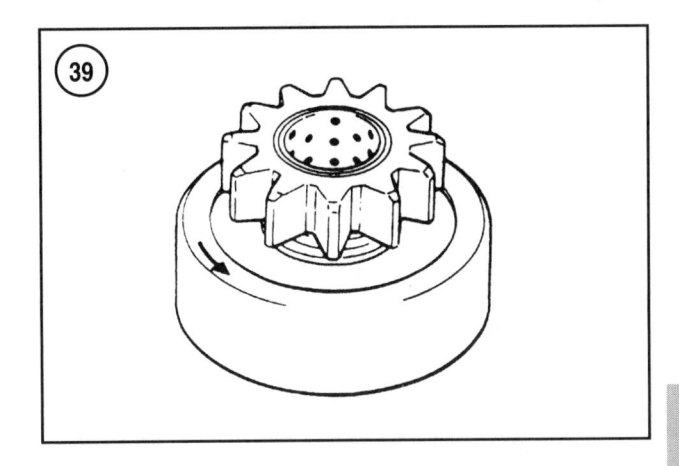

fully pry the locking clip from the armature shaft. Remove the stopper and spring from the armature shaft.

3. Turn the pinion drive counterclockwise to remove it from the helical splines of the armature.

4. Make reference marks (**Figure 34**) on the top and bottom cover to the frame. Support both ends of the starter motor and remove the throughbolts (**Figure 35**).

5. Carefully pull the bottom cover from the armature (**Figure 36**). If necessary, carefully tap on the bottom cover with a plastic mallet to free it from the frame. Remove and discard the O-ring, if so equipped.

6. Lay the frame assembly on its side. Grasp the frame and lightly tap on the end of the armature to free the top cover from the frame. Do not tap on the commutator part of the armature.

7. Pull the armature from the frame assembly. Note the orientation of the composite and metal washers on the armature shaft. Remove them from the armature and wire them together to ensure they are installed in the same order and position during assembly.

8. Remove the nut (**Figure 37**) then pull the washers, bushing or insulator from the starter terminal.

9. Mark the brush plate and lower cover to ensure correct orientation during assembly. Remove the screws (**Figure 38**), then lift the brush plate from the lower cover.

10. Use compressed air to remove debris from the starter motor components. Use a mild solvent to remove oily material from the armature, covers, frame assembly and pinion drive. Do not clean the brushes in solvent.

Component inspection

1. Place the pinion drive on a flat work surface. Attempt to rotate the pinion drive in the clockwise and counterclockwise directions (**Figure 39**). Replace the pinion drive if it does not turn freely when rotated in the clock-

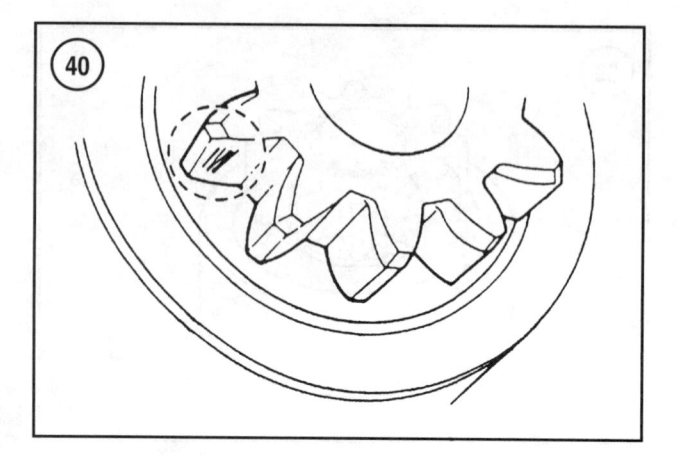

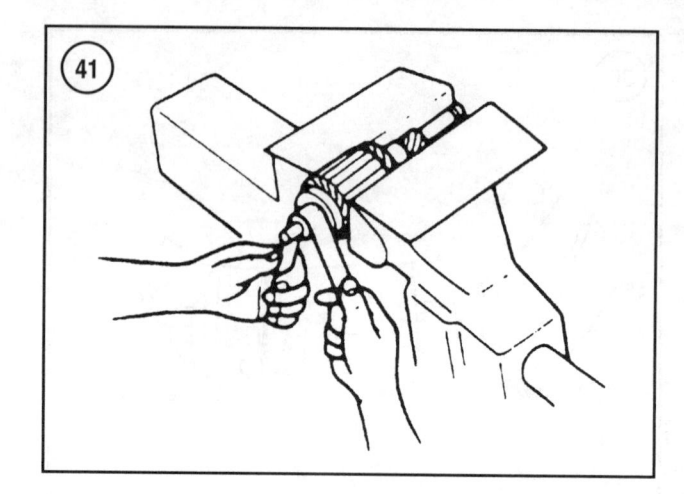

wise direction and lock to the center hub when rotated in the counterclockwise direction.

2. Inspect the pinion drive teeth (**Figure 40**) for cracked, chipped or excessively worn teeth. Replace the pinion drive if any of the teeth are damaged or if a step has worn on the contact surfaces. Inspect the helical splines at the pinion drive end of the armature. Replace the armature if there are chipped areas or the pinion drive will not thread smoothly onto the shaft.

3. Carefully secure the armature in a vise with protective jaws. Tighten the vise only enough to secure the armature. Excessive force will damage the armature. Use 600 grit carburundum (wet or dry polishing cloth) to remove corrosion deposits and glazed surfaces from the commutator (**Figure 41**). Work the area enough to just clean the surfaces. Avoid removing too much material. Rotate the armature to polish the surfaces evenly.

4. Calibrate a multimeter to the 1 ohm scale. Connect the negative meter test lead to one of the commutator contacts and the positive test lead to the laminated section of the armature (**Figure 42**). If the meter indicates continuity, the armature is shorted and must be replaced.

5. Connect the negative meter test lead to one of the commutator contacts and positive test lead to the armature shaft (**Figure 42**). If the meter indicates continuity, the armature is shorted and must be replaced.

6. Connect the negative meter test lead to one of the commutator contacts. Connect the positive test lead to each of the remaining contacts (**Figure 43**). If the meter indicates no continuity for any contact-to-contact connection, the armature has failed open and must be replaced.

7. Use an accurate caliper or micrometer to measure the diameter of the commutator (**Figure 44**). Replace the armature if the measurement is less than the minimum specification in **Table 5**.

8. Use a disposable nail file or a suitable small file (**Figure 45**) to remove metal and mica particles from the undercut, or the area between and below the commutator contacts.

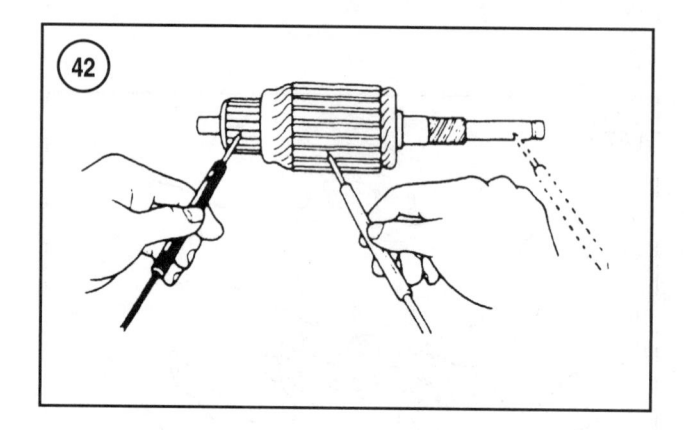

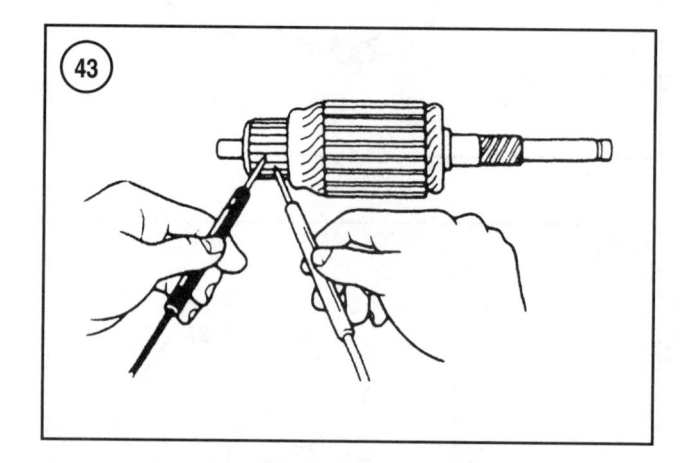

9. Use compressed air to blow away any loose particles and use a depth micrometer to measure the depth of the undercut (**Figure 46**). Replace the armature if the measurement is less than the minimum specification in **Table 5**.

IGNITION AND ELECTRICAL SYSTEMS

⑭

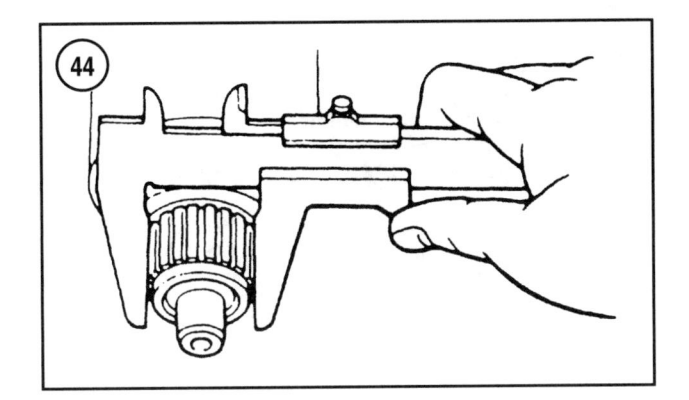

㊺

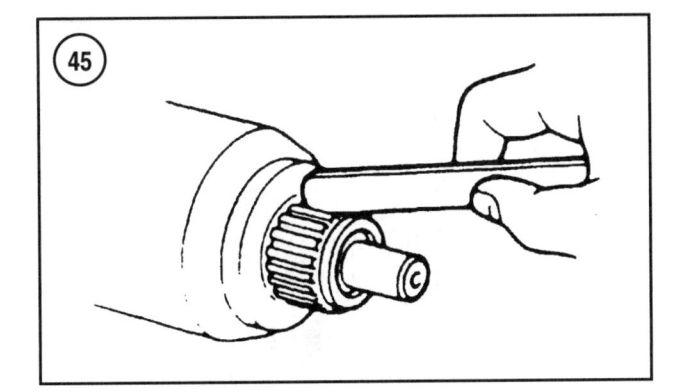

㊻

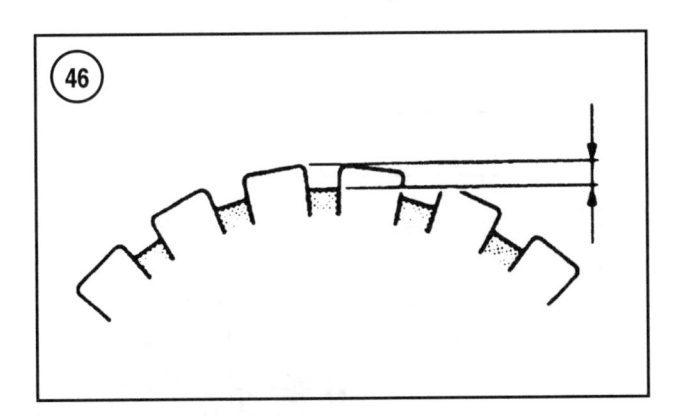

㊼

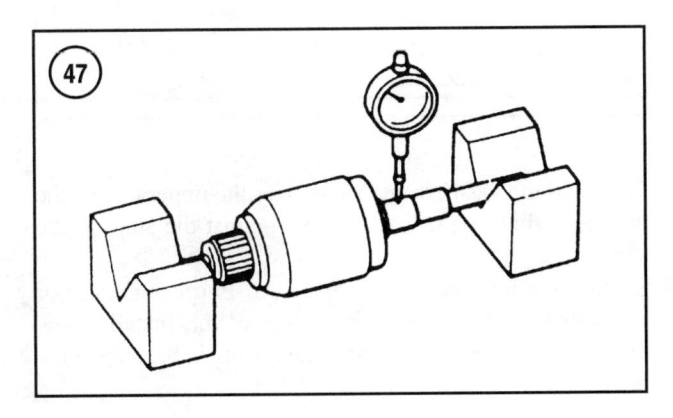

㊽

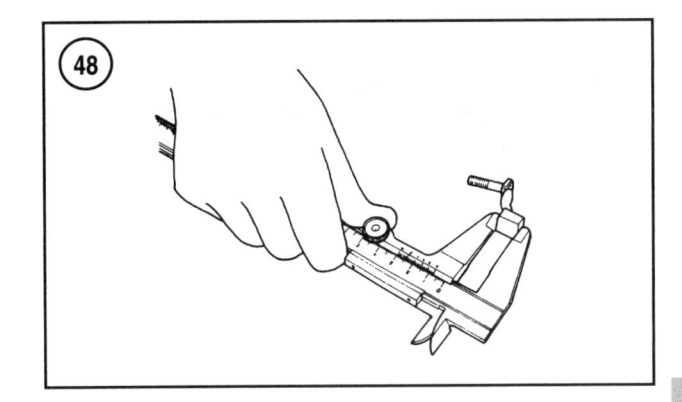

10. Support the end of the armature shaft on V-blocks or other suitable supports. Position a dial indicator with the plunger in direct contact with the upper bushing contact surface (**Figure 47**). Slowly rotate the armature while reading the deflection on the dial indicator. Replace the armature if the measurement exceeds the specification in **Table 5**.

11. Inspect the brushes for corroded, chipped or oil contaminated surfaces. Replace the brushes if any of these conditions are present. Use an accurate caliper to measure the length of each of the brushes (**Figure 48**). Replace both brushes if either of them has worn to less than the minimum specification in **Table 5**.

12. Inspect the brush springs for corroded or distorted loops and replace them as needed. Corroded or damaged springs will not apply adequate pressure for the brushes, resulting in poor starter motor performance.

13. Inspect the magnets in the frame assembly for corrosion or other contaminants. Inspect the frame assembly for loose or cracked magnets. Replace the frame assembly if it cannot be adequately cleaned or if the magnets are damaged.

14. Inspect the bushings in the upper and lower covers and the bushing contact surfaces on the armature for discoloration and excessive or uneven wear. Replace the armature if the bushing surfaces are rough or unevenly worn. Replace the cover(s) if the bushing is worn. The bushing is not available separately.

15. Temporarily install the brush plate, brushes, bushing and washers into the lower cover. Do not install the brush springs. Test the brush plate and bottom cover as follows:
  a. Calibrate a multimeter to the 1 ohm scale.
  b. Touch the positive and negative test leads to the brush holders as shown in **Figure 49**. If the meter indicates continuity, the brush plate is shorted and must be replaced.
  c. On 6-70 hp models, touch the positive meter test lead to the positive brush. The positive brush con-

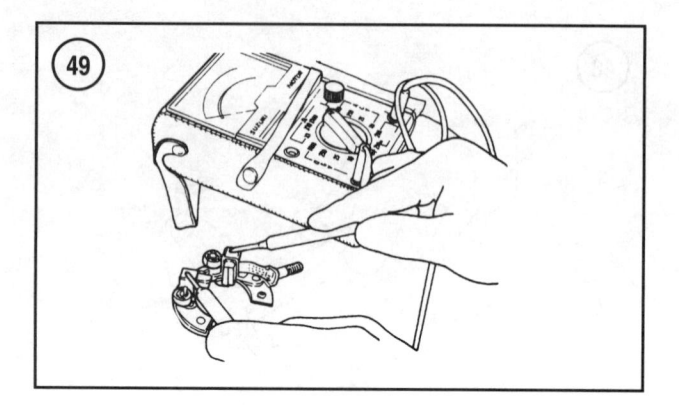

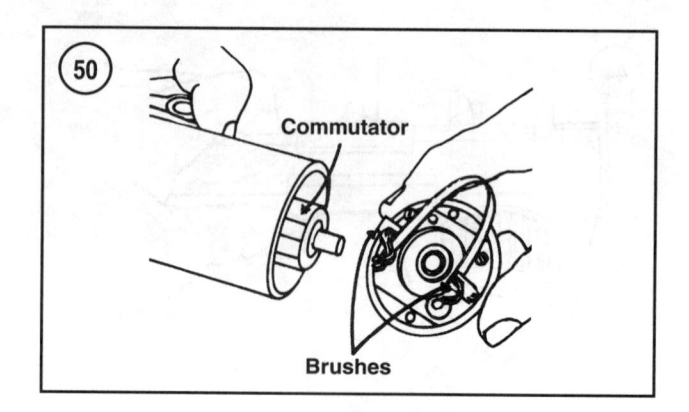

nects to the starter terminal post. Touch the negative meter test lead to the lower cover. If the meter indicates continuity, the brush plate is shorted and must be replaced.

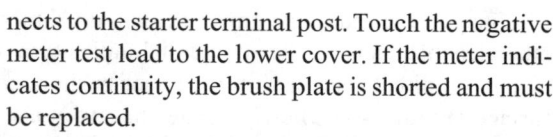

d. Remove the brush plate and related components.

Assembly

Apply a light coat of Yamaha All-Purpose Grease or equivalent to the bushing in the covers and the helical splines on the armature during assembly. Do not allow grease to contact the brushes or the commutator surfaces. Replace grease contaminated brushes. Refer to **Figures 29-32** for component identification and orientation.

1. Align the marks and install the brush plate and brushes into the bottom cover. Securely tighten the brush plate screws. Insert the springs, then the brushes, into the brush holders.
2. Apply a light coat of Yamaha All-Purpose Grease or equivalent to the lower cover bushing. Install the thrust washer over the lower end of the armature and seat it against the commutator.
3. Fabricate a brush retaining tool by bending a stiff piece of wire into a U shape. Manually push the brushes into the holders and insert the installation tool as shown in **Figure 50**.
4. Guide the armature shaft into the bushing while fitting the lower cover over the commutator. Carefully remove the brush retaining tool. Make sure the brushes contact the commutator contacts (**Figure 51**).
5. Install a new O-ring onto the lower cover. Seat the O-ring into the step in the cover, then carefully slide the frame assembly over the armature. Maintain pressure on the opposite end of the armature shaft to prevent the armature from pulling from the lower cover. The magnets are quite strong.
6. Align the reference marks (**Figure 34**) and antirotation structures (**Figure 52**). 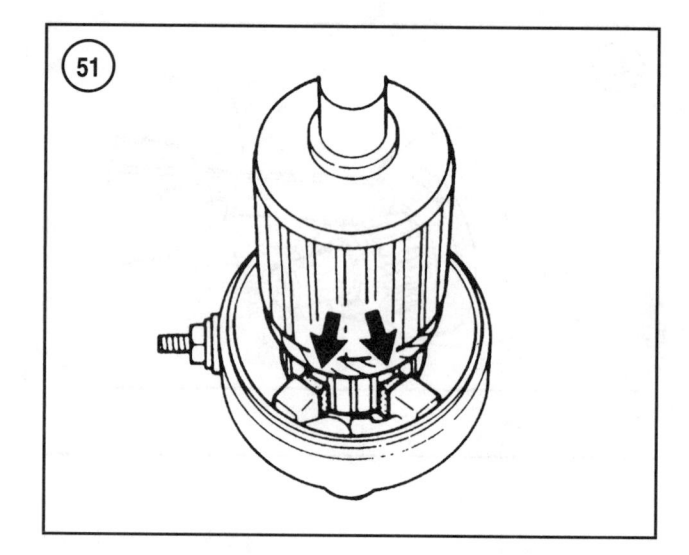 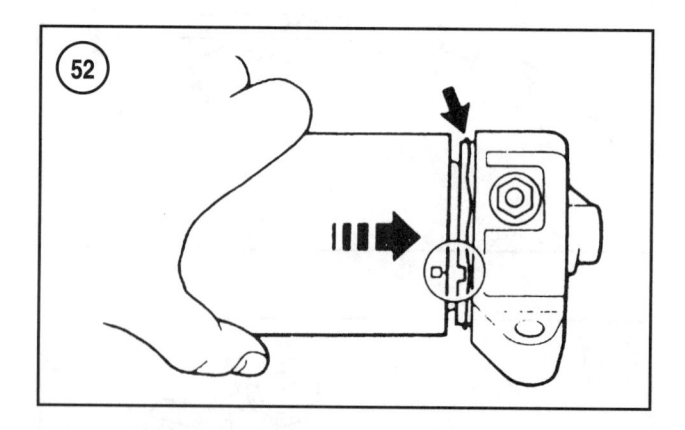
7. Install the washers and rings over the upper end of the armature shaft. Seat the washers against the step on the shaft.
8. Apply a light coat of Yamaha All-Purpose Grease or equivalent to the bushing in the top cover. Install a new O-ring onto the top cover. Seat the O-ring in the step in the cover.

IGNITION AND ELECTRICAL SYSTEMS

53 LOCKING CLIP/PINION STOPPER ASSEMBLY

1. Spring
2. Pinion stopper
3. Locking clip

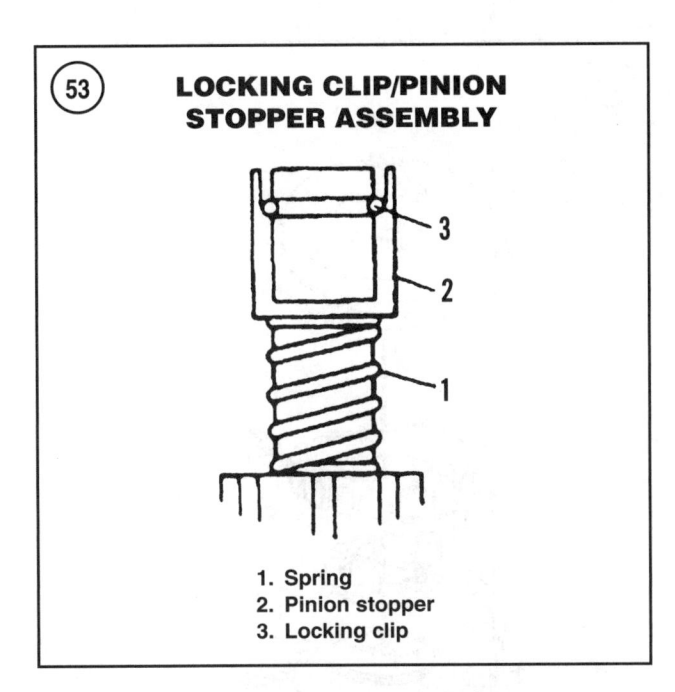

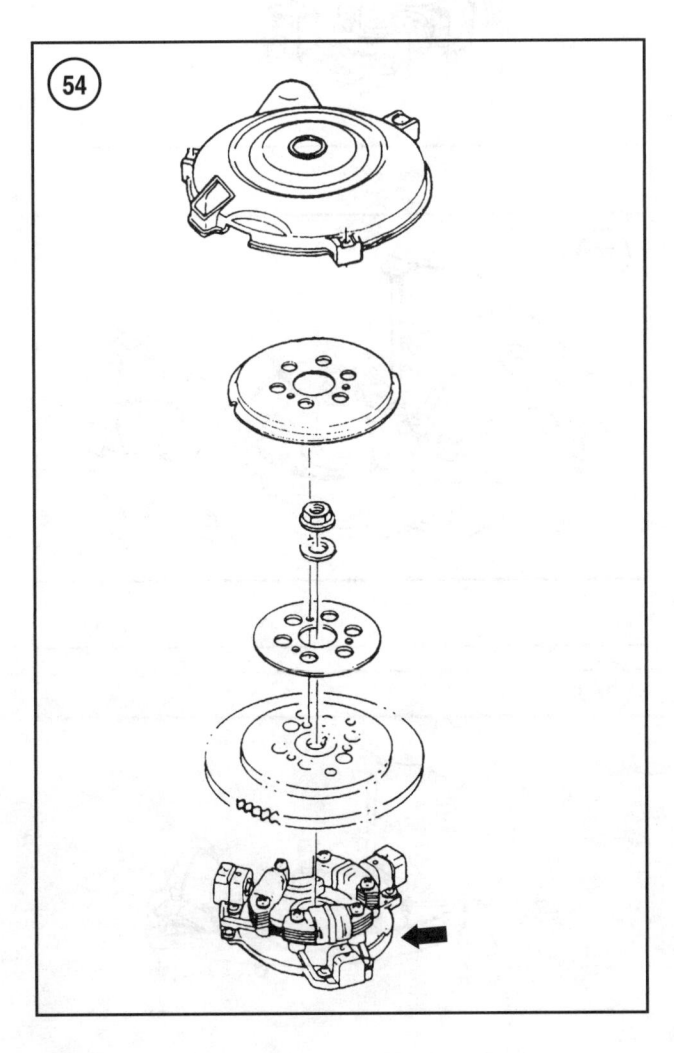

54

9. Slide the top cover over the armature shaft. Align the reference marks (**Figure 34**) and seat the cover in the frame assembly.

10. Guide the throughbolts through the bottom cover and frame, then hand-thread them into the top cover. Tighten the throughbolts evenly to the standard torque specifications in Chapter One.

11. Apply a light coat of Yamaha All-Purpose Grease or equivalent to the helical splines in the armature shaft. Thread the pinion drive onto the armature shaft.

12. Install the spring (1, **Figure 53**) and pinion stopper (2) onto the shaft. Push the pinion stopper toward the starter to expose the locking clip groove. Snap the locking clip (3, **Figure 53**) into the groove. Use pliers to form the locking clip if it is distorted during installation.

13. Slowly release the pinion stopper. Inspect the stopper and locking clip for proper installation. The locking clip must be positioned in the pinion stopper opening as shown in **Figure 53**.

14. Install the starter motor as described in this chapter.

CHARGING SYSTEM COMPONENTS

This section includes removal and installation procedures for the battery charge coil, ignition charge coil, lighting coil, rectifier and rectifier/regulator.

Battery Charge/Lighting Coil

Before removing the coil(s), make a drawing or take a photograph of the wire routing and coil mounting location. This will help ensure proper wire routing and charge coil positioning during installation.

Battery charge/lighting coil appearance and mounting arrangements vary by model.

On 6-70 hp (except 65 jet) models, the battery charge or lighting coil is fastened to a mounting base (**Figure 54**) alongside the ignition charge coil.

On 65 jet and 75-90 hp models, the battery charging and ignition charging coils are integrated into a single unit (**Figure 55**). If either coil fails, the unit must be replaced.

Removal

CAUTION
The ignition charge and battery charge/lighting coils are almost identical on some 6-50 hp models. Use the wiring diagrams and illustrations to identify the proper coil.

Refer to the wiring diagrams at the end of the manual to identify the wire colors for the battery charge/lighting coil. Trace the wires from to the coil mounting location under the flywheel.

1. Disconnect the battery cables. Disconnect and ground the spark plug leads to prevent accidental starting.

2. On manual start models, remove the starter as described in Chapter Ten.

3. Remove the flywheel as described in Chapter Seven.

4A. On 6-70 hp (except 65 jet) models, use the wire colors to identify the battery charge/lighting coil(s). Some models use two coils. Do not inadvertently select the ignition charge coil. Mark the wire terminals and take note of wire routing and connection points, then disconnect the coil wires from the rectifier terminals, rectifier/regulator terminals or engine mounted terminal block.

4B. On 65 jet and 75-90 hp models, mark the wire terminals and take note of the wire routing and connection points, then disconnect the battery charge/ignition coil wires from the rectifier/regulator and CDI unit.

5. Make reference marks on the battery charge/lighting coil(s) and the mounting base or power head. This will help ensure proper orientation of the coil on assembly.

CAUTION
It may be necessary to use an impact driver to loosen the battery charge/lighting coil and ignition charge coil screws. Work carefully and avoid using excessive force. The coil mounting base can sustain considerable damage if excessive force is used.

6A. On 6-70 hp (except 65 jet) models, remove the screws (**Figure 56**) for the battery charge coil(s). Mark each screw to indicate its mounting location upon removal. On some models, the mounting screws are different lengths. Route the charge coil wires through any openings while lifting the coil from the mounting base.

6B. On 65 jet and 75-90 hp models, make reference marks on the charge coil and the power head to ensure correct orientation during installation. Remove all of the screws (**Figure 57**), then carefully lift the component from the power head. If necessary, carefully tap on the coil laminations with a plastic hammer to free the coil. Do not pry the coil loose. The coils can be easily damaged if the pry bar contacts the windings.

7. Clean corrosion and other debris or contaminants from the coil mounting location. Clean, inspect and repair, if necessary, the threads for the coil mounting screws.

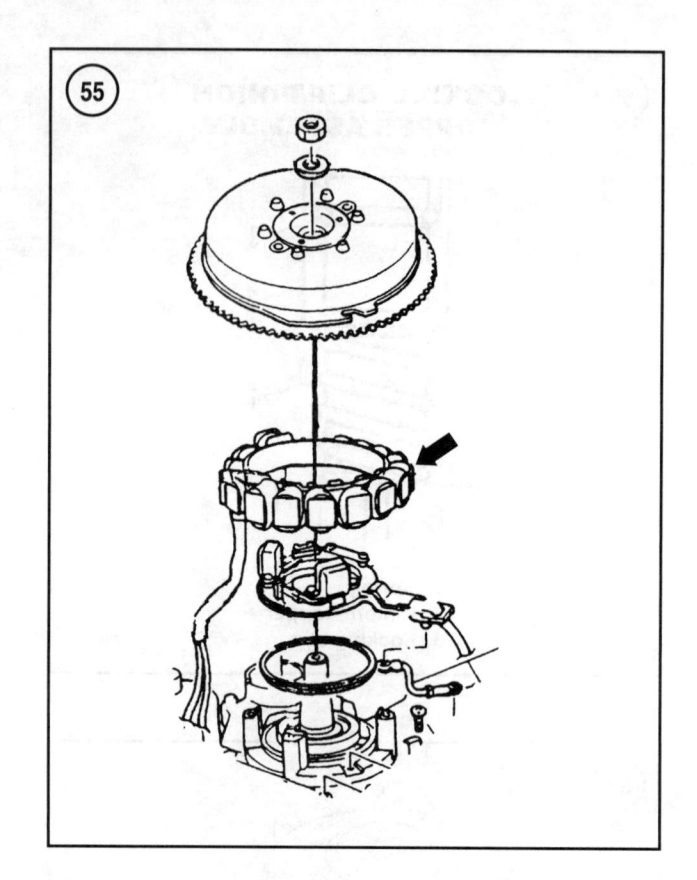

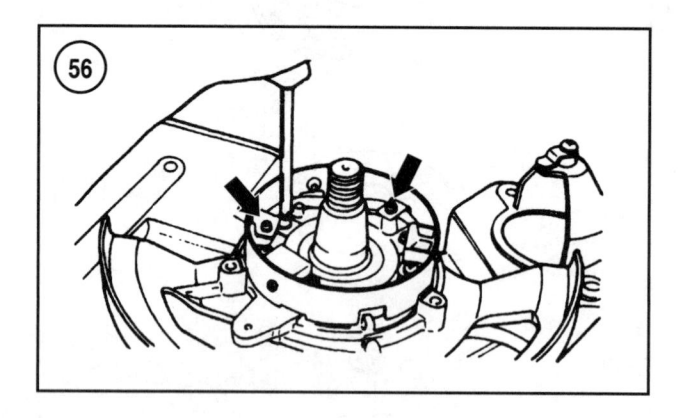

IGNITION AND ELECTRICAL SYSTEMS

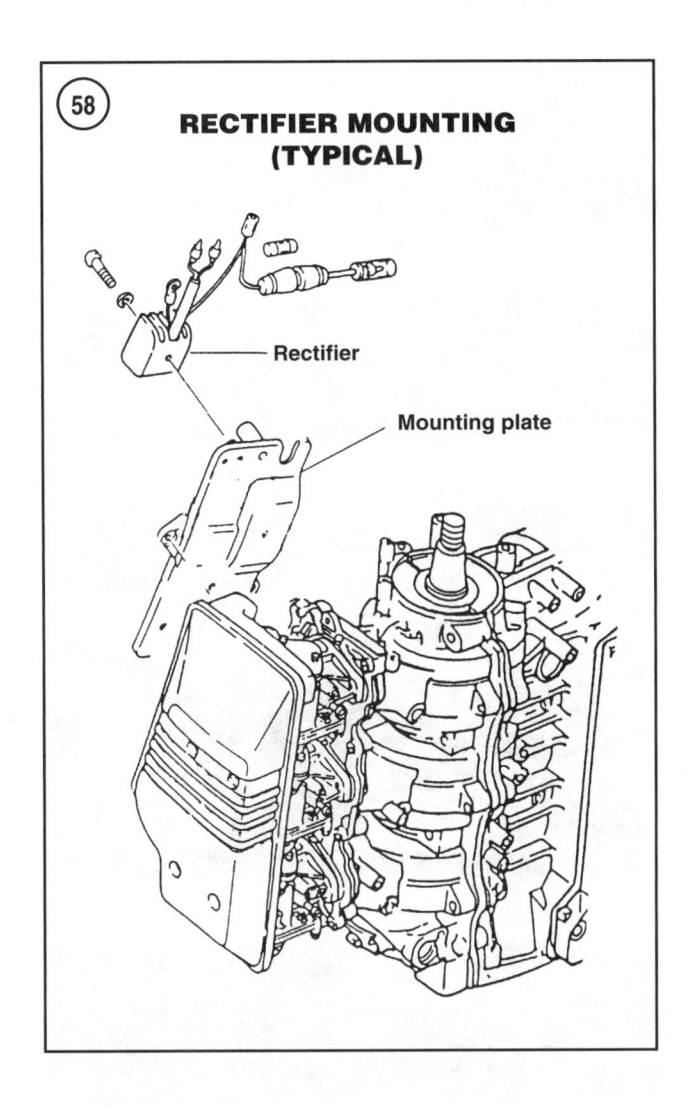

58 RECTIFIER MOUNTING (TYPICAL)
- Rectifier
- Mounting plate

Installation

CAUTION
On models with the ignition charge coil integrated into the battery charge coil, the assembly must be installed with the correct orientation for proper phasing of the ignition system. Always align the reference marks on the coil and power head during coil installation. Poor ignition system performance can occur if the engine is operated with an out of phase ignition charge coil.

1. When replacing the coil, transfer the reference mark to the replacement coil.

2. Carefully route the battery charge/lighting coil wires through any openings while installing the coil onto the mounting base or power head.

3. Align the reference mark and seat the coil on the mounting base or mounting bosses on the power head.

4. If so equipped, install all spacers and washers into the original location on the coil. Apply a light coat of Loctite 271 to the threads, then thread the mounting screws into the coil and mounting base. Verify proper seating and reference mark alignment, then securely tighten the screws.

5A. On 6-70 hp (except 65 jet) models, connect the battery charge/lighting coil wires to the rectifier, rectifier/regulator or terminal block connections.

5B. On 65 jet and 75-90 hp models, connect the battery/ignition charge coil assembly wires to the CDI unit and rectifier/regulator connections.

6. Route the wires to avoid interference with moving components. Clamp the wires with plastic locking type clamps as necessary.

7. Install the flywheel as described in Chapter Seven. Manually rotate the flywheel while checking for interference with the coil. Remove the flywheel and check the installation if there is binding or rubbing.

8. On manual start models, install the starter as described in Chapter Ten.

9. Connect the battery cables and spark plug leads.

Rectifier and Rectifier/Regulator

All Yamaha outboards with battery charging capability are equipped with either a rectifier (**Figure 58**, typical) or rectifier/regulator (**Figure 59**). The type of control and starting system on the engine determines which component is used. Either component contains circuits that change the AC current from the battery charge coil to DC current for charging the battery. The rectifier/regulator contains additional circuits that limit current flow to the battery when it reaches full charge. Refer to the wiring diagrams located at the end of the manual to determine which component is used on the engine.

Removal and installation procedures for either component are similar. Refer to the following information and the wiring diagrams to help locate the rectifier or rectifier regulator.

1. On 6 and 8 hp models, the rectifier is mounted on the rear starboard side of the power head and directly aft of the starter motor. The rectifier/regulator is mounted on the front and port side of the power head.

2. On 9.9 and 15 hp models, the rectifier or rectifier/regulator is mounted on the front side of the power head and to the port side of the carburetor.

3. On 20 and 25 hp two-cylinder models, the rectifier is mounted on the electrical component bracket on the port side of the power head.

4. On 25 hp three-cylinder and 30 hp models, the rectifier is mounted on the electrical component bracket on the

59 RECTIFIER/REGULATOR MOUNTING (TYPICAL)

Rectifier/regulator

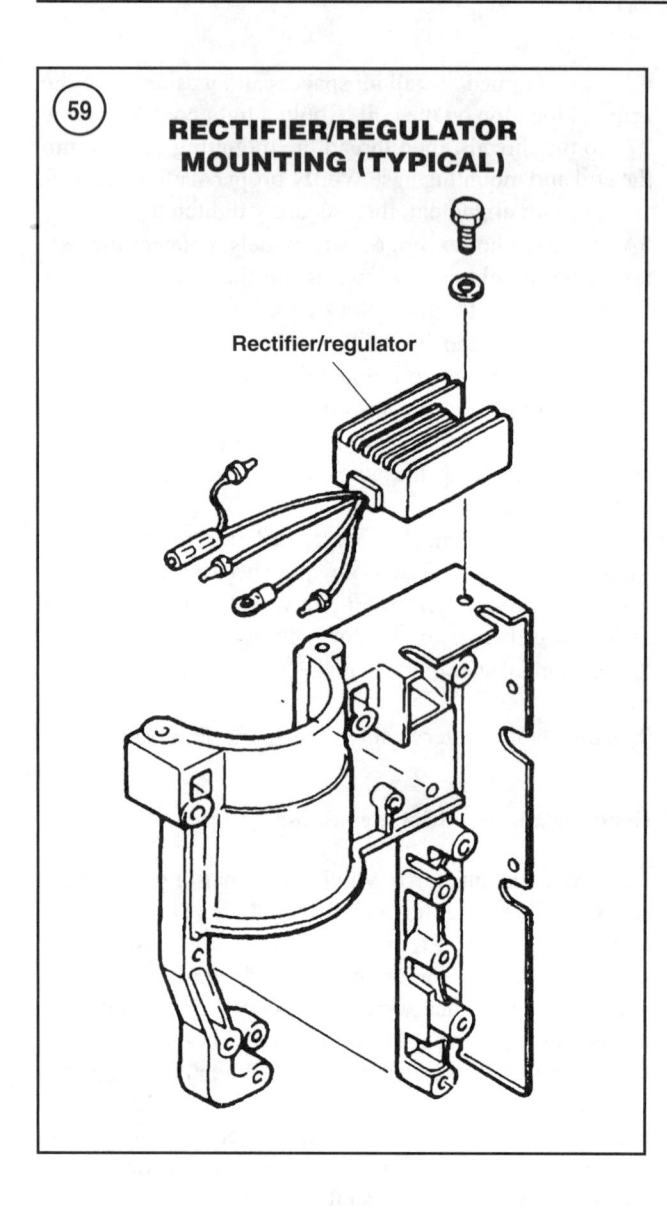

starboard side of the power head. The rectifier is located directly below the starter motor.

5. On 28 jet, 35 jet, 40 hp and 50 hp models, the rectifier/regulator is mounted on top of the electrical component mounting bracket on the rear starboard side of the power head.

6. On 60-90 hp models, the rectifier/regulator is mounted on the electrical component cover on the starboard side of the power head. The plastic electrical component cover (**Figure 60**) must be removed to access the rectifier/regulator.

Removal/installation

1. Disconnect the battery cables. Disconnect and ground the spark plug leads to prevent accidental starting.

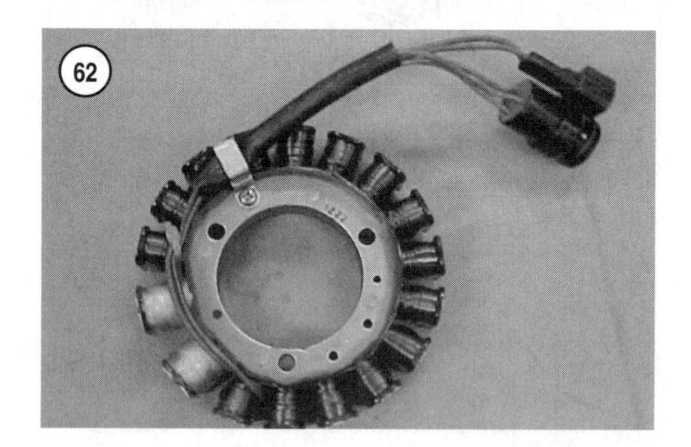

2. Disconnect the rectifier or rectifier/regulator wires from the battery charge/lighting coil wires and the starter relay.

3. Remove the mounting screw(s) and pull the component from the mount. If so equipped, remove the screw to disconnect the ground wire for the component. On some models, the mounting screw secures the ground wire terminal.

4. Clean corrosion and contamination from the rectifier mounting and ground screw openings.

IGNITION AND ELECTRICAL SYSTEMS

63

**IGNITION CHARGE COIL
(2 HP MODEL)**

1. Screw
2. Pulley
3. Plate
4. Flywheel nut
5. Washer
6. Flywheel
7. Bolt
8. Lockwasher
9. Washer
10. Mounting base
11. Ignition charge coil
12. Screw

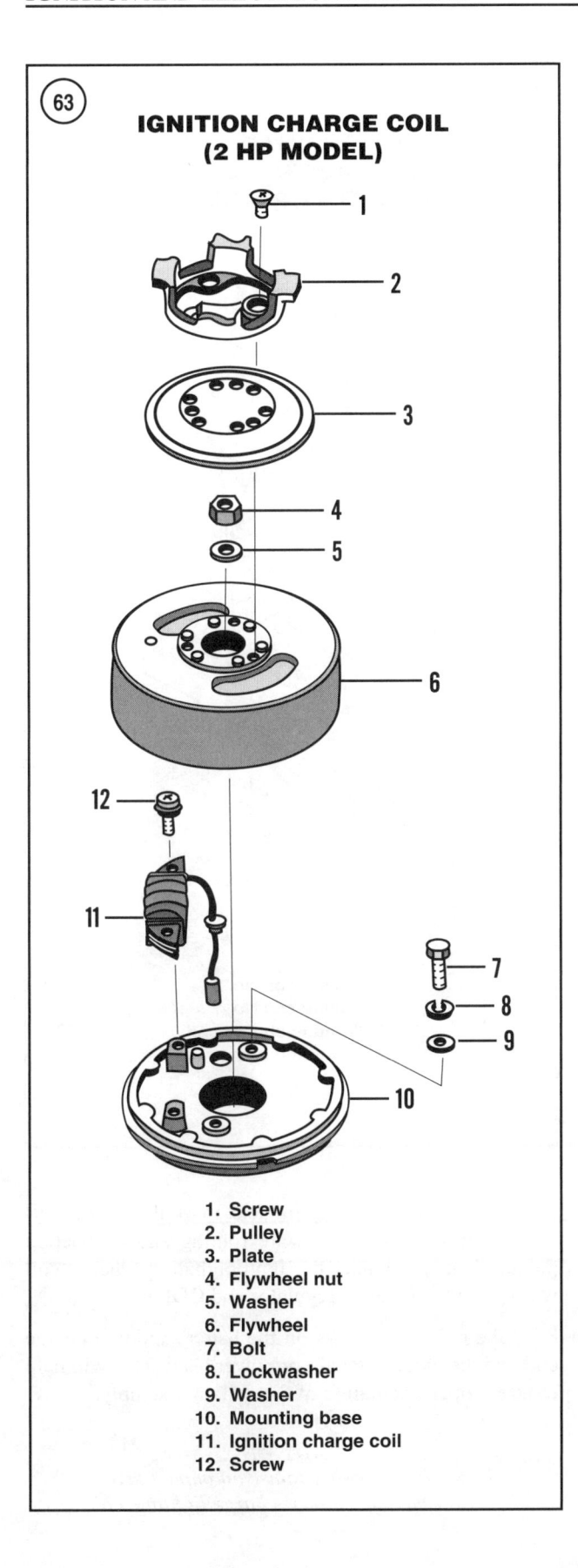

5. Installation is the reverse of removal. Note the following:
   a. Make sure bullet connectors are properly plugged together.
   b. Make sure the components grounding wire (black) terminal is attached to the component mounting screw or separate grounding screw.
   c. Route the wiring to avoid interference with moving components. Clamp the wiring with plastic locking type clamps as necessary.
6. Connect the battery cables and spark plug leads.

IGNITION SYSTEM COMPONENTS

This section describes removal and installation for the ignition charge coil, pulser coil, crankshaft position sensor, CDI unit and the ignition coil(s).

Ignition Charge Coil

Before removing the coil, make a drawing or take a photograph of the wire routing and coil mounting location. This will help ensure proper wire routing and charge coil positioning during installation.

Ignition charge coil appearance and mounting arrangements vary by model. On 6-50 hp models, the ignition charge coil appearance (**Figure 61**) is very similar to the battery charge/lighting coil(s). Verify by wire color that the correct coil is selected.

The ignition charge coil and pulser coils used on 25 hp three-cylinder and 30 hp models share a common wiring harness. Replace the assembly if one pulser coil or the ignition charge coil is faulty.

On 60-90 hp models, the ignition charge and battery charge coils are integrated into a single component (**Figure 62**). If either coil fails, replace the assembly.

Refer to **Figures 63-73** and the wiring diagrams located at the end of the manual to identify the ignition charge coil.

Removal

CAUTION
The ignition charge and battery charge/lighting coils are almost identical on some 6-50 hp models. Use the wiring diagrams and illustrations to identify the proper coil.

1. On electric start models, disconnect the battery cables.
2. On manual start models, remove the starter as described in Chapter Ten.

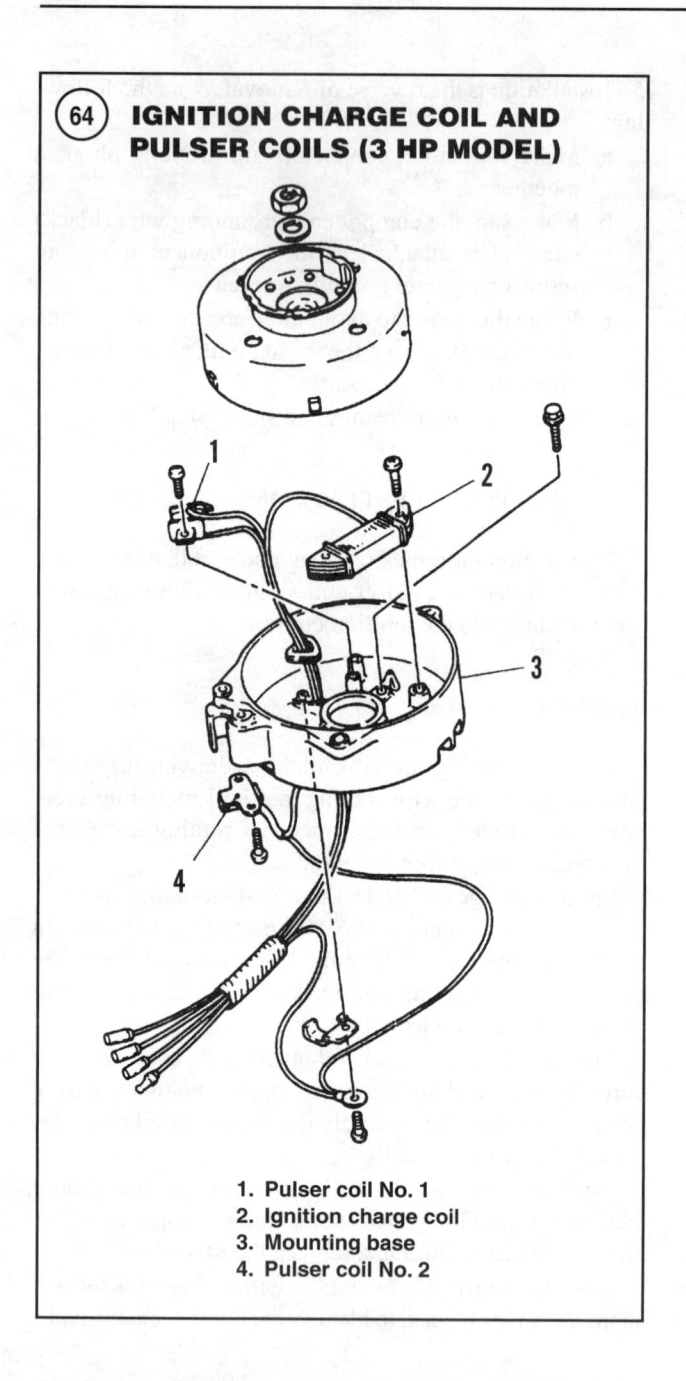

64 IGNITION CHARGE COIL AND PULSER COILS (3 HP MODEL)

1. Pulser coil No. 1
2. Ignition charge coil
3. Mounting base
4. Pulser coil No. 2

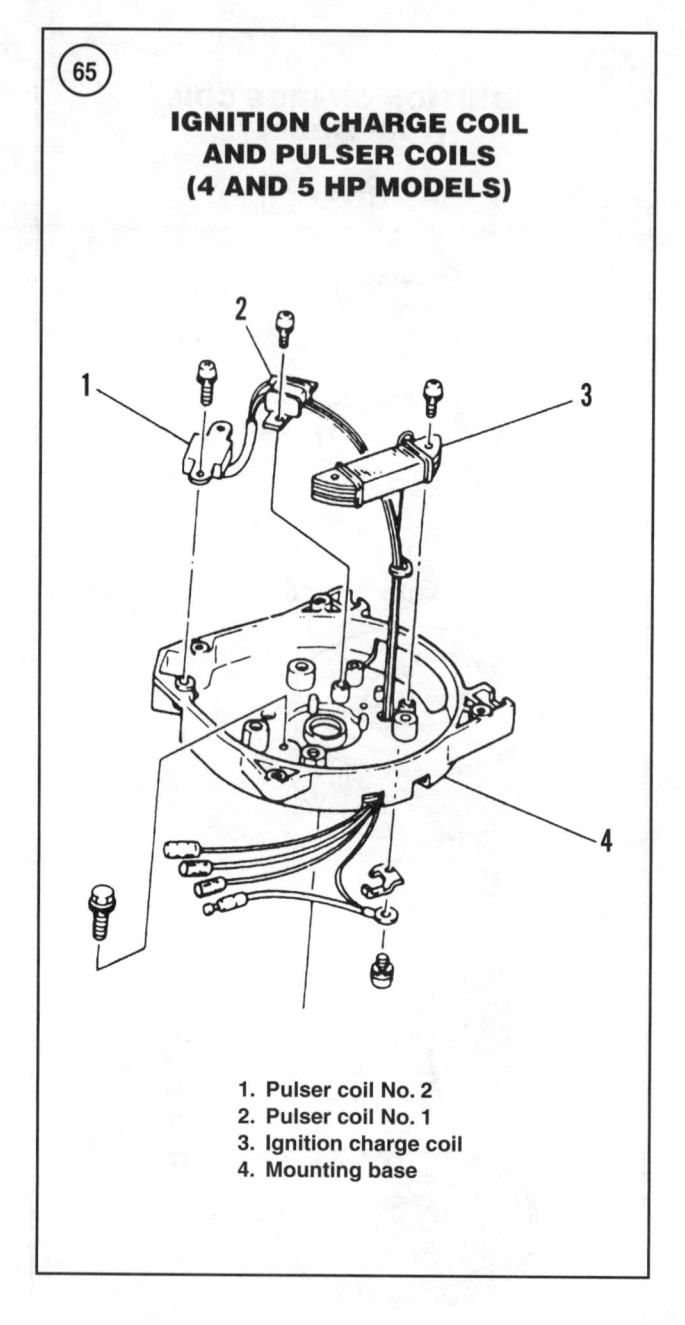

65 IGNITION CHARGE COIL AND PULSER COILS (4 AND 5 HP MODELS)

1. Pulser coil No. 2
2. Pulser coil No. 1
3. Ignition charge coil
4. Mounting base

3. Disconnect and ground the spark plug lead(s) to prevent accidental starting.

4. Remove the flywheel as described in Chapter Seven.

5. On 2-70 hp (except 65 jet) models, use the wire colors to identify the ignition charge coil. Do not inadvertently select the battery charge coil. Mark the wire terminals and take note of wire routing and connection points, then disconnect the coil wires CDI unit.

6. On 25 hp three-cylinder and 30 hp models, remove the pulser coil mounting screws as described in *Pulser Coil* and *Crankshaft Position Sensor* in this chapter.

7. On 65 jet and 75-90 hp models, mark the wire terminals and take note of the wire routing and connection points, then disconnect the ignition/battery charge coil wires from the rectifier/regulator and CDI unit.

8. Make reference marks on the battery ignition charge coil and the mounting base or power head. This will help ensure proper orientation of the coil on assembly.

CAUTION
It may be necessary to use an impact driver to loosen the battery charge/lighting coil

IGNITION AND ELECTRICAL SYSTEMS

66 IGNITION CHARGE, BATTERY CHARGE/LIGHTING AND PULSER COILS (6 AND 8 HP MODELS)

1. Pulser coil
2. Battery charge/lighting coil
3. Ignition charge coil
4. Mounting base
5. Base plate
6. Bearing
7. Bushing

67 IGNITION CHARGE, BATTERY CHARGE/LIGHTING AND PULSER COILS (9.9 AND 15 HP MODELS)

- Lighting coil
- Ignition charge coil
- Pulser coil

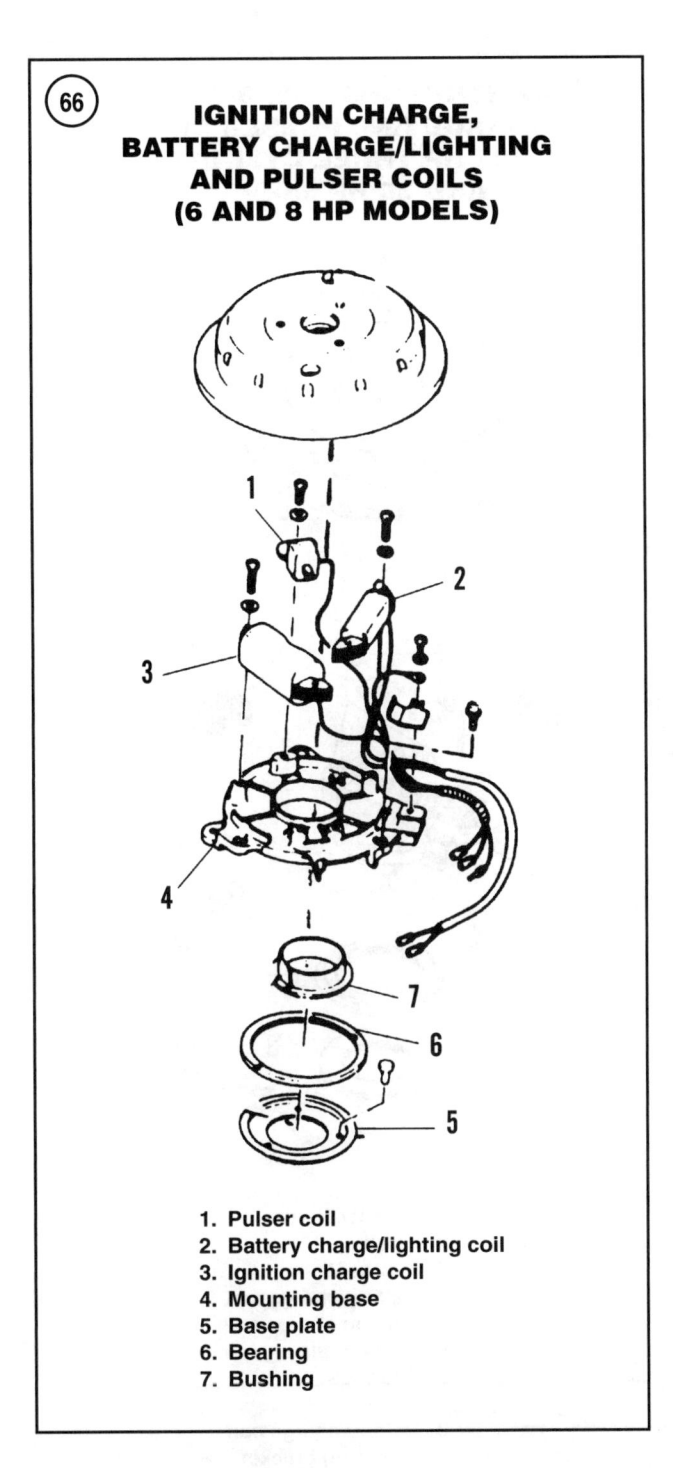

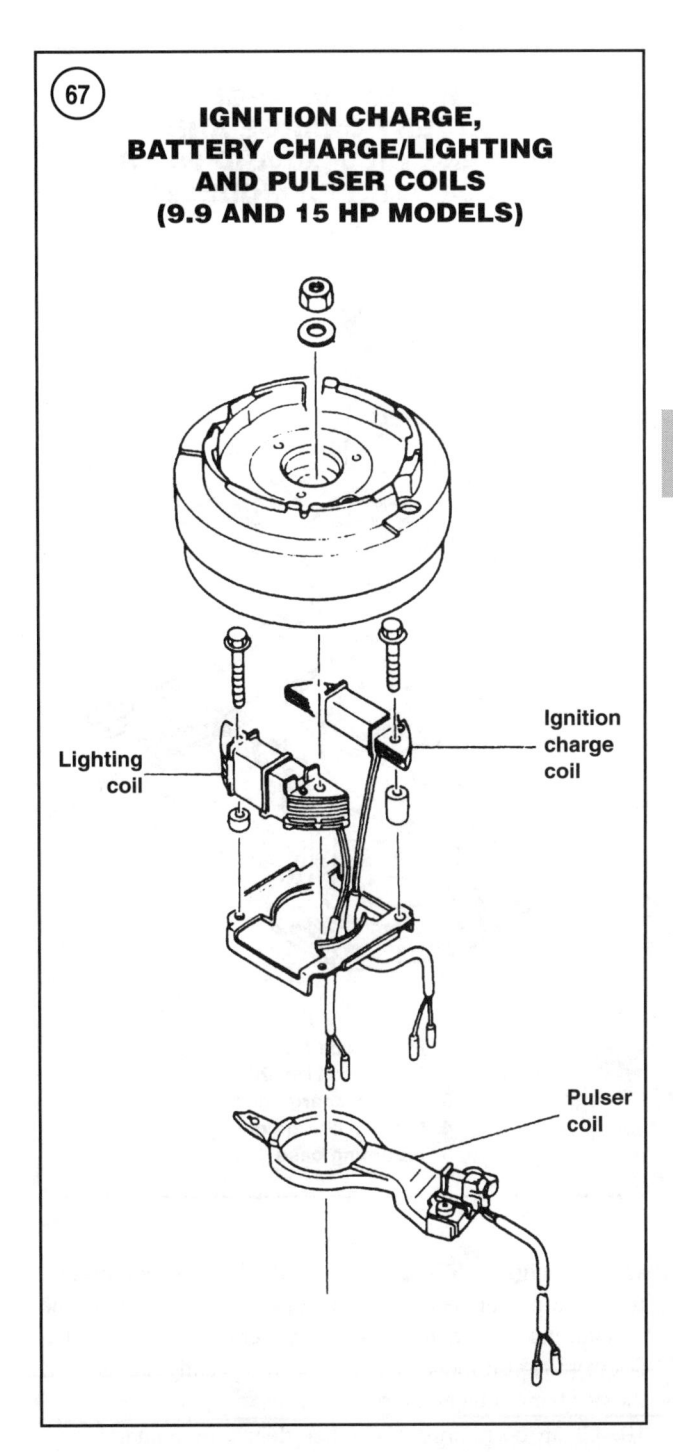

and ignition charge coil screws. Work carefully and avoid using excessive force. The coil mounting base can sustain considerable damage if excessive force is used.

9A. On 2-70 hp (except 65 jet) models, remove the screws (**Figure 56**) for the ignition charge coil. Mark each screw to indicate its mounting location upon removal. On some models the mounting screws are different lengths. Remove any clamps, then route the coil wiring through any openings or grommets while lifting the coil from the mounting base.

9B. On 65 jet and 75-90 hp models, make reference marks on the charge coil and the power head to ensure correct orientation during installation. Remove all of the

68 IGNITION CHARGE, BATTERY CHARGE AND PULSER COILS (20 AND 25 HP TWO-CYLINDER MODELS)

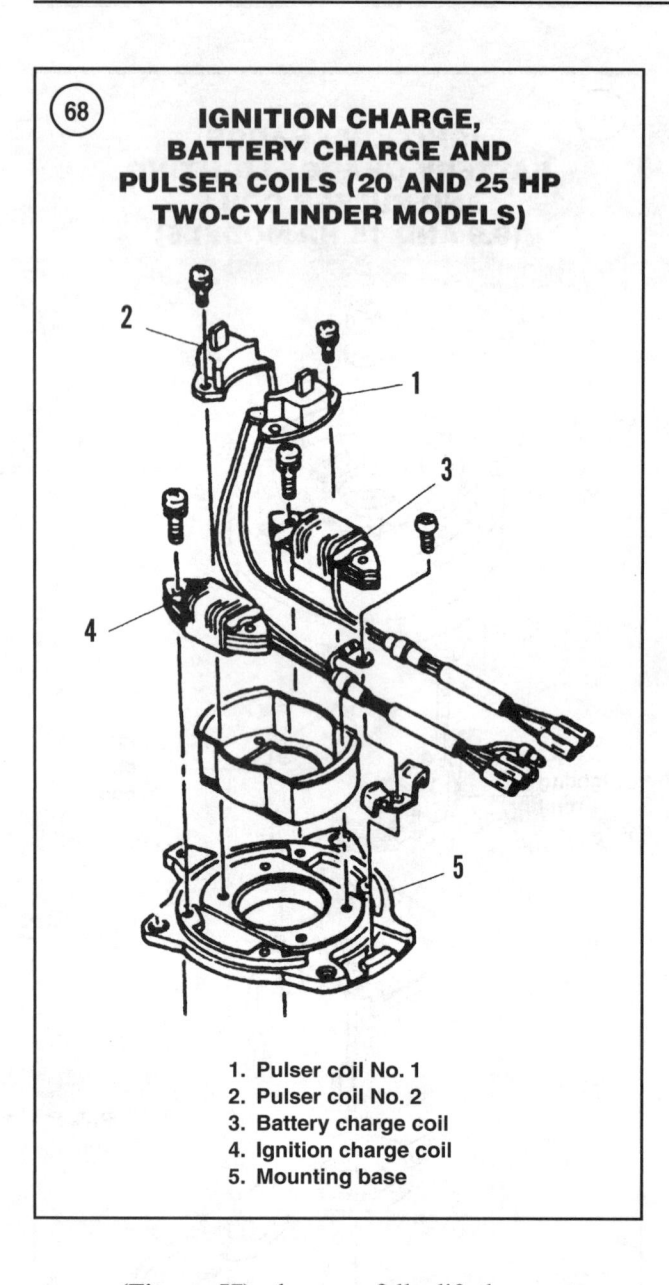

1. Pulser coil No. 1
2. Pulser coil No. 2
3. Battery charge coil
4. Ignition charge coil
5. Mounting base

69 IGNITION CHARGE, BATTERY CHARGE AND PULSER COILS (25 HP THREE-CYLINDER AND 30 HP MODELS)

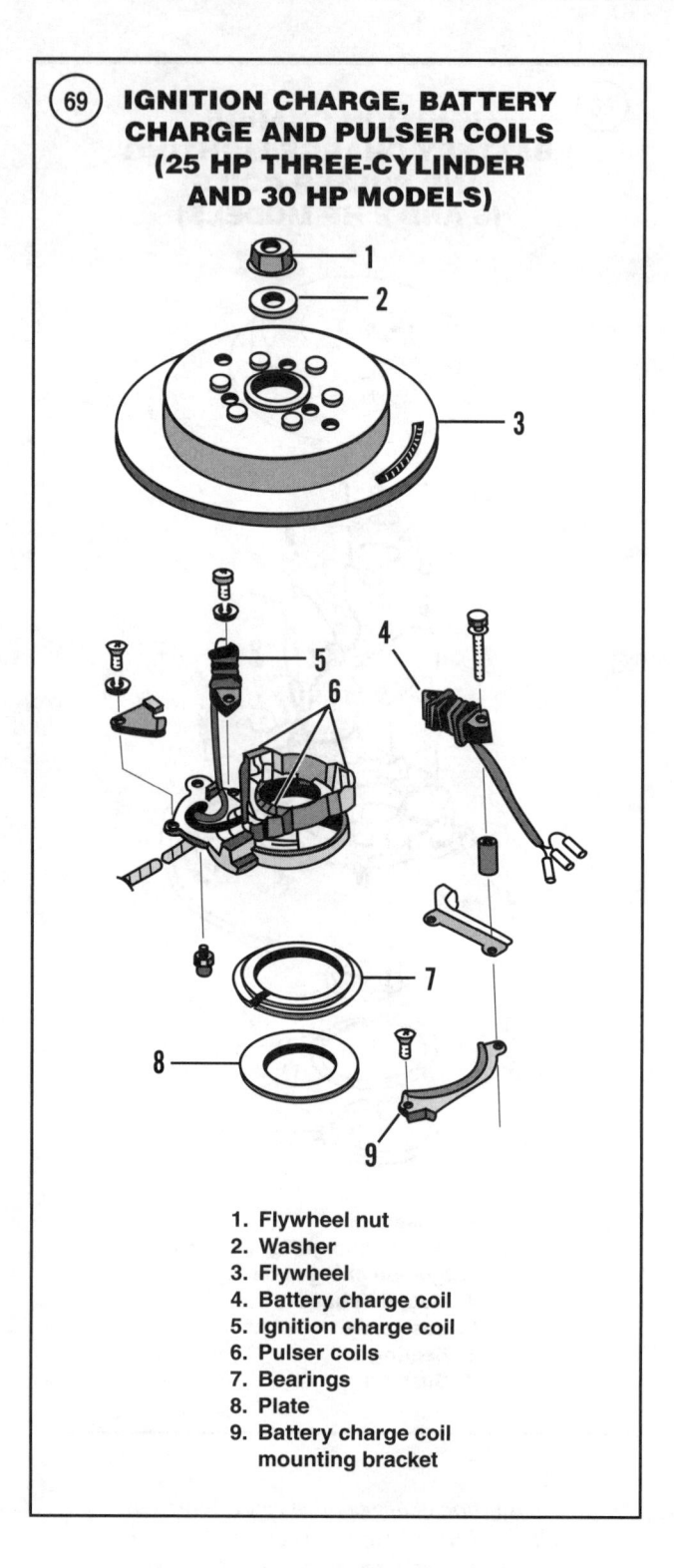

1. Flywheel nut
2. Washer
3. Flywheel
4. Battery charge coil
5. Ignition charge coil
6. Pulser coils
7. Bearings
8. Plate
9. Battery charge coil mounting bracket

---

screws (**Figure 57**), then carefully lift the component from the power head. If necessary, carefully tap on the coil laminations with a plastic hammer to free the coil. Do not pry the coil loose. The coils can be easily damaged if the pry bar contacts the windings.

10. Clean corrosion, and other debris or contaminants from the coil mounting location. Clean, inspect and repair, if necessary, the threads for the coil mounting screws.

Installation

CAUTION
On models with the ignition charge coil integrated into the battery charge coil, the assembly must be installed with the correct orientation for proper phasing of the ignition system. Always align the reference marks on the coil and power head during coil installation. Poor ignition sys-

IGNITION AND ELECTRICAL SYSTEMS

70

IGNITION CHARGE, BATTERY CHARGE AND PULSER COILS (28 JET, 35 JET, 40 HP AND 50 HP MODELS)

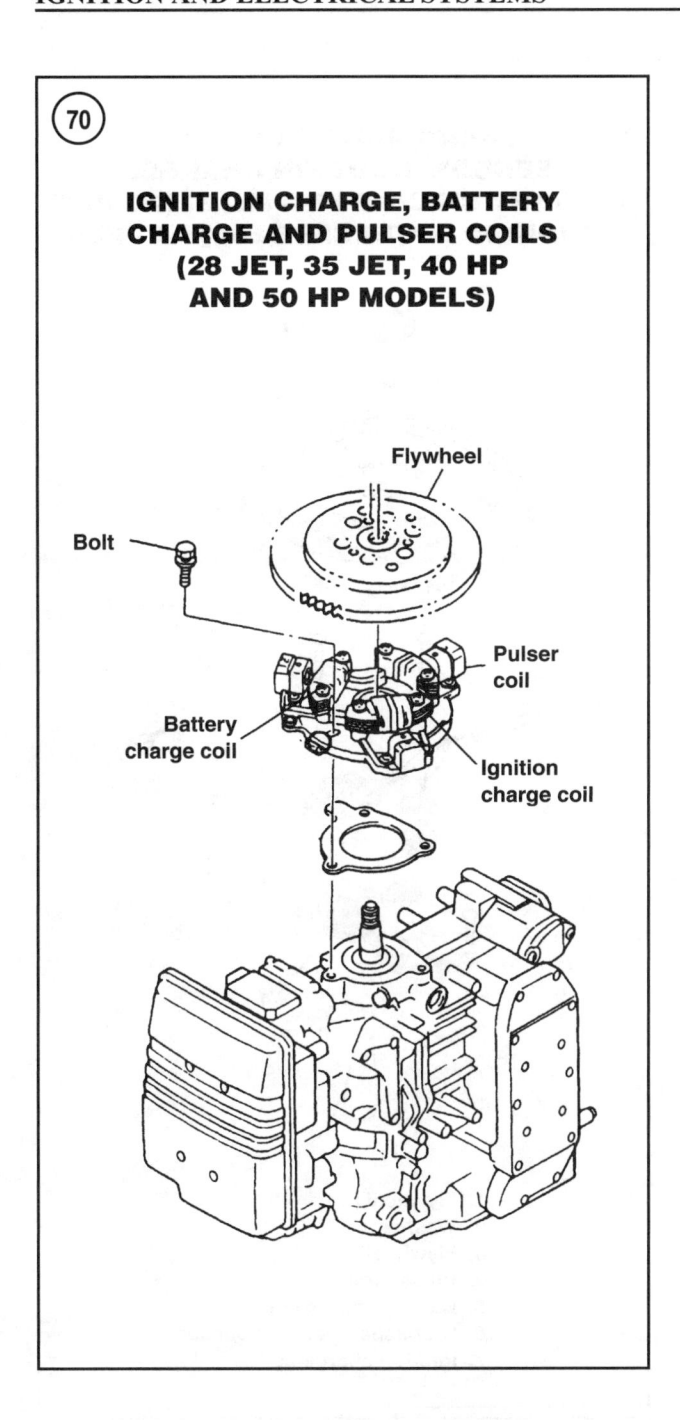

- Flywheel
- Bolt
- Pulser coil
- Battery charge coil
- Ignition charge coil

71

IGNITION CHARGE AND PULSER COILS (E60 MODEL)

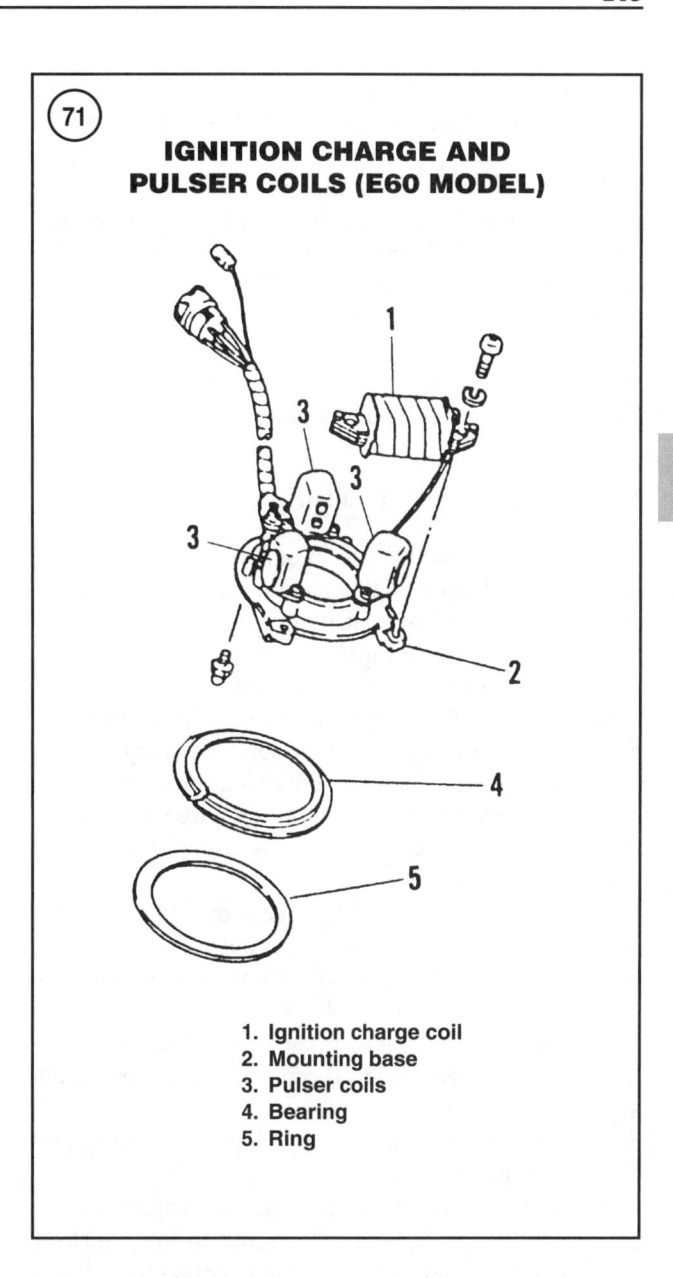

1. Ignition charge coil
2. Mounting base
3. Pulser coils
4. Bearing
5. Ring

tem performance can occur if the engine operates with an out of phase ignition charge coil.

1. When replacing the coil, transfer the reference mark to the replacement coil.

2. Carefully route the battery charge/lighting coil wires through any openings or grommets while installing the coil onto the mounting base or power head. If so equipped, install the clamps onto the coil wiring.

3. Align the reference mark and seat the coil on the mounting base or mounting bosses on the power head.

4. If so equipped, install all spacers and washers into the original location on the coil. Apply a light coat of Loctite 271 to the threads, then thread the mounting screws into the coil and mounting base. Verify proper seating and reference mark alignment, then securely tighten the screws.

5A. On 6-70 hp (except 65 jet) models, connect the battery charge/lighting coil wires to the CDI unit connections.

5B. On 65 jet and 75-90 hp models, connect the battery/ignition charge coil assembly wires to the CDI unit and rectifier wires.

6. Route the wires to avoid interference with moving components. Clamp the wires with plastic locking type clamps as necessary.
7. Install the flywheel as described in Chapter Seven. Manually rotate the flywheel while checking for interference with the coil. Remove the flywheel and check the installation if there is binding or rubbing.
8. On manual start models, install the starter as described in Chapter Ten.
9. On electric start models, connect the battery cables.
10. Connect the spark plug lead(s).

Pulser Coil Removal/Installation

Pulser coil appearances and mounting locations vary by model. Refer **Figures 64-73** and the wiring diagrams located at the end of the manual to identify the coil.

The pulser coils and ignition charge coil used on 25 hp three-cylinder and 30 hp models share a common wiring harness. Replace the charge coil/pulser coil assembly if one pulser coil or the ignition charge coil is faulty. The pulser coils used on 28 jet, 35 jet, 40 hp, 50 hp and E60 models share a common wire harness. Replace the three pulser coils as an assembly if one of the coils is faulty.

Before removing the coil, make a drawing or take a photograph of the wire routing and pulser coil mounting locations. This will help ensure proper wire routing and coil positioning during installation.

1. On electric start models, disconnect the battery cables.
2. On manual start models, remove the starter as described in Chapter Ten.
3. Disconnect and ground the spark plug lead(s) to prevent accidental starting.
4. Remove the flywheel as described in Chapter Seven.
5A. On 3 hp models, remove the screw to free the No. 1 pulser coil (1, **Figure 64**) from the mounting base. Use a short screwdriver to remove the screws that hold the No. 2 pulser coil (4, **Figure 64**). If the screw is inaccessible with the tools available, remove the mounting base (3, **Figure 64**).
5B. On 4 and 5 hp models, remove the two screws to free the pulser coils (1 and 2, **Figure 65**) from the mounting base.
5C. On 6 and 8 hp models, remove the single screw to free the pulser coil (1, **Figure 66**) from the mounting base.
5D. On 9.9 and 15 hp models:
   a. Remove the battery charge/lighting coils as described in this chapter.
   b. Remove the spacers and coil mounting bracket from the power head.

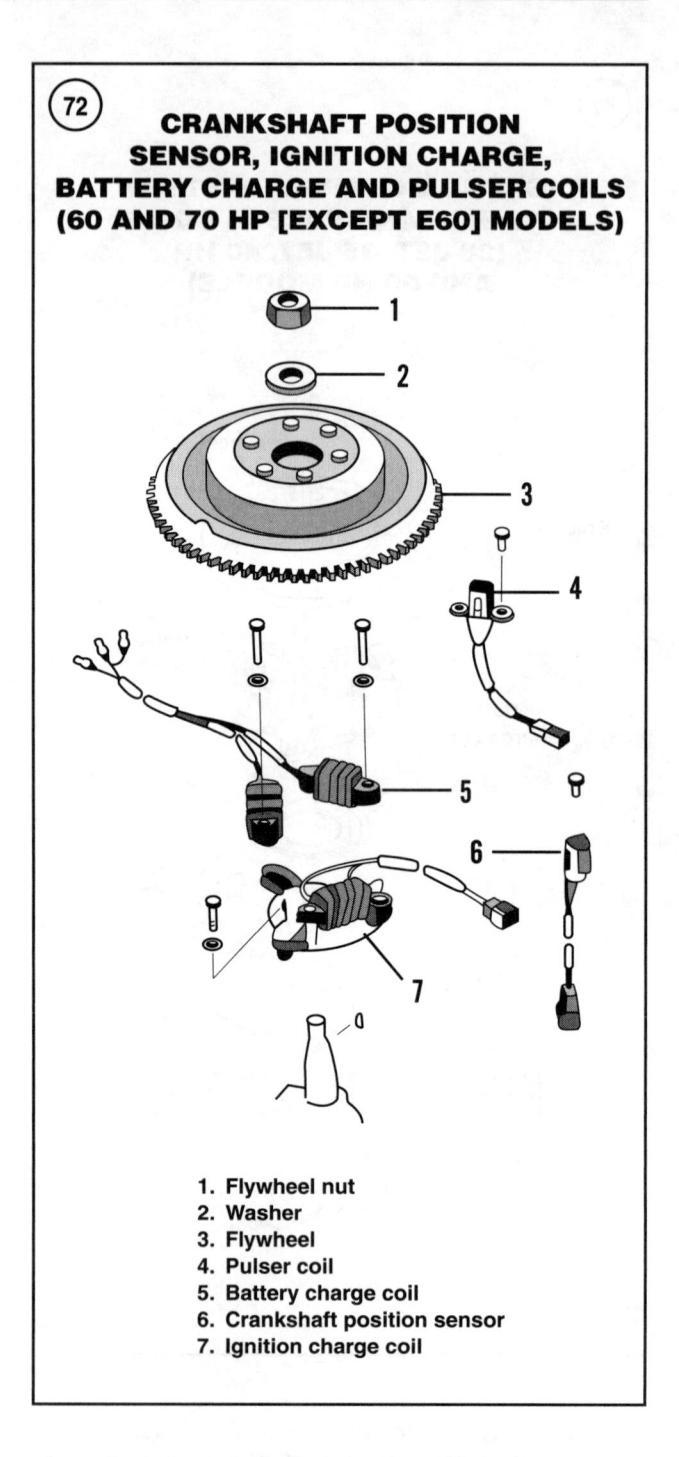

72 CRANKSHAFT POSITION SENSOR, IGNITION CHARGE, BATTERY CHARGE AND PULSER COILS (60 AND 70 HP [EXCEPT E60] MODELS)

1. Flywheel nut
2. Washer
3. Flywheel
4. Pulser coil
5. Battery charge coil
6. Crankshaft position sensor
7. Ignition charge coil

   c. Carefully disconnect the throttle arm linkage from the pulser coil assembly (**Figure 67**).

5E. On 20 and 25 hp two-cylinder models, remove the screws that hold the selected pulser coil (1 or 2, **Figure 68**) to the mounting base.
5F. On 25 hp three-cylinder and 30 hp models, remove the ignition charge coil from the mounting plate as described in this chapter. Remove the three screws to free

IGNITION AND ELECTRICAL SYSTEMS

73

IGNITION/BATTERY CHARGING AND PULSER COILS (65 JET AND 75-90 HP MODELS)

1. Bearing
2. Pulser coil assembly
3. Ignition/battery charge coil
4. Linkage connection point

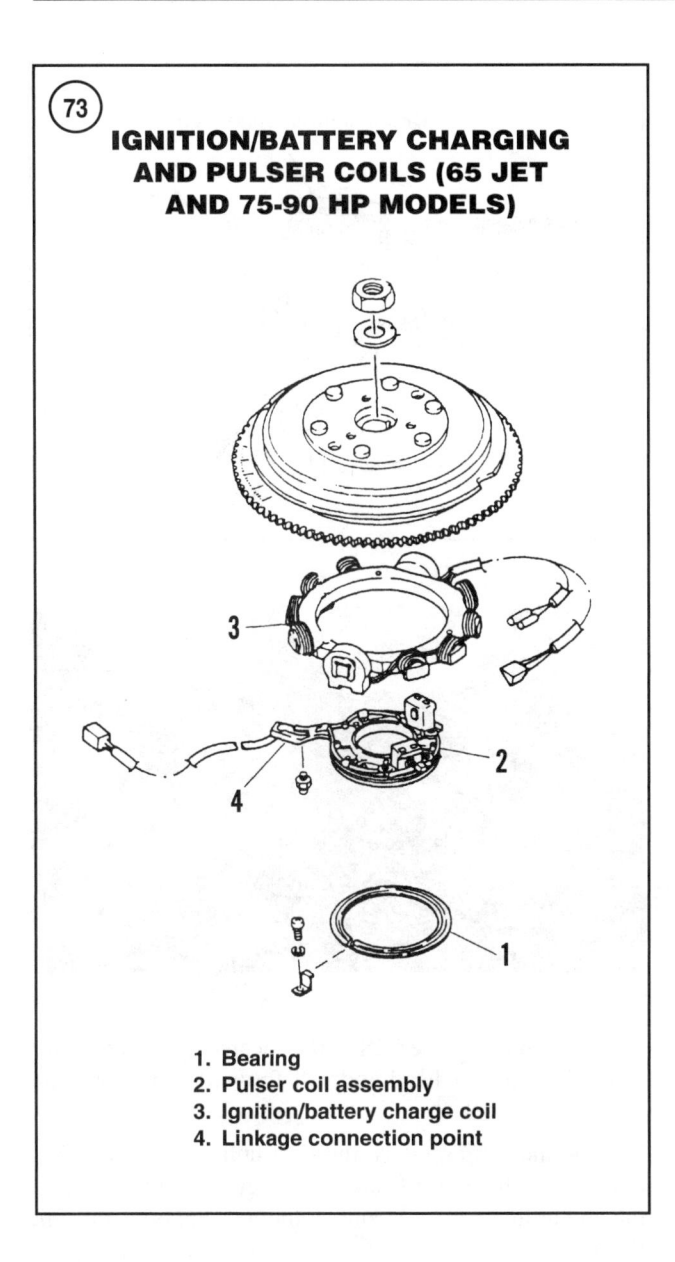

the pulser coils (6, **Figure 69**) from the mounting base. The pulser coils and ignition charge coil share a common wire harness and must be replaced as an assembly.

5G. On 28 jet, 35 jet, 40 hp and 50 hp models, remove the two screws that hold each pulser coil (**Figure 70**) to the mounting base. The three pulser coils share a common wire harness. Replace all three coils if one coil is faulty.

5H. On E60 models, remove the screws that hold the pulser coils (3, **Figure 71**) to the mounting base. The three pulser coils share a common wire harness. Replace all three coils if one coil is faulty.

5I. On 60 and 70 hp (except E60) models, remove the two screws to free the pulser coil (4, **Figure 72**) from the power head boss.

5J. On 65 jet and 75-90 hp models, remove the ignition charge coil as described in this chapter. Disconnect the throttle arm linkage from the connection point (4, **Figure 73**) on the trigger.

6. On 60-90 hp models, remove the plastic electrical component cover (**Figure 60**).

7. Disconnect the pulser coil wires from the CDI unit. Note the wiring positioning, then remove any clamps from the pulser coil wiring.

8. Guide the wiring through any openings or grommets while lifting the pulser coil(s) from the power head.

9. Clean corrosion or other contaminants from the coil mount and screw openings.

10. Pulser coil installation is the reverse of removal. Perform the following during installation.
   a. On 6-50 hp and E60 models, apply a light coat of Yamaha All-Purpose Grease or equivalent to the bottom of the mounting base or pulser coil mount. Lift the base or trigger mount slightly to access the surfaces. The mounting base must pivot freely for proper ignition timing control.
   b. Route all wiring to prevent interference with moving components. Clamp the wiring with plastic locking type clamps as needed.
   c. Check for proper pivoting action of the mounting base. Remove unnecessary clamps or correct binding before operating the engine.
   d. Apply a light coat of 271 Loctite to the pulser coil mounting screw threads prior to installation. Securely tighten the screws.

11. Install the flywheel as described in Chapter Seven. Manually rotate the flywheel while checking for interference with the coil. Remove the flywheel and check the installation if there is binding or rubbing.

12. On manual start models, install the starter as described in Chapter Ten.

13. On electric start models, connect the battery cables.

14. Connect the spark plug lead(s).

15. Perform all applicable timing adjustments as described in Chapter Four.

Crankshaft Position Sensor Removal/Installation

The crankshaft position sensor (**Figure 74**) is positioned in the cover recess next to the flywheel.

Air gap adjustment is not required. However, the sensor must not contact the flywheel at any point of flywheel rotation. Check for incorrect sensor installation if it contacts the flywheel.

Remove the flywheel cover to provide the best access to the crankshaft position sensor screws. On manual start models, also remove the rewind starter. Refer to Chapter Ten for manual starter removal and installation procedures.

Before removing the sensor, make a drawing or take a photograph of the wire routing and sensor mounting locations. This will help ensure proper wire routing and sensor positioning during installation.

Refer to the wiring diagrams at the end of the manual to identify the wire colors for the pulser coil(s). Trace the wires from to the coil mounting location under the flywheel.

1. On electric start models, disconnect the battery cables.
2. On manual start models, remove the manual starter as described in Chapter Ten.
3. Disconnect and ground the spark plug lead(s) to prevent accidental starting.
4. Remove the plastic electrical component cover (**Figure 60**) to access the wire connections.
5. Disconnect the sensor wires from the CDI unit.
6. Remove the two mounting screws, then carefully pull the sensor from the mount. Carefully guide the sensor wiring through any openings or grommets during removal.
7. Clean corrosion or other contaminants from the coil mount and screw openings.
8. Position the sensor on the mount. Apply a light coat of Loctite 271 to the threads, then install the mounting screw and washers. Securely tighten the screws.
9. Manually rotate the flywheel while checking for contact with the sensor. Remove the sensor and check the installation if it contacts the flywheel.
10. Route the wires to their connections on the CDI unit harness. Plug the sensor harness into the CDI harness.
11. Route the wiring to prevent interference with moving components. Secure the wires with plastic locking type clamps as needed.
12. On manual start models, install the starter as described in Chapter Ten.
13. On electric start models, connect the battery cables.
14. Connect the spark plug lead(s).
15. Perform all applicable timing adjustments as described in Chapter Four.

CDI Unit Removal/Installation

CDI unit (**Figure 75**, typical) appearance and mounting locations vary by model. Refer to the wiring diagrams located near the end of the manual to identify the wire colors connecting to the unit. Use the wire colors and the following information to locate the CDI unit.

On 2 hp models, the CDI unit is located on the starboard side of the power head and just below the fuel tank.

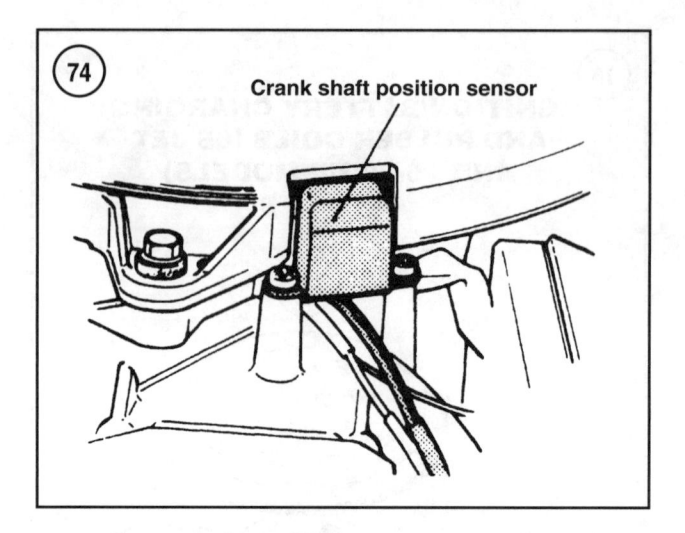

On 3 hp models, the CDI unit is located on the starboard side of the power head and just forward of the ignition coil.

On 4 and 5 hp models, the CDI unit is located on the port side of the power head. Two screws secure the coil to the mounting plate. A rubber mount supports the unit (**Figure 76**).

On 6 and 8 hp models, the CDI unit is located on the top of the power head and just to the rear of the flywheel.

On 9.9 and 15 hp models, the CDI unit is located on the port side of the power head and just below the flywheel.

On 20 and 25 hp two-cylinder models, the CDI unit is located on the port side of the power head and just below the flywheel. The unit is often hidden behind the bundle of wires extending from under the flywheel.

On 25 hp three-cylinder and 30 hp models, the CDI unit is located on the starboard side of the power head and just to the rear of the throttle linkages.

On 28 jet, 35 jet, 40 hp and 50 hp models, the CDI unit is located on the starboard side of the power head and just

IGNITION AND ELECTRICAL SYSTEMS

below the flywheel. A throttle arm linkage connects to the CDI unit pointer.

On 60-90 hp models, the CDI unit is located on the electrical component mounting bracket. The bracket is mounted on the starboard side of the power head. Remove the plastic electrical component cover to access the CDI unit connections. A throttle arm linkage connects to the CDI unit pointer.

Note the size and location of all plastic locking type clamps that must be removed.

1. On electric start models, disconnect the battery cables.
2. Disconnect and ground the spark plug(s) leads to prevent accidental starting.
3. On 28 jet, 35 jet and 40-90 hp models, carefully disconnect the throttle arm linkage from the CDI unit pointer.
4. On 60-90 hp models, remove the plastic electrical component cover (**Figure 60**) to access the CDI unit connectors.
5. Note the wire routing and connection points, then disconnect all wires from the CDI unit.
6. Locate and remove the screws and washers that hold the CDI unit to the attaching point. Make note of any grounding wires. Grounding wires must be connected during assembly.

7. Remove the CDI unit, then clean corrosion or other contaminants from the CDI unit mount and screw openings.
8. Install the CDI mount and secure it with the fasteners. Make sure any ground wires are connected during installation. Tighten the fasteners to the specification in **Table 1** or Chapter One.
9. Connect the CDI unit wires to the engine harness, ignition charge coil, pulser coil and crankshaft position sensor wires.
10. Route wiring to prevent contact with other components. Secure wiring with plastic locking type clamps as needed.
11. On 28 jet, 35 jet and 40-90 hp models, carefully connect the throttle arm linkage to the CDI unit pointer.
12. On 60-90 hp models, install the plastic electrical component cover (**Figure 60**).
13. On electric start models, connect the battery cables.
14. Connect the spark plug lead(s).
15. Perform all applicable timing adjustments as described in Chapter Four.

Ignition Coil Removal/Installation

Ignition coil (**Figure 77**, typical) appearance, quantity and mounting locations vary by model. Refer to the wiring diagrams located near the end of the manual to identify the wire colors connecting to the coil(s). Use the wire colors and the following information to locate the coil(s).

On 2 hp models, the single ignition coil is located on the starboard side of the power head and below the flywheel.

On 3 hp models, the single ignition coil is located on the lower starboard side of the power head and just below the fuel tank.

On 4 and 5 hp models, the single ignition coil is located on the lower port side of the power head.

On 6 and 8 hp models, a single ignition coil (**Figure 77**) is located on the rear and port side of the power head. The coil contains two secondary windings and provides spark for both cylinders.

9.9 and 15 hp models use two ignition coils. The ignition coil for the No. 1 cylinder is located on the upper port side of the power head. The coil for the No. 2 cylinder is located on the upper starboard side of the power head.

On 20 and 25 hp two-cylinder models, the two ignition coils are located on the rear and port sides of the power head.

On 25 hp three-cylinder and 30 hp models, the three ignition coils are located on the rear and starboard sides of the power head.

On 28 jet, 35 jet and 40-90 hp models, the three ignition coils are located on the aft end of the electrical component mounting bracket. The bracket is mounted on the starboard side of the power head.

Mark the cylinder number on the spark plug lead(s) before removing multiple coils. Note the size and location of all plastic locking type clamps that must be removed.

1. On electric start models, disconnect the battery cables.
2. Disconnect and ground the spark plug(s) leads to prevent accidental starting.
3. On 60-90 hp models, remove the plastic electrical component cover (**Figure 60**) to access the ignition coil and CDI unit wires.
4. Note the wire routing and connection points, then disconnect the coil wires from the CDI unit or engine harness wires (**Figure 78**, typical).
5. Locate and remove the screws and washers that retain the coil to the attaching point. Make note of any grounding wires.
6. Remove the ignition coil, then clean corrosion or other contaminants from the mount and screw openings.
7. Carefully unthread the spark plug cap from the secondary lead (**Figure 79**). Test the spark plug cap as described in Chapter Two.
8. Thread the spark plug cap onto the secondary lead of the replacement coil (**Figure 79**).
9. Install the coil and secure it with the fasteners. Make sure any ground wires are connected during installation. Tighten the fasteners to the specification in **Table 1** or Chapter One.
10. Connect the ignition coil leads to the engine harness or CDI unit wires.
11. Route wiring to prevent contact with other components. Secure wiring with plastic locking type clamps as needed.
12. On 60-90 hp models, install the plastic electrical component cover (**Figure 60**).
13. On electric start models, connect the battery cables.
14. Connect the spark plug lead(s) to the spark plug(s).
15. Perform all applicable timing adjustments as described in Chapter Four.

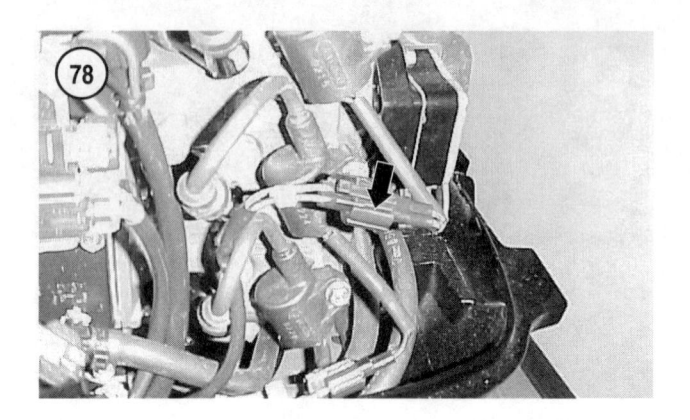

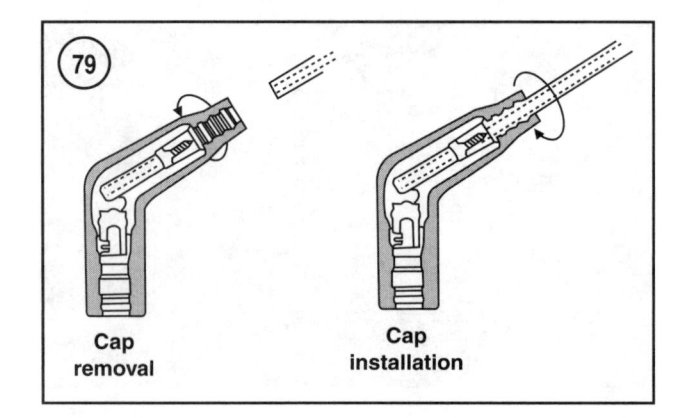

Engine Stop and Lanyard Switch Replacement

An engine stop switch or combination stop/lanyard switch (**Figure 80**) is mounted on the front of the lower cover (**Figure 81** or **Figure 82**) on 2-30 hp (except 28 jet) tiller control models. A combination stop/lanyard switch is mounted on the tiller arm (**Figure 83**) on 28 jet, 25 jet and 40-90 hp models. The engine stop and combination engine stop/lanyard appearance and replacement procedures are very similar.

Refer to **Figures 81-83** for this procedure.
1. On electric start models, disconnect the battery cables.
2. Disconnect and ground the spark plug leads to prevent accidental starting.
3. Remove the retaining nut from the stop switch or stop/lanyard switch.
4. Disconnect the stop switch/lanyard switch wires from the engine wire harness. Remove the switch from the lower engine cover or tiller arm.
5. Fit the replacement switch into the engine cover opening. Thread the nut onto the switch and securely tighten it.

IGNITION AND ELECTRICAL SYSTEMS

81 STARTER BUTTON AND STOP/LANYARD SWITCH (2-15 HP MODELS [TYPICAL])

1. Stop switch
2. Washer
3. Stop switch nut
4. Start switch nut
5. Bracket
6. Starter button and harness

82 STARTER BUTTON AND STOP/LANYARD SWITCH (20-30 HP [EXCEPT 28 JET] MODELS)

Stop switch
Starter button

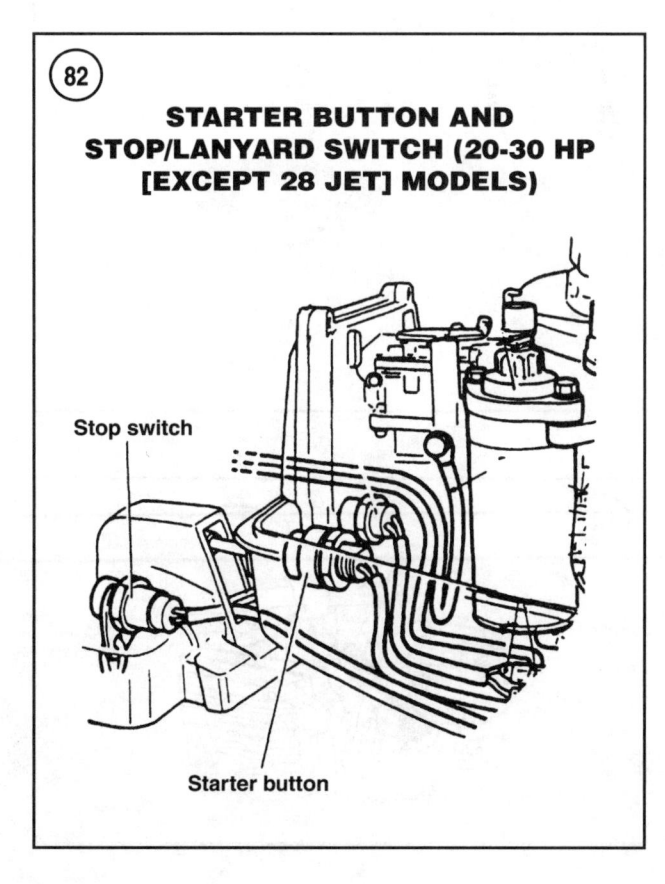

6. Route the stop/lanyard switch wire harness to the connections on the engine wire harness. Position the wiring to prevent contact with moving components. Secure the harness with plastic locking type clamps as needed.
7. Connect the battery cables and spark plug leads.

WARNING SYSTEM COMPONENTS

This section includes removal and installation procedures for the thermoswitch, warning horn and warning light. Refer to Chapter Twelve for oil level sensor replacement procedures.

Thermoswitch Removal/Installation

A thermoswitch is used on all 20-90 hp models. The switch mounts into the bore in the upper section of the cylinder head or water jacket cover (**Figure 84**).
1. On electric start models, disconnect the battery cables.
2. Disconnect and ground the spark plug leads to prevent accidental starting.
3. Locate the switch on the cylinder head or water jacket cover. Disconnect the switch wires from the engine wire harness.
4. Carefully pull the switch from the bore in the cylinder head or water jacket. Thoroughly clean debris or oily contaminants from the switch surfaces and bore.
5. Carefully insert the replacement thermoswitch into the bore. Do not apply sealant or lubricant. Sealant or lubricant may insulate the switch and hinder its operation. Press the switch fully into the bore.
6. Connect the thermoswitch wires to the engine harness wires. Route the wiring to avoid interference with moving components. Secure the wiring with plastic locking clamps as needed.
7. Connect the spark plug leads.
8. On electric start models, connect the battery cables.

Warning Horn Removal/Installation

The warning horn is located in the control box, within the engine cover, within the tiller control housing or behind the dash mounted instruments.
1. Disconnect the battery cables. Disconnect and ground the spark plug leads to prevent accidental starting.
2. If the warning horn is mounted in the remote control, disassemble the remote control and replace the horn as described in Chapter Thirteen.
3. If the horn is mounted behind the dash or on the engine, replace the warning horn as follows:

272

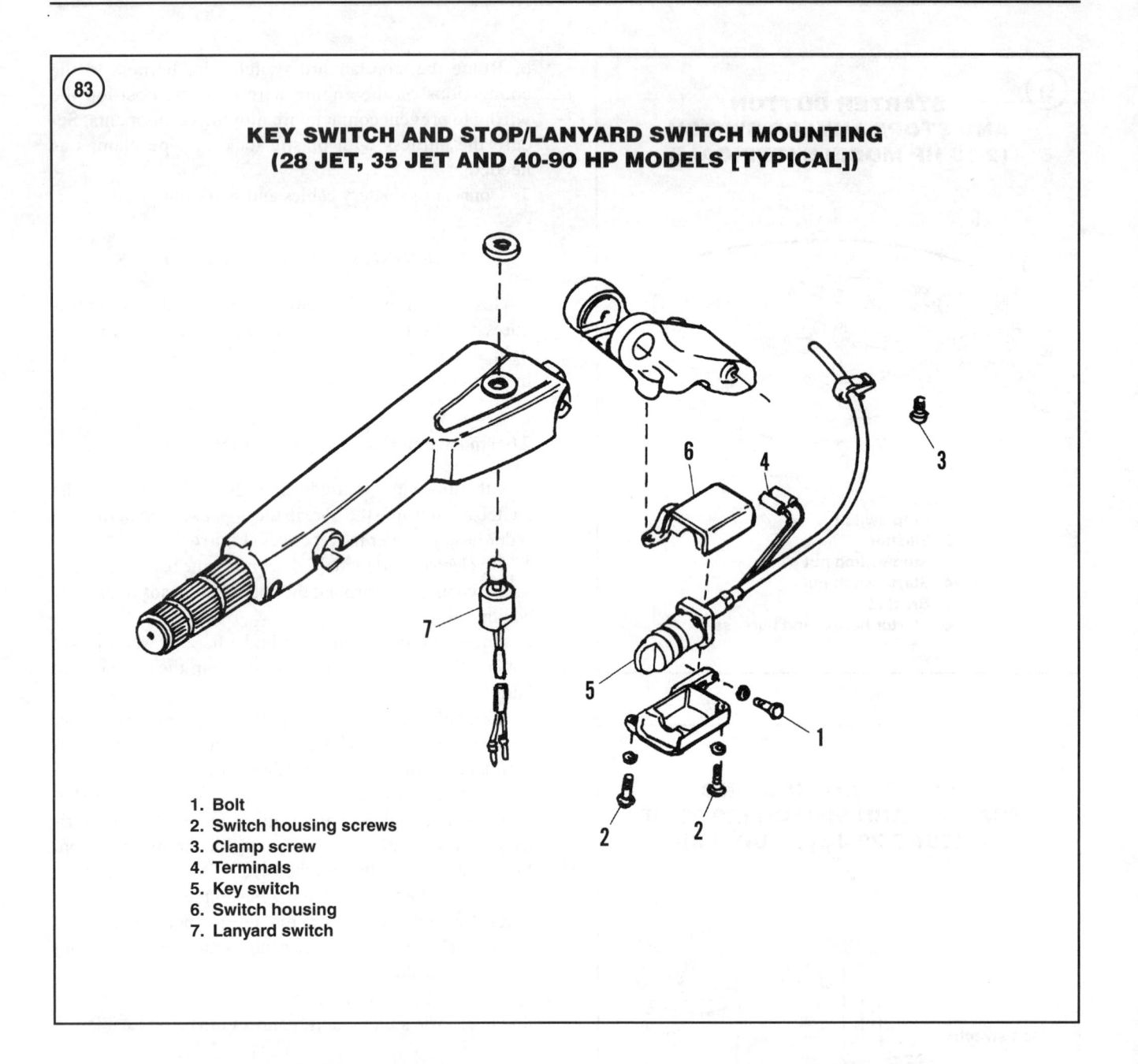

CHAPTER SIX

83

**KEY SWITCH AND STOP/LANYARD SWITCH MOUNTING
(28 JET, 35 JET AND 40-90 HP MODELS [TYPICAL])**

1. Bolt
2. Switch housing screws
3. Clamp screw
4. Terminals
5. Key switch
6. Switch housing
7. Lanyard switch

   a. Disconnect the warning horn wires and clean them.
   b. Remove the clamp to free the warning horn from the wiring.
   c. Connect the warning horn wire to the appropriate instrument or engine harness wires.
   d. Position the wiring to prevent interference with moving components.
   e. Secure the warning horn to the wiring with a plastic locking type clamp.
4. On electric start models, connect the battery cables.
5. Connect the spark plug leads.

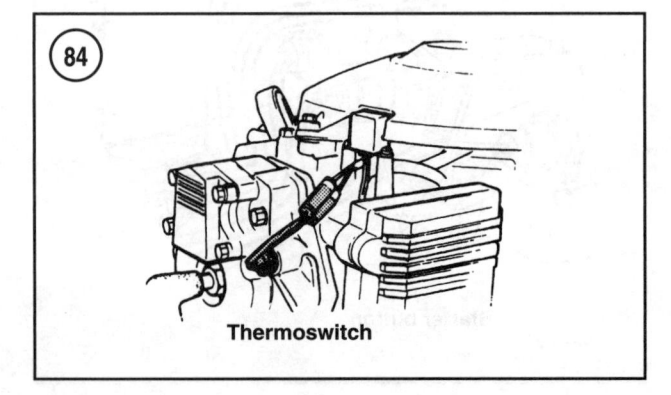

84

Thermoswitch

IGNITION AND ELECTRICAL SYSTEMS

6. Check the warning horn operation as described in Chapter Two.

Warning Light Removal/Installation

The warning light (**Figure 85**) is mounted on the front of the lower engine cover. This component is used on 20-50 hp models with tiller control and some 20-30 hp models with remote control.

1. On electric start models, disconnect the battery cables.
2. Disconnect and ground the spark plug leads to prevent accidental starting.
3. Disconnect the warning light wires from the engine wire harness leads.
4. Remove the retainer, then remove the light from the lower engine cover.
5. Insert the replacement warning light into the opening in the lower cover. Install the retainer into the groove in the light to secure the light.
6. Connect the warning light wires to the appropriate engine wire harness connections. Route the wiring to prevent interference with moving components. Secure the wiring with plastic locking type clamps as needed.
7. On electric start models, connect the battery cables.
8. Connect the spark plug leads.

Table 1 IGNITION AND ELECTRICAL SYSTEMS TORQUE SPECIFICATIONS

Fastener	N•m	in.-lb.	ft.-lb.
CDI unit			
4 and 5 hp	5	44	–
6 and 8 hp	4	36	–
Ignition coil			
4 and 5 hp	8	70	–
6 and 8 hp	7	62	–
Starter button retainer	5	44	–
Starter cable to starter relay	9	80	–
Starter motor mounting bolts			
6-50 hp	18	–	13
60-90 hp	20	–	15

Table 2 BATTERY CHARGE PERCENTAGE

Specific gravity reading	Percentage of charge remaining
1.120-1.140	0
1.135-1.155	10
1.150-1.170	20
1.160-1.180	30
1.175-1.195	40
1.190-1.210	50
1.205-1.225	60
1.215-1.235	70
1.230-1.250	80
1.245-1.265	90
1.260-1.280	100

Table 3 BATTERY CAPACITY

Accessory draw	Provides continuous power for:	Approximate recharge time
80 amp-hour battery		
5 amps	13.5 hours	16 hours
15 amps	3.5 hours	13 hours
25 amps	1.6 hours	12 hours
105 amp-hour battery		
5 amps	15.8 hours	16 hours
15 amps	4.2 hours	13 hours
25 amps	2.4 hours	12 hours

Table 4 BATTERY REQUIREMENTS

Model	Minimum CCA rating	Amp hour rating
6-30 hp (except 28 jet)	210	40-70
35 jet and 50-90 hp	380	70-100

Table 5 STARTER MOTOR SPECIFICATIONS

Model	Specification
Brush length	
6-25 hp two-cylinder	4.5-7.5 mm (0.177-0.295 in.)
25 hp three-cylinder and 30-70 hp (except 65 jet)	9.0-12.5 mm (0.354-0.492 in.)
65 jet and 75-90 hp	12.0-16.0 mm (0.472-0.630 in.)
Commutator diameter	
6-25 hp two-cylinder	19.4-20.0 mm (0.764-0.787 in.)
25 hp three-cylinder and 30-70 hp (except 65 jet)	29.0-30.0 mm (1.142-1.181 in.)
65 jet and 75-90 hp	31.0-33.0 mm (1.220-1.299 in.)
Commutator undercut	0.20 mm-0.80 mm (0.008-0.0.031 in.)
Maximum armature deflection	0.05 mm (0.002 in.)

Chapter Seven

Power Head

This chapter includes power head removal/installation, disassembly/reassembly, and cleaning and inspection procedures for 2-90 hp models. The power head can be removed from the outboard engine without the entire outboard being removed from the boat.

Since this chapter covers a large range of models, spanning several model years, the power heads from different model groups will differ in construction and require different service procedures. Whenever possible, engines with similar service procedures have been grouped together.

The components shown in the accompanying illustrations are generally from the most common models. While the components shown in the illustrations may not be identical to those being serviced, the step-by-step procedures cover each model in this manual. Illustrations, typical of each power head model group, are located in the appropriate *Disassembly* section and are helpful references for many service procedures.

This chapter is arranged in a disassembly/assembly sequence. When only a partial repair is required, follow the procedure(s) to the point where the faulty parts can be replaced, then go to the reassembly section.

Many procedures require special tools, which can be purchased from a Yamaha outboard dealership.

Power head work stands and holding fixtures (**Figure 1**) are available from specialty shops or marine and industrial product distributors.

Make sure the work bench, work station, engine stand or holding fixture is of sufficient capacity to support the size and weight of the power head. This is especially important when working on larger engines.

SERVICE CONSIDERATIONS

Performing internal service procedures on the power head requires considerable mechanical ability. Carefully consider your capabilities before attempting any operation involving major disassembly of the engine.

If, after studying the text and illustrations in this chapter, you decide not to attempt major power head disassembly or repair, it may be financially beneficial to perform certain preliminary operations yourself. Consider separating the power head from the outboard and removing the fuel, ignition and electrical systems and all accessories, then taking only the power head to the dealership for the actual overhaul or major repair.

Since most marine dealerships often have lengthy waiting lists for service, especially during the spring and summer, this practice can reduce the time the unit is in the shop. If much of the preliminary work is already done, repairs can be scheduled and performed much quicker. Always discuss the options with the dealership before taking a disassembled engine to the dealership. Dealerships will often want to install, adjust and test run the engine in order to be comfortable providing warranty coverage for the overhaul or repair.

No matter who is doing the work, repair will be quicker and easier if the engine is clean before service procedures are started. There are many special cleaners available from automotive supply stores. Most of these cleaners are simply sprayed on, then rinsed off with a garden hose after the recommended time period. Always follow all instructions provided by the manufacturer. Never apply cleaning solvent to electrical and ignition components or spray it into the induction or exhaust system.

WARNING
Never use gasoline as a cleaning agent. Gasoline presents an extreme fire and explosion hazard. Work in a well-ventilated area when using cleaning solvent. Keep a large fire extinguisher rated for gasoline and oil fires nearby in case of an emergency.

If you have decided to do the job yourself, thoroughly read this chapter to understand what is involved in completing the repair satisfactorily. Make arrangements to buy or rent the necessary special tools and obtain a source for replacement parts *before* starting. It is frustrating and time-consuming to start a major repair and then be unable to finish because the necessary tools or parts are not available.

NOTE
Take a series of at least five photographs from the front, rear, top and both sides of the power head before removal to help during reassembly and installation. The photographs are especially useful for routing electrical harnesses, and fuel, primer and recirculation lines. They will also be helpful during the installation of accessories, control linkages and brackets.

Before beginning the job, review Chapter One of this manual.

Table 1 lists specific torque specifications for most power head fasteners. Chapter One lists standard torque specifications. Use the standard torque specifications for fasteners not listed in **Table 1**. **Tables 2-5** list the required dimensional specifications. All tables are located at the end of this chapter.

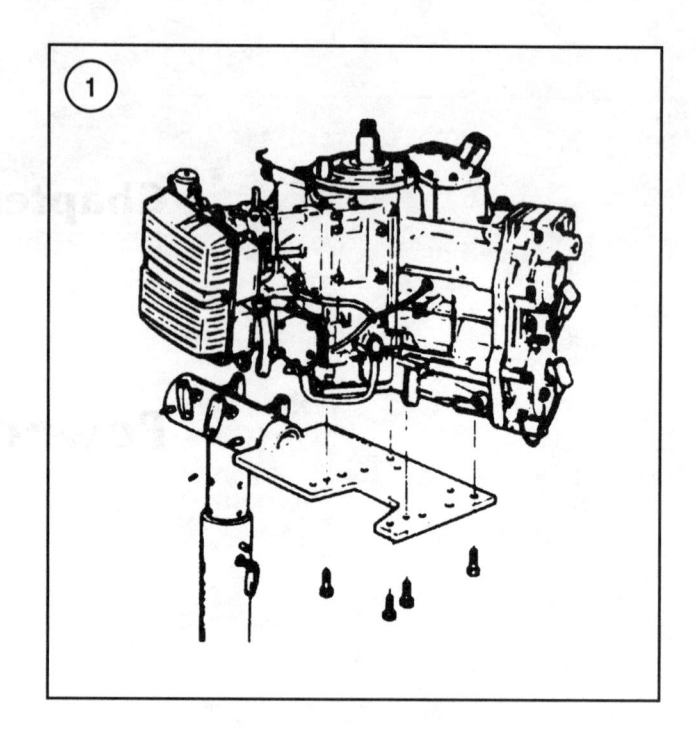

POWER HEAD BREAK-IN

Whenever a power head has been rebuilt or replaced, or if *any* new internal parts have been installed, it must be treated as a new engine. Run the engine on the specified fuel/oil mixture and operated it in accordance with the recommended break-in procedure described in Chapter Three.

CAUTION
Failure to follow the recommended break-in procedure will result in premature power head failure.

SERVICE RECOMMENDATIONS

If the engine has experienced a power head failure, make every attempt to determine the cause of the failure. Refer to the *Power Head* section in Chapter Three for troubleshooting procedures.

Many failures are caused by using the incorrect or stale fuel, and incorrect lubricating oil. Refer to Chapter Three for all fuel and oil recommendations.

POWER HEAD

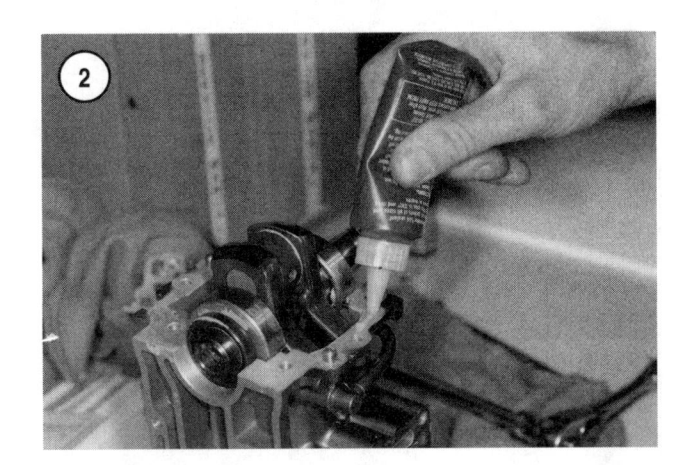

When rebuilding or performing a major repair on the power head, consider performing the following steps to prevent the failure from reoccurring.

1. Service the water pump. Replace the impeller, all seals and all gaskets. See Chapter Eight.
2. Replace the thermostat(s) and remove and inspect the water pressure relief valve, on models so equipped, as described in this chapter. Replace suspect components.
3. Drain the fuel tank(s) and dispose of the old fuel in an approved manner.
4. Fill the fuel tank with fresh fuel and add the recommended oil to the fuel tank at the *break-in* ratio as described in Chapter Three.
5. Replace or clean all fuel filters. See Chapter Three.
6. Clean and adjust the carburetors. See Chapter Five.
7. Drain and clean the oil reservoir(s). Dispose of the old oil in an approved manner. Then refill the oil system with the specified oil (Chapter Three) and bleed the oil system as described in Chapter Twelve.
8. Install new spark plugs. Only use the recommended spark plugs listed in Chapter Three. Make sure the spark plugs are correctly tightened. Incorrect torque can lead to spark plug overheating.
9. Perform *all* of the synchronization and linkage adjustments as described in Chapter Four before returning the engine to service.

LUBRICANTS, SEALANTS AND ADHESIVES

The manufacturer recommended lubricants, sealants and adhesives are listed in the repair procedures. Equivalent products are acceptable, as long as they meet or exceed the specifications.

During power head assembly, lubricate all internal engine components with two-cycle (TCW-3) outboard engine oil. Lubricate all seal lips and O-rings with Yamaha All-Purpose Grease or equivalent.

Use Yamaha Combustion Chamber Cleaner to efficiently remove the carbon from the pistons and combustion chambers. Allow ample time for the cleaner to soak into and soften carbon deposits.

Unless otherwise specified, do not apply gasket sealing compound to gasket surfaces. Many of the gaskets used on Yamaha outboards are designed to cure and seal after reaching operating temperature. Gasket sealing compound may prevent proper curing of the gasket. If no other sealant or adhesive is specified, coat the threads of all external fasteners with a light coat of two-cycle outboard engine oil to help prevent corrosion and ease future removal.

Before sealing the crankcase cover/cylinder block, make sure both mating surfaces are free of sealant residue, dirt, oil or other contamination. Locquic Primer, lacquer thinner, acetone or similar solvents work well when used with a plastic scraper. Never use solvents with an oil, wax or petroleum base.

CAUTION
*Clean all mating surfaces carefully to avoid nicks and gouges. A plastic scraper can be improvised from a common household electrical outlet cover or a piece of Lucite with one edge ground to a 45° angle. Be extremely careful when using a metal scraper, such as a putty knife. Nicks and gouges may prevent the sealant from curing. Do **not** lap or machine the crankcase cover-to-cylinder block surface.*

Loctite Gasket Maker is the only sealant recommended for sealing the crankcase cover-to-cylinder block mating surface. Apply the sealant bead to the inside (crankshaft side) of all crankcase cover bolt holes (**Figure 2**).

Apply Loctite 271 threadlocking adhesive to the outer diameter of all seals before pressing them into place. Also apply this adhesive to the threads of all internal fasteners if no other adhesive is specified.

Before using a Loctite product, always clean the surface to be sealed or threads to be secured with Locquic Primer. Locquic Primer cleans and primes the surface and ensures a quick secure bond by leaving a thin film of catalyst on the surface or threads. Allow the primer to air dry, as blow drying disables the catalyst.

Sealing Surfaces

Use a plate glass or a machinist's surface plate or straightedge for surface checking. Ordinary window glass does not have a uniform surface and will give false readings. Plate glass has a very uniform surface.

Once the surfaces are clean, check the component for warp by placing the component on a piece of plate glass or a machinist's surface plate. Apply uniform downward pressure and try to insert a selection of feeler gauges between the plate and the component.

A machinist's straightedge can be used to check areas that cannot be accessed using the glass or surface plate. See **Figure 3**. Unless otherwise specified, replace the component if warp exceeds 0.1 mm (0.004 in.).

CAUTION
Do not lap the cylinder block-to-crankcase cover all models.

To remove minor warp, minor nicks or scratches, or traces of sealant or gasket material, place a large sheet of 320-400 grit wet sandpaper on the plate glass or surface plate. Apply light downward pressure and move the component in a figure-eight pattern as shown in **Figure 4**. Use a light oil, such as WD-40, to keep the sandpaper from loading up. Remove the component from the sandpaper and recheck the sealing surface.

It may be necessary to repeat the lapping process several times to achieve the desired results. Never remove any more material than is absolutely necessary. Before reassembly, thoroughly wash the component to remove all grit.

FASTENERS AND TORQUE

Always replace a worn or damaged fastener with one of equal size, type and torque requirement. Power head torque values are in **Table 1**. If a specification is not provided for a given fastener, use the standard torque values in Chapter One according to fastener size. Fastener measurement is described in Chapter One.

Damaged threads in components and castings can be repaired using a Heli-Coil (or an equivalent) stainless steel threaded insert (**Figure 5**, typical). Heli-coil kits are available at automotive or marine and industrial supply stores. Never run a thread tap or thread chaser into a hole equipped with a Heli-coil. Replace damaged Heli-coils by gripping the outermost coil with needlenose pliers and unthreading the coil from the hole. Do not pull the coil straight out. Doing so damages the opening.

CAUTION
Metric fasteners are used on these engines. Always match a replacement fastener to the original. Do not run a tap or thread chaser into a hole or over a bolt without first verifying the thread size and pitch.

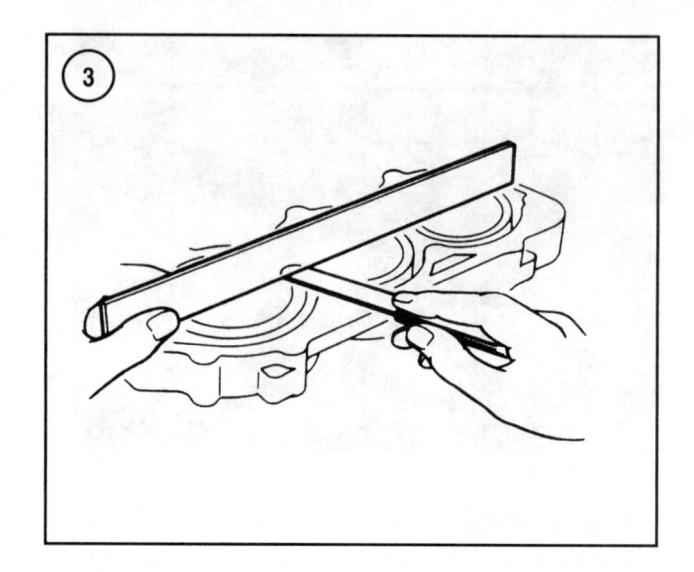

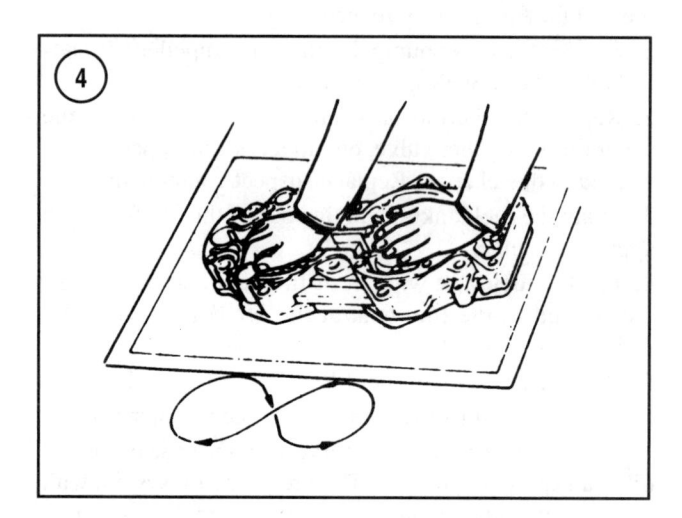

Unless otherwise specified, components secured by more than one fastener should be tightened in a *minimum* of three steps. First, evenly tighten all fasteners hand-tight. Then, evenly tighten all fasteners to 50% of the specified torque value. Finally, evenly tighten all fasteners to 100% of the specified torque value.

Be sure to follow torque sequences as directed. If no sequence is specified, start at the center of the component and tighten fasteners in a circular pattern, working outward. Torque sequences are in the appropriate *Assembly* section of this chapter.

POWER HEAD REMOVAL/INSTALLATION

The removal and installation procedures in this chapter are the most efficient sequence for removing the power

POWER HEAD

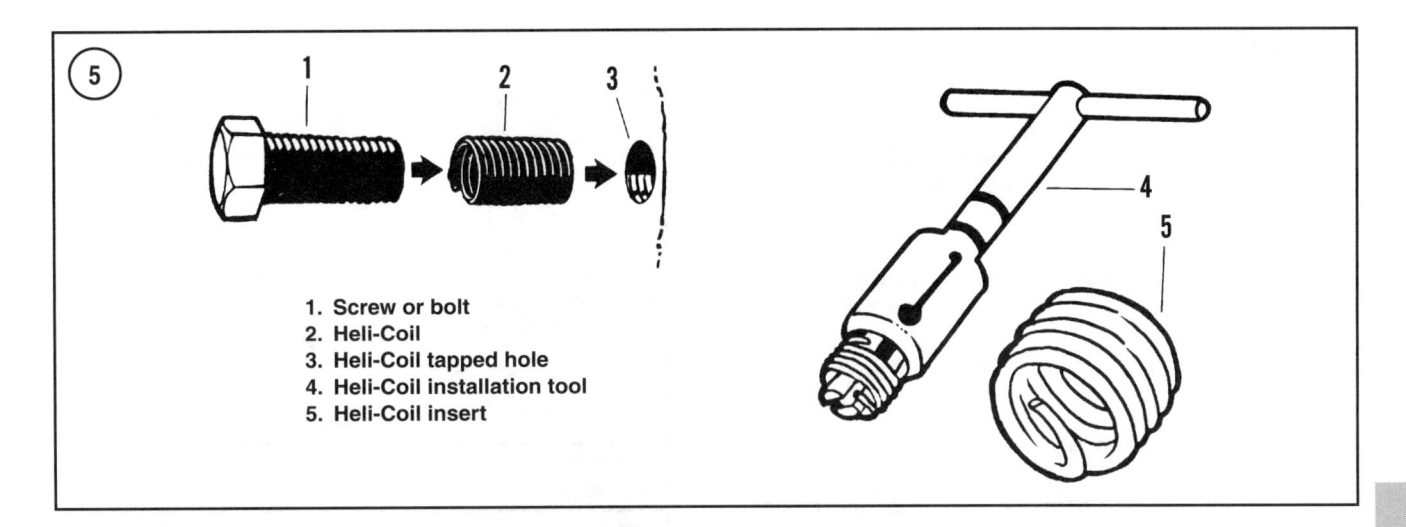

5
1. Screw or bolt
2. Heli-Coil
3. Heli-Coil tapped hole
4. Heli-Coil installation tool
5. Heli-Coil insert

head while preparing for complete disassembly. If complete disassembly is not necessary, stop disassembly at the appropriate point, then begin reassembly where disassembly stopped. Remove the power head as an assembly if major repair must be performed. Power head removal is not required for certain service procedures, such as cylinder head removal, intake and exhaust cover removal, ignition component replacement, fuel system component replacement and reed block/intake manifold removal.

Preparation for Removal

Visually inspect the engine to locate the fuel supply hose, control cables and battery connections. Virtually all hoses and wire connections must be removed for a complete power head repair. In such instances, disconnect only the hoses and wires necessary to remove the power head from the engine. Many of the hoses and wires will be more accessible after the power head is removed.

Diagrams of the fuel and electrical systems are provided in Chapter Five and Chapter Six to assist with hose and wire routing.

To speed up installation and ensure correct connections, take several pictures of each side of the power head *before* beginning the power head removal process. Make notes and sketches of wire and hose routing, connection points and linkage orientation. This will save a great deal of time during the assembly procedure.

Secure the proper lifting equipment before attempting to remove the power head. It is not difficult to lift a 20 hp engine and small power head with some assistance. Larger engines will require an overhead hoist. A complete power head may weigh nearly 200 lb. (91 kg).

Have an assistant help lift or move any power head. Attach the hoist to the lifting hook located on the top of the power head (**Figure 6**) when lifting all 25 hp and larger engines. A lifting hook is not used on 2-20 hp models. Grasp the power head on the cylinder head and intake manifold when lifting 2-20 hp models.

WARNING
The power head may abruptly separate from the mid-section during removal with an overhead hoist. Avoid using excessive force when lifting the power head. Use pry bars to carefully separate the power head from its mount before lifting it with a hoist.

CAUTION
To avoid damaging the power head mounting machined surfaces, check for overlooked fasteners before attempting to pry the power head from the mid-section.

NOTE
Corrosion may prevent easy removal of the power head. Apply a penetrating oil to the mating surface and allow it to soak into the

gasket before attempting power head removal.

NOTE
Power head mounting fastener location and quantity vary with the models. Refer to the illustrations for assistance in locating the fasteners. Which components must be removed before removing the power head also varies. Make sure all required fasteners and components are removed before attempting to lift the power head from the mid-section.

Removal (2-15 hp Models)

1. On 2-5 hp models, drain the fuel from the engine mounted fuel tank.
2. On 3-5 hp models, loosen the screw, then pull the throttle rod from the carburetor lever.
3. On 4-15 hp models, disconnect the black and white stop switch wires from the engine ground and engine wire harness connections.
4. On 4-15 hp models, disconnect the lockout cable (neutral only start) from the shift linkages or manual starter. Refer to Chapter Ten for procedures.
5. On 4 and 5 hp models, remove the two screws to free the ignition coil bracket from the power head. The screws are located on the bottom side of the lower engine cover.
6. On 5-15 hp models with a remote fuel tank, disconnect the fuel supply hose (**Figure 7**) from the quick connector. Drain all fuel from the hoses.
7. On 6-15 hp models with electric starting, disconnect both cables from the battery. Disconnect the battery cable from the starter relay and the ground terminal from the power head.
8. On 6 and 8 hp models, remove the two screws, then pull the throttle plate from the starboard side of the power head. Remove the throttle cable bracket.
9A. On 6-15 hp electric start tiller control models, disconnect the red and brown starter button wires from the starter relay and neutral safety switch.
9B. On 6-15 hp electric start remote control models, unplug the remote control harness from the engine wire harness.
10. On 9.9 and 15 hp models:
    a. Remove the screw, then pull the shift selector lever from the opening on the starboard side of the engine cover.
    b. Carefully disconnect the choke knob linkage from the carburetor lever.
    c. Loosen the screw, then pull the throttle linkage from the carburetor lever.
    d. Remove the bolt and washer, then pull the throttle and shift bracket away from its mount on the starboard side of the power head.
    e. Disconnect the shift linkage coupler from the lower shift shaft. Refer to Chapter Eight for instructions.
11. If so equipped, disconnect the ground wire (A, **Figure 8**) from the power head. Disconnect the water stream hose (B, **Figure 8**) from the engine cover fitting.

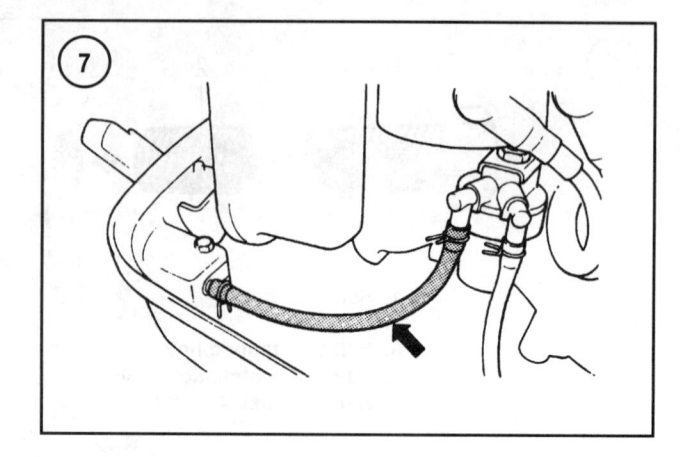

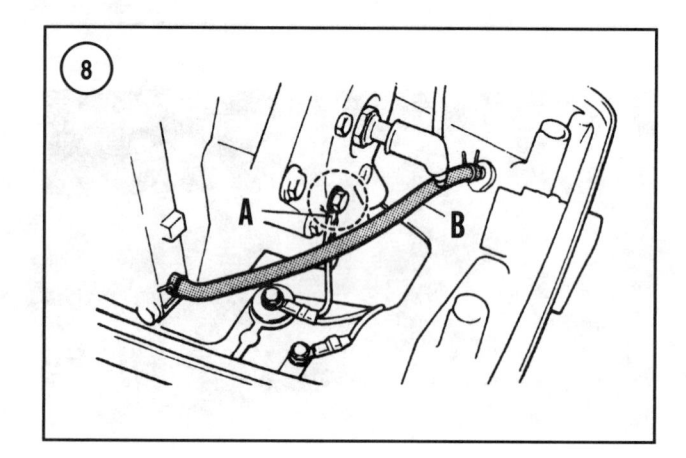

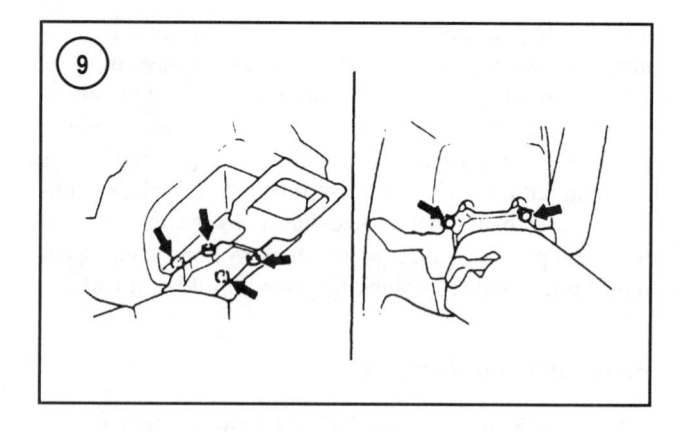

POWER HEAD

Figure 10
Mounting bolts

Figure 11
1. Locating pins
2. Power head mounting gasket

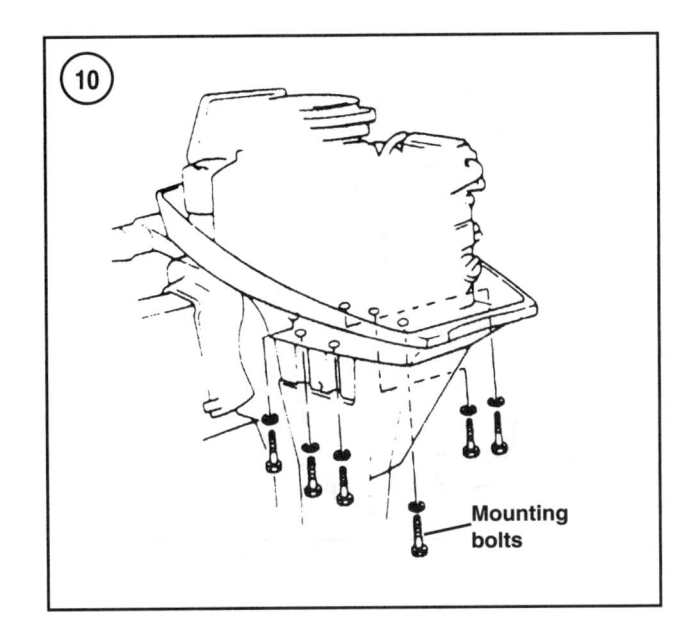

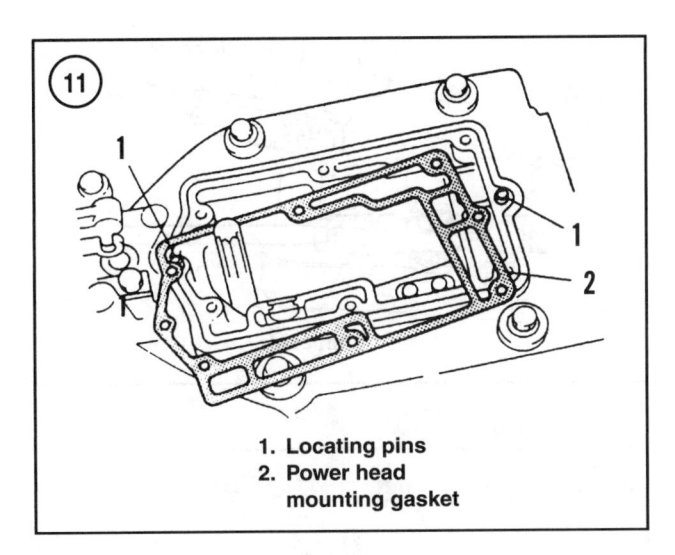

12. Thoroughly inspect the power head for attached wires, linkages or hoses. Remove or disconnect them if necessary for power head removal.
13. Locate and remove the power head mounting bolts.
    a. 2 and 3 hp models use six bolts. See **Figure 9**.
    b. 4 and 5 hp models use seven bolts. Four bolts are located on the lower starboard side. Three are located on the lower port side.
    c. 6-15 hp models use six bolts. See **Figure 10**.
14. Slightly rock the power head on the mount to break the gasket bond. Then carefully lift the power head from the midsection. Place the power head on a stable work surface.
15. Remove and discard the power head mounting gasket (2, **Figure 11**). Clean the power head mounting surfaces, then inspect them for deep scratches or extensive corrosion damage. Replace the housing if there are defects.
16. Inspect the locating pins (1, **Figure 11**) for damaged or missing pins. Inspect the pin holes in the midsection and power head for elongation or cracked areas. Replace defective components as required. If the pins are found in the power head openings, remove them and place them in the corresponding opening in the midsection.

Installation (2-15 hp Models)

1. Move all hoses, wires, cables and linkages remaining on the engine away from the power head mating surfaces. Tie them back with plastic locking type clamps as needed.
2. Apply a coat of Loctite Gasket Maker to both surfaces of the mounting gasket.
3. Install the new mounting gasket (2, **Figure 11**) onto the mid-section and fit the corresponding openings over the locating pins (1).
4. Coat the lower drive shaft seal lips and the drive shaft splines with Yamaha All-Purpose Grease or equivalent.
5. With assistance, slowly lower the power head onto the midsection. Guide the drive shaft into the crankshaft seal opening. Keep the flywheel as level as possible to avoid damaging the drive shaft, gasket and mating surfaces. Rotate the flywheel to align the crankshaft and drive shaft splines, then lower the power head onto the mating surface.
6. Apply Loctite 572 to the mounting bolt threads.
7. Thread the mounting bolts into the power head.
    a. 2 and 3 hp models use six bolts. See **Figure 9**.
    b. 4 and 5 hp models use seven bolts. Four bolts are located on the lower starboard side. Three are located on the lower port side.
    c. 6-15 hp models use six bolts. See **Figure 10**.
8A. On 2 hp, 6 hp and 8 hp models, tighten the mounting bolts in a crossing pattern to the standard tightening torque specification in Chapter One.
8B. On 3-5 hp, 9.9 hp and 15 hp models, tighten the mounting bolts in a crossing pattern, starting from the center bolts, to the specification in **Table 1**.
9. If so equipped, connect the ground wire (A, **Figure 8**) and water stream hose (B).
10. On 9.9 and 15 hp models:
    a. Connect the shift linkage coupler to the lower shift shaft. Refer to Chapter Eight for procedures.
    b. Mount the throttle and shift bracket on the starboard side of the power head. Install the bolt and washer to hold the bracket. Tighten the bolt to the standard tightening torque specification in Chapter One.
    c. Insert the throttle linkage into the clamp opening on the throttle lever. Securely tighten the clamp screw.

d. Connect the choke knob linkage to the carburetor lever.
e. Insert the shift selector lever and related bushings and washers into the opening in the starboard side of the engine. Tighten the screw to secure the shift linkage onto the lever.

11. On 6-15 hp with electric starting models, connect the battery cable to the starter relay and the ground terminal on the power head.

12A. On 6-15 hp electric start tiller control models, connect the red and brown starter button wires to the starter relay terminals.

12B. On 6-15 hp electric start remote control models, plug the remote control harness into the engine wire harness.

13. On 6 and 8 hp models, install the throttle plate onto the starboard side of the power head and secure it with the two screws. Install the throttle cable bracket and two screws. Securely tighten the four screws.

14. On 4 and 5 hp models, mount the coil ignition bracket on the lower engine cover. Insert the two coil bracket screws through the openings in the lower engine cover. Securely tighten the screws.

15. On 3-5 hp models, insert the throttle rod into the clamp opening on the carburetor lever. Securely tighten the clamp screw.

16. On 4-15 hp models, connect the black and white stop switch wires to the engine ground and engine wire harness connections.

17. On 4-15 hp models, connect the lockout cable (neutral only start) to the shift linkages or manual starter. Refer to Chapter Ten for procedures.

18. On 5-15 hp models with a remote fuel tank, connect the fuel supply hose (**Figure 7**) to the quick connector fitting. Secure the hose with a suitable clamp.

19. On 6-15 hp models with electric starting, connect the cables to the battery.

20. Perform all applicable adjustments as described in Chapter Four. Start the engine and immediately check for fuel, water or exhaust leaks. Correct any leaks before putting the engine into service.

Removal (20-90 hp Models)

1. On electric start models, disconnect both cables from the battery. Disconnect the battery cable from the starter relay and the ground terminal from the power head.
2. Disconnect the fuel supply hose (**Figure 7**) from the quick connector. Drain all fuel from the hoses.
3. On 20-30 hp tiller control models, disconnect the black and white stop switch wires from the CDI module engine ground connections.

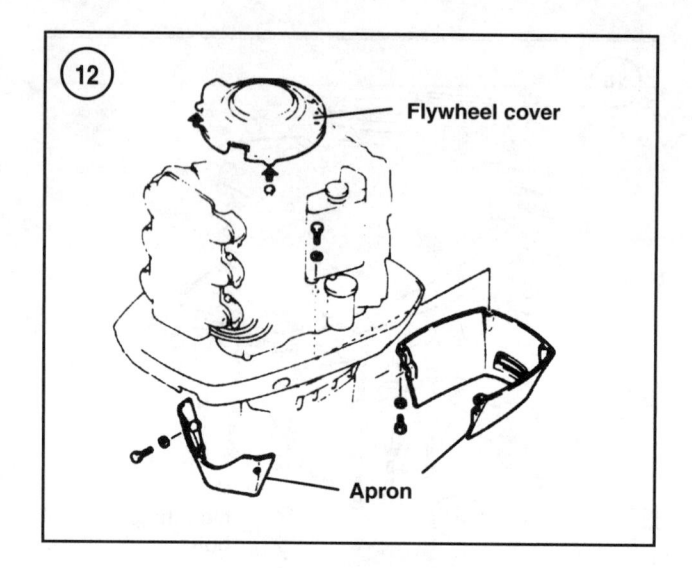

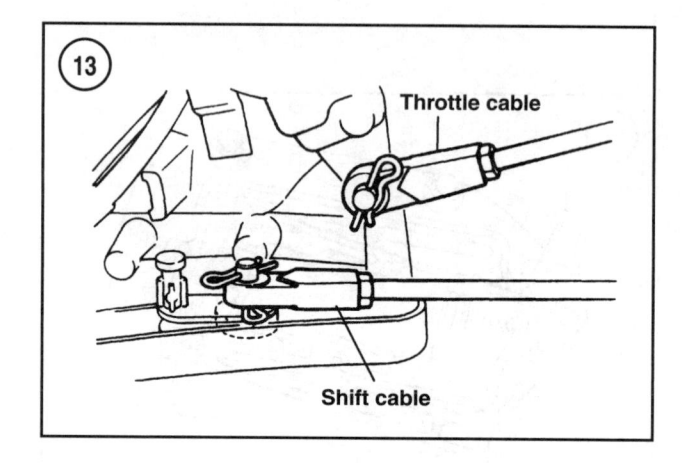

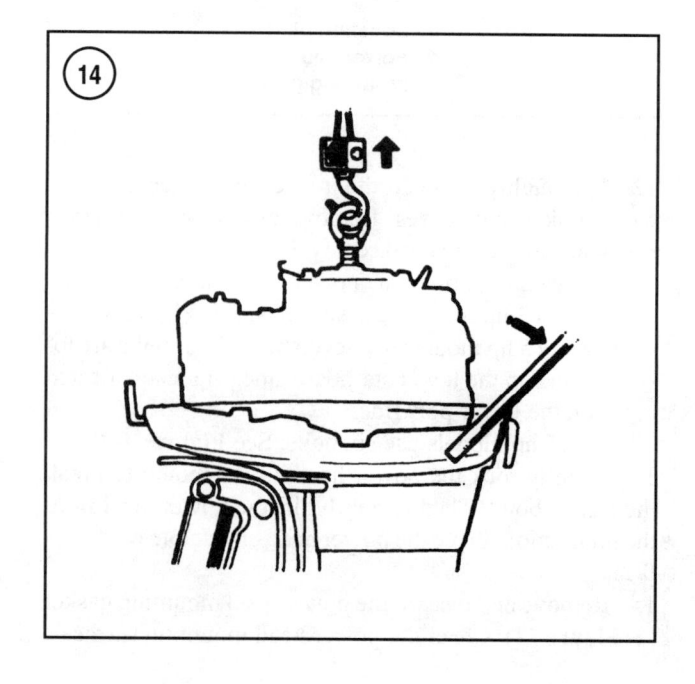

6. On remote control models:
   a. Unplug the remote control harness from the engine wire harness.
   b. Disconnect the throttle and shift cables from the linkages (**Figure 13**, typical). Refer to Chapter Four to identify the linkages.
7. On 20-75 hp manual start models, disconnect the lockout cable (neutral only start) from the shift linkages or manual starter. Refer to Chapter Ten for procedures.
8. On 20 hp two-cylinder models:
   a. On tiller control models, remove the bolt and carefully pull the throttle arm and cables away from the power head.
   b. On manual start models, disconnect the choke knob linkage from the carburetor.
9. If so equipped, disconnect the ground wire (A, **Figure 8**) from the power head. Disconnect the water stream hose (B, **Figure 8**) from the engine cover fitting.
10. On 25-90 hp models with power tilt and trim, disconnect the electric trim motor wires from the trim relays. Disconnect the trim position sender harness from the engine wire harness.
11. On 20-50 hp tiller control models with oil injection, disconnect the oil warning light harness from the engine wire harness.
12. On 40-75 hp tiller control models:
   a. Unplug the tiller control harness from the engine harness.
   b. Disconnect the throttle and shift cables and linkages.
13. Thoroughly inspect the power head for attached wires, linkages or hoses. Remove or disconnect them if necessary for power head removal.
14. Attach an overhead hoist to the lifting hook (**Figure 14**) and provide enough force to take all slack from the lifting cable or chain.
15. Locate and remove the power head mounting bolts.
   a. 20-50 hp models use six bolts. See **Figure 9**.
   b. 60 and 70 hp models use eight bolts. See **Figure 15**.
   c. 75-90 hp models use eleven bolts. Five bolts are located on each side of the mid-section (**Figure 16**). One bolt is located under the aft end of the power head.
16. Locate an area where a pry bar can be inserted between the power head and mid-section. Notches are provided on most models. Carefully pry and rock the power head to separate it from the mid-section (**Figure 17**).

CAUTION
Lift the power head slowly and maintain support to ensure the power head lifts straight off the mid-section. The drive shaft and other components may be damaged if the power head is lifted or lowered at an angle.

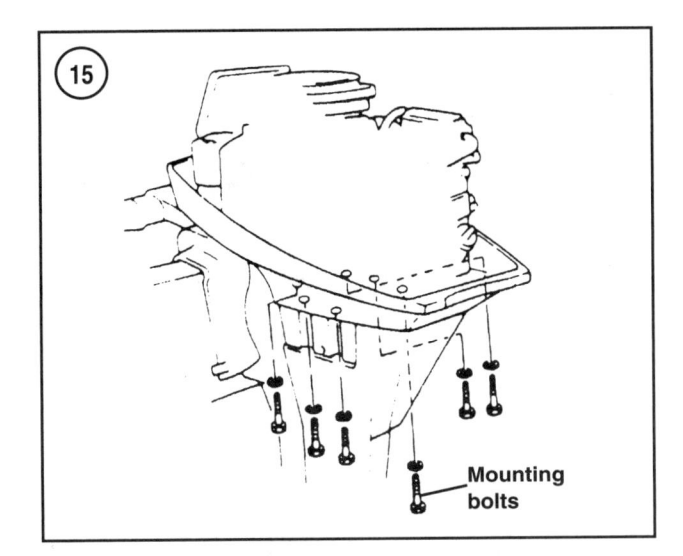

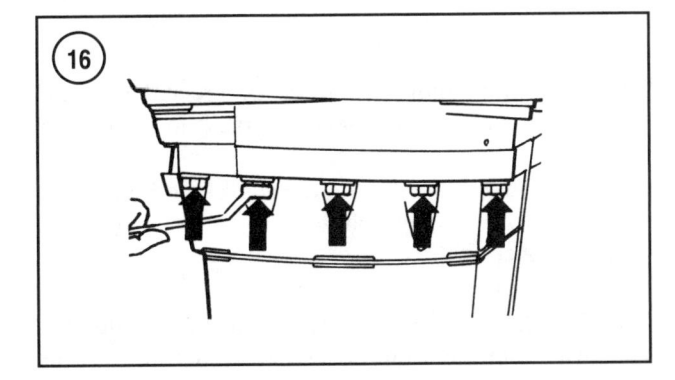

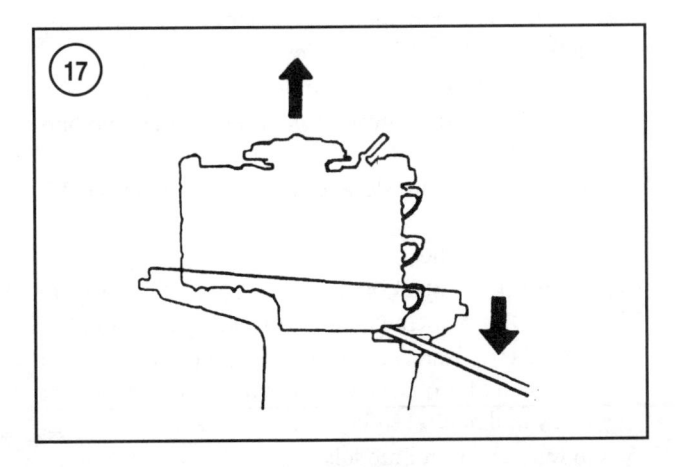

4. On 25 hp three-cylinder and 30-90 hp models, remove the screws and pull both aprons (**Figure 12**) from the drive shaft housing.

5. On 20-30 hp electric start tiller control models, disconnect the red and brown starter button wires from the starter relay and neutral safety switch wires.

17. Slowly lift the power head from the mid-section. Mount the power head securely on a suitable work stand (**Figure 1**).
18. Remove and discard the power head mounting gasket (2, **Figure 11**). Clean the power head mounting surfaces, then inspect them for deep scratches or extensive corrosion damage. Replace the housing if there are defects.
19. Inspect the locating pins (1, **Figure 11**) for damaged or missing pins. Inspect the pin holes in the mid-section and power head for elongation or cracked areas. Replace defective components as required. If the pins are found in the power head openings, remove them and place them in the corresponding opening in the mid-section.

Installation (20-90 hp Models)

1. Move all hoses, wires, cables and linkages remaining on the engine away from the power head mating surfaces. Tie them back with plastic locking type clamps as needed.
2. Attach an overhead hoist to the lifting hook (**Figure 6**). Lift the power head enough to take all slack out of the lifting cable or chain. Remove the fasteners to free the power head from the work stand. Position the power head directly over the midsection.
3. Apply a coat of Loctite Gasket Maker to both surfaces of the mounting gasket.
4. Install the new mounting gasket (2, **Figure 11**) onto the mid-section and fit the corresponding openings over the locating pins (1).
5. Coat the lower drive shaft seal lips and the drive shaft splines with Yamaha All-Purpose Grease or equivalent.
6. With assistance, slowly lower the power head onto the midsection (**Figure 14**). Guide the drive shaft into the crankshaft seal opening. Keep the flywheel as level as possible to avoid damaging the drive shaft, gasket and mating surfaces. Rotate the flywheel to align the crankshaft and drive shaft splines, then lower the power head onto the mating surface.
7. Apply Loctite 572 to the mounting bolt threads.
8. Thread the mounting bolts into the power head.
    a. 20-50 hp models use six bolts. See **Figure 9**.
    b. 60 and 70 hp models use eight bolts. See **Figure 15**.
    c. 75-90 hp models use eleven bolts. Five bolts are located on each side of the midsection (**Figure 16**). One bolt is located under the aft end of the power head.
9A. On 20 hp, 25 hp two-cylinder and 40-90 hp models, tighten the mounting bolts in a crossing pattern, starting from the center bolts, to the specification in **Table 1**.
9B. On 25 hp three-cylinder and 30 hp models, tighten the mounting bolts in a crossing pattern to the standard torque specification in Chapter One.

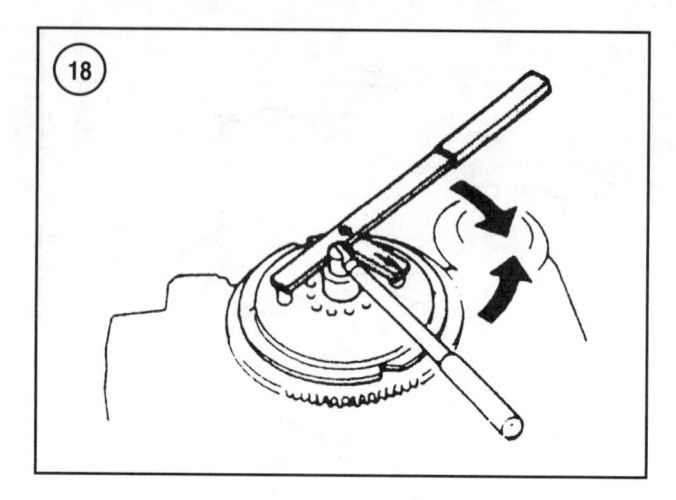

10. If so equipped, connect the ground wire (A, **Figure 8**) to the power head. Connect the water stream hose (B, **Figure 8**) to the engine cover fitting.
11. On 25-90 hp models with power tilt and trim, connect the electric trim motor wires to the trim relay harnesses. Connect the trim position sender harness to the engine wire harness.
12. On 20-50 hp tiller control models with oil injection, connect the oil warning light harness to the engine wire harness connector.
13. On 20 hp two-cylinder models:
    a. On tiller control models, mount the throttle arm with cables onto the power head. Secure the arm with the bolt and washer.
    b. On manual start models, connect the choke knob linkage to the carburetor lever.
14. On 40-75 hp tiller control models:
    a. Plug the tiller control harness into the engine harness connector.
    b. Connect the throttle and shift cables (**Figure 13**, typical).
15. On 20-30 hp tiller control models:
    a. Connect the black and white stop switch wires to the CDI module and engine ground connections.
    b. On electric start models with tiller control, connect the red and brown starter button wires to the starter relay and neutral safety switch wires.
16. On remote control models:
    a. Plug the remote control harness into the engine wire harness connector.
    b. Connect the throttle and shift cables to the linkages (**Figure 13**, typical). Refer to Chapter Four to identify the linkages.
17. Connect the fuel supply hose (**Figure 7**) to the quick connector fitting. Secure the hose with a suitable clamp.

POWER HEAD

of the engine. Never use a hammer without using protective eyewear.

CAUTION
Use only the appropriate tools and procedures to remove the flywheel. Never strike the flywheel. The magnets may break and result in poor ignition system performance or potential damage to other engine components.

Removal

Make sure the engine or power head is securely mounted before attempting to remove the flywheel. A suitable flywheel holder (Yamaha part No. YB-06139-90890-06522) and a flywheel removal tool (Yamaha part No. YB-06117/90890-06521) are required to remove the flywheel.

1. On manual start models, remove the manual starter as described in Chapter Ten.
2. Disconnect the spark plug lead(s). Connect the lead(s) to a suitable engine ground to prevent arcing.
3. On electric start models, disconnect both cables from the battery. Remove the flywheel cover (**Figure 12**).
4. Install the pins of the flywheel holder into the openings in the flywheel (**Figure 18**). Install an appropriate size socket and breaker bar on the flywheel nut. Hold the flywheel stationary and rotate the breaker bar counterclockwise to loosen the flywheel nut.
5. Loosen the flywheel nut until the top edge is flush or slightly below the threads on the crankshaft. Install the flywheel removal tool onto the flywheel. Secure the puller to the flywheel with the included bolts. Make sure the puller bolts are threaded several turns into the flywheel and the puller is level with the flywheel surface (**Figure 19**). Make sure the large puller bolt is contacting the top end of the crankshaft and not the flywheel nut.
6. Use the flywheel holder to keep the flywheel from rotating (**Figure 20**). Turn the puller bolt clockwise until the bolt is difficult to turn.
7. Support the flywheel and lightly tap on the puller bolt (**Figure 21**). Tighten the puller bolt and again tap on the puller bolt. Continue until the flywheel pops free from the crankshaft.
8. Remove the flywheel puller. Remove and discard the flywheel nut and washer. Remove the woodruff key from the slot in the crankshaft (**Figure 22**). Retrieve the key from the flywheel magnets if it is not found in the key slot. Inspect the woodruff key for corroded, bent or marked surfaces. Replace the key if it is not in excellent condition.
9. Use a solvent soaked shop towel to clean debris and contaminants from the crankshaft threads, key slot and

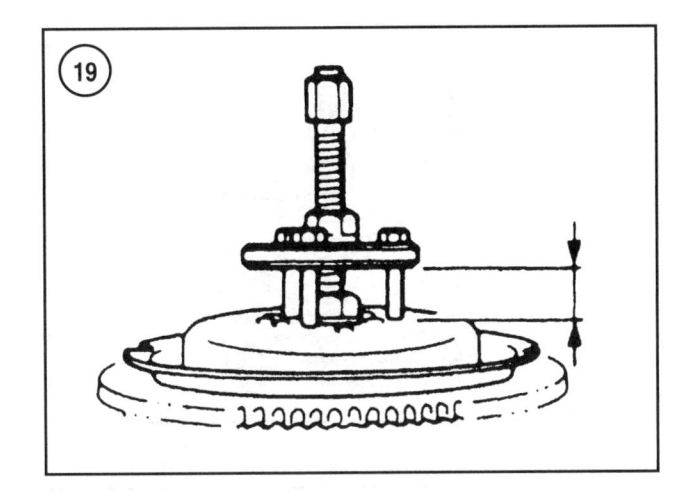

18. On 20-75 hp manual start models, connect the lockout cable (neutral only start) to the shift linkages or manual starter. Refer to Chapter Ten for instructions.
19. On electric start models, connect the battery cables to the starter relay and power head ground terminal. Connect both cables to the battery.
20. On 25 hp three-cylinder and 30-90 hp models, install both aprons (**Figure 12**) onto the drive shaft housing. Securely tighten the apron screws.
21. Perform all applicable adjustments as described in Chapter Four. Start the engine and immediately check for fuel, water or exhaust leaks. Correct any leaks before returning the engine into service.

FLYWHEEL REMOVAL/INSTALLATION

WARNING
Wear protective eyewear when removing or installing the flywheel or other components

flywheel taper. Use compressed air to remove debris or contaminants from the flywheel. Do not use solvent to clean the flywheel. Solvent may soften the magnet adhesive. Wipe oily deposits from the flywheel with a shop towel.

10. Inspect the flywheel for cracked or damaged magnets, rough surfaces in the tapered opening, and worn or damaged flywheel teeth. Replace the flywheel if these or other defects are noted.

11. Inspect the crankshaft taper for corroded, worn or rough surfaces. Remove minor surface corrosion by light polishing with crocus cloth. Replace the crankshaft if the taper is discolored, deeply pitted or has rough surfaces.

12. Inspect the crankshaft threads for corroded or damaged threads. Repair minor thread damage with an appropriate die. Replace the crankshaft if the threads cannot be returned to like-new condition.

Installation

Make sure the engine or power head is securely mounted before attempting to install the flywheel. A suitable flywheel holder (Yamaha part No. YB-01639-90890-06522) is required to install the flywheel.

1. Place the woodruff key into the key slot as shown in **Figure 22**.

2. Position the flywheel on the crankshaft taper. Slowly rotate the flywheel to align the flywheel key slot with the woodruff key. The flywheel drops when the key slot aligns with the key. Rotate the flywheel clockwise while observing the threaded end of the crankshaft. If the crankshaft does not rotate with the flywheel, remove the flywheel, reposition the woodruff and repeat the process.

3. Apply a light coat of outboard engine oil to the crankshaft threads. Place a new washer on the crankshaft and seat it against the flywheel. Hand-thread the new flywheel nut onto the crankshaft.

4. Install the pins of the flywheel holder into the openings in the flywheel (**Figure 18**). Install an appropriate size socket and torque wrench on the flywheel nut. Hold the flywheel stationary and tighten the flywheel nut to the specification in **Table 1**.

5. Connect the spark plug lead(s).

6. On electric start models, install the flywheel cover (**Figure 12**). Connect the cables onto the battery.

7. On manual start models, install the starter as described in Chapter Ten.

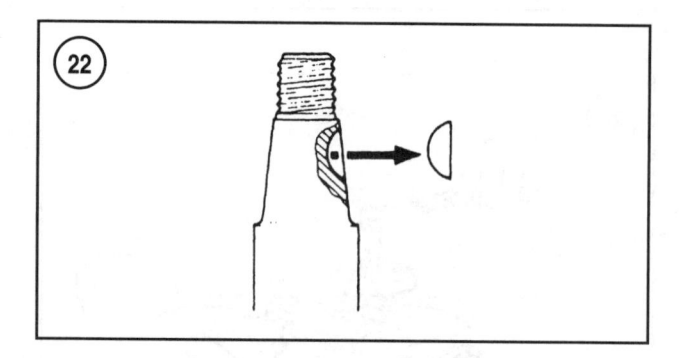

POWER HEAD DISASSEMBLY

Power head overhaul gasket sets are available for all models. It is often more economical and simpler to order the gasket set instead of each component individually. Replace *every* gasket, seal and O-ring during power head reassembly.

Dowel pins position the crankcase halves to each other and position some crankshaft bearings. The dowel pins do not have to be removed if they are securely seated in a bore on either side of the crankcase halves or in the bearing. However, they must not be lost during disassembly and reassembly. If a dowel pin can be easily removed from its bore, remove and secure it, and stored it with the other internal components until reassembly begins.

Clean and inspect all power head components before reassembly. If the power head has had a major failure, it may be more economical to replace the basic power head as an assembly.

Special tools are required for power head repair. The part numbers are listed in the repair procedures. Parts damaged by not using the correct tool can often be more expensive than the original cost of the tool.

A large number of fasteners of different lengths and sizes are used in a power head. Plastic sandwich bags and/or cupcake tins are excellent methods of keeping small parts organized. Tag all larger internal parts for lo-

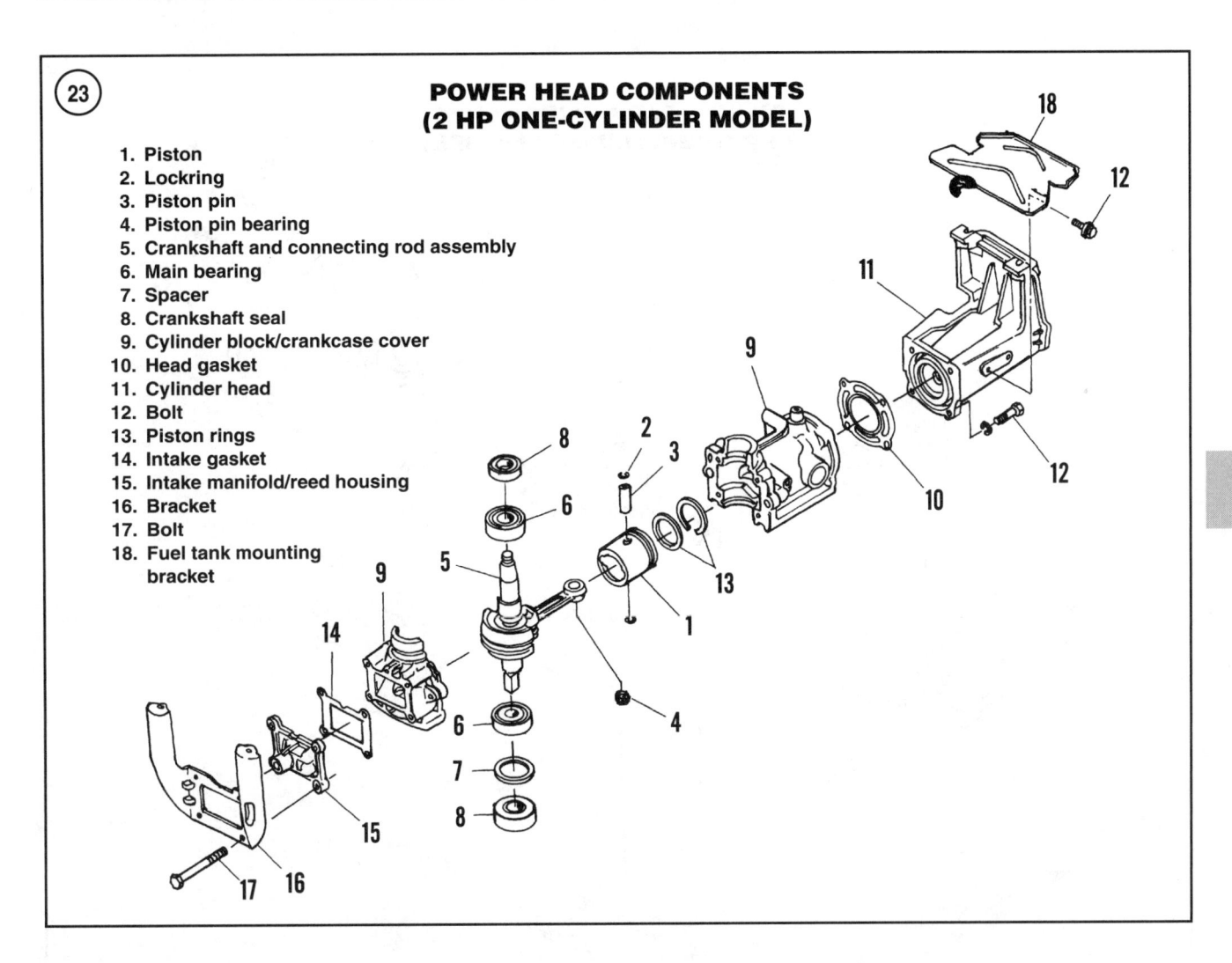

POWER HEAD

23 POWER HEAD COMPONENTS
(2 HP ONE-CYLINDER MODEL)

1. Piston
2. Lockring
3. Piston pin
4. Piston pin bearing
5. Crankshaft and connecting rod assembly
6. Main bearing
7. Spacer
8. Crankshaft seal
9. Cylinder block/crankcase cover
10. Head gasket
11. Cylinder head
12. Bolt
13. Piston rings
14. Intake gasket
15. Intake manifold/reed housing
16. Bracket
17. Bolt
18. Fuel tank mounting bracket

cation and orientation. Use a felt-tipped permanent marker to mark components after they have been cleaned. Avoid scribing or stamping internal components as the marking process may damage or weaken the component.

Always make notes, drawings or photographs of all external power head components *before* beginning the disassembly process. Although illustrations are provided throughout this manual, drawings and photographs will save a great deal of time during the assembly process. Correct wire and hose routing is important for proper engine operation. An incorrectly routed wire or hose may interfere with linkage movement and result in a dangerous lack of throttle or shift control. Hoses or wires may chafe and short circuit if they contact sharp edges or moving parts. Other components, such as fuel pumps, can often be mounted in two or more positions. Mark or make note of the top and forward direction *before* removing such components.

If possible, remove components that share a common wires or hoses in a cluster. This will reduce the time required to disassemble and assemble the power head and reduce the chance of improper connection on assembly.

Bearings and some other internal components of the power head can be removed and reused if they are in good condition. *Component Inspection* in this chapter describes which components must be replaced. If needle bearings must be reused, make sure they are installed in the same location on assembly.

Replace the piston rings and hone the cylinder bore if the piston(s) are taken out of the cylinder bore. Always replace piston pin lockrings if they are removed. The cost of many of these components is small compared to the expense of repairing the damage to other components if they fail.

2-5 hp One-Cylinder Models

For help with component orientation, refer to **Figures 23-25** during the disassembly procedure.

1. Remove the flywheel as described in this chapter.

CHAPTER SEVEN

(24) POWER HEAD COMPONENTS (3 HP ONE-CYLINDER MODEL)

1. Piston
2. Lockring
3. Piston pin
4. Piston pin bearing
5. Crankshaft and connecting rod assembly
6. Main bearing
7. Spacer
8. Crankshaft seal
9. Cylinder block/crankcase cover
10. Head gasket
11. Cylinder head
12. Water jacket cover
13. Gasket
14. Bolt
15. Bolt
16. Exhaust tube
17. Piston rings
18. Thermostat
19. Gasket
20. Thermostat cover

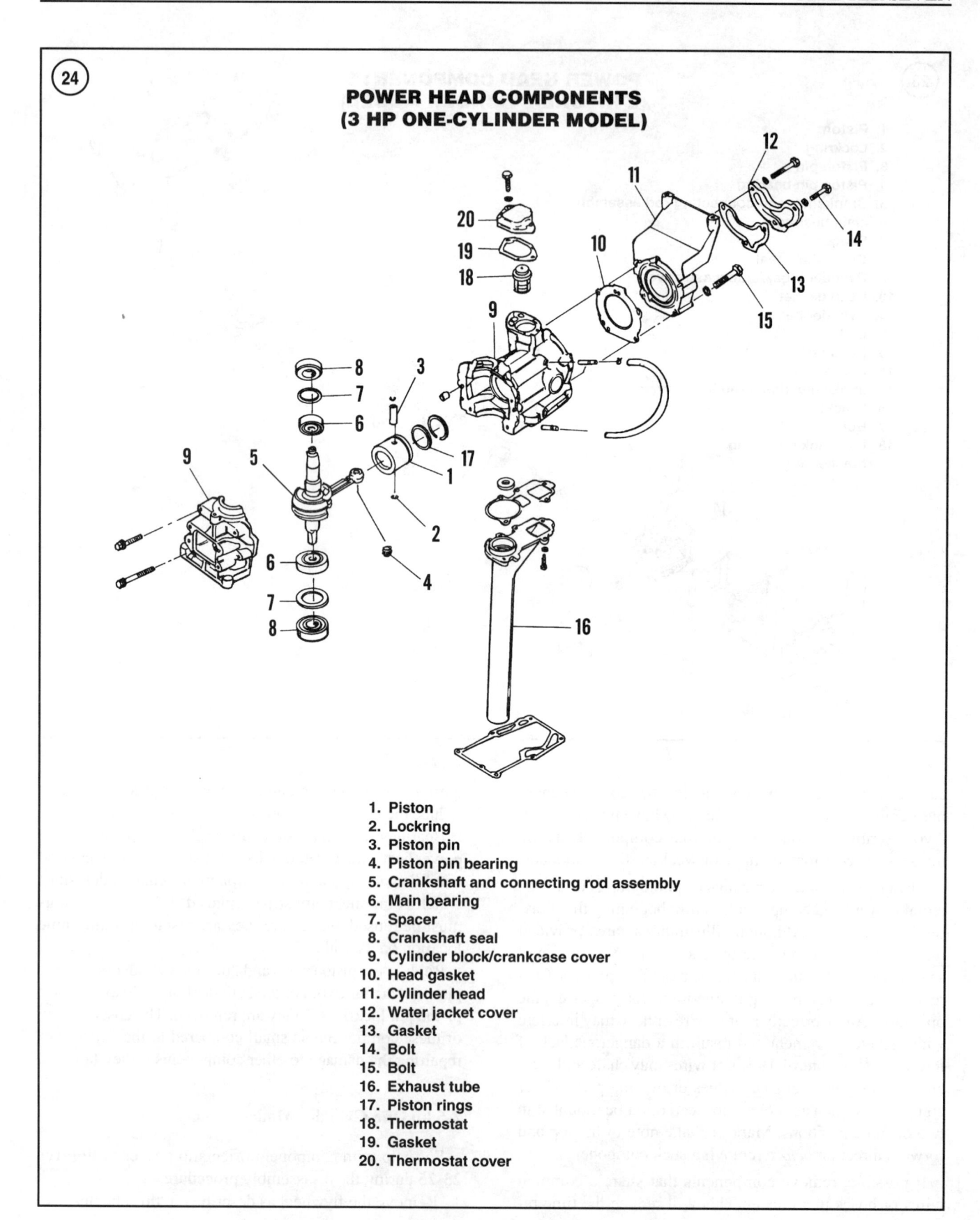

POWER HEAD

**POWER HEAD COMPONENTS
(4 AND 5 HP ONE-CYLINDER MODELS)**

1. Piston
2. Lockring
3. Piston pin
4. Piston rings
5. Cylinder block/crankcase cover
6. Piston pin bearing
7. Crankshaft and connecting rod assembly
8. Main bearing
9. Spacer*
10. Crankshaft oil seal
11. Locating pin
12. Bolt and washer
13. Seal carrier
14. Mounting gasket
15. Exhaust plate
16. Exhaust cover
17. Gasket
18. Gasket
19. Water jacket cover
20. Bolt
21. Bolt
22. O-ring
23. Crankshaft seal

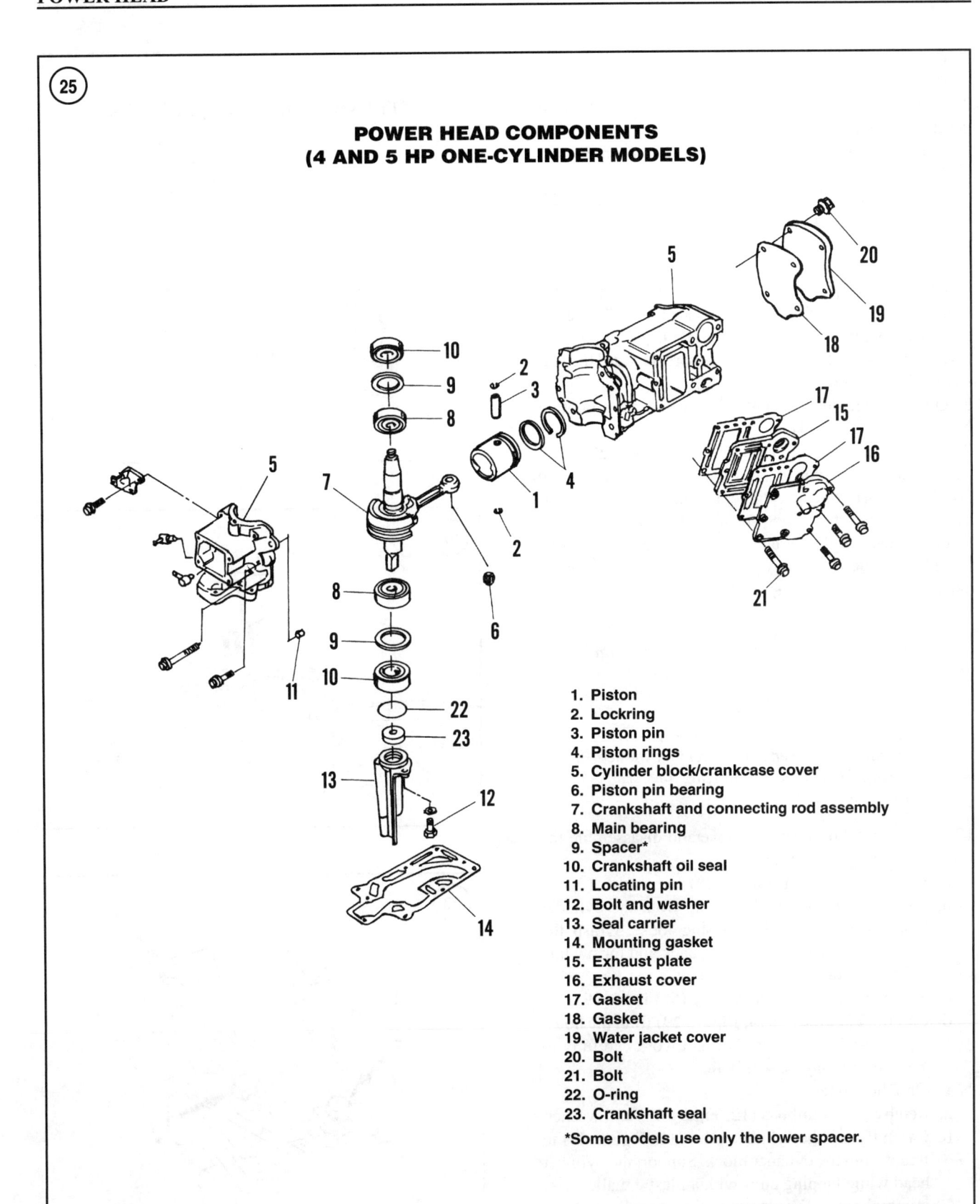

*Some models use only the lower spacer.

2. On 2 and 3 hp models, remove the fuel tank as described in Chapter Five.

3. Remove the fuel pump, carburetor and all fuel hoses as described in Chapter Five.

4. Remove the wire harness and all electrical components as described in Chapter Six.

5. Remove the intake manifold/reed housing (**Figure 26**, typical) as described in Chapter Five.

6. Remove the ignition charge coil mounting base (**Figure 27**, typical).

7. On 4 and 5 hp models, remove the O-ring from the mounting base. Carefully pry the oil seal (10, **Figure 25**) from the mounting base. Use a blunt tip pry bar and work carefully to avoid damaging the seal bore. Discard the seal and O-rings.

8. On 2 hp models, remove the fuel tank mounting bracket (18, **Figure 23**).

9. On 3 hp models, remove the bolts (**Figure 28**), then use a blunt tip pry bar to carefully pry the exhaust tube (16, **Figure 24**) from the cylinder block. Work carefully to avoid damaging the mating surfaces. Remove the gasket from the tube or cylinder block. Discard the gasket. Use a blunt tip pry bar to carefully pry the two seals from the exhaust tube. Do not damage the seal bore.

CAUTION
Do not use excessive force when prying the lower seal housing from the power head. Excessive force may break the housing or damage the mating surfaces. If removal is difficult, remove the housing after removing the crankcase cover. Always remove the seal housing bolts before removing the crankcase cover.

10. On 4 and 5 hp models, remove and disassemble the lower seal housing as follows:
    a. Remove the bolt (1, **Figure 29**) and washer (2).
    b. Carefully pull the seal housing from the cylinder block. Do not pry the housing loose. Grasp the housing and work the housing back and forth while pulling it from the cylinder block.
    c. Remove and discard the O-ring (5, **Figure 29**).
    d. Carefully pry the seal (4, **Figure 29**) from the housing. Use a blunt tip pry bar and work carefully to avoid damaging the seal bore.

11A. On 2 hp models:
    a. Remove the four bolts (12, **Figure 23**) and washer.
    b. Carefully tap the cylinder head (11, **Figure 23**) to free it from the cylinder block. Support the cylinder head while tapping on it with a plastic mallet. Use minimal force. Do not pry the cylinder head loose. The delicate gasket surfaces are easily damaged.

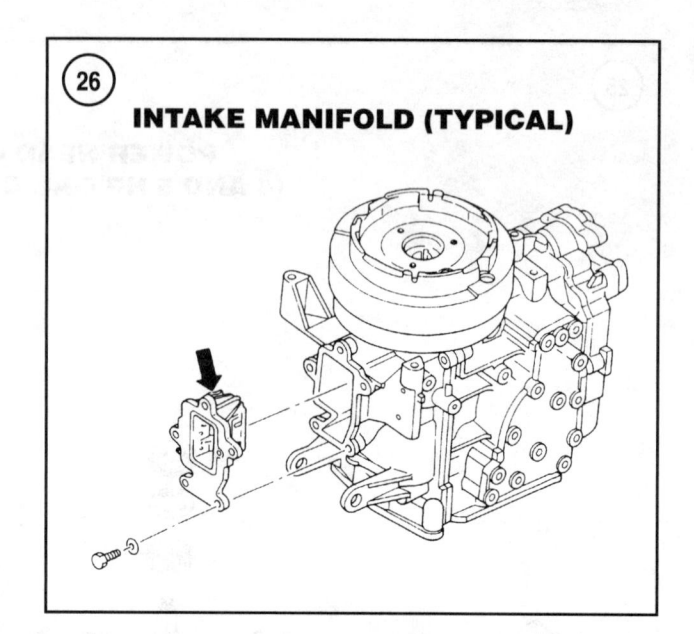

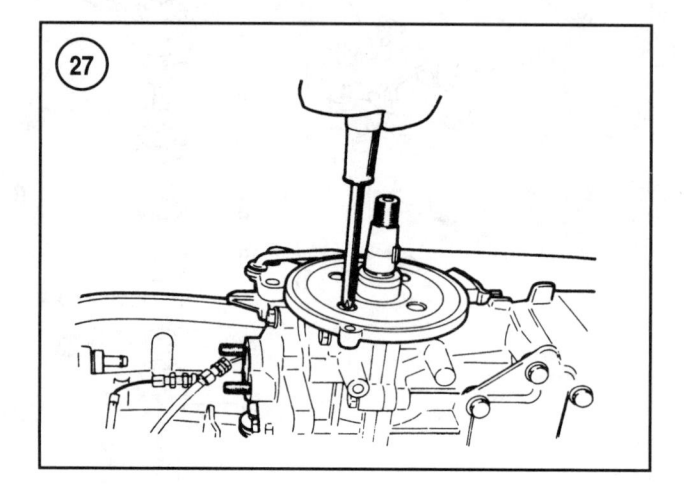

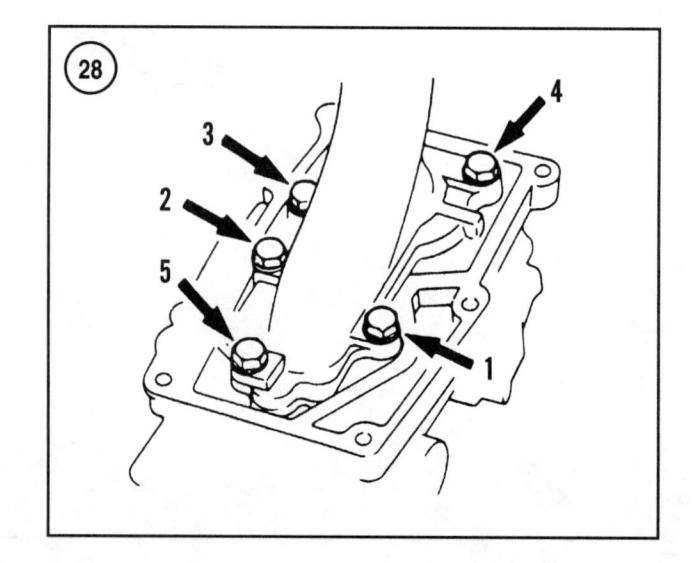

POWER HEAD

29 LOWER SEAL HOUSING (4 AND 5 HP MODELS)

1. Bolt
2. Washer
3. Seal housing
4. Seal
5. O-ring
6. Main bearing*
7. Spacer*

*These components are located on the crankshaft.

30

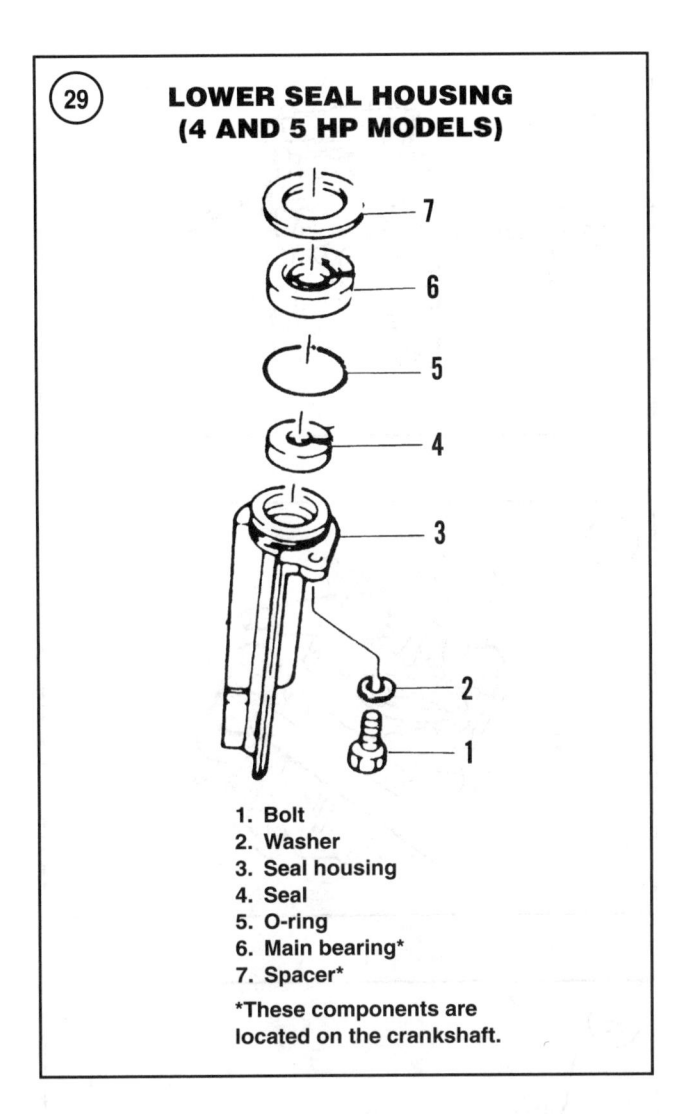

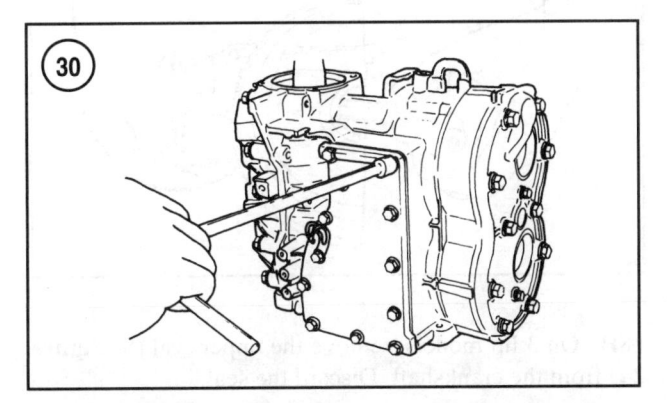

c. Remove and discard the head gasket (10, **Figure 23**).

11B. On 3 hp models:
  a. Remove the three bolts (14, **Figure 24**) from the water jack cover (12).

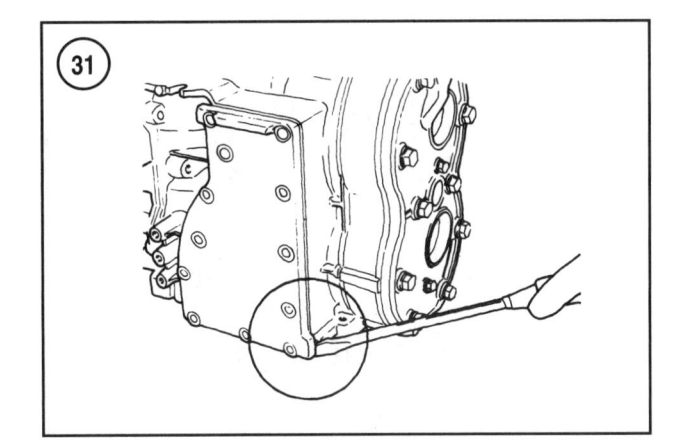

31

  b. Carefully pry the water jacket cover from the cylinder head (11, **Figure 24**). Use a blunt tip pry bar and work carefully to avoid damaging the mating surfaces. Remove and discard the gasket (13, **Figure 24**).
  c. Remove the three bolts (15, **Figure 24**) and washers from the cylinder head.
  d. Carefully tap the cylinder head (11, **Figure 24**) to free it from the cylinder block. Support the cylinder head while tapping on it with a plastic mallet. Use minimal force. Do not pry the cylinder head loose. The delicate gasket surfaces are easily damaged.
  e. Remove and discard the head gasket (10, **Figure 24**).

11C. On 4 and 5 hp models, remove the five bolts (20, **Figure 25**), then carefully pry the water jack cover (19) from the cylinder block. Use a blunt tip pry bar and work carefully to avoid damaging the mating surfaces. Remove and discard the gasket (18, **Figure 25**).

12. On 3 hp models, remove the cover and thermostat as follows:
  a. Remove the bolts, then carefully pry the thermostat cover (20, **Figure 24**) from the cylinder block. Use a blunt tip pry bar and work carefully to avoid damaging mating surfaces.
  b. Pull the thermostat from the opening. Test the thermostat as described in Chapter Two. Replace the thermostat if it is corroded or coated with salt or mineral deposits.
  c. Remove and discard the gasket (19, **Figure 24**).

13. On 4 and 5 hp models, remove the exhaust cover and plate as follows:
  a. Remove the nine bolts from the exhaust cover (**Figure 30**).
  b. Locate a pry point near the bottom of the cover (**Figure 31**). Use a blunt tip pry bar to carefully pry the cover loose. Do not damage the mating surfaces.

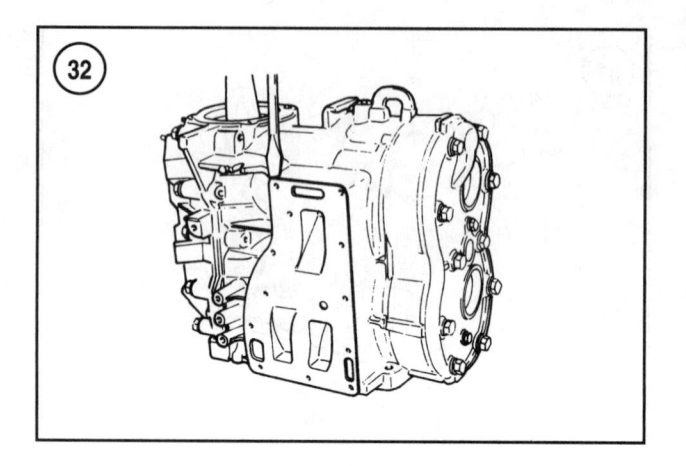

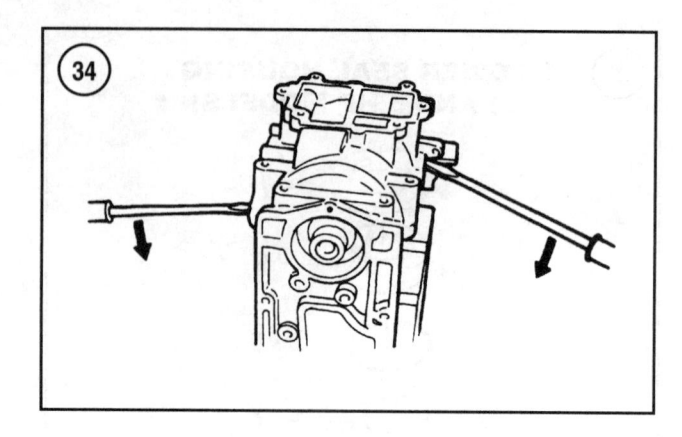

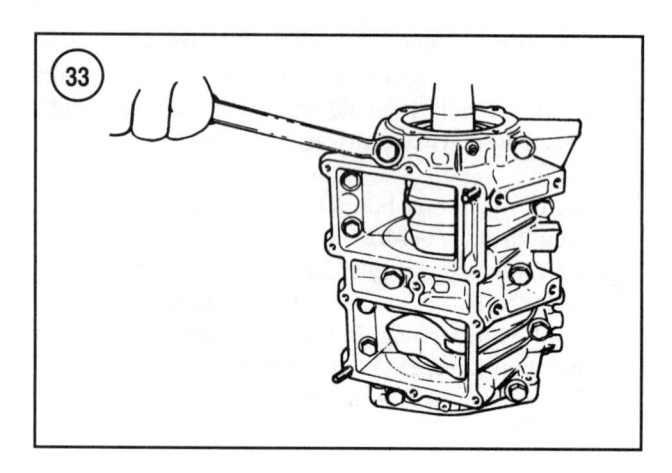

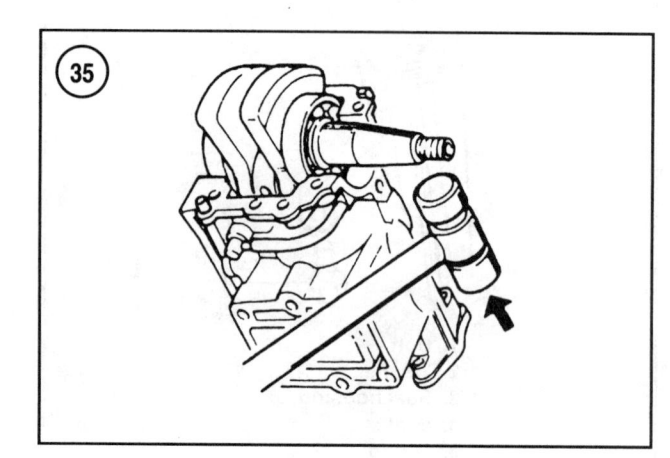

c. Locate a pry point near the top of the exhaust plate (**Figure 32**). Carefully pry the plate from the cylinder block. Do not damage the mating surfaces.

d. Carefully scrape the gaskets (17, **Figure 25**) from the cylinder block, cover and plate. Never reuse the cover or plate gasket.

14. Locate and remove all six of the fasteners on the crankcase cover (**Figure 33**). On 2 hp models, four of the bolts are removed when the intake manifold is removed.

15. Locate suitable pry points (**Figure 34**) and carefully pry the crankcase cover from the cylinder block. Take all necessary precautions to prevent damage to the mating surfaces.

16. Lightly tap on the end of the crankshaft with a plastic mallet (**Figure 35**) to free the main bearings from the cylinder block.

17. Grasp the crankshaft and cylinder block (**Figure 36**). Pull the crankshaft, connecting rod and piston as an assembly from the cylinder block.

18A. On 2 hp models, remove the two seals from the crankshaft (**Figure 37**) and discard them.

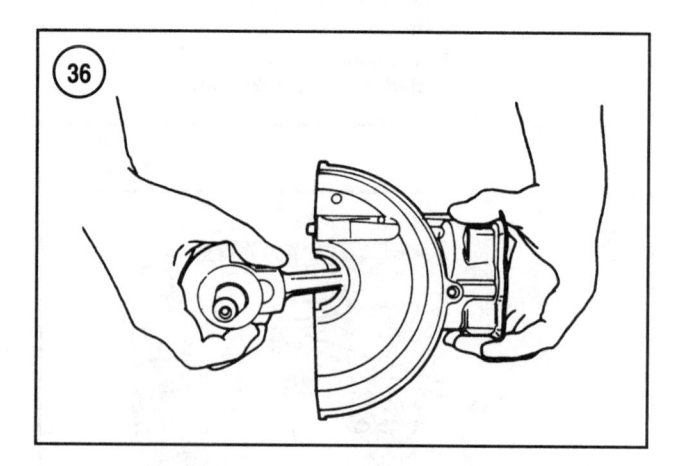

18B. On 3 hp models, remove the upper seal (8, **Figure 24**) from the crankshaft. Discard the seal.

19. Clamp the crankshaft in a vise with protective jaws. Clamp on the flyweight part of the crankshaft.

20. Locate the *UP* or arrow mark on the piston (**Figure 38**). The marking must face toward the tapered end of the crankshaft. If the original mark is illegible or cannot be found, mark the up direction on the underside of the piston

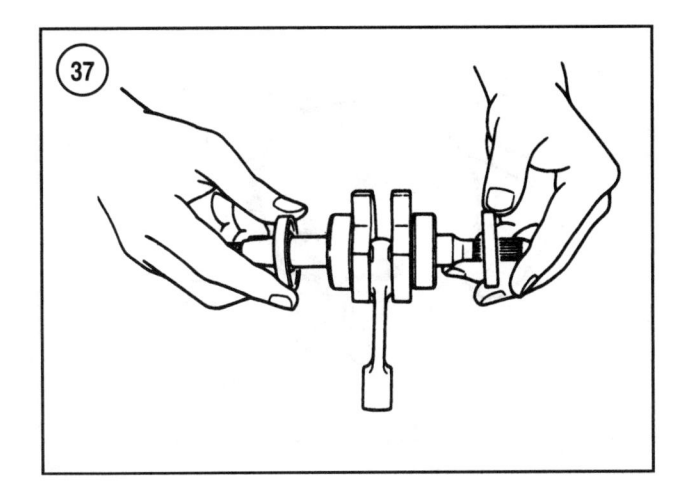

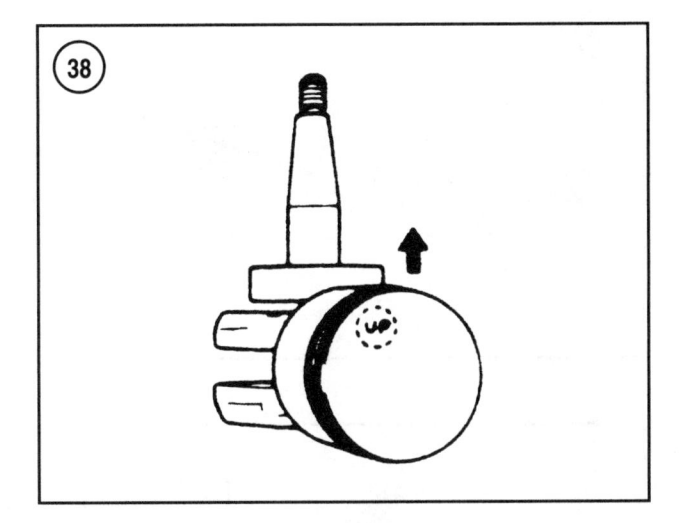

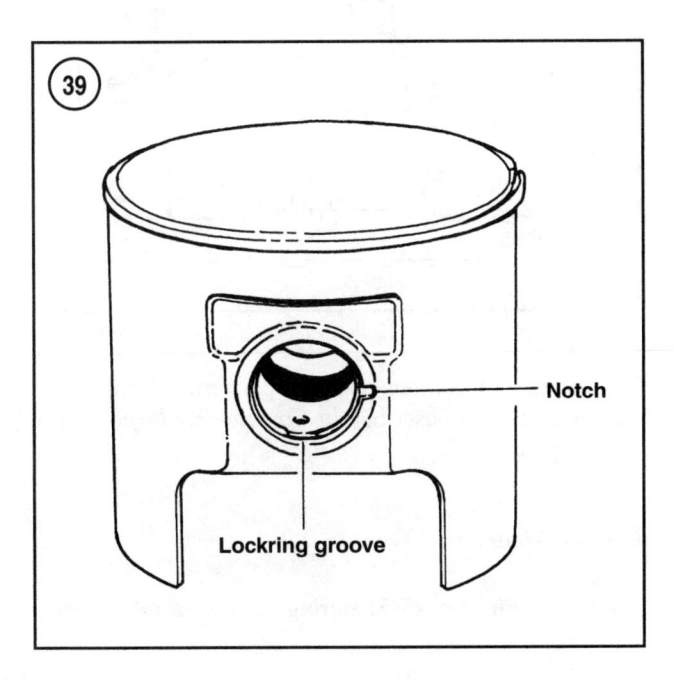

dome. Use a permanent marker or scribe. Do not scribe the piston skirt.

WARNING
Use protective eyewear when working with the power head. Piston pin lockrings and other components may unexpectedly spring free and cause an injury.

CAUTION
*Insert the removal tool into the notch in the lockring groove (**Figure 39**) when removing the lockring. The lockring groove can easily damaged by the removal tool. Work carefully and avoid any unnecessary contact with the piston surfaces.*

21. Use a small screwdriver or scribe to carefully pry the lockrings from the piston (**Figure 40**). Hold a glove protected thumb over the lockring to prevent it from springing free upon removal. Use the notch opposite the lockring gap on models with two notches in the lockring groove.

NOTE
If piston pin removal is difficult, heat the piston to approximately 60° C (140° F) with a portable hair dryer. The piston bore expands when heated, allowing easier pin removal.

22. Remove the piston from the connecting rod as follows:

   a. Select a suitable steel rod, socket or section of tubing to push the piston pin from the piston. The removal tool must be slightly smaller in diameter than the piston pin. Piston pin diameters are listed in **Table 3**.

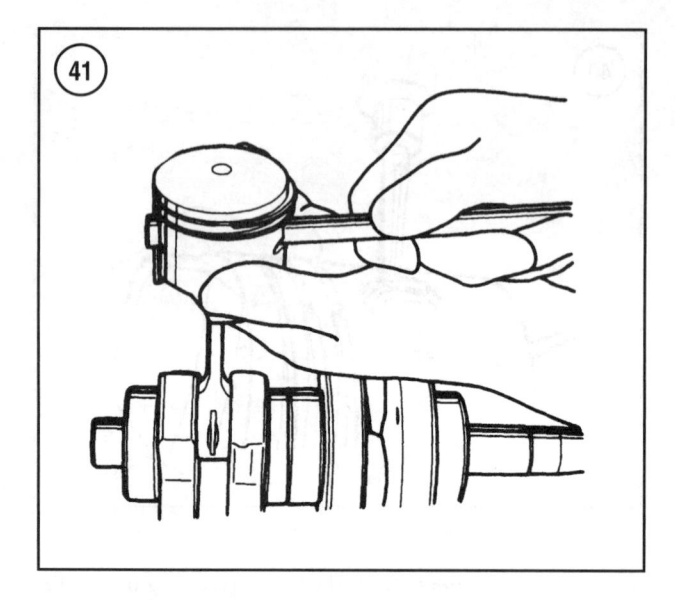

b. Insert the removal tool into the pin bore (**Figure 41**). Push on the tool until the pin extends from the opposite side and is clear of the connecting rod.

c. Hold a hand under the piston and carefully remove the removal tool.

d. Pull the piston from the rod.

e. Retrieve the piston pin bearing from the connecting rod.

23. Before removing the piston rings, mark the top side and note the groove in which the ring is installed. Spread the piston rings (**Figure 42**) just enough to clear the ring grooves then slide them from the piston. Avoid scratching or damaging the piston while removing the rings. Do not discard the rings at this time.

24. Remove the crankshaft main bearing(s) only if they must be replaced. The removal process damages the bearing. Refer to *Components Inspection* to determine the need for replacement. Remove the bearing as follows:

a. Put the sharp edge of a bearing separator between the crankshaft and bearing as shown in **Figure 43**.

b. When removing the upper bearing, thread the used flywheel nut onto the crankshaft to protect the threads.

c. When removing the lower bearing, use a socket or section of tubing to press against the crankshaft. The socket tubing must pass through the bearing bore during the removal process.

d. Rest the bearing on the table of a press. Support the crankshaft and press on the flywheel nut, socket or tubing until the bearing is free (**Figure 44**).

e. Discard the bearing(s).

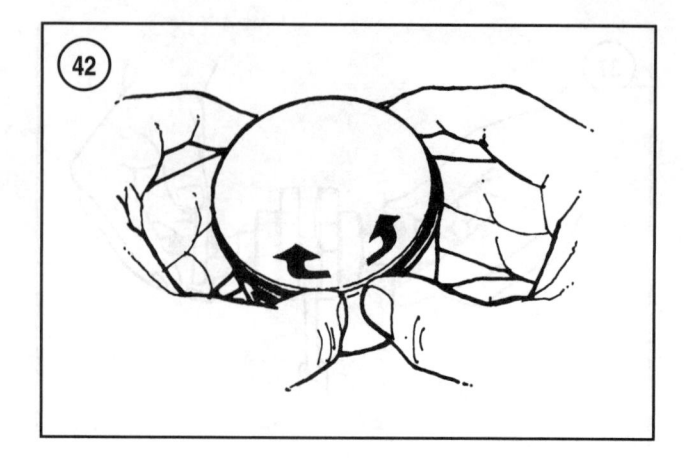

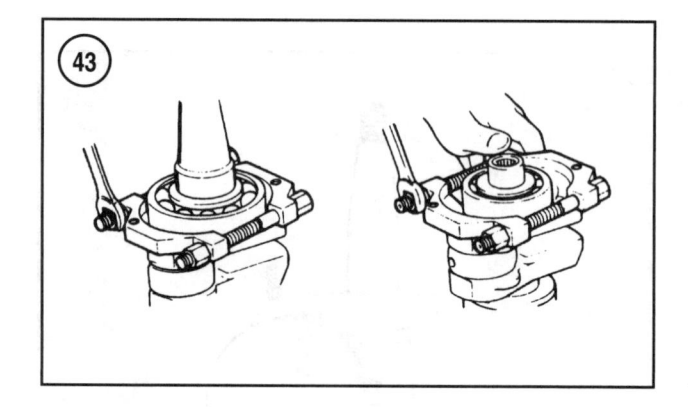

25. Inspect all components and perform all applicable measurements as described in *Components Inspection* in this chapter.

6-90 hp Models

Refer to **Figures 45-51** during the disassembly procedure.

POWER HEAD

POWER HEAD COMPONENTS
(6 AND 8 HP TWO-CYLINDER MODELS)

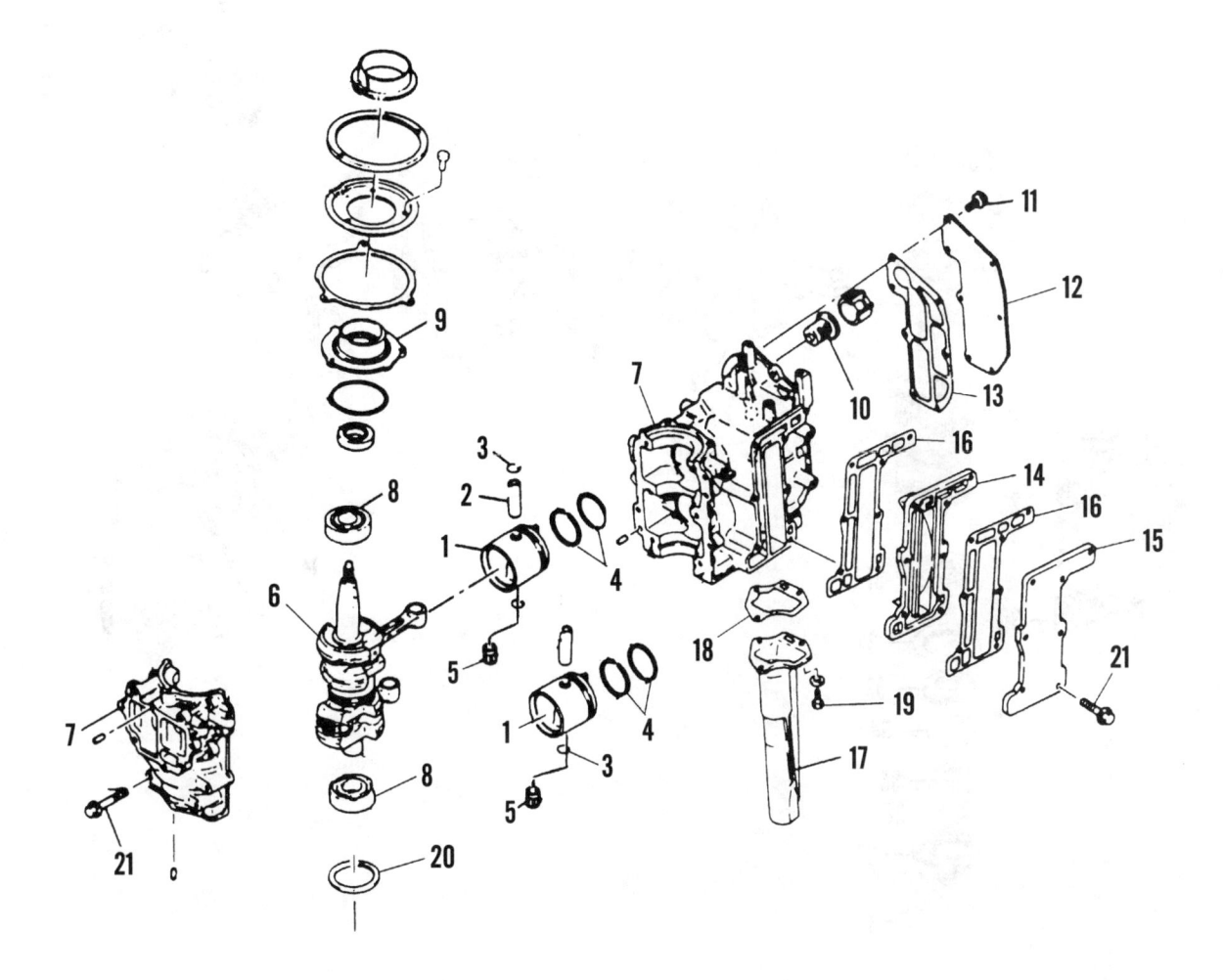

㊺

1. Piston
2. Piston pin
3. Lockring
4. Piston rings
5. Piston pin bearing
6. Crankshaft and connectin rods assembly
7. Cylinder block/crankcase cover
8. Main bearing
9. Top cover
10. Thermostat
11. Bolt
12. Water jacket cover
13. Gasket
14. Exhaust plate
15. Exhaust cover
16. Gasket
17. Exhaust tube
18. Gasket
19. Bolt and washer
20. O-ring
21. Bolt

POWER HEAD COMPONENTS
(9.9 AND 15 HP TWO-CYLINDER MODELS)

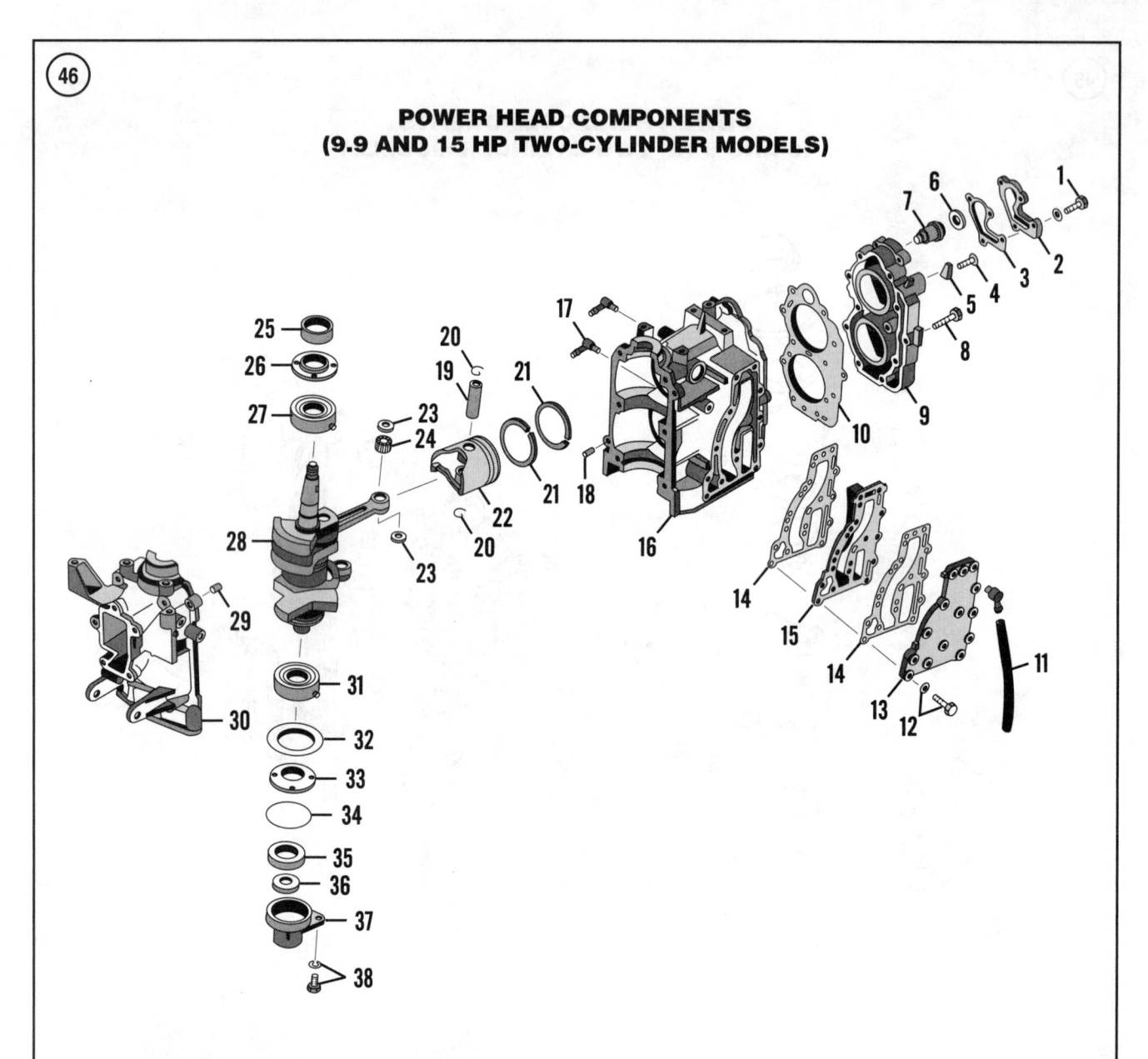

1. Bolt and washer
2. Thermostat cover
3. Gasket
4. Screw
5. Anode
6. Washer
7. Thermostat
8. Bolt
9. Cylinder head
10. Head gasket
11. Water stream hose
12. Bolt and washer
13. Exhaust cover
14. Gasket
15. Exhaust plate
16. Cylinder block
17. Fittings
18. Locating pin
19. Piston pin
20. Lockring
21. Piston rings
22. Piston
23. Thrust washer
24. Piston pin bearing
25. Crankshaft seal
26. Upper seal housing and cover
27. Upper main bearing
28. Crankshaft and connecting rods assembly
29. Locating pin
30. Crankcase cover
31. Lower main bearing
32. Spacer
33. Plate
34. O-ring
35. Crankshaft seal
36. Drive shaft seal
37. Lower seal housing and cover
38. Bolt and washer

Power Head

POWER HEAD COMPONENTS
(20 AND 25 HP TWO-CYLINDER MODELS)

1. Bolt
2. Bolt
3. Water stream hose
4. Bolt
5. Thermostat cover
6. Gasket
7. Thermostat
8. Bolt
9. Gasket
10. Water jacket cover
11. Gasket
12. Exhaust plate
13. Gasket
14. Exhaust cover
15. Cylinder head
16. Head gasket
17. Cylinder block/crankcase cover
18. Piston rings
19. Lockring
20. Piston pin
21. Piston
22. Thrust washer
23. Piston pin bearing
24. Crankshaft and connecting rods assembly
25. Upper main bearing
26. Crankshaft seal
27. O-ring
28. Oil pump drive gear
29. Lower main bearing
30. Spacer
31. Seal
32. Seal
33. O-ring
34. Lower seal housing and cover
35. Bolt and washer

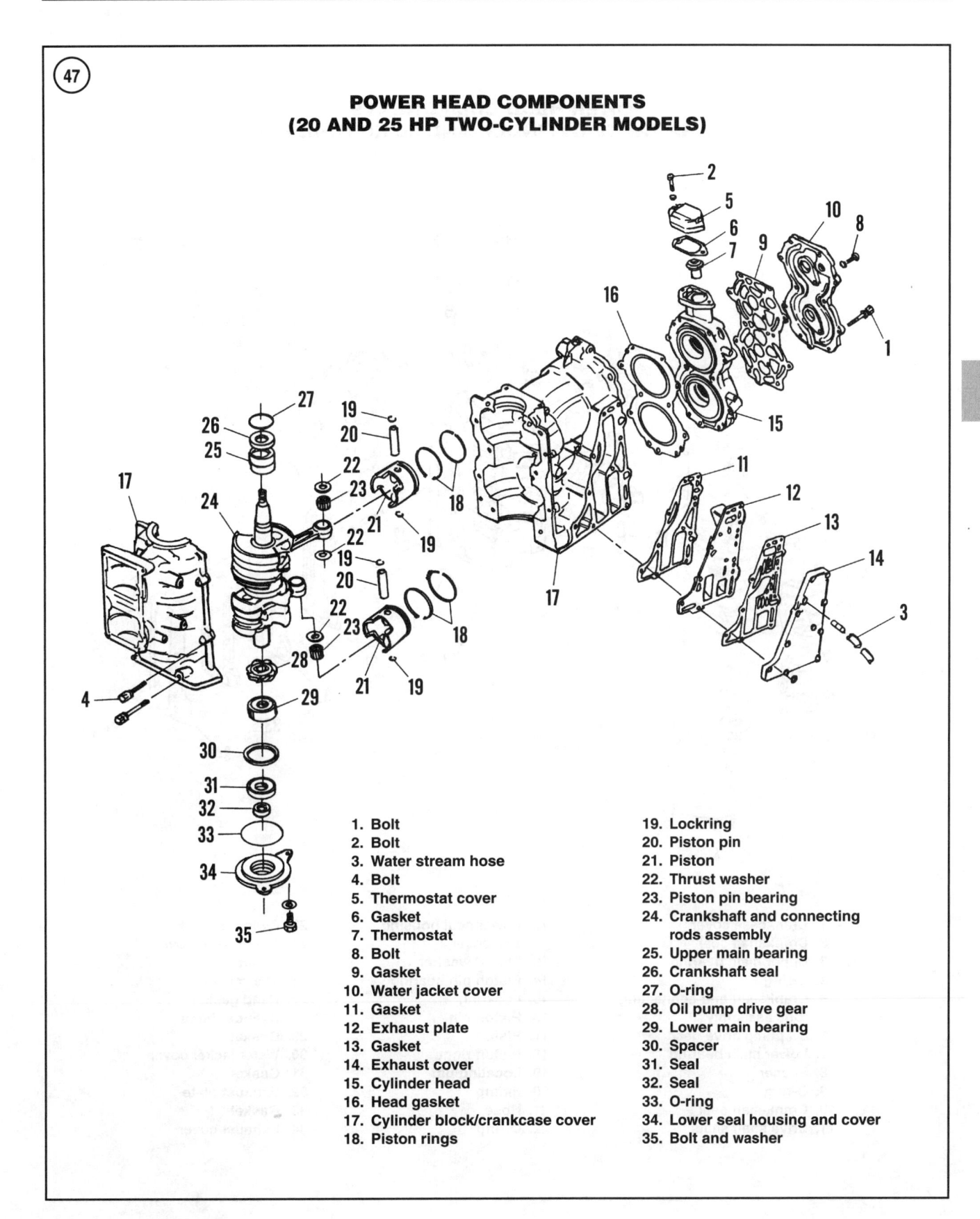

POWER HEAD COMPONENTS
(25 HP THREE-CYLINDER AND 30 HP MODELS)

1. Crankcase cover
2. Crankshaft seal
3. Upper main bearing
4. O-ring
5. Crankshaft and connecting rods assembly
6. Oil pump drive gear
7. Lower main bearing
8. Spacer
9. O-ring
10. Crankshaft seal
11. Drive shaft seals
12. Lower seal housing and cover
13. Thrust washer
14. Piston pin bearing
15. Lockring
16. Piston pin
17. Piston
18. Piston rings
19. Locating pin
20. Fitting
21. Hose
22. O-ring
23. Cylinder block
24. Thermostat cover
25. Gasket
26. Thermostat
27. Head gasket
28. Cylinder head
29. Gasket
30. Water jacket cover
31. Gasket
32. Exhaust plate
33. Gasket
34. Exhaust cover

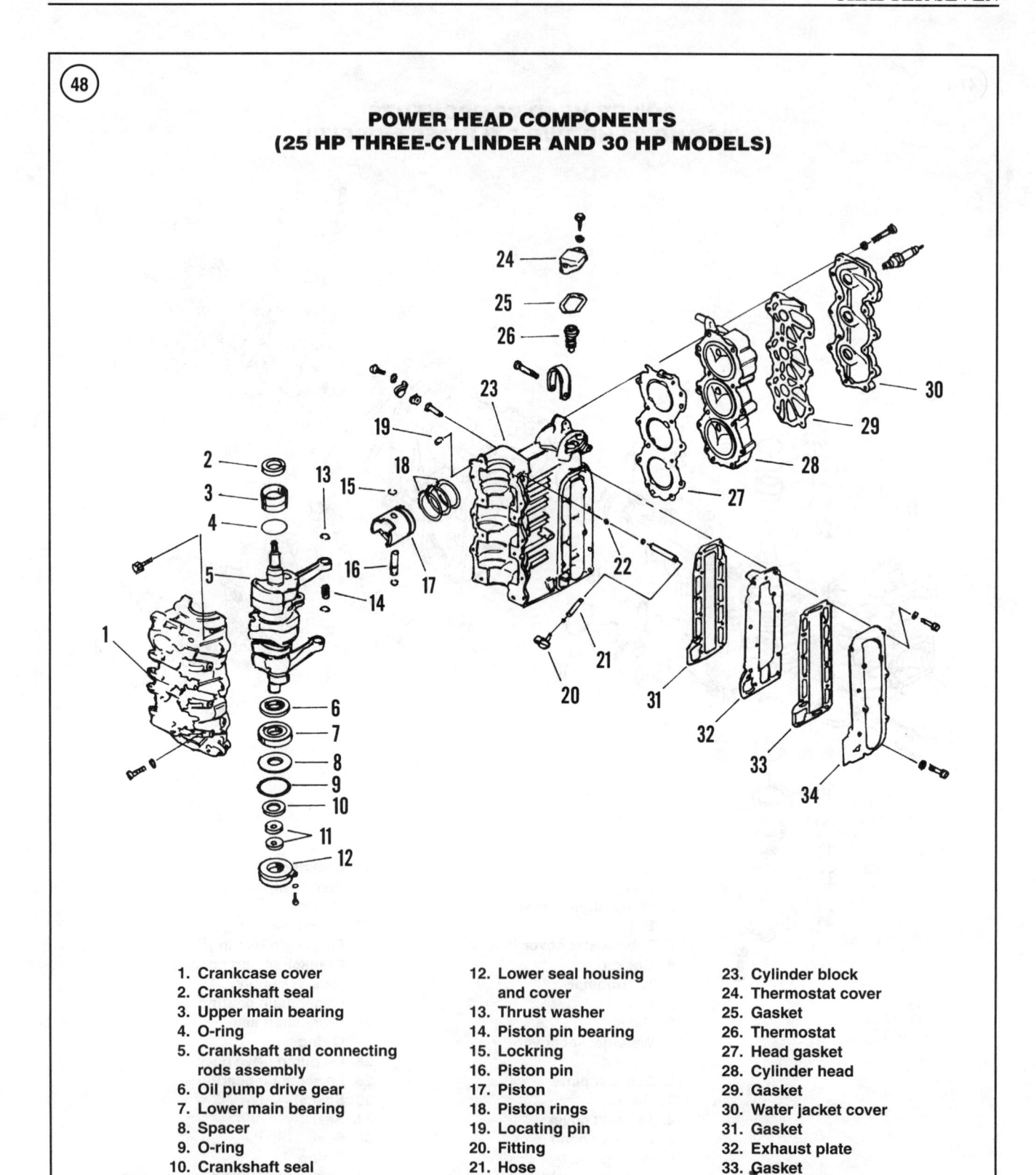

Power Head

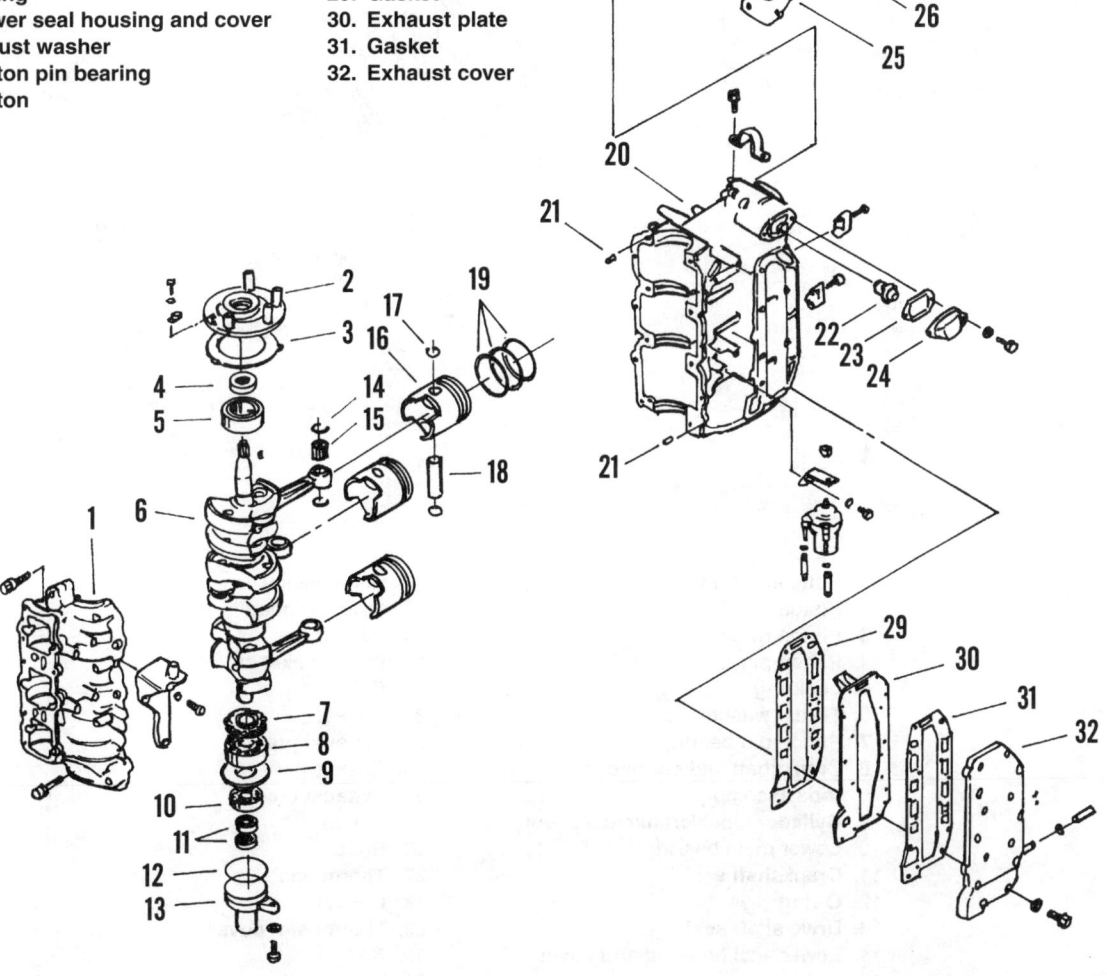

POWER HEAD COMPONENTS
(28 JET, 35 JET, 40 AND 50 HP THREE-CYLINDER MODELS)

1. Crankcase cover
2. Upper seal housing
3. Gasket
4. Crankshaft seal
5. Upper main bearing
6. Crankshaft and connecting rods assembly
7. Oil pump drive gear
8. Lower main bearing
9. Spacer
10. Crankshaft seal
11. Drive shaft seals
12. O-ring
13. Lower seal housing and cover
14. Thrust washer
15. Piston pin bearing
16. Piston
17. Lockring
18. Piston pin
19. Piston rings
20. Cylinder block
21. Locating pin
22. Thermostat
23. Gasket
24. Thermostat cover
25. Head gasket
26. Cylinder head
27. Gasket
28. Water jacket cover
29. Gasket
30. Exhaust plate
31. Gasket
32. Exhaust cover

CHAPTER SEVEN

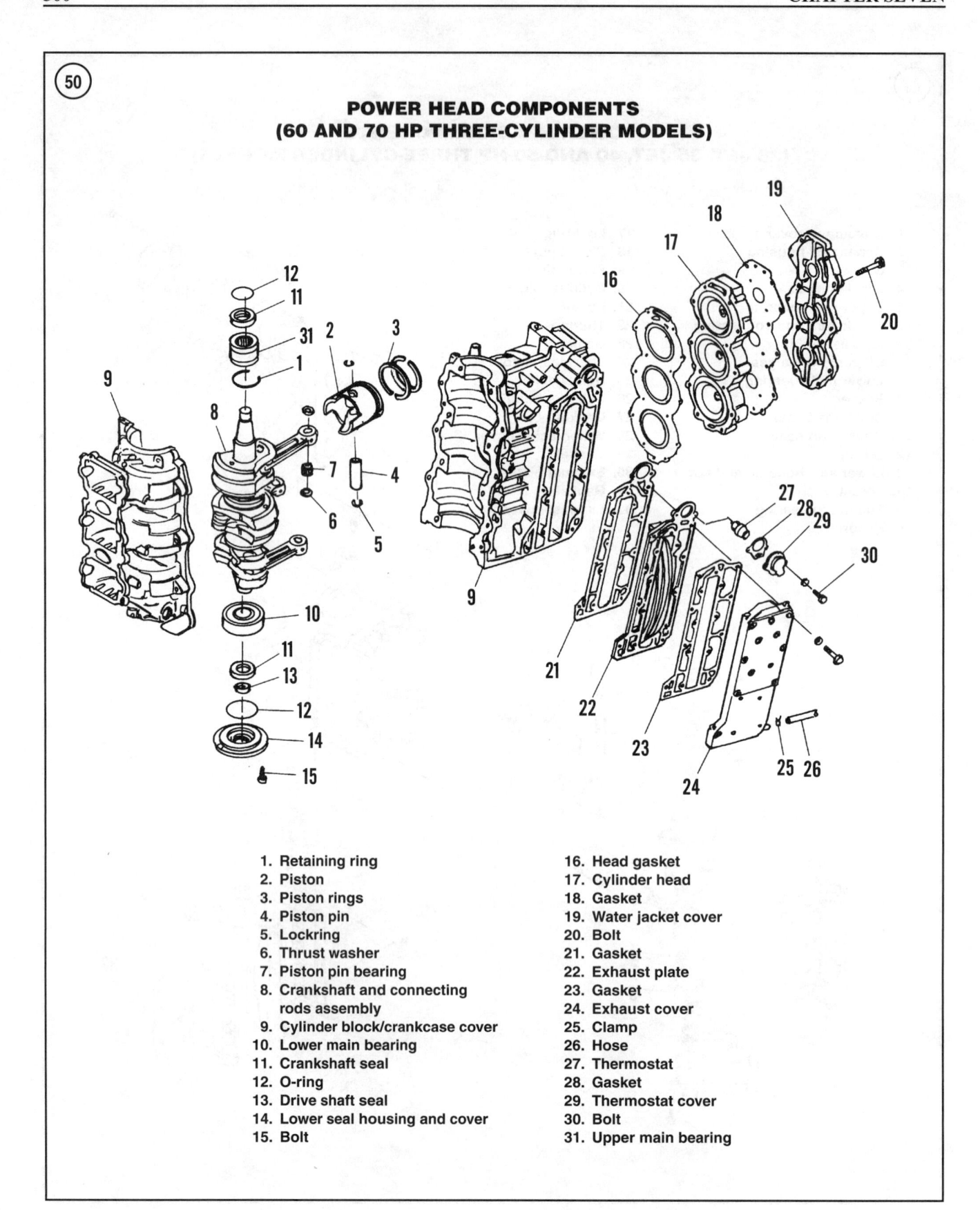

50 POWER HEAD COMPONENTS (60 AND 70 HP THREE-CYLINDER MODELS)

1. Retaining ring
2. Piston
3. Piston rings
4. Piston pin
5. Lockring
6. Thrust washer
7. Piston pin bearing
8. Crankshaft and connecting rods assembly
9. Cylinder block/crankcase cover
10. Lower main bearing
11. Crankshaft seal
12. O-ring
13. Drive shaft seal
14. Lower seal housing and cover
15. Bolt
16. Head gasket
17. Cylinder head
18. Gasket
19. Water jacket cover
20. Bolt
21. Gasket
22. Exhaust plate
23. Gasket
24. Exhaust cover
25. Clamp
26. Hose
27. Thermostat
28. Gasket
29. Thermostat cover
30. Bolt
31. Upper main bearing

POWER HEAD

301

POWER HEAD COMPONENTS
(65 JET AND 75-90 HP THREE-CYLINDER MODELS)

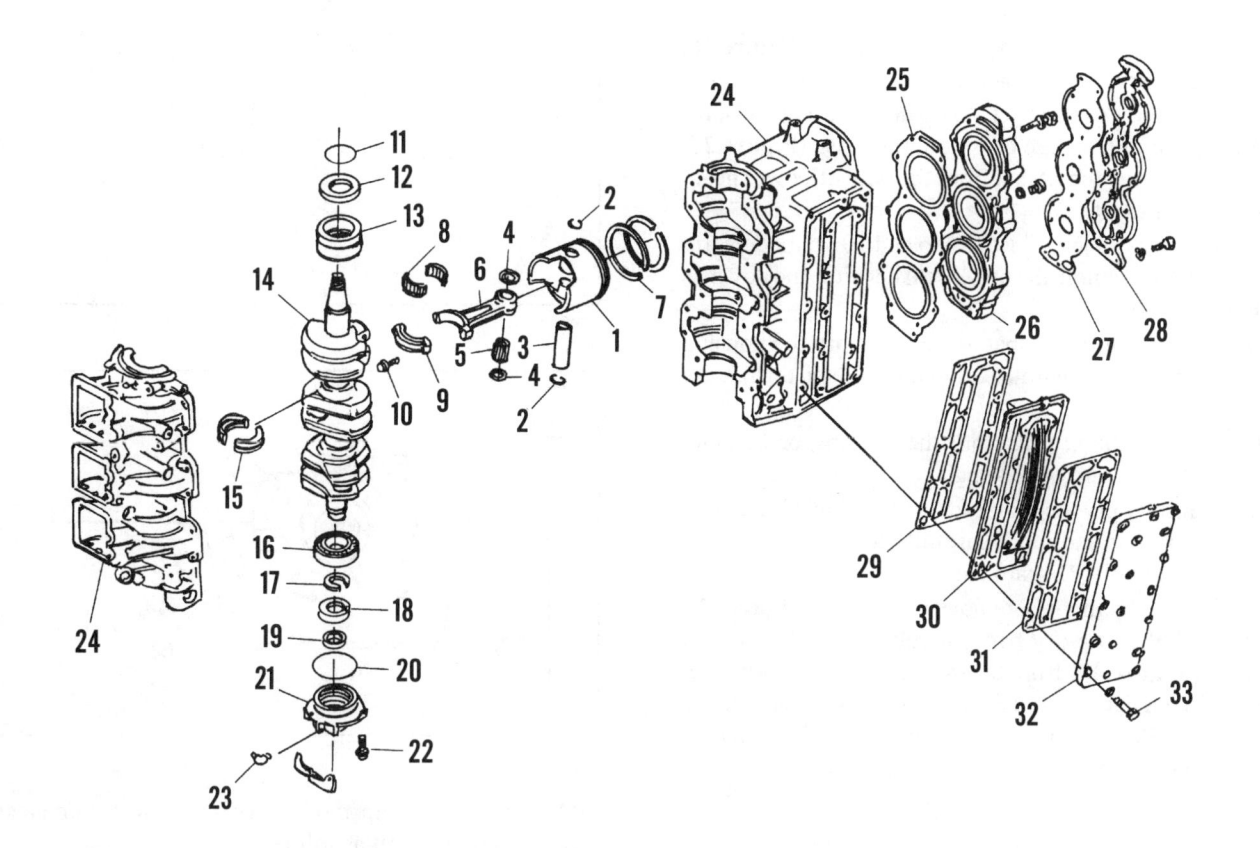

1. Piston
2. Lockring
3. Piston pin
4. Thrust washer
5. Piston pin bearing
6. Connecting rod
7. Piston rings
8. Bearing set
9. Rod cap
10. Rod bolt
11. O-ring
12. Crankshaft seal
13. Upper main bearing
14. Crankshaft
15. Center main bearing
16. Lower main bearing
17. Snap ring
18. Seal
19. Seal
20. O-ring
21. Lower bearing cover and seal housing
22. Bolt
23. Fitting
24. Cylinder block/crankcase cover
25. Head gasket
26. Cylinder head
27. Gasket
28. Water jacket cover
29. Gasket
30. Exhaust plate
31. Gasket
32. Exhaust cover
33. Bolt

1. Remove the flywheel as described in this chapter.
2. On oil injected models, remove all oil injection components as described in Chapter Twelve.
3. Remove the fuel pump, carburetor and all fuel hoses as described in Chapter Five.
4. Remove the wire harness and all electrical components as described in Chapter Six.
5. Remove the intake manifold/reed housing (**Figure 26**, typical) as described in Chapter Five.
6. On 6-15 hp, 28 jet, 35 jet, 40 hp and 50 hp models, remove the ignition charge coil mounting base (**Figure 27**, typical). Remove the gasket from the base or power head. Discard the gasket.
7. On 6-15 hp, 28 jet, 35 jet, 40 hp and 50 hp models, remove and disassemble the upper seal housing and cover as follows:
   a. Use a blunt tip pry bar to carefully pry the housing from the cylinder block. Do not damage the mating surface.
   b. Remove the O-ring from the housing or cylinder block. Discard the O-ring.
   c. Carefully pry the seal from the housing. Use a blunt tip pry bar and work carefully to avoid damaging the seal bore. Discard the seal.
8. On 6 and 8 hp models, remove the screws (**Figure 52**), then use a blunt tip pry bar to carefully pry the exhaust tube (17, **Figure 45**) from the cylinder block. Work carefully to avoid damaging the mating surfaces. Remove the gasket (18, **Figure 45**) from the tube or cylinder block. Discard the gasket.

CAUTION
Do not use excessive force when prying the lower seal housing and cover from the power head. Excessive force may break the housing or damage the mating surfaces. If removal is difficult, remove the housing after removing the crankcase cover. Always remove the seal housing bolts before removing the crankcase cover.

9. Remove and disassemble the seal housing as follows:
   a. On 65 jet and 75-90 hp models, note the orientation of the deflector and mounting bolts (**Figure 53**). Mark the deflector and seal housing as needed.
   b. Remove all of the seal housing bolts (**Figure 54**).
   c. Use a blunt tip pry bar to carefully pry the housing from the cylinder block. Work carefully to avoid damaging the mating surfaces.
   d. Carefully pry the seals from the housing. Use a blunt tip pry bar and work carefully to avoid damaging the seal bore. Discard the seals.

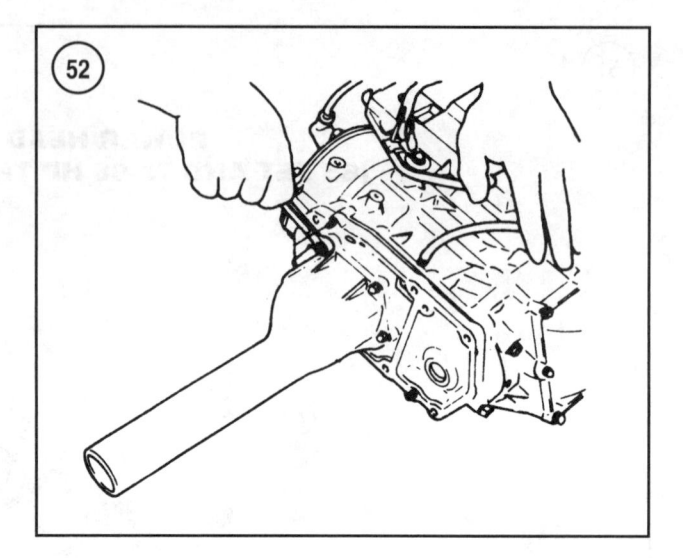

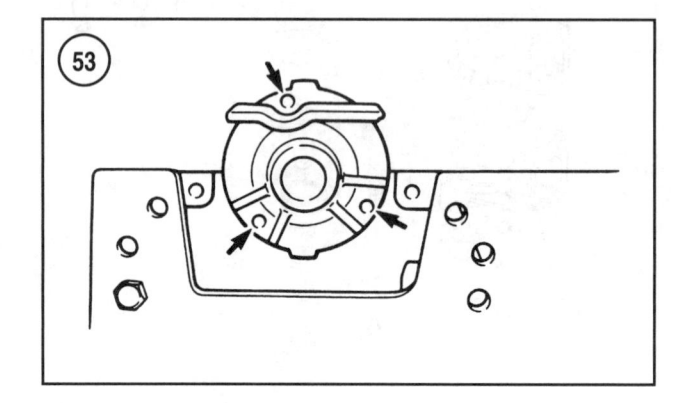

10A. On 6 and 8 hp models, remove the water jacket cover and thermostat as follows:
   a. Remove the bolts (11, **Figure 45**).
   b. Carefully pry the water jack cover (12, **Figure 45**) from the cylinder block. Use a blunt tip pry bar and work carefully to avoid damaging the mating surfaces. Do not use excessive force. If removal is difficult, check for overlooked bolts. Apply moderate heat to the mating surface if the cover is seized.
   c. Remove and discard the gasket (13, **Figure 45**).
   d. Pull the sleeve, then the thermostat (10, **Figure 45**), from the cylinder block or water jacket cover.

10B. On 9.9-70 hp models, remove the thermostat cover and thermostat. Refer to the **Figures 46-50** to identify and locate the thermostat cover, gaskets and related components. Remove them as follows:
   a. Remove the two bolts from the thermostat cover.
   b. Carefully pry the thermostat cover from the cylinder head, cylinder block or exhaust cover. Use a

POWER HEAD

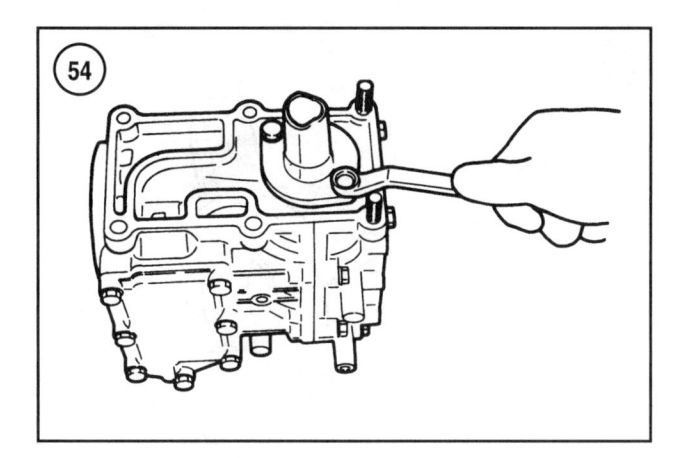

Figure 54

blunt tip pry bar and work carefully to avoid damaging the mating surfaces.

c. Pull the thermostat and related components from the cylinder head, cylinder block or exhaust cover.

d. Remove the thermostat cover gasket. Discard the gasket.

10C. On 75-90 hp models, remove the thermostat cover, thermostat and water pressure relief valve from the rear of the cylinder head as follows:

a. Remove the four bolts, then carefully pry the thermostat cover from the cylinder head water jacket.

b. Pull the water pressure relief valve and thermostat from the water jacket.

c. Remove the relief valve spring. Replace the spring if it is damaged, is corroded or has lost spring tension.

d. Remove the thermostat cover gasket. Discard the gasket.

11. Test the thermostat as described in Chapter Two. Replace the thermostat if it is faulty, corroded, or coated with salt or mineral deposits.

12. Remove the exhaust cover and exhaust plate. Refer to **Figure 45-51** to identify and locate the cover, plate and gaskets. Remove them as follows:

a. Remove the bolts from the exhaust cover (**Figure 30**).

b. Locate a pry point near the bottom of the cover (**Figure 31**). Use a blunt tip pry bar to carefully pry the cover loose. Do not damage the mating surfaces. If removal is difficult, check for overlooked bolts. Apply moderate heat to the mating surface if the cover or plate is seized to the cylinder block.

c. Locate a pry point near the top of the exhaust plate (**Figure 32**). Carefully pry the plate from the cylinder block. Do not damage the mating surfaces.

d. Carefully scrape the gaskets from the cylinder block, cover and plate. Never reuse the cover or plate gasket.

13. Locate and remove all of the fasteners on the crankcase cover (**Figure 33**).

a. 6 and 8 hp models use ten bolts.

b. 9.9 and 15 hp models use six bolts.

c. 20 and 25 hp two-cylinder models use ten bolts.

d. 25 hp three-cylinder and 30 hp models use twelve bolts.

e. 28 jet, 35 jet, and 40-70 hp models use fourteen bolts.

f. 65 jet and 75-90 hp models use twenty bolts.

14. Locate suitable pry points (**Figure 34**) and carefully pry the crankcase cover from the cylinder block. Take all necessary precautions to prevent damage to the mating surfaces.

CAUTION
Avoid using excessive force when removing the crankshaft from the cylinder block. Excessive force may dislodge or damage the main bearing locating pins or damage the cylinder block.

15. Lightly tap on the threaded end of the crankshaft with a plastic mallet (**Figure 35**) to free the main bearings from the cylinder block.

16. Have an assistant hold the cylinder block down, then carefully lift the crankshaft and pistons from the cylinder block.

17. On 20-30 and 60-90 hp models, remove and disassemble the upper main bearing and seal assembly. Refer to **Figures 47-51** to identify and locate the components.

a. Slide the upper main bearing and seal assembly from the threaded end of the crankshaft.

b. Carefully pry the seal from the bearing case. Use a blunt tip pry bar and work carefully to avoid damaging the seal bore. Discard the seal.

c. Remove the O-ring from the bearing. Discard the O-ring.

18. On 9.9-50 hp models, remove any loose washer, spacer or plate from the lower end of the crankshaft. Refer to **Figures 46-49** to identify and locate these components.

19. Clamp the crankshaft in a vise with protective jaws. Clamp on the flyweight part of the crankshaft.

20. Locate the *UP* or arrow mark on the piston (**Figure 38**). The mark must face toward the tapered end of the crankshaft. If the original mark is illegible or cannot be found, mark the up direction on the underside of the piston dome. Use a permanent marker or scribe. Do not scribe the piston skirt. Mark the cylinder number on the underside of the dome of each piston. Install the pistons, if re-

used, into their original cylinders. The number one cylinder is always closest to the flywheel end of the crankshaft.

> *WARNING*
> *Use protective eyewear and gloves when working with the power head. Piston pin lockrings and other components may unexpectedly spring free and cause an injury.*

> *CAUTION*
> *Insert the removal tool into the notch in the lockring groove (**Figure 39**) when removing the lockring. The lockring groove can be easily damaged by the removal tool. Work carefully and avoid any unnecessary contact with the piston surfaces.*

> *NOTE*
> *Some models use loose needle bearings at the piston pin end of the connecting rod. Work carefully and take all necessary precautions to prevent lost needles during the removal process. If the needle bearings must be reused, install them onto the same connecting rod and piston pin as removed.*

21. Use a small screwdriver or scribe to carefully pry the lockrings from the piston (**Figure 40**). Hold a thumb over the lockring to prevent it from springing free upon removal. Use the notch opposite the lockring gap on models with two notches in the lockring groove.

> *NOTE*
> *If piston pin removal is difficult, heat the piston to approximately 60° C (140° F) with a portable hair dryer. The piston bore expands when heated, allowing easier pin removal.*

22. Remove the pistons from the connecting rod as follows:
    a. Select a suitable steel rod, socket or section of tubing to push the piston pin from the piston. The removal tool must be slightly smaller in diameter than the piston pin. Piston pin diameters are listed in **Table 3**.
    b. Insert the removal tool into the pin bore (**Figure 41**). Push on the tool until the pin extends from the opposite side and is clear of the connecting rod.
    c. Hold a hand under the piston and carefully remove the removal tool.
    d. Pull the piston from the rod.
    e. On 6-8 hp models, retrieve the piston pin bearing(s) from the connecting rod.

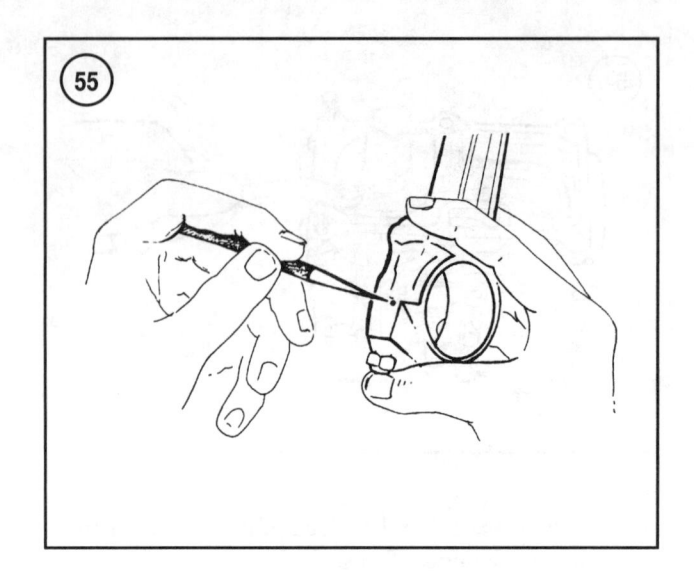

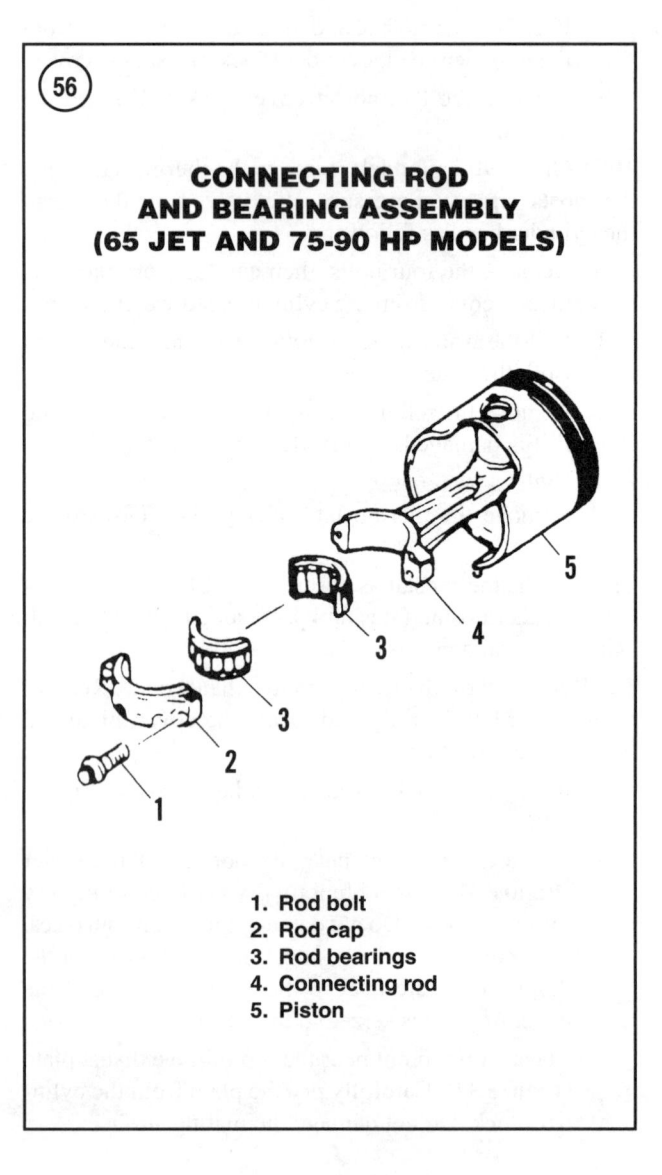

CONNECTING ROD AND BEARING ASSEMBLY (65 JET AND 75-90 HP MODELS)

1. Rod bolt
2. Rod cap
3. Rod bearings
4. Connecting rod
5. Piston

POWER HEAD

Figure 57 — Main bearing, Retaining ring, Awl

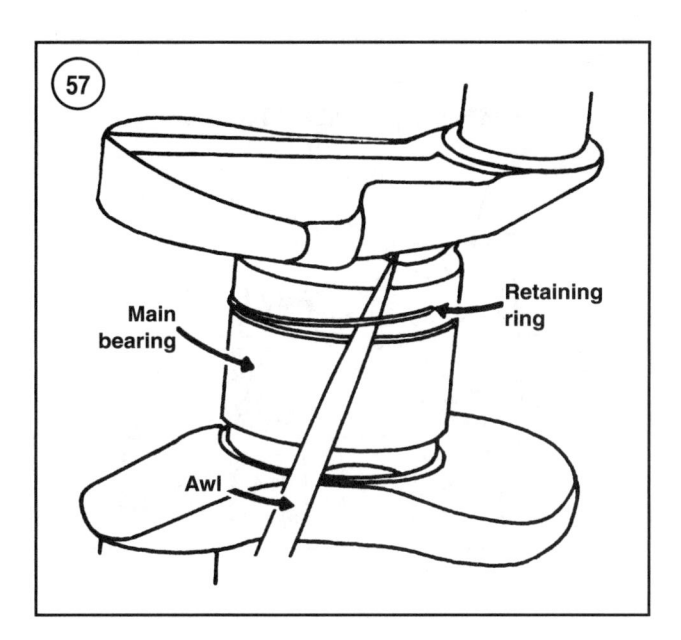

  f. On 9.9-90 models, retrieve the piston pin bearing(s) and two thrust washers.

  g. For loose needle bearings, count the number of needle bearings upon removal. If the same number is not removed from each connecting rod, inspect the crankshaft and cylinder block until the missing bearing(s) are found.

  h. Repeat this step for each piston. Mark the cylinder number on each piston prior to removal. If the piston pin bearing or thrust washers must be reused, store them in containers that identify the cylinder number.

23. Mark the top side of each piston ring and note the groove in which the ring is installed prior to removal. Spread the piston rings (**Figure 42**) just enough to clear the ring grooves then slide them from the piston. Avoid scratching or damaging the piston while removing the rings. Tag the rings to indicate the original cylinder number. Do not discard the rings at this time.

24. On 75-90 hp models, remove the rod cap and connecting rod bearings as follows:

  a. Carefully scribe marks on the side of the rod cap and connecting rod mating surfaces (**Figure 55**) to identify the cap position on the rod and the cylinder number. Use one line for the No. 1 cylinder, two lines for the No. 2 cylinder and three lines for the No. 3 cylinder.

  b. Mark the flywheel side of the connecting rod to ensure proper orientation of the rod on assembly.

  c. Remove the rod bolts (1, **Figure 56**), then carefully pull the rod cap (2) from the connecting rod.

  d. Remove the rod bearings (3, **Figure 56**). If the bearings must be reused, mark the flywheel side to ensure they turn in the same direction after assembly.

  e. Remove the connecting rod from the crankshaft. Align the marks and install the rod cap onto the connecting rod. Thread the rod bolts into the rod to secure the cap.

25. On 28 jet, 35 jet and 40-90 hp models, use an awl to carefully remove the retaining ring from the center main bearings (**Figure 57**). If the center main bearings must be reused, place the bearing cage halves and roller bearings into containers marked with the cylinder number in which they were originally installed.

26. Remove pressed-on crankshaft main bearings only if replacement is required or if the bearing must be removed to access the oil pump drive gear. The removal process damages the bearing. Refer to *Components Inspection* in this chapter to determine if the bearings must be replaced. Remove the bearing as follows:

  a. On 75-90 hp models, remove the snap ring (17, **Figure 51**), then carefully slide the oil pump drive gear from the crankshaft. If necessary, pry the gear from the crankshaft. Do not pry against the teeth of the gear. The teeth can be easily bent or broken when excessive force is applied.

  b. Engage the sharp edge of a bearing separator between the crankshaft and bearing as shown in **Figure 43**.

  c. To remove the upper bearing on 6-15 hp, 28 jet, 35 jet, 40 hp and 50 hp models, thread the used flywheel nut onto the crankshaft to protect the threads.

  d. To remove the lower bearing on 6-90 hp models, use a socket or section of tubing to press against the crankshaft. The socket tubing must pass through the bearing bore during the removal process.

  e. Rest the bearing on the table of a press. Support the crankshaft and press on the flywheel nut, socket or tubing until the bearing is free (**Figure 44**). Discard the bearing(s).

  f. On 20-70 hp models, carefully remove the spacer or oil injection drive gear from the crankshaft. If necessary, pry the gear or spacer from the crankshaft. Do not pry against the teeth of the gear. The teeth can be easily bent or broken if excessive force is applied.

27. Inspect all components and perform all applicable measurements as described in *Components Inspection* in this chapter.

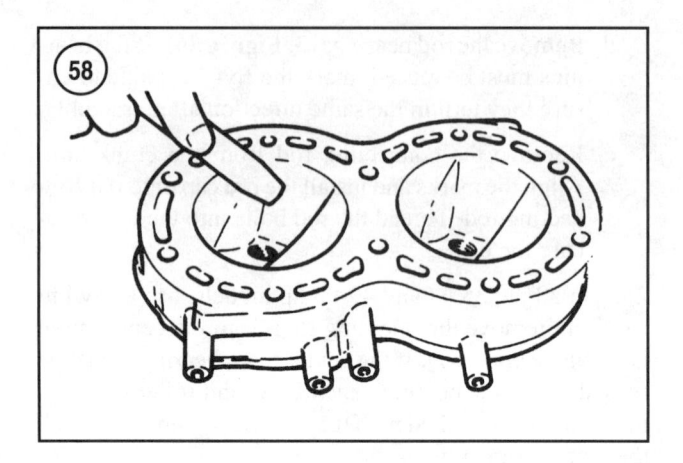

POWER HEAD COMPONENTS CLEANING AND INSPECTION

This section includes procedures for component cleaning, inspecting for visual defects and measuring the components.

Take all precautions necessary to maintain the marks indicating the original position of each component. If reused, all components must be installed into the same cylinder or position on the power head. Wear patterns form on any contacting surfaces. Maintaining the wear patterns help ensure a durable and reliable repair.

Review *Lubricants, Sealants and Adhesives*; *Sealing Surfaces*; and *Fasteners and Torque* in this chapter.

Replace the seals, O-rings, gaskets, piston pin lock rings, piston rings and all piston pin bearings any time a power head is disassembled.

Perform the cleaning and inspection procedures in each of the following sections that applies to your engine *before* beginning assembly procedures.

Cylinder Block and Crankcase

Yamaha outboard cylinder blocks and crankcase covers are matched, align-bored assemblies. Do not attempt to assemble an engine with parts salvaged from other blocks. If the following inspection procedure indicates that the block or cover requires replacement, replace the cylinder block and crankcase cover as an assembly.

NOTE
Remove all fuel bleed components, such as hoses, T-fittings, threaded fittings, check valves and check valve carriers, if it is necessary to submerge the block and/or cover in a strong cleaning solution. See **Recirculation** *in Chapter Six.*

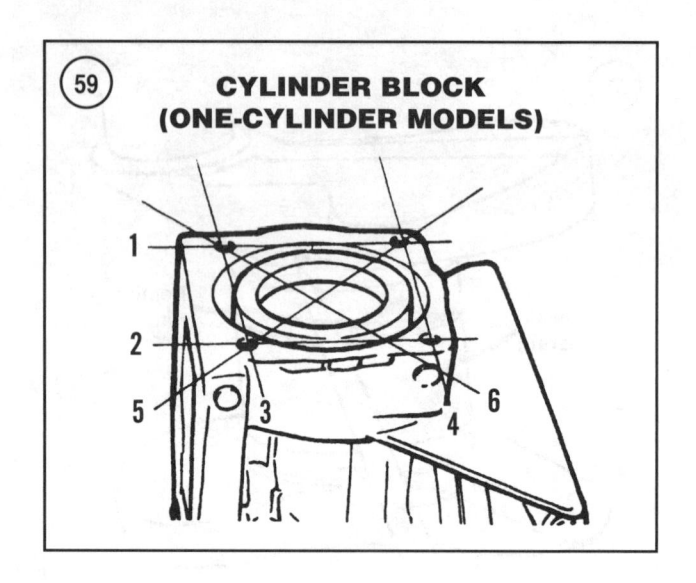

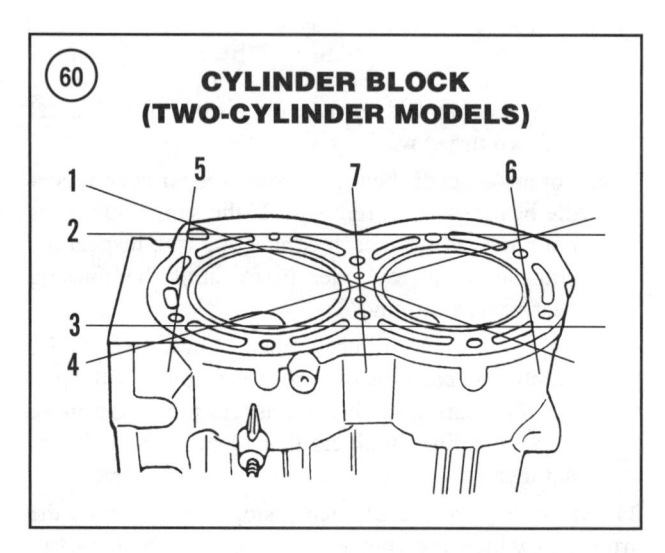

1. Clean the cylinder block and crankcase cover thoroughly with clean solvent using a parts washing brush. Carefully remove all gasket and sealant material from mating surfaces.

2. Remove all carbon and varnish deposits from the combustion chambers, exhaust ports and exhaust cavities with a carbon removing solvent, such as Yamaha Combustion Chamber Cleaner. Use a hardwood dowel or plastic scraper to remove stubborn deposits. See **Figure 58**. Do not scratch, nick or gouge the combustion chambers or exhaust ports.

WARNING
Use suitable hand and eye protection when using muriatic acid products. Avoid breathing the vapors. Use muriatic acid products only in a well-ventilated area.

POWER HEAD

61 CYLINDER BLOCK (THREE-CYLINDER MODELS)

62 CYLINDER HEAD (ONE-CYLINDER MODELS)

63 CYLINDER HEAD (TWO-CYLINDER MODELS)

64 CYLINDER HEAD (THREE-CYLINDER MODELS)

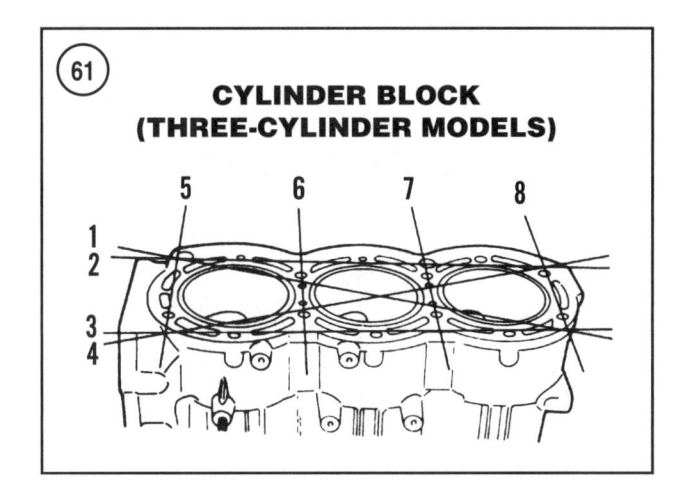

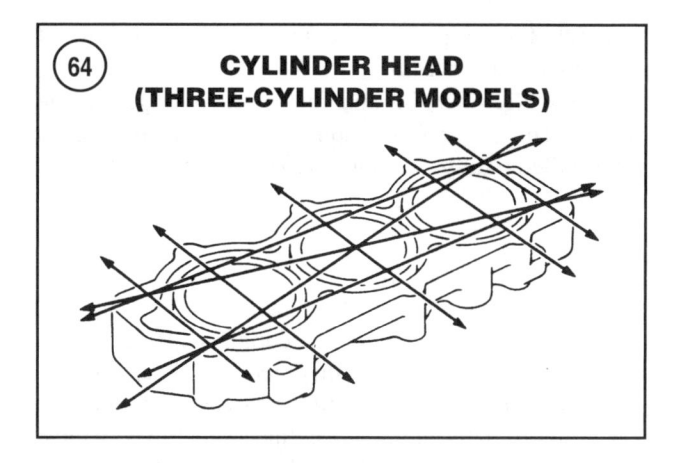

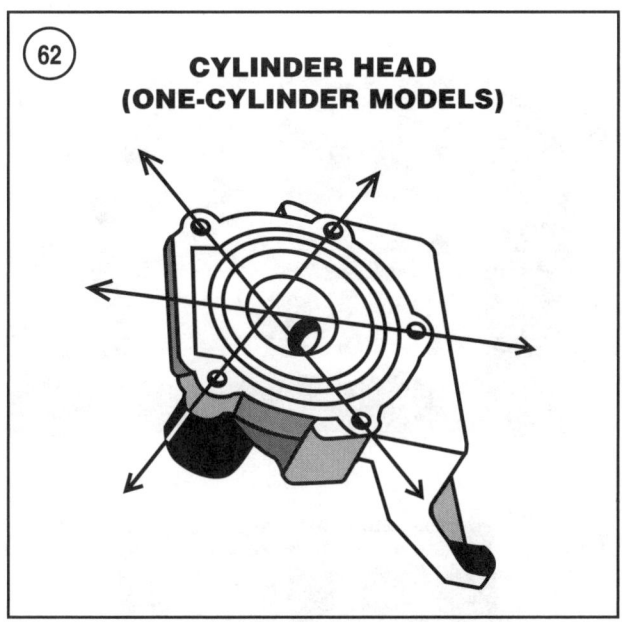

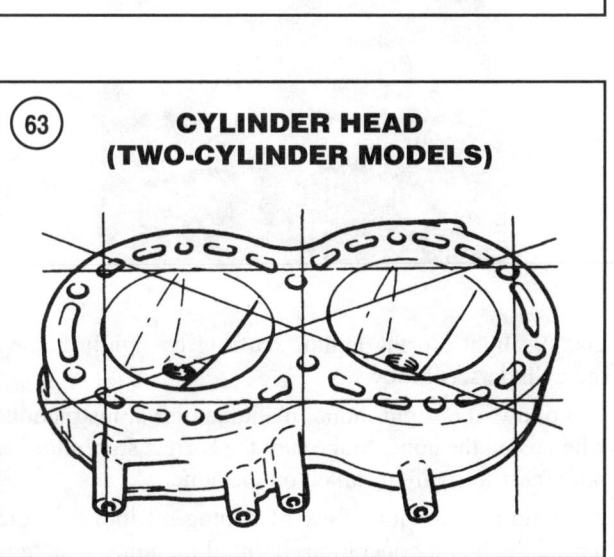

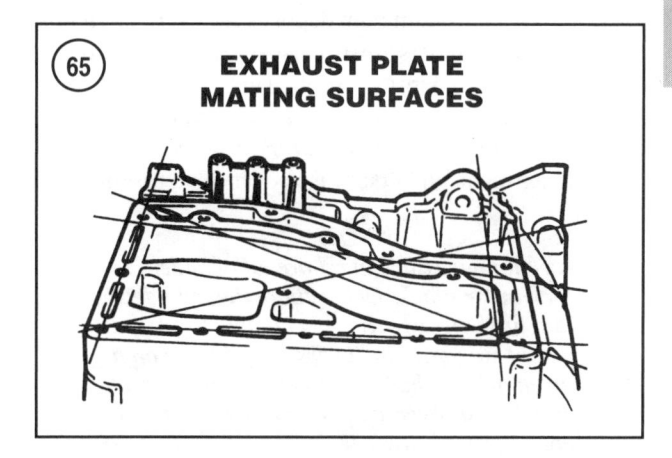

65 EXHAUST PLATE MATING SURFACES

CAUTION
Do not allow muriatic acid to come into contact with the aluminum surfaces of the cylinder block.

3. If the cylinder bore(s) has aluminum transfer from the piston(s), clean loose deposits using a stiff bristle brush. Apply a *small* quantity of diluted muriatic acid to the aluminum deposits. A bubbling action indicates that the aluminum is dissolving. Wait 1-2 minutes, then thoroughly wash the cylinder with hot water and detergent. Repeat this procedure until the aluminum deposits have been removed. Lightly oil the cylinder wall to prevent rusting.

4. Check the cylinder block and crankcase cover for cracks, fractures, stripped threads or other damage.

5. Inspect gasket mating surfaces for nicks, grooves, cracks or distortion. Any defects may allow leaking. Check the surfaces for warp as described in *Sealing Surfaces* in this chapter. Unless otherwise specified, replace components if the warp exceeds 0.1 mm (0.004 in.). Smaller imperfections can be removed by lapping the component as described under *Sealing Surfaces* in this chapter. **Figures 59-65** show typical directions in which

to check for warp on the cylinder head and exhaust cover/manifold surfaces.

6. Check all water, oil and fuel bleed passages in the block and cover for obstructions. Make sure all pipe plugs are installed tightly. Seal pipe plugs with Loctite 567 PST pipe sealant.

Cylinder bore inspection

Inspect the cylinder bores for scoring, scuffing, grooving, cracks, bulging or any other mechanical damage. Inspect the cylinder block casting and cast-iron liner for separation from the aluminum cylinder block. There must be no gaps or voids between the aluminum casting and the liner. Remove any aluminum deposits as described in this chapter. If the cylinders are in a visually acceptable condition, hone the cylinders as described in *Cylinder wall honing* in this section. If the cylinders are in an unacceptable condition, rebore the defective cylinder bore(s) or replace the cylinder block and crankcase cover as an assembly.

NOTE
It is not necessary to rebore all cylinders in a cylinder block. Only rebore the cylinders that are defective. It is acceptable to have a mix of standard and oversize cylinders on a given power head as long as the correct standard or oversize piston is used to match each bore. Always check the manufacturer's parts catalog for oversize piston availability and bore sizes before over-boring the cylinder(s).

Cylinder bore honing

The manufacturer recommends using only a rigid type cylinder hone to deglaze the bore to aid in the seating of new piston rings. If the cylinder has been bored oversize, the rigid hone is used in two steps. First, a deburring hone is used to remove the machining marks, then a finish hone is used to establish the correct cross-hatch pattern in the cylinder bore.

Flex hones and spring-loaded hones are not acceptable as they will not produce a true (straight and perfectly round) bore.

CAUTION
Have a machine shop or dealership perform the cylinder bore honing if you are not proficient with the use of a rigid cylinder hone.

If the cylinders are in a visually acceptable condition, prepare the cylinder bore for new piston rings and remove glazing, light scoring and/or scuffing by lightly honing the cylinders as follows:

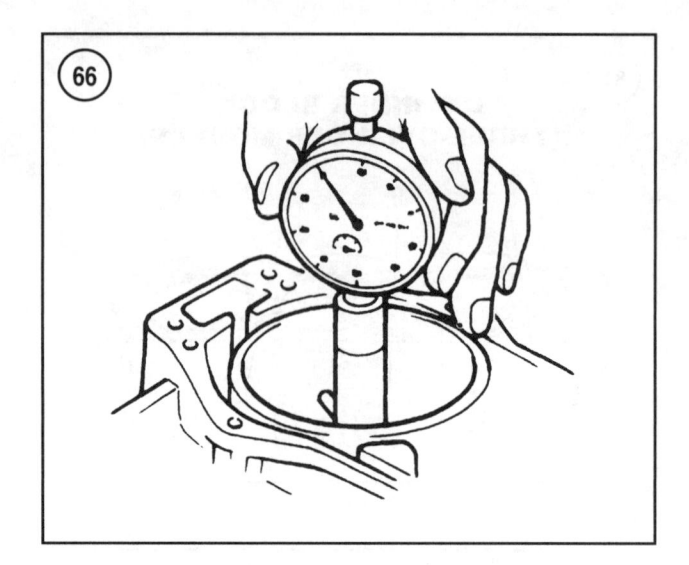

1. Follow the rigid hone manufacturer's instructions when using the hone. Make sure the correct stones for the bore (cast-iron) are installed on the hone.

2. Pump a continuous flow of honing oil into the bore during the honing operation. If an oil pumping system is

POWER HEAD

Cylinder bore measurements

Oversize bore specifications are simply the standard bore specification *plus* the oversize dimension. Check the parts catalog for available oversize dimensions. All standard bore, maximum taper and out-of-round specifications are in **Table 2**.

Use a cylinder bore gauge (**Figure 66**), inside micrometer (**Figure 67**), or a telescoping gauge (**Figure 68**) and a regular micrometer (**Figure 69**) to measure the entire area of ring travel in the cylinder bore. Take three sets of readings at the top, middle and bottom of the ring travel area (**Figure 70**). Measure each cylinder bore as follows:

1. Take the first reading at the top of the ring travel area, approximately 12.7 mm (1/2 in.) from the top of the cylinder bore, with the gauge aligned with the crankshaft centerline. Record the reading. Then, turn the gauge 90° to the crankshaft centerline and record the reading.
2. The difference between the two or the highest and lowest readings is the cylinder out-of-round. The reading should not exceed the specification in **Table 2**.
3. Take a second set of readings at the midpoint of the ring travel area just above the ports using the same alignment points described in Step 1. Record the readings. Calculate the cylinder out-of-round by determining the difference between the two or the highest and lowest readings. The reading should not exceed the specification in **Table 2**.
4. Take a third set of readings at the bottom of the ring travel area near the bottom of the cylinder bore using the same alignment points described in Step 1. Record the readings. Calculate the cylinder out-of-round by determining the difference between the two or the highest and lowest readings. The reading should not exceed the specification in **Table 2**.
5. To determine the cylinder taper, subtract the readings taken at the top of the cylinder bore (Step 1) from the readings taken at the bottom of the cylinder bore (Step 4). The difference in these readings is the cylinder taper. The reading should not exceed the specification in **Table 2**.
6. Repeat Steps 1-5 for each remaining cylinder.
7. If any cylinder out-of-round, taper or maximum bore diameter measurement exceeds specification, bore the cylinder(s) oversize or replace the cylinder block and crankcase cover as an assembly.

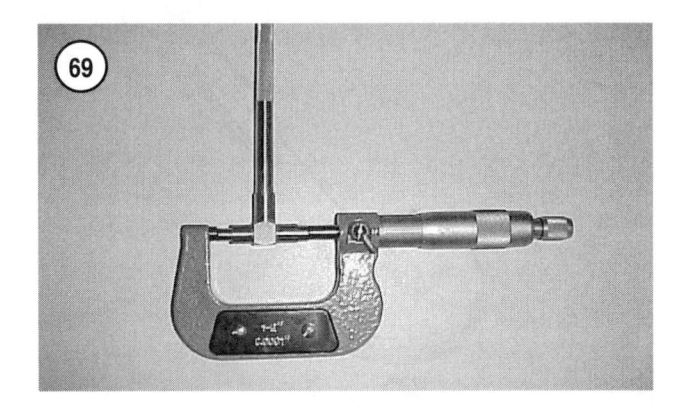

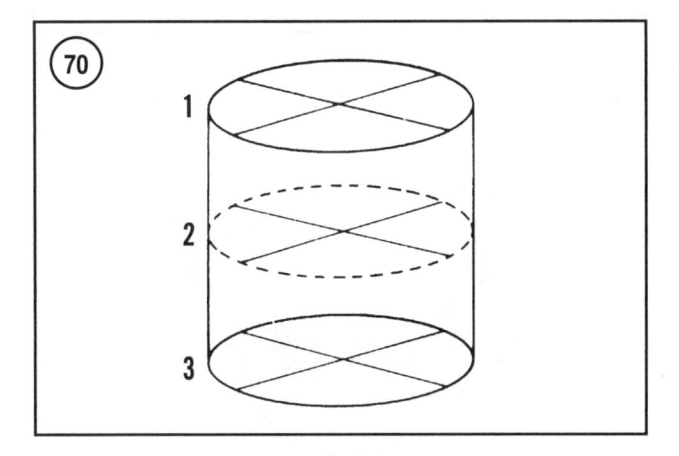

not available, have an assistant use an oil can to keep the cylinder walls flushed with honing oil.

3. If the hone loads (slows down) at one location in the bore, this is the narrowest portion of the bore. Localize the stroking in this location to remove stock until the hone maintains the same speed and load throughout the entire bore.
4. Frequently remove the hone from the cylinder bore and inspect the bore. Do not remove any more material than necessary.
5. Attempt to achieve a stroke rate of approximately 30 cycles per minute, adjusting the speed of the hone to achieve a cross-hatch pattern with an intersecting angle of approximately 30°. Do not exceed a cross-hatch of more than 45°.
6. After honing, thoroughly clean the cylinder block using hot water, detergent and a stiff bristle brush. Remove all abrasive material from the honing process. After washing and flushing the cylinder block, coat the cylinder walls with a film of outboard motor oil to prevent rusting.
7. Proceed to *Cylinder bore measurements* in this section to determine if the cylinder bores are within the manufacturer's specifications for wear, taper and out-of-round.

Piston

Service the piston and piston pin as an assembly. If either is damaged, replace them as an assembly. Reinstall piston pins in the pistons from which they were removed.

CAUTION
Do not use an automotive ring groove cleaning tool as it can damage the ring grooves and loosen the ring locating pins.

Cleaning the piston(s)

1. Clean the piston(s), piston pin(s), thrust (locating) washers and the piston pin needle bearing assemblies thoroughly with clean solvent using a parts washing brush. Do not use a wire brush as metal from the wire can be imbedded in the piston. This can lead to preignition and detonation damage.
2. Remove all carbon and varnish deposits from the top of the piston, piston ring groove(s) and under the piston crown with a carbon removing solvent, such as Yamaha combustion chamber cleaner. Use a piece of hardwood or a plastic scraper (**Figure 71**) to remove stubborn deposits. Do not scratch, nick or gouge any part of the piston. Do not remove any stamped or cast identification marks.

CAUTION
The locating pin in the ring grooves can be loosened within its bore if care is not taken when cleaning the ring grooves. If the pin is loosened, it may dislodge during operation and result in serious power head damage. Use solvent and a small plastic brush to remove carbon deposits from the locating pin.

3. Clean stubborn deposits from the ring groove(s) as follows:
   a. Fashion a ring cleaning tool from the original piston ring(s). Rings are shaped differently for each ring groove. Use the correct original ring for each ring groove.
   b. Break off approximately 1/3 of the original ring. Grind a beveled edge onto the broken end of the ring.

NOTE
On keystone and semi-keystone rings, grind off enough of the ring taper to allow the inside edge of the broken ring to reach the inside diameter of the ring groove.

   c. Use the ground end of the ring to gently scrape the ring groove clean (**Figure 72**). Be careful to only remove the carbon. Do not gouge the metal and do not damage or loosen the piston ring locating pin(s).

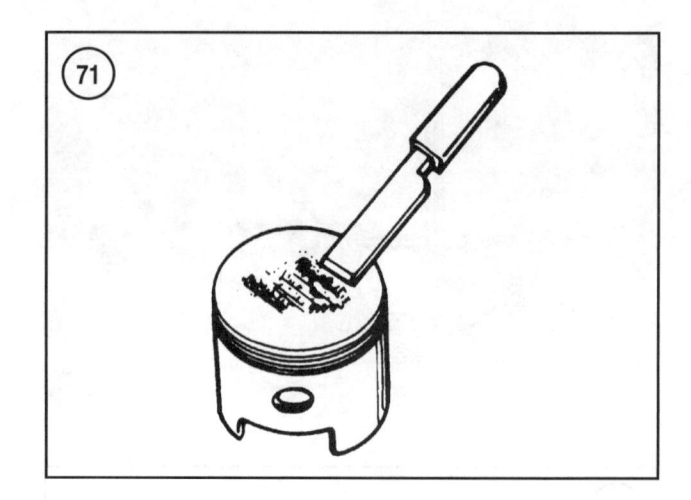

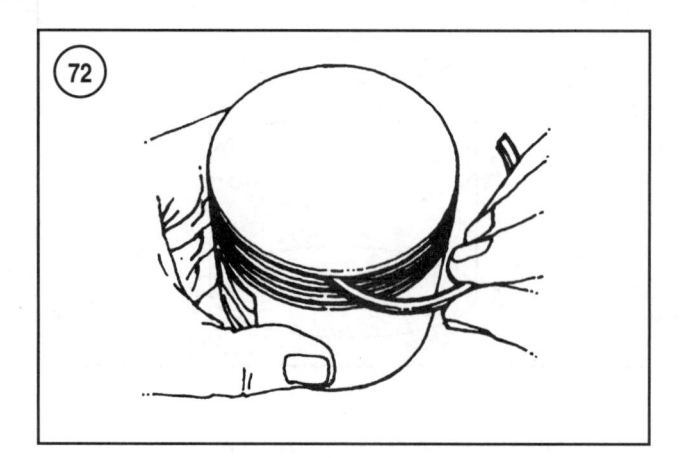

4. Polish off nicks, burrs or sharp edges on and around the piston skirt with crocus cloth or 320 grit carborundum cloth. Do not remove cast or stamped identification marks. Wash the piston thoroughly to remove all abrasive grit.
5. Inspect the piston(s) overall condition for scoring (**Figure 73**), cracks, worn or cracked piston pin bosses and any other mechanical damage. Carefully inspect the

POWER HEAD

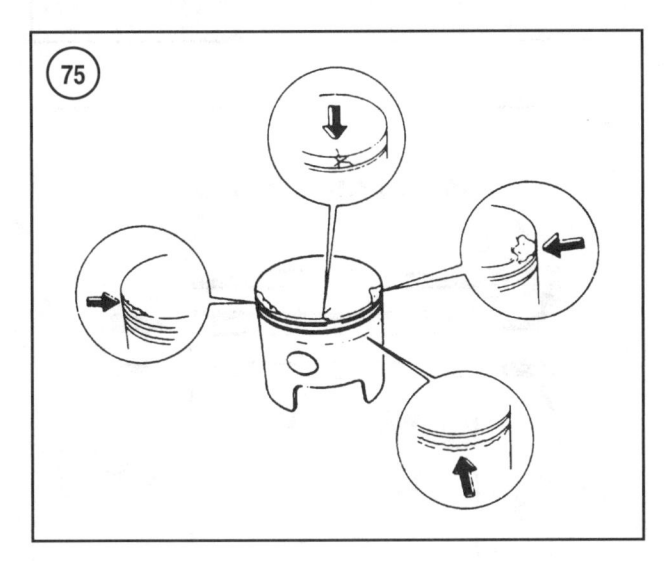

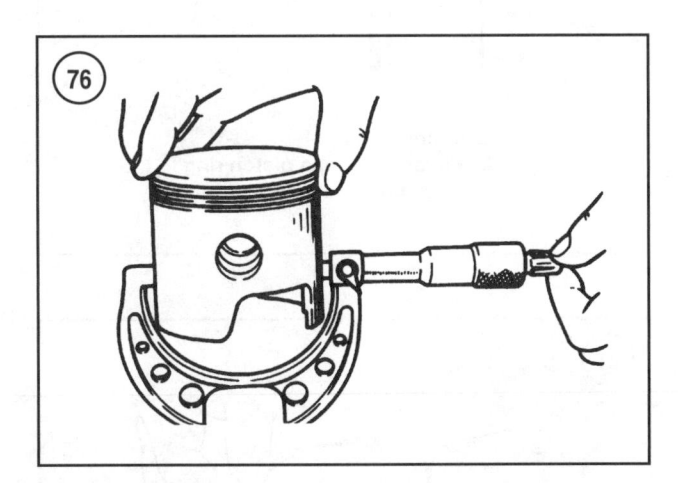

crown and the top outer diameter for burning (**Figure 74**), erosion, evidence of ring migration and mechanical damage (**Figure 75**). Replace the piston and pin as necessary.

6. Check piston ring grooves for wear, erosion, distortion and loose ring locating pins.

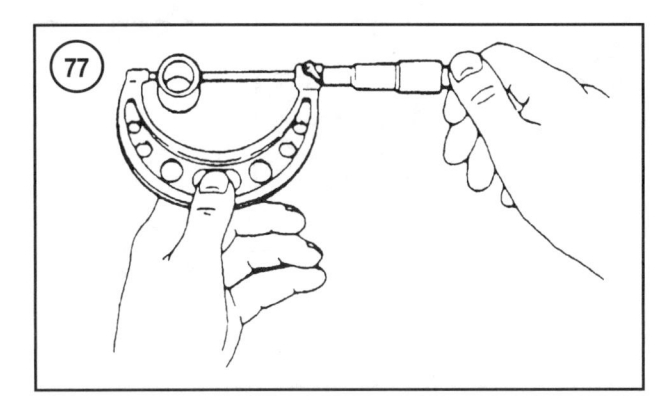

7. Inspect the piston pin for water etching, pitting, scoring, heat discoloration, excessive wear, distortion and mechanical damage. Roll the pin across a machinist's surface plate to check the pin for distortion. Replace the piston and piston pin as necessary.

8. Inspect the thrust (locating) washers and needle bearings for water damage, pitting, scoring, overheating, wear and mechanical damage. Replace damaged washers and needle bearings.

Piston measurements

The pistons used in Yamaha engines are cam shaped or out-of-round. The piston is engineered to fit the bore perfectly when at operating temperature and fully expanded, which makes the engine run more quietly and efficiently. Measure the piston at the specified point(s) or the readings will be inaccurate.

Measure each piston skirt with a micrometer as described in the following procedure and compare the readings to the specifications in **Table 3**.

To calculate the specified skirt dimension on oversize pistons, simply add the oversize dimension to the standard skirt diameter listed in **Table 3**.

1. Use a micrometer to measure each piston skirt diameter at a 90° angle to the piston pin bore (**Figure 76**) and at the distance of 10 mm (0.39 in.) from the bottom of the piston skirt. Measure all pistons and record each measurement by cylinder number. If a piston is not within the specification, replace the piston(s).

2A. On 3 hp and 60-90 hp models, measure the piston pin and pin bore as follows:

  a. Measure the piston pin diameter (**Figure 77**) at the pin bore and needle bearing contact surfaces. If the pin diameter is not within the specification in **Table 3** at all locations, replace the piston and piston pin assembly.

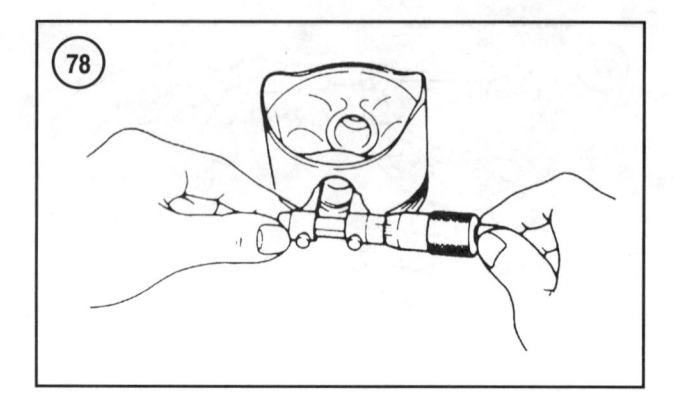

b. Measure the piston pin bore diameter (**Figure 78**) on both sides of the piston and at several locations around the diameter. If the pin bore diameter is not within the specification in **Table 3** at all locations, replace the piston and piston pin assembly. Perform these measurements for each piston and pin.

2B. On 3 hp and 60-90 hp models, check for excessive piston pin and pin bore wear as follows:

   a. Insert the piston pin into the pin bore (**Figure 79**) to approximately the same depth as the pin diameter.
   b. Move the piston pin in the direction indicated (**Figure 79**).
   c. Replace the piston and pin if it wobbles.
   d. Perform this check for each piston and pin.

3. Measure the piston ring side clearance as follows:

   a. Note the shape of the rings and ring grooves in the piston (**Figure 80**).
   b. Carefully install new rings onto the pistons (**Figure 81**). Install the bottom ring first, then install the top ring. Do not scratch the piston surfaces. Make sure the piston shape matches the ring groove and the ring mark (**Figure 82**) faces toward the piston dome.
   c. Rotate the ring to align the ring gap with the locating pin as indicated in **Figure 83**.
   d. Insert a feeler gauge between the piston ring and the side of the piston ring groove (**Figure 84**). The feeler gauge must contact the square side of the piston ring (**Figure 85**) for an accurate measurement.
   e. The ring side clearance equals the thickness of the feeler gauge that can be passed between the ring and the side of the groove with a slight drag. Measure and record the side clearance for each piston ring groove.
   f. Replace the piston if either of the side clearance measurements is greater or less than the specification in **Table 4**.
   g. Repeat this step for each piston.

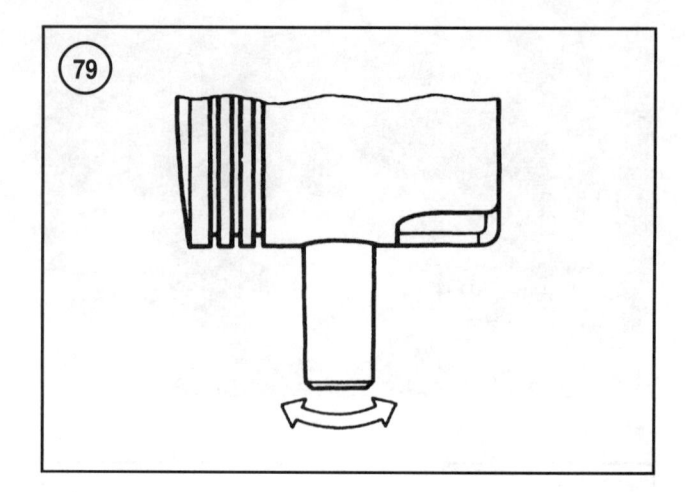

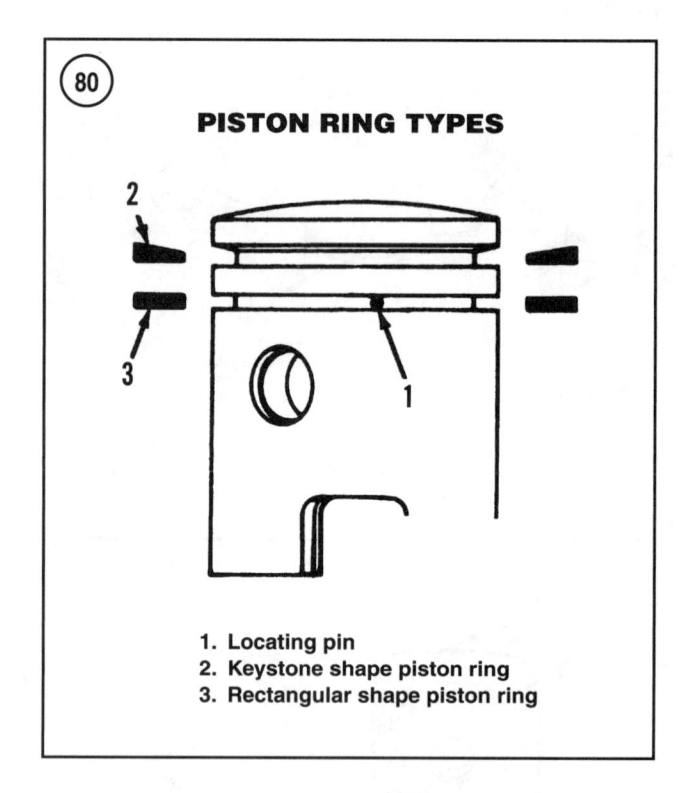

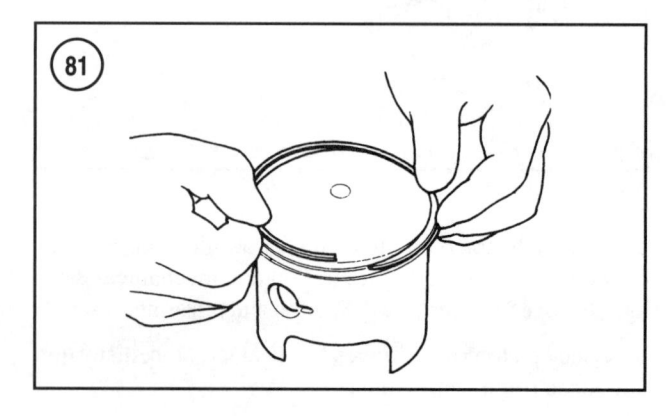

PISTON RING TYPES

1. Locating pin
2. Keystone shape piston ring
3. Rectangular shape piston ring

POWER HEAD

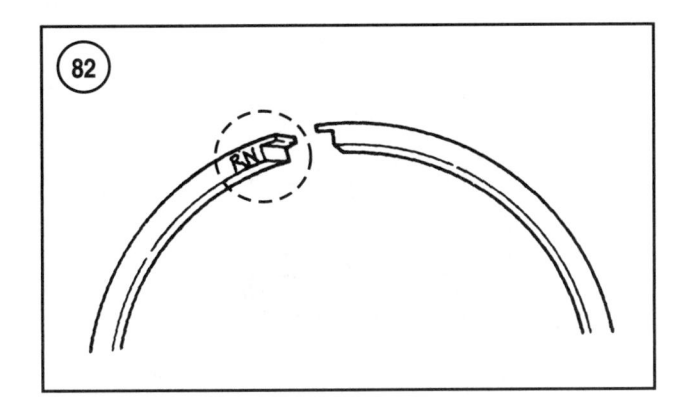

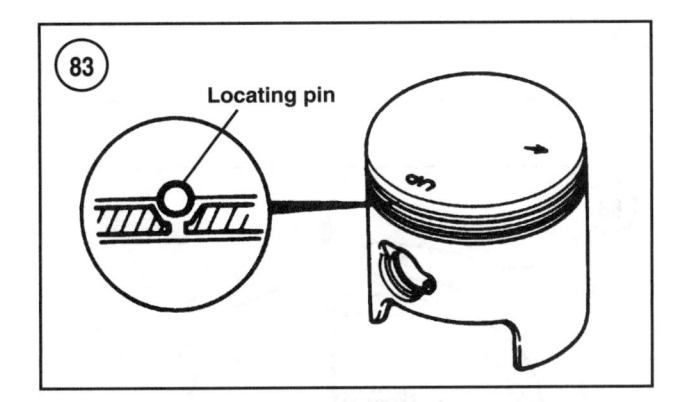

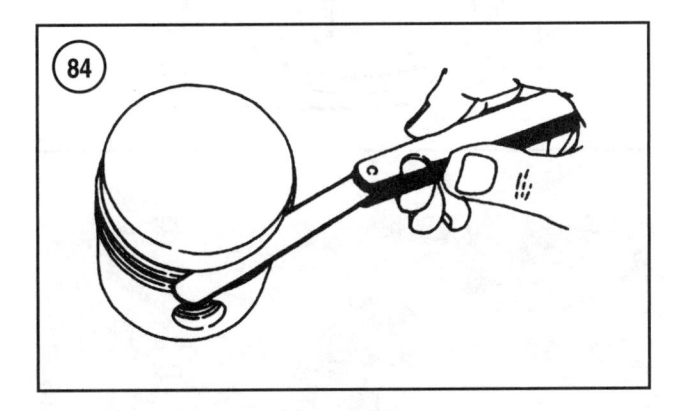

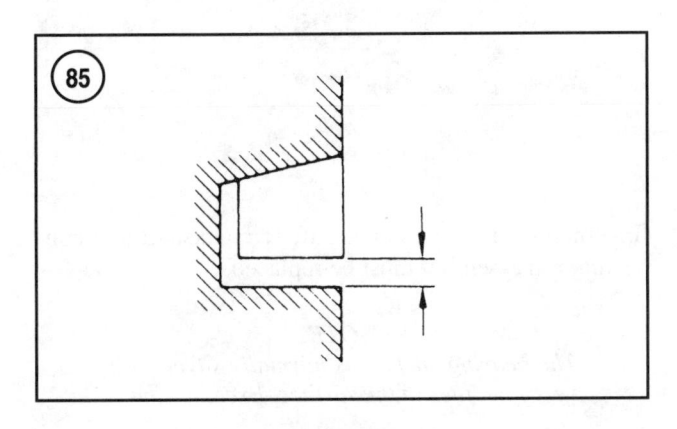

h. Carefully remove the rings from the piston. Do not scratch the piston surfaces.

4. Determine the piston skirt clearance (**Figure 86**) by subtracting the measured piston diameter from the smallest bore diameter measurement for the corresponding cylinder. The skirt clearance should be within the specification in **Table 3**.

   a. If the skirt clearance is less than the specification, repeat the piston and cylinder bore measurements. If the piston measurement is correct, have a machinist hone the cylinder to attain the specified skirt clearance.
   b. If the skirt clearance is greater than the specification, repeat the piston and cylinder bore measurements. If both measurements are correct, repeat the measurements using a new piston. New pistons usually measure at the upper limit of the specification. If the skirt clearance remains greater than the specification, bore the cylinder and install the next larger oversize piston.

5. After the cylinder bore and piston diameter are confirmed to be correct, measure the piston ring end gap as follows:

   a. Carefully compress and install the ring into the cylinder bore. Use a piston without rings to push the new ring to the depth specified in **Table 4**. See **Figure 87**.
   b. Use a feeler gauge to measure the ring end gap (**Figure 88**).
   c. Compare the feeler gauge measurement to the specification in **Table 4**.
   d. If the gap is within the specification, tag the ring to identify the cylinder number.
   e. If the gap is not within the limit, try a different, new ring in the cylinder and re-measure the gap. If the gap is correct, tag the ring with the cylinder number. If it is not correct, make sure the cylinder bore measurements are correct, then try a different, new ring.

f. Continue until rings with the correct gap have been selected for each piston. Tag all rings to identify the cylinder number.

Crankshaft and Connecting Rod

WARNING
Never allow bearings or other components to spin while being dried with compressed air. The bearings or other components may rotate at extremely high speeds and fly apart.

CAUTION
Never spin the bearings with compressed air. Spinning the bearings at high speed without lubrication will result in overheating and serious damage to bearings and the surfaces they contact.

Thoroughly wash the crankshaft and the main and connecting rod bearing assemblies with clean solvent and a parts washing brush. Thoroughly dry the crankshaft with compressed air.

All 2-70 hp models use a non-serviceable crankshaft. The connecting rods, crankpin journals and flyweights are pressed together using specialized equipment. Replace the crankshaft and connecting rod assembly if any of these components require replacement. The center main bearings are serviceable on 28 jet, 35 jet, 40 hp and 50 hp models. On 6-30 hp models, the center main bearings are non-serviceable and the crankshaft must be replaced if the bearings are faulty. The oil pump drive gear, upper main bearing and lower main bearing are serviceable on all models.

On 65 jet and 75-90 hp models, crankshaft specifications are not available from the manufacturer; however, inspect the crankshaft for worn or discolored components. Replace any suspect components. Contact a marine dealership for information on crankshaft repair facilities. Crankshaft repair is usually more economical than purchasing a new assembly.

Perform the following inspections and measurements.

Crankshaft visual inspection

1. Inspect the drive shaft splines, flywheel taper, flywheel key groove and flywheel nut threads for corrosion, cracks, excessive wear and mechanical damage. Replace the crankshaft and connecting rod assembly if these defects are noted.
2. Inspect the upper and lower seal and all bearing surfaces for excessive grooving, pitting, nicks or burrs. The seal surfaces can be polished with crocus cloth if necessary. If the defect can be felt by dragging a pencil lead or a fingernail over it, the crankshaft or crankshaft and connecting rod assembly must be replaced.

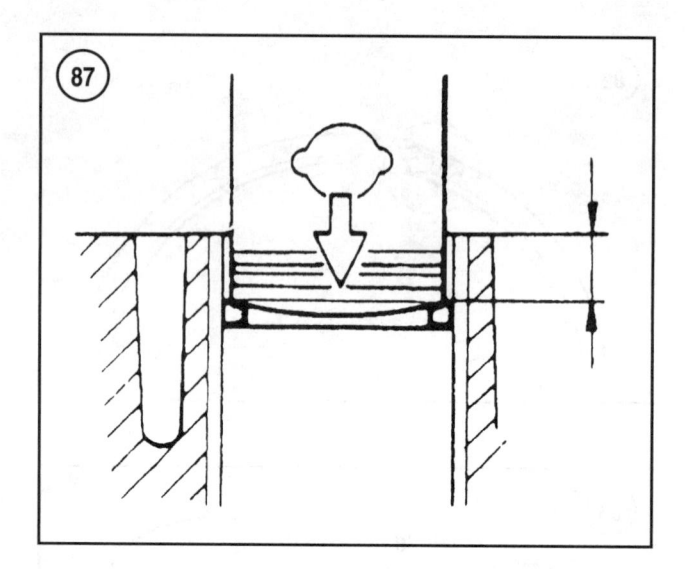

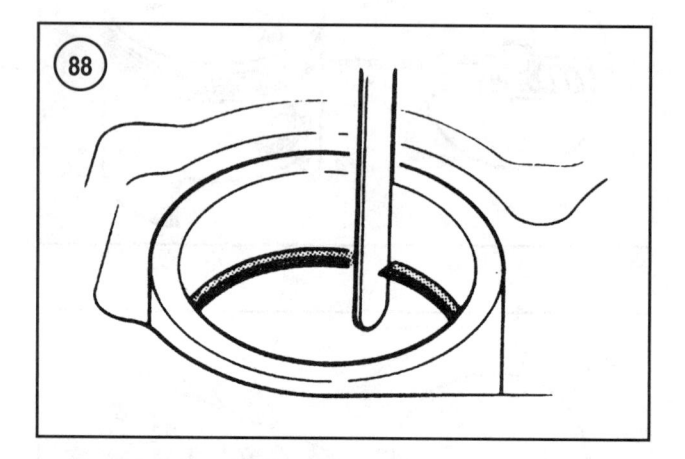

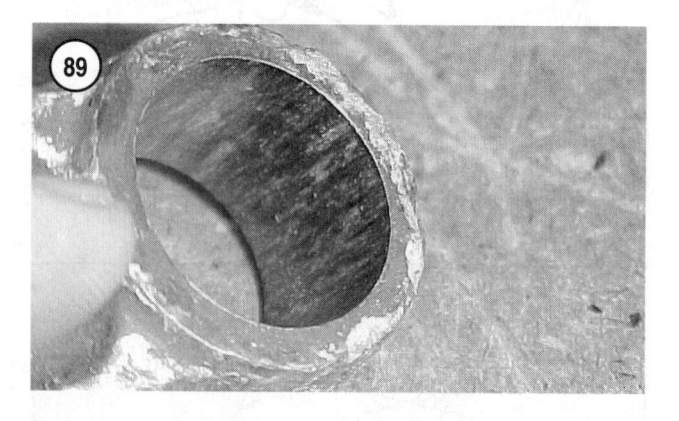

NOTE
The bearing surface is normally silver with very fine lines in the surface. Excessive heat

POWER HEAD

marks, heat discoloration and excessive or uneven wear (**Figure 90**). If the defect can be felt by dragging a pencil lead or a fingernail over it, replace the crankshaft and connecting rod assembly. Stains or marks that cannot be felt can be polished off with crocus cloth. Do not remove any more material than absolutely necessary.

4. On 2-70 hp models, move the connecting rod(s) repeatedly in the directions shown in **Figure 91**. A very small amount of movement is normal and is present on new assemblies. Significant movement indicates the big end bearing of the connecting rod has probably failed and the assembly must be replaced.

5. Visually check for bending or twisting of the I-beam section of the connecting rod(s). See **Figure 92**. Replace the connecting rod or crankshaft and connecting rod assembly if it is defective.

6. Inspect the oil pump drive gear for worn or chipped teeth, heat damage or any other damage. Replace the oil pump drive if it is damaged. Replace the oil pump driven gear (Chapter Twelve) when replacing the drive gear.

7. If the crankshaft is in a visually acceptable condition, lightly oil the crankshaft to prevent rusting.

Crankshaft bearings inspection

CAUTION
Some bearing cages are designed to hold the rollers, while others are not. The bearing cages should either hold all or none of the rollers. If some rollers fall out of the cage, but some do not, replace the bearing assembly. If the condition of any bearing is questionable, replace it.

Inspect the crankshaft main bearings as follows:

1. *Ball bearing*—Rotate the bearing. The bearing should rotate smoothly with no rough spots, catches or noise. There should be no discernible end or axial play (**Figure 93**) between the inner and outer races of the bearing. If the bearing shows any visible signs of wear, corrosion or deterioration, replace it.

2. *Roller/needle bearings*—Inspect the rollers and/or needles for water etching, pitting, chatter marks, heat discoloration and excessive or uneven wear. Inspect the cages for wear and mechanical damage. Replace bearings as an assembly. Do not attempt to replace individual rollers or needles.

Crankshaft and connecting rods measurement

All 2-70 hp models use a non-serviceable crankshaft and measurements are made with the connecting rods on the crankshaft.

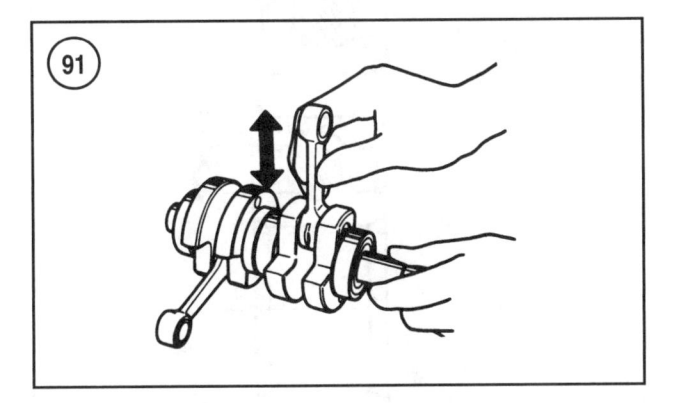

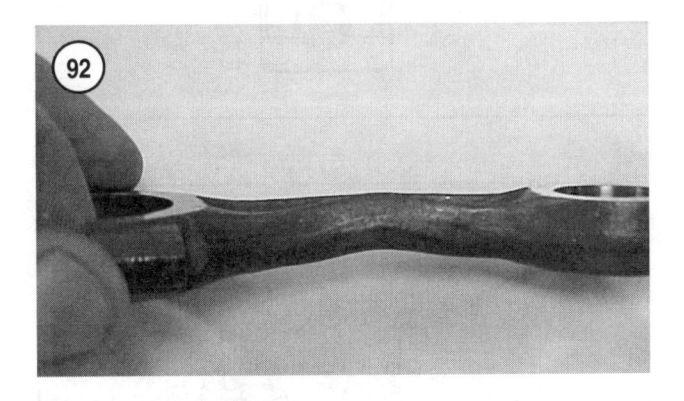

causes discoloration. Highly polished surfaces are caused by inadequate lubrication, excessive engine operating speed or excessive bearing wear. Chatter marks may occur where the needle bearings contact the bearing surfaces. Chatter marks resemble the surface of a washboard. Replace the crankshaft or crankshaft and connecting rod assembly if there are chatter marks or other defects on bearing surfaces.

3. Check the connecting rod bearing surfaces for rust, water damage (**Figure 89**), pitting, spalling, chatter

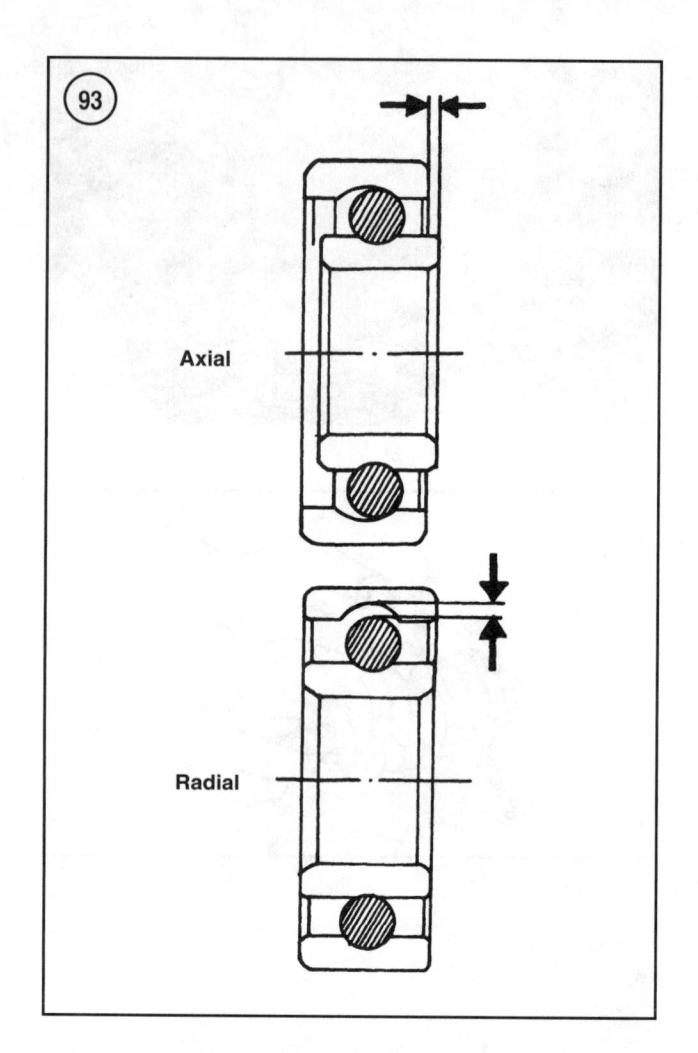

1A. On 2-5 hp models, measure the crankshaft run-out as follows:
   a. Support the crankshaft on V-block as shown in **Figure 94**. Rest the upper and lower main bearings on the V-blocks. If the bearings have been removed, rest the bearing contact surfaces on the blocks.
   b. Use a suitable mount to position the dial indicator pointer in direct contact with the crankshaft at the point indicated in **Figure 94**.
   c. Read the dial indicator while slowly rotating the crankshaft. The needle movement indicates the amount of crankshaft run-out. Record the run-out measurement.
   d. Position the dial indicator pointer in direct contact with the crankshaft near the seal contact surfaces at the bottom of the crankshaft. Measure and record the crankshaft run-out.
   e. Replace the crankshaft and connecting rod assembly if either run-out measurement exceeds the maximum specification in **Table 5**.

1B. On 6-25 hp two-cylinder models, measure the crankshaft run-out as follows:
   a. Support the crankshaft on V-blocks as shown in **Figure 94**. Rest the upper and lower main bearings on the V-blocks. If the bearings have been removed, rest the bearing contact surfaces on the blocks.
   b. Use a suitable mount to position the dial indicator pointer in direct contact with the crankshaft center main bearing (**Figure 95**).
   c. Read the dial indicator while slowly rotating the crankshaft. The needle movement indicates the amount of crankshaft run-out. Record the run-out measurement.
   d. Position the dial indicator pointer in direct contact with the crankshaft near the seal contact surfaces at the bottom of the crankshaft. Measure and record the crankshaft run-out.
   e. Position the dial indicator pointer in direct contact with the crankshaft near the seal contact surfaces at the top of the crankshaft. Measure and record the crankshaft run-out.
   f. Replace the crankshaft and connecting rod assembly if any run-out measurement exceeds the maximum specification in **Table 5**.

1C. On 25 hp three-cylinder and 30-90 hp models, measure the crankshaft run-out as follows:
   a. Support the crankshaft on V-block as shown in **Figure 96**. Rest the upper and lower main bearings on the V-blocks. If the bearings have been removed, rest the bearing contact surfaces on the blocks.

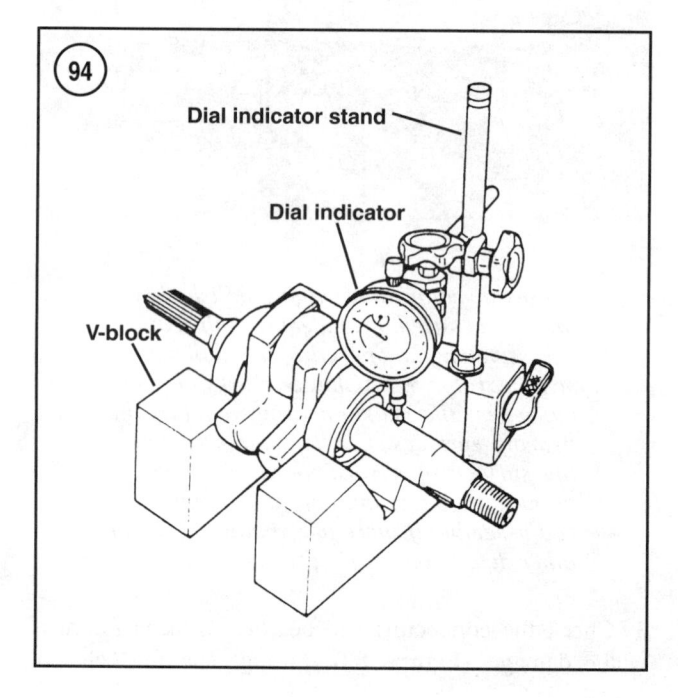

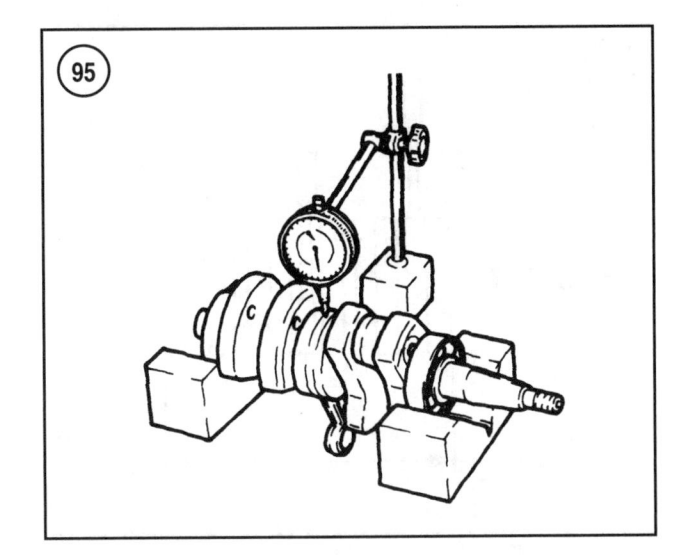

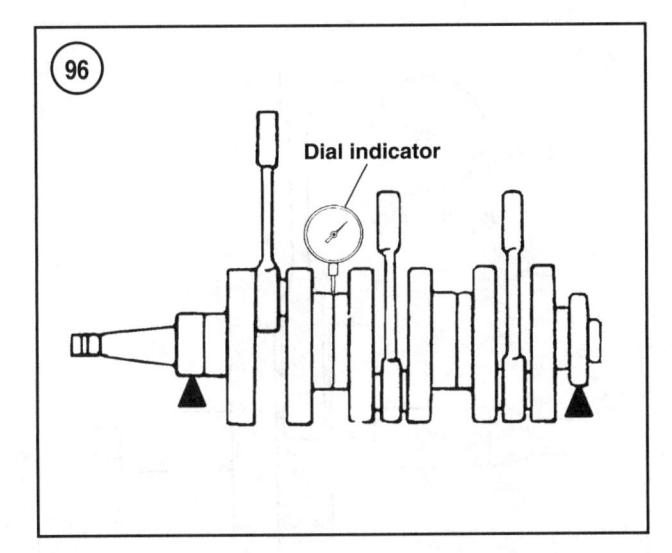

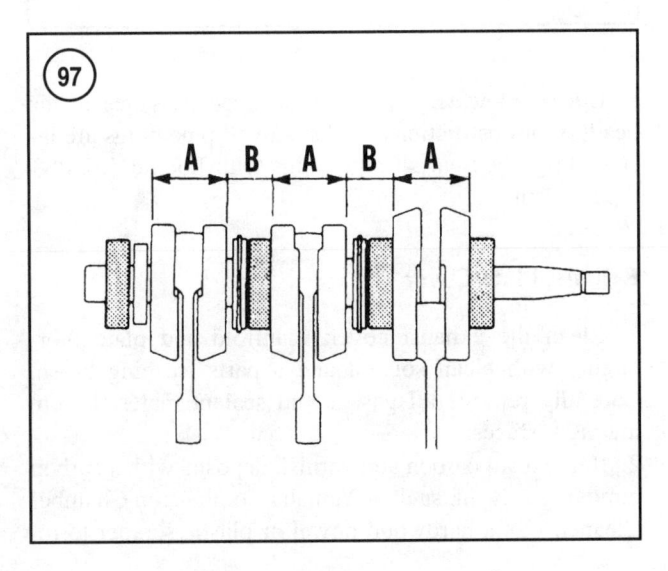

b. Use a suitable mount to position the dial indicator pointer in direct contact with the upper crankshaft center main bearing or bearing contact surfaces (**Figure 96**).
c. Read the dial indicator while slowly rotating the crankshaft. The needle movement indicates the amount of crankshaft run-out. Record the run-out measurement.
d. Position the dial indicator in direct contact with the lower center main bearing. Measure and record the crankshaft run-out.
e. Position the dial indicator pointer in direct contact with the crankshaft near the seal contact surfaces at the bottom of the crankshaft. Measure and record the crankshaft run-out.
f. Position the dial indicator pointer in direct contact with the crankshaft near the seal contact surfaces at the top of the crankshaft. Measure and record the crankshaft run-out.
g. Replace the crankshaft or crankshaft and connecting rod assembly if any run-out measurement exceeds the maximum specification in **Table 5**.

2. On 2-70 hp models, use an accurate caliper to measure the distance from the outer edge of one flyweight to the outer edge of the corresponding flyweight (A, **Figure 97**). Record the flyweight width and repeat the measurement for each pair of flyweights. If any measurement is not within the specification in **Table 5**, replace the crankshaft and rod assembly.

3. On 6-70 hp (except 65 jet) models, use an accurate caliper to measure the spacing between the edges of the flyweights for adjacent cylinders (B, **Figure 97**). Record the measurement and measure the spacing for the next adjacent cylinder (three-cylinder models). If any flyweight spacing measurement is not within the specification in **Table 5**, replace the crankshaft and rod assembly.

4. On 25 hp three-cylinder and 30-70 hp models, use an accurate caliper to measure the distance from the edge of the upper flyweight to the edge of the lower flyweight (**Figure 98**). If the measurement is not within the specification in **Table 5**, replace the crankshaft and connecting rod assembly.

5. On 2-70 hp models, measure the connecting rod axial play as follows:
    a. Secure the crankshaft and rod assembly in a horizontal position.
    b. Use a sturdy mount to position a dial indicator perpendicular to the connecting rod as shown in **Figure 99**. Place the pointer in contact with the connecting rod on the flat surface closest to the piston pin boss.
    c. Observe the dial indicator while moving the connecting rod in the direction shown. Note the dial

indictor reading when the rod reaches each limit of its travel. The amount of needle movement indicates the axial play measurement.

d. Record the measurement. Measure the axial play of each connecting rod.

e. Compare the measurements with the specification in **Table 5**. Replace the crankshaft and connecting rod assembly if any measurement exceeds the maximum specification in **Table 5**.

6. On 2-70 hp models, use feeler gauges to measure the connecting rod side clearance (**Figure 100**) for each cylinder. Select the feeler gauge that can be passed between the flyweight and the connecting rod with a slight drag. If all side clearance measurements are not within the specification in **Table 5**, replace the crankshaft and connecting rod assembly.

Seal Housing/Covers

1. Clean the seal housing/covers(s) thoroughly with clean solvent and a parts washing brush. Carefully remove all sealant material from mating surfaces.

2. Inspect the seal bore(s) for nicks, gouges or corrosion that would cause the seal to leak around its outer diameter. Replace the housing or cover if the seal bore is damaged.

3. Inspect the end cap mating surface and O-ring groove for nicks, grooves, cracks, corrosion or distortion. Replace the end cap(s) if the defect could cause a leak.

Cylinder Head(s)

1. Clean the cylinder head(s) or block cover thoroughly with clean solvent and a parts washing brush. Carefully remove all gasket and sealant material from mating surfaces.

2. Remove all carbon and varnish deposits from the combustion chambers of the cylinder head(s) with a carbon removing solvent, such as Yamaha Combustion Chamber Cleaner. Use a sharpened hardwood dowel or plastic scraper to remove stubborn deposits. Do not scratch, nick or gouge the combustion chambers.

3. Check the cylinder head(s) and block cover for cracks, fractures, distortion or other damage. Check the cylinder head(s) for stripped or damaged threads. Refer to *Sealing Surfaces* at the beginning of this chapter and check the cylinder head(s) for warp. Remove minor imperfections as described in *Sealing Surfaces*.

4. Inspect all gasket surfaces or O-ring and water seal grooves for nicks, grooves, cracks, corrosion or distortion. Replace the cylinder head or block cover if the defect is severe enough to cause a leak.

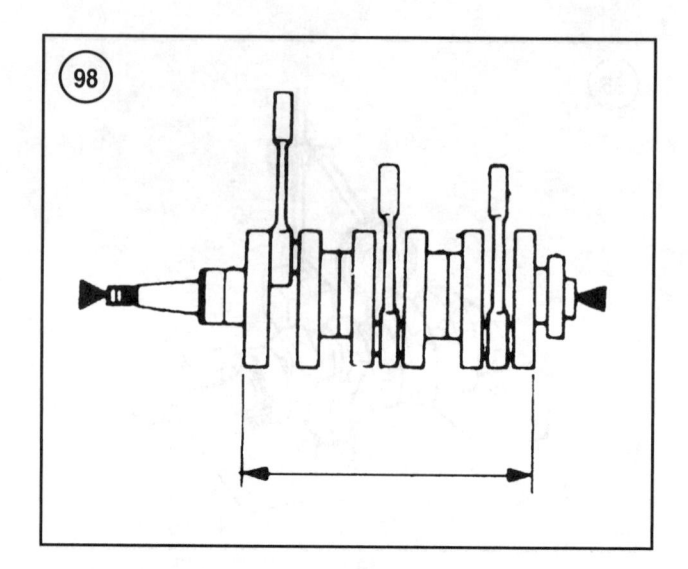

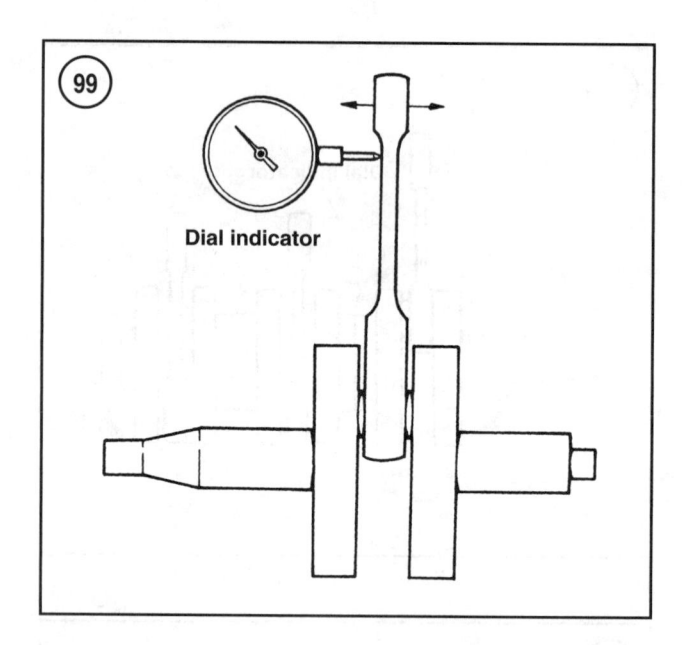

5. Check all water, oil and fuel bleed passages in the head(s) for obstructions. Make sure all pipe plugs are installed tightly. Seal all pipe plugs with Loctite 567 PST pipe sealant.

Exhaust Plate/Cover

1. Clean the exhaust cover, manifold and plate thoroughly with clean solvent and a parts washing brush. Carefully remove all gasket and sealant material from mating surfaces.

2. Remove all carbon and varnish deposits with a carbon removing solvent, such as Yamaha Combustion Chamber Cleaner. Use a hardwood dowel or plastic scraper to re-

POWER HEAD

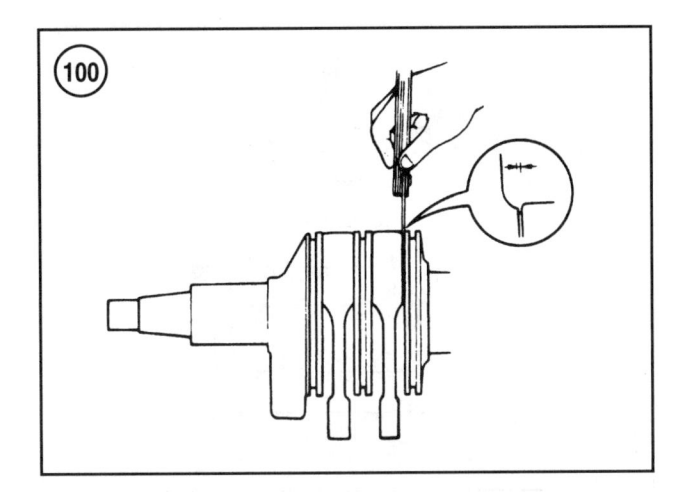

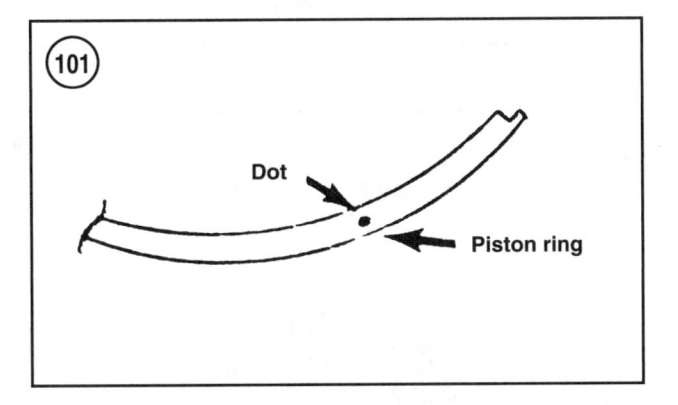

100

101 Dot — Piston ring

move stubborn deposits. Do not scratch, nick or gouge the mating surfaces.

3. Inspect the component and all gasket surfaces for nicks, grooves, cracks, corrosion or distortion. Replace the cover/manifold/plate if the defect is severe enough to cause a leak.

Thermostat Cover

1. Clean the thermostat cover and mating surface with a suitable solvent and a stiff plastic bristle brush. Carefully remove all mineral deposits, gasket material and sealant from the cover.

2. Inspect the cover for corrosion, cracking or other damage. Replace the cover as necessary.

POWER HEAD ASSEMBLY

Before beginning assembly, complete all applicable sections of the *Components Inspection* in this chapter.

Review *Sealing Surfaces*; *Fasteners and Torque*; and *Lubricants, Sealants and Adhesives* in this chapter.

Replace all seals, O-rings, gaskets, piston pin lock rings, piston rings and all needle bearings any time a power head is disassembled. If the original needle bearings must be reused, reinstall them in their original positions.

Any identification mark on a piston ring (**Figure 101**) must face up when installed. Some pistons use a combination of ring styles. Rings may be rectangular, semi-keystone, or full-keystone.

Rectangular and full-keystone rings fit their grooves in either direction, but they must be installed with their identification mark facing up.

Semi-keystone rings are beveled 7°-10° on the upper surface only. These rings will not fit their groove correctly if they are installed upside down. Carefully examine the construction of the rings and look for identification marks before installation. The beveled side must face up, matching the ring groove, and is identified by the mark on the upper surface.

Lubricate the needle and roller bearings, pistons, rings and cylinder bores with two-stroke outboard engine oil during assembly.

A selection of torque wrenches is essential for correct assembly and to ensure maximum longevity of the power head assembly. Failing to torque items as specified will cause premature power head failure.

Most power head torque specifications are in **Table 1**. Standard torque specifications are in Chapter One. Use the standard torque specifications for fasteners not listed in **Table 1**.

Make sure the mating surfaces are free of gasket material, sealant residue, dirt, oil, grease or any other contaminant. Use oil, petroleum and wax-free solvents, such as lacquer thinner, acetone, and isopropyl alcohol for the final preparation of mating surfaces.

2-5 hp One-Cylinder Models

To assist with component orientation, refer to **Figures 23-25** during the assembly procedure.

> *CAUTION*
> *Use a slot in the table of the press to support the flyweight nearest the bearing when pressing bearings onto the crankshaft. The crankshaft and rod assembly may bend if the opposite end of the crankshaft is resting on the table. Use suitable blocks to support the flyweight if the slot in the table will not accommodate the crankshaft and rod assembly.*

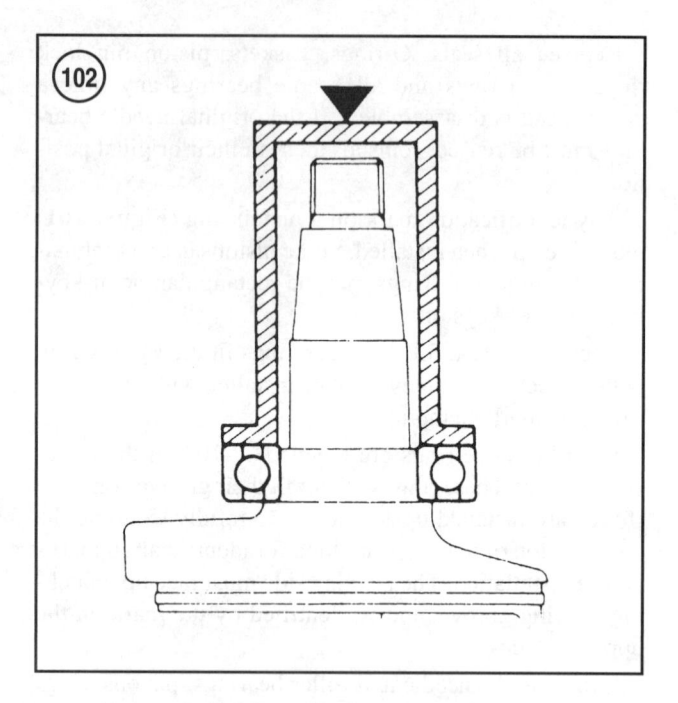

1. If the upper main bearings were removed, install them onto the crankshaft as follows:
   a. Select a section of tubing or another suitable tool to press the upper main bearing onto the crankshaft. The tool must slide freely over the crankshaft, but only contact the inner race of the bearing. The tool must be of sufficient length to prevent the press from contacting the crankshaft threads.
   b. Support the upper flyweight of the crankshaft on the table of a press with the flywheel end facing up.
   c. Apply two-stroke outboard engine oil to the surfaces, then slide the bearing over the crankshaft taper. The numbered side of the bearing must face up. Rest the bearing on the step.
   d. Slide the installation tool over the crankshaft and seat it against the inner bearing race (**Figure 102**).
   e. Press on the tool until the bearing seats against the step on the crankshaft.
2. If the lower main bearing was removed, install it onto the crankshaft as follows:
   a. Select a section of tubing or another suitable tool to press the lower main bearing onto the crankshaft. The tool must slide over the crankshaft, but only contact the inner race of the bearing. The tool must be of sufficient length to prevent the press from contacting the end of the crankshaft.
   b. Support the lower flyweight on the table of a press with the flywheel end facing downward.
   c. Apply two-stroke outboard engine oil to the surfaces, then slide the bearing over the crankshaft. The numbered side of the bearing must face up. Rest the bearing on the step.
   d. Slide the installation tool over the crankshaft and seat it against the inner bearing race (**Figure 103**).
   e. Press on the tool until the bearing seats against the step on the crankshaft.
3. Clamp the crankshaft in a vise with protective jaws. The flywheel end of the crankshaft must face up. Clamp on the flyweight part of the crankshaft.
4. Locate the UP or arrow mark on the piston. When installed on the connecting rod, the mark must face toward the flywheel end of the crankshaft (**Figure 104**).

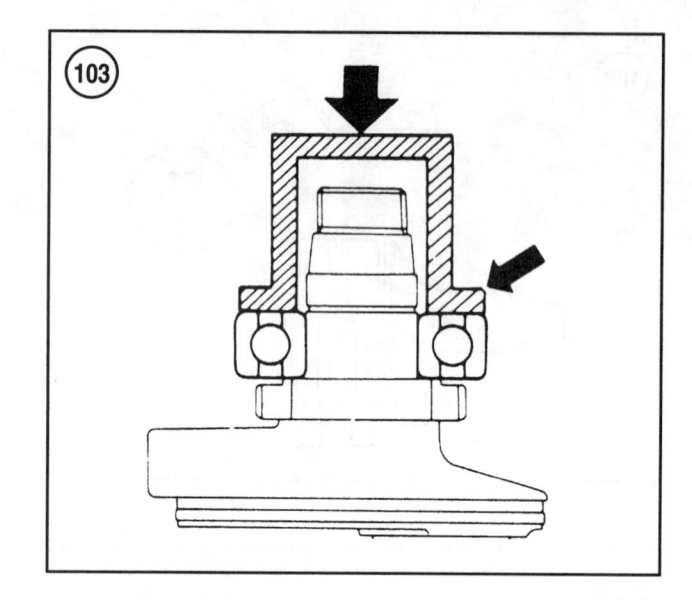

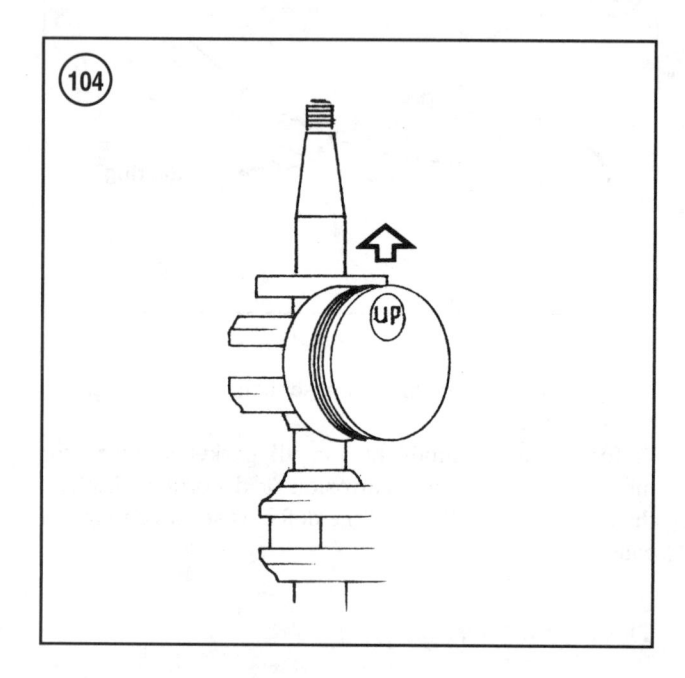

POWER HEAD

105

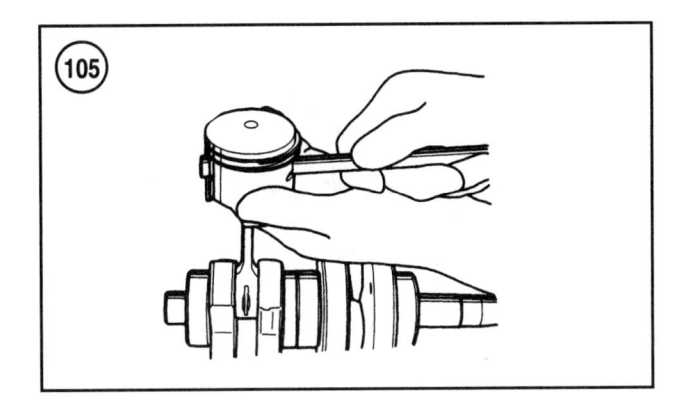

106

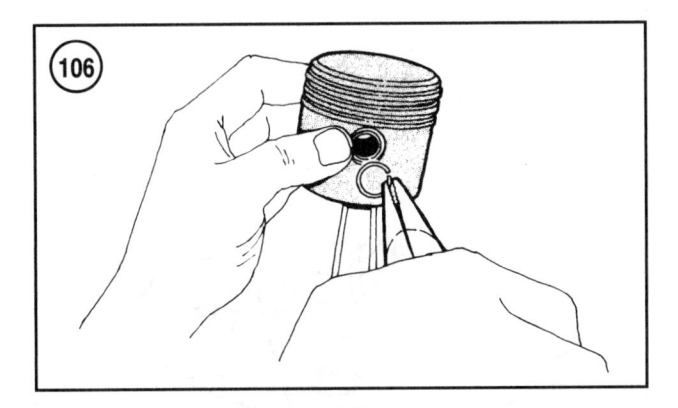

107 PISTON RING INSTALLATION

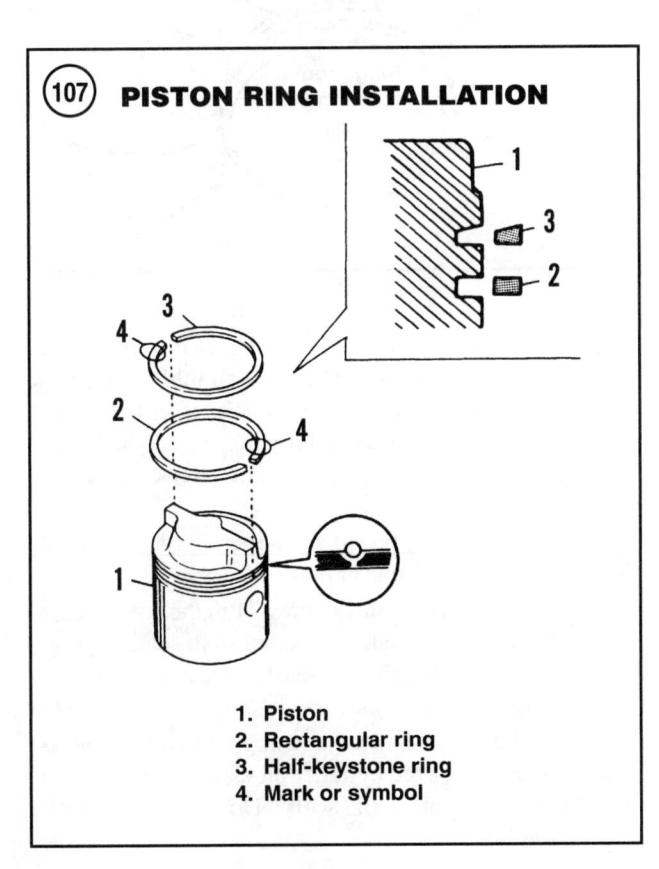

1. Piston
2. Rectangular ring
3. Half-keystone ring
4. Mark or symbol

WARNING
Use protective eyewear when working with the power head. Piston pin lockrings and other components may unexpectedly spring free.

NOTE
If piston pin installation is difficult, heat the piston to approximately 60° C (140° F) with a portable hair dryer. The piston bore expands when heated, allowing easier pin installation.

5. Install the piston onto the connecting rod as follows:
   a. Select a suitable steel rod, socket or section of tubing to install the piston pin into the piston. The installation tool must be slightly smaller in diameter than the piston pin. Piston pin diameters are listed in **Table 3**.
   b. Lubricate the caged needle bearing with two-stroke outboard oil, then slide the bearing into the connecting rod bore.
   c. Install the piston over the connecting rod and align the piston pin bores in the piston and connecting rod. Make sure the caged needle bearing remains centered in the connecting rod bore.
   d. Lubricate the piston pin with two-stroke outboard oil. Maintain pin bore alignment and use the installation tool to push the piston pin into the bores (**Figure 105**). Work carefully to avoid damaging the bearing. Push the piston pin in enough to fully expose the lockring groove on each side of the piston.
   e. Use needlenose pliers to insert the lockring into the groove in the piston pin bore (**Figure 106**). Repeat this step to install the lockring into the groove on the other side of the piston.
   f. Inspect the piston to make sure the lockrings are fully seated into the grooves.

CAUTION
Be careful when spreading the rings for installation onto the piston. Spread the gap ends only enough to allow the ring to slide over the piston. The ring will break or crack if it is spread too much.

NOTE
Various types of piston rings are used. A rectangular ring (2, Figure 107), full-keystone or half-keystone (3) may be used. The piston may use one or a combination of types. Inspect the piston ring and ring groove before installing any of the rings to ensure the proper ring is installed. The mark

7

on the ring (4, **Figure 107**) must face upward the piston dome.

6. Install the piston rings onto the piston as follows:
   a. Use a ring expander to spread the bottom ring enough to clear the top of the piston (**Figure 108**). The mark on the ring (4, **Figure 107**) must face up. Avoid scratching the piston. Slide the ring over the piston and release the ring into the bottom ring groove.
   b. Repeat this procedure for the top ring. The mark on the top ring must face up.
   c. Apply a coat of two-stroke outboard engine oil to all surfaces of the piston.

CAUTION
Work carefully and patiently when installing the piston into the cylinder bore. Never use excessive force to insert the piston. Excessive force can break the piston ring(s) or damage other components.

NOTE
Install the piston, connecting rod and crankshaft into the cylinder block as an assembly. A ring compressor is not required. A taper in the crankcase near the bottom of the bore compresses the rings during piston installation.

7. Install the piston, rod and crankshaft assembly into the cylinder block as follows:
   a. Apply a generous coat of two-stroke outboard oil to the cylinder bores, crankshaft bearings and connecting rod bearings.
   b. Position the ring gaps over the locating pins as indicated in **Figure 109**. The gaps must remain over the locating pins during piston installation.
   c. Position the crankshaft over the crankcase with the flywheel taper end facing the top of the cylinder block. Carefully lower the crankshaft and insert the piston into the bore.
   d. Guide the piston into the bore while carefully and gently rocking the piston to compress the rings. Do not rotate the piston in the bore. If the piston will not enter the bore, remove the assembly and inspect the ring gap position.
   e. Carefully guide the crankshaft main bearings into their recesses in the cylinder block while lowering the crankshaft into the cylinder block.

8. Maintain downward pressure on the crankshaft to prevent the crankshaft from moving out of the cylinder block. Look into the exhaust opening and slowly rotate the crankshaft until the piston rings span the exhaust port (**Figure 110**). Use a blunt tip screwdriver to carefully press *in* on each ring. The rings should spring back when the screwdriver is pulled back. If either of the rings does not spring back, remove the crankshaft, connecting rod and piston assembly, and check for broken piston rings.

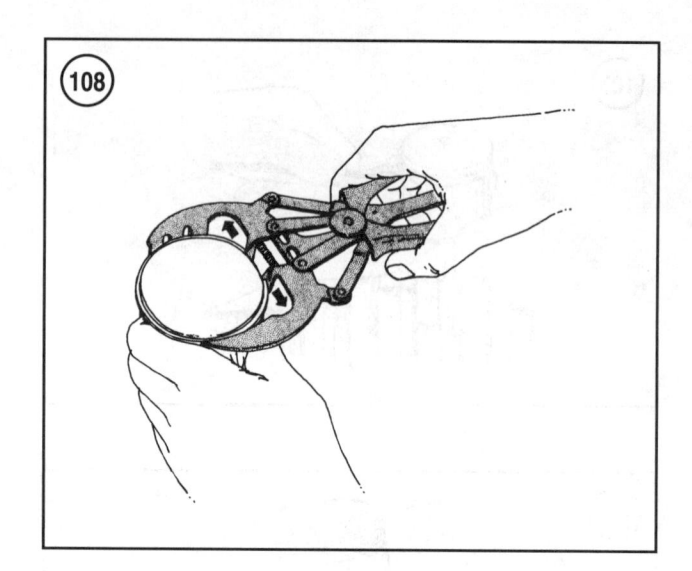

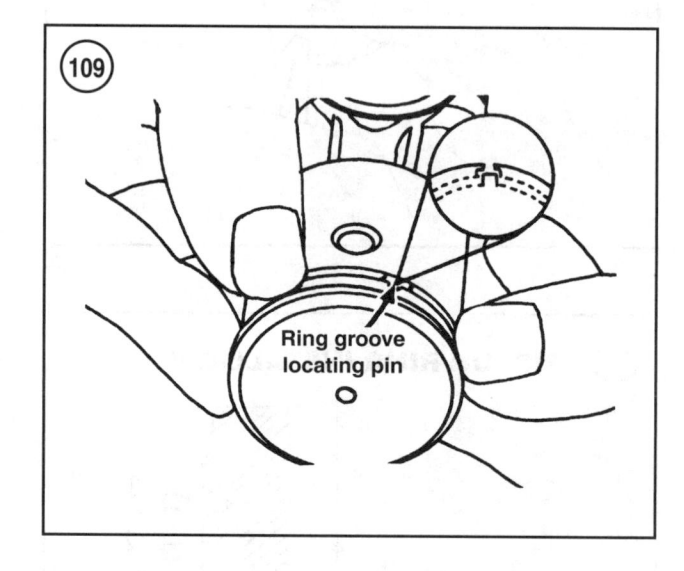

9A. On 2 hp models, install the upper and lower crankshaft seals onto the crankshaft as follows:
   a. Apply a light coat of Loctite 271 to the outer diameter of the upper and lower crankshaft seals. Apply a coat of Yamaha All-Purpose Grease or equivalent to the lips of both seals.
   b. Pull the crankshaft connecting rod and piston assembly out of the cylinder block just enough to install the crankshaft seals. Do not remove the assembly.

POWER HEAD

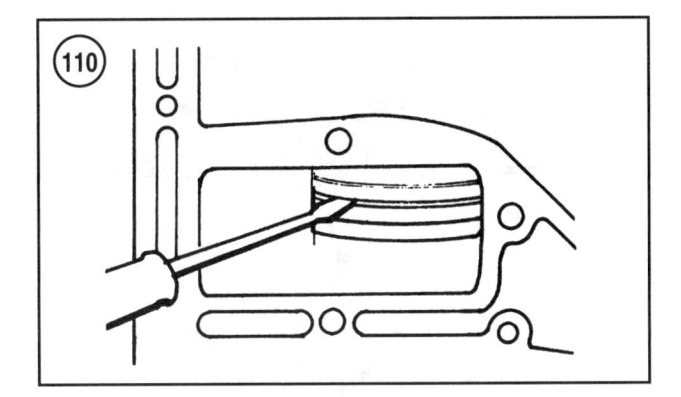

c. Slide the upper crankshaft seal over the tapered end of the crankshaft. The lip (open) side of the seal must face *toward* the connecting rod.

d. Slide the lower crankshaft seal over the square lower end of the crankshaft. The lip (open) side of the seal must face *away from* the connecting rod.

e. Guide both seals into their respective recesses in the cylinder block while lowering the crankshaft into the block. Seat both bearings and seals into the cylinder block.

9B. On 3 hp models, install the upper crankshaft seal onto the crankshaft as follows:

  a. Apply a light coat of Loctite 271 to the outer diameter of the upper crankshaft seal. Apply a coat of Yamaha All-Purpose Grease or equivalent to the seal lip.

  b. Pull the crankshaft connecting rod and piston assembly out of the cylinder block just enough to install the upper crankshaft seal and spacer. Do not remove the assembly.

  c. Slide the spacers (7, **Figure 24**) onto the upper and lower ends of the crankshaft. Seat the spacers against the main bearings.

  d. Slide the upper crankshaft seal over the tapered end of the crankshaft. The lip (open) side of the seal must face *toward* the connecting rod.

  e. Guide the upper seal and both spacers into their respective recesses in the cylinder block while lowering the crankshaft into the block. Seat both main bearings, both spacers and the upper seal into the cylinder block.

9C. On 4 and 5 hp models, install the lower crankshaft seal onto the crankshaft as follows:

  a. Apply a light coat of Loctite 271 to the outer diameter of the lower crankshaft seal. Apply a coat of Yamaha All-Purpose Grease or equivalent to the seal lip.

  b. Pull the crankshaft connecting rod and piston assembly out of the cylinder block just enough to install the lower crankshaft seal and spacer. Do not remove the assembly.

  c. Slide the spacers (9, **Figure 25**) onto the upper and lower ends of the crankshaft. Seat the spacers against the main bearings.

  d. Slide the lower crankshaft seal over the square lower end of the crankshaft. The lip (open) side of the seal must face *away from* the connecting rod.

  e. Guide the lower seal and both spacers into their respective recesses in the cylinder block while lowering the crankshaft into the block. Seat both main bearings, both spacers and the lower seal into the cylinder block.

10A. On 3 hp models, install new lower crankshaft seals into the exhaust tube as follows:

  a. Select sections of tubing or sockets to use as seal installation tools. The tools must contact the outer case of the seal, but not contact the seal bore during installation.

  b. Apply a light coat of Loctite 271 to the outer diameter of both seals and their respective bores in the exhaust tube.

  c. Lightly clamp the exhaust tube (16, **Figure 24**) in a vise with protective jaws. The seal openings must face up.

  d. Insert the smaller diameter (lower) seal into the bore opening with the lip side facing down. Use the tool to drive the seal into the bore until it is fully seated.

  e. Insert the larger diameter seal (8, **Figure 24**) into the bore opening with the lip side facing down. Use the tool to drive the seal into the bore until it is fully seated.

  f. Apply a generous coat of Yamaha All-Purpose Grease or equivalent to the seal lips.

10B. On 4 and 5 hp models, install a new drive shaft seal and O-ring into the lower seal housing as follows:

  a. Select a section of tubing or a socket to use as seal installation tool. The tool must contact the outer case of the seal, but not contact the seal bore during installation.

  b. Apply a light coat of Loctite 271 to the outer diameter of the seal and its bore in the seal housing.

  c. Lightly clamp the seal housing (3, **Figure 29**) in a vise with protective jaws. The seal openings must face up.

  d. Insert the seal (4, **Figure 29**) into the bore opening with the lip side facing down. Use the tool to drive the seal into the bore until it is fully seated.

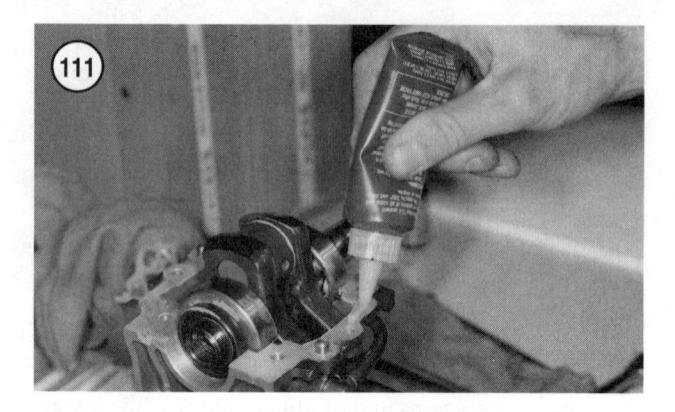

e. Lubricate the O-ring (5, **Figure 29**) with Yamaha All-Purpose Grease or equivalent. Install the O-ring into the groove in the seal housing.

f. Apply a generous coating of Yamaha All-Purpose Grease onto the seal lip.

11. Install the crankcase cover onto the cylinder block as follows:

   a. Apply a continuous bead of Loctite Gasket Maker to the mating surfaces of the cylinder block (**Figure 111**). Apply the sealant bead on the inside of the crankcase bolt opening as shown in **Figure 112**.

   b. Install the crankcase cover and seat it on the cylinder block.

   c. On 2 hp models, install the intake manifold/reed housing as described in Chapter Five. Do not install the mounting bolts at this time.

   d. Apply Loctite 572 to the six crankcase cover bolts. Hand-thread the bolts into the cover.

   e. Tighten the bolts in two steps to the specification in **Table 1**. Use the tightening sequence shown in **Figure 113**.

   f. Slowly rotate the crankshaft. Remove the cover and check for improper bearing, seal or spacer installation if there is binding or roughness. Check for broken piston rings if there is a clicking noise. Clean the mating surface and apply a new bead of sealant each time the crankcase is removed.

12A. On 3 hp models, install the exhaust tube as follows:

   a. Install a new gasket onto the exhaust tube mating surface.

   b. Install the seals over the crankshaft while seating the exhaust tube onto the cylinder block. Align the bolt openings.

   c. Apply Loctite 572 to the threads, then hand-thread the six bolts and washers into the exhaust tube and cylinder block.

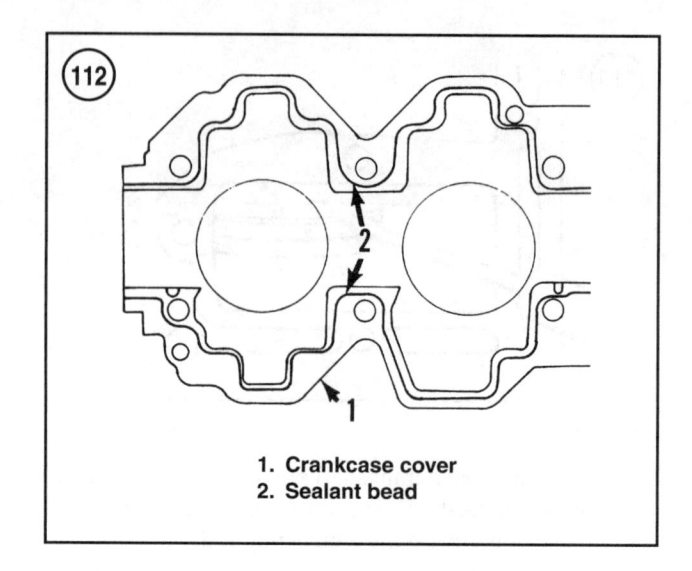

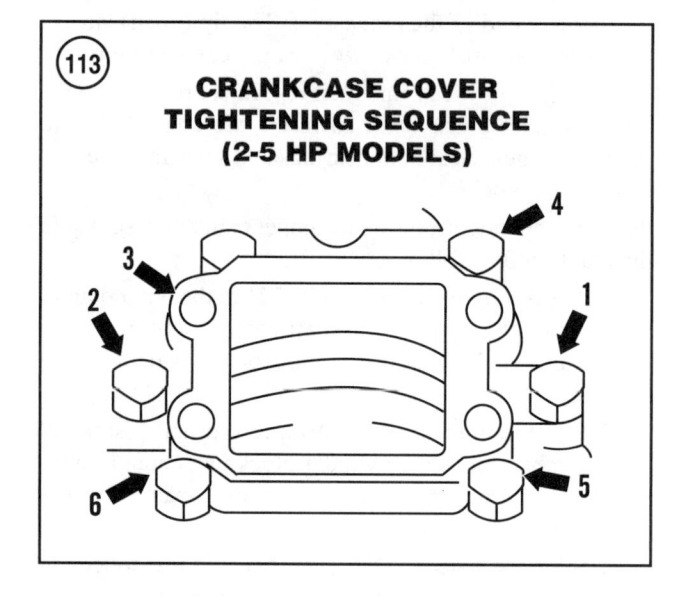

   d. Tighten the bolts in two steps to the specification in **Table 1**. Use the tightening sequence shown in **Figure 114**.

12B. On 4 and 5 hp models, install the lower seal housing as follows:

   a. Install the seal over the crankshaft while seating the seal housing (3, **Figure 29**) onto the cylinder block. Align the bolt opening.

   b. Install the bolt and washer (1 and 2, **Figure 29**). Tighten the bolt to the specification in **Table 1**.

13A. On 2 hp models, install the cylinder head as follows:

   a. Install a new head gasket (10, **Figure 23**) onto the cylinder head. The tab on the gasket must face up.

POWER HEAD 325

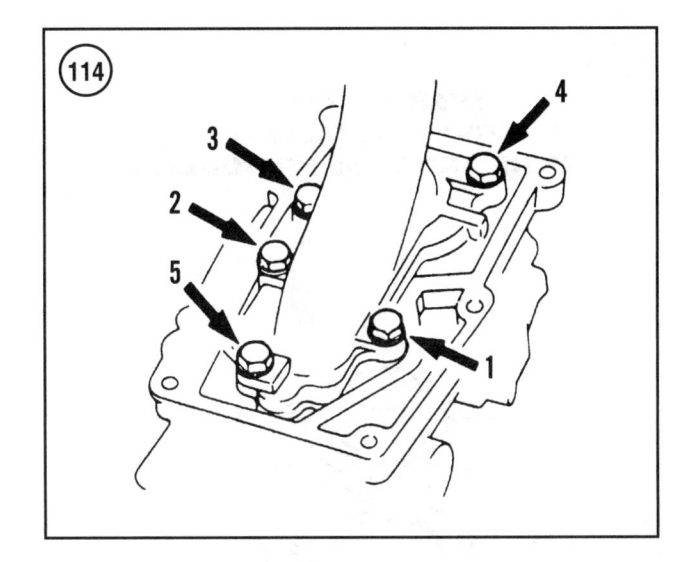

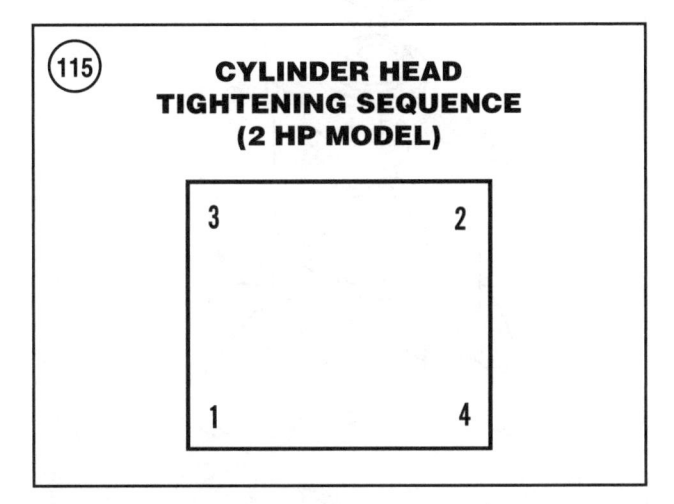

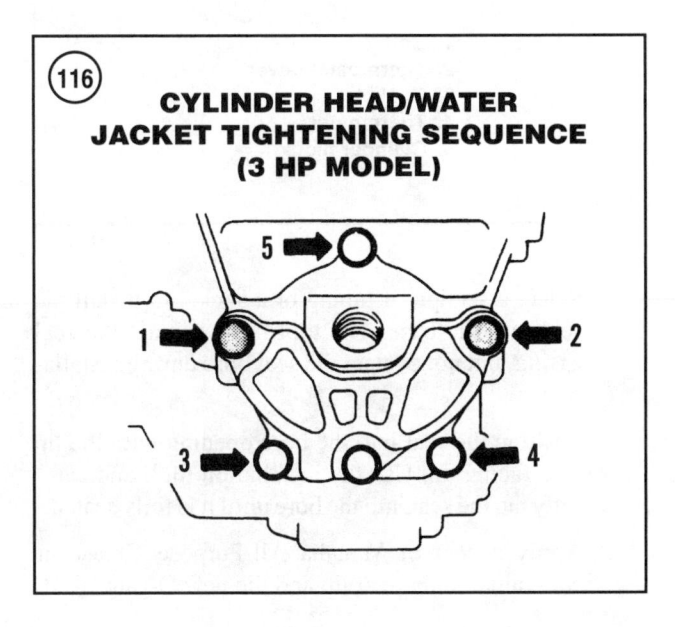

114

115 CYLINDER HEAD TIGHTENING SEQUENCE (2 HP MODEL)

```
3         2


1         4
```

116 CYLINDER HEAD/WATER JACKET TIGHTENING SEQUENCE (3 HP MODEL)

b. Install the cylinder head (11, **Figure 23**) onto the cylinder block. The fuel tank support casting must face up.

c. Apply a light coat of Loctite 572 to the threads of the four mounting bolts. Hand-thread the bolts into the cylinder head and block.

d. Tighten the bolts in two steps to the specification in **Table 1**. Use the tightening sequence shown in **Figure 115**.

13B. On 3 hp models, install the cylinder head and water jacket cover as follows:

a. Install a new gasket (13, **Figure 24**) onto the water jacket cover (12). Install the water jacket cover onto the cylinder head (11, **Figure 24**).

b. Apply a light coat of two-stroke engine oil to the threads then insert the three longer bolts (14, **Figure 24**) into the water jacket and cylinder head.

c. Install a new head gasket (10, **Figure 24**) onto the cylinder head. Make sure the three bolts pass through the bolt openings in the gasket.

d. Mount the cylinder head on the cylinder block. The fuel tank support casting must face up. Hand-thread the three bolts into the cylinder block to secure the head.

e. Apply a light coat of two-stroke engine oil to the threads, then hand-thread the two bolts (14, **Figure 24**) and washers into the cylinder head and cylinder block.

f. Tighten the five bolts in two steps to the specification in **Table 1**. Use the tightening sequence shown in **Figure 116**.

13C. On 4 and 5 hp models, install the water jacket covers onto the cylinder block as follows:

a. Install a new gasket (18, **Figure 25**) onto the rear water jacket cover (19).

b. Install the water jacket cover with the gasket onto the cylinder block. Hold the jacket in firm contact with the cylinder head, then hand-thread the five bolts (20, **Figure 25**) into the water jacket.

c. Tighten the water jacket bolts in two steps to the specification in **Table 1**. Use the tightening sequence shown in **Figure 117**.

14. On 3 hp models, install the thermostat and cover as follows:

a. Insert the thermostat (4, **Figure 118**) into the cylinder block opening. The copper colored cylindrical end of the thermostat must face toward the cylinder block. Seat the thermostat against the step in the bore.

b. Install a new gasket (3, **Figure 118**) onto the cylinder block (5). Install the thermostat cover (2, **Figure 118**) onto the gasket.

7

117 REAR WATER JACKET COVER TIGHTENING SEQUENCE (4 AND 5 HP MODELS)

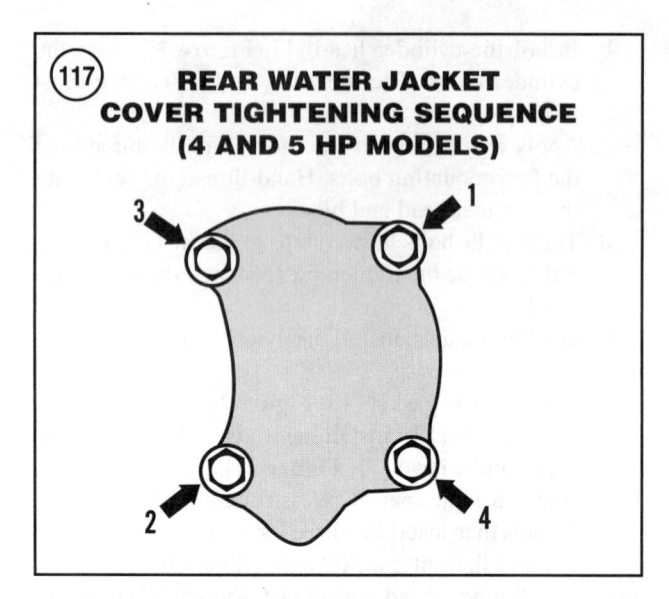

118 THERMOSTAT AND COVER INSTALLATION (3 HP AND 20-50 HP MODELS)

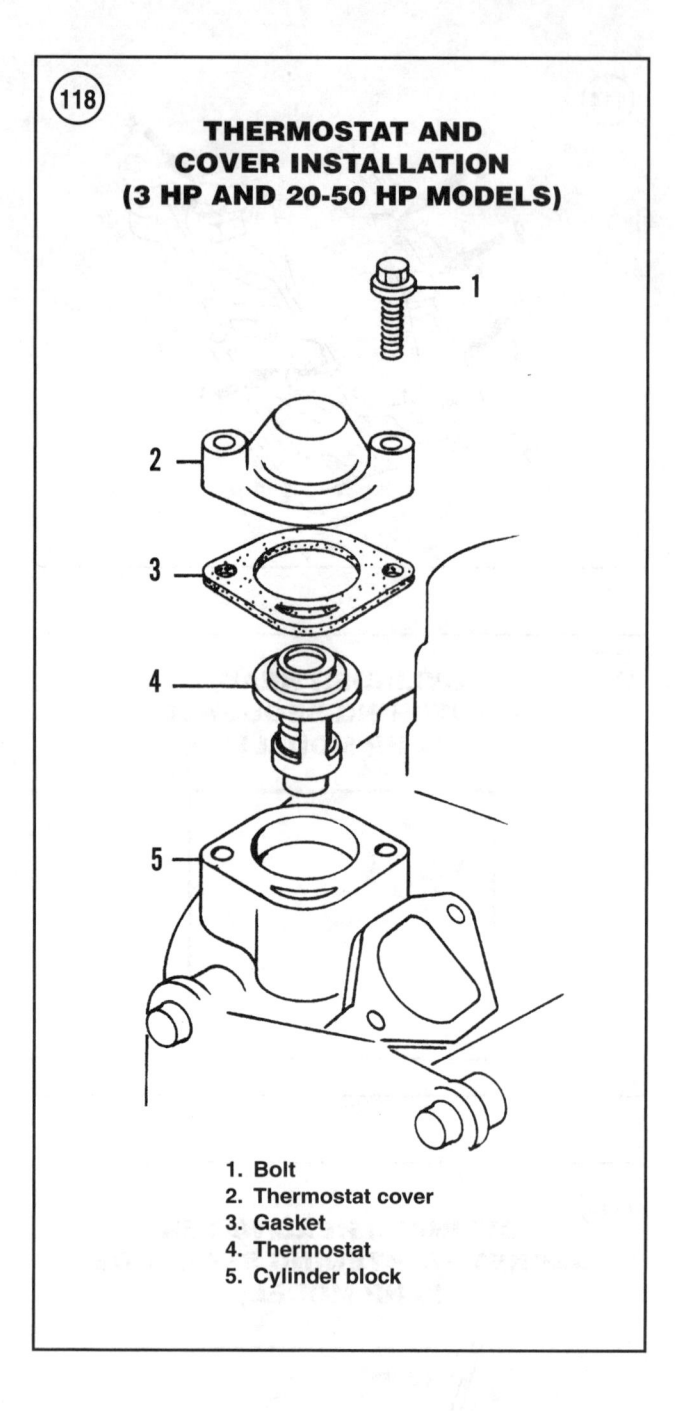

1. Bolt
2. Thermostat cover
3. Gasket
4. Thermostat
5. Cylinder block

c. Install and securely tighten the two bolts (1, **Figure 118**).

15. On 4 and 5 hp models, install the exhaust plate, exhaust cover and thermostat as follows:
   a. Place the exhaust cover (16, **Figure 25**) on a work surface with the external surface facing down.
   a. Install a new gasket (17, **Figure 25**) onto the inner side of the exhaust cover (16).
   b. If so equipped, install the thermostat into the opening in the exhaust plate (15, **Figure 25**). The copper colored cylindrical shaped end must face toward the cylinder block.
   c. Install a new gasket onto the inner surface of the exhaust cover.
   d. Position the exhaust plate on the exhaust cover and gasket. Temporarily insert two of the mounting bolts into the cover to align the bolt openings.
   e. Align the mounting bolts openings while fitting the exhaust plate and cover onto the cylinder block.
   f. Apply a light coat of Loctite 572 to the nine mounting bolt threads. Hand-thread the bolts into the cover and cylinder block.
   g. Tighten the bolts in two steps to the specification in **Table 1**. Use the tightening sequence shown in **Figure 119**.

16. On 4 and 5 hp models, install a new seal and O-ring into the charge coil mounting base as follows:
   a. Place the ignition charge coil on a sturdy work surface with the flywheel side facing down.
   b. Apply a light coat of Loctite 271 to the outer diameter of the new oil seal and the corresponding bore in the mounting base.
   c. Select a section of tubing or a socket to install the seal into the base. The tool must contact the seal casing, but not contact the seal bore during installation.
   d. Position the seal into the bore opening with the lip side facing up. Use the installation tool, and carefully tap the seal into the bore until it is fully seated.
   e. Apply a coat of Yamaha All-Purpose Grease or equivalent to the seal lip and the new O-ring.

POWER HEAD

119 EXHAUST COVER TIGHTENING SEQUENCE (4 AND 5 HP MODELS)

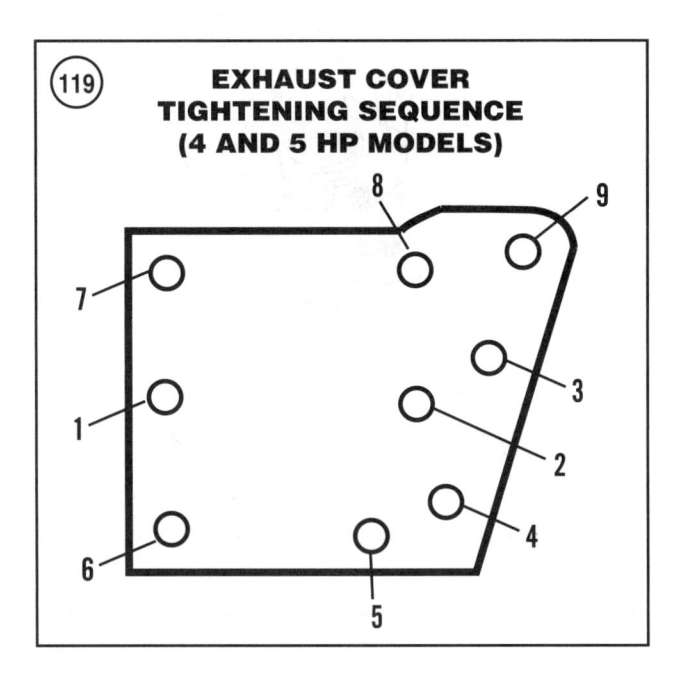

120

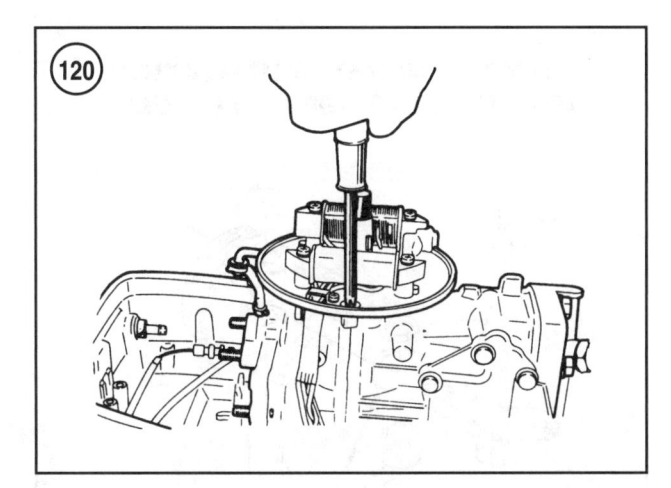

121

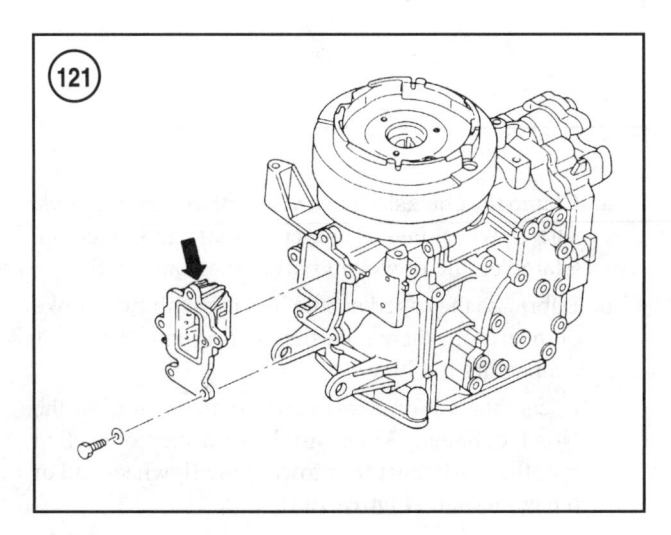

f. Install the new O-ring over the crankshaft taper and seat it into the recess in the cylinder block.

g. Guide the crankshaft taper through the seal while installing the mounting base onto the cylinder block. Rotate the mounting base to align the mounting screw openings. Install and securely tighten the screws (**Figure 120**).

17. On 2 hp models, install the fuel tank mounting bracket (18, **Figure 23**). Securely tighten the screws.

18. Install the intake manifold/reed housing (**Figure 121**, typical) as described in Chapter Five.

19. Install the wire harness and all electrical components as described in Chapter Six.

20. On 2 and 3 hp models, install the fuel tank as described in Chapter Five.

21. On 2-5 hp models, install the fuel pump, carburetor and all fuel hoses as described in Chapter Five.

22. Install the flywheel as described in this chapter.

23. Install the power head as described in this chapter. Perform all necessary adjustments as described in Chapter Four.

24. Perform the break-in procedures as described in Chapter Four.

6-90 hp Models

To assist with component orientation, refer to **Figures 45-51** during the assembly procedure.

1. On 6-15 hp, 28 jet, 35 jet, 40 hp and 50 hp models, if the upper main bearings were removed, install them onto the crankshaft as follows:

   a. Select a section of tubing or another suitable tool to press the upper main bearing onto the crankshaft. The tool must slide freely over the crankshaft, but only contact the inner race of the bearing. The tool must be of sufficient length to prevent the press from contacting the crankshaft threads.

   b. Support the upper flyweight of the crankshaft on the table of a press with the flywheel end facing upward.

   c. Apply two-stroke outboard engine oil to the surfaces, then slide the bearing over the crankshaft taper. On 6-15 hp models, install the bearing with its locating pin closest to the crankshaft flyweight. On 28 jet, 35 jet, 40 hp and 50 hp models, install the bearing with the open side closest to the crankshaft flyweight.

   d. Rest the bearing on the step. Slide the installation tool over the crankshaft and seat it against the inner bearing race (**Figure 102**).

   e. Press on the tool until the bearing seats against the step on the crankshaft.

2. If the lower main bearing was removed, install it onto the crankshaft as follows:
   a. Select a section of tubing or another suitable tool to press the lower main bearing onto the crankshaft. The tool must slide over the crankshaft, but only contact the inner race of the bearing. The tool must be of sufficient length to prevent the press from contacting the end of the crankshaft.
   b. On 20-70 hp models, apply two-stroke outboard oil to the surfaces, then slide the oil injection drive gear onto the crankshaft. The stepped side of the gear hub must face away from the crankshaft flyweight. This positions the gear teeth closer to the flyweight.
   c. Support the lower flyweight on the table of a press with the flywheel end facing down.
   d. Apply two-stroke outboard engine oil to the surfaces, then slide the bearing over the crankshaft. The numbered side of the bearing must face up. Rest the bearing on the step.
   e. Slide the installation tool over the crankshaft and seat it against the inner bearing race (**Figure 103**).
   f. Press on the tool until the bearing seats against the step on the crankshaft.
   g. On 75-90 hp models, apply two-stroke outboard oil to the surfaces, then slide the oil injection drive gear onto the crankshaft. The stepped side of the gear hub must contact the lower main bearing. Install the snap ring into the groove in the crankshaft (**Figure 122**).

WARNING
Use protective eyewear when working with the power head. Piston pin lockrings and other components may unexpectedly spring free.

NOTE
Some models use loose needle bearings at the piston pin end of the connecting rod. Do not lose the needles during installation. If the needle bearings must be reused, install them onto the same connecting rod and piston pin as they were removed.

NOTE
If piston pin installation is difficult, heat the piston to approximately 60° C (140° F) with a portable hair dryer. The piston bore expands when heated, allowing easier pin installation.

3A. On 6 and 8 hp models, install the pistons onto the connecting rods as follows:

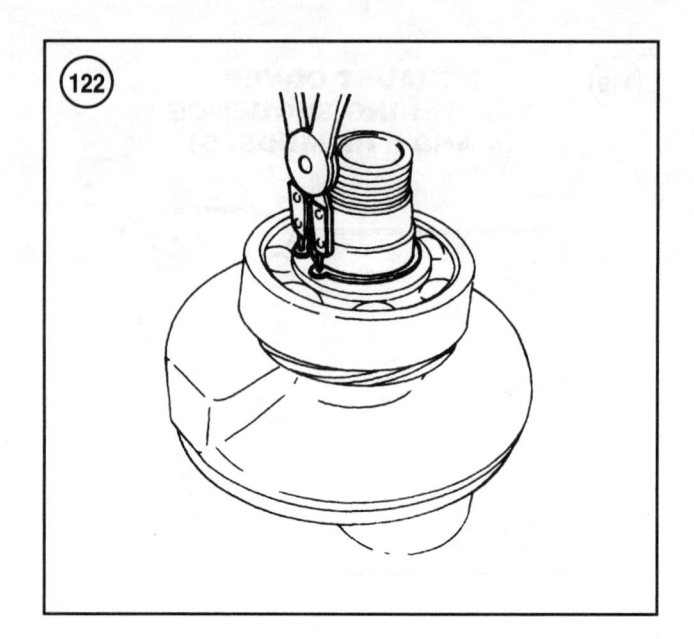

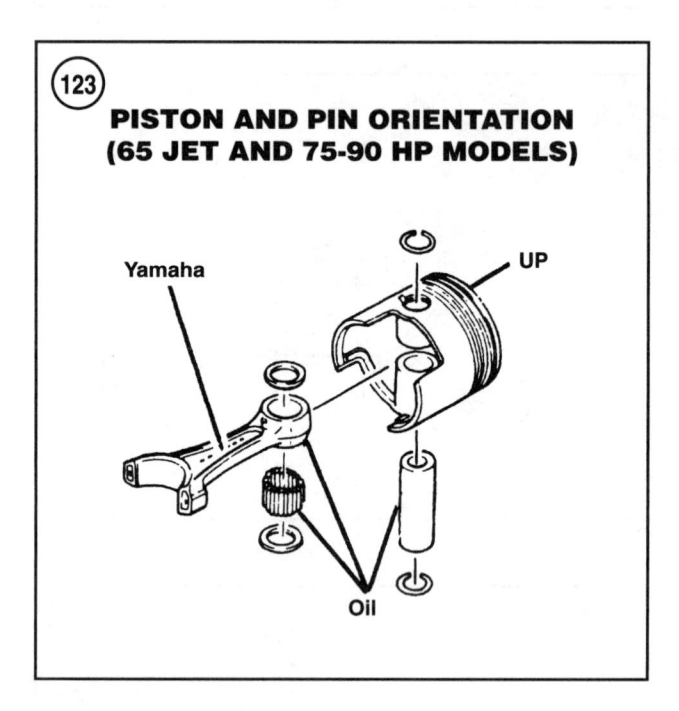

a. Clamp the crankshaft in a vise with protective jaws. The flywheel end of the crankshaft must face up. Clamp on the flyweight part of the crankshaft.
b. Lubricate the caged needle bearing with two-stroke outboard oil, then slide the bearing into the No. 1 connecting rod bore.
c. Locate the UP or arrow mark on the piston for the No. 1 cylinder. When installed on the connecting rod, the mark must face toward the flywheel end of the crankshaft (**Figure 104**).

POWER HEAD

124 Needle bearings / Piston pin installation tool

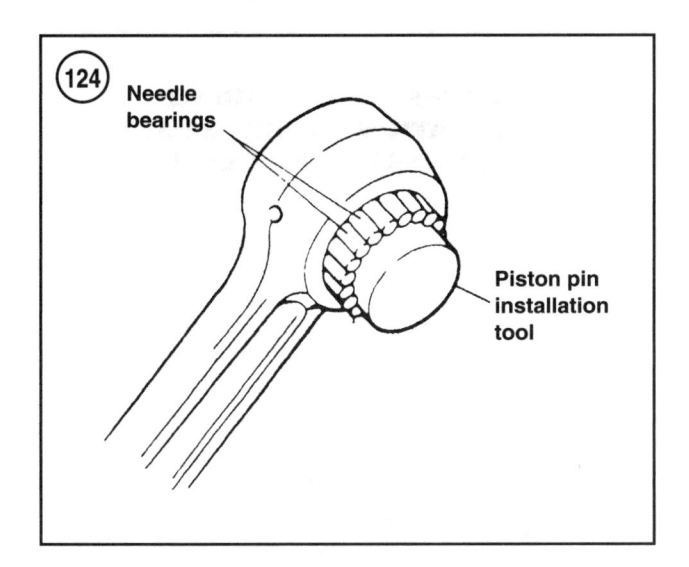

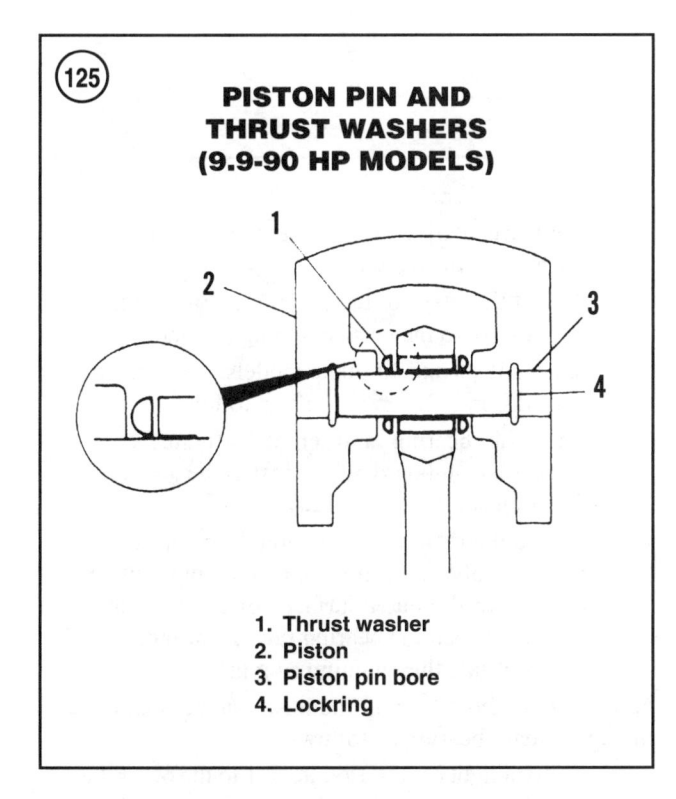

125 PISTON PIN AND THRUST WASHERS (9.9-90 HP MODELS)

1. Thrust washer
2. Piston
3. Piston pin bore
4. Lockring

d. Select a suitable steel rod, socket or section of tubing to install the piston pin into the piston. The installation tool must be slightly smaller in diameter than the piston pin. Piston pin diameters are listed in **Table 3**.

e. Install the piston over the connecting rod and align the piston pin bores in the piston and connecting rod. The UP mark on the piston must face toward the flywheel end of the crankshaft. Make sure the caged needle bearing remains centered in the connecting rod bore.

f. Lubricate the piston pin with two-stroke outboard oil. Maintain pin bore alignment and use the installation tool to push the piston pin into the bores (**Figure 105**). Work carefully to avoid damaging the bearing. Push the piston pin in enough to fully expose the lockring groove on each side of the piston.

g. Use needlenose pliers to insert the lockring into the groove in the piston pin bore (**Figure 106**). Repeat this step to install the lockring into the groove on the other side of the piston.

h. Repeat Step 3A for the No. 2 cylinder.

i. Inspect the pistons to make sure the lockrings are fully seated in the grooves.

3B. On 20-90 hp models, install the pistons onto the connecting rods as follows:

a. On 20-70 hp models, clamp the crankshaft into a vise with protective jaws. The flywheel end of the crankshaft must face up. Clamp on the flyweight part of the crankshaft.

b. On 65 jet and 75-90 hp models, clamp the No. 1 connecting rod in a vise with protective jaws. The Yamaha mark on the connecting rod (**Figure 123**) must face up.

c. Insert the piston pin installation tool into the small end of the No. 1 connecting rod (**Figure 124**). Use only the manufacturer recommended tool for this operation. On 9.9 and 15 hp models, use Yamaha part No. YB-06104/90890-06543. On 20 and 25 hp two-cylinder models, use Yamaha part No. YB-06107/90890-06526. On 25 hp three-cylinder and 30 hp models, use Yamaha part No. YB-6105/90890-06525. On 28 jet, 35 jet, 40 hp and 50 hp models, use Yamaha part No. YB-6106/90890-06526. On 60 and 70 hp models, use Yamaha part No. YB-6287/90890-06527. On 65 jet and 75-90 hp models, use Yamaha part No. YB-6107/90890-06527.

d. On 9.9-90 hp models, place a thumb under the connecting rod and insert the needle bearings between the tool and the connecting rod bore. On 9.9 and 15 hp models, insert 25 needle bearings. On 20 and 25 hp two-cylinder models, insert 31 needle bearings. On 25 hp three-cylinder and 30 hp models, insert 28 needle bearings. On 28 jet, 35 jet, 40 hp and 50 hp models, insert 31 needle bearings. On 60-90 hp models, insert 28 needle bearings.

e. Make sure no more needle bearings can be installed into the rod. Position the thrust washers (1, **Figure 125**) on each side of the connecting rod bore. The flat side of the thrust washer must contact the connecting rod.

   f. Install the No. 1 piston over the connecting rod and align the piston pin bores in the piston and connecting rod. The UP mark on the piston must face toward the flywheel end of the crankshaft. Make sure the needle bearings, thrust washer and installation tool remains centered in the connecting rod bore.

   g. Lubricate the piston pin with two-stroke outboard oil. Maintain pin bore alignment and carefully push the piston pin into the bores (**Figure 105**). Work carefully to avoid damaging the bearings. Push the piston pin in until the installation tool exits the bore on the other side of the piston and the lockring grooves are exposed on each side.

   h. Use needlenose pliers to insert the lockring into the groove in the piston pin bore (**Figure 106**). Repeat this step to install the lockring into the groove on the other side of the piston.

   i. Inspect the piston to make sure the lockrings are fully seated in the grooves.

   j. Repeat Step 3B for the No. 2 and No. 3 pistons. Install each piston onto its corresponding connecting rod.

CAUTION
Be careful when spreading the rings for installation onto the piston. Spread the gap ends only enough to allow the ring to slide over the piston. The ring will break or crack if it is spread too much.

NOTE
*Various types of piston rings are used. A rectangular ring (2, **Figure 107**), full-keystone or half-keystone (3) may be used. The piston may use one or a combination of types. Inspect the piston ring and ring groove before installing any of the rings to ensure the proper ring is installed. The mark on the ring (4, **Figure 107**) must face up toward the piston dome.*

4. Install the piston rings onto the piston as follows:
   a. Select the rings for the No. 1 cylinder and the No. 1 piston.
   b. Use a ring expander to spread the bottom ring enough to clear the top of the No. 1 piston (**Figure 108**). The mark on the ring (4, **Figure 107**) must face up. Avoid scratching the piston. Slide the ring over the piston and release the ring in the bottom ring groove.
   c. Repeat this procedure for the top ring. The mark on the top ring must face up.

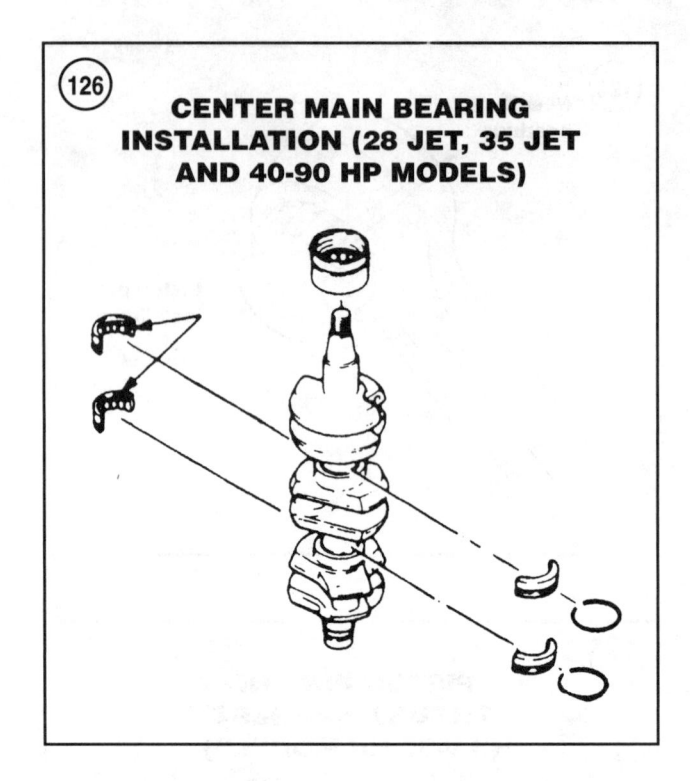

126
CENTER MAIN BEARING INSTALLATION (28 JET, 35 JET AND 40-90 HP MODELS)

   d. Apply a coat of two-stroke outboard engine oil to all surfaces of the piston.
   e. Repeat this step for the remaining piston(s). Install the rings onto the corresponding piston(s).

5. On 28 jet, 35 jet and 40-90 hp models, install the center main bearings onto the crankshaft as follows:
   a. Coat the bearing and crankshaft surfaces with two-stroke outboard oil and install the bearings onto the crankshaft (**Figure 126**).
   b. Spread the retaining ring enough to slip it over the bearing halves. Position the retaining ring in the grooves in the outer surfaces of the bearings. The ring must span the bearing mating surfaces. If necessary, rotate the retaining ring in the groove.

6. On 20-30 and 60-90 hp models, assemble and install the upper main bearing as follows:
   a. Apply a light coat of Loctite 271 to the outer diameter of the new crankshaft seal and the seal bore in the upper main bearing. See **Figure 127**. Do not allow any Loctite into the roller bearings.
   b. Select a section of tubing or a socket to install the seal. The tool must contact the seal casing, but not contact the seal bore in the bearing.
   c. Place the main bearing (**Figure 127**) on a sturdy work surface with the seal bore facing up.
   d. Insert the seal into the bore opening. The seal (**Figure 127**) lip must face down.

POWER HEAD

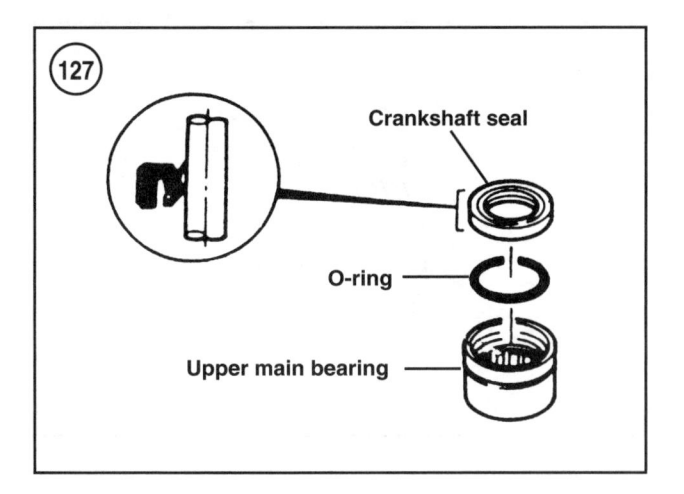

127
Crankshaft seal
O-ring
Upper main bearing

e. Using the tool, carefully tap the seal into the bore until it is fully seated.
f. Apply a coat of Yamaha All-Purpose Grease or equivalent to the seal lip and the new O-ring (**Figure 127**).
g. Slide the O-ring over the bearing and set it into the groove on the bearing case.
h. Slide the main bearing over the crankshaft taper. The seal side of the bearing must face away from the crankshaft flyweight. Do not allow the bearing to slip from the crankshaft during other operations.

7. On 6-15 hp, 28 jet, 35 jet, 40 hp and 50 hp models, install a new seal into the upper seal housing as follows:
   a. Place the upper seal housing on a sturdy work surface with the seal bore facing up. The larger diameter side of the housing must face down.
   b. Apply a coat of Loctite 271 to the outer diameter of the seal casing.
   c. Insert the seal into the bore with the seal lip facing down.
   d. Select a section of tubing or a socket to install the seal. The tool must contact the seal casing, but not contact the seal bore during installation.
   e. Use the tool to push the seal into the bore until it is fully seated.

8. Install new seals into the lower seal housing as follows:
   a. Select sections of tubing or sockets to use as seal installation tools. The tools must contact the outer case of the seal, but not contact the seal bore during installation.
   b. Apply a light coat of Loctite 271 to the outer diameter of the seals and the seal bores in the seal housing.
   c. Lightly clamp the seal housing in a vise with protective jaws. The seal openings must face up.
   d. Insert the smaller diameter (lower) seal into the bore opening. On 6-50 hp models, the lip side of the seal must face down. On 60-90 hp models, the lip side of the seal must face up.
   e. Use the tool to push the seal into the bore until it is fully seated.
   f. Insert the larger diameter (upper) seal into the bore opening with the lip side facing downward.
   g. Use the tool to push the seal into the bore until it is fully seated.
   h. Lubricate the O-ring with Yamaha All-Purpose Grease or equivalent. Position the O-ring in the groove in the seal housing.
   i. Apply a generous coat of Yamaha All-Purpose Grease or equivalent to the seal lip.

CAUTION
Work carefully and patiently when installing the piston into the cylinder bore. Never use excessive force to insert the piston. Excessive force can break the piston ring(s) or damage other components.

CAUTION
***Do not** force the pistons into the bore. Excessive force will damage the piston, rings or cylinder bore. Remove the piston and check for improper ring gap alignment, excessive ring compressor pressure or inadequate ring compressor pressure if the piston(s) will not slide easily into the bore.*

NOTE
On 2-70 hp models, the pistons, connecting rods and crankshaft are installed in the cylinder block as an assembly. A ring compressor is not required. A taper in the crankcase near the bottom of the bore compresses the rings during piston installation.

9A. On 6-70 hp models, install the pistons, connecting rods and crankshaft assembly into the cylinder block as follows:
   a. On 6-50 hp models, install the washer, spacer or plate onto the lower end of the crankshaft. Refer to **Figures 45-49** to identify and locate these components.
   b. Apply a generous coat of two-stroke outboard oil to the cylinder bores, crankshaft bearings and connecting rod bearings.
   c. Position the ring gaps over the locating pins as indicated in **Figure 109**. The gaps must remain over the locating pins during piston installation.
   d. Position the crankshaft over the crankcase with the flywheel taper end facing the top of the cylinder

7

block. Carefully lower the crankshaft and insert the pistons into the bore.

e. Guide the pistons into the bore while carefully and gently rock the pistons to compress the rings. Do not rotate the pistons within the bore. If any of the pistons will not enter the bore, remove the assembly and inspect the ring gap positioning.

f. Carefully guide the locating pins on the crankshaft main bearings into their recesses in the cylinder block while lowering the crankshaft into the cylinder block. Use hand pressure to seat the crankshaft main bearings into the cylinder block. Do not strike the crankshaft, bearings, connecting rods or other components.

9B. On 65 jet and 75-90 hp models, install the crankshaft into the cylinder block as follows:

a. Position the crankshaft over the crankcase with the flywheel taper end facing the top of the cylinder block.

b. Carefully guide the locating pins on the crankshaft main bearings into their recesses in the cylinder block while lowering the crankshaft into position.

c. Use hand pressure to seat the crankshaft main bearings into the cylinder block. Do not strike the crankshaft.

d. Slowly rotate the crankshaft within the cylinder block. Remove the crankshaft and inspect all bearing and alignment pins for damage if there is any binding or roughness.

10. Apply a light coat of Loctite Gasket Maker to the mating surface of the lower seal housing. Guide the lower end of the crankshaft through the seal openings while installing the lower seal housing onto the cylinder block. Rotate the seal housing to align the bolt openings. Install the bolts (**Figure 128**) and hand tighten them to help hold the crankshaft.

11. On 65 jet and 75-90 hp models, install the piston and connecting rods into the cylinder block as follows:

a. Apply a generous coat of two-stroke outboard oil to the cylinder bores, crankshaft bearings and connecting rod bearings.

b. Rotate the crankshaft until the No. 1 crankshaft journal is at the bottom of the stroke.

c. Position the ring gaps over the locating pins as indicated in **Figure 109**. The gaps must remain over the locating pins during piston installation.

d. Select the piston, rings, bearings and rod assembly for the No. 1 cylinder. Use a standard automotive type ring compressor to compress the piston rings. The ring gaps must remain in position over the locating pins.

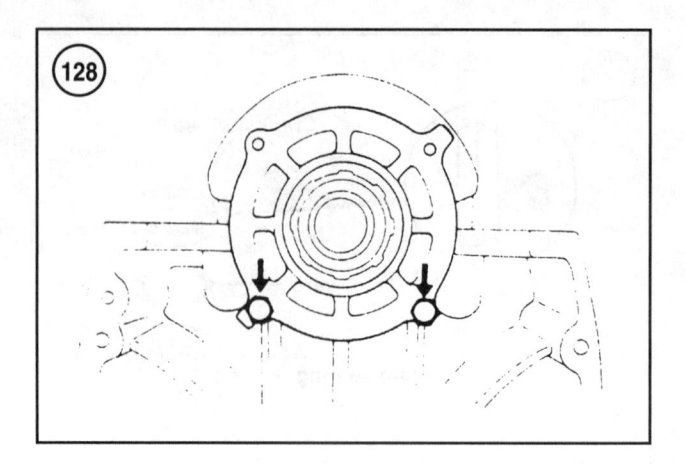

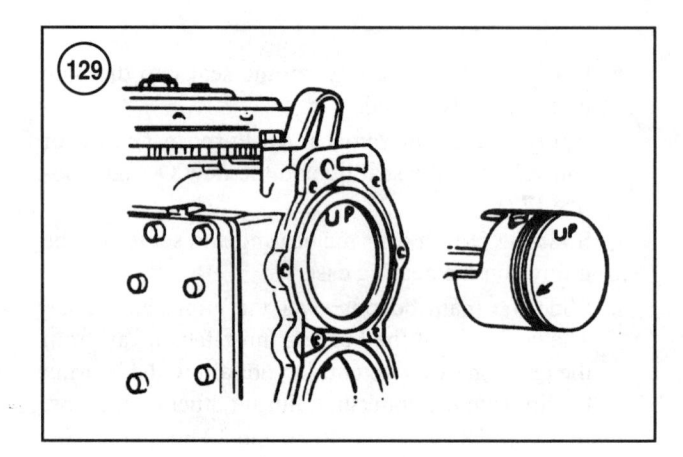

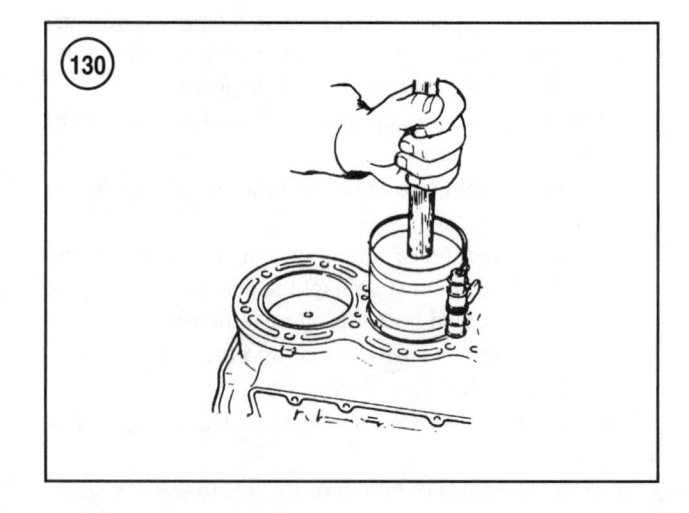

e. Mark the rod cap for orientation and remove it from the rod. Insert the piston skirt into the bore at the cylinder head mating surface (**Figure 129**). The UP mark on the piston must face toward the flywheel.

f. Hold the ring compressor firmly against the cylinder block. To avoid damaging the block, crankshaft

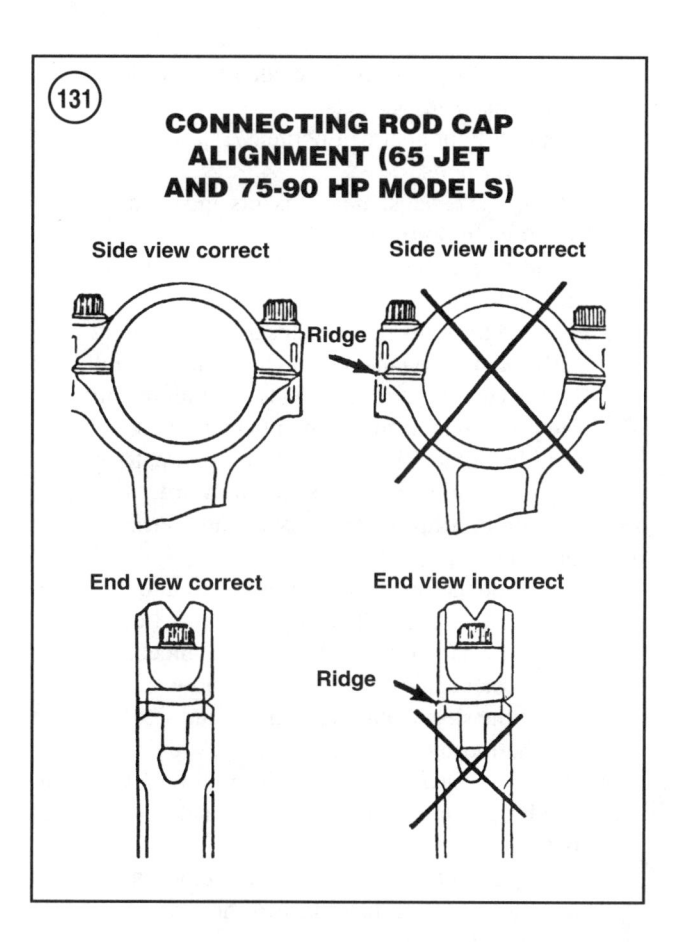

131

CONNECTING ROD CAP ALIGNMENT (65 JET AND 75-90 HP MODELS)

Side view correct — Side view incorrect (Ridge)

End view correct — End view incorrect (Ridge)

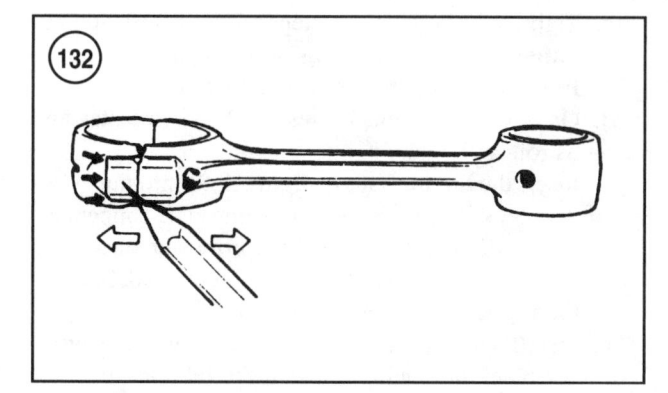

132

or connecting rod, guide the connecting rod into position on the crankshaft while installing the piston. Use a large wooden dowel to push the piston into the bore (**Figure 130**).

g. Apply two-stroke outboard oil to the crankshaft journal and install both halves of the bearing onto the crankshaft. Pull the rod into the crankcase until it contacts the bearing.

h. Install the rod cap onto the connecting rod. Make sure the connecting rod is oriented correctly and install the used rod bolts. Torque the rod bolts in two steps to the specification in **Table 1**.

i. Check the alignment as indicated in **Figure 131**. Pass a sharp pencil point or other pointed object across the rod and cap mating surfaces (**Figure 132**). If the point catches an edge, the rod is not aligned properly. If the rod is misaligned, remove the cap and check for debris between the mating surfaces. Carefully align the rod while reinstalling the cap and bolts. If the rod is still misaligned, replace the connecting rod.

j. Loosen and remove one of the rod bolts. Install a new rod bolt and tighten it in two steps to the specification in **Table 1**. Then remove, replace and tighten the other rod bolt.

k. Rotate the crankshaft until the No. 2 cylinder is at the bottom of its stroke. Repeat Step 11 for the remaining two cylinders.

12. On 65 jet and 75-90 hp models, use feeler gauges to measure the connecting rod side clearance (**Figure 100**) for each cylinder. Select the feeler gauge that can be passed between the flyweight and the connecting rod with a slight drag. The connecting rod side clearance must be within the specification in **Table 5**.

  a. If the side clearance exceeds the specification, replace the connecting rod and repeat the measurement. Replace the crankshaft if the clearance exceeds the specification with the new connecting rod.

  b. If the side clearance is below the specification, check the rod cap to connecting rod alignment. If the alignment is correct, replace the connecting rod, then repeat the measurement. Replace the crankshaft if the clearance is below the specification with the new connecting rod.

13. Maintain downward pressure on the crankshaft to prevent the crankshaft from moving out of the cylinder block during this procedure. Look into the exhaust opening and slowly rotate the crankshaft until the piston rings for the No. 1 cylinder span the exhaust port (**Figure 110**). Use a blunt tip screwdriver to carefully press *in* on each ring. The ring should spring back when the screwdriver is pulled back. If either of the rings fail to spring back, remove the crankshaft, connecting rod and piston assembly, and check for broken piston rings. Repeat this step for the remaining cylinder(s).

14. Install the crankcase cover onto the cylinder block as follows:

  a. Apply a continuous bead of Loctite Gasket Maker to the mating surfaces of the cylinder block (**Figure 111**). Apply the sealant bead on the inside of the crankcase bolt opening as shown in **Figure 112**.

b. Install the crankcase cover and seat it onto the cylinder block.
c. On 6-15 hp models, install the intake manifold/reed housing as described in Chapter Five. Do not install the mounting bolts at this time.
d. Apply Loctite 242 to the crankcase cover bolts. Hand-thread the bolts into the cover.
e. Slowly rotate the crankshaft. Remove the cover and check for improper bearing, seal or spacer installation if there is binding or roughness. Check for broken piston rings if there is a clicking noise. Clean the mating surface and apply a new bead of sealant each time the crankcase is removed.
f. Tighten the bolts in two steps to the specification in **Table 1**. Tighten the bolts in the sequence indicated by the cast-in numbers next to the bolt openings. If the tightening sequence numbers are missing or illegible, tighten the bolts in a crossing pattern starting in the middle and working outward.
g. Install any remaining bolts into the lower seal housing. On 65 jet and 75-90 hp models, install the deflector (**Figure 53**) onto the bottom of the housing and position it as noted before removal.
h. Tighten all of the seal housing bolts to the general torque specification in Chapter One.

15. On 6 and 8 hp models, install a new gasket (18, **Figure 45**) onto the exhaust tube (17), then install the tube onto the bottom of the cylinder block. Install the bolts and washers. Tighten the bolts evenly to the general torque specification in Chapter One.

16. On 9.9-70 hp models, install the cylinder head onto the cylinder block as follows:
    a. Install the anodes into the cylinder water jacket if they were removed. Position a new head gasket and the cylinder head on the cylinder block.
    b. Install a new gasket and the water jacket cover onto the cylinder head if the cylinder head bolts pass through it.
    c. Sealant or adhesive is not required on these gaskets. Apply a light coat of two-stroke outboard engine oil to the bolt threads. Hand-thread the bolts into the cylinder head and block.
    d. Check the alignment of the components. Tighten the bolts in two steps to the specification in **Table 1**. Tighten the bolts in the sequence indicated by the cast-in numbers next to the bolt openings. If the tightening sequence numbers are missing or illegible, tighten the bolts in a crossing pattern starting in the middle and working outward.

17. Install the exhaust plate and exhaust cover onto the cylinder block as follows:
    a. Refer to **Figures 45-51** to identify and locate the cover, plate and gaskets.
    b. Apply a light coat of Loctite 572 to the threads of the cover bolts.
    c. Mount the exhaust plate, gaskets and exhaust cover as shown in **Figures 45-51**.
    d. Hand-thread the bolts into the cover, plate and cylinder block.
    e. Tighten the bolts in two steps to the specification in **Table 1**. Tighten the bolts in the sequence indicated by the cast-in numbers next to the bolt openings. If the tightening sequence numbers are missing or illegible, tighten the bolts in a crossing pattern starting in the middle and working outward.

18A. On 6 and 8 hp models, install the thermostat and rear water jacket cover as follows:
    a. Insert the thermostat (10, **Figure 45**) into the cylinder block opening. The copper colored cylindrical end must face toward the cylinder block. Seat the thermostat against the step in the bore.
    b. Insert the sleeve into the opening and seat it against the thermostat.
    c. Position a new gasket (13, **Figure 45**) on the cylinder block, then install the water jacket cover (12) onto the gasket.
    d. Apply a light coat of two-stroke outboard oil to the bolt threads, then hand-thread the seven bolts into the cylinder block.
    e. Tighten the bolts in two steps to the specification in **Table 1**. Use a crossing tightening sequence starting from the center and working outward.

18B. On 9.9-70 hp models, install the thermostat and cover as follows:
    a. Insert the thermostat (4, **Figure 118**) into the cylinder block or cylinder head opening. The copper colored cylindrical end of the thermostat must face toward the cylinder block or cylinder head. Seat the thermostat against the step in the bore.
    b. Install a new gasket (3, **Figure 118**) onto the cylinder block or head (5). Install the thermostat cover (2, **Figure 118**) onto the gasket.
    c. Apply a light coat of Loctite 572 to the bolt threads, then install the two cover bolts (1, **Figure 118**). Tighten the bolts to the general torque specification in Chapter One.

18C. On 75-90 hp models, install the thermostat, water pressure relief valve and thermostat cover into the rear of the cylinder head as follows:
    a. Insert the thermostat into the cylinder block opening. The copper colored cylindrical end of the thermostat must face toward the cylinder block. Seat the thermostat against the step in the bore.

b. Insert the grommet, then water pressure relief valve, into the cylinder head opening.

c. Install the spring onto the stem of the relief valve.

d. Install a new gasket onto the cover mating surface. Install the cover over the spring and seat it against the gasket.

e. Install the four bolts and tighten them to the standard torque specification in Chapter One.

19. On 20-90 hp models, install the intake manifold/reed housing as described in Chapter Five.

20. Install the fuel pump, carburetor and all fuel hoses as described in Chapter Five.

21. On oil injected models, install all oil injection components as described in Chapter Twelve.

22. Install the wire harness and all electrical components as described in Chapter Six.

23. Install the flywheel as described in this chapter.

24. Install the power head as described in this chapter. Perform all necessary adjustments as described in Chapter Five.

25. Perform the break-in procedures as described in Chapter Four.

Table 1 POWER HEAD TORQUE SPECIFICATIONS

Fastener	N•m	in.-lb.	ft.-lb.
Crankcase cover			
2 hp			
First step	5	44	–
Second step	10	86	–
3 hp			
First step	5	44	–
Second step	11	97	–
4 and 5 hp			
First step	6	53	–
Second step	12	–	9
6 and 8 hp			
First step	6	53	–
Second step	11	97	–
9.9 and 15 hp			
First step	15	–	11
Second step	30	–	22
20-50 hp			
First step			
6 mm bolts	5	44	–
8 mm bolts	15	–	11
Second step			
6 mm bolts	11	97	–
8 mm bolts	28	–	21
60 and 70 hp			
First step			
8 mm bolts	10	86	–
10 mm bolts	20	–	15
Second step			
8 mm bolts	20	–	15
10 mm bolts	40	–	30
65 jet and 75-90 hp			
First step			
6 mm bolts	4	36	–
10 mm bolts	20	–	15
Second step			
6 mm bolts	12	–	9
10 mm bolts	40	–	30
(continued)			

Table 1 POWER HEAD TORQUE SPECIFICATIONS (continued)

Fastener	N•m	in.-lb.	ft.-lb.
Connecting rod bolts			
65 jet and 75-90 hp			
First step	12	–	9
Second step	35	–	26
Cylinder head bolts			
2 hp			
First step	5	44	–
Second step	10	86	–
3 hp			
First step	5	44	–
Second step	11	97	–
9.9 and 15 hp			
First step	8	70	–
Second step	17	–	13
20-50 hp			
First step	15	–	11
Second step	28	–	21
60 and 70 hp			
First step	15	–	11
Second step	32	–	24
65 jet and 75-90 hp			
First step	15	–	11
Second step	30	–	22
Exhaust cover/plate			
4 and 5 hp			
First step	3	26	–
Second step	9	80	–
6 and 8 hp			
First step	4	36	–
Second step	8	70	–
9.9 and 15 hp			
First step	6	53	–
Second step	12	–	9
20- 30 hp			
First step	3	26	–
Second step	8	70	–
28 jet, 35 jet, 40 hp and 50 hp			
First step	4	36	–
Second step	8	70	–
60 and 70 hp			
First step	3	26	–
Second step	8	70	–
65 jet and 75-90 hp			
First step	9	80	–
Second step	18	–	13
Exhaust tube			
3 hp			
First step	3	26	–
Second step	8	70	–
Flywheel nut			
2-8 hp	45	–	33
9.9 and 15 hp	105	–	78
20 and 25 hp two-cylinder	100	–	74
25 hp three-cylinder and 30-50 hp	110	–	81
60-90 hp	160	–	118
Lower seal housing			
4 and 5 hp			
First step	6	53	–
Second step	12	–	9

(continued)

POWER HEAD

Table 1 POWER HEAD TORQUE SPECIFICATIONS (continued)

Fastener	N•m	in.-lb.	ft.-lb.
Power head mounting bolts			
3 hp	8	70	–
4 and 5 hp			
First step	3	26	–
Second step	8	70	–
20 and 25 hp two-cylinder	21	–	15
40-90 hp	21	–	15
Water jacket cover			
4 and 5 hp			
First step	3	26	–
Second step	9	80	–
6 and 8 hp			
First step	4	36	–
Second step	8	70	–

Table 2 CYLINDER BORE SPECIFICATIONS

Model	Specification
Standard bore diameter	
2 hp	39.0-39.10 mm (1.535-1.540 in.)
3 hp	46.0-46.10 mm (1.811-1.815 in.)
4 hp	50.00-50.10 mm (1.9685-1.9724 in.)
5 hp	54.00-54.10 mm (2.1260-2.129 in.)
6 and 8 hp	50.00-50.10 mm (1.9685-1.9724 in.)
9.9 and 15 hp	56.00-56.10 mm (2.2047-2.2087 in.)
20 and 25 hp two-cylinder	67.00-67.10 mm (2.6378-2.6417 in.)
25 hp three-cylinder and 30 hp	59.50-59.60 mm (2.3425-2.3465 in.)
28 jet, 35 jet, 40 hp and 50 hp	67.00-67.10 mm (2.6378-2.6417 in.)
60 and 70 hp	72.00-72.02 mm (2.8346-2.8354 in.)
65 jet and 75-90 hp	82.00-82.02 mm (3.2283-3.2291 in.)
Maximum cylinder taper	0.08 mm (0.003 in.)
Maximum cylinder out-of-round	0.05 mm (0.002 in.)

Table 3 PISTON SPECIFICATIONS

Model	Specification
Standard piston diameter	
2 hp	38.967-38.986 mm (1.5341-1.5349 in.)*
3 hp	45.965-45.990 mm (1.8096-1.8106 in.)*
4 hp	49.970-50.000 mm (1.9673-1.9685 in.)*
5 hp	53.970-54.000 mm (2.1248-2.1260 in.)*
6 and 8 hp	49.955-49.980 mm (1.9667-1.9677 in.)*
9.9 and 15 hp	55.940-55.985 mm (2.2024-2.2041 in.)*
20 and 25 hp two-cylinder	66.955-66.980 mm (2.6360-2.6370 in.)*
25 hp three-cylinder and 30 hp	59.455-59.480 mm (2.3407-2.3417 in.)*
28 jet, 35 jet, 40 hp and 50 hp	66.940-67.000 mm (2.6354-2.6378 in.)*
60 and 70 hp	71.945-71.970 mm (2.8325-2.8335 in.)*
65 jet and 75-90 hp	81.935-81.960 mm (3.2258-3.2268 in.)*

(continued)

Table 3 PISTON SPECIFICATIONS (continued)

Model	Specification
Piston skirt to cylinder clearance	
2 hp	0.030-0.085 mm (0.0012-0.0033 in.)
3-5 hp	0.030-0.035 mm (0.0012-0.0014 in.)
6 and 8 hp	0.040-0.045 mm (0.0016-0.0018 in.)
9.9 and 15 hp	0.035-0.040 mm (0.0014-0.0016 in.)
20-30 hp	0.040-0.045 mm (0.0016-0.0018 in.)
28 jet, 35 jet, 40 hp and 50 hp	0.060-0.065 mm (0.0024-0.0026 in.)
60 and 70 hp	0.050-0.055 mm (0.0020-0.0022 in.)
65 jet and 75-90 hp	0.060-0.065 mm (0.0024-0.0026 in.)
Piston pin bore	
2 hp	10.004-10.015 mm (0.3939-0.3943 in.)
4-8 hp	12.004-12.015 mm (0.4726-0.4730 in.)
9.9 and 15 hp	14.000-14.015 mm (0.5512-0.5518 in.)
20 and 25 hp two-cylinder	18.008-18.015 mm (0.7090-0.7093 in.)
25 hp two-cylinder and 30 hp	15.974-15.985 mm (0.6289-0.6293 in.)
28 jet, 35 jet, 40 hp and 50 hp	18.008-18.015 mm (0.7090-0.7093 in.)
Piston pin diameter	
2 hp	9.996-10.000 mm (0.3935-0.3937 in.)
4-8 hp	11.996-12.000 mm (0.4723-0.4724 in.)
9.9 and 15 hp	13.996-14.000 mm (0.5510-0.5512 in.)
20 and 25 hp two-cylinder	17.995-18.000 mm (0.7085-0.7087 in.)
25 hp three-cylinder and 30 hp	15.965-15.970 mm (0.6285-0.6287 in.)
28 jet, 35 jet, 40 hp and 50 hp	17.995-18.000 mm (0.7085-0.7087 in.)

*Measured 10 mm (0.39 in.) from the bottom of the piston skirt.

Table 4 PISTON RING SPECIFICATIONS

Model	Specification
Side clearance	
2 hp	
Top ring	0.03-0.07 mm (0.0012-0.0028 in.)
Second ring	0.03-0.07 mm (0.0012-0.0028 in.)
3-8 hp	
Top ring	0.02-0.06 mm (0.0008-0.0024 in.)
Second ring	0.03-0.07 mm (0.0012-0.0028 in.)
9.9 and 15 hp	
Top ring	0.02-0.06 mm (0.0008-0.0024 in.)
Second ring	0.04-0.08 mm (0.0016-0.0032 in.)
20 and 25 hp two-cylinder	
Top ring	0.02-0.06 mm (0.0008-0.0024 in.)
Second ring	0.03-0.07 mm (0.0012-0.0028 in.)
25 hp three-cylinder and 30 hp	
Top ring	0.05-0.09 mm (0.0020-0.0035 in.)
Second ring	0.05-0.09 mm (0.0020-0.0035 in.)
28 jet, 35 jet, 40 hp and 50 hp	
Top ring	0.04-0.08 mm (0.0016-0.0032 in.)
Second ring	0.03-0.07 mm (0.0012-0.0028 in.)
60 and 70 hp	
Top ring	0.03-0.07 mm (0.0012-0.0028 in.)
Second ring	0.03-0.07 mm (0.0012-0.0028 in.)
65 jet and 75-90 hp	
Top ring	0.03-0.06 mm (0.0012-0.0024 in.)
Second ring	0.03-0.06 mm (0.0012-0.0024 in.)

(continued)

POWER HEAD

Table 4 PISTON RING SPECIFICATIONS (continued)

Model	Specification
Ring end gap	
2 and 3 hp	0.10-0.30 mm (0.004-0.012 in.)
4-8 hp	0.15-0.35 mm (0.006-0.014 in.)
9.9 and 15 hp	0.15-0.55 mm (0.006-0.022 in.)
20 and 25 hp two-cylinder	0.40-0.80 mm (0.016-0.031 in.)
25 hp three-cylinder and 30 hp	0.15-0.30 mm (0.006-0.012 in.)
28 jet, 35 jet, 40 hp and 50 hp	0.40-0.80 mm (0.016-0.031 in.)
60 and 70 hp	0.30-0.50 mm (0.012-0.020 in.)
65 jet and 75-90 hp	0.40-0.60 mm (0.016-0.024 in.)
Ring end gap measuring depth	
2 and 3 hp	20 mm (0.787 in.)[1]
4 and 5 hp	70 mm (2.756 in.)[2]
6 and 8 hp	60 mm (2.362 in.)[1]
9.9-90 hp	20 mm (0.787 in.)[1]

1. Measuring point from top (head side) of the cylinder bore.
2. Measuring point from bottom (crankcase side) of the cylinder bore.

Table 5 CRANKSHAFT SPECIFICATIONS

Model	Specification
Maximum crankshaft run-out	
2 hp	0.02 mm (0.0008 in.)*
3-70 hp (except 65 jet)	0.03 mm (0.0012 in.)*
65 jet and 75-90 hp	0.05 mm (0.0020 in.)*
Flyweight to flyweight width	
2 hp	27.90-27.95 mm (1.098-1.100 in.)
3 hp	35.90-36.00 mm (1.413-1.417 in.)
4-8 hp	39.90-39.95 mm (1.571-1.573 in.)
9.9 and 15 hp	46.90-46.95 mm (1.846-1.848 in.)
20-30	49.90-49.95 mm (1.965-1.967 in.)
28 jet, 35 jet, 40 hp and 50 hp	53.90-53.95 mm (2.122-2.124 in.)
60 and 70 hp	57.90-57.95 mm (2.280-2.282 in.)
Flyweight to flyweight spacing	
6 and 8 hp	21.90-22.10 mm (0.862-0.870 in.)
9.9 and 15	25.90-26.10 mm (1.020-1.028 in.)
20 and 25 hp two-cylinder	38.90-39.10 mm (1.531-1.539 in.)
25 hp three-cylinder and 30 hp	28.90-29.10 mm (1.138-1.146 in.)
28 jet, 35 jet, 40 hp and 50 hp	32.88-33.10 mm (1.294-1.303 in.)
60 and 70 hp	35.90-36.10 mm (1.413-1.421 in.)
Upper flyweight to lower flyweight	
25 hp three-cylinder and 30 hp	207.50-208.10 mm (8.169-8.193 in.)
28 jet, 35 jet, 40 hp and 50 hp	227.50-228.10 mm (8.957-8.980 in.)
60 and 70 hp	245.50-246.10 mm (9.665-9.689 in.)
Connecting rod axial play	2.0 mm (0.079 in.)*
Connecting rod side clearance	
2 and 3 hp	0.30-0.60 mm (0.012-0.024 in.)
4-8 hp	0.20-0.70 mm (0.008-0.028 in.)
9.9 and 15	0.30-0.80 mm (0.012-0.031 in.)
20-50 hp	0.20-0.70 mm (0.008-0.028 in.)
60 and 70 hp	0.20-0.70 mm (0.008-0.028 in.)
65 jet and 75-90 hp	0.12-0.26 mm (0.005-0.010 in.)

*This is maximum allowable specification.

Chapter Eight

Gearcase

This chapter provides lower gearcase removal/installation, rebuilding and resealing procedures for all 2-90 hp Yamaha outboards. Water pump maintenance and repair are also included in this chapter.

Table 1 lists torque specifications for most gearcase fasteners. Use the general torque specifications in Chapter One for fasteners not listed in **Table 1**. **Table 2** lists gearcase backlash specifications. **Table 1** and **Table 2** are located at the end of this chapter.

Expanded illustrations of each gearcase are located in the appropriate *Disassembly* section and are helpful references for many service procedures.

The lower gearcase can be removed from the outboard without the entire outboard being removed from the boat.

The various gearcases covered in this chapter differ in construction and require different service procedures. The chapter is arranged in a normal disassembly/assembly sequence. When only partial repair is required, follow the procedure(s) to the point where the faulty parts can be replaced, then jump ahead to reassemble the gearcase.

Since the chapter covers a large range of models, the gearcases shown in the accompanying illustrations are the most common models. While the components shown in the pictures may not be identical to those being serviced, the step-by-step procedures cover each model in the manual.

GEARCASE OPERATION

A drive shaft transfers engine torque from the engine crankshaft to the lower gearcase. See **Figure 1**. A pinion (drive) gear on the drive shaft is in constant mesh with forward and reverse (driven) gears in the lower gearcase housing. These gears are spiral bevel cut to change the vertical power flow into the horizontal flow required by the propeller shaft. The spiral bevel design also makes operation quiet.

All gearcases use precision shimmed gears. This means that the gears are precisely located in the gear housing by very thin metal spacers called shims (**Figure 2**). After assembly, check for correct shimming of the gears by measuring the *gear lash*, also called *backlash*. Gear lash is the measurement of the clearance or air gap between a tooth on the pinion gear and two teeth on the forward or reverse gear.

If the gear lash is excessive, the gear teeth are too far apart. This causes excessive gear noise and a reduction in

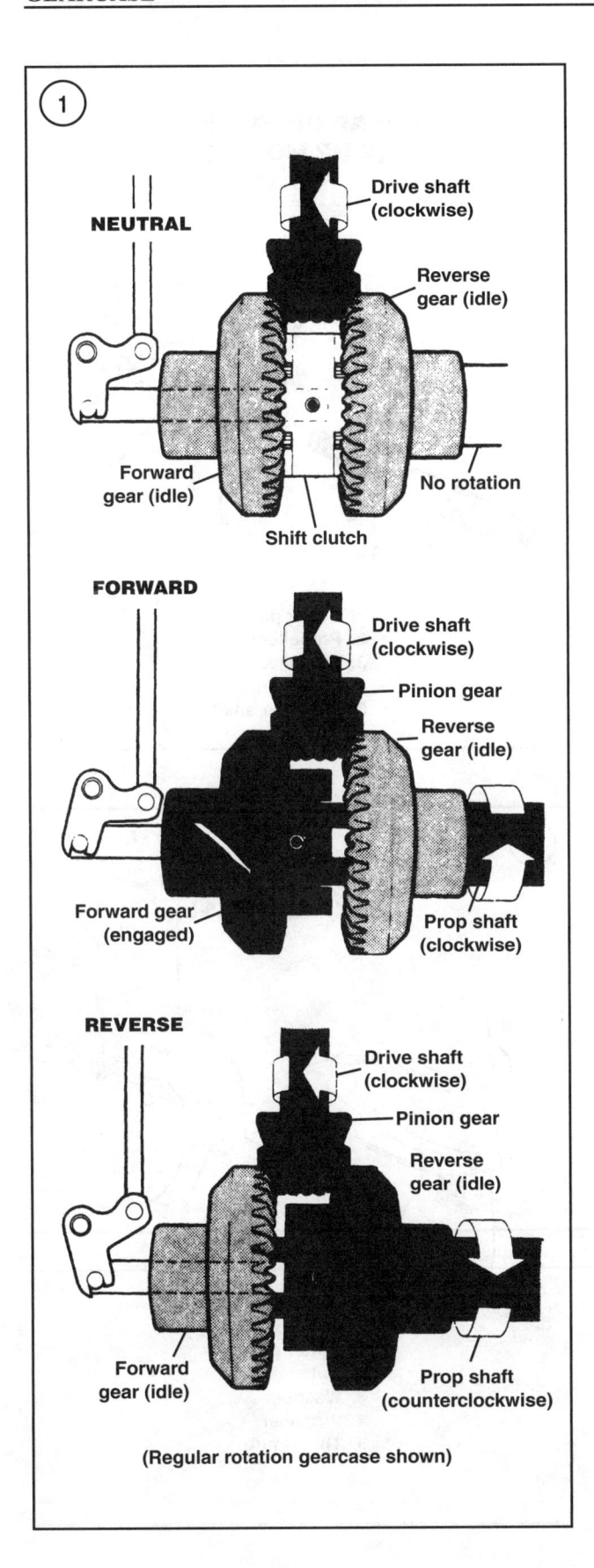

GEARCASE

1

NEUTRAL
- Drive shaft (clockwise)
- Reverse gear (idle)
- Forward gear (idle)
- No rotation
- Shift clutch

FORWARD
- Drive shaft (clockwise)
- Pinion gear
- Reverse gear (idle)
- Forward gear (engaged)
- Prop shaft (clockwise)

REVERSE
- Drive shaft (clockwise)
- Pinion gear
- Reverse gear (idle)
- Forward gear (idle)
- Prop shaft (counterclockwise)

(Regular rotation gearcase shown)

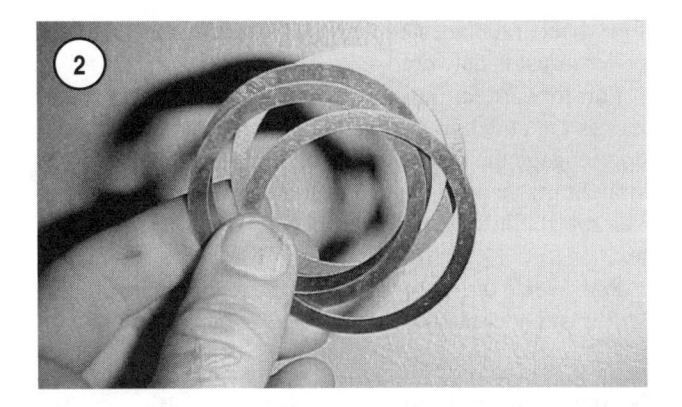

2

gear strength and durability since the gear teeth are not sufficiently overlapping.

If the gear lash is insufficient, the gear teeth are too close together. Insufficient gear lash leads to gear failure since there is not enough clearance to maintain a film of lubricant. Heat expansion only compounds the problem.

All lower gearcases incorporate a water pump to supply cooling water to the power head. All models require gearcase removal to service the water pump. Water pump removal and installation procedures are covered in this chapter.

All models (except 2 and 3 hp models) have full shifting capability. A sliding clutch, splined to the propeller shaft, engages the forward or reverse gear. This creates a direct coupling of the drive shaft to the propeller shaft. Since this is a straight mechanical engagement, only shift the engine at idle speed. Shifting at higher speeds causes gearcase failure.

Non-shifting Units

The 2 hp gearcase only has a pinion and driven gear. The propeller shaft is directly connected to the driven gear at all times. This is a direct drive gearcase. Anytime the engine is cranked or running, the propeller shaft turns and delivers thrust.

For reverse thrust, the entire engine must be pivoted to direct the propeller thrust under the boat. For neutral operation, the engine is switched OFF.

Forward and Neutral Shifting Units

The 3 hp gearcase also only has a pinion and driven gear, but the propeller shaft has a sliding clutch to allow neutral and in-gear operation. Both the pinion and driven gear rotate when the engine is running.

When neutral is selected, the clutch is positioned away from the driven gear. This allows the propeller shaft to freewheel or remain stationary as the gears rotate. No propeller thrust is delivered.

For forward or reverse thrust, the shift mechanism moves the clutch to engage the driven gear as the clutch dogs engage the bosses on the driven gear. Since this is a straight mechanical engagement, only shift the engine at idle speed. Shifting at higher speeds causes gearcase failure.

For reverse thrust, pivot the engine to direct the propeller thrust under the boat.

Neutral, Forward and Reverse Shifting Units

All 4-90 hp models have full shifting capability. A sliding clutch, splined to the propeller shaft, engages the forward or reverse gear. See **Figure 1**. This creates a direct coupling of the drive shaft to the propeller shaft. Since this is a straight mechanical engagement, only shift the engine at idle speed. Shifting at higher speeds causes gearcase failure.

When neutral is selected (**Figure 1**), the shift mechanism positions the clutch midway between the driven gears. This allows the propeller shaft to freewheel or remain stationary. No propeller thrust is delivered.

When forward is selected (**Figure 1**), the shift mechanism moves the clutch to engage the front mounted gear. This mechanical engagement results in clockwise rotation of the propeller. The right-hand propeller then produces forward propeller thrust.

When reverse is selected (**Figure 1**), the shift mechanism moves the clutch to engage the rear-mounted gear. This mechanical engagement results in counterclockwise rotation of the propeller. The right-hand propeller then produces reverse propeller thrust is delivered.

CAUTION
Never use a left-hand propeller on a gearcase designed to only use a right-hand propeller. Continued operation in the wrong direction for forward thrust can cause gearcase component failure.

PROPELLER

Two methods are used to absorb shock and mount the propeller. 2 hp models use a shear pin. 3-90 hp models use a thrust hub.

With the shear pin design, the propeller nut (2, **Figure 3**) and cotter pin (1) secure the propeller to the propeller shaft. The shear pin (4, **Figure 3**) engages and drives the propeller. The shear pin is designed to break during an un-

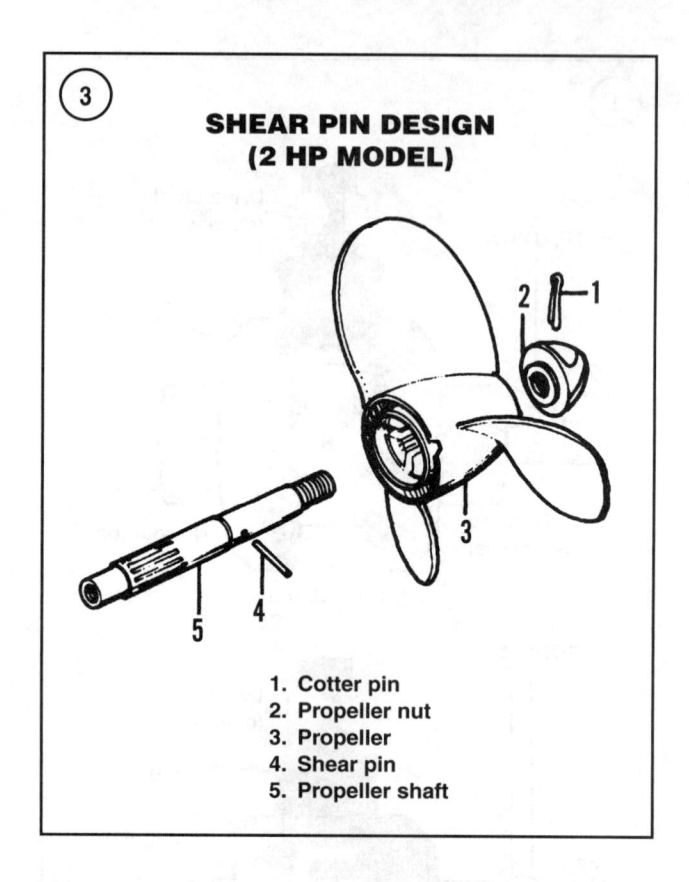

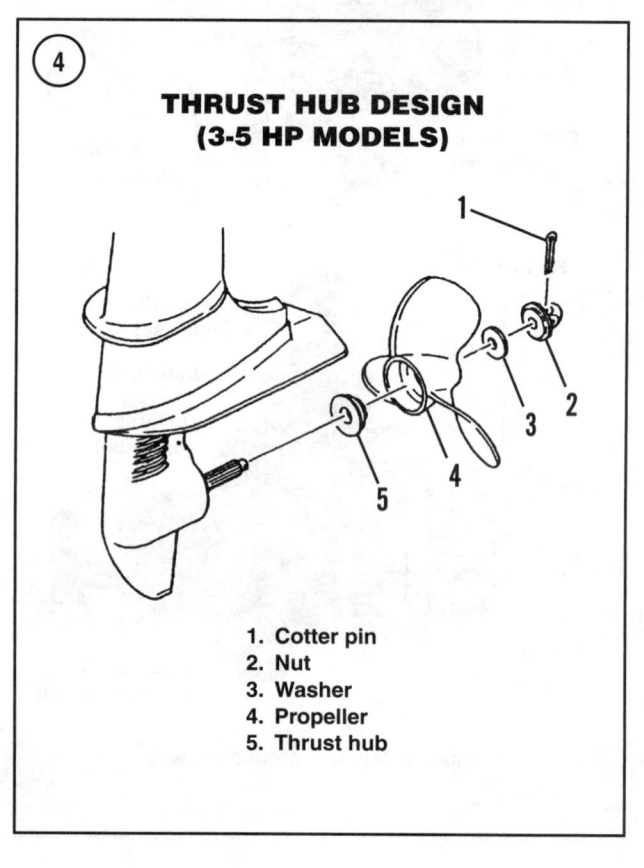

SHEAR PIN DESIGN (2 HP MODEL)

1. Cotter pin
2. Propeller nut
3. Propeller
4. Shear pin
5. Propeller shaft

THRUST HUB DESIGN (3-5 HP MODELS)

1. Cotter pin
2. Nut
3. Washer
4. Propeller
5. Thrust hub

GEARCASE

5

**THRUST HUB DESIGN
(6-90 HP MODELS)**

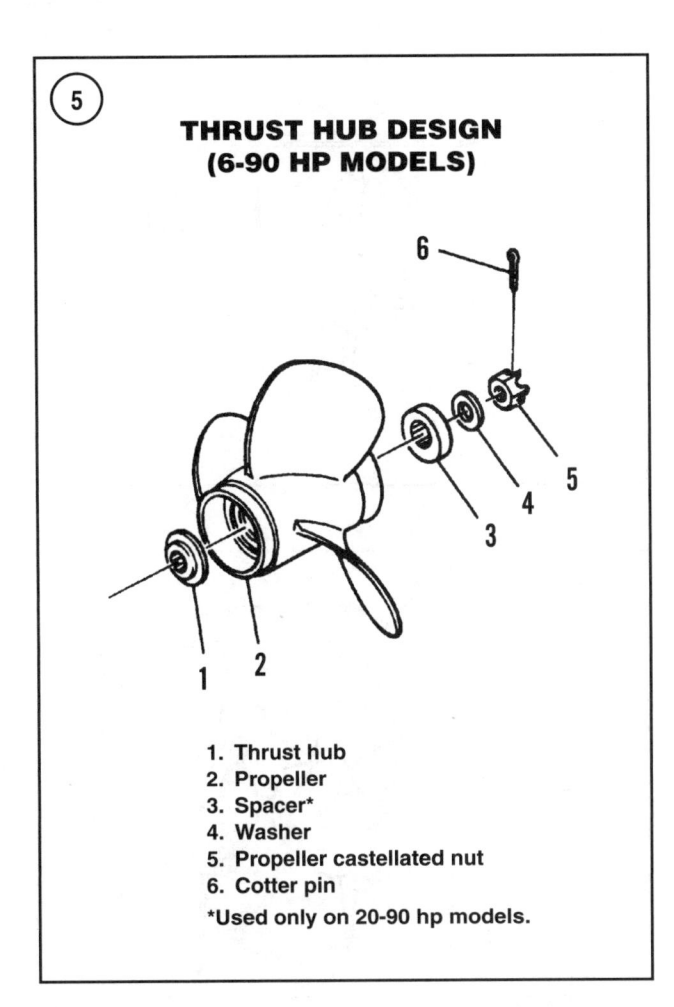

1. Thrust hub
2. Propeller
3. Spacer*
4. Washer
5. Propeller castellated nut
6. Cotter pin

*Used only on 20-90 hp models.

6

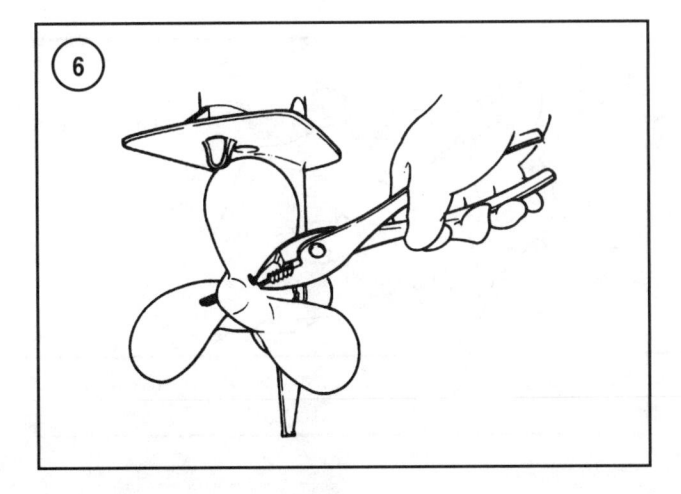

derwater impact, providing some protection for the gearcase components.

With the thrust hub design, the propeller is driven by a splined connection of the propeller shaft to the rubber thrust hub. The rubber thrust hub is pressed into a bore in the propeller and provides a cushion for shifting. It also provides some protection for the gearcase components during an underwater impact. The front-mounted thrust hub (5, **Figure 4**) directs the propeller thrust to a tapered area on the propeller shaft.

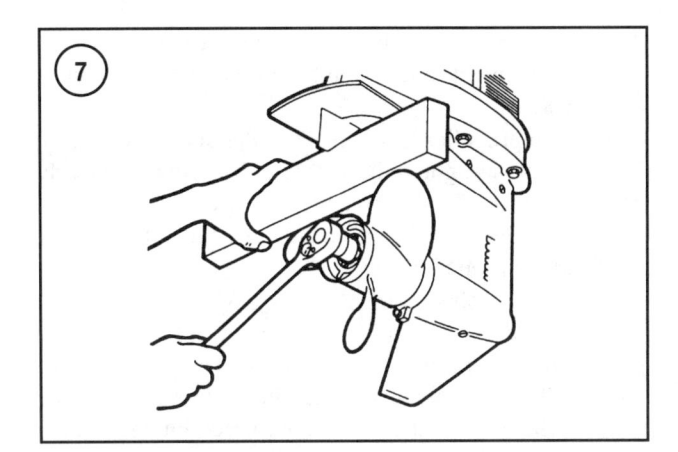

Three different methods are used to secure the propeller to the propeller shaft.

2 hp models use a cone shaped propeller nut (2, **Figure 3**) and cotter pin (1).

3-5 hp models use a cone shaped propeller nut (2, **Figure 4**) cotter pin (1) and washer (3).

6-90 hp models use a castellated nut (5, **Figure 5**), cotter pin (6), washer (4) and spacer (3).

CAUTION
If necessary, use light force to remove the propeller from the propeller shaft. Excessive force will damage the propeller, propeller shaft and internal components of the gearcase. If the propeller cannot be removed by normal means, have a reputable marine repair shop or propeller repair shop remove the propeller.

Always replace the cotter pin and shear pin during installation. Purchase the replacement pins at a marine dealership and select the proper size and material. The cotter pin is made with stainless steel. Use a shear pin designed for the correct model to ensure it will shear at the designated load.

Removal (2 hp Models)

1. Disconnect the spark plug lead.
2. Use pliers to straighten and remove the cotter pin (**Figure 6**). To prevent propeller rotation, place a block of wood between the propeller and the gearcase as shown in **Figure 7**.

3. Engage a wrench to the two flat surfaces of the propeller nut and turn the nut counterclockwise to remove it (**Figure 8**).
4. Pull the propeller from the propeller shaft (**Figure 9**). Use pliers to straighten the shear pin if necessary. Gently drive one end of the shear pin until it is flush with one side of the propeller shaft. Use pliers to twist and pull the shear pin from the propeller shaft.
5. Inspect the shear pin hole for burrs or elongation. Dress burrs down with a file. Attempt to fit the new shear pin into the shear pin hole (**Figure 10**). The pin should fit tightly. Check the pin size if the pin fits loosely. Replace the propeller shaft if the pin size is correct, but the pin fits loosely in the shaft.
6. Clean all surfaces of the propeller and propeller bore for the shaft. Inspect the pin engagement slot in the propeller for wear or damage. Replace the propeller if there are defects in these areas.

Installation (2 hp Models)

1. Position a new shear pin in the hole (**Figure 10**). Use a hammer to gently drive the pin into the propeller shaft until the same amount of the pin protrudes from each side of the propeller shaft.
2. Apply a light coat of Yamaha All-Purpose Grease or its equivalent to the shear pin and propeller shaft threads. Apply grease to the propeller shaft and the shaft bore in the propeller.
3. Slide the propeller onto the propeller shaft. Rotate the propeller while pushing forward until the shear pin engages the slot in the propeller.
4. Maintain engagement of the shear pin in the slot while threading the propeller nut onto the shaft. Tighten the propeller nut hand tight at this time.
5. To prevent propeller rotation, place a block of wood between the propeller and the gearcase as shown in **Figure 7**. Securely tighten the propeller nut.
6. Check for alignment of the cotter pin hole in the propeller nut with the hole in the propeller shaft. Tighten the propeller nut an additional amount as necessary to align the holes. Do not over tighten the nut. Never loosen the nut to align the cotter pin holes.
7. Insert a new cotter pin into the holes and bend the ends over.
8. Reconnect the spark plug lead.

Removal (3-90 hp Models)

After removing the propeller, inspect it for the presence of black rubber material in the driver hub area (**Figure 11**).

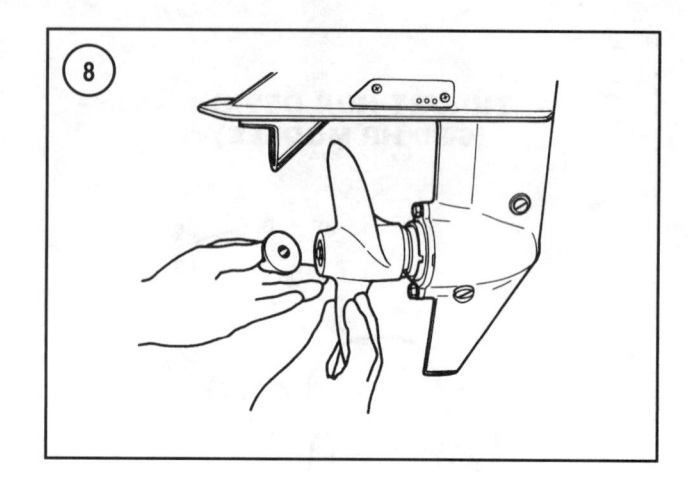

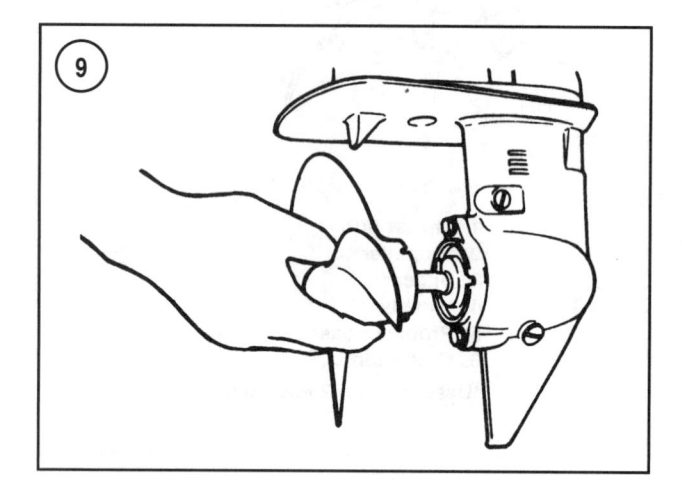

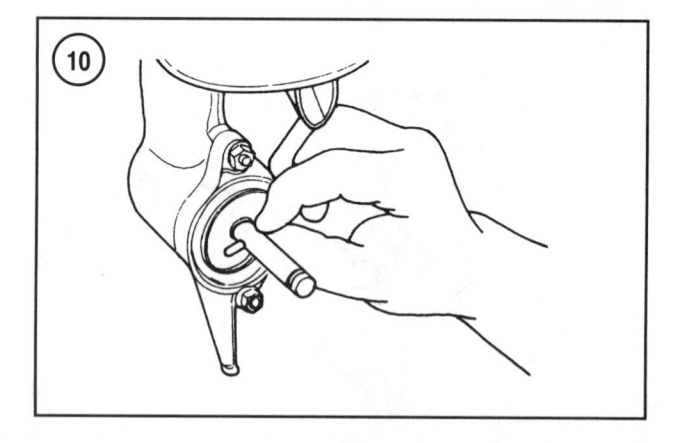

Have the hub inspected or replaced at a propeller repair facility if this material is present. It normally indicates the hub has spun in the propeller bore.

1. Disconnect the spark plug leads.
2. On electric start models, disconnect the cables from the battery.

GEARCASE

6. Mark the propeller side of the thrust hub. Remove the thrust hub (**Figure 12**). Tap the hub lightly if it is seized on the propeller shaft.
7. Clean all debris and old grease from the propeller shaft. Inspect the propeller shaft for twisted splines or excessively worn surfaces. Pay particular attention to the tapered surface that contacts the thrust washer. Rotate the propeller shaft while observing for shaft deflection. Replace the propeller shaft if there are worn surfaces, twisted splines or shaft deflection.
8. Inspect the thrust hub (1, **Figure 5**) for worn or cracked surfaces and replace as necessary.

CAUTION
Never use a damaged, worn or cracked propeller thrust hub. An excessively worn hub may allow the propeller to contact the gearcase during operation. A cracked hub may unexpectedly fail, allowing the propeller to contact the gearcase. The gearcase will be irreparably damaged if the engine operates with the propeller contacting the gearcase.

Installation (3-90 hp Models)

1. Apply a light coat of Yamaha All-Purpose Grease or its equivalent to the propeller shaft tapered surface and threaded end. Apply grease to the propeller shaft and the shaft bore in the propeller.
2. Slide the thrust hub onto the propeller shaft. The tapered surface of the thrust hub must contact the tapered surface of the propeller shaft.
3. Slide the propeller onto the propeller shaft. Rotate the propeller to align the propeller splines with the propeller shaft splines. Seat the propeller against the thrust hub.
4. Refer to **Figure 4** or **Figure 5** and install the washer and spacer (20-90 hp models only). Thread the propeller nut hand-tight onto the propeller shaft.
5. To prevent propeller rotation, place a block of wood between the propeller and the gearcase as shown in **Figure 7**.
   a. On 3-5 hp models, securely tighten the propeller nut.
   b. On 6-90 hp models, tighten the propeller nut to the specification in **Table 1**.
6. Check for alignment of the cotter pin slot in the propeller nut with the hole in the propeller shaft. Tighten the propeller nut an additional amount as necessary to align the holes. Do not over tighten the nut. Never loosen the nut to align the cotter pin holes.
7. Insert a new cotter pin into the holes and bend the ends over.

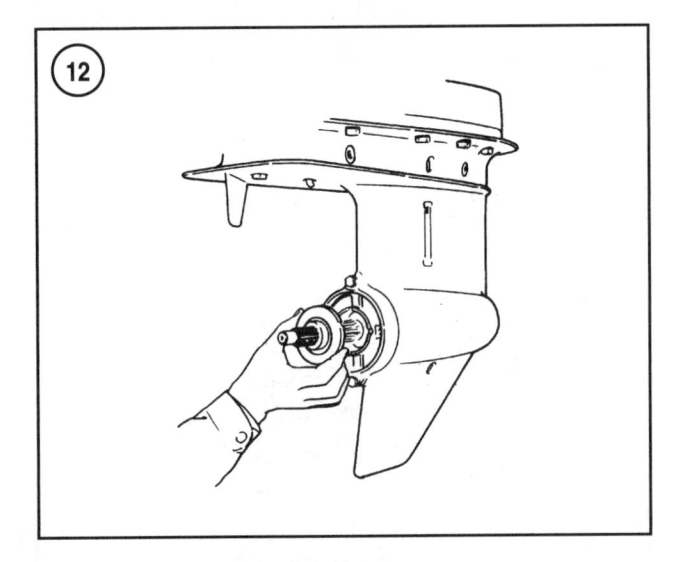

3. Use pliers to straighten and remove the cotter pin (**Figure 6**). To prevent propeller rotation, place a block of wood between the propeller and the gearcase as shown in **Figure 7**.
4A. On 3-5 hp models, engage a wrench to the two flat surfaces of the propeller nut and turn the nut counterclockwise to remove it (**Figure 8**). Remove the washer (3, **Figure 4**).
4B. On 6-15 hp models, engage a socket wrench to the propeller nut. Turn the nut counterclockwise to remove the propeller nut. Remove the washer (4, **Figure 5**).
4C. On 20-90 hp models, engage a socket wrench to the propeller nut. Turn the nut counterclockwise to remove the propeller nut. Remove the washer (4, **Figure 5**) and spacer (3).
5. Carefully pull the propeller from the propeller shaft. Use a block of wood as a cushion and carefully drive the propeller from the shaft if necessary. Only use light force to avoid damaging the propeller or gearcase components.

8. On electric start models, connect the cables to the battery.
9. Reconnect the spark plug leads.

GEARCASE REMOVAL/INSTALLATION

Always remove the propeller before removing or installing the gearcase. Refer to the procedures described in this chapter. To prevent accidental starting or starter engagement, disconnect all spark plug leads and the battery cables (electric start models) before gearcase removal.

Drain the gearcase lubricant before removal if the gearcase will require disassembly. Refer to Chapter Four for procedures.

Gearcase removal and installation procedures vary by model. Refer to the procedures specified for the model requiring service.

CAUTION
Work carefully when using a pry bar to separate the gearcase from the drive shaft housing. Always make sure all fasteners are removed before attempting to pry the housings apart. Use a blunt tip pry bar and locate a pry point near the front and rear mating surfaces.

CAUTION
Never apply grease to the top of the drive shaft or fill the connection at the crankshaft. The grease may cause a hydraulic lock on the shaft that can cause failure of the gearcase and/or power head. Apply a light coat of Yamaha All-Purpose Grease or equivalent to the sides of the splines on the upper end of the drive shaft.

CAUTION
Work carefully when installing the upper end of the drive shaft into the crankshaft. The lower seal on the crankshaft can be dislodged or damaged by the drive shaft. Make sure the shafts are properly aligned before inserting the drive shaft into the crankshaft. Never attempt to force the gearcase into position. Rotate the drive slightly and attempt to install the gearcase again if necessary.

NOTE
Apply moderate heat to the gearcase and drive shaft housing mating surfaces if corrosion prevents easy removal of the gearcase.

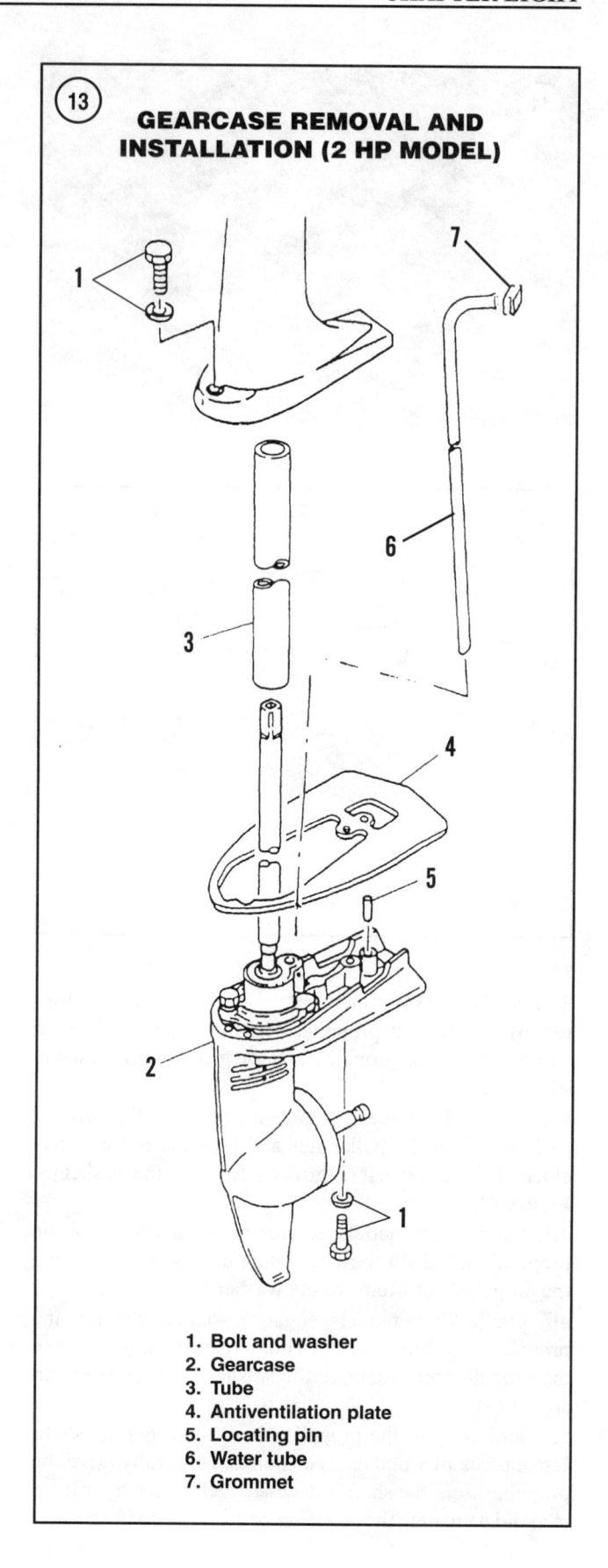

GEARCASE REMOVAL AND INSTALLATION (2 HP MODEL)

1. Bolt and washer
2. Gearcase
3. Tube
4. Antiventilation plate
5. Locating pin
6. Water tube
7. Grommet

GEARCASE

4. Retrieve the locating pin (5, **Figure 13**) if it was dislodged. Install the pin into the opening provided in the gearcase.
5. Clean corrosion and other contaminants from the gearcase-to-drive shaft housing mating surfaces and upper end of the drive shaft.

Installation (2 hp Models)

1. Apply a very light coat of Yamaha All-Purpose Grease or its equivalent to the locating pin and the upper end of the drive shaft.
2. Place the antiventilation plate (4, **Figure 13**) on the gearcase. The locating pin (5, **Figure 13**) must fit into the opening in the plate.
3. Install the tube (3, **Figure 13**) over the drive shaft. Align the lower end of the water tube (6, **Figure 13**) with its opening in the water pump while guiding the drive shaft into the drive shaft housing. Align the tube (3, **Figure 13**) and attempt to seat the gearcase against the drive shaft housing. Do not force the gearcase into position. If seating the gearcase is difficult, lower the gearcase and slightly rotate the drive shaft clockwise. Repeat this step until the square drive shaft connection engages the square opening in the crankshaft and the gearcase seats against the drive shaft housing. Check for proper alignment of the water tube to the water pump opening during each installation attempt. Make sure the locating pin enters its opening in the drive shaft housing.
4. Apply Loctite 572 to the threads of the mounting bolts (1, **Figure 13**). With the gearcase held in position, install both bolts and washers. Tighten the bolts to the general torque specification in Chapter One.
5. Connect the spark plug lead. Run the engine and check for correct cooling system operation. If water does not exit the tell-tale opening, remove the gearcase and check for a dislodged water tube or grommet (7, **Figure 13**).

Removal (3-8 hp Models)

1. On electric start models, disconnect both cables from the battery.
2. To prevent accidental starting, disconnect the spark plug lead(s).
3. Locate the shift lever (1, **Figure 14**) on the starboard side lower engine cover.
   a. On 3 hp models, shift the lever into FORWARD.
   b. On 4-8 hp models, shift the lever into REVERSE.
4A. On 3-5 hp models, carefully pry the rubber grommet (2, **Figure 14**) from the drive shaft housing. This allows access to the shift shaft connector (**Figure 15**). Scribe or mark the connector position on the lower shift

14
1. Shift lever
2. Rubber grommet
3. Bolt

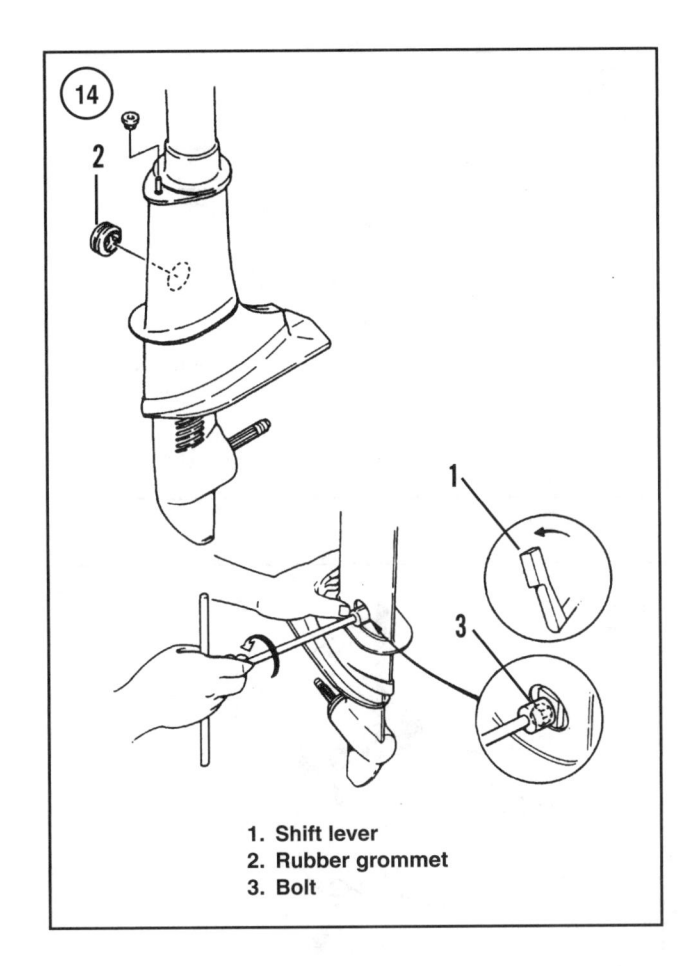

15

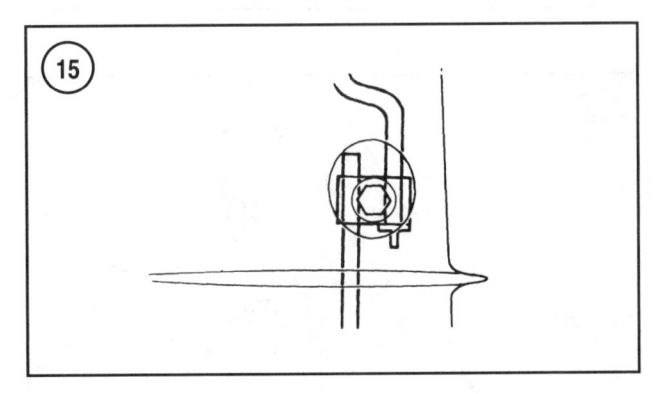

Removal (2 hp Models)

1. Disconnect the spark plug lead.
2. Support the gearcase while removing the bolts and washers (1, **Figure 13**).
3. Carefully tug or pry the gearcase from the drive shaft housing. Remove the antiventilation plate (4, **Figure 13**) and tube (3). Install the water tube (6, **Figure 13**) and grommet (7) into the drive shaft housing if they were dislodged during gearcase removal.

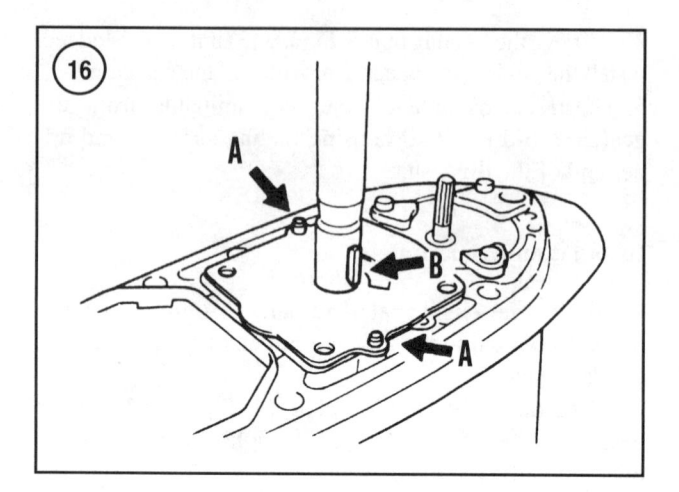

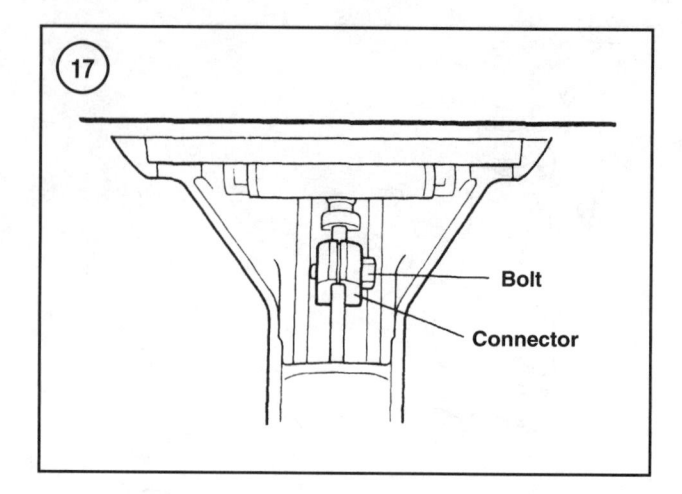

shaft (**Figure 16**). This will reduce the time needed to adjust the shift linkage after gearcase installation. Loosen the bolt on the shift shaft connector (**Figure 16**) three complete turns.

4B. On 6 and 8 hp models, tilt the engine fully up and engage the tilt lock mechanism. Trace the lower shift shaft up to the connector (**Figure 17**). Scribe or mark the connector position on the shift shafts (**Figure 16**). This will reduce the time needed to adjust the shift linkage after gearcase installation. Remove the bolt and connector from the shift shafts.

5. Support the gearcase and remove the bolts that secure the gearcase to the drive shaft housing.
   a. On 3 hp models, four bolts (**Figure 18**) secure the gearcase.
   b. On 4 and 5 hp models, two bolts secure the gearcase. One bolt is located on the under side of the antiventilation plate and directly above the propeller shaft. The remaining bolt is located on the front of the gearcase just below the gearcase-to-drive shaft housing mating surface.
   c. On 6 and 8 hp models, four bolts secure the gearcase. Two bolts are located on each side of the gearcase (**Figure 19**).

6. Make sure the lower shift shaft is free from the shift shaft connector, then lower the gearcase from the drive shaft housing. If necessary, carefully tug or pry the gearcase from the housing.

7. Reposition the water tube and sealing grommet if they were dislodged during gearcase removal.

8. Clean corrosion and other contaminants from the gearcase mating surfaces, shift shafts and drive shaft.

9. Inspect the grommet that connects the water tube to the water pump for damage or deterioration. Replace the grommet if it is faulty or in questionable condition.

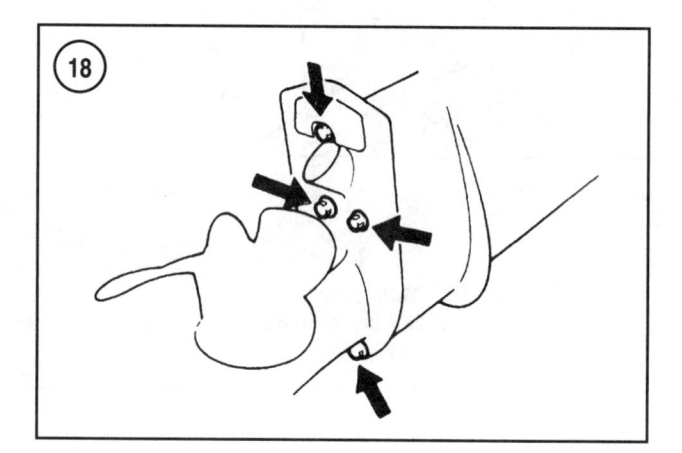

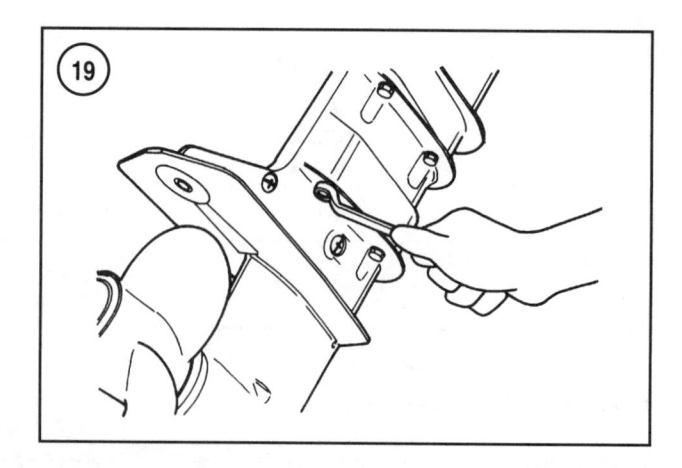

Installation (3-8 hp Models)

1. Apply a light coat of Yamaha All-Purpose Grease or its equivalent to the splined section at the upper end of the drive shaft and the grommet that connects the water tube into the water pump (**Figure 20**).

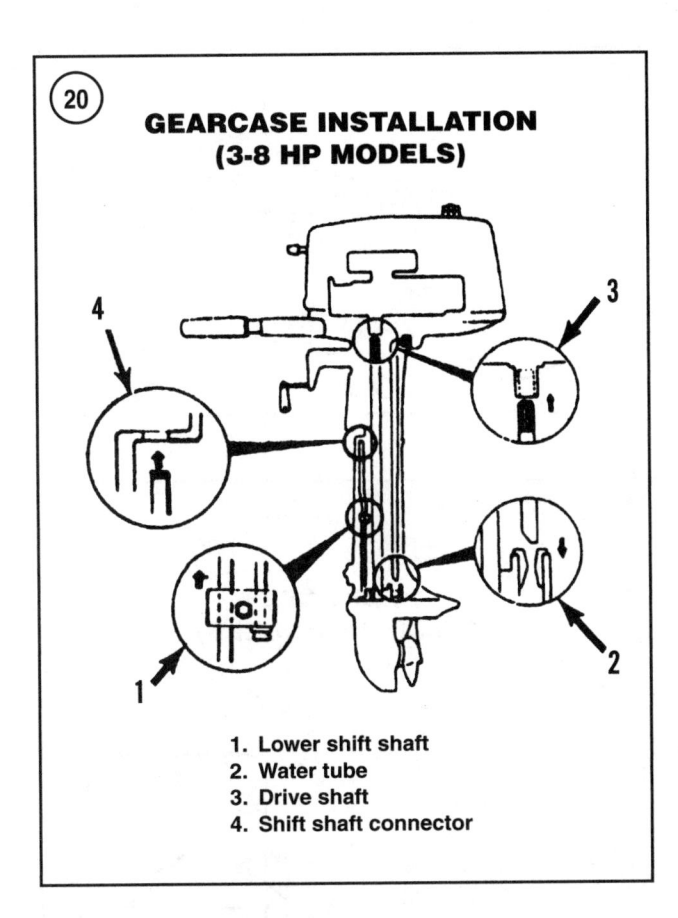

GEARCASE

20 GEARCASE INSTALLATION
(3-8 HP MODELS)

1. Lower shift shaft
2. Water tube
3. Drive shaft
4. Shift shaft connector

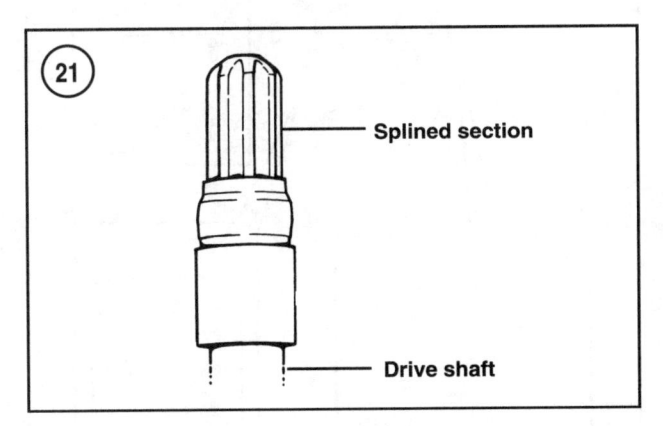

21
- Splined section
- Drive shaft

CAUTION
*Never rotate the propeller shaft to align the drive shaft splined connection (**Figure 21**) with the crankshaft splines. The water pump impeller can be damaged, leading to overheating of the engine.*

2. Rotate the drive shaft clockwise (**Figure 22**) while observing the propeller shaft. Push the lower shift shaft up or down until the propeller shaft direction matches the position of the shift lever.

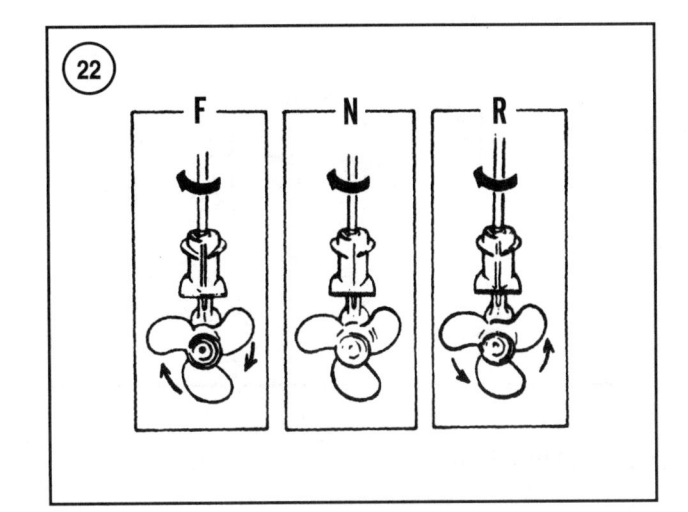

22 F N R

3. Make sure all locating pins are in their respective bores within the gearcase and drive shaft housings.
4. Align the lower end of the water tube (2, **Figure 20**) with its opening in the water pump while guiding the drive shaft into the drive shaft housing. Align the drive shaft with the crankshaft and attempt to seat the gearcase against the drive shaft housing. Do not force the gearcase into position. If the gearcase is difficult to seat, lower the gearcase and slightly rotate the drive shaft clockwise. Repeat this step until the splined drive shaft connection engages the splined opening in the crankshaft and the gearcase seats against the drive shaft housing. Check for proper alignment of the water tube to the water pump opening during each installation attempt. Make sure the locating pins enter the openings in the drive shaft housing.
5. Check for proper alignment of the upper shift shaft and connector (4, **Figure 20**) with the lower shift shaft. Lower the gearcase and align the shaft before proceeding. Apply Loctite 572 to the threads of the mounting bolts. With the gearcase held in position, install both bolts and washers. Tighten the bolts to the general torque specification in Chapter One.
6. Position the shaft connector over the shift shaft and align it with the marks made prior to gearcase removal. Slowly rotate the flywheel clockwise as viewed from the top to make sure the propeller shaft rotates in the direction that matches the shift lever. Tighten the shift shaft connector bolt to the torque specification in **Table 1** or Chapter One.
7. Adjust the shift linkages as described in Chapter Four. Connect the spark plug lead. Run the engine and check for correct cooling system operation. If water does not exit the tell-tale opening, remove the gearcase and check for a dislodged water tube or grommet.

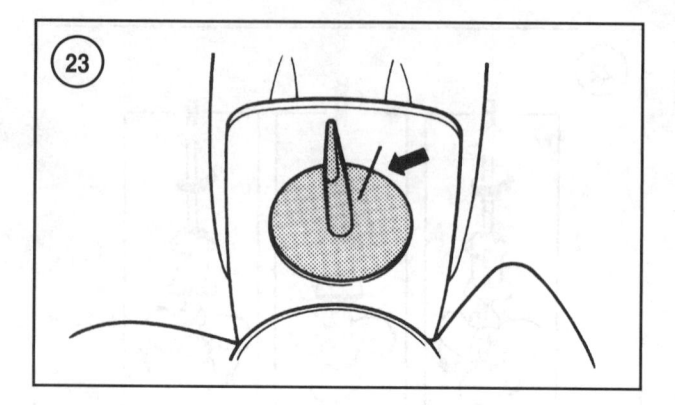

Removal (9.9-30 hp Models)

1. To prevent accidental starting, disconnect the spark plug leads.
2. On electric start models, disconnect both cables from the battery.
3. Use a marker to reference the trim tab setting (**Figure 23**). Do not use a scribe as the gearcase will corrode where the paint is scratched. Remove the bolt (**Figure 24**). Carefully tap the anode or trim tab loose, then remove it from the gearcase. Inspect the anode as described in *Sacrificial Anodes* in this chapter.
4. On 25 hp three-cylinder and 30 hp models, cut the plastic locking type clamp and disconnect the speedometer hose from the connector (1, **Figure 25**). Heat the speedometer hose with a portable hair dryer for easier removal from the connector.
5. Place the shift lever into REVERSE gear. Locate the shift shaft coupling (**Figure 26**) on the forward side of the drive shaft housing. Mark the upper and lower shift shafts where they align with reference points on the engine. This will reduce the time needed to adjust the shift linkages after gearcase installation.
6. Hold the shift coupling with a wrench while loosening the jam nut (**Figure 27**). Unthread the coupling from the lower shift shaft.
   a. On 20 and 25 hp two-cylinder models, unthread the jam nut from the lower shift shaft.
   b. On all other models, the jam nut remains threaded on the lower shift shaft during gearcase removal.
7. Support the gearcase and remove the bolts that secure the gearcase to the drive shaft housing.
   a. On 9.9-25 hp two-cylinder models, four bolts secure the gearcase. Two bolts are located on each side of the gearcase (**Figure 19**).
   b. On 25 hp three-cylinder and 30 hp models, five bolts secure the gearcase. One bolt is located in the trim tab cavity directly above the propeller shaft.

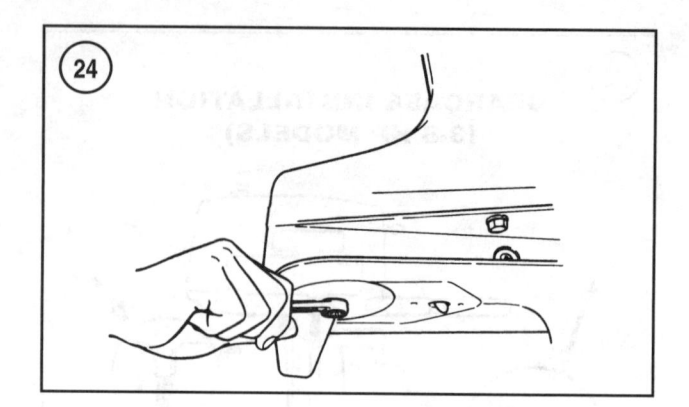

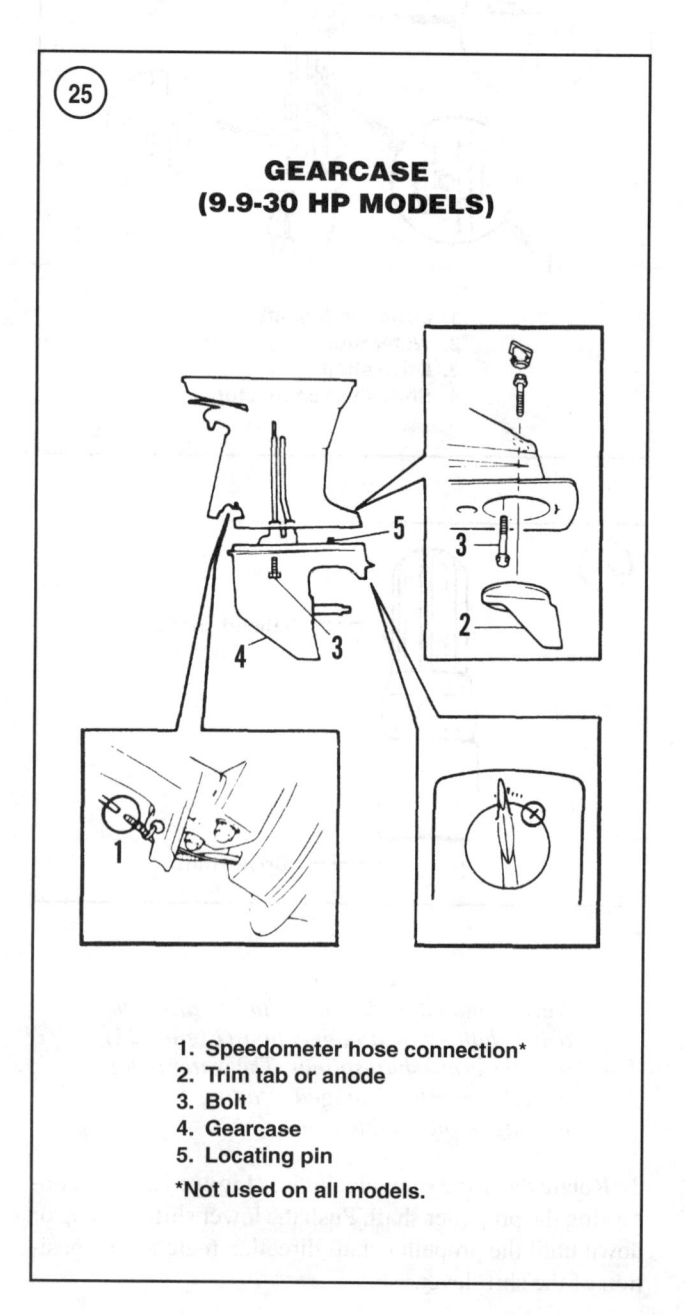

GEARCASE (9.9-30 HP MODELS)

1. Speedometer hose connection*
2. Trim tab or anode
3. Bolt
4. Gearcase
5. Locating pin

*Not used on all models.

GEARCASE

26

Bolt

27

28

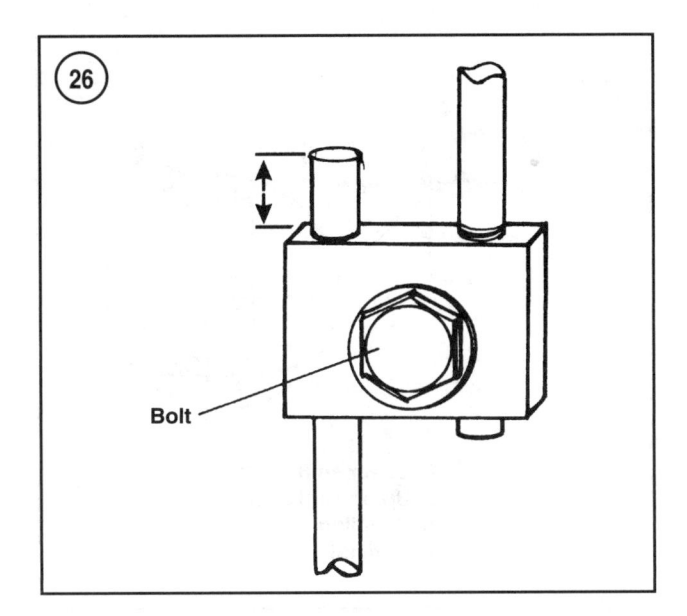

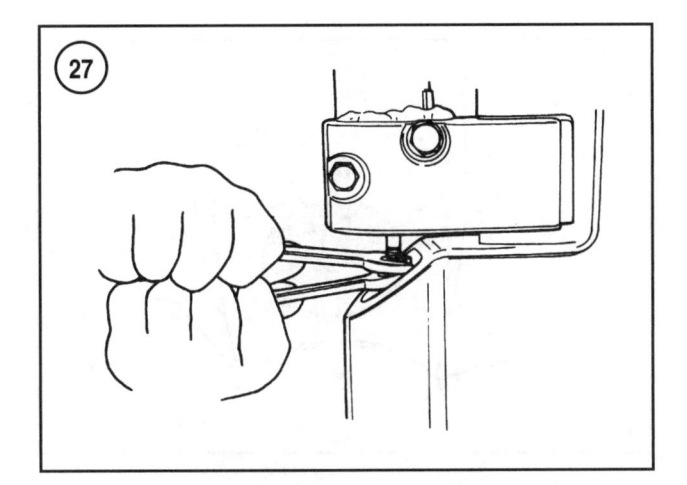

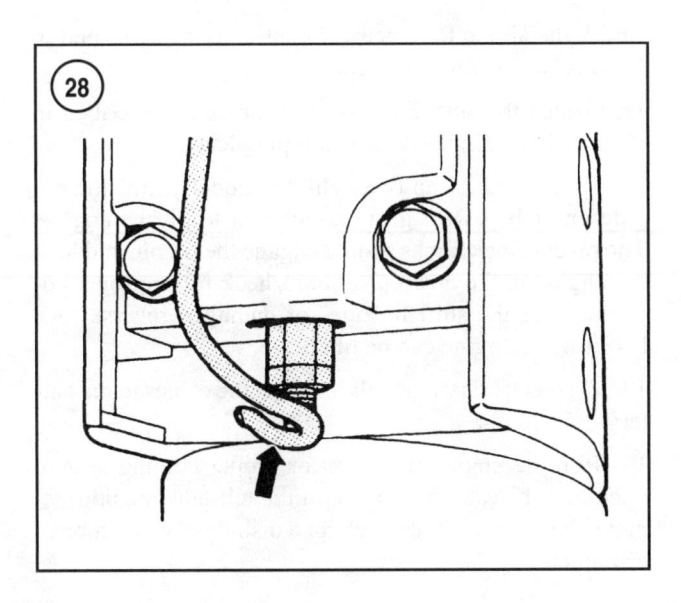

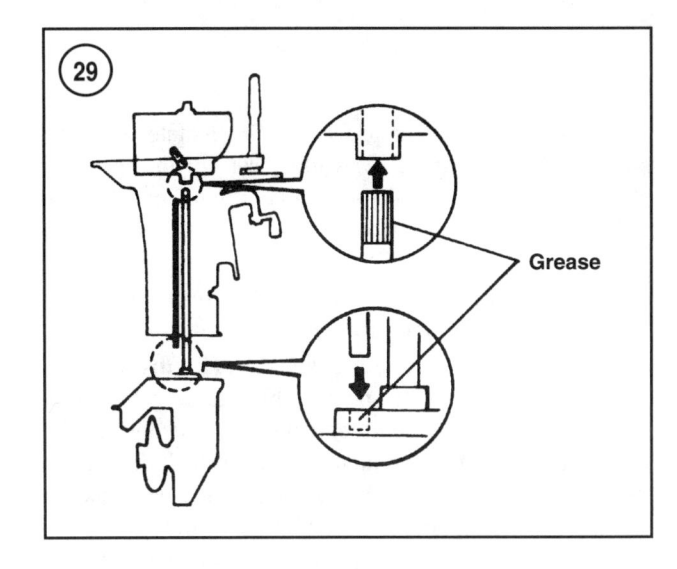

29

Grease

Two bolts are located on each side of the gearcase (**Figure 19**).

8. Make sure the lower shift shaft is free from the shift shaft connector, then lower the gearcase from the drive shaft housing. If necessary, carefully tug or pry the gearcase from the housing. On 20 and 25 hp two-cylinder models, guide the lower shift shaft from the reverse lock linkage (**Figure 28**) during gearcase removal.

9. Reposition the water tube and upper sealing grommet if they were dislodged during gearcase removal.

10. Clean corrosion and other contaminants from the gearcase mating surfaces, shift shafts and drive shaft.

11. Inspect the grommet that connects the water tube to the water pump for damage or deterioration. Replace the grommet if it is faulty or in questionable condition.

Installation (9.9-30 hp Models)

CAUTION
Never apply grease to the top of the drive shaft or fill the connection at the crankshaft. The grease may cause a hydraulic lock on the shaft that can cause failure of the gearcase, power head or both.

1. Apply a light coat of Yamaha All-Purpose Grease or its equivalent to the splined section at the upper end of the drive shaft and the grommet that connects the water tube to the water pump (**Figure 29**).

CAUTION
Never rotate the propeller shaft to align the drive shaft splined connection with the crankshaft splines. The water pump impel-

ler can be damaged, leading to overheating of the engine.

2. Move the shift lever to REVERSE. Rotate the drive shaft clockwise (**Figure 22**) while observing the propeller shaft. Push the lower shift shaft up or down until the propeller shaft direction matches the position of the shift lever.

3. Make sure all locating pins are in their respective bores within the gearcase and drive shaft housings.

4. Align the lower end of the water tube (**Figure 29**) with its opening in the water pump while guiding the drive shaft into the drive shaft housing. On 20 and 25 hp two-cylinder models, guide the lower shift shaft through the reverse lock linkage (**Figure 28**) during gearcase installation. Align the drive shaft with the crankshaft and attempt to seat the gearcase against the drive shaft housing. Do not force the gearcase into position. If the gearcase is difficult to seat, lower the gearcase and slightly rotate the drive shaft clockwise. Repeat this step until the splined drive shaft connection engages the splined opening in the crankshaft and the gearcase seats against the drive shaft housing. Check for proper alignment of the water tube to the water pump opening during each installation attempt. Make sure the locating pins enter the openings in the drive shaft housing.

5. Apply Loctite 572 to the threads of the gearcase mounting bolts. Hold the gearcase in position and install the bolts.

   a. On 9.9 and 15 hp models, evenly tighten the bolts to the general torque specification in Chapter One.
   b. On 20 and 30 hp models, evenly tighten the bolts to the specification in **Table 1**.

6. On 25 two-cylinder and 30 hp models, heat the end of the speedometer hose with a portable hair dryer and quickly slip it fully over the connector (1, **Figure 25**). Secure the hose on the connector with a plastic locking type clamp.

7. On 20 and 25 hp two-cylinder models, thread the jam nut onto the lower shift shaft.

8. Align the upper and lower shift shaft as indicated in **Figure 30**. Thread the upper shift shaft coupling onto the lower shift shaft until the marks on the shift shafts align with the reference points (**Figure 26**) made before removal.

9. Make sure the coupler makes several turns of engagement onto the lower shift shaft. Hold the coupling with a wrench (**Figure 27**) and tighten the jam nut until it is firmly locked against the coupling.

10. Install the trim tab or anode and bolt. Align the reference mark (**Figure 23**) and securely tighten the bolt.

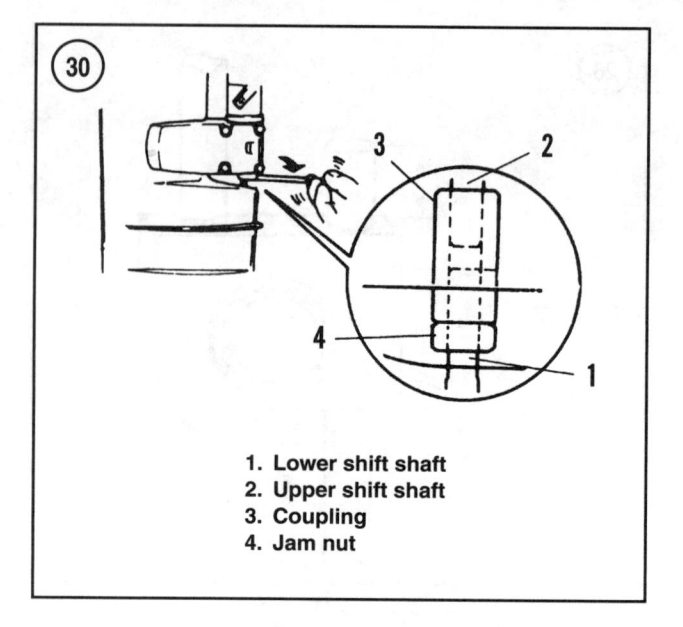

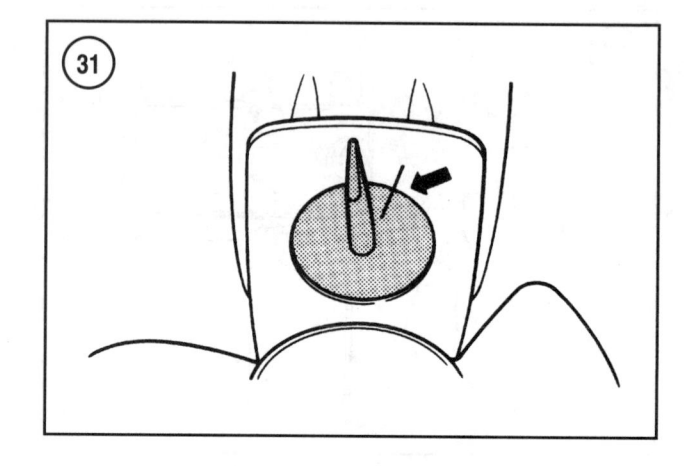

30

1. Lower shift shaft
2. Upper shift shaft
3. Coupling
4. Jam nut

31

Check the anode for electrical continuity as described in *Sacrificial Anodes* in this chapter.

11. Adjust the shift linkages and cables as described in Chapter Four. Connect the spark plug leads.

12. On 20 and 25 hp two-cylinder models, shift the engine into REVERSE gear and attempt to tilt the engine. The reverse lock hooks should engage the tilt pin and lock the engine in the down position. Check for improper adjustment of the shift linkages or damaged reverse lock hooks if the engine can be tilted.

13. On electric start models, connect the cables to the battery.

14. Run the engine to check for proper cooling system operation. If water does not exit the tell-tale opening, remove the gearcase and check for a dislodged water tube or grommet.

GEARCASE

fully tug or pry the gearcase from the housing. Pry at points near the front and rear of the gearcase-to-drive shaft housing mating surface.

8. Reposition the water tube and upper sealing grommet if they were dislodged during gearcase removal.

9. Clean corrosion and other contaminants from the gearcase mating surfaces, shift shafts and drive shaft.

10. Inspect the grommet that connects the water tube to the water pump for damage or deterioration. Replace the grommet if it is faulty or in questionable condition.

Installation (40-90 hp Models)

1. Apply a light coat of Yamaha All-Purpose Grease or its equivalent to the splined section at the upper end of the drive shaft and the grommet that connects the water tube into the water pump (**Figure 29**).

CAUTION
Never rotate the propeller shaft to align the drive shaft splined connection with the crankshaft splines. The water pump impeller can be damaged leading to overheating of the engine.

2. Install the shift handle (Yamaha part No. YB-6052) onto the lower shift shaft (**Figure 33**). If this tool is not available, grip the lower shift shaft with pliers and a shop towel (**Figure 34**).

3. Move the shift lever to REVERSE. Rotate the drive shaft clockwise while observing the propeller shaft. Rotate the lower shift shaft until the propeller shaft rotates in the forward, then the reverse, direction. Note the shift shaft position for each gear. Position the shift shaft at the point midway between the forward and reverse gear positions. Rotate the drive shaft to make sure the gearcase is in neutral gear. Remove the shift handle.

4. Make sure all locating pins are in their respective bores within the gearcase and drive shaft housings.

5. Align the lower end of the water tube (**Figure 29**) with its opening in the water pump while guiding the drive shaft into the drive shaft housing.

6. Align the drive shaft with the crankshaft and both shift shafts while attempting to seat the gearcase against the drive shaft housing. Never force the gearcase into position. This could result in damage to the shift shafts and drive shaft seal. If the gearcase is difficult to seat, lower the gearcase and slightly rotate the drive shaft clockwise. Repeat this step until the splined drive shaft connection engages the splined opening in the crankshaft and the gearcase seats against the drive shaft housing. If the shift shaft is difficult to align, have an assistant slightly toggle the shift selector to align the shift shaft splines. Check for

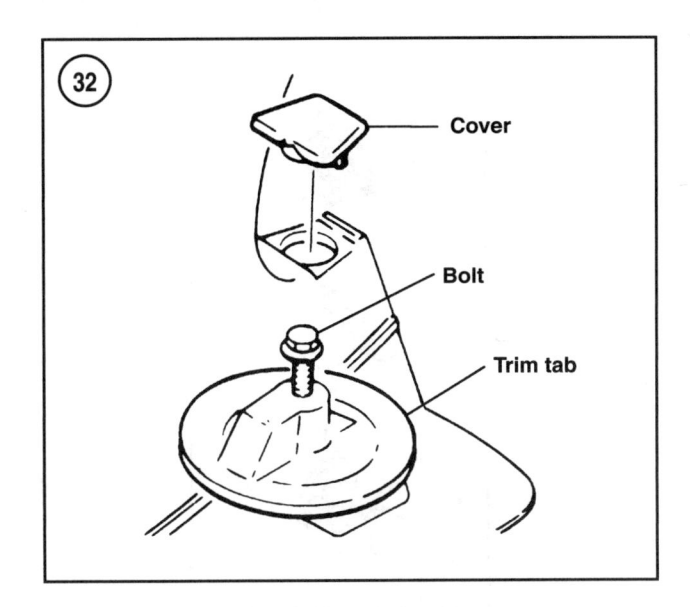

15. Move the shift lever to the FORWARD, NEUTRAL and REVERSE gear positions to verify correct shift operation. Adjust the shift linkages if the shift does not operate correctly.

Removal (40-90 hp Models)

1. To prevent accidental starting, disconnect the spark plug leads.

2. On electric start models, disconnect both cables from the battery.

3. Use a marker to reference the trim tab setting (**Figure 31**). Do not use a scribe as the gearcase will corrode where the paint is scratched.
   a. On 40 and 50 hp models, remove the bolt (**Figure 24**). Carefully tap the trim tab loose, then remove it from the gearcase.
   b. On 60-90 hp models, locate and remove the bolt access cover (**Figure 32**). Use a socket and extension to remove the trim tab bolt. Carefully tap the trim tab loose, then remove it from the gearcase.

4. Cut the plastic locking type clamp and disconnect the speedometer hose from the connector (1, **Figure 25**). Heat the speedometer hose with a portable hair dryer for easier removal from the connector.

5. Shift the engine into NEUTRAL gear.

6. Support the gearcase and remove the five bolts that secure the gearcase to the drive shaft housing. One bolt is located in the trim tab cavity directly above the propeller shaft. Two bolts are located on each side of the gearcase (**Figure 19**).

7. Make sure all bolts are removed, then lower the gearcase from the drive shaft housing. If necessary, care-

33

Shift handle

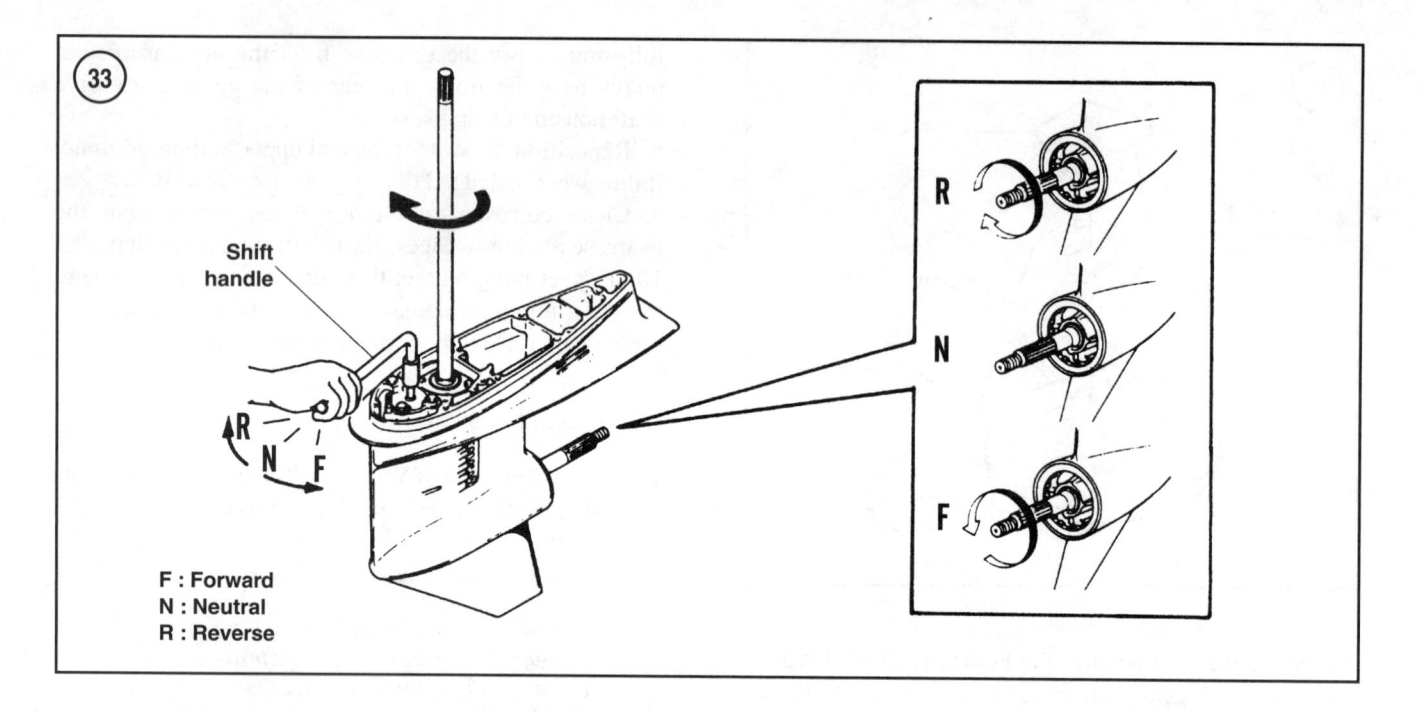

F : Forward
N : Neutral
R : Reverse

proper alignment of the water tube to the water pump opening during each installation attempt. Make sure the locating pins enter the openings in the drive shaft housing.

7. Apply Loctite 572 to the threads of the gearcase mounting bolts. Have an assistant hold the gearcase in position and install the bolts. Tighten the bolts evenly to the specification in **Table 1**.

8. Heat the end of the speedometer hose with a portable hair dryer and quickly slip it fully over the connector (1, **Figure 25**). Secure the hose to the connector with a plastic locking type clamp.

9. Install the trim tab onto the gearcase and hold it in position. Align the reference mark (**Figure 31**) made before removal.

   a. On 40 and 50 hp models, securely tighten the trim tab bolt (**Figure 24**).

   b. On 60-90 hp models, use a socket and extension to install and securely tighten the trim tab bolt (**Figure 32**). Install the bolt access cover into the opening in the drive shaft housing.

10. Adjust the shift linkages and cables as described in Chapter Four. Connect the spark plug leads.

11. On electric start models, connect the cables to the battery.

12. Run the engine to check for proper shifting and cooling system operation. If water does not exit the tell-tale opening, remove the gearcase and check for a dislodged water tube or grommet. Check and correct the linkage adjustment if it does not shift correctly.

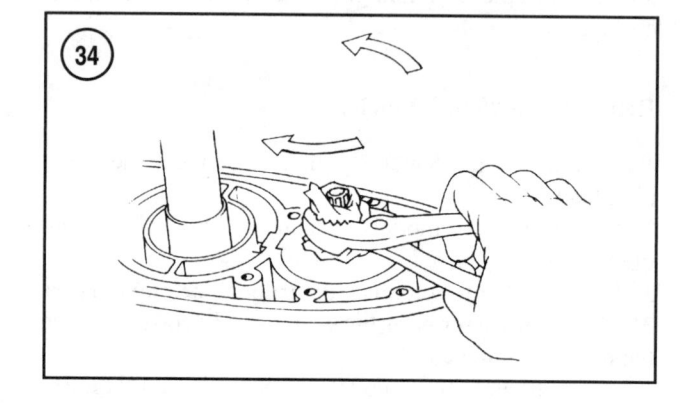

34

WATER PUMP

Service the water pump when the engine is running warmer than normal and at the service intervals listed in Chapter Three.

Always replace the impeller, seals, O-rings and all gaskets when servicing the water pump. Never compromise the operation of the water pump. Overheating and extensive power head damage can result from operation with faulty water pump components.

Component appearances and mounting arrangements vary by model. To assist with component identification and orientation, refer to the illustration that applies to the selected model. The appearance of the components may differ slightly from the illustration. Four different water pumps are used on the models covered in this manual. Refer to the procedures for the engine model.

GEARCASE

Figure 35: WATER PUMP COMPONENTS (2 HP MODEL)

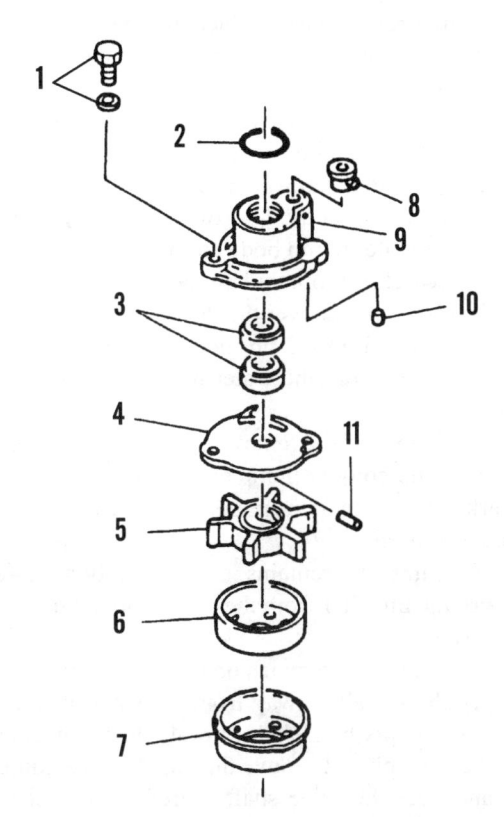

1. Screw and washer
2. O-ring
3. Seals
4. Wear plate
5. Impeller
6. Insert
7. Seal protector
8. Water tube grommet
9. Pump cover
10. Locating pin
11. Drive key

Disassembly (2 hp Models)

Refer to **Figure 35** for this procedure.

1. Remove the gearcase as described in this chapter. To ease impeller removal and reduce the chance of contaminating the gearcase, clean all corrosion and debris from the exposed surfaces of the drive shaft.

2. Carefully pry the water tube grommet (8, **Figure 35**) from the pump cover (9). Slide the O-ring (2, **Figure 35**) over the drive shaft. Discard the O-ring.

3. Remove both screws and washers (1, **Figure 35**), then lift the pump cover (9) from the gearcase. If necessary, pry the cover from the gearcase with two small screwdrivers. Work carefully to avoid damaging the cover mating surfaces. Remove the wear plate (4, **Figure 35**) from the cover or gearcase.

4. Mark the UP side of the impeller if it must be reused. Carefully pry the impeller (5, **Figure 35**) from the insert. Remove the impeller by sliding it up and over the drive shaft.

5. Remove the water pump insert and protector only if they must be replaced. Refer to *Component Inspection* in this chapter to determine the need for replacement. Use two screwdrivers to carefully pry the insert (6, **Figure 35**) from the gearcase. Use the same method to remove the seal protector (7, **Figure 35**).

6. Remove the seals (3, **Figure 35**) from the pump cover only if they must be replaced. Refer to *Component Inspection* in this chapter to determine the need for replacement. Remove the seals as follows:
   a. Place the pump cover on a flat work surface with the impeller side facing down.
   b. Use a small punch to carefully drive the lower seal from the bore.
   c. Place the pump cover on a flat work surface with the impeller side facing up.
   d. Use a small screwdriver to carefully pry the upper seal from the bore. Work carefully to avoid damaging the seal bore.

7. Clean all corrosion and contaminants from the water pump cover, wear plate and seal protector bore in the gearcase.

8. Inspect all water pump components as described in *Component Inspection* in this chapter.

Assembly (2 hp Models)

Refer to **Figure 35** for this procedure.

1. Install the seal protector and insert into the gearcase, if they were removed, as follows:
   a. Insert the seal protector into the gearcase. Align the protrusion on the seal protector lip with the notch in the protector bore.
   b. Press down on the protector until it fully seats in the gearcase.
   c. Align the protrusion on the insert with the notch in the seal protector. Then press the insert into the seal protector until it is fully seated.

2. Apply a light coat of Yamaha All-Purpose Grease or its equivalent to the inner bore of the insert. Install the drive key (11, **Figure 35**) into its slot in the drive shaft.

3. Slide the new impeller over the drive shaft until it contacts the insert. Rotate the drive shaft clockwise as viewed from the top while pushing down lightly on the impeller. Continue rotating the drive shaft until the impeller engages the drive key and completely enters the insert.

4. Apply a light coat of Yamaha All-Purpose Grease or its equivalent to the impeller contact surfaces of the wear plate. Slide the wear plate over the drive shaft and seat it against the insert.

5. Install the seals (3, **Figure 35**) into the water pump cover (9), if they were removed, as follows:
   a. Select a section of tubing or a socket to use as a seal installation tool. The tool must contact the seal casing, but not contact the seal bore in the pump cover.
   b. Apply a light coat of Loctite 271 to the seal bore and outer diameter of the seals.
   c. Place the pump cover on a flat work surface with the impeller side facing up. Install the upper seal into the bore with the lip side toward the impeller side of the cover.
   d. Use the installation tool to seat the seal fully into the bore.
   e. Press the lower seal into the bore using the same method. The lower seal lip must face the impeller.

6. Apply a light coat of Loctite Gasket Maker to the mating surface of the water pump cover.

7. Apply a bead of Yamaha All-Purpose Grease or equivalent to the lips of the seals in the pump cover. Slide the pump cover over the drive shaft. Rotate the pump cover to align the locating pin (10, **Figure 35**) with the opening in the cover. Then seat the cover onto the insert.

8. Apply a light coat of Loctite 572 to the screw threads. Install both screws and washers (1, **Figure 35**), and evenly tighten them to the general torque specification in Chapter One.

9. Apply Yamaha All-Purpose Grease or equivalent to the contact surfaces. Then slide the O-ring (2, **Figure 35**) over the drive shaft. Seat the O-ring against the pump cover.

10. Apply Yamaha All-Purpose Grease or equivalent to the surfaces, then insert the water tube grommet (8, **Figure 35**) into the pump cover. Install the protrusion on the grommet into the corresponding opening in the cover.

11. Install the gearcase as described in this chapter. Run the engine to check for proper cooling system operation. If water does not exit the tell-tale opening, remove the gearcase and check for a dislodged water tube or grommet. If no fault is found with the tube or grommet, disassemble the water pump and check for improperly assembled or damaged components.

Disassembly (3-5 hp and 6-25 hp Two-Cylinder Models)

Refer to **Figure 36** for this procedure.

1. Remove the gearcase as described in this chapter. To ease impeller removal and reduce the chance of contaminating the gearcase, clean all corrosion and debris from the exposed surfaces of the drive shaft.

2. Carefully pry the water tube grommet (3, **Figure 36**) from the water pump body (4).

3. Remove the four screws (1, **Figure 36**) and two plates (2) from the pump body. Use two screwdrivers to carefully pry the water pump body from the base (11, **Figure 36**). Work carefully to avoid damaging mating surfaces. Slide the body up and over the drive shaft.

4A. On 3 hp and 9.9-25 hp models, remove the O-ring (15, **Figure 36**) from the water pump body. Discard the O-ring.

4B. On 4-8 hp models, remove the gasket (7, **Figure 36**) from the pump body or pump base. Discard the gasket.

5. Mark the UP side of the impeller (6 or 14, **Figure 36**) if it must be reused.
   a. If the impeller remains in the pump body, carefully pry the impeller from the insert. Do not damage the insert.
   b. If the impeller remains on the drive shaft, carefully pry the impeller away from the wear plate using a blunt tip pry bar. Work carefully to avoid damaging the wear plate. Remove the impeller by sliding it up and over the drive shaft. Carefully split the inner hub of the impeller with a sharp chisel if the impeller is seized on the drive shaft. Work carefully to avoid damaging the drive shaft surfaces. To help prevent drive shaft damage, cut the impeller hub at the drive key slot.

6. Remove the drive key (10, **Figure 36**) from the slot in the drive shaft.

7. Only remove the water pump insert (5, **Figure 36**) if it must be replaced. The removal process damages the insert. Refer to *Component Inspection* in this chapter to determine the need for replacement. Use a punch to drive the insert from the water pump body through the drive shaft bore. Discard the insert after removal.

8. Remove the wear plate as follows:
   a. If the wear plate must be reused, mark the impeller side of the wear plate with a permanent marker. Do not scratch the plate.
   b. On 9.9 and 15 hp models, remove the two screws (13, **Figure 36**) from the wear plate and shift shaft retainer. Do not disturb the shift shaft while removing the screws.
   c. Carefully pry the wear plate (8 or 12, **Figure 36**) loose from the pump base. Work carefully to avoid

GEARCASE

**WATER PUMP COMPONENTS
(3-5 HP AND 6-25 HP TWO-CYLINDER MODELS)**

1. Screw
2. Plate
3. Water tube grommet
4. Water pump body
5. Insert (except 9.9 and 15 hp models)
6. Impeller (except 9.9 and 15 hp models)
7. Gasket (4-8 hp models)
8. Wear plate (except 9.9 and 15 hp models)
9. Locating pin
10. Drive key
11. Water pump base and seal carrier
12. Wear plate (9.9 and 15 hp models)
13. Screw
14. Impeller (9.9 and 15 hp models)
15. O-ring (3 hp and 9.9-25 hp models)

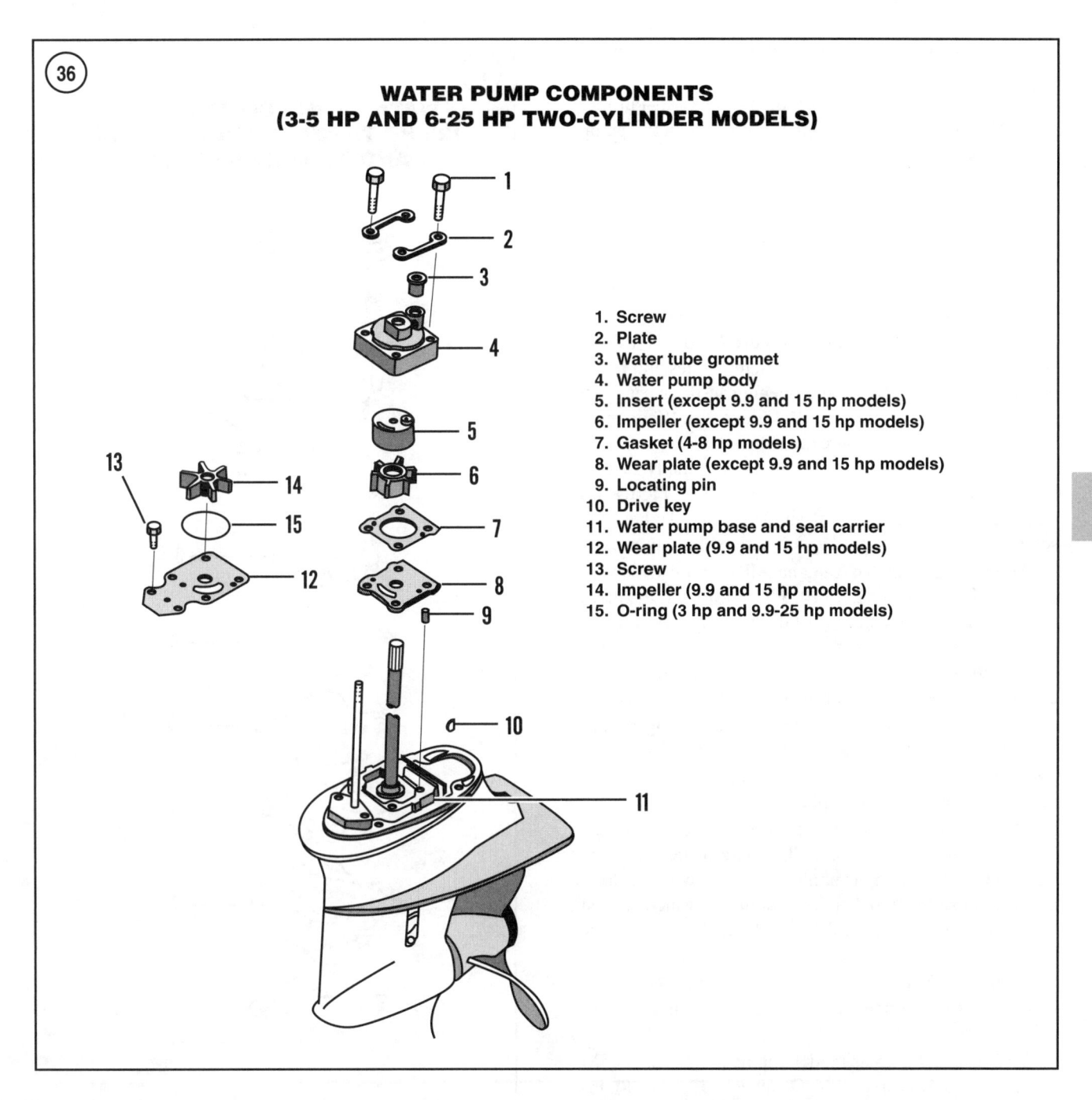

damaging the pump base. Slide the wear plate up and over the drive shaft.

9. If the locating pin (9, **Figure 36**) was dislodged, insert it into its respective opening in the water pump base.

10. Clean all corrosion and contaminants from the water pump cover, wear plate and water pump base.

11. Inspect the water pump base (11, **Figure 36**) for cracked, damaged or melted surfaces. Replace the pump base if there are any defects. Damaged surfaces on the base prevent efficient operation of the water pump. Refer to *Gearcase Repair* in this chapter for replacement procedures.

12. Inspect all water pump components as described in *Component Inspection* in this chapter.

Assembly (3-5 hp and 6-25 hp Two-Cylinder Models)

Refer to **Figure 36** for this procedure.

1. Install a new water pump insert, if it was removed, as follows:
    a. Apply a very light coat of Yamaha All-Purpose Grease or equivalent to the insert bore in the pump body.
    b. Slide the insert slightly into the water pump body. The open side must face out.
    c. Rotate the insert to align the tab or protrusion on the insert with its respective opening in the pump body.
    d. Guide the tab or protrusion into the pump body opening while seating the insert in the bore.

2. Slide the wear plate (8 or 12, **Figure 36**) over the drive shaft. Rotate the plate to align the screw holes and rest it on the water pump base. The opening in the wear plate must fit over the locating pin (9, **Figure 36**). When reusing the wear plate, make sure the UP mark made before removal faces up. On 9.9 and 15 hp models, apply Loctite 572 to the threads, then install both screws (13, **Figure 36**) into the wear plate and shift shaft retainer. Tighten the screws to the general torque specification in Chapter One.

3. Apply a light coat of Yamaha All-Purpose Grease or equivalent to the drive key (10, **Figure 36**) and the drive key slot in the drive shaft. Install the drive key into the slot. The curved side of the drive key must fit into the drive shaft slot. Apply a light coat of grease to the impeller contact surfaces of the wear plate.

4. On 4-8 hp models, slide a new gasket (7, **Figure 36**) over the drive shaft and rest it on the wear plate. Rotate the gasket to align the screw and locating pin openings, then seat the gasket on the wear plate.

5. Slide the new impeller over the drive shaft. When reusing the impeller, make sure the UP mark made before removal faces up. Align the impeller key slot with the drive key, then push the impeller down until it is seated against the wear plate. Rotate the drive shaft clockwise to verify correct drive key engagement.

6. Apply a light coat of Yamaha All-Purpose Grease or equivalent to the impeller contact surfaces in the water pump insert.

7. On 3 hp and 9.9-25 hp models, apply a light coat of 3M Weather-strip Adhesive to the O-ring (15, **Figure 36**). Install the O-ring into its groove in the water pump body (4). Allow the O-ring to firmly adhere to the water pump body before proceeding.

8. Slide the water pump body over the drive shaft and rest it on the impeller. Rotate the pump body to align the screw and locating pin opening. Press down lightly on the pump body while rotating the drive shaft clockwise as viewed from the top. Maintain the screw and pin opening alignment. Continue until the impeller enters the water pump body and the body seats on the wear plate.

37

WATER PUMP COMPONENTS (25 HP THREE-CYLINDER, 30 HP AND 60-90 HP MODELS)

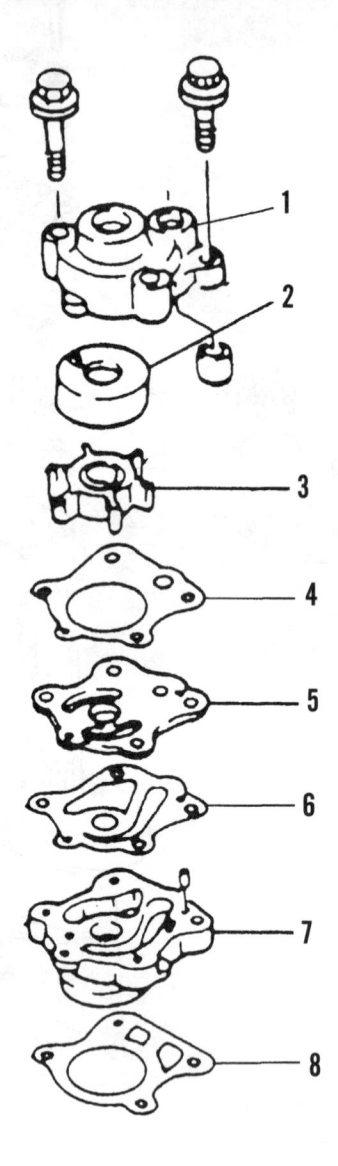

1. Water pump body
2. Insert
3. Impeller
4. Upper gasket
5. Wear plate
6. Lower gasket
7. Pump base
8. Base gasket

GEARCASE

38

Wear plate
Drive key
Locating pin

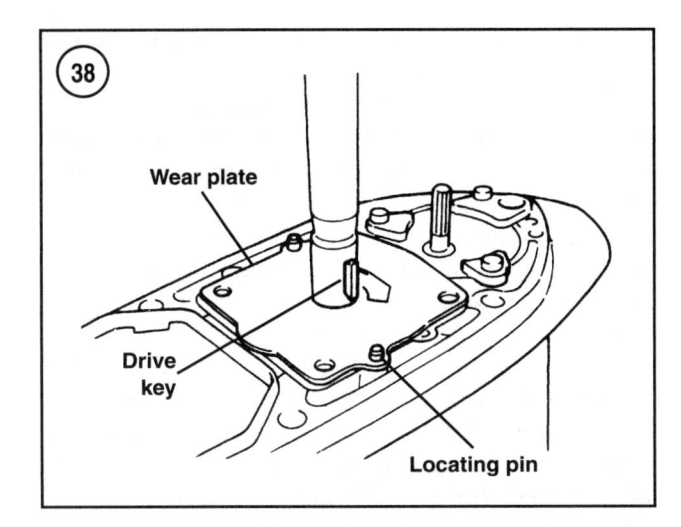

9. Pull up on the water pump body just enough to inspect the gaskets and O-rings. Do not allow the impeller to exit the pump body. Replace any damaged or dislodged gaskets or O-rings.

10. Apply Loctite 572 to the threads of the four screws (1, **Figure 36**). Install both plates (2, **Figure 36**) and the four screws (1). On 20 and 25 hp models, washers are used on the screws. Tighten the screws to the specification in **Table 1** or Chapter One.

11. Apply Yamaha All-Purpose Grease to the surfaces, then insert the water tube grommet (3, **Figure 36**) into the pump cover. Install the protrusion on the grommet into its corresponding opening in the cover.

12. Install the gearcase as described in this chapter. Run the engine to check for proper cooling system operation. If water does not exit the tell-tale opening, remove the gearcase and check for a dislodged water tube or grommet. If no fault is found with the tube or grommet, disassemble the water pump and check for improperly assembled or damaged components.

Disassembly (25 hp Three-Cylinder, 30 hp and 60-90 hp Models)

Refer to **Figure 37** for this procedure.

1. Remove the gearcase as described in this chapter. To ease impeller removal and reduce the chance of contaminating the gearcase, clean all corrosion and debris from the exposed surfaces of the drive shaft.

2. Remove the two screws and retainer, then carefully pry the water tube grommet from the water pump body (1, **Figure 37**).

3. Remove the four screws and washers from the pump body. Use two screwdrivers to carefully pry the water pump body from the base (7, **Figure 37**). Work carefully to avoid damaging mating surfaces. Slide the body up and over the drive shaft.

4. Remove the upper gasket (4, **Figure 37**) from the pump body or wear plate (5). Discard the gasket.

5. Mark the UP side of the impeller (3, **Figure 37**) if it must be reused.

   a. If the impeller remains in the pump body, carefully pry the impeller from the insert. Do not damage the insert.

   b. If the impeller remains on the drive shaft, carefully pry the impeller away from the wear plate using a blunt tip pry bar. Work carefully to avoid damaging the wear plate (**Figure 38**). Remove the impeller by sliding it up and over the drive shaft. Carefully split the inner hub of the impeller with a sharp chisel if the impeller is seized on the drive shaft. Work carefully to avoid damaging the drive shaft surfaces. To help prevent drive shaft damage, cut the impeller hub at the drive key slot.

6. Remove the drive key (**Figure 38**) from the slot in the drive shaft.

7. Only remove the water pump insert (2, **Figure 37**) if it must be replaced. The removal process damages the insert. Refer to *Component Inspection* in this chapter to determine the need for replacement. Use a punch to drive the insert from the water pump body through the drive shaft bore. Discard the insert after removal.

8. If the wear plate must be reused, mark the impeller side of the wear plate with a permanent marker. Do not scratch the plate. Carefully pry the wear plate (5, **Figure 37**) loose from the pump base. Work carefully to avoid damaging the pump base or dislodging the locating pin(s) (**Figure 38**). Slide the wear plate up and over the drive shaft. Remove the gasket (6, **Figure 37**) from the wear plate or pump base (7). Discard the gasket.

9. If the locating pin(s) (**Figure 38**) were dislodged, insert them into their respective opening(s) in the water pump base.

10. Clean all corrosion and contaminants from the water pump body, wear plate and pump base.

11. Inspect the water pump base (7, **Figure 37**) for cracked, damaged or melted surfaces. Replace the pump base if there are any defects. Damaged surfaces on the base prevent efficient operation of the water pump. Refer to *Gearcase Repair* in this chapter for replacement procedures.

12. Inspect all water pump components as described in *Component Inspection* in this chapter.

Assembly (25 hp Three-Cylinder, 30 hp and 60-90 hp Models)

Refer to **Figure 37** for this procedure.

1. Install a new water pump insert, if it was removed, as follows:
    a. Apply a very light coat of Yamaha All-Purpose Grease or equivalent to the insert bore in the pump body.
    b. Slide the insert slightly into the water pump body. The open side must face out.
    c. Rotate the insert to align the tab or protrusion on the insert with its respective opening in the pump body.
    d. Guide the tab or protrusion into the pump body opening while seating the insert in the bore.
2. Slide a new lower gasket (6, **Figure 37**) over the drive shaft. Rotate the gasket to align the screw holes and rest it on the water pump base. The opening(s) in the lower gasket must fit over the locating pin(s) (**Figure 38**).
3. Slide the wear plate (5, **Figure 37**) over the drive shaft. Rotate the plate to align the screw holes and rest it on the water pump base. The opening in the wear plate must fit over the locating pin (**Figure 38**). When reusing the wear plate, make sure the up mark made prior to removal faces up.
4. Apply a light coat of Yamaha All-Purpose Grease or equivalent to the drive key and the drive key slot in the drive shaft. Install the drive key into the slot as indicated in **Figure 38**. The curved side of the drive key must fit into the drive shaft slot. Apply a light coat of grease to the impeller contact surfaces of the wear plate.
5. Slide a new upper gasket (4, **Figure 37**) over the drive shaft and rest it on the wear plate. Rotate the gasket to align the screw and locating pin opening(s), then seat the gasket on the wear plate.
6. Slide the new impeller over the drive shaft. When reusing the impeller, make sure the up mark made prior to removal faces up. Align the impeller key slot with the drive key, then push the impeller down until it is seated against the wear plate. Rotate the drive shaft clockwise to verify correct drive key engagement.
7. Apply a light coat of Yamaha All-Purpose Grease or equivalent to the impeller contact surfaces in the water pump insert.
8. Slide the water pump body over the drive shaft and rest it on the impeller. Rotate the pump body to align the screw and locating pin opening(s). Press down lightly on the pump body while rotating the drive shaft clockwise as viewed from the top. Maintain the screw and pin opening alignment. Continue until the impeller enters the water pump body and the body seats on the wear plate.
9. Pull up on the water pump body just enough to inspect the gaskets. Do not allow the impeller to exit the pump body. Replace any damaged or dislodged gaskets.
10. Apply Loctite 572 to the threads of the four screws and washers. Install the screws and washers, and tighten them to the general torque specification in Chapter One.
11. Apply Yamaha All-Purpose Grease or equivalent to the surfaces, then insert the water tube grommet into the pump cover. The larger tapered opening must face out. Secure the grommet with the plate and two screws.
12. Install the gearcase as described in this chapter. Run the engine to check for proper cooling system operation. If water does not exit the tell-tale opening, remove the gearcase and check for a dislodged water tube or grommet. If no fault is found with the tube or grommet, disassemble the water pump and check for improperly assembled or damaged components.

Disassembly (40 and 50 hp Models)

Refer to **Figure 39** for this procedure.

1. Remove the gearcase as described in this chapter. To ease impeller removal and reduce the chance of contaminating the gearcase, clean all corrosion and debris from the exposed surfaces of the drive shaft.
2. Carefully pry the water tube grommet (4, **Figure 39**) and sleeve (5) from the water pump body (3).
3. Remove the four screws (1, **Figure 39**) and special washers (2) from the pump body. Use two screwdrivers to carefully pry the water pump body from the wear plate (10, **Figure 39**). Work carefully to avoid damaging mating surfaces. Slide the body up and over the drive shaft.
4. Remove the O-ring (8, **Figure 39**) from the water pump body. Discard the O-ring.
5. Mark the UP side of the impeller (7, **Figure 39**) if it must be reused.
    a. If the impeller remains in the pump body, carefully pry the impeller from the insert. Do not damage the insert.
    b. If the impeller remains on the drive shaft, carefully pry the impeller away from the wear plate using a blunt tip pry bar. Work carefully to avoid damaging the wear plate. Remove the impeller by sliding it up and over the drive shaft. Carefully split the inner hub of the impeller with a sharp chisel if the impeller is seized on the drive shaft. Work carefully to avoid damaging the drive shaft surfaces. To help prevent drive shaft damage, cut the impeller hub at the drive key slot.
6. Remove the drive key (**Figure 38**) from the slot in the drive shaft.

GEARCASE

Figure 39 — WATER PUMP COMPONENTS (40 AND 50 HP MODELS)

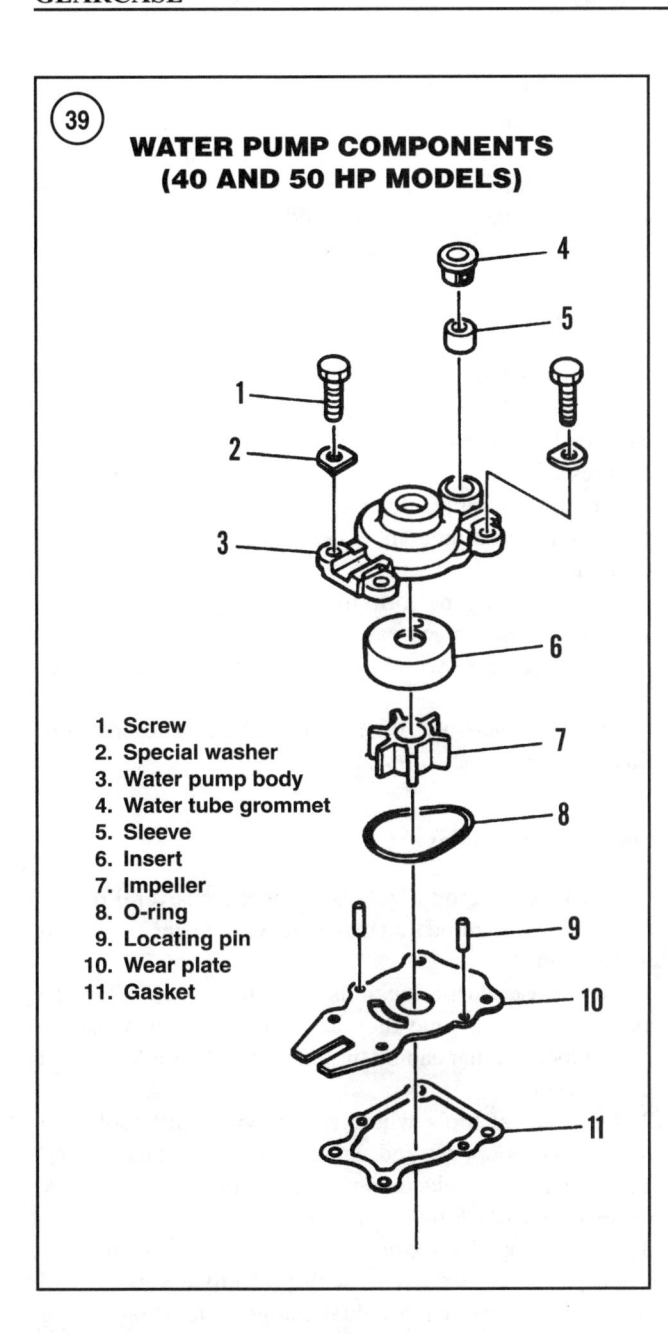

1. Screw
2. Special washer
3. Water pump body
4. Water tube grommet
5. Sleeve
6. Insert
7. Impeller
8. O-ring
9. Locating pin
10. Wear plate
11. Gasket

7. Only remove the water pump insert (6, **Figure 39**) if it must be replaced. The removal process damages the insert. Refer to *Component Inspection* in this chapter to determine the need for replacement. Use a punch to drive the insert from the water pump body through the drive shaft bore. Discard the insert after removal.

8. If the wear plate must be reused, mark the impeller side of the wear plate with a permanent marker. Do not scratch the plate. Carefully pry the wear plate (10, **Figure 39**) loose from the pump base. Work carefully to avoid damaging the gearcase housing. Slide the wear plate up and over the drive shaft.

9. Remove the gasket (11, **Figure 39**) from the wear plate or gearcase housing. Discard the gasket.

10. If the locating pins (9, **Figure 36**) were dislodged, insert them into the respective openings in the gearcase housing.

11. Clean all corrosion and contaminants from the water pump cover, wear plate and gearcase. Clean all old adhesive from the O-ring groove in the pump body.

12. Inspect all water pump components as described in *Component Inspection* in this chapter.

Assembly (40 and 50 hp Models)

Refer to **Figure 39** for this procedure.

1. Install a new water pump insert, if it was removed, as follows:
   a. Apply a very light coat of Yamaha All-Purpose Grease or equivalent to the insert bore in the pump body.
   b. Slide the insert slightly into the water pump body. The open side must face out.
   c. Rotate the insert to align the tab or protrusion on the insert with its respective opening in the pump body.
   d. Guide the tab or protrusion into the pump body opening while seating the insert in the bore.

2. Slide a new gasket (11, **Figure 39**) over the drive shaft. Rotate the gasket to align the screw holes and rest it on the gearcase housing. The openings in the gasket must fit over the locating pins (9, **Figure 39**).

3. Slide the wear plate (10, **Figure 39**) over the drive shaft. The slot in the wear plate must straddle the shift shaft retainer. Rotate the plate to align the screw holes and rest it on the gasket. The openings in the wear plate must fit over the locating pins (**Figure 38**). When reusing the wear plate, make sure the UP mark made prior to removal faces up.

4. Apply a light coat of Yamaha All-Purpose Grease or equivalent to the drive key and the drive key slot in the drive shaft. Install the drive key into the slot as indicated in **Figure 38**. The curved side of the drive key must fit into the drive shaft slot. Apply a light coat of grease to the impeller contact surfaces of the wear plate.

5. Slide the new impeller over the drive shaft. When reusing the impeller, make sure the UP mark made prior to removal faces up. Align the impeller key slot with the drive key, then push the impeller down until it is seated against the wear plate. Rotate the drive shaft clockwise to verify correct drive key engagement.

6. Apply a light coat of Yamaha All-Purpose Grease or equivalent to the impeller contact surfaces in the water pump insert.

7. Apply a light coat of 3M Weather-strip Adhesive to the O-ring (8, **Figure 39**). Install the O-ring into its groove in the water pump body (3, **Figure 39**). Allow the O-ring to firmly adhere to the water pump before proceeding.

8. Slide the water pump body over the drive shaft and rest it on the impeller. Rotate the pump body to align the screw and locating pin opening. Press down lightly on the pump body while rotating the drive shaft clockwise as viewed from the top. Maintain the screw and pin opening alignment. Continue until the impeller enters the water pump body and the body seats on the wear plate.

9. Pull up on the water pump body just enough to inspect the gasket and O-ring. Do not allow the impeller to exit the pump body. Replace the O-ring or gasket if it is damaged or dislodged.

10. Apply Loctite 572 to the threads of the four screws (1, **Figure 39**). Install the screws and special washers (2, **Figure 39**). Rotate the washers to match the contour of the water pump body. Tighten the screws to the general torque specification in Chapter One.

11. Apply Yamaha All-Purpose Grease or equivalent to the surfaces, then insert the sleeve (5, **Figure 39**) and water tube grommet (4) into the pump cover.

12. Install the gearcase as described in this chapter. Run the engine to check for proper cooling system operation. If water does not exit the tell-tale opening, remove the gearcase and check for a dislodged water tube or grommet. If no fault is found with the tube or grommet, disassemble the water pump and check for improperly assembled or damaged components.

GEARCASE DISASSEMBLY/ASSEMBLY

This section covers complete gearcase disassembly, inspection and reassembly for each engine covered in this manual. Once the gearcase is disassembled, refer to *Component Inspection* in this chapter to determine the need to replace gearcase components.

On larger models, shim the gears and verify the gear lash between the forward gear and the pinion gear before continuing with assembly. The assembly procedures describe the shimming operation.

Special gauging fixtures and precision measuring instruments are required to shim the gearcase. Have the shimming operation performed by a qualified technician if you do not have access to the special tools or are unfamiliar with their use. The cost of the special tools is far greater than the cost of having a professional perform the procedure.

Many of the disassembly and assembly operations require special service tools. The Yamaha part numbers of required tools are listed in the model specific disassembly/assembly procedures. Purchase or rent any required special tool from a Yamaha outboard dealership.

Note the mounting location and orientation of all components before removing them from the gearcase. Mark components that can be installed in different directions accordingly. Perform the following before gearcase disassembly:

Remove the propeller, then the gearcase, as described in this chapter.

Remove all water pump components as described in this chapter. Do not remove the water pump base, if so equipped, until instructed to do so in the disassembly procedures.

After disassembly, clean and inspect all gearcase components as described in *Component Inspection* in this chapter.

After assembly, perform the following:

Pressure test the gearcase as described in this chapter.

Fill the gearcase with lubricant as described in Chapter Three.

Install the gearcase, then the propeller, as described in this chapter.

Service Precautions

When working on a gearcase, there are several procedures to keep in mind that make the work easier, faster and more accurate.

1. Never use elastic locknuts more than twice. Replace elastic nuts each time they are removed. Never use an elastic locknut that can be turned by hand without the aid of a wrench.

2. Use special tools where noted. Makeshift tools can damage components and cause serious personal injury. The expense to replace damaged components can easily exceed the cost of the special tool.

3. Use appropriate fixtures to hold the gearcase housing when possible. Use a vise with protective jaws to hold smaller housings or individual components. If protective jaws are not available, insert blocks of wood or similar padding on each side of the housing or component before clamping.

4. Remove and install pressed-on parts with an appropriate mandrel, support and arbor or hydraulic press. Do not attempt to pry or hammer components on or off unless otherwise specified in the procedure.

5. Proper torque is essential to ensure long life and satisfactory service from gearcase components. Use the general torque specifications in Chapter One for fasteners not listed in **Table 1**.

6. To help reduce corrosion, especially in saltwater areas, apply Yamaha Marine Grease or its equivalent to all exter-

GEARCASE

nal surfaces of bearing carriers, housing mating surfaces and fasteners when no other sealant, adhesive or lubricant is recommended. Do not apply grease where it can get into gears or bearings.

7. Discard all O-rings, seals and gaskets during disassembly. Apply Yamaha All-Purpose Grease or its equivalent to new O-rings and seal lips to provide initial lubrication.

8. Tag all shims with the location and thickness of each shim as it is removed from the gearcase. Shims are reusable as long as they are not damaged or corroded. Follow shimming instructions closely and carefully. Shims control gear location and/or bearing preload. Incorrectly shimming a gearcase will cause failure of the gears and/or bearings.

9. Work in an area with good lighting and sufficient space for component storage. Keep an ample number of clean containers available for parts storage. Cover parts and assemblies that are not being worked on with clean shop towels or plastic bags.

10. When a threadlocking adhesive is specified, first spray the threads of the threaded hole or nut and the screw with Locquic primer. Allow the primer to air dry before proceeding. Locquic primer cleans the surfaces and allows better adhesion. Locquic primer also accelerates the cure rate of threadlocking adhesives from an hour or longer to 15-20 minutes.

11. Note the mounting location and orientation of all components before removing them. Mark the front and/or upper side of components that can be installed in different directions. This is necessary to maintain the existing wear patterns on sliding or bearing surfaces.

Disassembly (2 hp Models)

Refer to **Figure 40** for this procedure.

1. Drain the gearcase lubricant (**Figure 41**) as described in Chapter Three.

CAUTION
Never heat the gearcase housing to the point that the finish is burned. Continually move the flame around the mating surface to apply heat evenly. Excessive heat can distort or melt the gearcase.

NOTE
To assist with removal of the gearcase cap where corrosion has seized the components, use a torch to apply moderate heat to the gearcase. Heat the area near the gearcase housing-to-gearcase cap mating surfaces.

2. Remove the two bolts and washers (**Figure 42**). Use a blunt tip pry bar to carefully pry the gearcase cap loose from the gearcase housing (**Figure 43**). Work carefully to avoid damaging the mating surfaces. Pull the gearcase cap from the gearcase and propeller shaft. Remove the O-ring (27, **Figure 40**) from the cap. Discard the O-ring.

3. Use needlenose pliers to remove the E-clip from the groove on the drive shaft (**Figure 44**).

4. Pull up slightly on the drive shaft to free the pinion gear from the shaft. Remove the pinion gear from the gearcase (**Figure 45**). Retrieve the thrust washer (22, **Figure 40**) and shim (23) from the gearcase.

5. Carefully draw the drive shaft from the gearcase (**Figure 46**). Pull the propeller shaft and driven gear assembly from the gearcase (**Figure 47**).

6. Remove the driven gear shim (2, **Figure 48**) from the front of the propeller shaft (3) or the driven gear bearing (1). Slide the gearcase cap (28, **Figure 40**) from the propeller shaft.

7. Only remove the propeller shaft seal (29, **Figure 40**) if it must be replaced. The seal is damaged during the removal process. Refer to *Component Inspection* in this chapter to determine the need for replacement. Remove the seal as follows:
   a. Place the gearcase cap on a suitable work surface with the seal bore opening facing down. Block the cap to provide adequate clearance under the seal bore for the seal. Support the cap on the open jaws of a vise if necessary.
   b. Use a suitable punch or blunt tip screwdriver to drive the seal from the bore. Direct the driving tool against the seal casing. Work carefully to avoid contacting the seal bore in the gearcase cap. Discard the seal.

8. Only remove the driven gear bearing (24, **Figure 40**) if it must be replaced. The removal process damages the bearing. Refer to *Component Inspection* in this chapter to determine the need for replacement. Remove the bearing as follows:
   a. Clamp the gearcase in a vise with protective jaws. Engage the jaws of a slide hammer to the propeller shaft bore in the bearing (**Figure 49**).
   b. Use short hammer strokes to remove the bearing from the gearcase.
   c. Discard the bearings.

9. Clamp the gearcase in a vise with protective jaws. Engage the jaws of a slide hammer under the drive shaft seal casing (**Figure 50**). Use short hammer strokes to remove the seal. Discard the seal.

10. Only remove the drive shaft bushings (15-17, **Figure 40**) if they must be replaced. The removal process usually damages the bushings. Refer to *Component Inspection* in

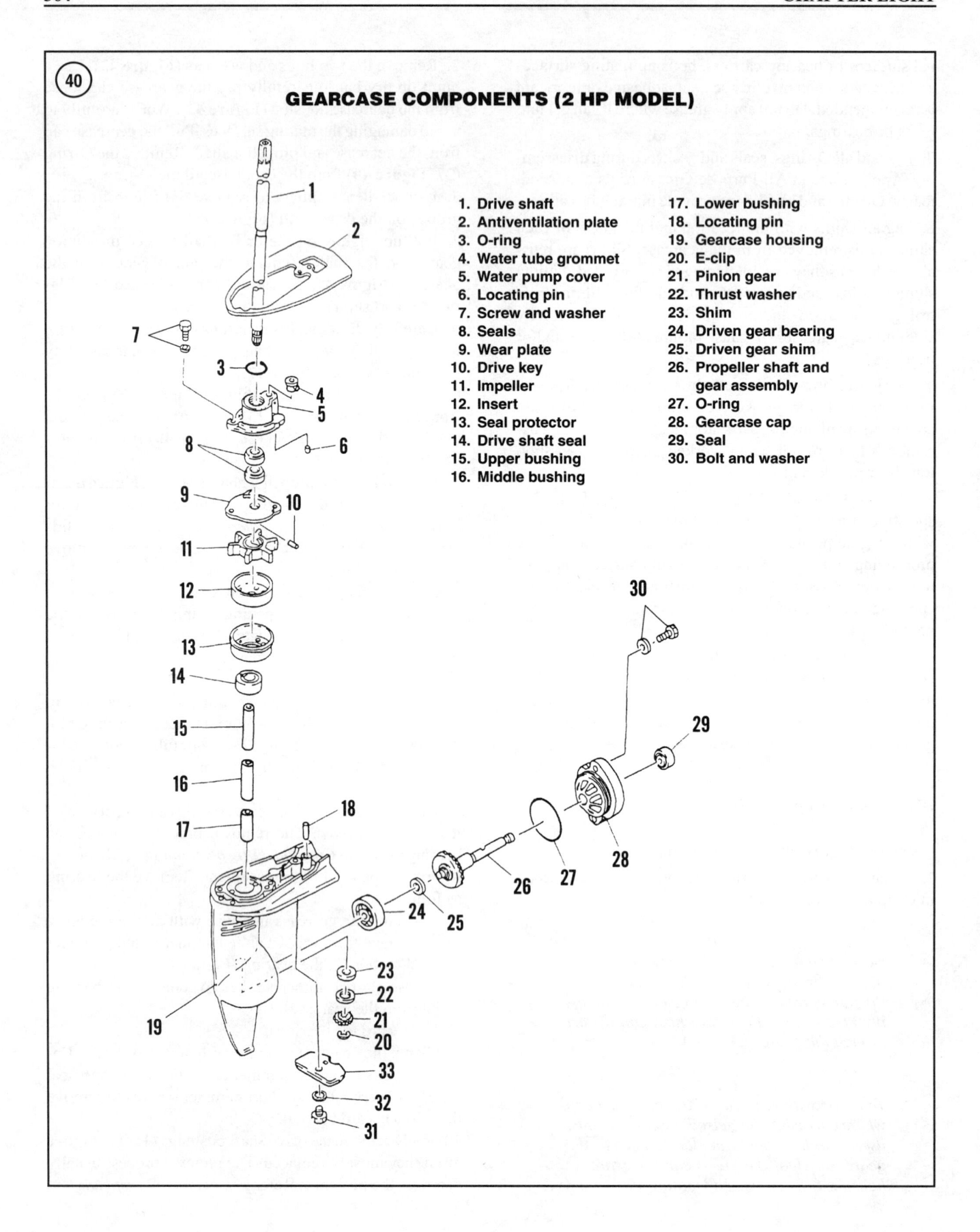

CHAPTER EIGHT

GEARCASE COMPONENTS (2 HP MODEL)

1. Drive shaft
2. Antiventilation plate
3. O-ring
4. Water tube grommet
5. Water pump cover
6. Locating pin
7. Screw and washer
8. Seals
9. Wear plate
10. Drive key
11. Impeller
12. Insert
13. Seal protector
14. Drive shaft seal
15. Upper bushing
16. Middle bushing
17. Lower bushing
18. Locating pin
19. Gearcase housing
20. E-clip
21. Pinion gear
22. Thrust washer
23. Shim
24. Driven gear bearing
25. Driven gear shim
26. Propeller shaft and gear assembly
27. O-ring
28. Gearcase cap
29. Seal
30. Bolt and washer

GEARCASE

41

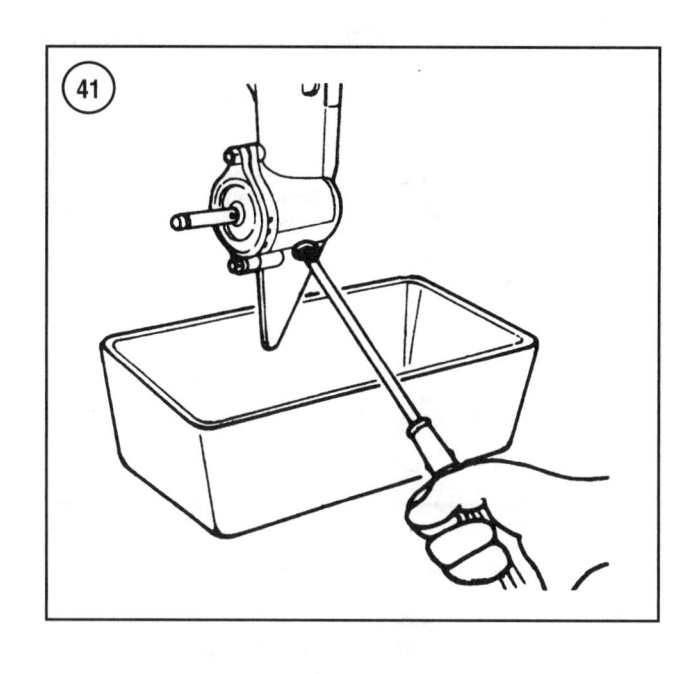

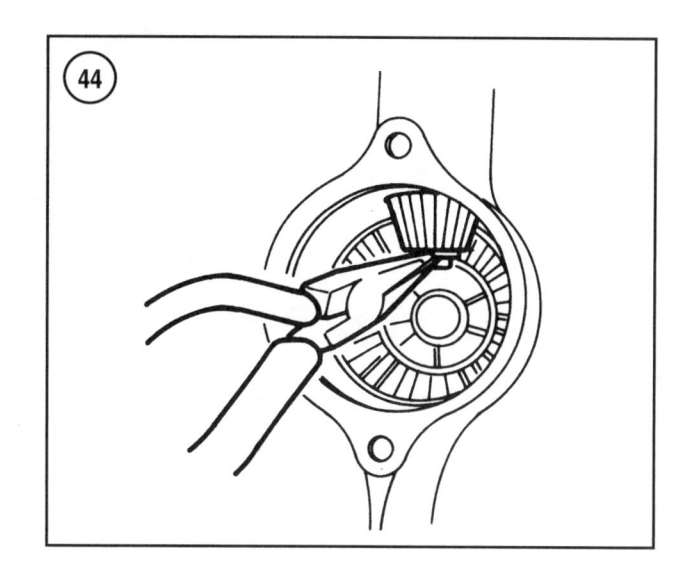

42

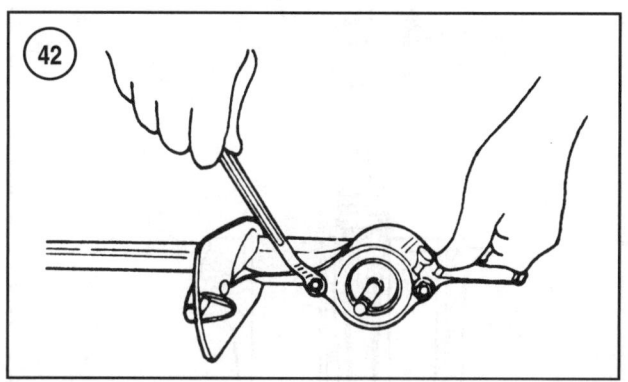

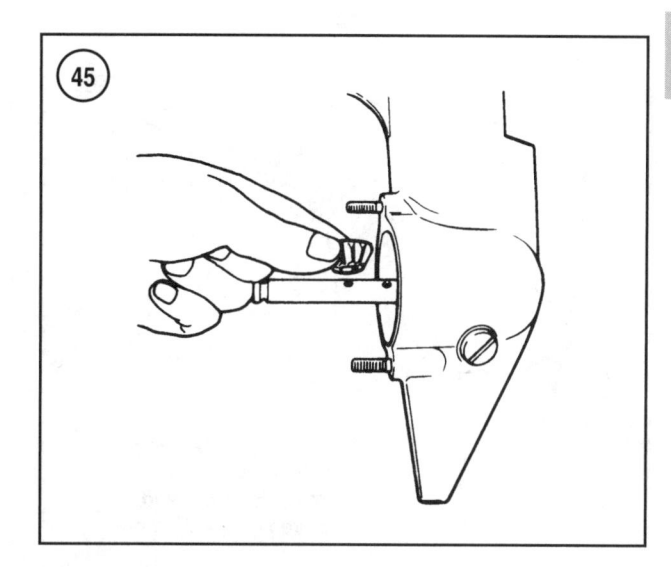

43

44

45

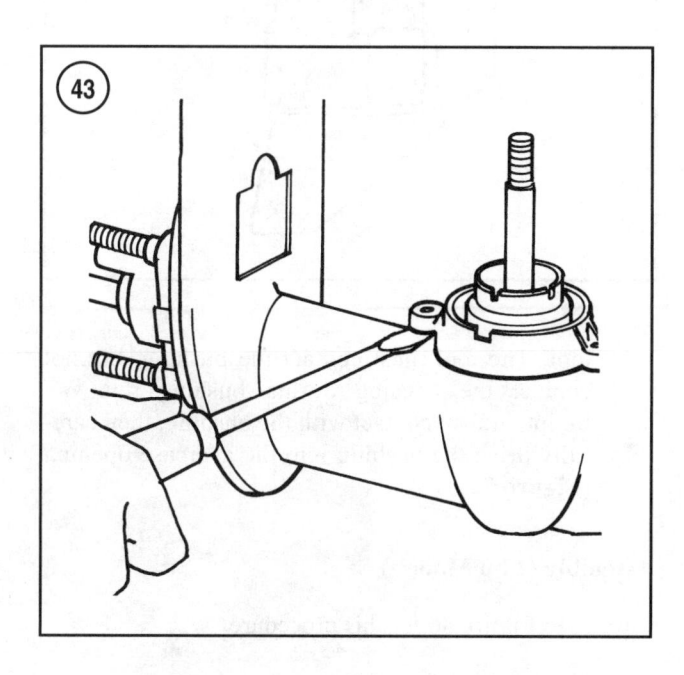

46

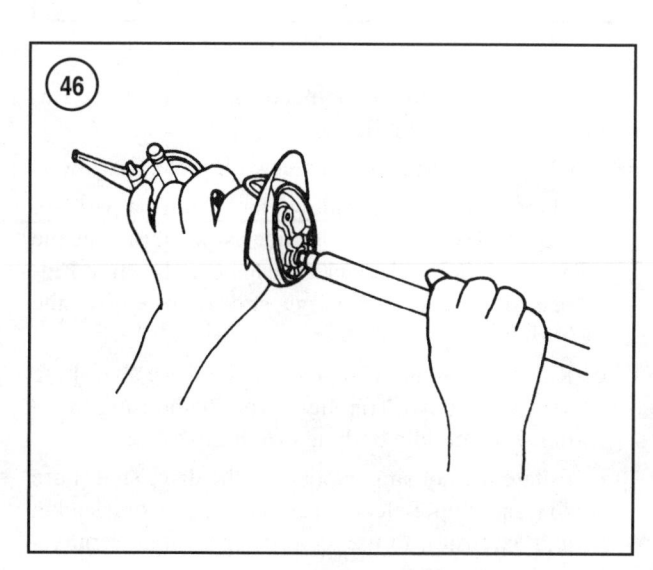

366

Figure 47

Figure 48
1. Driven gear bearing 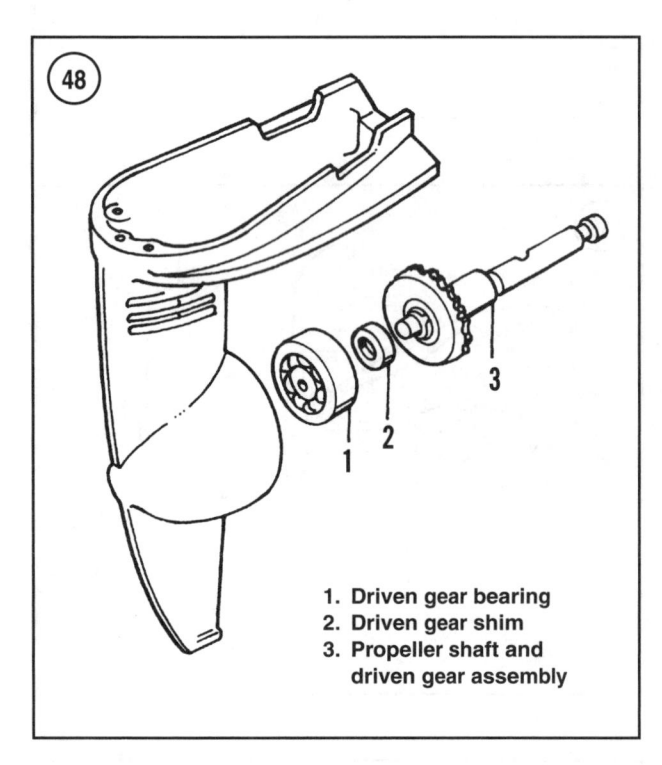
2. Driven gear shim
3. Propeller shaft and driven gear assembly

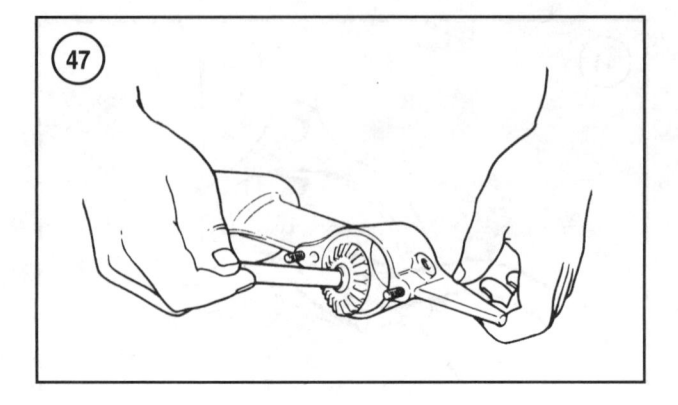

Figure 49 — Slide hammer puller

Figure 50 — Slide hammer puller

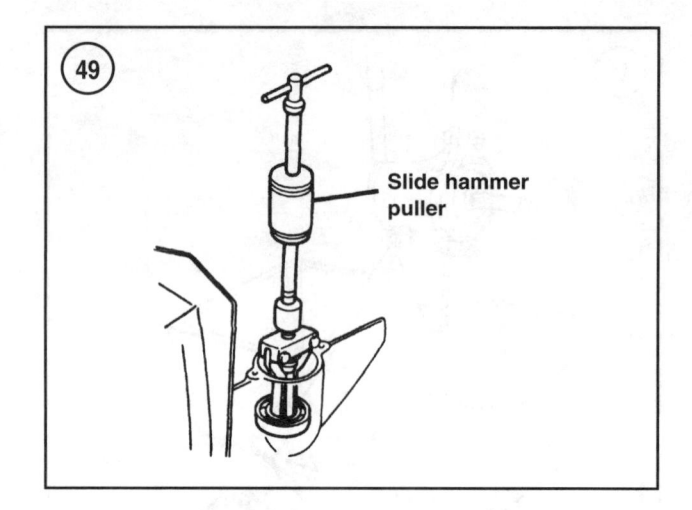

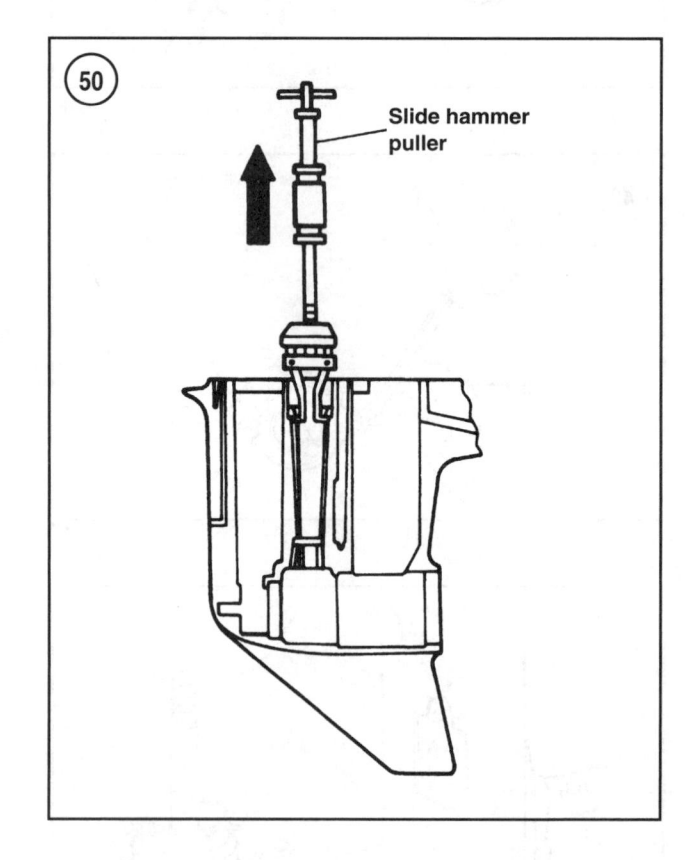

this chapter to determine the need for replacement. Remove the bushings as follows:

   a. Clamp the gearcase in a vise with protective jaws.

   b. Thread the bushing removal tool (Yamaha part No. YB-6178) onto a suitable slide hammer. Engage the removal tool to the upper bushing as shown in **Figure 51**. Use short hammer strokes to remove the bushing.

   c. Rotate the housing to position the drive shaft bore so it faces down. Tap lightly on the housing to remove the middle bushing (16, **Figure 40**).

   d. Rotate the housing to position the drive shaft bore so it faces up. Select a section of tubing or a socket and extension to use as a lower bushing removal tool. The tool must contact the bushing, but not contact the housing during bushing removal. Maintain firm contact with the bushing, then carefully drive the bushing into the gearcase opening (**Figure 52**).

Assembly (2 hp Models)

Refer to **Figure 40** for this procedure.

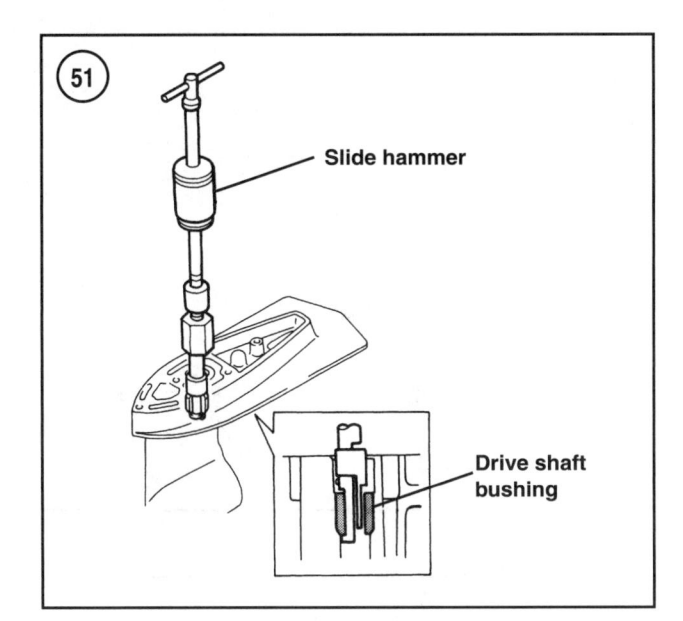

GEARCASE

51
Slide hammer

Drive shaft bushing

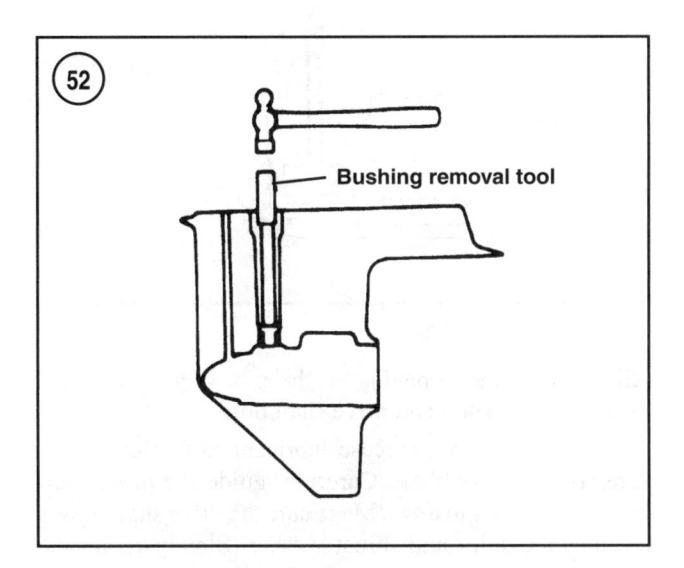

52
Bushing removal tool

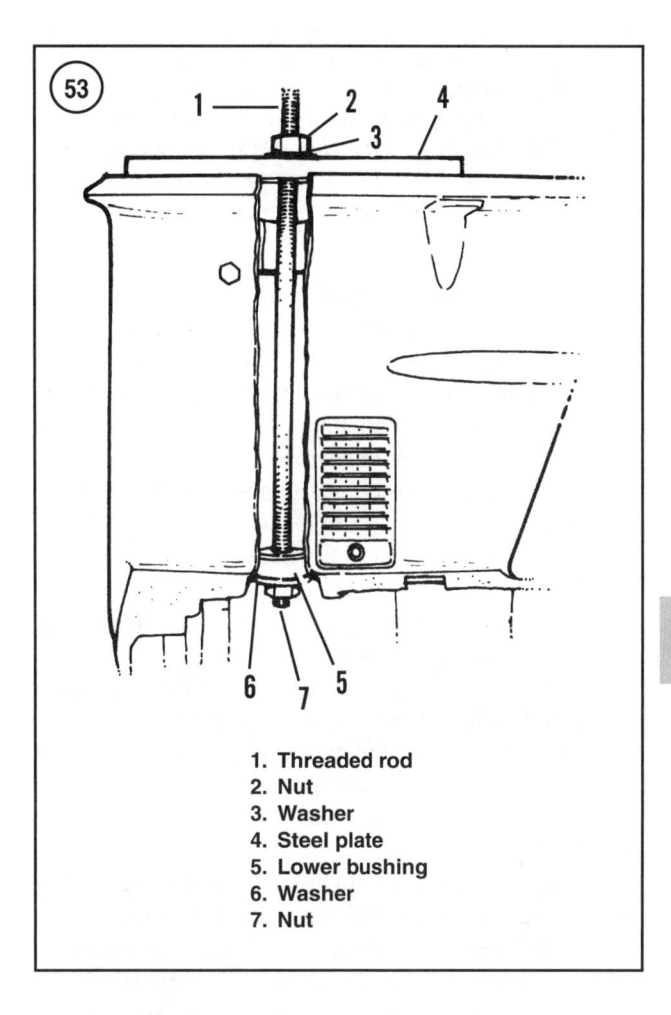

53
1. Threaded rod
2. Nut
3. Washer
4. Steel plate
5. Lower bushing
6. Washer
7. Nut

1. Install the new drive shaft bushings, if they were removed, as follows:
   a. Apply a light coat of gearcase lubricant to the bushings and bushing bore in the gearcase housing.
   b. Working through the gearcase opening, insert the lower bushing into the bore. The flanged side of the bushing must face down.
   c. Select a washer with an outer diameter slightly smaller than the bushing flange. The washer must be of sufficient diameter to adequately support the bushing. Select a washer of sufficient diameter to span the drive shaft bore at the top of the housing. If a suitable washer is not available, use a steel plate with a hole to span the bore. A threaded rod of an adequate length with a diameter that matches the washers and two hex nuts are also required.
   d. Arrange the washers, threaded rod and nuts in the gearcase as shown in **Figure 53**. Tighten the nuts until the flange on the lower bushing seats against the step in the bore. Remove the installation tools.
   e. Insert the middle bushing (16, **Figure 40**) into the drive shaft bore. Seat the middle bushing against the lower bushing.
   f. Select a section of tubing or a socket and extension to use as a bushing installation tool. The tool must contact the end of the bushing, but not contact the gearcase during bushing installation.
   g. Insert the bushing into the drive shaft bore. Maintain firm contact with the bushing (**Figure 54**) during the installation process. Gently drive the bushing into the bore until it just contacts the step in the bore.

NOTE
When driving a bearing or bearing race into the gearcase housing, strike the driver hard

enough to slightly move the bearing or race. Stop driving when the pitch changes or a sharp ring is heard as the driver is struck. This indicates the bearing or race is seated. Continued driving may bounce the bearing or race out of the bore.

2. Install the new driven gear bearing (24, **Figure 40**) into the housing, if it was removed, as follows:
   a. Select a piece of tubing to use as a bearing installation tool. The tool must contact only the outer race of the bearing, and not contact the gear housing during bearing installation.
   b. Apply a light coat of gearcase lubricant to the bearing surfaces and the bearing bore in the gearcase housing.
   c. Clamp the housing in a vise with protective jaws. The gearcase opening must face up.
   d. Place the new bearing in the bore with the number marks facing out. Maintain firm contact with the bearing while gently driving it into the bore (**Figure 55**). Use light force and do not allow the bearing to tilt in the bore. Continue driving until the bearing fully seats in the housing.
3. Install a new drive shaft seal (14, **Figure 40**) into the gearcase as follows:
   a. Apply a light coat of Loctite 271 to the outer casing of the seal and the seal bore in the gearcase housing.
   b. Select a piece of tubing or socket and an extension to use as a seal installation tool. The tool must contact the seal casing, but not contact the gear housing during seal installation.
   c. Insert the seal into the bore with the lip side facing up. Carefully drive the seal into the bore until it is seated against the step. Wipe excess Loctite from the drive shaft bore before proceeding.
   d. Apply a bead of Yamaha All-Purpose Grease or equivalent to the seal lip.
4. Install the shim (2, **Figure 48**) onto the driven gear and propeller shaft assembly (3). To keep the shim in position, apply a light coat of Yamaha All-Purpose Grease or equivalent to the shim and shaft mating surfaces. Install the gear and propeller shaft assembly into the gearcase housing. Guide the propeller shaft into the driven gear bearing during installation. Seat the gear and shim against the bearing.
5. Apply a very light coat of Yamaha All-Purpose Grease or equivalent to the shim (23, **Figure 40**) and thrust washer (22). Install these components into the housing. Align the shim and washer with the drive shaft bore.
6. Install the pinion gear into the gearcase (**Figure 45**). Mesh the pinion gear teeth with the driven gear teeth.

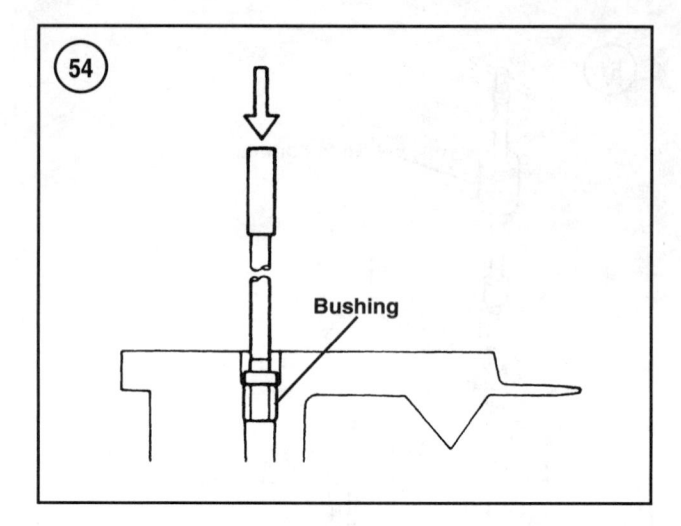

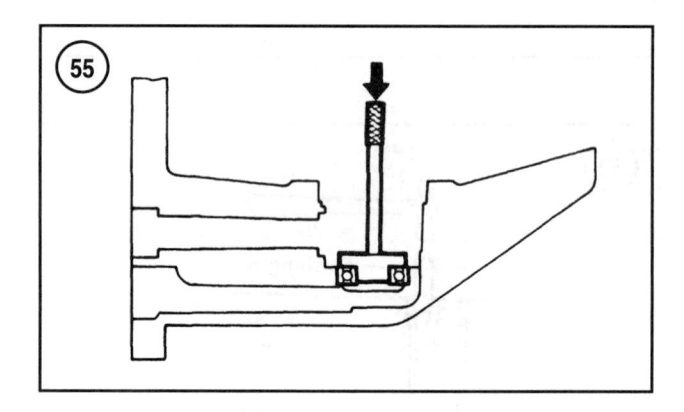

Align the splined opening in the pinion gear with the thrust washer, shim and drive shaft bore.

7. Apply a coat of gearcase lubricant to the lower surfaces of the drive shaft. Carefully guide the drive shaft into the bore (**Figure 46**). Make sure the drive shaft passes through the shim and thrust washer. Slowly rotate the drive shaft to align the drive shaft splines with the pinion gear splines. The shaft drops into the pinion gear when the splines align.

8. Use needlenose pliers (**Figure 44**) to install the E-clip into the drive shaft groove. Pull up on the drive shaft to verify groove engagement.

9. Install a new seal (29, **Figure 40**) into the gearcase cap, if the seal was removed, as follows:
   a. Apply a coat of Loctite 271 to the outer diameter of the seal casing and the seal bore in the gearcase cap.
   b. Select a section of tubing or a socket and extension to use as a seal installation tool. The tool must contact the seal casing, but not contact the seal bore in the gearcase cap.

GEARCASE

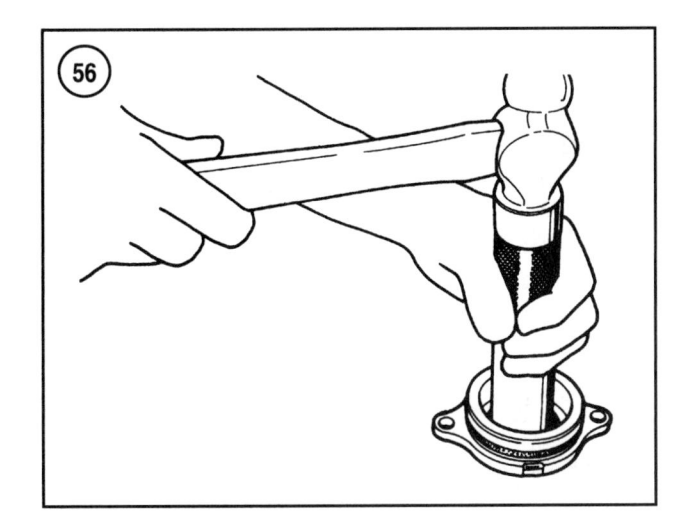

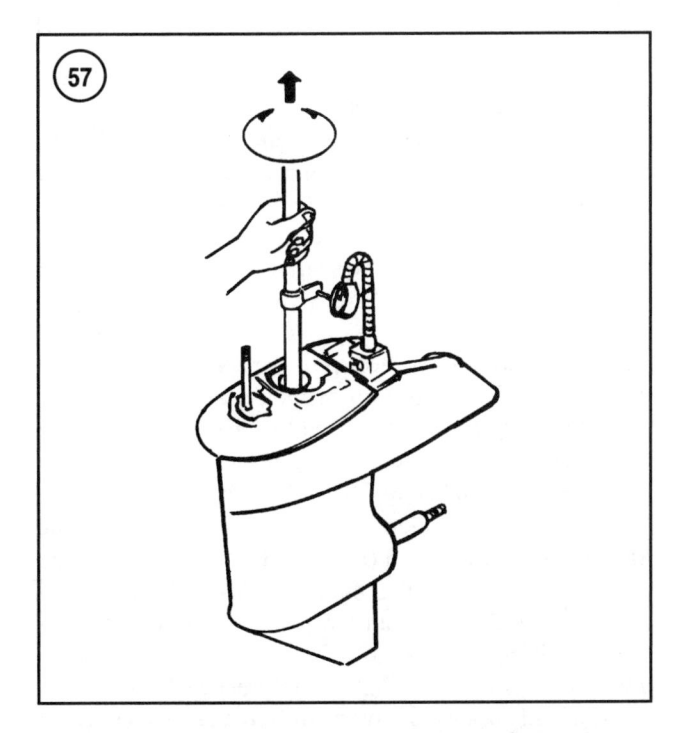

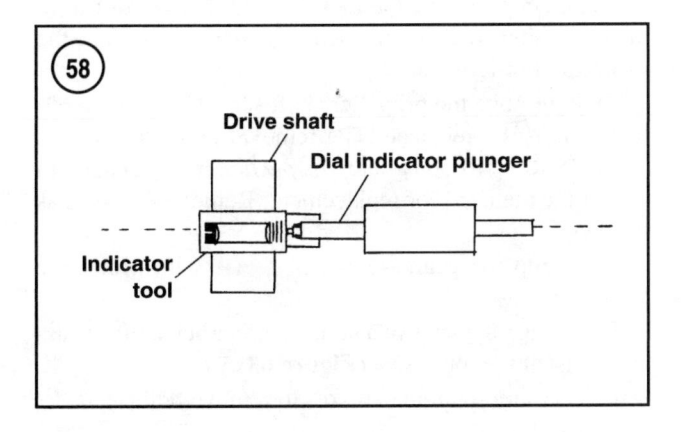

c. Place the new seal in the bore with the lip side facing in. Carefully drive the seal into the bore until it is fully seated (**Figure 56**).

d. Apply a coat of Yamaha All-Purpose Grease or equivalent to the seal lip.

10. Apply a coat of Yamaha All-Purpose Grease or equivalent to the surfaces, then install the new O-ring (27, **Figure 40**) into the groove in the gearcase cap.

11. Slip the gearcase cap over the propeller shaft. Align the mounting bolt holes while inserting the cap into the gearcase housing. Push on the cap until it seats against the gearcase housing.

12. Apply Loctite 572 to the threads of the bolts (30, **Figure 40**). Thread the bolts and washers into the cap and gearcase housing. Evenly tighten the bolts to the general torque specification in Chapter One.

CAUTION
Use very light force when moving the drive shaft during the backlash measurement. The readings will be inaccurate if excessive force is applied to the drive shaft.

NOTE
Remove all water pump components before measuring gear backlash. The drag created by the water pump components will prevent accurate measurement. Temporarily remove the drive shaft seal carrier or water pump base during backlash measurements.

NOTE
Make sure all gearcase lubricant has been drained from the gearcase before measuring gear backlash. The readings will be inaccurate due to the cushion effect of the lubricant on the gear teeth.

13. Measure and correct the gear backlash if a new gearcase housing, driven gear and propeller shaft, pinion gear or driven gear bearing was installed during the gearcase repair. Measure and correct the gearcase backlash as follows:

a. Attach a dial indicator to the gearcase using a suitable clamping device (**Figure 57**). Dial indicators and mounts are available from most tool suppliers. The mount must remain rigid during the measurement, otherwise the backlash measurement will be inaccurate.

b. Clamp the backlash indicator tool (Yamaha part No. YB-06265-90890-06265) onto the drive shaft. Arrange the dial indicator mount to position the dial indicator plunger at the same height as the indicator tool (**Figure 58**) and with the plunger at a 90° angle to the indicator arm (**Figure 59**). Reposition the dial indicator to place the plunger in line with the mark on the indicator tool.

c. Have an assistant push in on the propeller shaft during this procedure. Pull up on the drive shaft (**Figure 57**) while lightly rotating the drive shaft clockwise and counterclockwise. Note the dial indicator reading when the drive shaft reaches its free movement limit in each direction. Record the amount of dial indicator movement as gear backlash. Remove the backlash measuring instruments.

d. If the backlash is below the specification in **Table 2**, disassemble the gearcase and install a thinner shim (25, **Figure 40**) between the driven gear and the bearing. If the backlash is above the specification, install a thicker shim. Reassemble the gearcase and repeat the backlash measurement. Several shim changes may be required to obtain the correct gear backlash.

14. Install new seals (8, **Figure 40**) into the water pump cover (5), then install all water pump components as described in this chapter.

Disassembly (3 hp Models)

Refer to **Figure 60** for this procedure.

1. Drain the gearcase lubricant (**Figure 41**) as described in Chapter Three.

CAUTION
Never heat the gearcase housing to the point that the finish is burned. Continually move the flame around the mating surface to apply heat evenly. Excessive heat can distort or melt the gearcase.

NOTE
To assist with removal of the gearcase cap where corrosion has seized the components, use a torch to apply moderate heat to the gearcase. Heat the area near the gearcase housing-to-gearcase cap mating surfaces.

2. Remove the two bolts and washers (**Figure 42**). Use a blunt tip pry bar and carefully pry the gearcase cap loose from the gearcase housing (**Figure 43**). Work carefully to avoid damaging the mating surfaces.

3. Grasp the propeller shaft (**Figure 61**), then pull the shaft and cap from the gearcase. If the cam follower (12, **Figure 60**) becomes dislodged from the propeller shaft during removal, retrieve it from the gearcase.

4. Pull the gearcase cap from the propeller shaft. Mark the orientation, then remove the thrust washer (16, **Figure 60**) from the propeller shaft or gearcase cap. Remove the O-ring (17, **Figure 60**) from the cap. Discard the O-ring.

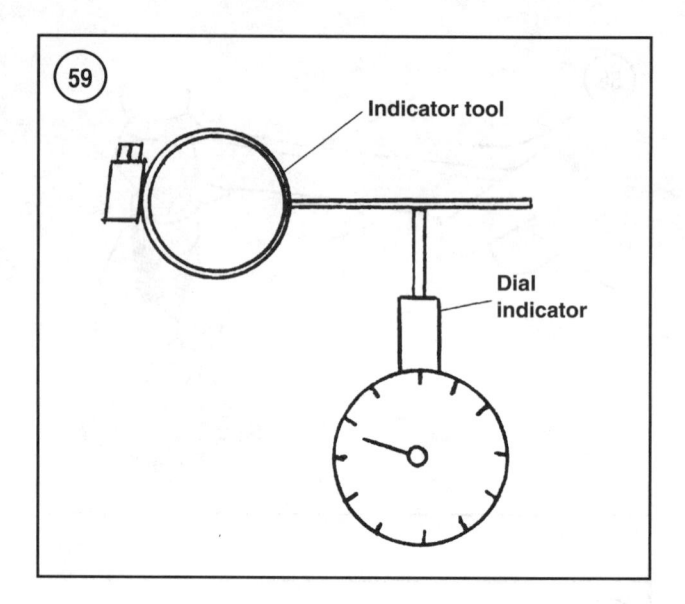

5. Carefully pry the water pump base (36, **Figure 60**) from the gearcase. Work carefully to avoid damaging the mating surfaces. Slide the base and lower shift shaft assembly up and over the drive shaft. Carefully pull the shift shaft bellows (**Figure 62**) from the opening in the water pump base. Work carefully to avoid tearing the bellows. Slide the bellows over the top of the shift shaft. Replace the bellows if they are torn or look weathered. Pull the shift shaft (**Figure 62**) from the lower side of the pump base. Remove the gasket (37, **Figure 60**) from the pump base or gearcase housing. Discard the gasket.

6. Use needlenose pliers to remove the E-clip from the groove on the drive shaft (**Figure 44**). Pull up slightly on the drive shaft to free the pinion gear from the shaft. Remove the pinion gear from the gearcase (**Figure 45**). Remove the shim (5, **Figure 60**) from the gearcase. Mark the pinion gear side of the shim for reference during assembly. Carefully draw the drive shaft from the gearcase (**Figure 46**). Only remove the lockring (27, **Figure 60**) from the drive shaft if it is corroded or damaged. Discard the lockring after removal.

7. Only remove the propeller shaft seals (19, **Figure 60**) if they must be replaced. The removal process damages the seals. Refer to *Component Inspection* in this chapter to determine the need for replacement. Remove the seals as follows:

a. Clamp the gearcase cap in a vise with protective jaws.

b. Engage the jaws of a slide hammer beneath the casing of the inner seal (**Figure 63**).

c. Use short hammer strokes to remove both seals.

GEARCASE

371

⑥⓪

GEARCASE COMPONENTS (3 HP MODEL)

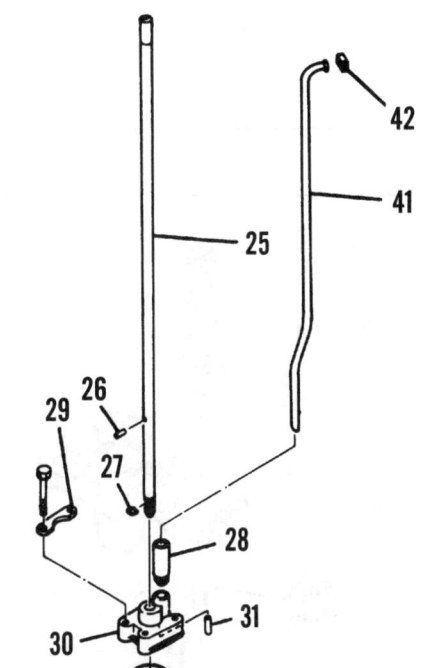

1. Gearcase housing
2. Vent plug
3. Sealing washer
4. Fill plug
5. Shim (pinion gear)
6. Pinion gear
7. E-clip
8. Anode
9. Shim (forward gear)
10. Bearing (forward gear)
11. Forward gear
12. Cam follower
13. Clutch
14. Spring
15. Propeller shaft
16. Thrust washer
17. O-ring
18. Gearcase cap
19. Seals
20. Thrust hub
21. Propeller
22. Washer
23. Propeller nut
24. Cotter pin
25. Drive shaft
26. Drive key
27. Lockring
28. Water tube grommet
29. Plate
30. Water pump body
31. Locating pin
32. O-ring
33. Insert
34. Impeller
35. Wear plate
36. Water pump base
37. Gasket
38. Drive shaft seal
39. Locating pin
40. Shift shaft bellows
41. Water tube
42. Water tube seal

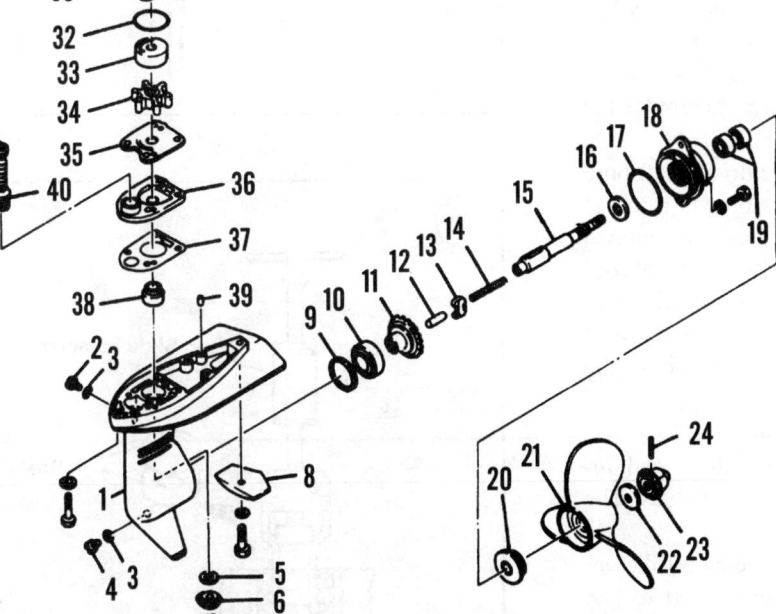

8

d. Discard the seals.

8. Remove the forward gear from the housing (**Figure 64**). If necessary, tap lightly on the front of the housing to free the gear from the bearing.

9. Only remove the driven gear bearing (10, **Figure 60**) if it must be replaced. The removal process damages the bearing. Refer to *Component Inspection* in this chapter to determine the need for replacement. Remove the bearing as follows:
   a. Clamp the gearcase in a vise with protective jaws. Engage the jaws of a slide hammer into the propeller shaft bore in the bearing (**Figure 49**).
   b. Use short hammer strokes to remove the bearing from the gearcase. Discard the bearing.
   c. Remove the forward gear shim (9, **Figure 60**) from the bearing or bearing bore. Do not discard the shim.

10. Clamp the gearcase in a vise with protective jaws. Engage the jaws of a slide hammer under the drive shaft seal casing (**Figure 50**). Use short hammer strokes to remove the seal. Discard the seal.

11. Only remove the drive shaft bushings if they must be replaced. The removal process usually damages the bushings. Refer to *Component Inspection* in this chapter to determine the need for replacement. Remove the bushings as follows:
   a. Clamp the gearcase in a vise with protective jaws.
   b. Thread the bushing removal tool (Yamaha part No. YB-6178) onto a suitable slide hammer. Engage the removal tool into the upper bushing as shown in **Figure 51**. Use short hammer strokes to remove the bushing.
   c. Rotate the housing to position the drive shaft bore so it faces up. Select a section of tubing or a socket and extension to use as a lower bushing removal tool. The tool must contact the bushing, but not contact the housing during bushing removal. Maintain firm contact with the bushing during the removal process. Carefully drive the bushing into the gearcase opening (**Figure 52**).

12. Disassemble the propeller shaft as follows:
   a. If the cam follower (**Figure 65**) was dislodged, insert it into the opening in the propeller shaft. The pointed end must face out.
   b. Use the propeller shaft and push the cam follower against a solid surface. Use enough effort to just collapse the spring. (**Figure 65**).
   c. With the spring collapsed, carefully pull the clutch (**Figure 65**) from the propeller shaft slot.
   d. Release the pressure, then remove the cam follower and spring.

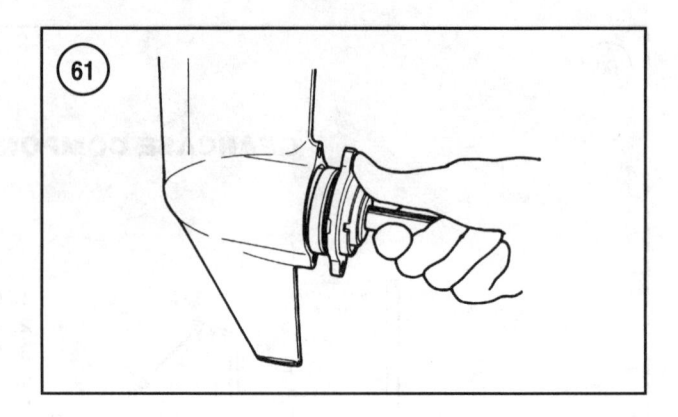

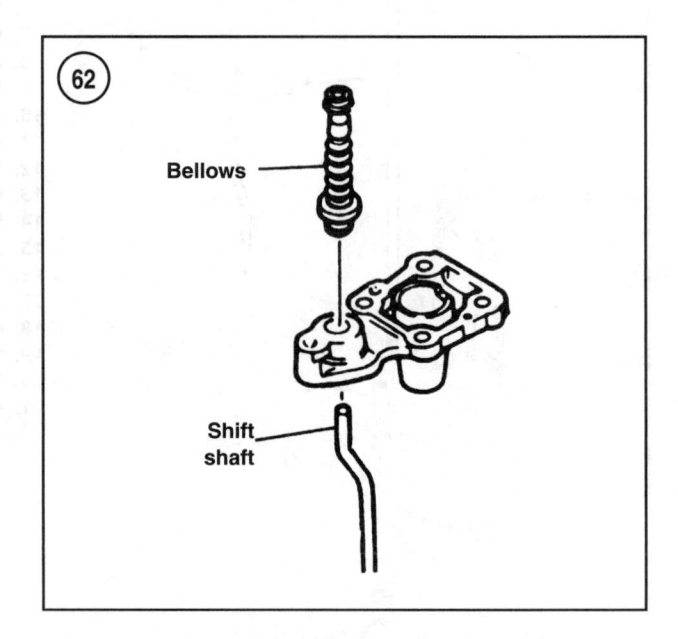

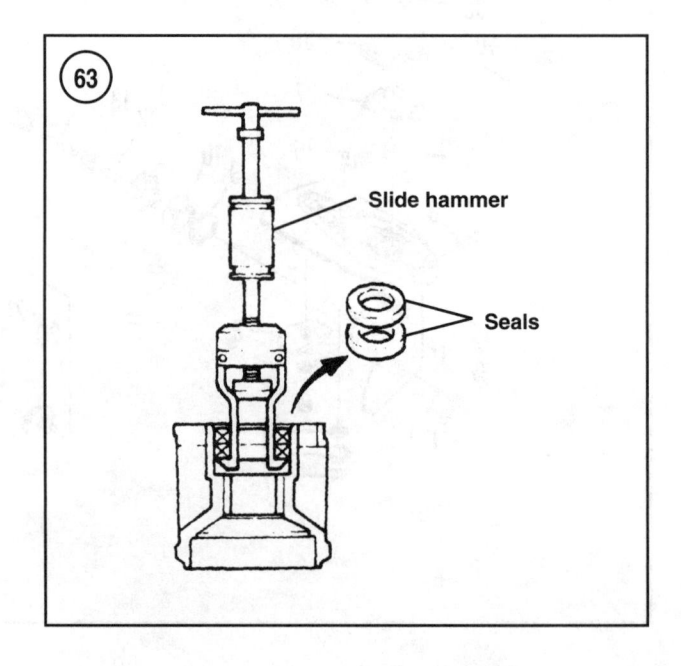

GEARCASE

quate length with a diameter that matches the washers and two hex nuts are also required.

    d. Arrange the washers, threaded washers and nuts in the gearcase as shown in **Figure 53**. Tighten the nuts until the flange on the lower bushing seats against the step in the bore. Remove the installation tools.

    e. Select a section of tubing or a socket and extension to use as a bushing installation tool. The tool must contact the end of the bushing, but not contact the gearcase during bushing installation.

    f. Insert the bushing into the drive shaft bore. Maintain firm contact with the bushing (**Figure 54**) during the removal process. Gently drive the bushing into the bore until it just contacts the step in the bore.

NOTE
When driving a bearing or bearing race into the gearcase housing, strike the driver hard enough to slightly move the bearing or race. Stop driving when the pitch changes or a sharp ring is heard as the driver is struck. This indicates the bearing or race is seated. Continued driving may bounce the bearing or race out of the bore.

2. Install the new driven gear bearing (10, **Figure 60**) into the housing, if it was removed, as follows:

    a. Select a piece of tubing to use as a bearing installation tool. The tool must contact only the outer race of the bearing, but not contact the gear housing during bearing installation.

    b. Apply a light coat of gearcase lubricant to the bearing surfaces and the bearing bore in the gearcase housing.

    c. Clamp the housing in a vise with protective jaws. The gearcase opening must face up.

    d. Install the forward gear shim (9, **Figure 60**) into the gearcase. Position the shim in the bearing recess in the housing.

    e. Place the new bearing in the bore with the number marks facing out. Maintain firm contact with the bearing while gently driving it into the bore (**Figure 55**). Use light force and do not allow the bearing to tilt in the bore. Continue driving until the bearing fully seats in the housing.

3. Install a new drive shaft seal (38, **Figure 60**) into the gearcase as follows:

    a. Apply a light coat of Loctite 271 to the outer casing of the seal and the seal bore in the gearcase housing.

    b. Select a piece of tubing or a socket and extension to use as a seal installation tool. The tool must contact

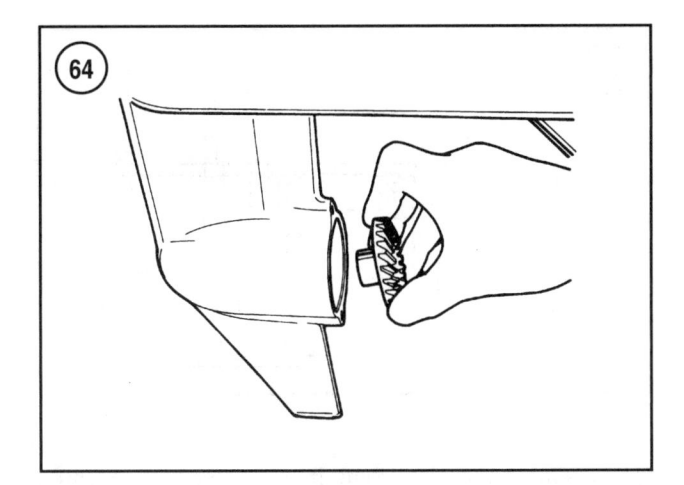

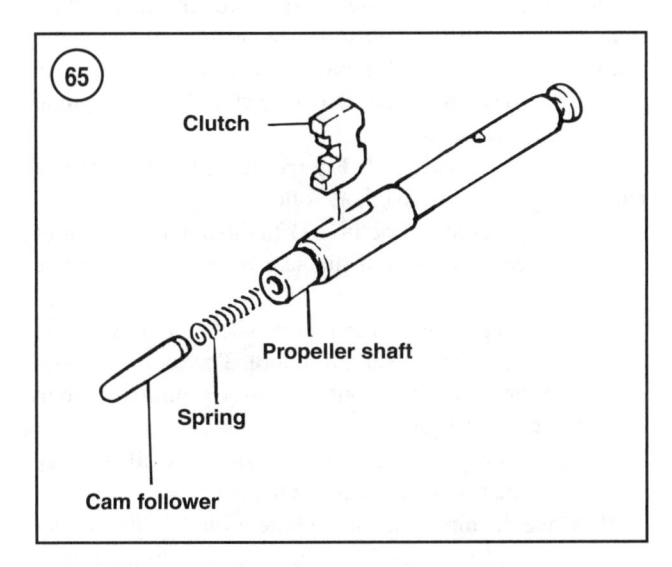

Assembly (3 hp Models)

Refer to **Figure 60** for this procedure.

1. Install the new drive shaft bushings, if they were removed, as follows:

    a. Apply a light coat of gearcase lubricant to the bushings and bushing bore in the gearcase housing.

    b. Working through the gearcase opening, insert the lower bushing into the bore. The flanged side of the bushing must face down.

    c. Select a washer with an outer diameter slightly smaller than the bushing flange. The washer must be of sufficient diameter to adequately support the bushing. Select a washer of sufficient diameter to span the drive shaft bore at the top of the housing. If a suitable washer is not available, use a steel plate with a hole to span the bore. A threaded rod of ade-

the seal casing, but not contact the gear housing during seal installation.

   c. Insert the seal into the bore with the lip side facing up. Carefully drive the seal into the bore until the upper edge of the seat is recessed 1.5-2.0 mm (0.06-0.08 in.) below the seal bore opening (**Figure 66**). Wipe excess Loctite from the drive shaft bore before proceeding.

   d. Apply a bead of Yamaha All-Purpose Grease or equivalent to the seal lip.

4. Install the forward gear into the housing (**Figure 64**). The hub of the gear must enter the opening in the bearing. Seat the gear against the inner race of the bearing.

5. Apply a very light coat of gearcase lubricant to the shim (5, **Figure 60**). Install the shim into the housing. If the original shim is used, the mark made during removal must face the pinion gear. Align the shim with the drive shaft bore.

6. Install the pinion gear into the gearcase (**Figure 45**). Mesh the pinion gear teeth with the driven gear teeth. Align the splined opening in the pinion gear with the shim and drive shaft bore.

7. Apply a coat of gearcase lubricant to the lower surfaces of the drive shaft. If the lockring was removed, install a new lockring (27, **Figure 60**) into its groove in the drive shaft. Do not install the lockring into the lowest groove.

8. Carefully guide the drive shaft into the bore (**Figure 46**). Make sure the drive shaft passes through the shim. Slowly rotate the drive shaft to align the drive shaft splines with the pinion gear splines. The shaft will drop into the pinion gear when the splines align. Use needlenose pliers (**Figure 44**) to install the E-clip into the drive shaft groove. Pull up on the drive shaft to verify groove engagement.

9. Insert the straight end of the shift shaft (**Figure 62**) into its opening in the bottom of the water pump base. The curved end of the shift shaft must be at the bottom. Apply a light coat of Yamaha All-Purpose Grease or equivalent to the upper end of the shift shaft. Carefully slide the shift shaft bellows (**Figure 62**) over the top of the shift shaft. Insert the lower end of the bellows fully into the opening in the water pump base. If the bellows does not fit tightly in the opening, it is old and must be replaced.

10. Apply Loctite Gasket Maker to the gasket contact surfaces of the water pump base and the gearcase housing. Install a new gasket (37, **Figure 60**) onto the water pump base. The lower end of the shift shaft must pass through the opening in the gasket.

11. Rotate the shift shaft to position the outward curving side of the shift shaft toward the aft end of the gearcase. When installed, this surface must contact the cam follower. Guide the shift shaft into the gearcase opening while sliding the water pump base over the drive shaft. Seat the base on the housing. Thread one of the water pump screws through the base and into the housing to temporarily hold the base. Do not install the water pump components at this time.

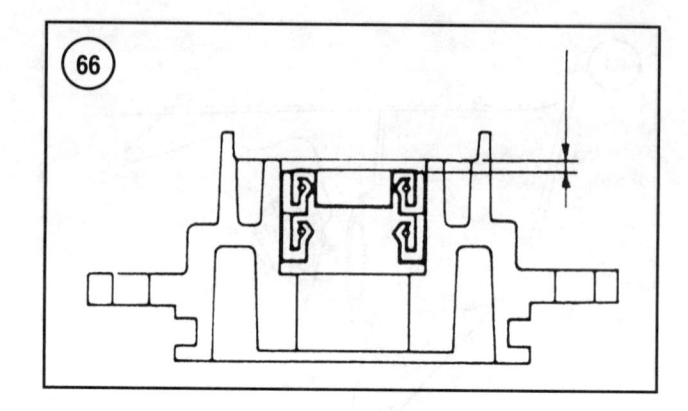

12. Install new seals (19, **Figure 60**) into the gearcase cap, if they were removed, as follows:

   a. Apply a coat of Loctite 271 to the outer diameter of the seal casings and the seal bore in the gearcase cap.

   b. Select a section of tubing or a socket and extension to use as a seal installation tool. The tool must contact the seal casing, but not contact the seal bore in the gearcase cap.

   c. Place the gearcase cap on a sturdy work surface with the propeller side facing up.

   d. Place the inner seal in the bore with the lip side facing out. Carefully drive the inner seal into the bore until its outer surface is just below the seal bore opening.

   e. Place the outer seal into the bore with the lip side facing outward. Carefully drive the outer seal into the bore until its outer surface is 1.0-1.5 mm (0.04-0.06 in.) recessed in the seal bore opening.

   f. Wipe excess Loctite from the seal bore. Apply a coat of Yamaha All-Purpose Grease or equivalent to the seal lips.

13. Reassemble the propeller shaft as follows:

   a. Insert the spring (**Figure 65**) into the propeller shaft opening.

   b. Working from the opening, use a small punch to collapse the spring.

   c. With the spring collapsed, slip the clutch into the propeller shaft slot. The clutch dogs must face forward as indicated in **Figure 65**.

   d. Release the spring to hold the clutch. The spring should fit into the notch in the clutch. Move the

GEARCASE

position the washer as indicated by the mark made before removal. Slide the gearcase cap over the propeller shaft. Seat the cap against the thrust washer.

16. Position the gearcase with the drive shaft facing up. Install the propeller shaft into the gearcase (**Figure 61**). Keep the shaft horizontal and work carefully to avoid dislodging the cam follower (**Figure 65**). The cam follower must pass through the opening in the forward gear and contact the shift shaft.

17. Align the mounting bolt holes while inserting the cap into the gearcase housing. Push on the cap until it seats against the gearcase housing. Apply Loctite 572 to the threads of the gearcase cap bolts. Thread the bolts and washers into the cap and gearcase housing. Evenly tighten the bolts (**Figure 42**) to the general torque specification in Chapter One.

CAUTION
Use very light force when moving the drive shaft during the backlash measurement. The readings will be inaccurate if excessive force is applied to the drive shaft.

NOTE
Remove all water pump components before measuring gear backlash. The drag created by the water pump components will prevent accurate measurement. Temporarily remove the drive shaft seal carrier or water pump base during backlash measurements.

NOTE
Make sure all gearcase lubricant has been drained from the gearcase before measuring gear backlash. The readings will be inaccurate due to the cushion effect of the lubricant on the gear teeth.

18. Measure and correct the gear backlash if a new gearcase housing, driven gear, pinion gear, drive shaft or driven gear bearing was installed during the repair. Measure and correct the gearcase backlash as follows:
   a. Pull up on the shift shaft to shift the gearcase into forward gear (**Figure 67**).
   b. Attach a dial indicator to the gearcase using a suitable clamping device (**Figure 68**). Dial indicators and mounts are available from most tool suppliers. The mount must remain rigid, otherwise the backlash measurement will be inaccurate.
   c. Clamp the backlash indicator tool (Yamaha part No. YB-06265-90890-06265) onto the drive shaft. Arrange the dial indicator mount to position the dial indicator plunger at the same height as the indicator tool (**Figure 58**) and with the plunger at a 90° angle

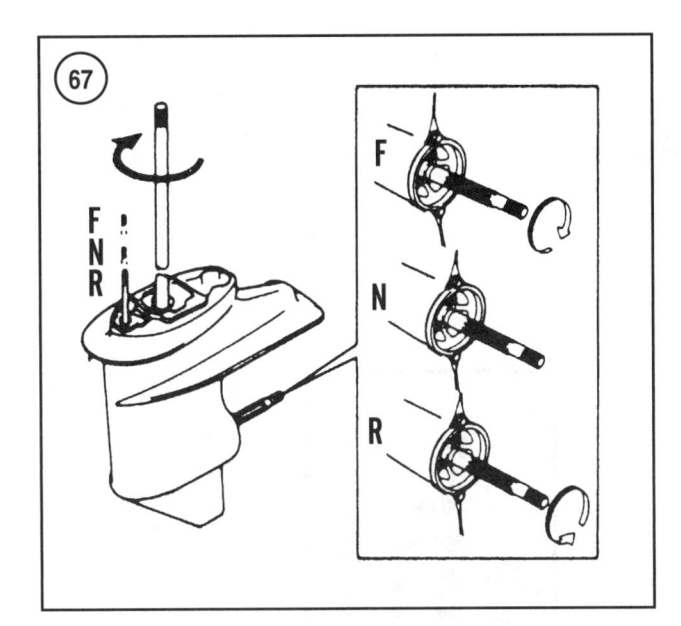

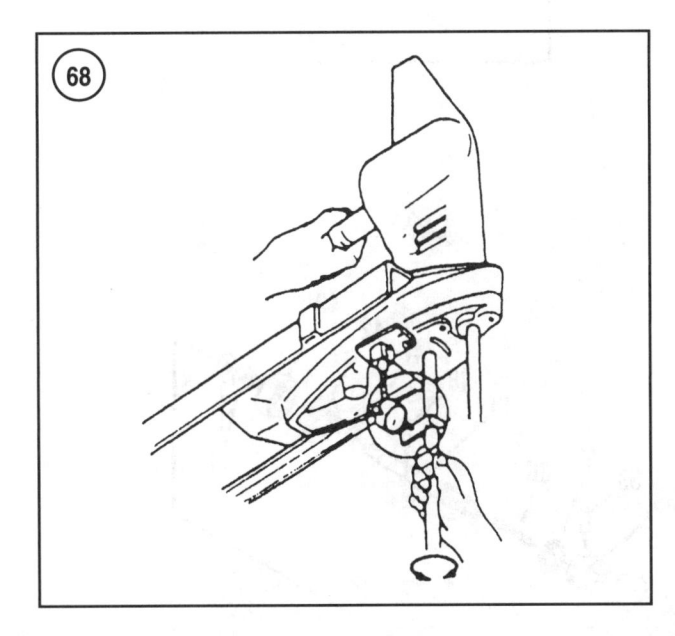

clutch in the slot to verify spring engagement. The clutch should protrude the same amount on both sides of the shaft. Correct as necessary.

   e. Apply a coat of Yamaha All-Purpose Grease or equivalent to the cam follower. Insert the cam follower into the propeller shaft opening. The pointed end of the follower must face outward.

14. Apply a coat of Yamaha All-Purpose Grease or equivalent to the surfaces, then fit the new O-ring (17, **Figure 60**) into the groove in the gearcase cap.

15. Slip the thrust washer (16, **Figure 60**) over the propeller end of the propeller shaft. When reusing the washer,

CHAPTER EIGHT

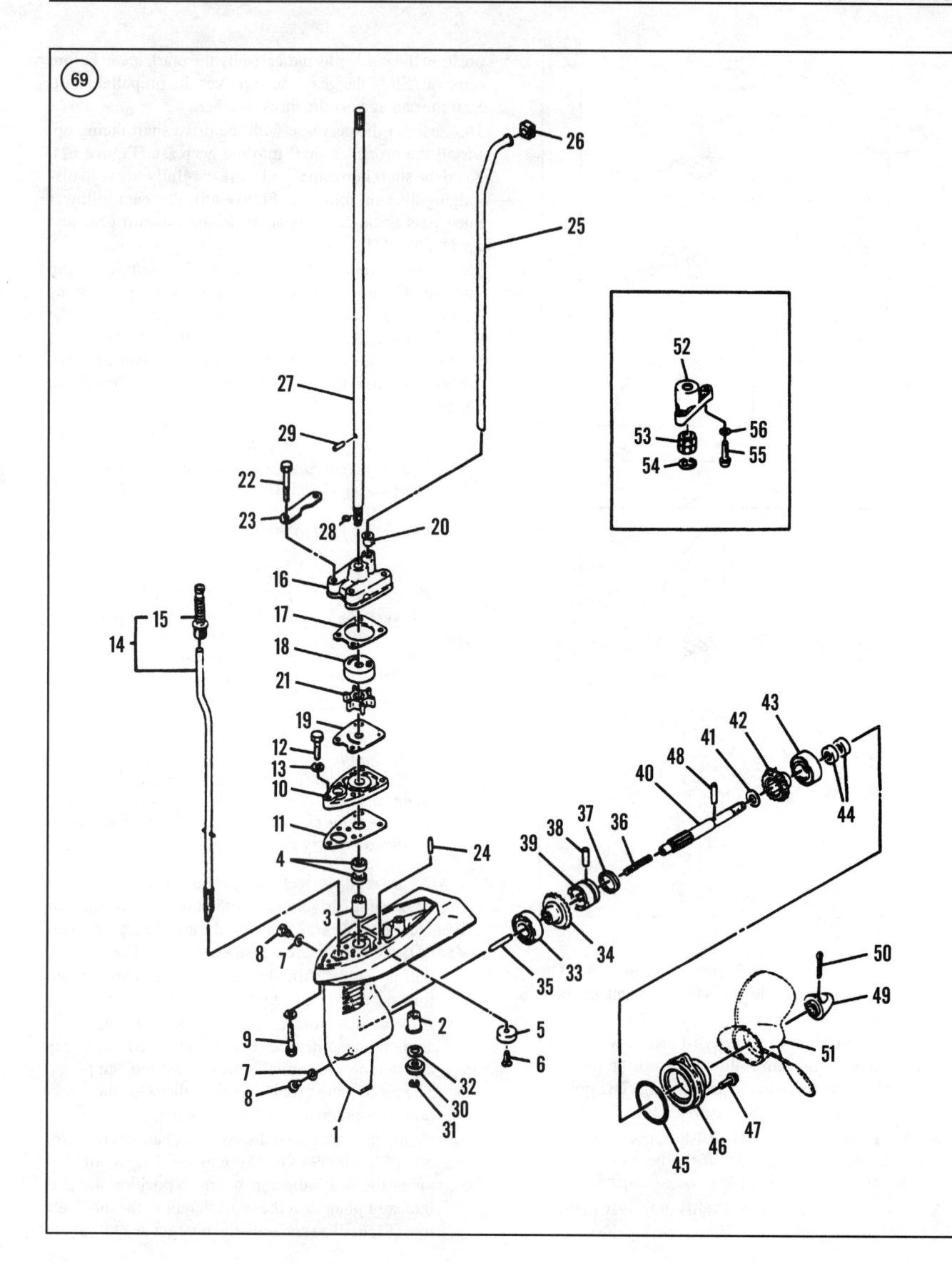

GEARCASE

**GEARCASE COMPONENTS
(4 AND 5 HP MODELS)**

1. Gearcase housing
2. Lower drive shaft bushing
3. Upper drive shaft bushing
4. Drive shaft seals
5. Anode
6. Bolt
7. Sealing washer
8. Drain/fill/vent plugs
9. Mounting bolt
10. Water pump base
11. Gasket
12. Screw
13. Lockwasher
14. Shift shaft assembly
15. Shift shaft bellows
16. Water pump body
17. Gasket
18. Insert
19. Wear plate
20. Water tube grommet
21. Impeller
22. Screw
23. Plate
24. Locating pin
25. Water tube
26. Grommet/seal
27. Drive shaft
28. Lockring
29. Drive key
30. Pinion gear
31. E-clip
32. Pinion gear shim
33. Forward gear bearing
34. Forward gear
35. Cam follower
36. Cam follower spring
37. Clutch spring
38. Cross pin
39. Clutch
40. Propeller shaft
41. Thrust washer
42. Reverse gear
43. Reverse gear bearing
44. Propeller shaft seals
45. O-ring
46. Gearcase cap
47. Bolt
48. Shear pin (earlier models only)
49. Propeller nut
50. Cotter pin
51. Propeller
52. Bushing housing*
53. Bushing*
54. Clip*
55. Screw*
56. Washer*

*Used only on long shaft models.

to the indicator arm (**Figure 59**). Reposition the dial indicator to place the plunger in line with the mark on the indicator tool.

d. Rotate the drive shaft so that the drive shaft points down (**Figure 68**). Have an assistant push in on the propeller shaft during this procedure. Observe the dial indicator while lightly rotating the drive shaft clockwise and counterclockwise. Do not push up on the drive shaft. Note the dial indicator reading when the drive shaft reaches its free movement limit in each direction. Record the amount of dial indicator movement as gear backlash. Remove the backlash measuring instruments.

e. If the backlash is below the specification in **Table 2**, disassemble the gearcase and install a thinner shim (5, **Figure 60**) above the pinion gear (6). If the backlash is above the specification, install a thicker shim. Reassemble the gearcase and repeat the backlash measurement. If a high backlash cannot be corrected with the shim change, check for a missing or damaged forward gear shim (9, **Figure 60**). If a low backlash cannot be corrected with the shim change, check for an improperly installed driven gear bearing (10, **Figure 60**) or debris in the bearing bore. The forward gear shim is not available in alternate sizes. Do not proceed until the backlash is correct.

19. Remove the screw from the water pump base. Install all water pump components as described in this chapter.

Disassembly (4 and 5 hp Models)

Refer to **Figure 69** for this procedure.

1. Drain the gearcase lubricant (**Figure 70**) as described in Chapter Three.

CAUTION
Never heat the gearcase housing to the point that the finish is burned. Continually move the flame around the mating surface to apply heat evenly. Excessive heat can distort or melt the gearcase.

NOTE
To assist with removal of the gearcase cap when corrosion has seized the components, use a torch to apply moderate heat to the gearcase. Heat the area near the gearcase housing-to-gearcase cap mating surfaces.

2. Remove the two bolts and washers (**Figure 71**). Use a blunt tip pry bar and carefully pry the gearcase cap loose from the gearcase housing (**Figure 72**). Use the two pry

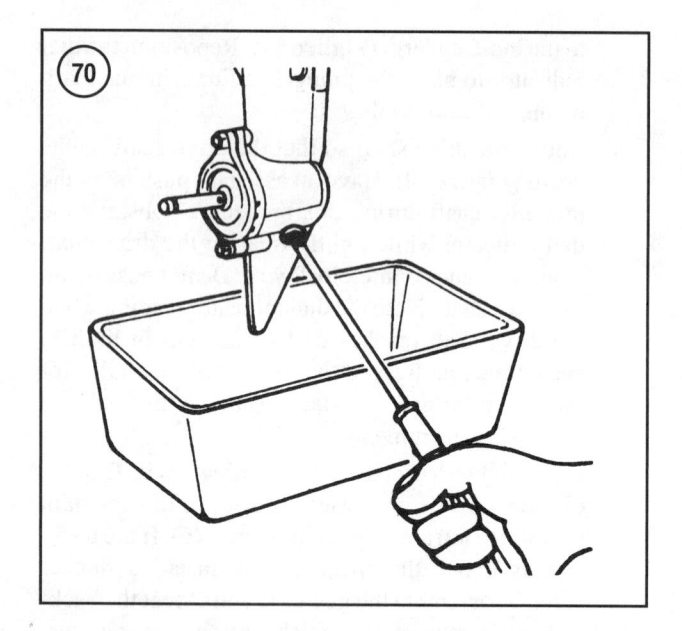

slots and work carefully to avoid damaging the mating surfaces.

3. Grasp the propeller shaft (**Figure 61**), then pull the shaft and cap from the gearcase. If the cam follower (35, **Figure 69**) becomes dislodged from the propeller shaft during removal, promptly retrieve it from the gearcase.

4. Pull the gearcase cap (46, **Figure 69**) from the aft end of the propeller shaft. Mark the orientation, then remove the thrust washer (41, **Figure 69**) from the propeller shaft (40) or inner race of the reverse gear bearing (43). Remove the O-ring (45, **Figure 69**) from the cap. Discard the O-ring.

5. Pull the reverse gear from the gearcase cap. If necessary, carefully pry the reverse gear from the bearing (**Figure 73**). Use two blunt tip pry bars and work carefully to avoid damaging the components.

6. Only remove the reverse gear bearing (43, **Figure 69**) if the bearing or propeller shaft seals must be replaced. The removal process may damage the bearing. Refer to *Component Inspection* in this chapter to determine the need for replacement. Remove the bearing as follows:
   a. Clamp the gearcase cap in a vise with protective jaws.
   b. Engage the jaws of a slide hammer beneath the inner bearing race (**Figure 74**).
   c. Use short hammer strokes to remove the bearing.

7. Only remove the propeller shaft seals (44, **Figure 69**) if they must be replaced. The removal process damages the seals. Refer to *Component Inspection* in this chapter to determine the need for replacement. Remove the seals as follows:

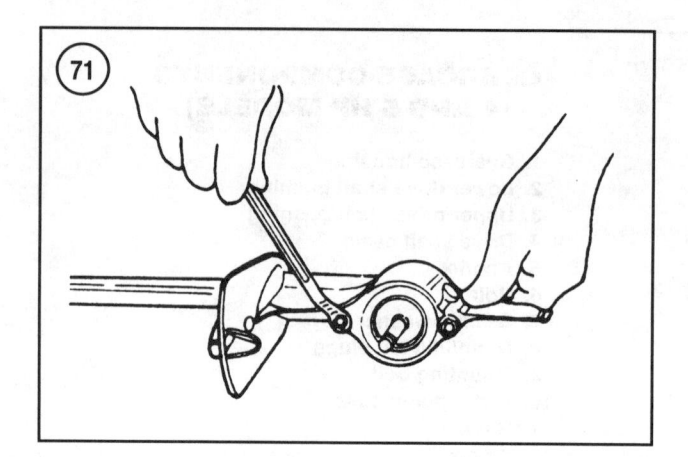

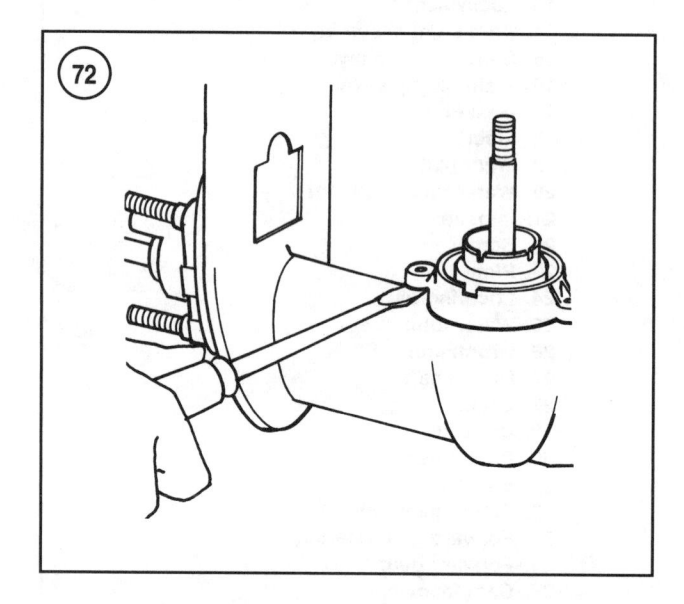

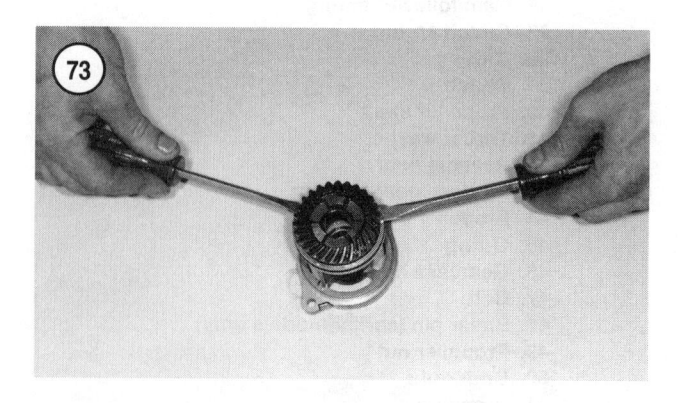

   a. Clamp the gearcase cap in a vise with protective jaws. The gear side of the cap must face up.
   b. Engage the jaws of a slide hammer beneath the casing of the inner seal (**Figure 63**).
   c. Use short hammer strokes to remove the seals.

GEARCASE

⑦④ Reverse gear bearing / Slide hammer

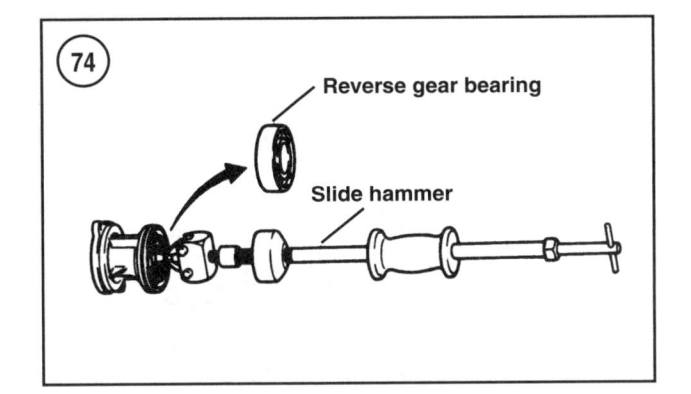

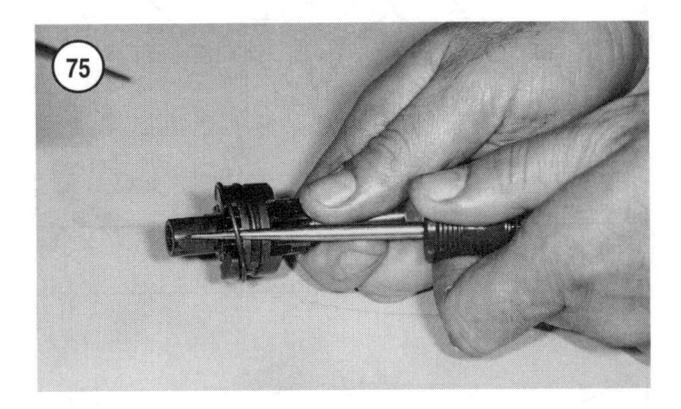

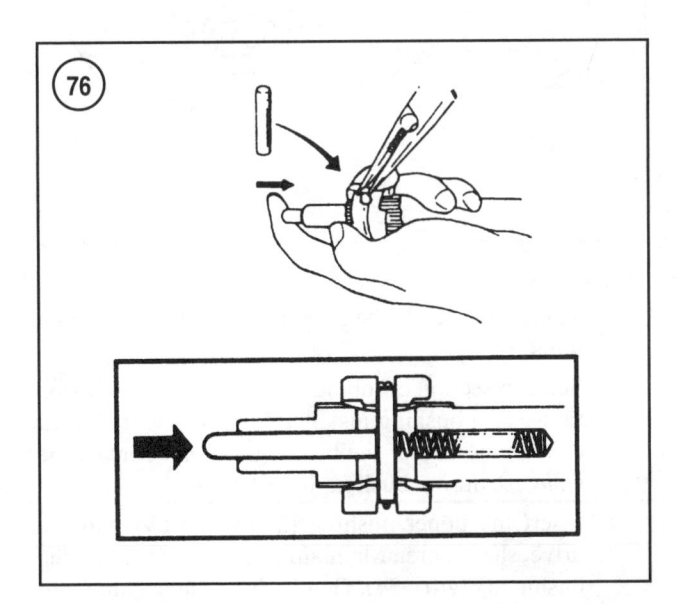

⑦⑤

⑦⑥

d. Discard the seals.
8. Disassemble the propeller shaft as follows:
   a. Carefully unwind the spring from the clutch (**Figure 75**).
   b. Push in on the cam follower to collapse the follower spring (**Figure 76**).
   c. Grip the cross pin with needlenose pliers and pull it from the clutch.
   d. Release the spring tension, then pull the cam follower (35, **Figure 69**) and spring (36) from the propeller shaft bore.
   e. Slide the clutch (39, **Figure 69**) from the front end of the propeller shaft.

9. Carefully pry the water pump base (10, **Figure 69**) loose from the gearcase. Work carefully to avoid damaging the mating surfaces. Slide the base and lower shift shaft assembly up and over the drive shaft. Remove the gasket (11, **Figure 69**) from the pump base or gearcase housing. Discard the gasket.

10. Carefully pull the shift shaft bellows (**Figure 62**) from the opening in the water pump base. Work carefully to avoid tearing the bellows. Slide the bellows over the top of the shift shaft. Replace the bellows if they are torn or look weathered.

11. Only remove the shift shaft from the water pump base if the shift shaft, shift cam or water pump base require replacement. Refer to *Component Inspection* in this chapter to determine the need for replacement. Remove the shift shaft as follows:
   a. Use a small punch to carefully drive the upper pin from the shift shaft. The upper pin protrudes evenly from both sides of the shaft. If the pin does not fit tightly in the shift shaft, replace the pin. If the fit is still loose, replace the shift shaft.
   b. Use a small pin punch to drive the lower pin from the shift cam and shift shaft. If the pin does not fit tightly in the shift shaft and shift cam, replace the pin. If the fit is still loose, replace the shift cam, shift shaft or both components.
   c. Carefully pull the shift shaft from the top side of the water pump base.

12. Use needlenose pliers to remove the E-clip from the groove on the drive shaft (**Figure 77**). Pull up slightly on the drive shaft to free the pinion gear from the shaft. Remove the pinion gear from the gearcase (**Figure 78**), then remove the shim (32, **Figure 69**) from the gearcase. Mark the pinion gear side of the shim for reference during assembly. Carefully draw the drive shaft from the gearcase. Only remove the lockring (28, **Figure 69**) from the drive shaft if it is corroded or damaged. Discard the lockring after removal.

13. Remove the forward gear from the housing (**Figure 78**). If necessary, tap lightly on the front of the housing to free the gear from the bearing.

14. Only remove the forward gear bearing (33, **Figure 69**) if it must be replaced. The removal process damages the bearing. Refer to *Component Inspection* in this chap-

ter to determine the need for replacement. Remove the bearing as follows:
   a. Clamp the gearcase in a vise with protective jaws. Engage the jaws of a slide hammer in the propeller shaft bore in the bearing (**Figure 49**).
   b. Use short hammer strokes to remove the bearing from the gearcase. Discard the bearing.
15. Clamp the gearcase in a vise with protective jaws. Engage the jaws of a slide hammer under the casing of the lower seal (**Figure 50**). Use short hammer strokes to remove both seals. Discard the seals.
16. Remove the drive shaft bushings only if they must be replaced. The removal process usually damages the bushings. Refer to *Component Inspection* in this chapter to determine the need for replacement. Remove the bushings as follows:
   a. Clamp the gearcase in a vise with protective jaws.
   b. Thread the bushing removal tool (Yamaha part No. YB-6178) onto a suitable slide hammer. Engage the removal tool in the upper bushing as shown in **Figure 51**. Use short hammer strokes to remove the bushing.
   c. Rotate the housing to position the drive shaft bore so it faces up. Select a section of tubing or a socket and extension to use as a lower bushing removal tool. The tool must contact the bushing, but not contact the housing during bushing removal. Maintain firm contact with the bushing, then carefully drive it into the gearcase opening (**Figure 52**).

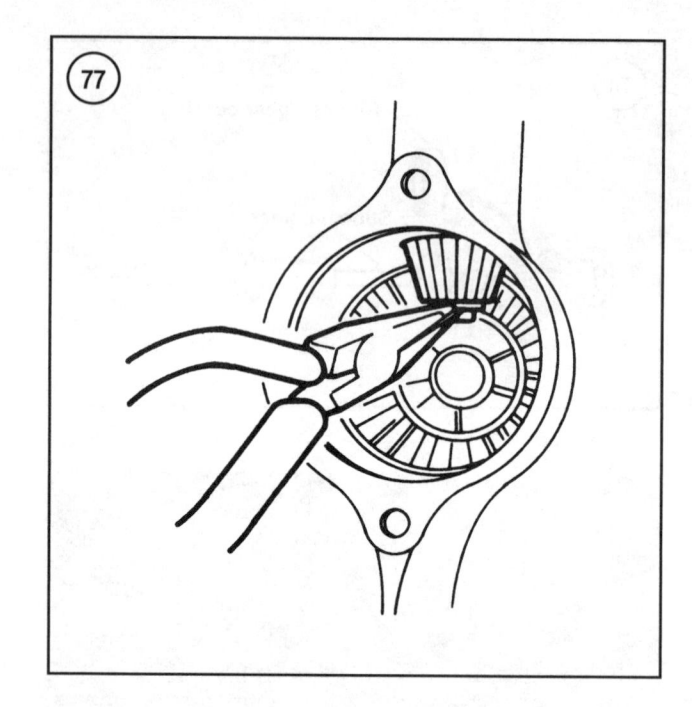

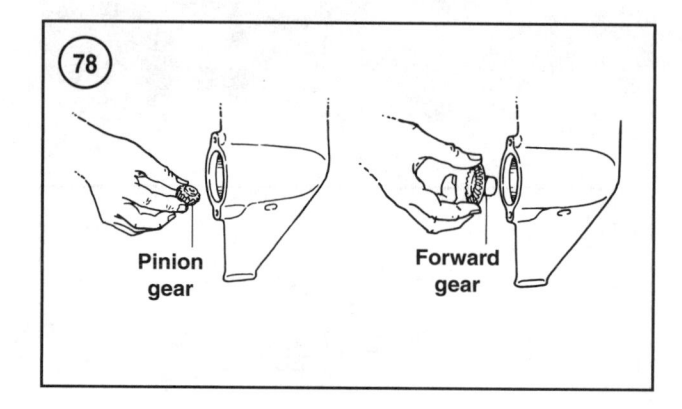

Assembly (4 and 5 hp Models)

Refer to **Figure 69** for this procedure.
1. Install new drive shaft bushings, if they were removed, as follows:
   a. Apply a light coat of gearcase lubricant to the bushings and bushing bore in the gearcase housing.
   b. Working through the gearcase opening, insert the lower bushing (2, **Figure 69**) into the bore. The flanged side of the bushing must face down.
   c. Select a washer with an outer diameter slightly smaller than the bushing flange. The washer must be of sufficient diameter to adequately support the bushing. Select a washer of sufficient diameter to span the drive shaft bore at the top of the housing. If a suitable washer is not available, use a steel plate with a hole to span the bore. A threaded rod of adequate length with a diameter that matches the washers and two hex nuts are also required.
   d. Arrange the washers, threaded washers and nuts in the gearcase as shown in **Figure 53**. Tighten the nuts until the flange on the lower bushing seats against the step in the bore. Remove the installation tools.
   e. Select a section of tubing or a socket and extension to use as a bushing installation tool. The tool must contact the end of the bushing, but not contact the gearcase during bushing installation.
   f. Insert the upper bushing (3, **Figure 69**) into the drive shaft bore. Maintain firm contact with the bushing (**Figure 54**). Gently drive the bushing into the bore until it just contacts the step in the bore.

NOTE
When driving a bearing or bearing race into the gearcase housing, strike the driver just enough to slightly move the bearing or race. Stop driving when the pitch changes or a sharp ring is heard as the driver is struck.

GEARCASE

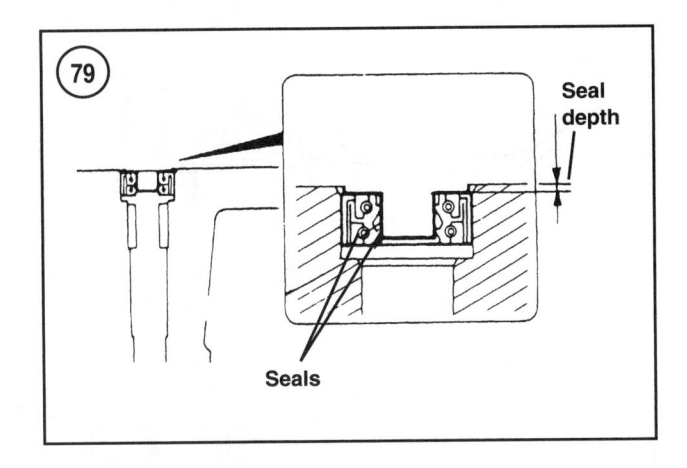

79

Seal depth

Seals

This indicates the bearing or race is seated. Continued driving may bounce the bearing or race out of the bore.

2. Install a new driven gear bearing (33, **Figure 69**) into the housing, if it was removed, as follows:
   a. Select a piece of tubing to use as a bearing installation tool. The tool must contact only the outer race of the bearing, but not contact the gear housing during bearing installation.
   b. Apply a light coat of gearcase lubricant to the bearing surfaces and the bearing bore in the gearcase housing.
   c. Clamp the housing in a vise with protective jaws. The gearcase opening must face up.
   d. Place the new bearing in the bore with the number marks facing out. Maintain firm contact with the bearing while gently driving it into the bore (**Figure 55**). Use light force and do not allow the bearing to tilt in the bore. Continue driving until the bearing fully seats in the housing.

3. Install new drive shaft seals (4, **Figure 69**) into the gearcase as follows:
   a. Apply a light coat of Loctite 271 to the outer casing of the seals and the seal bore in the gearcase housing.
   b. Select a piece of tubing or a socket and extension to use as a seal installation tool. The tool must contact the seal casing, but not contact the gear housing during seal installation.
   c. Insert the inner seal into the bore with the lip side facing up. Carefully drive the seal into the bore until the upper edge of the seal is slightly recessed in the bore.
   d. Insert the outer seal into the bore with the lip side facing up. Carefully drive the outer seal into the bore until it just contacts the inner seal.
   e. Drive both seals into the bore until the casing of the outer seal is recessed 1.0-1.5 mm (0.04-0.06 in.) below the seal bore opening (**Figure 79**). Wipe excess Loctite from the drive shaft bore before proceeding.
   f. Apply a bead of Yamaha All-Purpose Grease or equivalent to the seal lips.

4. Install the forward gear into the housing (**Figure 78**). The hub of the gear must enter the opening in the bearing. Seat the gear against the inner race of the bearing.

5. Apply a very light coat of gearcase lubricant to the shim (32, **Figure 69**). Install the shim into the housing. If the original shim is reused, the mark made during removal must face the pinion gear. Align the shim with the drive shaft bore.

6. Install the pinion gear into the gearcase (**Figure 78**). Mesh the pinion gear teeth with the forward gear teeth. Align the splined opening in the pinion gear with the shim and the drive shaft bore.

7. Apply a coat of gearcase lubricant to the lower surfaces of the drive shaft. If the lockring was removed, install a new lockring (28, **Figure 69**) into its groove in the drive shaft. Do not install the lockring into the lowest groove.

8. Carefully guide the drive shaft into the bore. Make sure the drive shaft passes through the shim. Slowly rotate the drive shaft to align the drive shaft splines with the pinion gear splines. The shaft drops into the pinion gear when the splines align. Use needlenose pliers (**Figure 77**) to install the E-clip into the drive shaft groove. Pull up on the drive shaft to verify groove engagement.

9. Install the shift shaft into the water pump base as follows:
   a. Slide the shift shaft (straight end first) into its opening in the top of the water pump base (10, **Figure 69**).
   b. Drive the upper pin into its opening in the shift shaft. Do not drive the pin into the opening near the bottom of the shaft. The pin must fit tightly in the opening and protrude equal amounts on each side of the shaft.
   c. Rotate the shift shaft so the curved end would be facing forward if the base was mounted on the gearcase.
   d. Install the shift cam onto the lower end of the shift shaft. The slanted end must face towards the rear if the base was mounted on the gearcase.
   e. Carefully drive the lower pin through the shift cam and shift shaft. The pin must protrude or be recessed the same amount on each side of the shift cam.
   f. Apply a light coat of Yamaha All-Purpose Grease or equivalent to the upper end of the shift shaft. Care-

8

fully slide the shift shaft bellows (**Figure 62**) over the top of the shift shaft. Insert the lower end of the bellows fully into the opening in the water pump base. If the bellows does not fit tightly in the opening, it must be replaced.

10. Install a new gasket (11, **Figure 69**) onto the water pump base. The lower end of the shift shaft must pass through the opening in the gasket.

11. Rotate the shift shaft to position the slanted side of the shift cam toward the aft end of the gearcase. When installed, this surface must contact the cam follower. Guide the shift shaft into the gearcase opening while sliding the water pump base over the drive shaft. Seat the base on the housing. Thread one of the water pump screws through the base and into the housing to temporarily hold the base. Do not install the water pump components at this time.

12. Install new seals (44, **Figure 69**) into the gearcase cap, if they were removed, as follows:
   a. Apply a coat of Loctite 271 to the outer diameter of the seal casings and the seal bore in the gearcase cap.
   b. Select a section of tubing or a socket and extension to use as a seal installation tool. The tool must contact the seal casing, but not contact the seal bore in the gearcase cap.
   c. Place the gearcase cap on a sturdy work surface with the reverse gear side facing up.
   d. Place the first seal in the bore with the lip side facing down. Carefully drive the seal into the bore until it is fully seated (**Figure 80**).
   e. Place the second seal in the bore with the lip side facing down. Carefully drive the seal into the bore until it is seated against the first seal.
   f. Wipe excess Loctite from the seal bore. Apply a coat of Yamaha All-Purpose Grease or equivalent to the seal lips.

13. If the reverse gear bearing was removed, install a new reverse gear bearing (43, **Figure 69**) into the gearcase cap as follows:
   a. Select a piece of tubing to use as a bearing installation tool. The tool must contact only the outer race of the bearing, but not contact the gearcase cap during bearing installation.
   b. Apply a light coat of gearcase lubricant to the bearing surfaces and the bearing bore in the gearcase cap.
   c. Place the gearcase cap on a sturdy work surface with the bearing bore facing up.
   d. Place the new bearing in the bore with the number marks facing up. Maintain firm contact with the bearing while gently driving it into the bore (**Figure 81**). Use light force and do not allow the bearing to

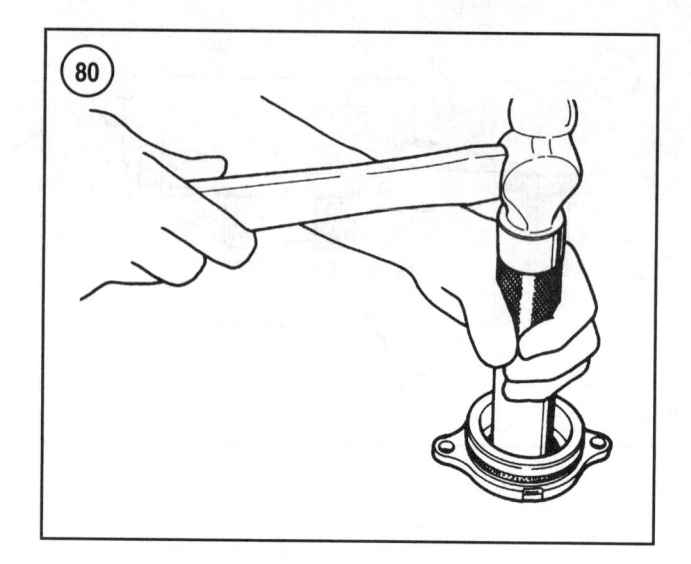

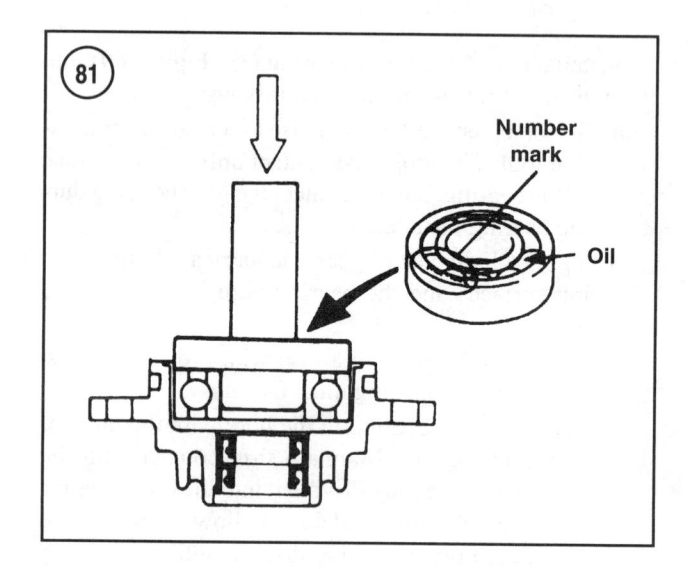

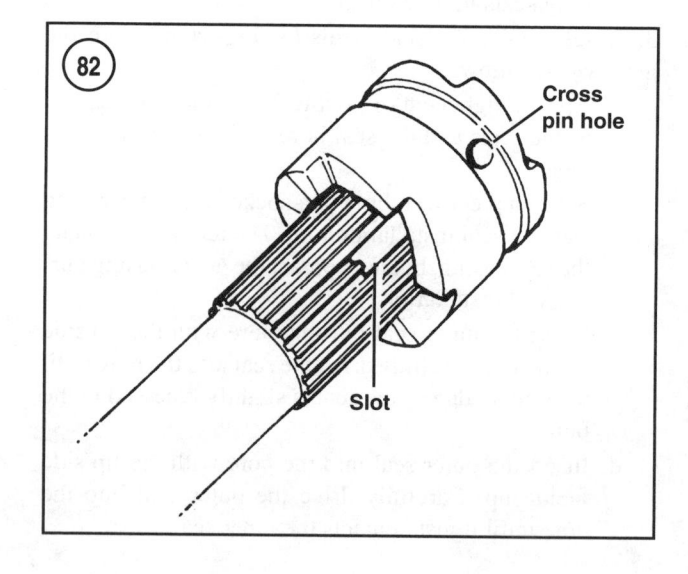

GEARCASE

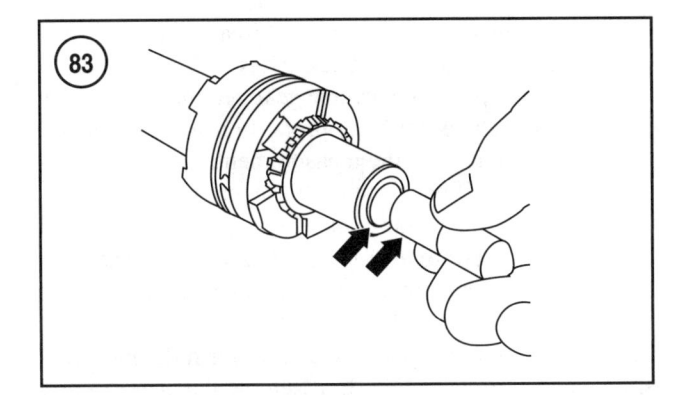

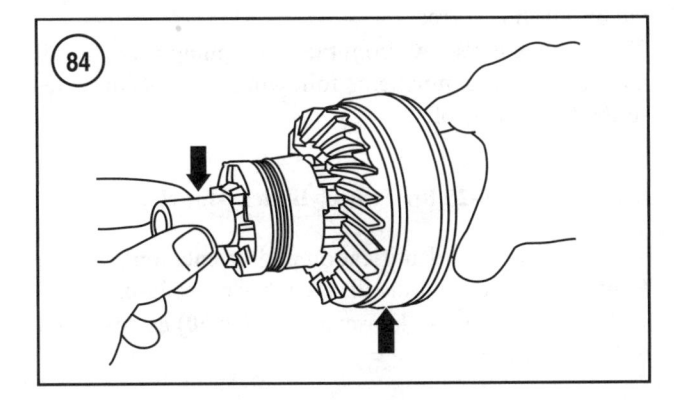

83

84

tilt in the bore. Continue driving until the bearing fully seats in the bore.

14. Apply a coat of Yamaha All-Purpose Grease or equivalent to the surfaces, then install the new O-ring (45, **Figure 69**) into the groove in the gearcase cap.
15. Reassemble the propeller shaft as follows:
    a. Align the cross pin opening in the clutch with the slot in the propeller shaft (**Figure 82**), then slide the clutch over the forward side of the propeller shaft. The F mark on the clutch must face forward.
    b. Insert the spring (36, **Figure 69**) into the propeller shaft opening.
    c. Working from the opening, use a small punch to collapse the spring.
    d. With the spring collapsed, insert the cross pin (38, **Figure 69**) through the clutch and propeller slot.
    e. Release the spring to hold the cross pin. Carefully wind the clutch spring onto the clutch (**Figure 75**). The spring must fit tightly on the clutch and loops must span both ends of the cross pin. Each loop must lay flat against the clutch.
    f. Apply a coat of Yamaha All-Purpose Grease or equivalent to the cam follower. Insert the cam follower into the propeller shaft opening (**Figure 83**). The pointed end of the follower must face out.

16. Slip the thrust washer (41, **Figure 69**) over the propeller end of the propeller shaft. If the washer is reused, position it as indicated by the mark made before removal.
17. Insert the hub of the reverse gear (42, **Figure 69**) into the bore of the reverse gear bearing (43). Seat the gear in the bearing. Slide the propeller shaft through the reverse gear and gearcase cap (**Figure 84**). Seat the propeller shaft against the thrust washer and reverse gear bearing.
18. Position the gearcase with the drive shaft facing up. Install the propeller shaft into the gearcase (**Figure 61**). Keep the shaft horizontal and work carefully to avoid dislodging the cam follower. The cam follower must pass through the opening in the forward gear and contact the shift cam.
19. Align the mounting bolt holes while inserting the cap into the gearcase housing. Push on the cap until it seats against the gearcase housing. Apply Loctite 572 to the threads of the gearcase cap bolts. Thread the bolts and washers into the cap and gearcase housing. Evenly tighten the bolts (**Figure 71**) to the first tightening sequence specification in **Table 1**. Then tighten the bolts to the second tightening sequence specification in **Table 1**.

CAUTION
Use very light force when moving the drive shaft during the backlash measurement. The readings will be inaccurate if excessive force is applied to the drive shaft.

NOTE
Remove all water pump components before measuring gear backlash. The drag created by the water pump components will hinder accurate measurement. Temporarily remove the drive shaft seal carrier or water pump base during backlash measurements.

NOTE
Make sure all gearcase lubricant has been drained from the gearcase before measuring gear backlash. The readings will be inaccurate due to the cushion effect of the lubricant on the gear teeth.

20. Measure and correct the gear backlash if a new gearcase housing, gear, drive shaft, pinion gear shim or bearing was installed during the repair. Measure and correct the gearcase backlash as follows:
    a. Pull up or push down on the shift shaft to shift the gearcase into neutral gear (**Figure 67**).
    b. Attach a dial indicator to the gearcase using a suitable clamping device (**Figure 68**). Dial indicators and mounts are available from most tool suppliers. The mount must remain rigid for the dial indicator,

otherwise the backlash measurement will be inaccurate.

c. Clamp the backlash indicator tool (Yamaha part No. YB-06265-90890-06265) onto the drive shaft. Arrange the dial indicator mount to position the dial indicator plunger at the same height as the indicator tool (**Figure 58**) and with the plunger at a 90° angle to the indicator arm (**Figure 59**). Reposition the dial indicator to place the plunger in line with the mark on the indicator tool.

d. Rotate the drive shaft so that it is pointing down (**Figure 68**).

e. During this procedure, have an assistant push in on the propeller shaft with enough effort to prevent shaft rotation. Observe the dial indicator while lightly rotating the drive shaft clockwise and counterclockwise. Do not push up on the drive shaft. Note the dial indicator reading when the drive shaft reaches its free movement limit in each direction. Record the amount of dial indicator movement as forward gear backlash.

f. During this procedure, have an assistant pull out on the propeller shaft with enough effort to prevent shaft rotation. Observe the dial indicator while lightly rotating the drive shaft clockwise and counterclockwise. Do not push up on the drive shaft. Note the dial indicator reading when the drive shaft reaches its free movement limit in each direction. Record the amount of dial indicator movement as reverse gear backlash. Remove the backlash measuring instruments.

21. The forward and reverse gear backlash measurements should be within the specification in **Table 2**. If both backlash measurements are correct, proceed to Step 23. If either backlash reading is incorrect, refer to the following:

a. If the forward and reverse gear backlash is greater than specified, install a thicker pinion gear shim (32, **Figure 69**).

b. If the forward and reverse gear backlash is less than specified, install a thinner pinion gear shim (32, **Figure 69**).

c. If the forward gear backlash is greater than specified and the reverse gear backlash is within the specification, replace the forward gear bearing (33, **Figure 69**) and repeat the measurement. Replace the pinion and forward gear if the backlash is still incorrect.

d. If the forward gear backlash is less than specified and the reverse gear backlash is within the specification, check for an improperly installed forward gear bearing (33, **Figure 69**).

e. If the reverse gear backlash is greater than specified and the forward gear backlash is within the specification, replace the reverse gear bearing (43, **Figure 69**) and check for an improperly installed gearcase cap (46). Repeat the measurement. Replace the reverse gear if backlash is still incorrect.

f. If the reverse gear backlash is less than specified and the forward gear backlash is within the specification, check for an improperly installed reverse gear bearing (43, **Figure 69**).

22. Disassemble the gearcase and perform the indicated shim change or inspection. Reassemble the gearcase and repeat the backlash measurements. Do not proceed until the backlash is correct.

23. Remove the screw from the water pump base. Install all water pump components following the procedure described in this chapter.

Disassembly (6-25 hp Two-Cylinder Models)

For component identification and orientation, refer to **Figures 85-87** during the disassembly procedure.

1. Drain the gearcase lubricant (**Figure 70**) as described in Chapter Three.

CAUTION
Never heat the gearcase housing to the point that the finish is burned. Continually move the flame around the mating surface to apply heat evenly. Excessive heat can distort or melt the gearcase.

NOTE
To ease removal of the gearcase cap where corrosion has seized the components, use a torch to apply moderate heat to the gearcase. Heat the area near the gearcase housing-to-gearcase cap mating surfaces.

2. Remove the two bolts and washers from the bearing carrier flange (**Figure 88**). Use a blunt tip pry bar to carefully pry the bearing carrier away from the gearcase housing (**Figure 89**). Grasp the propeller shaft and pull the bearing carrier and propeller shaft as an assembly from the housing (**Figure 90**). If the carrier is seized, pull the carrier from the housing with a two-jaw puller (Yamaha part No. YB-06234/90890-06501, 06503 or 06504) or an equivalent. Engage the jaws to the carrier and position the puller bolt against the end of the propeller shaft (**Figure 91**). Tighten the puller bolt to loosen the bearing carrier.

3. Remove the large O-ring (**Figure 92**) from the bearing carrier. Discard the O-ring. Slide the propeller shaft assembly from the bearing carrier. Remove the thrust

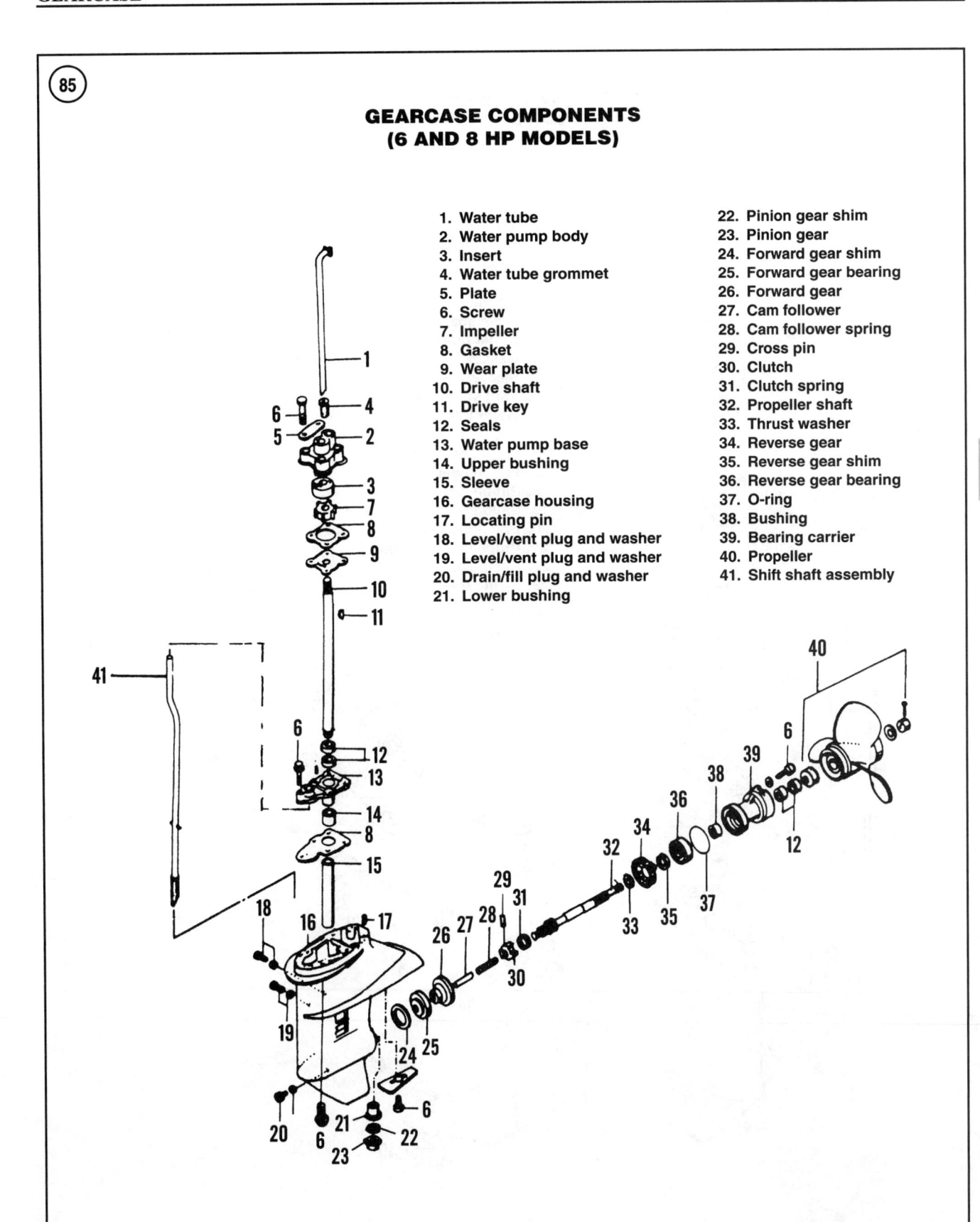

GEARCASE

385

(85)

GEARCASE COMPONENTS
(6 AND 8 HP MODELS)

1. Water tube
2. Water pump body
3. Insert
4. Water tube grommet
5. Plate
6. Screw
7. Impeller
8. Gasket
9. Wear plate
10. Drive shaft
11. Drive key
12. Seals
13. Water pump base
14. Upper bushing
15. Sleeve
16. Gearcase housing
17. Locating pin
18. Level/vent plug and washer
19. Level/vent plug and washer
20. Drain/fill plug and washer
21. Lower bushing
22. Pinion gear shim
23. Pinion gear
24. Forward gear shim
25. Forward gear bearing
26. Forward gear
27. Cam follower
28. Cam follower spring
29. Cross pin
30. Clutch
31. Clutch spring
32. Propeller shaft
33. Thrust washer
34. Reverse gear
35. Reverse gear shim
36. Reverse gear bearing
37. O-ring
38. Bushing
39. Bearing carrier
40. Propeller
41. Shift shaft assembly

8

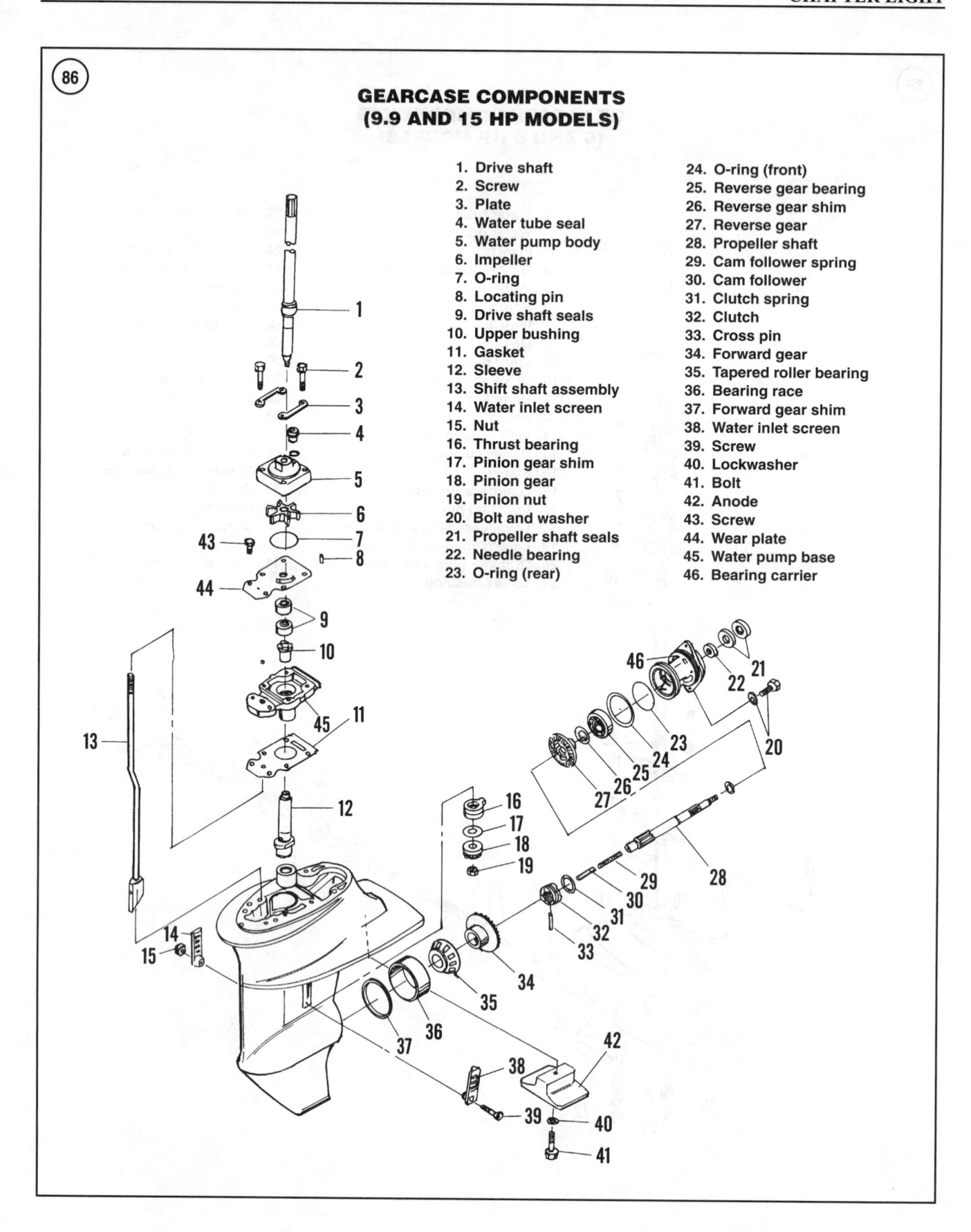

GEARCASE COMPONENTS (9.9 AND 15 HP MODELS)

1. Drive shaft
2. Screw
3. Plate
4. Water tube seal
5. Water pump body
6. Impeller
7. O-ring
8. Locating pin
9. Drive shaft seals
10. Upper bushing
11. Gasket
12. Sleeve
13. Shift shaft assembly
14. Water inlet screen
15. Nut
16. Thrust bearing
17. Pinion gear shim
18. Pinion gear
19. Pinion nut
20. Bolt and washer
21. Propeller shaft seals
22. Needle bearing
23. O-ring (rear)
24. O-ring (front)
25. Reverse gear bearing
26. Reverse gear shim
27. Reverse gear
28. Propeller shaft
29. Cam follower spring
30. Cam follower
31. Clutch spring
32. Clutch
33. Cross pin
34. Forward gear
35. Tapered roller bearing
36. Bearing race
37. Forward gear shim
38. Water inlet screen
39. Screw
40. Lockwasher
41. Bolt
42. Anode
43. Screw
44. Wear plate
45. Water pump base
46. Bearing carrier

GEARCASE

washer from the propeller shaft or reverse gear (**Figure 93**). Retrieve the cam follower from the housing if it was dislodged from the propeller shaft during the removal process. Insert the follower (**Figure 83**) into the opening in the propeller shaft.

4A. On 6-15 hp models, pull the reverse gear from the bearing carrier. If necessary, carefully pry the reverse gear from the bearing (**Figure 94**). Use two blunt tip pry bars and work carefully to avoid damaging the components. If the gear cannot be removed by this method, remove the gear using the procedure described in Step 4B.

4B. On 20 and 25 hp two-cylinder models, remove the reverse gear if the reverse gear, reverse gear bearing or reverse gear shim must be replaced. The removal process may damage the bearing. Refer to *Component Inspection* in this chapter to determine the need for replacement. Remove the reverse gear as follows:
   a. Clamp the bearing carrier in a vise with protective jaws.
   b. Engage the jaws of a slide hammer to the hub of the reverse gear (**Figure 95**).
   c. Use short hammer strokes to remove the reverse gear from the carrier.

5. The bearing may be pulled from the carrier along with the gear. Separate the bearing and gear as follows:
   a. Insert the sharp edge of a bearing separator between the reverse gear and the bearing.
   b. Place the gear and bearing on the table of a press with the gear facing down (**Figure 96**).
   c. Block the bearing separator to allow adequate clearance for gear removal.
   d. Press the gear from the bearing using a section of tubing or a socket as a removal tool. The tool must contact the hub of the gear, but not contact the bearing bore.

6. Remove the reverse gear shim (**Figure 92**) from the hub of the gear or the reverse gear bearing.

7. Only remove the reverse gear bearing if the bearing must be replaced. The removal process may damage the bearing. Refer to *Component Inspection* in this chapter to determine the need for replacement. Remove the reverse gear bearing as follows:
   a. Clamp the bearing carrier in a vise with protective jaws.
   b. Engage the jaws of a slide hammer beneath the inner bearing race (**Figure 97**).
   c. Use short hammer strokes to remove the bearing.

8. Only remove the propeller shaft seals if they must be replaced. The removal process damages the seals. Refer to *Component Inspection* in this chapter to determine the need for replacement. Remove the seals as follows:

   a. Clamp the bearing carrier in a vise with protective jaws. The gear side of the carrier must face down.
   b. Engage the jaws of a slide hammer beneath the casing of the inner seal (**Figure 98**).
   c. Use short hammer strokes to remove the seals.
   d. Discard the seals.

9. Only remove the needle bearing or bushing from the bearing carrier if it must be replaced. The removal process damages the component. Refer to *Component Inspection* in this chapter to determine the need for replacement. Remove the needle bearing or bushing as follows:
   a. Place the carrier on the table of a press with the gear side facing up. Block the carrier or place it over an opening to ensure adequate clearance for the bearing or bushing during removal.
   b. Select a section of tubing or a socket and extension for a removal tool. The tool must contact the casing of the bearing or bushing, but not contact the bearing carrier during removal.
   c. Seat the tool against the bearing or bushing, then carefully push the component from the bore (**Figure 99**).
   d. Discard the bearing or bushing.

10. Disassemble the propeller shaft as follows:
    a. Pull the cam follower from the propeller shaft (**Figure 83**).
    b. Carefully unwind the spring from the clutch groove (**Figure 100**).
    c. Push the cam follower from the clutch and propeller shaft (**Figure 101**).
    d. Slide the clutch over the forward end of the propeller shaft (**Figure 102**).
    e. Pull the follower spring from the propeller shaft opening. If necessary, tap the end of the propeller shaft against a block of wood to remove the spring.

11A. On 6 and 8 hp models, remove the screw (6, **Figure 85**) that secures the front of the water pump base to the gearcase housing.

11B. On 9.9 and 15 hp models, remove the two screws (43, **Figure 86**) and the wear plate (44) from the water pump base. Remove the jam nut from the shift shaft (13, **Figure 86**).

11C. On 20 and 25 hp two-cylinder models, remove the jam nut (6, **Figure 87**) from the shift shaft (23).

12. Carefully pry the water pump base loose from the gearcase. Work carefully to avoid damaging the mating surfaces. Slide the base and lower shift shaft assembly up and over the drive shaft. Remove the gasket from the pump base or gearcase housing. Discard the gasket.

13. On 20 and 25 hp two-cylinder models, remove the screws then lift the retainer (**Figure 103**) from the water pump base.

388

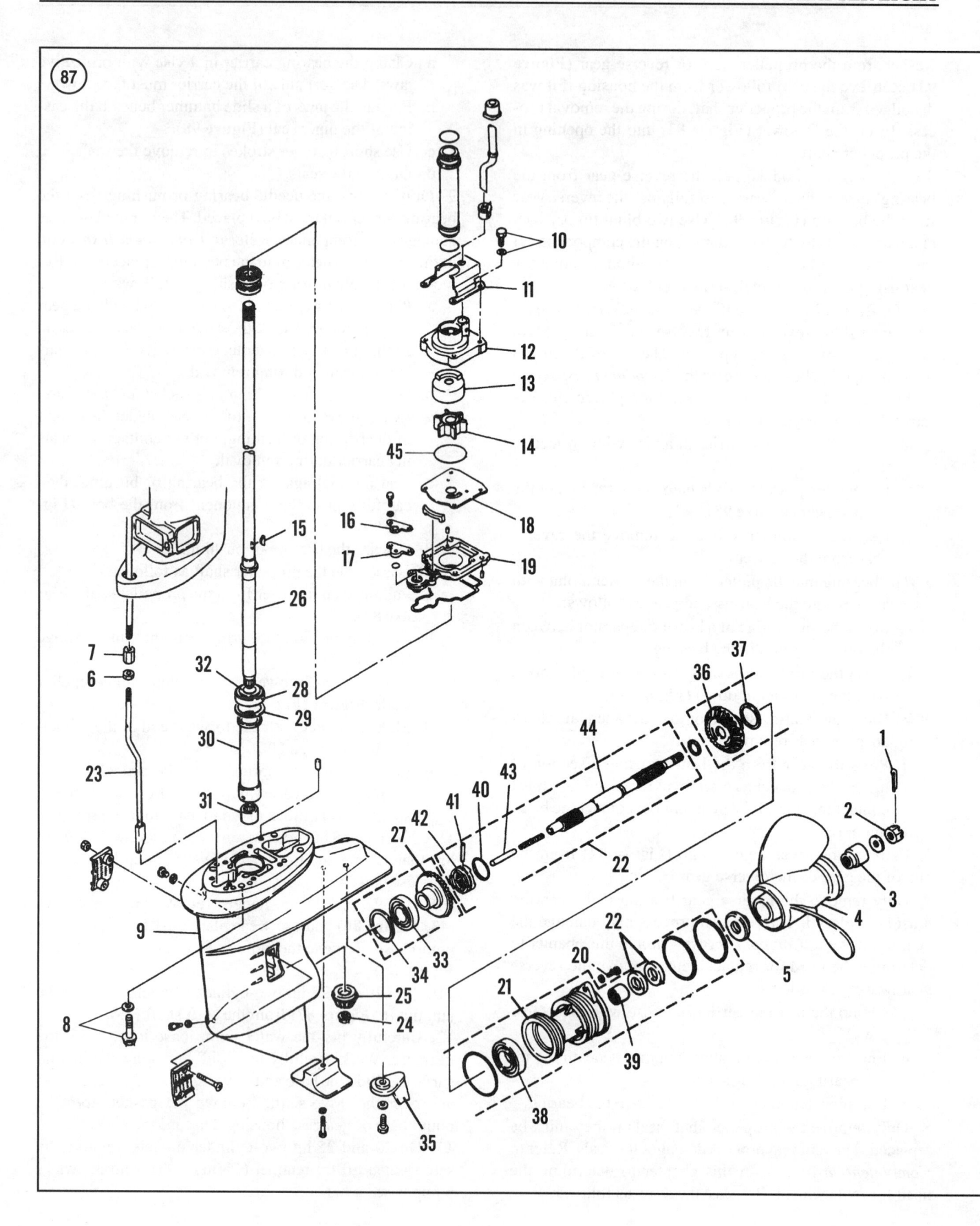

CHAPTER EIGHT

GEARCASE

389

GEARCASE COMPONENTS (20 AND 25 HP TWO-CYLINDER MODELS)

1. Cotter pin
2. Propeller nut
3. Spacer
4. Propeller
5. Thrust hub
6. Jam nut
7. Shift shaft coupling
8. Mounting bolt and washer
9. Gearcase housing
10. Screw and washer
11. Cover*
12. Water pump body
13. Insert
14. Impeller
15. Drive key
16. Plate
17. Shift shaft bellows retainer
18. Wear plate
19. Water pump base
20. Bolt and washer
21. Bearing carrier
22. Propeller shaft seals
23. Shift shaft assembly
24. Pinion nut
25. Pinion gear
26. Drive shaft
27. Forward gear
28. Thrust bearing
29. Pinion gear shim
30. Sleeve
31. Lower drive shaft bearing
32. Bearing race
33. Forward gear bearing
34. Forward gear shim
35. Trim tab
36. Reverse gear
37. Reverse gear shim
38. Reverse gear bearing
39. Propeller shaft needle bearing
40. Clutch spring
41. Cross pin
42. Clutch
43. Cam follower
44. Propeller shaft
45. O-ring

*Not used on all models

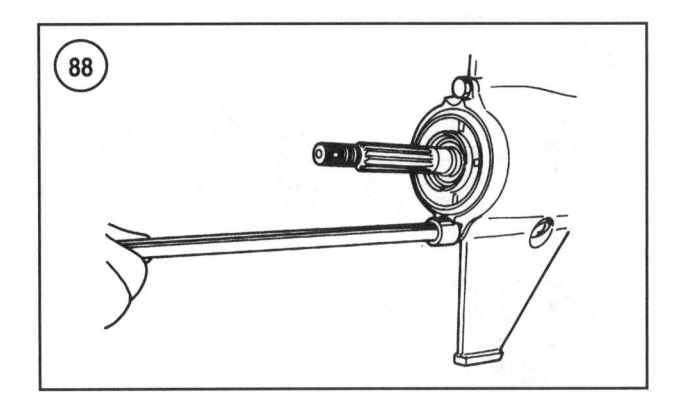

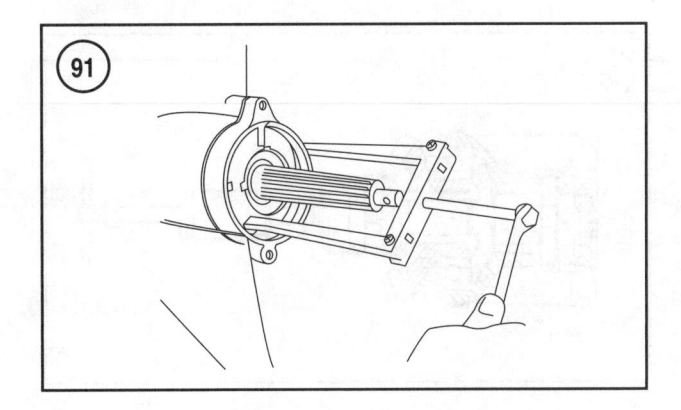

8

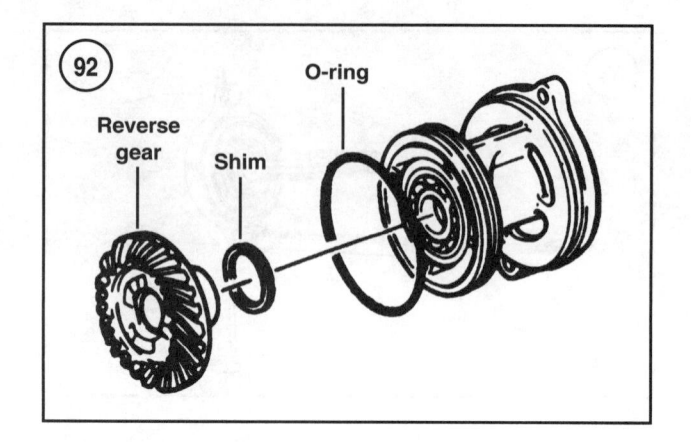

390

CHAPTER EIGHT

92 Reverse gear — Shim — O-ring

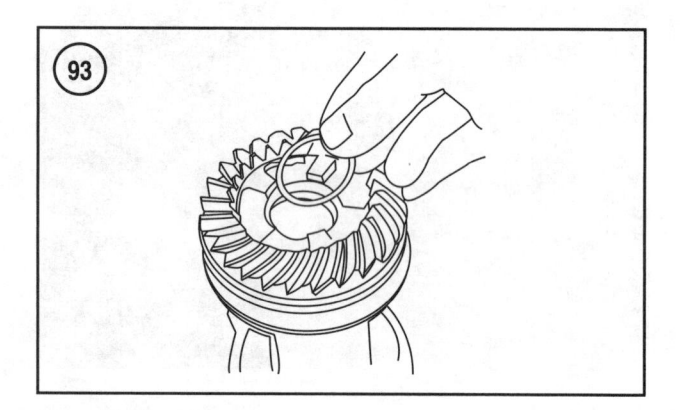

93

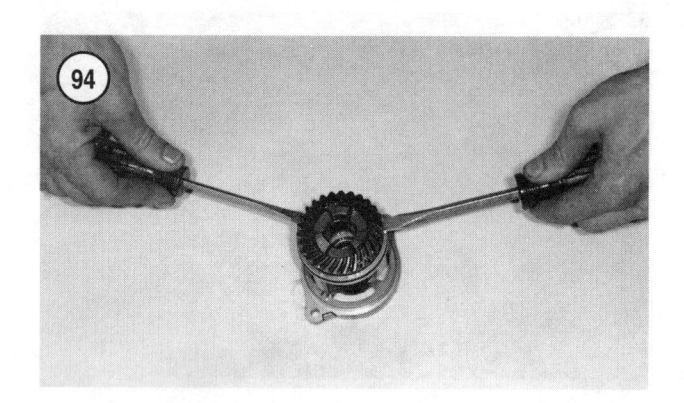

94

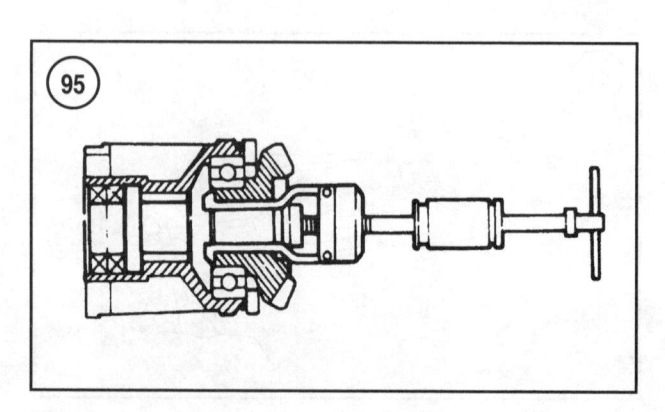

95

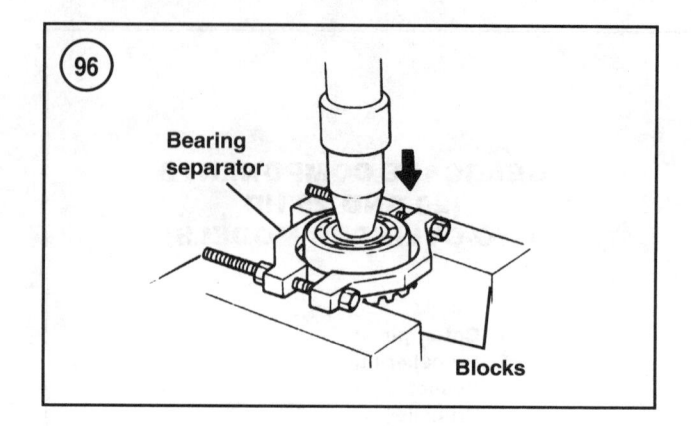

96 Bearing separator — Blocks

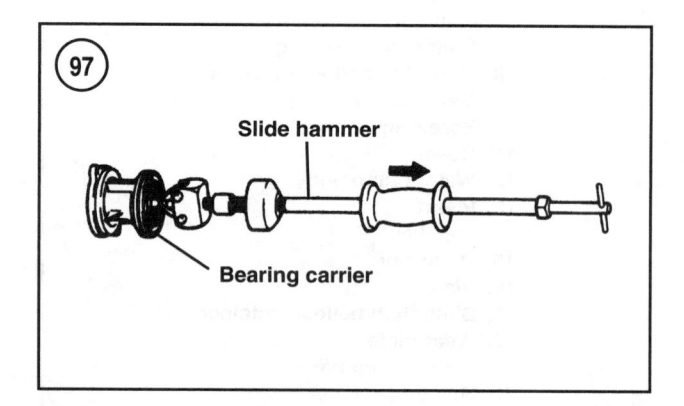

97 Slide hammer — Bearing carrier

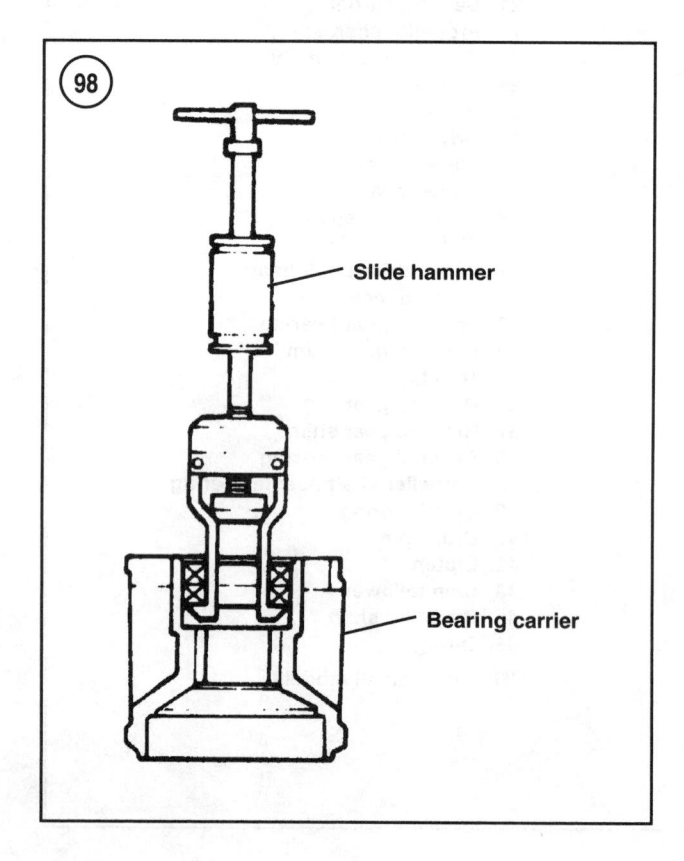

98 Slide hammer — Bearing carrier

GEARCASE

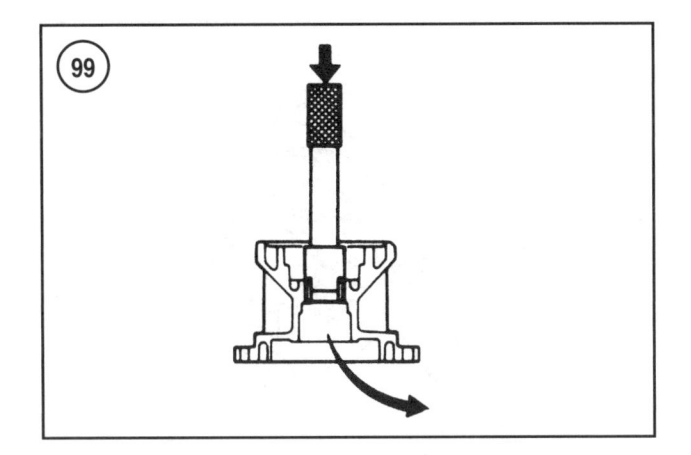

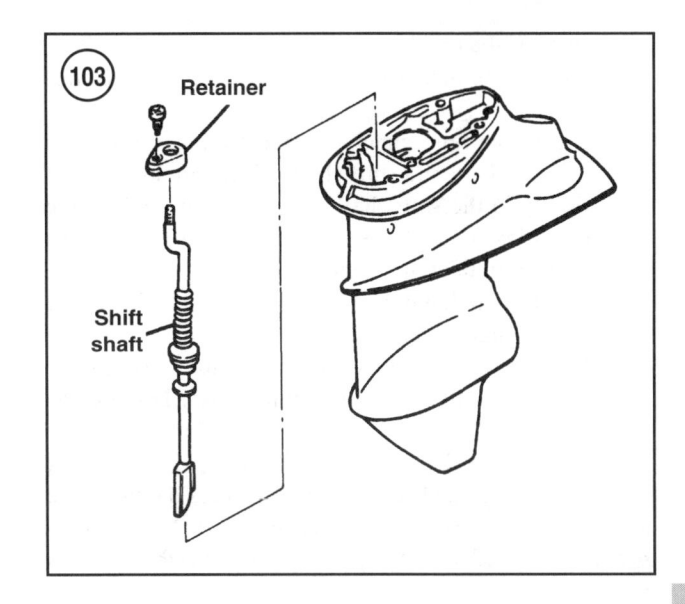

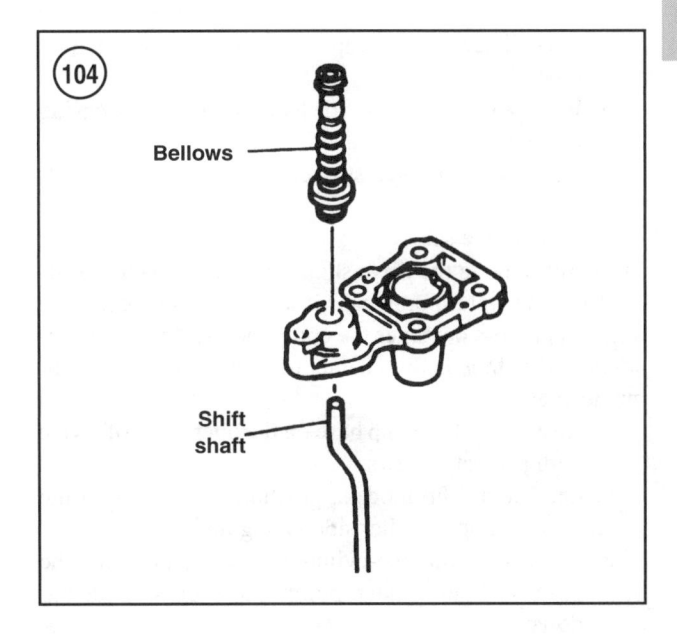

14. Carefully pull the shift shaft bellows (**Figure 104**) from the opening in the water pump base. Work carefully to avoid tearing the bellows. Slide the bellows over the top of the shift shaft. Replace the bellows if it is torn or looks weathered.

15. Only remove the shift shaft from the water pump base if the shift shaft, shift cam or water pump base require replacement. Refer to *Component Inspection* in this chapter to determine the need for replacement. Remove the shift shaft as follows:

   a. On 6 and 8 hp models, use a small punch and carefully drive the upper pin from the shift shaft. The upper pin protrudes evenly from both sides of the

shaft. If the pin does not fit tightly in the shift shaft, replace the pin. If it is still loose, replace the shift shaft.
  b. Use a small pin punch to drive the lower pin from the shift cam and shift shaft. If the pin does not fit tightly in the shift shaft and shift cam, replace the pin. If it is still loose, replace the shift cam, shift shaft or both components.
  c. Carefully pull the shift shaft from the top side of the water pump base.
  d. On 9.9 and 15 hp models, remove the O-ring from the shift shaft bore in the pump base. Discard the O-ring.

16. Only remove the seals from the water pump base if they must be replaced. The removal process damages the seals. Refer to *Component Inspection* in this chapter to determine the need for replacement. Remove the seals as follows:
  a. Clamp the water pump base in a vise with protective jaws. The water pump impeller side of the base must face up.
  b. Engage the jaws of a slide hammer below the casing of the inner seal.
  c. Use short hammer strokes to remove both seals from the base.
  d. Discard the seals.

17. Only remove the drive shaft bushing or needle bearing from the water pump base if it must be replaced. The removal process damages the components. Refer to *Component Inspection* in this chapter to determine the need for replacement.
  a. Rest the water pump base on the open jaws of a vice with protective jaws.
  b. On 6 and 8 hp models, position the base with the water pump impeller side facing up.
  c. On 9.9-25 hp two-cylinder models, position the base with the water pump impeller side facing down.
  d. Select a section of tubing or a socket and extension to use as a bushing or bearing removal tool. The tool must contact the bushing or bearing, but not contact the water pump base housing during removal.
  e. Insert the removal tool into the drive shaft bore of the water pump base. Seat the tool against the bushing or bearing. Maintain firm contact with the bushing or bearing and gently drive the component from the base.

18A. On 6 and 8 hp models, use needlenose pliers to remove the E-clip from the groove on the drive shaft (**Figure 105**).

18B. On 9.9-25 hp two-cylinder models, remove the pinion nut as follows:

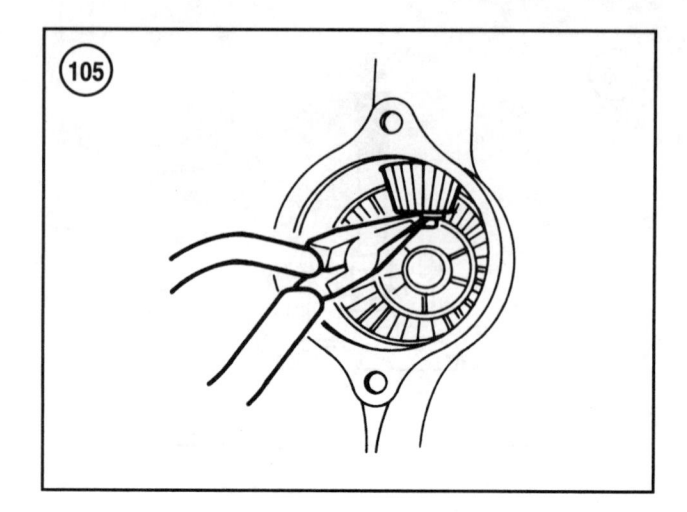

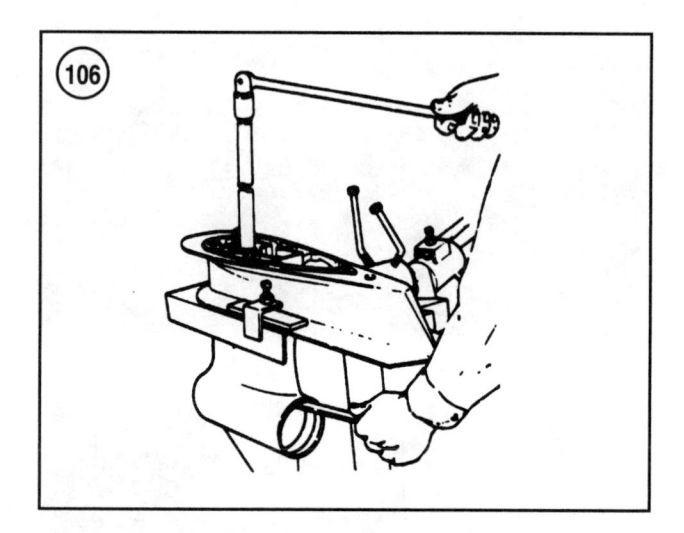

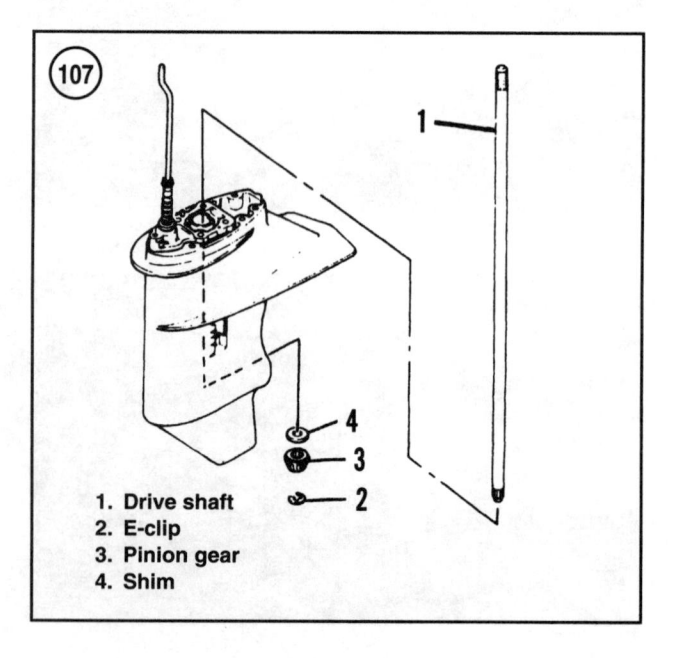

1. Drive shaft
2. E-clip
3. Pinion gear
4. Shim

GEARCASE

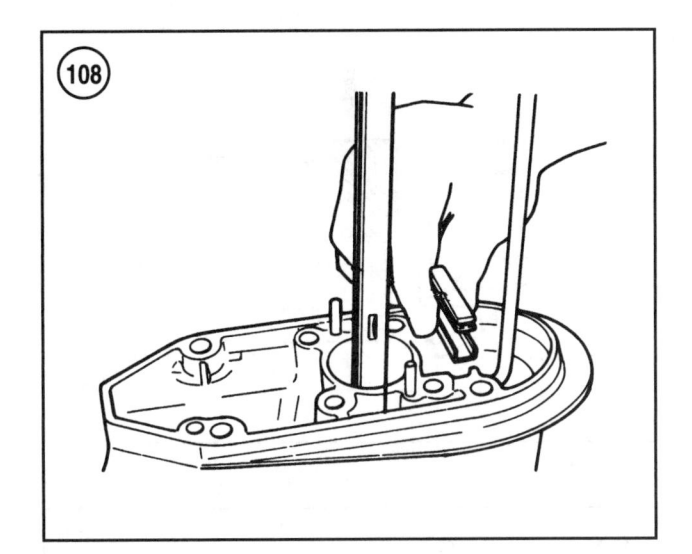

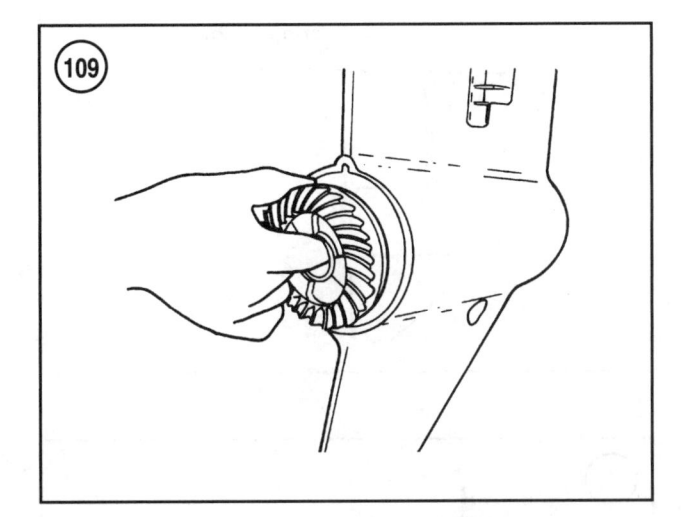

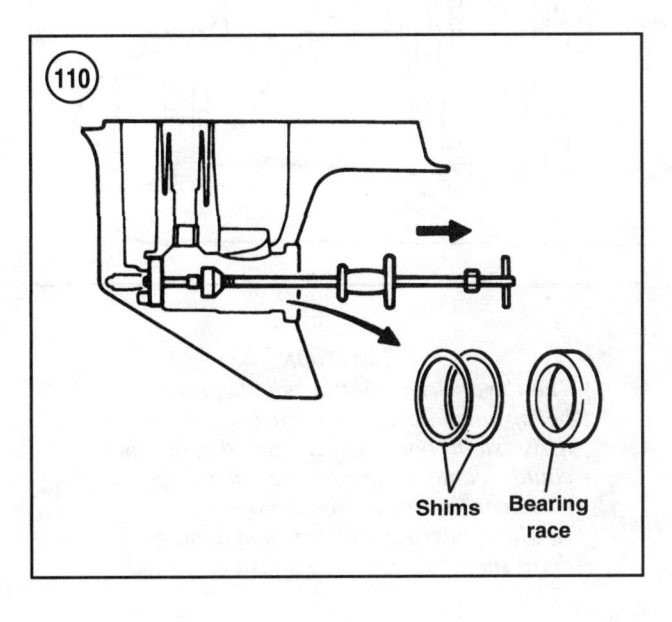

a. Install the splined drive shaft adapter onto the upper end of the drive shaft. For 9.9 and 15 hp models, use Yamaha part No. YB-06228-90890-6515. For 20 and 25 hp two-cylinder models, use Yamaha part No. YB-06368/90890-6516.

b. Use a suitable socket wrench to engage the pinion nut (**Figure 106**). Use shop towels to protect the housing surface from the socket wrench.

c. Rotate the drive shaft counterclockwise as viewed from the top to loosen the nut. Continue until the pinion nut is free from the drive shaft.

19A. On 6 and 8 hp models, carefully pull the drive shaft (1, **Figure 107**) from the gearcase. Reach into the housing and remove the pinion gear (3, **Figure 107**) and shim (4). Mark the pinion gear side of the shim. Use a permanent marker. Do not scratch the shim. Only remove the small lockring from the drive shaft if it is corroded or damaged. Discard the lockring after removal. Carefully draw the sleeve (15, **Figure 85**) from the drive shaft bore.

19B. On 9.9 and 15 hp models, remove the filler block seal (**Figure 108**). Carefully pull the drive shaft from the gearcase. Reach into the housing and remove the pinion gear (18, **Figure 86**), shim (17) and thrust bearing (16). Mark the pinion gear side of the shim. Use a permanent marker. Do not scratch the shim. Carefully draw the sleeve (12, **Figure 86**) from the drive shaft bore.

19C. On 20 and 25 hp two-cylinder models, carefully pull the drive shaft from the gearcase. Reach into the housing and remove the pinion gear (25, **Figure 87**), shim (29), thrust bearing (28) and bearing race (32). Carefully draw the sleeve (30, **Figure 87**) from the drive shaft bore.

20. Remove the forward gear from the housing (**Figure 109**). If necessary, tap lightly on the front of the housing to free the gear from the bearing race.

21. Only remove the forward gear bearing race to replace the forward gear bearing or the forward gear shims. Remove the bearing as follows:

a. Engage the jaws of a slide hammer to the inner surface of the bearing race (**Figure 110**).

b. Use short hammer strokes to remove the bearing race and shim(s) from the gearcase.

c. Inspect the shim(s) for bent or corroded surfaces. Replace damaged shims with new ones of the same thickness.

22. Only remove the tapered roller bearing from the forward gear if the bearing or forward gear must be replaced. The removal process damages the bearing. Refer to *Component Inspection* in this chapter to determine the need for replacement. Remove the bearing as follows:

a. Engage the sharp edge of a bearing separator between the bearing and forward gear (**Figure 111**).

b. Block the sides of the separator to ensure adequate travel for the gear.

c. Select a section of tubing or a socket to use as a removal tool. The tool must contact the gear hub, but not contact the inner race of the bearing.

d. Press on the tool to remove the gear from the bearing. Discard the bearing.

23. Only remove the lower drive shaft bushing or bearing if it must be replaced. The removal process damages the component. Refer to *Component Inspection* in this chapter to determine the need for replacement. Remove the lower drive shaft bushing or bearing as follows:

a. Select a section of tubing or a socket and extension to use as a bushing/bearing removal tool. The tool must contact the case of the bearing or bushing, but not contact the drive shaft bore in the gearcase housing.

b. Insert the removal tool into the drive shaft bore and seat it against the bushing or bearing (**Figure 112**).

c. Gently drive the bushing or bearing into the gearcase housing. Discard the component after removal.

Assembly (6-25 hp Two-Cylinder Models)

For component identification and orientation, refer to **Figures 85-87** during the assembly procedure.

1A. On 6 and 8 hp models, install the new lower drive shaft bushing, if it was removed as follows:

a. Apply a light coat of gearcase lubricant to the bushing or bearing and the bore in the gearcase housing.

b. Working through the gearcase opening, insert the lower bushing (21, **Figure 85**) into the bore. The flanged side of the bushing must face down.

c. Select a washer with an outer diameter slightly smaller than the bushing flange. The washer must be of sufficient diameter to adequately support the bushing. Select a washer of sufficient diameter to span the drive shaft bore at the top of the housing. If a suitable washer is not available, use a steel plate with a hole to span the bore. A threaded rod of an adequate length, with a diameter that matches the washers, and two hex nuts are also required.

d. Arrange the washers, threaded washers and nuts into the gearcase as shown in **Figure 113**. Tighten the nuts until the flange on the lower bushing seats against the step in the bore.

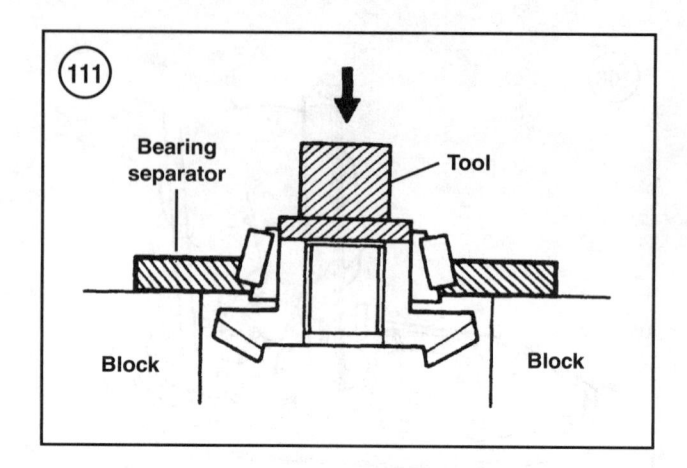

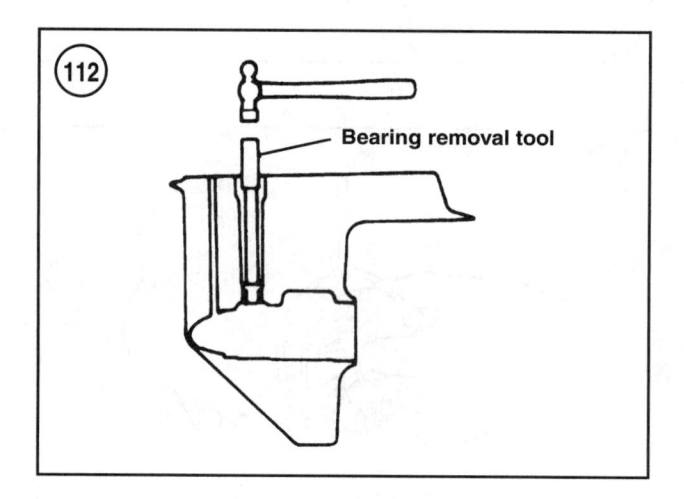

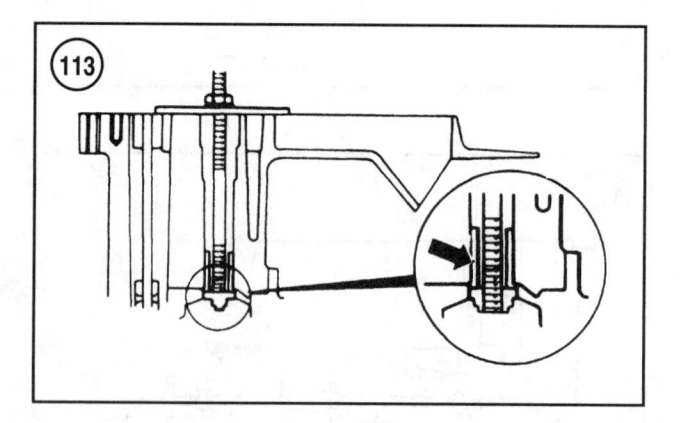

CAUTION
The lower drive shaft needle bearing must be installed to the specified depth in the drive shaft bore. Otherwise, the bearing could contact the drive shaft on a non-bearing surface during operation. The resulting bearing failure would damage the drive shaft and gearcase housing.

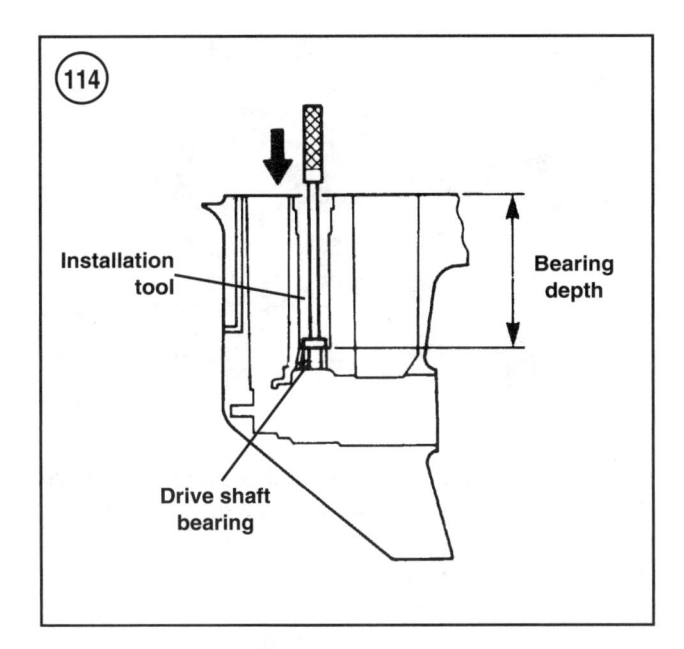

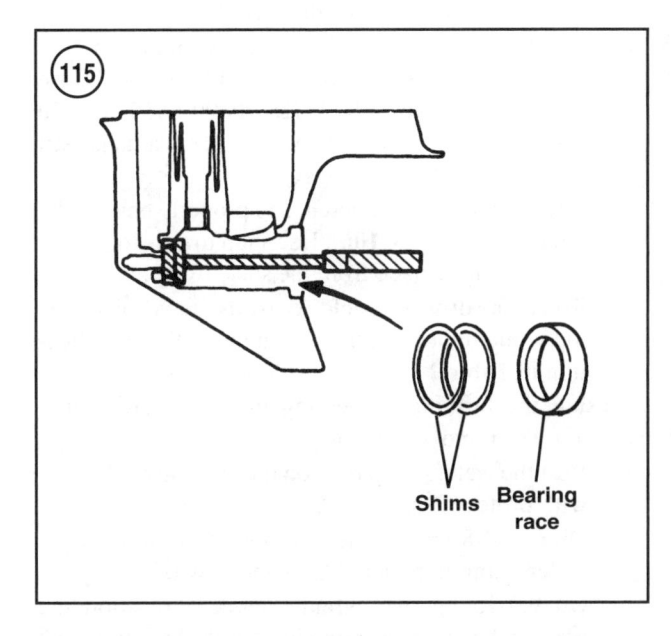

GEARCASE

Figure 114 — Installation tool, Drive shaft bearing, Bearing depth

Figure 115 — Shims, Bearing race

1B. On 9.9-25 hp two-cylinder models, install a new lower drive shaft needle bearing, if it was removed, as follows:

a. Select a section of tubing or a socket and extension to use as a bearing installation tool. The tool must contact the bearing case, but not contact the drive shaft bore during installation.

b. Working through the drive shaft bore opening, insert the needle bearing into the drive shaft bore. The numbered side of the bearing case must face up or toward the water pump when installed.

c. Insert the installation tool into the drive shaft bore (**Figure 114**) and seat it against the numbered side of the bearing.

d. Slowly tap the bearing into the bore. Stop frequently and measure the depth.

e. On 9.9 and 15 hp models, stop when the bearing reaches a depth of 172.7-173.2 mm (6.80-6.82 in.) at the points indicated in **Figure 114**.

f. On 20 and 25 hp two-cylinder models, stop when the bearing reaches a depth of 162.0-163.0 mm (6.38-6.42 in.) at the points indicated in **Figure 114**.

NOTE
When driving a bearing race into the gearcase housing, strike the driver just enough to slightly move the bearing or race. Stop driving when the pitch changes or a sharp ring is heard as the driver is struck. This indicates the bearing or race is seated. Continued driving may bounce the bearing or race out of the bore.

2. Install the bearing race and shim(s) into the housing, if they were removed as follows:

a. Use the manufacturer recommended tool for this procedure. On 6 and 8 hp models, YB-06085/90890-06628 and YB-6085- 90890-06605. On 9.9-25 hp two-cylinder models: YB-06085/90890-06625 and YB-6085-90890-06605. If the tool is not available, use a section of tubing or a suitable mandrel and driver. The tool must contact near the outer diameter of the bearing race, but not contact the gear housing during installation.

b. Apply a light coat of gearcase lubricant to the race surfaces and the corresponding bore in the gearcase housing.

c. Place the shim(s) into the housing. The shim(s) must rest in the bearing race bore.

d. Install the bearing race into the bore with the tapered opening facing out. Maintain firm contact with the bearing race while gently driving it into the bore (**Figure 115**). Use light force and do not allow the race to tilt in the bore. Continue driving until the race is fully seated in the housing.

3. Install a new tapered roller bearing onto the forward gear, if it was removed, as follows:

a. Place the forward gear on the table of a press with the gear teeth side facing down.

b. Select a section of tubing or a large diameter socket to use as a bearing installation tool. The tool opening must only contact the inner race of the bearing.

c. Install the bearing on the hub of the gear with the tapered side facing up. Place the installation tool on the bearing (**Figure 116**).

d. Press the bearing onto the gear hub until it is fully seated.

4. Install the forward gear and bearing into the housing (**Figure 109**). Seat the gear and bearing against the bearing race.

5A. On 6 and 8 hp models, if the lockring was removed, install a new lockring into the groove in the drive shaft. Do not install the lockring into the lowest groove. Insert the sleeve (15, **Figure 85**) into the drive shaft bore. Seat the sleeve against the lower bushing. Install the shim (4, **Figure 107**) into the gearcase. If the original shim is being reused, the mark made upon removal must face toward the pinion gear. Align the shim with the lower drive shaft bushing. Install the pinion gear (3, **Figure 107**) into the housing.

5B. On 9.9 and 15 hp models, insert the sleeve (12, **Figure 86**) into the drive shaft bore. Insert the protrusion near the bottom of the sleeve into the recess in the bore. Seat the sleeve against the lower drive shaft bearing. Working through the gearcase opening, install the thrust bearing (16, **Figure 86**) into the drive shaft bore. The tab on the upper race of the bearing must fit into the recess in the drive shaft bore. Install the shim (17, **Figure 86**) into the gearcase. If the original shim is being reused, the mark made upon removal must face toward the pinion gear. Align the shim with the thrust washer and the drive shaft bore. Install the pinion gear (18, **Figure 86**) into the housing.

5C. On 20 and 25 hp two-cylinder models, insert the sleeve (30, **Figure 87**) into the drive shaft bore. Insert the tab near the bottom of the sleeve into the slot in the bore. Install the bearing race (32, **Figure 87**), thrust bearing (28) and shim (29) into the housing. If the original shim is being reused, the mark made upon removal must face toward the pinion gear. Align the race, bearing and shim with the drive shaft bore. Install the pinion gear (25, **Figure 87**) into the housing.

6. Mesh the pinion gear teeth with the driven gear teeth. Align the splined opening in the pinion gear with the shim, thrust bearing and the drive shaft bore.

7. Apply a coat of gearcase lubricant to the lower surfaces of the drive shaft. Carefully guide the drive shaft into the bore. Make sure the drive shaft passes through the lower bushing/bearing and applicable shims, race and thrust bearing. Slowly rotate the drive shaft to align the drive shaft splines with the pinion gear splines. The shaft drops into the pinion gear when the splines align.

8A. On 6 and 8 hp models, use needlenose pliers (**Figure 105**) to install the E-clip into the drive shaft groove. Pull up on the drive shaft to verify groove engagement.

8B. On 9.9-25 hp two-cylinder models, install and tighten the new pinion nut as follows:

a. Apply Loctite 271 to the threads, then hand-thread a new pinion nut onto the drive shaft.

b. Install the splined drive shaft adapter onto the upper end of the drive shaft. On 9.9 and 15 hp models, use Yamaha part No. YB-06228-90890-6515. On 20 and 25 hp two-cylinder models, use Yamaha part No. YB-06368/90890-6516.

c. Use a suitable socket wrench to properly engage the pinion nut (**Figure 106**). Use shop towels to protect the housing surface from the socket wrench.

d. Rotate the drive shaft clockwise as viewed from the top while tightening the pinion nut to the specification in **Table 1**.

9. Install the bushing or bearing into the water pump base, if it was removed, as follows:

a. Rest the water pump base on the open jaws of a vice with protective jaws.

b. On 6 and 8 hp models, position the base with the water pump impeller side facing down.

c. On 9.9-25 hp two-cylinder models, position the base with the water pump impeller side facing up.

d. Select a section of tubing or a socket and extension to use as a bushing or bearing installation tool. The tool must contact the bushing or bearing, but not contact the drive shaft bore during installation.

e. On 6 and 8 hp models, insert the bushing into the opening. Using the installation tool, slowly tap the bushing into the bore until it reaches a depth of 5.0 mm (0.20 in.) as measured at the points indicated (**Figure 117**).

f. On 9.9 and 15 hp models, insert the bushing into the opening with the larger diameter side facing up. Using the installation tool, slowly tap the bushing

GEARCASE

Figure 117 — Seal depth / Bearing depth

Figure 118 — Bearing depth

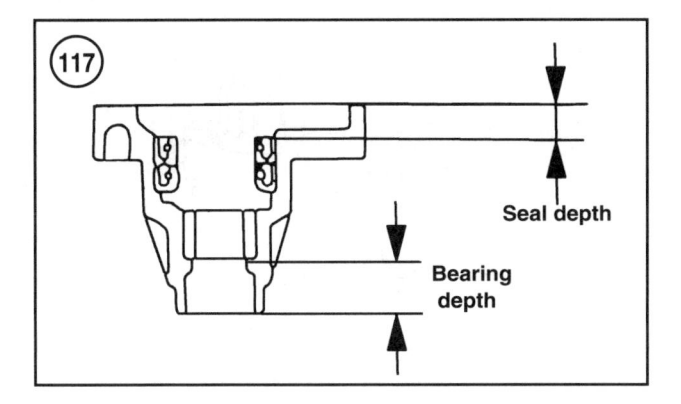

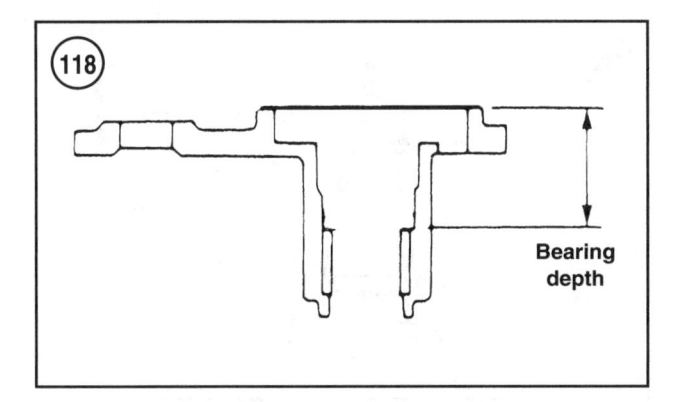

into the bore until the step seats against the bore opening.

   g. On 20 and 25 hp two-cylinder models, insert the needle bearing into the opening with the numbered side facing up. Using the installation tool, slowly tap the bearing into the bore until it reaches a depth of 31.0-31.5 mm (1.22-1.24 in.) at the points indicated (**Figure 118**).

10. Install the drive shaft seals into the water pump base, if they were removed, as follows:

   a. Apply a light coat of Loctite 271 to the outer casing of the seals and the seal bore in the pump base.

   b. Rest the water pump base on the open jaws of a vice with protective jaws. The impeller side of the base must face up.

   c. Select a piece of tubing or a socket and extension to use as a seal installation tool. The tool must contact the seal casing, but not contact the seal bore during seal installation.

   d. Insert the inner seal into the bore with the lip side facing up. Carefully drive the seal into the bore until the upper edge of the seal is slightly recessed in the bore.

   e. Insert the outer seal into the bore with the lip side facing up. Carefully drive the outer seal into the bore until it just contacts the inner seal.

   f. Drive both seals into the bore until the casing of the outer seal just reaches the specified depth at the points indicted in **Figure 117**. On 6 and 8 hp models, the seal depth must be 3.0-3.5 mm (0.12-0.14 in.). On 9.9 and 15 hp models, the seal depth must be 7.0-8.0 mm (0.28-0.31 in.). On 20 and 25 hp two-cylinder models, the seal depth must be 8.5-9.0 mm (0.33-0.35 in.).

   g. Wipe excess Loctite from the drive shaft bore before proceeding.

   h. Apply a bead of Yamaha All-Purpose Grease or equivalent to the seal lips.

11. Install the shift shaft into the water pump base, if it was removed, as follows:

   a. On 9.9 and 15 hp models, insert a new O-ring into the shift shaft bore in the water pump base. Seat the O-ring into the recess in the base.

   b. Slide the shift shaft straight end first into its opening in the top of the water pump base.

   c. On 6 and 8 hp models, drive the upper pin into its opening in the shift shaft. Do not drive the pin into the opening near the bottom of the shaft. The pin must fit tightly in the opening and protrude equal amounts on each side of the shaft.

   d. Rotate the shift shaft so the curved end would face forward if the base were mounted on the gearcase.

   e. Install the shift cam onto the lower end of the shift shaft. The slanted end must face rearward.

   f. Carefully drive the lower pin through the shift cam and shift shaft. The pin must protrude or be recessed the same amount on each side of the shift cam.

   g. Apply a light coat of Yamaha All-Purpose Grease or equivalent to the upper end of the shift shaft. Carefully slide the shift shaft bellows (**Figure 104**) over the top of the shift shaft. Insert the lower end of the bellows fully into the opening in the water pump base. If the bellows does not fit tightly in the opening, it must be replaced.

   h. On 20 and 25 hp two-cylinder models, install the retainer (**Figure 103**) over the bellows. Secure the retainer with the two screws.

12. Install a new gasket onto the water pump base. The lower end of the shift shaft must pass through the opening in the gasket.

13. Rotate the shift shaft to position the slanted side of the shift cam toward the aft end of the gearcase. When installed, this surface must contact the cam follower. Guide the shift shaft into the gearcase opening while sliding the water pump base over the drive shaft. Seat the base on the housing. Hand-thread one of the water pump screws into the base and housing to temporarily secure the base. Do

not install the remaining water pump components at this time.

14A. On 6 and 8 hp models, install and securely tighten the screw (6, **Figure 85**) that secures the front of the water pump base to the gearcase housing.

14B. On 9.9 and 15 hp models, install the wear plate (44, **Figure 86**) onto the water pump base. Secure the wear plate with the two screws (43, **Figure 86**). Thread the jam nut onto the shift shaft (13, **Figure 86**).

14C. On 20 and 25 hp two-cylinder models, thread the jam nut (6, **Figure 87**) onto the shift shaft (23).

15. Reassemble the propeller shaft as follows:
    a. Align the cross pin opening in the clutch with the slot in the propeller shaft (**Figure 102**), then slide the clutch over the forward side of the propeller shaft. The *F* mark on the clutch face must face forward.
    b. Insert the follower spring into the propeller shaft opening.
    c. Working from the opening, use a small punch to collapse the spring.
    d. With the spring collapsed, insert the cross pin through the clutch and propeller slot (**Figure 119**).
    e. Release the spring to secure the cross pin. Carefully wind the clutch spring onto the clutch (**Figure 100**). The spring must fit tightly on the clutch and the loops must span both ends of the cross pin. Each loop must lay flat against the clutch.
    f. Apply a coat of Yamaha All-Purpose Grease or equivalent to the cam follower. Insert the cam follower into the propeller shaft opening (**Figure 119**). The pointed end of the follower must face out.

16A. On 6-15 hp models, install a new bushing or needle bearing into the bearing carrier, if it was removed, as follows:
    a. Apply a light coat of gearcase lubricant to the outer surfaces of the bushing or bearing bore in the bearing carrier.
    b. Place the bearing carrier on a sturdy work surface with the propeller side facing up.
    c. On 6 and 8 hp models, insert the bushing into the bore. The bushing can be installed in either direction.
    d. On 9.9 and 15 hp models, insert the needle bearing into the bore with the numbered side facing up.
    e. Select a socket and extension or another suitable driver to use as an installation tool. The tool must be 0.25-0.50 mm (0.010-0.020 in.) larger in diameter than the bushing or bearing case.
    f. Slowly tap the bushing or bearing into the bore until the installation tool seats against the step. The end of the bearing or bushing must be flush with the step in the bore.

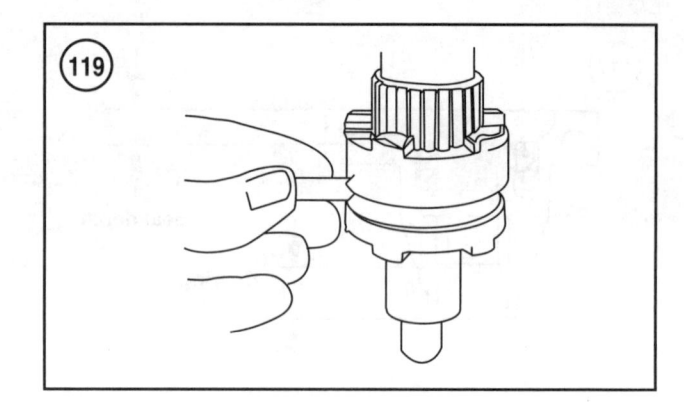

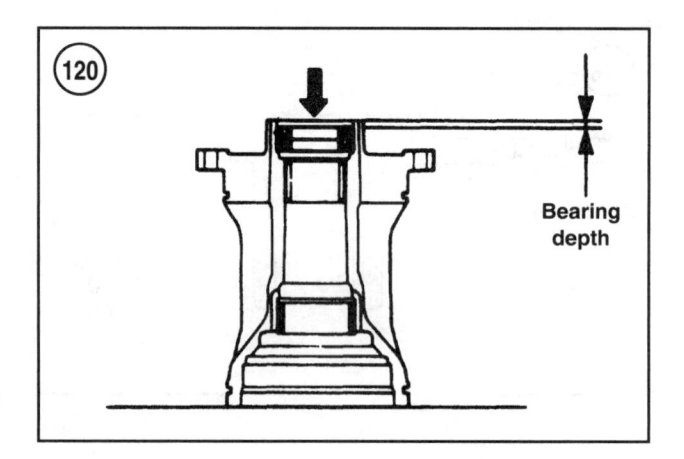

16B. On 20 and 25 hp two-cylinder models, install a new needle bearing into the bearing carrier, if it was removed, as follows:
    a. Apply a light coat of gearcase lubricant to the outer surfaces of the bushing or bearing bore in the bearing carrier.
    b. Place the bearing carrier on a sturdy work surface with the propeller side facing down.
    c. Insert the needle bearing into the bore with the numbered side facing up.
    d. Select a section of tubing, socket and extension or another tool to use as an installation tool. The tool must be 0.25-0.50 mm (0.010-0.020 in.) smaller in diameter than the bearing case.
    e. Use the tool to slowly tap the bearing into the bore. Stop when the bearing reaches a depth of 35.5-36.0 mm (1.40-1.42 in.) from the bearing carrier surface to the bearing case. The bearing case should be flush with the step in the bore.

17. Install new propeller shaft seals into the bearing carrier, if they were removed, as follows:

GEARCASE

121

Bearing
Bearing carrier

122

Bearing carrier

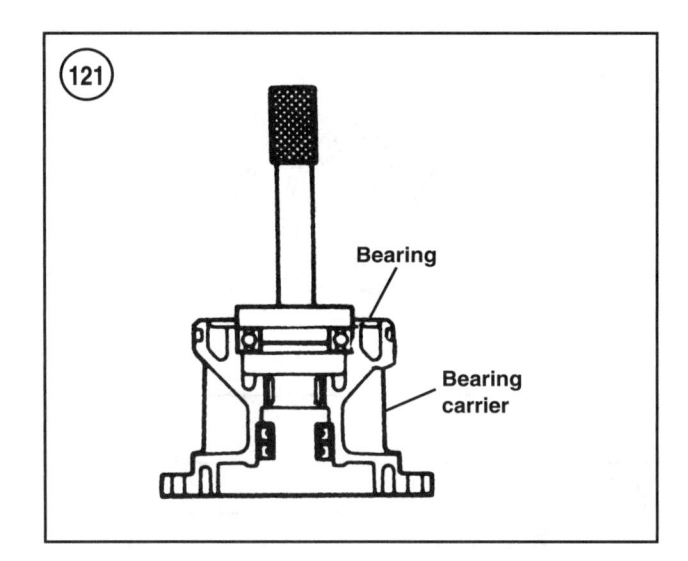

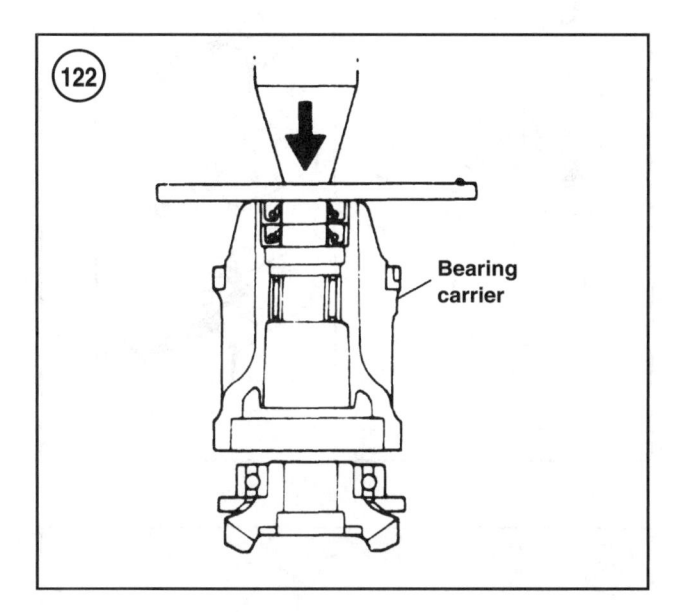

a. Apply a coat of Loctite 271 to the outer diameter of the seal casings and the seal bore in the gearcase cap.
b. Select a section of tubing, socket and extension or another suitable tool to use as a seal installation tool. The tool must contact the seal casing, but not contact the seal bore in the bearing carrier.
c. Place the gearcase cap on a sturdy work surface with the propeller side facing up.
d. Place the first seal into the bore with the lip side facing up. Carefully drive the seal into the bore until the seal case is just below the bore opening.
e. Place the second seal into the bore with the lip side facing up. Carefully drive the seal into the bore until it is seated against the first seal.

f. Slowly tap both seals into the bore until the outer seal is the specified distance below the bore opening (**Figure 120**). Stop frequently to measure the distance. On 6-15 hp models, the seal must be recessed 3.0-3.5 mm (0.12-0.14 in.). On 20 and 25 hp two-cylinder models, the seal must be recessed 4.5-5.0 mm (0.18-0.20 in.).
g. Wipe excess Loctite from the seal bore. Apply a coat of Yamaha All-Purpose Grease or equivalent to the seal lips.

18. Install the new reverse gear bearing into the bearing carrier, if it was removed, as follows:
    a. Select a piece of tubing or another suitable driver to use as a bearing installation tool. The tool must only contact the outer race of the bearing, and not contact the bearing carrier during installation.
    b. Apply a light coat of gearcase lubricant to the bearing surfaces and the bearing bore in the gearcase cap.
    c. Place the gearcase cap on a sturdy work surface with the bearing bore facing up.
    d. Place the new bearing into the bore with the number marks facing up. Maintain firm contact with the bearing while gently driving it into the bore (**Figure 121**). Use light force and do not allow the bearing to tilt in the bore. Continue driving until the bearing fully seats in the bore.

19A. On 6-15 hp models, install the reverse gear shim (**Figure 92**) over the hub of the reverse gear. Insert the hub of the gear into bore of the bearing. Seat the gear against the bearing. If the gear cannot be hand-pressed into the gear, install the gear using the method described in Step 19B.

19B. On 20 and 25 hp two-cylinder models, install the reverse gear as follows:
    a. Install the reverse gear shim (**Figure 92**) over the hub of the reverse gear.
    b. Place the reverse gear on the table of a press with the gear teeth facing down. Place a block of wood under the gear to protect the gear teeth.
    c. Place the bearing carrier on the reverse gear as shown in **Figure 122**. Align the hub of the gear with the bore in the bearing.
    d. Place a block of wood on the bearing carrier to protect the surface from the press.
    e. Press the carrier onto the gear until the gear fully seats against the bearing.

20. Apply a coat of Yamaha All-Purpose Grease or equivalent to the surfaces, then install the new O-ring into the groove in the bearing carrier.

21. Install the thrust washer onto the reverse gear (**Figure 93**). If the washer is being reused, position the washer as

indicated by the mark made before removal. Center the washer with the propeller shaft bore in the gear.

22. Carefully slide the propeller shaft into the reverse gear and bearing carrier (**Figure 123**).

23. Position the gearcase with the drive shaft facing up. Install the propeller shaft, then the bearing carrier, into the gearcase. Keep the shaft horizontal and work carefully to avoid dislodging the cam follower. The cam follower must pass through the opening in the forward gear and contact the shift cam.

24. Align the mounting bolt holes while inserting the bearing carrier into the gearcase housing. The cast-in arrow on the carrier must face up. Push on the carrier until it seats against the gearcase housing. Apply Loctite 572 to the threads of the bearing carrier bolts. Thread the bolts and washers into the carrier and gearcase housing. Evenly tighten the bolts to the general torque specification in Chapter One.

CAUTION
Use very light force when moving the drive shaft during backlash measurement. The readings will be inaccurate if excessive force is applied to the drive shaft.

NOTE
Remove all water pump components before measuring gear backlash. The drag created by the water pump components will hinder accurate measurement. Temporarily remove the drive shaft seal carrier or water pump base during backlash measurements.

NOTE
Make sure all gearcase lubricant is drained from the gearcase before measuring gear backlash. The cushion effect of the lubricant on the gear teeth will cause inaccurate readings.

25. Measure and correct the gear backlash if a new gearcase housing, gear, drive shaft, pinion gear shim or bearing was installed during the repair. Measure and correct the gearcase backlash as follows:
  a. Pull up or push down on the shift shaft to shift the gearcase into neutral gear (**Figure 124**).
  b. Attach a dial indicator to the gearcase using a suitable clamping device (**Figure 125**). Dial indicators and mounts are available from most tool suppliers. The mount must remain rigid for the dial indicator, otherwise the backlash measurements will be inaccurate.
  c. Clamp the backlash indicator tool onto the drive shaft. On 6 and 8 hp models, use Yamaha part No.

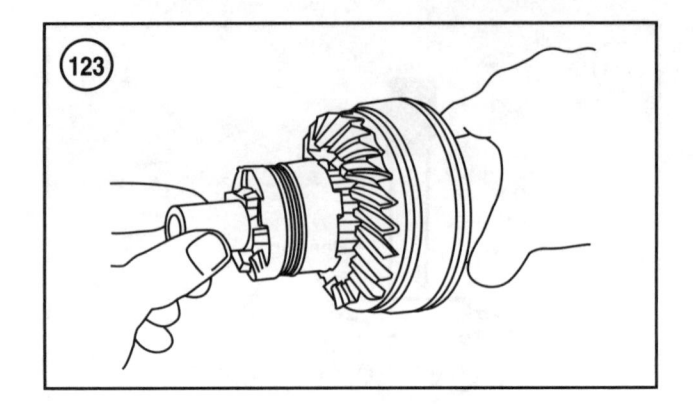

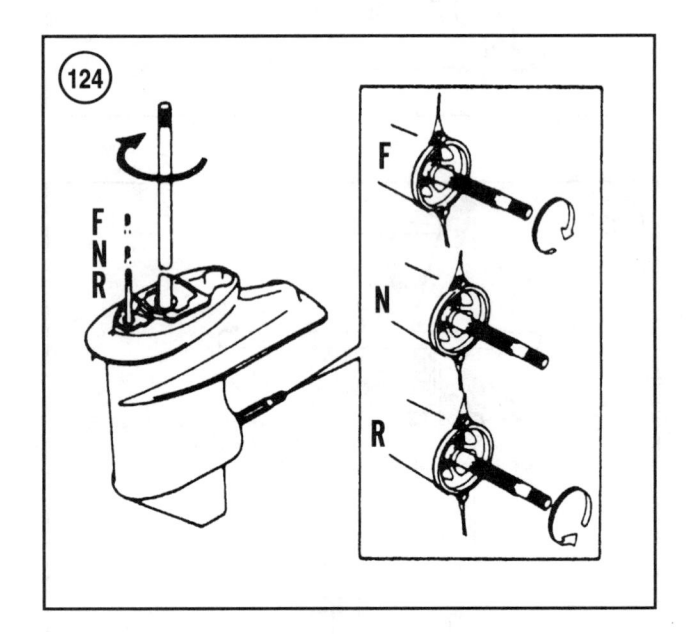

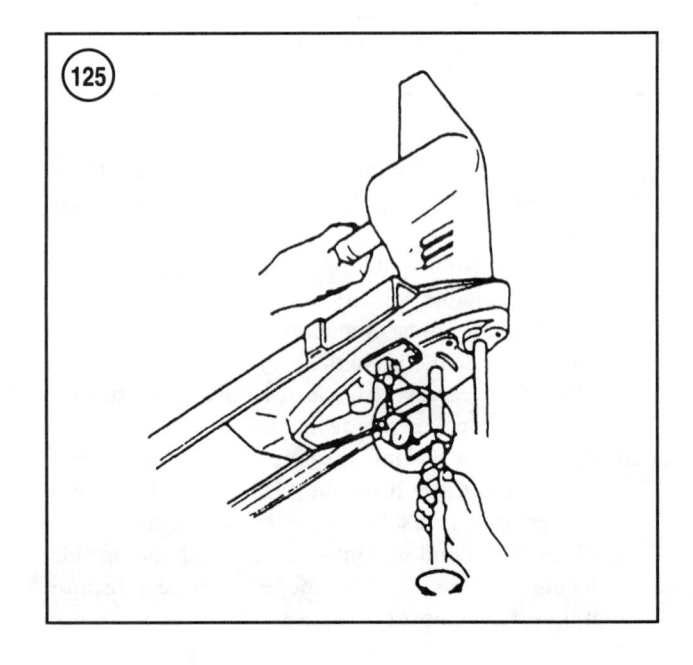

GEARCASE

126
Drive shaft
Dial indicator plunger
Indicator tool

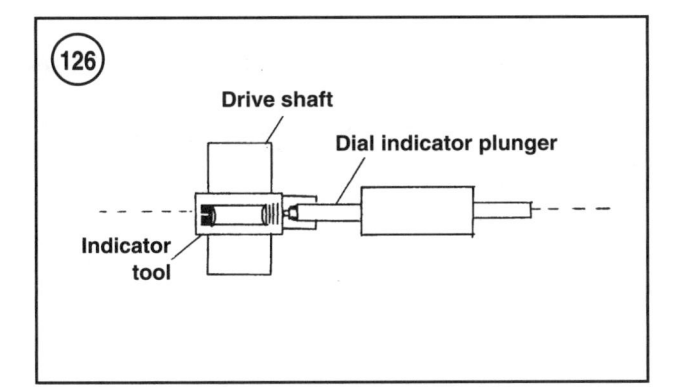

127
Indicator tool
Dial indicator

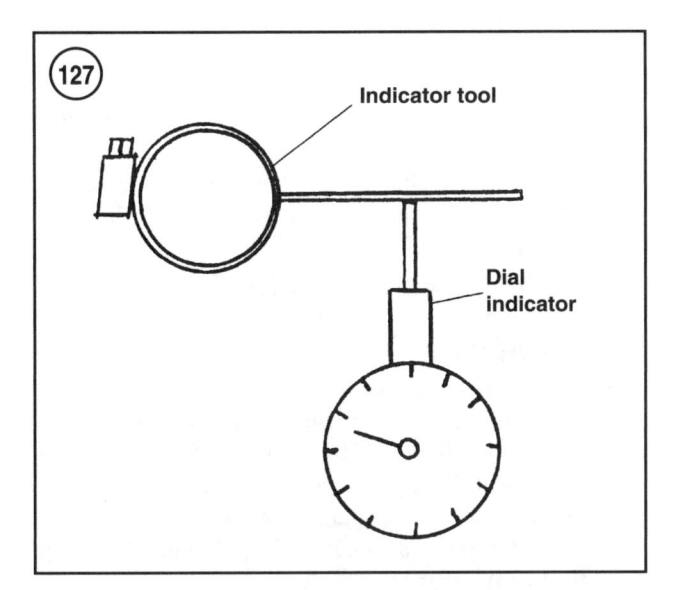

128

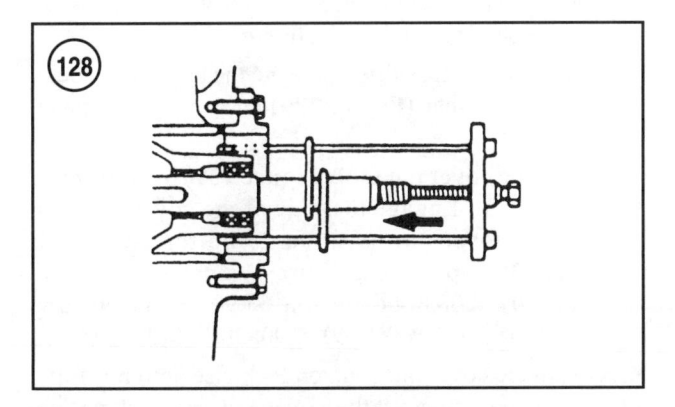

YB-06265/90890-6265. On 9.9-25 hp two-cylinder models, use Yamaha part No. YB-06265/90890-6706.

d. Arrange the dial indicator mount to position the dial indicator plunger at the same height as the indicator tool (**Figure 126**) with the plunger at a 90° angle to

129
Drive shaft
Propeller

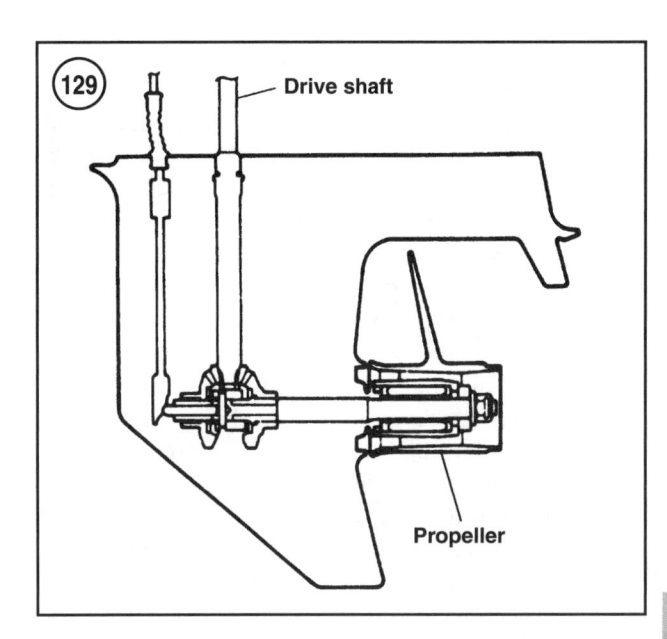

the indicator arm (**Figure 127**). Reposition the dial indicator to place the plunger in line with the mark on the indicator tool.

e. Install a two-jaw puller onto the bearing carrier and propeller shaft as shown in **Figure 128**. Use Yamaha part Nos. YB-06234/90890-06501, 06503 and 06504 or an equivalent. Engage the jaws to the carrier and position the puller bolt against the end of the propeller shaft. Tighten the puller bolt to 5.0 N•m (71 in.-lb.).

f. Rotate the drive shaft so it is pointing down (**Figure 125**).

g. Observe the dial indicator while lightly rotating the drive shaft clockwise and counterclockwise. Do not push up on the drive shaft. Note the dial indicator reading when the drive shaft reaches its free movement limit in each direction. Record the amount of dial indicator movement as forward gear backlash.

h. Remove the two-jaw puller. Install the propeller backwards onto the propeller shaft (**Figure 129**). Do not install the thrust washer between the propeller and the gearcase. Install the thrust washer, then the propeller nut, onto the propeller shaft. Tighten the propeller nut to 5.0 N•m (71 in.-lb.). Shift the gearcase into reverse gear and hold the drive shaft while tightening the propeller nut.

i. Observe the dial indicator while lightly rotating the drive shaft clockwise and counterclockwise. Do not push up on the drive shaft. Note the dial indicator reading when the drive shaft reaches its free movement limit in each direction. Record the amount of dial indicator movement as reverse gear backlash.

Remove the propeller and backlash measuring instruments.

26. The forward and reverse gear backlash measurements should be within the specification in **Table 2**. If both backlash measurements are correct, proceed to Step 28. If either backlash reading is incorrect, refer to the following:
   a. If the forward and reverse gear backlash is greater than specified, install a thicker pinion gear shim.
   b. If the forward and reverse gear backlash is less than specified, install a thinner pinion gear shim.
   c. If the forward gear backlash is greater than specified and the reverse gear backlash is within the specification, install a thicker forward gear shim and repeat the measurement.
   d. If the forward gear backlash is less than specified and the reverse gear backlash is within the specification, check for an improperly installed forward gear bearing race. If the race is installed correctly, install a thinner forward gear shim.
   e. If the reverse gear backlash is greater than specified and the forward gear backlash is within the specification, install a thicker reverse gear shim.
   f. If the reverse gear backlash is less than specified and the forward gear backlash is within the specification, check for an improperly installed reverse gear bearing. If the bearing is installed correctly, install a thinner reverse gear shim.

27. Disassemble the gearcase and perform the indicated shim change or inspection. Reassemble the gearcase and repeat the backlash measurements. Do not proceed until the backlash is correct.

28. Remove the screw from the water pump base. Install all water pump components following the procedure described in this chapter.

Disassembly (25 hp Three-Cylinder and 30-90 hp Models)

For component identification and orientation, refer to **Figures 130-132** during the disassembly procedure.

CAUTION
Never heat the gearcase housing to the point that the finish is burned. Continually move the flame around the mating surface to apply heat evenly. Excessive heat can distort or melt the gearcase.

NOTE
To ease removal of the gearcase cap where corrosion has seized the components, use a torch to apply moderate heat to the gearcase. Heat the area near the gearcase housing-to-gearcase cap mating surfaces.

1. On 75-90 hp models, remove the two screws (**Figure 133**) and carefully pry the shift shaft seal housing from the gearcase. Grip the shift shaft, then pull the shift shaft and seal housing from the gearcase (**Figure 134**). Remove the E-clip, then pull the seal housing from the shift shaft. Carefully pry the shift shaft seal from the housing. Work carefully to avoid damaging the housing. Discard the seal.

2A. On 40 and 50 hp models, remove the bearing carrier as follows:
   a. Remove the two bolts and washers from the bearing carrier flange (**Figure 135**).
   b. Use a blunt tip pry bar to carefully pry the bearing carrier away from the gearcase housing (**Figure 136**).
   c. Grasp the propeller shaft and pull the bearing carrier and propeller shaft as an assembly from the housing (**Figure 137**).
   d. On 25 hp three-cylinder, 30 hp and 60-90 hp models, remove the locating key from the slot in the gearcase (**Figure 138**) or bearing carrier.
   e. If the carrier is seized in the housing, loosen the carrier using a two-jaw puller (Yamaha part Nos. YB-06234/90890-06501, 06503, 06504) or an equivalent. Engage the jaws to the carrier and position the puller bolt against the end of the propeller shaft (**Figure 128**). Tighten the puller bolt to loosen the bearing carrier.

2B. On 25 hp three-cylinder, 30 hp and 60-90 hp models, remove the bearing carrier as follows:
   a. Use a large screwdriver to bend the tabs on the locking tab washer (**Figure 139**) away from the cover nut lugs.
   b. Slip the cover nut tool (**Figure 139**) over the propeller nut. Engage the lugs of the cover nut tool to the cover nut lugs. On 25 hp three-cylinder and 30 hp models, use Yamaha part No. YB-6075/90890-06509. On 60-90 hp models, use Yamaha part No. YB-6075/90890-06513.
   c. Turn the cover nut counterclockwise until it is fully loosened. Remove the cover nut and locking tab washer.
   d. Loosen the carrier using a two-jaw puller (Yamaha YB-06234/90890-06501, 06503, 06504) or an equivalent. Engage the jaws to the carrier and position the puller bolt against the end of the propeller shaft (**Figure 128**). Tighten the puller bolt to loosen the bearing carrier.

GEARCASE

**GEARCASE COMPONENTS
(25 HP THREE-CYLINDER AND 30 HP MODELS)**

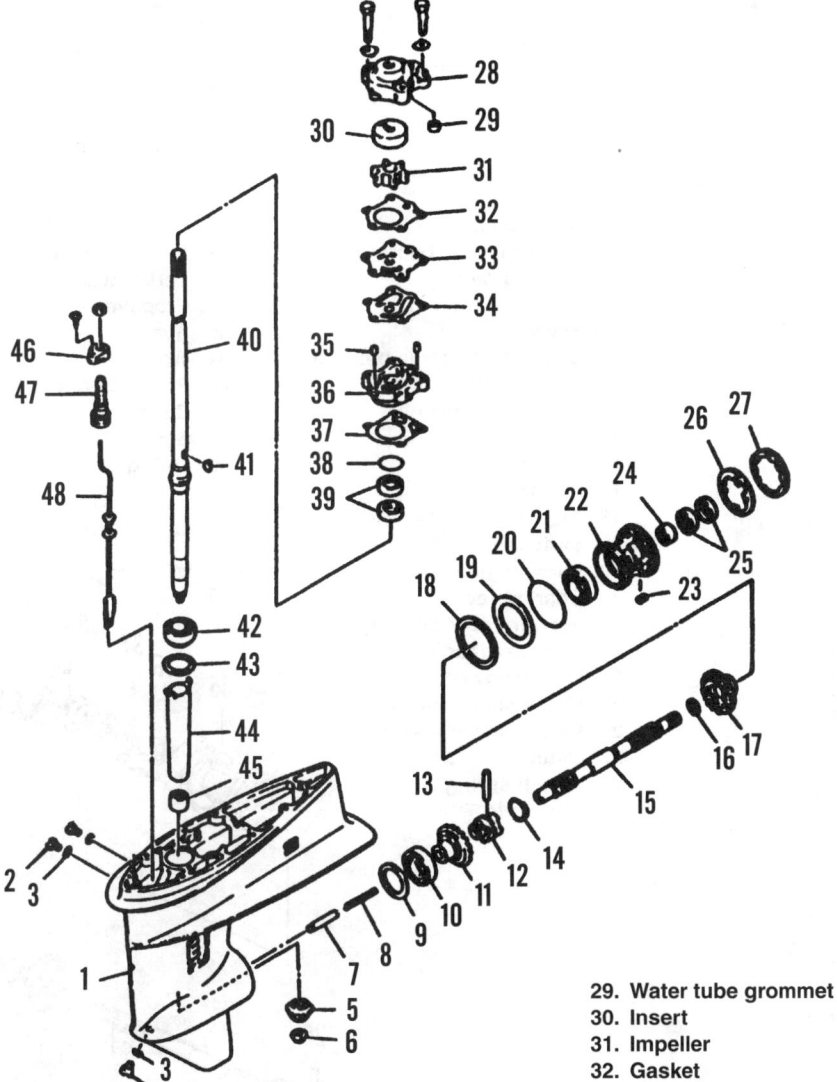

1. Gearcase housing
2. Level/vent plug
3. Sealing washer
4. Fill/drain plug
5. Pinion gear
6. Pinion nut
7. Cam follower
8. Spring
9. Forward gear shim
10. Forward gear bearing
11. Forward gear
12. Clutch
13. Cross pin
14. Clutch spring
15. Propeller shaft
16. Thrust washer
17. Reverse gear
18. Reverse gear shim
19. Thrust washer
20. O-ring
21. Reverse gear bearing
22. Bearing carrier
23. Locating key
24. Needle bearing
25. Propeller shaft seals
26. Locking tab washer
27. Cover nut
28. Water pump body
29. Water tube grommet
30. Insert
31. Impeller
32. Gasket
33. Wear plate
34. Gasket
35. Locating pin
36. Water pump base
37. Gasket
38. O-ring
39. Drive shaft seals
40. Drive shaft
41. Drive key
42. Drive shaft tapered roller bearing
43. Pinion gear shim
44. Sleeve
45. Drive shaft needle bearing
46. Retainer
47. Shift shaft bellows
48. Shift shaft

404 CHAPTER EIGHT

(131)

GEARCASE COMPONENTS
(40 AND 50 HP MODELS)

1. Water pump assembly
2. Seal cover
3. Seal carrier
4. O-ring
5. Drive shaft seals
6. Spacer
7. Drive shaft
8. Tapered roller bearing
9. Bearing race
10. Pinion gear shim
11. Sleeve
12. Drive shaft needle bearing
13. Shift shaft assembly
14. Gearcase housing
15. Trim tab
16. Pinion gear
17. Pinion nut
18. Anode
19. Shift cam
20. Forward gear shim
21. Bearing race
22. Forward gear bearing
23. Forward gear
24. Cam follower
25. Cross pin connector
26. Cam follower spring
27. Clutch
28. Clutch spring
29. Cross pin
30. Propeller shaft
31. Thrust washer
32. Reverse gear
33. Reverse gear shim
34. Reverse gear shim
35. Bearing carrier
36. Propeller shaft needle bearing
37. Propeller shaft seals
38. Thrust washer
39. Propeller
40. Spacer
41. Washer
42. Propeller nut
43. Cotter pin
44. Spacer
45. O-ring

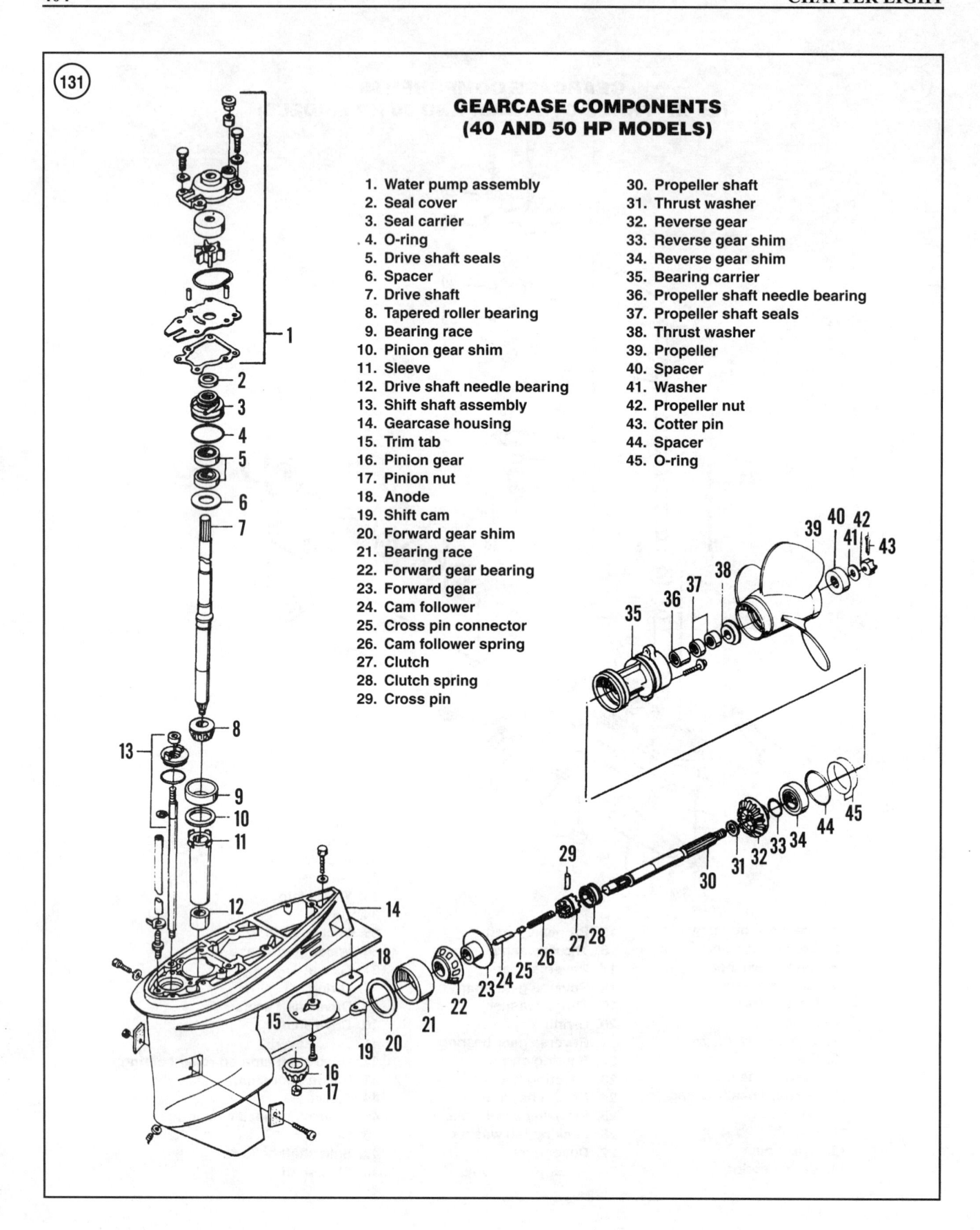

GEARCASE

405

GEARCASE COMPONENTS
(60-90 HP MODELS)

1. Gearcase housing
2. Drive shaft
3. Drive key
4. Drive shaft bearing
5. Shim
6. Sleeve
7. Drive shaft needle bearing
8. Water pump assembly
9. Propeller shaft
10. Clutch
11. Clutch spring
12. Cross pin
13. Forward gear
14. Forward gear bearing
15. Cam follower and springs
16. Pinion gear
17. Pinion nut
18. Trim tab
19. Shift shaft assembly
20. Fill/drain plug and sealing washer
21. Bolt and washer
22. Reverse gear
23. Reverse gear bearing
24. O-ring
25. Bearing carrier
26. Propeller shaft needle bearing
27. Propeller shaft seals
28. Locking tab washer
29. Cover nut
30. Propeller assembly

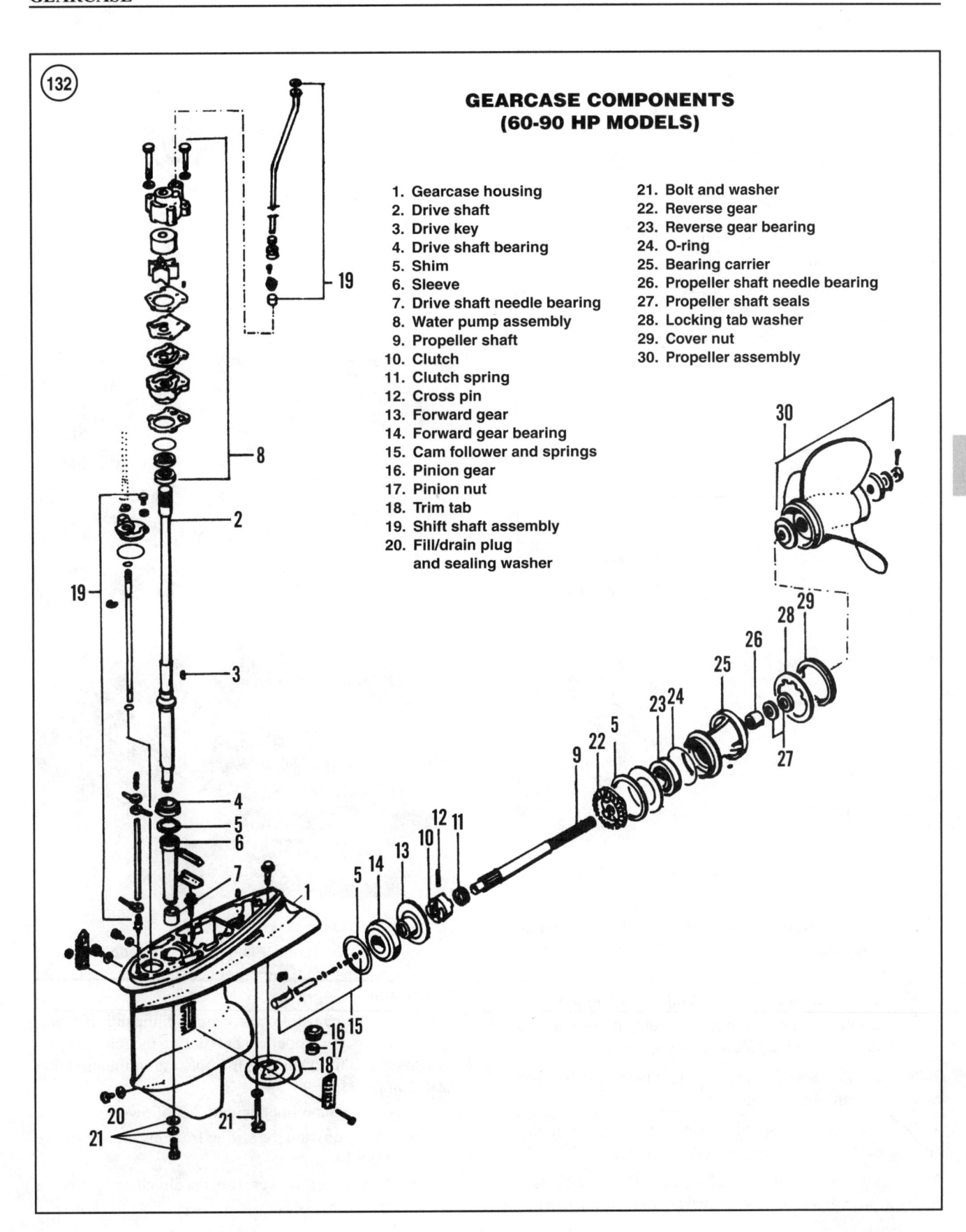

8

133

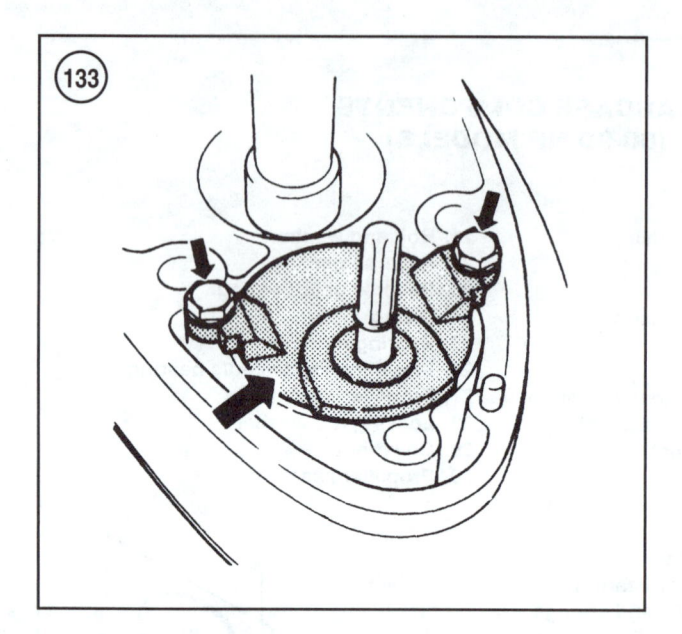

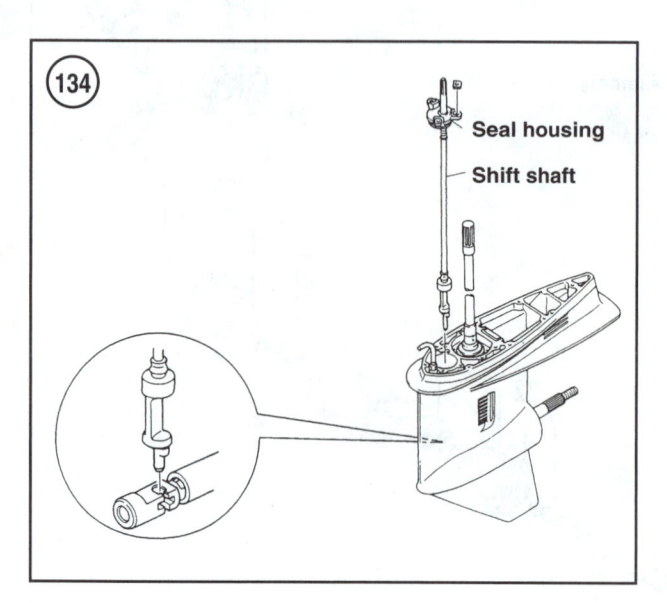

134
Seal housing
Shift shaft

135

136

137

e. Grasp the propeller shaft and pull the bearing carrier and propeller shaft as an assembly from the housing (**Figure 137**).

f. On 25 hp three-cylinder, 30 hp and 60-90 hp models, remove the locating key from the slot in the gearcase (**Figure 138**) or bearing carrier.

3. Remove the large diameter O-ring(s) from the bearing carrier. Discard the O-ring(s).

4. Remove any loose shims, O-rings or spacers from the bearing carrier or gearcase housing opening.

5. Grasp the front of the propeller shaft (**Figure 123**) and slide the propeller shaft assembly from the bearing carrier.

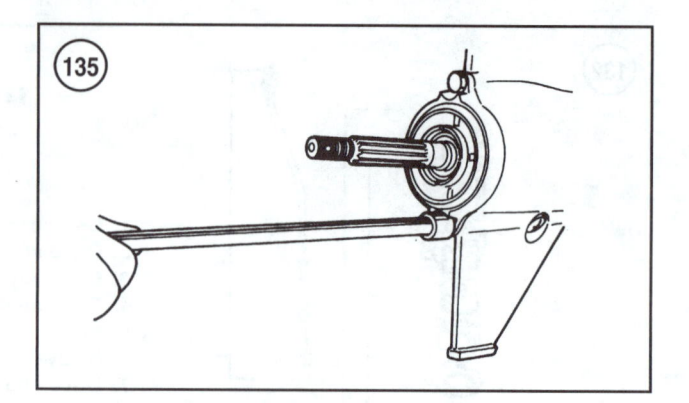

6. On 25 hp three-cylinder and 30-50 hp models, remove the thrust washer from the propeller shaft or reverse gear (**Figure 140**).

7. Retrieve the cam follower from the housing if it was dislodged from the propeller shaft during the removal process. Insert the follower into the opening in the propeller shaft (**Figure 119**).

8. Disassemble the propeller shaft as follows:
   a. Carefully unwind the spring from the clutch groove (**Figure 141**).
   b. Push the cam follower from the clutch and propeller shaft (**Figure 142**).

GEARCASE

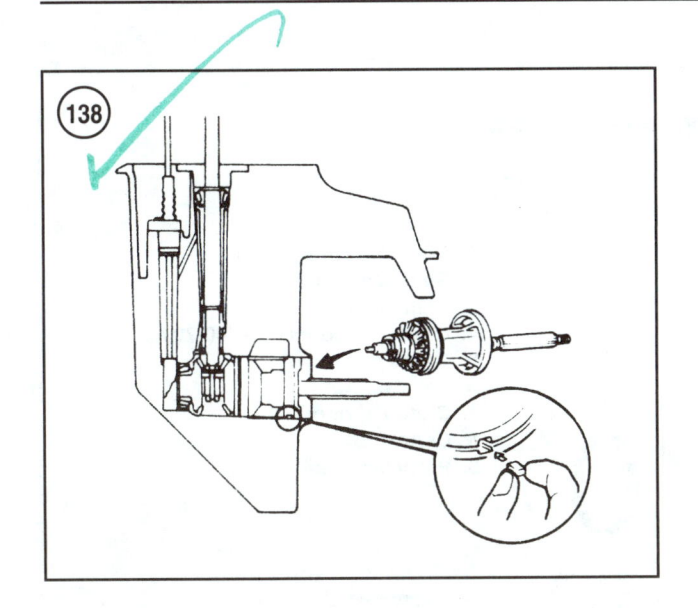

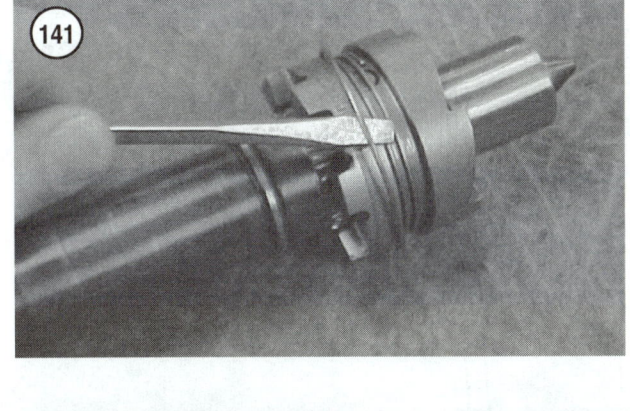

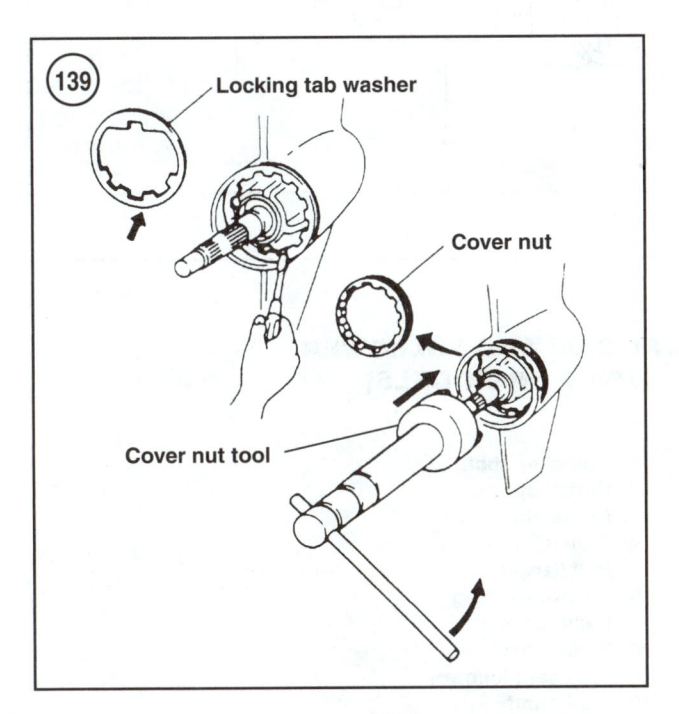

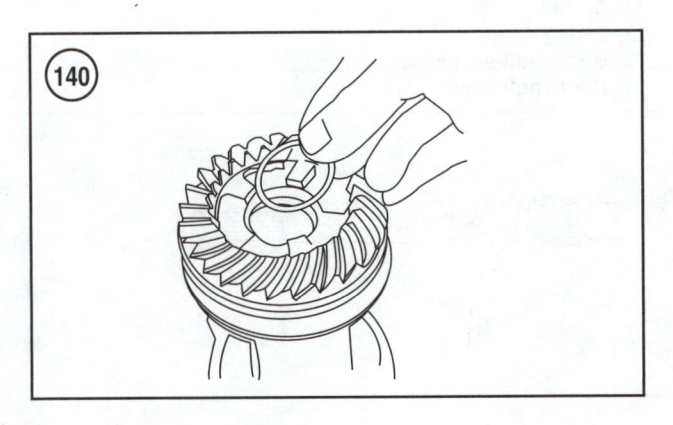

407

138

139 Locking tab washer / Cover nut / Cover nut tool

140

141

142

143

c. Slide the clutch over the forward end of the propeller shaft (**Figure 143**).

d. On 25 hp three-cylinder and 30-70 hp models, pull the cam follower (3, **Figure 144**) from the propeller shaft.

e. On 40 and 50 hp models, pull the cross pin connector (4, **Figure 144**) from the propeller shaft opening.

f. On 25 hp three-cylinder and 30-70 hp models, pull the follower spring (6, **Figure 144**) from the propeller shaft opening. If necessary, tap the end of the propeller shaft to dislodge the spring.

8

CHAPTER EIGHT

144 SHIFT CAM AND FOLLOWER

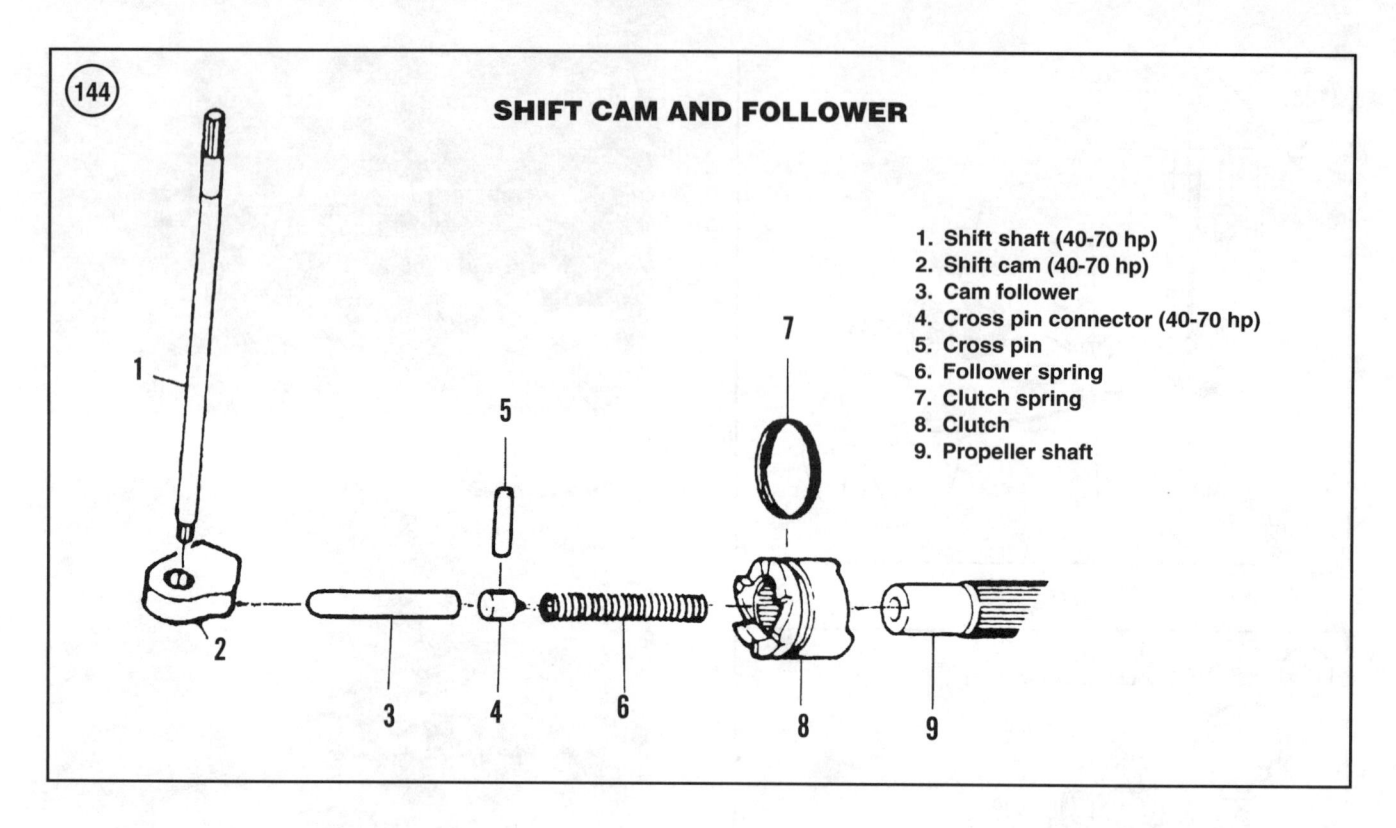

1. Shift shaft (40-70 hp)
2. Shift cam (40-70 hp)
3. Cam follower
4. Cross pin connector (40-70 hp)
5. Cross pin
6. Follower spring
7. Clutch spring
8. Clutch
9. Propeller shaft

145 SHIFT CAM AND FOLLOWER (75-90 HP MODELS)

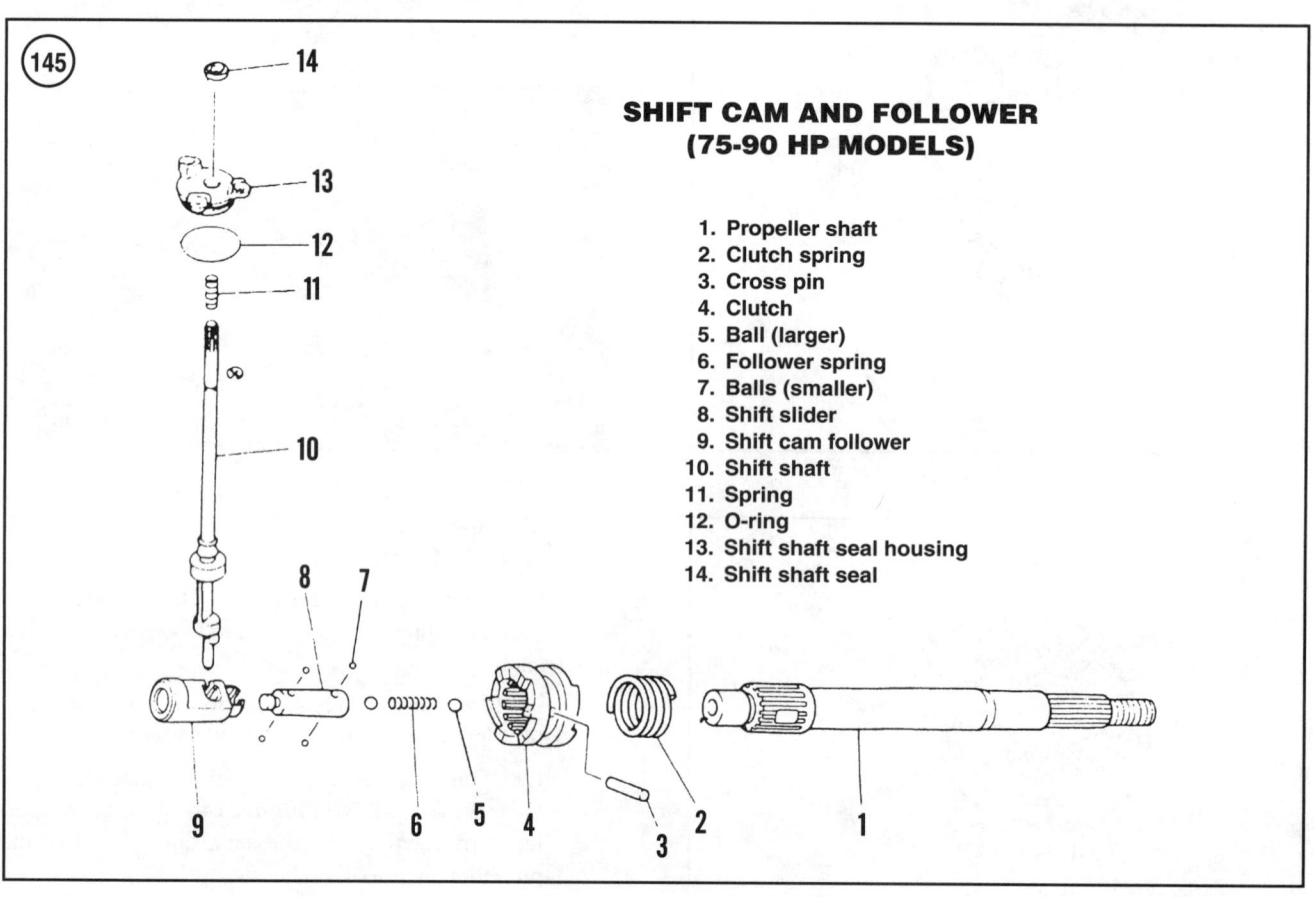

1. Propeller shaft
2. Clutch spring
3. Cross pin
4. Clutch
5. Ball (larger)
6. Follower spring
7. Balls (smaller)
8. Shift slider
9. Shift cam follower
10. Shift shaft
11. Spring
12. O-ring
13. Shift shaft seal housing
14. Shift shaft seal

GEARCASE

146

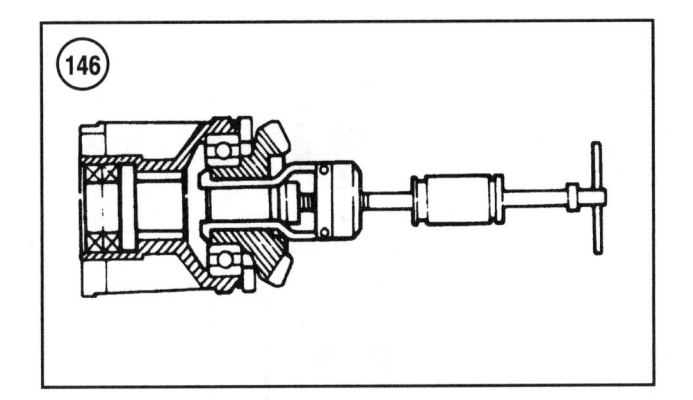

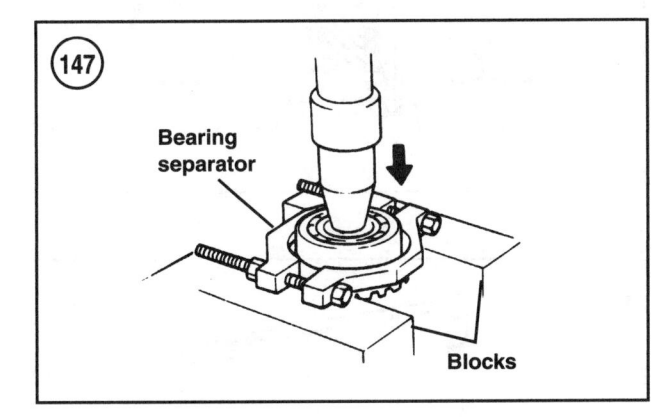

147 Bearing separator / Blocks

148 Slide hammer / Bearing carrier

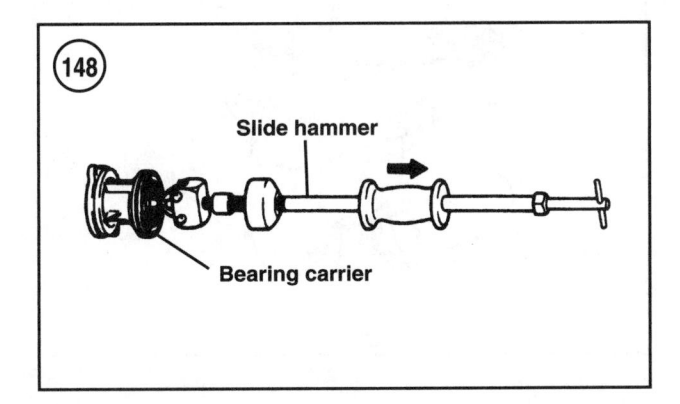

g. On 75-90 hp models, position the shift shaft over a container to capture small components that may fall during disassembly. Pull the shift cam follower (9, **Figure 145**) forward to draw the shift slider (8) from the propeller shaft. Capture the four balls (7, **Figure 145**). Remove the two larger balls (5, **Figure 145**) and follower spring (6). If necessary, tap the end of the propeller shaft to dislodge the spring.

9. On 23 hp three-cylinder, 30 hp and 60-90 hp models, remove the locating key (**Figure 138**) from the slot in the carrier.

10. Only remove the reverse gear if the reverse gear, reverse gear bearing or reverse gear shim (40 and 50 hp models) must be replaced. The removal process may damage the bearing. Refer to *Component Inspection* in this chapter to determine the need for replacement. Remove the reverse gear as follows:
   a. Clamp the bearing carrier in a vise with protective jaws.
   b. Engage the jaws of a slide hammer to the hub of the reverse gear (**Figure 146**).
   c. Use short hammer strokes to remove the reverse gear from the carrier.

11. In some instances, the bearing will be pulled from the carrier along with the gear. Separate the bearing and gear as follows:
   a. Insert the sharp edge of a bearing separator between the reverse gear and the bearing.
   b. Place the gear and bearing on the table of a press with the gear facing down (**Figure 147**).
   c. Block the bearing separator to allow adequate clearance for gear removal.
   d. Press the gear from the bearing using a section of tubing or a socket as a removal tool. The tool must contact the hub of the gear, but not contact the bearing bore.

12. On 40 and 50 hp models, remove the reverse gear shim (33, **Figure 131**) from the hub of the gear or the reverse gear bearing.

13. Only remove the reverse gear bearing if the bearing must be replaced. The removal process may damage the bearing. Refer to *Component Inspection* in this chapter to determine the need for replacement. Remove the bearing as follows:
   a. Clamp the bearing carrier in a vise with protective jaws.
   b. Engage the jaws of a slide hammer beneath the inner bearing race (**Figure 148**).
   c. Use short hammer strokes to remove the bearing.
   d. On 25 hp three-cylinder, 30 hp and 60-90 hp models, remove the thrust spacer from the reverse gear or bearing.

14. Only remove the propeller shaft seals if they must be replaced. The removal process damages the seals. Refer to *Component Inspection* in this chapter to determine the need for replacement. Remove the seals as follows:
   a. Clamp the bearing carrier in a vise with protective jaws. The gear side of the carrier must face down.
   b. Engage the jaws of a slide hammer beneath the casing of the inner seal (**Figure 149**).
   c. Use short hammer strokes to remove the seals.
   d. Discard the seals.

15. Only remove the needle bearing from the bearing carrier if it must be replaced. The removal process damages the bearing. Refer to *Component Inspection* in this chapter to determine the need for replacement. Remove the bearing as follows:

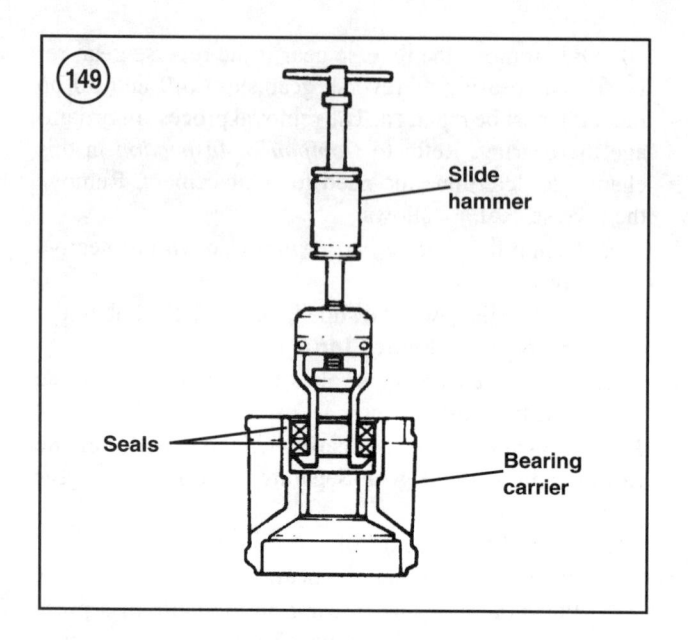

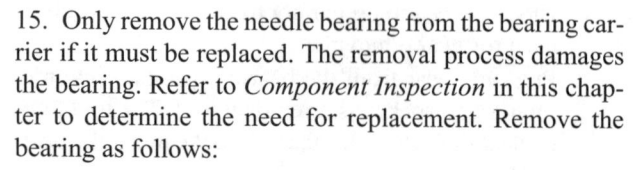

   a. Place the carrier on the table of a press with the gear side facing up. Block the carrier or place it over an opening to ensure adequate clearance for the bearing or bushing during removal.
   b. Select a section of tubing or a socket and extension to use as a removal tool. The tool must contact the casing of the bearing, but not contact the bearing carrier bore during removal.
   c. Seat the tool against the bearing or bushing, then slowly tap the bearing from the bore (**Figure 150**).
   d. Discard the bearing or bushing.

16A. On 25 hp three-cylinder, 30 hp and 60-90 hp models, use a blunt tip pry bar to carefully pry the water pump base from the gearcase. Avoid damaging the mating surfaces. Slide the base up and over the drive shaft. Remove the gasket and O-ring. Discard the gasket and O-ring.

16B. On 40 and 50 hp models, carefully pry the drive shaft seal carrier (3, **Figure 131**) out of the drive shaft bore. Remove the O-ring (4, **Figure 131**) from the seal carrier. Discard the O-ring.

17. Only remove the drive shaft seals from the water pump base or seal carrier if they must be replaced. The removal process damages the seals. Refer to *Component Inspection* in this chapter to determine the need for replacement. Remove the seals as follows:

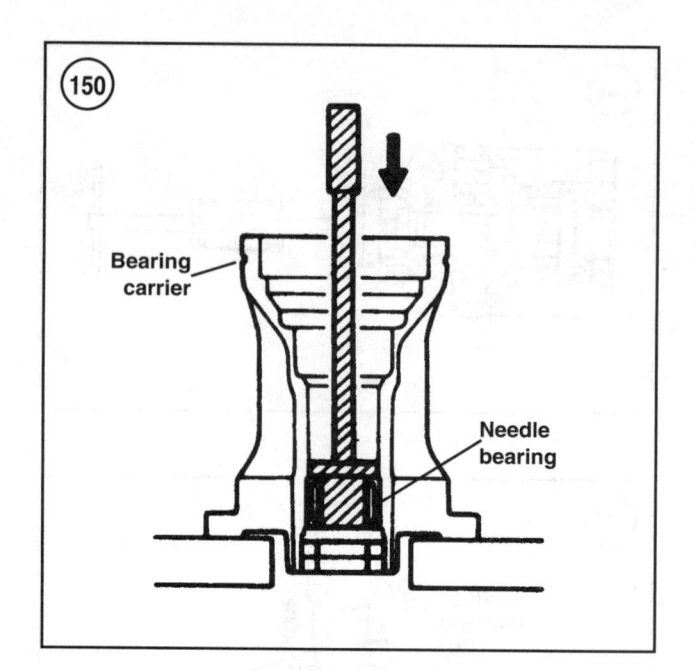

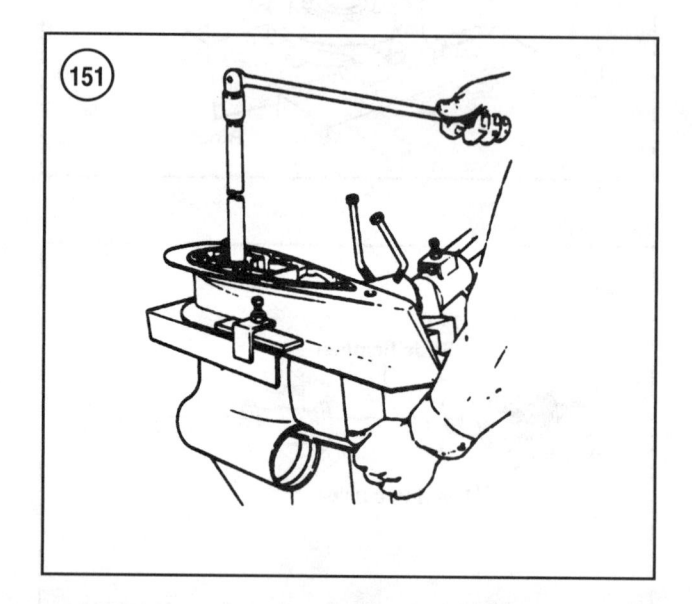

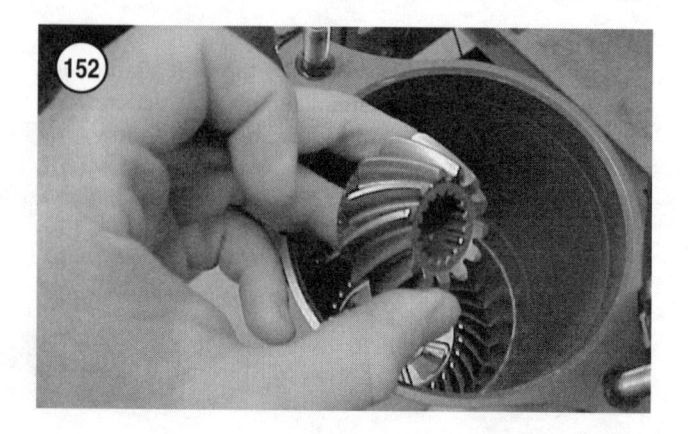

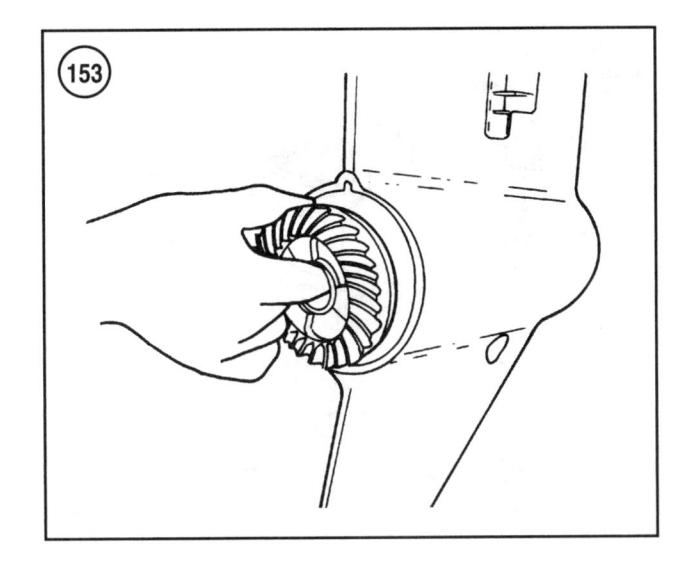

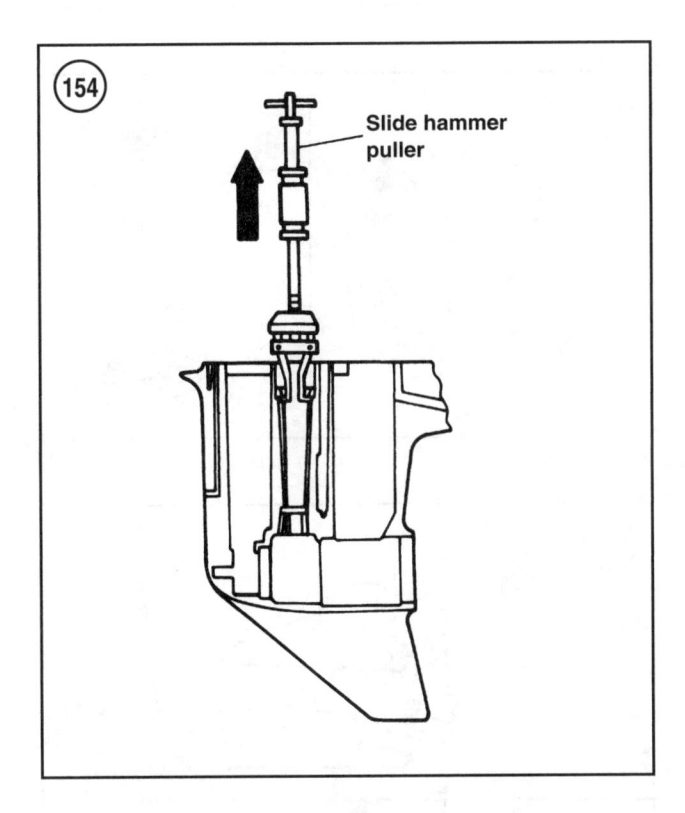

GEARCASE

153

154

Slide hammer puller

155

a. Clamp the water pump base or seal carrier in a vise with protective jaws. The larger diameter opening must face up.
b. Engage the jaws of a slide hammer below the casing of the inner seal.
c. Use short hammer strokes to remove both seals from the base.
d. Discard the seals.

18. Remove the pinion nut as follows:

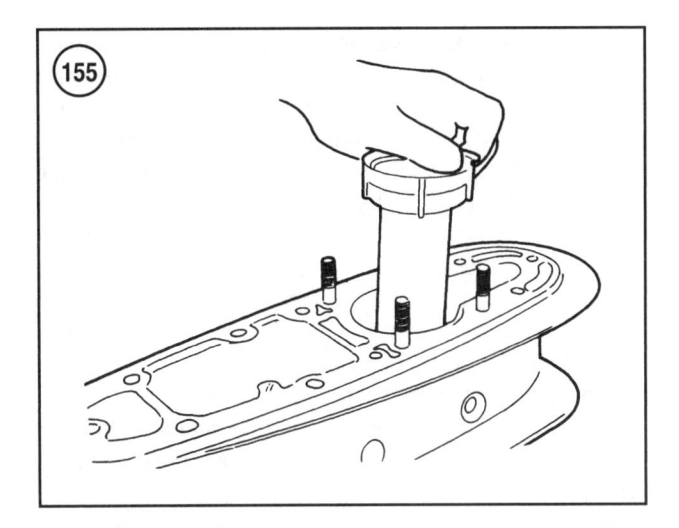

a. Install the splined drive shaft adapter onto the upper end of the drive shaft. On 25 hp three-cylinder and 30-50 hp models, use Yamaha part No. YB-67079-A/90890-06517. On 60 and 70 hp models, use Yamaha part No. YB-6049/90890-06518. On 75-90 hp models, use Yamaha part No. YB-6151/90890-06519.
b. Use a suitable socket wrench to properly engage the pinion nut (**Figure 151**). Use shop towels to protect the housing surface from the socket wrench.
c. Rotate the drive shaft counterclockwise as viewed from the top to loosen the nut. Continue until the pinion nut is free from the drive shaft.

19. Support the pinion gear and carefully pull the drive shaft from the gearcase. Remove the pinion gear (**Figure 152**).

20. Remove the forward gear from the housing (**Figure 153**). If necessary, tap lightly on the front of the housing to free the gear from the bearing race.

21. Engage the jaws of a slide hammer beneath the tapered roller bearing race (**Figure 154**). Use short hammer strokes to remove the race and pinion gear shims.

22. Remove the sleeve from the drive shaft bore (**Figure 155**).

23. On 25 hp three-cylinder and 30 hp models, remove the screws, then lift the retainer (**Figure 156**) from the gearcase. Pull the shift shaft from the gearcase housing.

24. On 25 hp three-cylinder and 30 hp models, remove the jam nut, then pull the shift cable bellows over the top of the shift shaft. Work carefully to avoid tearing the bellows. Replace the bellows if it is torn or looks weathered.

25. On 25 hp three-cylinder and 30 hp models, only remove the shift cam from the lower end of the shift shaft if it must be replaced. Refer to *Component Inspection* in this chapter to determine the need for replacement. Use a

small pin punch to drive the pin from the shift cam and shift shaft. If the pin does not fit tightly in the shift shaft and shift cam, replace the pin. If the pin is still loose, replace the shift cam, shift shaft or both components.

26. On 40-70 hp models, remove the two screws (**Figure 157**), then carefully pry the shift shaft seal housing from the gearcase. Grip the top of the shift shaft and pull the assembly from the gearcase (**Figure 157**). Remove the E-clip, then carefully pull the seal housing from the shift shaft. Pry the seal from the housing. Work carefully to avoid damaging the housing. Discard the seal after removal. Remove the shift cam (**Figure 158**).

27. Only remove the forward gear bearing race when the forward gear bearing or the forward gear shims are being replaced. Remove the bearing race as follows:
   a. Engage the jaws of a slide hammer to the inner surface of the bearing race (**Figure 159**).
   b. Use short hammer strokes to remove the bearing race and shim(s) from the gearcase.
   c. Inspect the shim(s) for bent or corroded surfaces. Replace damaged shims with new ones of the same thickness.

28. Only remove the tapered roller bearing from the forward gear if the bearing or forward gear must be replaced. The removal process damages the bearing. Refer to *Component Inspection* in this chapter to determine the need for replacement. Remove the bearing as follows:
   a. Insert the sharp edge of a bearing separator between the bearing and forward gear (**Figure 160**).
   b. Block the sides of the separator to ensure adequate travel for the gear.
   c. Select a section of tubing or a socket to use as a removal tool. The tool must contact the gear hub, but not contact the inner race of the bearing.
   d. Press on the tool to remove the gear from the bearing. Discard the bearing.

29. Only remove the lower drive shaft bearing if it must be replaced. The removal process damages the bearing. Refer to *Component Inspection* in this chapter to determine the need for replacement. Remove the bearing as follows:
   a. Select a section of tubing or a socket and extension to use as a removal tool. The tool must contact the case of the bearing, but not contact the drive shaft bore in the gearcase housing.
   b. Insert the removal tool into the drive shaft bore and seat it against the bearing (**Figure 161**).
   c. Carefully tap the bearing into the gearcase housing. Discard the component after removal.

30. Only remove the tapered roller bearing from the drive shaft if it must be replaced. The removal process damages the bearing. Refer to *Component Inspection* in this chapter to determine the need for replacement. Remove the bearing as follows:
   a. Insert the drive shaft into a bearing separator. Seat the inner race of the bearing against the shoulder on the crankshaft side of the bearing.

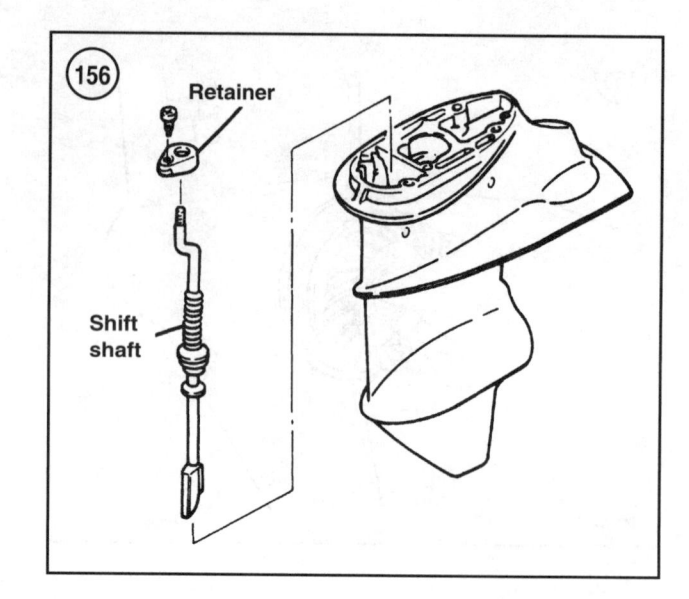

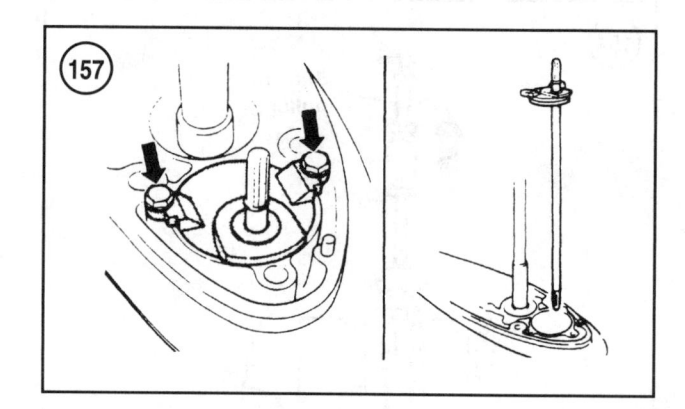

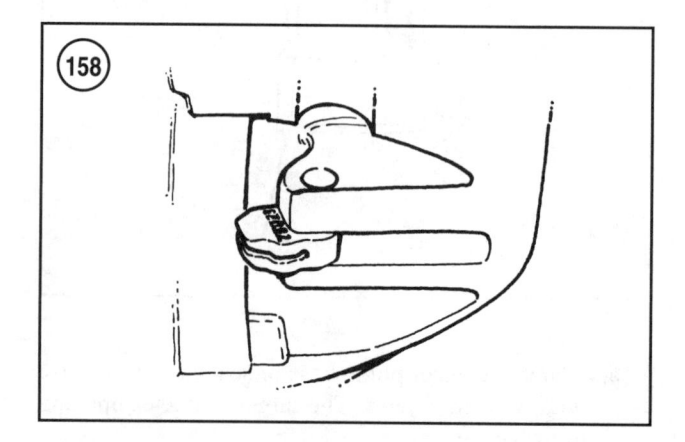

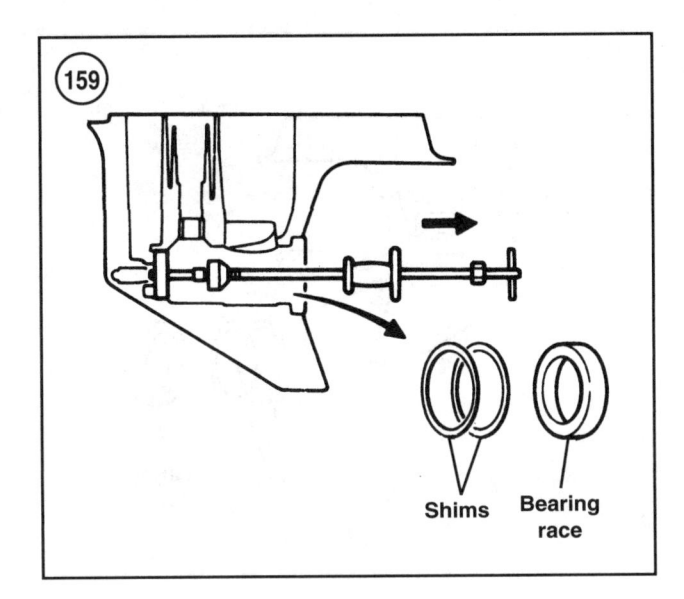

GEARCASE

Figure 159 — Shims, Bearing race

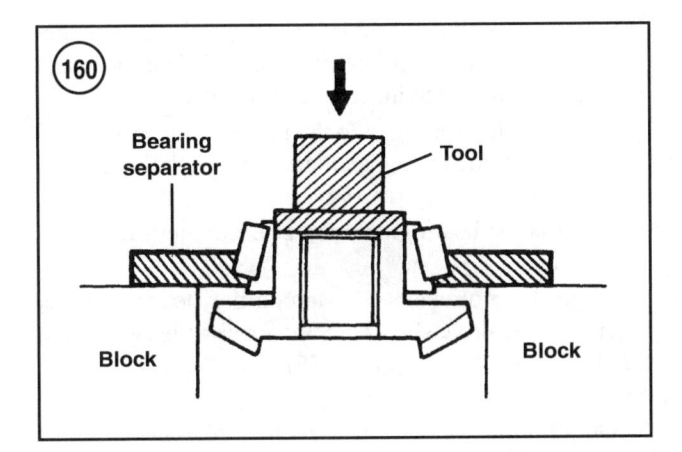

Figure 160 — Bearing separator, Tool, Block, Block

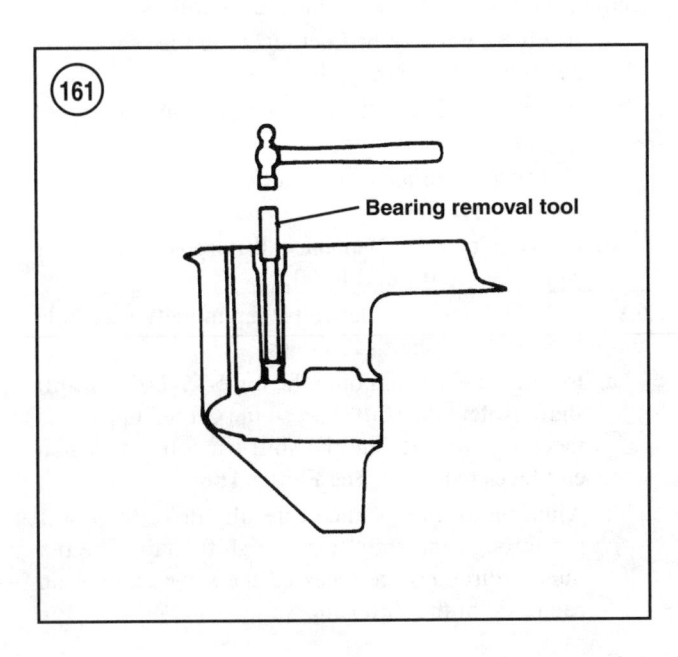

Figure 161 — Bearing removal tool

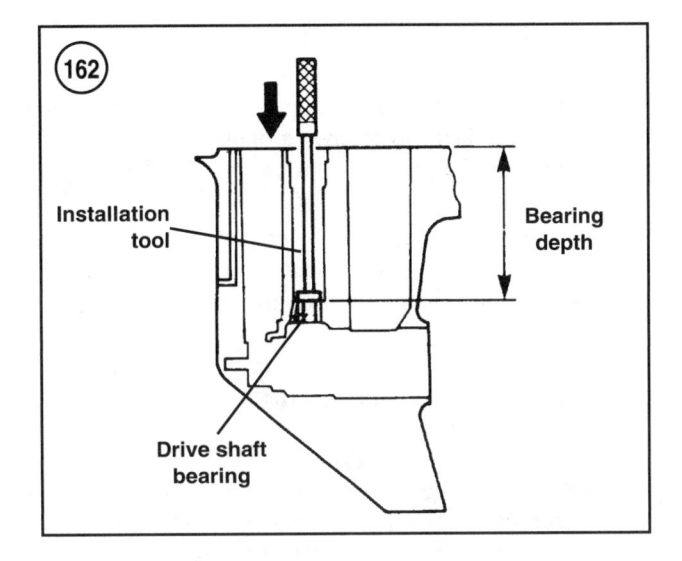

Figure 162 — Installation tool, Drive shaft bearing, Bearing depth

b. Place the drive shaft and bearing separator on the table of a press with the pinion gear side facing up. Thread the used pinion nut onto the shaft to protect the threads.
c. Support the lower end of the drive shaft while pressing the shaft from the bearing bore.
d. Discard the bearing.

Assembly (25 hp Three-Cylinder and 30-90 hp Models)

For component identification and orientation, refer to **Figures 130-132** during the disassembly procedure.

CAUTION
The lower drive shaft needle bearing must be installed to the specified depth in the drive shaft bore. Otherwise, the bearing may contact the drive shaft on a non-bearing surface during operation. The resulting bearing failure could damage the drive shaft and gearcase housing.

1. Install a new lower drive shaft needle bearing, if it was removed, as follows:
    a. Select a section of tubing or a socket and extension to use as a bearing installation tool. The tool must contact the bearing case, but not contact the drive shaft bore during installation.
    b. Working through the drive shaft bore opening, insert the needle bearing into the drive shaft bore. The numbered side of the bearing case must face up or toward the water pump when installed.
    c. Insert the installation tool into the drive shaft bore (**Figure 162**) and seat it against the numbered side of the bearing.

d. Slowly tap the bearing into the bore. Stop frequently to measure the depth.
e. On 25 hp three-cylinder and 30 hp models, stop when the bearing reaches a depth of 196.5-197.5 mm (7.74-7.78 in.) at the points indicated in **Figure 162**.
f. On 40 and 50 hp models, stop when the bearing reaches a depth of 182.5-183.0 mm (7.19-7.20 in.) at the points indicated in **Figure 162**.
g. On 60-90 hp models, stop when the bearing reaches a depth of 187.6-188.6 mm (7.39-7.43 in.) at the points indicated in **Figure 162**.

NOTE
When driving a bearing race into the gearcase housing, always use very light taps and listen to the noise when the driver is struck. Only strike the driver hard enough to slightly move the bearing or race. Stop driving when the pitch changes or a sharp ring is heard as the driver is struck. This indicates the bearing or race is seated. Continued driving may bounce the bearing or race out of the bore.

2. Install the bearing race and shim(s) into the housing, if they were removed, as follows:
    a. Use the manufacturer recommended tool for this procedure. On 25 hp three-cylinder and 30 hp models: YB-06085/90890-06627 and YB-6071-90890-06605. On 40 and 50 hp models: YB-41446/90890-06626 and YB-6071-90890-06605. On 60-90 hp models: YB-6276B/90890-06621 and YB-6071-90890-06605. If these tools are not available, use a section of tubing or a suitable mandrel and driver. The tool must contact near the outer diameter of the bearing race, but not contact the gear housing during installation.
    b. Apply a light coat of gearcase lubricant to the race surfaces and the corresponding bore in the gearcase housing.
    c. Place the shim(s) in the housing. The shim(s) must rest in the bearing race bore.
    d. Install the bearing race into the bore with the tapered opening facing out. Maintain firm contact with the bearing race while gently driving it into the bore (**Figure 163**). Use light force and do not allow the race to tilt in the bore. Continue driving until the race fully seats in the housing.
3. Install a new tapered roller bearing onto the forward gear, if it was removed, as follows:
    a. Place the forward gear on the table of a press with the gear teeth side facing down.
    b. Select a section of tubing or a large diameter socket to use as a bearing installation tool. The tool must only contact the inner race of the bearing.
    c. Install the bearing onto the hub of the gear with the tapered side facing up. Place the installation tool on the bearing (**Figure 164**).
    d. Press the bearing onto the gear hub until it is fully seated.
4. Align the protrusion(s) or tab on the sleeve with the notches in the drive shaft bore, then insert the sleeve into the drive shaft bore (**Figure 155**). Seat the sleeve in the bore.
5. On 40-90 hp models, install a new seal into the shift shaft seal housing, if it was removed, as follows:
    a. Apply a light coat of Loctite 271 to the seal casing and the seal bore in the housing.
    b. Insert the seal into the bore with the open side facing down.
    c. Use an appropriately sized socket and carefully seat the seal in the bore.
    d. Apply a coat of Yamaha All-Purpose Grease or equivalent to the seal lip(s).
6A. On 25 hp three-cylinder and 30 hp models, assemble and install the shift shaft as follows:
    a. Install the shift cam onto the lower end of the shift shaft. Rotate the shift shaft so the curved upper end faces forward. Rotate the shift cam so the slanted end faces rearward. See **Figure 156**.
    b. Align the openings, then carefully drive the lower pin through the shift cam and shift shaft. The pin must protrude or be recessed the same amount on each side of the shift cam.

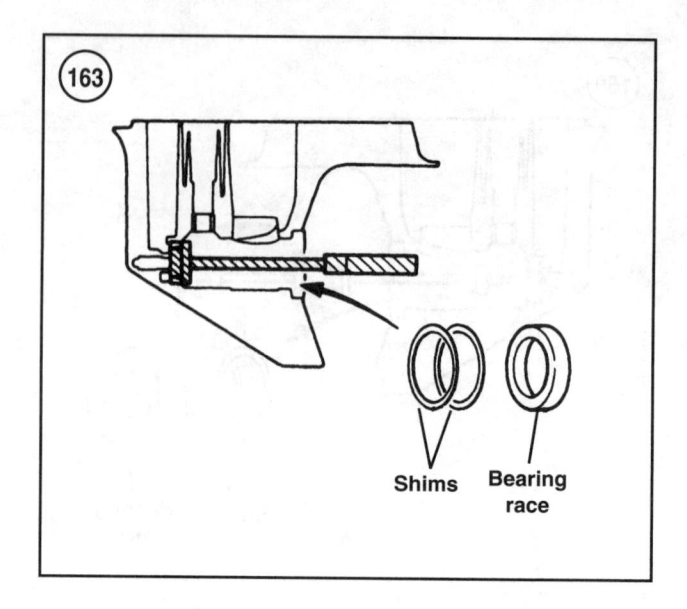

GEARCASE

164

c. Apply a light coat of Yamaha All-Purpose Grease or equivalent to the upper end of the shift shaft. Carefully slide the shift shaft bellows over the top of the shift shaft.

d. Guide the shift shaft assembly into its opening in the housing. The slanted side of the shift cam must face rearward (**Figure 156**).

e. Insert the lower end of the bellows fully into the opening in the housing. If the bellows does not fit tightly in the opening, it is old and must be replaced.

f. Install the retainer (**Figure 156**) over the bellows. Secure the retainer with the two screws.

g. Thread the jam nut onto the shift shaft.

6B. On 40 and 50 hp models, install the shift cam and shift shaft as follows:

a. Install the shift cam into the gearcase (**Figure 158**). The mark on the shift cam must face up. Align the spline opening in the shift cam with the shift shaft bore in the housing.

b. Apply a light coat of Yamaha All-Purpose Grease or equivalent to the O-ring, then install the O-ring into the groove in the shift shaft seal housing.

c. Slide the seal housing over the top of the shift shaft. Insert the E-clip(s) into the shift shaft groove(s).

d. Grip the top of the shift shaft, then insert the shift shaft into its bore (**Figure 157**). Guide the shift shaft into the splined opening in the shift cam (**Figure 158**). Rotate the shift shaft to align the splines. The shaft will drop into position when the splines align.

e. Carefully push the lower end of the shift shaft seal carrier into the bore. Align the openings then install the screws and retainers (**Figure 157**). Tighten the screws to the general torque specification in Chapter Three.

7. Install a new tapered roller bearing onto the drive shaft, if it was removed, as follows:

a. Lubricate the bearing and lower drive shaft surfaces with gearcase lubricant.

b. Slide the bearing over the lower end of the drive shaft. The tapered side of the bearing must face toward the pinion gear end of the shaft.

c. Select a section of tubing to use as a bearing installation tool. The tool must be long enough and have an inner diameter large enough to slide over the drive shaft and contact only the inner race of the bearing.

d. Slide the crankshaft end of the drive shaft through the opening of a bearing separator. Adjust the separator opening to contact the step on the shaft.

e. Place the bearing separator and plate on the table of a press. The pinion gear end of the shaft must face up.

f. Slide the installation tool over the pinion gear end of the drive shaft and seat it against the inner race of the bearing.

g. Press on the end of the installation tool until the bearing seats against the step on the drive shaft.

NOTE
When driving a bearing race into the gearcase housing, strike the driver just enough to slightly move the bearing or race. Stop driving when the pitch changes or a sharp ring is heard as the driver is struck. This indicates the bearing or race is seated. Continued driving may bounce the bearing or race out of the bore.

8. Install the drive shaft bearing race as follows:

a. Apply a coat of gearcase lubricant to the bearing race and the race bore in the housing.

b. Insert the pinion gear shims into the drive shaft bore. The shims must rest on the step in the bore.

c. Install the race into the bore with the tapered side facing out.

d. Select a section of tubing or a suitable driver to use as an installation tool. The tool must only contact on the flat surface of the race, and not contact the housing during installation.

e. Maintain firm contact with the race while slowly tapping the race into the bore (**Figure 165**). Continue until the race seats against the shims. Do not allow the race to tilt in the bore.

9. Install the forward gear and bearing into the housing (**Figure 153**). Seat the gear and bearing against the bearing race.

10. Install the pinion gear into the housing (**Figure 152**). Mesh the pinion gear teeth with the driven gear teeth.

Align the splined opening in the pinion gear with the drive shaft bore.

11. Apply a coat of gearcase lubricant to the lower surfaces of the drive shaft. Carefully guide the drive shaft into the bore. Make sure the drive shaft passes through the lower bearing. Slowly rotate the drive shaft to align the drive shaft splines with the pinion gear splines. The shaft will drop into the pinion gear when the splines align.

12. Install the pinion nut as follows:
   a. Apply Loctite 271 to the threads of the new pinion nut. Hand-thread the nut onto the drive shaft.
   b. Install the splined drive shaft adapter onto the upper end of the drive shaft. On 25 hp three-cylinder and 30-50 hp models, use Yamaha part No. YB-67079-A/90890-06517. On 60 and 70 hp models, use Yamaha part No. YB-6049/90890-06518. On 75-90 hp models, use Yamaha part No. YB-6151/90890-06519.
   c. Use a suitable socket wrench to properly engage the pinion nut (**Figure 151**). Use shop towels to protect the housing surface from the socket wrench.
   d. Rotate the drive shaft clockwise as viewed from the top while tightening the pinion nut to the specification in **Table 1**.

13. Install the drive shaft seals into the water pump base or seal carrier (40 and 50 hp models), if it was removed, as follows:
   a. Apply a light coat of Loctite 271 to the outer casing of the seals and the seal bore in the base or seal carrier.
   b. Place the water pump base or seal carrier on a sturdy work surface with the larger diameter opening facing up. The impeller side must face down.
   c. Select a piece of tubing or socket and extension to use as a seal installation tool. The tool must contact the seal casing, but not contact the seal bore during installation.
   d. Insert the inner seal into the bore with the lip side facing down. Carefully drive the seal into the bore until the upper edge of the seal is slightly recessed in the bore.
   e. Insert the outer seal into the bore with the lip side facing down. Carefully drive the outer seal into the bore until it just contacts the inner seal.
   f. Drive both seals into the bore until the casing of the outer seal just reaches the correct depth at the points indicted in **Figure 166**. On 25 hp three-cylinder and 30 hp models, the inner seal must seat in the bore. The outer seal must seat against the inner seal. On 40 and 50 hp models, the seal depth must be 0-0.5 mm (0-0.20 in.). On 60-90 hp models, the inner seal must seat in the bore. The outer seal must seat against the inner seal.
   g. Wipe excess Loctite from the drive shaft bore before proceeding.
   h. Apply a bead of Yamaha All-Purpose Grease or equivalent to the seal lips.

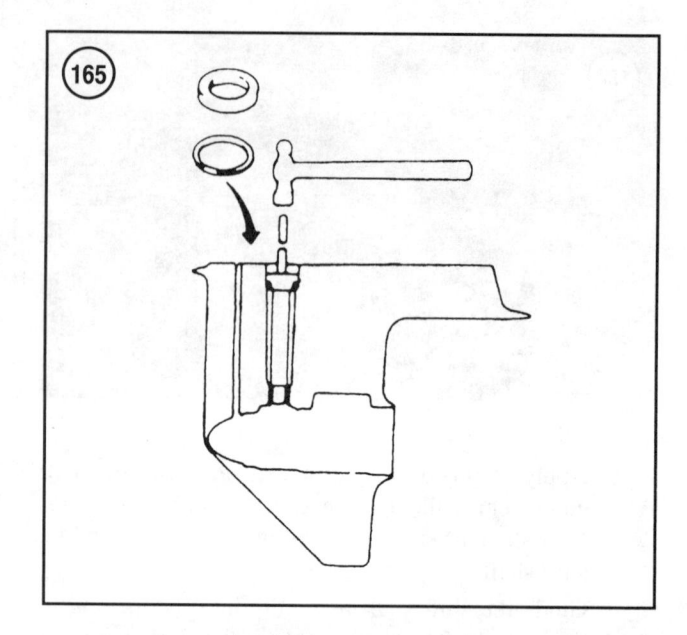

14. Apply a light coat of Yamaha All-Purpose Grease or equivalent to the O-ring. Install the O-ring into the groove in the water pump base or seal carrier (40 and 50 hp models).

15A. On 25 hp three-cylinder, 30 hp and 60-90 hp models, install a new gasket onto the water pump base. Slide the water pump base over the drive shaft and seat it into

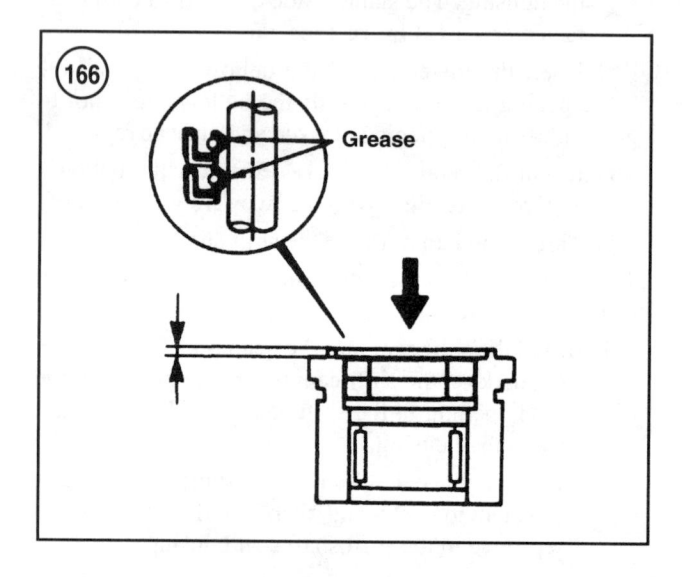

GEARCASE

the gearcase housing bore. Temporarily install one of the water pump screws to secure the base.

15B. On 40 and 50 hp models, slide the seal carrier over the drive shaft. Rotate the carrier so the two projections face forward. Push on the top of the carrier until it fully seats in the housing.

16A. On 25 hp three-cylinder and 30-70 hp models, reassemble the propeller shaft as follows:

   a. Align the cross pin opening in the clutch with the slot in the propeller shaft (**Figure 143**), then slide the clutch over the forward side of the propeller shaft. The *F* mark on the clutch face must face forward.
   b. Insert the follower spring (6, **Figure 144**) into the propeller shaft opening.
   c. On 40-70 hp models, insert the cross pin connector (4, **Figure 144**) into the propeller shaft opening. The pointed end must face the cross pin spring. Rotate the connector until the connector opening aligns with the propeller shaft slot (**Figure 167**) and the cross pin opening.
   d. Insert the cam follower (3, **Figure 144**) into the propeller shaft opening. The pointed end of the follower must face out.
   e. On 40 and 70 hp models, use the propeller shaft to push the follower against a solid object until the connector opening aligns with the clutch opening. Insert the cross pin through the openings (**Figure 168**).
   f. On 25 hp three-cylinder and 30 hp models, push in on the follower to fully collapse the spring. Insert a scribe or another suitable object through the cross pin opening to hold the spring (**Figure 142**). Guide the cross pin (5, **Figure 144**) into one opening while slowly withdrawing the scribe from the other. The spring must fit below the cross pin in the propeller shaft opening.
   g. Release the spring to hold the cross pin. Carefully wind the clutch spring onto the clutch (**Figure 141**). The spring must fit tightly on the clutch and the loops must span both ends of the cross pin. Each loop must lay flat against the clutch.
   h. Apply a coat of Yamaha All-Purpose Grease or equivalent to the cam follower.

16B. On 75-90 hp models, assemble the propeller shaft as follows:

   a. Align the cross pin opening in the clutch with the slot in the propeller shaft (**Figure 143**), then slide the clutch over the forward side of the propeller shaft. The *F* mark on the clutch face must face forward.
   b. Insert the larger diameter ball (5, **Figure 145**) into the propeller shaft opening. Insert the spring (6, **Figure 145**), then the second larger diameter ball, into the opening.
   c. Insert the protrusion on the shift slider (8, **Figure 145**) into the slot in the cam follower.
   d. Apply Yamaha All-Purpose Grease or equivalent to the smaller diameter balls (7, **Figure 145**), then place them into the four recesses in the shift slider (8).
   e. Align the cross pin opening in the shift slider with the corresponding opening in the clutch. Then insert the slider into the propeller shaft opening. Do not allow the smaller diameter balls to become dislodged from the recesses.
   f. Push the slider with the cam follower to collapse the spring (6, **Figure 145**). Rotate and push the slider until the cross pin openings in the slider and clutch align.
   g. Insert the cross pin through the clutch and slider opening.
   h. Carefully wind the clutch spring onto the clutch (**Figure 141**). The spring must fit tightly on the clutch and the loops must span both ends of the cross pin. Each loop must lay flat against the clutch.

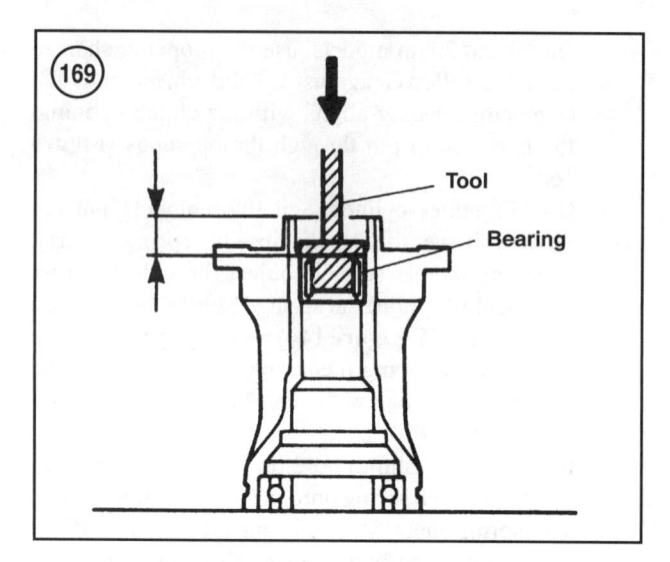

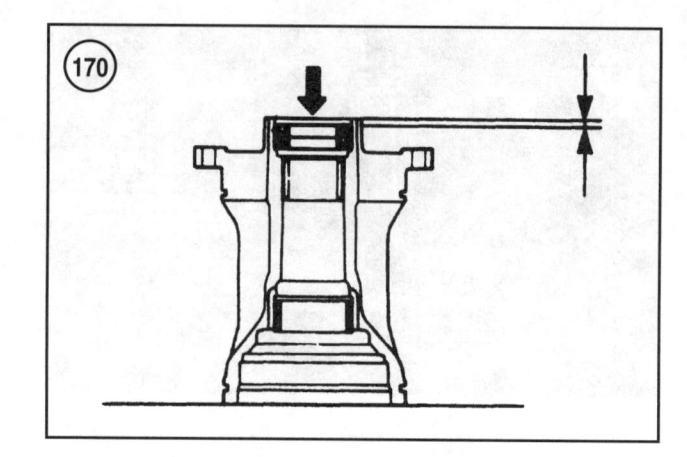

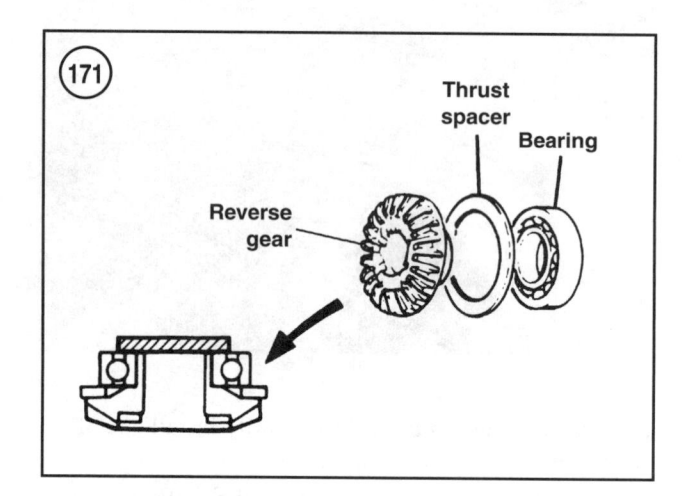

i. Apply a coat of Yamaha All-Purpose Grease or equivalent to the cam follower. Install the shift cam into the recess in the follower.

17. Install a new needle bearing into the bearing carrier, if it was removed, as follows:

   a. Apply a light coat of gearcase lubricant to the outer surfaces of the bushing or bearing bore in the bearing carrier.
   b. Place the bearing carrier on a sturdy work surface with the propeller side facing up.
   c. Insert the needle bearing into the bore with the numbered side facing up.
   d. Select a section of tubing, socket and extension or another tool to use as an installation tool. The tool must be 0.25-0.50 mm (0.010-0.020 in.) smaller in diameter than the bearing case.
   e. Slowly tap the bearing into the bore. Stop frequently to measure the depth. Stop when the bearing reaches the specified depth from the bearing carrier surface to the bearing case (**Figure 169**). The bearing case should be flush with the step in the bore. On 25 hp three-cylinder and 30 hp models, the bearing depth must be 24.0 mm (0.94 in.). On 40 and 50 hp models, the bearing depth must be 23.0-23.5 mm (0.91-0.93 in.). On 60-90 hp models, the bearing depth must be 25.5 mm (1.004 in.).

18. Install new propeller shaft seals into the bearing carrier, if they were removed, as follows:

   a. Apply a coat of Loctite 271 to the outer diameter of the seal casings and the seal bore in the gearcase cap.
   b. Select a section of tubing, a socket and an extension or another suitable tool to use as a seal installation tool. The tool must contact the seal casing, but not contact the seal bore in the bearing carrier.
   c. Place the gearcase cap on a sturdy work surface with the propeller side facing up.
   d. Place the first seal into the bore with the lip side facing up. Carefully drive the seal into the bore until the seal case is just below the bore opening.
   e. Place the second seal into the bore with the lip side facing up. Carefully drive the seal into the bore until it is seated against the first seal.
   f. Slowly tap both seals into the bore until the outer seal is recessed the specified distance below the bore opening (**Figure 170**). Stop frequently to measure the depth. On 25 hp three-cylinder and 30 hp models, the seal depth must be 6.85-6.90 mm (0.270-0.272 in.). On 40 and 50 hp models, the seal depth must be 4.0-4.5 mm (0.16-0.18 in.). On 60-90 hp models, the seal depth must be 5.0 mm (0.20 in.).
   g. Wipe excess Loctite from the seal bore. Apply a coat of Yamaha All-Purpose Grease or equivalent to the seal lips.

GEARCASE

172

Installation tool
Bearing
Gear

173

Carrier
Reverse gear and bearing

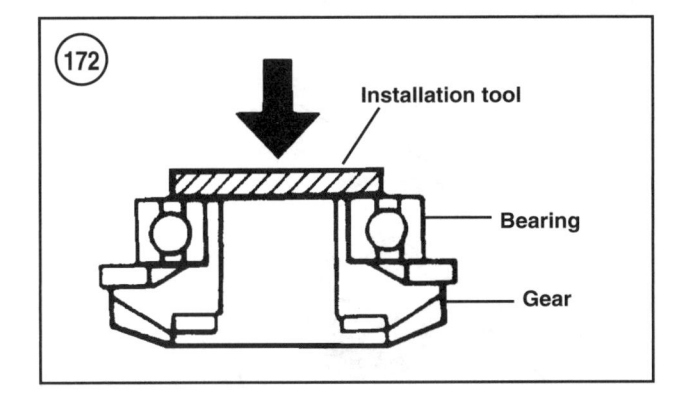

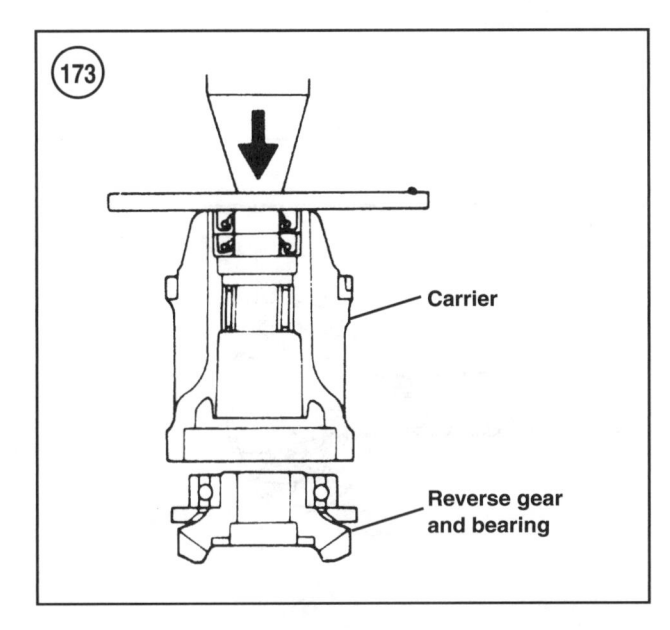

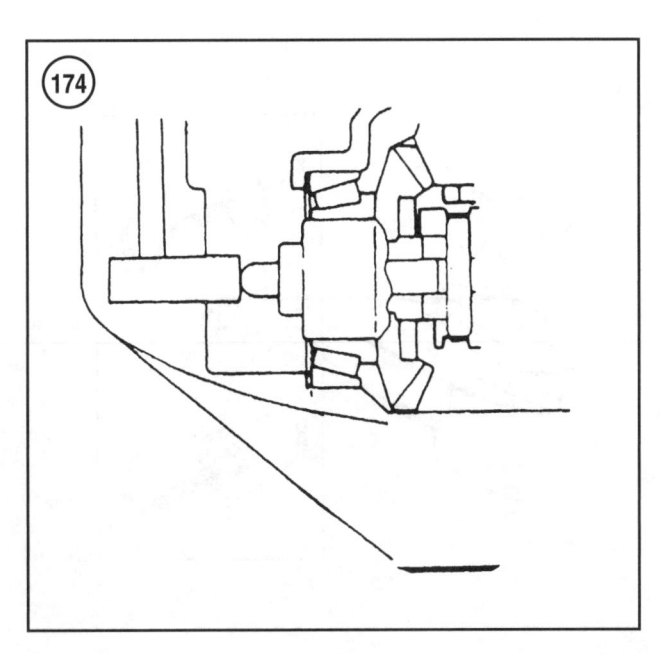

174

19. Install the reverse gear and bearing into the bearing carrier, if they were removed, as follows:
   a. Place the reverse gear on the table of a press with the gear teeth facing down. Apply a light coat of gearcase lubricant to the hub of the reverse gear.
   b. On 40 and 50 hp models, install the reverse gear shim (33, **Figure 131**) onto the hub of the reverse gear.
   c. On 25 hp three-cylinder, 30 hp and 60-90 hp models, install the thrust spacer (**Figure 171**) over the hub of the reverse gear. The beveled side must face toward the reverse gear.
   d. Select a flat piece of steel or another suitable drive to use as a bearing installation tool. The tool must only contact the inner race of the bearing (**Figure 172**).
   e. Install the bearing onto the hub of the gear. Press the bearing onto the gear until it is fully seated.
   f. Apply a light coat of gearcase lubricant to the bearing bore in the bearing carrier. Position the bearing carrier on the bearing as shown in **Figure 173**.
   g. Place a block on the propeller side of the bearing carrier for protection, then press the carrier onto the reverse gear bearing until the bearing fully seats in the bore. Do not allow the carrier to tilt on the bearing.

20. Apply a coat of Yamaha All-Purpose Grease or equivalent to the surfaces, then install the new O-ring into the groove in the bearing carrier.

21A. On 25 hp three-cylinder and 30-70 hp models, install the propeller shaft as follows:
   a. Position the gearcase so the drive shaft faces up.
   b. Guide the propeller shaft into the opening in the forward gear. Seat the propeller shaft against the gear. The cam follower must contact the shift cam (**Figure 174**).
   c. On 25 hp three-cylinder and 30-50 hp models, install the thrust washer over the propeller shaft. Seat the washer against the step on the propeller shaft. If the washer is being reused, position the washer as indicated by the mark made before removal.

21B. On 75-90 hp models, install the propeller shaft and shift shaft as follows:
   a. Position the gearcase so the drive shaft faces up. Install the E-clip into the groove in the shift shaft.
   b. Apply Yamaha All-Purpose Grease or equivalent to the shift cam recess in the shift follower. Insert the shift cam into the recess as indicated in **Figure 175**.
   c. Guide the shift follower through the opening in the forward gear. Do not rotate the propeller shaft during installation. The shift cam must remain horizontal.

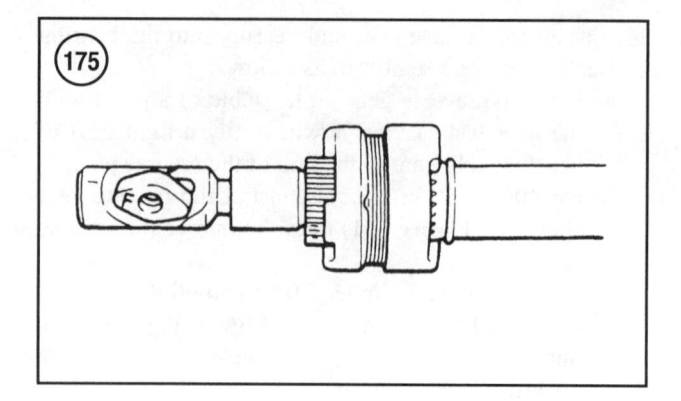

d. Install the shift shaft into the gearcase bore. Guide the tip on the bottom of the shaft into the opening in the shift cam. Seat the shift shaft into the shift cam. Rotate the shift shaft to check for correct engagement. The clutch must move with the shift shaft.

e. Install a new O-ring into the groove in the seal carrier. Slide the seal carrier over the shift shaft. Push on the carrier until it fully seats in the gearcase.

f. Secure the carrier with the two screws (**Figure 133**). Tighten the screws to the general torque specification in Chapter One. On 25 hp three-cylinder, 30 hp and 60-90 hp models, install the large diameter shim into the gearcase. Seat the shim against the step.

22. Carefully slide the bearing carrier and reverse gear over the propeller shaft. Rotate the drive shaft while guiding the carrier into the gearcase opening.

23. On 25 hp three-cylinder, 30 hp and 60-90 hp models, secure the bearing carrier as follows:

a. Seat the carrier in the gearcase.

b. Rotate the carrier to align the slots for the locating key (**Figure 176**). Insert the key into the slot.

c. Install the locking tab washer onto the bearing carrier. The raised areas on the carrier must fit into the slots in the washer.

d. Hand-thread the cover nut into the gearcase.

e. Slip the cover nut tool over the propeller nut. Engage the lugs of the cover nut tool onto the cover nut lugs. On 25 hp three-cylinder and 30 hp models, use Yamaha part No. YB-6075/90890-06509. On 60-90 hp models, use Yamaha part No. YB-6075/90890-06513.

f. Turn the cover nut clockwise and tighten it to the specification in **Table 1**.

g. Use a pair of slip joint pliers to bend at least one of the locking tabs (**Figure 177**) into a slot between the cover nut lugs. Bend down tabs that do not align with the slots. Tighten the cover nut slightly if nec-

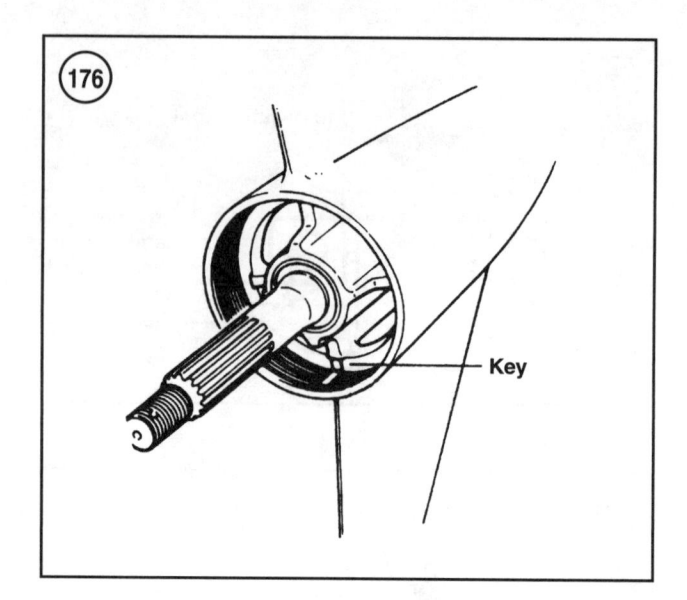

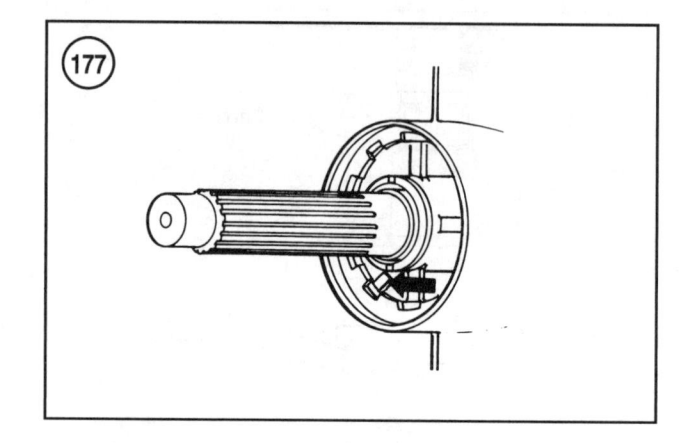

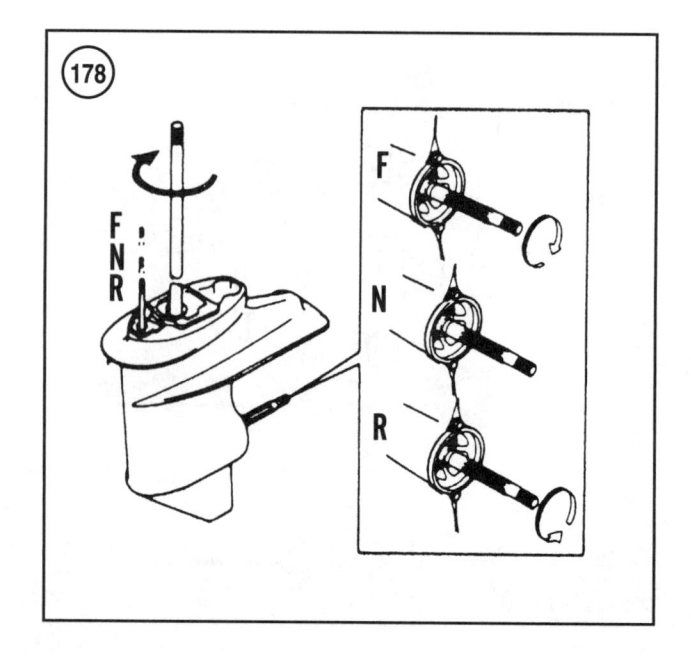

GEARCASE

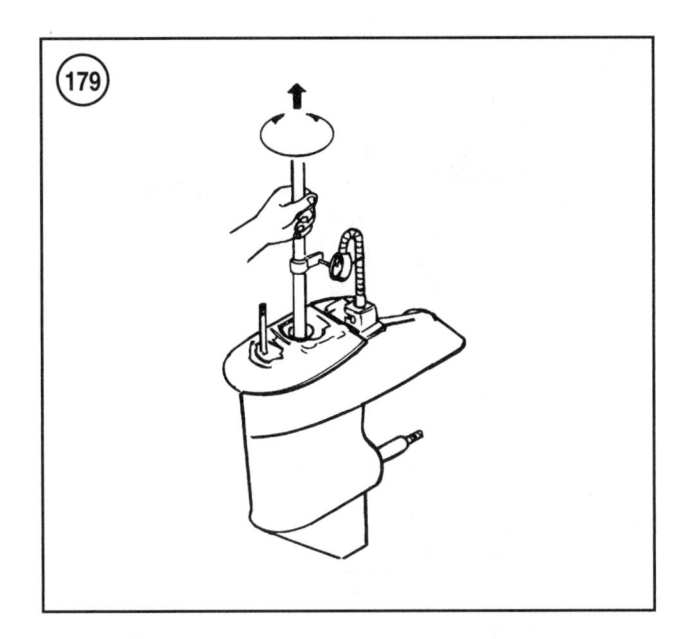

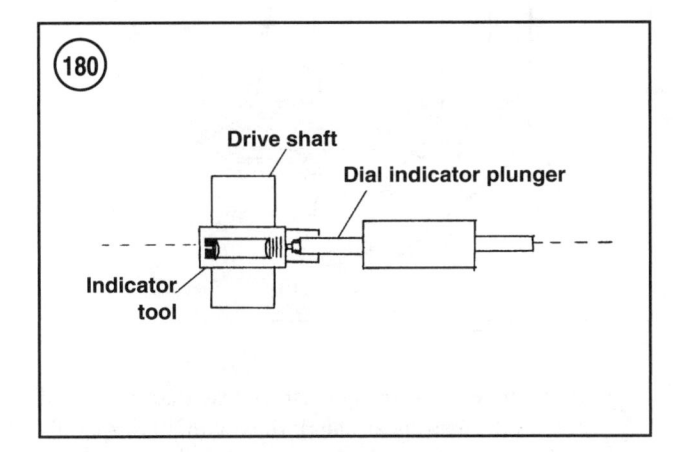

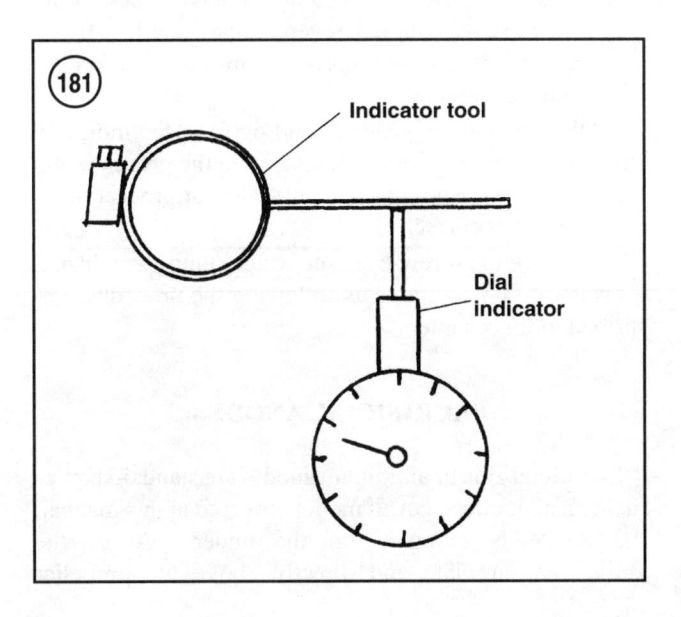

essary to align the tab and slot. Never loosen the cover nut to align the tab.

CAUTION
Use very light force when moving the drive shaft during backlash measurement. Readings will be inaccurate if excessive force is applied to the drive shaft.

NOTE
Remove all water pump components before measuring gear backlash. The drag created by the water pump components will hinder accurate measurement. Temporarily remove the drive shaft seal carrier or water pump base during backlash measurements.

NOTE
Make sure all gearcase lubricant is drained from the gearcase before measuring gear backlash. The cushion effect of the lubricant on the gear teeth will cause the readings to be inaccurate.

24. Measure and correct the gear backlash if a new gearcase housing, gear, drive shaft, pinion gear shim or bearing was installed during the repair. Measure and correct the gearcase backlash as follows:

   a. Pull up, push down or rotate the shift shaft to shift the gearcase into neutral gear (**Figure 178**).
   b. Attach a dial indicator to the gearcase with a suitable clamping device (**Figure 179**). Dial indicators and mounts are available from most tool suppliers. The mount must remain rigid for the dial indicator, or the backlash measurements will be inaccurate.
   c. Clamp the backlash indicator tool (Yamaha part No. YB-06265/90890-06706) to the drive shaft.
   d. Arrange the dial indicator mount so the dial indicator plunger is at the same height as the indicator tool (**Figure 180**) and the plunger is at a 90° angle to the indicator arm (**Figure 181**). Reposition the dial indicator so the plunger is in line with the mark on the indicator tool.
   e. Install a two-jaw puller onto the bearing carrier and propeller shaft as shown in **Figure 182**. Use Yamaha part Nos. YB-06234/90890-06501, 06503 and 06504 or an equivalent. Engage the jaws to the carrier and position the puller bolt against the end of the propeller shaft. Tighten the puller bolt to 5.0 N•m (71 in.-lb.).
   f. Rotate the drive shaft so the drive shaft points down.
   g. Push down on the drive and observe the dial indicator while lightly rotating the drive shaft clockwise

and counterclockwise. Note the dial indicator reading when the drive shaft reaches its free movement limit in each direction. Record the amount of dial indicator movement as forward gear backlash.

h. Remove the two-jaw puller. Install the propeller backward onto the propeller shaft (**Figure 183**). Do not install the thrust washer between the propeller and the gearcase. Install the thrust washer, then the propeller nut, onto the propeller shaft. Tighten the propeller nut to 5.0 N•m (71 in.-lb.). Shift the gearcase into reverse gear and hold the drive shaft while tightening the propeller nut.

i. Push down on the drive shaft and observe the dial indicator while lightly rotating the drive shaft clockwise and counterclockwise. Note the dial indicator reading when the drive shaft reaches its free movement limit in each direction. Record the amount of dial indicator movement as reverse gear backlash. Remove the propeller and backlash measuring instruments.

25. The forward and reverse gear backlash measurements should be within the specification in **Table 2**. If both backlash measurements are correct, proceed to Step 28. If either backlash reading is incorrect, refer to the following:

   a. If the forward and reverse gear backlash is greater than specified, install a thinner pinion gear shim.
   b. If the forward and reverse gear backlash is less than specified, install a thicker pinion gear shim.
   c. If the forward gear backlash is greater than specified and the reverse gear backlash is within the specification, install a thicker forward gear shim and repeat the measurement.
   d. If the forward gear backlash is less than specified and the reverse gear backlash is within the specification, check for an improperly installed forward gear bearing race. If the race is installed correctly, install a thinner forward gear shim.
   e. If the reverse gear backlash is greater than specified and the forward gear backlash is within the specification (only 40 and 50 hp models), install a thicker reverse gear shim.
   f. If the reverse gear backlash is less than specified and the forward gear backlash is within the specification (only 40 and 50 hp models), check for an improperly installed reverse gear bearing. If the bearing is installed correctly, install a thinner reverse gear shim.
   g. If the reverse gear backlash is greater than specified and the forward gear backlash is within the specification (25, 30 and 60-90 hp models), install a thinner reverse gear shim.
   h. If the reverse gear backlash is less than specified and the forward gear backlash is within the specification (25, 30 and 60-90 hp models), check for an improperly installed reverse gear bearing. If the bearing is installed correctly, install a thicker reverse gear shim.

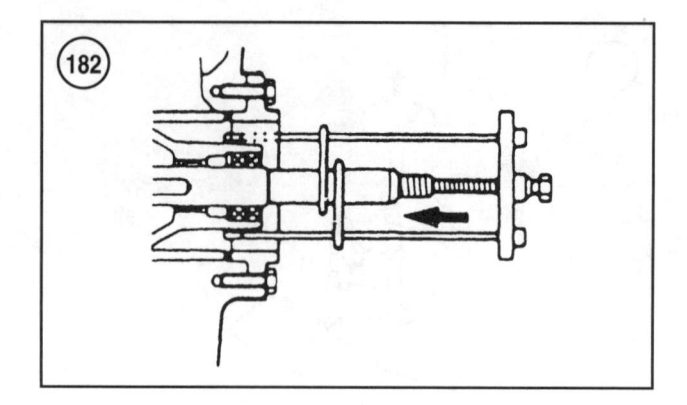

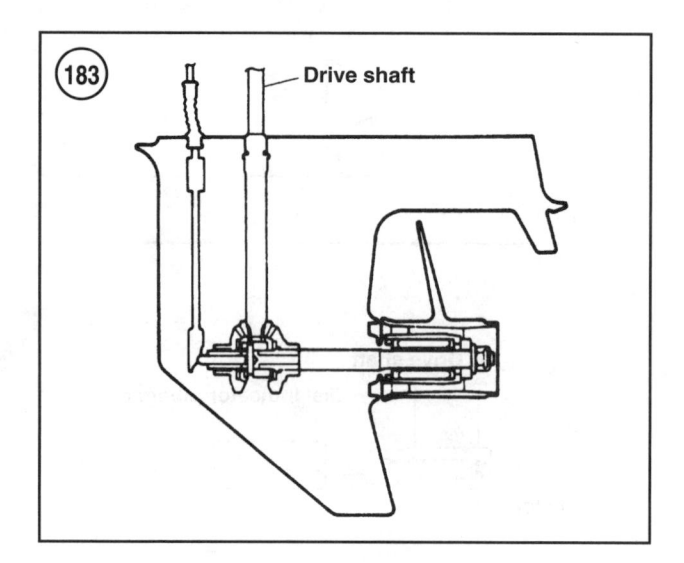

26. Disassemble the gearcase and perform the indicated shim change or inspection. Reassemble the gearcase and repeat the backlash measurements. Do not proceed until the backlash is correct.

27. Remove the screw from the water pump base. Install all water pump components following the procedure described in this chapter.

SACRIFICIAL ANODES

Sacrificial zinc or aluminum anodes are standard equipment on all models. On all models covered in this manual, the anode is mounted on the under side of the antiventilation plate and directly above the propeller

GEARCASE

Figure 184

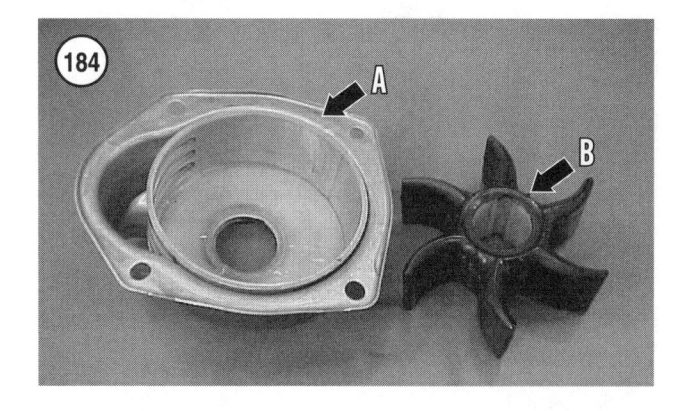

shaft. A flat anodic plate is used on 2-15 hp models. The trim tab is the anode on 20-90 hp models. Refer to the expanded illustration of each gearcase in the appropriate disassembly procedure in this chapter for exact anode mounting locations.

Inspect the anode anytime the gearcase is serviced and at the intervals listed in Chapter Three. Anodes are inspected visually and tested electrically. The anodes must have good electrical continuity to ground or they will not function. Anodes cannot be painted or coated with any material.

Visual Inspection

Check for loose mounting hardware. Make sure the anodes are not painted and check the amount of deterioration. Replace anodes if they are 1/2 their original size (1/2 gone). Test the electrical continuity of each anode after installation as described in this chapter.

Electrical Test

This test requires an ohmmeter.

1. Calibrate the ohmmeter on the R × 1 scale.
2. Connect one ohmmeter lead to the anode being tested. Connect the other ohmmeter lead to a good ground point on the gearcase on which the anode is mounted. The meter should indicate continuity.
3. If the meter indicates an open circuit, remove the anode and clean the mounting surfaces of the anode, gearcase and mounting hardware. Reinstall the anode and retest the continuity.
4. Test the continuity of the gearcase to the engine and negative battery post by connecting one ohmmeter lead to the negative battery cable and the other ohmmeter lead to a good ground point on the lower gearcase. The meter should indicate continuity.
5. If the meter indicates an open circuit, check the electrical continuity of the lower gearcase to the drive shaft housing, the upper drive shaft housing to the power head and the power head to the negative battery terminal. Check for loose mounting hardware, broken or missing ground straps, or excessive corrosion. Repair as necessary to establish a good electrical ground path.

COMPONENT INSPECTION

Never compromise a proper repair by using damaged or questionable components.

Prior to inspection, thoroughly clean all components using clean solvent. Note component orientation before cleaning when necessary. Use compressed air to dry all components then arrange them in an orderly fashion on a clean work surface. Never allow bearings to spin when drying them with compressed air.

Make sure all components have been removed, then use pressurized water to clean the gearcase housing. Inspect all passages and crevices for debris or contaminants. Use compressed air to thoroughly dry the gearcase.

WARNING
Never allow bearings to spin when drying them with compressed air. The bearing may fly apart or explode and cause personal injury.

Gearcase Housing

Inspect the gearcase for cracked, dented or excessively pitted surfaces. Damage to the skeg can be economically repaired by a propeller shop. Damage to other surfaces may allow water leaks and subsequent failure of the internal components.

Inspect the locating pins for bent pins and worn or elongated openings. Replace a housing with elongated openings. Otherwise, the drive shaft may be operated with improper alignment. This could cause the failure of the drive shaft and other engine components.

Water Pump Inspection

1. Inspect the impeller (B, **Figure 184**) for brittle, missing or burnt vanes. Squeeze the vanes toward the hub and release the vanes. The vanes should spring back to the extended position. Replace the impeller if there are damaged, burnt, brittle or stiff vanes.
2. Inspect the water tube, grommets and seals for a burned appearance, cracks or brittle material. Replace the water tube, grommets and seals if there are any defects.

3. Inspect the wear plate for warp, wear grooves, melted plastic or other damage. Replace the wear plate if a groove is worn in the plate or there are any other defects.
4. Inspect the water pump insert (A, **Figure 184**) for a burned, worn or damaged surface. Replace the insert or water pump body if there are any defects.
5. Inspect the water pump body for melted plastic or other indications of overheating. Replace the water pump body and the water pump base if there are any defects.

Propeller Shaft Inspection

1. Position the propeller shaft on V blocks (**Figure 185**). Rotate the shaft and check for deflection or wobble. Replace the propeller shaft if there is visible deflection or wobble.
2. Inspect the propeller shaft for corrosion, and damaged or worn surfaces (**Figure 186**). Inspect the propeller shaft splines and threaded area (B, **Figure 187**) for twisted splines or damaged propeller nut threads.
3. Inspect the bearing contact areas (A, **Figure 187**) at the front and midpoint of the propeller shaft. Replace the propeller if there are discolored areas, rough surfaces, transferred bearing material or other defects.
4. Inspect the propeller shaft at the seal contact areas. Replace the propeller shaft if deep grooves are worn in the surface.
5. Place V blocks at the points indicated in **Figure 185**. Use a dial indicator to measure the shaft deflection at the rear bearing support area. Securely mount the dial indicator. Observe the dial indicator movement and slowly rotate the propeller shaft. Replace the propeller shaft if the needle movement exceeds 0.15 mm (0.006 in). Propeller straightening is not recommended.

Gear and Clutch Inspection

1. Inspect the clutch (B, **Figure 188**) and gears for chips, damage, wear or rounded surfaces. Replace the clutch and gears if these conditions are found on either component.
2. Inspect the gear (A, **Figure 188**) for worn, broken or damaged teeth. Check for pitted, rough or excessively worn highly polished surfaces. Replace all of the gears if any of these conditions are found. This is especially important on engines with high operating hours.

NOTE
Replace all gears if any of the gears must be replaced. A wear pattern forms on the gears in a few hours of use. The wear patterns will be disturbed if a new gear is installed with used gears.

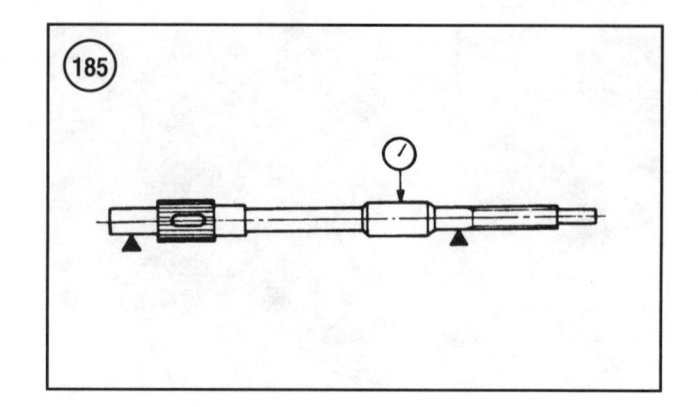

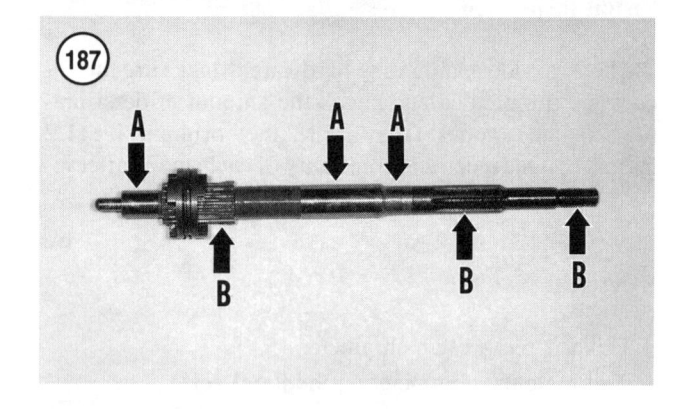

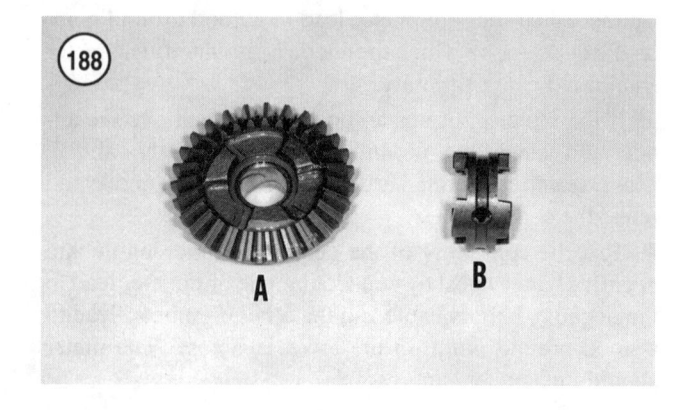

GEARCASE

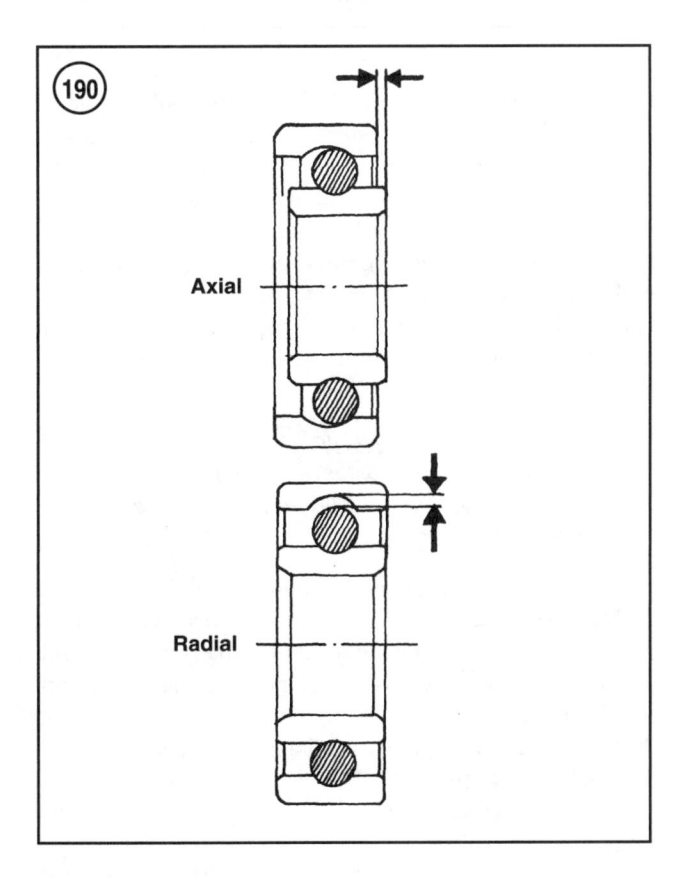

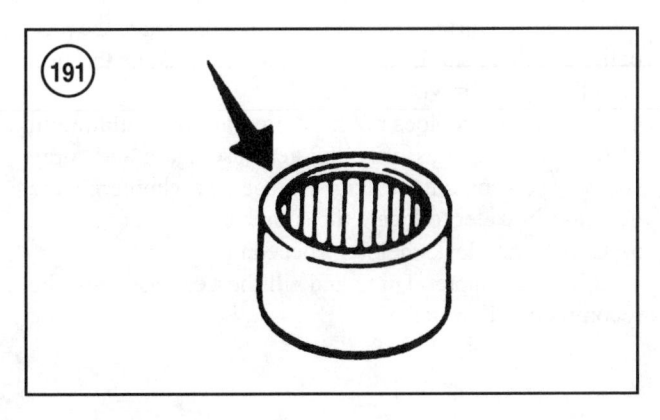

Bearing Inspection

1. Clean all bearings thoroughly in solvent and air dry them before inspection. Replace the bearings if the gear lubricant drained from the gearcase is heavily contaminated with metal particles. The particles tend to collect inside the bearings.
2. Inspect the roller bearings and bearing races (**Figure 189**) for pitting, rusting, discoloration or roughness. Inspect the bearing race for highly polished or unevenly worn surfaces. Replace the bearing assembly if any of these defects are found.
3. Rotate the ball bearings and check for rough operation. Move the bearing in the directions shown in **Figure 190**. Check for *axial* or *radial* looseness. Replace the bearing if the operation is rough or if the bearing is loose.
4. Inspect the needle bearings (**Figure 191**) located in the bearing carrier, forward gear and drive shaft seal, and bearing housing. Replace the bearing if there are flattened rollers, discoloration, rusting, roughness or pitting.
5. Inspect the propeller shaft and drive shaft at the bearing contact area. Replace the drive shaft or propeller shaft and the needle bearing if there is discoloration, pitting, transferred bearing material or roughness.

Shift Cam and Related Components Inspection

1. Inspect the bore in the propeller shaft for debris, damage or excessive wear. Clean debris from the bore.
2. Inspect the clutch spring for damage, corrosion or weak spring tension and replace it if it is defective.
3. Inspect the cross pin for damage, roughness or excessive wear. Replace as required. Inspect the cam follower and spring for damage or corrosion and replace as required.
4. Inspect the cam follower for cracked, broken or worn areas. Replace any worn or defective components.
5. Inspect the shift cam located at the lower end of the shift shaft for wear, chips, cracks or corrosion.
6. Inspect the shift shaft for excessive wear and a bent or twisted condition. Inspect the shift shaft bushing for cracks or a worn shift shaft bore. Replace the bushing or shift shaft if there are defects.

Shims, Spacers, Fasteners and Washers Inspection

1. Inspect all shims for bent, rusted or damaged surfaces. Replace any shim that does not appear to be like new.
2. Spacers are used in various locations in the gearcase. Some function as thrust bearings. Replace them if there

are worn areas or if they are bent, corroded or damaged. Only replace them with the correct part. In most cases, they are of a certain dimension and made with a specified material.

3. Replace locking nuts unless they are in excellent condition. Always replace the pinion nut during final assembly.

4. Replace any worn or damaged washers on the pinion gear. These washers are sometimes used as a thrust loaded surface and are subject to wear.

Seals, O-rings and Gaskets

Replace seals when they are removed and when a shaft that contacts the seal is replaced. If the seal must be reused, inspect it for a bent or damaged casing and a worn, weathered, cracked or damaged seal lip. Never use a damaged or questionable seal. A damaged seal will probably leak and cause extensive damage to internal gearcase components.

Replace O-rings when they are removed. If an O-ring must be reused, inspect it for torn, deteriorated or flattened surfaces. Never use a damage or questionable O-ring.

Never reuse gaskets. A gasket is made of a material that forms into small imperfections in a mating surface. With a few exceptions, gaskets are not designed to maintain good seal after the initial installation.

Bushings

Inspect the bushings for worn, elongated or discolored surfaces. Always replace the bushing when replacing the shaft or components that contact the bushing.

Grommets

Replace grommets that are split, deformed or hard and brittle. Check for improper installation if the removed grommet is deformed.

GEARCASE PRESSURE TEST

Pressure test the gearcase anytime the gearcase has been disassembled. If the gearcase fails the pressure test, find and correct the source of the leak. Failure to correct a leak will result in major gearcase damage from water entering the gearcase or lubricant leaking out.

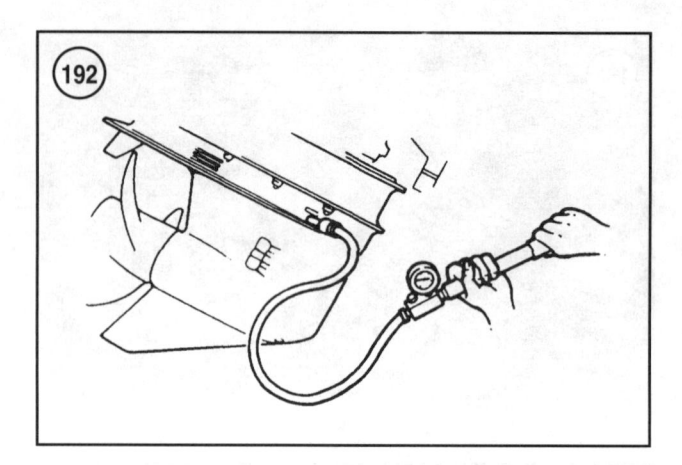

Pressure testers are available from most tool suppliers. If necessary, a pressure tester can be fabricated using a common fuel primer bulb, air pressure gauge, fittings and hoses. If necessary, use the fitting from a gearcase lubricant pump. When using a fabricated pressure tester, clamp the hoses shut with locking pliers after applying pressure with the primer bulb. Otherwise, air may leak past the check valve in the primer bulb, giving a false indication of a leak. If possible, use a commercially available gearcase pressure tester.

NOTE
Drain the gearcase lubricant before pressure testing. Refer to Chapter Four if necessary.

Pressure test the gearcase as follows:

1. Make sure the gearcase lubricant has been completely drained. Then make sure the fill/drain plug is installed and properly tightened. Always use a new sealing washer on the fill plug.

2. Remove the vent plug. Install a pressure tester into the vent hole. See **Figure 192**. Tighten the tester securely. Always use a new sealing washer on the pressure tester fitting.

3. Pressurize the gearcase to 10 psi (69 kPa) for at least five minutes. During this time, periodically rotate the propeller and drive shafts, and move the shift linkage through its full range of travel.

4. If the gearcase does not hold pressure for a minimum of five minutes, pressurize the gearcase again and spray soapy water on all sealing surfaces or submerge the gearcase in water to locate the source of the leak.

5. Correct any leaks before proceeding.

6. Refer to Chapter Three and fill the gearcase with the recommended lubricant.

GEARCASE

Table 1 GEARCASE TORQUE SPECIFICATIONS

Fastener	N•m	in.-lb.	ft.-lb.
Bearing carrier bolts			
40 and 50 hp	16	–	12
Cover nut			
25 three-cylinder and 30 hp	90	–	66
60-90 hp	145	–	107
Drain/fill/vent plugs			
3 hp	7	62	–
Gearcase cap bolts			
4 and 5 hp			
First sequence	3	27	–
Second sequence	8	71	–
Gearcase mounting			
20-90 hp	40	–	30
Pinion nut			
9.9 and 15 hp	26	–	19
20 and 25 hp two-cylinder	51	–	38
25 three-cylinder and 30 hp	50	–	37
40-70 hp	75	–	55
75-90 hp	95	–	70
Propeller nut			
6-15 hp	17	–	13
20-30 hp	35	–	26
40 and 50 hp	30	–	22
60-90 hp	35	–	26
Shift shaft connector			
4-8 hp	10	89	–
Water inlet screen			
9.9 and 15 hp	5	44	–
40 and 50 hp	5	44	–
Water pump housing			
6 and 8 hp	11	97	–

Table 2 GEAR BACKLASH SPECIFICATIONS

Model	Specification
2 hp	0.27-0.99 mm (0.011-0.039 in.)
3 hp	
Forward gear	0.15-1.22 mm (0.006-0.048 in.)
4 and 5 hp	
Forward gear backlash	0.28-0.71 mm (0.011-0.028 in.)
Reverse gear backlash	0.28-0.71 mm (0.011-0.028 in.)
6 and 8 hp	
Forward gear backlash	0.25-0.75 mm (0.010-0.029 in.)
Reverse gear backlash	0.25-0.75 mm (0.010-0.029 in.)
9.9 and 15 hp	
Forward gear backlash	0.19-0.86 mm (0.007-0.034 in.)
Reverse gear backlash	0.95-1.65 mm (0.037-0.065 in.)
20 and 25 hp two-cylinder	
Forward gear backlash	0.32-0.53 mm (0.013-0.021 in.)
Reverse gear backlash	0.85-1.17 mm (0.033-0.046 in.)
25 two-cylinder and 30 hp	
Forward gear backlash	0.20-0.50 mm (0.008-0.020 in.)
Reverse gear backlash	0.70-1.00 mm (0.028-0.039 in.)
40 and 50 hp	
Forward gear backlash	0.18-0.45 mm (0.007-0.018 in.)
Reverse gear backlash	0.71-0.98 mm (0.028-0.038 in.)

(continued)

Table 2 GEAR BACKLASH SPECIFICATIONS (continued)

Model	Specification
60 and 70 hp	
Forward gear backlash	0.09-0.28 mm (0.004-0.011 in.)
Reverse gear backlash	0.75-1.13 mm (0.030-0.044 in.)
75-90 hp	
Forward gear backlash	0.08-0.25 mm (0.003-0.010 in.)
Reverse gear backlash	0.67-1.00 mm (0.026-0.39 in.)

Chapter Nine

Jet Drive

Jet drives (**Figure 1**) offer significant advantages for shallow water operation. The absence of the propeller and gearcase allows the engine to operate in areas much too shallow for a standard propeller drive gearcase.

A drawback of having excellent shallow water running ability is a substantial reduction in efficiency. Jet drive model descriptions reflect the reduction in performance associated with the installation of a jet drive. The performance is generally equivalent to 70 percent of the same basic engine with a standard propeller drive gearcase. Refer to the following for comparison.

When a jet drive is installed:
1. A 40 hp model becomes a 28 jet.
2. A 50 hp model becomes a 35 jet.
3. A 90 hp model becomes a 65 jet.

Service to the power head, ignition system, electrical system, fuel system and power trim and tilt system is the same as on propeller-driven outboard models. Refer to the appropriate chapter and service section for the engine model using a propeller gearcase. Refer to **Table 1** for specific torque specifications and Chapter One for general torque specifications. Use the general torque specifications for fasteners not listed in **Table 1**.

JET DRIVE OPERATION

Jet Drive Components

The major components of the jet drive include the impeller (1, **Figure 2**), intake opening (2), volute tube (3) and the outlet nozzle (4). The impeller is connected to a shaft supported by bearings on one end and the crankshaft on the other end. When the engine is running the impeller turns.

The rotating impeller pulls water through the intake opening and pushes it through the volute tube (3, **Figure 2**). The volute tube directs the water toward the outlet nozzle (4, **Figure 2**). The water flowing from the outlet nozzle provides thrust to move the boat. Thrust increases with increased impeller speed.

Thrust Control

Operational direction is controlled by a thrust gate. The thrust gate is controlled by an engine-mounted directional control cable. When the directional control lever is placed in the full forward position (**Figure 3**), the thrust gate should completely uncover the jet drive housing outlet nozzle opening and seat securely against the rubber pad on the jet drive pump housing. This gate position allows full water flow from the outlet nozzle for maximum forward thrust. When the directional control lever is placed in full reverse position (**Figure 4**), the thrust gate should completely block the pump housing outlet nozzle opening. This directs water under the pump for reverse thrust. Reverse thrust is far less efficient than forward thrust, resulting in less power in the reverse direction. The neutral thrust gate position is midway between full forward and full reverse (**Figure 5**). In neutral, some of the water exiting the nozzle is directed under the jet drive to balance the thrust and there is little if any boat movement.

The boat is steered by pivoting the engine port or starboard as with the standard propeller drive gearcases.

CAUTION
Steering response is limited and unpredictable in reverse. Practice common backing maneuvers in open water until you are comfortable with the jet drive backing characteristics.

Mounting Height

A jet drive outboard must be mounted higher on the transom plate than an equivalent propeller-driven outboard. However, if the jet drive is mounted too high, air enters the jet drive resulting in cavitation and power loss. If the jet drive is mounted too low, excessive drag, water spray and loss in speed occur.

Set the initial height of the outboard motor as follows:
1. Place a straightedge against the boat bottom (not the keel) with the end of the straightedge against the jet drive intake. See **Figure 2**.
2. The fore edge of the water intake housing must align with the top edge of the straightedge (**Figure 2**).
3. Secure the outboard at this setting, then test run the boat.
4. If the outboard over-revs or has a loss of thrust due to cavitation, lower the outboard in 6.35 mm (1/4 in.) increments until operation is uniform.
5. If operation is uniform at the initial setting, raise the outboard in 6.35 mm (1/4 in.) increments until cavitation occurs. Then lower the motor to the last uniform setting.

NOTE
A slight amount of cavitation in rough water and during turns is normal. However, excessive cavitation damages the impeller and can cause the power head to overheat.

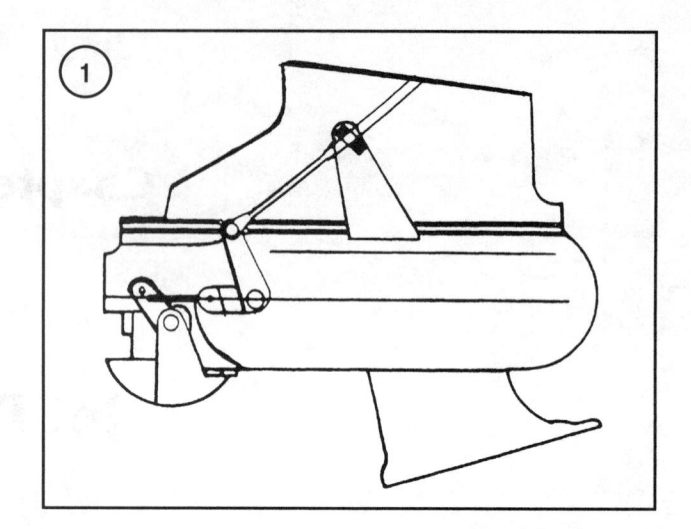

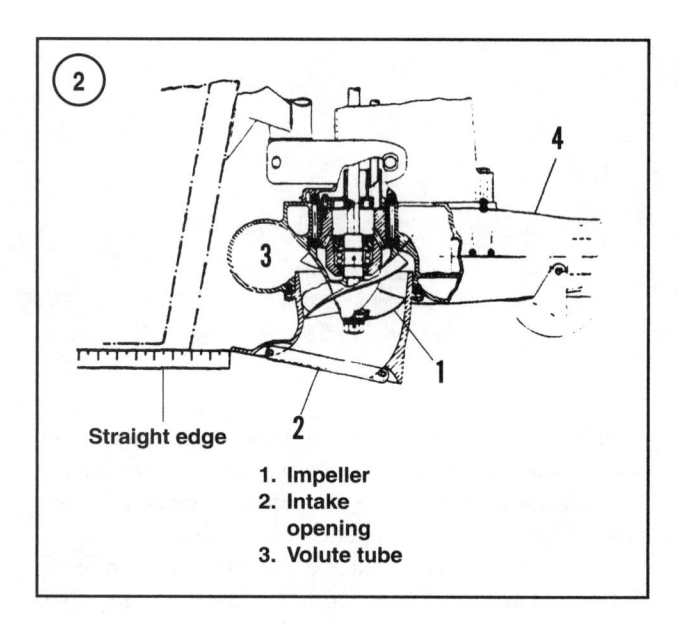

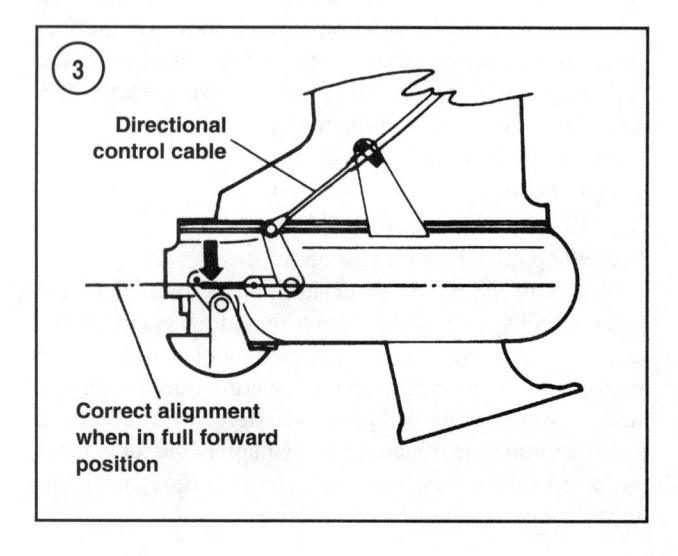

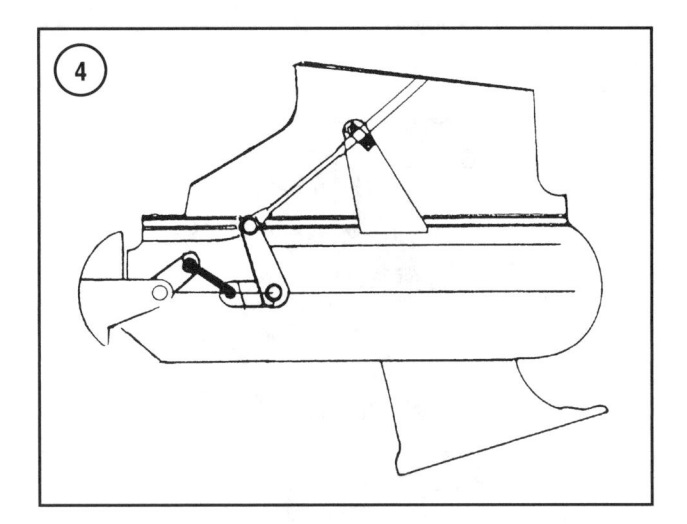

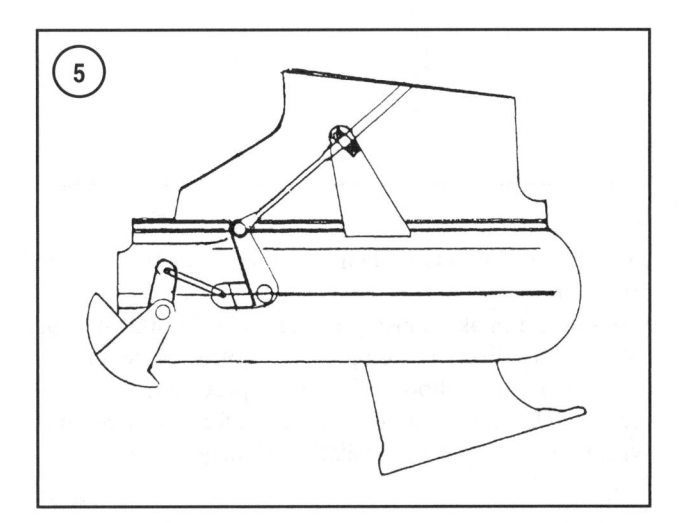

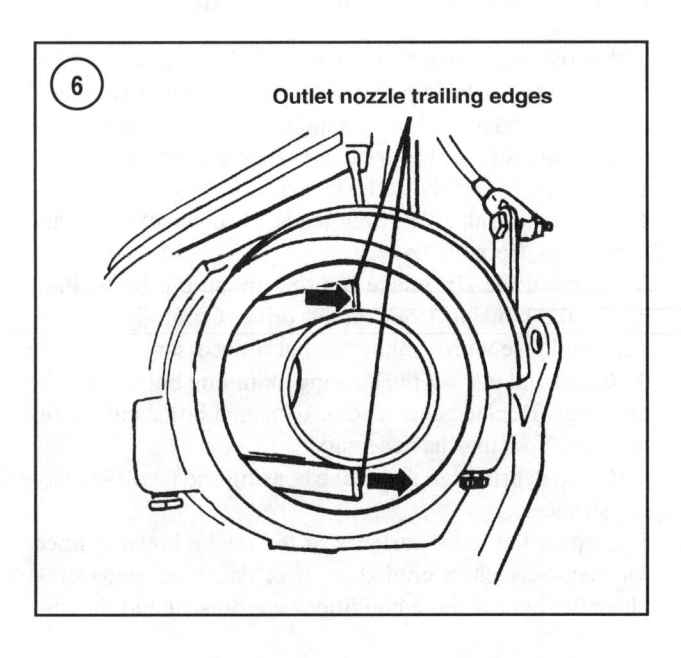

JET DRIVE

NOTE
The outboard should be vertical when the boat is on plane. Adjust the trim setting as needed. If the outboard trim setting is altered, check the outboard height and adjust it if necessary as previously described.

Steering Torque

A minor adjustment to the trailing edge of the drive outlet nozzle may be made if the boat pulls in one direction when the boat and outboard are pointed straight-ahead. If the boat pulls to the starboard side, bend the top and bottom trailing edge of the jet drive outlet nozzle 1.6 mm (1/16 in.) toward the starboard side of the jet drive. See **Figure 6**.

JET DRIVE REPAIR

Since outboards with jet drives typically operate in very shallow water, certain components are susceptible to wear. A jet drive may ingest a considerable amount of sand, rock and other debris during normal operation. Components that require frequent inspection are the engine water pump, impeller and intake housing liner. Other components that may require frequent inspection or repair include the bearing housing, drive shaft bearings and drive shaft.

Water Pump

The water pump used to cool the power head is virtually identical to the pump used on standard propeller drive gearcases. Like the standard propeller drive gearcase, the water pump is connected to and driven by the drive shaft.

Refer to *Water Pump* in Chapter Nine for water pump inspection and repair procedures. Use the procedures for the horsepower the engine would be rated at if a propeller drive gearcase were installed.

Flushing the Cooling System

Sand and other debris will quickly wear the impeller and other components of the water pump. Frequently inspect the water pump if the engine is operated in sand or silt laden water. Sand and other debris may collect in the power head cooling water passages. These deposits will eventually lead to overheating and increased corrosion. Flush the power head after each period of operation. This can add years to the life of the outboard. Refer to Chapter

Three for power head flushing procedures and water pump maintenance intervals.

Bearing Lubrication

Lubricate the jet pump bearing(s) after *each* operating period, after every 10 hours of operation and prior to storage. Also, pump additional grease into the bearing(s) to purge moisture after every 30 hours of operation. Refer to Chapter Three for bearing housing lubrication procedures.

Impeller-to-Housing Clearance

Worn or damaged surfaces on the impeller or the intake housing allow water to slip past the impeller and cause decreased efficiency. Measure the impeller clearance if engine rpm increases and there is a loss in top speed or power.

1. Remove all spark plug leads and disconnect both battery cables from the battery.
2. Locate the intake grate on the bottom of the jet drive. Use long feeler gauges to measure the clearance between the impeller edges and the intake housing as indicated in **Figure 7**. Carefully rotate the flywheel and check the clearance in several locations. Determine the *average* clearance measured.
3. Correct average clearance is approximately 0.8 mm (0.030 in.). Small variations are acceptable as long as the impeller is not contacting the intake housing and the engine is not exceeding the maximum rated engine speed. Refer to *Shimming the Impeller* in this chapter if the clearance is excessive or the impeller is contacting the intake housing.
4. Attach the spark plug leads. Connect the battery cables to the battery.

Removal and Installation

> **WARNING**
> *Always disconnect all spark plugs and both battery cables at the battery terminals before working with the jet drive to prevent accidental starting.*

Disconnect the directional control cable (**Figure 3**) from the thrust gate lever. Remove the intake housing to access the jet drive mounting bolts. Refer to *Intake Housing Removal and Installation* in this chapter for procedures. Refer to Chapter Nine for removal and installation procedures for the propeller drive gearcase and remove the jet drive from the engine. Disregard the references to the shift shaft when removing or installing a jet drive unit.

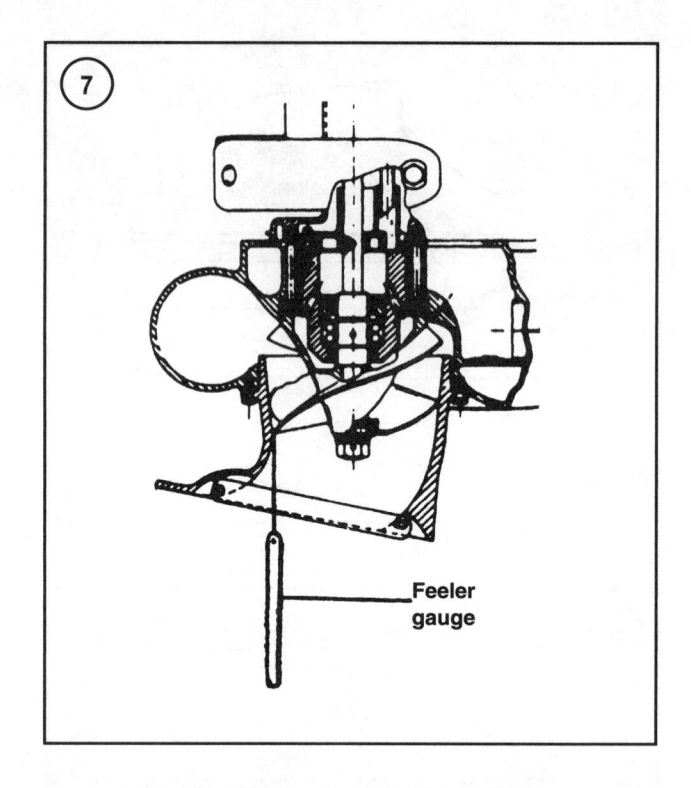

Install the intake housing as described in this chapter. Check and correct the directional control cable adjustment after installation. Adjustment procedures are described in Chapter Four. Always check for proper cooling system operation after installation of the jet drive.

Intake Housing Removal and Installation

Remove the intake housing when shimming the impeller or to inspect the impeller and housing for worn or damaged components. For component identification and orientation, refer to **Figure 8** or **Figure 9** during the disassembly and assembly of the jet drive.

1. Disconnect all spark plug leads. Disconnect both battery cables from the battery.
2. Remove the six intake housing mounting bolts. Pull the intake housing from the jet drive. Carefully tap the housing loose with a rubber mallet if necessary.
3. Clean and inspect the housing mounting bolts and bolt openings. Replace corroded or damaged bolts and repair threaded openings as necessary.
4. Clean debris from the intake housing and jet drive mating surfaces.
5. Inspect the inner surfaces of the intake housing liner for deep scratches, eroded areas or damaged areas. Replace the liner if these conditions are present and the im-

JET DRIVE

peller-to-housing clearance is excessive. Refer to *Intake Housing Liner Replacement* in this chapter for procedures.

6. Install the intake housing onto the jet drive housing with the lower end facing the rear. Apply Yamaha All-Purpose Grease or equivalent to the threads of the bolts. Tighten them to the specification in **Table 1**.

7. Connect all spark plug leads. Connect the battery leads to the battery. Run the engine and check for proper operation before putting the engine into service.

Intake Housing Liner Replacement

Removal of the intake grate may be necessary for proper access to the liner.

1. Refer to *Intake Housing Removal and Installation* in this chapter for procedures, then remove the intake housing from the jet drive.

2. Locate the bolts on the side of the intake housing that hold the liner in the housing. Note the locations, then remove the bolts.

3. Tap the liner loose with a long punch through the intake grate opening. Position the punch tip on the edge of the liner and carefully drive it from the housing.

4. Apply a light coat of Yamaha All-Purpose Grease or equivalent to the liner bore in the intake housing. Carefully slide the new liner into position. Align the bolt holes in the liner with the bolt holes in the housing.

5. Apply Yamaha All-Purpose Grease or equivalent to the threads of the bolts. Install the bolts and evenly tighten them to the specification in **Table 1**. Use a file to remove any burrs or bolt material protruding into the intake housing.

6. Install the intake housing onto the jet as described in this chapter.

Impeller Removal and Installation

Access to the upper end of the drive shaft is required to remove and install the impeller nut.

1. Remove the jet drive from the engine as described in this chapter.

2. Remove the intake housing as described in this chapter.

3. Select the drive shaft adapter for the engine model. For 28 jet and 35 jet models, use Yamaha part No. YB-6079. For 65 jet models, use Yamaha part No. YB-6151.

4. Use the drive shaft adapter to grip the splined end of the drive shaft when removing or installing the impeller nut.

5. Use a screwdriver to bend the tabs of the tab washer (8, **Figure 8** or 8, **Figure 9**) away from the impeller nut. Note the mounting location and orientation of all components prior to removal. Use a suitable socket and adapter to remove the impeller nut, tab washer and lower shims. Discard the tab washer.

6. Carefully pull the impeller, drive key, sleeve and upper shims from the drive shaft. Use a rubber mallet to carefully tap the impeller loose from the shaft if necessary.

7. Inspect the impeller for worn or damaged surfaces and replace the impeller if it has defects.

8. Place the sleeve and drive key (4 and 5, **Figure 8** or 4 and 5, **Figure 9**) onto the drive shaft. Apply Yamaha All-Purpose Grease or equivalent to the drive key and the impeller bore. Carefully slide the upper shims, then the impeller onto the drive shaft.

9. Place the lower shims, new tab washer (8, **Figure 8** or 8, **Figure 9**) and impeller nut onto the drive shaft. Make sure the shims and tab washer are in the proper position. Use the drive shaft adapter and a suitable socket to tighten the impeller nut to the specification in **Table 1**.

10. Bend the tabs up to secure the impeller nut. Install the intake housing onto the jet drive as described in this chapter. Refer to *Impeller-to-Housing Clearance* for procedures, then measure and correct the clearance. Install the jet drive onto the engine as described in this chapter.

Shimming the Impeller

The impeller must be shimmed to ensure proper impeller-to-housing clearance. Remove the intake housing and impeller for each shim change. Refer to the appropriate section in this chapter for removal and installation procedures. For component identification and orientation, refer to **Figure 8** or **Figure 9**.

Refer to *Impeller-to-Housing Clearance* in this chapter after each shim change for measurement procedures. Repeat the process until the clearance is correct.

Eight shims are used on 28 jet and 35 jet models. Nine shims are used on 65 jet models. All shims are 0.8 mm (0.030 in.) thick. Normally shims are located both above and below the impeller.

1. Remove the jet drive as described in this chapter.

2. Remove the intake housing from the jet drive as described in this chapter.

3. Note the location and orientation of all components, then remove the impeller from the drive shaft. Refer to *Impeller Removal and Installation* in this chapter for procedures.

4. If there is too much impeller clearance, remove a shim from below the impeller and place it above the impeller.

434

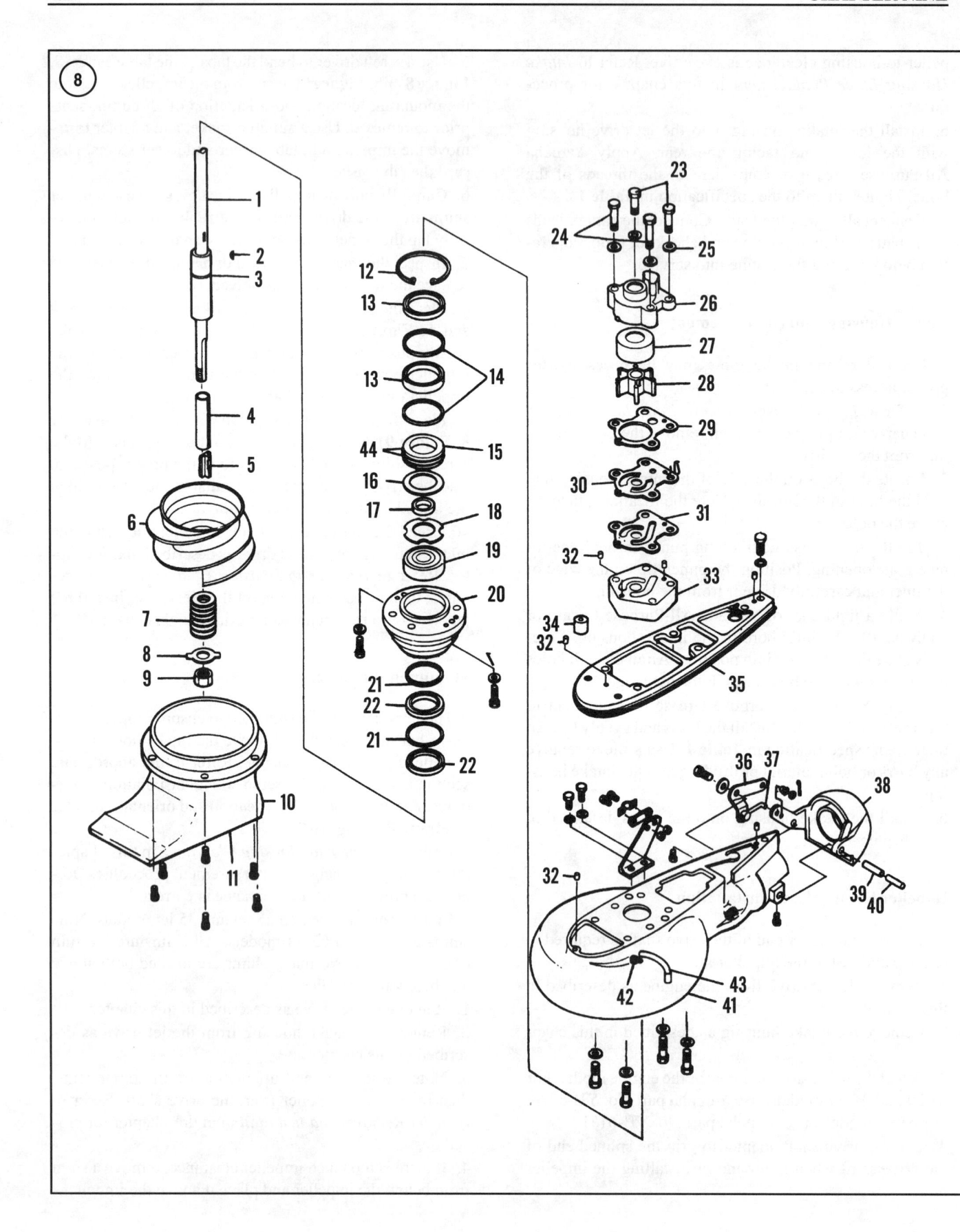

CHAPTER NINE

JET DRIVE COMPONENTS
(28 JET AND 35 JET MODELS)

1. Drive shaft
2. Drive key (engine water pump)
3. Thrust ring (flange)
4. Sleeve
5. Impeller drive key
6. Impeller
7. Shims
8. Tab washer
9. Impeller nut
10. Intake housing
11. Intake grate opening
12. Snap ring
13. Seal
14. Retaining ring
15. Seal carrier
16. Washer
17. Collar
18. Thrust washer
19. Bearing
20. Bearing housing
21. Seal retainer
22. Seal
23. Bolts (rear)
24. Bolts (front)
25. Washers
26. Water pump cover
27. Insert
28. Impeller
29. Gasket
30. Wear plate
31. Gasket
32. Locating pin
33. Spacer plate
34. Rubber sleeve
35. Adapter plate
36. Gate lever
37. Linkage
38. Gate
39. Bushing
40. Pin
41. Jet drive housing
42. Grease fitting
43. Vent hose
44. O-rings

436

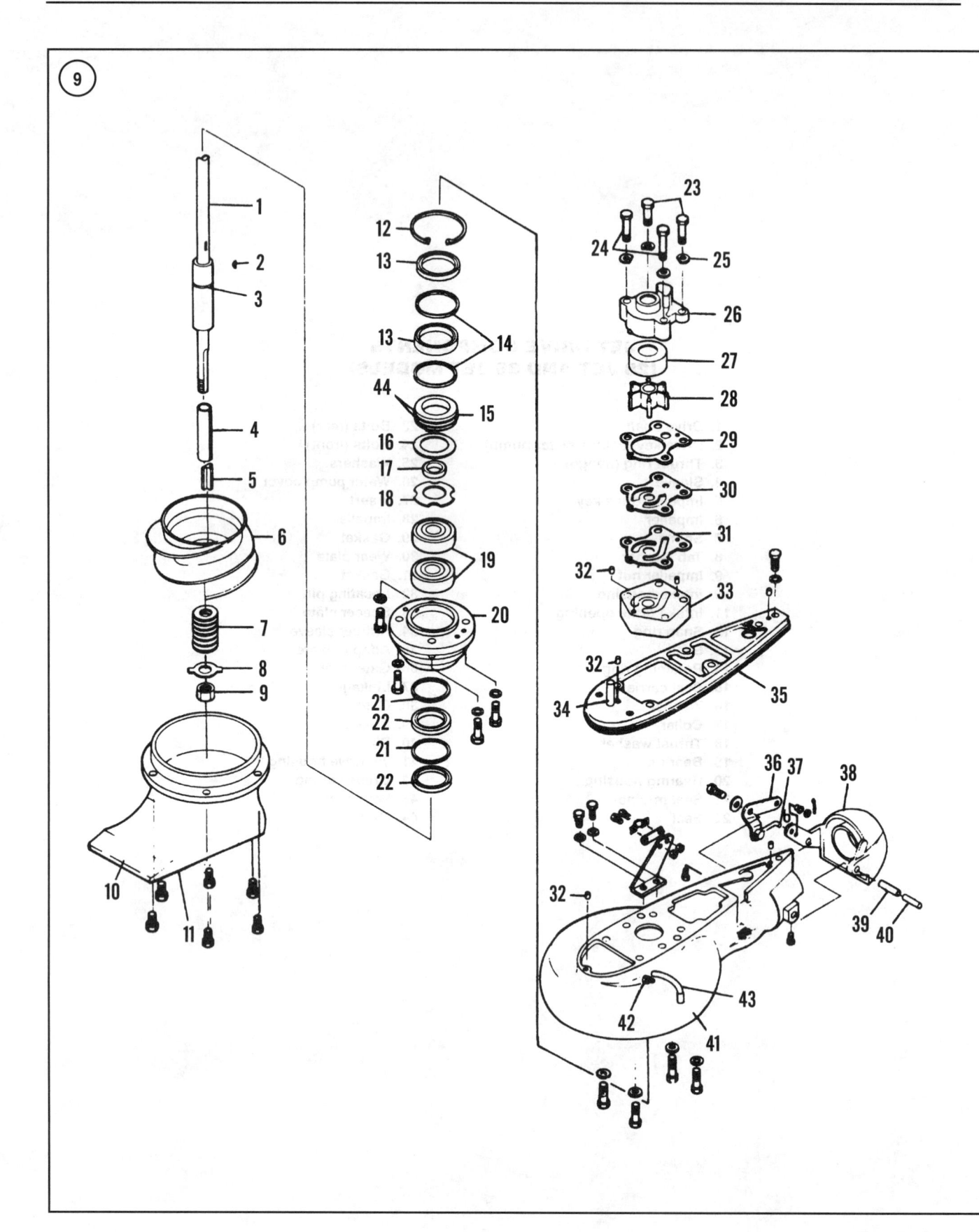

CHAPTER NINE

JET DRIVE COMPONENTS
(65 JET MODEL)

1. Drive shaft
2. Drive key (engine water pump)
3. Thrust ring
4. Sleeve
5. Impeller drive key
6. Impeller
7. Shims
8. Tab washer
9. Impeller nut
10. Intake housing
11. Intake grate opening
12. Snap ring
13. Seal
14. Seal retainer
15. Seal carrier
16. Washer
17. Collar
18. Thrust washer
19. Bearings
20. Bearing housing
21. Seal retainer
22. Seal
23. Bolts (rear)
24. Bolts (front)
25. Washer
26. Water pump cover
27. Insert
28. Impeller
29. Gasket
30. Wear plate
31. Gasket
32. Locating pin
33. Spacer plate
34. Locating pin
35. Adapter plate
36. Gate lever
37. Linkage
38. Gate
39. Sleeve
40. Pin
41. Jet drive housing
42. Grease fitting
43. Vent hose
44. O-rings

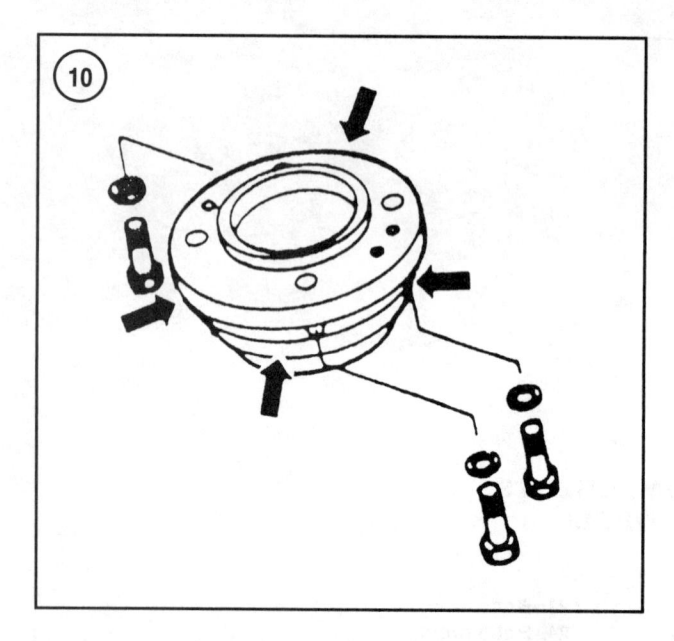

5. If there is too little clearance, remove a shim from above the impeller and place it below the impeller.

6. Install the impeller and intake housing onto the jet drive as described in this chapter. Refer to *Impeller-to-Housing Clearance* and measure the clearance. Repeat Steps 1-7 until the clearance is correct.

Bearing Housing Removal

Inspect and/or replace the drive shaft bearing if contaminants or a significant amount of water is found during routine maintenance to the jet drive. Replace all seals, gaskets and O-rings anytime they are removed. Remove the bearing housing to access bearings, shafts, seals and other components.

1. Remove the jet drive from the engine as described in this chapter.

2. Remove the intake housing and impeller as described in this chapter.

3. Remove all engine water pump components. Refer to *Water Pump* in Chapter Nine for procedures. Use the procedures for the horsepower the engine would be rated as if a propeller drive gearcase were installed.

4. Remove the spacer plate (33, **Figure 8** or 33, **Figure 9**) from the jet drive housing. Locate and remove the bolts and washer securing the bearing housing (**Figure 10**) to the jet drive housing.

5. Carefully pull the bearing housing from the jet drive housing and place it on a clean work surface.

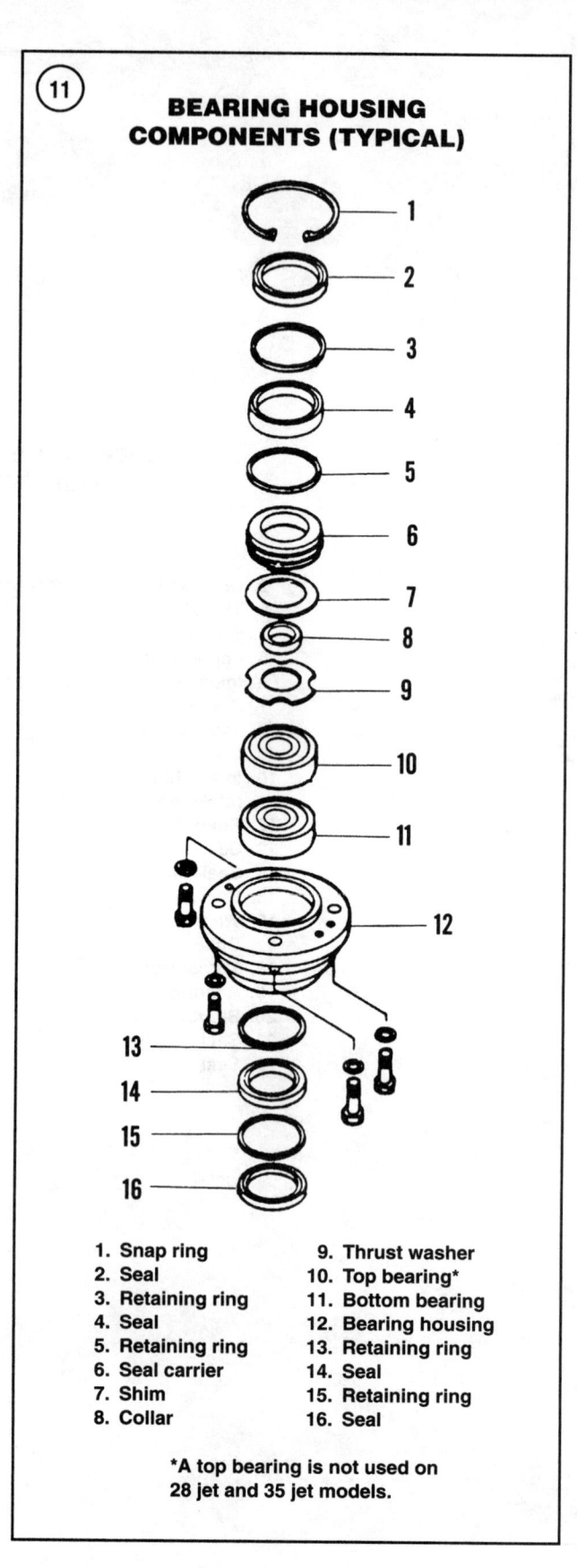

BEARING HOUSING COMPONENTS (TYPICAL)

1. Snap ring
2. Seal
3. Retaining ring
4. Seal
5. Retaining ring
6. Seal carrier
7. Shim
8. Collar
9. Thrust washer
10. Top bearing*
11. Bottom bearing
12. Bearing housing
13. Retaining ring
14. Seal
15. Retaining ring
16. Seal

*A top bearing is not used on 28 jet and 35 jet models.

JET DRIVE

(12)

Drive shaft
Bearing
Bearing separator

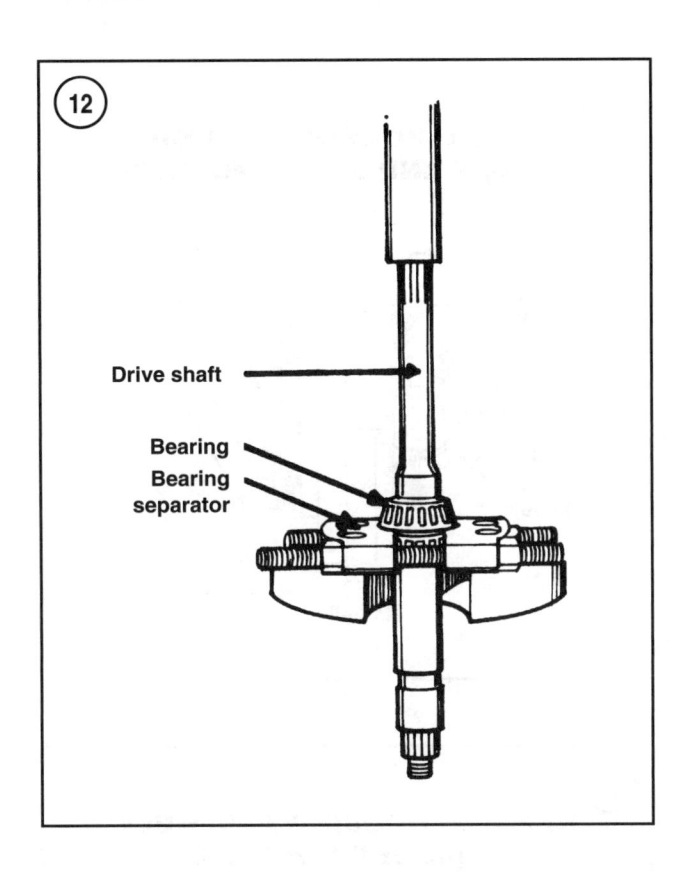

Drive Shaft Bearing Removal and Installation

WARNING
The components of the bearing housing become very hot during disassembly and assembly. Take all necessary precautions to protect yourself and others from injury.

WARNING
Never use a flame or allow sparks in an area where combustible material is present. Always have a suitable fire extinguisher nearby when using a flame or another heat producing device.

CAUTION
Note the direction the bearings are installed on the drive shaft. The inner race surfaces are wider on one side. The inner race surfaces must be installed correctly to ensure durable repair. Refer to the illustrations before assembling the drive shaft.

NOTE
A single bearing is used on the drive shaft for 28 jet and 35 jet models. Two bearings are used on 65 jet models.

For component identification, refer to **Figure 8** or **Figure 9** during disassembly and assembly procedures. Note the location and orientation of all components before removing them from the bearing housing. Rotate the drive shaft to check the bearings for rough operation. Replace the bearings if operation is rough or the bearings feel loose.

Do not remove the bearing from the drive shaft unless it must be replaced. The removal process may damage the bearings. Removal of the bearings requires heat to be applied to the bearing housing. The seals must be replaced as they are usually damaged from the heat or removal process.

1. Carefully pry the snap ring (1, **Figure 11**) from the groove in the bearing housing (12) bore.

2. Secure the bearing housing in a vise with protective jaws. The impeller end of the housing must face up. Thread the impeller nut onto the drive shaft to protect the threads. Apply moderate heat to the areas noted with arrows (**Figure 10**). Use a block of wood and a hammer to tap on the installed nut end while applying heat. Continue until the shaft and bearing slide from the housing.

3. Remove the seal carrier (6, **Figure 11**) from the drive shaft. Note the orientation of the seal lips, then carefully pry the grease seals (2 and 4, **Figure 11**) and both retaining rings (3 and 5) from the carrier. Remove the O-rings from the seal carrier and discard them.

4. Note the location and orientation of the shim, collar and thrust washer (7-9, **Figure 11**), then remove them from the bearing housing bore.

5. Note the seal lip direction, then carefully pry the retaining rings and both seals (13-16, **Figure 11**) from the bearing housing bore. Discard the seals. Press the bearing(s) from the drive shaft. See **Figure 12**, typical.

6. Inspect the drive shaft for damaged surfaces or excessive wear on the seal contact areas. Replace the drive shaft if there are any defects. A deeply grooved shaft will allow water into the bearings and eventually cause component failure.

7. Place the thrust washer (9, **Figure 11**) onto the drive shaft. Note the correct orientation of the bearing thrust surfaces (wide side of the inner race) as indicated in **Figure 13** or **Figure 14**, and slide the bearings(s) onto the shaft. Use a section of tubing or pipe to press the new bearing(s) onto the drive shaft. The tool must only contact the inner bearing race.

8. Use Loctite Primer T to clean all contaminants from the seal bore in the bearing housing. Select a large socket or a section of tubing to install the seals into the housing. The tool must contact the seal, but not contact the housing during seal installation.

9

9. Apply Loctite Primer T to the outer surface of the seal. When it is dry, apply Loctite 271 to the seal bore in the housing and the outer diameter of the seal. Place the seal into the housing with the seal lip facing the direction noted prior to removal or indicated in **Figure 13** or **Figure 14**. Use the selected tool to press the seal into the bearing housing until it is fully seated.

10. Install the retaining ring into the groove in the housing bore. Apply Loctite 271 to the outer diameter of the second seal. Place the seal into the housing with the seal lip facing the direction noted prior to removal or indicated in **Figure 13** or **Figure 14**. Use the selected tool to press the seal into the bearing housing until it is fully seated against the retainer. Place the second retaining ring into the groove in the housing bore. The notched area must align with the small hole in the retaining ring groove. Wipe excess Loctite from the seal area.

11. Apply Yamaha All-Purpose Grease or equivalent to the seal lips and retaining ring before installing of the drive shaft and bearings.

CAUTION
Only apply enough heat to the bearing housing to allow it to expand and slide over the bearing(s). Excessive heat damages the seal and retainers. Use an appropriately sized section of tubing and a press, if necessary, to fully seat the bearing(s) into the housing. Only press on the outer race of the bearing. Only use light pressure. Never drive the bearing(s) into the housing.

12. Place the drive shaft in a vise with protective jaws. The impeller side of the drive shaft must face up. Set the bearing housing on the drive shaft. Use a heat lamp or torch to heat the bearing housing in the areas indicated in **Figure 10**. Remove the heat and use heavy gloves to push the bearing housing over the drive shaft bearings. Apply heat gradually until the bearing housing slides fully onto the bearing(s) and the bearing(s) seat in the housing.

13. Install the thrust washer (9, **Figure 11**) on the drive shaft with the gray side facing the impeller. Place the collar (8, **Figure 11**) onto the drive shaft. Place the shim (7, **Figure 11**) into the housing in the direction noted prior to removal.

14. Apply Loctite Primer T to the seal bore surfaces in the carrier (6, **Figure 11**) and the outer diameter of the seals (2 and 4). Install the first retaining ring into the groove in the seal carrier bore.

15. Place the seal into the seal bore opening with the seal lip facing the direction noted prior to removal or indicated in **Figure 13** or **Figure 14**. Use an appropriately sized socket or a section of tubing to push the first seal into the carrier. The tool must contact the seal, but not contact the seal bore during installation. Push until the seal seats fully against the retainer.

16. Place the second retainer into the groove in the seal carrier bore. Push the second seal into the seal carrier bore as described in Step 15. Place new O-rings on the seal carrier. Lubricate the seal lips and all seal carrier surfaces with Yamaha All-Purpose Grease or equivalent. Slide the seal carrier over the drive shaft and carefully press it into

BEARING HOUSING ASSEMBLY (28 JET AND 35 JET MODELS)

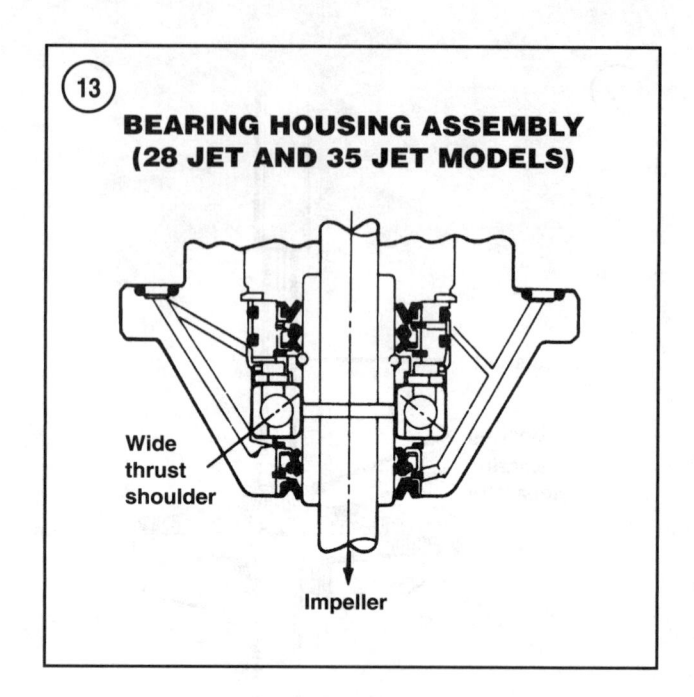

BEARING HOUSING ASSEMBLY (65 JET MODEL)

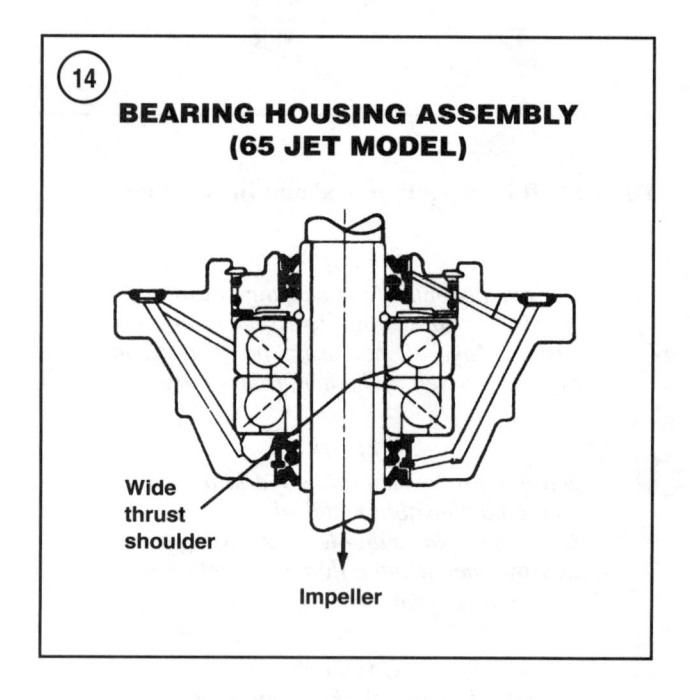

JET DRIVE

the bearing housing bore. The carrier must seat fully in the bearing housing.

17. Use snap ring pliers to install the snap ring (1, **Figure 11**) into the groove in the bearing housing bore.

Bearing Housing Installation

1. Make sure the mating surfaces of the bearing housing and jet drive housing are free of debris and contaminants.

2. Carefully slide the drive shaft and bearing housing into the jet drive housing. Apply Yamaha All-Purpose Grease or equivalent to the threads of the bolts that hold the bearing housing. Install the bolts and evenly tighten them to the specification in **Table 1**.

3. Install the aluminum spacer plate (33, **Figure 8** or 33, **Figure 9**) onto the jet drive housing. Refer to Chapter Nine for procedures to install the engine water pump onto the jet drive. Use the procedures listed for the horsepower the engine would be rated if a propeller drive gearcase were installed.

4. Install the impeller and intake housing as described in this chapter.

5. Measure the impeller-to-housing clearance as described in this chapter. Correct the clearance as required.

6. Install the jet drive onto the engine as described in this chapter. Removal of the intake housing may be required to access the mounting fasteners on some models.

7. Perform the lubrication procedures as described in Chapter Three. Adjust the jet drive thrust gate as described in Chapter Four.

Table 1 JET DRIVE TORQUE SPECIFICATIONS

Fastener	N.m	in.-lb.	ft.-lb.
Bearing housing mounting bolts	7.9	70	–
Impeller nut	23	–	17
Intake housing mounting bolts	10.9	96	–
Intake housing liner bolts	11.3	100	–
Jet drive mounting bolts	31.2	–	23

Chapter Ten

Manual Starter

This chapter includes repair procedures for all manual starter assemblies. **Table 1** lists torque specifications for most manual starter fasteners. Use the standard torque specifications in Chapter Four for fasteners not listed in **Table 1**. **Table 2** lists rewind rope length. **Table 1** and **Table 2** are located at the end of this chapter.

Some electric start models are equipped with a manual starter (**Figure 1**). An electric or manual starter is used on 9.9-50 hp models.

The major components of the manual starter include:
1. Starter rope.
2. Sheave.
3. Drive pawl.
4. Rewind spring.
5. Starter housing.
6. Rope guide.

Except for the rope guide and lockout assembly, all of the above components are in the housing.

As the rope (1, **Figure 2**, typical) is pulled, the sheave (2) rotates clockwise as viewed from the top. Rotation of the sheave causes the drive pawl (3, **Figure 2**) to pivot from its normal position and engage the starter pulley which is mounted on the flywheel. The starter spring winds up within the housing as the rope is pulled.

As the rope is released, the starter spring unwinds causing the sheave to rotate counterclockwise as viewed from the top. Counterclockwise sheave rotation causes the drive pawl spring (10, **Figure 2**) to pivot the drive pawl to its normal position, releasing the starter from the flywheel. Further sheave rotation winds the rope around the sheave.

The rope guide (7, **Figure 2**, typical) is supported by a bracket on most models and protrudes into an opening on the top engine cover.

To prevent the engine from starting in gear, all 4-75 hp models are equipped with a lockout assembly (**Figure 3**, typical). The lockout is cable actuated and mechanically prevents the starter sheave from rotating when the shift engages forward or reverse gear. The gear shift linkage(s) operates the lockout assembly. Adjust the lockout assem-

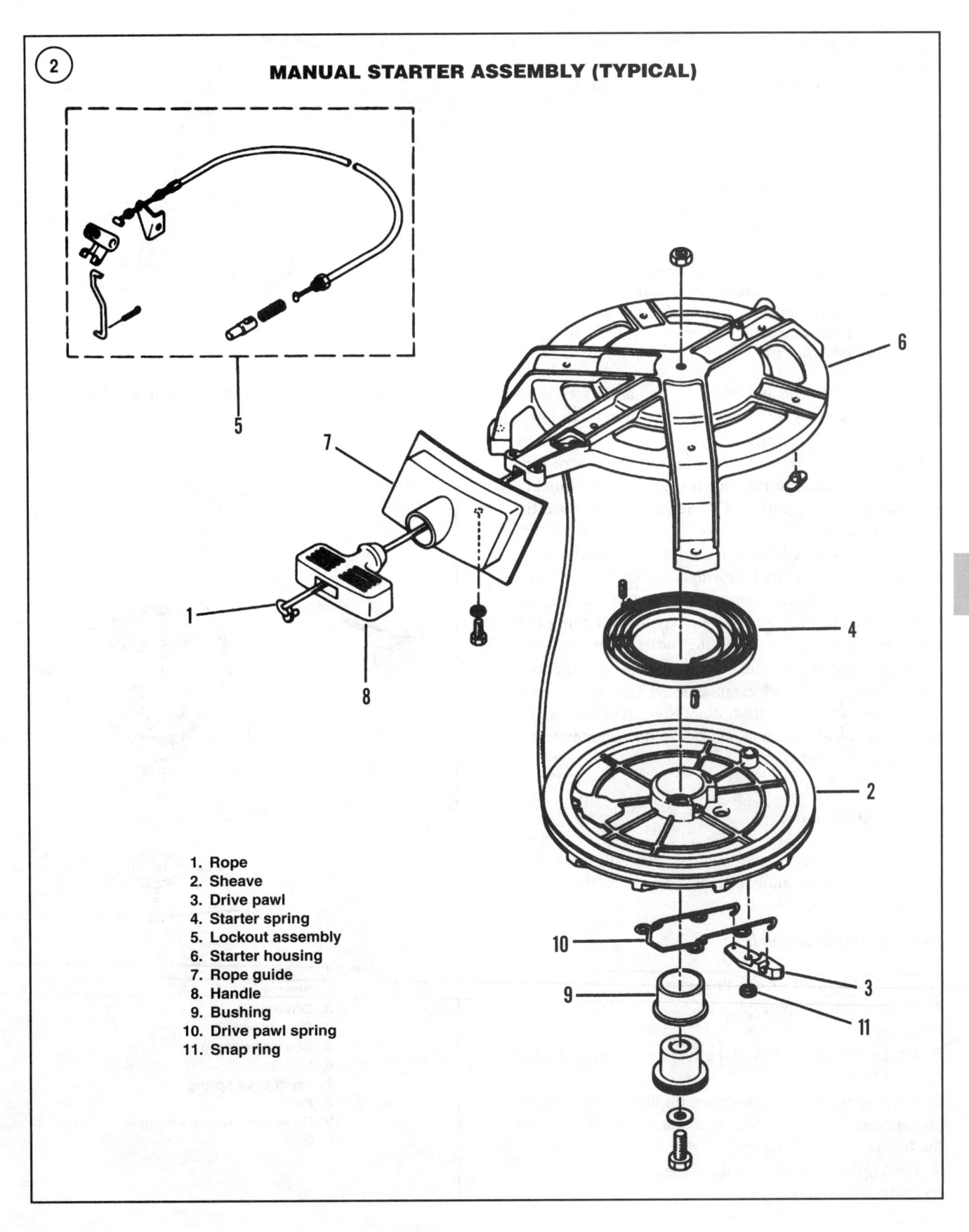

MANUAL STARTER

MANUAL STARTER ASSEMBLY (TYPICAL)

1. Rope
2. Sheave
3. Drive pawl
4. Starter spring
5. Lockout assembly
6. Starter housing
7. Rope guide
8. Handle
9. Bushing
10. Drive pawl spring
11. Snap ring

bly anytime the manual starter, lockout assembly, lockout assembly components, or related linkages are removed. Refer to Chapter Four for adjustment procedures.

REPAIR

WARNING
When servicing the manual starter, wear suitable eye protection, gloves and adequate covering over the entire body. The starter spring may unexpectedly release from the starter housing with considerable force and cause an injury. Follow all instructions and wear suitable protection to minimize the risk.

Disassemble, clean and lubricate the starter if the drive pawl fails to engine the flywheel or the starter binds as the rope is pulled.

Only use the correct starter rope. Other types of rope will not withstand the rigorous use and will fail quickly. Contact a Yamaha outboard dealership to purchase the correct starter rope.

Apply Yamaha All-Purpose Grease or its equivalent to all bushings, drive pawls, springs and sliding surfaces. Also apply grease to the starter spring and spring housing. Use Loctite 271 or 572 on the starter shaft retaining bolt and other fasteners that secure the starter to the engine.

Refer to the illustrations for component identification and orientation. The appearance of the components may differ slightly from the illustration. Note all of the component locations and orientation prior to disassembly to ensure proper assembly.

2 and 3 hp Models

Three screws secure the manual starter to the power head. A lockout assembly is not used on these models.

Removal and disassembly

Refer to **Figure 4** for this procedure.
1. Disconnect the spark plug lead to prevent the engine from starting.
2. On 2 hp models, remove the fuel tank as described in Chapter Five.
3. Remove the three screws, then lift the starter from the power head. Place the starter on a clean work surface with the flywheel side facing up.
4. On 3 hp models, remove the three grommets from the mounting screw holes.

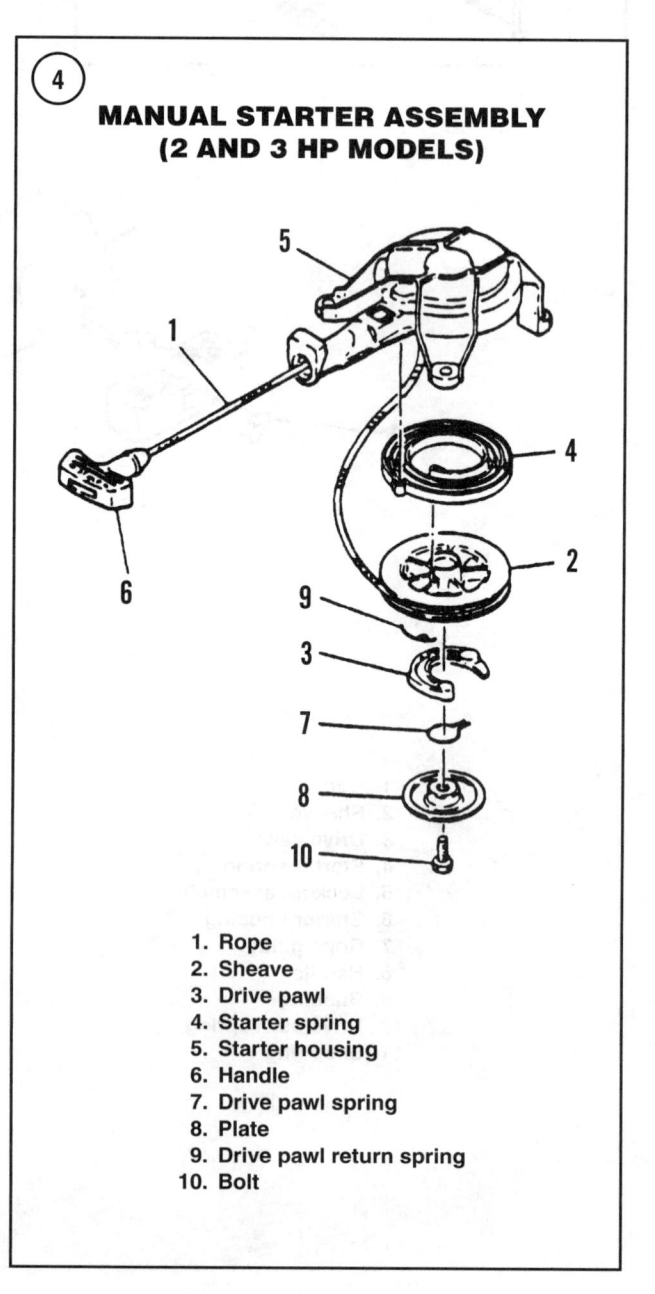

MANUAL STARTER ASSEMBLY (2 AND 3 HP MODELS)

1. Rope
2. Sheave
3. Drive pawl
4. Starter spring
5. Starter housing
6. Handle
7. Drive pawl spring
8. Plate
9. Drive pawl return spring
10. Bolt

MANUAL STARTER

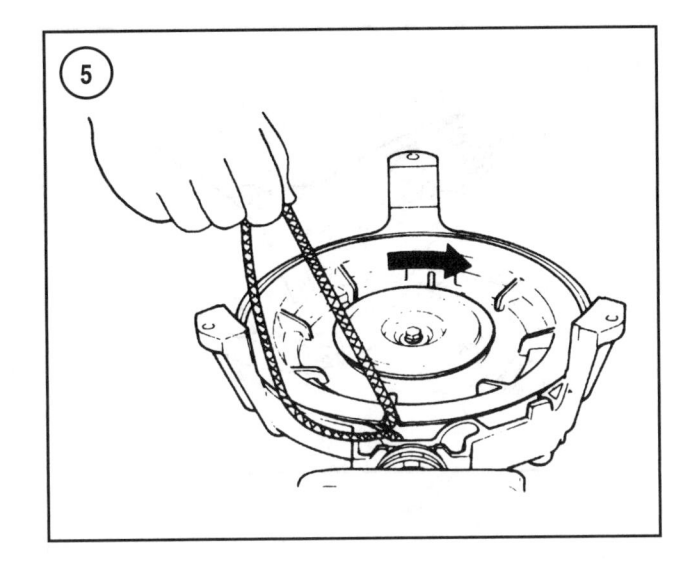

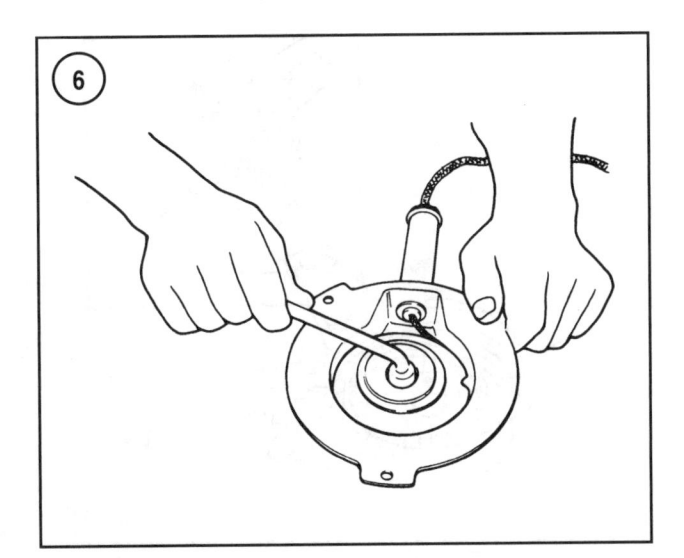

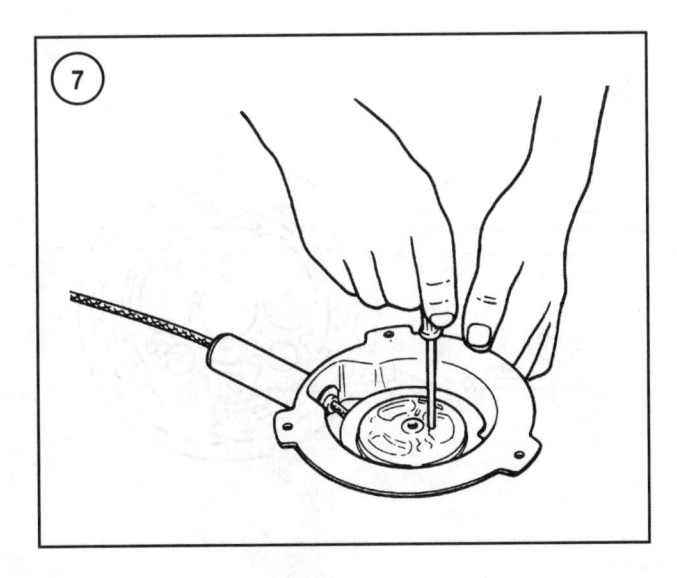

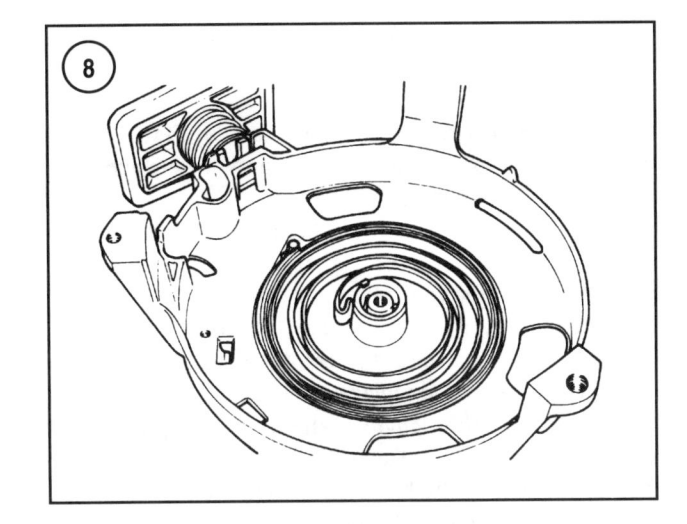

445

5. Rotate the sheave until the notch aligns with the rope guide. Grasp a loop of the rope and fit it into the notch as shown in **Figure 5**. Hold the rope in the notch while rotating the sheave clockwise until the spring is fully relaxed.

6. Carefully pry the plug and rope knot from the handle. Untie the knot, then pull the handle from the rope.

7. Remove the bolt and plate (**Figure 6**). Lift the drive pawl (3, **Figure 4**) and springs (7 and 9) from the sheave.

8. Insert a small tip screwdriver into the opening in the starter spring (**Figure 7**). Press down on the screwdriver to hold the spring in the housing. Maintain constant downward pressure and carefully lift the sheave and rope from the housing. Remove the screwdriver when the sheave clears the housing.

9. Loosen the knot and remove the rope from the sheave.

10. Inspect the starter spring (4, **Figure 4**) for corroded, distorted or cracked surfaces. If the spring is defective, remove it as follows:

   a. Note the direction the spring winds into the housing (**Figure 8**) before removing it.
   b. Wear eye protection, heavy gloves and protective clothing when removing the spring. Place a heavy piece of cloth or a towel over the spring to help contain the spring.
   c. Pull one loop of the spring at a time from the housing (**Figure 9**).

Component inspection

Clean all components except the rope in a solvent suitable for composite or plastic material. Use hot soapy water if a suitable solvent is not available. Dry all components with compressed air.

1. Inspect the plate (8, **Figure 4**) and drive pawl (3) for worn, damaged or cracked surfaces and replace it if necessary.
2. Inspect the drive pawl springs (7 and 9, **Figure 4**) for broken or bent springs and corroded or worn surfaces. Replace them if there are any defects.
3. Inspect the entire length of the starter spring, if it was removed, for cracked, corroded or damaged surfaces. Pay particular attention to the hook or bent end of the spring. Replace the spring if there are any defects.
4. Inspect the sheave (2, **Figure 4**) for warped, worn or damaged surfaces and replace as necessary.
5. Inspect the entire length of the rope (1, **Figure 4**) for cuts and worn or frayed areas. Pay particular attention to the length nearest the handle. Replace the rope with the proper type and length if it is not in excellent condition.
6. Inspect the rope guide in the housing for worn or damaged surfaces. To prevent rapid wear of the replacement rope, replace the housing if there are sharp surfaces or if a deep groove has worn in the rope guide.

Starter assembly and installation

Measure the length of the starter rope and compare it to the specification in **Table 2**. Trim the rope to the *exact* length as specified. To keep the end of the rope from unraveling, carefully melt the cut end of the rope with a small flame. While it is still molten, use thick gloves and shape the end of the rope into a compact nub. Trim loose pieces from the end when it has cooled.

Refer to **Figure 4** for this procedure.
1. Apply Yamaha All-Purpose Grease or its equivalent to the spring contact surfaces in the housing.

CAUTION
Do not *remove the retainer from a replacement starter spring until the spring is properly installed in the housing.*

2. Install the hooked or bent end of the spring over the tab in the housing as indicated in **Figure 10**. Carefully wind the spring counterclockwise into the housing until all loops are installed and the spring is fully positioned in the housing.
3. Slip one end of the rope through the hole in the sheave and tie a knot as indicated in **Figure 11**. Press the knot into the recess in the sheave. Position the sheave so the flywheel side faces up.
4A. On 2 hp models, wrap the rope 3 1/2 turns counterclockwise around the sheave groove.
4B. On 3 hp models, wrap the rope 1 1/2 turns counterclockwise around the sheave groove.

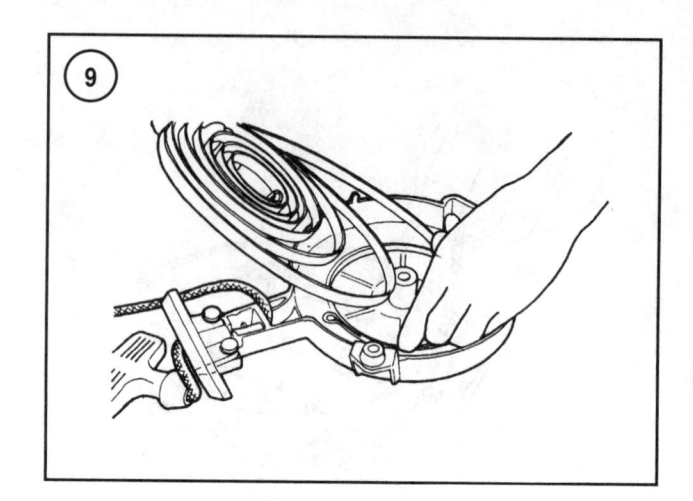

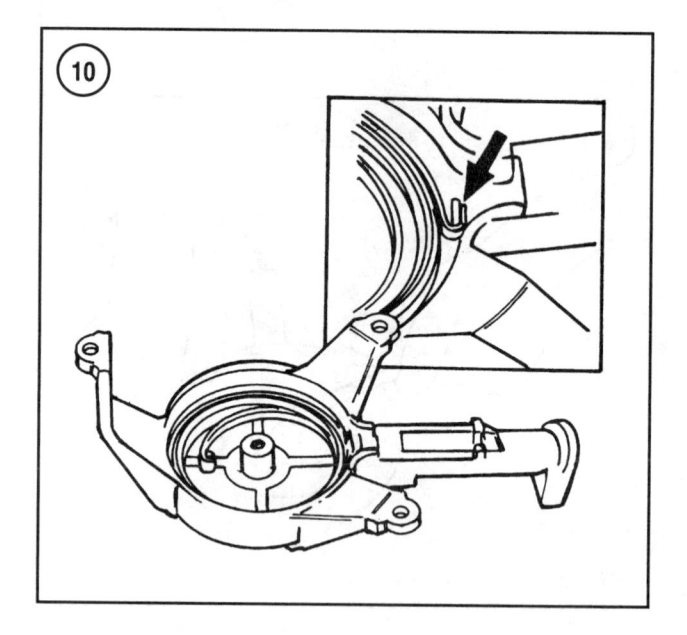

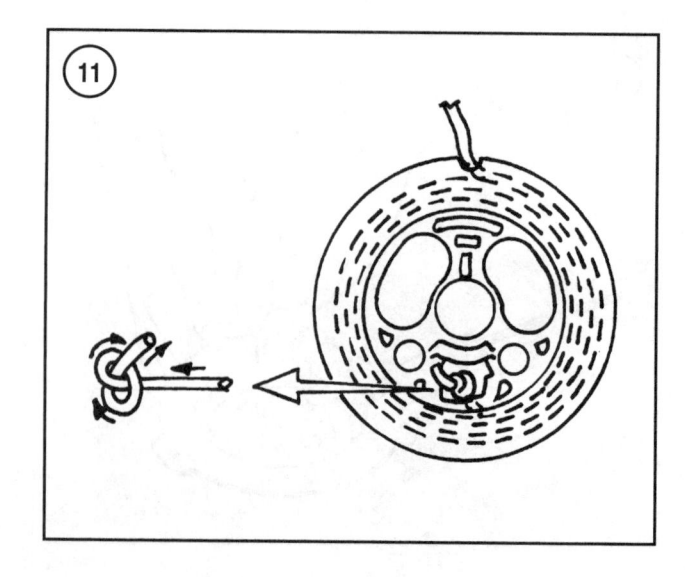

MANUAL STARTER

7. Hold the sheave into the housing and rotate the sheave slightly counterclockwise. If there is no spring tension, the spring is not engaging the tab and the sheave must be removed and reinstalled.

8. Apply a light coat of Yamaha All-Purpose Grease or its equivalent to the drive pawl and springs. Install the drive pawl return spring (9, **Figure 4**), drive pawl (3) and drive pawl spring (7).

9. Install the plate (8, **Figure 4**) onto the sheave. Make sure the open ends of the drive pawl spring fit over the tab on the drive pawl.

10. Apply Loctite 271 or 572 to the thread of the bolt (10, **Figure 4**). Install and securely tighten the bolt (**Figure 6**).

11. Place the starter on a work surface with the flywheel end facing up. Install the rope into the notch in the sheave as indicated in **Figure 13**.

12A. On 2 hp models, keep the rope in the notch while rotating the sheave three complete turns counterclockwise.

12B. On 3 hp models, keep the rope in the notch while rotating the sheave six complete turns counterclockwise.

13. Have an assistant maintain light downward pressure on the sheave to prevent rotation. Route the rope through the handle. Tie a knot in the handle as indicated in **Figure 14**. Push the knot into the opening in the handle.

14. Pull on the handle to remove slack from the rope. Have the assistant release the sheave while slowly allowing the rope to feed into the housing. Press the plug to the handle.

15. Operate the starter several times to check for proper operation. The drive pawl must pivot out as the rope is pulled and pivot in as the rope is released. Disassemble and inspect the starter if it binds or does not operate correctly.

16. On 3 hp models, install the grommets into the mounting screw openings in the housing. Position the larger diameter side of the grommets so they face the power head side of the housing.

17. Install the manual starter onto the power head. Install and securely tighten the three mounting screws.

18. On 2 hp models, install the fuel tank as described in Chapter Five.

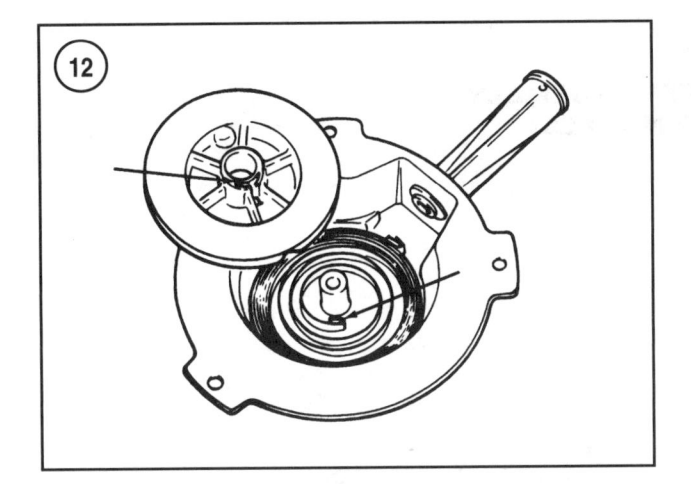

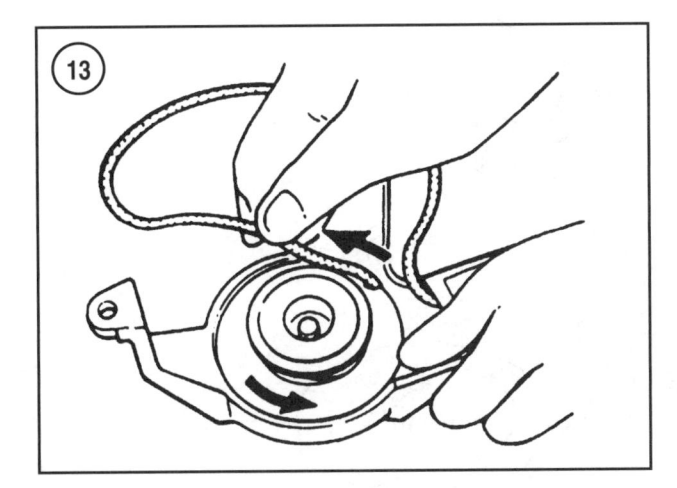

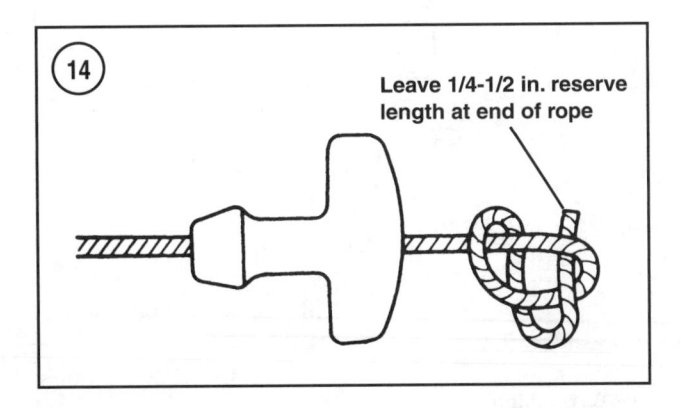

5. Apply Yamaha All-Purpose Grease or its equivalent to the flat surfaces of the sheave that contact the spring. Pass the free end of the rope through the rope guide.

6. Engage the hook or bent end of the spring over the tab on the sheave (**Figure 12**) while installing the sheave into the housing. Insert a screwdriver into the opening in the sheave to engage the spring to the tab if necessary.

4-8 and 20-50 hp Models

Three screws secure the starter to the power head. A plunger type cable actuated lockout assembly is used on these models. For component identification and orientation, refer to **Figures 15-18** during the disassembly and assembly procedures.

448

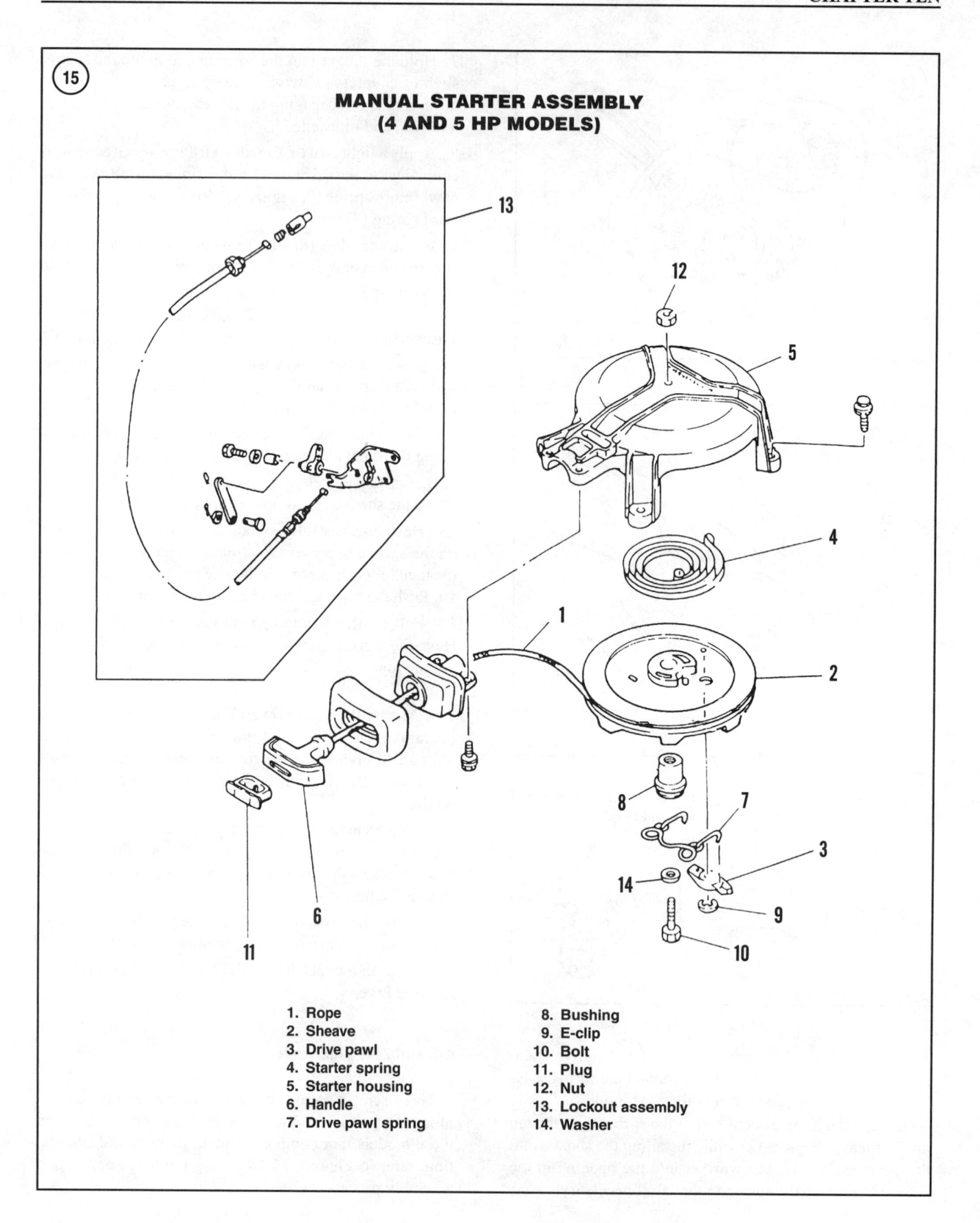

CHAPTER TEN

⑮ **MANUAL STARTER ASSEMBLY (4 AND 5 HP MODELS)**

1. Rope
2. Sheave
3. Drive pawl
4. Starter spring
5. Starter housing
6. Handle
7. Drive pawl spring
8. Bushing
9. E-clip
10. Bolt
11. Plug
12. Nut
13. Lockout assembly
14. Washer

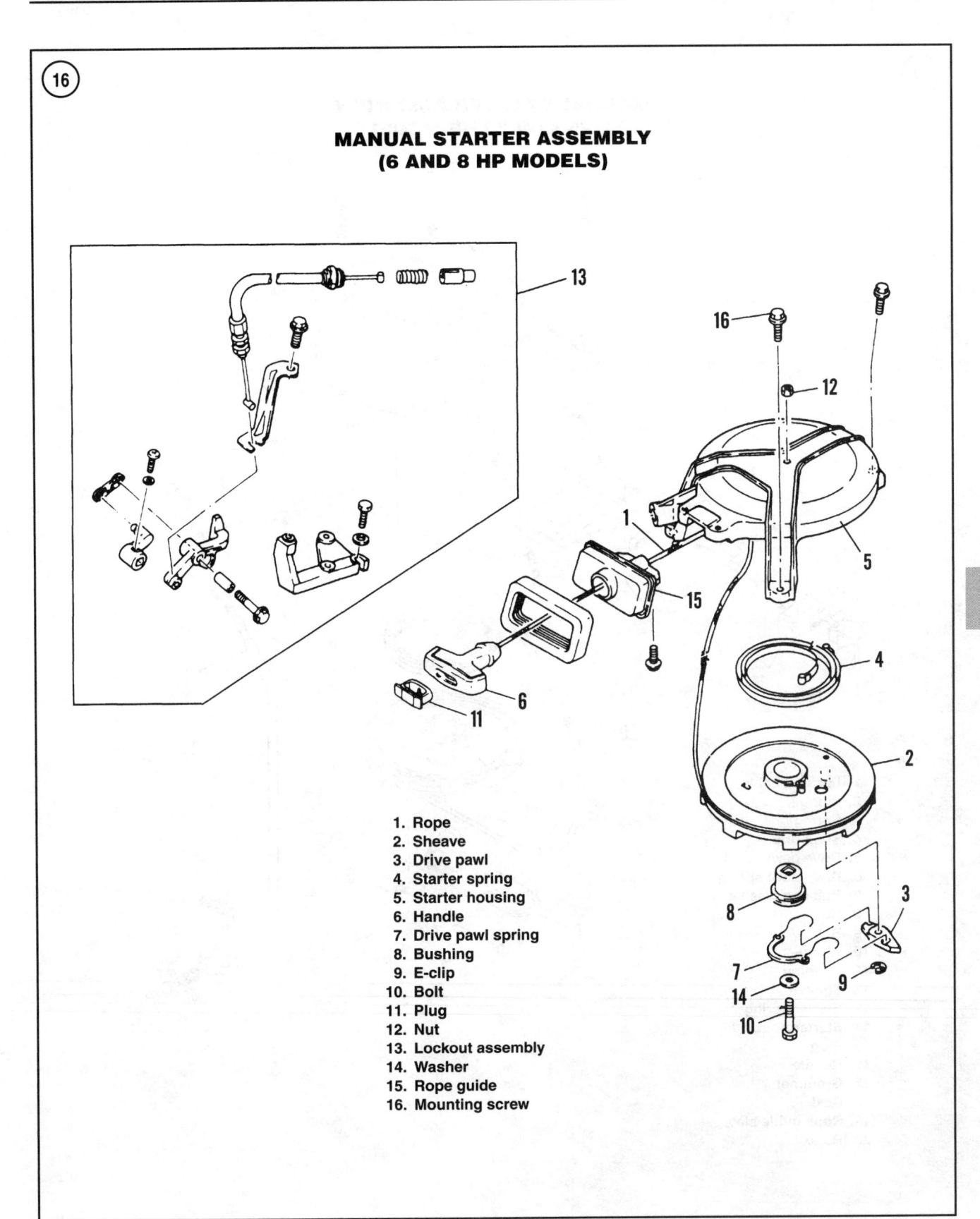

MANUAL STARTER

449

⑯

**MANUAL STARTER ASSEMBLY
(6 AND 8 HP MODELS)**

1. Rope
2. Sheave
3. Drive pawl
4. Starter spring
5. Starter housing
6. Handle
7. Drive pawl spring
8. Bushing
9. E-clip
10. Bolt
11. Plug
12. Nut
13. Lockout assembly
14. Washer
15. Rope guide
16. Mounting screw

10

MANUAL STARTER ASSEMBLY
(20, 25 AND 30 HP MODELS)

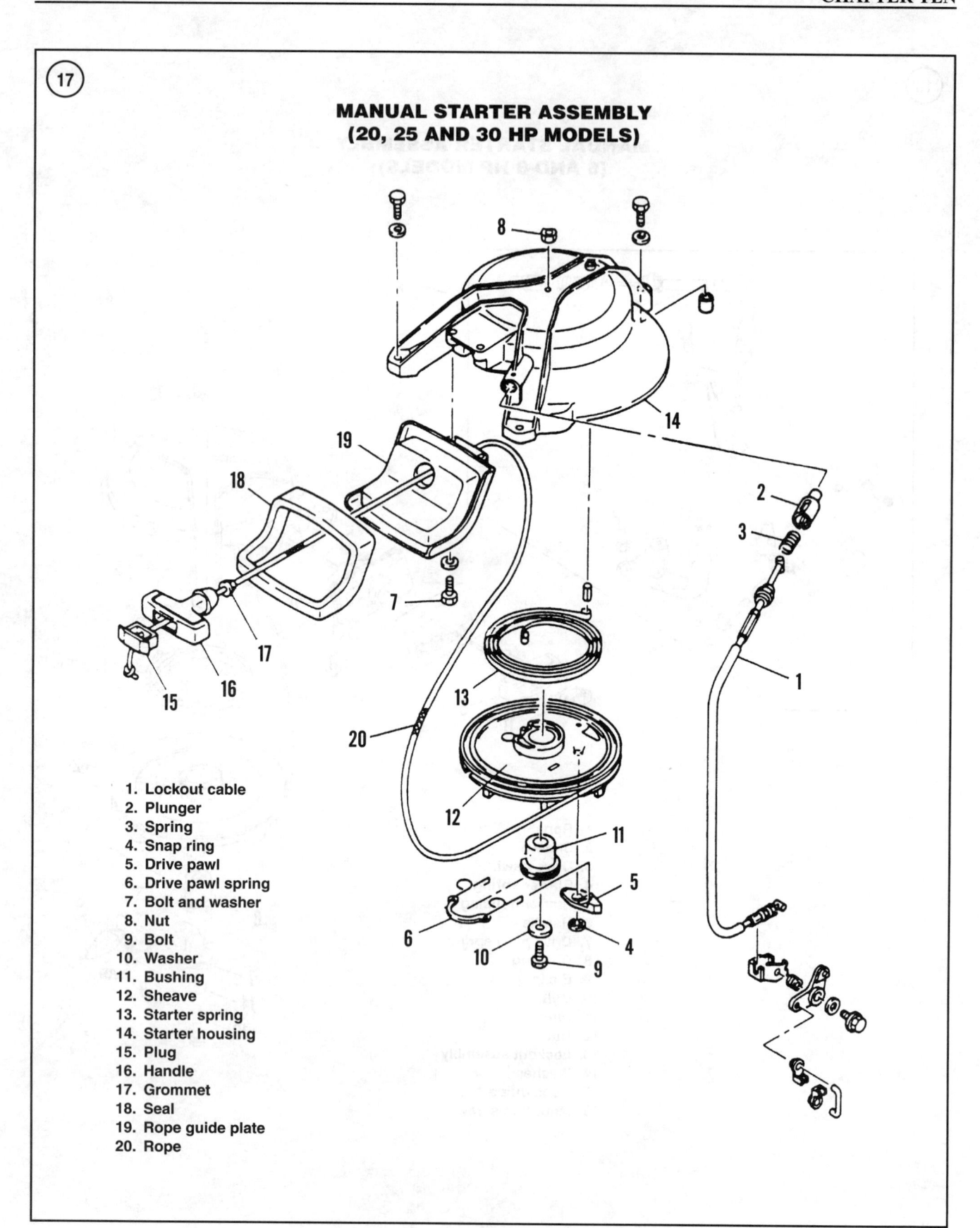

1. Lockout cable
2. Plunger
3. Spring
4. Snap ring
5. Drive pawl
6. Drive pawl spring
7. Bolt and washer
8. Nut
9. Bolt
10. Washer
11. Bushing
12. Sheave
13. Starter spring
14. Starter housing
15. Plug
16. Handle
17. Grommet
18. Seal
19. Rope guide plate
20. Rope

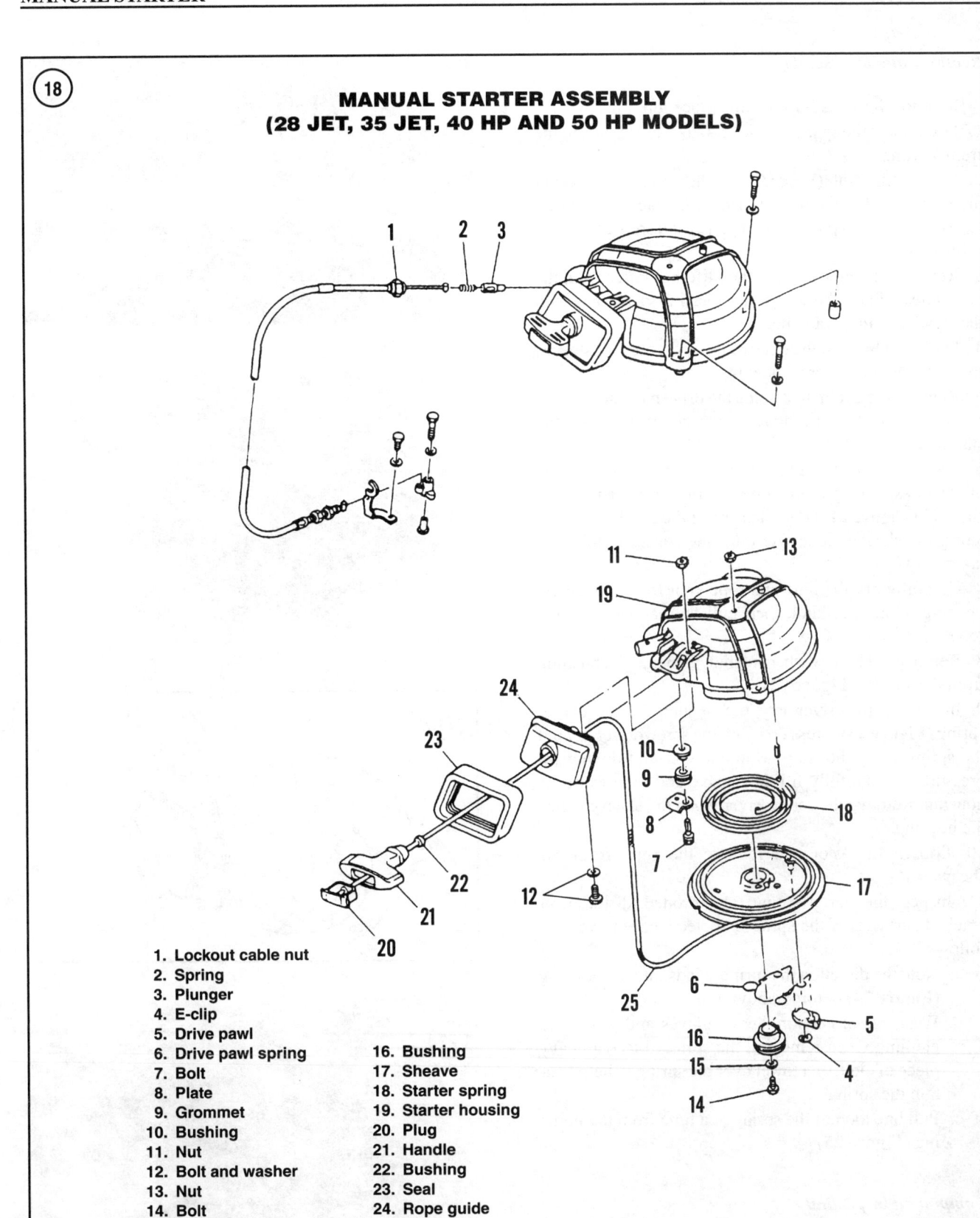

MANUAL STARTER

451

MANUAL STARTER ASSEMBLY
(28 JET, 35 JET, 40 HP AND 50 HP MODELS)

1. Lockout cable nut
2. Spring
3. Plunger
4. E-clip
5. Drive pawl
6. Drive pawl spring
7. Bolt
8. Plate
9. Grommet
10. Bushing
11. Nut
12. Bolt and washer
13. Nut
14. Bolt
15. Washer
16. Bushing
17. Sheave
18. Starter spring
19. Starter housing
20. Plug
21. Handle
22. Bushing
23. Seal
24. Rope guide
25. Starter rope

Removal and disassembly

Refer to **Figures 15-18** for this procedure.

1. Disconnect the spark plug lead(s) to prevent the engine from starting.
2. Loosen the nut (**Figure 19**), then pull the lockout plunger assembly from the housing. Collapse the spring (3, **Figure 17**) and pull the plunger (2) and spring from the cable end.
3. Remove the three screws, then lift the starter from the power head. Place the starter on a clean work surface with the flywheel side facing up.
4. On 20-50 hp models, remove the grommets or sleeves from the mounting screw openings.
5. Remove the E-clip that holds the drive pawl and spring to the sheave. Lift the drive pawl and spring from the starter (**Figure 20**).
6. Rotate the sheave until the notch aligns with the rope guide. Grasp a loop of the rope and fit it into the notch as shown in **Figure 21**. Hold the rope in the notch while rotating the sheave clockwise until the spring is fully relaxed.
7. Carefully pry the plug and rope knot from the handle opening. Untie the knot, then pull the handle from the rope.
8. Remove the bolt, washer and nut, then pull the bushing from the sheave (**Figure 22**).
9. Insert a screwdriver into the opening in the starter spring (**Figure 23**). Press down on the screwdriver to hold the spring in the housing. Maintain constant downward pressure and carefully lift the sheave and rope from the housing. Remove the screwdriver when the sheave clears the housing.
10. Loosen the knot and remove the rope from the sheave.
11. Inspect the starter spring for corroded, distorted or cracked surfaces. If the spring is defective, remove it as follows:
    a. Note the direction the spring winds into the housing (**Figure 24**) before removing it.
    b. Wear eye protection, heavy gloves and protective clothing when removing the spring. Place a heavy piece of cloth or a towel over the spring to help contain the spring.
    c. Pull one loop of the spring at a time from the housing (**Figure 25**).

Component inspection

Clean all components except the rope in a solvent suitable for composite or plastic material. Use hot soapy wa-

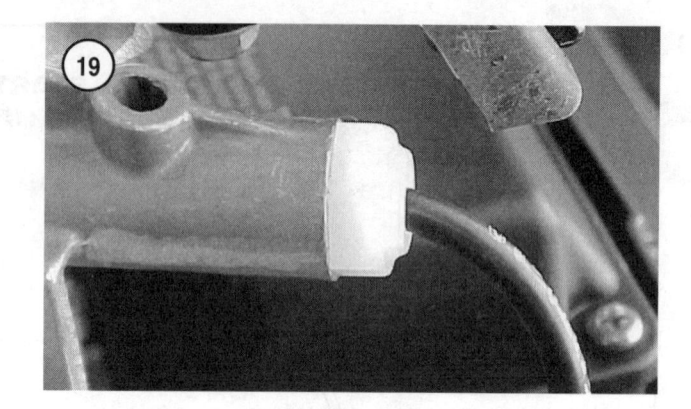

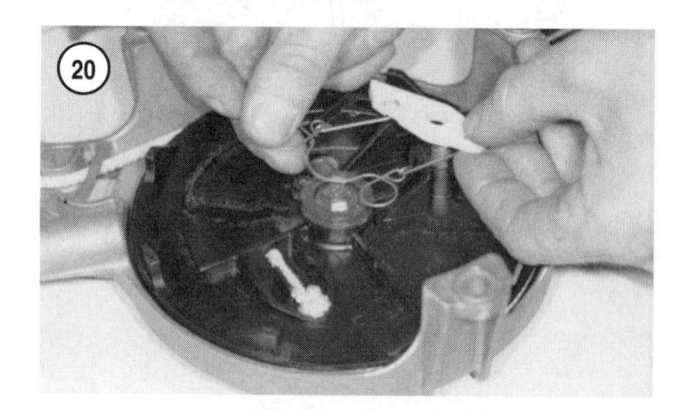

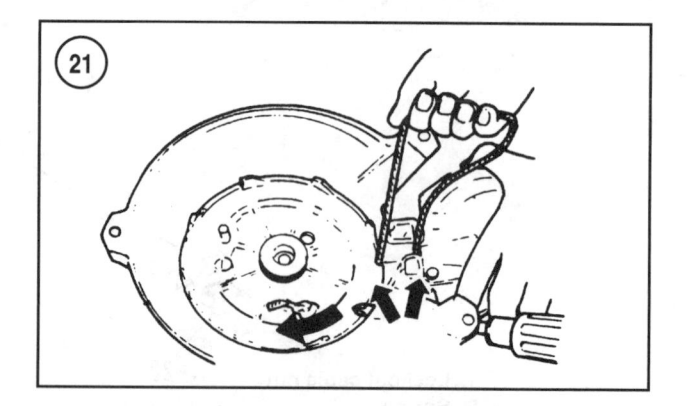

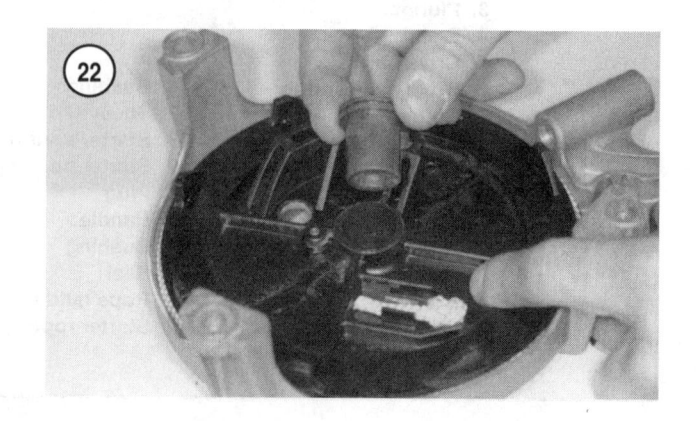

MANUAL STARTER

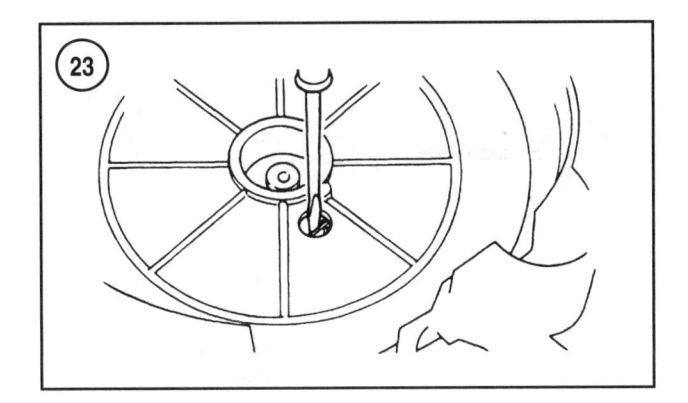

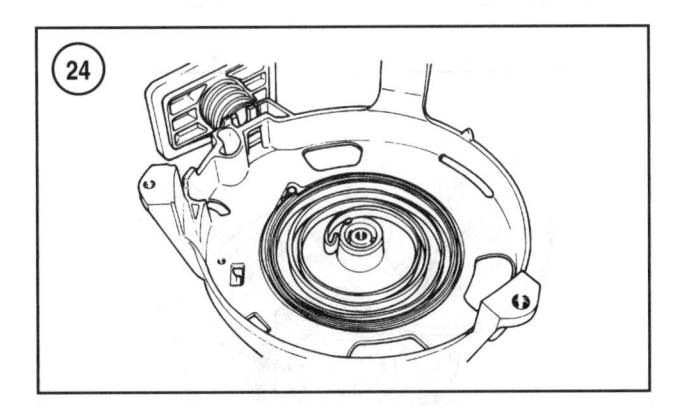

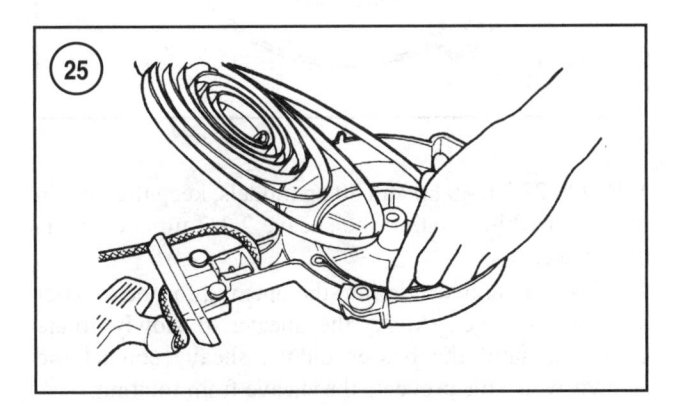

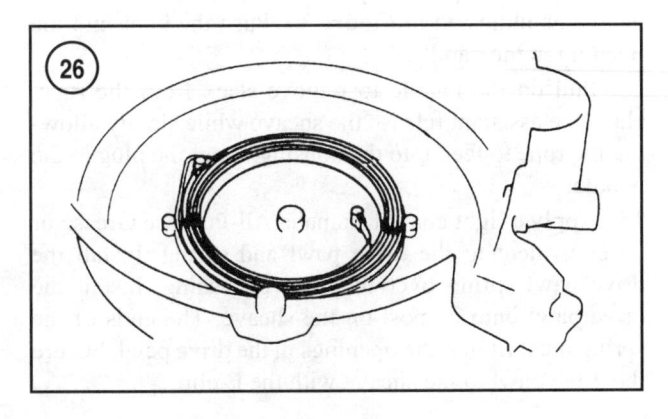

ter if a suitable solvent is not available. Dry all components with compressed air.

1. Inspect the drive pawl for worn, damaged or cracked surfaces and replace it if necessary.
2. Inspect the drive pawl spring for broken or bent springs and corroded or worn surfaces. Replace it if there are any defects.
3. Inspect the entire length of the starter spring, if it was removed, for cracked, corroded or damaged surfaces. Pay particular attention to the hook or bent end. Replace the spring if there are any defects.
4. Inspect the sheave for warped, worn or damaged surfaces and replace as necessary.
5. Inspect the entire length of the rope for cuts and worn or frayed areas. Pay particular attention to the length nearest the handle. Replace the rope with the proper type and length if it is not in excellent condition.
6. Inspect the rope guide and roller for worn or damaged surfaces. To prevent rapid wear of the replacement rope, remove and replace the guide or roller if they have sharp surfaces or if a deep groove has worn in the rope guide or roller.
7. Inspect the plunger portion (2, **Figure 17**, typical) for worn or damaged surfaces and replace as necessary. Inspect the lockout cable, spring and linkages for defects. Replace any defective or questionable components.

Assembly and installation

Measure the length of the starter rope and compare it to the specification in **Table 2**. Trim the rope to the *exact* length as specified. To prevent the end of the rope from unraveling, carefully melt the cut end of the rope with a small flame. While it is still molten, use thick gloves and shape the end of the rope into a compact nub. Trim loose pieces from the end when it has cooled.

Refer to **Figures 15-18** for this procedure.

1. Apply Yamaha All-Purpose Grease or its equivalent to the spring contact surfaces in the housing.

CAUTION
***Do not** remove the retainer from a replacement starter spring until the spring is properly installed in the housing.*

2A. For a new starter spring, install the spring fully into the housing (**Figure 26**). Place the loop on the outer end of the spring over the post in the housing. Hold the spring firmly into the housing with a glove protected hand and carefully remove the spring retainers.
2B. For a used starter spring, clamp the housing to a stable work surface. Place the loop on the outer end of the

spring over the post in the housing. Carefully wind the spring counterclockwise into the housing until all loops are installed and the spring is fully positioned in the housing.

3. Slip one end of the rope through the hole in the sheave and tie a knot as indicated in **Figure 27**. Make sure the rope end equals the dimension indicated in **Figure 27**. Press the knot into the recess in the sheave. Position the sheave so the flywheel side faces up.

4A. On 4-8 hp models, wrap the rope 2 1/2 turns counterclockwise around the sheave groove.

4B. On 20 hp and 25 hp two-cylinder models, wrap the rope 1 9/10 turns counterclockwise around the sheave groove.

4C. On 25 hp three-cylinder and 30 hp models, wrap the rope 2 1/4 turns counterclockwise around the sheave groove.

4D. On 28 jet, 40 hp and 50 hp models, wrap the rope 1 9/10 turns counterclockwise around the sheave groove.

5. Apply Yamaha All-Purpose Grease or its equivalent to the flat surfaces of the sheave that contact the spring. Pass the free end of the rope through the rope guide.

6. Engage the loop on the inner end of the spring over the post on the sheave (**Figure 28**) while installing the sheave into the housing. Insert a screwdriver into the opening in the sheave to guide the loop onto the post if necessary.

7. Hold the sheave into the housing and rotate the sheave slightly counterclockwise. If there is no spring tension, the loop at the end of the spring is not over the post and the sheave must be removed and reinstalled.

8. Apply a light coat of Yamaha All-Purpose Grease or equivalent to the outer surfaces of the bushing and bushing opening in the sheave. Insert the bushing into the sheave so the wider diameter side faces out.

9. Apply Loctite 271 or 572 to the threads of the sheave bolt and nut. Install the bolt, washer and nut, then tighten it to the specification in **Table 1** or Chapter One.

10. Place the starter on a work surface with the flywheel end facing up. Install the rope into the notch in the sheave as indicated in **Figure 29**.

11A. On 4 and 5 hp models, keep the rope in the notch while rotating the sheave two complete turns counterclockwise.

11B. On 6 and 8 hp models, keep the rope in the notch while rotating the sheave three complete turns counterclockwise.

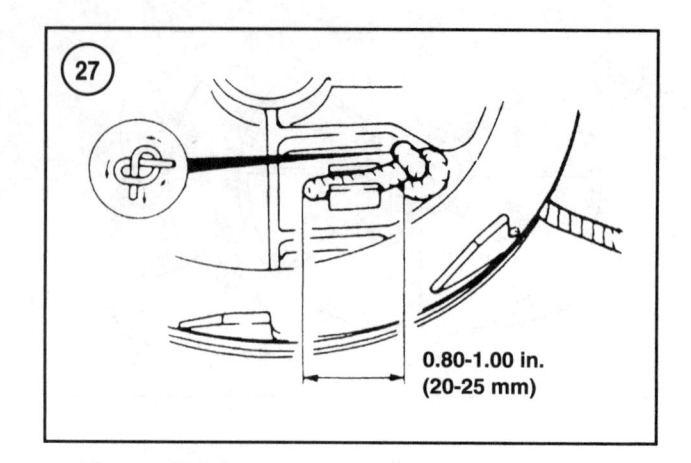

11C. On 20 hp and 25 hp two-cylinder models, keep the rope in the notch while rotating the sheave 2 1/2 turns counterclockwise.

11D. On 25 hp three-cylinder and 30 hp models, keep the rope in the notch while rotating the sheave two complete turns counterclockwise.

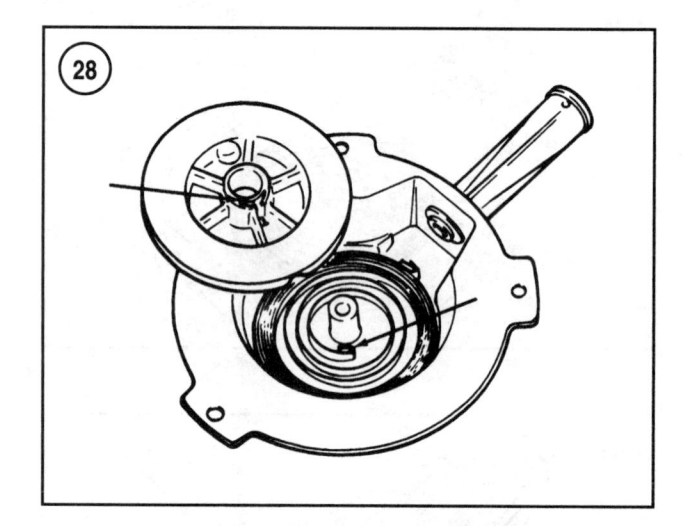

11E. On 28 jet, 40 hp and 50 hp models, keep the rope in the notch while rotating the sheave 2 1/2 turns counterclockwise.

12. Insert a screwdriver into the opening for the lockout assembly plunger. Allow the sheave to slowly rotate clockwise until the bosses on the sheave contact the screwdriver. This prevents the sheave from rotating.

13. Route the rope through the handle. Tie a knot in the handle as indicated in **Figure 30**. Push the knot into the opening in the handle.

14. Pull on the handle to remove slack from the rope. Have the assistant release the sheave while slowly allowing the rope to feed into the housing. Press the plug to the handle.

15. Apply a light coat of Yamaha All-Purpose Grease or its equivalent to the drive pawl and spring. Install the drive pawl spring over the sheave bushing. Install the drive pawl onto its post on the sheave. The ends of the spring must fit into the openings in the drive pawl. Secure the drive pawl to the sheave with the E-clip.

MANUAL STARTER

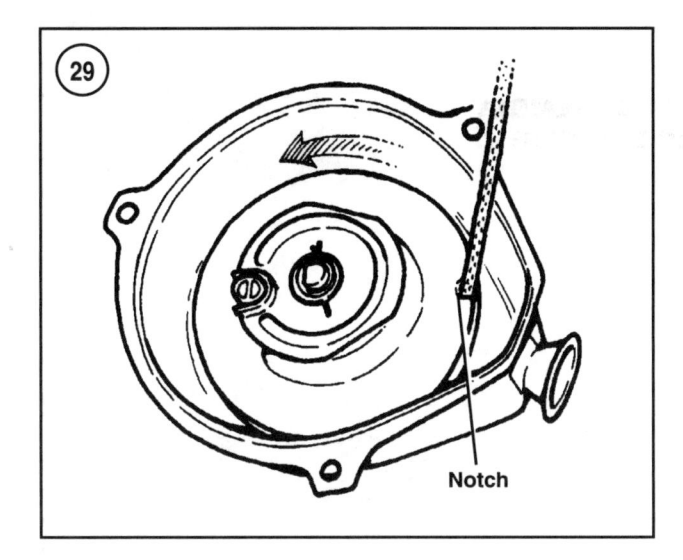

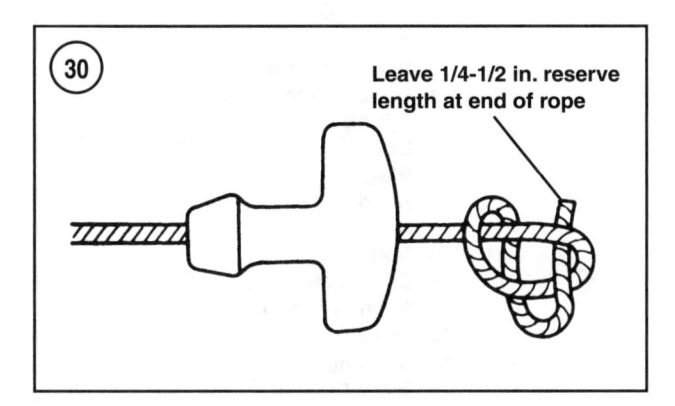

Figure 29 — Notch

Figure 30 — Leave 1/4-1/2 in. reserve length at end of rope

16. Operate the starter several times to check for proper operation. The drive pawl should pivot out as the rope is pulled and pivot in as the rope is released. Disassemble and inspect the starter if it binds or operates incorrectly.

17. Slip the spring (3, **Figure 17**, typical) over the lockout assembly cable. Collapse the spring, then insert the cable end into the opening in the side of the plunger (2, **Figure 17**, typical). The protrusion on the plunger must face away from the spring. Release the spring to hold the plunger to the cable.

18. On 20-50 hp models, install the grommets or sleeves into the mounting screw openings.

19. Install the manual starter onto the power head. Apply Loctite 271 or 572 to the threads of the mounting screws. Install the three mounting screws. Install and securely tighten the three mounting screws.

20. Insert the lockout assembly plunger into its opening in the manual starter housing. Tighten the nut to secure the cable in the manual starter housing.

21. Adjust the lockout assembly as described in Chapter Four. Connect the spark plug lead(s). Check for proper operation of the lockout assembly before putting the engine into service.

9.9 and 15 hp Models

Three screws secure the manual starter to the power head. A lever type cable actuated lockout assembly is used on these models.

Removal and disassembly

Refer to **Figure 31** for this procedure.

1. Disconnect the spark plug leads to prevent the engine from starting.
2. Loosen the adjusting nuts (**Figure 32**), then pull the lockout cable from the bracket and shift linkage.
3. Remove the three screws, then lift the starter from the power head. Place the starter on a clean work surface with the flywheel side facing up.
4. Remove the bushings from the mounting screw openings.
5. Rotate the sheave until the notch aligns with the rope guide. Grasp a loop of the rope and fit it into the notch as shown in **Figure 33**. Hold the rope in the notch while rotating the sheave clockwise until the spring is fully relaxed.
6. Carefully pry the plug (7, **Figure 31**) and rope knot from the handle opening. Untie the knot, then pull the handle from the rope.
7. Remove the bolt (**Figure 34**), then lift the drive plate and friction spring from the sheave (**Figure 35**).
8. Insert a screwdriver into the opening in the starter spring (**Figure 23**). Press down on the screwdriver to hold the spring in the housing. Maintain constant downward pressure and carefully lift the sheave and rope from the manual housing. Remove the screwdriver when the sheave clears the manual housing.
9. Remove the bushing (14, **Figure 31**) from the boss in the housing. Loosen the knot and remove the rope from the sheave.
10. Remove the link and spring (19 and 20, **Figure 31**) from the sheave and drive pawl. Remove the E-clip (17, **Figure 31**), then pull the drive pawl (18) from the sheave.
11. Remove the cotter pin (**Figure 36**). Pull the stopper lever and cable from the housing. Pull the stopper lever from the spring side of the housing (**Figure 37**).
12. Inspect the starter spring for corroded, distorted or cracked surfaces. If the spring is defective, remove it as follows:

MANUAL STARTER ASSEMBLY (9.9 AND 15 HP MODELS)

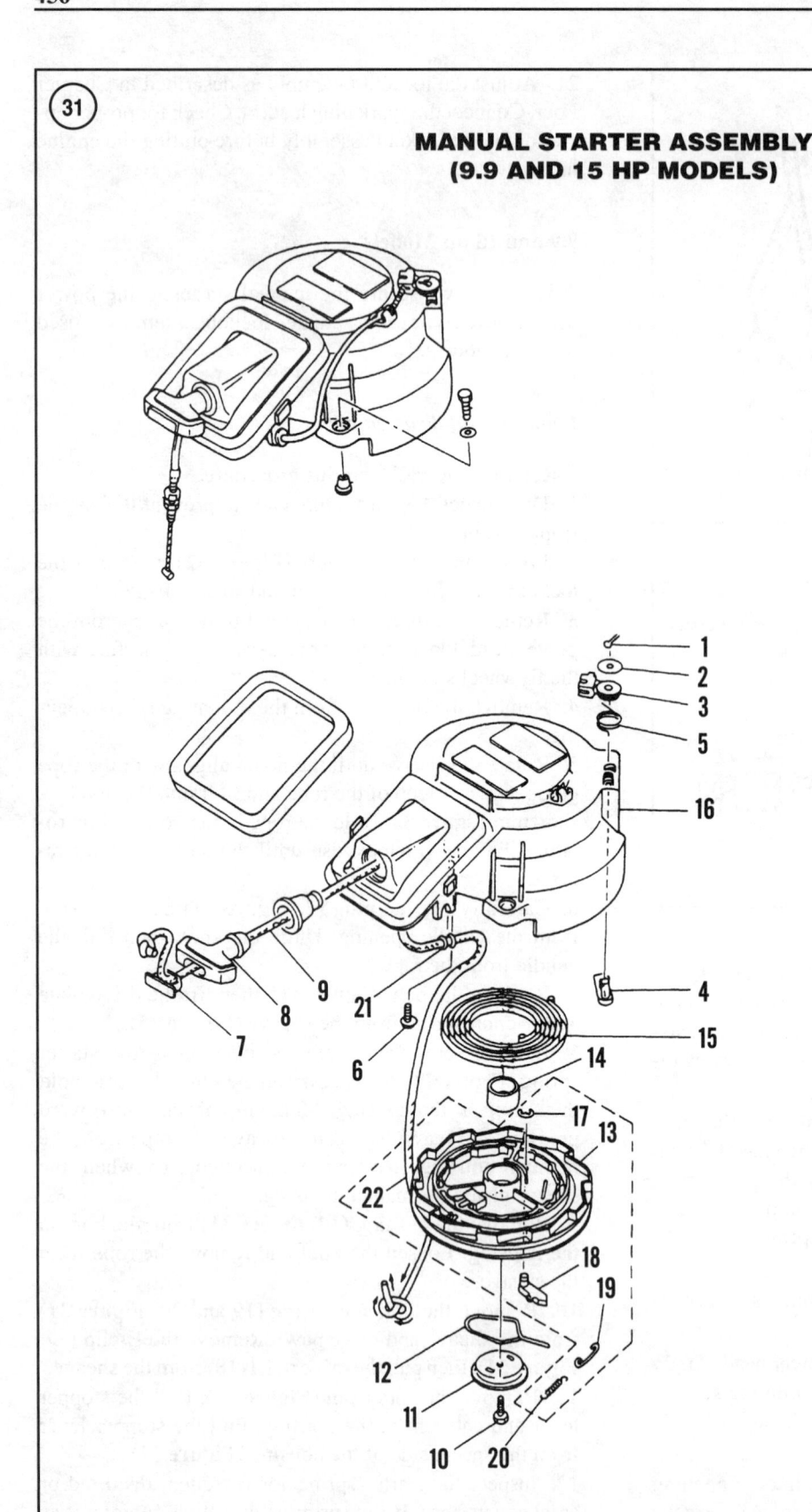

1. Cotter pin
2. Washer
3. Upper stopper lever
4. Lower stopper lever
5. Spring
6. Bolt
7. Plug
8. Handle
9. Rope
10. Bolt
11. Drive plate
12. Friction spring
13. Sheave
14. Bushing
15. Starter spring
16. Starter housing
17. E-clip
18. Drive pawl
19. Link
20. Drive pawl spring
21. Guide bushing
22. Rope guide

MANUAL STARTER

457

32

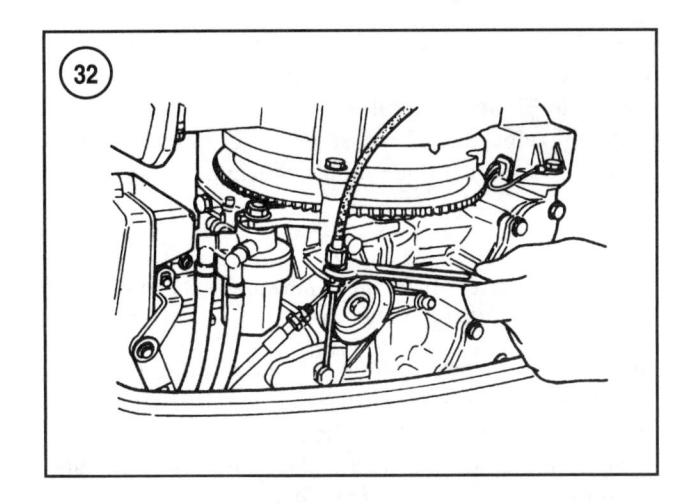

33

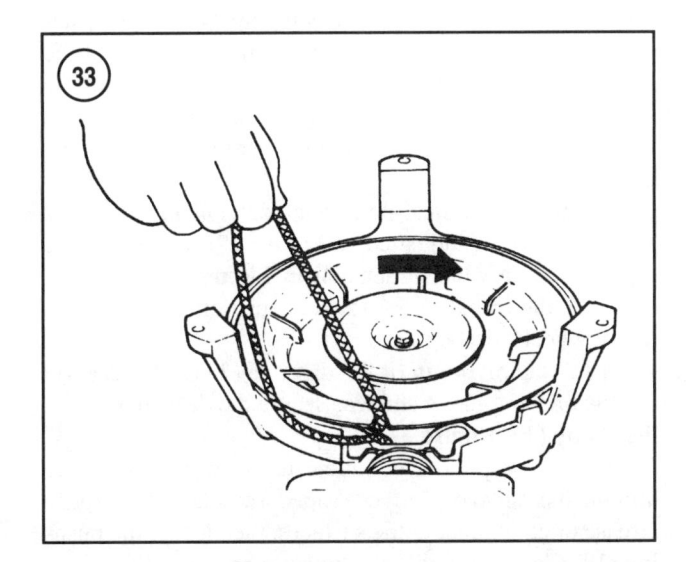

34

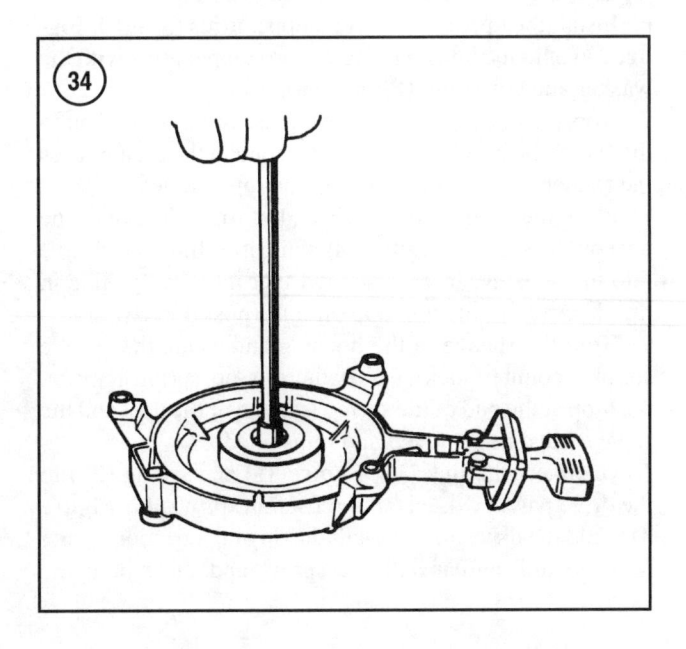

35 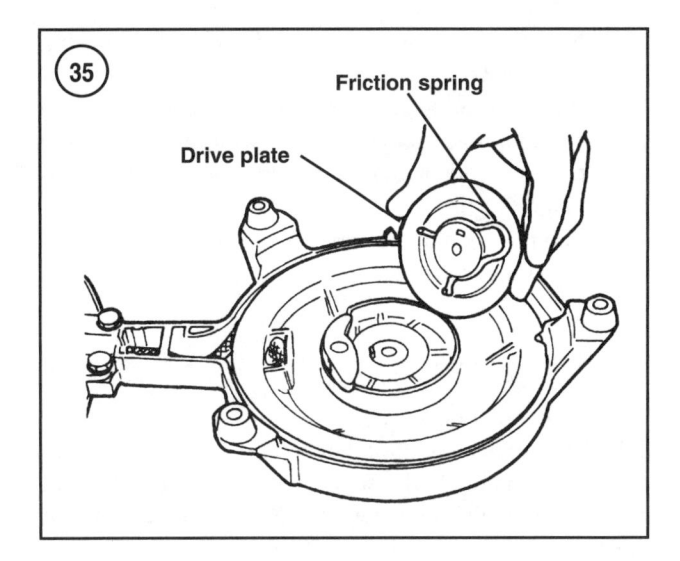 Friction spring
Drive plate

36 Stopper lever
Stopper arm

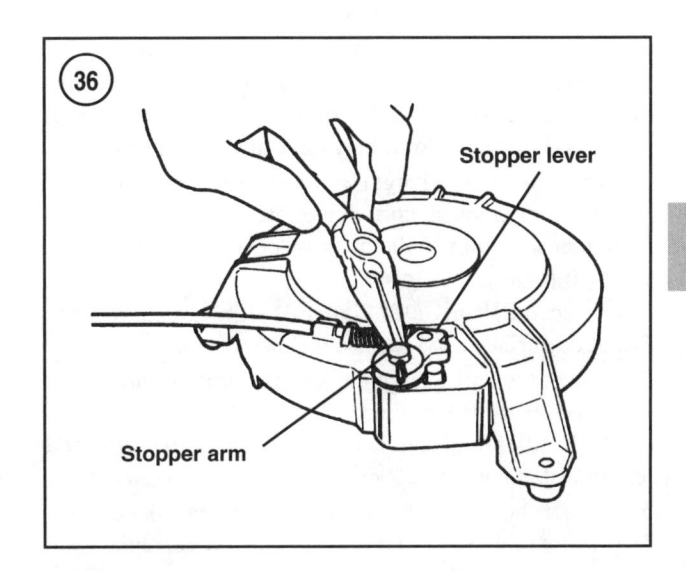

37

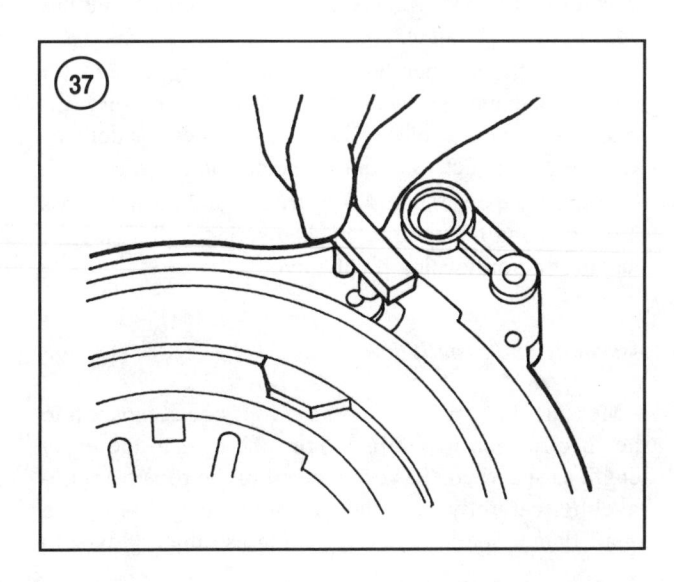

a. Note the direction the spring winds into the housing (**Figure 24**) before removing it.
b. Wear eye protection, heavy gloves and protective clothing when removing the spring. Place a heavy piece of cloth or a towel over the spring to help contain the spring.
c. Pull one loop of the spring at a time from the housing (**Figure 25**).

Component inspection

Clean all components except the rope in a solvent suitable for composite or plastic material. Use hot soapy water if a suitable solvent is not available. Dry all components with compressed air. Refer to **Figure 31** for this procedure.

1. Inspect the drive pawl (18, **Figure 31**) for worn, damaged or cracked surfaces and replace it if necessary.
2. Inspect the link and drive pawl spring (19 and 20, **Figure 31**) for broken or bent springs and corroded or worn surfaces. Replace them if they have any defects.
3. Inspect the entire length of the starter spring, if it was removed, for cracked, corroded or damaged surfaces. Pay particular attention to the hook or bent end. Replace the spring if it has any defects.
4. Inspect the sheave (13, **Figure 31**) for warped, worn or damaged surfaces and replace it if necessary.
5. Inspect the entire length of the rope for cuts and worn or frayed areas. Pay particular attention to the length nearest the handle. Replace the rope with the proper type and length if it is not in excellent condition.
6. Inspect the rope guide for worn or damaged surfaces. To prevent rapid wear of the replacement rope, replace the housing if it has sharp surfaces or if a deep groove has worn in the rope guide.
7. Inspect the stopper levers (3 and 4, **Figure 31**) for worn or damaged surfaces and replace as necessary. Inspect the lockout cable, spring and linkages for defects. Replace any defective or questionable components.
8. Inspect the bushing (14, **Figure 31**) and bushing boss in the housing for worn or cracked surfaces. Replace the bushing and/or housing if defective.

Assembly and installation

Measure the length of the starter rope and compare it to the specification in **Table 2**. Trim the rope to the *exact* length as specified. To keep the end of the rope from unraveling, carefully melt the cut end of the rope with a small flame. While it is still molten use thick gloves to shape the end of the rope into a compact nub. Trim loose pieces from the end when it has cooled.

Refer to **Figure 31** for this procedure.

1. Apply Yamaha All-Purpose Grease or its equivalent to the spring contact surfaces in the housing.

CAUTION
Do not remove the retainer from a replacement starter spring until the spring is properly installed in the housing.

2A. For a new starter spring, install the spring fully into the housing (**Figure 26**). Install the loop on the outer end of the spring over the post in the housing. Hold the spring firmly into the housing with a glove protected hand and carefully remove the spring retainers.
2B. For a used starter spring, clamp the housing to a stable work surface. Install the loop on the outer end of the spring over the post in the housing. Carefully wind the spring counterclockwise into the housing until all loops are installed and the spring is fully positioned in the housing.
3. Slip one end of the rope through the hole in the sheave and tie a knot as indicated in **Figure 27**. Make sure the rope end equals the dimension in **Figure 27**. Press the knot into the recess in the sheave. Position the sheave so the flywheel side faces up.
4. Install the pivot pin of the drive pawl (18, **Figure 31**) into its opening in the sheave. Secure the drive pawl with the E-clip (17, **Figure 31**).
5. Wrap the rope two complete turns counterclockwise around the sheave groove. Apply Yamaha All-Purpose Grease or equivalent to the surfaces, then install the bushing (14, **Figure 31**) onto the housing boss.
6. Install the upper and lower stopper arms (3 and 4, **Figure 31**) onto the housing. Secure the stopper arms with the washer and cotter pin (**Figure 36**).
7. Apply Yamaha All-Purpose Grease or its equivalent to the flat surfaces of the sheave that contact the spring. Pass the free end of the rope through the rope guide.
8. Place the loop on the inner end of the spring over the post on the sheave (**Figure 28**) while installing the sheave into the housing. Insert a screwdriver into the opening in the sheave to guide the loop onto the post if necessary.
9. Hold the sheave in the housing and rotate the sheave slightly counterclockwise. If there is no spring tension, the loop at the end of the spring is not over the post and the sheave must be removed and reinstalled.
10. Connect the link (19, **Figure 31**) and spring (20) to the drive pawl (18). Install the friction spring (12, **Figure 31**) onto the drive plate. Install the tip of the friction spring into the link and install the spring and plate onto the sheave.

MANUAL STARTER

11. Apply Loctite 271 or 572 to the threads of the sheave bolt (10, **Figure 31**). Install the bolt and tighten it to the specification in or Chapter One.

12. Place the starter on a work surface with the flywheel end facing up. Install the rope into the notch in the sheave as indicated in **Figure 29**.

13. Keep the rope in the notch while rotating the sheave 2 1/2 turns counterclockwise direction.

14. Have an assistant maintain light downward pressure on the sheave to prevent rotation. Route the rope through the handle. Tie a knot in the handle as indicated in **Figure 30**. Push the knot into the opening in the handle.

15. Pull on the handle to remove slack from the rope. Have the assistant release the sheave while slowly allowing the rope to feed into the housing. Press the plug into the handle.

16. Move the upper stopper lever to release the lockout assembly. Operate the starter several times to check for proper operation. The drive pawl should pivot out as the rope is pulled and pivot in as the rope is released. Disassemble and inspect the starter if it binds or does not operate correctly.

17. Collapse the spring, then insert the end of the lockout cable into the slot in the upper stopper lever. Press the cable into the retaining groove in the housing.

18. Install the bushing into the mounting screw openings. Install the manual starter onto the power head. Apply Loctite 271 or 572 to the threads of the mounting screws. Install the three mounting screws and washers. Install and securely tighten the three mounting screws.

19. Connect the end of the lockout cable to the shift linkage and bracket. Secure the cable with the adjusting nuts (**Figure 32**).

20. Adjust the lockout assembly as described in Chapter Four. Connect the spark plug leads. Check for proper operation of the lockout assembly before putting the engine into service.

E60 and E75 Models

Three screws secure the manual starter to the power head. A lever type cable actuated lockout assembly is used on these models.

Removal and disassembly

Refer to **Figure 38** for this procedure.

1. Disconnect the spark plug leads to keep the engine from starting.

2. Remove the screw and cotter pin, then disconnect the lockout cable from the slide (33, **Figure 38**) and housing (18).

3. Remove the three screws, then lift the starter from the power head. Place the starter on a clean work surface with the flywheel side facing up. Remove the bushings from the mounting screw openings.

4. Rotate the sheave until the notch aligns with the rope guide. Grasp a loop of the rope and insert it into the notch as shown in **Figure 33**. Hold the rope in the notch while rotating the sheave clockwise until the spring is fully relaxed.

5. Carefully pry the plug (19, **Figure 38**) and rope knot from the handle opening. Untie the knot, then pull the handle from the rope.

6. Remove the bolt (**Figure 34**), then lift the washers (2, **Figure 38**), drive plate (3) and springs (4 and 5) from the sheave.

7. Use snap ring pliers to remove the snap ring (8, **Figure 38**). Lift the washer (9, **Figure 38**) from the sheave. Remove the lower plate (12, **Figure 38**) from the spring.

8. Insert a screwdriver into the opening in the starter spring (**Figure 23**). Press down on the screwdriver to hold the spring in the housing. Maintain constant downward pressure and carefully lift the sheave and rope from the housing. Remove the screwdriver when the sheave clears the housing.

9. Remove the bushing (10, **Figure 38**) from the boss in the housing. Loosen the knot and remove the rope from the sheave. Pull the drive pawl (6, **Figure 38**) and collar (7) from the sheave.

10. Remove the pivot screw (29, **Figure 38**), then lift the lever (30) and spring (31) from the housing. Pull the slide (33, **Figure 38**) and spring (32) from the housing.

11. Inspect the starter spring for corroded, distorted or cracked surfaces. If the spring is defective, remove it as follows:
    a. Note the direction the spring winds into the housing (**Figure 24**) before removing it.
    b. Wear eye protection, heavy gloves and protective clothing when removing the spring. Place a heavy piece of cloth or a towel over the spring to help contain the spring.
    c. Pull one loop of the spring at a time from the housing (**Figure 25**).
    d. Remove the upper plate (14, **Figure 38**) from the housing.

Component inspection

Clean all components except the rope in a solvent suitable for composite or plastic material. Use hot soapy wa-

460

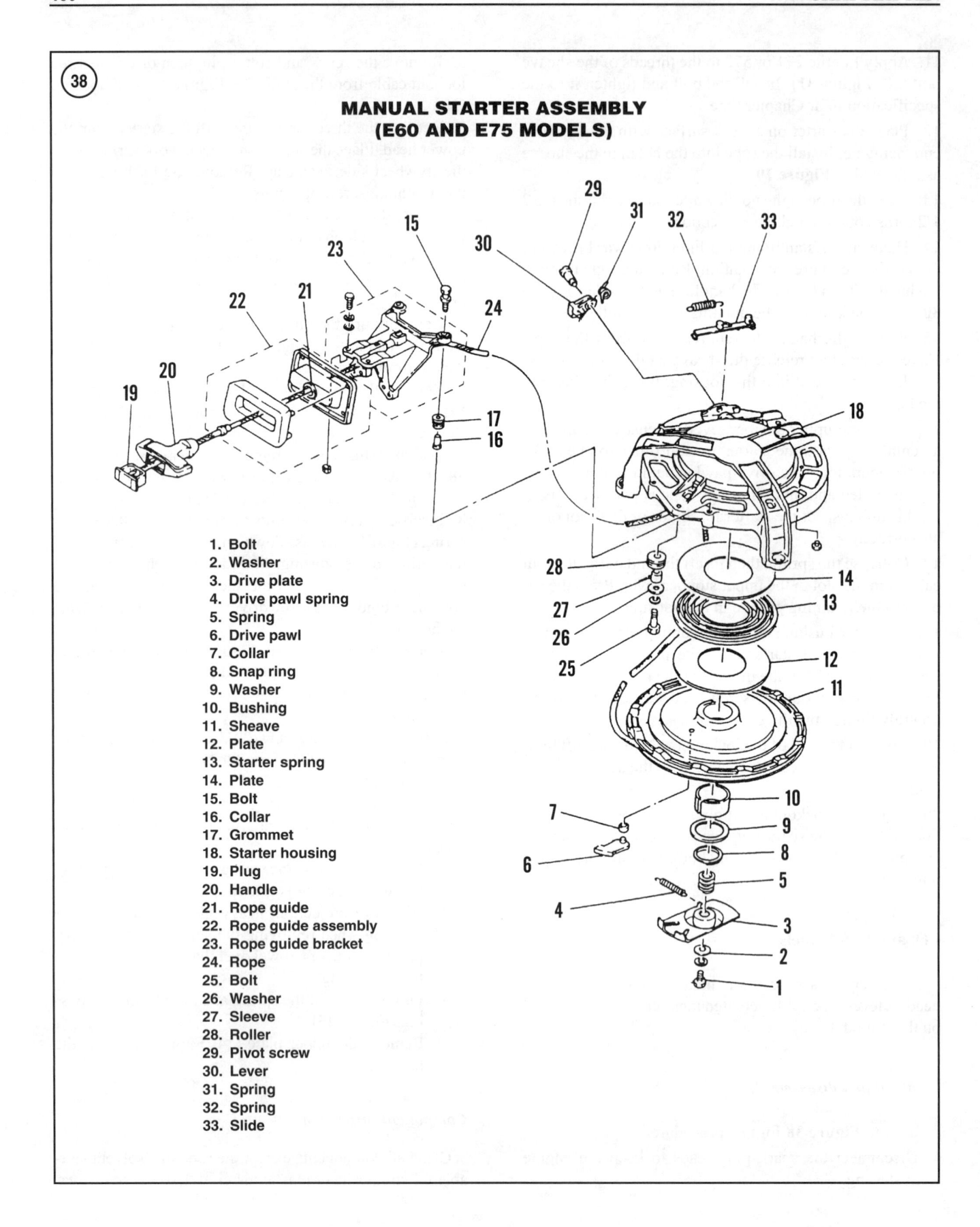

CHAPTER TEN

MANUAL STARTER ASSEMBLY (E60 AND E75 MODELS)

1. Bolt
2. Washer
3. Drive plate
4. Drive pawl spring
5. Spring
6. Drive pawl
7. Collar
8. Snap ring
9. Washer
10. Bushing
11. Sheave
12. Plate
13. Starter spring
14. Plate
15. Bolt
16. Collar
17. Grommet
18. Starter housing
19. Plug
20. Handle
21. Rope guide
22. Rope guide assembly
23. Rope guide bracket
24. Rope
25. Bolt
26. Washer
27. Sleeve
28. Roller
29. Pivot screw
30. Lever
31. Spring
32. Spring
33. Slide

MANUAL STARTER

ter if a suitable solvent is not available. Dry all components with compressed air. Refer to **Figure 38** for this procedure.

1. Inspect the drive pawl (6, **Figure 38**) for worn, damaged or cracked surfaces and replace it if necessary.
2. Inspect the drive pawl spring (4, **Figure 38**) for broken, bent, corroded or worn surfaces. Replace it if it has any defects.
3. Inspect the entire length of the starter spring, if it was removed, for cracked, corroded or damaged surfaces. Pay particular attention to the hook or bent end. Replace the spring if it has any defects.
4. Inspect the sheave (11, **Figure 38**) for warped, worn or damaged surfaces and replace it if necessary.
5. Inspect the entire length of the rope for cuts and worn or frayed areas. Pay particular attention to the length nearest the handle. Replace the rope with the proper type and length if it is not in excellent condition.
6. Inspect the rope guide and roller for worn or damaged surfaces. To prevent rapid wear of the replacement rope, replace the rope guide and/or roller if there are sharp surfaces or if a deep groove has worn in the rope guide or roller.
7. Inspect the lockout lever (30, **Figure 38**) for worn or damaged surfaces and replace it if necessary. Inspect the lockout cable, springs and linkages for defects. Replace any defective or questionable components.
8. Inspect the bushing (10, **Figure 38**) and bushing boss in the housing for worn or cracked surfaces. Replace the bushing and/or housing if there are defects.
9. Inspect the spring plates (12 and 14, **Figure 38**) for worn, corroded or damaged surfaces and replace them if they have defects.

Assembly and installation

Measure the length of the starter rope and compare it to the specification in **Table 2**. Trim the rope to the *exact* length as specified. To prevent the end of the rope from unraveling, carefully melt the cut end of the rope with a small flame. While it is still molten use thick gloves to shape the end of the rope into a compact nub. Trim loose pieces from the end when it has cooled.

Refer to **Figure 38** for this procedure.

1. Insert the upper plate (14, **Figure 38**) into the housing. Apply Yamaha All-Purpose Grease or its equivalent to the spring contact surfaces on the plate.

CAUTION
Do not *remove the retainer from a replacement starter spring until the spring is properly installed in the housing.*

2A. For a new starter spring, install the spring fully into the housing (**Figure 26**). Place the loop on the outer end of the spring over the post in the housing. Hold the spring firmly into the housing and carefully remove the spring retainers.

2B. For a used starter spring, clamp the housing to a stable work surface. Place the loop on the outer end of the spring over the post in the housing. Carefully wind the spring counterclockwise into the housing until all loops are installed and the spring is fully positioned into the housing.

3. Apply Yamaha All-Purpose Grease or equivalent to the spring contact surfaces of the lower plate (14, **Figure 38**). Insert the lower plate into the housing with the greased side toward the spring. Seat the plate against the spring.
4. Slip one end of the rope through the hole in the sheave and tie a knot as indicated in **Figure 27**. Make sure the rope end equals the dimension indicated in **Figure 27**. Press the knot into the recess in the sheave. Position the sheave so the flywheel side faces up.
5. Wrap the rope 1 1/2 turns counterclockwise around the sheave groove. Apply Yamaha All-Purpose Grease or equivalent to the surfaces, then install the bushing (10, **Figure 38**) onto the housing boss.
6. Pass the free end of the rope through the rope guide.
7. Place the loop on the inner end of the spring over the post on the sheave (**Figure 28**) while installing the sheave into the housing. Insert a screwdriver into the opening in the sheave to guide the loop onto the post if necessary.
8. Hold the sheave into the housing and rotate the sheave slightly counterclockwise. If there is no spring tension, the loop at the end of the spring is not over the post and the sheave must be removed and reinstalled.
9. Install the washer (9, **Figure 38**) over the sheave. Use snap ring pliers to install the snap ring (8, **Figure 38**). The snap ring must seat fully into the groove in the housing boss.
10. Place the starter on a work surface with the flywheel end facing up. Insert the rope into the notch in the sheave as indicated in **Figure 29**.
11. Keep the rope in the notch while rotating the sheave six complete turns counterclockwise direction.
12. Have an assistant maintain light downward pressure on the sheave to prevent rotation. Route the rope through the handle. Tie a knot in the handle as indicated in **Figure 30**. Push the knot into the opening in the handle.
13. Pull on the handle to remove slack from the rope. Have the assistant release the sheave while slowly allowing the rope to feed into the housing. Press the plug to the handle.

14. Press the collar (7, **Figure 38**) into its opening in the sheave. Install the pivot of the drive pawl (6, **Figure 38**) into the collar. Install the spring (5, **Figure 38**) into its opening in the sheave. Apply a light coat of Yamaha All-Purpose Grease or equivalent to the drive pawl surfaces.

15. Connect the drive pawl spring (4, **Figure 38**) to the drive pawl. Connect the drive pawl spring to the drive plate, then install the drive plate onto the sheave. The slot in the drive plate must align with the raised surfaces on the sheave.

16. Install the thrust washers (2, **Figure 38**). Then apply Loctite 271 or 572 to the threads of the bolt (1, **Figure 38**). Install the bolt and tighten it to the specification in **Table 1**.

17. Apply a light coat of Yamaha All-Purpose Grease or equivalent to the surfaces, then install the slide (33, **Figure 38**) and spring (32) into its slot in the housing. Apply a light coat of Yamaha All-Purpose Grease or equivalent to the surfaces of the lever (30, **Figure 38**). Install the spring (31, **Figure 38**), then the lever (30), into the housing. The ends of the spring must fit into the slot in the housing and the opening in the lever. Install and securely tighten the pivot screw (29, **Figure 38**) to secure the lever. Connect the spring (32, **Figure 38**) to the lever and the tab on the housing.

18. Move the lever to release the lockout assembly. Operate the starter several times to check for proper operation. The drive pawl should pivot out as the rope is pulled and pivot in as the rope is released. Disassemble and inspect the starter if it binds or does not operate correctly.

19. Install the bushing into the mounting screw openings. Install the manual starter onto the power head. Apply Loctite 271 or 572 to the threads of the mounting screws. Install and securely tighten the three mounting screws.

20. Install the end of the lockout cable over the pin on the slide. Secure the cable to the pin with the cotter pin. Install the lockout cable into the groove in the housing. Secure the cable to the housing with a screw.

21. Adjust the lockout assembly as described in Chapter Four. Connect the spark plug leads. Check for proper operation of the lockout assembly before putting the engine into service.

Table 1 MANUAL STARTER TORQUE SPECIFICATIONS

Fastener	N•m	in.-lb.	ft.-lb.
Rope guide/bracket bolts			
4 and 5 hp	6	53	–
6 and 8 hp	5	44	–
Starter sheave bolt/nut			
4 and 5 hp	3	26	–
6 and 8 hp	4	35	–
E48, E60 and E75	8	70	–

Table 2 STARTER ROPE LENGTH

Model	Rope length
2 hp	1300 mm (51.2 in.)
3 hp	1650 mm (65.0 in.)
4-8 hp	1850 mm (72.8 in.)
9.9 and 15 hp	1800 mm (70.9 in.)
20 hp	1950 mm (76.8 in.)
25 hp two-cylinder	1950 mm (76.8 in.)
25 hp three-cylinder	1925 mm (75.8 in.)
28 jet, 35 jet, 40 hp and 50 hp	2095 mm (82.5 in.)
E60 and E75	2300 mm (90.6 in.)

Chapter Eleven

Tilt/Trim and Midsection

This chapter includes removal, installation and minor repair procedures for the hydraulic tilt and trim systems. Procedures for removal, inspection and assembly of the midsection and tiller control components are also in this chapter.

Table 1 lists torque specifications for most trim, midsection and tiller control components. Use the general torque specifications in Chapter One for fasteners not listed in **Table 1**. **Table 2** lists electric trim motor specifications. **Table 1** and **Table 2** are located at the end of the chapter.

WARNING
*Never work under any part of the engine without providing suitable support. The engine-mounted tilt lock or hydraulic system may unexpectedly collapse and allow the engine to drop. Support the engine with suitable blocks or an overhead cable **before** working under the engine.*

MANUAL TILT SYSTEM REMOVAL AND INSTALLATION

WARNING
The trim system may contain fluid under high pressure. Always use protective eyewear and gloves when working with the trim system. Never remove components or plugs without first bleeding the pressure from the system. Follow the instructions carefully.

Mounting fastener location and component appearance vary by model. Mark or make note of component mounting location and orientation prior to removal to ensure proper assembly.

Apply Yamaha All-Purpose Grease or its equivalent to all bushings (5, **Figure 1**, typical), pivot points and sliding surfaces during assembly. Apply Loctite 572 to the threads of the tilt lever (2, **Figure 1**, typical) bolt and the mounting bolt (6).

464

CHAPTER ELEVEN

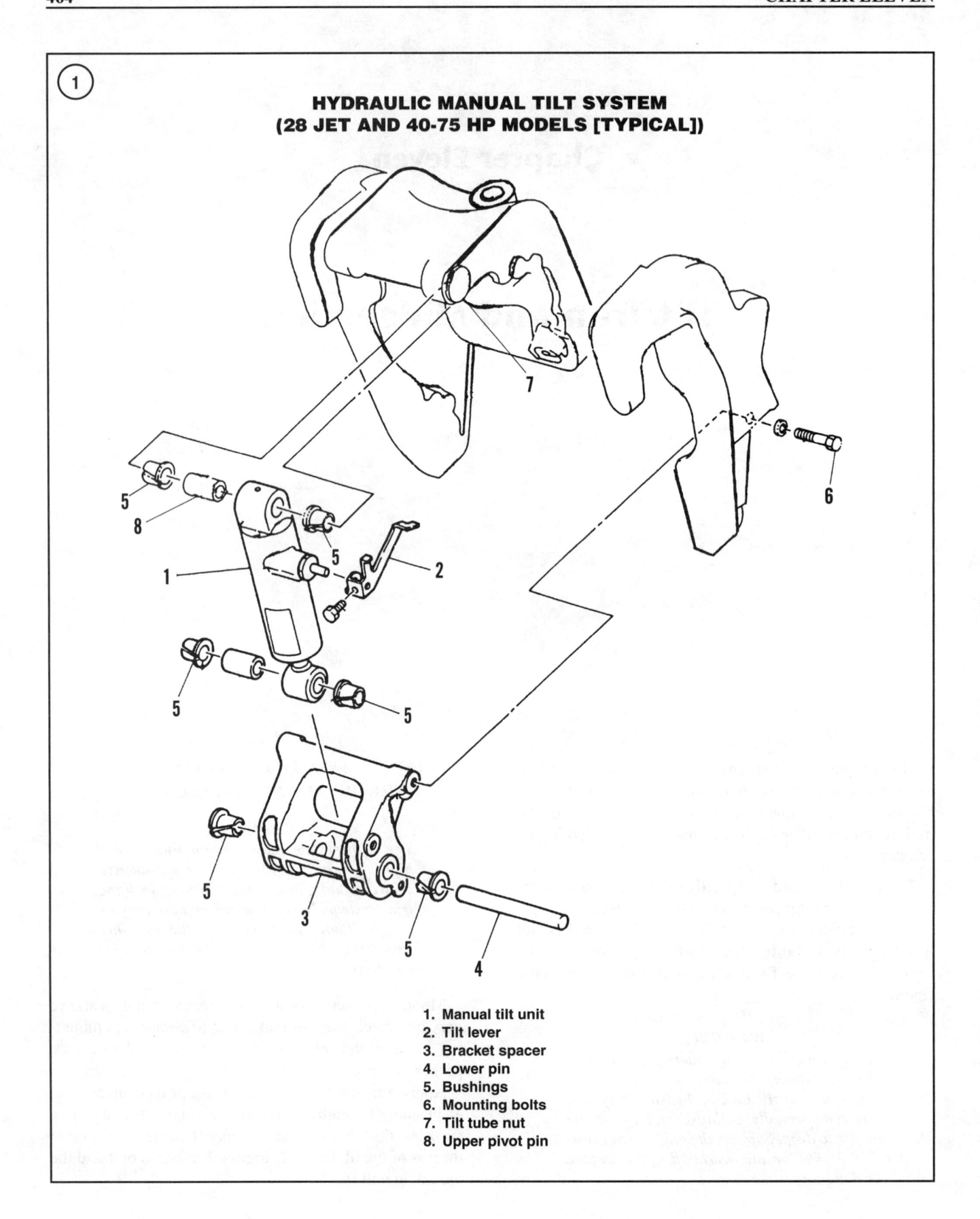

① **HYDRAULIC MANUAL TILT SYSTEM (28 JET AND 40-75 HP MODELS [TYPICAL])**

1. Manual tilt unit
2. Tilt lever
3. Bracket spacer
4. Lower pin
5. Bushings
6. Mounting bolts
7. Tilt tube nut
8. Upper pivot pin

TILT/TRIM AND MIDSECTION

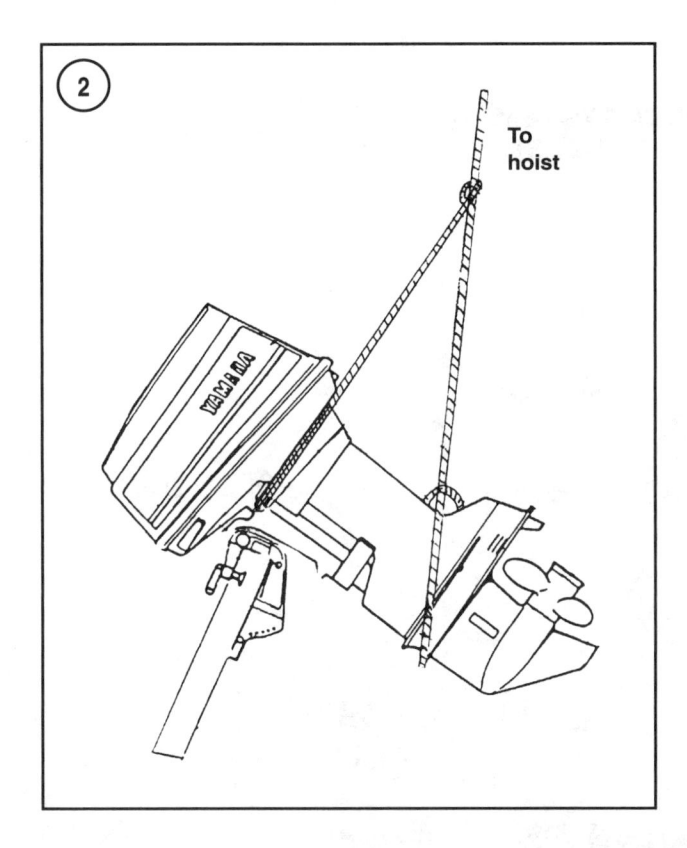

The manual tilt unit (1, **Figure 1**) is non-serviceable and must be replaced if it is defective. The tilt lever, pivot pins and bushings are the only replaceable components of the system. Refer to **Figure 1** during the removal and installation procedures.

1. Disconnect the battery cables. Disconnect *all* spark plug leads.
2. Move the tilt lever to the UNLOCK position and pivot the engine to the full UP position. Use an overhead hoist or other secure means to support the engine as indicated in **Figure 2**.
3. Remove the bolts (6, **Figure 1**) from the clamp brackets.
4. Pivot the bracket spacer (3, **Figure 1**) out of the clamp brackets and carefully drive the lower pin (4) from the assembly. Be careful to avoid damaging the pivot surfaces or bushings.
5. Remove the snap ring, then carefully drive the upper pivot pin (8, **Figure 1**) from the swivel bracket and tilt unit cylinder. Remove the tilt unit from the engine.
6. Inspect the snap ring for corrosion or weak spring tension and replace it if its condition is questionable. Inspect all bushings and pins for damaged or worn surfaces and replace them as necessary.
7. Remove the tilt lever (2, **Figure 1**) by loosening the bolt and slipping the lever from the control valve rod. To reinstall the tilt lever, align the bolt opening in the lever with the flat surface on the control valve rod. Apply Loctite 572 to the threads of the tilt lever bolt. Install and securely tighten the bolt.
8. Installation is the reverse of removal. Apply Loctite 572 to the threads of the bracket spacer bolts (6, **Figure 1**). Apply Yamaha All-Purpose Grease or equivalent to the pivot surfaces of all bushings and pivot pins. Tighten all fasteners to the specification in **Table 1** or Chapter One.
9. Connect the battery cables to the battery. Check for proper operation before putting the engine into service.

POWER TILT/TRIM SYSTEM REMOVAL/INSTALLATION

Fastener location and component appearance vary by model. Mark the mounting location and orientation of all components prior to removal to ensure proper assembly. Make a sketch of the trim motor wire routing before removal. Improper routing may allow the wire to become pinched during engine operation. Apply Yamaha All-Purpose Grease or equivalent to all bushings, pivot points and sliding surfaces on assembly. Apply Loctite 242 to the threads of the trim system fasteners. Remove all corrosion, paint or foreign material from the terminal, mounting screw threads, and terminal contact surfaces.

25 and 25 hp Models

Refer to **Figure 3** for this procedure.

1. Disconnect the battery cables. Disconnect *all* spark plug leads.
2. Locate the access opening for the manual release valve (**Figure 4**) in the starboard side clamp bracket. Rotate the manual release valve 3-4 turns counterclockwise. Tilt the engine to the full up position and securely tighten the manual release valve.
3. Use an overhead hoist or other suitable means to support the engine as indicated in **Figure 2**.
4. Trace the wires from the electric tilt/trim motor (21, **Figure 3**) to the connections at the power head and disconnect the wires. Route the wires out of the lower cover opening to allow for removal of the tilt/trim system. Cut the plastic tie clamp (3, **Figure 3**) to free the wires from the clamp bracket.
5. Remove the screws (16, **Figure 3**), grounding wires (14 and 17) and anode (15) from the tilt/trim unit. Replace the anode if it has lost a significant amount of material, is deeply pitted, or coated with marine growth or other foreign material.

CHAPTER ELEVEN

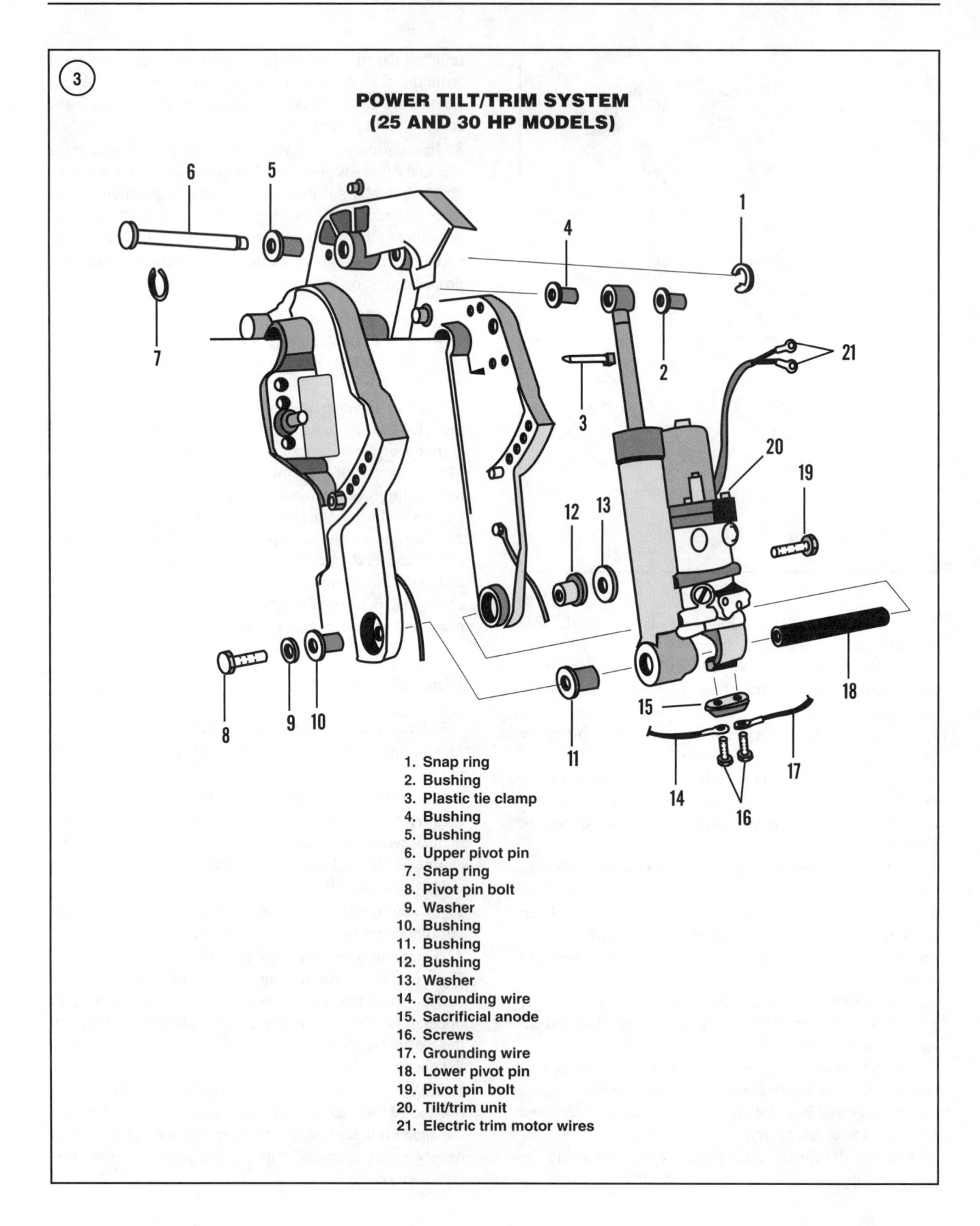

③ **POWER TILT/TRIM SYSTEM (25 AND 30 HP MODELS)**

1. Snap ring
2. Bushing
3. Plastic tie clamp
4. Bushing
5. Bushing
6. Upper pivot pin
7. Snap ring
8. Pivot pin bolt
9. Washer
10. Bushing
11. Bushing
12. Bushing
13. Washer
14. Grounding wire
15. Sacrificial anode
16. Screws
17. Grounding wire
18. Lower pivot pin
19. Pivot pin bolt
20. Tilt/trim unit
21. Electric trim motor wires

TILT/TRIM AND MIDSECTION

Route the wires out of the lower cover opening to allow for removal of the tilt/trim system. Cut the plastic tie clamp (2, **Figure 5**) to free the wires from the clamp bracket.

5. Remove the bolts (3 and 5, **Figure 5**) and ground wires (4 and 6) from the clamp brackets.
6. Remove the nuts (8 and 13, **Figure 5**), washers (9) and stud bolt (10). Pivot the bracket spacer (11, **Figure 5**) out of the clamp brackets.
7. Pull the bracket spacer from the tilt/trim system and remove the bushings (12, **Figure 5**).
8. Remove the snap ring (14, **Figure 5**) from the upper pivot pin (15). Support the tilt/trim system and carefully drive the upper pivot pin from the swivel housing.
9. Lower the tilt/trim system and remove the bushings (17, **Figure 5**) and sleeve (18) from the cylinder ram.
10. Inspect the snap rings for corrosion and weak spring tension. Replace the snap rings if they are in questionable condition. Inspect all bushings and pivot pins for worn, corroded or damaged surfaces. Replace as necessary.
11. Installation is the reverse of removal. Tighten all fasteners to the specification in **Table 1** or Chapter One. Apply Loctite 242 to the threads of the stud bolt (10, **Figure 5**) before installation. Route the trim motor wires carefully to avoid interference with other components. Secure the wires to the clamp bracket with a new plastic tie clamp (2, **Figure 5**).
12. Check for proper tilt/trim system operation before putting the engine into service.

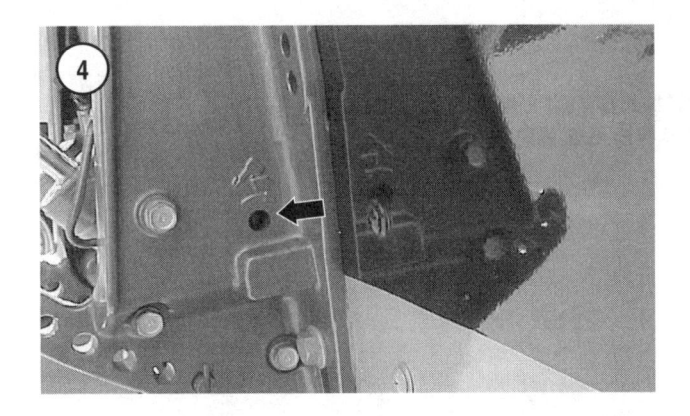

6. Remove the starboard snap ring (1, **Figure 3**) from the upper pivot pin (6). Carefully drive the upper pin from the swivel housing and tilt/trim unit. Only remove and replace the port snap ring (7, **Figure 3**) if it is damaged or if the upper pivot pin is being replaced.
7. Remove the pivot pin bolts (8 and 19, **Figure 3**) along with the washers (9) and external bushings (10). Carefully pivot the tilt/trim unit from the clamp brackets. Remove the bushings (11 and 12, **Figure 3**), washer (13) and lower pivot pin (18) from the clamp brackets and tilt/trim unit.
8. Inspect the snap rings for corrosion and weak spring tension. Replace the snap rings if they are in questionable condition. Inspect all bushings and pivot pins for worn, corroded or damaged surfaces. Replace as necessary.
9. Installation is the reverse of removal. Tighten all fasteners to the specification in **Table 1** or Chapter One. Apply Loctite 242 to the threads of the pivot pin bolts (8 and 19, **Figure 3**) before installation. Route the trim motor wires carefully to avoid interference with other components. Secure the wires to the clamp bracket with a new plastic tie clamp (3, **Figure 3**).
10. Check for proper tilt/trim system operation before putting the engine into service.

28 Jet, 35 Jet, 40 hp and 50 hp Models

Refer to **Figure 5** for this procedure.
1. Disconnect the battery cables. Disconnect *all* spark plug leads.
2. Locate the access opening for the manual release valve (**Figure 4**) in the port side clamp bracket. Rotate the manual release valve 2-3 turns counterclockwise. Move the engine to the full up position and securely tighten the manual release valve.
3. Use an overhead hoist or other suitable means to support the engine as indicated in **Figure 2**.
4. Trace the wires from the electric tilt/trim motor to the connections at the power head and disconnect the wires.

65 Jet and 60-90 hp Models

Refer to **Figure 6** for this procedure.
1. Disconnect the battery cables. Disconnect *all* spark plug leads.
2. Trace the wires (1, **Figure 6**) leading from the electric trim motor to the connections on the power head. Disconnect the wires from the relays or engine wire harness and route them out of the lower engine cover. Remove the plastic tie clamps (3, **Figure 6**) from along the wire.
3. Locate the access opening for the manual release valve (**Figure 4**) in the starboard side clamp bracket. Rotate the valve counterclockwise 2-3 turns (**Figure 7**). Carefully tilt the engine to the full up position. Use an overhead hoist or other suitable means to support the engine as indicated in **Figure 2**. Securely tighten the manual release valve.
4. Disconnect the grounding wires (2, **Figure 6**). Clean and inspect the grounding wire mounting locations and screw threads. Replace damaged wires and repair corroded or damaged threaded openings.

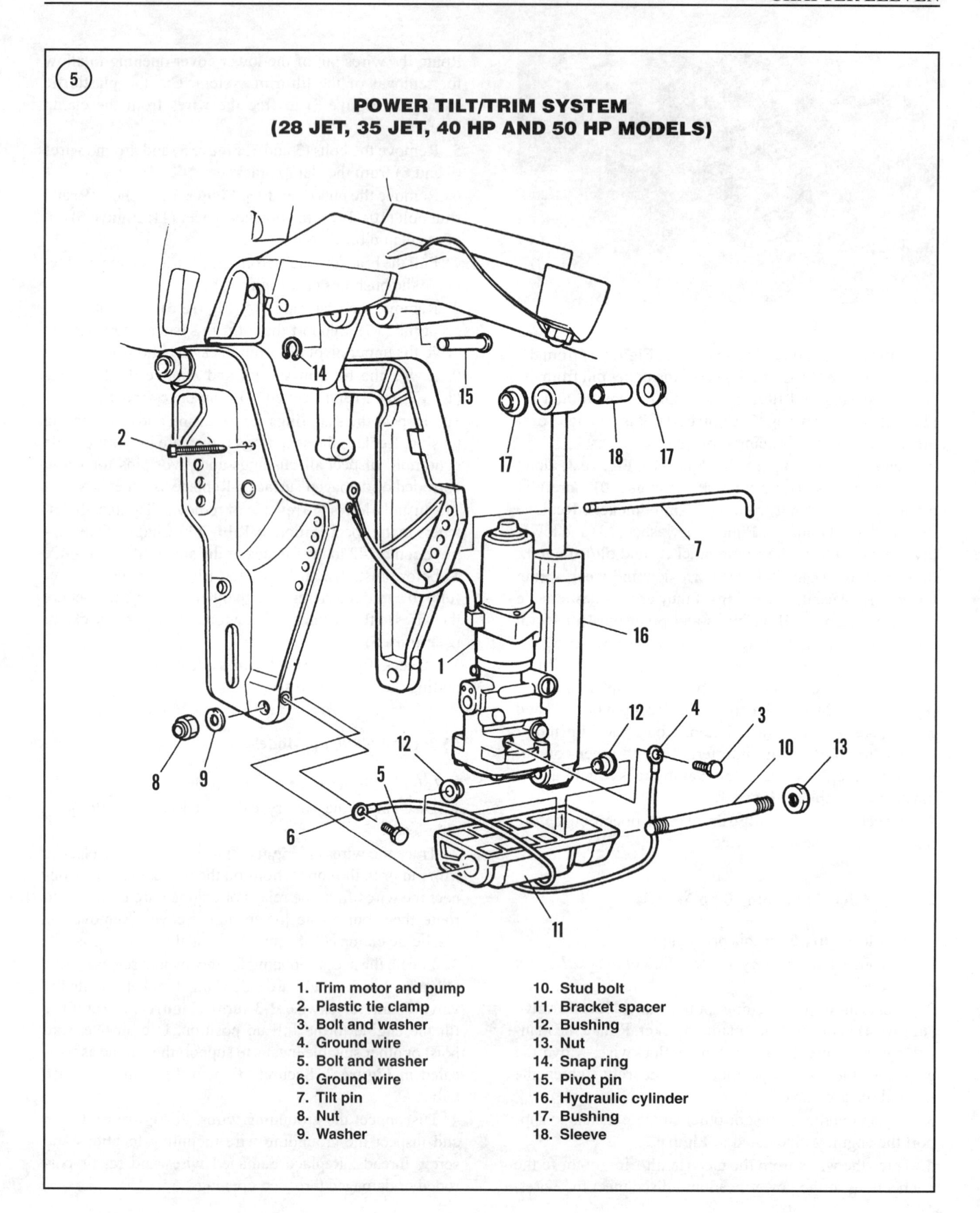

POWER TILT/TRIM SYSTEM
(28 JET, 35 JET, 40 HP AND 50 HP MODELS)

1. Trim motor and pump
2. Plastic tie clamp
3. Bolt and washer
4. Ground wire
5. Bolt and washer
6. Ground wire
7. Tilt pin
8. Nut
9. Washer
10. Stud bolt
11. Bracket spacer
12. Bushing
13. Nut
14. Snap ring
15. Pivot pin
16. Hydraulic cylinder
17. Bushing
18. Sleeve

TILT/TRIM AND MIDSECTION

(6) POWER TILT/TRIM SYSTEM (65 JET AND 60-90 HP MODELS)

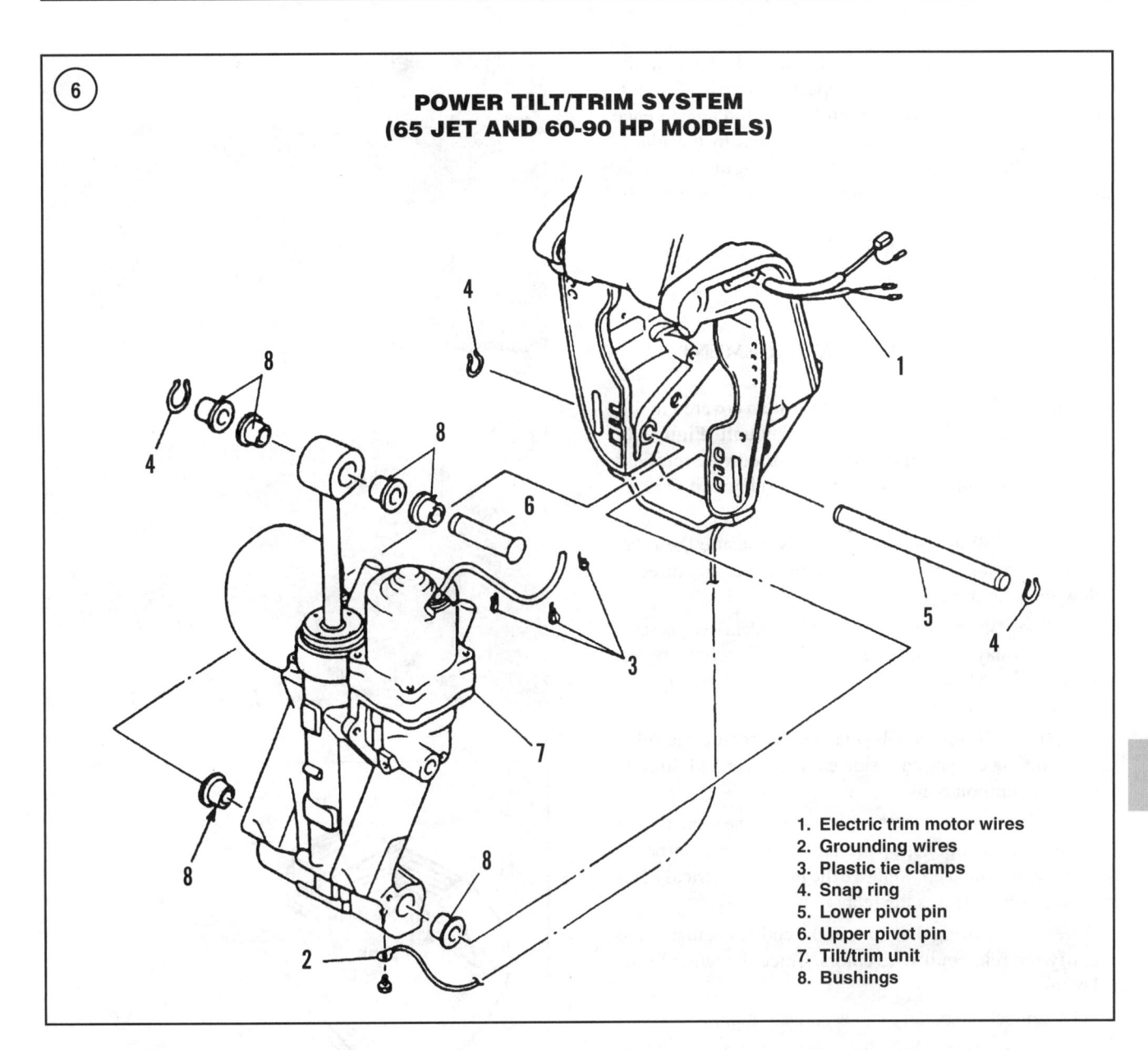

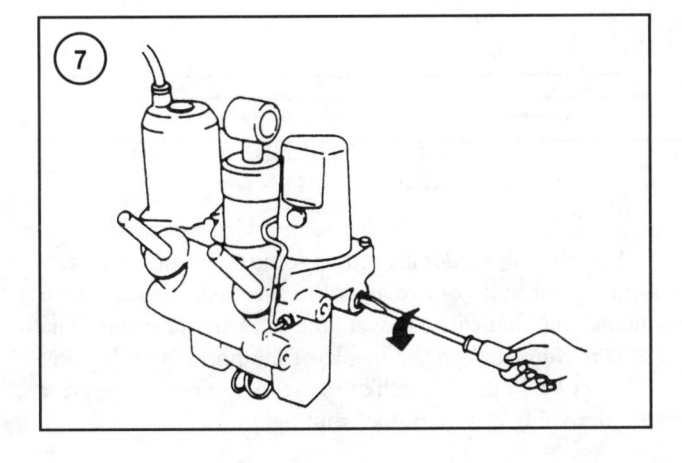

1. Electric trim motor wires
2. Grounding wires
3. Plastic tie clamps
4. Snap ring
5. Lower pivot pin
6. Upper pivot pin
7. Tilt/trim unit
8. Bushings

5. Remove the snap rings (4, **Figure 6**) from the lower pivot pin. Carefully drive the pivot pin from the clamp brackets and tilt/trim system.

6. Remove the snap ring (4, **Figure 6**) from the port side of the upper pivot pin (6). Support the tilt/trim system and carefully drive the upper pivot pin from the swivel housing. Pull the trim system from the clamp brackets.

7. Remove the bushings (8, **Figure 6**) from the tilt/trim system, swivel housing and clamp brackets.

8. Inspect the snap rings for corrosion and weak spring tension. Replace the snap rings if they are in questionable condition. Inspect all bushings and pivot pins for worn, corroded or damaged surfaces. Replace as necessary.

9. Installation is the reverse of removal. Tighten the grounding wire screws to the specification in **Table 1**. Route the trim motor wires carefully to avoid interference with other components. Secure the wires to the clamp bracket with new plastic tie clamps (3, **Figure 6**). Make sure the snap rings (4, **Figure 6**) fit snugly into the grooves in the pivot pins.

10. Check for proper tilt/trim system operation before putting the engine into service.

TILT/TRIM RELAY REPLACEMENT

All models with a power tilt/trim system covered in this manual are equipped with a single relay unit (**Figure 8**). Replace the relay unit if either the up or down circuit has failed. The mounting locations for the relay unit vary by model.

On 25 and 30 hp models, two screws secure the relay unit to the lower starboard side engine cover and directly below the starter motor.

On 28 jet, 35 jet, 40 hp and 50 hp models, two screws secure the relay unit to the electrical component bracket on the starboard side of the power head. The relay unit mounts below the starter motor.

On 60 and 70 hp models, two screws secure the relay unit to the lower starboard side engine cover and directly below the ignition coils.

On 75-90 hp models, two screws secure the relay unit to the electrical component plate on the rear and starboard side of the power head. Remove the plastic electrical component cover to access the relay unit.

Refer to the wiring diagrams at the end of the manual to identify the relay unit wire colors. Trace the wires to the relay unit.

1. Disconnect the battery cables at the battery.

2. Trace the wires to the component on the engine. Mark the connection location and orientation of each wire before removal. Disconnect all relay wires.

3. Remove the screws and lift the relay from the engine. Clean the mounting locations and the threaded holes for the mounting screws. Clean and inspect all terminal connections.

4. Reconnect the relay unit wires. Reinstall the relay and secure it with the two screws. Tighten the screws to the standard torque specification in Chapter One. Route all wires to avoid interference with other components.

5. Connect the battery cables to the battery. Check for proper operation of the tilt/trim system before putting the engine into service.

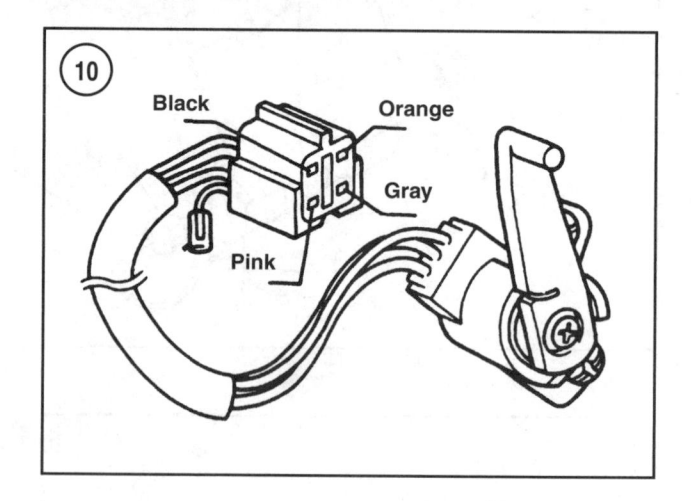

TILT/TRIM SENDER REPLACEMENT

The tilt/trim sender is used on some 60-90 hp models. It sends a varying voltage signal to the dash-mounted trim gauge that indicates the engine tilt/trim position. The sender is located on the inside of the port clamp bracket (**Figure 9**). Make a sketch of the sender wire routing prior to removal to ensure proper routing.

TILT/TRIM AND MIDSECTION

(11)

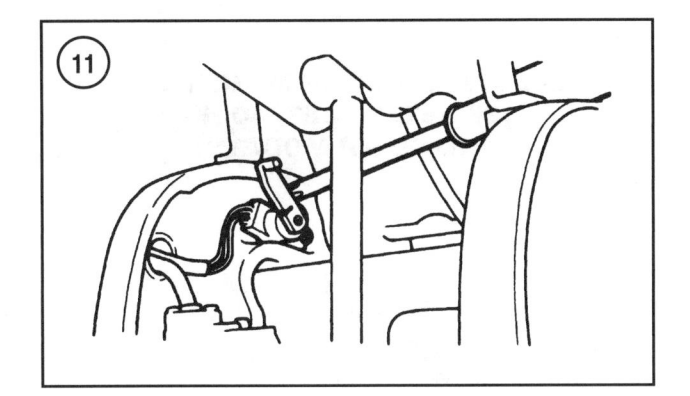

(12) ELECTRIC MOTOR MOUNTING (25 AND 30 HP MODELS)

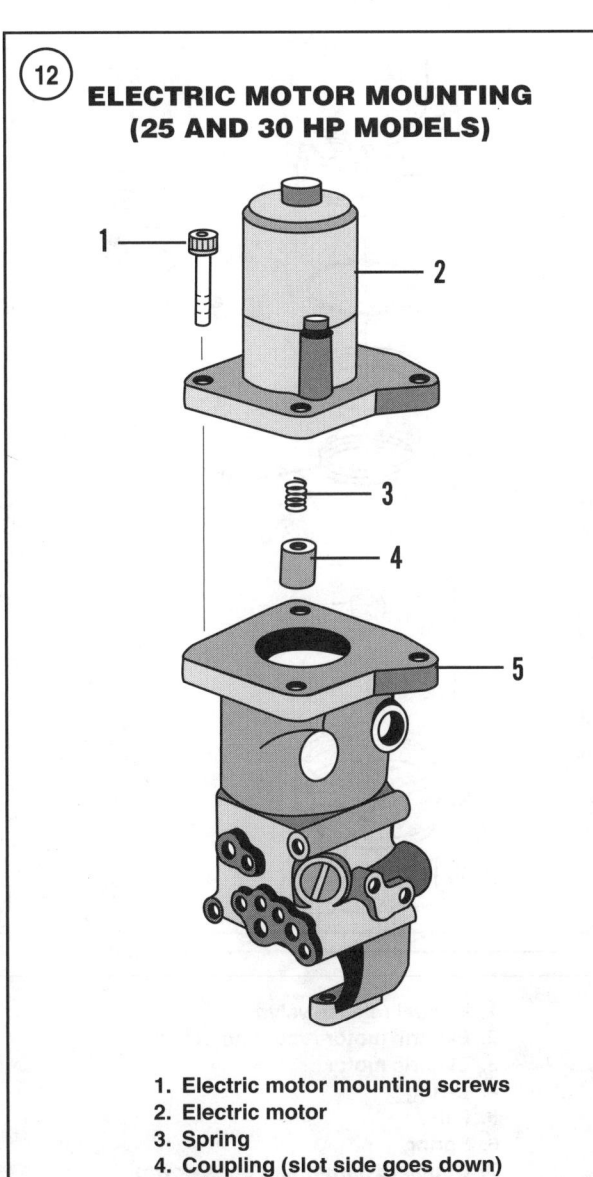

1. Electric motor mounting screws
2. Electric motor
3. Spring
4. Coupling (slot side goes down)
5. Hydraulic pump assembly

NOTE
Always adjust the tilt/trim sender after replacement. An improperly adjusted tilt/trim sender will cause inaccurate gauge readings.

1. Tilt the engine to the full up position and engage the tilt lock lever. Support the engine with blocks or a suitable overhead cable (**Figure 2**).
2. Trace the sender wires (**Figure 10**) to the engine wire harness connection. Disconnect the sender wires. Route the wires out of the lower engine cover. Remove the plastic tie clamps so the sender can be removed.
3. Use a felt tip marker to trace the outline of the sender on the clamp bracket. This will make the replacement sender adjustment quicker.
4. Remove both mounting screws (**Figure 11**) and the sender. Route the wires through the opening in the port clamp bracket and remove the assembly.
5. Clean corrosion and contamination from the sender mounting location and mounting screw openings.
6. Install the replacement sender onto the clamp bracket. Install and lightly tighten the mounting screws. Align the sender with the traced line and securely tighten the screws.
7. Route the sender wire through the clamp bracket and lower engine cover opening. Connect the sender wire to the engine wire harness.
8. Route the wires so they do not interfere with other components. Secure the sender wires to the clamp bracket with new plastic tie clamps.
9. Adjust the sender as described in Chapter Four.

ELECTRIC TRIM MOTOR REMOVAL/INSTALLATION

WARNING
The trim system may contain fluid under high pressure. Always use protective eyewear and gloves when working with the trim system. Never remove components or plugs without first bleeding the pressure from the system. Follow the instructions carefully.

The electric trim motor appearance, mounting arrangement and replacement procedures vary by model. Refer to **Figures 12-14** and the model specific instructions during the removal and installation procedures. The appearance of the components may vary slightly from the illustrations.

The port clamp bracket usually has to be removed for the electric motor on the triple hydraulic system used on 60-90 hp models to be removed. It is easier to remove the entire trim system than the clamp bracket. Clamp bracket or trim system removal and installation procedures are located in this chapter.

Removal and installation procedures vary by model. Model specific procedures are provided.

CAUTION
Never direct pressurized water at the seal surfaces when cleaning debris or contaminants from the trim system. The water may pass by the seal surface and contaminate the fluid.

The trim system must be operated with clean fluid. Small amounts of contaminants can wreak havoc with the trim system operation. Thoroughly clean the trim system external surfaces with soapy water before disassembly. Use compressed air to dry the trim system.

Work in a clean area and use lint-free towels to wipe debris or fluid from the components. Cover any openings to prevent accidental contamination of the fluid.

CAUTION
To avoid unnecessary disassembly and potential wire interference, always note the orientation of the electric trim motor and wire harness before disassembly. Use a paint dot or piece of tape to mark the location. Never scratch the housings as it will promote corrosion.

25 and 30 hp Models

Apply a light coat of Dextron II automatic transmission fluid to the O-ring on the base of the motor during assembly. Refer to **Figure 12** for this procedure.

1. Disconnect the battery cables. Disconnect *all* spark plug leads.

2. Locate the access opening for the manual release valve (**Figure 4**) in the starboard side clamp bracket. Rotate the manual release valve 3-4 turns counterclockwise (**Figure 7**). Tilt the engine to the full up position and securely tighten the manual release valve.

3. Use an overhead hoist or other suitable means to support the engine as indicated in **Figure 2**.

4. Trace the wires from the electric tilt/trim motor (21, **Figure 3**) to the connections at the power head and disconnect the wires. Route the wires out of the lower cover opening to allow the tilt/trim system to be removed. Cut the plastic tie clamp (3, **Figure 3**) to free the wires from the clamp bracket.

---

⑬ ELECTRIC MOTOR MOUNTING (28 JET, 35 JET, 40 HP AND 50 HP MODELS)

1. Manual release valve
2. Electric motor mounting screws
3. Electric motor
4. O-ring
5. Filter
6. Spring
7. Coupling (larger slot goes down)
8. Hydraulic pump assembly

TILT/TRIM AND MIDSECTION

14 ELECTRIC MOTOR MOUNTING (65 JET AND 60-90 HP MODELS)

1. Electric motor mounting screws
2. Electric motor
3. O-ring
4. Coupling (protrusion goes down)
5. Filter

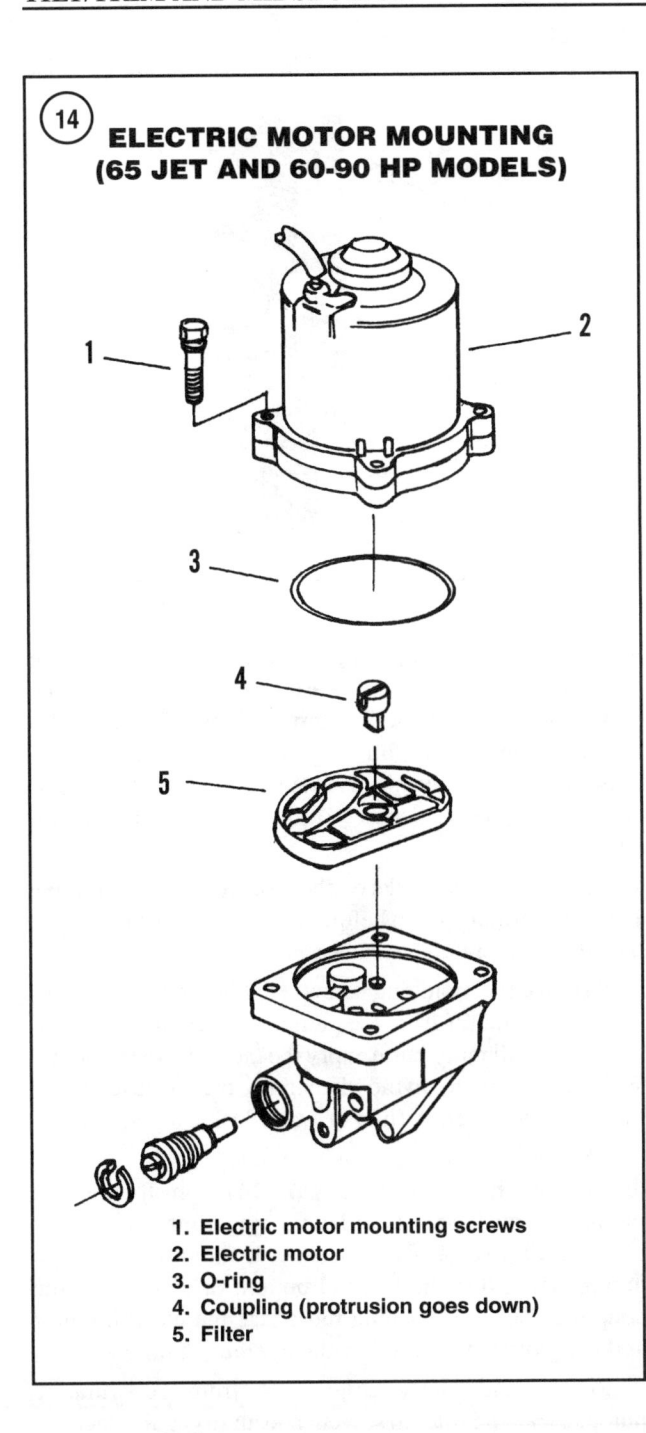

5. Make reference marks on the electric motor (2, **Figure 12**) and hydraulic pump (5) before removal. Use a paint dot or tape. Do not scratch the surfaces.

6. Remove the mounting screws (1, **Figure 12**) and carefully lift the motor from the pump. If necessary, use a flat scraper or dull putty knife to pry the motor from the pump. Work carefully to avoid damaging the electric motor mounting surfaces. A fluid or water leak can occur if the surfaces are damaged.

7. Remove the O-ring from the electric motor or pump base. Discard the O-ring. Retrieve the coupling (4, **Figure 12**) and spring (3) from the electric motor or hydraulic pump shaft. Note the top and bottom orientation of the coupling. The star-shaped opening must face the electric motor and the slotted side must face the hydraulic pump.

8. Clean and inspect the trim motor mounting surfaces for corroded, pitted or scratched surfaces. Replace any components that have scratches that can be felt with a fingernail.

9. Apply a light coat of Yamaha All-Purpose Grease or equivalent to a new O-ring and install it onto the electric motor-to-hydraulic pump mating surfaces. Apply a light coat of grease to the coupling. Install the spring, then the coupling, onto the electric motor shaft. Place the electric motor on the pump and rotate it until the coupling aligns with the pump and the motor drops into position.

10. Slowly rotate the electric motor until the wiring orientation is correct and install the electric motor mounting screws (1, **Figure 12**). Tighten the screws to the specification in **Table 1**.

11. Fill and bleed the hydraulic system as described in this chapter. Check for proper operation before putting the engine into service.

28 Jet, 35 Jet, 40 hp and 50 hp Models

Apply Loctite 572 to the threads of the electric motor mounting screw during assembly. Apply a light coat of Yamaha All-Purpose Grease or equivalent to the O-ring during assembly. Refer to **Figure 13** for this procedure.

1. Disconnect the battery cables. Disconnect *all* spark plug leads.

2. Locate the access opening for the manual release valve (**Figure 4**) in the port side clamp bracket. Rotate the manual release valve 3-4 turns counterclockwise (**Figure 7**). Tilt the engine to the full up position and securely tighten the manual release valve.

3. Use an overhead hoist or other suitable means to support the engine as indicated in **Figure 2**.

4. Trace the wires from the electric tilt/trim motor to the connections at the power head and disconnect the wires. Route the wires out of the lower cover opening so the tilt/trim system can be removed. Cut the plastic tie clamp (2, **Figure 5**) to free the wires from the clamp bracket.

5. Make reference marks on the electric motor (3, **Figure 13**) and hydraulic pump (8) before removal. Use a paint dot or tape. Do not scratch the surfaces.

6. Remove the mounting screws (2, **Figure 13**) and carefully lift the motor from the pump. If necessary, use a flat scraper or dull putty knife to pry the motor from the pump. Work carefully to avoid damaging the electric motor

mounting surfaces. A fluid or water leak can occur if the surfaces are damaged.

7. Remove the O-ring (4, **Figure 13**) from the electric motor or pump base. Discard the O-ring. Retrieve the coupling (7, **Figure 13**) from the electric motor or hydraulic pump shaft. Note the top and bottom orientation of the coupling. The smaller slot opening must face the electric motor and the larger slot opening side must face the hydraulic pump.

8. Remove the filter (5, **Figure 13**) and spring (6) from the hydraulic pump. Clean the filter and spring in solvent and air dry them. Replace the filter if it is damaged or if debris remains on the filter after cleaning. Replace the spring if it is corroded or damaged.

9. Clean and inspect the trim motor mounting surfaces for corroded, pitted or scratched surfaces. Replace any components that have scratches that can be felt with a fingernail.

10. Apply a light coat of Yamaha All-Purpose Grease or equivalent to a new O-ring (4, **Figure 13**) and install it onto the electric motor-to-hydraulic pump mating surface. Apply a light coat of grease to the coupling. Install the coupling onto the electric motor shaft. The smaller slot in the coupling must fit over the electric motor shaft.

11. Insert the spring, then the filter, into the hydraulic pump. The spring must fit onto the hydraulic pump body and the filter must be centered on the spring.

12. Position the electric motor on the pump and rotate it until the coupling aligns with the pump and the motor drops into position.

13. Slowly rotate the electric motor until the wiring orientation is correct. Apply Loctite 572 to the threads the mounting screws (2, **Figure 13**) then install them. Tighten the screws to the specification in Chapter One.

14. Fill and bleed the hydraulic system as described in this chapter. Check for proper operation before putting the engine into service.

65 Jet and 60-90 hp Models

Refer to **Figure 14** for this procedure. Remove the port clamp bracket or the complete tilt/trim system if the mounting arrangement does not allow easy access to the trim motor mounting screws.

1. Disconnect the battery cables. Disconnect *all* spark plug leads.

2. Trace the wires (1, **Figure 6**) leading from the electric trim motor to the connections on the power head. Disconnect the wires from the relays or engine wire harness and route them out of the lower engine cover. Remove the plastic tie clamps (3, **Figure 6**) from along the wire.

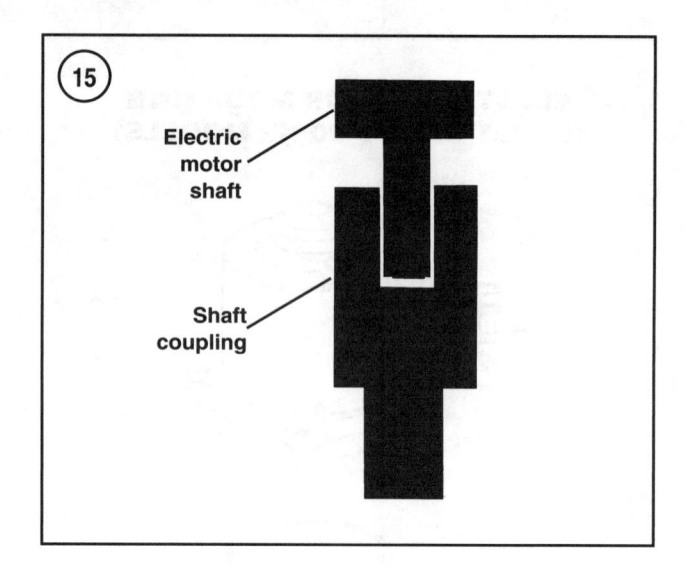

15
Electric motor shaft
Shaft coupling

3. Locate the access opening for the manual release valve (**Figure 4**) in the starboard side clamp bracket. Rotate the valve counterclockwise 2-3 turns (**Figure 7**). Carefully tilt the engine to the full up position. Use an overhead hoist or other suitable means to support the engine as indicated in **Figure 2**. Securely tighten the manual release valve.

4. Make reference marks on the electric motor (2, **Figure 14**) and hydraulic pump before removal. Use a paint dot or tape. Do not scratch the surfaces.

5. Remove the mounting screws (1, **Figure 14**) and carefully lift the motor from the pump. If necessary, use a flat scraper or dull putty knife to pry the motor from the pump. Work carefully to avoid damaging the electric motor mounting surfaces. A fluid or water leak can occur if the surfaces are damaged.

6. Remove the O-ring (3, **Figure 14**) from the electric motor or pump base. Discard the O-ring. Retrieve the coupling (4, **Figure 14**) from the electric motor or hydraulic pump shaft. Note the top and bottom orientation of the coupling. The slot opening must face the electric motor and the protrusion must face the hydraulic pump.

7. Remove the filter (5, **Figure 14**) from the hydraulic pump. Clean the filter in solvent and air dry it. Replace the filter if it is damaged or if debris remains on the filter after cleaning.

8. Clean and inspect the trim motor mounting surfaces for corrosion, pitting or scratches. Replace any components that have scratches that can be felt with a fingernail.

9. Apply a light coat of Yamaha All-Purpose Grease or equivalent to a new O-ring (3, **Figure 14**) and install it onto the electric motor-to-hydraulic pump mating surface. Apply a light coat of grease to the coupling. Install the

TILT/TRIM AND MIDSECTION

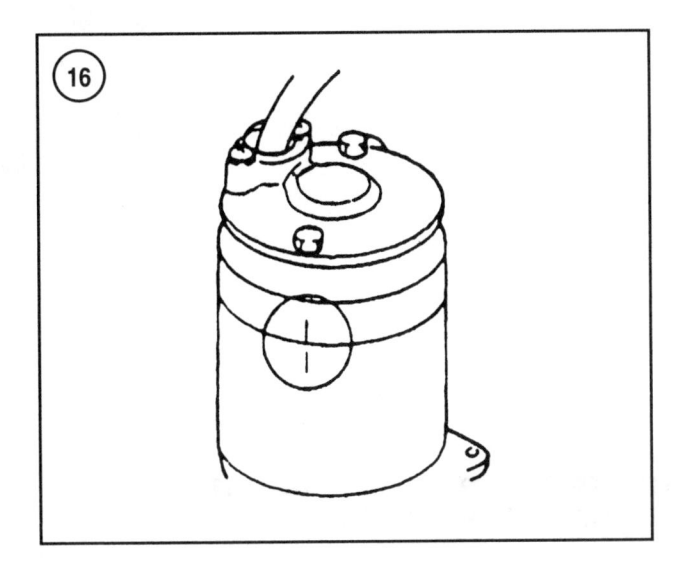

coupling onto the electric motor shaft as indicated in **Figure 15**.

10. Insert the filter into the hydraulic pump. The flat side of the filter must align with the flat side in the filter bore.

11. Position the electric motor on the pump and rotate it until the protrusion on the coupling aligns with the slot in the hydraulic pump shaft. When it is aligned, the motor drops into position.

12. Slowly rotate the electric motor until the wiring orientation is correct.

13. Apply Loctite 572 to the threads of the mounting screws (1, **Figure 14**), then install them. Tighten the screws to the specification in **Table 1**.

14. Fill and bleed the hydraulic system as described in this chapter. Check for proper operation before putting the engine into service.

TILT/TRIM SYSTEM ELECTRIC MOTOR REPAIR

This section includes disassembly, inspection and assembly procedures for the tilt/trim electric motor. The procedures vary slightly by models. Instructions are provided for the individual models.

Work in a clean environment to avoid contaminants. Use electrical cleaner to remove contaminants and debris from the motor components. Electrical contact cleaner is available at most electrical supply sources. It evaporates rapidly and leaves no residue to contaminate components. Avoid touching the brushes and commutator after cleaning. Natural oils on your fingertips will contaminate these components.

NOTE
*Mark the upper cover, frame and lower cover of the electric motor (**Figure 16**) prior to repair. Use paint dots or removal tape. Never scratch the components as it will promote corrosion of the metal components.*

The electric trim motor component appearance, disassembly and assembly procedures vary by model. Refer to **Figures 17-19** and the model specific instructions during the disassembly and assembly procedures. The appearance of the components may vary slightly from the illustration.

CAUTION
Be careful when working around the permanent magnets in the frame assembly. These magnets are quite powerful. Fingers can be easily pinched between components by the magnetic force. Never drop or strike the frame assembly. The magnets may break and damage other components during operation.

Electric Motor Disassembly

1. Remove the electric motor as described in this chapter.
2. Mark all components (**Figure 16**) before disassembly to ensure proper orientation on assembly.
3. Remove the screws that hold the frame on the lower cover.

NOTE
The magnets in the frame assembly are quite powerful. Considerable effort may be required to remove the frame assembly from the armature. Make sure all fasteners have been removed before removing the armature.

4. Grasp the armature shaft with pliers and a shop towel as shown in **Figure 20**. Pull the armature and lower cover from the frame. Remove and discard the O-ring from the frame or lower cover.

5A. On 25 and 30 hp models, remove the screws (8, **Figure 17**) to free the brush plate (9), and brush wires (6) from the lower cover. Remove the screw (5, **Figure 17**), then carefully pull the armature (4) and brush plate from the lower cover (10).

5B. On 28 jet, 35 jet, 40 hp and 50 hp models, use two screwdrivers to carefully push the brushes to collapse the brush springs (12, **Figure 18**). With the spring collapsed, pull the armature (3, **Figure 18**) from the lower cover (13). Work carefully to avoid damaging the brushes or commutator. Remove the thrust washer (4, **Figure 18**) from the armature shaft or lower cover. Remove the

476   CHAPTER ELEVEN

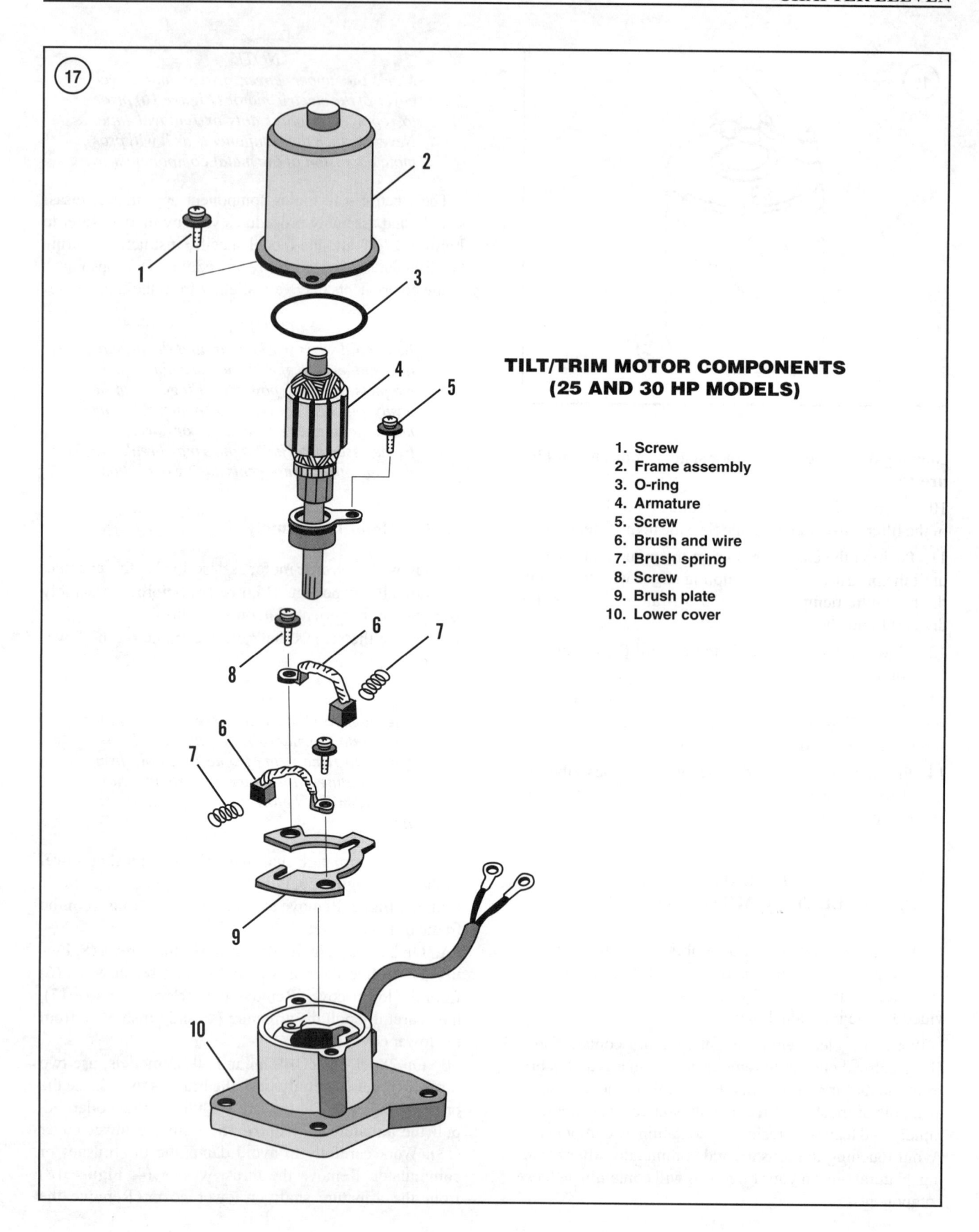

⑰

**TILT/TRIM MOTOR COMPONENTS
(25 AND 30 HP MODELS)**

1. Screw
2. Frame assembly
3. O-ring
4. Armature
5. Screw
6. Brush and wire
7. Brush spring
8. Screw
9. Brush plate
10. Lower cover

TILT/TRIM AND MIDSECTION

⑱

**TILT/TRIM MOTOR COMPONENTS
(28 JET, 35 JET, 40 HP AND 50 HP MODELS)**

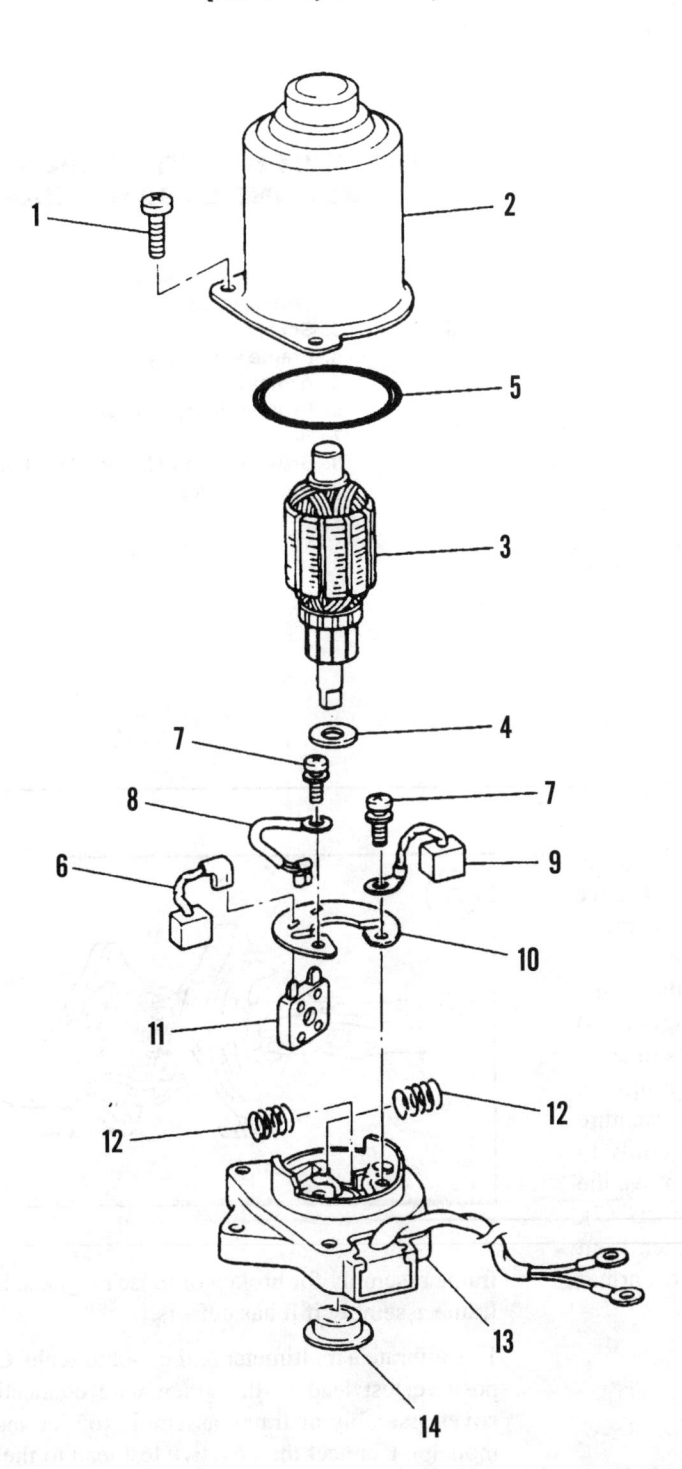

1. Screw
2. Frame assembly
3. Armature
4. Thrust washer
5. O-ring
6. Brush and wire
7. Screw
8. Wire
9. Brush and wire
10. Brush plate
11. Bi-metal switch
12. Brush springs
13. Lower cover
14. Coupling

19

**TILT/TRIM MOTOR COMPONENTS
(65 JET AND 60-90 HP MODELS)**

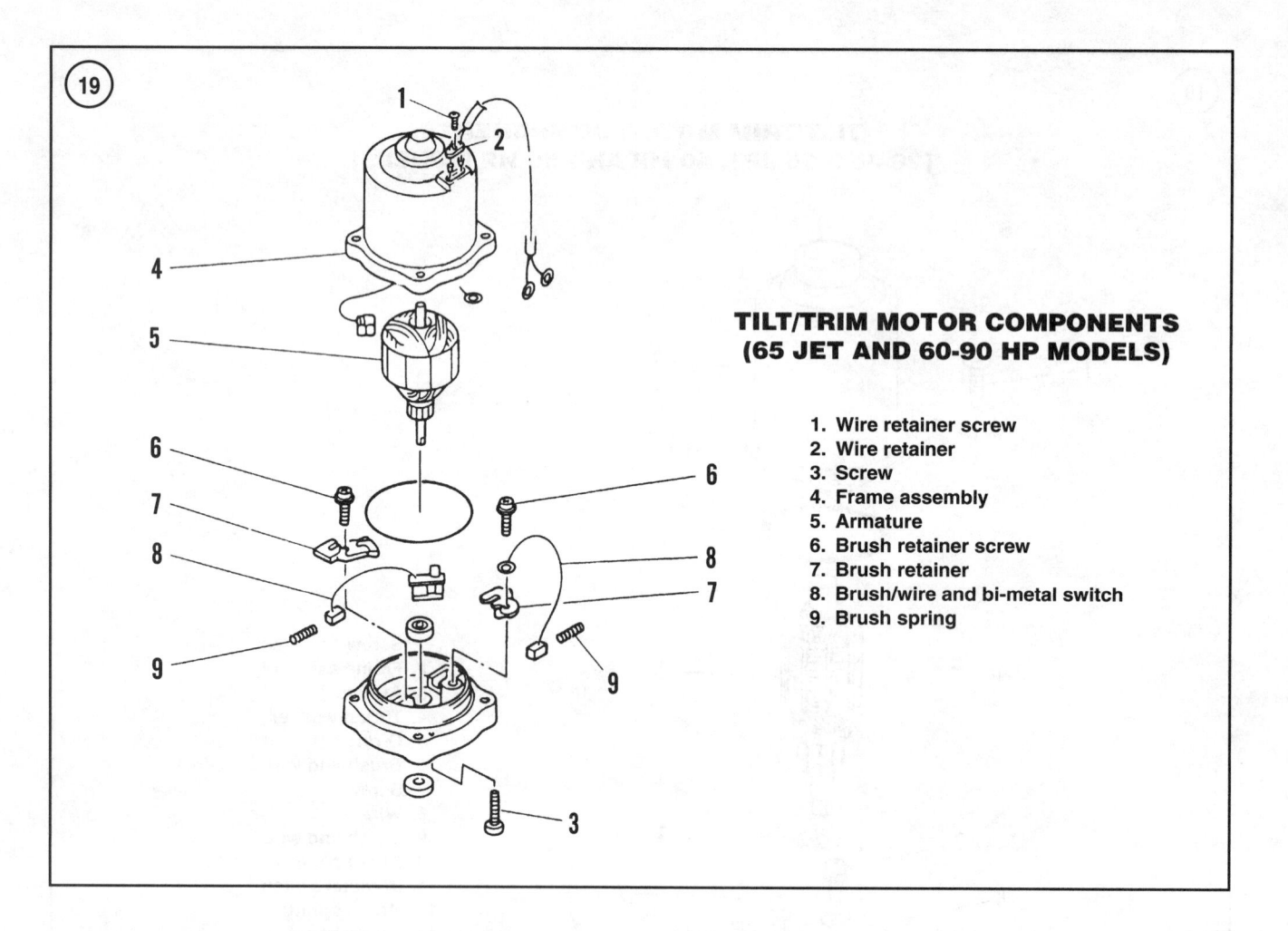

1. Wire retainer screw
2. Wire retainer
3. Screw
4. Frame assembly
5. Armature
6. Brush retainer screw
7. Brush retainer
8. Brush/wire and bi-metal switch
9. Brush spring

---

screws (7, **Figure 18**), then pull the brush plate (10) away from the lower cover. Unplug the brush wire (6, **Figure 18**) from the bi-metal switch (11). Remove the plate, brushes, springs and bi-metal switch.

5C. On 65 jet and 60-90 hp models, unplug the frame wire connector from the bi-metal switch (8, **Figure 19**) and remaining brush wire. Use two screwdrivers to carefully push the brushes to collapse the brush springs (9, **Figure 19**). With the springs collapsed, pull the armature (5, **Figure 19**) from the lower cover. Work carefully to avoid damaging the brushes or commutator. Remove the screws (6, **Figure 19**), then lift the brush retainers (7), brushes and wires, springs (9) and bi-metal switch from the lower cover. Remove the thrust washer from the armature shaft or lower cover.

**Electric Motor Component
Inspection and Tests**

Before performing any test or measurement, clean debris and contaminants from all components. Inspect the

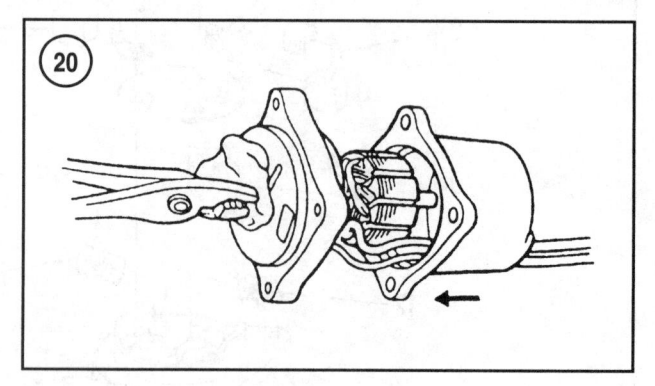

20

frame assembly for broken or loose magnets. Replace the frame assembly if it has defects.

1. Calibrate a multimeter to the 1-ohm scale. Connect the positive test lead to the green wire connection on the cover assembly or frame assembly (65 jet and 60-90 hp models). Connect the negative test lead to the respective brush wire, bi-metal switch connector or brush screw terminal for that wire (**Figure 21**, typical). Repeat the test

TILT/TRIM AND MIDSECTION

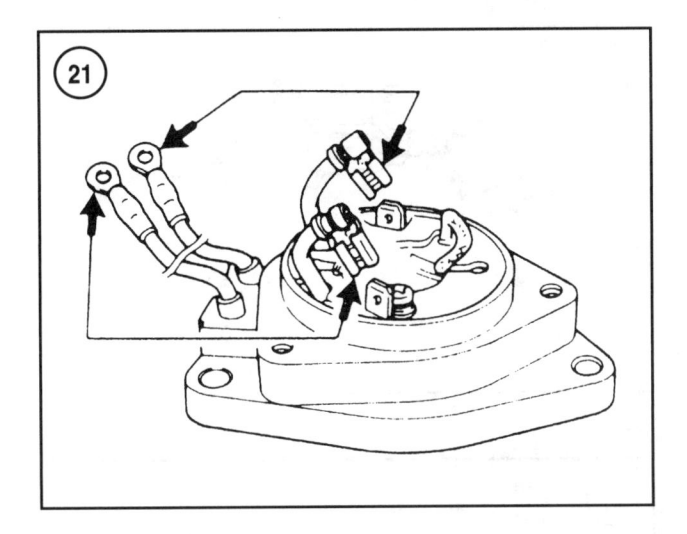

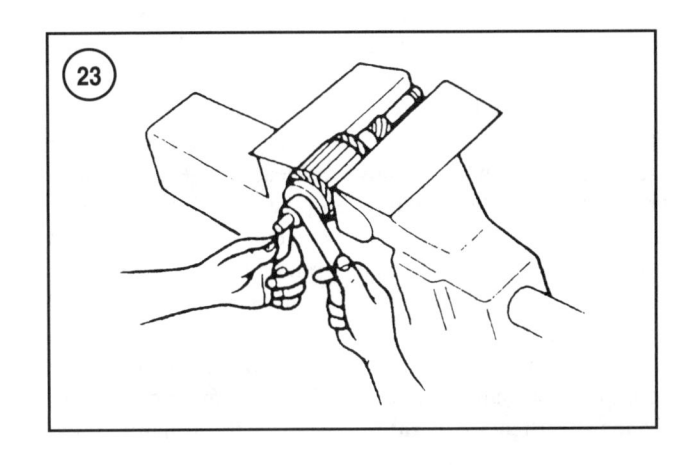

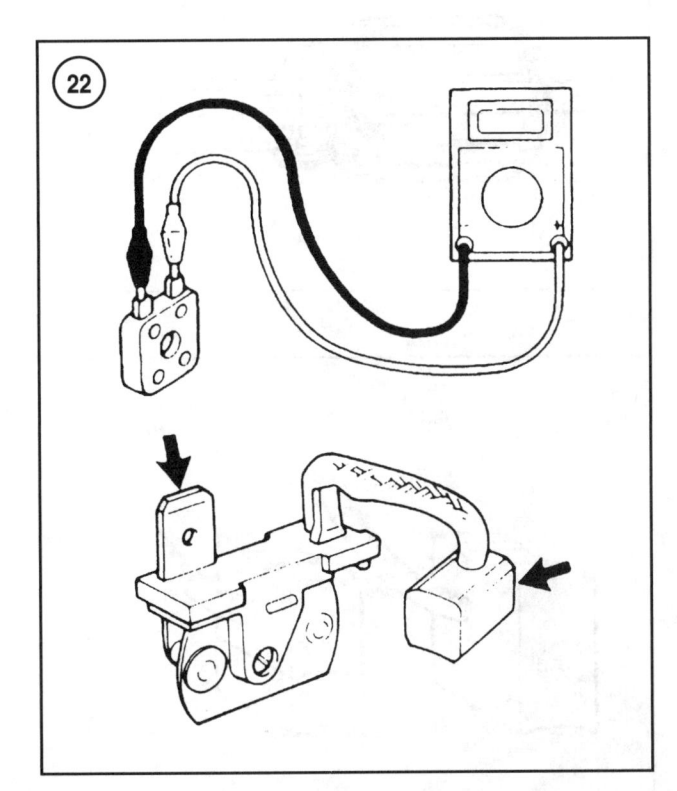

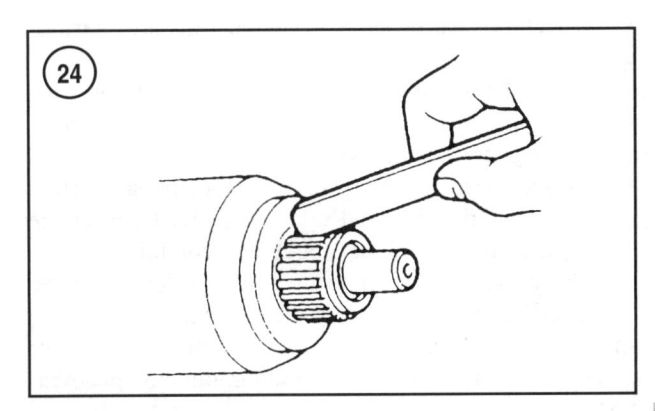

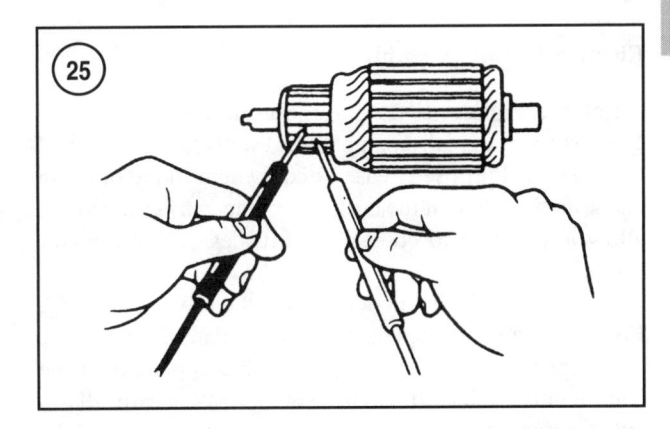

with the blue wire and respective connection. If the meter indicates no continuity for any test, the lower frame or cover is faulty and must be replaced.

2. Connect the positive test lead to one of the terminals or brush lead connection at the bi-metal switch (**Figure 22**). Connect the negative test lead to the other terminal of the bi-metal switch. If the meter indicates no continuity, the switch is faulty and must be replaced.

3. Carefully grip the armature in a vise with protective jaws (**Figure 23**). Excessive clamping force will damage the armature. Only use enough force to lightly hold the component. Polish the commutator surfaces with 600 grit wet or dry carburundum. Periodically rotate the armature to polish it evenly. Avoid removing too much material.

4. Use a disposable fingernail file to remove mica and brush material from the undercut surfaces (**Figure 24**).

5. Calibrate a multimeter to the 1-ohm scale. Touch the positive test lead to one of the segments on the commutator (**Figure 25**). Touch the negative test lead to a different segment. Repeat this test until all segments have been

tested. If the meter indicates no continuity between any pair of commutator segments, the commutator is faulty and must be replaced.

6. Touch the positive test lead to one of the commutator segments. Touch the negative test lead to one of the laminated areas of the armature (**Figure 26**). Note the meter reading. Touch the negative test lead to the armature shaft (**Figure 26**) and note the meter reading. If the meter indicates continuity for any test, the armature is shorted and must be replaced.

7. Use a micrometer or vernier caliper to measure the commutator diameter (**Figure 27**). Compare the diameter to the specification in **Table 2**. Replace the armature if the diameter is less than the minimum specification.

8. Inspect the bearing surfaces on the armature shaft for wear or damage and replace as necessary.

9. Inspect the bushings in the lower cover and frame assembly. Replace the lower cover and/or frame assembly if the bushings are worn or damaged.

10. Inspect the brush spring for corrosion, lost spring tension from overheating and other damage. Replace the springs if there is any doubt about their condition.

11. Use a vernier caliper to measure the length of the brushes (**Figure 28**). Compare the measurement with the specification in **Table 2**. Replace both brushes if either brush measurement is less than the minimum specification.

Electric Motor Assembly

Refer to **Figures 17-19** during this procedure.

1. Clean and dry all components. Apply a light coat of Yamaha All-Purpose Grease or equivalent to the bushing and armature shaft at the bushing contact surfaces. Do not allow any grease to contact the brushes or commutator surfaces.

2A. On 25 and 30 hp models, install the brush springs (7, **Figure 17**) and brushes onto the brush plate. Collapse the brush springs and carefully slide the brush plate over the commutator. Release the brush springs. Work carefully to avoid damaging the brushes and commutator. Insert the armature and brush plate into the lower cover. The tab on the brush plate must align with the respective slot in the cover. Align the screw openings, then install and securely tighten the screw (5, **Figure 17**). Slip the screws (8, **Figure 17**) through the terminals on the brush wires. Thread the screws into the terminal openings in the lower cover. Securely tighten the screws.

2B. On 28 jet, 35 jet, 40 hp and 50 hp models, install the bi-metal switch (11, **Figure 18**) into the recess in the lower cover. Install the brush plate (10, **Figure 18**), springs (12) and brush and wire (6 and 9) into the lower cover. The brush springs and brushes must fit into the slots. Connect the wire (8, **Figure 18**) to the bi-metal switch terminal. Secure the brush wire, wire terminal and brush plate to the lower cover with the screw (7, **Figure 18**). Securely tighten the screws. Slip the thrust washer (4, **Figure 18**) over the armature shaft. Collapse the brush springs and carefully slip the armature into the lower

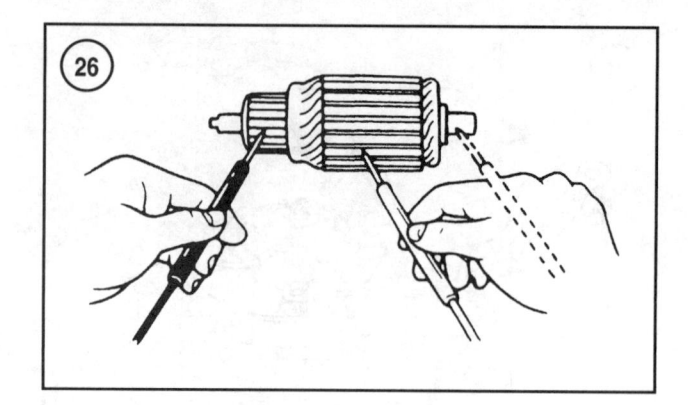

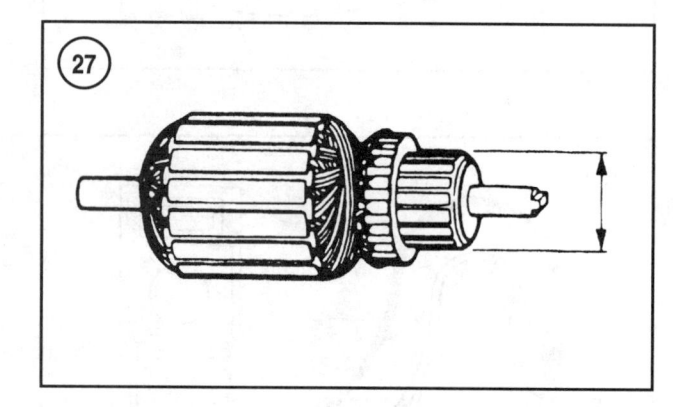

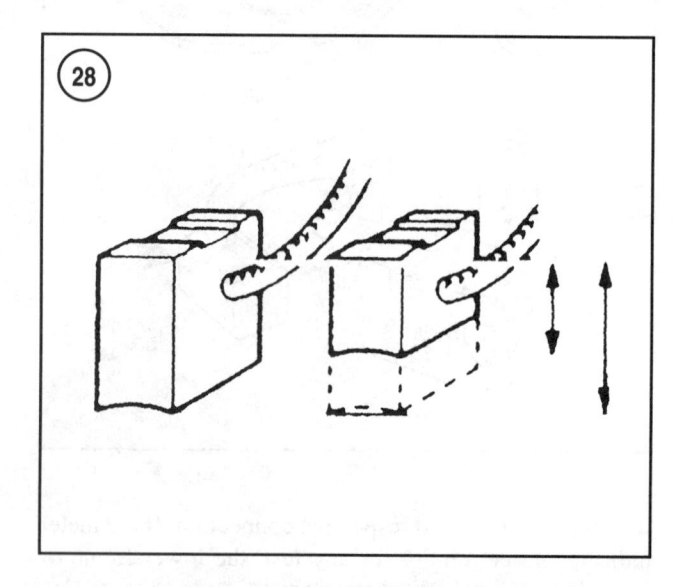

TILT/TRIM AND MIDSECTION

brush springs. Work carefully to avoid damaging the brushes and commutator.

3. On 65 jet and 60-90 hp models, connect the push-on terminal extending from the frame to the terminal of the bi-metal switch. Connect the remaining ring terminal frame lead to the terminal provided on the remaining brush retainer.

4. Install a new O-ring onto the lower cover. Use pliers and a shop towel to maintain the position of the armature and the lower cover (**Figure 20**) while carefully guiding the armature into the frame. The upper end of the armature shaft must enter the bushing at the top of the frame.

5. Seat the frame against the lower cover. Make sure the O-ring is still in position and not damaged. A water leak could occur if the O-ring is out of position or damaged.

6. Align the marks made before disassembly (**Figure 16**). Install the screws that secure the lower cover to the frame assembly. Tighten the screws to the specification in **Table 1** or Chapter One. Rotate the armature shaft and check for binding. Disassemble the motor and check for improper assembly if it binds.

7. Install the electric trim motor as described in this chapter.

MANUAL RELEASE VALVE REMOVAL AND INSTALLATION

Replacing the manual release valve is simple if the screwdriver slot is intact. If it is not, the valve can usually be removed by other means. Heat the tip of a screwdriver and hold it against the remnants of the valve. The valve material will melt into the shape of the screwdriver tip. Allow the material to cool and use the same screwdriver to remove the valve. Never drill the valve out or the seating surfaces for the O-ring will be irreparably damaged.

Inspect the O-rings on the valve even though they will be discarded. Large portions missing or torn from the O-rings could cause problems. They usually migrate to a valve or other component with the tilt/trim system and cause the system to malfunction.

1. Tilt the engine to the full up position. Engage the tilt lock lever and support the engine with blocks or an overhead cable (**Figure 29**).

2. Locate the access opening for the manual release valve (**Figure 30**).
    a. On 25 and 30 hp models, the opening is located in the starboard side clamp bracket.
    b. On 28 jet, 35 jet, 40 hp and 50 hp models, the opening is located in the port side clamp bracket.
    c. On 65 jet and 60-90 hp models, the opening is located in the starboard side clamp bracket.

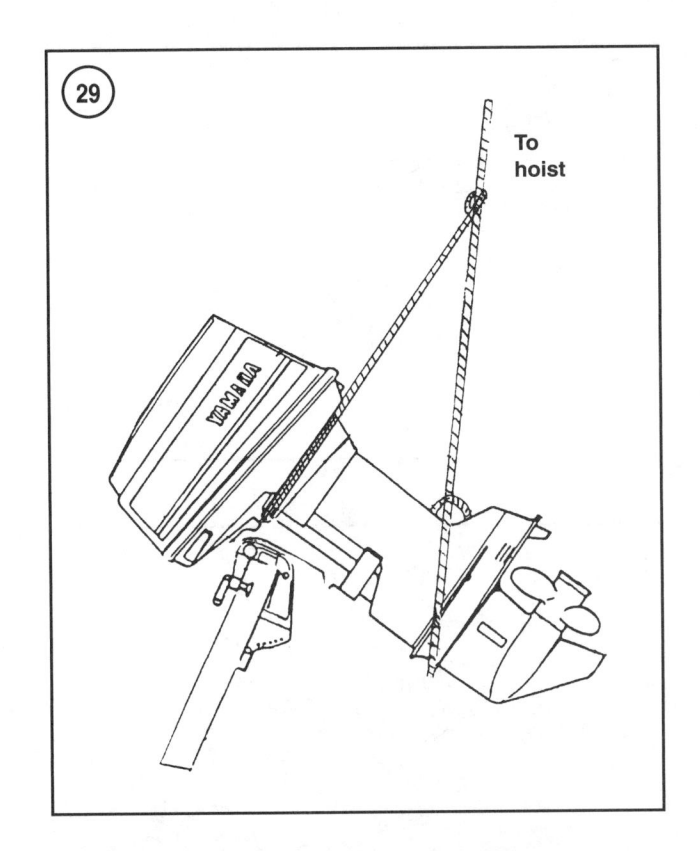

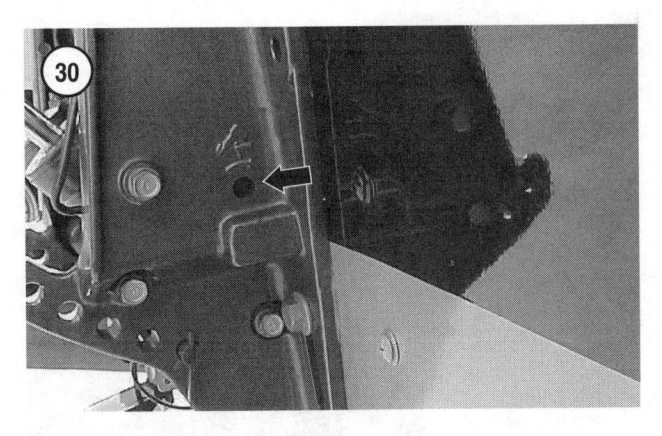

cover. The armature must seat against the thrust washer and lower cover. Release the brush springs. Work carefully to avoid damaging the brushes and commutator.

2C. On 65 jet and 60-90 hp models, install the bi-metal switch into the recess in the lower cover. Insert the brush springs (9, **Figure 19**) and brushes into the slots in the lower cover. Install the brush retainers (7, **Figure 19**). Secure the retainers into the cover with the screws (6, **Figure 19**). Slip the thrust washer over the armature shaft. Collapse the brush springs and carefully slip the armature into the lower cover. The armature must seat against the thrust washer and lower cover. Release the

3. Slowly loosen the valve by rotating it 2-3 turns counterclockwise (**Figure 31**). Remove the locking ring from the valve (**Figure 32**) and unthread the valve from the trim system. Remove the valve through the access opening (**Figure 30**).

4. Use a suitable light and small pick or screwdriver to remove any remnants of O-ring from the opening. Avoid damaging any of the machined surfaces in the opening.

5. Lubricate the new manual release valve with Dextron II automatic transmission fluid and install *new* O-rings onto the valve. Lubricate the new O-rings with Dextron II automatic transmission fluid and thread the valve into the opening. *Do not* tighten the valve at this time.

6. Rotate the valve clockwise until there is a slight resistance. Rotate the valve 1/4 turn clockwise then 1/8 turn counterclockwise. Repeat this process until the valve seats. Finally tighten the valve to the specification in **Table 1**.

7. Fill the system with fluid and bleed air from the system as described in this chapter.

HYDRAULIC SYSTEM FILLING AND BLEEDING

Refer to the filling procedure if the unit has lost a large amount of fluid or after a major component has been replaced.

Refer to the bleeding procedure if the tilt/trim system shows symptoms of air in the fluid.

> *WARNING*
> *Never work under any part of the engine without providing suitable support. The engine-mounted tilt lock or hydraulic system may unexpectedly collapse and allow the engine to drop. Support the engine with suitable blocks or an overhead cable **before** working under the engine.*

Filling Procedure

The system should not require filling unless completely disassembled. In such cases, add fluid to all fluid cavities during the assembly. This procedure is used to add the small amount of fluid lost when performing the procedures described in this chapter. This procedure can be used to fill a completely empty system; it just takes longer than when the system is pre-filled during assembly.

The air bleeding procedure is very similar to the fluid filling procedure. It is used to remove air that may form in the system during some conditions.

1. Use the power tilt/trim system or open the manual release valve (**Figure 31**) to place the engine in the full up position. Engage the tilt/lock lever and support the engine with suitable blocks or an overhead cable (**Figure 29**). Close the manual release valve.

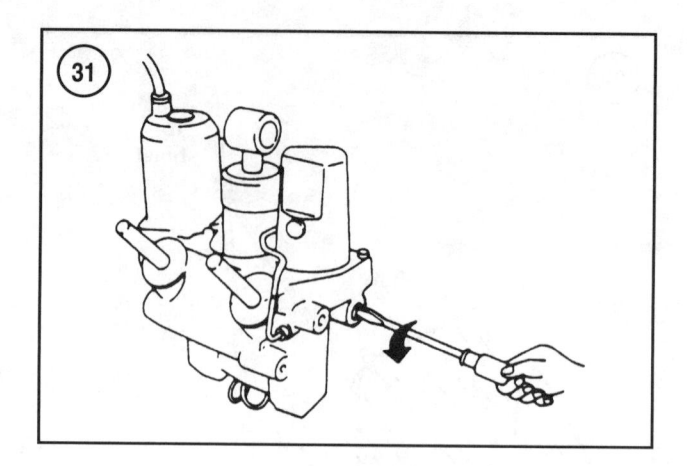

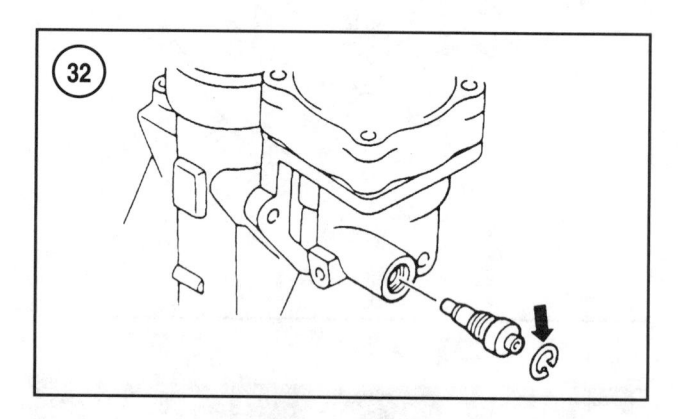

2. Locate and clean the area around the fluid reservoir plug.
   a. On 25 and 30 hp models, the plug is located on the rear starboard side of the system and below the electric tilt/trim motor (**Figure 33**).
   b. On 28 jet, 35 jet, 40 hp and 50 hp models, the plug is located on the rear port side of the system (**Figure 34**).
   c. On 65 jet and 60-90 hp models, the plug is located on the fluid reservoir on the rear starboard side of the system (**Figure 35**).

TILT/TRIM AND MIDSECTION

7. Tighten the reservoir plug to the specification in **Table 1** or Chapter One.

Bleeding Procedure

A spongy feel or inability to hold the trim position under load is a common symptom when air is present in the internal passages. The engine will usually tuck under when load is applied and tilt out when power is reduced.

Minor amounts of air are usually purged from the system during normal operation. When major components have been removed, a significant amount of air can enter the system. Then the air must be bled from the system.

1. Operate the tilt/trim system or open the manual release valve to place the engine in the full up position. Support the engine with suitable blocks or an overhead hoist (**Figure 29**). Correct the fluid level as indicated in Step 4 of *Filling procedure*. Install the plug and tighten the manual release valve.

2. Operate the tilt/trim system until the engine is in the fully DOWN position. Then operate the trim in the up direction while listening to the electric motor. Stop immediately if the electric pump motor begins to run faster or sounds different. The pump is ventilating. Then open the manual release valve and manually lift the engine to the full UP position. Support the engine with suitable blocks or an overhead hoist (**Figure 29**). Correct the fluid level as indicated in Step 4 of *Filling procedure*. Install the plug and tighten the manual release valve.

3. Continue to repeat Step 2 until the motor reaches the full up position without ventilating the pump. If a large amount of foam is in the reservoir, allow the engine to sit for one hour and repeat the process.

4. Cycle the tilt/trim system fully UP and DOWN several times to purge the remaining air from the system.

MIDSECTION

Minor repairs to the midsection usually involve replacing worn motor mounts or bushings. Major repairs involve replacing broken components such as the clamp bracket and swivel bracket. Broken midsection components are usually caused by impact with underwater objects.

Unless otherwise specified, apply Loctite 572 to the threads of all fasteners. Apply Yamaha All-Purpose Grease onto all bushings and pivoting or sliding surfaces. Apply a *marine grade* sealant into the drilled holes that attach the clamp brackets to the vessel. Tighten all fasteners to the specification in **Table 1** or Chapter One.

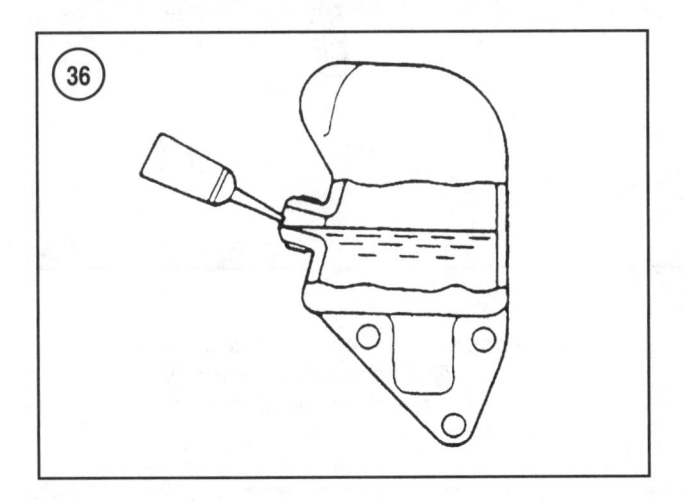

3. Slowly loosen and remove the fluid fill plug. Inspect the plug gasket for damage and replace it if necessary.

4. Fill the unit to the bottom of the plug opening (**Figure 36**) with the engine in the full up position. Install the plug.

5. Remove the blocks or overhead cable. Disengage the tilt lock lever.

6. Cycle the system to the full DOWN, then the full UP, positions several times. Check and correct the fluid level as necessary.

484　　CHAPTER ELEVEN

(37) MID-SECTION COMPONENTS (2 HP MODEL)

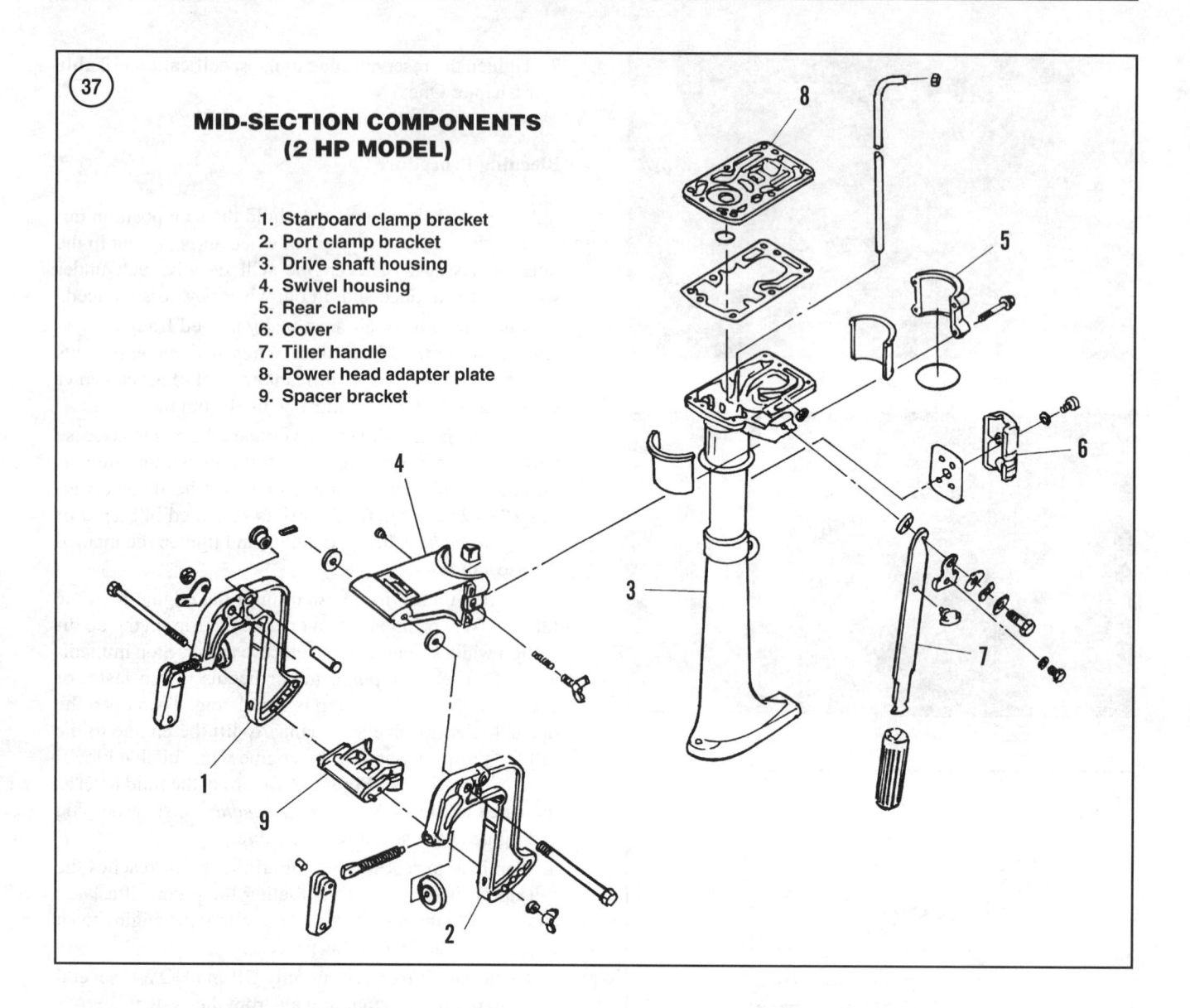

1. Starboard clamp bracket
2. Port clamp bracket
3. Drive shaft housing
4. Swivel housing
5. Rear clamp
6. Cover
7. Tiller handle
8. Power head adapter plate
9. Spacer bracket

Component appearance and mounting orientation vary by model. Refer to **Figures 37-43** and locate the illustration that applies to your model.

Refer to the illustration for fastener location and component orientation. Component appearance may vary slightly from the illustration. Note the location and orientation of all components before removing them.

Inspect all components and fasteners for wear or damage. Never use a questionable component. Replace all gaskets and seals in the exhaust portion of the drive shaft housing on assembly.

WARNING
*Never work under any part of the engine without providing suitable support. The engine mounted tilt lock or hydraulic system may unexpectedly collapse and allow the engine to drop. Support the engine with suitable blocks or and overhead cable **before** working under the engine.*

Motor Mounts

On 2-5 hp models, the engine mounts are easy to access and relatively easy to replace. Bolt-on clamps secure the drive shaft housing onto the swivel bracket. The mounts fit between the rear clamp, swivel bracket and the drive shaft housing. A split in the upper and lower mount bushing allows them to slip over the drive shaft housing.

On 6 and 8 hp models, the upper and lower mounts are located under covers on the sides of the drive shaft hous-

TILT/TRIM AND MIDSECTION

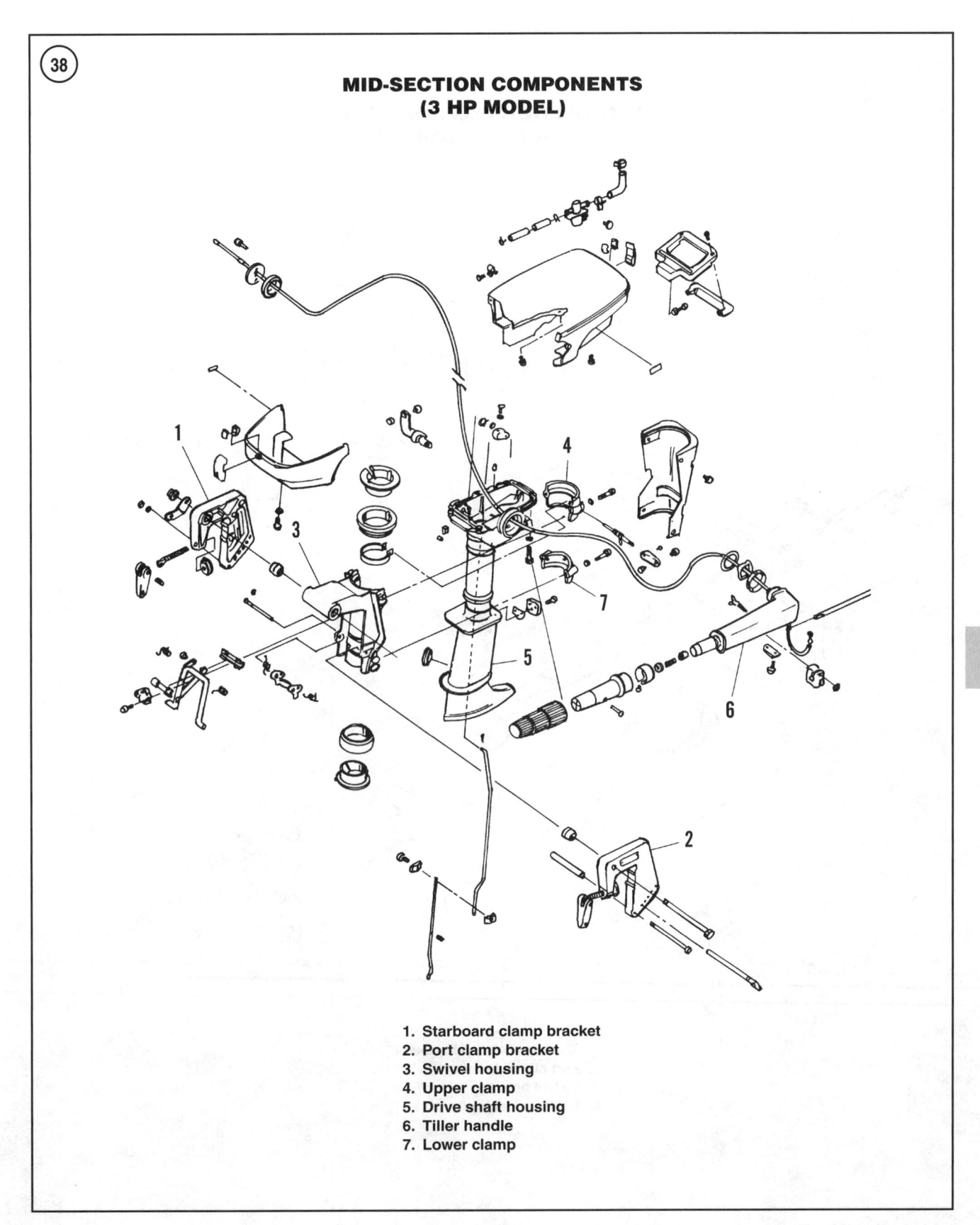

(38)

MID-SECTION COMPONENTS
(3 HP MODEL)

1. Starboard clamp bracket
2. Port clamp bracket
3. Swivel housing
4. Upper clamp
5. Drive shaft housing
6. Tiller handle
7. Lower clamp

MID-SECTION COMPONENTS
(4 AND 5 HP MODELS)

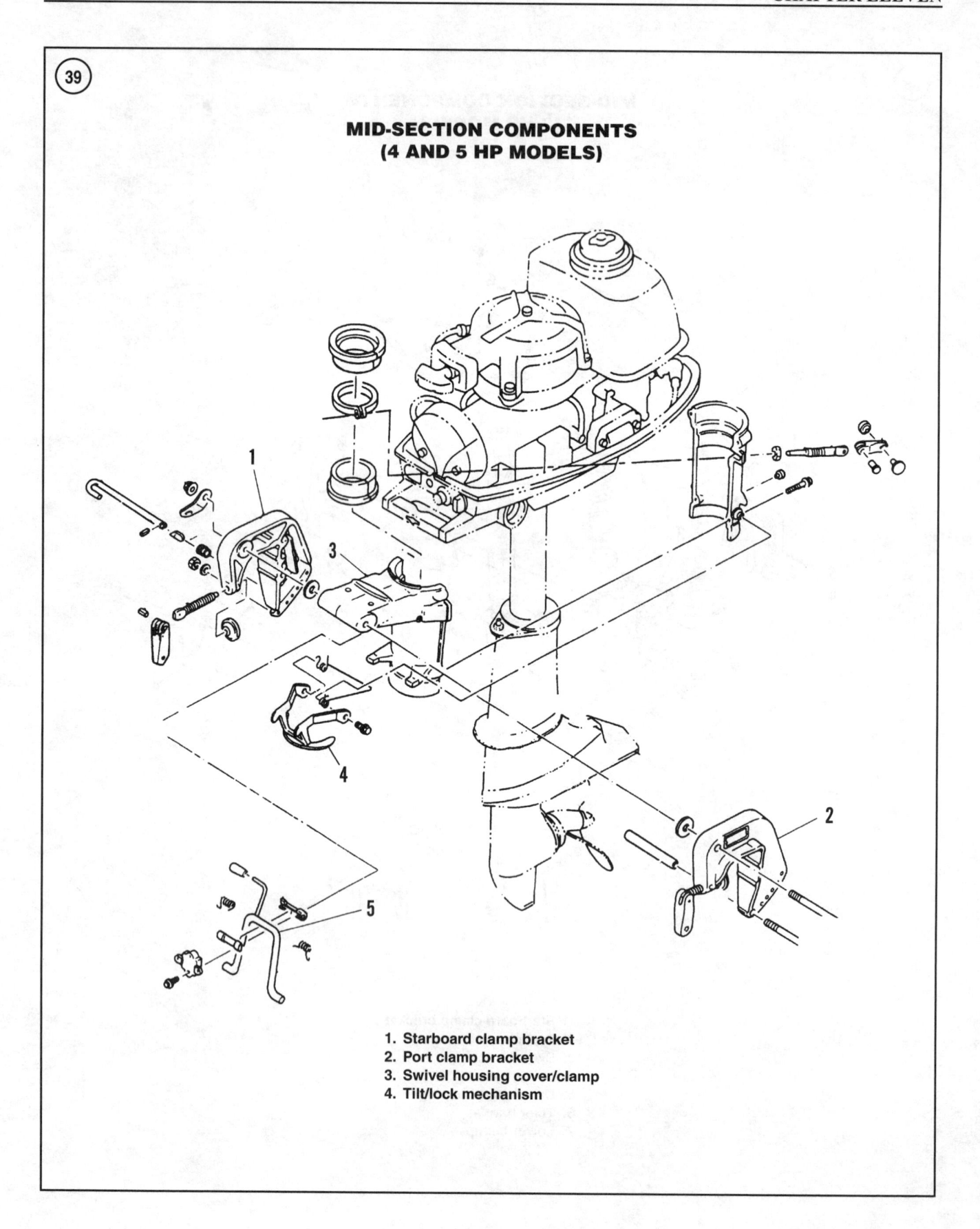

1. Starboard clamp bracket
2. Port clamp bracket
3. Swivel housing cover/clamp
4. Tilt/lock mechanism

TILT/TRIM AND MIDSECTION

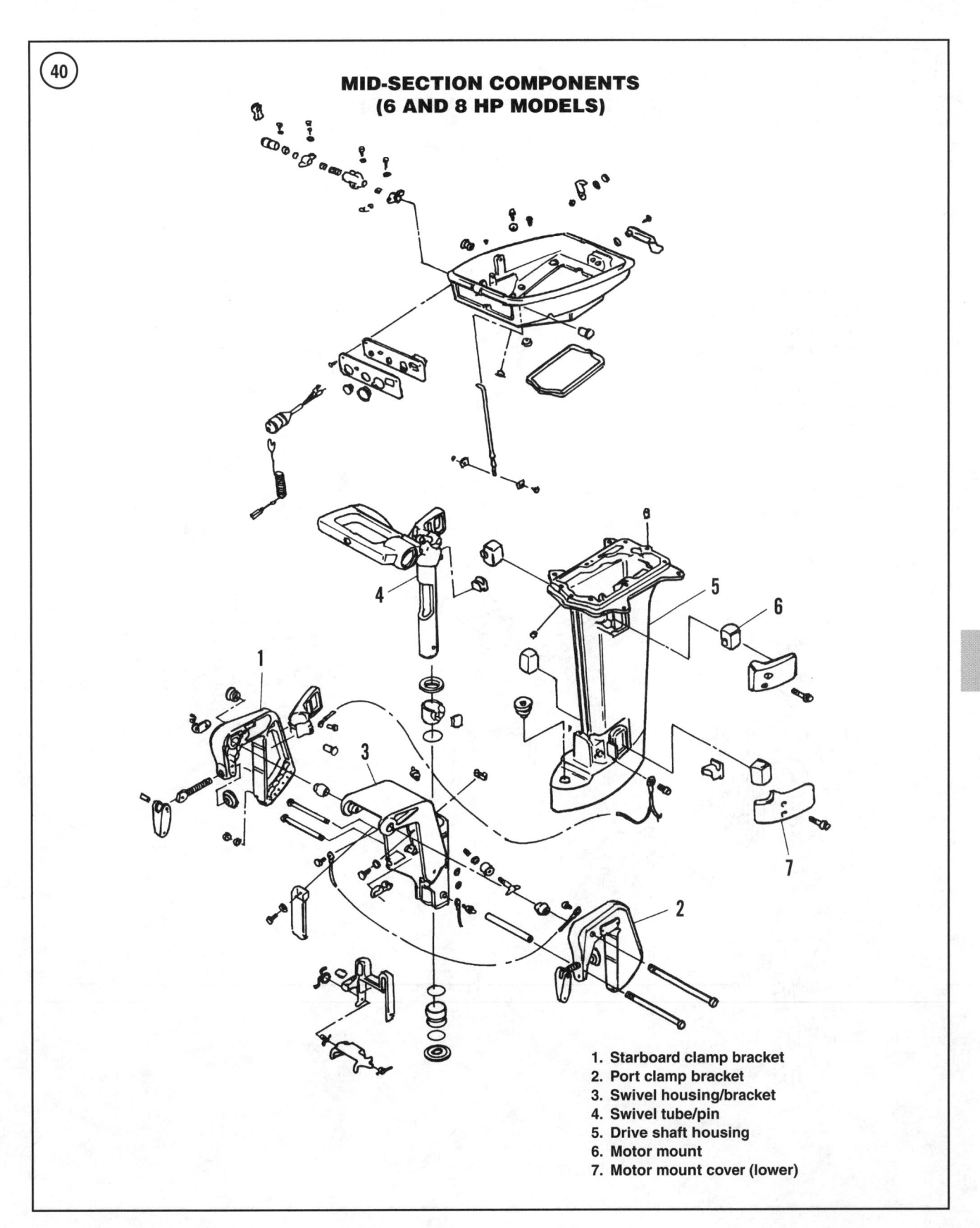

MID-SECTION COMPONENTS (6 AND 8 HP MODELS)

1. Starboard clamp bracket
2. Port clamp bracket
3. Swivel housing/bracket
4. Swivel tube/pin
5. Drive shaft housing
6. Motor mount
7. Motor mount cover (lower)

488

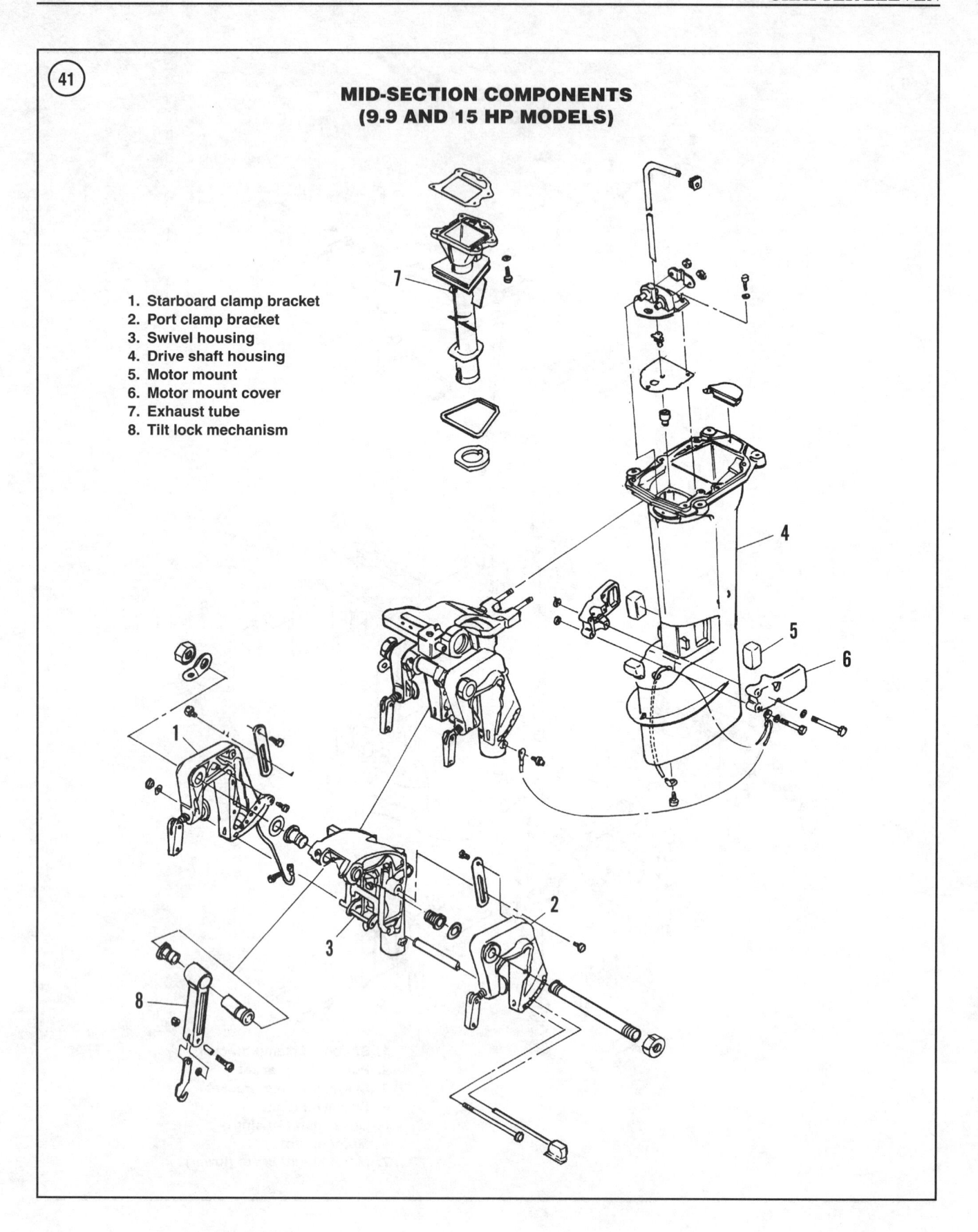

CHAPTER ELEVEN

(41)

**MID-SECTION COMPONENTS
(9.9 AND 15 HP MODELS)**

1. Starboard clamp bracket
2. Port clamp bracket
3. Swivel housing
4. Drive shaft housing
5. Motor mount
6. Motor mount cover
7. Exhaust tube
8. Tilt lock mechanism

TILT/TRIM AND MIDSECTION

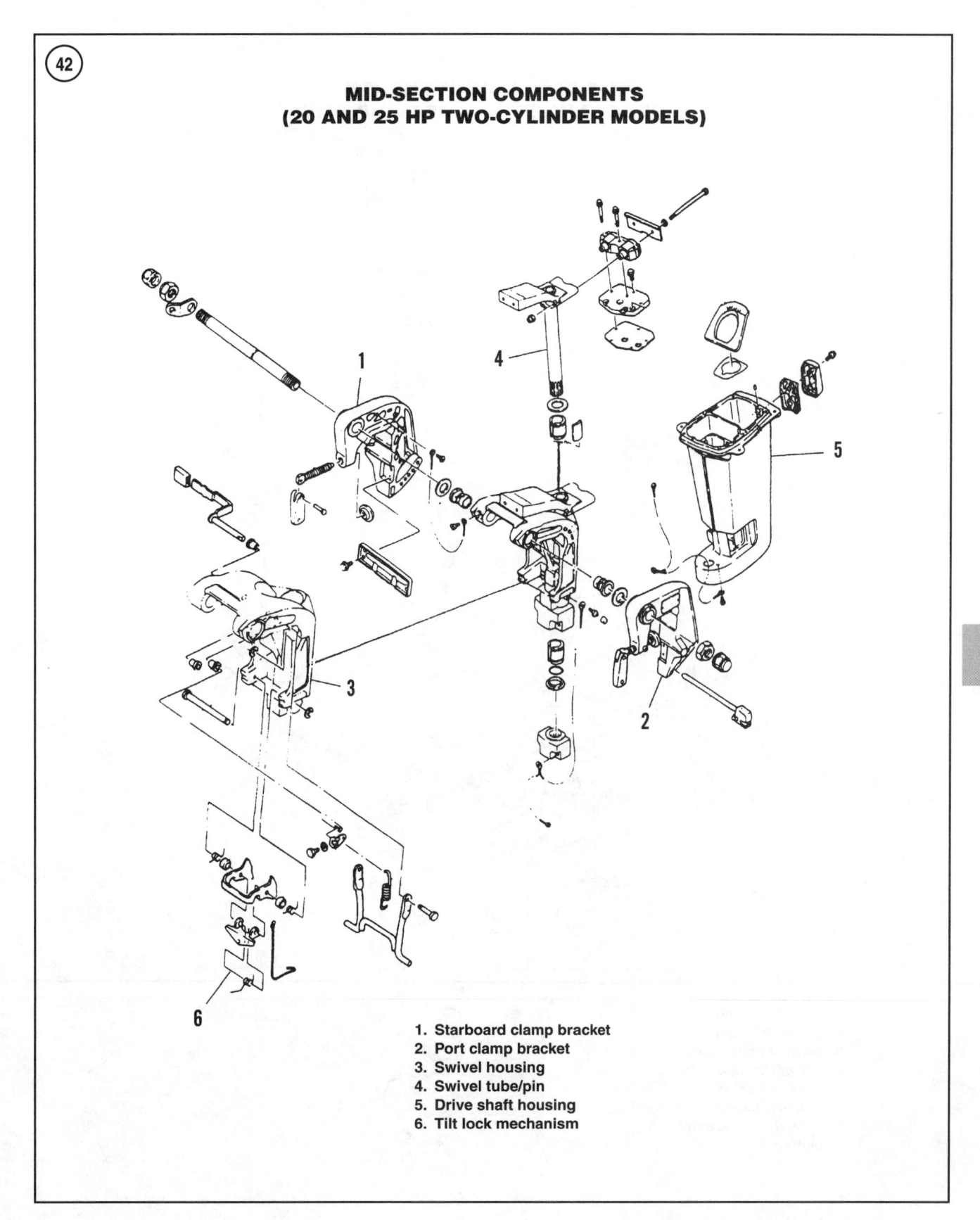

**MID-SECTION COMPONENTS
(20 AND 25 HP TWO-CYLINDER MODELS)**

1. Starboard clamp bracket
2. Port clamp bracket
3. Swivel housing
4. Swivel tube/pin
5. Drive shaft housing
6. Tilt lock mechanism

490

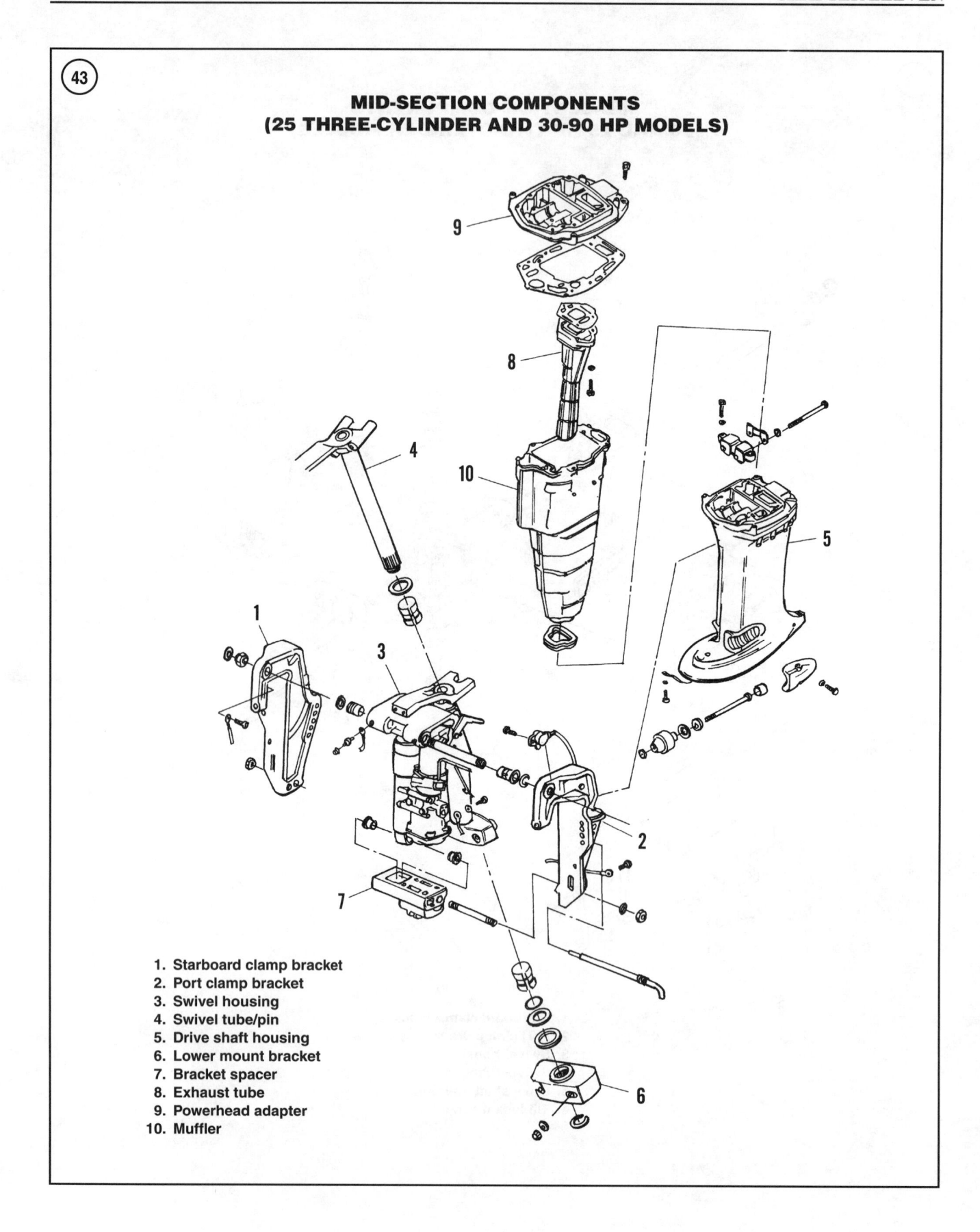

CHAPTER ELEVEN

(43)

**MID-SECTION COMPONENTS
(25 THREE-CYLINDER AND 30-90 HP MODELS)**

1. Starboard clamp bracket
2. Port clamp bracket
3. Swivel housing
4. Swivel tube/pin
5. Drive shaft housing
6. Lower mount bracket
7. Bracket spacer
8. Exhaust tube
9. Powerhead adapter
10. Muffler

TILT/TRIM AND MIDSECTION

44

**TILLER HANDLE COMPONENTS
(4 AND 5 HP MODELS)**

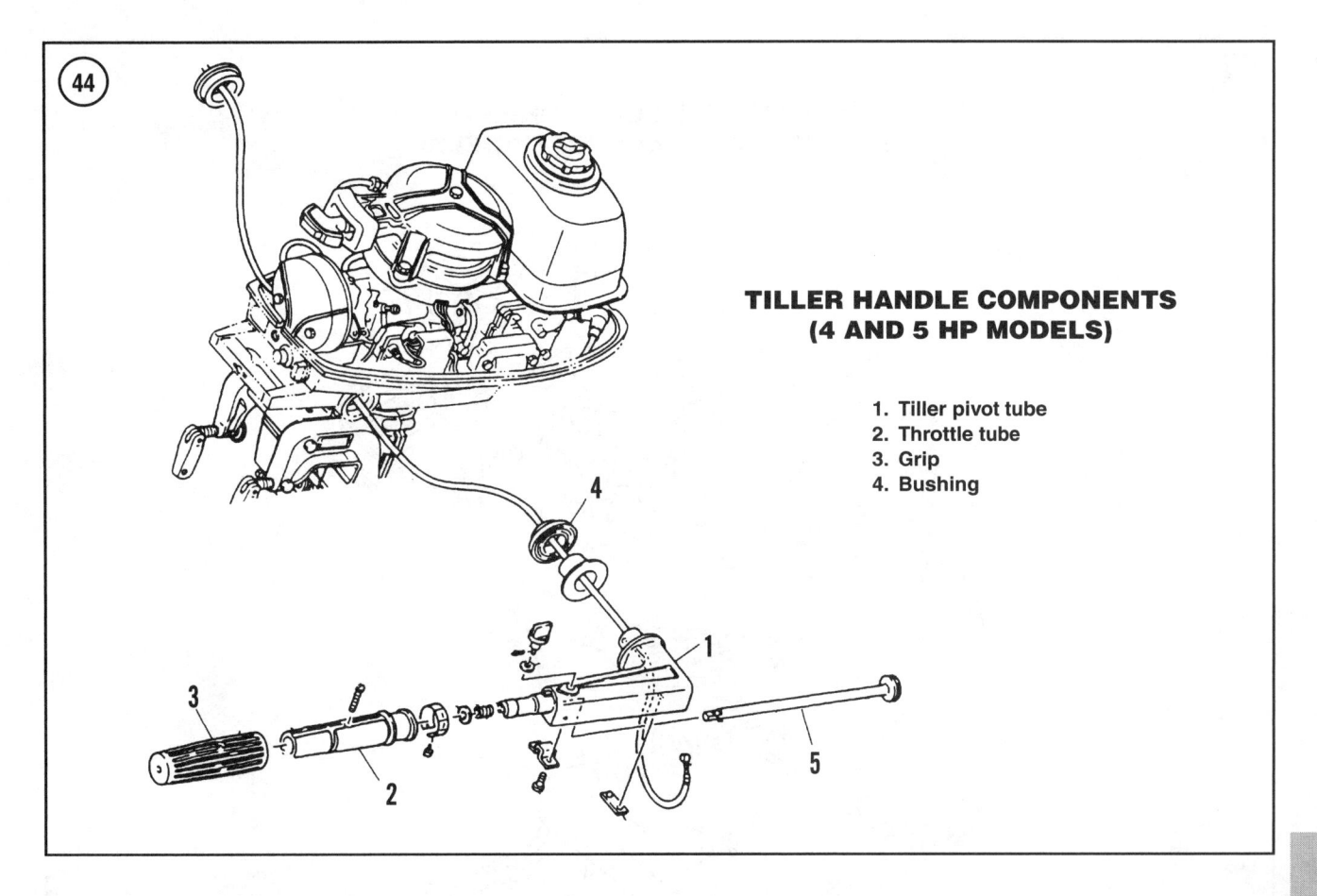

1. Tiller pivot tube
2. Throttle tube
3. Grip
4. Bushing

ing. The mount can be replaced without the power head or other major components being removed.

On 9.9-60 hp models, the upper mounts are located beneath the power head to drive shaft housing mating surface. Remove the power head to access the upper mounts. The lower mounts are located beneath covers on the lower side of the drive shaft housing and can be replaced without major disassembly.

Refer to **Figures 37-43** and remove the components necessary to access the worn or damaged component(s). Tighten all fasteners to the specification in **Table 1** or Chapter One during assembly. Check for proper tilting and steering operation before operating the engine. Check for damaged or improperly assembled components if there is binding or looseness. Never operate the engine if the steering or tilting components are binding.

Clamp Bracket and Swivel Bracket

Component appearance and mounting orientation vary by model. Refer to **Figures 37-43** and locate the illustration that applies to your model. Refer to the illustration for fastener location and component orientation. Component appearance may vary slightly from the illustration. Note the location and orientation of all components before removing them.

Remove the components necessary to access the worn or damaged component(s). When replacing the clamp bracket(s) without removing the power head, support the engine with suitable blocks or an overhead cable (**Figure 29**) during the process.

Tighten all fasteners to the specification in **Table 1** or Chapter One during assembly. Check for proper tilting and steering operation before operating the engine. Check for damaged or improperly assembled components if there is binding or looseness. Never operate the engine if the steering or tilting components are binding.

Tiller Handle Components

Tiller handle repair generally involves replacement of the throttle and/or shift cable or the replacement of worn or damaged bushings.

Component orientation and mounting location vary by model. Refer to **Figures 37-46** for location and orientation of the tiller handle components. Always make notes,

CHAPTER ELEVEN

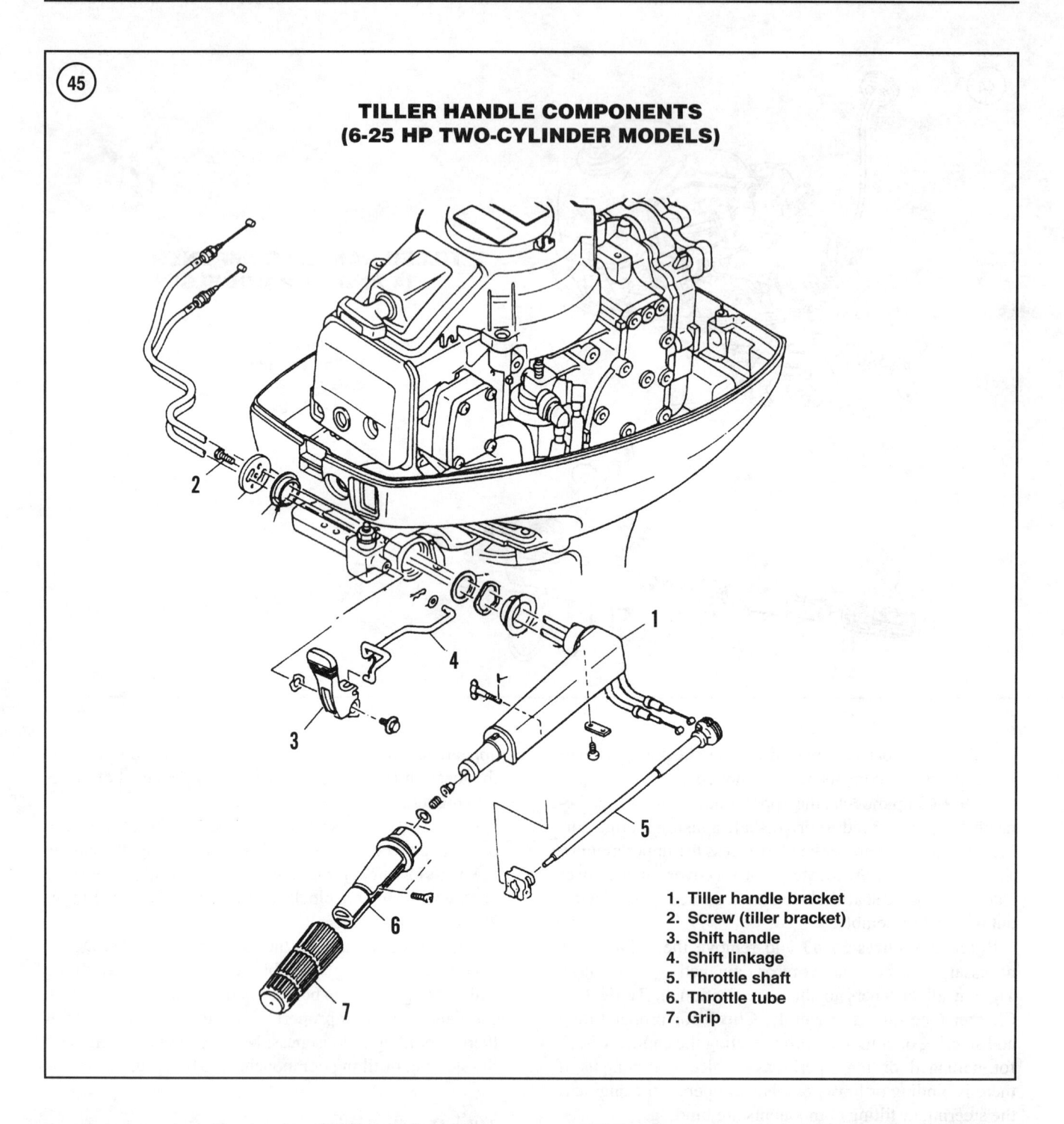

TILLER HANDLE COMPONENTS (6-25 HP TWO-CYLINDER MODELS)

1. Tiller handle bracket
2. Screw (tiller bracket)
3. Shift handle
4. Shift linkage
5. Throttle shaft
6. Throttle tube
7. Grip

drawings or marks indicating the orientation of each component before removing it.

Refer to the illustrations to determine which components must be removed to access the worn or damaged component(s).

Apply a light coat of Yamaha All-Purpose Grease or equivalent to the contact surfaces of all bushings, pivoting and sliding surfaces. Apply Loctite 572 to the threads of all tiller handle fasteners. Tighten all fasteners to the specifications in **Table 1** or Chapter One.

Check for proper steering, shift and throttle operation before operating the engine. Disassemble the tiller handle and check for damaged or improperly assembled components if there is binding, looseness or improper operation.

TILT/TRIM AND MIDSECTION

(46)

**TILLER HANDLE COMPONENTS
(25-75 HP THREE-CYLINDER MODELS)**

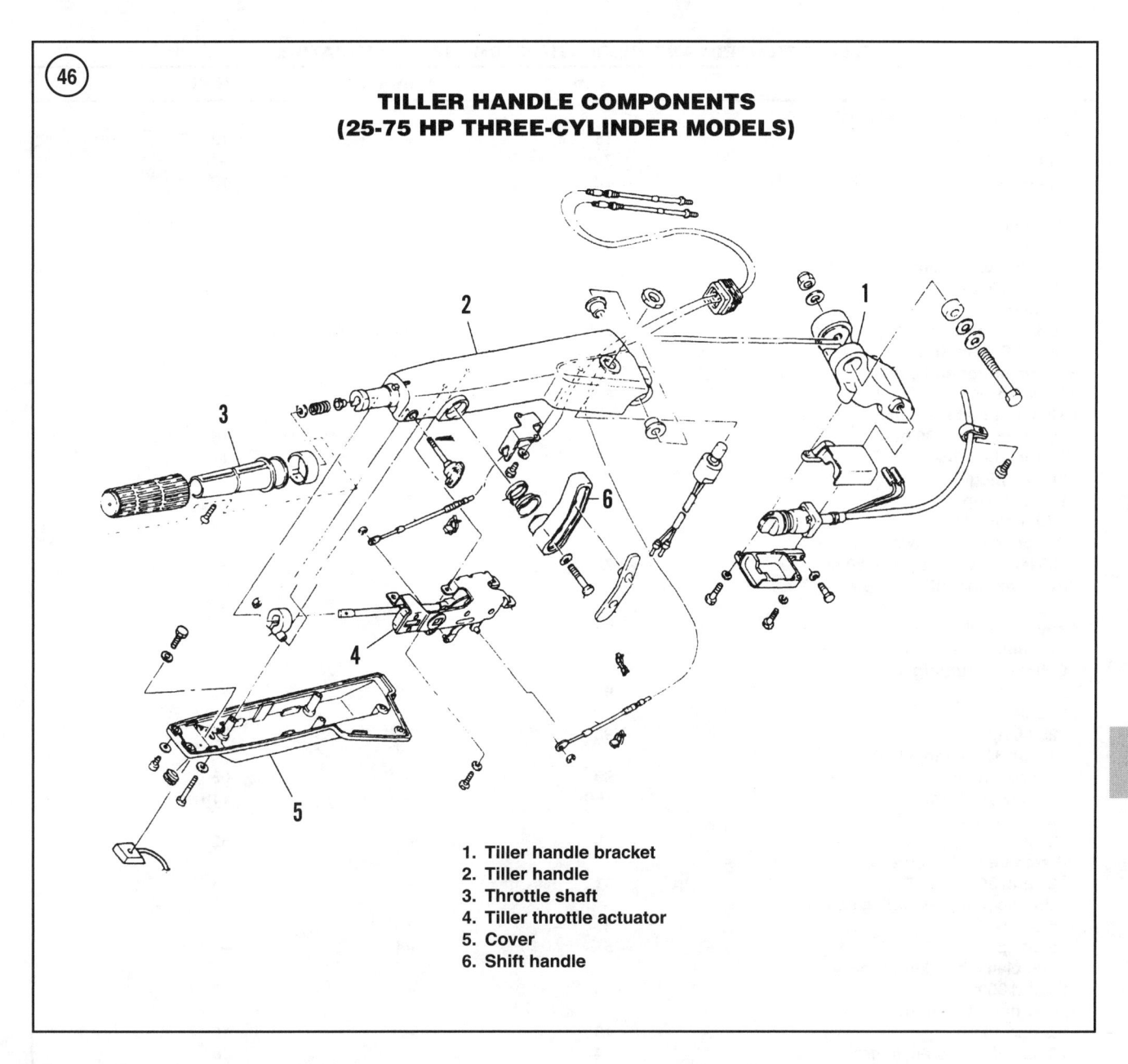

1. Tiller handle bracket
2. Tiller handle
3. Throttle shaft
4. Tiller throttle actuator
5. Cover
6. Shift handle

Never operate an outboard with a throttle control, shift control or steering system malfunction.

Shift/throttle cables

On 4-75 hp models, the throttle and/or shift cables are routed through the tiller handle. Replace any cables that have damaged or worn outer jacket surfaces. Push and pull the core wire in the outer jacket. Replace the cable if it does not move smoothly. Anytime the shift or throttle cables have been removed or even disturbed, adjust the throttle and shift linkages as described in Chapter Four.

Pivot points and bushings

Inspect all bushings and pivot bolts, tubes or shafts for worn, corroded or damaged surfaces and replace as necessary. To prevent corrosion and excessive wear, apply a light coat of Yamaha All-Purpose Grease or equivalent to the contact surfaces of all bushings, pivoting and sliding surfaces. Use 3M Weatherstrip Adhesive to glue the grip onto the throttle shaft. Thoroughly clean old adhesive or other contaminants from the grip and throttle shaft before applying the adhesive. Make sure the bond of the grip is secure before operating the engine.

Table 1 TILT/TRIM AND MIDSECTION TORQUE SPECIFICATIONS

Fastener	N•m	in.-lb.	ft.-lb.
Clamp bracket to swivel bracket			
2 hp	16	–	12
3 hp	7	62	–
4 and 5 hp	13	–	10
6 and 8 hp	7	62	–
Drive shaft housing cover/clamp			
3-5 hp	8	70	–
Electric motor mounting screws			
25 and 30 hp	7	62	–
60-90 hp			
6H308 stamping	6	53	–
6H1-15 stamping	7	62	–
Electric motor end cover			
60-90 hp	4	35	–
Exhaust tube to adapter			
28 jet, 35 jet, 40-90 hp	21	–	16
External fluid lines	15	–	11
Fluid fill plug			
25 and 30 hp	7	62	–
Fluid reservoir			
Bottom cover screws			
28 jet, 35 jet, 40 hp and 50 hp	7	62	–
Reservoir mounting screws			
60-90 hp	7	62	–
Grounding wire screws	8	70	–
Hydraulic cylinder			
Cylinder mounting screws			
25-50 hp	9	80	–
End cap			
25-50 hp	90	–	66
28 jet, 35 jet and 60-90 hp			
Tilt cylinder	90	–	66
Trim cylinders	160	–	118
Internal cylinder end cap			
28 jet, 35 jet, 40 hp and 50 hp	70	–	52
Piston mounting screws			
25 and 30 hp	61	–	45
Hydraulic pump mounting screws			
25-50 hp	4	35	–
60-90 hp	5	44	–
Lower clamp bracket spacer			
25 and 30 hp	18	–	13
Lower mount bolts/nuts			
9.9 and 15 hp	13	–	10
20 and 25 hp two-cylinder	24	–	18
25 and 30 hp three-cylinder	40	–	30
Lower mount cover/retainer			
20 and 25 hp two-cylinder	24	–	18
25 and 30 hp three-cylinder	18	–	13
Main shuttle valve plug			
25 and 30 hp	7	62	–
28 jet, 35 jet and 40-90 hp	11	98	–
Manual release valve			
25 and 30 hp	3	27	–
28 jet, 35 jet, 40 hp and 50 hp	2	18	–
60-90 hp	3	27	–
Power head adapter to drive shaft housing			
25-90 hp three-cylinder	21	–	16

(continued)

TILT/TRIM AND MIDSECTION

Table 1 TILT/TRIM AND MIDSECTION TORQUE SPECIFICATIONS (continued)

Fastener	N•m	in.-lb.	ft.-lb.
Pressure relief plug (bottom)			
25 and 30 hp	6	53	–
Reverse hook pivot			
9.9 and 15 hp	4	35	–
20 and 25 hp two-cylinder	5	44	–
Shift handle screw			
4-8 hp	6	53	–
Shift shaft bracket			
6 and 8 hp	6	53	–
Steering friction screw	5	44	–
Steering friction mount collar			
28 jet, 35 jet, 40 hp and 50 hp	20	–	15
Throttle shaft screw			
9.9 and 15 hp	4	35	–
Tiller handle bracket			
20 and 25 hp two-cylinder	40	–	30
28 jet, 35 jet, 40-75 hp	38	–	28
Tiller handle pivot			
28 jet, 35 jet, 40-75 hp	38	–	28
Tilt tube nut			
9.9 and 15 hp	13	–	10
20-50 hp	45	–	33
Tilt lock lever pivot			
9.9 and 15 hp	8	70	–
Upper mount bolts/nuts			
9.9 and 15 hp	21	–	15
20-90 hp	24	–	18
Upper mount bracket			
25 and 30 hp three-cylinder	18	–	13
Valve retaining plate screws	4	35	–

Table 2 TILT/TRIM MOTOR SPECIFICATIONS

Measurement	Specification
Minimum brush length	
25 and 30 hp	3 mm (0.12 in.)
28 jet, 35 jet, 40 hp and 50 hp	3.5 mm (0.14 in.)
60-90 hp	4.8 mm (0.19 in.)
Minimum commutator diameter	
25 and 30 hp	15.5 mm (0.61 in.)
28 jet, 35 jet and 40-90 hp	21.0 mm (0.83 in.)

Chapter Twelve

Oil Injection System

This chapter includes removal, inspection and installation procedures for all oil injection components. Air bleeding procedures are also included. **Table 1** lists torque specifications for most oil injection system fasteners. Use the standard torque specifications in Chapter One for fasteners not listed in **Table 1**. **Table 2** lists oil reservoir capacities. **Table 3** lists oil pump identification information. **Tables 1-3** are located at the end of this chapter.

All Yamaha outboards from 20-90 hp may be factory-equipped with oil injection. Most manual start tiller handle control and all models with a C in the model name are not equipped with oil injection. Enduro E60 and E75 models are designed for commercial use and are not equipped with oil injection. The oil and fuel must also be premixed with oil injected models during the initial break-in period and after a major power head repair. Refer to Chapter Three for oil and fuel premixing procedures.

Refer to Chapter Two for testing and troubleshooting procedures for the oil injection and warning system components.

SYSTEM OPERATION

Oil from the engine-mounted oil reservoir (1, **Figure 1**) is gravity fed to a crankshaft/gear driven oil injection pump (2). The oil pump is a variable ratio unit that provides the precise amount of oil at a given throttle setting. Fuel-to-oil ratio at idle is approximately 200 to 1 for 20-50 hp models and approximately 100 to 1 for 60-90 hp models. Fuel-to-oil ratio at wide-open throttle is approximately 100 to 1 for 20-50 hp models and approximately 50 to 1 for 60-90 hp models.

To change the oil level, a linkage connected to the carburetor(s) throttle linkage rotates the pump lever and shaft (1, **Figure 2**). This changes the pump stroke and changing the pump stroke increases or decreases the volume of oil supplied to the engine.

The oil is injected through hoses into the fittings on the carburetor mounting bases. The oil flows into the crankcase where it lubricates the internal power head components.

OIL INJECTION SYSTEM

① OIL INJECTION SYSTEM (20-90 HP MODELS [TYPICAL])

1. Oil reservoir
2. Oil injection pump
3. Carburetors
4. Fuel filter
5. Fuel pump

② GEAR DRIVEN VARIABLE RATIO OIL INJECTION PUMP

1. Pump lever shaft
2. Plunger shaft
3. Worm gear shaft
4. Pump cylinder
5. Outlet check valve
6. Pump identification number

③

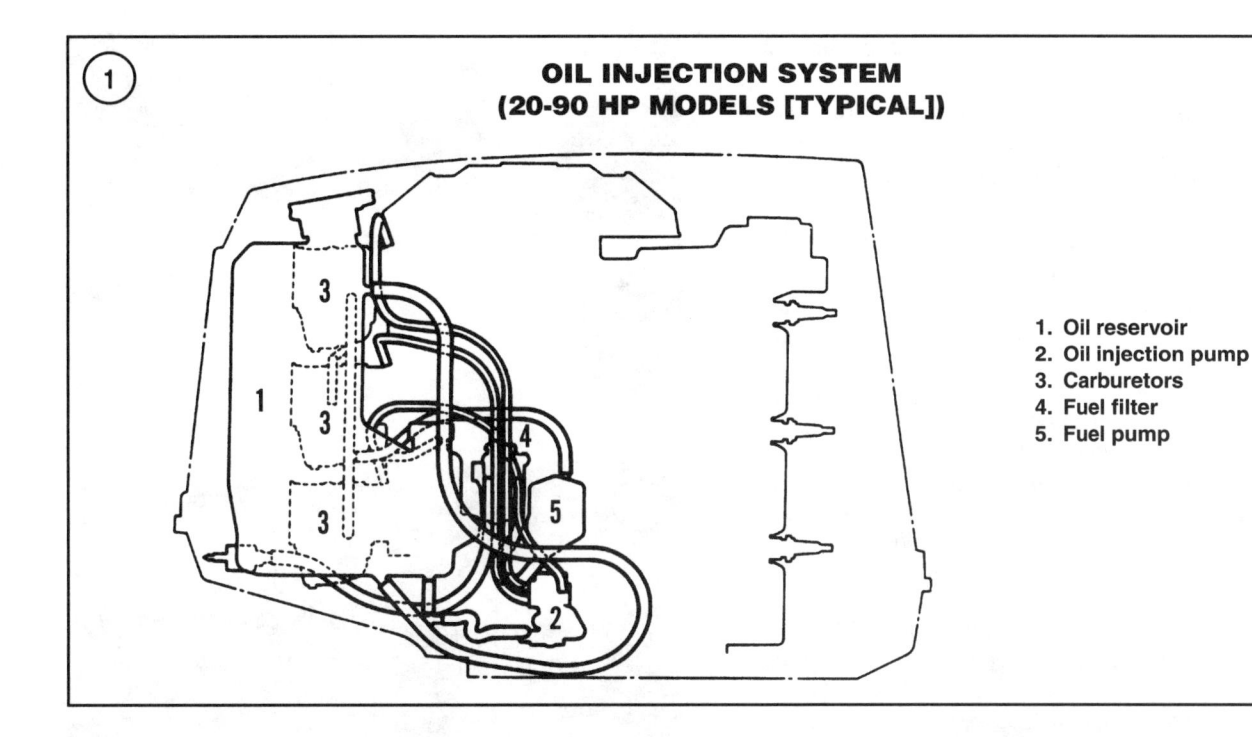

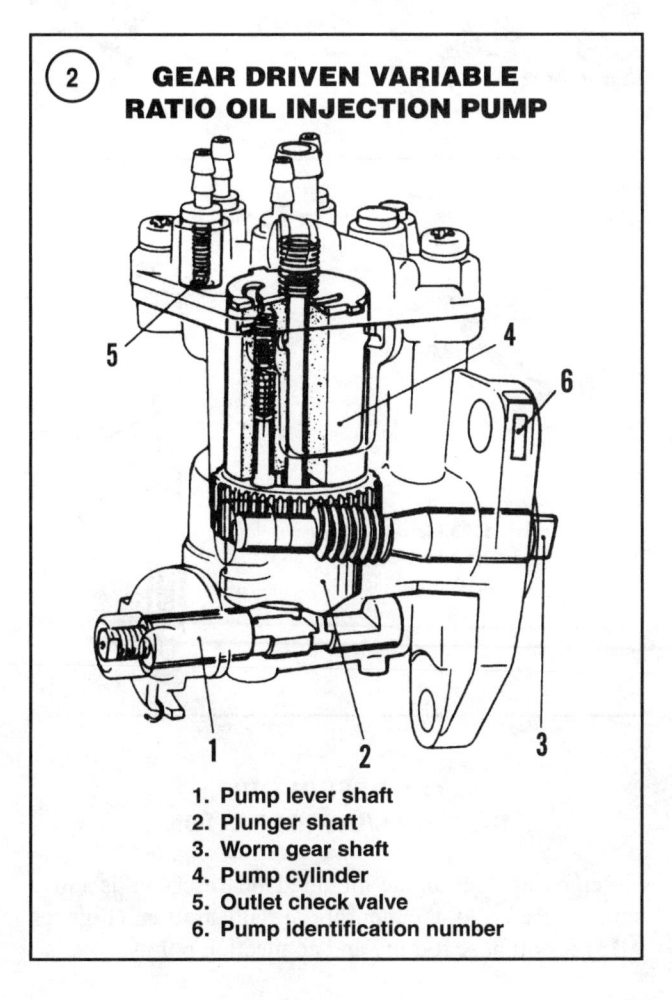

OIL LEVEL SENSOR REMOVAL/INSTALLATION

Refer to Chapter Two for troubleshooting and testing procedures for this component. Only work in a clean environment. Any debris in the system will eventually migrate to the oil pump or check valves and block oil flow or seize moving components in the oil pump, causing insufficient lubrication and eventual failure of the power head.

1. Locate the oil level sensor (**Figure 3**) at the top of the oil supply reservoir. Disconnect the sensor wires at the engine harness connector.

2. Grasp the oil level sensor between your forefinger and thumb (**Figure 4**). Squeeze the sensor and carefully pull the sensor from the reservoir (**Figure 5**). Inspect the

O-ring at the oil level sensor reservoir opening for damage and replace it if necessary.

3. Note the alignment of the oil strainer to the oil level sensor. Most models have alignment marks. If necessary, mark the sensor and strainer (2, **Figure 6**) to ensure proper alignment on assembly.

4. Carefully pull the strainer from the sensor. Clean the strainer with a suitable solvent and air dry it. Inspect the strainer and replace it if it has torn or damaged surfaces.

5. Inspect the gasket (3, **Figure 6**) and replace it if it has torn, deteriorated or deformed surfaces.

CAUTION
Improper installation of the strainer on the sensor will prevent air from venting from the strainer. Without proper venting, the float in the sensor may not operate properly and cause the warning system to malfunction.

6. Install the cleaned strainer onto the sensor. The vent hole (**Figure 7**) on the strainer must align with the flat area on the sensor.

CAUTION
*The rubber gasket (3, **Figure 6**) must fit tightly on the nipple on the bottom of the strainer (2). A loose fit can allow the gasket to drop off during sensor installation and lodge in the oil supply passage for the oil pump, possibly restricting oil flow to the oil pump.*

7. Install the gasket (3, **Figure 6**) over the nipple on the bottom of the strainer. Seat the gasket against the flat surface at the bottom of the strainer. If the gasket does not fit tightly on the nipple, replace the gasket.

CAUTION
Improper installation of the sensor can prevent oil flow to the oil pump and cause power head failure due to insufficient lubrication. Always align the sensor cap and reservoir mark during sensor installation.

8. Note the alignment mark on the cap and the oil reservoir (**Figure 8**). Lubricate the O-ring on the sensor with Yamalube or its equivalent. Avoid pinching the O-ring during sensor installation. Align the marks and carefully slip the sensor into the reservoir opening. The nipple on the bottom of the strainer must fit into the oil passage at the bottom of the reservoir. Carefully press the sensor into the reservoir until it is fully seated.

9. Connect the oil level sensor wires to the engine wire harness connector. Fill the reservoir with oil as described in Chapter Three. Bleed air from the system as described in this chapter.

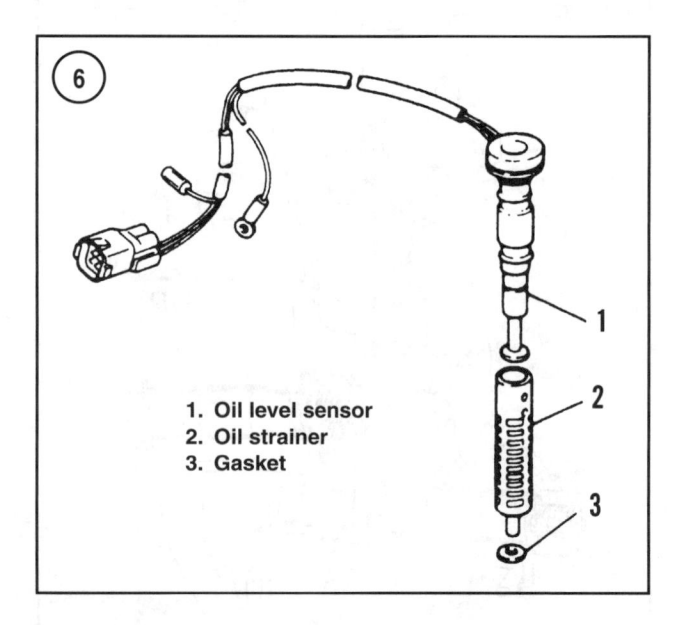

1. Oil level sensor
2. Oil strainer
3. Gasket

OIL RESERVOIR REMOVAL/INSTALLATION

Removing the engine-mounted oil reservoir is fairly simple. Refer to the appropriate illustration (**Figures 9-13**) for oil hose routing and connection points.

OIL INJECTION SYSTEM

the reservoir for cracked, leaking or abraded surfaces. Replace the reservoir if any fault is found.

9. Install the grommets into their respective openings in the reservoir. Carefully mount the reservoir onto the power head. Make sure no hoses wiring or other components are pinched between the reservoir and the power head. Install the sleeves, washers and mounting bolts. Again make sure no hoses, wiring or other components are pinched, then securely tighten the mounting bolts.

10. Refer to the appropriate illustration (**Figures 9-13**), sketch or marks and connect all hoses to the reservoir. Secure the hoses with the appropriate clamps.

11. Fill the reservoir with Yamalube or its equivalent as described in Chapter Three. Reconnect the battery cables and spark plug leads.

12. Bleed air from the system as described in this chapter.

OIL HOSES AND CHECK VALVES

Refer to the appropriate illustration (**Figures 9-13**) for hose routing and connection points. Always mark hose connection points and make sketches of hose routing before disconnecting them.

Clean all loose material and contaminants from hose fittings before disconnecting the hoses. The oil injection system must operate with clean oil. Even minute particles can wreak havoc with the oil injection system.

Hose Removal and Inspection

CAUTION
Work carefully when removing plastic tie clamps from the oil hoses. The hose can be inadvertently cut as the clamp is cut and the cut might not be visually apparent. The hose can leak or fail at the cut at a later time, causing an oil leak and/or insufficient lubrication of the power head. The power head will fail if the engine is operated with insufficient lubrication.

Carefully cut, remove and replace all plastic locking tie clamps when they have to be removed. Work carefully to avoid damaging hoses or hose fittings. Inspect spring type hose clamps for distortion, corrosion or weak spring tension. Replace damaged or questionable clamps.

Remove multiple hose connections in a cluster along with their oil injection system components when possible. This reduces oil leaks, incorrect hose connections during assembly and the time needed to bleed air from the system.

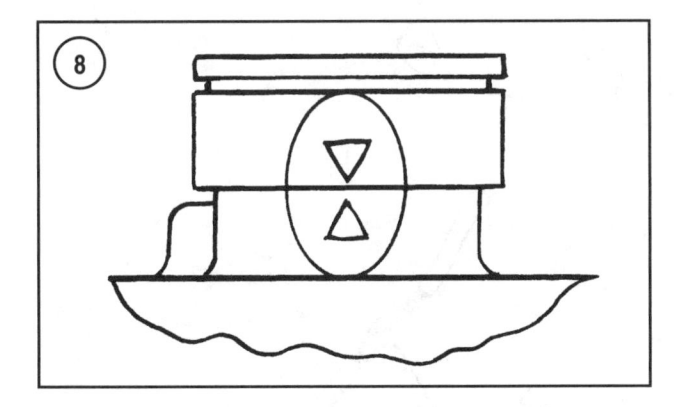

1. Disconnect the battery cables. Disconnect and ground all spark plug leads to prevent accidental starting.
2. Remove the oil level sensor as described in this chapter.
3. Remove the oil hose leading to the oil pump or the water drain hose (if so equipped) and quickly direct the hose into a container of suitable material and capacity to hold the oil. **Table 2** lists oil reservoir capacities.
4. Note the routing and connection points for all hoses connected to the reservoir. Mark or make a sketch of the hose routing and connection points as needed. Replace hose clamps that are corroded, distorted or have weak spring tension.
5. On 20 and 25 hp two-cylinder models, remove the screw and clamp that secure the sensor wire to the reservoir.
6. Note the orientation of the grommets, washers and sleeves. Then support the reservoir and remove the mounting bolts. Make sure all hoses are disconnected from the reservoir, then remove the reservoir.
7. Clean debris and the oil film from the reservoir and power head mating surfaces.
8. Clean the reservoir in a suitable solvent or warm soapy water and air dry it. If soap is used, thoroughly rinse the reservoir with clean water to remove soap residue. Inspect

500

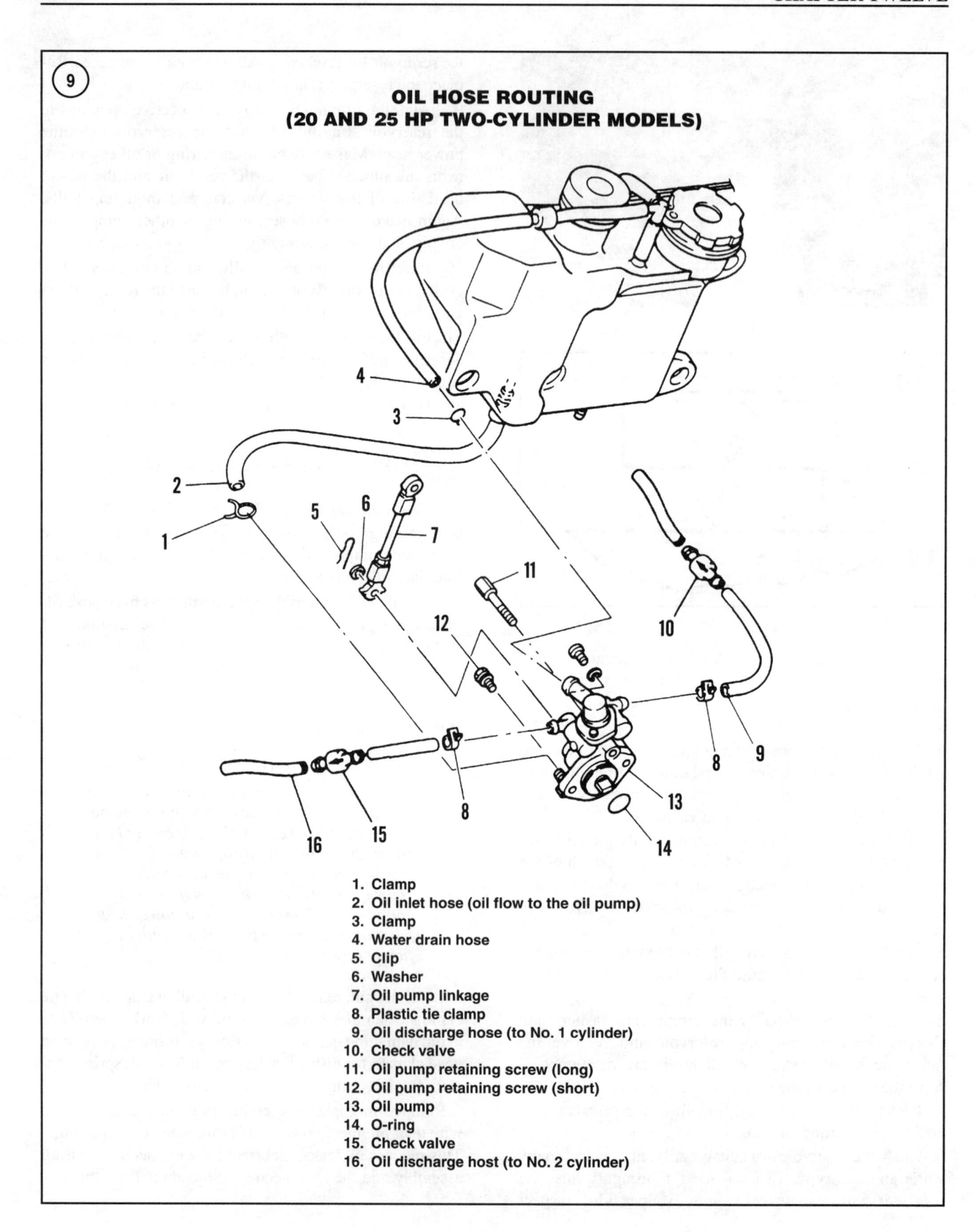

CHAPTER TWELVE

⑨

**OIL HOSE ROUTING
(20 AND 25 HP TWO-CYLINDER MODELS)**

1. Clamp
2. Oil inlet hose (oil flow to the oil pump)
3. Clamp
4. Water drain hose
5. Clip
6. Washer
7. Oil pump linkage
8. Plastic tie clamp
9. Oil discharge hose (to No. 1 cylinder)
10. Check valve
11. Oil pump retaining screw (long)
12. Oil pump retaining screw (short)
13. Oil pump
14. O-ring
15. Check valve
16. Oil discharge host (to No. 2 cylinder)

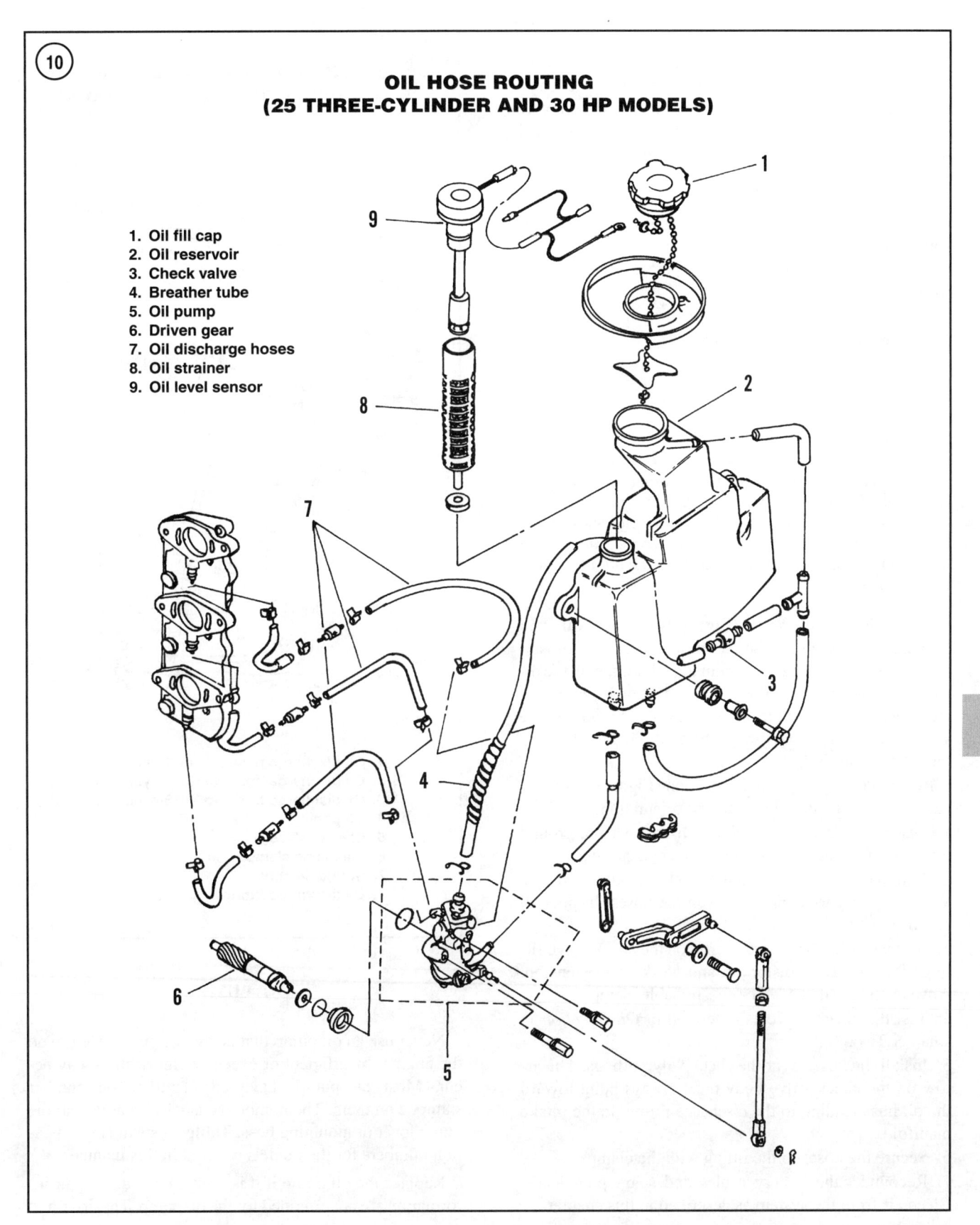

OIL INJECTION SYSTEM

10

**OIL HOSE ROUTING
(25 THREE-CYLINDER AND 30 HP MODELS)**

1. Oil fill cap
2. Oil reservoir
3. Check valve
4. Breather tube
5. Oil pump
6. Driven gear
7. Oil discharge hoses
8. Oil strainer
9. Oil level sensor

Inspect hoses for cut, cracked or abraded surfaces. Replace hoses that have any of these defects. Replace hoses that feel hard or brittle. Hard or brittle hoses will eventually break and leak oil. Replace hoses that feel excessively soft or spongy. Check the type of oil that is being used (Chapter Three). The wrong type of oil may promote softening of the oil hoses.

Clear hoses are often used at the oil pump. Inspect these hoses as described. These hoses must be transparent. Always replace clear hoses that have become cloudy. This is more common when the engine is operated or stored in a warmer climate.

After hose installation, bleed air from the oil injection system as described in this chapter.

Check Valves Removal/Installation

CAUTION
Be careful when installing oil hose check valves. The power head will be damaged if a check valve is installed in the wrong direction. The arrow on the check valve indicates the direction of oil flow. The arrow must point toward the hose leading to the oil discharge fitting on the intake manifold.

The oil line check valves (**Figure 14**) prevent oil from flowing out of the oil hoses when the engine is not running. Before removing them from the oil lines, note the direction of the arrow on the check valve body. The arrow indicates the direction the oil flows through the valve. The arrow must always lead toward the oil discharge fitting on the intake manifold.

Refer to the appropriate illustration (**Figures 9-13**) for check valve mounting location and orientation.
1. Disconnect the battery cables. Disconnect and ground the spark plug leads to prevent accidental starting.
2. Remove the clamps from the check valve fittings. Work carefully to avoid damaging the hoses. Inspect all oil hoses as described in this chapter.
3. Inspect spring type hose clamps on the check valve fittings for corrosion, distortion and weak spring tension. Always replace damaged or questionable clamps.
4. Test the check valve as described in *Oil Injection* in Chapter Two.
5. Install the hoses over the check valve fittings. The arrow on the check valve body must always point toward the oil hose leading to the discharge fitting on the intake manifold.
6. Secure the hoses to the fitting with the clamps.
7. Reconnect the battery cables and spark plug leads. Bleed air from the system as described in this chapter.

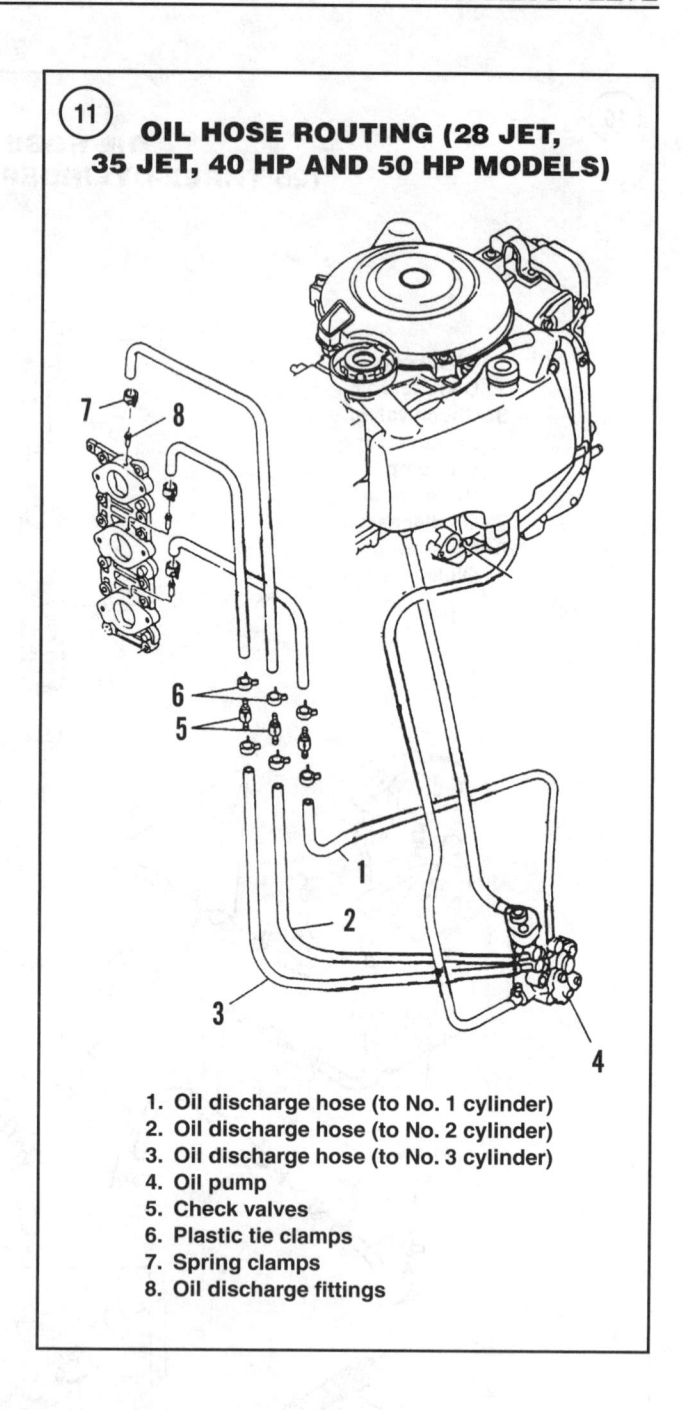

11 OIL HOSE ROUTING (28 JET, 35 JET, 40 HP AND 50 HP MODELS)

1. Oil discharge hose (to No. 1 cylinder)
2. Oil discharge hose (to No. 2 cylinder)
3. Oil discharge hose (to No. 3 cylinder)
4. Oil pump
5. Check valves
6. Plastic tie clamps
7. Spring clamps
8. Oil discharge fittings

OIL PUMP

Never use an oil pump that is not designated for use on the engine. Insufficient or excessive lubrication may occur. Most oil pumps have an identification number stamped on them. The number is usually located near the pump lever or mounting boss. **Table 3** lists the identification numbers for the models covered in this manual.

Replace the oil pump if it is faulty. Parts and repair information are not provided for the oil pump. The drive and

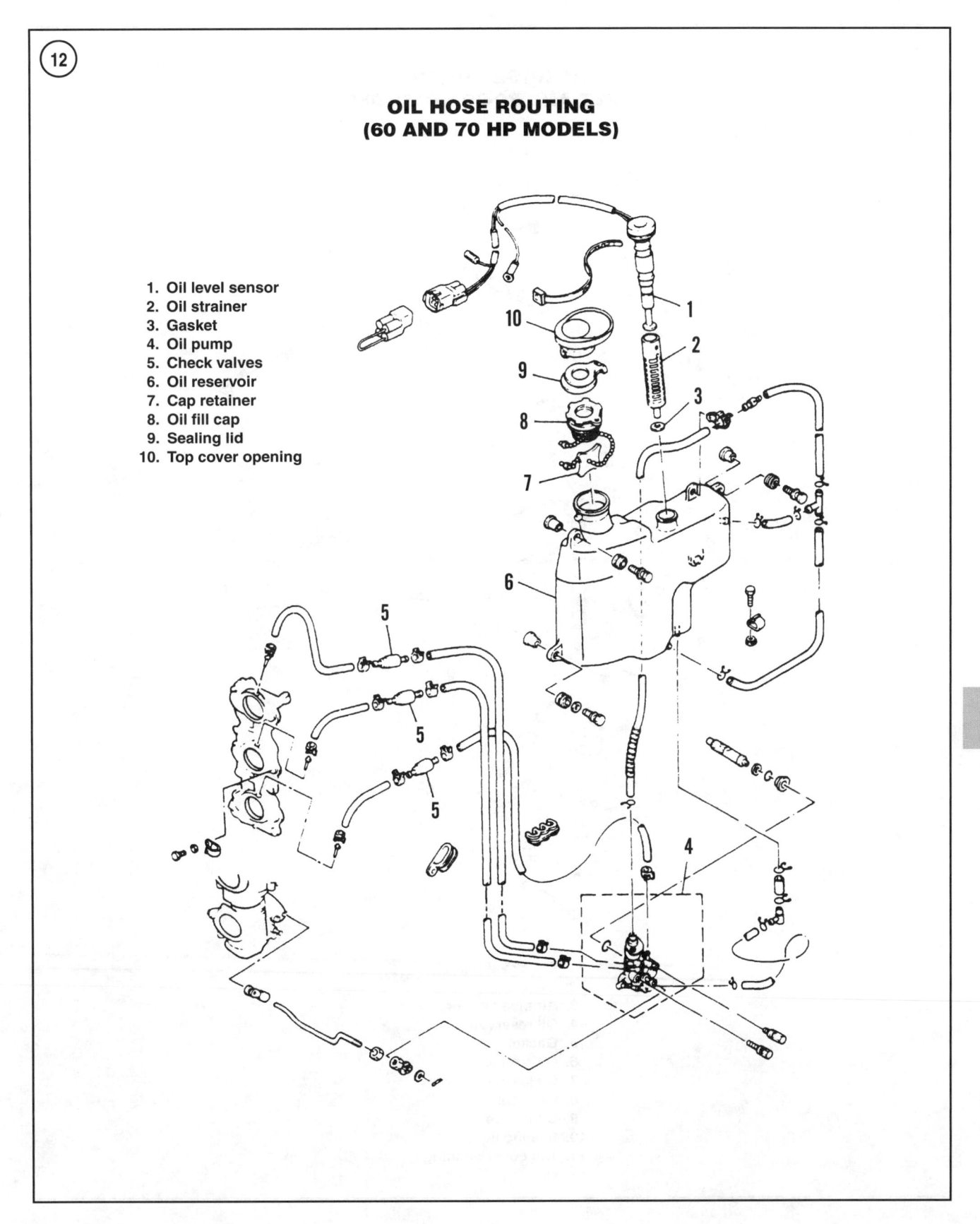

OIL INJECTION SYSTEM

503

**OIL HOSE ROUTING
(60 AND 70 HP MODELS)**

1. Oil level sensor
2. Oil strainer
3. Gasket
4. Oil pump
5. Check valves
6. Oil reservoir
7. Cap retainer
8. Oil fill cap
9. Sealing lid
10. Top cover opening

12

504

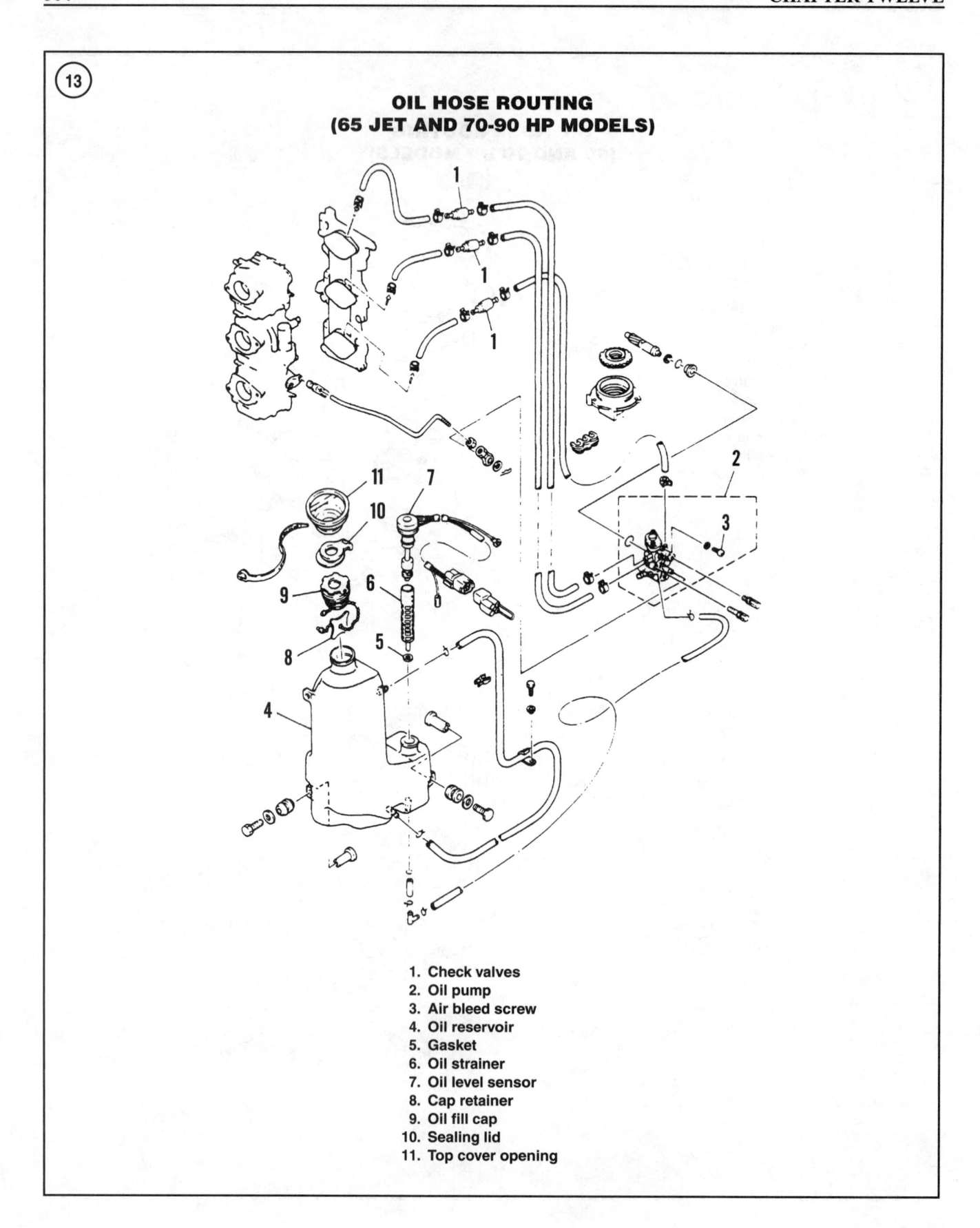

CHAPTER TWELVE

⑬

**OIL HOSE ROUTING
(65 JET AND 70-90 HP MODELS)**

1. Check valves
2. Oil pump
3. Air bleed screw
4. Oil reservoir
5. Gasket
6. Oil strainer
7. Oil level sensor
8. Cap retainer
9. Oil fill cap
10. Sealing lid
11. Top cover opening

OIL INJECTION SYSTEM

OIL PUMP MOUNTING (TYPICAL) — Figure 15

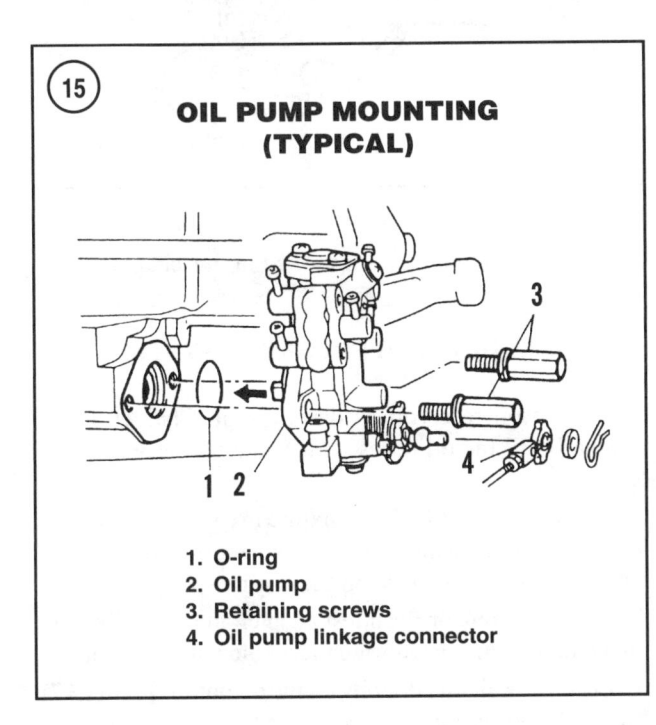

1. O-ring
2. Oil pump
3. Retaining screws
4. Oil pump linkage connector

OIL PUMP DRIVE COMPONENTS (TYPICAL) — Figure 16

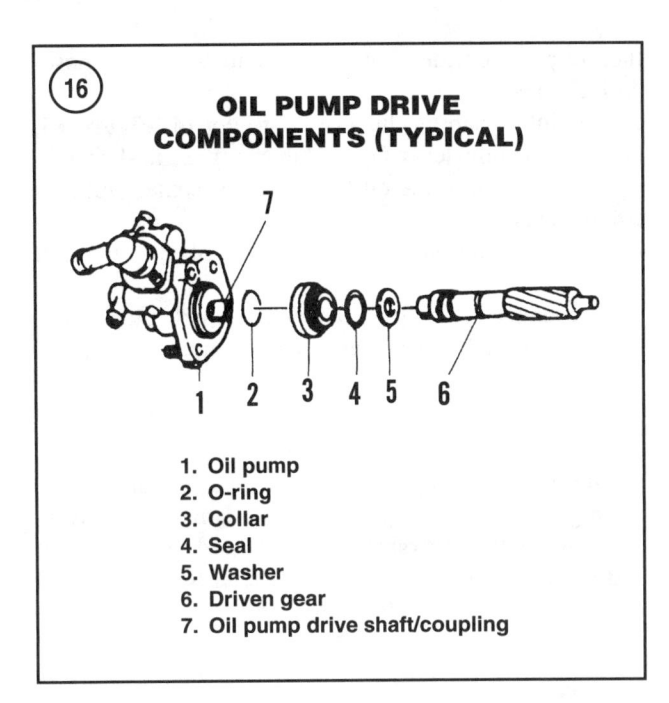

1. Oil pump
2. O-ring
3. Collar
4. Seal
5. Washer
6. Driven gear
7. Oil pump drive shaft/coupling

driven gears, seal, oil ring and mounting bolts are available.

Removal

Mark all hoses and make a sketch of hose routing before removal. Note the size and mounting location of all plastic locking tie clamps and replace them if they are removed.

1. Disconnect both cables from the battery. Disconnect all spark plug leads to prevent accidental starting.
2. Carefully pry the linkage connector (4, **Figure 15**) from the pump lever. Do not disturb the link rod adjustment.
3. Remove the clamp and carefully pull the inlet hose from the oil pump. Quickly plug the hose with a suitable object, such as a dowel rod or golf tee. Inspect spring type hose clamps for corrosion, distortion and weak spring tension. Replace faulty or suspect clamps.
4. Mark the cylinder number on all outlet hoses and pump fittings. Remove the clamps and carefully pull each outlet hose from the oil pump. Plug the hoses as described in Step 3.
5. Remove the two retaining screws (3, **Figure 15**) and carefully pull the pump (2) from the cylinder block. Remove and discard the O-ring (1, **Figure 15**). Wipe oil residue and other contaminants from the oil pump mounting surfaces.

Installation

1. Apply Yamalube or its equivalent to the surfaces of a new O-ring. Install the O-ring (1, **Figure 15**) onto the oil pump. The O-ring must seat against the step on the oil pump mounting surface.
2. Position the oil pump on the driven gear collar. Insert the oil pump drive shaft (7, **Figure 16**) into the driven gear (6). Rotate the pump on the collar until the oil pump shaft aligns with the slot in the driven gear. The oil pump seats against the collar when it is aligned. Never force the pump against the collar.
3. Keep the pump in contact with the collar while rotating the pump to align the retaining screw holes. Install the mounting screws (3, **Figure 15**) and tighten them to the specification in **Table 1**.
4. Remove the plugs and fill the disconnected hoses with Yamalube or equivalent. Quickly connect the oil hoses to

their respective fittings on the oil pump. Secure the hoses with clamps.

5. Carefully snap the linkage connector (4, **Figure 15**) onto the oil pump lever. Operate the throttle and shift linkages to make sure the oil hoses do not contact moving components.

6. Adjust the oil pump linkage as described in Chapter Four.

7. Reconnect the battery cables and spark plug leads. Bleed air from the system as described in this chapter.

DRIVEN GEAR

After removal, inspect the driven gear for damaged or worn gear teeth. If the gear teeth are damaged or excessively worn, the crankshaft mounted drive gear is suspect and must be inspected. Refer to Chapter Seven for drive gear removal and installation procedures.

Removal

1. Remove the oil pump as described in this chapter.
2. Note the mounting location and orientation of the driven gear components before their removal.
3. Carefully remove the collar (3, **Figure 16**) and seal (4) from the power head. If necessary, pry the collar loose. Work carefully to avoid damaging the mating surfaces. Remove and discard the seal. Mark the pump side, then remove the washer (5, **Figure 16**).
4. Use needlenose pliers to pull the driven gear from the power head. Pull the gear from the protruded coupling end. Wipe all oil residue and other contaminants from the oil pump and collar mounting surfaces.
5. Clean the collar and gear with a suitable solvent and air dry it. Replace any worn or damaged components.

Installation

1. Lubricate the driven gear, O-rings, seal and collar with Yamalube or its equivalent. Use needlenose pliers to carefully insert the driven gear into the power head. Slowly rotate the gear during installation to mesh the driven gear teeth with the drive gear teeth.
2. Install the washer, seal and collar as shown in **Figure 16**. Seat the collar against the mating surface. Check for improper driven gear installation if the collar will not seat. Never force the collar against the mating surface.

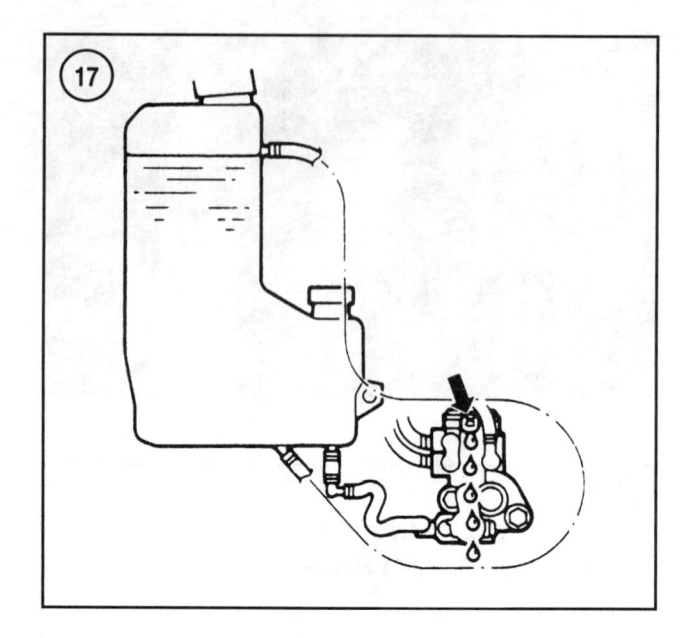

3. Install the oil pump as described in this chapter.

BLEEDING AIR FROM THE SYSTEM

1. Fill the oil reservoir as described in Chapter Three. Manually fill the oil hoses with Yamalube or its equivalent.

2. Prepare a 50 to 1 fuel/oil mixture in a portable fuel tank as described in Chapter Three. Connect the portable fuel tank to the fuel inlet hose on the engine.

3. Use a test tank or flush/test adapter and run the engine on the fuel/oil mixture during the air bleeding procedure.

4. Locate the air bleed screw on the oil pump (**Figure 17**). The air bleed screw has a gasket under the screw head.

5. Place a shop towel under the screw to catch spilled oil. With the engine running at idle speed, loosen the bleed screw 3 to 4 turns counterclockwise. Fully tighten the screw clockwise when oil begins flowing from the screw opening.

6. For transparent oil outlet hoses, visually inspect the oil outlet hoses for air bubbles. Repeat Steps 1-5 until there are no bubbles in the outlet hoses.

7. Run the engine for an additional 10 minutes on the fuel/oil mixture to purge any remaining air bubbles from the system. Continue to run the engine until all bubbles are purged from the hoses.

OIL INJECTION SYSTEM

Table 1 OIL INJECTION SYSTEM TORQUE SPECIFICATIONS

Fastener	N•m	in.-lb.	ft.-lb.
Oil pump retaining screws			
20-50 hp	6.5	57	–
60-90 hp	7.0	62	–

Table 2 OIL RESERVOIR CAPACITY

Model	Capacity
20 and 25 hp (two-cylinder)	0.7 L (0.74 qt.)
28 jet, 35 jet, 40 hp and 50 hp	1.5 L (1.6 qt.)
60 and 70 hp	2.8 L (2.96 qt.)
65 jet and 75-90 hp	3.3 L (3.49 qt.)

TABLE 3 OIL PUMP IDENTIFICATION

Model	Identification marking
20 and 25 hp (two-cylinder)	6L200
28 jet, 35 jet, 40 hp and 50 hp	63D00
60 and 70 hp	6H302
65 jet and 75-90 hp	6H102

Chapter Thirteen

Remote Control

The remote control allows an operator to control throttle, shifting and other engine operations from a location out of reach of the engine (**Figure 1**). This chapter includes neutral throttle operating instructions, shift cable replacement procedures and remote control disassembly/assembly procedures.

Table 1 lists torque specifications for most remote control fasteners. Use the standard torque specifications in Chapter One for fasteners not listed in **Table 1**. **Table 1** is located at the end of this chapter.

CAUTION
Always refer to the owner's manual for specific operating instructions for the remote control. Become familiar with all control functions before operating the engine.

NEUTRAL THROTTLE OPERATION

Two common types of controls are used with Yamaha outboards. The most commonly used type is the surface mount 703 control or *pull for neutral throttle control* (**Figure 2**). To activate neutral throttle operation, move the handle to NEUTRAL. Pull the handle straight out or away from the control (**Figure 3**). The throttle can then be advanced without the engine being shifted into gear. This allows for easier starting and quicker engine warm-up. To return to normal operation, move the handle to neutral and push the handle toward the control.

The less commonly used type is the 705 panel mounted (**Figure 4**) or binacle mount (**Figure 5**) *push for neutral throttle control*. This control is used primarily with higher horsepower engines. To activate neutral throttle operation, move the handle to NEUTRAL. Push in and hold the free accelerator button (**Figure 6**). Advance the throttle slightly and release the button. The button should remain depressed. Returning the handle to the neutral position should allow the button to spring up. The operator should be able to shift gears. No wiring diagrams are available for this model.

WARNING
A malfunction in the remote control can lead to lack of shift and throttle control. Never operate the outboard when there is a malfunction with the remote control. Check for proper remote control operation before operating the engine or after any service or repair.

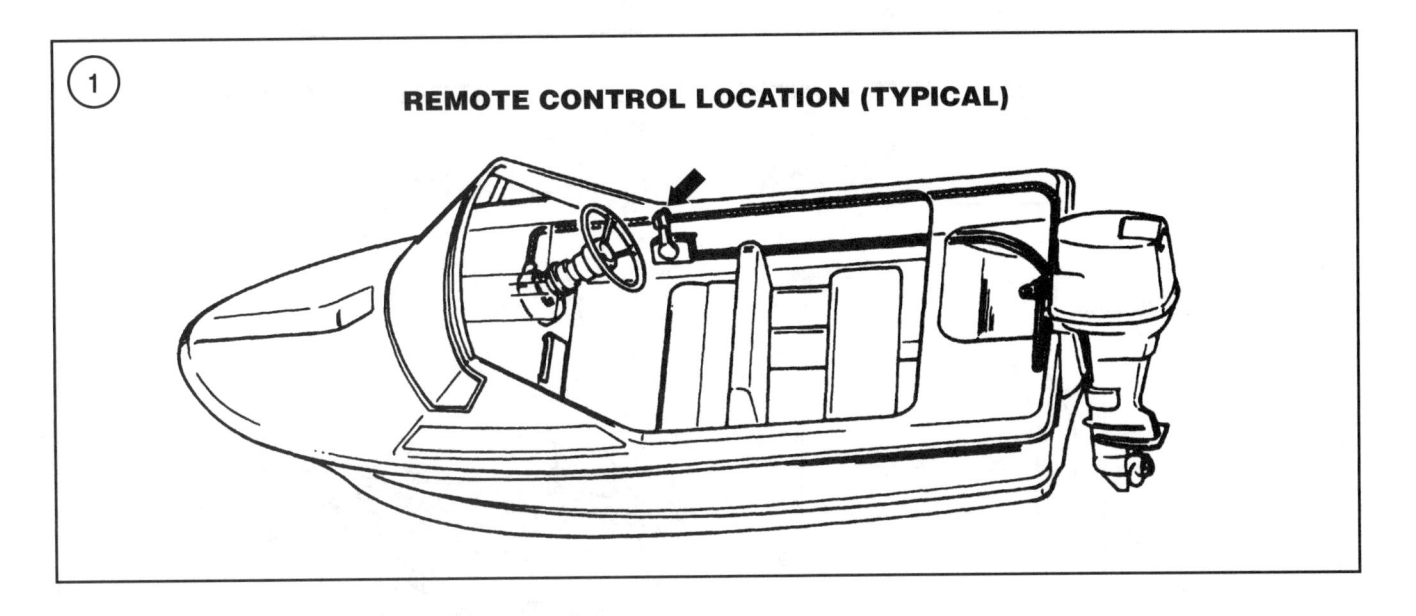

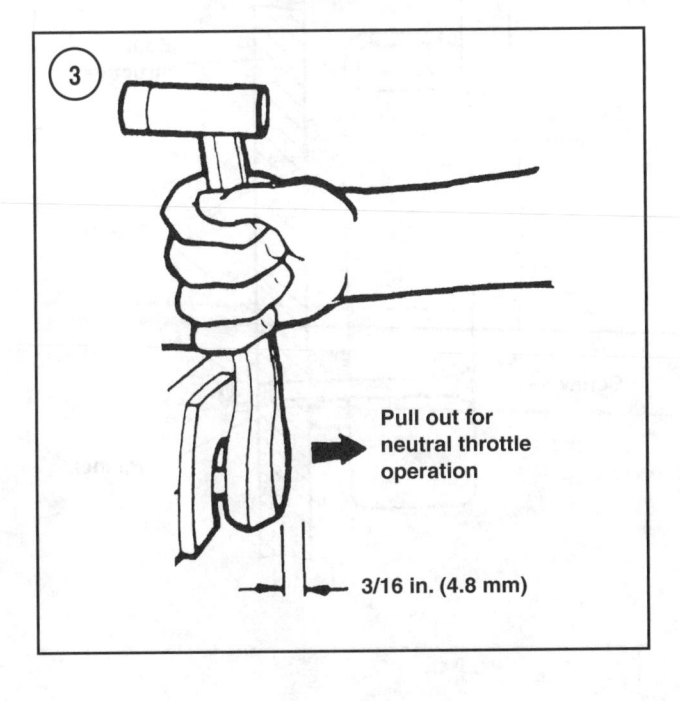

REMOTE CONTROL

① **REMOTE CONTROL LOCATION (TYPICAL)**

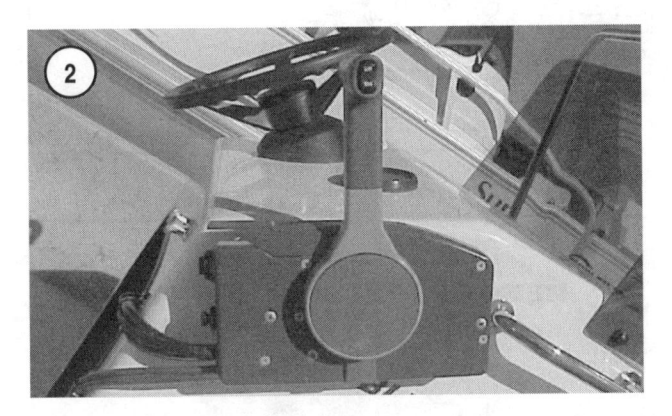

②

③ Pull out for neutral throttle operation
3/16 in. (4.8 mm)

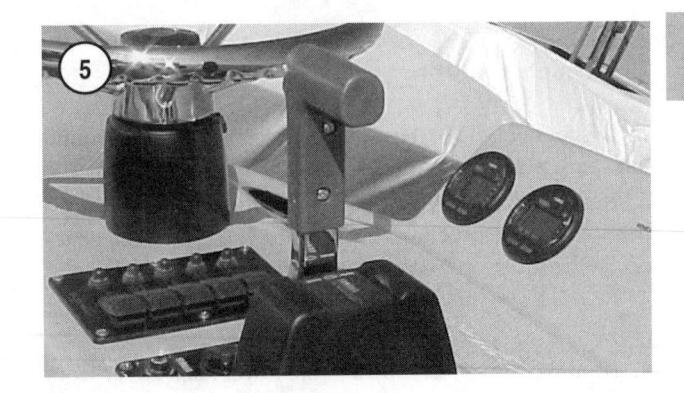

④

⑤

THROTTLE/SHIFT CABLE REMOVAL/INSTALLATION

Replace the cables if they are hard to move or have excessive play due to cable wear. Replace both the throttle and shift cables at the same time. The conditions that caused one cable to require replacement are probably

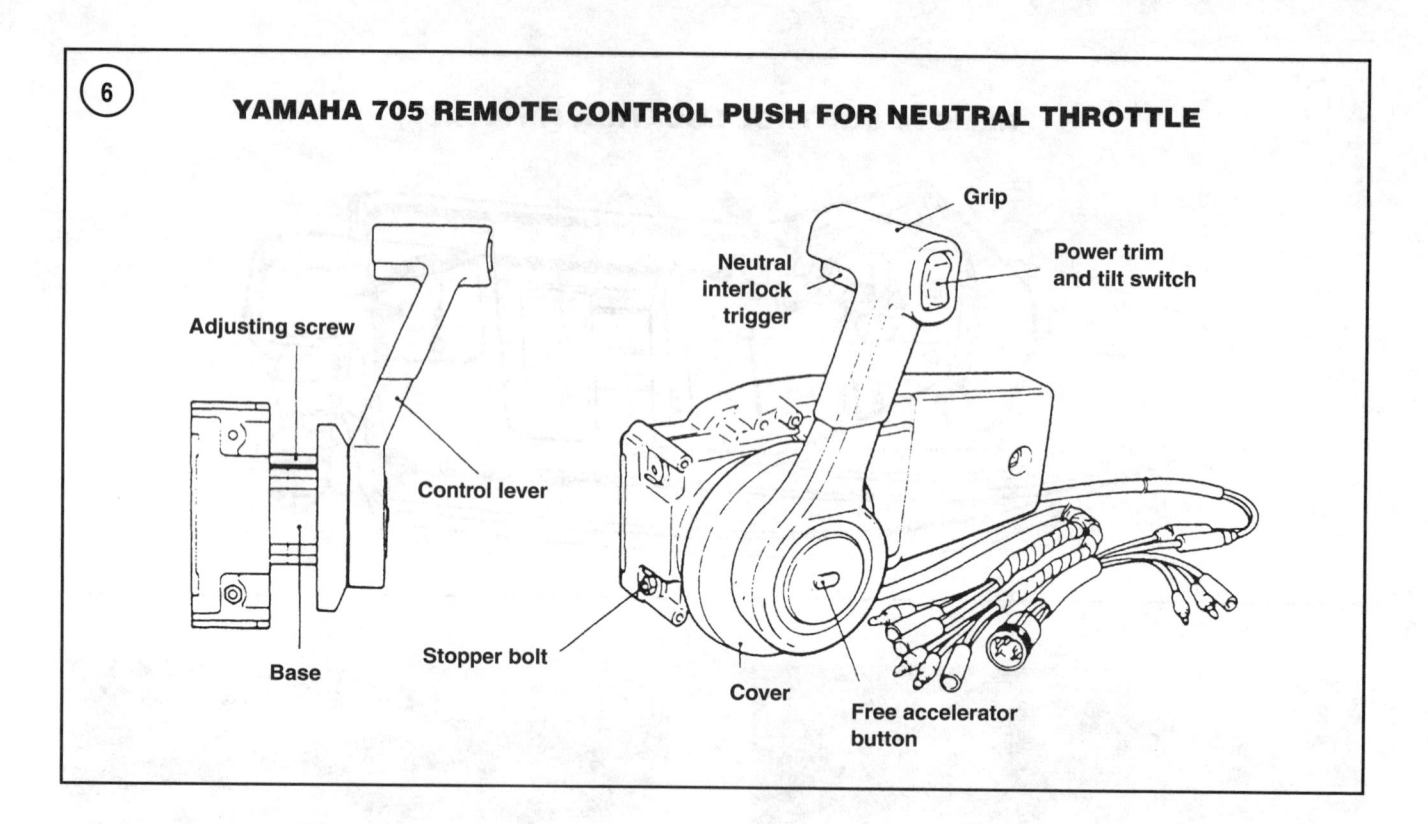

510 CHAPTER THIRTEEN

6 YAMAHA 705 REMOTE CONTROL PUSH FOR NEUTRAL THROTTLE

present in the other cable. Mark the cables before removal to ensure the cables are installed to the proper attaching points. Remove and attach one cable at a time to avoid confusion.

Procedures are provided for both the 703 and 705 remote controls. Refer to *Neutral Throttle Operation* in this chapter to identify the control box.

703 Remote Control

1. Disconnect the battery cables. Disconnect and ground the spark plug leads to prevent accidental starting.

2. Remove the screws or bolts attaching the remote control to the boat structure. See **Figure 7**. Capture the spacers as the mounting screws are removed.

3. Carefully pull the cover from the area below the handle (**Figure 8**).

4. Remove the two screws and the lower back cover from the control (**Figure 9**).

5. Identify the throttle and shift cables (**Figure 10**). Move the control handle to access the circlip on one of the cables.

6. Note and/or mark the position of the cable and cable grommet in the clamp groove (**Figure 11**). Remove the circlip (**Figure 10**), then lift the cable from the clamp groove and pin on the lever. Inspect the circlip for corro-

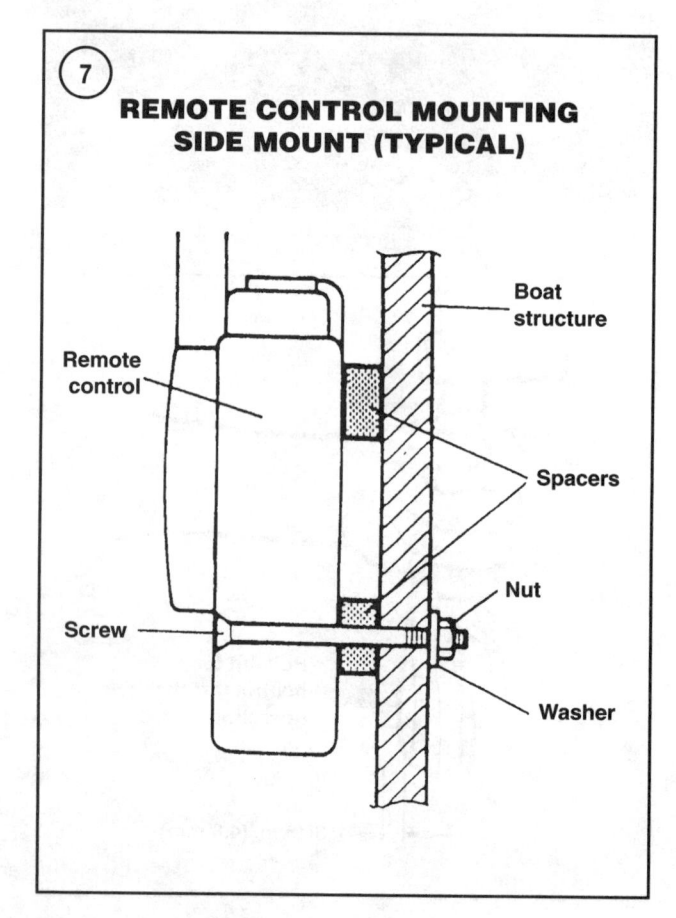

7 REMOTE CONTROL MOUNTING SIDE MOUNT (TYPICAL)

REMOTE CONTROL

8

9
Screw — Lower back cover — Screw

10
Remote control throttle cable
Circlip
Remote control shifting cable

11 YAMAHA 703 REMOTE CONTROL CABLE ATTACHMENT
Shift arm
Circlip
Grommet
Clamp groove

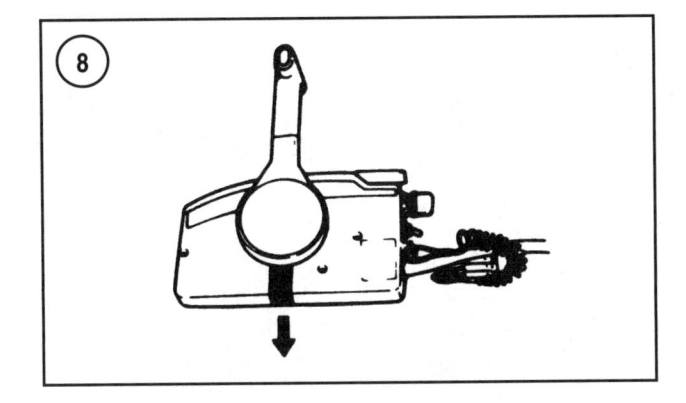

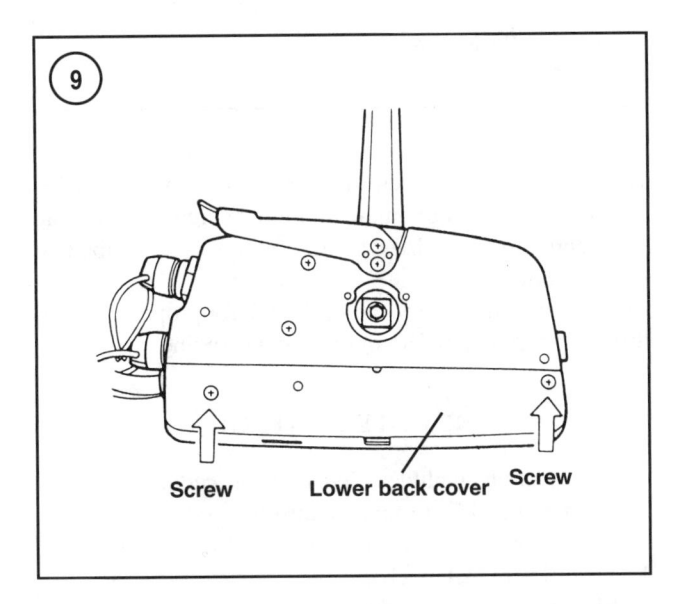

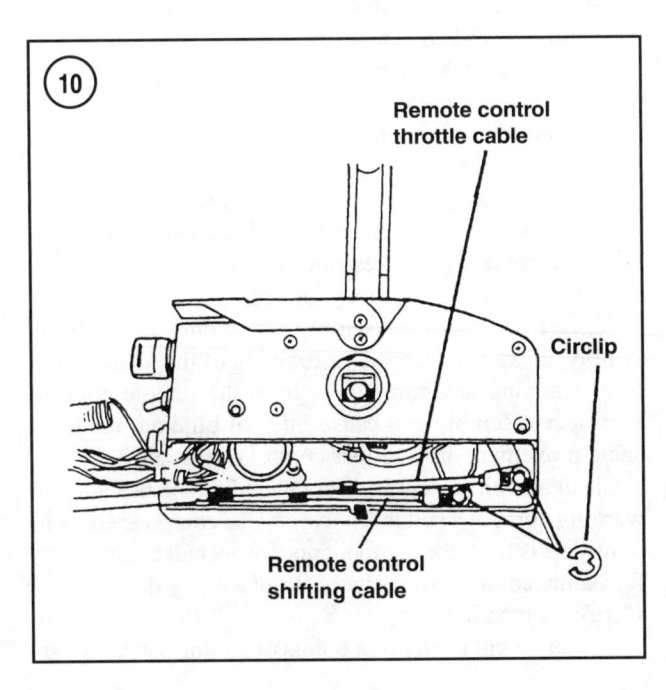

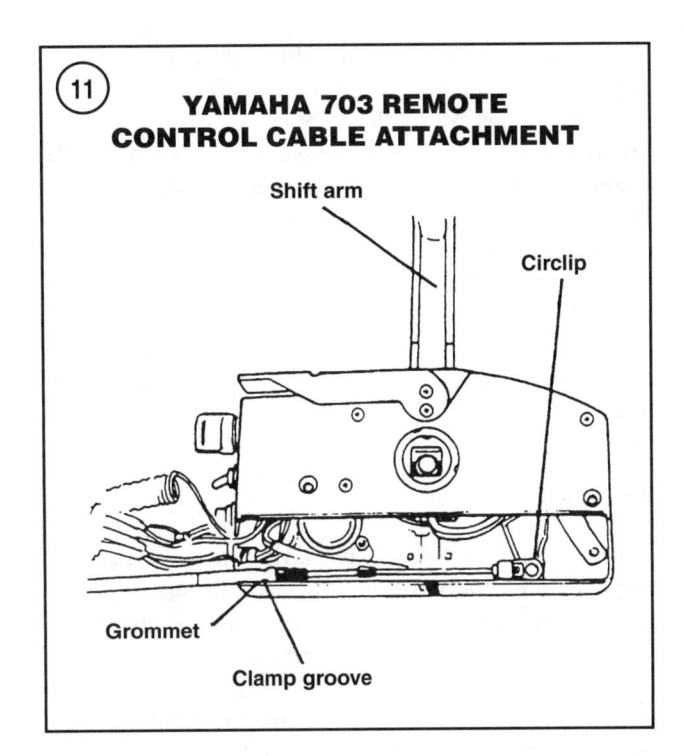

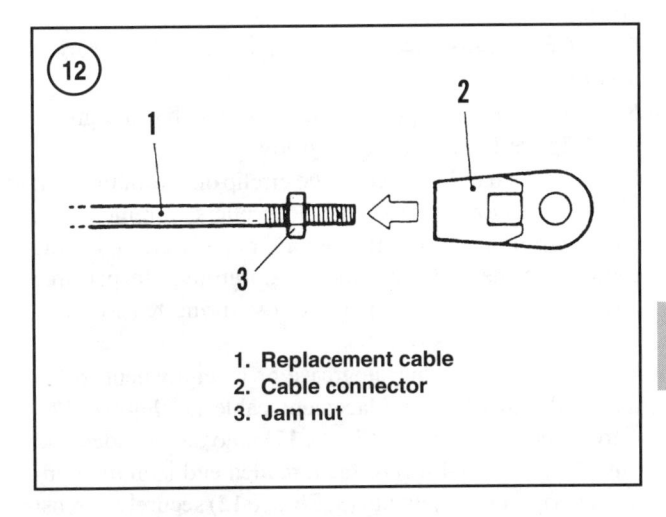

12
1. Replacement cable
2. Cable connector
3. Jam nut

sion, damage or lost spring tension. Replace it if it has any defects.

7. Apply Yamaha marine grease or its equivalent to the threaded end of the replacement cable (1, **Figure 12**). Thread the connector (2, **Figure 12**) onto the threaded end until 11.0 mm (0.4 in.) of the threaded end is in the connector. Tighten the jam nut (3, **Figure 12**) securely against the cable connector.

8. Place the cable and grommet in the clamp groove in the control box as indicated in **Figure 11**. Apply Yamaha marine grease or equivalent to the attaching points of the cables. Install the cable connector over the pin on the lever,

then install the circlip (**Figure 10**). Make sure the circlip is properly installed in the groove in the pin.

9. Repeat Steps 5-8 for the other cable.

10. Install the lower back cover and screws (**Figure 9**). Carefully slide the cover (**Figure 8**) into the slot below the handle. Install the control and attaching screws to the boat. Make sure the spacers are positioned as shown in **Figure 7**. Securely tighten the mounting screws.

11. Adjust the throttle and shift cables at the engine as described in Chapter Four. Connect the battery cables. Check for proper throttle and shift operation before operating the engine.

705 Remote Control

1. Disconnect the battery cables. Disconnect and ground the spark plug leads to prevent accidental starting.

2. Remove the screws or bolts attaching the control to the boat structure as necessary to access the back cover or the control.

3. Remove the five screws (**Figure 13**) from the back cover. Support the cables, then carefully pry the back cover from the control.

4. Refer to **Figure 14** to identify the shift cable. Mark it accordingly.

5. Make note of the position of the shift cable and grommet (**Figure 14**) in the clamp groove.

6. Move the handle to access the circlip on one of the shift cable connectors. Use needle nose pliers to remove the circlip from the shift arm attaching pin. Carefully lift the cable from the shift arm and clamp groove. Inspect the circlip for corrosion, damage or lost spring tension. Replace it if it has any defects.

7. Apply Yamaha marine grease or its equivalent to the threaded end of the replacement cable (1, **Figure 12**). Thread the connector (2, **Figure 12**) onto the threaded end until 11.0 mm (0.4 in.) of the threaded end is in the connector. Tighten the jam nut (3, **Figure 12**) securely against the cable connector.

8. Apply Yamaha marine grease or equivalent to the attaching points for the cable. Place the cable and grommet into the clamp groove as indicated in **Figure 14**. Install the cable connector over the pin on the shift arm. Install the circlip onto the pin. Make sure the circlip is properly installed in the groove in the pin.

9. Repeat Steps 5-8 for the throttle cable. The throttle cable must attach to the throttle arm (**Figure 14**). Inspect the cables to make sure both are properly aligned in the clamp groove (**Figure 14**). Place the back cover on the control. Hold the back cover firmly in position and install the five screws (**Figure 13**). Securely tighten the screws.

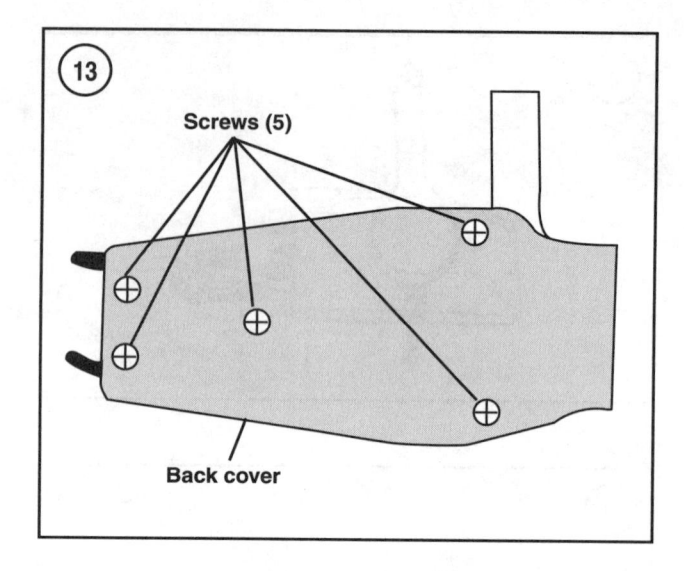

13
Screws (5)
Back cover

10. If the control was removed, install it to the boat structure and securely tighten the mounting screws. Adjust the shift and throttle cables at the engine as described in Chapter Four.

11. Connect the battery cables. Check for proper shift and throttle operation before operating the engine.

REMOTE CONTROL

This section includes separate procedures for the Yamaha 703 and 705 remote controls.

The major components of the control include the:

1. Throttle control mechanism.
2. Shift control mechanism.
3. Neutral throttle mechanism.
4. Tilt/trim switch.
5. Ignition/key switch.
6. Fuel enrichment switch.
7. Warning horn.

If complete disassembly is not required to access the faulty component(s), perform the disassembly until the desired component is accessible. Reverse the disassembly steps to assemble the remote control.

To save time during assembly and to ensure proper assembly, make a note, mark or drawing of the location before removing any component from the remote control. Improper assembly can cause internal binding, reversed cable movement or improper control operation.

Clean all components, except electric switches and the warning horn, in a suitable solvent. Use compressed air to blow debris from the components. Inspect all components for damaged or worn surfaces. Replace any defective or suspect components. Apply Yamaha All-Purpose Grease or its equivalent to all pivot points or sliding surfaces dur-

REMOTE CONTROL

(14) YAMAHA 705 REMOTE CONTROL CABLE ATTACHMENT

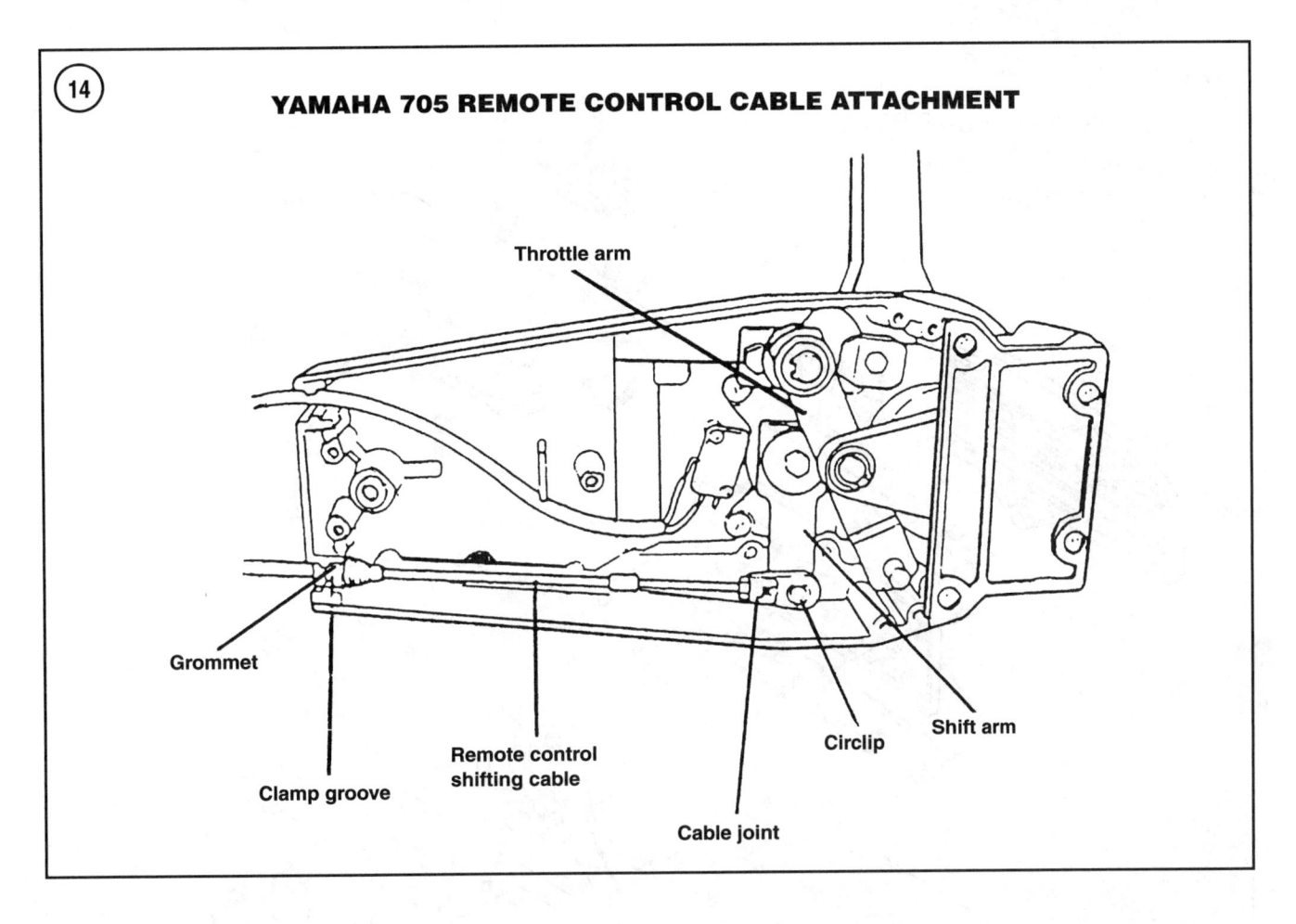

Labels: Throttle arm, Grommet, Clamp groove, Remote control shifting cable, Cable joint, Circlip, Shift arm

ing assembly. Test all electrical components that were removed to ensure proper operation after assembly. Test procedures for all electrical components are in Chapter Two.

703 Remote Control Disassembly and Assembly

1. Disconnect the battery cables. Disconnect and ground the spark plug lead to prevent accidental starting.
2. Remove the screws or bolts that attach the control to the boat structure. Mark all wires leading to the control to ensure proper connection on installation. Disconnect all wires. Place the control handle in the NEUTRAL position.
3. Mark the cable location for reference, then remove the throttle and shift cables as described in *Throttle/Shift Cable Removal/Installation*. Place the control on a clean work surface.
4. Remove the screws, then the back cover plates (1, **Figure 15**). Remove the throttle-only lever and shaft (13 and 4, **Figure 15**). Remove the retaining bolt, then lift the throttle arm and shift arm from the control housing. Remove any accessible bushings, grommets and retainers at this point.
5. Secure the retainer (5, **Figure 15**), then lift the retainer and neutral only key switch from the control housing.
6. Note the position of the gear (7, **Figure 15**), then carefully lift it from the control housing. Remove any accessible bushings, grommets and retainers. Note the tilt/trim switch wire routing, then remove the control handle.
7. Remove the neutral position lever from the handle. Note the wire routing, then pull the tilt/trim switch from the handle.
8. Note all wire routing and connections points before removal. Disconnect the wires, then remove the key switch, lanyard switch, warning horn and fuel enrichment switch. Note the location and orientation of any remaining components, then remove them from the control housing.
9. Assembly is the reverse of disassembly. Apply Yamaha All-Purpose Grease or equivalent to all bushings, pivot points and sliding surfaces. Apply Loctite 271 to the threads of all bolts and screws on assembly. Tighten all fasteners to the specifications in **Table 1** or Chapter One.

514

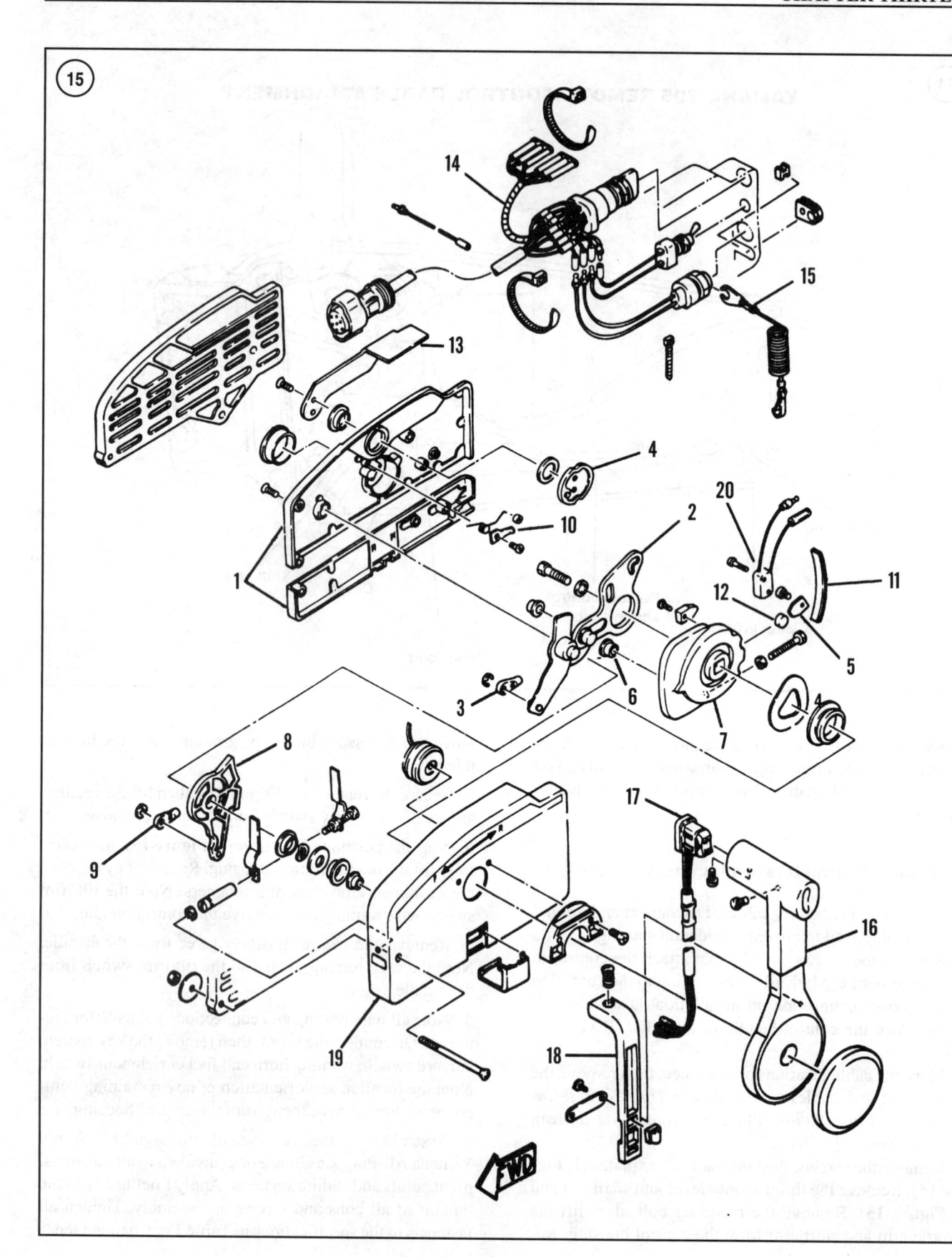

CHAPTER THIRTEEN

REMOTE CONTROL

YAMAHA 703 REMOTE CONTROL INTERNAL COMPONENTS

1. Back cover plates
2. Throttle arm/lever
3. Cable connector
4. Throttle only shaft/cam
5. Retainer
6. Bushing
7. Gear
8. Shift arm
9. Cable connector
10. Detent roller
11. Leaf spring
12. Throttle only roller
13. Throttle only lever
14. Start switch wires/connectors
15. Lanyard
16. Control handle
17. Tilt/trim switch*
18. Neutral position lever
19. Control housing
20. Neutral only start switch

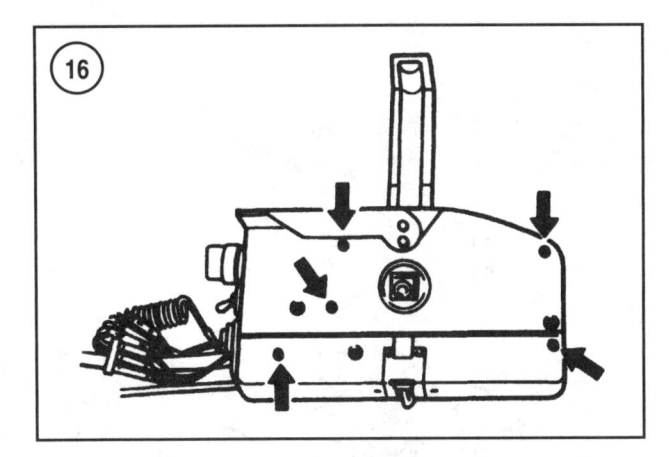

*Used only on tilt/trim models.

10. Install the throttle and shift cables as described in this chapter. Install both back covers (**Figure 16**). Re-attach all disconnected wires to the control. Connect the control cables to the battery. Adjust the cables at the engine as described in Chapter Four. Check for proper remote control operation before putting the engine into service.

705 Remote Control Disassembly and Assembly

For component identification and orientation, refer to **Figure 17**. Note the location and orientation of *all* components before removal.

1. Disconnect the battery cables. Disconnect and ground the spark plug lead to prevent accidental starting.
2. Remove the screws or bolts that attach the control to the boat structure. Place the control handle in the NEUTRAL position. Mark the cable location for reference, then remove the throttle and shift cables as described in *Throttle/Shift Cable Removal/Installation* in this chapter. Place the control on a clean work surface.
3. Mark all wires leading to the control to ensure proper connection on installation. Disconnect all wires.
4. Make a mark, note or drawing of the location and orientation of each component before removal.
5. Place the control handle in the NEUTRAL gear position. Remove the circlip (1, **Figure 18**) from the throttle lever pivot. Lift the cam plate (2, **Figure 18**) and dwell plate (3) from the control.
6. Slide the throttle lever toward the back of the control to access the two screws (1, **Figure 19**) that hold the drive plate (2) to the drive arm limiter (26, **Figure 17**). Remove the screws, then lift the drive plate, drive arm and the drive arm limiter from the control housing.
7. Count the number of turns while tightening the throttle friction to the fully seated position. Record the number of turns. Loosen the circlip (1, **Figure 20**). Note the orientation of the components, then lift the washer, throttle arm,

516

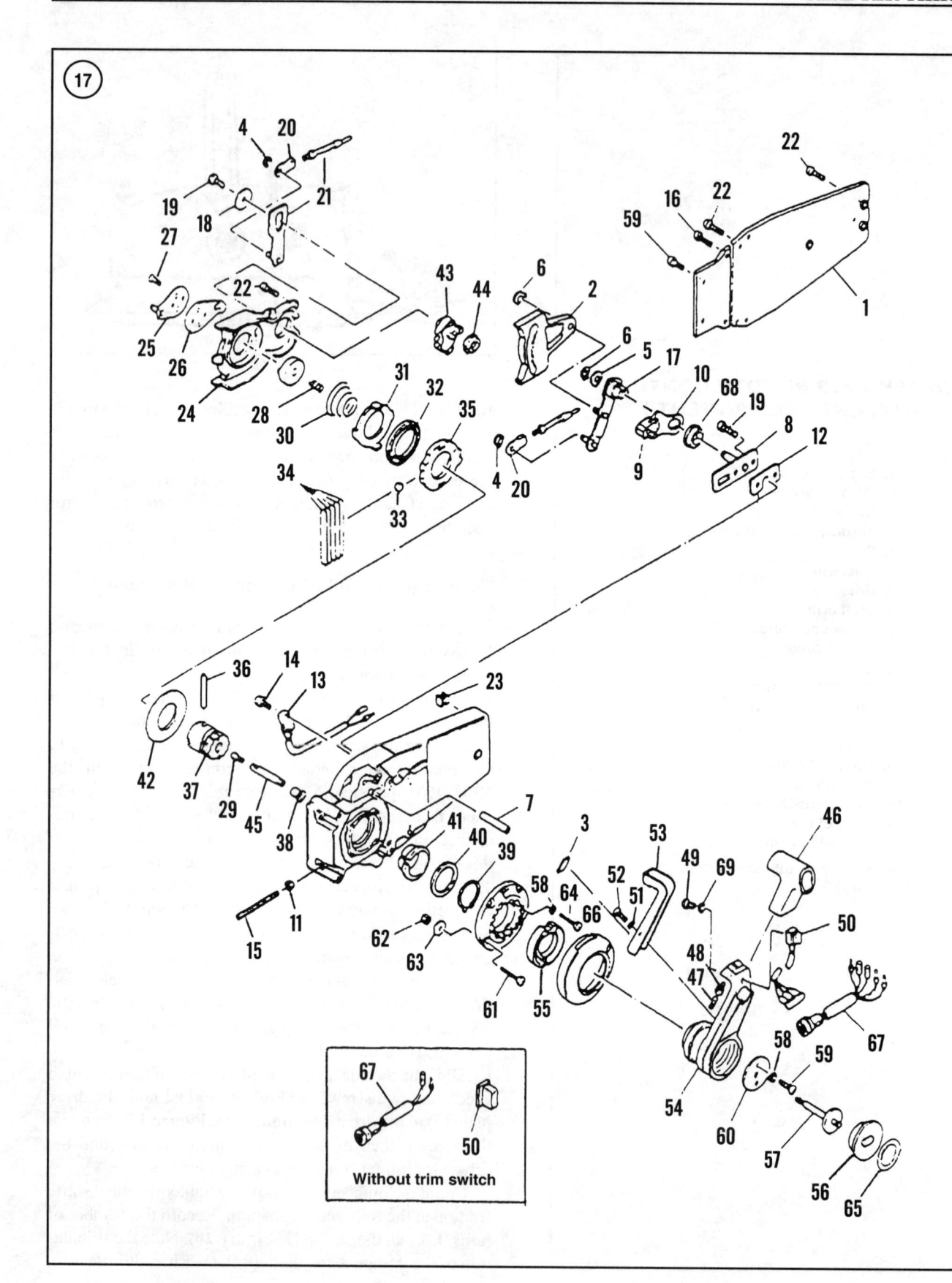

CHAPTER THIRTEEN

REMOTE CONTROL

YAMAHA 705 REMOTE CONTROL INTERNAL COMPONENTS

1. Back cover
2. Cam plate
3. Cap
4. Circlip
5. Washer
6. Circlip
7. Friction shaft
8. Throttle shaft
9. Throttle friction lever
10. Friction adjusting plate
11. Nut
12. Spacer
13. Neutral only key switch
14. Screw
15. Screw
16. Screw
17. Throttle lever
18. Washer
19. Bolt
20. Cable connector
21. Shift cable
22. Screw
23. Cable grommet
24. Gear cover
25. Drive arm
26. Drive arm limiter
27. Screw
28. Spring
29. Screw
30. Spring
31. Locking plate
32. Shifting plate
33. Throttle only roller
34. Spring
35. Gear
36. Pin
37. Shaft
38. Bushing
39. Circlip
40. Washer
41. Bushing
42. Washer
43. Gear
44. Bushing
45. Shaft
46. Handle grip
47. Spring
48. Screw
49. Screw
50. Tilt/trim switch*
51. Washer
52. Screw
53. Neutral lock lever
54. Control handle
55. Neutral lock plate
56. Cover
57. Throttle only shaft
58. Washer
59. Screw
60. Washer
61. Screw
62. Nut
63. Washer
64. Screw
65. Decal
66. Decal cover
67. Wire*
68. Bushing
69. Washer

*Used only on tilt/trim models.

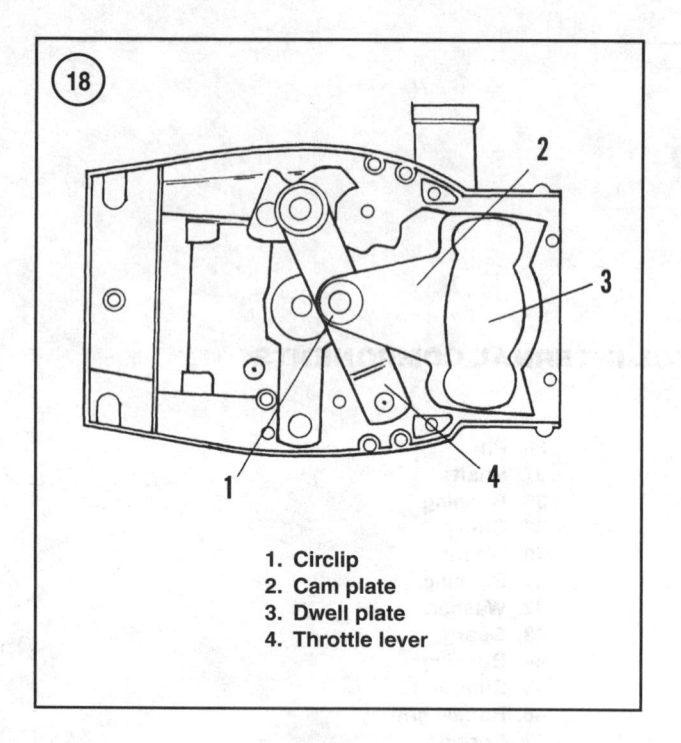

518

CHAPTER THIRTEEN

⑱

1. Circlip
2. Cam plate
3. Dwell plate
4. Throttle lever

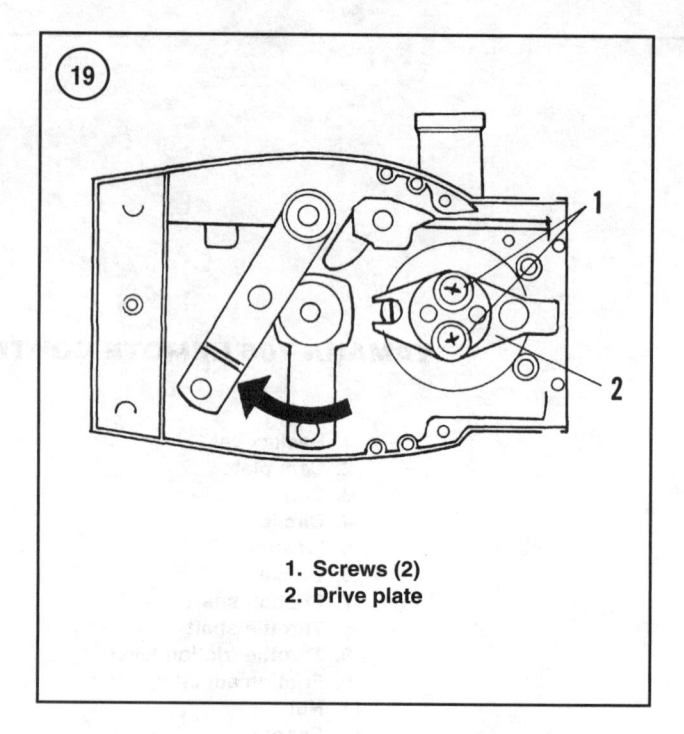

⑲

1. Screws (2)
2. Drive plate

⑳

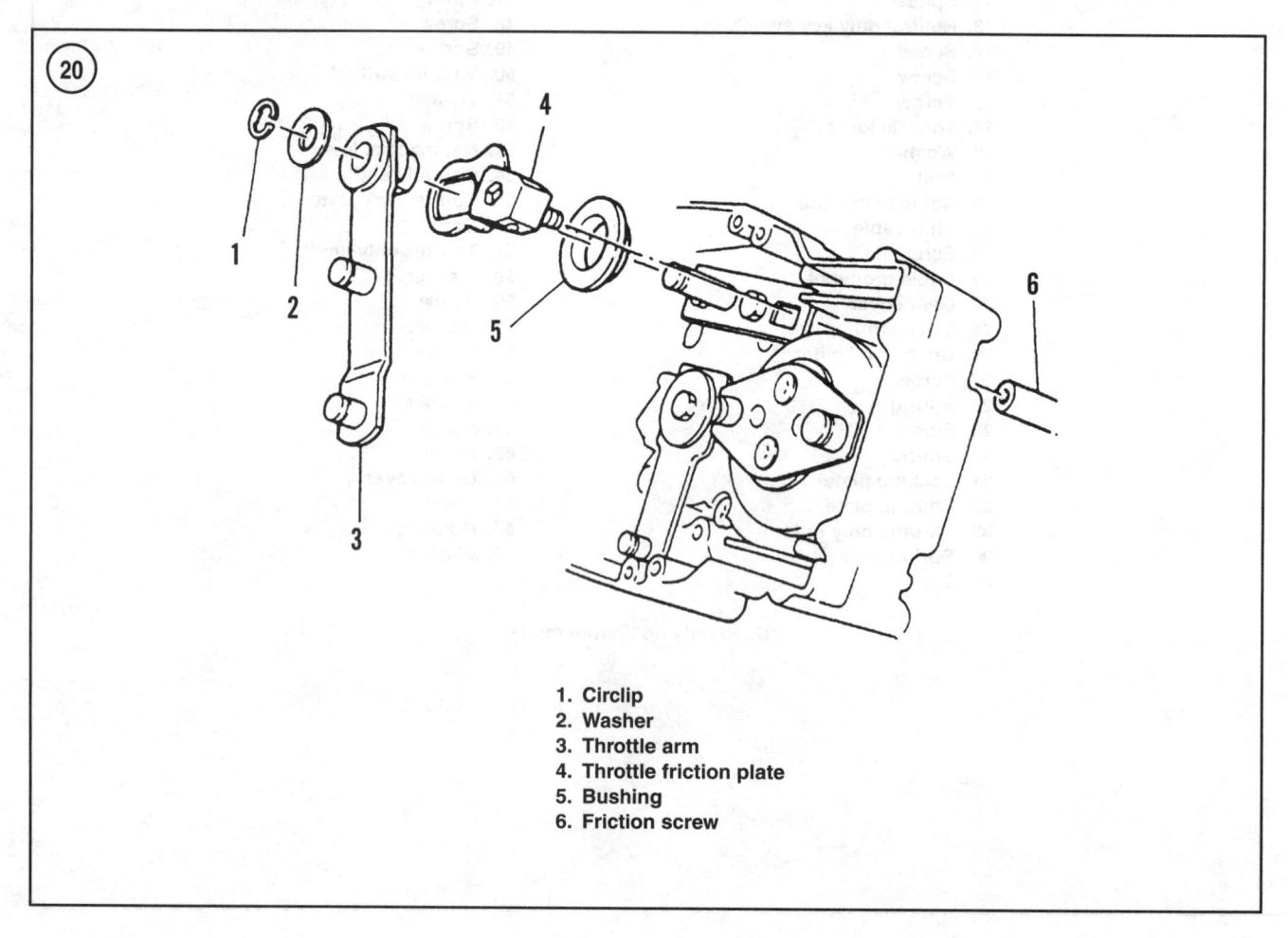

1. Circlip
2. Washer
3. Throttle arm
4. Throttle friction plate
5. Bushing
6. Friction screw

REMOTE CONTROL

21

Throttle shaft

22

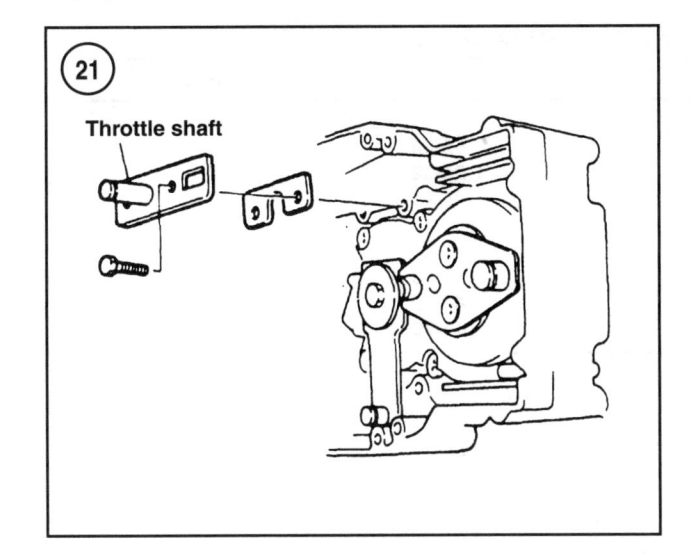

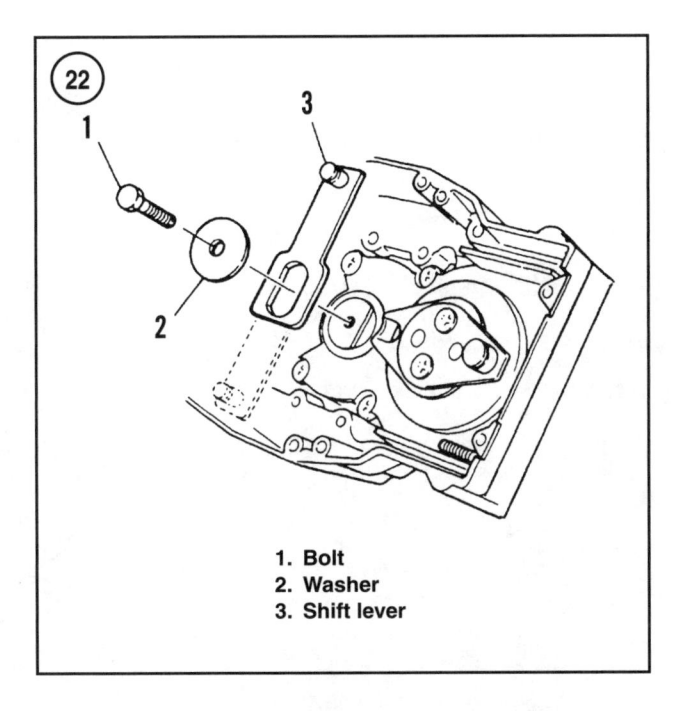

1. Bolt
2. Washer
3. Shift lever

throttle friction and bushing (2-5, **Figure 20**) from the control housing. Remove the friction screw (6, **Figure 20**) from the control housing.

8. Remove the two hex bolts, then lift the throttle shaft (**Figure 21**) from the control housing. Note the position of the shift lever (3, **Figure 22**). It must be installed in the same position as removed. Remove the bolt (1, **Figure 22**) and washer (2), then lift the throttle lever from the control housing.

9. Remove the screws (22, **Figure 17**), then carefully lift the gear cover (24) from the control housing. Loosen the locking nut (11, **Figure 17**) without turning the stopper screw (15). Count the turns while turning the stopper screw clockwise to the fully seated position. Record the number of turns then remove the screw and locking nut.

10. Carefully pry the throttle-only cover (56, **Figure 17**) from the throttle-only shaft (57). Use pliers to pull the throttle-only shaft from the control housing. The shaft may break during the removal procedure. Remove the two screws (59, **Figure 17**) from the washer (60). Note the routing of the tilt/trim switch wires, then pull the control handle and trim switch wires from the control. Disconnect the tilt/trim switch wires from the instrument harness. Remove the decal cover (66, **Figure 17**) and neutral lock plate (55).

11. Mark all components before removal. Remove the screws (61, **Figure 17**), and the cover/mount. Remove the circlip (39, **Figure 17**) from the drive shaft (37). Note the orientation of the lock plate, shift plate and gear (31, 32 and 35, **Figure 17**) then slide them from the drive shaft. Note the location and orientation of all remaining control components, then remove them.

12. Remove the neutral-only key switch (13, **Figure 17**), trim switch and wires (50 and 67) along with the key switch, fuel enrichment switch and warning horn. Refer to Chapter Two and test these components before assembly.

13. Assembly is the reverse of disassembly. Apply Yamaha All-Purpose Grease or equivalent to all pivot points and sliding surfaces. Install the throttle friction screw and stopper screw until they are seated, then back them out the recorded number of turns. Tighten the jam nut securely. Apply Loctite 271 to the threads of all fasteners, except the throttle friction and stopper screw. Tighten all fasteners to the specification in **Table 1** or Chapter One.

14. Install the throttle and shift cables as described in this chapter. Install the remote control to the boat and securely tighten the mounting screws.

15. Adjust the control cables at the engine as described in Chapter Four. Check for proper remote control operation and correct as necessary.

Table 1 is on the following page.

Table 1 REMOTE CONTROL TORQUE SPECIFICATIONS

Fastener	N•m	in.-lb.	ft.-lb.
Control handle screw			
703 control	6-6.5	52-56	–
705 control	3-4.5	26-39	–
Cover screws (705 control)	5-8	44-70	–
Drive plate screws (705 control)	5-8	44-70	–
Neutral lock holder (703 control)	1.2-1.5	11-13	–
Neutral throttle lever screws (703 control)	1.5-1.8	13-16	–
Throttle lever (705 control)	5-8	44-70	–
Throttle stopper locknut (705 control)	5-8	44-70	–

Index

A

Adhesives, sealants and lubricants
   power head 277-278
Adjustment
   and timing and synchronization,
      carburetor. 138-174
   general information 136
   jet drive thrust gate 178
   lockout assembly. 176-177
   maximum, full advance
      ignition timing 183-184
   oil pump linkage 174-176
   pilot screw specifications 184
   required equipment 137-138
   safety precautions 135-136
   shift
      cable. 180-182
      linkage 178-180
   specifications
      idle speed. 184
      idle/full retard timing 183
      pickup timing. 183
      pilot screw 184
   test propellers 182
   tilt/trim sender. 177-178
   wide open throttle speed 183
      verification. 137

Anodes sacrificial 422-423

B

Backlash specifications 427-428
Battery. 236-243
   charge coil test, specifications
      troubleshooting 104-105
   capacity 274
   charge percentage. 273
   requirements. 274
Bleeding air from
   the oil injection system 506
Break-in, power head 276

C

Cable removal/installation
   throttle/shift. 509-512
Carburetor 208-227
   choke solenoid 227
   electrothermal valve 226-227
   Prime-Start pump 227
   timing and synchronization
      adjustment 138-174
CDI unit output
   specifications, troubleshooting. . . . 108

Charging system
   capacity, troubleshooting 104
   components. 257-261
   troubleshooting. 57-63
Check valves and hoses 499-502
Choke solenoid 227
Components
   cleaning and inspection
      power head 306-319
Cooling system
   troubleshooting. 97-99
Corrosion, galvanic 10-12
Crankshaft specifications 339
   position sensor output
      troubleshooting 108
Cylinder bore specifications 337

D

Driven gear 506

E

Electric trim motor
   removal/installation 471-475
   repair. 475-481

15

Electrical system
  and ignition torque
    specifications................ 273
  battery................... 236-243
    capacity..................... 274
    charge percentage............ 273
    requirements................ 274
  fundamentals................ 28-30
  starting system
    components............. 243-248
    starter motor........... 248-257
    specifications................ 274
  warning system components ... 271-273
  wiring diagrams........... 525-549
Electrothermal valve......... 226-227
Engine
  break-in.................. 130-131
  identification codes.......... 36-37
  maximum operating speed
    troubleshooting.............. 108
  operation...................... 5

F

Fasteners.................... 5-8
  and torque................... 278
Filter, fuel.................. 203-204
Float height specifications....... 235
Flywheel removal/installation ... 285-286
Fuel and oil mixing rates.......... 133
Fuel system
  carburetor............... 208-227
    choke solenoid.............. 227
    electrothermal valve....... 226-227
    Prime-Start pump............. 227
  components service......... 185-208
    filter................... 203-204
    hoses.................... 191-192
      connectors............. 192-194
    primer bulb.............. 190-191
    pumps................... 194-203
    silencer cover
      removal/installation...... 204-208
    tank
      integral................ 187-189
      portable remote......... 185-186
      vessel mounted.......... 186-187
    valves....................... 194
  recirculation system............ 233
  reed housing/intake manifold... 228-233
  safety....................... 185
  specifications
    float height................. 235
    reed valve................... 234
    torque....................... 234
  troubleshooting......... 43, 102-103

Fuse and wire harness
  troubleshooting............. 63-64

G

Galvanic corrosion............. 10-12
Gearcase
  backlash specifications...... 427-428
  component inspection....... 423-426
  disassembly/assembly....... 362-422
  operation................ 340-342
  pressure test.................. 426
  propeller................ 342-346
  removal/installation....... 346-354
  sacrificial anodes.......... 422-423
  torque specifications........... 427
  troubleshooting........... 99-100
  water pump.............. 354-362
General information
  basic mechanical skills........ 30-36
  conversion formulas.......... 38-39
  electrical system fundamentals ... 28-30
  engine
    identification codes......... 36-37
    operation...................... 5
  fasteners..................... 5-8
  galvanic corrosion............ 10-12
  manual organization............. 1
  metric tap and drill sizes......... 38
  propellers................. 12-17
  safety....................... 2-3
  serial number and
    model identification.......... 3-5
  shop supplies................ 8-10
  technical abbreviations.......... 37
  tools
    basic.................... 17-20
    precision measuring......... 20-28
    special...................... 20
  torque specifications............ 39
  warnings, cautions and notes....... 2

H

Hoses
  and check valves.......... 499-502
  fuel..................... 191-192
    connectors............. 192-194
Hydraulic system
  filling and bleeding........ 482-483

I

Idle speed specifications......... 184
Idle/full retard timing
  specifications................ 183

Ignition system
  and electrical
    torque specifications.......... 273
  charging system
    components............. 257-261
  components.............. 261-271
  coil resistance specifications
    troubleshooting......... 106-107
  timing................... 136-137
    maximum, full advance 183-184
  troubleshooting...... 72-88, 103-104
  charge coil specifications
    output..................... 107
    resistance.................. 106
Inspection
  gearcase components....... 423-426
  preliminary, troubleshooting....... 41
Intake manifold/reed housing.... 228-233
Integral fuel tank............ 187-189

J

Jet drive
  operation................ 429-431
  repair................... 431-441
  thrust gate adjustment........... 178
  torque specifications........... 441

L

Lockout assembly adjustment... 176-177
Lubrication................ 109-118
  engine break-in............ 130-131
  fluid capacities................ 133
  lubricants, sealants and adhesives
    power head.............. 277-278
  oil and fuel mixing rates......... 133
  torque specifications........... 131

M

Maintenance............... 118-127
  engine break-in............ 130-131
  schedule................. 132-133
  torque specifications........... 131
Manual release valve
  removal and installation..... 481-482
Manual starter.............. 442-462
  repair................... 444-462
  rope length................... 462
  torque specifications........... 462
Manual tilt system
  removal and installation..... 463-465
Midsection................. 483-493
  and tilt/trim
    torque specifications....... 494-495

INDEX

Motor specifications, tilt/trim 495

N

Neutral throttle operation 508

O

Oil and fuel mixing rates 133
Oil injection system
  bleeding air from the system 506
  driven gear 506
  hoses and check valves 499-502
  level sensor
    removal/installation 497-498
  pump 502-506
    identification 507
    linkage adjustment 174-176
    output, specifications
      troubleshooting 106
  reservoir
    capacity 507
    removal/installation 498-499
  system operation 496
  torque specifications 507
  troubleshooting 70-72

P

Pickup timing specifications 183
Pilot screw
  adjustment specifications 184
Piston, specifications 337-338
  ring 338-339
Portable remote fuel tank 185-186
Power head
  assembly 319-335
  break-in 276
  components
    cleaning and inspection 306-319
    disassembly 286-305
    fasteners and torque 278
  flywheel
    removal/installation 285-286
  lubricants, sealants
    and adhesives 277-278
  removal/installation 278-285
  service
    considerations 275-276
    recommendations 276-277
  specifications
    crankshaft 339
    cylinder bore 337
    piston 337-338
      ring 338-339
    torque 335-337
  troubleshooting 95-97

Power tilt/trim system
  removal/installation 465-470
Pressure test, gearcase 426
Primer bulb 190-191
Prime-Start pump 227
Propellers 12-17, 342-346
  test 182
Pulser coil
  specifications, troubleshooting
    output 107
    resistance 106
Pumps
  fuel 194-203
  oil 502-506
  identification 507

R

Recirculation system 233
Reed
  housing/intake manifold 228-233
  valve specifications 234
Relay replacement, tilt/trim 470
Remote control 512-519
  neutral throttle operation 508
  throttle/shift cable
    removal/installation 509-512
  torque specifications 520
Reservoir capacity, oil 507
Rope length, manual starter 462

S

Sacrificial anodes 422-423
Sealants, lubricants and adhesives
  power head 277-278
Sender, tilt/trim
  adjustment 177-178
  replacement 470-471
Sensor removal/installation
  oil level 497-498
Shift adjustment
  cable 180-182
  linkage 178-180
Silencer cover
  removal/installation 204-208
Spark plug specifications 134
Specifications
  backlash 427-428
  crankshaft 339
  cylinder bore 337
  float height 235
  idle speed specifications 184
  idle/full retard timing 183
  pickup timing 183
  pilot screw adjustment 184
  piston 337-338

ring 338-339
reed valve 234
spark plug 134
tilt/trim motor 495
torque 131
  fuel system 234
  gearcase 427
  general 39
  ignition and electrical systems ... 273
  jet drive 441
  manual starter 462
  oil injection system 507
  power head 335-337
  remote control 520
  tilt/trim and midsection 494-495
troubleshooting
  battery charge coil test 104-105
  CDI unit output 108
  crankshaft position
    sensor output 108
  ignition, charge coil
    output 107
    resistance 106-107
  oil pump output 106
  pulser coil
    output 107
    resistance 106
  thermoswitch test 105
Starting system
  components 243-248
  motor 248-257
  specifications 274
  troubleshooting 51-57, 101-102
  starting difficulty 41-43
Supplies, shop 8-10
Synchronization
  adjustment
    jet drive thrust gate 178
    lockout assembly 176-177
    oil pump linkage 174-176
    shift
      cable 180-182
      linkage 178-180
    tilt/trim sender 177-178
    timing and carburetor 138-174
  general information 136
  maximum (full advance)
    ignition timing 183-184
  required equipment 137-138
  safety precautions 135-136
  specifications
    idle speed 184
    idle/full retard timing 183
    pickup timing 183
    pilot screw adjustment 184
    test propellers 182
    wide open throttle speed 183
    verification 137

T

Tank, fuel
- integral 187-189
- portable remote 185-186
- vessel mounted 186-187

Test propellers................. 182

Thermoswitch test
- specifications
  - troubleshooting 105

Throttle
- operation, neutral 508
- shift cable
  - removal/installation 509-512
- speed, wide open............... 183
- verification................... 137

Tilt and trim system
- electric motor
  - removal/installation 471-475
  - motor repair 475-481
- hydraulic system
  - filling and bleeding........ 482-483
- manual release valve
  - removal and installation 481-482
- manual system
  - removal and installation 463-465
- power system
  - removal/installation 465-470
- relay replacement 470
- sender replacement 470-471
- specifications
  - and midsection torque...... 494-495
  - motor 495
- troubleshooting............. 88-94

Timing
- adjustment
  - jet drive thrust gate............ 178
  - lockout assembly 176-177
  - oil pump linkage.......... 174-176
  - shift
    - cable.................. 180-182
- linkage................. 178-180
- synchronization
  - and carburetor 138-174
  - tilt/trim sender 177-178
- general information 136
- ignition 136-137
  - maximum, full advance 183-184
- required equipment 137-138
- safety precautions 135-136
- specifications
  - idle speed.................. 184
  - idle/full retard timing.......... 183
  - pickup timing................ 183
  - pilot screw adjustment 184
- synchronization and adjustments ... 135
  - carburetor 138-174
- test propellers................ 182
- wide open throttle speed........ 183
- verification................... 137

Tools
- basic 17-20
- precision measuring 20-28
- special..................... 20

Torque specifications 131
- gearcase 427
- ignition and electrical systems 273
- jet drive 441
- manual starter................. 462
- oil injection system............. 507
- power head 335-337
- remote control 520
- tilt/trim and midsection 494-495

Troubleshooting
- charging system.............. 57-63
  - capacity 104
- cooling system 97-99
- engine
  - maximum operating speed...... 108
- fuel system............. 43, 102-103
- fuse and wire harness........ 63-64
- gearcase................. 99-100
- ignition system....... 72-88, 103-104
- oil injection system 70-72
- operating requirements.......... 41
- power head 95-97
- preliminary inspection 41
- specifications
  - battery charge coil test 104-105
  - CDI unit output 108
  - crankshaft position
    - sensor output 108
  - ignition charge coil
    - output 107
    - resistance 106-107
  - ignition coil resistance 106-107
  - oil pump output 106
  - pulser coil
    - output 107
    - resistance................ 106
  - thermoswitch test............ 105
- starting
  - system 51-57, 101-102
  - difficulty................. 41-43
- tilt and trim system 88-94
- warning system 64-70

Tune-up 127-130
- spark plug specifications 134

V

Valves, fuel 194
Vessel mounted fuel tank 186-187

W

Warning system
- components............... 271-273
- troubleshooting............. 64-70

Water pump 354-362

Wide open throttle speed, ... 183
- verification................... 137

Wire harness and fuse
- troubleshooting.............. 63-64

Wiring diagrams 525-549

WIRING DIAGRAMS

2 HP MODEL (1999-ON)

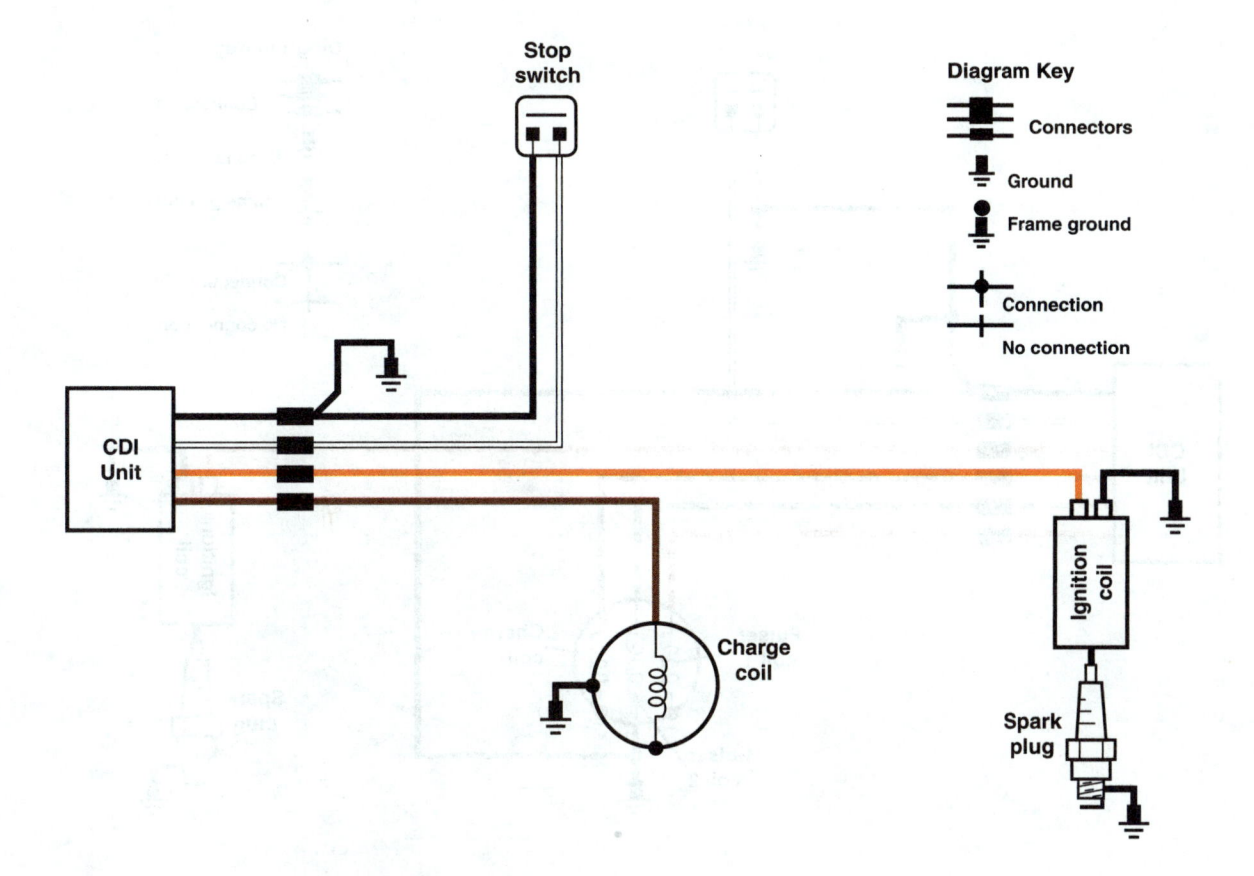

3 HP MODEL (1999-ON)

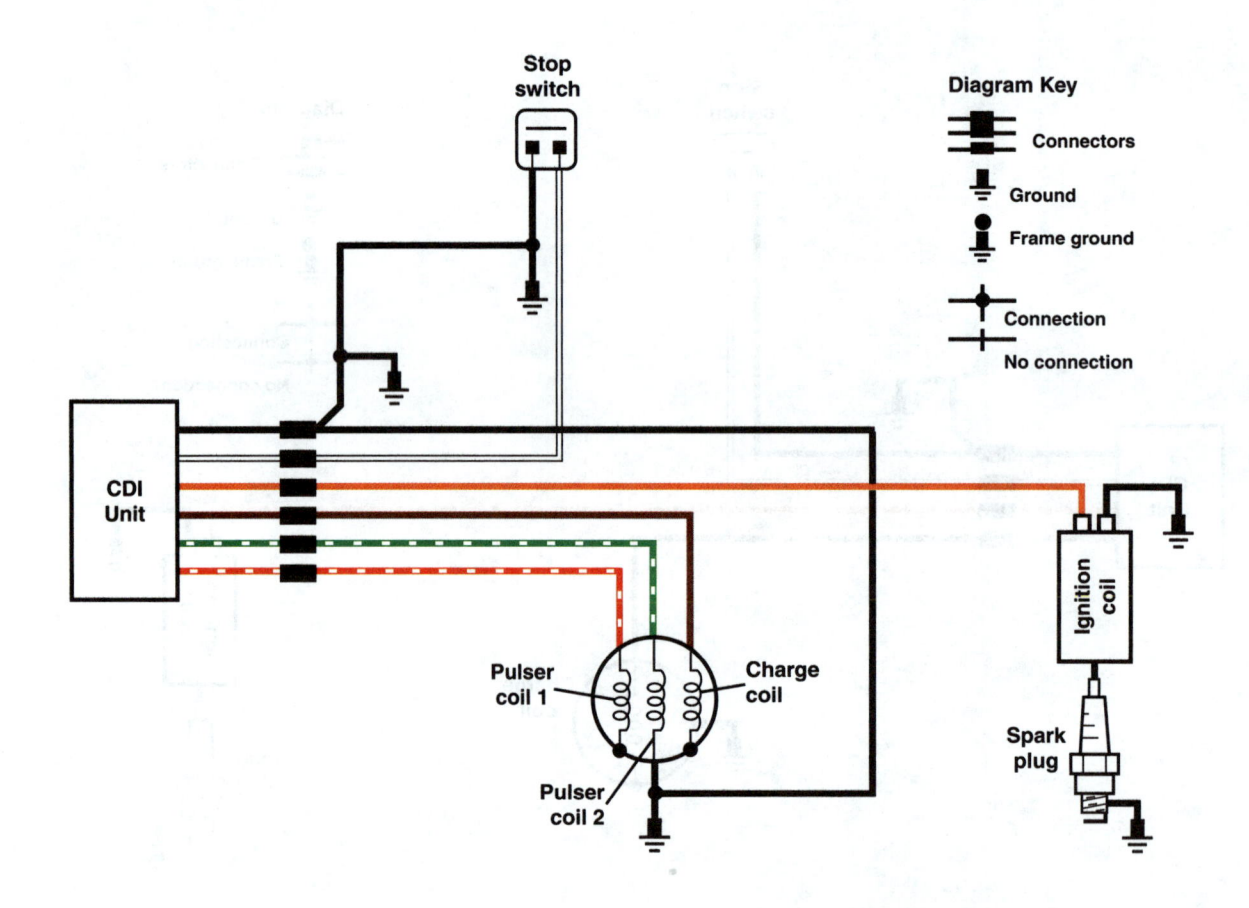

WIRING DIAGRAMS

4 AND 5 HP MODELS (1999-ON)

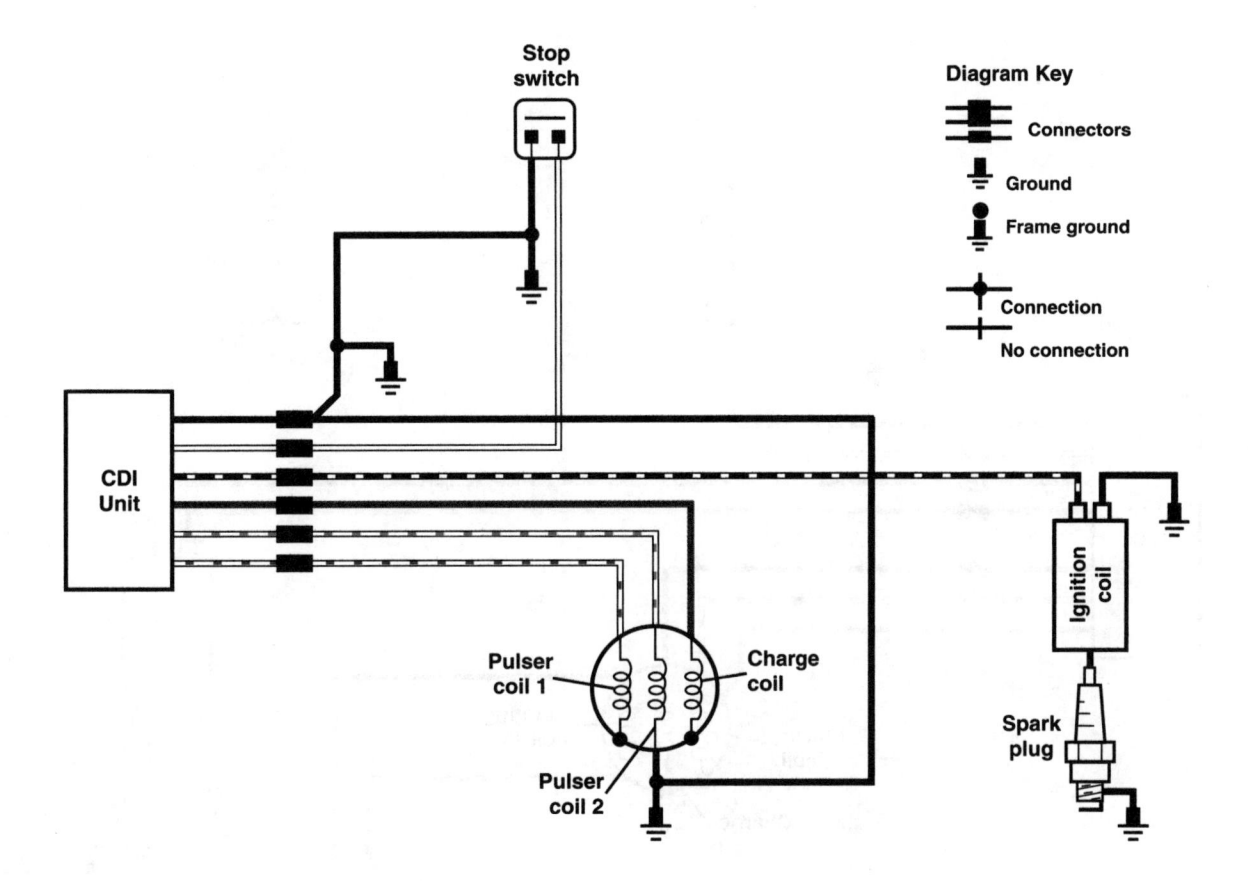

6 AND 8 HP MODELS
(MANUAL START WITH TILLER CONTROL [1999-ON])

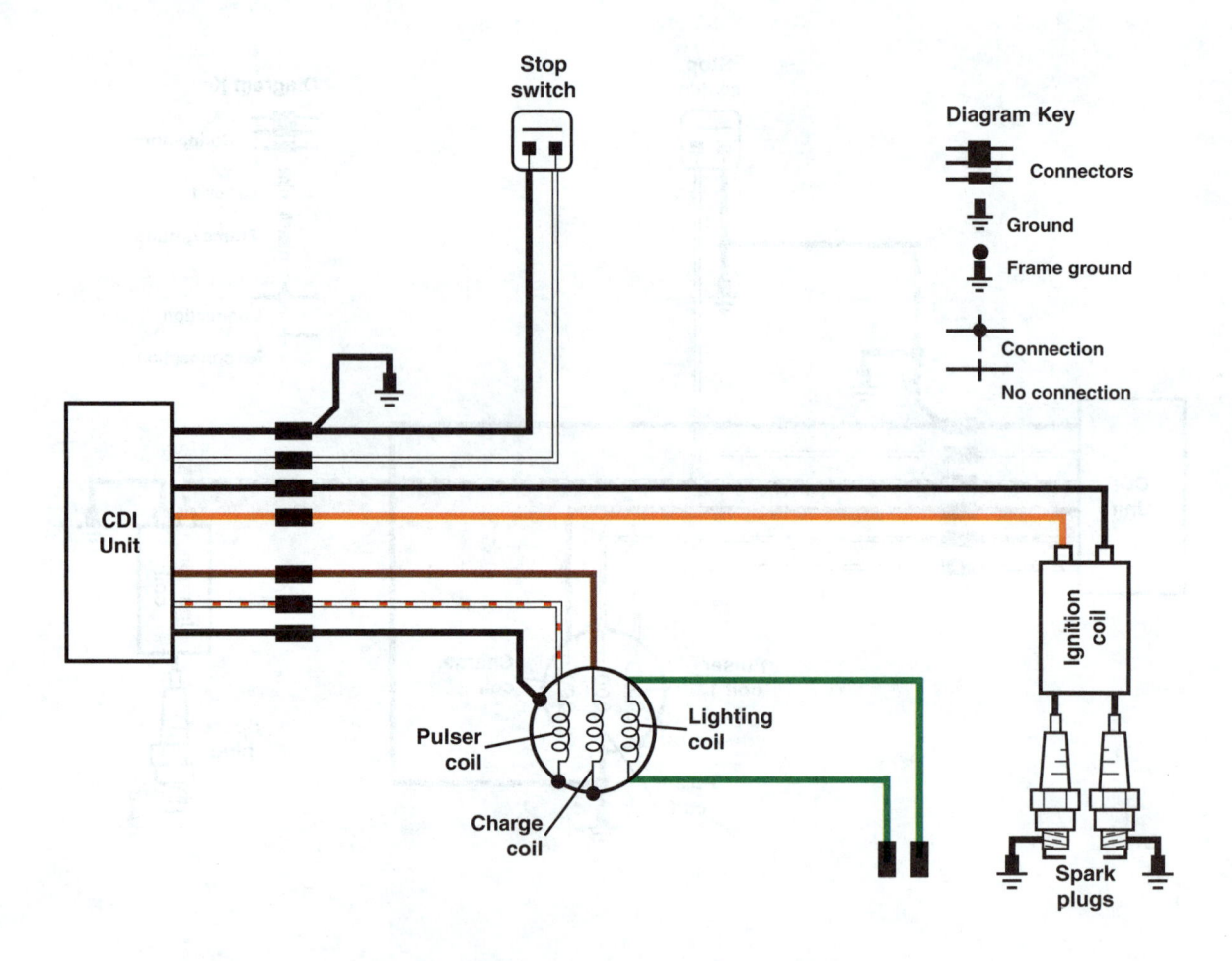

WIRING DIAGRAMS

6 AND 8 HP MODELS
(ELECTRIC START WITH TILLER CONTROL [1999-ON])

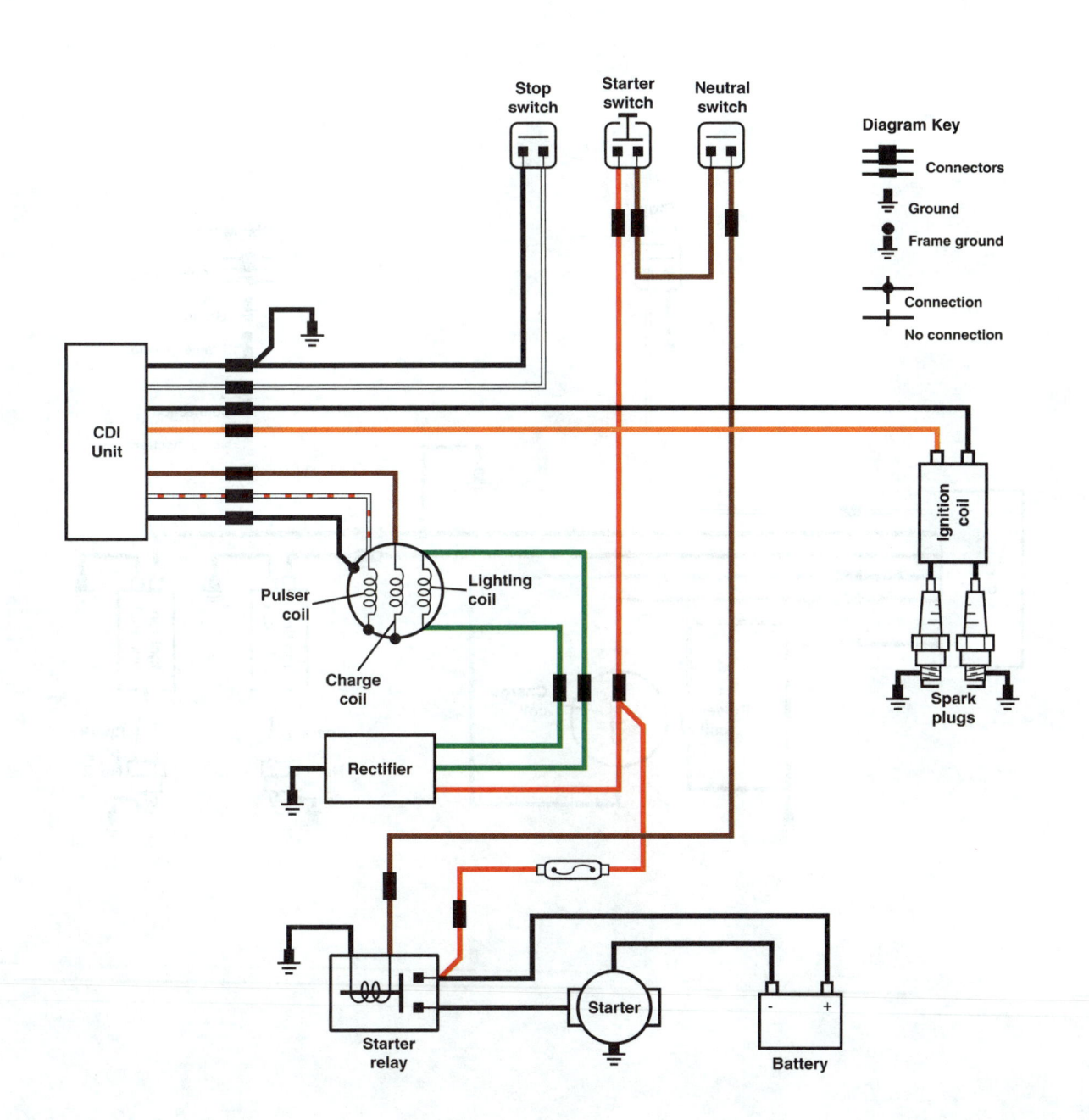

9.9 AND 15 HP MODELS
(MANUAL START WITH TILLER CONTROL [1999-ON])

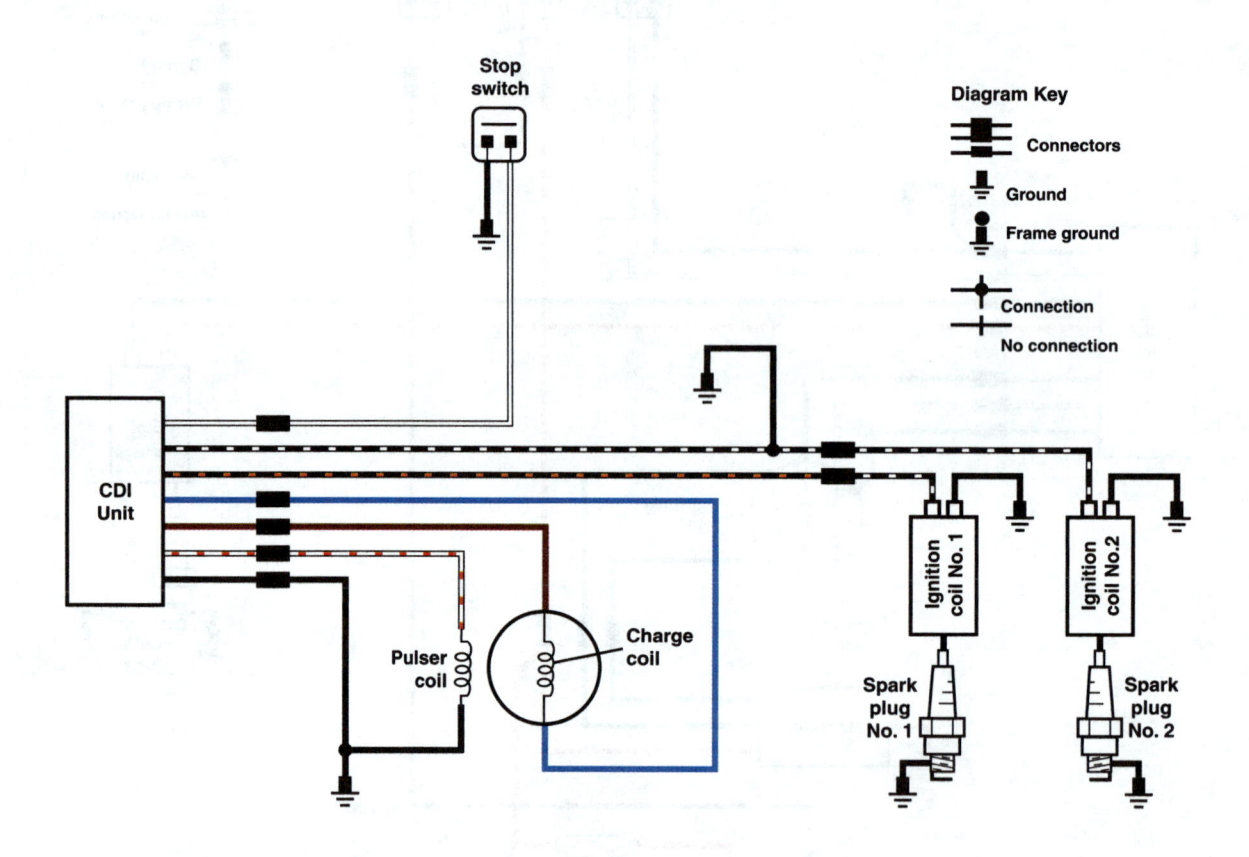

WIRING DIAGRAMS

531

9.9 AND 15 HP MODELS
(ELECTRIC START WITH TILLER CONTROL [1999-ON])

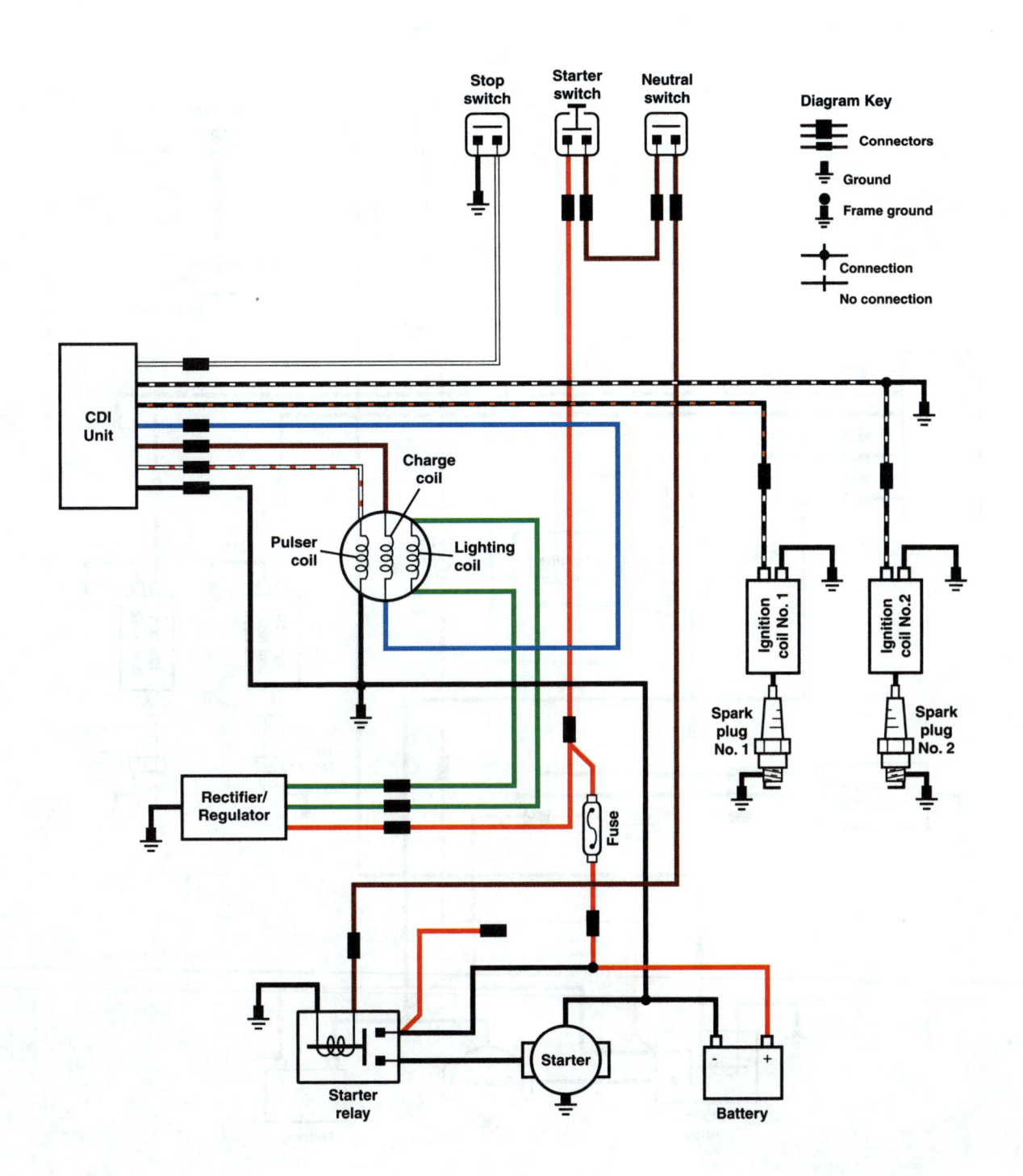

15

WIRING DIAGRAMS

9.9 AND 15 HP MODELS
(ELECTRIC START WITH REMOTE CONTROL [1999-ON])

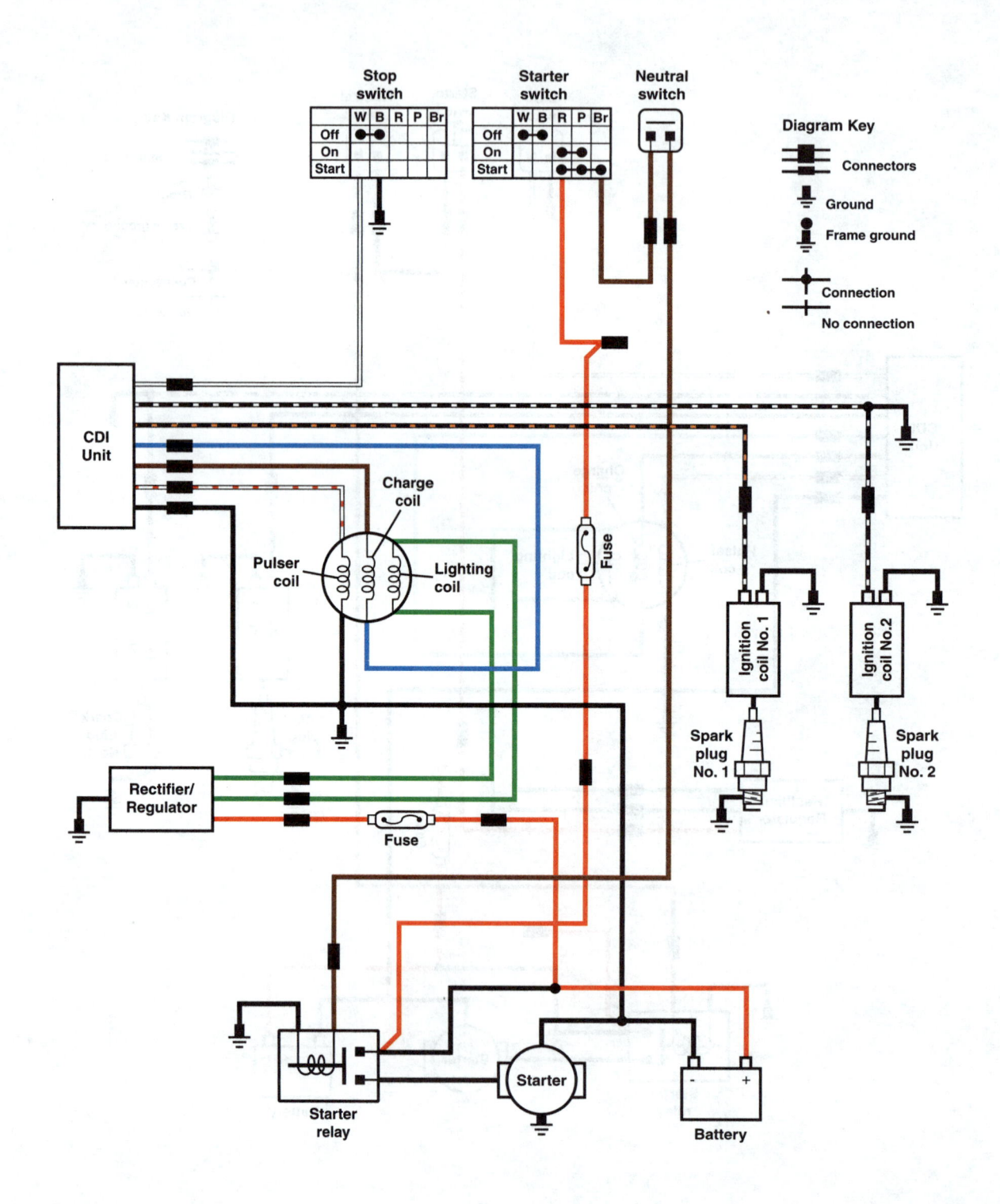

WIRING DIAGRAMS

20 AND 25 HP TWO-CYLINDER MODELS
(MANUAL START WITH TILLER CONTROL [1999-ON])

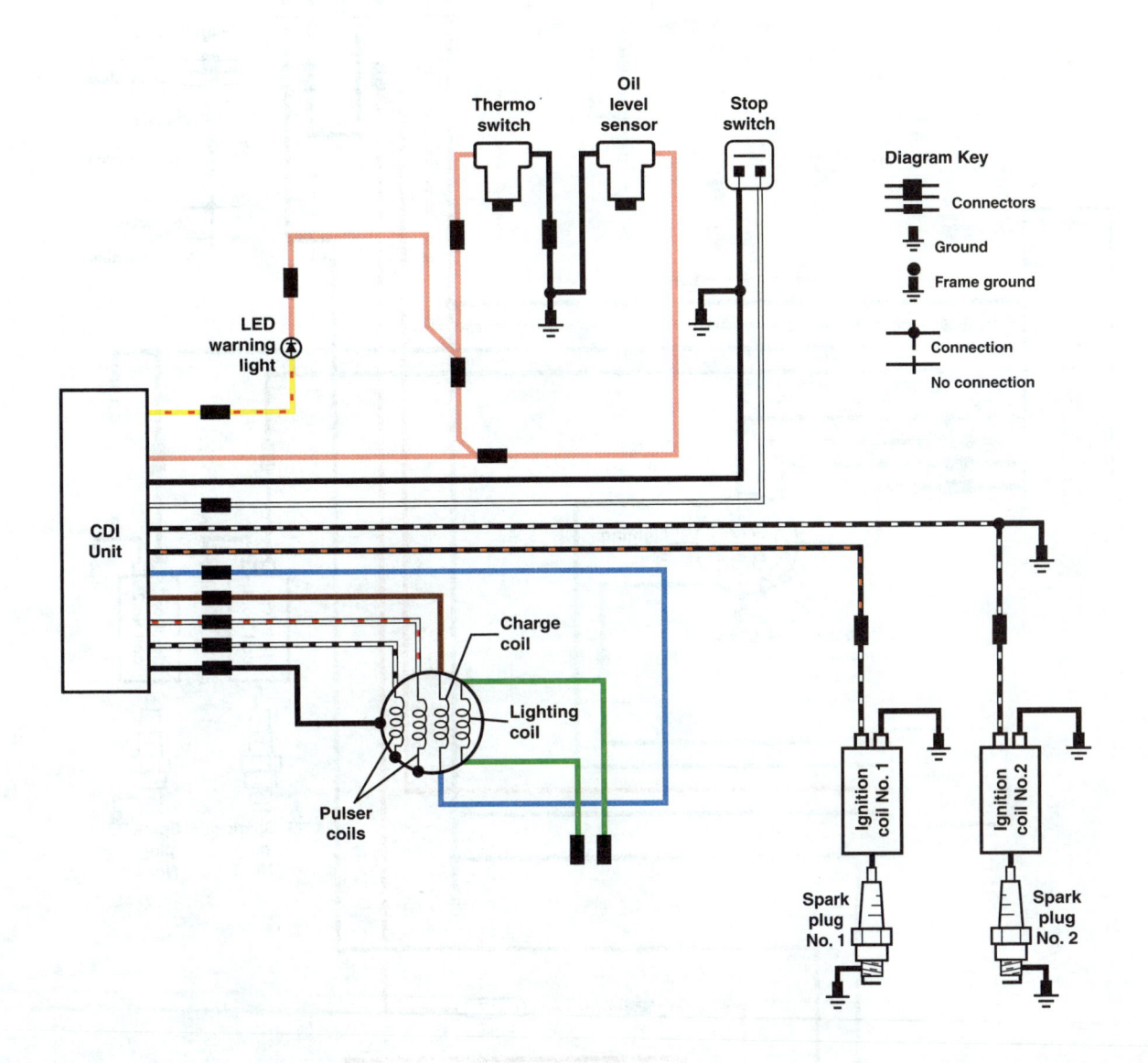

WIRING DIAGRAMS

20 AND 25 HP TWO-CYLINDER MODELS
(ELECTRIC START WITH TILLER CONTROL [1999-ON])

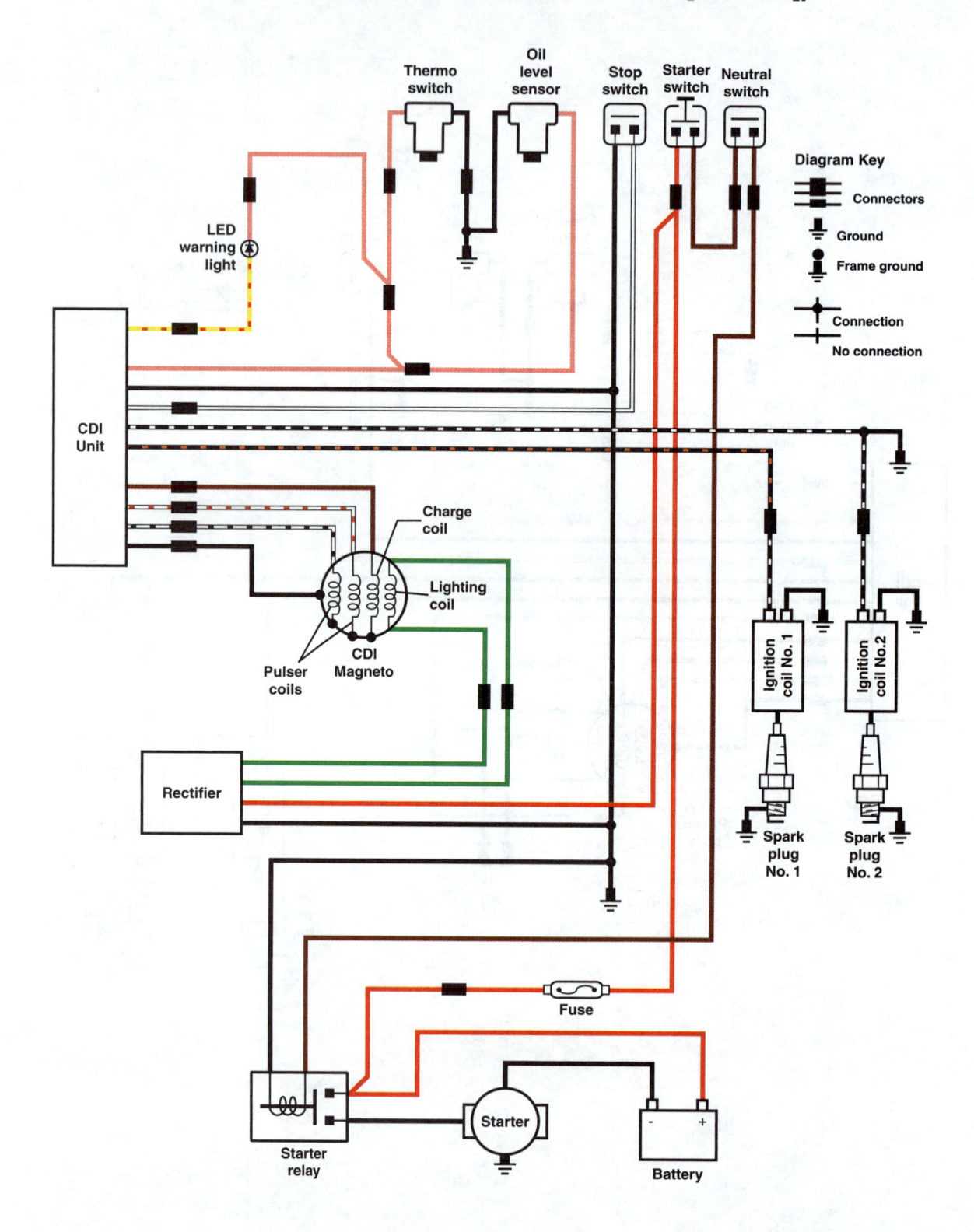

WIRING DIAGRAMS

20 AND 25 HP TWO-CYLINDER MODELS
(ELECTRIC START WITH REMOTE CONTROL [1999-ON])

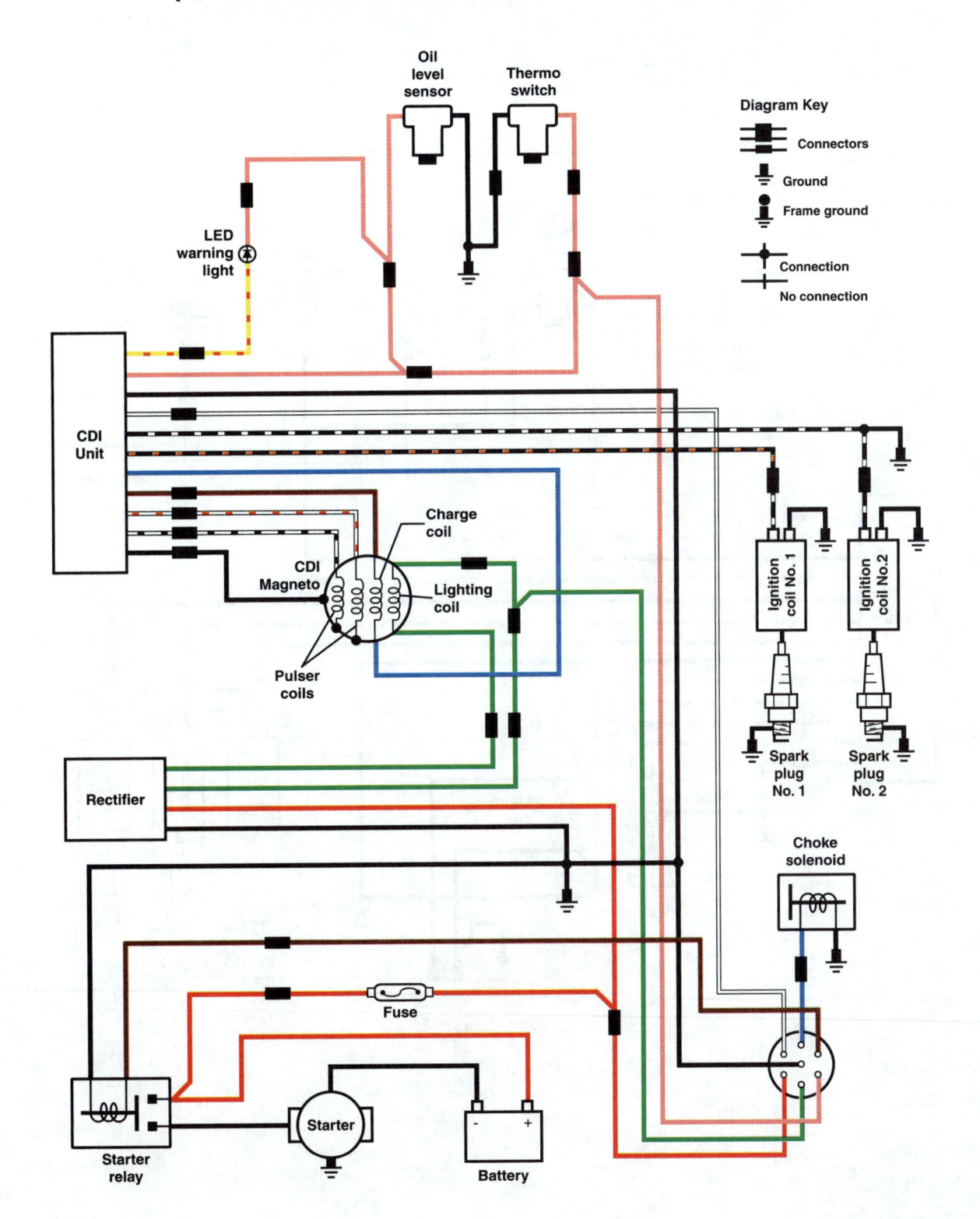

25 AND 30 HP THREE-CYLINDER MODELS
(MANUAL START WITH TILLER CONTROL [1999-ON])

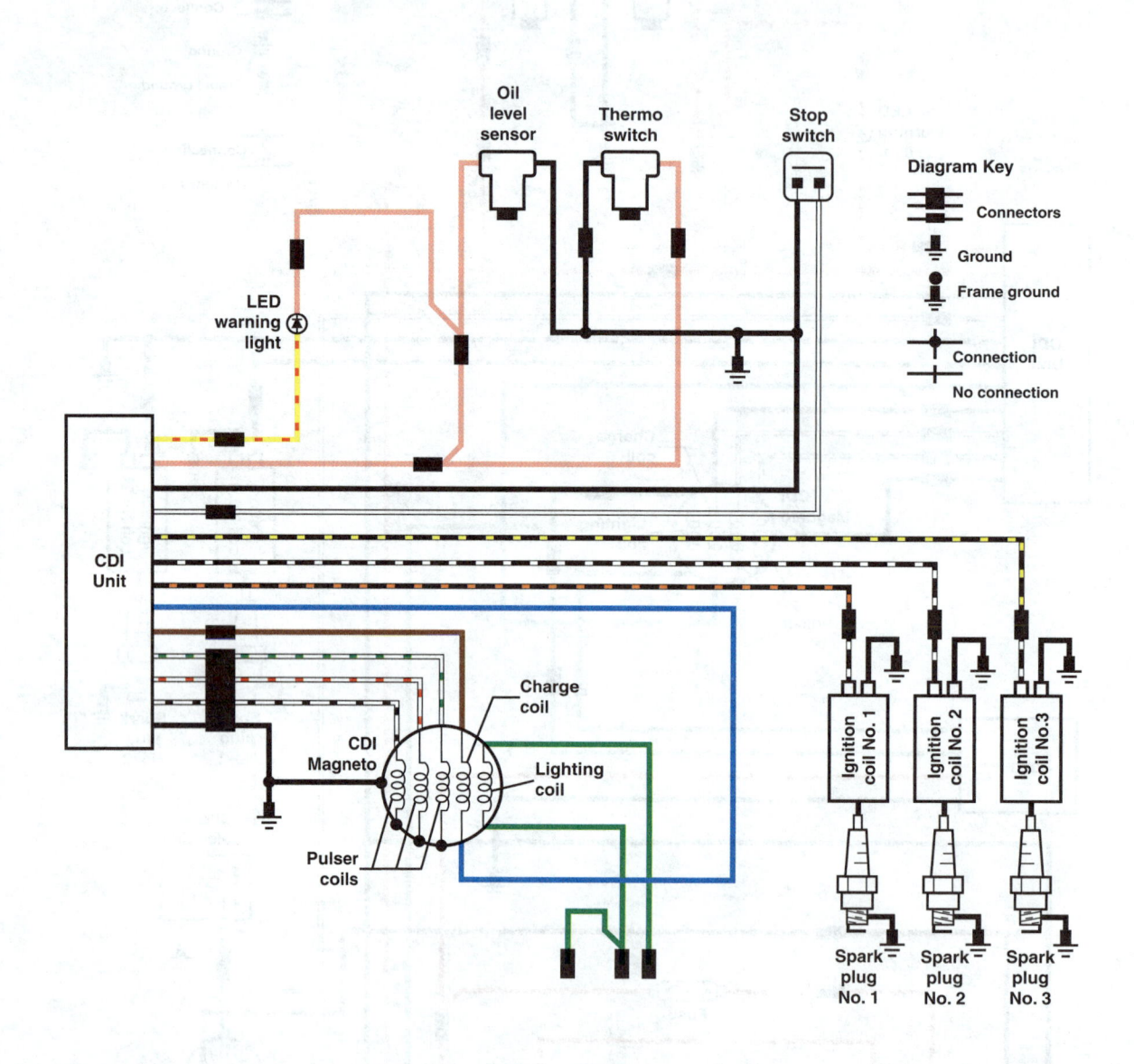

WIRING DIAGRAMS

25 AND 30 HP THREE-CYLINDER MODELS
(ELECTRIC START WITH TILLER CONTROL [1999-ON])

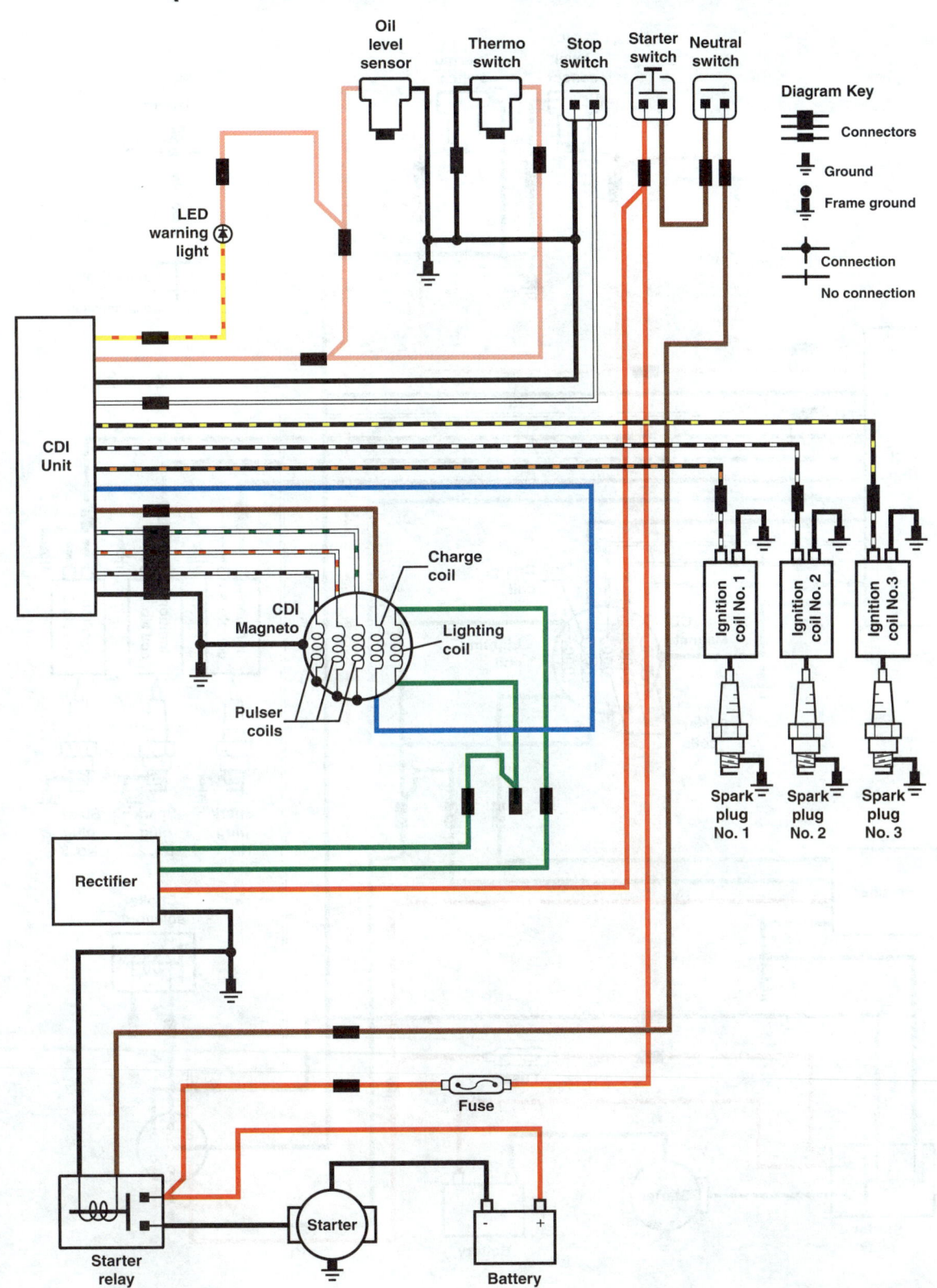

25 AND 30 HP THREE-CYLINDER MODELS
(ELECTRIC START WITH REMOTE CONTROL [1999-ON])

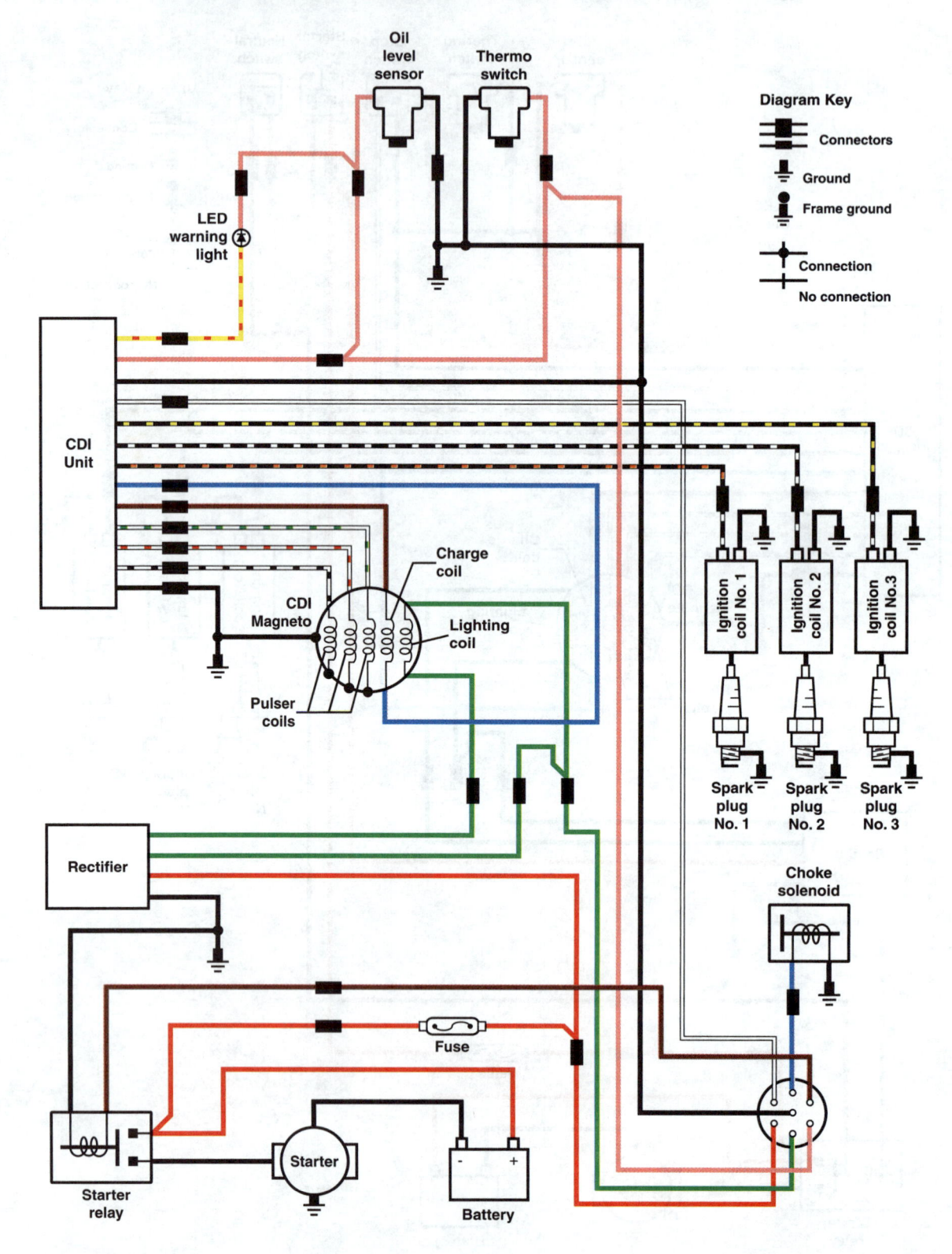

WIRING DIAGRAMS

539

28 JET, 35 JET, 40 HP AND 50 HP MODELS
(IGNITION SYSTEM [1999-ON])

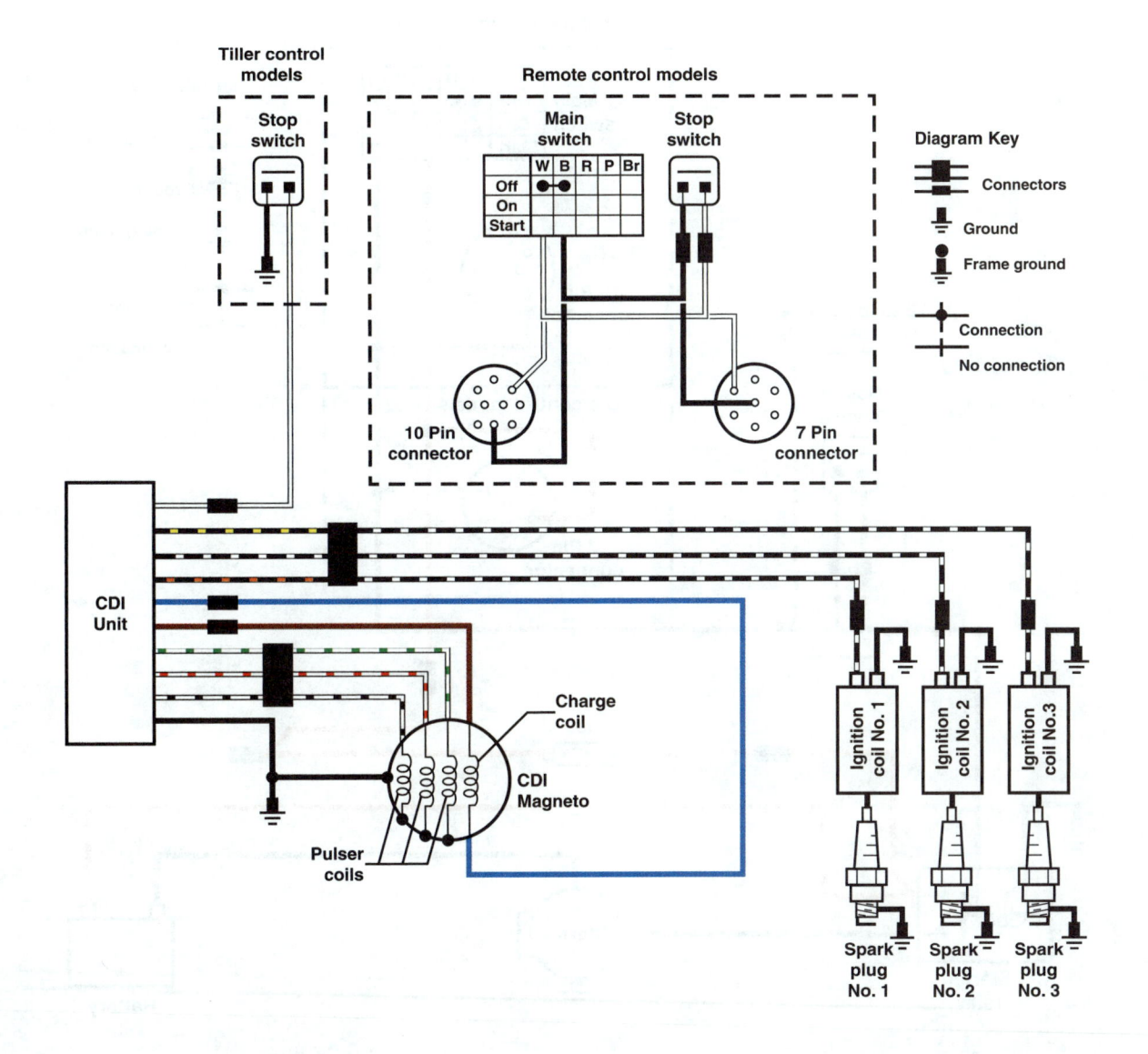

Tiller control models
- Stop switch

Remote control models
- Main switch

	W	B	R	P	Br
Off	●—●				
On					
Start					

- Stop switch
- 10 Pin connector
- 7 Pin connector

Diagram Key
- Connectors
- Ground
- Frame ground
- Connection
- No connection

- CDI Unit
- Charge coil
- CDI Magneto
- Pulser coils
- Ignition coil No. 1
- Ignition coil No. 2
- Ignition coil No. 3
- Spark plug No. 1
- Spark plug No. 2
- Spark plug No. 3

15

540

WIRING DIAGRAMS

28 JET, 35 JET, 40 HP AND 50 HP MODELS (ELECTRIC STARTING SYSTEM [1999-ON])

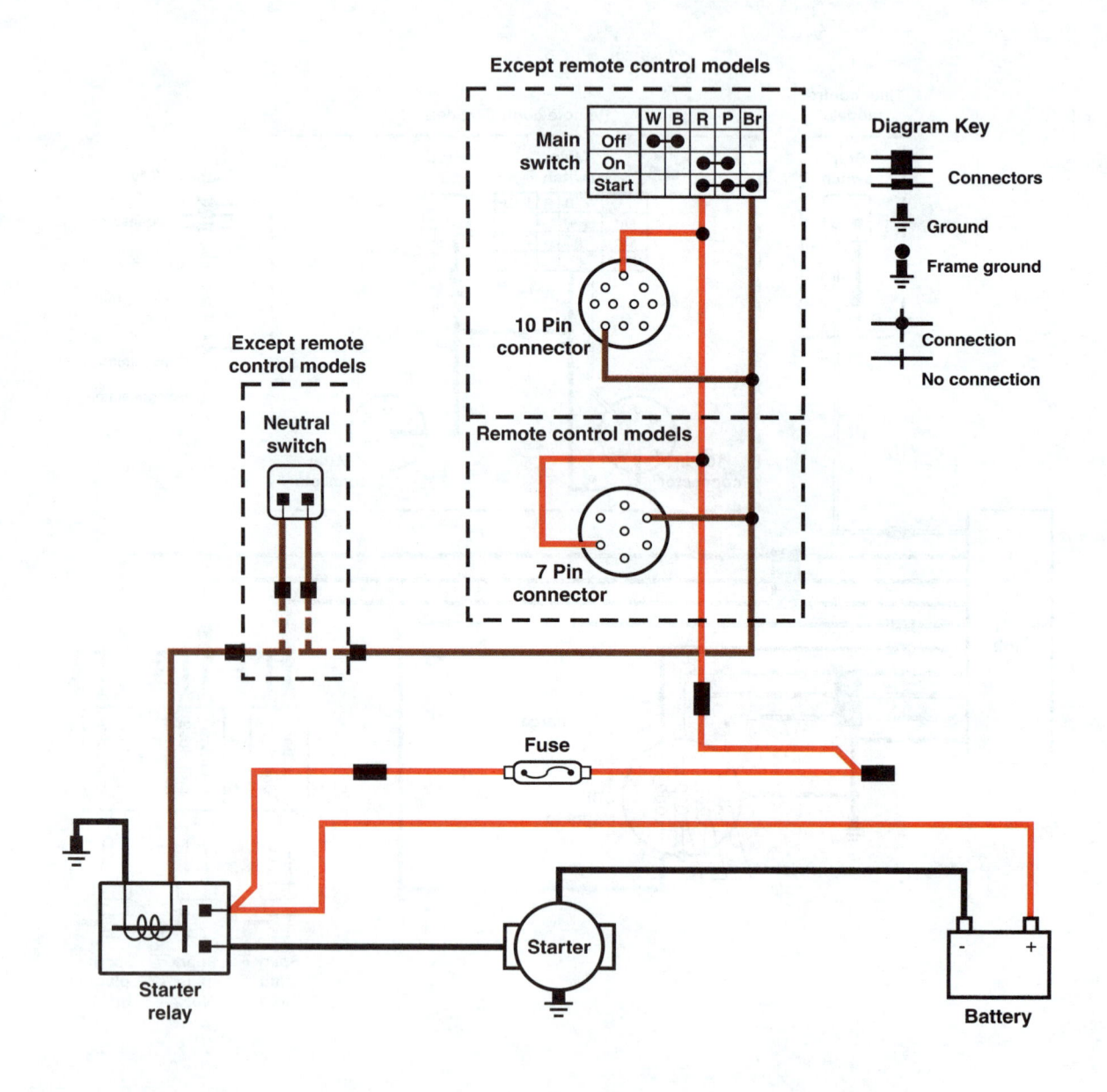

WIRING DIAGRAMS

28 JET, 35 JET, 40 HP AND 50 HP MODELS
(BATTERY CHARGING SYSTEM [1999-ON])

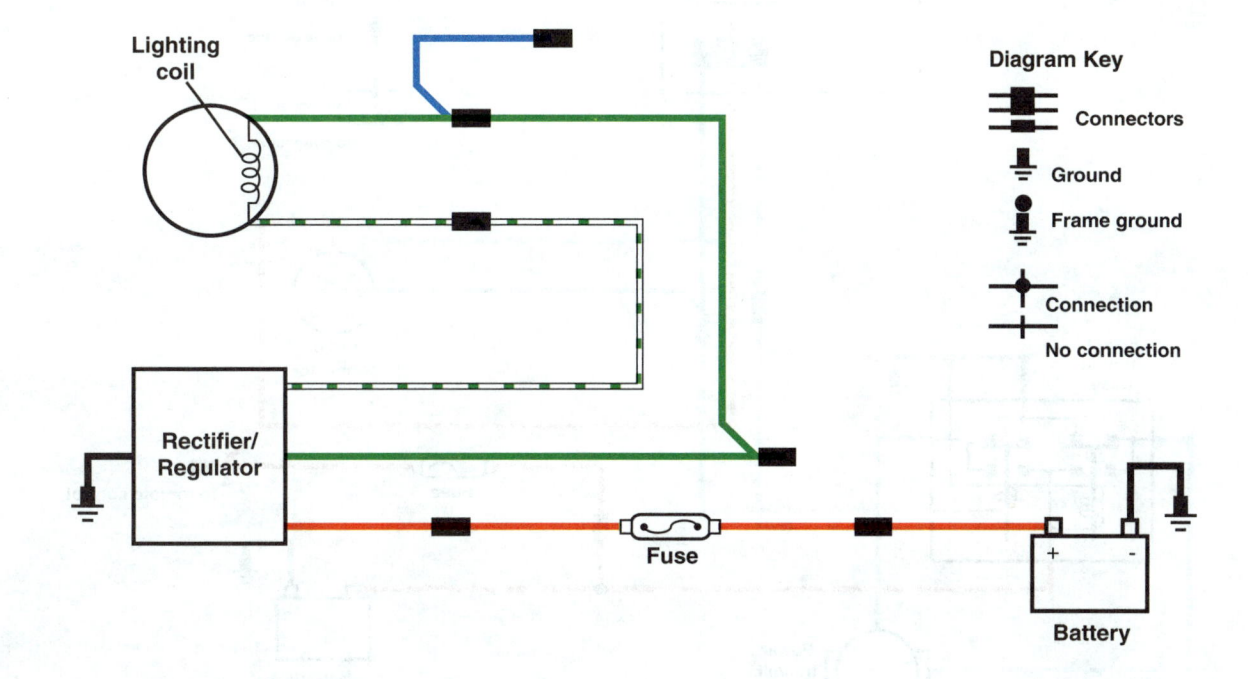

28 JET, 35 JET, 40 HP AND 50 HP MODELS (POWER TILT AND TRIM SYSTEM [1999-ON])

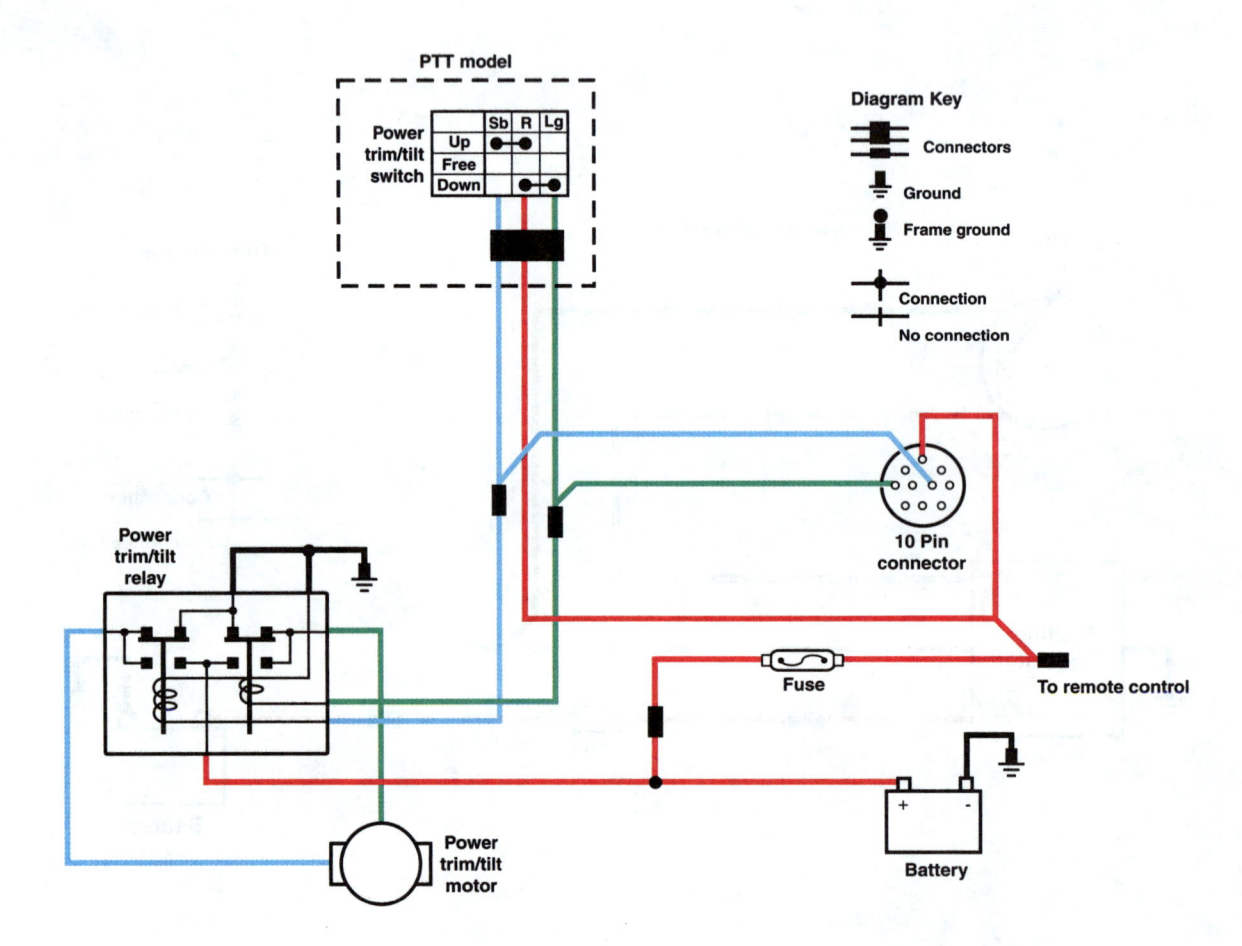

WIRING DIAGRAMS

543

28 JET, 35 JET, 40 HP AND 50 HP MODELS (WARNING SYSTEM [1999-ON])

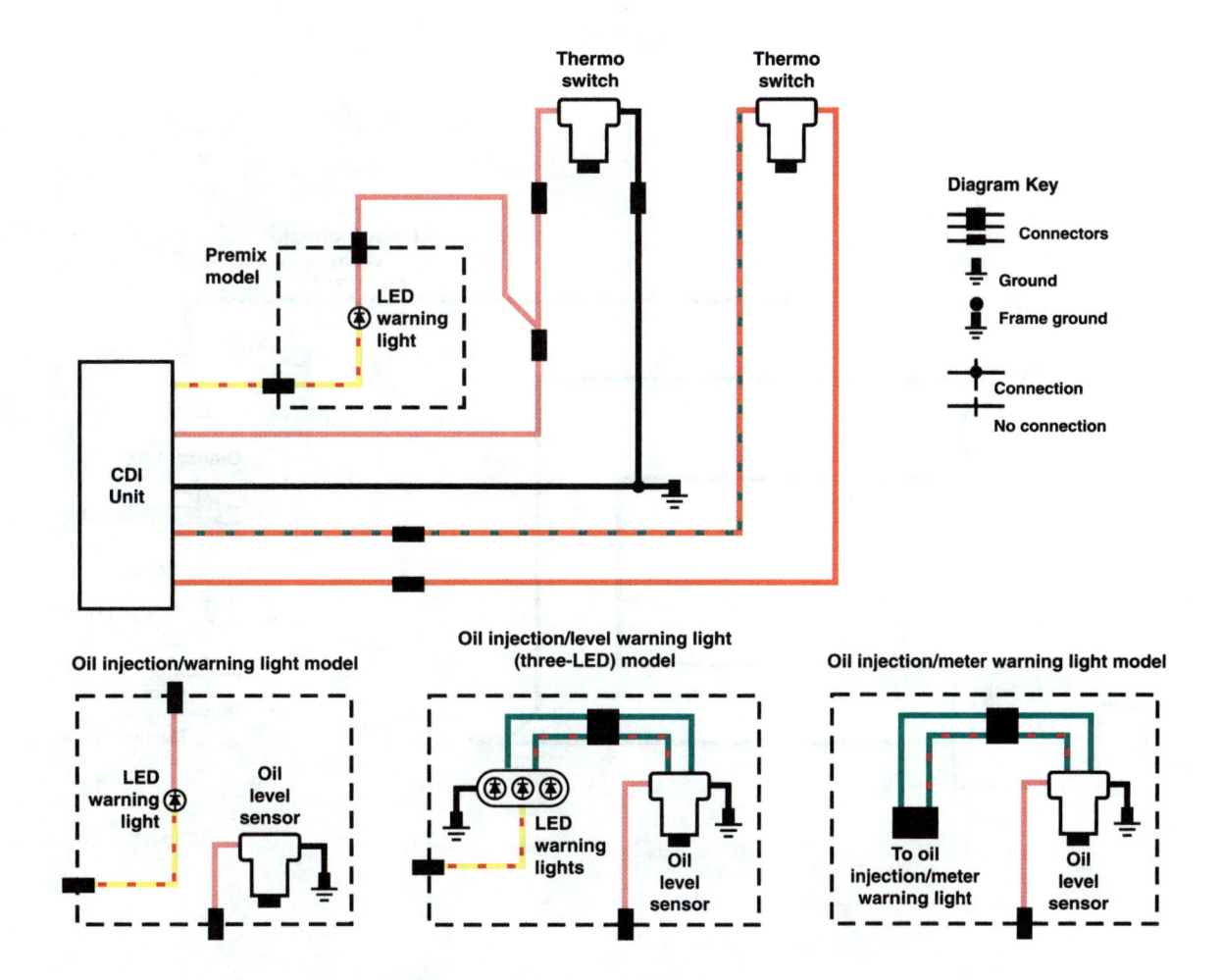

28 JET AND 30-50 HP MODELS
(PRIME-START SYSTEM)

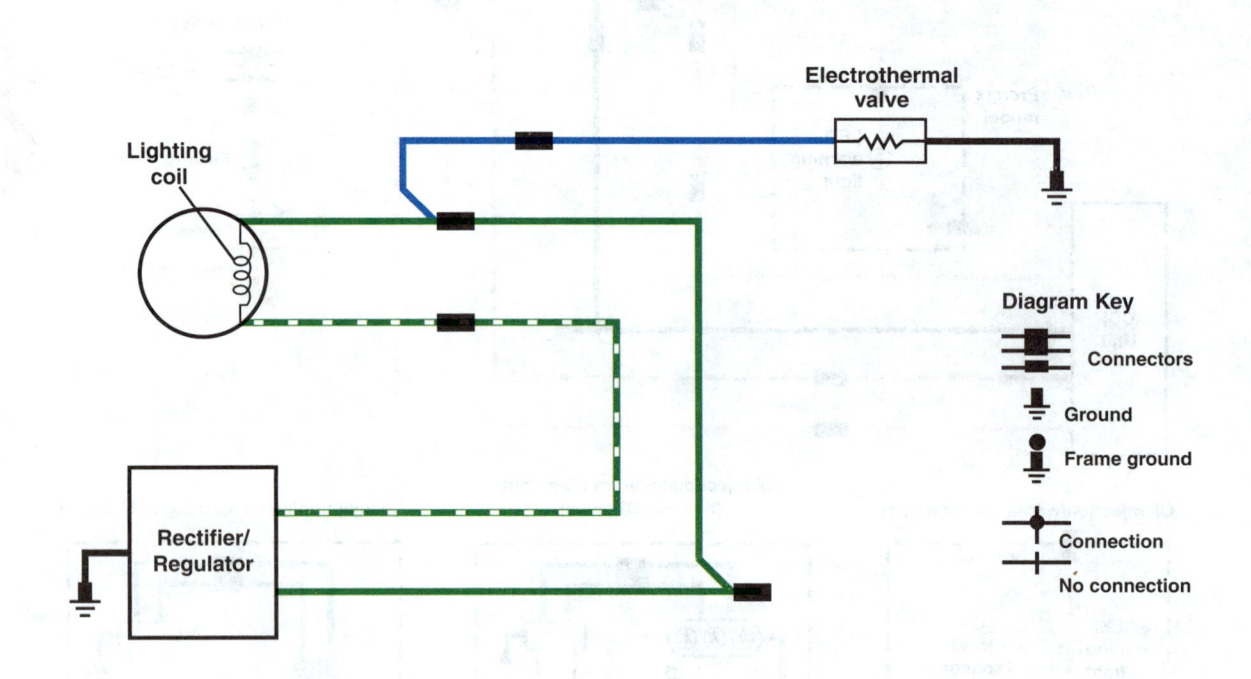

Lighting coil

Electrothermal valve

Rectifier/Regulator

Diagram Key
- Connectors
- Ground
- Frame ground
- Connection
- No connection

WIRING DIAGRAMS

545

60 AND 70 HP MODELS
(1999-ON [EXCEPT E60])

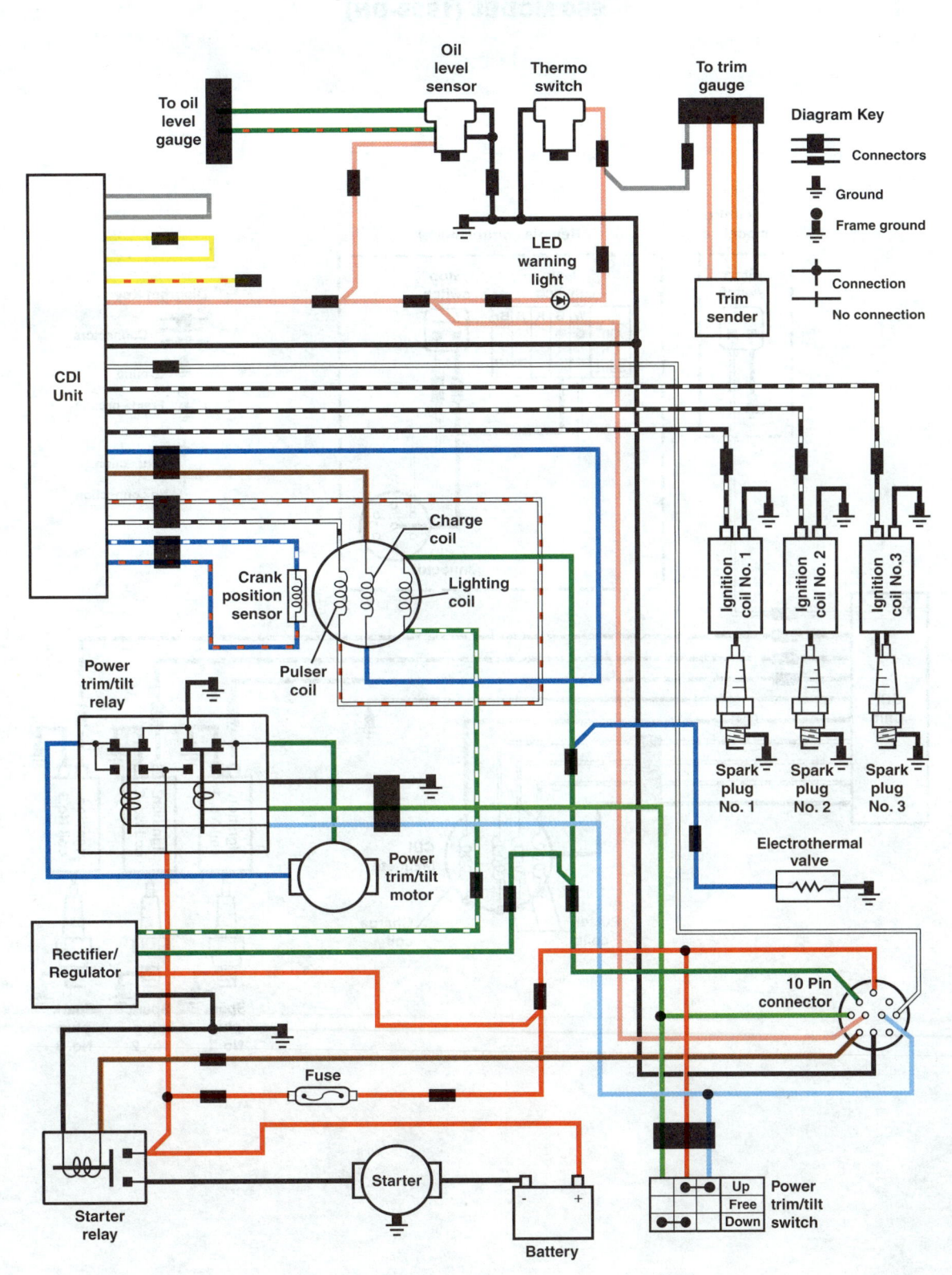

E60 MODEL (1999-ON)

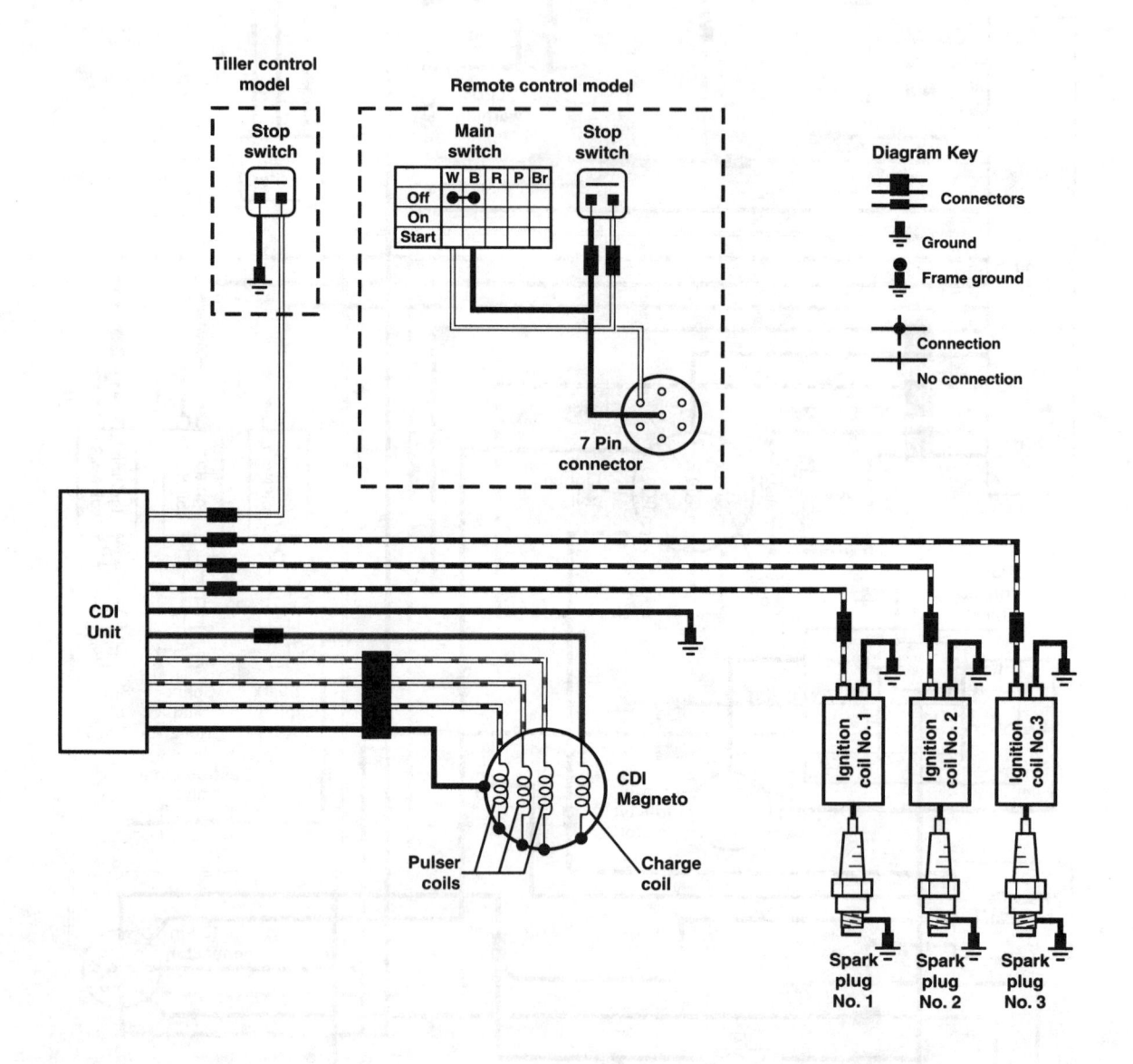

WIRING DIAGRAMS

547

65 JET AND 75-90 HP MODELS
(1999-ON [EXCEPT E75])

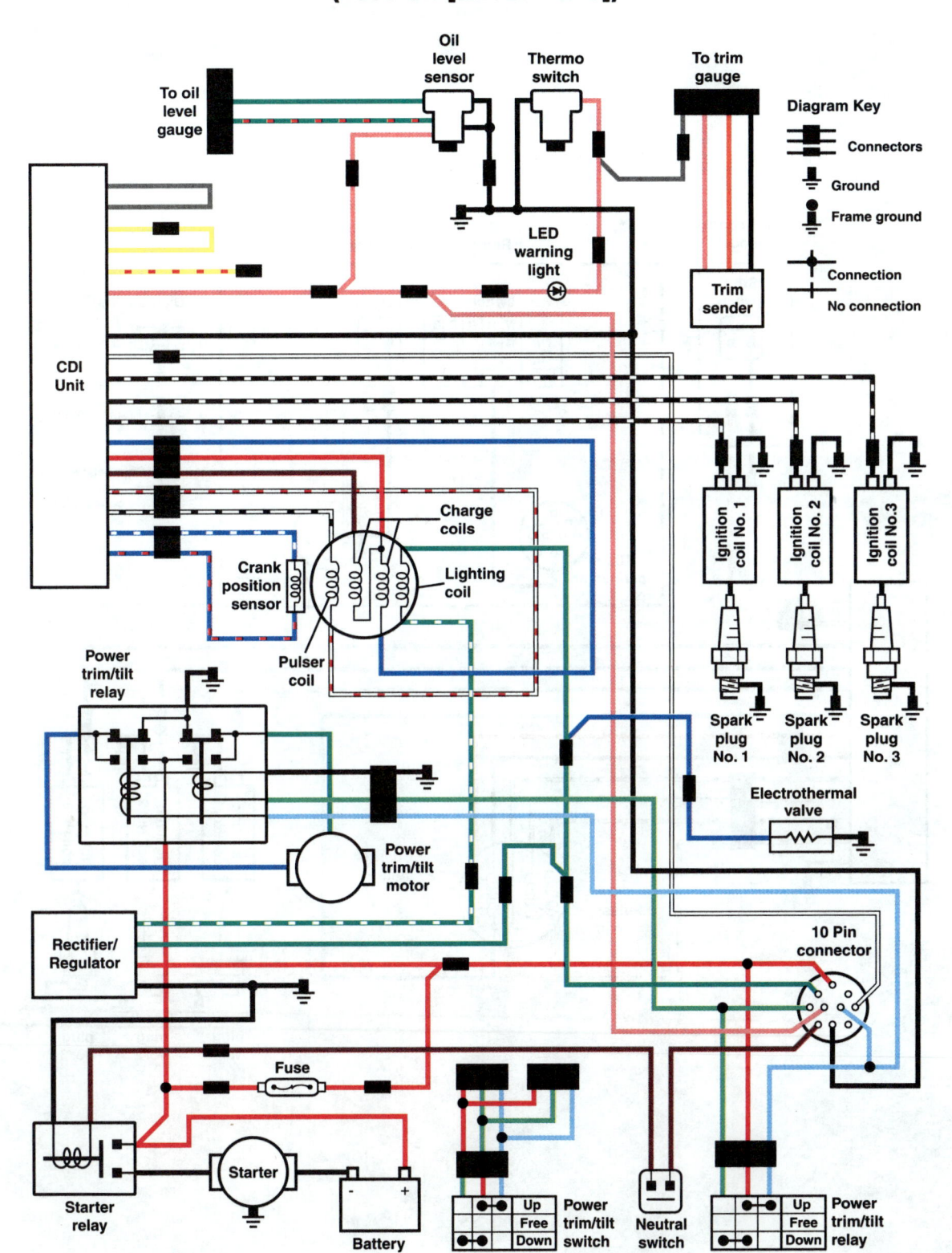

WIRING DIAGRAMS

E75 MODEL (1999-ON)

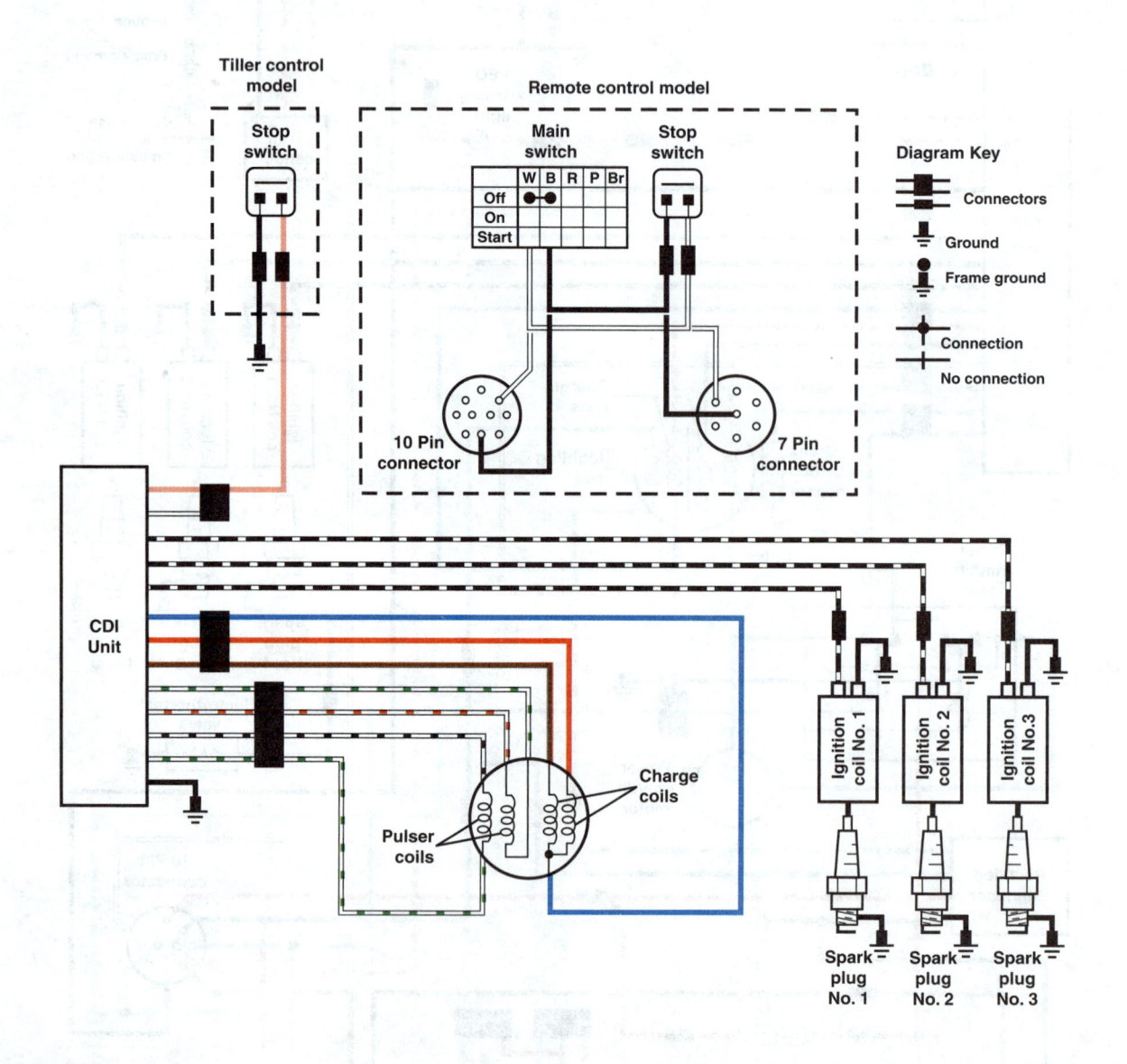

WIRING DIAGRAMS

549

REMOTE CONTROL WIRING DIAGRAM
(TYPICAL YAMAHA 703 CONTROL)

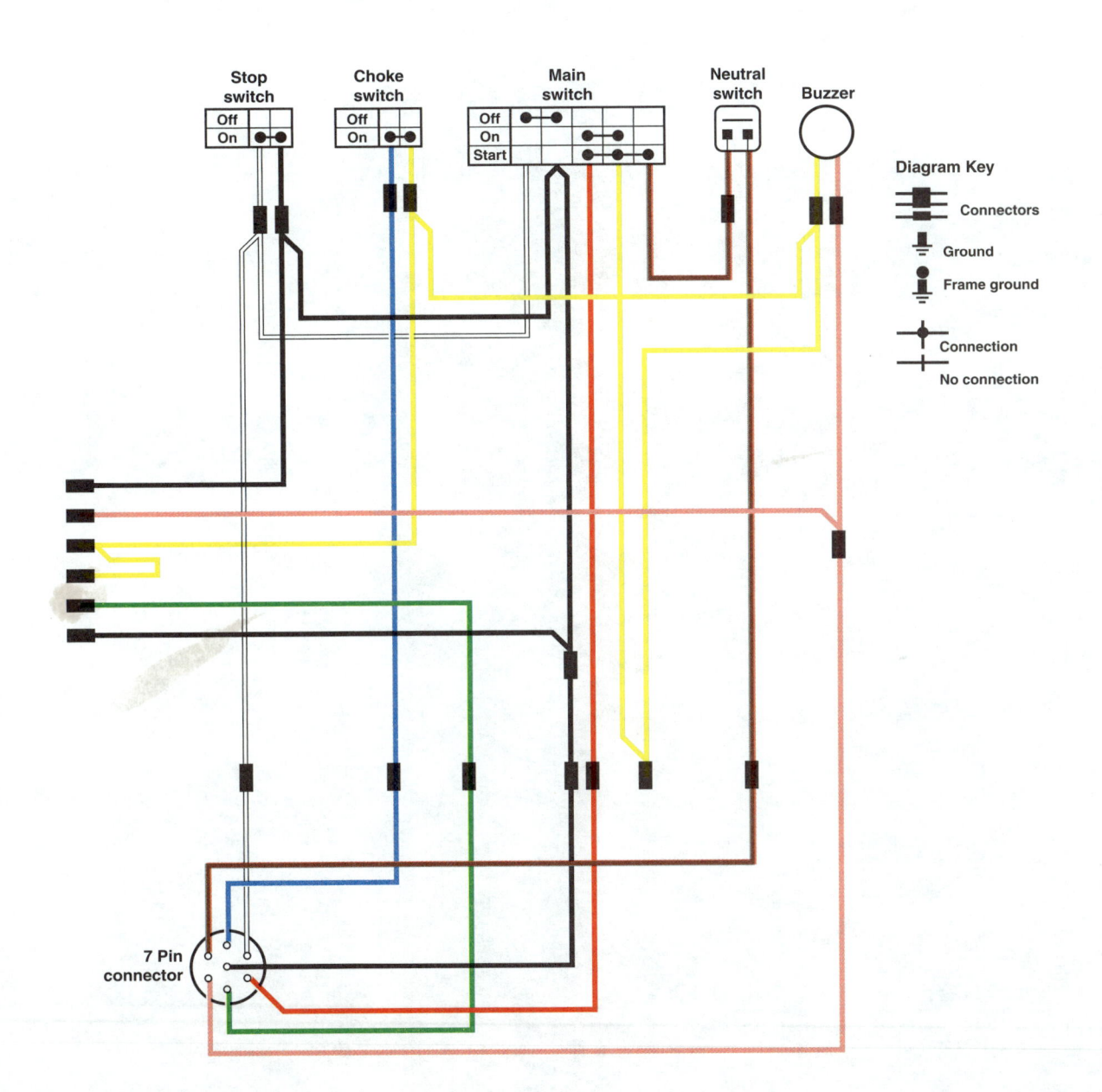

15

NOTES

NOTES

NOTES

NOTES

NOTES

NOTES

MAINTENANCE LOG

Date	Engine Hours	Type of Service